SECOND EDITION

PSYCHOLOGY

CONTEXTS OF BEHAVIOR

JANE S. HALONEN · **JOHN W. SANTROCK**
Alverno College · *The University of Texas at Dallas*

Brown & Benchmark
PUBLISHERS

Madison   Dubuque, IA   Guilford, CT   Chicago   Toronto   London
Caracas   Mexico City   Buenos Aires   Madrid   Bogota   Sydney

Book Team

Executive Publisher *Edgar J. Laube*
Acquisitions Editor *Steven Yetter*
Developmental Editor *Linda Falkenstein*
Production Editor *Debra DeBord*
Proofreading Coordinator *Carrie Barker*
Designer *Christopher E. Reese*
Art Editor *Rachel Imsland*
Photo Editor *Carol Judge*
Permissions Coordinator *Karen L. Storlie*
Production Manager *Beth Kundert*
Production/Costing Manager *Sherry Padden*
Marketing Manager *Carla Aspelmeier*
Copywriter *Jennifer Smith*

Basal Text *10/12 Minion*
Display Type *Minion*
Typesetting System *Macintosh/QuarkXPress*
Paper Stock *50# Mirror Matte*

President and Chief Executive Officer *Thomas E. Doran*
Vice President of Production and Business Development *Vickie Putman*
Vice President of Sales and Marketing *Bob McLaughlin*
Director of Marketing *John Finn*

A Times Mirror Company

The credits section for this book begins on page 785 and is considered an extension of the copyright page.

Cover images: © Top left/Lele/Mask/University of Iowa Museum of Art; © Top right/Third Coffin of Tutankhamen/Superstock; © Middle left/Gauguin/Ancestors of Tehamana/Art Institute of Chicago; © Middle right/Leonardo da Vinci/La Gioconda/Art Resource; © Bottom left/Paul Klee/Senecio/Art Resource; © Bottom right/Charles Craig/Portrait of an Indian/Superstock

Copyedited by Wendy Nelson; proofread by Francine Buda Banwarth

Printed in the United States of America by Times Mirror Higher Education Group, Inc., 2460 Kerper Boulevard, Dubuque, IA 52001

10 9 8 7 6 5 4 3 2 1

Brief Contents

CONTENTS

SECTION ONE
Psychology as Science and Story

---

*These sections appear in every chapter.

CHAPTER FIFTEEN
Personality   533

SECTION SEVEN
Abnormal Psychology and Therapy

CHAPTER SIXTEEN
Abnormal Psychology   573

CHAPTER SEVENTEEN
Therapies   613

LIST OF BOXES

Critical Thinking

Sociocultural Worlds

Applications in Psychology

Practical Knowledge About Psychology

Resources for Psychology and Improving Humankind

PREFACE

his preface especially highlights what is new to the second edition of *Contexts* and the book's extensive, extremely effective learning system.

NEW TO THE SECOND EDITION

The second edition of *Contexts* underwent an extremely thorough, substantive revision. The changes include a fine-tuning of the sociocultural approach, the addition of critical thinking as a major theme, the addition of a new coauthor, an extensive overhaul of the content and readability of every chapter, and the inclusion of four new chapters and a prechapter.

Modification of Sociocultural Contexts Material

The first edition of *Contexts* was a unique departure from the standard introductory psychology textbook. How the sociocultural contexts in which we live influence the way we think, feel, and behave was woven throughout the book. The emphasis on **sociocultural contexts**—culture, ethnicity, and gender—has been retained in the second edition of *Contexts*. We have carefully considered how and where the sociocultural material is presented with the help of extensive feedback from our expert consultants, reviewers, adopters, and students.

Critical Thinking as a Major Theme

Another important change in the book is the dramatic increase in emphasis on **critical thinking.** Many introductory psychology texts now include material on critical thinking. However, we believe the way critical thinking has been infused into *Contexts,* second edition, is truly a unique way of challenging students to stretch their minds.

Addition of Coauthor Jane Halonen

The addition of critical thinking as a new major theme of *Contexts,* second edition, was made possible by the contributions of new coauthor Jane Halonen. We emphasize various intellectual skills or outcomes that should be enhanced in an introductory psychology course oriented to improving critical thinking about behavior. This emphasis promotes active engagement with the concepts and principles of psychology throughout the text.

Dr. Halonen replaced Dr. LaRue Allen, coauthor on the first edition of *Contexts.* Unfortunately, LaRue's increasing academic commitments kept her from continuing as a coauthor on the book's second edition. Dr. Allen has recently become the chair of the Applied Psychology Program at New York University. She also is working extensively on a research grant that focuses on stress and coping in ethnic minority children in low-income urban areas. Fortunately, LaRue has stayed on the book as the expert consultant in the area of ethnicity, joining Richard Brislin (culture) and Florence Denmark (gender) as our three content advisors. We sincerely thank LaRue for her significant contributions to *Contexts.* Although no longer a coauthor because of her increasing academic commitments, LaRue's voice continues to permeate *Contexts,* second edition.

Overhaul of Content and Readability

In addition to the major changes in sociocultural contexts and critical thinking, *Contexts* underwent a substantial overhaul in content and readability. We left virtually no stone unturned in our effort to create a truly readable, up-to-date rendering of psychology at the introductory level. Every section, paragraph, sentence, figure, table, and legend went under a microscope and, whenever necessary, was amplified, trimmed, clarified, or tweaked with regard to content and readability.

New Chapters and Prechapter

The effort to make *Contexts,* second edition, the very best introductory text possible led to the creation of four new chapters—"Research and Reasoning," "Gender," "Sexuality," and "Culture and Ethnicity"—and a new prechapter on critical thinking.

Research and Reasoning

Coauthor Jane Halonen developed a truly unique chapter on research and reasoning that provides students with a solid grounding in how research in psychology is conducted. She also explores how knowledge of research methodology can be transferred to practical contexts to sharpen critical thinking skills.

Gender and Sexuality

Contexts, second edition, has separate chapters on gender and sexuality, whereas the first edition combined gender and sexuality in one chapter. We believe that both gender and sexuality deserve considerable coverage in an introductory psychology text. Further, splitting the chapters helps to uncouple gender and sexuality concepts so that they can be discussed independently. However, coverage of gender is not constrained only to a single chapter but also appears where appropriate throughout the book.

Culture and Ethnicity

The critical topics of culture and ethnicity, like gender, now have their own chapter. In the first edition, these ideas were presented in an epilogue. And as with gender, culture and ethnicity are not only discussed in a separate chapter but are also infused into discussions of psychological issues throughout *Contexts,* second edition.

Prechapter: Learning to Learn About Psychology

The study of psychology involves three things: (1) acquiring a specialized knowledge base, (2) learning to think critically about behavior, and (3) developing an attitude and motivation consistent with the science of psychology. The completely new prechapter creates a learning, motivational, and attitudinal framework that helps students understand what the study of psychology is and how to think about psychology.

THE LEARNING SYSTEM IN CONTEXTS, SECOND EDITION

Contexts, second edition, has the most extensive learning system of any introductory psychology text. It is both very effective and challenging.

Critical Thinking

Extremely important additions to the learning system in the book's second edition are the well-orchestrated **critical thinking** components. The critical thinking system includes

- A prechapter that provides students with an understanding of the importance of learning how to think critically and how to think more effectively about behavior
- Critical thinking boxes that are inserted periodically in each chapter to encourage students to stretch their minds
- More extensive "Critical Thinking About Behavior" end-of-chapter pieces that focus on topics related to the chapter's content
- A new chapter on research and reasoning that emphasizes how to think more effectively about the science of psychology
- Picture and graphics legends that encourage active learning by pushing students to think through implications of the concepts presented in the legends

Pedagogical System

We wanted not only to encourage students to think critically about psychology's subject matter but also to help them learn. The pedagogical system begins with a **visual student preface** (following this preface); the visual student preface portrays how the student can effectively learn from the text. A **section opening introduction** informs students what the section is about and lists its chapters. An **outline** at the beginning of each chapter reveals the organization of the material.

We believe that psychology can be best understood by combining scientific research with human stories. We implement this belief in two ways. First, following the outline is an easy-to-read, high interest introduction to the chapter called **The Story of . . . .** The **Preview** section links the story to the chapter's contents. Second, **quotations** also are sprinkled through the text to embellish the chapter contents with human voices.

Key terms appear in the text in boldfaced type, with their definitions following immediately within the text in *italics.* This is an important pedagogical feature that provides students with a very clear understanding of important psychological concepts. The key terms also are defined in a book-ending **glossary.**

Another key dimension of the learning system in contexts is the **Review** section that appears two to four times in each chapter. We designed reviews to activate students' memory and comprehension of main topics or important ideas that have been discussed to that point. This allows students to get a handle on complex concepts before they reach the end of the chapter. The review sections serve as a cognitive framework for organizing the most important information in that part of the book.

Figures, tables, photographs, and cartoons were carefully chosen for *Contexts,* second edition. The unique **visual figures** combine a description of important content information with a photograph(s) to illustrate the content. In a number of instances, the visual figures represent summaries or reviews of salient issues that have been discussed in the text. The visual figures enhance students' retention and make the book a more attractive one to study.

Two types of boxed features appear in each chapter. **Sociocultural Worlds** boxes give special attention to the cultural, ethnic, and gender dimensions of psychology. **Applications in Psychology** boxes feature discussion of a high interest applied topic related to the chapter's content.

A number of pedagogical features appear at the end of each chapter. The chapter-ending material begins with a section called **Critical Thinking About Behavior,** which highlights an aspect of critical thinking related to a particular dimension of the chapter's material. Next, an **Overview** section includes two parts: a cognitive map of the chapter's main topics along with a brief summary of the chapter's contents. The **Perspectives** section reviews which of psychology's six main perspectives have been emphasized in that particular chapter. Visual icons signal the perspectives to students. **Key terms** are defined again for the student at the end of each chapter and are page-referenced.

Two new chapter-ending features are unique to introductory psychology texts. First, the **Practical Knowledge About Psychology** section consists of practical book reviews (including a photograph of the book) designed to encourage students to read further about the chapter's contents. Second, the **Resources for Psychology and Improving Humankind** section lists books, brochures, agencies, telephone numbers, research journals, and psychological organizations that provide students with an extensive set of resources for learning more about psychology's many fields and practical information for improving humankind.

TEXT SUPPLEMENTS

We've tried to combine a student-oriented textbook with an integrated ancillary package designed to meet the unique needs of instructors and students. Our goal has been to create a teaching package that is as enjoyable to teach with as it is to study from.

The *Instructor's Course Planner* (ISBN 0–697–14910–2) was prepared by Steven A. Schneider of Pima Community College. This flexible planner provides many useful tools to enhance your teaching. For each chapter, learning objectives, an extended chapter outline, suggestions for teaching, lecture/discussion suggestions, video and film suggestions, classroom activities, and handout forms are provided. Suggestions for essay test questions focused on the "critical thinking" chapter endpieces from *Psychology: The Contexts of Behavior* are also included. The *Instructor's Course Planner* is available on disk for IBM, Apple, and Macintosh computers.

The Brown & Benchmark *Introductory Psychology Activities Handbook* offers additional activities, in-class and out-of-class projects, and discussion questions. The activities handbook will help you get your students actively engaged and thinking critically.

The *Student Study Guide* was also created by instructor's manual author Steven A. Schneider. For each chapter of the text, the student is provided with learning objectives, a detailed outline of the chapter, a guided review of terms and concepts, and two multiple-choice practice tests.

The Critical Thinker (second edition) by Richard Mayer and Fiona Goodchild, both of the University of California–Santa Barbara, explicitly teaches strategies for understanding and evaluating material in any introductory psychology textbook. This 70-page booklet is available free to adopters.

The AIDS Booklet, third edition, by Frank D. Cox of Santa Barbara City College, is a brief but comprehensive introduction to the Acquired Immune Deficiency Syndrome, HIV, and related viruses.

Two *Test Item Files* (TIF #1 ISBN 0–697–14922–6; TIF #2 0–697–27023–8) will be available to instructors who adopt the second edition of *Psychology: The Contexts of Behavior.* The first contains over 2,375 multiple-choice questions that are keyed to the text and the learning objectives. The second test item file will be available in early 1996.

Dr. Al Cohen, director of the Office of Testing and Evaluation Services at the University of Wisconsin–Madison, provides valuable feedback in the construction of all Brown & Benchmark test item files.

The questions in the test item file are also available on *MicroTest III,* a powerful but easy-to-use test-generating program by Chariot Software Group. MicroTest is available for your use in DOS (3.5 [ISBN 0–697–14916–1] and 5.25 [ISBN 0–697–14917–X] size disks), Windows (ISBN 0–697–14918–8), and Macintosh (ISBN 0–697–14920–X) versions. With MicroTest, instructors can easily select questions from the *Test Item File* and print tests and answer keys. Instructors can also customize questions, headings, and instructions; add or import their own questions; and print tests in a choice of printer-supported fonts.

Or take advantage of Brown & Benchmark's free call-in *Testing Service.* With 48 hours' notice, our Educational Resources Department will prepare your test and fax you the questions and the answer key. Simply select your questions in advance and call **1–800–338–5371** and our educational resources representatives will be glad to help you.

The CD-ROM *Explorations in Health and Psychology* by George B. Johnson of Washington University in St. Louis will help students actively investigate processes vital to their understanding of psychology as they should be explored—with movement, color, sound, and interaction. This set of 10 interactive animations on CD-ROM allows students to set and re-set variables in each (including modules on the life span, drug addiction, nerve conduction, AIDS, and more) and then evaluate those results. Contact your local Brown & Benchmark Representative for more information or call the Times Mirror Higher Education Group Customer Service at 1–800–338–5578.

A large selection of *videotapes* is also available to adopters based on the number of textbooks ordered. Consult your Brown & Benchmark Representative for ordering policies.

The Brain Modules on Videodisc created by WNET in New York, Antenne 2 TV/France, the Annenberg/CPB Foundation, and Professor Frank J. Vattano of Colorado State University, is based on the Peabody-award-winning series "The Brain." Thirty segments, averaging 6 minutes each, illustrate an array of topics in psychology. Consult your Brown & Benchmark Representative for details.

The Brown & Benchmark *Human Development Interactive Videodisc Set,* produced by Roger Ray of Rollins College, vividly introduces life-span development with instant access to over 30 brief video segments from the highly acclaimed *Seasons of Life* series. Consult your Brown & Benchmark Representative for details.

Sixty book-specific *transparencies* (ISBN 0–697–14921–8) or slides (ISBN 0–697–14924–2) accompany the text. The charts, graphs, and images were chosen by Jane Halonen to augment and aid the teaching of each chapter. In addition, Brown & Benchmark offers 132 additional transparencies illustrating key concepts in general psychology in the *Introductory Psychology Transparency Set*

(ISBN 0–697–17354–2) or slides (ISBN 0–697–17355–0) and accompanying handbook with specific suggestions for classroom use by Susan J. Shapiro of Indiana University East. *New! The Brown & Benchmark Introductory Transparency Set Electronic Image Bank Version* (ISBN 0–697–29647–4) provides you with the same outstanding graphics on a CD-ROM for presentation from your PC or Macintosh. We provide our own generic viewer, but the contents are .pict files, so they can be downloaded into your own favorite presentation program—for instance, PowerPoint.

Our *Custom Transparency Program* is also available to adopters of *Psychology: The Contexts of Behavior.* If there is any image in the book you would like to use as a transparency, which is not included in the set, we will create it for you. Consult your Brown & Benchmark Representative for further details.

The *Brown & Benchmark Reference Disks* are available free to adopters. The disks include over 15,000 journal and book references arranged in files by topic. The complete set of five disks is available on IBM (3.5″ or 5.25″), Apple, or Macintosh disks.

CourseKits/CourseWorks, our custom publishing service, also allows you to have your own notes, handouts, or other classroom materials printed and bound very inexpensively for your course use, either as part of a custom designed textbook or separately. Contact Kate Finn or Kathy Phelan at 1–800–446–8979 for further information.

Annual Editions: Psychology provides convenient, inexpensive access to a wide range of current, carefully selected articles from magazines, newspapers, and journals written by psychologists, researchers, and educators, providing useful perspectives on important and timely topics in psychology.

Taking Sides: Clashing Views on Psychological Issues (ISBN 1–56134–294–7) is a debate-style reader designed to introduce students to controversies in psychology. By requiring students to analyze opposing viewpoints and reach considered judgements, *Taking Sides* actively develops students' critical thinking skills.

Sources: Notable Selections in Psychology (ISBN 1–56134–263–7) brings together 46 selections including classic articles, book excerpts, and research studies that have shaped the study of psychology. If you want your students to gain greater background knowledge in reading and interpreting firsthand from source material, *Sources* collects a diverse array of accessible but significant readings in one place.

The Encyclopedic Dictionary of Psychology (ISBN 0–87967–885–2) provides easy reference access to the key figures, concepts, movements, and practices of the field of psychology.

ACKNOWLEDGMENTS

First, we owe a special debt to the three outstanding expert consultants for *Contexts,* second edition. **LaRue Allen, Florence Denmark,** and **Richard Brislin** provided us with invaluable material and feedback about what to include and what to exclude in the second edition of the book.

In addition the **Human Diversity Advisory Group** of almost 100 psychologists from North America and abroad continued to offer their expertise in our effort to present the topic of human diversity in the most competent and strategic way in the text.

No textbook of this size or scope is possible without the efforts and scrutiny of a large number of thoughtful and conscientious reviewers. They, along with the expert consultants and human diversity advisory group, played a crucial role in making this a better book than we could have achieved on our own. Many thanks to the following reviewers of the book's second edition:

Jeannette Altarriba, *SUNY–Albany*
Lou Banderet, *Northeastern University*
Eugene Butler, *Quinsigamond Community College*
Thomas Cadwallader, *Indiana State University*
Luetilla M. Carter, *Oakwood College*
Toby Klinger Connet, *Johnson City Community College*
Katherine Covell, *University College of Cape Breton*
Robert Cox, *Shelby State Community College*
Florence Denmark, *Pace University*
Nancy Denney, *University of Wisconsin–Madison*
Peter Flynn, *North Essex Community College*
Sandra Graham, *UCLA*
Algea Harrison, *Oakland University*
Morton Heller, *Winston-Salem State University*
Mary Kite, *Ball State University*
Claudia Kittock, *Cambridge Community College*
Lyla Maynard, *Des Moines Area Community College*
Jodi Mindell, *St. Joseph's University*
John Moritsugu, *Pacific Lutheran University*
Dirk W. Mosig, *University of Nebraska*
Linda Petioff, *Central Community College*
David Pittenger, *Marietta College*
Marilyn J. Reedy, *Alverno College*
Harriette W. Richard, *Northern Kentucky University*
Boika S. Twe, *Sinclair Community College*
Shirley A. Vaugh, *Henry Ford Community College*

We also benefitted enormously from the reviews of the first edition of *Contexts.* Many thanks also to the following individuals who served as reviewers of *Contexts'* first edition:

Bruce Bain, *University of Alberta, Edmonton*
Robert Bell, *Texarkana Community College*
Deborah Best, *Wake Forest University*
Richard Brislin, *East-West Center, University of Hawaii*
Jagannath P. Das, *University of Alberta*
Larry Dohrn, *San Antonio Community College*
Pauline Ginsberg, *Utica College of Syracuse University*
Randall Gold, *Cuesta College*
Peter Gram, *Pensacola Junior College*
James Hart, *Edison State Community College*

Janet E. Helms, *University of Maryland*
Nils Hovik, *Lehigh County Community College*
Jeannette Ickovics, *Yale University*
Rick Kribs, *Motlow State Community College*
Stan Kuczaj, *Southern Methodist University*
V. K. Kumar, *West Chester University*
Ed Lawson, *State University of New York, Fredonia*
David Matsumoto, *San Francisco State University*
Steve Myers, *Washburn University*
Mary Ellen O'Connor, *University of Tulsa*
Michele Paludi, *CUNY: Hunter College*
Paul Pederson, *Syracuse University*
Retta Poe, *Western Kentucky University*
Marshall Segall, *Syracuse University*

Tod Sloan, *University of Tulsa*
Martha Spiker, *University of Charleston*
Joseph Trimble, *Western Washington University*
Cynthia Whissell, *Laurentian University*

Finally, we wish to express our continued gratitude to the Human Diversity Advisory Group that was created at the start of this project. They continue to serve us and the other authors of Brown & Benchmark by lending their expertise to our efforts to infuse psychology textbooks with the sociocultural perspective. We gratefully acknowledge the ongoing help of the following individuals:

John Adamopoulos, *Indiana University at South Bend*
Leonore Loeb Adler, *Molloy College*
Rhoda L. Agin, *California State University, Hayward*
Jeannette Altarriba, *University of Massachusetts, Amherst*
James Anderson, *Indiana University of Pennsylvania*
Bobbie M. Anthony, *Chicago State University*
Yvonne Asamoah, *CUNY: Hunter College*
Roya Ayman, *Illinois Institute of Technology*
Bruce Bain, *University of Alberta, Edmonton*
Deborah L. Best, *Wake Forest University*
Hector Betancourt, *Loma Linda University*
Richard Brislin, *East-West Center, University of Hawaii*
Phyllis A. Bronstein, *University of Vermont*
John E. Carr, *University of Washington Medical Center*
Robert T. Carter, *Teachers' College, Columbia University*
Felipe G. Castro, *San Diego State University*
S. Andrew Chen, *Slippery Rock University*
George Cvetkovich, *Western Washington University*
Jagannath P. Das, *University of Alberta*
John M. Davis, *Southwest Texas State University*
J. Peter Denny, *University of Western Ontario*
Geri Anne Dino, *Frostburg State University*

Juris Draguns, *Pennsylvania State University*
Nadya Fouad, *University of Wisconsin, Milwaukee*
William K. Gabrenya, *Florida Institute of Technology*
Peter Gamlin, *Ontario Institute for Studies in Education*
Uwe P. Gielen, *St. Francis College*
Pauline Ginsberg, *Utica College of Syracuse University*
Bernadette Gray-Little, *The University of North Carolina*
George M. Guthrie, *Pennsylvania State University*
Janet E. Helms, *University of Maryland*
Jeannette Ickovics, *Yale University*
Martha D. John, *Marymount University*
James M. Jones, *University of Delaware*
Prabha Khanna, *Memphis State University*
W. M. Klein, *Princeton University*
Stan Kuczaj, *Southern Methodist University*
V. K. Kumar, *West Chester University*
Teresa D. LaFromboise, *University of Wisconsin*
Hope Landrine, *California State University, San Bernardino*
Leonard M. Lansky, *University of Cincinnati*
Edwin D. Lawson, *State University of New York, Fredonia*
D. John Lee, *Calvin College*
Walter J. Lonner, *Western Washington University*
Chalsa Loo, *University of Hawaii, Manoa*
Gerardo Marin, *University of San Francisco*
Carol Markstrom-Adams, *University of Guelph*

David Matsumoto, *San Francisco State University*
Ogretta V. McNeil, *College of the Holy Cross*
Martha T. Mednick, *Howard University*
Anita M. Meehan, *Kutztown University*
Peter F. Merenda, *The University of Rhode Island*
John Moritsugu, *Pacific Lutheran University*
Ruth Munroe, *Pitzer College*
Linda J. Myers, *The Ohio State University*
Mary Ellen O'Connor, *University of Tulsa*
Virginia E. O'Leary, *Indiana State University*
Esteban Olmedo, *California School of Professional Psychology*
Harry Osser, *Queen's University, Kingston*
Amado M. Padilla, *Stanford University*
Anita Wan-ping Pak, *Brock University*
Michele Paludi, *CUNY: Hunter College*
Paul B. Pederson, *Syracuse University*
Anthony D. Pellegrini, *University of Georgia*
W. Clinton Pettus, *Virginia State University*
Retta E. Poe, *Western Kentucky University*
Pamela T. Reid, *CUNY: Graduate School and University Center*
Charles L. Richman, *Wake Forest University*
Ronald P. Rohner, *University of Connecticut, Storrs*
Judy F. Rosenblith, *Wheaton College*
Rosellen M. Rosich, *University of Alaska, Anchorage*
Selma Sapir, *Bank Street College, Yonkers*

B. Mark Schoenberg, *Memorial University of Newfoundland*

Marshall H. Segall, *Syracuse University*

Jack A. Shaffer, *Humboldt State University*

Laura Sidorowicz, *Nassau Community College*

Andrei Simic, *University of Southern California*

Carolyn H. Simmons, *University of Colorado, Denver*

Tod Sloan, *University of Tulsa*

Margaret Beale Spencer, *Emory University*

Mary L. Spencer, CAS, *University of Guam*

Harold Stevenson, *University of Michigan*

Michael Stevenson, *Ball State University*

Norman D. Sundberg, *University of Oregon*

Harold Takooshian, *Fordham University*

Irmgard M. Thiessen, *Mount Royal College*

Donald L. Tollefson, *Canisius College*

Judith Torney-Purta, *University of Maryland*

Harry C. Triandis, *University of Illinois*

Joseph E. Trimble, *Western Washington University*

Oliver C. S. Tzeng, *Indiana University–Purdue University at Indianapolis*

Susana P. Urbina, *University of North Florida*

Emmy E. Werner, *University of California, Davis*

Cynthia Whissell, *Laurentian University*

Lisa Whitten, *SUNY–College at Old Westbury*

Daniel E. Williams, *Montclair State College*

Julian Wohl, *University of Toledo*

Frankie Y. Wong, *Texas A&M University*

Joe Yamamoto, *University of California, Los Angeles*

Lucy Yu, *Pennsylvania State University*

We owe special thanks to our former editor Michael Lange, who helped to create *Contexts,* first and second editions, for his vision, competence, and friendship. We miss you. Steven Yetter, our new editor and former marketing manager in psychology, has successfully carried on where Michael left off and is deeply committed to the philosophy of *Contexts.* Thank you, Steven, for orchestrating the book's many facets so smoothly. We also thank Linda Falkenstein, developmental editor, for shepherding the book through many stages of development.

Thanks also go to Steven A. Schneider, who prepared a very useful instructor's course planner and student study guide, and to Eric Landrum for his hard work in constructing a new test item file.

A final note of thanks go to our spouses—Brian Halonen and Mary Jo Santrock—for their enthusiastic support of our work, for their patient tolerance of our single-minded work habits, and for their companionship and unfailing humor.

Contexts' Consulting Advisors

To improve the coverage of ethnicity, gender, and culture in *Contexts,* second edition, three consulting advisors provided valuable advice and suggestions. These experts' recommendations and insights have considerably improved the coverage of sociocultural contexts in the book.

LaRue Allen is chair of the Applied Psychology Program at New York University. She has also taught in the Psychology Department at Michigan State University. She received her B.A. in social relations from Radcliffe College in 1972 and her Ph.D. in clinical/community/developmental psychology from Yale in 1980. She has taught graduate and undergraduate courses in introductory psychology, developmental psychopathology, child and adolescent development, community psychology, psychology of women, ecological assessment, and mental health consultation methods. Her areas of research interest include stress and coping in ethnic-minority children in low-income urban areas, prevention of psychopathology in ethnically diverse children, and sociocultural influence (including competence and humor responsiveness as a measure of adaptive behavior). She was coauthor of the first edition of *Psychology: The Contexts of Behavior.*

Florence L. Denmark is an internationally recognized scholar, administrator, leader, researcher, and policy maker. She received her Ph.D. in Social Psychology from the University of Pennsylvania and has since made many contributions in that area, particularly to the psychology of women. Denmark has authored more than 75 articles and 15 books, presented over 100 talks and invited addresses, and appeared on numerous radio and television shows. Denmark has also served as a leader in psychology in many capacities, among them president of the American Psychological Association and president of the Council of International Psychologists. She is also the recipient of numerous other prestigious distinctions, including the APA's Distinguished Contributions to Psychology in the Public Interest/Senior Career Award as well as APA's Division 35's (Psychology of Women) Carolyn Wood Sherif Award. Denmark has been the Thomas Hunter Professor of Psychology at Hunter College of the City University of New York and at present is the Robert Scott Pace Distinguished Professor of Psychology at Pace University, where she is chair of the Department of Psychology.

Richard Brislin is the Senior Fellow and Director of Intercultural Programs at the East-West Center in Honolulu, Hawaii. He has taught courses in cross-cultural psychology, intercultural communication, cross-cultural counseling, and cross-cultural research methods. He is the author of several books which have been used as texts in college courses, including *Cross-Cultural Research Methods* (1973), *Cross-Cultural Encounters: Face to Face Interaction* (1981), *Intercultural Interactions: A Practical Guide* (1986), *Understanding Culture's Influence on Behavior* (1993), and *Intercultural Communication Training: An Introduction* (1994). Since 1975 he has organized a wide variety of workshops at the East-West center for researchers, college professors, practitioners, and cross-cultural trainers. He was a G. Stanley Hall Lecturer for the American Psychological Association and is coeditor of *Improving Intercultural Interactions: Modules for Cross-Cultural Training Programs* (1994).

VISUAL STUDENT PREFACE
How the Learning System Works

his book contains an extensive and very effective learning system that will both challenge you to think critically and help you to learn the material more competently.

CRITICAL THINKING

Prechapter

Read the prechapter "Learning to Learn in Psychology." The prechapter will not only help you learn how to think critically about psychology but will also provide you with a learning system that will help you in any course you take in college.

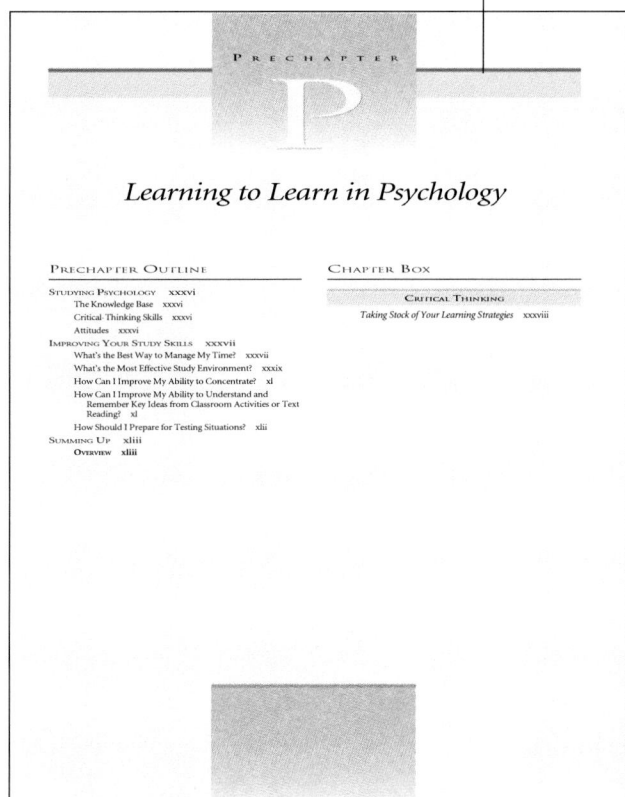

Critical Thinking Boxes

These boxes are inserted periodically in each chapter to encourage you to stretch your mind about a topic in that particular section of the chapter.

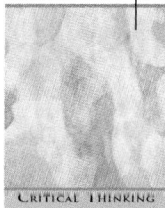

Critical Thinking About Behavior

This section appears at the end of each chapter and usually involves a more elaborate exploration of critical thinking than the boxed inserts.

CRITICAL THINKING ABOUT BEHAVIOR
Labeling and Justice

When you began this chapter, you constructed a list of characteristics that you thought captured your personality. We challenged you to think about whether the traits you selected were representative, enduring, consistent, and realistic. We questioned whether others would describe you in the same way.

Compassion could have been one of the traits you selected. Suppose we wanted to develop a simple self-report inventory that would allow the measurement of some aspects of compassion. Walter Mischel suggests that traits interact with situations. Suppose, to measure your compassion, we asked you which of the following acts you would perform:

· Agreeing to a request to sponsor a child in a technologically disadvantaged country
· Intervening in a friend's drug or alcohol problem
· Offering money to the homeless when they confront you personally
· Taking in stray animals
· Sacrificing your own plans to help a friend
· Volunteering assistance to a driver with a disabled car
· Alerting a friend who has some lunch stuck between his teeth
· Letting a sick friend copy your homework
· Giving away all your possessions to a needy organization

As you can see, measuring the trait of compassion with this inventory would be extremely difficult. The actions listed in this self-report checklist could all be compassionate in some circumstances, but it would certainly be difficult to evaluate a person's compassion using responses to this list. For example, you could endlessly adopt stray animals, but there are practical constraints on how much compassion you could show using this behavior. You could let a friend copy your homework in the compassion of the moment, but that judgment might be far from compassionate in the long run because your friend will be unlikely to learn something that could be useful in the future. Could we rule out your having any compassion if you indicated you wouldn't perform any of the actions on the list? Probably not. Although our compassion self-report checklist has face validity (that is, each item relates to compassion), it is unlikely that we could use it as it stands to conduct valid research on the trait.

Making judgments about traits is difficult not only in research situations; it can be surprisingly challenging in life. Although we regularly make trait attributions to help us understand situations, we might not sufficiently capture the complexity of the situation. The use of traits to explain behavior can help us be efficient processors of reality, but it is doubtful that it helps us make accurate or fair-minded interpretations. Sometimes the labels lead us to make premature judgments and turn our attention elsewhere—we assign a trait as the reason for an action and move on.

How can this knowledge help us to be more effective critical thinkers in relation to judgments about personality? We should be able to *apply psychological concepts to enhance personal adaptation* by incorporating the following skills:

1. **Reserve judgment, particularly when making negative attributions.**
   How important is it to resolve a behavioral question by attributing someone's actions to a trait? In many situations, labeling requires making a judgment that we may later regret. In the tradition of Skinner, it may be more helpful to think about and describe specific behaviors involved in the situation than dispense with the situation by assigning dysfunctional traits as the cause. For example, marriage therapists often help couples learn to describe the behaviors that are upsetting to them rather than continue to use hurtful and unhelpful labeling (such as "You are inconsiderate and insecure").

2. **Recognize the boundaries of labels.**
   When we feel compelled to make trait judgments, it is still helpful to remember the context in which the behavior occurred and confine the judgment to that circumstance. For example, if you think of your father as "mean," it will be useful to identify the circumstances in which he is mean. He might be mean when he has not gotten enough sleep or when he is trying to watch his weight. This restricted use of the label recognizes that there are likely to be many circumstances in which he is not mean, which brings into question the fairness of the use of the term.

3. **Abandon expectations about consistency.**
   As you read in this chapter, many other cultures may be less intense about defining, categorizing, and judging personality features. This attitude may be a function of living in collectivistic cultures where there is no particular advantage in labeling others' traits. Richard Brislin (1993) believes that enduring relationships in collectivistic cultures may show greater tolerance about inconsistencies in human behavior. Even if we don't live in a collectivistic culture, we can save some frustration if, like collectivists, we do not expect human beings to be consistent across all situations.

The very purpose of existence is to reconcile the glowing opinion we hold of ourselves with the appalling things that other people think about us.

Quentin Crisp

564   *Motivation, Emotion, Health, and Personality*

PEDAGOGICAL SYSTEM

Not only do we want to challenge you to think critically about psychology but we also want to help you learn the material. The following representation of the pedagogical system is organized by beginning, interior, and ending of chapter.

Beginning of Sections and Chapters
Section Opening Introduction

This beautiful two-page spread with an artpiece informs you about the section's contents and chapters.

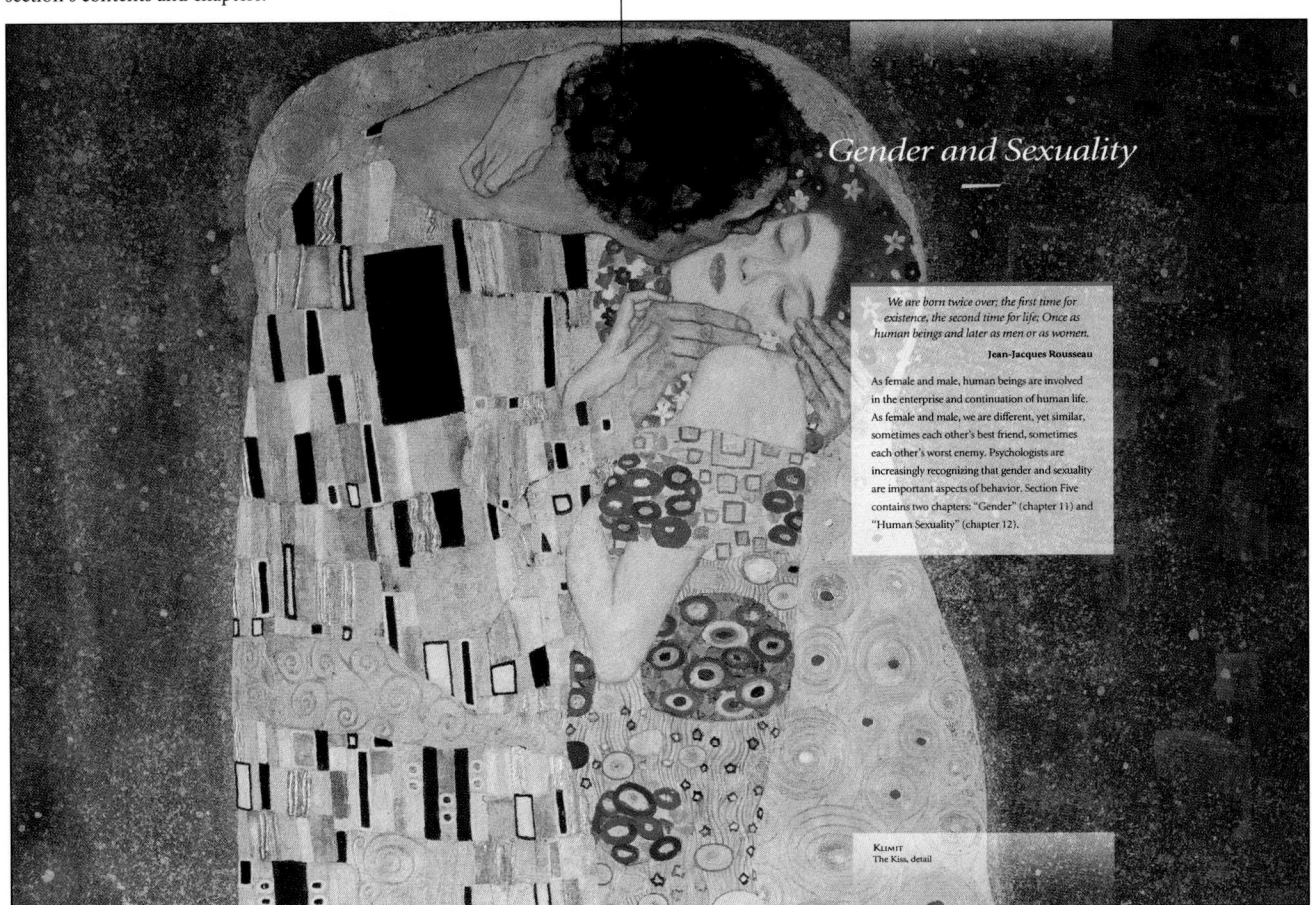

Gender and Sexuality

We are born twice over; the first time for existence, the second time for life; Once as human beings and later as men or as women.

Jean-Jacques Rousseau

As female and male, human beings are involved in the enterprise and continuation of human life. As female and male, we are different, yet similar, sometimes each other's best friend, sometimes each other's worst enemy. Psychologists are increasingly recognizing that gender and sexuality are important aspects of behavior. Section Five contains two chapters: "Gender" (chapter 11) and "Human Sexuality" (chapter 12).

KLIMT
The Kiss, detail

Research and Reasoning

> *Science is not an inhuman or
> superhuman activity. It's something
> that humans invented and it speaks
> to one of our great needs—to
> understand the world around us.*
> **Maxine Singer**

Chapter-Opening Outline

Each chapter begins with an outline that reveals the organization of topics. The outline gives you an overview of the arrangement and structure of the chapter.

The Story of . . .

This easy-to-read, high-interest piece introduces you to some aspect of the chapter's contents.

THE STORY OF ALICE WALKER: DISADVANTAGE AND TRIUMPH

In the summer of 1966, Alice Walker, who would later win a Pulitzer Prize for *The Color Purple*, spent her days battling racism in Mississippi. She had recently won her first writing fellowship and could have chosen to follow her dream of moving to Senegal, Africa, but instead she put herself in the heart and heat of the civil rights movement. Walker grew up knowing the brutal effects of poverty and racism. Born in 1944, she was the eighth child of Georgia sharecroppers who earned about $300 a year. When she was 8, her brother accidentally shot her in the left eye with a BB gun. By the time her parents got her to the hospital a week later (they had no car), she was blind in that eye and it had developed a disfiguring layer of scar tissue. Despite the counts against her, Walker has become an essayist, poet, award-winning novelist, short-story writer, and social activist, who, like her characters (especially the women), has overcome pain and anger to celebrate the human spirit. As Walker puts it, she writes about people who "make it, who come out of nothing. People who triumph."

Alice Walker won the Pulitzer Prize for her book *The Color Purple*. Like the characters in her book (especially the women), Walker overcame pain and anger to triumph and celebrate the human spirit.

PREVIEW

What leads a person like Alice Walker to turn poverty and trauma into a rich harvest of adjustment and achievement? How can we explain why one person can pick up the pieces of a life shattered by tragedy, such as a loved one's death, while another seems to come unhinged by life's minor hassles? Why is it that some people are real whirlwinds—successful at work, maintaining good relationships with their friends and family, and active participants in community organizations—while others hang out on the sidelines, mere spectators in life? Understanding such individual differences is an important goal of psychology. In this first chapter, we will introduce and define psychology, explore psychology's history and contemporary perspectives, and evaluate how psychology is practiced.

Preview

This section tells you what the chapter's contents are.

INTRODUCING PSYCHOLOGY

If you have ever wondered what makes people tick, you have asked yourself psychology's central question. In this book, you will explore the fascinating terrain of personality, motivation, the inner workings of the brain, and much, much more. You will learn about the methods psychologists use to explain human nature, as well as the progress psychology has made. In addition, you will see how cultural and ethnic background, gender, sexual orientation, economic circumstances, and other factors influence what people think and how they behave. However, psychology is still a young science and these are very complex issues; psychologists do not have all the answers.

Even so, psychology is uniquely qualified to help us make sense of our increasingly complex and challenging world. It isn't just your imagination; the world is getting tougher and tougher to keep up with. For example, one day's edition of the *New York Times* is packed with more information than a person who lived in the Middle Ages acquired during a lifetime, and gone are the days when the United States was an undisputed industrial giant. As the need to both import and export goods increases, so does global interdependence and the need to understand other cultures in order to develop good international relationships. We also live in a nation where the workforce is increasingly diverse. By the year 2000, for example, over 80 percent of the people entering the job market will be women and members of ethnic minority groups.

that such training works only on a superficial level and is ineffective unless the child is at a transitional point from one stage to the next.

Culture and education exert stronger influences on children's development than Piaget believed. Earlier in the chapter, we studied how the age at which individuals acquire conservation skills is associated to some extent with the degree to which their culture provides relevant practice. And in many developing countries, formal operational thought is a rare occurrence. And as you will learn shortly, there has been a wave of interest in how children's cognitive development progresses through interaction with skilled adults and peers, and how the children's embeddedness in a culture influences their cognitive growth. Such views stand in stark contrast to Piaget's view of the child as a solitary little scientist.

Vygotsky's Theory of Cognitive Development

Children's cognitive development does not occur in a social vacuum. Lev Vygotsky (1896–1934), a Russian psychologist, recognized this important point about children's minds more than half a century ago. Vygotsky's theory is increasingly receiving attention as we move toward the close of the twentieth century (Belmont, 1989; Light & Butterworth, 1993; Rogoff, 1993).

One of Vygotsky's (1962) most important concepts is that of the **zone of proximal development (ZPD)**, *which refers to tasks that are too difficult for children to master alone but that can be mastered with the guidance and assistance of adults or more-skilled children.* Thus, the lower limit of the ZPD is the level of problem solving reached by a child working independently. The upper limit is the level of additional responsibility the child can accept with the assistance of an able instructor (see figure 9.16). Vygotsky's emphasis on the ZPD underscored his belief in the importance of social influences on cognitive development. The practical teaching involved in ZPD begins toward the zone's upper limit, where the child is able to reach the goal only through close collaboration with an instructor. With continued instruction and practice, the child depends less and less on explanations, hints, and demonstrations, until she masters the skills necessary to perform the task alone. Once the goal is achieved, it may become the foundation for a new ZPD.

Many researchers who work in the field of culture and development find themselves comfortable with Vygotsky's theory, which focuses on sociocultural contexts (Pellegrini & others, 1990; Rogoff & Morelli, 1989). Vygotsky emphasized how the development of higher mental processes, such as reasoning, involve learning to use the inventions of society, such as language and mathematical systems. He also stressed the importance of teachers and role models in children's mental development. Vygotsky's emphasis on the importance of social interaction and culture

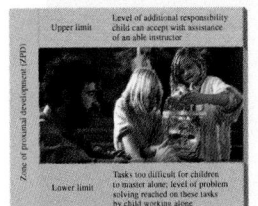

FIGURE 9.16

Vygotsky's Zone of Proximal Development
Vygotsky's zone of proximal development has a lower limit and an upper limit. Tasks in the ZPD are too difficult for the child to perform alone. They require assistance from an adult or a skilled child. As children experience the verbal instruction or demonstration, they organize the information in their existing mental structures so they can eventually perform the skill or task alone. *What implications does the ZPD have for school design?*

in children's cognitive development contrasts with Piaget's description of the child as a solitary young scientist.

American developmental psychologist Barbara Rogoff (1990) also believes that social interaction and culture play important roles in children's cognitive development. She argues that a child's cognitive development should involve an "apprenticeship" with companions who will strengthen the child's written and oral language skills, math skills, and memory strategies to preserve information over time. In mastering these skills, a child would use all sorts of tools—everything from notches on sticks to calculators and computers—that would be consistent with the culture in which the tools were developed and used.

Piaget once observed that children's cognitive development is a continuous creation of increasingly complex forms. As we will see next, this observation applies to children's social development as well.

If a child is to keep alive his inborn sense of wonder without any such gift from the fairies, he needs the companionship of at least one adult who can share it, rediscovering with him the joy, excitement and mystery of the world we live in.

Rachel Carson

Interior of Chapter

Visual Figures

Visual figures combine a description of important content information with a photograph(s) to illustrate the content. In a number of instances, the visual figures represent summaries of key ideas in the text to enhance your retention.

Key Terms

Key terms appear in the text in boldfaced type, with their definitions following immediately within the text in *italics*.

Quotations

Quotations are sprinkled through each chapter to stimulate further thought about a topic.

Applications in Psychology

This boxed feature focuses on a high-interest topic related to the chapter's content.

APPLICATIONS IN PSYCHOLOGY 7.2

I'll Never Forget What's-His-Name

Have you ever had trouble remembering someone's name? Probably so. A face might look familiar, but the name escapes you. This problem can be helped with the use of mnemonics.

Remembering someone's name can be broken down into three subproblems: remembering the face, remembering the name, and remembering the connection between the two. To remember the face, look at it closely while focusing on a distinctive feature, such as a large nose. To remember the name, try to find a meaning in it, and assign this a key word. As with a foreign language, you might think about a part of the name that sounds like an English word.

Finally, to remember the connection between the face and the name, think of an image that links the key word and the distinctive feature in the face. If you have just been introduced to Mr. Clausen, a man with the large nose, you might think of the English word *claws* as a key word for *Clausen*. Now imagine a large lobster claw tearing away at Clausen's large nose. When you see Mr. Clausen the next time, recall this image and the name *Clausen* should come to mind.

Another technique for remembering someone's name involves an expanded pattern of rehearsal. When you are introduced to someone, repeat the person's name immediately. You might say, "Tom Naylor? Hello, Tom." About 10 to 15 seconds later, look at the individual and rehearse his name silently. Do it again after 1 minute and then again after 3 minutes. The name will have a good chance of being retained in your long-term memory. One reason this spacing strategy works is that most forgetting occurs within a very short time after you first learn a fact (Loftus, 1980).

How might you effectively remember someone's name, such as Mr. Clausen?

Review

The review sections are a key dimension of the learning system. They appear two to four times in each chapter and are designed to activate your memory and comprehension of main topics or important ideas that have been discussed to that point. This allows you to get a handle on key concepts before you reach the end of the chapter.

REVIEW

The Nature and Nurture of Memory, and Mnemonics and Memory Strategies

The nature and nurture of memory involve the neurobiological basis of memory (nature) and the cultural dimensions of memory (nurture). In the study of the neurobiological basis of memory, a major issue is the extent to which memory is localized or distributed. Single neurons are involved in memory, but some neuroscientists believe that most memories are stored in circuits of about 1,000 neurons. There is no specific memory center in the brain; many parts of the brain participate in the memory of an event.

A culture sensitizes its members to certain objects and events in the environment, and these cultural experiences can influence the nature of memory. Bartlett's schema theory and Hirsch's ideas about cultural literacy reflect the role of culture in memory.

Mnemonics are techniques that improve memory. Many of these involve imagery, including the method of loci and the peg method. Systems based on a number of aspects of our knowledge about memory have been developed, including ARESIDORI, to improve memory.

SOCIOCULTURAL WORLDS 3.2

Race and Ethnicity

Race, which originated as a biological concept, is a system for classifying plants and animals into subcategories according to specific physical and structural characteristics. *Race* is one of the most misused and misunderstood words in the English language (Atkinson, Morten, & Sue, 1993; Root, 1992). Loosely, it has come to mean everything from a person's religion to skin color.

Scholars have difficulty even determining how many races the human species comprises. Skin color, head shape, facial features, stature, and the color and texture of body hair are the physical characteristics most widely used to determine race. Racial classifications presumably were created to define and clarify the differences among groups of people; however, they have not been very useful. Many people argue that racial groupings are socially constructed on the basis of physical differences and are not biologically defensible (Van den Berghe, 1978).

One approach to classification specifies three main races: Mongoloid, or Asian; Caucasoid, or European; and Negroid, or African. However, some groups, such as Native Americans, Australians, and Polynesians, do not fit into any of the three main categories. Also, obvious differences

within groups are not adequately explained. Arabs, Hindus, and Europeans, for instance, are physically different, yet they are all called Caucasian. Although there are some physical characteristics that distinguish "racial" groups, there are, in fact, more similarities than differences among such groups.

Too often we are socialized to accept as facts many myths and stereotypes about people whose skin color, facial features, and hair texture differ from ours. For example, some people still believe that Asians are inscrutable, Jews are acquisitive, and Hispanics are lazy. What people believe about race has profound social consequences. Until recently, for instance, African Americans were denied access to schools, hospitals, churches, and other social institutions attended by Whites.

Although scientists are supposed to be a fair-minded lot, some also have used racial distinctions to further their own biases. Some even claim that one racial group has a biological inheritance that gives it an adaptive advantage over other racial groups. Nineteenth-century biologist Louis Agassiz, for example, asserted that God had created Blacks and Whites as separate species. Also, in Nazi Germany, where science and death made their grisliest alliance, Jews and other "undesirables" were attributed with whatever characteristics were necessary to reinforce the conclusion that "survival of the fittest" demanded their elimination.

Social psychologist James Jones (1990, 1993, 1994) points out that thinking in racial terms has become embedded in cultures as an important factor in human interactions. For example, people often consider what race they will associate with when they decide on such things as where to live, who will make a suitable spouse, where to go to school, and what kind of job they want. Similarly, people often use race to judge whether or not another person is intelligent, competent, responsible, or socially acceptable. Children tend to adopt their parents' attitudes about race as they grow up, often perpetuating stereotypes and prejudice.

Physical and psychological characteristics vary not only across ethnic groups but also within them.

Sociocultural Worlds

This boxed feature gives special attention to the cultural, ethnic, and gender dimensions of psychology.

End of Chapter

Overview

The overview section consists of two parts: (1) a cognitive map that provides you with a visual organization of the chapter's main topics and (2) a brief summary of the chapter's main contents.

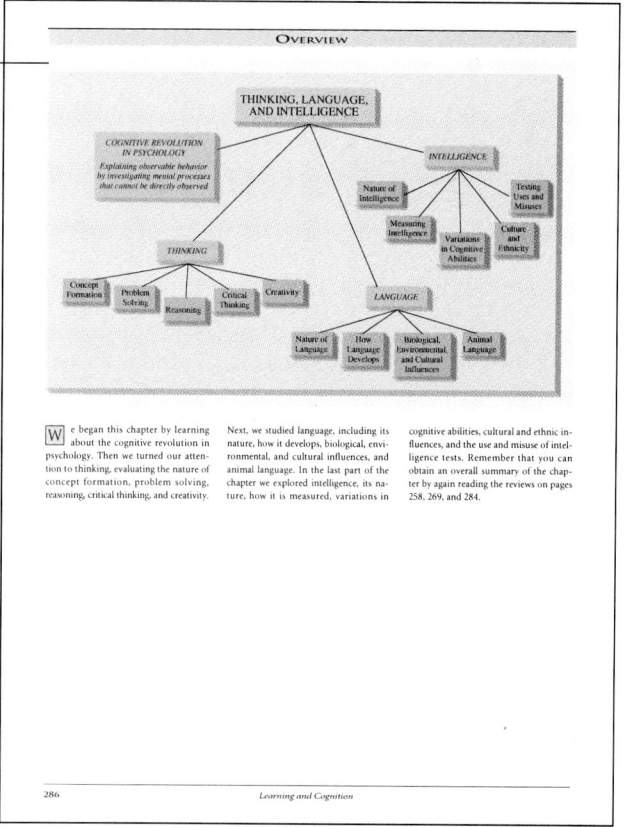

OVERVIEW

W e began this chapter by learning about the cognitive revolution in psychology. Then we turned our attention to thinking, evaluating the nature of concept formation, problem solving, reasoning, critical thinking, and creativity.

Next, we studied language, including its nature, how it develops, biological, environmental, and cultural influences, and animal language. In the last part of the chapter we explored intelligence, its nature, how it is measured, variations in

cognitive abilities, cultural and ethnic influences, and the use and misuse of intelligence tests. Remember that you can obtain an overall summary of the chapter by again reading the reviews on pages 258, 269, and 284.

Perspectives

This section reviews which of psychology's six main perspectives are highlighted in the chapter and page references them.

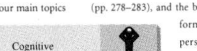
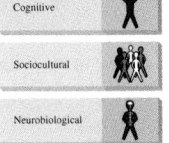
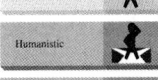
Key Terms

Key terms are defined in the order in which they appeared in the chapter and are page-referenced.

Practical Knowledge About Psychology

This section consists of practical book reviews (including a photograph of the book). We hope that some of the books will interest you and that you will be motivated to read further about some of psychology's topics.

This section lists books, brochures, agencies, phone numbers, research journals, and psychological organizations. The extensive description of resources is designed to provide you with more information about psychology's many domains and practical information for improving people's lives.

RESOURCES FOR PSYCHOLOGY AND IMPROVING HUMANKIND

Anxiety Disorders and Phobias: A Cognitive Perspective (1985)
by Aaron Beck and Gary Emery
New York: Basic Books

This book provides information about different types of anxiety and how people can change their thinking to overcome the anxiety that is overwhelming them.

Depression and Related Affective Disorders
Johns Hopkins Hospital, Meyer 3-181
600 N. Wolfe Street
Baltimore, MD 21205
410–955–4647

This is an organization for individuals with affective disorders and their families, friends, and mental health professionals. The organization provides support, referrals, and educational programs, and it publishes a quarterly newsletter, *Smooth Sailing.*

International Society for the Study of Multiple Personality and Dissociation
5700 Old Orchard Road, 1st Floor
Skokie, IL 60077-1024
708–966–4322

This organization of mental health professionals and students promotes a greater understanding of dissociation.

National Foundation for Depressive Illness
P.O. Box 2257
New York, NY 10116
800–248–4344

This foundation provides information and education about recent medical advances in affective mood disorders; it also has a referral service.

National Mental Health Association
1021 Prince Street
Alexandria, VA 22314-2971
800–969–NMHA

This consumer advocacy organization is devoted to promoting mental health and improving the lives of individuals with a mental disorder. It publishes NMHA Focus four times a year, as well as pamphlets on mental health issues.

National Mental Health Consumers Association
P.O. Box 1166
Madison, WI 53701

This organization seeks to protect the rights of mental health clients in housing, employment, and public benefits; it encourages the creation of self-help groups and aids them in acquiring funding and networking with other organizations.

Youth Suicide National Center
204 E. 2nd Ave Suite 203
San Mateo, CA 94401
415–347–3961

This is a national clearinghouse that develops and distributes educational materials on suicide and reviews current youth suicide prevention and support programs. Publications include *Suicide in Youth and What You Can Do About It* and *Helping Your Child Choose Life: A Parent's Guide to Youth Suicide.*

610   *Abnormal Psychology and Therapy*

End of Book
Glossary

Key terms are defined alphabetically in a book-ending glossary, along with their page references.

GLOSSARY

A

abnormal behavior Behavior that is maladaptive, harmful, statistically unusual, personally distressing, and/or designated as abnormal by the culture. 575

absolute threshold The minimum amount of energy that we can detect. 95

accommodation (cognitive) An individual's adjustment to new information. 307

accommodation (optical) An increase in the curvature of the lens in the eye. 100

acculturation Change that results from continuous, firsthand contact between two distinctive cultural groups that preserves the identities of both. 511, 700

acculturative stress The negative consequences of acculturation. 511

accurate empathy Rogers's term for the therapist's ability to identify with the client. 622

acetylcholine (ACh) A neurotransmitter that produces contractions of skeletal muscles by acting on motor nerves. 71

achievement motivation (need for achievement) The desire to accomplish something, to reach a standard of excellence, and to expend effort to excel. 460

action potential The brief wave of electrical charge that sweeps down the axon. 69

action therapy Therapy that promotes direct changes in behavior; insight is not essential for change to occur. 617

activation-synthesis view The view that dreams have no inherent meaning. Rather they reflect the brain's efforts to make sense out of or find meaning in the neural activity that takes place during REM sleep. In this view, the brain has considerable random activity during REM sleep, and dreams are an attempt to synthesize the chaos. 148

active-behavioral strategies Coping responses in which individuals take some type of action to improve their problem situation. 514

active-cognitive strategies Coping responses in which individuals actively think about a situation in an effort to adjust more effectively. 514

active listening Rogers's term for the ability to listen to another person with total attention to what the person says and means. 622

activity theory The theory that the more active and involved older people are, the more satisfied they will be with their lives and the more likely it is that they will stay healthy. 365

actor-observer hypothesis In attribution theory, differences in the interpretation of motives based on point of view. 658

acupuncture A technique in which thin needles are inserted at specific points in the body to produce effects such as local anesthesia. 111

adaptation Behavioral changes in response to challenges in the environment that enhance the organism's likelihood of survival. 63

addiction Physical dependence on a drug. 152

additive mixture The mixing of light beams from different parts of the color spectrum. 103

adolescence The transition from childhood to adulthood, which involves physical, cognitive, and socioemotional changes. In most cultures adolescence begins at about 10 to 13 years of age and ends at about 18 to 21 years of age. 335

adolescent egocentrism The adolescent's belief that others are as preoccupied with the adolescent as she herself is, the belief that one is unique, and the belief that one is indestructible. 338

adrenal glands Glands whose secretions play an important role in our moods, energy level, and ability to cope with stress; each adrenal gland secretes epinephrine (also called adrenaline) and norepinephrine (also called noradrenaline). 77

aerobic exercise Sustained exercise — jogging, swimming, or cycling, for example —that stimulates heart and lung activity. 491

affectionate love Also called companionate love; a type of love that occurs when an individual desires to have the other person near and has a deep, caring affection for the person. 666

afferent nerves Sensory nerves that carry information to the brain. 67

afterimages Sensations that remain after a stimulus is removed. 104

ageism Prejudice against people based on their age. 365

agoraphobia The fear of entering unfamiliar situations, especially open or public spaces; the most common phobic disorder. 584

AIDS A sexually transmitted disease that is caused by the human immunodeficiency virus (HIV), which destroys the body's immune system. 436

algorithms Procedures that guarantee an answer to a problem. 252

all-or-none principle The principle that once the electrical impulse reaches a certain level of intensity, it fires and moves all the way down the axon, remaining at the same strength throughout its travel. 69

alpha waves The EEG pattern of individuals who are in a relaxed or drowsy state. 41

altered state of consciousness A mental state that is noticeably different from normal awareness. Drugs, meditation, traumas, fatigue, hypnosis, and sensory deprivation produce altered states of consciousness. 137

739

Learning to Learn in Psychology

PRECHAPTER OUTLINE

CHAPTER BOX

CRITICAL THINKING

STUDYING PSYCHOLOGY

The study of psychology involves three things: acquiring a specialized knowledge base about behavior, learning to think critically about behavior, and developing attitudes and motivations consistent with the science of psychology.

The Knowledge Base

Psychology is rich in language that communicates findings about patterns of behavior. Concepts and terms deftly communicate complex behavior patterns. You will find that in this text we have printed key concepts in bold type to make them stand out and help you organize your reading.

As a scientific enterprise, psychology systematically explores behavior, generating principles to explain behavior. What regularities and irregularities exist in behavior, and how do we account for them? Psychologists search for the factors (or variables) that could most plausibly account for behavior. They create hypotheses that propose explanations, and they design research in various formats to test their hypotheses, seeing if they can generate evidence to confirm them. Sometimes psychologists will propose complex explanations of behavior, called theories, based on the research evidence. Where one theory does not sufficiently account for behavior, psychologists may offer competing explanations and criticism of positions other than their own.

In addition to specialized content areas of psychology, certain perspectives in psychology have dominated the development of psychological research since the foundation of the discipline. Six important perspectives in psychology are the behavioral, psychoanalytic, humanistic, neurobiological, cognitive, and sociocultural. Chapter 1, "What Is Psychology?" describes each of these approaches in more detail. What is important is that you recognize that these perspectives foster multiple explanations for behavior, a hallmark of psychological thinking.

Psychologists organize the knowledge in their discipline in specialized fields of psychology. This book is no exception. We will explore the major subfields of psychology in separate chapters, citing relevant research studies and human stories as we discuss psychological concepts and principles.

Psychological researchers specialize in selected fields and contribute to the knowledge in that field through creative research designs. In addition to books and popular articles, psychologists publish in professional journals for their specialized interest areas. The "literature" of psychology is organized and accessible through an indexing system published as *Psychological Abstracts*, which can assist you in tracking down information relevant to specific questions you have about behavior. The index in *Psychological Abstracts* is organized according to psychological concepts.

Critical Thinking Skills

What exactly is critical thinking? Experts differ on a precise definition; however, critical thinking generally involves such abilities as *asking questions, making accurate inferences, creating and defending arguments, evaluating validity, solving problems,*

TABLE P.1

Critical Thinking Skills in Psychology

Make accurate observations, descriptions, and inferences about behavior

Pursue alternative explanations to explain behavior comprehensively

Demonstrate appreciation for individual differences

Develop psychological arguments using evidence

Evaluate the validity of conclusions about behavior

Demonstrate awareness of underlying values that motivate behavior

Actively take the perspective of others in solving problems

Practice standards of ethical treatment toward individuals and groups

Apply psychological concepts and skills to enhance personal adaptation

Use psychological knowledge to promote human welfare

and *making value judgments.* All of us show various forms of critical thinking on a regular basis. However, when we begin to learn new disciplines, we have an opportunity to refine the critical thinking skills that the discipline emphasizes.

Psychologists think critically in order to observe, describe, explain, and predict behavior more effectively. They use critical thinking in a variety of ways in professional settings. Clinical psychologists analyze complex human stories and develop strategies for influencing new behaviors that may provide relief. Applied psychologists use psychological principles in a variety of other contexts in which knowledge of behavior is crucial. Research psychologists study the literature of psychology and design additional research to uncover more knowledge about systematic patterns of behavior. They may challenge existing results and create new theories to explain behavior. Psychologists who are teachers think critically about how to help their students learn the concepts and skills in the discipline.

How should your critical-thinking skills change as a result of your completing your first course in psychology? In addition to building a strong knowledge base comprised of psychological concepts, principles, and perspectives, you should be able to develop more effective critical thinking skills in the ten areas that characterize psychology, described in table P.1.

You will find that this text takes seriously the obligation to improve your critical thinking skills. Throughout the text, you will encounter many opportunities to enhance your ability to think like a psychologist and to improve your grasp of the concepts and principles you are learning.

Attitudes

Critical thinking in psychology goes beyond specific cognitive skills used to understand behavior. It also entails certain attitudes and motivations that characterize psychological ways of thinking.

For example, psychologists enjoy analyzing behavior. They are curious about what makes people tick. They like to think about what motivates people to act or refrain from acting. As a result of your studies in your first course in psychology, you may discover that you will be more routinely observant and have more questions about the behavior of others. (Your friends might also feel pestered by the questions that you generate!)

Psychologists believe that it is easy to fall into the trap of thinking that there is only one answer to a problem or one side to an issue. For example, when you witness your niece laughing in a manner that reminds you of your sister, you may be inclined to think of the laugh as "inherited." Your interpretation favors "nature," the contribution made from genes. However, it is quite likely that your sister has raised your niece, exposing your niece to her distinctive laugh all her life. The effect of the environment on behavior is referred to as the "nurture" side of the argument. How do we know which is the more powerful influence? We won't. Both influences are involved, and we would be hard pressed to determine which has greater impact. The *nature-nurture controversy* is complex, and we will revisit it throughout the text. However, it effectively illustrates the tendency we may have to produce simplistic explanations that don't completely account for complex problems.

According to psychologists, most behaviors are complex occurrences and simple explanations rarely account for them fully. For example, a friend might tell you, "My marriage didn't work because he couldn't let go of his mother." The husband's inability to relinquish his strong attachment to his mother may have been one cause of the divorce, but there were probably others as well—perhaps economic problems, religious differences, sexual difficulties, personality conflicts, and so on. One of psychology's great lessons is that behavior is multiply determined.

Most psychologists maintain a skeptical or disbelieving stance about simplistic behavioral claims. Psychologists seek to sort fact from fantasy by critically questioning the nature of mind and behavior. They prefer to rely on objective or research-based evidence to support behavioral claims rather than subjective accounts or personal testimony. They often seek multiple points of view in order to comprehend complex behavior. They actively pursue alternate explanations as a way of expanding the factors that might be implicated.

We might not discover some answers to behavioral questions until some time in the distant future. Psychologists refer to this acceptance of unresolved questions as *tolerance of ambiguity*. Psychologists not only expect and tolerate ambiguity, but enjoy the challenge of it.

Psychologists also try hard to avoid being judgmental. Because we can't be completely confident of identifying all of the causes of behavior, psychologists believe that there is value in slowing down and being extremely careful when forming conclusions, especially when determining blame. We routinely won't have all the information we need to be 100 percent confident in our conclusions. Therefore, the judgments we pose are *tentative* rather than definite. Psychologists often begin their answers to queries about behavior with the phrase *It depends on* as a reflection of these qualities. This response can be frustrating, until you recognize that this tentative approach is a hallmark of psychological ways of thinking.

Despite the nonjudgmental attitude, psychologists are unwilling to accept information at face value. They challenge the positions of others, whether to seek clarification, to suggest improvements, to identify inadequacies in stated positions, or propose alternatives. Psychology is a changing discipline; in the 1990s, psychologists continue to contribute new ideas, concepts, and theories about mind and behavior. It is through such critical thinking that psychology continues to advance as a science.

IMPROVING YOUR STUDY SKILLS

Let's examine a story that may be particularly relevant to you as you embark on your study of psychology and apply psychological ways of thinking in order to solve the problem posed in the story.

> A student named Tom came to his professor's office about 2 weeks before the final exam in an introductory psychology course. He had a *D* average in the course and wanted to know what was causing him to get such a low grade. It turned out that he wasn't doing well in any of his classes. What questions would you ask to discover the causes of his poor performance?

Several *hypotheses* may come to mind. Each question below highlights a possible *variable* that influences Tom's academic performance:

- Is Tom doing his reading? (preparation)
- Is he getting enough sleep? (fatigue)
- Does he like the professor? (emotion)

The following sections address several possibilities for improving your study skills. This may be your very first exposure to the scientific study of behavior called psychology. You may feel some anxiety about performing well in the course. On the other hand, you may have had the opportunity to study psychology before in another context so you have greater confidence about what lies ahead. The critical thinking exercise gives you an opportunity for you to identify your academic strengths as well as areas in which you can improve.

What's the Best Way to Manage My Time?

Did you guess Tom managed his time poorly? You would be right. Eventually the conversation between Tom and his professor turned to his study techniques and what he could do to get better grades on his final exams.

The professor asked Tom to put together a study schedule for the four final exams he was getting ready to take

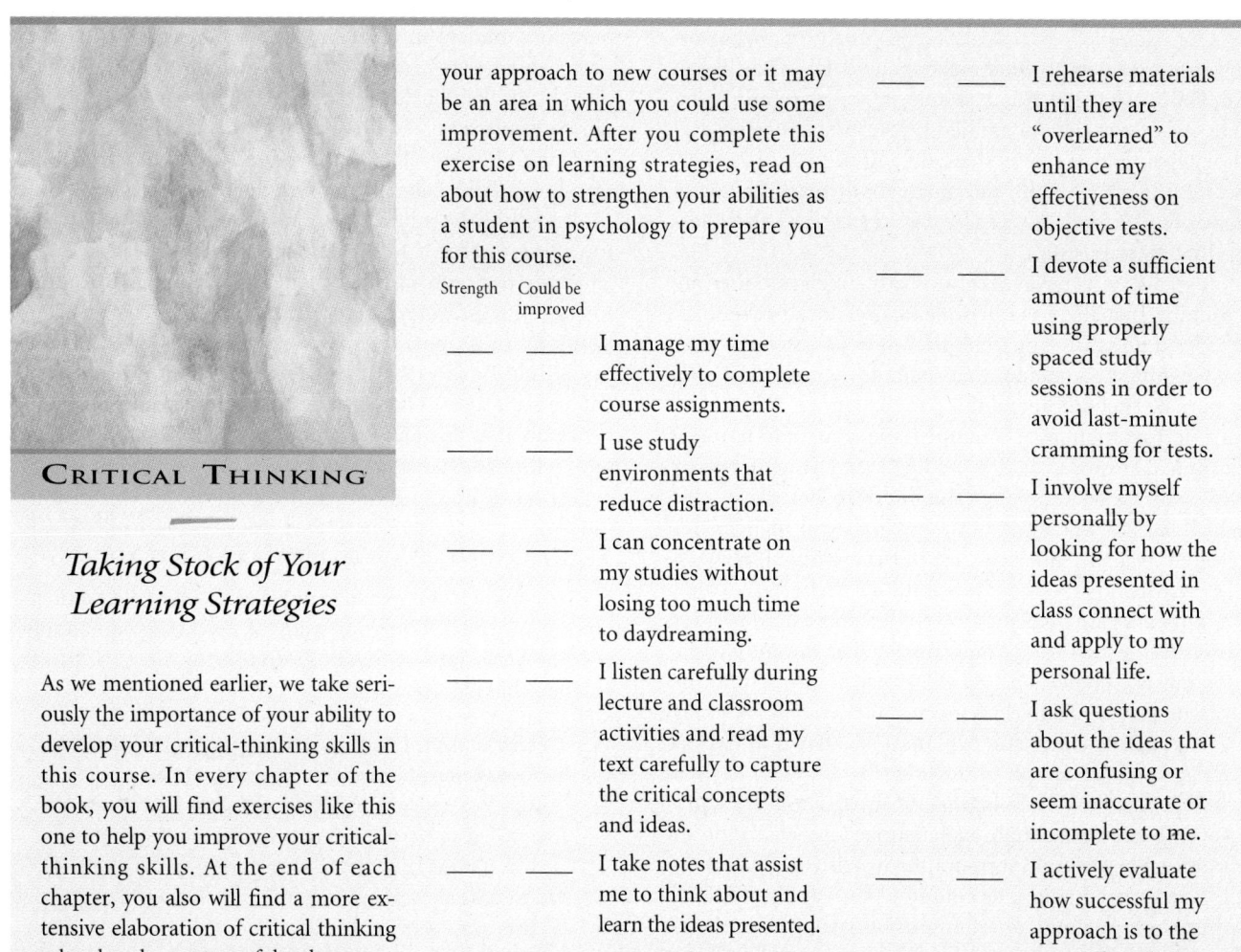

Taking Stock of Your Learning Strategies

As we mentioned earlier, we take seriously the importance of your ability to develop your critical-thinking skills in this course. In every chapter of the book, you will find exercises like this one to help you improve your critical-thinking skills. At the end of each chapter, you also will find a more extensive elaboration of critical thinking related to the content of the chapter.

In this first critical thinking exercise, review the elements of effective learning and, for each of them, indicate whether you think it is an area of strength you already demonstrate in your approach to new courses or it may be an area in which you could use some improvement. After you complete this exercise on learning strategies, read on about how to strengthen your abilities as a student in psychology to prepare you for this course.

Strength   Could be improved

_____ _____ I manage my time effectively to complete course assignments.

_____ _____ I use study environments that reduce distraction.

_____ _____ I can concentrate on my studies without losing too much time to daydreaming.

_____ _____ I listen carefully during lecture and classroom activities and read my text carefully to capture the critical concepts and ideas.

_____ _____ I take notes that assist me to think about and learn the ideas presented.

_____ _____ I organize and reorganize ideas to help me grasp main points and key concepts rather than memorize everything I read or hear.

_____ _____ I rehearse materials until they are "overlearned" to enhance my effectiveness on objective tests.

_____ _____ I devote a sufficient amount of time using properly spaced study sessions in order to avoid last-minute cramming for tests.

_____ _____ I involve myself personally by looking for how the ideas presented in class connect with and apply to my personal life.

_____ _____ I ask questions about the ideas that are confusing or seem inaccurate or incomplete to me.

_____ _____ I actively evaluate how successful my approach is to the course, based on feedback from my instructor, and make corrections to improve my effectiveness.

in 2 weeks. He planned to study a total of 4 hours for his psychology exam; he scheduled only 1 of those hours for the night before the exam and allotted no study time to the morning before the exam (the exam was in the late afternoon).

The professor assured Tom that although the psychology exam probably was not the most difficult one he would ever take in college, learning the material would require more than 4 hours of study time if he wanted to improve his grade for the course. Tom wasn't just bad at managing time—he was terrible! True, he had a part-time job in addition to the credit hours he was taking, but as he mapped out how he used his time during the day, Tom quickly became aware that he was wasting big chunks of it.

One week is 168 hours. Students vary in how they invest those hours. A typical full-time college student sleeps 50 hours, attends class between 12 and 20 hours, and eats 11 hours in every week. Students divide the remaining hours between study, work and family obligations, and leisure pursuits.

Tom attends class for 19 hours. In his situation, we must also allot 15 hours a week for his part-time job and 6 hours a week for transportation to and from school, work, and home. Tom finds that his main activities account for 101 hours of the week. Even though he works, he still has 67 hours in which to strike a balance between study and his other commitments.

The degree of success that you experience depends on how much time you allocate to study as well as how efficiently you use that time. One rule of thumb that you may find helpful is to spend 1 hour outside of class for every hour in class. Although this strategy doesn't guarantee success, it definitely serves as an improvement over Tom's approach to study. If you have fewer competing obligations, you may find a 2:1 ratio of study hours to classroom hours will be even more powerful in enhancing your success as a student.

You may find it helpful to fill out a weekly schedule of your activities to see where your time goes. Figure P.1 provides

Time Start	End	Time used	Activity-Description
7:45	8:15	:30	Dress
8:15	8:40	:25	Breakfast
8:40	9:00	:20	Nothing
9:00	10:00	1:00	Psychology-Lecture
10:00	10:40	:40	Coffee-Talking
10:40	11:00	:20	Nothing
11:00	12:00	1:00	Economics-Lecture
12:00	12:45	:45	Lunch
12:45	2:00	1:15	Reading-Magazine
2:00	4:00	2:00	Biology-Lab
4:00	5:30	1:30	Recreation-Volleyball
5:30	6:00	:30	Nothing
6:00	7:00	1:00	Dinner
7:00	8:00	1:00	Nap
8:00	8:50	:50	Study-Statistics
8:50	9:20	:30	Break
9:20	10:00	:40	Study-Statistics
10:00	10:50	:50	Rap session
10:50	11:30	:40	Study-Accounting
11:30	11:45	:15	Ready for bed
11:45	7:45	8:00	Sleep

Annotations (right side):

- Paste on mirror 3 × 5 cards. Laws of economics; psychological terms; statistical formulas–study while brushing teeth, etc.

- Look over textbook assignment and previous lecture notes to establish continuity for today's psychology lecture.

- Break too long and too soon after breakfast. Should work on psychology notes just taken; also should look over economics assignment.

- Should re-work the lecture notes on economics while still fresh in mind. Also, look over biology assignment to recall the objective of the coming lab.

- Use this time for reading a magazine or newspaper.

- Not a good idea. Better finish work, then get a good night's sleep.

- Break—too long.

- Good as a reward if basic work is done.

- Insufficient time allotted, but better than no time.

- While brushing teeth, study the 3 × 5 cards. Replace cards that have been mastered with new ones.

FIGURE P.1

Record of One Day's Activities and Suggestions for Better Time Management

an example of one student's daily time schedule, along with comments about how and where time could be used more effectively, based on the ideas presented in this chapter. Examine this schedule and then construct your own model in figure P.2. Where are there opportunities to reshape how you use your time more effectively? Researchers have found that most effective study often involves shorter, well-spaced study sessions than one intensive period of study. Where can you schedule shorter periods of study into your busy life?

Some students object to the use of a study schedule. They are afraid that a schedule will make them too rigid; however, more successful students usually follow organized schedules in order to manage their time efficiently. One compelling advantage in scheduling your time is the enhanced sense of control you will feel over your life; if you waste less time, you will have much more free time for personal activities and will spend fewer hours feeling guilty or unproductive.

How can you learn to live with a schedule? Try taking 5 minutes every morning to chart your plan for the day. Before you go to bed at night, review your day to see how well you met your schedule. Try to make this review a regular part of your routine. Your review will help you pinpoint problems that need to be solved or changes that must be made in your schedule to ensure your success. With a few weeks of practice, you should notice that this review becomes a more natural part of your daily routine.

What happens if you blow it? Like any new healthy habit, effective time management takes some time to learn. Don't let a minor deviation from the plan derail your good intentions to improve your study skills. Don't be too harsh in your evaluation. Recommit yourself to better time management tomorrow. As each week goes by, you may notice less strain in managing your time effectively.

What's the Most Effective Study Environment?

There are many distractions that keep you from studying or remembering what you have studied. Select your place of study carefully, paying close attention to the features of the environment that will allow you to do your best work.

Some students find that they work best if they consistently study in the same place. Ideally, this area should be well lighted without glare and should be a comfortable temperature.

Most individuals find that a quiet environment is more conducive to effective concentration than a noisy environment. Noise is one of the main distractions to effective

| Time | | Time | |
Start	End	used	Activity-Description

FIGURE P.2

Constructing Your Own Time Management Schedule
Make up a time management schedule for one day in your life. If
you need more lines, transfer the schedule to another sheet of
paper and add them. After creating the schedule, reflect on what
you learned about how efficient you are in organizing your time.

study. It is usually a good idea to turn off the stereo, radio,
or television while you are studying, to minimize distraction. However, your options about where you study may be
limited. If your situation involves interruption and noise,
you may find soft music and earphones will mask many of
these distractions. When you read chapter 14, "Health,
Stress, and Coping," you may find other ideas that will help
you in selecting a stress-reduced environment that will promote your best efficiency and productivity.

The library may be just the right place to maximize
your ability to concentrate. Go there to study, especially if
there are people where you live who are likely to distract
you. If you live on campus, you may want to explore other
quiet areas that you can adopt for your study purposes. For
example, some residence halls maintain quiet rooms that
will promote a nondistracting environment. However,
don't rule out other, less obvious possibilities. Some students report success in studying while riding on public
transportation and find this practice a reliable one to increase their study time, especially if long rides are required.

Some individuals need a private, personal study area
to maximize their efficiency. This area often includes your
own desk—a specific place for pens, paper, and books. If
you plan to organize your studies around your desk, you
may find it helpful to use your desk *only* for studying. If you
nap or daydream extensively at your desk, it can act as a cue
for more napping and daydreaming. Use your desk as a cue
for studying. When you choose to nap or spend some time
daydreaming, go somewhere else.

How Can I Improve My Ability to Concentrate?

So far we have talked about the physical aspects of the environment that may help or hinder your ability to concentrate
on what you are studying. Psychological and personal situations can also interfere with your ability to concentrate.

Daydreaming is a natural occurrence that takes you
away from the task at hand. As you will read in chapter 5
"States of Consciousness," some amount of daydreaming
may be inevitable in any period set aside for work. However,
daydreaming can sometimes get out of hand. Even though
daydreaming can be pleasant and restful, the consequences
of extensive daydreaming can be poor test or course grades.

How can you reduce the amount of time you spend
daydreaming? Analyze the trends in your daydreaming. Are
you trying to solve some problem? Or are you spending
time thinking about something over which you have virtually no control? Promise yourself that you will pursue specific problems more intently after your study period is over.

When daydreaming problems are serious, some students have found a mild punishment technique to be helpful. Wear a rubber band around your wrist. When you
recognize that you are off-task, snap the rubber band and
refocus your attention on the task at hand. Then congratu-
late yourself at the end of a successful study period for your
improved self-discipline.

If the problems that prompt you to daydream seem
overwhelming and you simply cannot avoid thinking about
them, you may want to contact the student counseling service at your college or university. Most college and university counseling centers not only have counselors who help
students with personal problems, but they often have study
skills counselors who help students personalize more successful approaches to their studies.

How Can I Improve My Ability to Understand and Remember Key Ideas from Classroom Activities or Text Reading?

Unfortunately, much of the knowledge offered in the
course of your education passes through your mind like
grains of sand washed through a sieve. In other words, it
goes in one ear and out the other. You need to do more
than just memorize or passively absorb new information.
You must read and listen carefully. You need to take notes
that serve you well outside the class.

Reading Carefully

Your instructor has selected a textbook that will compliment her or his approach to teaching psychology. Many students approach the challenge of reading the text as just so many pages to plow through. There is a difference between *reading to read* (to complete the required number of pages) and *reading to learn*. Reading to learn from a text is enhanced if you approach the text as a conversation the author is having with you about the concepts and principles in psychology. As in any effective conversation, you must pay attention, figure out how the parts of the conversation fit together, and make some judgments as you go about acquiring other information you need in order to understand the author's intent.

There is a specific study technique for improving comprehension of text materials that is in the spirit of this approach. This technique, called the SQ3R method, was developed by Frances Robinson more than 40 years ago. *S* stands for Survey, *Q* stands for Question, and *3R* stands for Read, Recite, and Review. We organized this text based on the SQ3R technique.

To *survey*, glance over the headings in each chapter to find the main points that will be developed. This text provides an outline at the beginning of each chapter that will help you anticipate what will follow. This structure will also help you organize the ideas as you read them.

To *question*, anticipate what major questions drive the construction of passages in the text. What major question does each section attempt to answer? What specific questions does each paragraph address? As you find information that answers your questions, you may find it helpful to underline or highlight it. Now put these principles into practice by anticipating what question the next paragraph will attempt to address and write it out in the margin. Are you right?

To accomplish the third step in the SQ3R method, you begin *reading* the book as you normally would. In the SQ3R method, though, your reading should be more efficient because you have already built a foundation for understanding the material by surveying and questioning.

The fourth step in the SQ3R method involves *reciting* information periodically as you go through a chapter. To help you use this strategy, reviews appear several times per chapter; they encourage you to recite what you have read in particular parts of the chapter. In many chapters, you will want to do this more than two or three times. We have included critical thinking challenges in the text to help you stop and think about what you have read.

After you have used the techniques suggested so far, you need to *review* the material you have read at least several times before you take a test. Just because you have read a chapter, do not think that you will be able to recall all of its information. By reciting the information, thinking critically about the key ideas, and continuing to review the material, you will improve your test performance. At the end of each chapter in this book, we will encourage you to go back and once again read the in-chapter reviews to obtain an overall summary of the chapter.

Listening Carefully

What goes on in the classroom is just as important as what is in this textbook. Listening to lecture or attending to other kinds of class activities can also be regarded as a conversation in which you are an active participant, if you are going to reap maximum benefits for your learning.

In preparing for a lecture, motivate yourself by telling yourself that it is important for you to stay alert and listen carefully. Make sure that you get sufficient rest and have eaten recently enough that your body won't distract you from listening. A regular exercise program can also heighten your alertness.

One approach to improve your involvement with the lecture is to listen with the intention of making connections between what you already know and what you are listening to in the lecture. As you listen to lecture or class discussion, actively process the ideas being presented. To assist you in developing this ability, the following questions may help:

- *Did I understand this portion?*
- *What's the main point?*
- *Does this remind me of anything in my own personal experience?*
- *Does this content relate to other ideas I've learned in this or other courses?*
- *Do the points seem accurate and valid, or is something missing?*
- *Do I like or agree with the ideas proposed?*

Initially, this approach may feel cumbersome; however, this deeper level of processing will help you build a more enduring content base for future testing and future life applications. It may even be time-saving; it makes more sense to read intensively than continually reread the same material with limited retention. This approach will also prepare you effectively to participate in any class discussions.

What about attendance? Instructors vary in the importance they place on your regular attendance; however, the vast majority are likely to treat each and every class hour as an important learning experience they have carefully planned to assist your learning. You would not skip a chapter in this book if you knew that you were responsible for the chapter on a later test, so it is not a good idea to skip a class just to reach the allowed number of cuts or to cram for an exam. Some students believe that, because they go to class and listen passively, they can get by in test situations without devoting further study time. However, by preparing for the lecture, using learning strategies actively during the lecture, and doing simple follow-up work on what you have heard, you should be able to improve your performance in the course.

Taking Effective Notes

Note taking can serve as an effective method to focus your attention. Some students approach taking notes as a stenographer might. They try to record every word without evaluating its significance or importance. They assume that the material will make more sense to them later if they have as much as possible of the material verbatim. This approach does work for a few students; however, most feel frustrated later when they review the massive quantity of information that they have recorded, because it might not make sense and will feel overwhelming.

Instead, you may wish to experiment with note-taking forms to see which serves you best. Some students find that recording notes in a simple narrative paragraph serves very well to capture key ideas and stimulate further questions. Others may find that mapping or outlining helps to organize the content and clarify how each point relates to others in the lecture. Striving to capture general ideas rather than minute details tends to be more effective.

There is no one right way to take notes. You need to develop a system that feels comfortable for you. For example, you can leave a wide margin to make your own notes or ask questions that you wish to follow up on later. You can skip lines to show the end of one idea and the beginning of another. Use abbreviations to save time so you can listen more. Draw pictures if they help you personalize what you hear. Regardless of the specific features that you incorporate into your own note-taking style, write legibly so that, when you review, you will know what you have written.

In addition, some students rewrite and reorganize their notes as a method of rehearsing main ideas. You may want to consolidate your notes during your first free time after class by underlining the key ideas. Reviewing these highlights before the next class period will improve your ability to recall the information. You will also prepare yourself effectively for what will be said in the coming class or questions that the instructor may pose.

How Should I Prepare for Testing Situations?

In most cases, your grade in this course will depend on how well you do on the exams spaced periodically throughout the semester. Well-constructed tests can serve as very accurate representations of the quality of your learning, although even well-constructed examinations won't be able to reflect everything that you have learned.

Students tend to have mixed feelings about tests. Tests can be time-consuming, nerve-wracking, and "tricky"; however, doing well on a test for which you have prepared well provides a special thrill. To enhance your course performance, we will address several areas.

Identifying the Test Format

You need to find out what kind of testing you will be confronting. Will the challenge be an objective test comprised of multiple choice questions? How many questions? What kind of format? Usually such tests emphasize term recognition and information recall. Therefore, preparation for such tests relies most heavily on memorization.

On the other hand, some instructors will evaluate your knowledge using *productive* measures, such as essay tests. In this kind of challenge, the teacher may emphasize *higher-order* thinking skills. Teachers may ask you to construct or defend an argument, to make comparisons between two approaches, to find flaws in an experiment, or to identify underlying values in a theoretical position. These tasks are appropriate critical thinking challenges for those just learning the discipline.

Preparing the Content

Regardless of the examination format, your grade in this course will depend on how well you perform in testing situations. You should complete all of your textbook reading several days before an examination. All of your classroom notes should be in order so you can review them easily. You should complete and hand in all term papers or projects so that you are free to concentrate on organizing and consolidating the information in the manner that fits the testing format.

If you have been following an effective routine for managing your time, taking notes, keeping up, and building in opportunities to recite and review what you have learned, you should be well positioned to consolidate what you have learned for the examination. You may want to develop a summary system, which would follow closely what you did for each chapter or lecture. Several days before the exam, you probably will have to review several chapters and a number of lectures. Try putting them together in an overall system the last day or so before the exam.

Some students find it helpful to develop their own multiple-choice questions for practice. This experience may help you think about the content as your professor might.

Should you cram for an exam? If you have not studied much until several days before the exam, you will probably have to do some intensive studying prior to the test. However, be aware that cramming can never replace methodical, consistent study throughout the course. Studying in shorter sessions that are distributed over time will produce superior results compared to cramming.

Practicing the Test Skills

Memorizing new ideas is a foundation skill in this and other courses you will be taking. How can you remember course terms and principles more effectively?

First, make up your mind to remember. If you really want to improve your memory, you can; but you must motivate yourself to improve. Second, keep refreshing your memory of the content you are trying to learn. Almost everything tends to fade unless you periodically think about it. Periodic rehearsal of what you have heard in class or read in this book will help you store the information and retrieve it not just for testing situations but for other practical purposes as well. Third, organize, outline, or otherwise structure what you want to remember. Pick out the main points in the material you are studying and arrange them in a meaningful pattern, outline, or image. Recite and repeat them until you can recall them on command. Select, organize, and repeat—these are time-tested steps for helping you remember.

You can adopt a number of strategies for improving your memory in learning psychology. One powerful approach is to relate what you have read to your own life. By drawing more connections to unfamiliar material, you make the ideas more accessible and more interesting. Chapter 7, "Memory," will address several other approaches to improving memory. If this approach intrigues you, you may want to skip ahead to that chapter and read how these techniques can help you organize and recall psychological concepts.

If you will be confronting testing situations that require more than memorization, you need ot/her preparation strategies. If your teacher asks you to write essay questions, you may want to ask the instructor for sample questions. Ask what kinds of thinking will be required. Try to anticipate what kinds of questions could be crafted by the instructor to fit the material. If you practice thinking about these potential questions, you aren't likely to be surprised by the particular combinations of ideas that your instructor may develop. In addition, you may find it helpful to write out some questions for practice to increase your rehearsal time and build your confidence.

Preparing Yourself

To ensure success on an exam, you need to be physically and psychologically ready in addition to having facts, ideas, and principles in mind. First, you need to be rested; second, you need to feel confident. If you create mountains of work for yourself, especially by not studying until the last minute, you will rob yourself of sleep, food, and exercise, leaving both your mind and your body in poor shape to perform well on an exam. In addition, if you find that anxiety significantly interferes with your performance, you may want to seek assistance from the student counseling center to develop strategies to minimize this interference. On the other hand, if you have managed more systematic approaches to your studies, you will be less likely to panic and will be more likely to develop a confident attitude about the test.

Learning from the Test

Some students believe that when the test is over, the learning is over. However, reviewing the test results and listening to instructor feedback will help you develop your study skills in several ways. First, you can determine which strategies were truly helpful in organizing the better features of your test performance. Second, you have the opportunity to revise incorrect ideas for future testing challenges or other practical uses. Finally, your review will also suggest other approaches you might take to increase the quality of your future performance. These alternatives may include seeking additional tutoring, asking for a conference with the instructor to seek further feedback, or developing a study group with your peers in the class.

SUMMING UP

Through planning, study, and review, you will be able to learn psychology efficiently and effectively. We will encourage you to use your critical-thinking skills as you read your text and study, as you participate in class, and as you go about your everyday activities. Critical thinking is crucially involved in academic study and life outside the classroom. By increasing your knowledge in psychology, you will not only build an impressive knowledge base but improve the skills that will help you observe, describe, explain, and predict behavior.

OVERVIEW

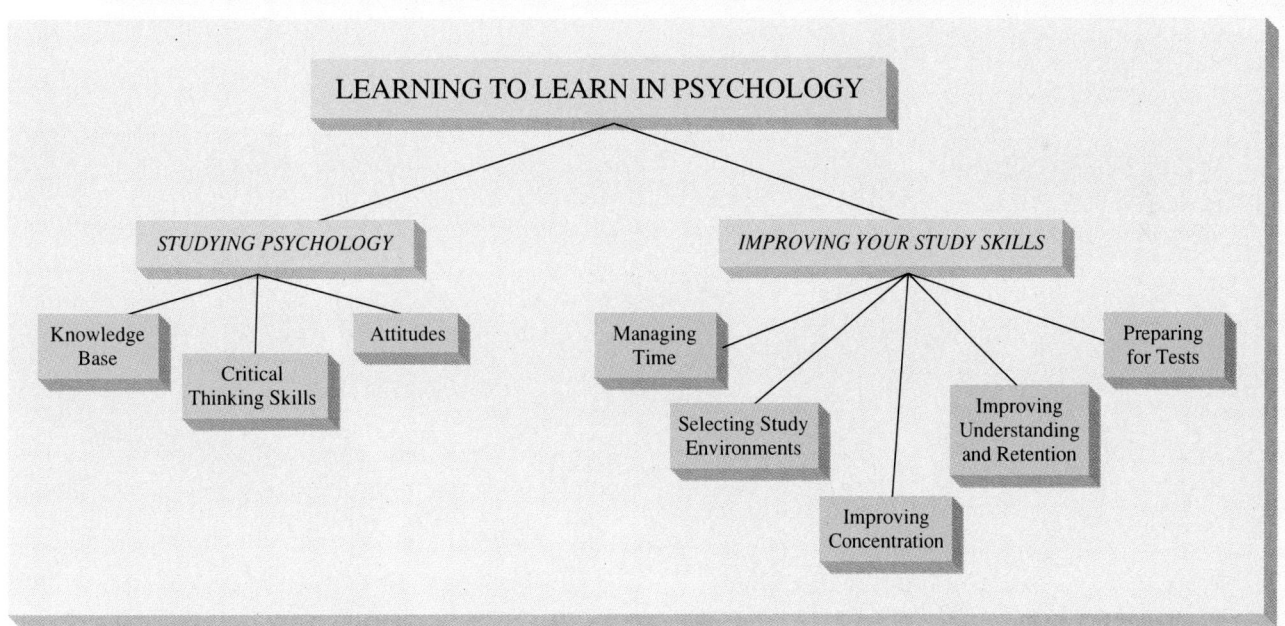

In this prechapter, "Learning to Learn in Psychology," you initially read about studying psychology, with an emphasis on three things: acquiring a specialized knowledge base about psychology, learning to think critically about behavior, and developing attitudes and motivations consistent with the science of psychology. Then you read about ways to improve your study skills, which included managing time, selecting study environments, improving concentration, improving understanding and retention, and preparing for tests.

PROLOGUE

The Flowers of a Garden

Consider the flowers of a garden: though differing in kind, colour, form and shape, yet, inasmuch as they are refreshed by the waters of one spring, revived by the breath of one wind, invigorated by the rays of one sun, this diversity increaseth their charm, and addeth unto their beauty. . . . How unpleasing to the eye if all the flowers and plants, the leaves and blossoms, the fruits, the branches and the trees of that garden were all of the same shape and colour! Diversity of hues, form and shape, enricheth and adorneth the garden, and heighteneth the effect thereof.

'Abdu'l-Bahá

Psychology as Science and Story

> *My friend . . . care for your psyche, and . . .*
> *make it as good as possible . . .*
> *Know thyself,*
> *for once we know ourselves,*
> *we may learn how to care for ourselves,*
> *but otherwise we never shall.*
>
> **Socrates**

For centuries, human beings have been curious about who they are and what they are all about. As we approach the twenty-first century, our curiosity about mind and behavior has, if anything, intensified. This book is about the questions and the answers, the knowns and the unknowns, of human behavior. In this first section, you will read two chapters. Chapter 1, "What Is Psychology?," introduces you to the field of psychology, systematically examined and explained in science and expressed in human stories and quotations. Chapter 2, "Research and Reasoning," informs you about the strategies used in designing research in psychology and lets you see how research principles promote better reasoning about everyday problems related to psychology.

MICHIO TAKAYAMA
Inner Peace, detail

What Is Psychology?

CHAPTER OUTLINE

CHAPTER BOXES

> Some things are very important
> and some are very unimportant. To
> know the difference is what
> we are given life to find out.
>
> **Anna F. Trevisan**

THE STORY OF ALICE WALKER: DISADVANTAGE AND TRIUMPH

In the summer of 1966, Alice Walker, who would later win a Pulitzer Prize for *The Color Purple,* spent her days battling racism in Mississippi. She had recently won her first writing fellowship and could have chosen to follow her dream of moving to Senegal, Africa, but instead she put herself in the heart and heat of the civil rights movement. Walker grew up knowing the brutal effects of poverty and racism. Born in 1944, she was the eighth child of Georgia sharecroppers who earned about $300 a year. When she was 8, her brother accidentally shot her in the left eye with a BB gun. By the time her parents got her to the hospital a week later (they had no car), she was blind in that eye and it had developed a disfiguring layer of scar tissue. Despite the counts against her, Walker has become an essayist, poet, award-winning novelist, short-story writer, and social activist, who, like her characters (especially the women), has overcome pain and anger to celebrate the human spirit. As Walker puts it, she writes about people who "make it, who come out of nothing. People who triumph."

Alice Walker won the Pulitzer Prize for her book *The Color Purple.* Like the characters in her book (especially the women), Walker overcame pain and anger to triumph and celebrate the human spirit.

PREVIEW

What leads a person like Alice Walker to turn poverty and trauma into a rich harvest of adjustment and achievement? How can we explain why one person can pick up the pieces of a life shattered by tragedy, such as a loved one's death, while another seems to come unhinged by life's minor hassles? Why is it that some people are real whirlwinds—successful at work, maintaining good relationships with their friends and family, and active participants in community organizations—while others hang out on the sidelines, mere spectators in life? Understanding such individual differences is an important goal of psychology. In this first chapter, we will introduce and define psychology, explore psychology's history and contemporary perspectives, and evaluate how psychology is practiced.

INTRODUCING PSYCHOLOGY

If you have ever wondered what makes people tick, you have asked yourself psychology's central question. In this book, you will explore the fascinating terrain of personality, motivation, the inner workings of the brain, and much, much more. You will learn about the methods psychologists use to explain human nature, as well as the progress psychology has made. In addition, you will see how cultural and ethnic background, gender, sexual orientation, economic circumstances, and other factors influence what people think and how they behave. However, psychology is still a young science and these are very complex issues; psychologists do not have all the answers.

Even so, psychology is uniquely qualified to help us make sense of our increasingly complex and challenging world. It isn't just your imagination; the world is getting tougher and tougher to keep up with. For example, one day's edition of the *New York Times* is packed with more information than a person who lived in the Middle Ages acquired during a lifetime, and gone are the days when the United States was an undisputed industrial giant. As the need to both import and export goods increases, so does global interdependence and the need to understand other cultures in order to develop good international relationships. We also live in a nation where the workforce is increasingly diverse. By the year 2000, for example, over 80 percent of the people entering the job market will be women and members of ethnic minority groups.

PEANUTS reprinted by permission of UFS, Inc.

These shifts raise questions that are extremely important to the future of our society. Psychology can help us reduce conflict and meet the challenges that lie ahead by seeking answers to such questions as these: What social distance is appropriate between American and Latin American business colleagues? Why do the Japanese have one of the lowest homicide rates in the world, despite the fact that their metropolitan areas are among the most crowded? Is intelligence understood in the same way in developing countries as it is in ours? Are women absent from work more often than men are because they are less committed to their jobs, or is it their child-care responsibilities that produce the gender difference in absentee rates? Why does the United States have one of the highest teen pregnancy rates among the industrialized nations? As you can see, theories of behavior need to reflect the experience of all people, both within and across national boundaries.

Not only can psychology help us grapple with some of the largest issues we face, but it can also help guide us in our daily lives. For example, consider these findings, which have important implications:

- Stressful events place individuals at risk for psychological and physical problems. For example, both divorced and unhappily married people are more vulnerable to disease than are happily married people (Kiecolt-Glaser & others, 1993).
- Women are making strides in many areas relative to men, but researchers continue to find that men outperform women in some tests of math skill, including the Scholastic Aptitude Test (SAT) (Hyde & Plant, 1995).
- Moderate aerobic exercise not only improves most people's physical health but also improves their self-concept and reduces their anxiety (Moses & others, 1989).

Psychology is not a cure-all for every knotty problem, and it doesn't tell us the meaning of life. It does, however, contribute enormously to our knowledge about why people are the way they are, why they think and act the way they do, and how they can cope more effectively with their lives. Psychologists are enthusiastic about psychology's potential to improve our lives as we approach the twenty-first century. This is an exciting time of discovery in the field of psychology.

DEFINING PSYCHOLOGY

Which finding would you predict to be true?
Finding 1: Couples who live together before marriage have a better chance of making the marriage last.
Finding 2: Couples who do not live together before marriage tend to have a lower divorce rate.

Even though the commonsense notion that "practice makes perfect" suggests that the first finding is the more likely, researchers have found a higher marriage success rate for couples who legally marry initially rather than live together before marriage (Teachman & Polonko, 1990). As you can see, psychology doesn't accept assumptions about human nature at face value, however reasonable they sound. It is a rigorous discipline that tests assumptions and gathers evidence to support explanations of behavior.

Psychology *is the scientific study of behavior and mental processes in contexts.* Psychology emphasizes observing, describing, explaining, and predicting behavior. There are four aspects of this definition that need elaboration: behavior, mental processes, science, and contexts. Let's examine behavior first.

Behavior *is everything we do that can be directly observed*—such as two people *kissing,* a baby *crying,* a student *studying.* Psychologists strive to distinguish behavior from inferences we draw about behavior. Behaviors are usually described using verb forms that communicate observable actions. In contrast, **inferences** *are conclusions that we draw from observing behavior.*

Mental processes are trickier to define and describe than behavior is. They *encompass thoughts, feelings, and motives that each of us experiences privately but that cannot be observed directly.* Although we cannot directly observe and describe thoughts and feelings, they are no less real because of that. For example, mental processes include *thoughts* about kissing someone, *feelings* a baby experiences when its mother leaves the room, and *memories* a college student has about a fine afternoon on a motorcycle.

Because we can't observe these processes directly in others, we often *infer* the mental processes that support observable behavior. For example, what would you infer Alice Walker might have felt when she won the Pulitzer

Describe the behaviors you see in these photographs. What verbs accurately describe them? What kinds of inferences can we draw about the meanings of these behaviors? Did you observe the behaviors closely by taking into account the contexts in which they are occurring?

This example illustrates the fact that interpreting behavior involves three steps: (1) *making accurate observations,* (2) *describing the behavior,* and (3) *drawing inferences about the behavior that reflect the contexts in which the behavior occurs.*

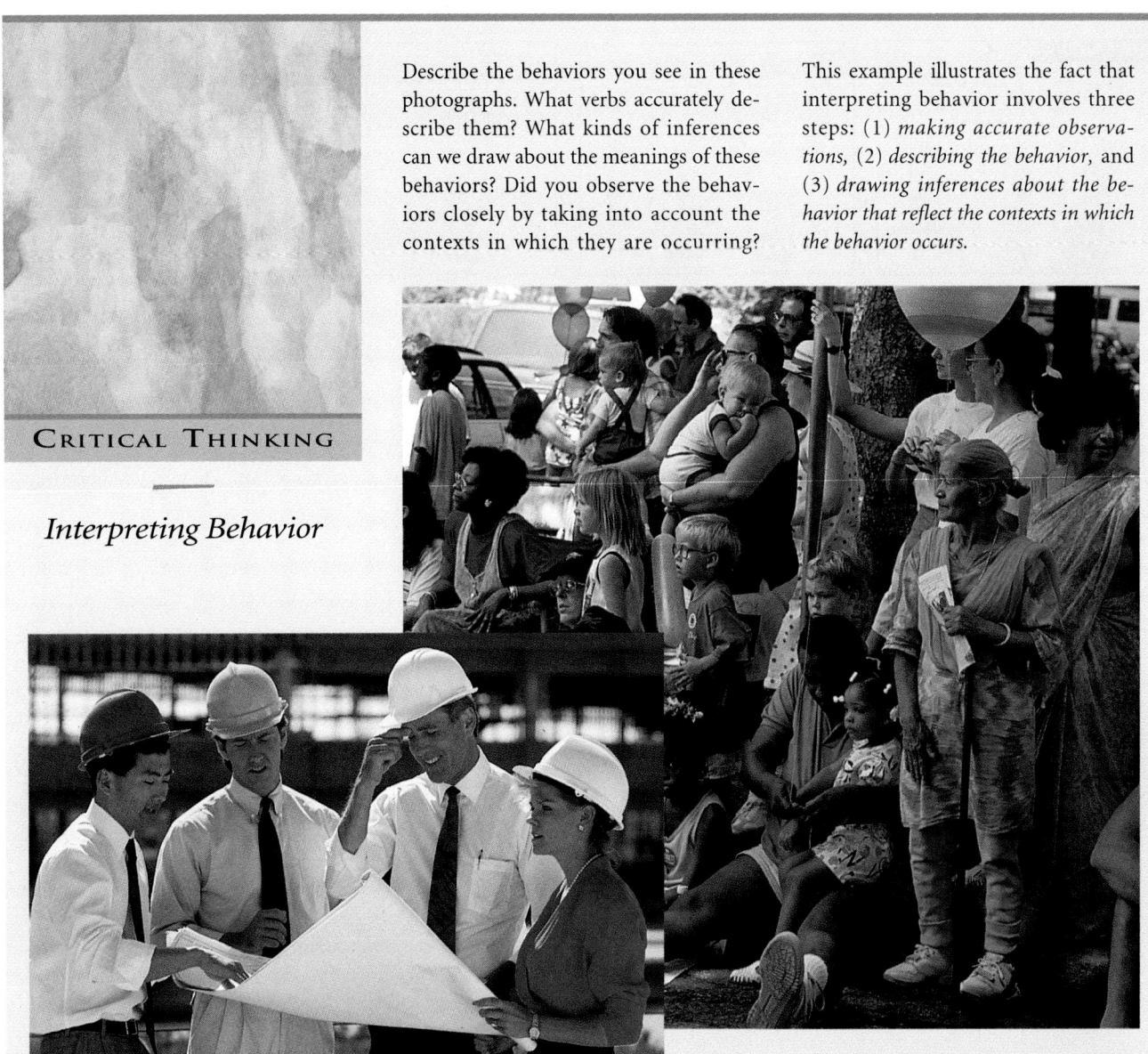

Prize? If we had been with her when she received the good news, we might have observed her *smiling* or *crying,* but we would have had to infer her mental processes. Would she have been overjoyed? stunned? relieved? thinking about how long it had taken to receive the recognition? planning on calling her loved ones? We would infer the impact of the news from our observations of her behavior.

Describing behavior is a relatively straightforward process; drawing inferences about unobservable mental processes is not. Our inferences can be right or wrong. Inferences can also vary from person to person. We can usually reach agreement about how to describe behavior we observe, but our inferences often reflect wide variations in how we each experience and interpret behavior.

The **science of psychology** *uses systematic methods to observe, describe, explain, and predict behavior.* Psychology's

methods are not casual; psychologists carefully plan and conduct research to generate meaningful data about behavior. Psychologists *observe* behavior in natural and laboratory environments. They *describe* these regular patterns of behavior using psychological terminology or concepts. After psychologists gather data, they want to *explain* what they have found. As is true of all sciences, psychology strives to establish cause-and-effect relationships, in this case about behavior. Why do behaviors occur? What factors or variables influence behavior? Answers to these questions enable psychologists to *predict* behavior.

The fourth key aspect of our definition of psychology is contexts. **Contexts** *refer to the historical, economic, social, and cultural factors that influence mental processes and behavior.* People do not act, or react, in a vacuum. Everything we think, say, or do is influenced by where we come from, whom we have spent time with, and what has happened to

Context is an important dimension of psychology. *Contexts* are settings that involve historical, economic, social, and cultural factors. Without reference to context, the racial tolerance of the college students shown here cannot be fully understood. *In this context, how would you describe the degree of racial tolerance shown by these students? What cues are you interpreting to come to this conclusion? What historical, economic, social, and cultural factors might account for this interaction?*

us. All human behavior occurs in a cultural context. These contexts—or settings—include homes, schools, churches, cities, neighborhoods, communities, university laboratories, the United States, China, Mexico, Egypt, and many others, each with important historical, economic, social, and cultural legacies (Bronfenbrenner, 1995).

Psychology itself is also influenced by social and historical contexts. For example, during one phase of American psychology, most psychologists restricted their studies to observable behavior. Psychologists widely believed that we really didn't need to understand mental processes in order to understand behavior. This practice dominated American psychology from its earliest years through the 1950s, when many psychologists began to argue for a broader definition of psychology. This shift took place during a period in which the United States had to cope with national discontent over an unpopular war, government corruption, and declining American influence and power in the world. The antiwar, civil rights, and women's

movements reflected increasing social awareness. One result of this social turmoil was renewed interest in how contexts influence behavior. The scope of research in psychology broadened to include examination of how people think and behave in real-world settings.

As our society continues to change, psychologists need to address new concerns, such as the dramatic increase in ethnic minority populations, increased interaction with cultures around the world, and expanded women's roles in society (Helmreich, 1995; McLoyd & Ceballo, 1995). As you read this book, you will discover that we stress the influence of contexts on behavior and mental processes. We believe that this emphasis will enhance your sensitivity to the important role of context in shaping behavior and mental processes. We will also examine other forces that influence behavior. Throughout the text we explore ways to improve your critical-thinking skills as you encounter complex and controversial questions about behavior. You are likely to learn to understand yourself and the people in your life better.

To explore psychology, we journey through a historical overview of psychology and examine contemporary perspectives.

A Historical Overview of Psychology

Ever since our ancestors first gathered around fires to create and embellish myths, we've been trying to explain why things are the way they are. Myths attributed most events to the pleasure or displeasure of the gods: When a volcano erupted, the gods were angry; if two people fell in love, they were the target of Cupid's arrows. As we became more sophisticated, myth and superstition gave way to philosophy, the rational investigation of the underlying principles of being and knowledge.

Forerunners of Psychology

Although psychology has predominantly been an enterprise of Western cultures (Lonner & Malpass, 1994), influences in contemporary psychology have come from many parts of the globe and from many disciplines. For example, the first recorded evidence of behavior's being measured for an applied purpose comes from China. Ta Yu, a Chinese emperor in 2000 B.C., developed methods for testing the competence of government officials before making promotion decisions.

Empathic interest in others, another characteristic of many applications of psychology, is noteworthy in many religious traditions around the world. The Chinese philosopher Confucius (551–479 B.C.) expounded the principle of *jen,* which means to love all people. The Confucian tenet that benevolence and concern for others are the most important aspects of human behavior is evident in many Asian cultures (Kagitcibasi, 1988, in press; Triandis, 1994).

Of the early Greek philosophers, Socrates (469–399 B.C.) urged us to know ourselves, and Aristotle (384–322 B.C.) urged us to use logic to make inferences about mind, and to observe behavior systematically. Aristotle argued that an empirical approach (direct observation), rather than dialogue, was the best route to knowledge. Direct observation remains an important dimension of psychology today.

Philosophical traditions in the Western world began to challenge early Greek assumptions about the nature of knowledge. Especially in the sixteenth and seventeenth centuries, philosophers debated a variety of issues relevant to psychology. For example, they questioned whether knowledge is inborn or a product of our environment, beginning psychology's enduring interest in the *nature-nurture controversy.* Although such speculation fueled a great deal of intellectual passion among the British associationists, it did not yield many concrete answers until scientific methods were used.

In the sixteenth century, Francis Bacon introduced the scientific method, arguing that direct observation alone is not adequate for understanding nature. According to

FIGURE 1.1

The Beginning of Psychology as a Science
Wilhelm Wundt established the first research laboratory in psychology at Germany's University of Leipzig in 1879. To help you place Wundt's achievement in history, consider that Alexander Graham Bell invented the telephone in 1876.

Bacon, all assumptions about nature should be questioned and tested whenever possible. He promoted the need to reproduce observations. His ideas earned him the designation "the father of science." It was not until the late nineteenth century that the traditions of philosophy and science converged in the systematic examination of behavior. In the late nineteenth century, Darwin's theory of evolution and biological adaptation also molded the thinking of early psychologists.

The Birth of Psychology as a Science

Imagine that you are in a room in Leipzig, Germany, in the year 1879. A bearded man with a wrinkled forehead and pensive expression is also sitting in the room. His head turns toward a soft sound coming from the far side of the room. After several minutes his head turns once again, this time toward a loud sound. The scenario is repeated with sounds of varying intensity. The man is Wilhelm Wundt, who is credited with developing the first scientific psychology laboratory (see figure 1.1). By exposing himself to environmental conditions that he systematically varied, and then recording his reactions to different stimuli, Wundt

The Problem with Being Hardheaded

Psychology is a discipline with a rich history representing many points of view. However, most people who have not formally studied psychology tend to lump all psychologists together as clinicians (the "soft-hearted"). This is a source of endless frustration for experimentalists (the "hardheaded"), who must continually explain why they are not in private practice. How do you think it would feel for others to constantly misunderstand your occupation? What ideas do you have for helping experimentalists with their public relations problem? Your answers will demonstrate an ability to *take the perspective of others actively in solving problems.*

years, but they had never varied conditions so systematically. The technique of introspection, however, came under heavy fire. The introspectionists thought they were studying immediate experience, but, in reality, it takes time to introspect. Introspection was actually retrospection; thus, the act of introspection changed the observer's experience, thereby modifying or contaminating the observation.

Behaviorists like John Watson (1913) began to challenge the method of introspection and argue that psychologists should observe behavior directly rather than make inferences about what is going on in a person's mind. Behaviorists emphasize the power of the environment in shaping behavior and minimize the importance of biological influences. Behaviorism dominated American psychology from the 1920s until the 1950s.

investigated the elements, or "structures," of the mind. His attempts to classify the structures of the mind were not unlike the work of a chemist breaking down chemicals into their component parts—water into hydrogen and oxygen, for example. Wundt's approach became quite logically known as **structuralism,** *the early theory of psychology developed by Wundt that emphasized the importance of conscious thought and classification of the mind's structures.*

Psychology Moves to North America

William James, one of the first American psychologists, argued against analyzing consciousness into Wundt's "structures." Instead, James emphasized the dynamic nature of mental activity; he was more interested in the *how* of behavior. James argued that our minds are characterized by a continuous flow of information about our experiences rather than by discrete components. Following in the steps of Darwin, James emphasized the mind's ability to continuously evolve as it adapts to information about the environment. This approach became known as **functionalism,** *William James's theory that psychology's role is to study the functions of the mind and behavior in adapting to the environment.*

Many of the early psychologists, such as Wundt and James, used introspection to discover information about conscious experiences. **Introspection** *is a technique whereby specially trained people carefully observe and analyze their own mental experiences.* It is a process of turning inward in search of mind's nature. Wundt was the master of introspection training. Before his students were permitted to describe their images and perceptions, they had to participate in a minimum of 10,000 practice observations. Philosophers had used introspection for several thousand

Two distinct breeds of psychologists became apparent early in the twentieth century. They have been referred to as the "hardheaded" and the "soft-hearted" (Kimble, 1984). The hardheaded are experimental psychologists, who generate knowledge through research; the soft-hearted are psychologists who use the principles of psychology to help others in clinical and applied settings.

Rival schools of thought to behaviorism developed in both the clinical arena and the experimental arena. On the clinical side, two alternative approaches to helping individuals with their psychological problems emerged—psychoanalysis and humanism. Both of these approaches have gained considerable popularity in the twentieth century. At the beginning of this century in Vienna, Austria, Sigmund Freud introduced a method of treatment, called *psychoanalysis,* that emphasizes detecting an individual's unconscious motivation. Freud had individuals talk at length in therapy sessions as he probed their minds for the unconscious nature of their statements. Freud's "talking cure" eventually earned him an influential following on both sides of the Atlantic. Although Freud's theory is controversial today, he is recognized as one of the most important thinkers of the twentieth century.

The humanistic perspective emerged in the middle of this century as a more optimistic view of human nature than Freud's perspective. Humanists believe that individuals are motivated to achieve their maximum potential. Humanistic therapists regard clients as capable of positive self-development with support from a warm and caring therapist. A number of therapists continue to use humanistic techniques today.

Behaviorism, psychoanalysis, and humanism offer three sharply contrasting views of human nature as well as of interventions to address human problems. Behaviorism views the individual as being like a "blank tablet," and holds that environmental experiences contribute to whether outcomes are positive or negative. Freud's psychoanalytic view stresses that individuals are conflicted beings, born into the world with a bundle of evil instincts. Humanism emphasizes that the person is basically good and competent.

In the experimental arena, some psychologists began to challenge the intellectual dominance of behaviorism during the second half of the twentieth century. Progress in the development of new research technology led to a better appreciation of the neurobiological contributions to behavior. Along these lines, excitement about the possibilities of the neurobiological perspective even heralded the 1990s as "the decade of the brain," because of the potential for understanding the brain's important role in behavior.

Behaviorism also has been challenged by cognitive psychology in the last half of the twentieth century. Dissatisfied with the restricted view of studying only observable behavior, cognitive psychologists adopted computers as models for human intelligence and studied the way human beings process information. The shift to the cognitive perspective was apparent not only in the experimental arena, but also in clinical circles, where cognitive therapies have become widely practiced.

A study of the history of experimental and clinical arenas in psychology makes it clear that some serious biases have characterized psychology in the twentieth century. Psychology has not fully credited the contributions made by women or by members of ethnic minority groups (Adler & Rieber, 1995). Sociocultural Worlds 1.1 explores these omissions. For a comprehensive and more inclusive review of the important pioneers and dates in the history of psychology, see figure 1.2.

Beginning with Wundt's formal studies of conscious experience, the enterprise of psychology has grown enormously. On the research side, the amount of research conducted in any specialized area in a single year is extensive. On the clinical side, hundreds of therapies have emerged as treatment alternatives for human problems. Next we will explore in more detail the current perspectives that influence how psychologists observe, describe, explain, and predict behavior.

REVIEW

Introducing Psychology, Defining and Exploring the History of Psychology

Psychology can serve many functions, among them providing a better understanding of how people behave and think. Psychology is the scientific study of behavior and mental processes in contexts. Behavior is everything we do that can be directly observed. Mental processes are the thoughts, feelings, and motives that we experience privately but that cannot be directly observed. As a science, psychology uses systematic methods to observe, describe, explain, and predict behavior. Contexts are the settings in which mental processes and behavior occur, settings that involve historical, economic, social, and cultural factors. Recently there has been a renewed interest in contexts in psychology. The contexts of mental processes and behavior are discussed extensively in this text.

Thinking about psychological concepts began with the early Greek philosophers, such as Socrates and Aristotle, and Chinese philosophers, such as Confucius. Darwin's theory of evolution and biological adaptation also molded the thinking of early psychologists. Psychology began as a science when Wilhelm Wundt developed the first scientific laboratory of psychology in 1879 in Leipzig, Germany. His approach was called structuralism. William James, one of the first American psychologists, developed an approach that became known as functionalism. Many of the early psychologists, such as Wundt and James, used introspection, the technique whereby specially trained individuals carefully observe and analyze their own mental experience.

Behaviorists, such as John Watson, began to challenge introspection and argue that psychologists should observe behavior more directly. Behaviorism dominated American psychology from the 1920s until the 1950s. Two distinct branches of psychology became apparent early in the twentieth century—"hardheaded" research and "soft-hearted" clinical psychology. Two rival schools to behaviorism developed in the clinical arena: Freud's psychoanalysis and the humanistic approach. And behaviorism was challenged in the experimental arena by another two rival perspectives: neurobiological and cognitive psychology. The history of psychology has included biases against females and ethnic minority groups.

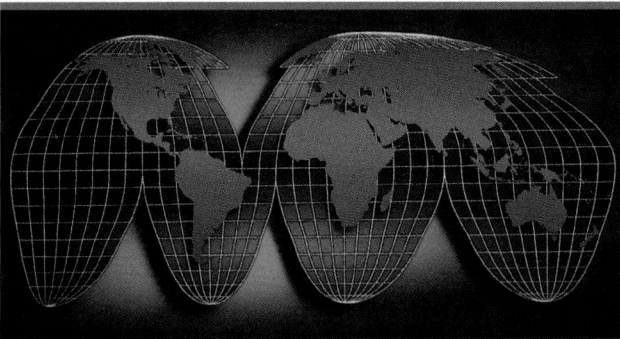

Women and Ethnic Minorities in Psychology

Until recently psychology, like so many professions, kept women out (Kimmel, 1992). During its first 75 years, few women broke through to psychology's inner sanctum. In fact, the first American woman to complete requirements for a doctorate in psychology, Christine Ladd-Franklin, was denied the degree in 1892 simply because she was a woman. Mary Calkins's history is another example of the barriers women faced. In 1891 she introduced psychology into Wellesley College's curriculum and established its first psychology laboratory. In 1892 she returned to Harvard for additional training. By 1894 Mary Calkins had developed a technique for investigating memory and had completed the requirements for a doctoral degree. Her Harvard psychology professors enthusiastically recommended that she be awarded the degree, but the administration refused because Calkins was a woman (Furumoto, 1989).

The first woman actually to be awarded a doctorate in psychology was Margaret Washburn in 1894. By 1906 about 1 in every 10 psychologists was a woman. In the mid-1980s in the United States, the number of men and women receiving a doctorate in psychology was approximately equal (Furumoto & Scarborough, 1986). In 1992, more women than men earned doctorates in psychology: 1,914 women earned doctorates, compared to 1,338 men.

Similarly, discrimination has barred many individuals from ethnic minority groups from entering the field of psychology. The first African American to become a professor of psychology was Gilbert Jones, who obtained his doctorate at the University of Jena in Germany in 1909. Ethnic minority women, especially, faced overwhelming odds. It wasn't until 1934 that an African American woman, Ruth Howard at the University of Minnesota, finally received a doctorate in psychology. Over a period of about 50 years, the 10 universities with the most prestigious programs in psychology granted several thousand doctoral degrees, yet by 1969 these universities had awarded only 8 doctoral degrees to African American students (Albee, 1988). Few Latinos have been awarded doctoral degrees—recent surveys indicate that less than 2 percent of all psychologists are Latino (Cervantes, 1987). George Sanchez is one of the few. His pioneering research demonstrated that intelligence tests are culturally biased against ethnic minority children. There are also very few Native American psychologists (McShane, 1987).

Over the past 25 years, the women's movement and the civil rights movement helped put the rights and needs of women and ethnic minorities on politicians' agendas and led to social change (Bronstein & Quina, 1988). Similarly psychologists, especially those belonging to these groups, began to reexamine psychology's basic premises and to question its relevance to their own experiences and concerns. This reexamination sparked new inquiry into populations that previously had been omitted from psychological research and the mainstream theories of psychology. Such journals as *Psychology of Women Quarterly, Sex Roles,* the *Hispanic Journal of Behavioral Science,* and the *Journal of Black Psychology* address the growing interest in gender and ethnic minority issues.

In recognizing the dearth of ethnic minority psychologists, the American Psychological Association has formed the Committee on Ethnic Minority Affairs to ensure that the concerns of its ethnic group members are heard. The Association of Black Psychologists directly involves its members in issues that are important to the African American community (Jones, 1987). The Asian American Psychological Association identifies resources, develops ideas for education and training, and fosters scientific research on issues of importance to the Asian American community (Suinn, 1987).

Contemporary Perspectives

In addition to specialized content areas of psychology, certain paradigms or systems of thinking have dominated the development of psychology research. Six important perspectives in psychology are the behavioral, psychoanalytic, humanistic, neurobiological, cognitive, and sociocultural. Each framework represents a distinctive way of looking at behavior. Each tends to emphasize certain elements in explaining behavior and might also omit or diminish other factors that might contribute to behavior. We will briefly describe here each of these approaches in turn, and we will also discuss them in much greater detail in later chapters.

Abstract principles of psychology can be difficult to remember. As we will do throughout the book, we will illustrate the perspectives of psychology through an example or story. In this case, we will apply each approach to

Wilhelm Wundt
(1832–1920)

William James
(1842–1910)

Alfred Binet
(1857–1911)

Ivan Pavlov
(1849–1936)

Ruth Howard
(1900–)

B. F. Skinner
(1904–1990)

Erik Erikson
(1902–1994)

Abraham Maslow
(1908–1970)

Carl Rogers
(1902–1987)

Albert Bandura
(1925–)

Sandra Bem
(1944–)

Eleanor Maccoby
(1917–)

1879: Wilhelm Wundt develops the first psychology laboratory at the University of Leipzig.

1890: William James publishes *Principles of Psychology,* which promotes functionalism.

1891: Mary Calkins establishes a laboratory for psychology at Wellesley.

1892: E. B. Titchener popularizes structuralism in the United States. G. Stanley Hall founds the American Psychological Association at Clark University.

1900: Sigmund Freud publishes *The Interpretation of Dreams*, reflecting his psychoanalytic view.

1905: Alfred Binet (with Theodore Simon) develops the first intelligence test to assess French schoolchildren.

1906: The Russian Ivan Pavlov publishes the results of his learning experiments with dogs.

1908: Margaret Washburn becomes the first woman to receive a Ph.D. in psychology.

1913: John Watson publishes his volume on behaviorism, promoting the importance of environmental influences.

1934: Ruth Howard becomes the first African American woman to receive a Ph.D. in psychology.

1938: B. F. Skinner publishes *The Behavior of Organisms*, expanding the view of behaviorism.

1939: Mamie Phipps Clark and Kenneth Clark conduct research on African American children's self-conceptions and identity. Later, in 1971, Kenneth Clark becomes the first African American president of the American Psychological Association.

1945: Karen Horney criticizes Freud's psychoanalytic theory as male-biased and presents her sociocultural approach.

1950: Erik Erikson publishes *Childhood and Society*, a psychoanalytic revision of Freud's views.

1954: Abraham Maslow presents the humanistic view, emphasizing the positive potential of the individual.

1954: Gordon Allport writes his now classic book, *The Nature of Prejudice*.

1958: Herbert Simon presents his information-processing view.

1961: Carl Rogers publishes *On Becoming a Person,* highlighting the humanistic approach.

1961: Albert Bandura presents ideas about social learning theory, emphasizing the importance of imitation.

1964: Roger Sperry publishes his split-brain research, showing the importance of the brain in behavior.

1969: John Berry, a Canadian psychologist, presents his ideas on the importance of cross-cultural research in psychology.

1974: Sandra Bem and Janet Spence develop tests to assess androgyny and promote the competence of females; Eleanor Maccoby (with Carol Jacklin) calls attention to the importance of sex and gender in understanding behavior and analyzing gender similarities and differences.

1977: Judith Rodin (with Ellen Langer) conducts research showing the powerful influence of perceived control over one's environment on behavior.

Mary Calkins
(1863–1930)

G. Stanley Hall
(1844–1924)

Margaret
Washburn
(1871–1939)

John B. Watson
(1878–1958)

Mamie Clark
(1917–)

Karen Horney
(1885–1952)

Gordon Allport
(1897–1967)

Sigmund Freud
(1856–1939)

Roger Sperry
(1913–1994)

John Berry
(1939–)

Judith Rodin
(1944–)

Herbert Simon
(1916–)

FIGURE 1.2

Important Pioneers and Theorists in Psychology's History

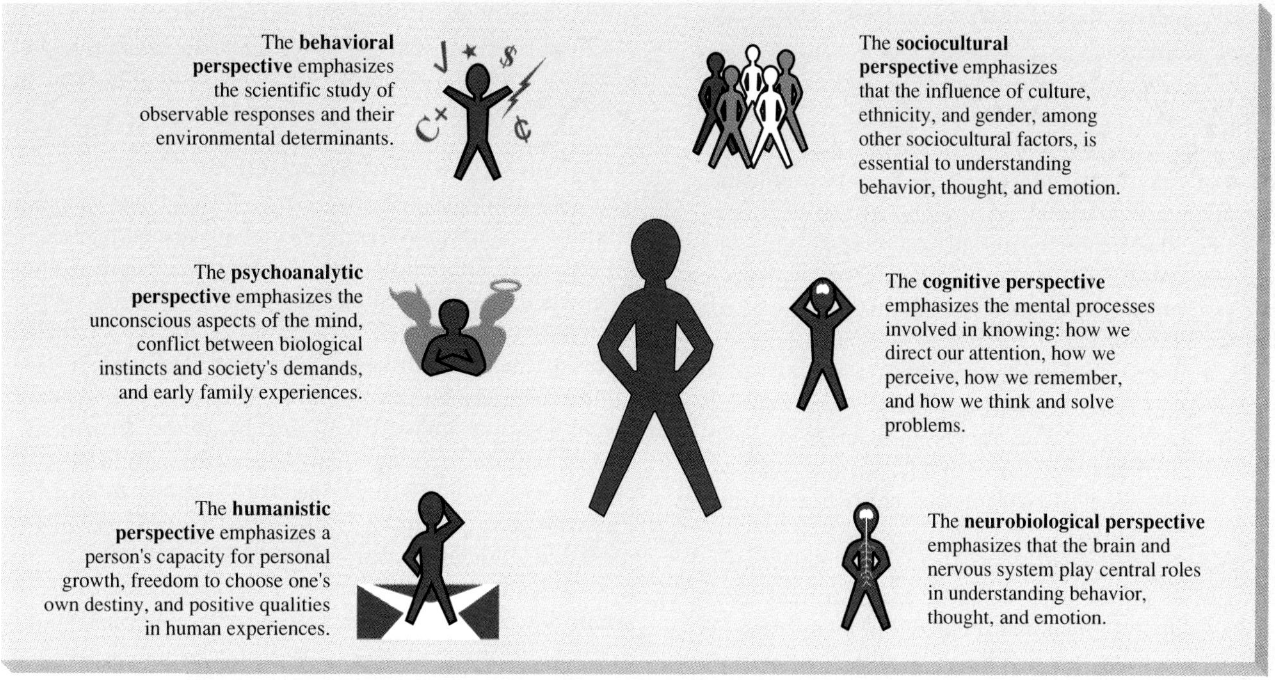

FIGURE 1.3

Six Contemporary Psychological Perspectives
These six contemporary psychological perspectives will be woven through our discussion of psychology at various points in the remainder of the text. At the end of each chapter, we will point out which contemporary perspectives have been emphasized and their location in the chapter. To signal the perspectives to you, we will use the logos shown here. Remember that each perspective emphasizes a particular domain of psychology.

something most of us have done in our lives—dating. Meet Ron and Angela, freshmen at the same campus. They're bright, attractive, and outgoing. We will discover how each psychological perspective explains what draws Ron and Angela to one another. A visual representation of the six contemporary perspectives is shown in figure 1.3.

There are few things more exciting to me than a psychological reason.

William James

The Behavioral Perspective

The **behavioral perspective** *emphasizes the scientific study of observable behavioral responses and their environmental determinants.* According to behaviorists, the only appropriate subject matter for psychological investigation is observable, measurable behavior. Under the intellectual leadership of John B. Watson and B. F. Skinner, behaviorism dominated ways of thinking about psychology during the first half of this century.

Behaviorists emphasize that what we *do* is the ultimate test of who we are, and that rewards and punishments determine our behavior. For example, we behave in a well-

mannered fashion for our parents because of the controls they place on us. We work hard at our jobs because of the money we receive for our effort. We don't do these things, say behaviorists, because of an inborn motivation to be competent people. We do them because of the environmental conditions we have experienced and continue to experience (Skinner, 1938).

What can the behavioral perspective tell us about dating? The behavioral perspective tells us not to look inside a person for clues about dating behavior. Inner motives and feelings about another person cannot be directly observed, so they will be of no help in understanding dating. Behaviorists wouldn't deny that we might experience feelings; however, they emphasize that feedback from the environment is more important in determining behavior. The behaviorists would encourage us to examine what goes on before and after a date, searching for the rewards and punishments people experience.

According to behaviorists, Ron might ask Angela out because of her engaging smile or because she's beautiful. If Ron receives attention for being with Angela, he might ask her out again, even if his date with her is just so-so. Being seen with Angela also increases Ron's status in the group, which provides a further reward.

The Psychoanalytic Perspective

The **psychoanalytic perspective** *emphasizes the unconscious aspects of the mind, conflict between biological instincts and society's demands, and early family experiences.* Stemming from the ideas of Sigmund Freud (1856–1939), the psychoanalytic perspective stresses that unlearned biological instincts, especially sexual and aggressive impulses, influence the way people think, feel, and act. These instincts, buried deep within the unconscious mind, are often at odds with society's demands. Society's job is to keep these instincts in check. For example, in Freud's view, a child who once ran wildly through a neighbor's flower garden but who grows up to be a successful surgeon or comedian has learned to channel her aggressive instincts in positive ways. Although Freud saw much of psychological development as instinctually based, he argued that our early relationships with our parents are the chief environmental contributions that shape our personality.

What can the psychoanalytic perspective tell us about dating? Above all, the psychoanalytic approach tells us we will have a difficult time understanding our own dating behavior. The reasons we behave in a given way lie deep within our unconscious mind and are primarily sexual. Sex is an unlearned human instinct that dominates our dating behavior. Society's job, which conflicts with our inner sexual motivation, is to keep this instinct in check. Our dating behavior can also be traced to our experiences with our parents during our childhood.

According to the psychoanalytic perspective, Angela might have dated Ron because something about his appearance or behavior unconsciously reminded her of her early relationship with her father. She might attempt to work through an earlier crisis with her father in her dating life with Ron.

The Humanistic Perspective

The **humanistic perspective** *emphasizes a person's capacity for personal growth, freedom to choose one's own destiny, and positive qualities.* Humanistic psychologists criticize the behavioral approach, stressing that people have the ability to control their lives rather than be manipulated by the environment (Maslow, 1971; Rogers, 1961). They also criticize the psychoanalytic approach, stressing that people are not driven by unconscious sexual and aggressive impulses. Humanists believe we have the ability to live by higher human values, such as altruism, aesthetics, and free will. They also think we have a tremendous potential for conscious self-understanding and that we can help others achieve this self-understanding by being warm, nurturant, and supportive.

What can the humanistic perspective tell us about dating? Humanistic psychologists do not believe that dating is based on sexual instinct. Rather, it is a natural tendency of human beings to be loving toward each other. Humanistic psychologists believe that each of us has the potential to be a loving person if only we would recognize it.

According to the humanists, Ron might ask Angela out because he is trusting, warm, and open to loving her. He might pursue her company in order to realize his greatest potential, to meet his need to belong, and to achieve intimacy.

The Neurobiological Perspective

The **neurobiological perspective** *emphasizes that the brain and nervous system play central roles in understanding behavior, thought, and emotion.* Neurobiologists believe that thoughts have a physical basis in the brain (Squire, 1992). Electrical impulses zoom throughout the brain's cells, releasing chemical substances as we think, feel, and act. Our remarkable capacities as human beings would not be possible without our brains. The human brain and nervous system constitute the most complex, intricate, and elegant system imaginable. This perspective continues to grow in importance in psychology, supported by progress in remarkable technologies that unlock the body's secrets.

What can the neurobiological perspective tell us about dating? The neurobiological perspective reminds us that underlying our thoughts, emotions, and behaviors in a dating situation are a physical brain, a nervous system, and hormones. Have you ever thought about how your brain changes when you are attracted to someone? When your heart throbs, we sometimes say, "the chemistry is right." When your feelings of attraction for someone increase, the chemistry of your brain changes. Chemical messengers in the body known as hormones also influence dating behavior. For example, subtle changes in pheromones (skin scents) can act as sexual attractants. In this manner, dating responses are wired into the circuitry of the brain.

In the neurobiological view, Ron and Angela are drawn to one another because their brains trigger chemical come-hithers. They pursue each other's company because of the powerful pleasant feelings their dating generates, governed in the brain by an elegantly coordinated system of sensation, perception, and interpretation as well as voluntary and involuntary responses.

The Cognitive Perspective

In the 1950s the cognitive sciences emerged as a significant way of thinking, specifically as a challenge to the narrow interests of behaviorism. The word *cognition* comes from the Latin word meaning "to know." The **cognitive perspective** *emphasizes the mental processes involved in knowing: how we direct our attention, how we perceive, how we remember, and how we think and solve problems.* For example, cognitive psychologists want to know how we solve algebraic equations, why we remember some things only for a short while and others for a lifetime, and how we can use mental images to plan for the future. A cognitive psychologist views the mind as an active and aware problem-solving system (Simon, 1990). This positive view of human capabilities shares the optimism of the humanistic perspective and contrasts with the pessimistic psychoanalytic view.

Harry Triandis *(above, left)* has been a pioneer in the field of cross-cultural psychology. He is past-president of the International Association of Cross-Cultural Psychology and has conducted insightful analyses of the individualistic and collectivistic dimensions of cultures.

What can the cognitive perspective tell us about dating? According to cognitive psychologists, our conscious thoughts are the key to understanding dating behaviors. Memories and images of people we want to date, or have dated, influence our behavior.

The cognitive perspective would look at the patterns of thinking and perception that influence dating. Angela might go out with Ron because she has *thought* about the engaging conversations they've had after class and *believes* that she would like to get to know him better. She *evaluates* his fitness as a potential partner and *decides* how much to invest in the relationship.

The Sociocultural Perspective

The sociocultural approach is one of psychology's newest frameworks for examining behavior. The **sociocultural perspective** *emphasizes that the influences of culture, ethnicity, and gender, among other sociocultural factors, are essential to understanding behavior, thought, and emotion.*

Culture *refers to the behavior patterns, beliefs, and other products of a particular group of people, such as the values, work patterns, music, dress, diet, and ceremonies, that are passed on from generation to generation.* A cultural group can be as small as the group of all inhabitants of a tiny island in the South Pacific or as large and complex as the group of all inhabitants of North America, but whatever its size, the group's culture influences the identity, learning, and social behavior of its members (Brislin, 1993; Lonner & Malpass, 1994; Triandis, 1994).

Ethnicity *is based on cultural heritage, nationality characteristics, race, religion, and language.* The word *ethnic* comes from the Greek word for "nation." Ethnicity involves descent from common ancestors, usually in a specifiable part of the world. Ethnicity is central to the development of an **ethnic identity,** *which is a sense of membership in an ethnic group, based on shared language, religion, customs, values, history, and race.* Ethnic identity involves the relative importance of one's ethnicity in comparison with the other aspects of the self that contribute to identity. We must distinguish between ethnicity and ethnic identity because individuals differ in the impact these characteristics have in their lives. For example, ethnicity is a prominent element of most Native Americans' day-to-day experiences, and their appreciation of their ethnic identity is quite strong. In contrast, consider the child adopted at birth with little information provided about her biological parents. She might grow up with a strong ethnic identity, but she might not have a clear idea about her ethnicity. To read further about ethnicity, turn to Applications in Psychology 1.1, where you will read about the increasing ethnic diversity in American Society.

A third important sociocultural factor is gender. Psychologists use the terms *sex* and *gender* in different ways. **Sex** *refers to the biological dimension of being female or male,* focusing on anatomical, reproductive, hormonal, and genetic aspects of being female or male. **Gender** *is the sociocultural dimension of being female or male, emphasizing how we learn to think and behave as females and males* (Caplan & Caplan, 1994; Denmark & Paludi, 1993; Unger & Crawford, 1992). Few aspects of our existence are more central to our identity and to our social relationships than our sex and gender are. Our gender-related attitudes and behavior seem to be changing, but how much change has actually occurred? How much change is desirable? Should there be a limit to society's influence on what constitutes appropriate behavior for males and females?

Other aspects of our identity are also important from a sociocultural perspective. Our age, socioeconomic class, physical characteristics, and sexual orientation also influence our experiences. For example, American culture tends to place a high value on youth, so growing older represents an emotional as well as a physical challenge. In contrast, a number of Asian cultures associate aging with increased wisdom and promote reverence of older members of the culture.

Access to financial resources determines socioeconomic class. A single mother on welfare faces challenges different from those facing a wealthy woman with income from a substantial family inheritance. Each will have opportunities and face constraints that the other will not experience because of her financial status.

APPLICATIONS IN PSYCHOLOGY 1.1

The Changing Tapestry of American Culture

In 1989 one-fifth of all children and adolescents in the United States under the age of 17 were members of ethnic minority groups—African American, Latino, Native American (American Indian), and Asian American. By the year 2000, one-third of all school-age children will fall into this category. This changing demographic tapestry promises national diversity, but it also carries the challenge of extending the American dream to people of all ethnic and minority groups. Historically ethnic minorities have found themselves at the bottom of the economic and social order. They have been disproportionately among the poor and the inadequately educated. Today, for instance, half of all African American children and one-third of all Latino children live in poverty, and the school dropout rate for minority youths is as high as 60 percent in some urban areas. Our social institutions can play an enormous part in helping correct these discrepancies. By becoming more sensitive to ethnic issues and by improving services to people of ethnic minority and low-income backgrounds, schools, colleges, social services, health and

mental health agencies, and the courts can help bring minorities into the mainstream of American life (Bennett, 1994; Jones, 1994; Lee & Hall, 1994; Marin, 1994).

An especially important fact for social planners to keep in mind is the tremendous diversity within each ethnic group. We're accustomed to thinking of American society as a melting pot of cultures—Anglo-Americans, African Americans, Latinos, Native Americans, Asian Americans, Italian Americans, Polish Americans, and so on. However, just as there are no cultural characteristics common *across* all American ethnic groups, there is no cultural characteristic common to all African Americans or all Latinos, for instance.

African Americans make up the largest ethnic minority group in the United States. African Americans are distributed throughout the social class structure, although a disproportionate number are poor.

Latinos also are a diverse group of individuals. Not all Latinos are Catholic. Many are, but some are not. Not all Latinos have a Mexican heritage. Many do, but others have cultural ties with South American countries, with Puerto Rico or other Caribbean countries, or with Spain.

Native Americans, with 511 distinct tribal units, also are an extremely diverse and complicated ethnic group (Trimble & Fleming, 1989). So are Asian Americans, with more than 30 distinct groups under this designation (Wong, 1982). Within each of these 511 Native American tribes and 30 Asian American groups, there is considerable diversity and individual variation (Ho, 1992).

America has embraced many cultures, and, in the process, the cultures have often mixed their beliefs and identities. Some elements of the cultures of origin are retained, some are lost, and some are mixed with the American culture. As the number of ethnic minority groups continues to increase rapidly in the next decade, one of psychology's most important agenda items is to understand better the role that culture and ethnicity play in the ways we think and act.

The tapestry of American culture has changed dramatically in recent years. Nowhere is the change more noticeable than in the increasing ethnic diversity of America's citizens. Ethnic minority groups—African American, Latino, Native American, and Asian American, for example—will make up approximately one-third of all individuals under the age of 17 in the United States by the year 2000. Two of psychology's challenges are to become more sensitive to race and ethnic origin and to provide improved services to ethnic minority individuals.

In Xinjiang, China, a woman prepares for horseback courtship. Her suitor must chase her, kiss her, and evade her riding crop—all on the gallop. A new marriage law took effect in China in 1981. The law sets a minimum age for marriage—22 years for males, 20 years for females. *What reasons can you propose that might account for such a comparatively late age restriction?* Late marriage and late childbirth are critical aspects of China's effort to control population growth (Engel, 1984).

brief, you can see how each perspective might offer a piece of the puzzle in understanding dating. All of these approaches to psychology are, in a sense, correct. They all have the potential to be valid or truthful ways of looking at human behavior, just as blueprints, floor plans, and photographs are all valid ways of looking at a house. Some approaches are better for some purposes. A floor plan, for instance, is more useful than a photograph for deciding how much lumber to buy, just as the neurobiological approach is probably more useful than the cognitive approach for understanding epilepsy. However, no single approach in explaining behavior is right or wrong.

Now let's turn our attention to the various areas in which psychologists specialize.

Physical characteristics can also enhance or constrain our experiences. For example, college students confined to wheelchairs sometimes face daunting obstacles in moving from class to class, yet they might also experience greater helpfulness from others than do those without physical challenges. In contrast to the obvious barriers that face the physically challenged, the limitations and opportunities faced by homosexuals may be far more subtle.

What can the sociocultural perspective tell us about dating? The sociocultural perspective tells us that dating behavior can vary according to sociocultural factors, such as one's ethnic, cultural, and gender background. For example, some cultural and ethnic groups have extremely conservative beliefs about dating, especially for women. The age at which young people first date varies from culture to culture. Cultures also differ in the value they place on dating as a precursor to marriage and regarding the importance of sexuality in dating.

Ron might not be able to go out on a car date with Angela until she is 18, because of her parents' cultural beliefs about appropriate dating behavior. On the other hand, suppose Ron and Angela are not traditional-age freshmen; their dating might be heartily endorsed by their grown children from prior relationships. Or suppose Ron and Angela are Ron and Andy? Each shift in scenario emphasizes the importance of sociocultural factors in determining experience.

Which Perspective Is Correct?

This question is likely to occur to you often throughout your studies in psychology. Although this introductory discussion of six major perspectives in psychology has been

PRACTICING PSYCHOLOGY

What careers are available to individuals with degrees in psychology? What are psychology's areas of specialization? What professional organizations are available to psychologists?

Careers in Psychology

You might already be wondering whether or not to major in psychology. Studying psychology as an undergraduate can give you a sound preparation for what lies ahead by helping you to more effectively understand, predict, and control the events in your own life. You will also gain a solid academic background that can enable you to enter various careers and go on to graduate programs, not just in psychology but in other areas as well, such as business and law (Woods & Wilkinson, 1987).

Many students hear that "you can't get a job with a degree in psychology" and forego psychology as a major. A bachelor's degree in psychology will not automatically lead to fame and fortune, but it is a highly marketable degree for a wide range of jobs, including parent educator, drug-abuse counselor, mental health aide, teacher for mentally retarded children, and staff member at a crisis hot-line center. An undergraduate degree in psychology also provides excellent training for many jobs in business, especially in the areas of sales, personnel, and training.

Although a master's degree or doctorate is not absolutely necessary to finding employment in psychology, you can greatly expand your opportunities and income by obtaining a graduate degree. Also, because there are so few ethnic minority psychologists, job opportunities are increasingly available to qualified ethnic minority applicants.

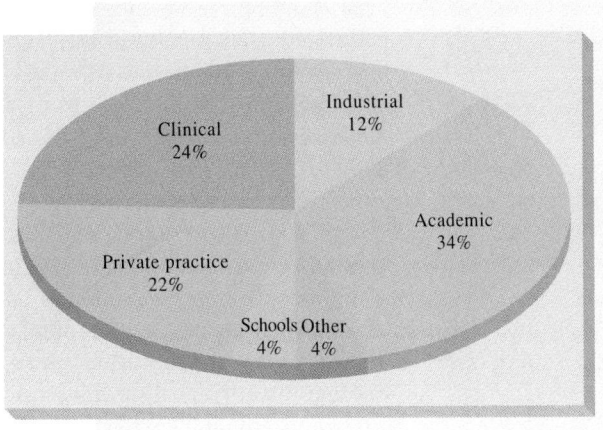

FIGURE 1.4

Settings in Which Psychologists Work

If you do go to graduate school, you will increase your options to work in a variety of settings that employ psychologists. Slightly more than one-third of individuals with graduate degrees in psychology are teachers, researchers, or counselors at colleges or universities. Most psychologists—almost half, in fact—work in clinical and private-practice settings (see figure 1.4). Although these careers represent the dominant activities of contemporary psychologists, psychology is a field with many areas of specialization. Psychologists also work in business and industry—for example, designing more efficient criteria for hiring. And they work in school and community settings.

Areas of Specialization in Psychology

In you enter graduate school, you will specialize in a particular area of psychology in order to focus your learning. We explore many categories of specialization. Sometimes the categories are not mutually exclusive. For example, some social psychologists are also experimental psychologists. In general, areas of specialization in psychology can be categorized as clinical, research, and applied.

Clinical Specializations

Clinical and counseling psychology *is the most widely practiced specialization in psychology; clinical and counseling psychologists diagnose and treat people with psychological problems.* The work of clinical psychologists often does not differ from that of counseling psychologists, although a counseling psychologist sometimes deals with people who have less serious problems. In many instances, counseling psychologists work with students, advising them about personal problems and career planning.

Clinical psychologists are different from psychiatrists. Typically a clinical psychologist has a doctoral degree in psychology, which requires 3 to 4 years of graduate work,

plus 1 year of internship in a mental health facility. **Psychiatry** *is a branch of medicine practiced by physicians with a doctor of medicine (M.D.) degree, who specialize in abnormal behavior and psychotherapy.* Clinical psychologists and psychiatrists both are interested in improving the lives of people with mental health problems. One important distinction is that psychiatrists can prescribe drugs, whereas clinical psychologists cannot. Clinical psychologists sometimes use psychological testing, which psychiatrists usually are not trained to do.

Research Specializations

Experimental and physiological psychology *are areas that often involve pure research. Although psychologists in other areas conduct experiments, virtually all experimental and physiological psychologists follow precise, careful experimental strategies.* These psychologists are more likely to work with animals, although many do not. Experimental psychologists explore the mental terrain of memory, sensation and perception, motivation, and emotion. Physiological psychologists investigate a range of topics—from the role of the brain in behavior to the influence of drugs on hormones. The neurobiological approach to psychology is closely aligned with physiological psychology.

Developmental psychology *is concerned with how we become who we are, from conception to death.* In particular, developmental psychologists focus on the biological and environmental factors that contribute to human development. For many years, the major emphasis was on child development. However, an increasing number of today's developmental psychologists show a strong interest in adult development and aging. Their inquiries range across the biological, cognitive, and social domains of life.

Social psychology *deals with people's social interactions, relationships, perceptions, and attitudes.* Social psychologists believe we can better understand mental processes and behavior if we know something about how people function in groups.

Personality psychology *focuses on the relatively enduring traits and characteristics of individuals.* Personality psychologists study such topics as self-concept, aggression, moral development, gender roles, and inner or outer directedness.

Cross-cultural psychology *examines the role of culture in understanding behavior, thought, and emotion. Cross-cultural psychologists compare the nature of psychological processes in different cultures, with a special interest in whether or not psychological phenomena are universal or culture-specific.* The International Association for Cross-Cultural Psychology promotes research on cross-cultural comparisons and awareness of culture's role in psychology.

The **psychology of women** *emphasizes the importance of promoting the research and study of women, integrating this information about women with current psychological knowledge and beliefs, and applying the information to society* *and its institutions*. The Division of the Psychology of Women in the American Psychological Association was formed in 1973.

Applied Specializations

Community psychology *focuses on providing accessible care for people with psychological problems. Community-based mental health centers are one means of providing such services as outreach programs to people in need, especially those who traditionally have been underserved by mental health professionals.* Community psychologists view human behavior in terms of adaptation to resources and to one's situation. They work to create communities that are more supportive of residents by pinpointing needs, by providing needed services, and by teaching people how to gain access to resources already available. Finally, community psychologists are also concerned about *prevention*. They try to prevent mental health problems by identifying high-risk groups and then intervening to provide appropriate services and by stimulating new opportunities in the community.

School and educational psychology *is concerned with children's learning and adjustment in school.* School psychologists counsel children and parents when children have problems in school. They often give children psychological tests to assess personality and intelligence. Most educational psychologists, like other academic psychologists, also teach and conduct research.

Industrial/organizational psychology *deals with the workplace, focusing on both the workers and the organizations that employ them.* Industrial/organizational psychologists are concerned with training employees, improving working conditions, and developing criteria for selecting employees. For example, an organizational psychologist might recommend that a company adopt a new management structure that would increase communication between managers and staff. The background of industrial and organizational psychologists often includes training in social psychology.

Professional Organizations

G. Stanley Hall founded the American Psychological Association (APA) at Clark University in 1892. He probably had no idea when he created the charter for the 32 original members that the APA would grow to a membership of over 124,000 by its centennial celebration in 1992 (Sokal, 1992). Currently, special interest areas are represented by forty-nine divisions within the APA: Teaching of Psychology, Military Psychology, and Psychology of Religion are just three examples that illustrate the breadth of topics of interest in psychology.

Some psychologists became dissatisfied with the dominance of clinicians in the APA. They established the American Psychological Society in 1988 as a parallel organization devoted primarily to the support and promotion of psychological research. Their membership, composed largely of research and academic psychologists, continues to grow every year.

Some organizations have been formed to address the special concerns of students. For example, your college or university might have a psychology club for students who are pursuing interests in psychology that go beyond the classroom. Some schools also offer exceptional students of psychology the opportunity to be accepted in a psychology honorary society. At many 4-year schools, Psi Chi honors students with strong academic and service records. Exceptional students at participating 2-year schools may be admitted to Psi Beta. Inquire about the opportunities for psychology students at your school.

REVIEW

Contemporary Perspectives and Practicing Psychology

The six main contemporary perspectives in psychology are the behavioral, psychoanalytic, humanistic, neurobiological, cognitive, and sociocultural. The behavioral approach emphasizes the scientific study of observable behavioral responses and their environmental determinants. The psychoanalytic approach focuses on the unconscious, conflicts between biological instincts and society's demands, and early family experiences. The humanistic approach emphasizes a person's capacity for growth, freedom to choose one's identity, and positive qualities. The neurobiological approach emphasizes that the brain and nervous system play central roles in understanding behavior, thought, and emotion. The cognitive approach emphasizes cognitive, or thought, processes, such as attention, perception, memory, thinking, and problem solving. The sociocultural approach emphasizes that culture, ethnicity, and gender are key dimensions of understanding behavior, thought, and emotion.

There are many ways to be a psychologist. Careers range from improving the lives of people with mental problems to teaching at a university and conducting research. Psychology's many specializations fall into three categories: clinical, research, and applied. Psychology also has a number of professional organizations, including the American Psychological Association and the American Psychological Society.

Not to know is bad; not to wish to know is worse.

Nigerian proverb

Why do we do what we do? This is the fundamental question that drives the study of psychology and fuels our curiosity about what we experience. This question is at the heart of day-to-day interactions with others. It also drives psychological research that establishes new knowledge about human behavior.

Curiosity about behavior is one of our most valuable human characteristics. We are natural question-askers. Sometimes human behavior is especially compelling. We might never before have seen anything like the behavior in question, so we don't have a ready explanation to account for what we see. The discrepancy from "business as usual" stimulates us to make sense of the behavior.

Once our curiosity is aroused, we typically go through reliable thinking processes that might seem rather scientific. We observe behavior carefully, make inferences about what we observe, and—if it still does not make sense—we go after more "data" to get to a point of understanding the behavior. We can get more information through research, through purposefully relating the behavior to general ideas we have acquired from observing more familiar behavior, and through asking questions.

Asking questions is evidence of an active curiosity. Children are remarkable for their ability to ask questions, sometimes even embarrassing ones. As strong as this behavior is early in our lives, most of us experience a decline in this ability as we get older. Sometimes we wish not to be rude. Sometimes our experiences in school favor "content loading" over exploring questions. Sometimes we may feel overwhelmed by the complexity or the mystery being proposed.

Psychological perspectives offer us tools for exploring behaviors that we don't understand. Each perspective encourages certain kinds of questions (and ignores others). The following are a few of the questions that are typical of the perspectives presented throughout this text.

The Behavioral Perspective

What role does learning play in the behavior?
Is the behavior performed because it is rewarded?
Is the behavior modeled after someone else's?

The Psychoanalytic Perspective

Does the behavior have unconscious underpinnings?
Does sexuality influence the behavior?
What early childhood experiences contributed to the behavior?

The Humanistic Perspective

How does the behavior fulfill needs?
How does the behavior enhance self-esteem?
How well does the behavior fit with character?

The Neurobiological Perspective

How does genetic endowment influence the behavior?
What role does the brain play in the behavior?
How do hormonal changes contribute to the behavior?

The Cognitive Perspective

How does judgment affect the behavior?
Does cognitive developmental change influence the behavior?
What is the role of emotion in the behavior?

The Sociocultural Perspective

Does socioeconomic status affect the behavior?
What role does ethnicity play in the behavior?
Is the behavior influenced by gender?

Try out these perspectives on a behavior that intrigues you. Is there some event in the news that seems especially perplexing? Could you clarify a friend's behavior by looking at it through the lens of different psychological perspectives? Systematic analysis of behavior can lead to some questions you had not considered and to a more complete picture of what accounts for behavior.

We hope that your study of psychology will enrich the way you look at behavior. As you complete each chapter, you will have more material to draw upon in understanding and explaining behavior. We hope that this increased awareness and knowledge will motivate you to *pursue alternative explanations that help to explain behavior more comprehensively.*

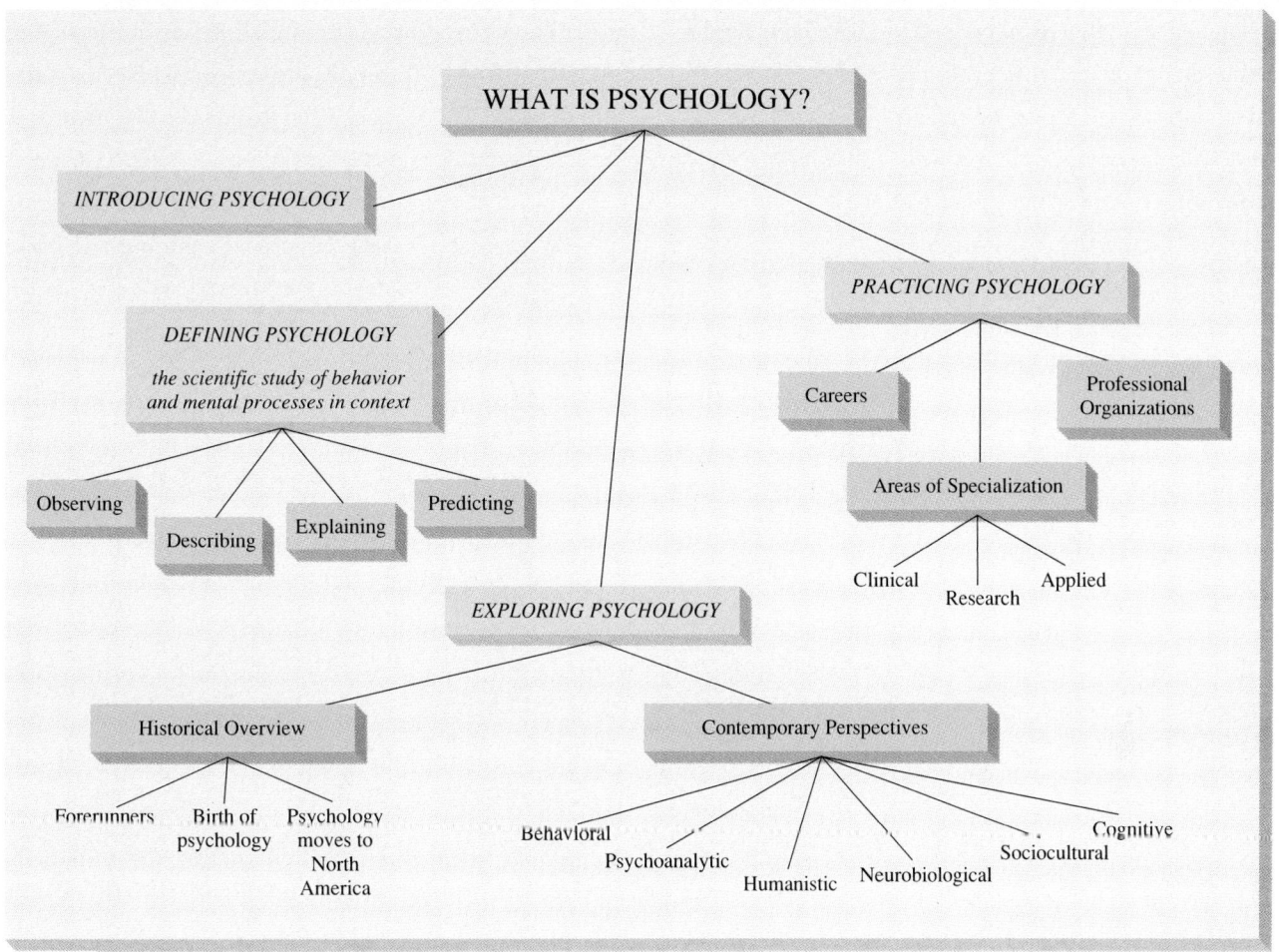

In this first chapter we explored what psychology is. Psychology is the scientific study of behavior and mental processes in context. As a science, psychology seeks to observe, describe, explain, and predict behavior. In the section on exploring psychology, we moved back in time and met the forerunners of psychology, studied the formal origin of psychology in Wundt's laboratory, and learned about psychology's coming to America, especially through William James's efforts. In the twentieth century, psychology has consisted of both clinical ("soft-hearted") and experimental ("hard-headed") domains. Behaviorism was challenged on the clinical front by both psychoanalysis and humanism, and on the experimental front by the neurobiological and cognitive perspectives. Six contemporary perspectives in psychology are the behavioral, psychoanalytic, humanistic, neurobiological, cognitive, and sociocultural. Practicing psychology involves careers in psychology, areas of specialization (clinical, research, and applied), and professional organizations. Don't forget that you can obtain a more detailed, complete summary of the chapter by again reading the two in-chapter reviews on pages 10 and 19.

At the end of each chapter, we will review which of the six contemporary psychological perspectives have been emphasized in that particular chapter. In this first chapter, we introduced the six main contemporary perspectives without favoring one over the other. The behavioral perspective is discussed on p. 13, the psychoanalytic perspective on p. 14, the humanistic perspective on p. 14, the neurobiological perspective on p. 14, the cognitive perspective on pp. 14–15, and the sociocultural perspective on pp. 15–17. In subsequent chapters not all perspectives will be emphasized as equally. Remember that each of the perspectives focuses more on some domains of psychology than on others. Each perspective contributes to understanding a part of psychology, but no one perspective can explain all of psychology's many parts.

Behavioral

Psychoanalytic

Humanistic

Neurobiological

Cognitive

Sociocultural

psychology The scientific study of behavior and mental processes in contexts. 5

behavior Everything we do that can be directly observed. 5

inferences Conclusions we draw from observing behavior. 5

mental processes Thoughts, feelings, motives, and so on, that each of us experiences privately but that cannot be observed directly. 5

science of psychology The use of systematic methods to observe, describe, explain, and predict behavior. 6

contexts The historical, economic, social, and cultural factors that influence mental processes and behavior. 6

structuralism The early theory of psychology developed by Wundt that emphasized the importance of conscious thought and classification of the mind's structures. 9

functionalism William James's theory that psychology's role is to study the functions of the mind and behavior in adapting to the environment. 9

introspection A technique whereby specially trained people carefully observe and analyze their own mental experiences. 9

behavioral perspective An emphasis on the scientific study of observable behavioral responses and their environmental determinants. 13

psychoanalytic perspective An emphasis on the unconscious aspects of the mind, conflict between biological instincts and society's demands, and early family experiences. 14

humanistic perspective An emphasis on a person's capacity for personal growth, freedom to choose one's own destiny, and positive qualities. 14

neurobiological perspective An emphasis that the brain and nervous system play central roles in understanding behavior, thought, and emotion. 14

cognitive perspective An emphasis on the mental processes involved in knowing: how we direct our attention, how we perceive, how we remember, and how we think and solve problems. 14

sociocultural perspective An emphasis on the influence of culture, ethnicity, and gender, among other sociocultural factors, as essential to understanding behavior, thought, and emotion. 15

culture The behavior patterns, beliefs, and other products of a particular group of people, such as their values, work patterns, music, dress, diet, and ceremonies, that are passed on from generation to generation. 15

ethnicity An aspect of human beings based on cultural heritage, nationality characteristics, race, religion, and language. 15

ethnic identity A sense of membership in an ethnic group, based on shared language, religion, customs, values, history, and race. 15

sex The biological dimension of being female or male. 15

gender The sociocultural dimension of being female or male, especially how we learn to think and behave as females and males. 15

clinical and counseling psychology The most widely practiced specialization in psychology. Clinical and counseling psychologists diagnose and treat people with psychological problems. 18

psychiatry A branch of medicine practiced by physicians with a doctor of medicine (M.D.) degree who specialize in abnormal behavior and psychotherapy. 18

experimental and physiological psychology Areas that involve pure research. Although psychologists in other areas conduct experiments, virtually all experimental and physiological psychologists follow precise, careful experimental strategies. 18

developmental psychology An area concerned with how we become who we are, from conception to death. 18

social psychology An area that deals with people's social interactions, relationships, perceptions, and attitudes. 18

personality psychology An area that focuses on relatively enduring traits and characteristics of individuals. 18

cross-cultural psychology An area that examines the role of culture in understanding behavior, thought, and emotion. 18

psychology of women An area that emphasizes the importance of promoting the research and study of women, integrating this information about women with current psychological knowledge and beliefs, and applying the information to society and its institutions. 18

community psychology An area that focuses on providing accessible care for people with psychological problems. Community-based mental health centers are one means of providing services like outreach programs to people in need, especially those who traditionally have been underserved by mental health professionals. 19

school and educational psychology An area concerned with children's learning and adjustment in school. 19

industrial/organizational psychology An area that deals with the workplace, focusing on both the workers and the organizations that employ them. 19

UNDERSTANDING CULTURE'S INFLUENCE ON BEHAVIOR

(1993) by Richard Brislin. San Diego: Harcourt Brace Jovanovich.

This very up-to-date book by a leading authority in cross-cultural psychology introduces you to cultural influences on behavior and ways we can communicate more effectively with people from cultural backgrounds different from our own. Among the topics covered are stereotyping, prejudice, tokenism, cultural flexibility, immersion in another culture, attention to people's feelings, how individualists can communicate more effectively with collectivists and vice versa, culture and gender, and culture's influence on health.

IS PSYCHOLOGY THE MAJOR FOR YOU?

(1987) by P. J. Woods and C. S. Wilkinson. Washington, DC: American Psychological Association.

This book is must reading for any student interested in a career in psychology. It shows how a degree in psychology can be valuable preparation for many diverse careers, including human services, management, and marketing. It also includes separate chapters on women in psychology, Native Americans and Alaska natives, Asian Americans, African Americans, Latinos, and the reentry of women and men into psychology. The book provides the names and addresses of various organizations and associations in psychology, including those involved in ethnic psychology and women's studies. Some of these organizations, including the American Psychological Association, have student memberships, which you might want to seek.

American Psychological Association
> 750 First Street, NE
> Washington, DC 20002-4242
> 202–336–5500

The American Psychological Association is the largest organization of psychologists in the United States. It publishes a number of journals on psychological topics and has books and brochures available. Undergraduate student members are welcome.

American Psychological Society
> 1010 Vermont Ave., NW
> Suite 1100
> Washington, DC 20005
> 202–783–2077

The American Psychological Society promotes and advances research and applications in psychology. Student affiliate memberships are available.

Canadian Psychological Association/Société canadienne de psychologie
> 151 Slater Street Suite 205
> Ottawa ON K1P 5H3 CANADA
> 613–237–2144
> e-mail: cpa@psychologyassoc.ca

The CPA is a national voluntary organization with over 4000 members, representing the interests of psychologists and advocating the development of national standards and ethical principles. National conferences, scientific journals and mainstream publications are used to disseminate information. Collaborative relationships are maintained with other provincial and national associations and with government departments in order to advance the objectives of the association.

Creating Community Anywhere (1993)
> by Carolyn Shaffer and Kristen Anundsen
> New York: Jeremy Tarcher/Perigree

This excellent book provides valuable information about how to develop successful communities, including what works and solutions for overcoming difficulties. Extensive lists of community resources are provided.

The Great Psychologists (1986)
> by Robert Watson
> Philadelphia: Lippincott

This fascinating book explores the early psychologists' views of mental processes and behavior.

Library Use: A Handbook for Psychology (2nd ed.) (1992)
> by Jeffrey Reed and Pam Baxter
> Washington, DC: American Psychological Association

From this book you will learn about selecting, defining, and locating topics for library search in psychology. The topics chosen appeal to the interests of many psychology students, and you don't need to have highly technical knowledge to use the book.

So You Want to Make a Difference
> 202–234–8494

This is a citizen's guide to taking action that is available through the Office of Management and Budget. The guide informs you about ways you can become an advocate for people's needs.

Volunteerism (3rd ed.) (1991)
> edited by Harriet Kipps
> New Providence, NJ: R. R. Bowker

This voluminous, well-organized book provides a huge listing of opportunities for volunteerism. It is an excellent resource for finding out how to make our communities better places in which to live and how to help improve humankind.

Research and Reasoning

CHAPTER OUTLINE

CRITICAL THINKING ABOUT BEHAVIOR

CHAPTER BOXES

> *Science is not an inhuman or
> superhuman activity. It's something
> that humans invented and it speaks
> to one of our great needs—to
> understand the world around us.*
>
> **Maxine Singer**

THE STORY OF JANE GOODALL: LIFE AMONG THE CHIMPS

J ane Goodall was a young woman when she made her first trip to the Gombe Research Center in Tanzania, Africa. Fascinated by chimpanzees, she dreamed about a career that would allow her to explore her hunches about the nature of chimpanzees. She embarked on a career in the bush that involved long and solitary hours of careful, patient observation. A specialist in animal behavior, her observations spanned 30 years, years that included her marriage, the birth of her son, untold hardship, and inestimable pleasure. Due to her efforts, our understanding of chimpanzees in natural settings dramatically improved.

Often I have gazed into a chimpanzee's eyes and wondered what was going on behind them. . . . For a time I never liked to look a chimpanzee straight in the eye— I assumed that, as is the case with most primates, this would be interpreted as a threat or at least as a breach of good manners. Not so. As long as one looks with gentleness, without arrogance, a chimpanzee will understand, and may even return the look. And then—or such is my fantasy—it is as though the eyes are windows into the mind. Only the glass is opaque so that the mystery can never be fully revealed.

Jane Goodall,
Through a Window

Insights from Jane Goodall's 30 years of research among the chimpanzees in Africa illustrate the process of scientific research.

PREVIEW

Not every psychologist shows the degree of commitment and sacrifice that animal behaviorist Jane Goodall demonstrated in her pursuit of more-thorough understanding of chimpanzee behavior. However, her efforts in understanding the social organization of chimpanzees are just one installment in the making of psychology. Her approach to exploring and explaining the chimpanzee's behavior illustrates one of many methods that psychologists use in solving psychological puzzles and understanding behavior. In this chapter we will explore the nature of the scientific method, strategic questions about research design in psychology, challenges in psychological research, and how to be a wise consumer of psychological knowledge.

THE SCIENTIFIC METHOD

Some people have difficulty thinking of psychology as being a science in the same way that physics, chemistry, and biology are sciences. Can a discipline that studies why people are attracted to each other, how they reason about moral values, and how ethnicity affects identity be equated with disciplines that examine gravity, the molecular structure of a compound, or the flow of blood in the circulatory system?

Science is defined not by *what* it investigates but by *how* it investigates. Whether you investigate photosynthesis, butterflies, Saturn's moons, or the reasons people bite their fingernails, it is the *way* you investigate that makes the approach scientific or not.

In psychology the **scientific method** *is an approach used to discover accurate information or establish meaningful relations about mind and behavior. It includes the following steps: analyze a problem, formulate a tentative explanation, collect data, draw conclusions, and confirm or revise theory.*

Analyze a Problem

What problem do you want to solve? You need to go beyond a general description of the problem by isolating, carefully defining, and focusing on what you hope to investigate.

Jane Goodall began her studies with chimpanzees out of her general interest in animal behavior. She questioned how chimps related to each other. She also wondered about what similarities existed between the chimp colonies and human culture.

Formulate a Tentative Explanation

What are the most important factors, or variables, involved in the problem? How do they relate to one another? In trying to figure out what the key factors are in understanding behavior, psychologists often construct theories and develop hypotheses. A **theory** *is a coherent set of ideas that helps to explain data and to make predictions. A theory has* **hypotheses,** *assumptions that can be tested to determine their accuracy.*

Goodall hypothesized that she would discover strong social networks in the chimp colonies she studied. She suspected there would be a dominance hierarchy among the chimps and began to plan how to obtain the **data,** *information from systematic observation,* to support her theory.

Collect Data

Psychologists use a variety of methods for collecting data in order to *confirm* or *disconfirm* a hypothesis. Regardless of the method, psychologists must identify what kind of *data* will support their ideas and what method of observation will produce the required data.

Many psychologists are biased toward conducting studies that have a *quantitative* foundation. Psychologists carefully define and measure various aspects of the research in order to analyze the numerical data using statistics. Some psychologists prefer *qualitative* research, which does not require such stringent attention to measurement issues.

Goodall's research represents the qualitative approach. Goodall carefully observed and recorded behaviors, inferring meanings about patterns she described.

Draw Conclusions

What do the data mean? (Note here that the word *data* is plural and takes plural verb forms.) Researchers must interpret their findings. After they analyze the data, they compare their findings with what others have discovered about the same issue or problem in order to establish confidence in their results or to determine the relative importance of their findings.

In her studies of chimpanzee social organization, Goodall described and explained the complex behaviors that established and maintained dominance in the chimp colony. Comparing individual chimp behaviors allowed her to draw conclusions about dominance, parenting, and other aspects of chimpanzee social life.

Confirm or Revise Theory

On the basis of the results of the investigation, your original hypothesis might be confirmed. (Psychologists tend not to use the word *prove* because it implies more permanence than research in behavior usually warrants.) If the data do *not* support the original hypothesis, you will have to revise your explanation.

Goodall confirmed many of her expectations about the social life of chimpanzees; yet she also reported surprises that prompted some changes in how the scientific community regarded chimpanzee behavior. For example, she discovered that chimps made and used tools in natural settings. They stripped the leaves from stems and poked the stems into deep holes in trees to extract and eat ants. This finding not only prompted her to revise theory, but also challenged the well-established idea that human beings are the only animals capable of making and using tools.

Over the years, some psychological theories and methods have been discarded, others revised. For example, Wundt's structuralist approach and introspective methods have been largely discarded, whereas psychologists have substantially revised behaviorism and psychoanalytic theory. The cognitive, neurobiological, and sociocultural explanations are undergoing revision as psychologists apply the scientific method to the questions these orientations stimulate. Figure 2.1 summarizes the main steps in the scientific method.

There is nothing quite as practical as a good theory

Kurt Lewin

STRATEGIC QUESTIONS ABOUT RESEARCH DESIGN IN PSYCHOLOGY

Several questions must be answered when applying scientific methods to solving problems in psychology:

1. *Who should be studied?* Is the focal behavior apparent only in humans? Can we study other animals and generalize to human behavior? Is the behavior demonstrated by only *some* humans? Is the behavior apparent in some cultures and not in others? Each of these questions shapes how research will be designed.
2. *In what kind of setting should the research be conducted?* This question concerns the degree of control we want to have over the behavior we are studying. If we use a laboratory setting, we will have a greater amount of control. Natural settings produce less control but offer other kinds of advantages, because we have access to more realistic behaviors outside the laboratory.
3. *Which research method will provide the most appropriate and satisfying depth of explanation?* Recall

---

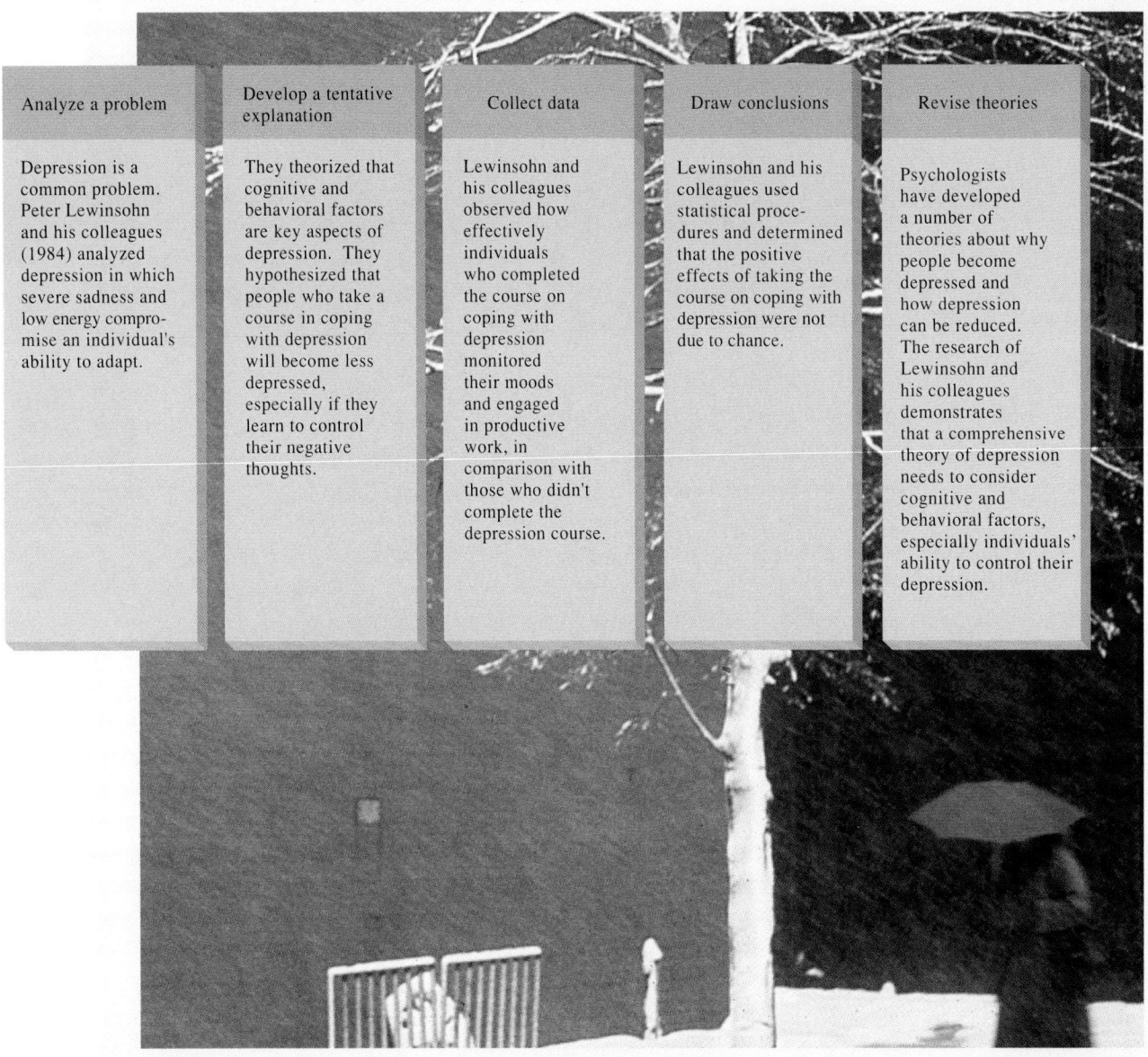

Analyze a problem	Develop a tentative explanation	Collect data	Draw conclusions	Revise theories
Depression is a common problem. Peter Lewinsohn and his colleagues (1984) analyzed depression in which severe sadness and low energy compromise an individual's ability to adapt.	They theorized that cognitive and behavioral factors are key aspects of depression. They hypothesized that people who take a course in coping with depression will become less depressed, especially if they learn to control their negative thoughts.	Lewinsohn and his colleagues observed how effectively individuals who completed the course on coping with depression monitored their moods and engaged in productive work, in comparison with those who didn't complete the depression course.	Lewinsohn and his colleagues used statistical procedures and determined that the positive effects of taking the course on coping with depression were not due to chance.	Psychologists have developed a number of theories about why people become depressed and how depression can be reduced. The research of Lewinsohn and his colleagues demonstrates that a comprehensive theory of depression needs to consider cognitive and behavioral factors, especially individuals' ability to control their depression.

FIGURE 2.1

Steps in the Scientific Method and an Application to Depression
In the text we applied the scientific method to Jane Goodall's research with chimpanzees. To help you understand the steps in the scientific method, here we apply the scientific method to the problem of depression. Peter Lewinsohn derived his theory about reducing depression from the behavioral/cognitive perspectives.

that the goals of psychology involve observing, describing, explaining, and predicting behavior. Some research offers a comprehensive description of a phenomenon with limited speculation about explaining or predicting the behavior. Other research emphasizes stronger controls over behavior to isolate cause-and-effect relationships, leading to more-precise explanations and more-accurate predictions of behavior.

4. *What measurement and research strategies will best serve the research question?* There are many options for selecting measures to assess behavior in the field of psychology. Choices will depend not only on the research questions, but also on time, space, and other resources that support research. We will examine various measures later in this chapter, including the advantages and disadvantages of the measures.

Predicting Aggression

Let's start with a familiar and important concept that generates a great deal of research attention in psychology—aggression. Why do you think some people are more likely than others to be aggressive? We will use this question as the basis for exploring research ideas that might help us to predict aggressive behaviors. All research design starts with curiosity. To assist you in exploiting your own curiosity, think about the last time you saw aggression erupt.

- Where did you last experience aggression?
- What environmental factors seemed to influence the aggressive behavior?

- What range of aggressive reactions did you witness?
- What factors or variables discouraged the aggressive behavior?
- Could aggressive individuals have higher hormone levels?
- What aspects of aggressive behavior interest you most?
- What other questions can you generate about predicting aggression?

Answering these questions demonstrates the ability to *make accurate observations, descriptions, and inferences about behavior* that can lead to the formulation of researchable questions.

Subject Selection

The choice of subjects to be studied is an important one. Although researchers can explore the experiences of one individual, most attempt to establish behavioral principles that can be generalized to large groups of individuals. For the most part, the more narrowly researchers define the subject population, the less generalizable the findings will be.

Psychology has had a long history of studying "the college sophomore" as its primary source of subjects, due to the availability of psychology students from various experimental subject pools. This practice has drawn appropriate criticism. We might not be able to generalize from this specialized group to people of other ages, education levels, and cultures.

Random Samples

Sometimes psychologists want information about a small set of people, such as all African American graduates of a particular high school in the past 5 years or all college students from your campus who participated in a civic protest. At other times, we want to know something about a large population of people, such as all people in the United States. In each instance, the people surveyed must represent the group to be described. Psychologists accomplish this important task by surveying a random sample of subjects. In a **random sample,** *every member of a population or group has an equal chance of being selected.*

Random samples are important because, in most instances, psychologists cannot survey everyone they are trying to describe. The National Crime Survey is an example of a random sample survey (U.S. Department of Justice,

1983). If we were to ask only people from a high-crime area of Miami, Florida, if they had been a victim of crime and use this information to project the frequency of crime in the United States, our projections would be inflated. Instead, the National Crime Survey uses a random sample, giving each household in the United States an equal chance of being surveyed; its results indicated that one third of the households surveyed were victimized by violence or theft.

How do researchers obtain a random sample of subjects? In studies like the National Crime Survey, sampling methods ensure that the samples are representative of the proportion of African American, Anglo-American, Latino, Asian American, Native American, low-income, middle-income, high-income, rural, and urban individuals in the United States. A national random sample of 5,000 subjects, for example, has fewer African Americans than Whites, fewer high-income than low-income persons, and fewer rural than urban subjects in order to be truly representative of the larger population.

Unfortunately, sometimes researchers do not follow appropriate sampling methods. Newspapers and magazines often conduct surveys of their readership, which can produce **selection bias,** or *lack of representativeness in the sample,* in their results. Those who participate by mailing or calling in their opinions probably feel more strongly about the issue in question than those who do not respond. Some issues, such as the morality of premarital sex, are likely to spur into action those with strong feelings. Surveys face some of the same problems as interviews—for example, individuals are not always willing to answer questions or do not always tell the truth.

Gender Bias

There is a growing consensus that science in general, and psychology in particular, has been oriented toward males and dominated by males. Research in psychology has predominantly studied males, sometimes assuming that the results could be generalized to females. Some researchers believe that we should challenge psychology to examine the world in a new way, one that incorporates not just gender but also other sociocultural factors, such as ethnicity, sexual orientation, age, and socioeconomic status (Beal, 1994; Matlin, 1993).

Gender bias influences subject selection but can also affect other stages in the research process (Denmark, 1994; Denmark & others, 1988; Gannon & others, 1992). For example, researchers who study contraceptives but use only female subjects reflect the assumption and stereotype that women alone are responsible for birth control. Studies of this type often carry titles, such as "Perceptions of Contraceptive Use," that imply a broader scope to the study than it has. We need to use more-precise titles and concluding statements, to clarify who was in the sample and whom the study results apply to (Denmark & others, 1988).

Florence Denmark *(shown here talking with a group of students)* has developed a number of guidelines for nonsexist research. Denmark and others believe that psychology needs to be challenged to examine the world in a new way, one that incorporates girls' and women's perspectives.

Cultural Bias

Researchers who are unfamiliar with the cultural and ethnic groups they are studying must take extra precautions to minimize any biases they bring with them from their own culture. For example, they must make sure they construct measures that are meaningful for each of the cultural or ethnic minority groups being studied (Berry, 1980; Berry & others, in press).

Let's go back to the study of aggression. Cross-cultural psychologists have found that aggression is universal; however, the expression of aggression might be culture-specific (Segall & others, 1990). For example, the !Kung of southern Africa actively dissuade one another from behaving aggressively, whereas the Yanomamo Indians of South America promote aggression. Yanomamo youths cannot achieve adult status unless they are capable of killing, fighting, and pummeling others (see figure 2.2). Researchers would need to be astute about the values and practices of the culture being studied in order to interpret behaviors accurately.

In a symposium on racism in research (Lee, 1992; Padilla & Lindholm, 1992), the participants concluded that we need to include more ethnic minority individuals in our research. Historically, most researchers discounted minorities from research, viewing them simply as variations from the norm. Nonmainstream individuals have been viewed as "confounds" or "noise" in data. Consequently, researchers have deliberately excluded them from their samples. Because research has excluded ethnic minority individuals for so long, there is likely to be more variation in people's real lives than our research data have indicated in the past (Graham, 1992).

Animal Studies

As Jane Goodall's research demonstrates, animal studies can be fascinating in their own right. However, if our primary interest is human behavior, animal studies might be a preferred method when research would be difficult to carry out with humans. These studies permit researchers to control their subjects' genetic background, diet, experiences during infancy, and many other factors (Catania, 1990). In addition, animal researchers can investigate the effects of treatments (such as brain implants) using controlled physiological studies that would be unethical with humans. Moreover, it is possible to track the entire life cycle of some animals over a relatively short period of time. Laboratory mice, for instance, have a life span of approximately 1 year.

FIGURE 2.2

Cultural Influences on Aggression

(a) The peaceful !Kung of Southern Africa discourage any kind of aggression; the !Kung are called the "harmless people." *(b)* Hardly harmless, the violent Yanomamo are called the "fierce people." Male Yanomamo youths are told that they cannot achieve manhood unless they are capable of killing, fighting, and pummeling others. *Can you imagine the difficulties researchers from Western cultures might have in overcoming their own expectations and biases about aggression to conduct research on cultures with such different values?*

With regard to aggression, researchers know that castration turns ferocious bulls into docile oxen by acting on the male hormone system, and, after a number of breedings of aggressive mice, researchers have created mice that are ferocious (Manning, 1989). Do these findings with animals apply to humans? Not always. Hormones and genes do influence human aggression, but the influence is less powerful than in animals because humans differ from animals in many important ways. One disadvantage to research with animals is that the results might not apply to humans.

Research Settings

Psychologists collect information systematically in a variety of settings. For example, we can watch aggression in the laboratory or in a more natural setting, such as a street corner. Observations of behavior in laboratories offer certain advantages. In laboratory settings we can *control* certain factors that influence behavior but aren't the direct focus of our research. **Laboratories** *are controlled settings with many of the complex factors of the "real world" removed.*

In a classic study on children's aggression, Albert Bandura (1965) had an adult model repeatedly hit a "Bobo doll," a plastic inflated clown doll about 3 feet tall. Bandura's research question was to examine under what conditions children would copy adult aggressive behavior. After the children saw the adult attack the Bobo doll on videotape, they also hit and kicked the inflated toy when given positive incentives to do so. By conducting his experiment in a laboratory with adult models and an adult experimenter the children did not know, Bandura had control over when the children witnessed aggression, how much aggression they saw, and what form the aggression took. Bandura could not have conducted his experiment as effectively if other factors, such as parents, siblings, friends, television, and a familiar room, had been present. We'll expand on other design features of Bandura's experiment later in this chapter.

Laboratory research has some drawbacks, however. First, it is almost impossible to conduct research without the participants' knowing they are being studied. Second,

Systematic observations in natural settings provide valuable information about behavior across cultures. For example, in one investigation, observations in different cultures revealed that American children often engage in less work and more play than children in many other cultures do (Whiting & Whiting, 1975). *Can you speculate about why such differences might exist between American children and those of other cultures? Can you identify some implications for this balance of work and play in American children?*

the laboratory setting is *unnatural* and therefore can cause the participants to behave unnaturally. Research participants usually show less aggressive behavior in a laboratory than in a more familiar or natural setting, such as at home or in a park. They also show less aggression when they are aware they are being observed than when they are unaware they are being observed. Third, people who are willing to go to a university laboratory are unlikely to represent groups from diverse cultural backgrounds. Those who are unfamiliar with university settings, or with the idea of "helping science," might be intimidated by the setting. Fourth, some aspects of mind and behavior are difficult, if not impossible, to examine in the laboratory. Certain types of stress are difficult (and unethical) to study in the laboratory. Alcohol, for instance, consistently increases aggression in individuals who are provoked, but laboratory investigations are not likely to fully capture how social factors and alcohol interact to enhance aggression.

Although laboratory research is a valuable tool for psychologists, naturalistic observation provides insight that cannot be achieved in the laboratory. In **naturalistic observation,** *psychologists observe behavior in real-world settings and make no effort to manipulate or control the situation.* Psychologists conduct naturalistic observations at soccer games, day-care centers, college residence halls, rest rooms, corporations, shopping malls, restaurants, dances, and other places people live in or frequent. In contrast to Bandura's laboratory observations, psychologists using naturalistic methods observe the aggression of children in nursery schools, of marital partners at home, and of people at sporting events and political protests (Bronfenbrenner, 1989; Patterson, 1991).

REVIEW

The Scientific Method and Strategic Questions About Research Design in Psychology

The scientific method is an approach used to discover accurate information about, and establish meaningful relationships between, mind and behavior. It consists of the following steps: (1) Analyze a problem; (2) formulate a tentative explanation—theories and hypotheses are often developed at this point;

(3) collect data; (4) draw conclusions; and (5) confirm or revise theory.

Four strategic questions about research design in psychology are these: (1) Who should be studied? This question raises questions about random samples, gender bias, culture bias, and animals as subjects. (2) In what kind of setting should the research be conducted? This question

often involves a choice between a laboratory setting and naturalistic observation. (3) Which research methods will provide the most appropriate and most satisfying depth of explanation? (4) Which measurement and research strategies will serve the research question best? We will explore these two questions next.

Psychology as Science and Story

Research Methods and Depth of Explanation

Researchers choose between three types of research methods with varying depths of explanation: descriptive, correlational, and experimental.

Descriptive Research Methods

Descriptive research methods *intend to provide an accurate portrayal of behavior. Descriptive statistics communicate basic qualities of the data being reported.* Descriptive methods provide less depth of explanation than do correlational and experimental methods. Consider an example. We might want to examine aggression in children's Saturday-morning cartoons. In this programming, researchers have observed, for example, an average of 20 to 25 aggressive episodes per hour and an absence of female leading characters in all cartoons (Goldstein, 1994; Signorielli, 1993). These descriptive findings are provocative and might encourage us to pursue more-rigorous studies that will enhance our understanding and the accuracy of our predictions in this area.

Correlational Research Methods

The second level of depth of explanation involves **correlational research methods,** *in which the goal is to describe the strength of the relation between two or more events or characteristics.* This is a useful research strategy because the more strongly events are related (associated or correlated), the more effectively we can predict one from the other. For example, researchers have shown that children's school performance and television watching appear to be related (Winn, 1987). If we find that academic effectiveness in school (as measured by grade point average) is strongly associated with minimal television watching, we can use the occurrence of a poor grade point average to predict extended television watching.

Can we then conclude that watching television causes poor school performance? Not necessarily. First of all, even a strong correlation between two events doesn't mean that one event causes the other. Some other factor or variable could be responsible for both. In our test case, we might speculate that the absence of parental supervision could be the causal factor for both poor school performance and extended television watching. A second possibility involves the direction of causation; perhaps poor performance in school causes increased television watching. Poor performers might seek passive, escapist entertainment to assuage their damaged self-esteem. A third possibility also exists. There could be a strong causal relation in the direction originally suspected. Unfortunately, the choice of a correlational research strategy will not allow us to verify cause-and-effect relationships. Throughout this text, you will read about numerous studies that used a correlational strategy. Keep in mind how easy it is to improperly assume causality when two events or characteristics are merely correlated. Figure 2.3 illustrates possible explanations of an observed correlation related to violence.

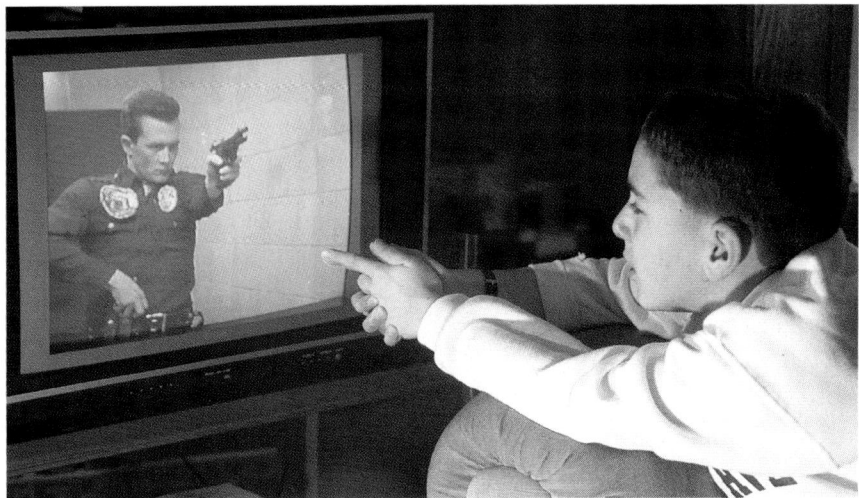

Correlational studies of extended television watching and children's grades cannot be used to say that watching television extensively causes students to obtain poor grades. *Why not?*

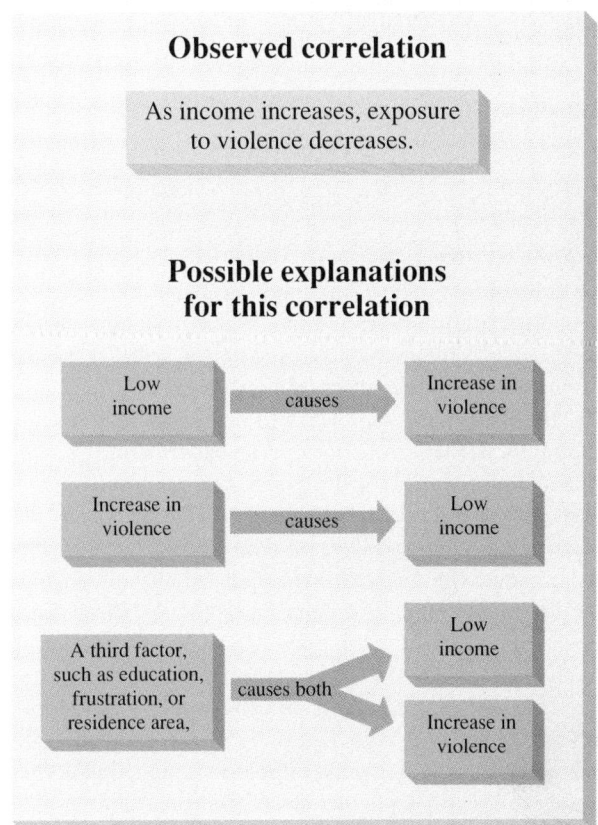

FIGURE 2.3

Possible Explanations of Correlational Data—Example of Income and Violence

Does Poverty Cause Violence?

Does poverty cause violence? Suppose we conduct a survey and find that people with lower incomes experience more episodes of violence than do people who make more money. Explain three reasons why we cannot interpret this finding to mean that making a great deal of money will cause us to have less violent lives.

1. There might be a third variable that causes both events. For example, education, self-esteem, social upbringing, and housing location might, plausibly, influence both one's money-making potential and the level of violence in one's life.

2. Perhaps the causal relationship is in the other direction: that violence causes poverty. Maybe lives teeming with aggression are too chaotic to sustain regular, high-paying employment. Court costs, weapon expense, and losses related to injury and death may also reduce economic resources.

3. There might, in fact, be a causal relationship between aggression intensity and amount of money; however, this connection cannot be confirmed on the basis of correlational data. We would have to use a different method, involving controlled comparison, to address causality.

In situations where we do not have control over the relevant variables, we must *pursue alternative explanations for behavior to explain behavior comprehensively,* instead of assuming, possibly erroneously, a simple causal relation. Adopting this stance encourages a more complete consideration of all the factors that might be involved.

Experimental Research Methods

The deepest level of explanation is provided by the experimental research method (see figure 2.4). Whereas correlational research methods allow us to say only that two events are related, **experimental research methods** *allow us to determine the causes of behavior with greater precision.* Psychologists accomplish this task by performing an **experiment,** *a carefully regulated procedure in which researchers manipulate one or more of the factors believed to influence the behavior being studied and hold all other factors constant.* If the behavior under study changes when a factor is manipulated, then the manipulated factor has caused the behavior to change. Psychologists use experiments to establish cause-and-effect relationships between events, something correlational studies cannot do. *Cause* reflects how the event is being manipulated, and *effect* is how the behavior changes because of the manipulation. Remember that *nothing* is manipulated in conducting correlational studies; in an experiment, the researcher actively intervenes to influence a behavior, manipulating some aspect of the experience to observe the effect on behavior.

> *Truth is arrived at by the painstaking process of eliminating the untrue.*
>
> **Arthur Conan Doyle, *Sherlock Holmes***

To illustrate the principles of the experimental strategy, let's return to Albert Bandura's (1965) classic study of children's aggression, sometimes referred to as the "Bobo doll" study. Earlier we commented about the degree of controlled observation that was possible in a laboratory setting versus natural environments. Bandura chose a controlled, laboratory setting to study children's imitation of videotaped aggression by adult models. He used an experimental strategy to establish more precise connections between the observation of aggression and performance of imitative aggressive acts (see figure 2.5).

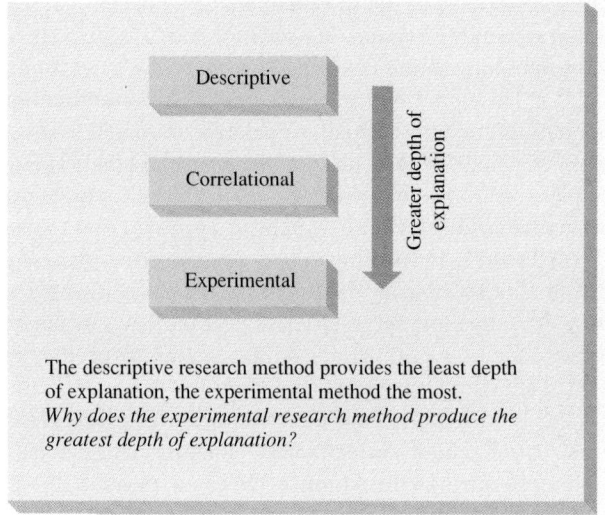

The descriptive research method provides the least depth of explanation, the experimental method the most. *Why does the experimental research method produce the greatest depth of explanation?*

FIGURE 2.4

Research Methods and Depth of Explanation

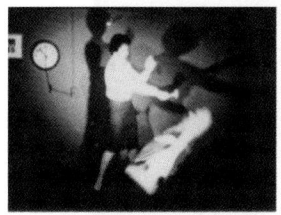
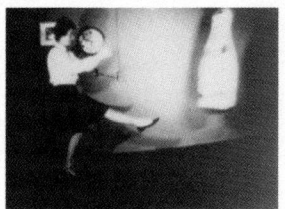

FIGURE 2.5

Bandura's Study of Imitation and Children's Aggression
The top two frames show the adult model behaving aggressively toward the Bobo doll by hitting it with a hammer and kicking it. In the bottom four frames, a boy and a girl are shown imitating the model's aggressive behaviors.

First, Bandura defined aggression and imitation. He videotaped a 5-minute sequence in which an adult male modeled four novel aggressive acts. For example, the model pounded the Bobo doll with a toy hammer and said, "Sockeroo . . . stay down." He kicked the Bobo doll repeatedly, saying, "Fly away." The other two acts involved punching the doll's nose and throwing balls at the doll while making similar distinctive verbal statements. Bandura trained observers to identify when children imitated one of these four novel acts. Because the aggressive acts were novel, Bandura reported a high level of agreement (99 percent) on which children's behaviors constituted imitation of the aggressive acts.

Bandura selected as subjects 33 male and 33 female children attending nursery school and randomly assigned them to one of three conditions. **Random assignment** *occurs when psychologists assign subjects to experimental and control conditions by chance. This practice reduces the likelihood that the results of the experiment will be due to preexisting differences between the two groups.* For example, random assignment greatly decreases the probability that the two groups will differ on such factors as health, intelligence, alertness, social class, and television-watching patterns.

The children watched an adult male model perform aggressive acts in one of three videotaped versions. At the end of the first videotape, another adult rewarded the aggressive model with candy and praised him for being a

"strong champion" for his aggression toward the Bobo doll. At the end of the second tape, the other adult punished the model for being a "bully" and spanked him. In the third condition, the adult aggressor received no consequences for aggressive behavior. In this example, the children who observed an aggressive adult being rewarded or punished were in the experimental groups. An **experimental group** *is a group whose experience is manipulated.* The children who observed the aggressive model receiving no consequences make up the **control group**—*a comparison group treated in every way like the experimental groups except for the manipulated factor.* The control group serves as a baseline against which psychologists can compare the effects found in the manipulated condition. All experiments involve controlled comparisons of some kind even if there is no formal control group.

The **independent variable** *is the manipulated, influential, experimental factor in an experiment.* We use the label *independent* because this variable can be changed independently of other factors. In Bandura's study, the type of consequence witnessed by the children (reward vs. punishment vs. no consequence) was the independent variable.

After the children observed the assigned model, trained observers counted how many acts of aggression showed up in the children's play. The **dependent variable** *is the factor that is measured in an experiment; it may change as the independent variable is manipulated.* We use the label *dependent* because the variable *depends on* the differences in treatment between the subject groups. The dependent variable depends on the independent variable. The independent variable (the cause) produces the dependent variable (the effect). In Bandura's study, the dependent variable was the number of imitative aggressive acts the children performed. An overview of Bandura's study of modeling and children's aggression is shown in figure 2.6.

Bandura reported that the children observing the aggressive model who had been punished for his acts showed less imitative aggression in subsequent free play than did children who observed the model who had been praised or given no consequences for aggression. When experimenters introduced positive incentives for imitating their aggressive acts after the free-play period was over, the differences among the groups disappeared. Bandura concluded that all of the children learned the aggressive responses regardless of the version of the videotape they viewed, but that the differences in the degree to which they demonstrated in free play what they had learned depended on the consequences they had witnessed. We will discuss the significance of Bandura's work when we study principles of learning in chapter 6.

Despite the power of the experimental paradigm, there are still some problems with this research strategy. For example, researchers must take great precautions to ensure that their own expectations don't influence the outcome of their research. In one study, college students were randomly assigned rats from the same litter, but half of the students were told that their rats were from a "maze bright" lineage and half were told that their rats were from a "maze dull" lineage (Rosenthal, 1976). The students then conducted

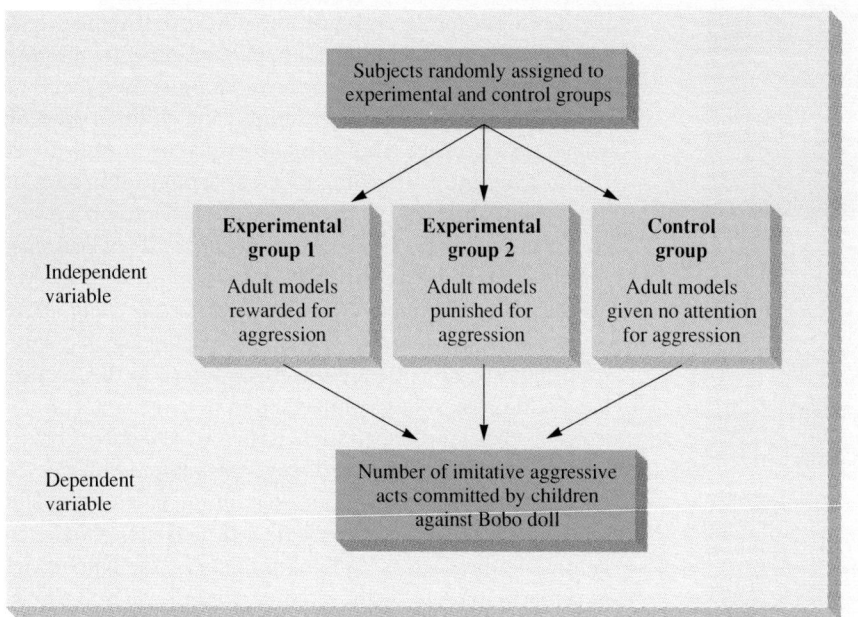

FIGURE 2.6

The Experimental Strategy in Psychology
Bandura's research demonstrated the effects of modeling (independent variable) on aggressive behavior (dependent variable).

"What it comes down to is you have to find out what reaction they're looking for, and you give them that reaction."

© 1991 by Sidney Harris—"You Want Proof? . . . " W. H. Freeman and Company.

experiments to determine their rat's ability to learn a maze. Remarkably, the reported performance of the rats on later maze runnings conformed to the labels that had been provided. No such difference should have occurred, due to the random assignment of the rats. The explanation: The experimenters' (students') expectancies influenced the outcome of the research results. For this reason, researchers often institute control procedures that prevent those measuring the dependent variable from knowing what kind of experimental treatment the participant received.

Another challenge involves participant expectations. Human subjects (participants) might actively attempt to help out the experimenter by guessing the hypothesis and conforming to the experimenter's expectations. Their heightened focus on expectations about their performance is sometimes referred to as a "placebo effect." Researchers try to guard against this effect by using control procedures that minimize participants' expectations about the outcome of research.

Although researchers believe that experimental research gives them the greatest amount of control, it might also require them to sacrifice generalizability. The more tightly controlled the procedure, the less likely it is that the results will apply in other contexts or with other participants.

Assessment Measures

In addition to selecting subjects, a research setting, and a research method, researchers in psychology also must choose one or more measures to assess the subjects' behavior. The measures used include observations, interviews, questionnaires, case studies, standardized tests, cross-cultural research, and research with ethnic minority individuals.

Observations

Sherlock Holmes chided Watson, "You see but you do not observe." We look at things all the time, but casually watching a friend cross the campus is not scientific observation. Unless you are a trained observer and practice your skills regularly, you might not know what to look for, you might not remember what you saw, what you are looking for might change from one moment to the next, and you might not communicate your observations effectively.

For observations to be effective, we have to know what we are looking for, whom we are observing, and when, where, and how we will observe. We must also decide what format to use when recording behavior. That is, we need to observe in a *systematic* way.

Consider aggression. Do we want to study verbal or physical aggression, or both? How will we know it when we see it? If one man punches another in the arm, will we mark that down as aggression? If both men are laughing and one punches the other, will that still count? An **operational definition** *is a definition of behavior in terms of observable features.* In our example of aggression, we might want to study several types of aggression—such as physical aggression, which might be operationally defined as "physical contact with an intent to harm," and verbal aggression, which might be operationally defined as "the use of language that contains insults, challenges, or swearing."

Measuring behavior is also tricky. At times it is appropriate to count occurrences of behavior, as in "How many times did the subject kick another during the observation period?" Time itself can serve as a measure. For example, we can compare the aggressive behavior of two nursery school children by timing how many minutes they spend in aggressive and in nonaggressive play.

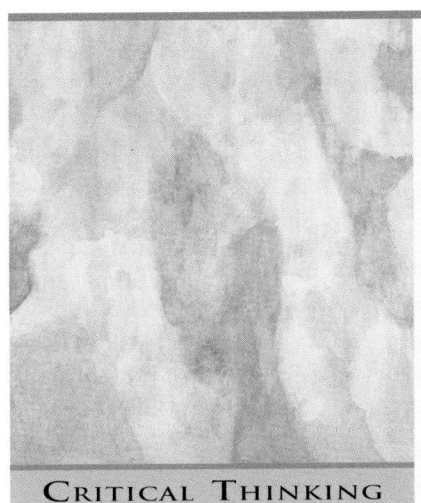

CRITICAL THINKING

Creating Aggression

Suppose that we wanted to experiment with the effects of steroids on aggressive behavior in college students. Steroids are drugs that enhance muscle development and improve the body's ability to cope with disease. However, steroids have been reported to have some danger-ous behavioral side effects, including increased irritability, and physical problems, including increased risk of cancer. Is it possible to create a stronger aggressive response in individuals as a consequence of taking steroids?

We enlist 100 volunteers who live on a college campus to be the participants in the experiment, which we will conduct for 8 weeks in the summer. We give half the students steroids and the other half gelatin capsules. We will hold all other aspects of the experimental situation constant.

What would your hypothesis be? _____

_____

Why would you randomly assign subjects to conditions? _____

_____

What aspects of subjects' lives would you have to control? _____

_____

What is the independent variable? _____

_____

How would you measure the dependent variable? _____

_____

Would you have any ethical concerns in conducting this study? _____

_____

How challenging would this experiment be to conduct? _____

_____

Designing an experiment should enhance your ability to *evaluate the quality of conclusions about behavior.* In addition, you probably recognized that such an experiment endangers the health and well-being of the participants. It is unlikely that your proposal would be approved by a review board without substantial reassurances that you would protect subjects from harm. When you recognize this difficulty, you are better able to propose research that *practices standards of ethical treatment toward individuals and groups.*

A common way to record observations is to write them down, using shorthand or symbols. Psychologists increasingly use tape recorders, video cameras, special coding sheets, and one-way mirrors to make observations more efficient.

Interviews

An **interview** *is a method in which questions are asked directly to an individual to find out about the person's experiences and attitudes.* Most interviews occur face-to-face, although they can take place over the telephone.

Interviews range from being highly unstructured to being highly structured. Examples of unstructured interview questions are the following: "How aggressive are you?" "How aggressive is your child?" These open-ended questions prompt answers in the subject's own words. Examples of structured interview questions include these: "In the past week, how often did you yell at your spouse?" "How often in the past year was your child involved in fights at school?" The questions themselves can impose structure, as when a question asks for a numerical estimate. The interviewer can also categorize answers by asking the respondent to choose from several options. For example, a researcher might ask you to answer a question by choosing among the options "highly aggressive," "moderately aggressive," "moderately unaggressive," and "highly unaggressive."

An experienced interviewer knows how to put respondents at ease and how to encourage them to open up. A competent interviewer pays attention to the way people respond to questions and might probe for more information. A person might respond to questions about the nature of marital conflict with fuzzy statements, such as "Well, I don't know whether we have a lot of conflict or not." A skilled interviewer pushes for more specific, concrete answers by making requests like "Tell me the worst things you and your husband said to each other in the past week." Using these strategies forces researchers to be involved with, rather than detached from, the people they interview and yields a better understanding of mind and behavior (Gregory, 1992).

Interviews also have shortcomings. Perhaps the most critical shortcoming is the factor of **social desirability,** *because of which participants tell interviewers what they think is most socially acceptable or desirable rather than what they truly think or feel.* When asked about her marital conflict, June might not want to disclose that arguments have been painfully tense in the past month. Sam, her husband, might not want to divulge his extramarital affair when asked about his sexual relationships. Skilled interviewing techniques and questions reduce defensiveness and secure more accurate information.

Questionnaires

Psychologists also find out information about people by using questionnaires or surveys. A **questionnaire** *is similar to a highly structured interview, except that respondents read*

Systematic, unbiased observation is a key feature of many good research studies. Here a researcher observes the behavior of young children in a preschool setting. *What advantages support the use of observation through a one-way mirror?*

he ran to a telephone booth to call his priest. This case reveals how depressive moods and bizarre thinking can precede violent acts, such as murder.

Although case histories provide dramatic, in-depth portrayals of people's lives, we need to exercise caution when generalizing from this information. The subject of a case study is unique, with a genetic makeup and experiences no one else shares. In addition, case studies involve judgments of unknown reliability. That is, psychologists who conduct case studies do not typically check to see if other psychologists agree with their conclusions.

Standardized Tests

Standardized tests *require people to answer a series of written or oral questions. They have two distinct features. First, psychologists usually total an individual's score to yield a single score, or a set of scores, that reflects something about the individual. Second, psychologists compare the individual's score to the scores of a large group of similar people to determine how the individual responded relative to others.* Scores are often described in percentiles. For example, perhaps you scored in the 92nd percentile on the SAT. This measure tells you that you scored higher than 92 percent of the large group of individuals who previously took the test.

To continue our look at how psychologists use various methods to evaluate aggression, consider the Minnesota Multiphasic Personality Inventory, or MMPI, which includes a scale to assess an individual's delinquent and antisocial tendencies. The items on this scale ask you to indicate whether you are rebellious and impulsive or if you have trouble with authority figures. The 26-year-old teacher who murdered his girlfriend would probably have scored high on a number of the MMPI scales, including one designed to measure how strange our thoughts and ideas are.

The main advantage of standardized tests is that they provide information about *individual differences* among people. However, information obtained from standardized tests might not always predict behavior in nontest situations. Psychologists base standardized tests on the belief that a person's behavior is consistent and stable. Although personality and intelligence, two of the primary targets of standardized tests, have some stability, they can vary with the situation. For example, a person might perform poorly on a standard intelligence test in an office setting but display a much higher level of intelligence at home, where she is less anxious. This criticism is especially relevant for individuals who have been inappropriately classified as mentally retarded on the basis of their scores on standardized

the questions and mark their answers on a sheet of paper rather than respond verbally to the interview. One major advantage of surveys and questionnaires is that psychologists can give them easily to a large number of people. Good surveys have concrete, specific, and unambiguous questions, and they assess the authenticity of the replies.

One example of the use of a questionnaire in psychological research is the National Crime Survey, described earlier in the chapter. Its subjects were asked to read questions and mark their answers related to the incidence of various crimes where they live.

Case Studies

A **case study** *provides an in-depth look at one individual; clinical psychologists use case studies when they cannot duplicate the unique aspects of an individual's life for study, for either practical or ethical reasons.* The case study is *descriptive,* providing a comprehensive accounting of one person's hopes, fears, fantasies, traumatic experiences, health, or anything else that helps the psychologist understand the person's mind and behavior.

Consider the following case study (Revitch & Schlesinger, 1978) involving aggressive behavior: A 26-year-old schoolteacher met a woman with whom he fell intensely in love. Several months after their love affair began, the schoolteacher became depressed, drank heavily, and talked about suicide. His actions became bizarre. On one occasion, he punctured the tires of his beloved's car. On another, he stood on the side of the road where she passed frequently in her car and extended his hand in his pocket so she would think he was holding a gun. His relationship with the woman vacillated between love and hate. Only 8 months after meeting her, the teacher shot and killed her while he was a passenger in the car she was driving. Soon after the act,

HERMAN © Jim Unger. Reprinted with permission of UNIVERSAL PRESS SYNDICATE. All rights reserved.

"Would you say you are, 'extremely happy,' 'happy,' 'average' or 'bored stiff'?"

intelligence tests. Also, many psychologists believe that standardized intelligence tests penalize ethnic minorities more than they do mainstream individuals.

Although many psychological tests work reasonably well in Western cultures, cross-cultural psychologists caution that the tests might not always be appropriate in cultures other than the one in which they were developed (Lonner, 1990). For example, individuals in other cultures simply might not have had as much exposure to the information in the test questions.

Cross-Cultural Research and Research with Ethnic Minority Groups

In conducting research on cultural and ethnic minority issues, investigators distinguish between the emic approach and the etic approach. In the **emic approach,** *the goal is to*
describe behavior in one culture or ethnic group in terms that are meaningful and important to the people in that culture or ethnic group, without regard to other cultures or ethnic groups. In the **etic approach,** *the goal is to describe behavior so that generalizations can be made across cultures.* That is, the emic approach is culture-specific; the etic approach is culture-universal. If researchers construct a questionnaire in an emic fashion, their concern is only that the questions be meaningful to the particular culture or ethnic group being studied. If, however, the researchers construct a questionnaire in an etic fashion, they want to include questions that reflect concepts familiar to all cultures involved (Berry, 1969). More information about the nature of cross-cultural research appears in Sociocultural Worlds 2.1.

How might emic and etic approaches be reflected in the study of family stress? In the emic approach, the researchers might choose to focus only on the stress experienced in middle-class White families, without regard to whether the information obtained in the study can be generalized or is appropriate for ethnic minority groups. In a subsequent study, the researchers might decide to adopt an etic approach by studying not only middle-class White family stress but also the stress in lower-income White families, African American families, Latino families, and Asian American families. In studying ethnic minority families, the researchers would likely discover that, in these families more frequently than in White American families, the extended family offers a support system that reduces stress. If so, the emic approach would reveal a different pattern of family stress than would the etic approach, documenting that research with middle-class White families cannot always be generalized to all other groups.

Now that we have considered the basic ways that psychologists conduct research, it is also important to examine continuing challenges to the quality of psychological research.

REVIEW

Research Methods, Depth of Explanation, and Assessment Measures

Researchers choose between three research methods with varying depths of explanation: descriptive, correlational, and experimental. The descriptive research method intends to provide accurate portrayals of behavior. Descriptive statistics communicate basic qualities of the data being reported. The descriptive research method provides less depth of explanation than the correlational and experimental strategies do. The second level of depth of explanation involves correlational research methods, in which the goal is to describe the strength of the relation between two or more events or characteristics. The correlational method does not allow causal statements. The deepest level of explanation involves the experimental research method, which allows us to determine behavior's causes.

The experimental research method involves the manipulation of influential factors—the independent variables—and the measurement of their effects on the dependent variables. In many studies, subjects are assigned randomly to experimental and control groups. Because the experimental method reveals how one event influences another, it can provide information about the causes of behavior.

The measures psychologists use to assess behavior include observations, interviews, questionnaires, case studies, standardized tests, cross-cultural research, and research with ethnic minority individuals.

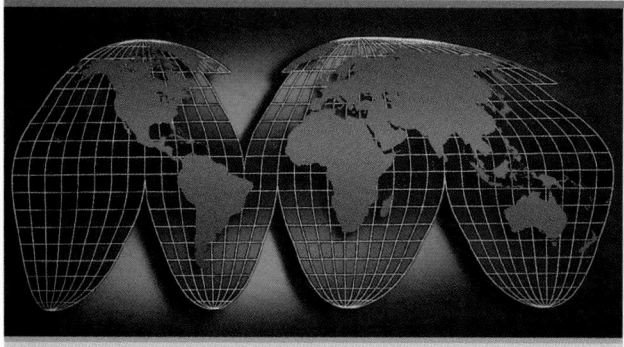

Cross-Cultural Research: The Benefits and the Challenges

Many researchers are becoming increasingly interested in the value of cross-cultural research in understanding human behavior (Scott-Jones, 1995; Stevenson, 1995). The increased interest is the result of many advantages that cross-cultural research confers. However, cross-cultural research also poses many problems.

Cross-cultural research affords the opportunity to analyze the contributions of the social context. When we are in our own culture, we often overlook the influence of the social context because we can so easily take it for granted. When researchers study behavior in a culture different from their own, the social context is often much more visible to them and easier to analyze, because it is fresher and less familiar.

A key feature of competent cross-cultural research is the intense effort to try to understand behavior from the point of view of those being studied (Coll & others, 1995; Entwisle & Astone, 1995). Researchers try not to impose the characteristics of their own culture on the cultures they are studying. They do not assume that the behaviors they examine are culture-universal. This sensitivity to others and the motivation to understand the cultural background of seemingly unusual, strange behaviors assist researchers in making culture-fair evaluations of the focal behaviors.

Cross-cultural research can sometimes enhance our understanding of how variables influence behavior. It is difficult to study the effects of one variable on another if there is not much range of experience with the variable or if there is little difference in the behavior of the subjects who participate in the study. For example, it would be very difficult to conduct a comprehensive study of the effects on school achievement of introducing a television set into the home if we confined the research to the United States—because almost all homes in the United States already have a television set. Rather, to carry out this study, we would have to conduct the research in cultures where television is just being introduced, such as rural Arctic villages in Canada. Thus, we often can understand the range of experience related to some variables only by studying them in other cultures (Brislin, 1993).

Cross-cultural research can sometimes help to unconfound variables (that is, tease them apart) to determine their relative contributions. For example, suppose that we want to study the relationship between diet and the propensity to develop certain genetic diseases. If individuals in a specific culture consume similar food, then it may be difficult to tease out the relative contribution of diet. If individuals from such a culture become *immigrants* to another culture and acquire the dietary habits of the new culture, we can separate the influence of the variables.

Cross-cultural psychologist Joseph Trimble (1989) has expressed concern about researchers' tendency to use ethnic gloss when they select and describe ethnic groups. By *ethnic gloss* Trimble means using an ethnic label, such as *Native American,* in a superficial way that assumes an ethnic group to be more homogeneous than it actually is. Trimble believes that ethnic gloss can cause researchers to obtain samples of ethnic groups and cultures that are not representative of their ethnic and cultural diversity, leading to overgeneralizations and stereotypes. Trimble proposes that researchers provide much more detail about the participants' country of origin, socioeconomic status, language, and ethnic self-identification to promote a richer understanding of diversity within culture.

CHALLENGES IN THE VALUES OF PSYCHOLOGICAL RESEARCH

Values involve standards about what is worthwhile and desirable. Psychologists share many values and have adopted a formal code of ethics to encourage clarity about the ethics of research practices. Despite these codes, challenges persist in several areas, including the nature of objectivity and the ethical treatment of human and animal subjects.

Objectivity

Some psychologists argue that psychology should be value free and morally neutral. From their perspective, the psychologist's role as a scientist is to present facts in as value-free a fashion as possible in order to achieve objective results (Kimble, 1989). Objectivity, defined as minimizing bias and distortion in research conclusions, is an important value in science. Although psychologists strive to be objective in their description, measurement, and interpretation of behavior, many critics suggest that true objectivity is not possible. Because psychologists are human, they are not value free, even if they try to be (Button & others, 1993).

Researchers' values influence their choice and execution of research strategies. For example, a divorced single parent might decide to study the inadequate involvement of male noncustodial parents in their children's development rather than the increased role of males in caring for children. Since each of us has preconceived ideas about behavior, selection of research that adheres to objective standards can be challenging.

Some people argue that psychologists should use the results of their objective research to promote action on value-laden issues. For example, if new research shows that poor-quality day care in the first year of life is harmful to children's development, shouldn't psychologists support reforms to improve the quality of day care? Perhaps. However, psychologists must evaluate new findings in the context of other studies to determine how much significance to attach to new findings. Often, issues are very complicated and courses of action about public policy are not likely to be clear-cut. Consider, for instance, the complexity of other value conflicts such as the right to own guns versus the gun control initiatives, bans on sexually explicit books versus freedom of literary expression and freedom to read, the public's right to know versus an individual's right to privacy, and retribution versus rehabilitation as the goal of criminal codes. Psychologists sometimes struggle to maintain an objective stance in evaluating research while being advocates in arenas of public policy.

Ethical Treatment of Human Subjects

When Anne and Pete, two 19-year-old college students, agreed to participate in an investigation of dating couples, they did not consider the possibility that the questionnaire they completed would stimulate them to think about issues that might lead to conflict in their relationship, and possibly end it. One year after the completion of the study, 9 of 10 participants said they had discussed their answers with their dating partner (Rubin & Mitchell, 1976). In most instances, the discussions helped strengthen the relationships, but in some cases the participants used the questionnaire as a springboard to discuss problems or concerns previously hidden. One participant said, "The study definitely played a role in ending my relationship with Larry." In this case, the couple had held different views about how long they expected to be together. She was thinking of a short-term dating relationship only, whereas he was thinking in terms of a lifetime. Their answers to the questions brought to the surface the disparity in their views and eventually led Larry to find someone who was more interested in marrying him.

At first glance, you would not imagine that a questionnaire on dating relationships would have any substantial impact on those who participate in such research. However, increasingly psychologists are recognizing that they need to take considerable caution to ensure the well-being of the participants in a psychological study. Today colleges and universities have review boards that evaluate the ethical nature of the research conducted at their institutions. Proposed research plans must pass the scrutiny of a research ethics committee before the research begins. In addition, the American Psychological Association (APA) has developed ethics guidelines for its members.

The code of ethics adopted by the APA instructs psychologists to protect their research subjects from mental and physical harm (Canter & others, 1994). The best interest of the subjects needs to be kept foremost in the researcher's mind. All subjects must give their informed consent to participate in research, which requires that subjects know what their participation will involve and any risks that might develop. For example, dating research subjects should be told beforehand that a questionnaire might stimulate thought about issues in their relationship that they haven't considered. Subjects also should be informed that, in some instances, a discussion of the issues raised can improve their dating relationship, whereas in other cases it can worsen the relationship or end it. Even after giving their informed consent, subjects retain the right to withdraw from a study at any time.

Deception is an ethical issue that psychologists have debated extensively (Koocher & Keith-Spiegel, 1996). In some circumstances, telling subjects beforehand what the research study is about substantially alters their behavior and destroys the investigator's data. For example, a psychologist wants to know whether a bystander will report a theft. A mock theft is staged, and the psychologist observes which bystanders report it. Had the psychologist informed the bystanders beforehand that the study intended to discover the percentage of bystanders who will report a theft, the intent of the study would have been lost. In all cases of deception, psychologists must ensure that the deception will not harm the subjects and must tell the subjects the complete nature of the study (this process is called *debriefing*) as soon as possible after the study is completed.

Researchers who conduct studies in communities and with various ethnic and cultural groups have ethical responsibilities to large groups of people. As researchers, psychologists have a responsibility to respect local morals and customs. They also should be honest with the community, ethnic, and cultural groups about the nature of the research agenda, especially if the research plans violate local sensibilities. As guests in another's setting, psychologists need to avoid the temptation to dispense wisdom and should resist trying to change situations they were not invited to change. As ethical professionals, psychologists have an obligation to write research findings in a nonjudgmental way that does not unfairly portray any particular group. They also should share such findings with interested representatives of the community, cultural, or ethnic group (Levine & Perkins, 1987).

Ethical Treatment of Animal Subjects

Over the past few decades, the annual meetings of the American Psychological Association have occasionally been the target of animal welfare and animal rights activists. The activists often chant slogans like "Psychologists Are Killing Our Animals" and "Stop the Pain and Abuse."

For generations, some psychologists have used animals in their research, research that has provided a better understanding of, and solutions for, many human problems. Neal Miller (1985), a leading figure in contemporary psychology who has made important discoveries about the

Animal welfare and rights activists believe that psychologists have been too abusive to animals in their research. Most psychologists believe that, although there have been isolated examples of abuse, the abuse has been exaggerated.

effects of biofeedback on health, listed the following areas in which animal research has benefited humans:

- Psychotherapy and behavioral medicine
- Rehabilitation of neuromuscular disorders
- Understanding and alleviating the effects of stress and pain
- Discovery and testing of drugs to treat anxiety and severe mental illness
- Knowledge about drug addiction and relapse
- Treatments to help premature infants gain weight so they can leave the hospital sooner
- Knowledge about memory used to alleviate deficits of memory in old age

How widespread is animal research in psychology? Only about 5 percent of all APA members use animals in their research. Rats and mice are by far the most widely used, accounting for 90 percent of all psychological research with animals.

How widespread is abuse to animals in psychological research? According to animal welfare and rights activists, it is extensive (Dawkins, 1990). It is true that researchers sometimes use procedures that would be unethical with humans, but they are guided by a stringent set of standards that addresses such matters as the housing, feeding, and psychological well-being of animals. Researchers are required to weigh the potential benefit of their research against the possible harm to the animal and to avoid inflicting unnecessary pain. Animal abuse is not as common as animal activists groups charge. However, stringent ethical guidelines must be followed when animals or humans are the subjects in psychological research (Driscoll & Bateson, 1988).

BEING A WISE CONSUMER OF PSYCHOLOGICAL KNOWLEDGE

"Eating jelly beans makes you smarter!"
"On Oprah—Secrets to make your marriage divorce-proof!"
"Scientists find Vitamin X extends life!"

Headlines and promotional announcements proclaim a variety of new insights about human behavior that are likely to be of interest to the general public. But how do you sort through the barrage of findings to distinguish believable claims from those that should be rejected and perhaps even ridiculed?

Not all psychological information presented for public consumption comes from professionals with excellent credentials and reputations at colleges, universities, and applied mental health settings. Because journalists, television reporters, and other personnel in media are not trained in psychology, it is not an easy task for them to make sound decisions about the best information to present to the public.

Unfortunately, the media often focus on sensational and dramatic psychological findings. Members of the media want you to read what they have written or stay tuned to their program. They hope to capture and keep your attention by presenting dramatic, sensational, and surprising information. As a consequence, media presentations of psychological information tend to misrepresent researchers' conclusions.

Even when the popular media present high-quality research findings to the public, it can be difficult for them to inform people adequately about the findings and the implications these findings have for their lives. They do not have the luxury of time and space to specify in detail the limitations of research findings. They might have only a few minutes on a few lines, and they will focus on making maximum impact rather than on elucidating the complexity of a study's findings.

Science is always profound. It is only the half-truths that are dangerous.
George Bernard Shaw, *The Doctor's Dilemma*, 1913

You can take several steps to improve your skills as a shrewd consumer by familiarizing yourself with typical problems that appear in popular press treatments of psychological knowledge. We will detail these for you in the following sections.

CRITICAL THINKING

The Role of Animals in Psychological Research

As you can tell from the foregoing section, the use of animals in psychological research is controversial. The conflict pits two value positions against each other. One side argues for the progress of science and the potential benefits for human beings of experimenting on animals. Because we are ethically bound in the kinds of manipulations we can make with humans, we require access to animals with fewer restrictions in order for knowledge to be discovered. On the other side, animal activists advocate for the value of the protection of life, regardless of its status in the evolutionary ladder. They advocate that the same constraints that limit research on human subjects should be applied to animal research.

Which side of the argument do you favor? _____
_____

On what values do you base your argument? _____
_____
_____
_____
_____

Your reflections on this important issue *demonstrate awareness of underlying values that motivate behavior and influence judgment about behavior.*

The Problem of Generalizing from Group Results to an Individual

To be a wise consumer of psychological information, one must understand the difference between nomothetic research and idiographic needs. Most psychological research is **nomothetic research,** *research conducted at the level of the group.* Individual variations in how subjects respond is often not a major focus of the research. For example, researchers interested in the effects of divorce on stress management might find that divorced women as a group cope more poorly with stress than married women do. This is a nomothetic finding that applies to divorced women as a group. In this particular study, some of the divorced women were probably coping better with stress than were some of their married counterparts—not as many, but some. Indeed, it is entirely possible that of the 100 women in the study, the 2 or 3 women who were coping the best with stress might have been well-adjusted divorced women. It would still be accurate to report the findings as showing that divorced women (as a group) cope more poorly with stress than married women do.

As a consumer of psychological information, you want to know what the information means for you *individually,* not necessarily what it means for a group of people. **Idiographic needs** *are needs that are important for the individual, not the group.* The failure of the media to distinguish adequately between nomothetic research and idiographic needs is not entirely their fault—researchers have not adequately done this either. Researchers too often fail to examine the overlap between groups and present only the differences between groups. When those differences are

reported, too often they are stated as if there is no overlap between the groups being compared, when in reality there is a substantial overlap. If you read a research treatment in the popular press that divorced women coped more poorly with stress than married women did, it does not mean that all divorced women coped more poorly than did all married women. It simply means that, as a group, married women coped better—it would not mean that you, if you are a divorced woman, cope less well than married women do.

The Problem of Overgeneralizing Based on a Small Sample

Often there isn't space or time in media presentations of psychological information to go into details about the nature of the sample. Sometimes you will get basic information about the sample's size—whether it is based on 10 subjects, 50 subjects, or 200 subjects, for example. In many cases, small or very small samples require that caution be exercised in generalizing to a larger population.

For example, if a study of divorced women is based on only 10 or 20 divorced women, the findings might not generalize to all divorced women, because the sample investigated might have some unique characteristics. The sample might have a high income, be White American, be childless, live in a small southern town, and be undergoing psychotherapy. In this study, then, we clearly would be making unwarranted generalizations if we thought the findings might automatically characterize divorced women who have moderate to low incomes, are from other ethnic backgrounds, have children, are living in different contexts, and are not undergoing psychotherapy.

The Problem of Accepting as Definitive Results Based on a Single Study

The popular press might identify an interesting piece of research or a clinical finding and claim that it is something phenomenal with far-reaching implications. Although such studies and findings do occur, it is rare for a single study to provide earth-shattering and conclusive answers, especially answers that apply to all people. In fact, in most psychological domains, where there are many investigations, finding conflicting results about a particular topic or issue is not unusual. Answers to questions in research usually emerge after many scientists have conducted similar investigations and have drawn similar conclusions. Thus, a report of one research study should not be taken as the absolute, final answer on an issue.

The Problem of Assuming Causality from Correlational Studies

Drawing causal conclusions from correlational studies is one of the most common mistakes made in the media. In an experiment, subjects are randomly assigned to treatments or experiences, and their responses are compared in order to establish cause-and-effect relationships. When true experiments are not conducted, research variables, or factors, might be only noncausally related to each other. Causal interpretations cannot be made when two or more factors are simply correlated with each other. We cannot say that one factor causes the other.

In the case of divorce, a headline might read "Low income causes divorced women to have a high degree of stress." We read the article and find out the headline was derived from the results of a research study. We obviously cannot, for ethical or practical purposes, randomly assign women to become divorced or stay married. For the same reasons, we cannot randomly assign divorced women to be poor or rich. So this questionable headline must be based on a correlational study, from which such causal claims cannot legitimately be inferred. Low income might have caused the divorced women to have low self-esteem, but in some cases their low self-esteem might have hurt their chances for having a higher income. Their low self-esteem likely is related to other factors as well, such as inadequate societal supports, a history of criticism from an ex-husband, and so on.

The Problem of Assuming Credibility from Questionable Sources

Studies conducted by psychologists and mental health professionals are not automatically accepted by the research and clinical community. Psychological research submitted to a research or clinical journal will be reviewed by other psychologists in that specialized area, who make a decision about the value of publishing the findings. The quality of research and clinical findings published in journals is not uniform, but in most cases these studies have undergone far greater scrutiny than much of the work that is reported in the media. Within the media, though, a distinction can usually be drawn between what is presented in respected newspapers, such as the *New York Times* and the *Washington Post,* as well as credible magazines, such as *Time* and *Newsweek,* and much less respected and less credible periodicals such as tabloids like the *National Enquirer* and *Star.*

Is *astrology*—the field that uses the position of the stars and the planets at the time of a person's birth to describe, explain, and predict a person's behavior—credible? Astrological predictions appear in some very respected newspapers—such as the *New York Times* and the *Washington Post.* Does that make them credible? When astrologers' predictions are successful, it is because they usually are so vague that they are virtually guaranteed to happen (for example, "Money is likely to be a concern for you this month" or "A tragic plane crash will occur in the southern United States this year"). Astrologers' more specific predictions ("An unidentified flying object will land on the field during the halftime of the ABC Monday Night Football game on October 21, 1996") never hold up. To read further about astrology and psychology's skepticism about it, see Applications in Psychology 2.1.

Let us be thankful for fools.
But for them the rest of us could not succeed.

Mark Twain

This concludes Section I, in which we studied two chapters: "What Is Psychology?" and "Research and Reasoning." Section II is entitled "Biological and Perceptual Processes." In the first chapter of that section you will read about biological foundations and the brain.

REVIEW

Challenges in the Values of Psychological Research and Being a Wise Consumer of Psychological Knowledge

Among the challenges related to the values of psychological research are those involved in objectivity and the ethical treatment of human and animal subjects. Objectivity is an important value in science. Although psychologists strive for objectivity, some experts believe that research cannot be value free. Researchers must ensure the well-being of subjects in psychological studies. The risk of mental and physical harm must be reduced, informed consent should occur, and deception should be used only with caution. Controversy surrounds the use of animals in psychological research, although abuse is not as extensive as some activists charge.

Being a wise consumer of psychological knowledge involves understanding a number of problems, including generalizing from group results to an individual, overgeneralizing based on a small sample, accepting as definitive results based on a single study, assuming causality from correlational studies, and assuming credibility from questionable sources.

APPLICATIONS IN PSYCHOLOGY 2.1

Astrology and Psychology's Skepticism

Let's examine some astrologers' comments:

> Astrology is a major influence in your life. It's not your only one. We do have environment, and we do have heredity. It's not the only influence. However, it's a major influence.
>
> Henry Weingarten,
> New York Astrology Center
> "Nightline," May 3, 1988

> I advise them (the Reagans) when to be careful. I don't make decisions for them. An astrologer just picks the best possible time to do something that someone else has already planned to do. It's like being in the ocean; you should go with the waves, not against them. I know his (President Reagan's) horoscope upside down, but I don't know him. I deal with Nancy.
>
> Joan Quigley,
> San Francisco astrologer
> *Time,* May 16, 1988

Could your belief in astrology be influenced by the way it is presented in the media? Consider the possibility that you were tuned in to a recent "Oprah Winfrey" television show. Popular showhost Winfrey included Roger Culver, an astronomer at Colorado State University, and a skeptic on her panel of experts, but the other three experts on the panel were astrologers, supported by an audience packed with believers. On a recent "Geraldo" show, the panel of experts consisted of five astrologers and no scientists. A recent "Donahue" show found host Phil Donahue's panel of experts to include an astrologer, a spiritual counselor, and two psychics; no scientists were present. Regrettably, following the lead of the *National Enquirer,* the media are often more interested in high audience ratings than in the truth of astrologers' claims.

On some responsible television shows, such as "Nightline," scientists were given adequate time to explain their view of astrology:

> It sounds a lot like science, it sounds like astronomy. It's got technical terms. It's got jargon. It confuses the public. The fact is that astrological beliefs go back at least 2500 years. Now that should be a sufficiently long time for astrologers to prove their case. They have not proved their case. It's just simply gibberish. The fact is, there's no theory for it, there are no observational data for it. It's been tested and tested over the centuries. Nobody's ever found any validity to it at all. It is not even close to a science. A science has to be repeatable, it has to have a logical foundation . . . astrology is really quite something else.
>
> Astronomer Richard Berendzen,
> President American University
> "Nightline," May 3, 1988

Science's battle against astrology is uphill. Despite the assertions of scientists that astrology is a false system of beliefs, the public's belief in astrology has increased. In 1976, 29 percent of the population said they believed in astrology, but in 1986 this figure increased to 36 percent. One reason for the increased interest in astrology is that astrology sells. It is a profitable business. Some kinds of horoscopes are sold in much the same manner as are cornflakes, candy, and beer. Another reason is that many television directors and producers either lack critical judgment about astrology or cater to public taste rather than exercising their responsibility to provide the public with facts.

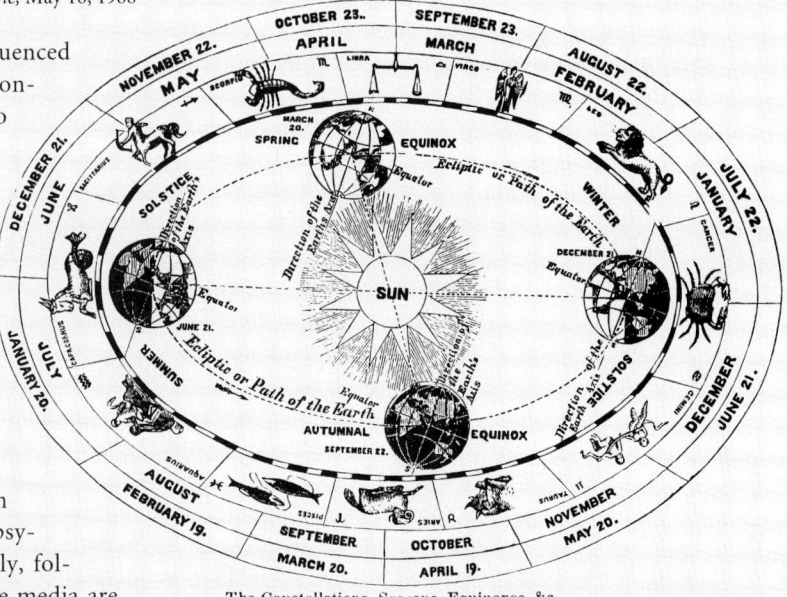

The Constellations, Seasons, Equinoxes, &c.

Why does the science of psychology urge you to be skeptical of astrology?

CRITICAL THINKING ABOUT BEHAVIOR

Personal Versus Psychological Evidence

What is needed is not the will to believe,
but the wish to find out.

Bertrand Russell

You have read about the history and scope of psychology and the current methods psychologists use in observing, describing, explaining, and predicting behavior. Just how different are psychology-based ways of thinking from the processes you go through when you are making judgments about behavior? There are some critical differences.

1. **Precise descriptions of behaviors.** Psychologists are exacting in how they define and describe behaviors, being especially careful to distinguish descriptions of behavior from other inferences or interpretations that can be made *about* behavior. We are constantly confronted with behaviors that we must examine and interpret, prompting us to come to conclusions, infer meanings, or make predictions about behavior; however, psychologists are inclined to be precise in their observations and cautious about their inferences. When confronted with a challenging behavior, critical thinkers trained in psychology are likely to ask, *"What exactly do you mean by . . . ?"*

2. **Reliance on systematic observation.** Nonscientific explanations of behavior correspond reasonably well to the first two stages of the scientific method: examining the problem (analyzing the behavior) and making interpretations (developing hypotheses or theories) about behavior. It is in the third stage of the scientific method that scientific and nonscientific ways of interpreting behavior diverge. Scientists collect data systematically, interpret the data, and revise their conclusions or beliefs, based on these interpretations.

    This procedure reflects a strong preference for conclusions that are based on objective data derived from carefully planned behavioral research rather than subjective conclusions that might not be carefully considered or are more likely to reflect unknown biases of the observer. When confronted with a conclusion about behavior, the critical thinker trained in psychology is likely to ask, *"What's your evidence for this conclusion?"*

3. **Pursuit of alternative explanations.** Many questions that we ponder about behavior might not lend themselves easily to objective research. In the absence of systematic observation and scientific interpretation, psychologists are likely to question whether there could be other explanations for the behavior being examined. They actively speculate about other variables that could influence the behavior, demonstrating a thinking characteristic that could be described as being *variable-minded.* Psychologists are likely to ask, *"Are there other plausible ways to explain the behavior?"*

You might already have formed some conclusions about the following examples of behaviors. What happens to your conclusions when you adopt psychological ways of examining behavior, when you ask 'for clarity, inquire about evidence, and look for alternative explanations?

- Magicians are well known for making objects disappear. *Do they really make objects vanish, or can you think of an alternative explanation for this compelling illusion?*
- Seeing a loved one ushering you through a tunnel toward a bright white light is an example of an experience commonly reported by people having a near-death experience. *Is this a confirmation of an afterlife, or could this phenomenon be explained in another way?*
- In psychotherapy, some individuals are startled by their recovery of memories that suggest they have been physically or emotionally abused in childhood. How could it be that something so horrifying isn't remembered until some point quite distant from the event? *How many variables or influences might be involved in understanding this phenomenon?*
- Some people are convinced that they have extrasensory powers. They claim to know in advance or from a distance when bad things happen to their relatives, to be able to predict songs that are about to come on the radio, and so on. *Is this phenomenon real? What evidence is there for extrasensory abilities? Are there other explanations that account for the behavior?*
- Two twins, separated at birth and raised apart, are reunited to discover that they have an uncanny number of similarities. Their reunion prompts strong speculation regarding the power of genetic influence in shaping behavior. *Is this research definitive "proof" of the power of inheritance, or are there other plausible ways to explain the remarkable number of similarities?*
- Many individuals believe that the growing problem of violence in our culture is a direct influence of violence portrayed in movies and television. *What evidence supports this position? Is violence really growing? What other factors might contribute to this important problem?*

You may have thought about some research strategies that could help you to *evaluate the quality of conclusions about behavior.* You will find out how these questions and others will be evaluated in the chapters that follow.

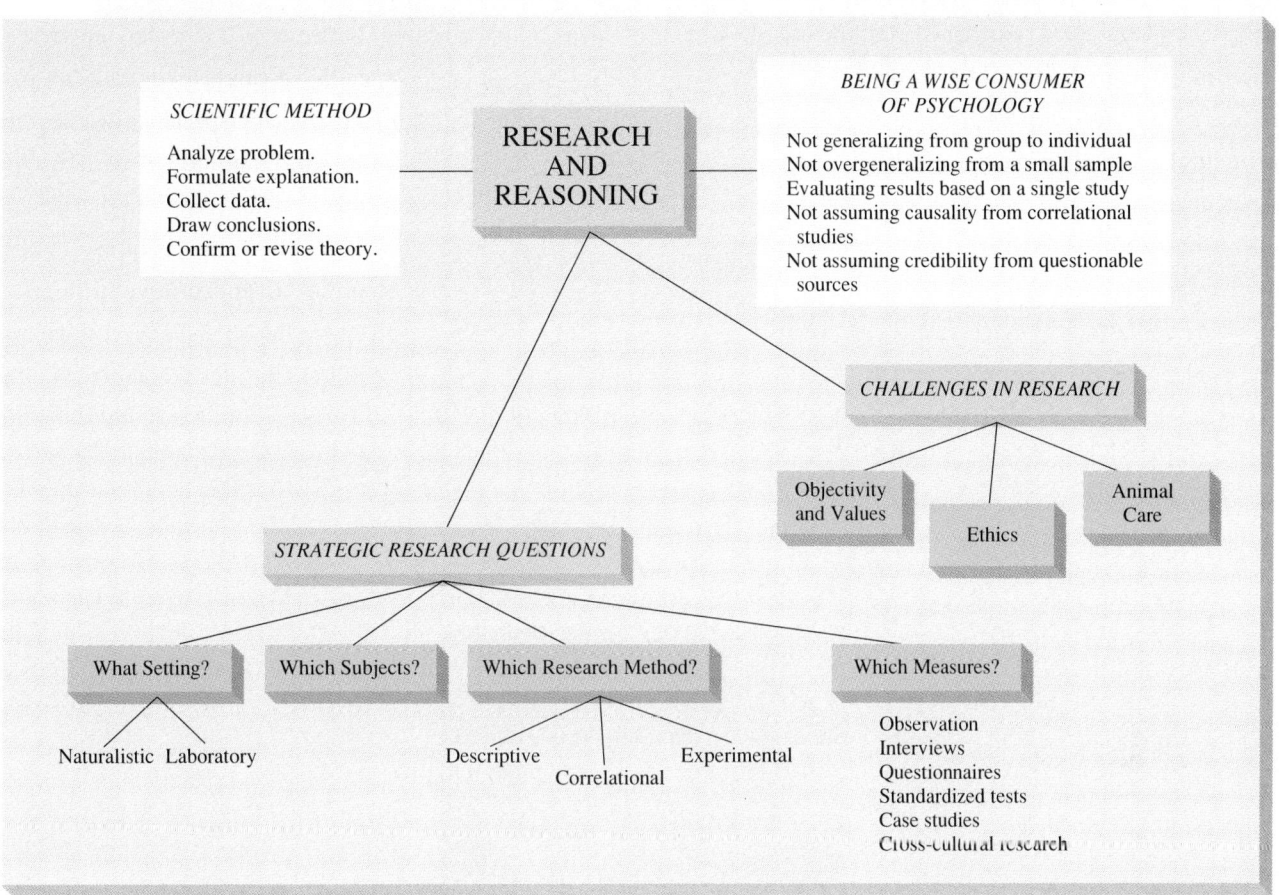

SCIENTIFIC METHOD

Analyze problem.
Formulate explanation.
Collect data.
Draw conclusions.
Confirm or revise theory.

RESEARCH AND REASONING

BEING A WISE CONSUMER OF PSYCHOLOGY

Not generalizing from group to individual
Not overgeneralizing from a small sample
Evaluating results based on a single study
Not assuming causality from correlational studies
Not assuming credibility from questionable sources

CHALLENGES IN RESEARCH

Objectivity and Values

Ethics

Animal Care

STRATEGIC RESEARCH QUESTIONS

What Setting?

Which Subjects?

Which Research Method?

Which Measures?

Naturalistic Laboratory

Descriptive   Correlational   Experimental

Observation
Interviews
Questionnaires
Standardized tests
Case studies
Cross-cultural research

I n this chapter on research and reasoning, we studied the scientific method and its steps of analyzing a problem, formulating a tentative explanation, collecting data, drawing conclusions, and confirming or revising theory. Then we evaluated four strategic questions about research design in psychology: Which subjects (and issues involving random samples, gender and culture bias, and animals)? Which setting (laboratory versus naturalistic observation)? Which research method (descriptive, correlational, or experimental)? and Which measures (observations, interviews, questionnaires, case studies, standardized tests, or cross-cultural or ethnic minority research)? Next, we studied value challenges in research related to objectivity and the ethical use of human and animal subjects in research. And we examined how to be a wise consumer of psychological knowledge by not generalizing from a group to an individual, not overgeneralizing from a small sample, evaluating results based on a single study, not assuming causality from correlational studies, and not assuming credibility from questionable sources. To obtain an overall summary of the chapter, you can again read the in-chapter reviews on pages 34, 41, and 46.

The behavioral perspective has always placed a strong emphasis on laboratory research (p. 33), the use of observation in assessing behavior (p. 34), and the importance of using the experimental method to discover the causes of behavior (pp. 36–38). The neurobiological and cognitive perspectives are also strong proponents of research methods. The sociocultural perspective is concerned about bias related to gender and culture (p. 32) and promotes cross-cultural research (p. 41). Although research is not as strongly emphasized in the psychoanalytic and humanistic perspectives, both perspectives show interest in specific research methods. The psychoanalytic perspective often uses the case-study method (p. 40). The humanistic perspective emphasizes research designs that help to establish therapeutic and intervention effectiveness. Each perspective, thus, emphasizes distinctive features of the scientific method and advocates the use of research to obtain a better understanding of behavior.

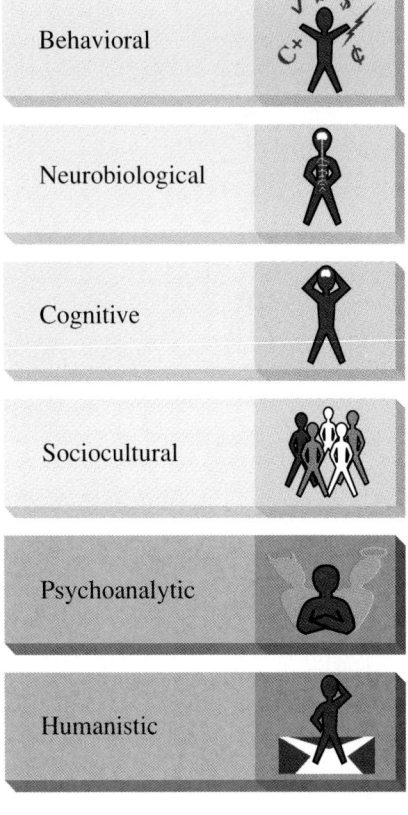

scientific method An approach used to discover accurate information or establish meaningful relations about mind and behavior. It includes the following steps: analyze a problem, formulate a tentative explanation, collect data, draw conclusions, and confirm or revise theory.   28

theory A coherent set of ideas that helps to explain data and to make predictions. A theory has hypotheses.   29

hypotheses Assumptions that can be tested to determine their accuracy.   29

data Information gathered through systematic observation.   29

random sample A sample in which every member of a population or group has an equal chance of being selected.   31

selection bias A lack of representativeness in a sample.   31

laboratories Controlled settings with many of the complex factors of the "real world" removed.   33

naturalistic observation Observation of behavior in real-world settings with no attempts to manipulate or control the situation.   34

descriptive research methods Methods intended to provide an accurate portrayal of behavior. Descriptive statistics communicate basic qualities of the data being reported.   35

correlational research methods Methods in which the goal is to describe the strength of the relation between two or more events or characteristics.   35

experimental research methods Methods that allow us to precisely determine the causes of behavior.   36

experiment A carefully regulated procedure in which researchers manipulate one or more factors believed to influence the behavior being studied and hold all other factors constant.   36

random assignment Assignment of subjects to experimental and control conditions by chance. This practice reduces the probability that the results of the experiment will be due to preexisting differences among the groups.   37

experimental group A group in an experiment whose experience is manipulated.   37

control group In an experiment, the comparison group that is treated like the experimental group in every way except for the manipulated factor.   37

independent variable The manipulated, influential, experimental factor in an experiment.   37

dependent variable The factor that is measured in an experiment; it may change when the independent variable is manipulated.   37

operational definition A definition of behavior in terms of observable features.   38

interview A descriptive method in which questions are asked directly to an individual to find out about the person's experiences and attitudes.   39

social desirability A factor that leads interview participants to tell interviewers what they think is socially desirable rather than what they really think or feel.   39

questionnaire A method similar to a highly structured interview, except respondents read the questions and mark their answers on a sheet of paper rather than respond directly to the interviewer.   39

case study A study that provides an in-depth look at one individual. Clinical psychologists use case studies when they cannot duplicate the unique aspects of an individual's life for study, for either practical or ethical reasons.   40

standardized tests Tests, consisting of a series of written or oral questions, that have two distinct features. First, psychologists usually total an individual's score to yield a single score, or set of scores, that reflects something about the individual. Second, psychologists compare the individual's score to the scores of a large group of similar people to determine how the individual responded relative to others.   40

emic approach An approach to research that has as its goal describing behavior in one culture or ethnic group in terms that are meaningful and important to the people in that culture or ethnic group, without regard to other cultures or ethnic groups.   41

etic approach An approach to research in which the goal is to describe behavior so that generalizations can be made across cultures.   41

nomothetic research Research that takes place at the level of the group.   45

idiographic needs Needs that are important for the individual, not for the group.   45

HOW TO THINK STRAIGHT ABOUT PSYCHOLOGY

(1992, 3rd ed.) by Keith E. Stanovich. New York: HarperCollins.

This charming text explores how psychologists think about behavior, with a special emphasis on creating and defending arguments about the validity of conclusions about cause-and-effect relations. The author offers many examples of classic research in psychology and also explores why psychologists struggle to gain respect from other sciences. The author refers to psychology as the "Rodney Dangerfield of the sciences" because of its image problem. Among the important psychological concepts examined by Stanovich are those of operationalism, converging evidence, experimental control, the role of statistics, correlation, and causation.

LIFTING THE VEIL: THE FEMININE FACE OF SCIENCE

(1993) by Linda Jean Shepherd. Boston: Shambhala.

In this provocative social criticism of contemporary science, biochemist Shepherd argues that we need to explore different models of science that encourage the feminine character in all scientists. She suggests that long-standing masculine traditions of science have produced remarkable achievements but these have been accompanied by many unanticipated and disastrous outcomes that threaten the existence of the world. She argues that an expanded model of "good science" emphasizing cooperation, intuition, connectedness, multiplicity, and subjectivity will create scientific progress that is more attuned to human needs and to the natural world.

***Even the Rat Was White: A Historical View of Psychology* (1976, 1994)**
> by Robert V. Guthrie
> New York: Harper & Row

This critique of psychology rests on the premise that in its first century, psychology has systematically excluded important sociocultural factors, particularly race and ethnicity. Guthrie offers suggestions for the promotion of a more inclusive science of human behavior.

***How to Lie with Statistics* (1954)**
> by Darrell Huff
> New York: W. W. Norton

This enduring text explores many ways statistics can be used to manipulate and distort information. The author includes many examples that help individuals improve their consumer skills.

***The Science Game* (1993)**
> by Sandra Pyke and Neil Agnew
> Englewood Cliffs, NJ: Prentice Hall

This popular book covers a number of important ideas about conducting research in psychology in an entertaining and informative way.

***Untold Lives: The First Generation of American Women Psychologists* (1987)**
> by Elizabeth Scarborough and Laurel Furumoto
> New York: Columbia University Press

This well-crafted volume uses a research method called historiography to capture the struggles of American's pioneering women psychologists. The authors constructed the stories of the earliest women in psychology from correspondence, archives, and interviews and concluded that their collective experience documented harsh discriminatory practices that placed obstacles in the paths of talented women. The authors also review what aspects have changed for women in psychology since that time.

Biological and Perceptual Processes

*There is a grandeur in this view of life . . .
whilst this planet has gone cycling on
according to the fixed law of gravity, from so
simple a beginning endless forms most
beautiful and wonderful have been, and
are being evolved.*

Charles Darwin

Nature has equipped us with a remarkable
brain to process information about our world,
with eyes, ears, nose, skin, and other senses to
perceive this world, and with different states of
consciousness to become aware of this world. In
this second section of *Psychology: The Contexts of
Behavior*, you will read three chapters: "Biological
Foundations and the Brain" (chapter 3),
"Sensation and Perception" (chapter 4), and
"States of Consciousness" (chapter 5).

JOHN SANTROCK
China Odyssey, detail

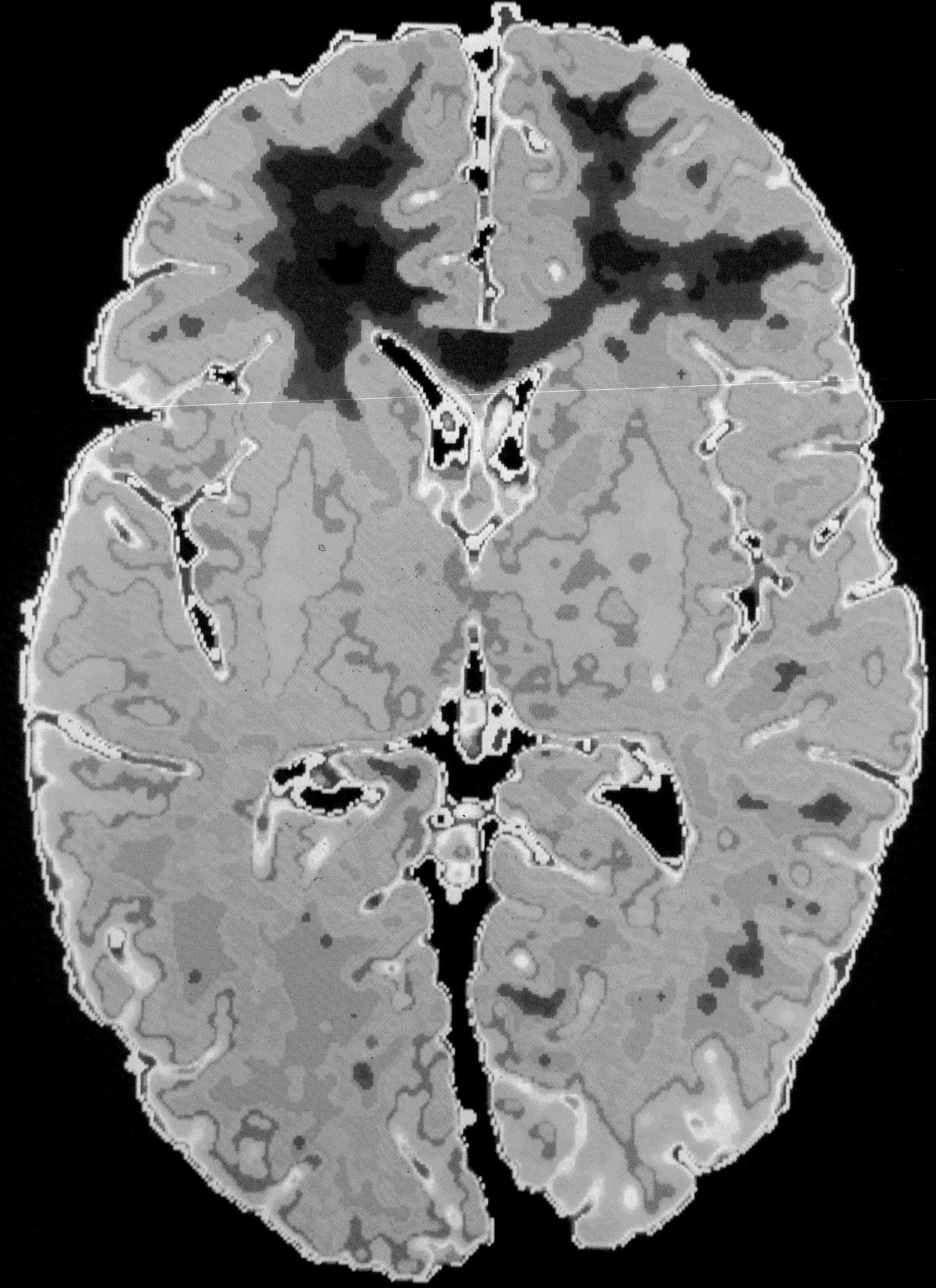

Biological Foundations and the Brain

The chess-board is the world. The pieces are the phenomena of the universe. The rules of the game are what we call laws of nature.

Thomas Huxley

THE STORY OF THE JIM AND JIM TWINS: GENETIC DETERMINISM OR MERE COINCIDENCE?

Jim Springer and Jim Lewis are identical twins. They were separated at the age of 4 weeks and didn't see one another again until they were 39 years old. Even so, they share uncanny similarities that read more like fiction than fact. For example, they have both worked as a part-time deputy sheriff, have vacationed in Florida, have driven Chevrolets, have had dogs named Toy, and have married and divorced women named Betty. In addition, one twin named his son James Allan, and the other named his son James Alan. Both like math but not spelling, and both enjoy carpentry and mechanical drawing. They have chewed their fingernails down to the nubs and have almost identical drinking and smoking habits. Both have had hemorrhoids, put on 10 pounds at about the same time, and first suffered headaches at the age of 18. They also have similar sleep patterns.

Jim and Jim have some differences as well. One wears his hair over his forehead, whereas the other wears it slicked back with sideburns. One expresses himself better verbally; the other is more proficient in writing. For the most part, however, they are more alike than different.

The Jim and Jim twins were part of the Minnesota Study of Twins Reared Apart, directed by Thomas Bouchard and his colleagues. The researchers brought identical (genetically identical because they come from the same egg) and fraternal (genetically dissimilar because they come from two eggs) twins from all over the world to Minneapolis to investigate the psychological aspects of the twins' lives. For example, the twins were interviewed and asked more than 15,000 questions about their family and childhood environment, personal interests, vocational orientation, values, and aesthetic judgments. Detailed medical histories were obtained, including information about their smoking, diet, and exercise habits. The researchers also took chest X rays and gave heart stress tests and EEGs (brain wave tests). The twins were also given a number of personality, ability, and intelligence tests (Bouchard & others, 1981; McGue & Bouchard, 1989). Many argue that the many uncommon

Jim Lewis (left) and Jim Springer (right).

similarities discovered in the twin study are evidence of a genetic basis for habits, tastes, and behavior.

Critics of the Minnesota twin study dispute this conclusion. They point out that some of the separated twins had been together several months prior to their adoption, that some twins had been reunited prior to their testing (in some cases a number of years earlier), that adoption agencies often place twins in similar homes, and that even strangers who spend several hours together and start comparing their lives are likely to come up with coincidental similarities (Adler, 1991). Still, even in the face of such criticism, the Minnesota study demonstrates the interest scientists have shown in the genetic basis of behavior.

PREVIEW

The bizarre similarities between the Jim and Jim twins raise questions about the role nature plays in human behavior and the biological foundations of our existence. How are characteristics transmitted from one generation to the next, for instance? How did the human species come to be? What exquisite systems give us our extraordinary ability to adapt to our world? These questions focus on biological perspectives and the nervous system, the main topics of this chapter.

PERSPECTIVES ON NATURE AND NURTURE

Biologists who study even the simplest animals agree that it is virtually impossible to separate the effects of an animal's genes from the effects of its environment (Mader, 1994). **Environment** *refers to all of the surrounding conditions and influences that affect the development of living things.* Environment includes the food that we eat, the air we breathe, and the many different physical and social contexts we experience—the cities and towns we live in; our relationships with parents, peers, and teachers; our continuing interactions at work, at home, and at play; and so on.

In an earlier chapter we introduced the concept of the nature-nurture controversy. The term **nurture** *is often used to describe an organism's environmental experiences.* The term **nature** *is often used to describe an organism's biological inheritance.* The interaction of nature *and* nurture, genes *and* environment, influences every aspect of mind and behavior to a degree. Neither factor operates alone (Plomin, 1993; Wadsworth & others, 1995; Waldman, Weinberg, & Scarr, 1995).

To illustrate how both genes and the environment mold human behavior, let's examine one of the first systematic studies ever undertaken to separate their effects. According to anthropologist Ashley Montagu (1971), Frederick II of Germany was curious about what kind of language humans would speak if they weren't brought up in a specific culture. He believed classic Greek would be the emerging language by nature without interference of the nurturing culture. He separated several infants from their mothers and placed them on an island with caretakers who had been rendered mute to insure that the infants would hear no language. The experiment had to be abandoned when the minimal care provided by the environment resulted in the death of all the infants.

Even though the king was unable to confirm his beliefs about language, his experiment illustrated several important characteristics about the interaction between nature and nurture. First, even if a trait is 100 percent *heritable* (determined by genetic endowment), an environment will considerably influence how the trait is expressed. Unfavorable environments can not only suppress the trait but disable the organism. Second, trying to determine how much of any characteristic can be attributed to nature or nurture is extremely challenging. You will read in later chapters about some approaches that rely on statistical methods to estimate the influence of heritability, especially on intelligence and abnormal behaviors. Third, psychologists do not permit experiments of this kind to be performed today because they clearly violate the ethical standards of caring for subjects.

Some psychologists wonder if the nature-nurture question is really worth an argument. For example, imagine that we could identify the precise genetic combination that predisposes a person to become either outgoing or shy.

Even with that information, we could not predict how shy a person might become, because shyness is also shaped by life's experiences. Parents, for example, can support and nurture a shy child in a way that encourages the child to feel comfortable in social situations. On the other hand, an initially outgoing child might experience a traumatic event and become shy and withdrawn in response to it.

> *With a good heredity, nature deals you a fine hand at cards; and with a good environment, you learn to play the hand well.*
>
> **Walter C. Alvarez**

More information about the environment's role in human behavior appears in Sociocultural Worlds 3.1, where we discuss the capacity of the human species to make culture.

Three major fields related to biology have contributed to our understanding of the influence of biological forces in the nature-nurture controversy: genetics, evolution, and sociobiology, each of which we will discuss in turn.

The Genetic Perspective

In the words of twentieth-century French essayist Antoine de Saint-Exupéry, "The seed of the cedar will become cedar, the seed of the bramble can only become bramble." An English proverb says, "That which comes of a cat will catch mice." Why does the bramble only become bramble? Why does the cat catch mice? No matter what the species, there must be a mechanism used to pass the message of inheritance from one generation to the next. That mechanism is genetics.

All humans begin life as a single cell, a fertilized human egg, weighing about one-twenty-millionth of an ounce. This single cell develops into a human being made of trillions of cells. The nucleus of each human cell contains 46 **chromosomes,** *which are threadlike structures that come in 23 pairs, one member of each pair coming from each parent.* Chromosomes contain the remarkable genetic

Drawing by Ziegler; © 1985 The New Yorker Magazine, Inc.

The Human Species Is a Culture-Making Species

Unlike other animal species, which evolve in response to random changes in their environment, humans change extensively through *cultural evolution*. For example, we've made astonishing accomplishments in the past 10,000 years or so, ever since we developed language. Most scientists believe that biological (Darwinian) evolution continues in our species, but its rate, compared with cultural evolution, is so slow that its impact seems almost negligible. There is no evidence, for example, that brain size or structure has changed since *Homo sapiens* appeared on the fossil record about 50,000 years ago.

As humans evolved, we acquired knowledge and passed it on from generation to generation. This knowledge, which originally instructed us how to hunt, make tools, and communicate, became our **culture.** The accumulation of knowledge has gathered speed—from a slow swell to a meteoric rise. Hunter-gatherer tribes, characteristic of early human society, changed over thousands of years into small agricultural communities. With people rooted in one place, cities grew and flourished. Life within those cities remained relatively unchanged for generations. Then industrialization put a dizzying speed on cultural change. Now technological advances in communication and transportation—computers, FAX machines, virtual reality—transform everyday life at a staggering pace.

Whatever one generation learns, it can pass to the next through writing, word of mouth, ritual, tradition, and a host of other methods humans have developed to assure their culture's continuity (Gould, 1981). By creating cultures, humans have built, shaped, and carved out their own environments. The human species is no longer primarily at nature's mercy. Rather, humans are capable of changing their environment to fit their needs (McCandless & Trotter, 1977).

More than 99 percent of all humans now live in a different kind of environment from that in which the species evolved. By creating cultures, humans have, in effect, built, shaped, and carved out their own environments.

---

substance **deoxyribonucleic acid, or DNA,** *a complex molecule that contains genetic information* (see figure 3.1). **Genes,** *the units of heredity information, are short segments of DNA. Genes act as a blueprint for cells to reproduce themselves through cell division called mitosis and manufacture the proteins that maintain life.* Chromosomes, DNA, and genes can be mysterious. To help you turn mystery into understanding, see figure 3.2.

The frightening part about heredity and environment is that we parents provide both.

Notebook of a Printer

Although we have a long way to go before we unravel all the mysteries about the way genes work, some aspects of heritability are well understood (Rose, 1995). Every person has two genes for each characteristic governed by heredity. When genes combine to determine our characteristics, some genes are dominant over others. According to the **dominant-recessive**

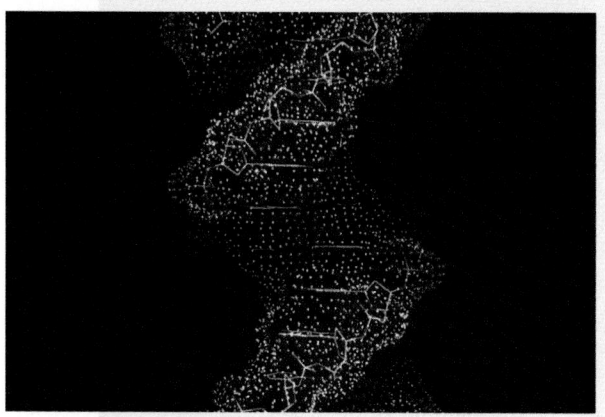

FIGURE 3.1

The Remarkable Substance Known as DNA
Notice that a DNA molecule is shaped like a spiral staircase. Genes are short segments of the DNA molecule. The horizontal bars that look like the rungs of a ladder play a key role in locating the identity of a gene.

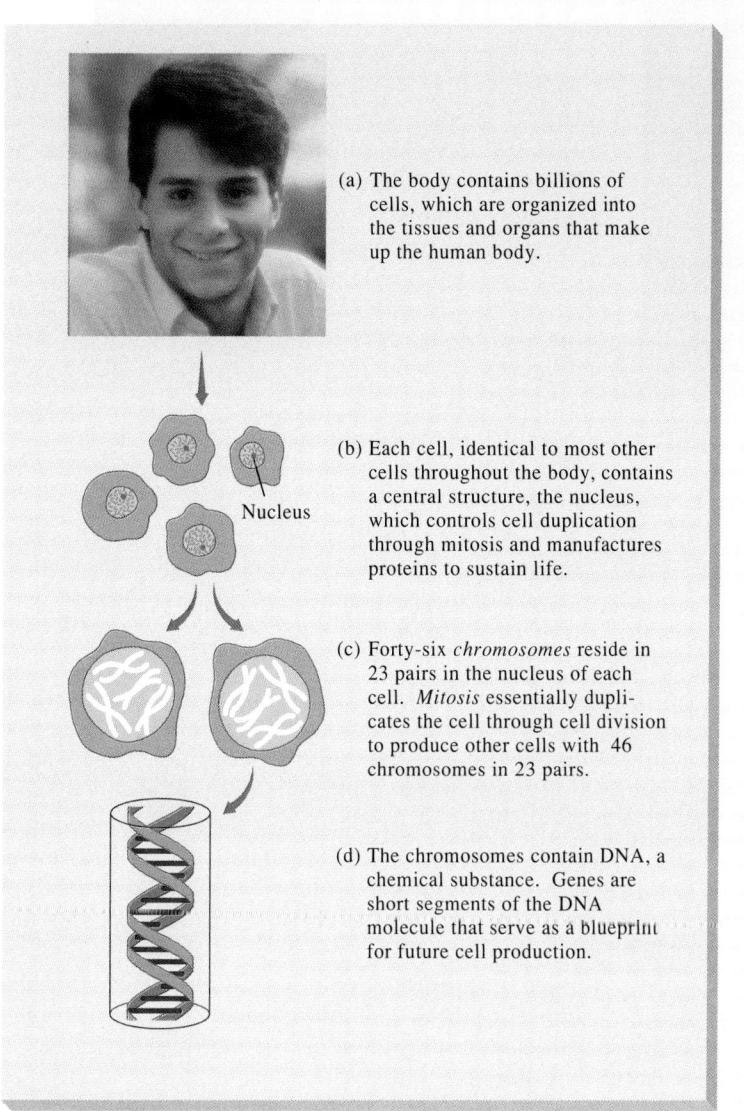

(a) The body contains billions of cells, which are organized into the tissues and organs that make up the human body.

Nucleus

(b) Each cell, identical to most other cells throughout the body, contains a central structure, the nucleus, which controls cell duplication through mitosis and manufactures proteins to sustain life.

(c) Forty-six *chromosomes* reside in 23 pairs in the nucleus of each cell. *Mitosis* essentially duplicates the cell through cell division to produce other cells with 46 chromosomes in 23 pairs.

(d) The chromosomes contain DNA, a chemical substance. Genes are short segments of the DNA molecule that serve as a blueprint for future cell production.

FIGURE 3.2

Concepts in Genetic Transmission

genes principle, *if one gene of a pair is dominant and one is recessive, the dominant gene exerts its effect, overriding the potential influence of the recessive gene. A recessive gene exerts its influence only if both genes of a pair are recessive.* If you inherit a recessive gene from only one parent, you may never know you carry the gene. In the world of dominant-recessive genes, brown eyes, far-sightedness, and dimples rule over blue eyes, near-sightedness, and freckles. If you inherit a recessive gene for a trait from both of your parents, you will show the trait. That's why two brown-eyed parents can have a blue-eyed child. In each parent, the genes that govern eye color include a dominant gene for brown eyes and a recessive gene for blue eyes. Since dominant genes override recessive genes, the parents have brown eyes; however, both can pass on their recessive genes for blue eyes. With no dominant gene to override them, the recessive genes make the child's eyes blue.

Long before people wondered how brown-eyed parents could possibly bear a blue-eyed child, they wondered what determined a child's sex. Aristotle believed that, as the father's sexual excitement increased, so did the odds of producing a son. He was wrong, of course, but it was not until the 1920s that researchers confirmed the existence of human sex chromosomes, the genetic material that determines sex. As already mentioned, humans normally have 46 chromosomes arranged in pairs. The 23rd pair may have two X-shaped chromosomes to produce a female, or it may have both an X-shaped and a Y-shaped chromosome to produce a male. The 23rd pair of chromosomes also carries some sex-linked characteristics, such as color blindness or hairy ear rims, both of which are more common in men. This mechanism is illustrated in figure 3.3 and is discussed more fully in chapter 9. To read further about X and Y chromosomes, turn to Applications in Psychology 3.1.

Most genetic transmission is more complex than these rather simple examples (McGue & Carmichael, 1995). Few psychological characteristics are the result of a single gene pair. Most are determined by the combination of different genes. Each of us has at least 50,000 genes in our chromosomes. When the 50,000 genes from one parent combine at conception with the 50,000 genes of the other parent, the number of possible combinations—in the trillions—is staggering. No wonder scientists are struck by the complexity of genetic transmission. Scientists have proposed the Human Genome Project (HGP), an international, 15-year project to map the human genome in order to unlock its mysteries. New discoveries of genetic linkages to disease have become a regular event due to the efforts of the HGP (Lee, 1991).

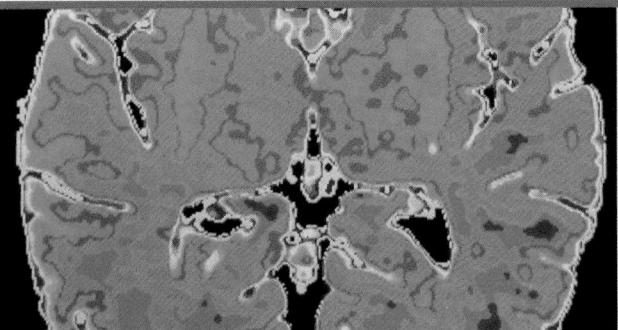

Heredity and Homosexuality

Are people born to be lesbian or gay? Or did they learn their homosexual orientation through experience? An increasing number of research investigators are seeking a biological explanation of homosexuality. In one recent study, gay men not only had unusually high numbers of gay brothers, but also had high numbers of gay uncles and cousins, but only on their mother's side of the family (Hamer & others, 1993). Families with two gay brothers have an even greater number of gay maternal uncles and cousins.

The researchers then examined the X chromosome— the sex chromosome men get from their mothers, along with the Y chromosome from their fathers. (Remember that women get two Xs, one from each parent.) What did they find? They discovered a region on the X chromosome that matched in 33 of 40 pairs of gay brothers. If the region played no role in the brothers' homosexuality, only 20 matches would be expected.

What kind of reactions has the study generated? Some gays welcome such studies' biologically oriented findings, saying they provide evidence that homosexuality is a naturally occurring and common sexual orientation. They hope that such information will dispel the idea that homosexuality is the result of "bad parenting" and promote recognition that it is part of the natural diversity of human existence. Some gays, though, believe that such data could lead to an unfortunate use of genetic engineering. They fear that some people will take the findings as showing a way to "cure" homosexuality, similar to the way German scientists in Nazi Germany performed brain surgery on gay men in an effort to change their sexual orientation.

Critics say the Hamer study does not prove that homosexuality has a genetic basis (Fausto-Sterling & Balaban, 1993). For one thing, the researchers could not find a specific genetic marker for homosexuality. Twin studies reveal that homosexuality is not exclusively genetic in nature. For example, half of the identical twins of gay men and lesbians are not gay, although they presumably have identical genes. Even if a genetic marker of homosexuality is found, it will interact with experiences the individual has to influence the course of sexual orientation and development. It also is important to recognize that the study focused only on gay men, so the results might not generalize to lesbians.

The researchers who conducted the study recognize that it is important for others to replicate their findings before any strong conclusions about heredity's role in homosexuality can be conclusively determined. More about the roles of heredity and environment, as well as the brain, in homosexuality appears in chapter 12, "Human Sexuality."

As you have seen, genes primarily determine our physical characteristics. The differences within a given species prompted biologists to develop a construct referred to as "race." In keeping with the sociocultural theme of this text, we will examine the concept of race and see how it has taken on elaborate, often unfortunate, social meanings in Sociocultural Worlds 3.2.

The Evolutionary Perspective

Humans are relative newcomers to Earth, according to evolution scientists. If we consider evolution in terms of Earth's history lasting a calendar year so far, then, scientists speculate, humans arrived on the planet on December 31 (Sagan, 1980). Despite our relatively brief existence, *Homo sapiens* has become the dominant species. How have our thinking and behavior changed as we evolved from our primitive ancestors?

> *Who are we? We find that we live on an insignificant planet of a humdrum star lost in a galaxy tucked away in some forgotten corner of a universe in which there are far more galaxies than people.*
>
> **Carl Sagan**

Nineteenth-century naturalist Charles Darwin addressed these concerns when he published his observations and thoughts in *On the Origin of Species* (1859). He sailed to South America to study a multitude of plant and animal species in their natural surroundings. He observed that most organisms reproduced at rates that should result in overpopulation, yet somehow populations remained nearly constant. Darwin reasoned that each new generation must engage in an intense, constant struggle for food, water, and other resources to account

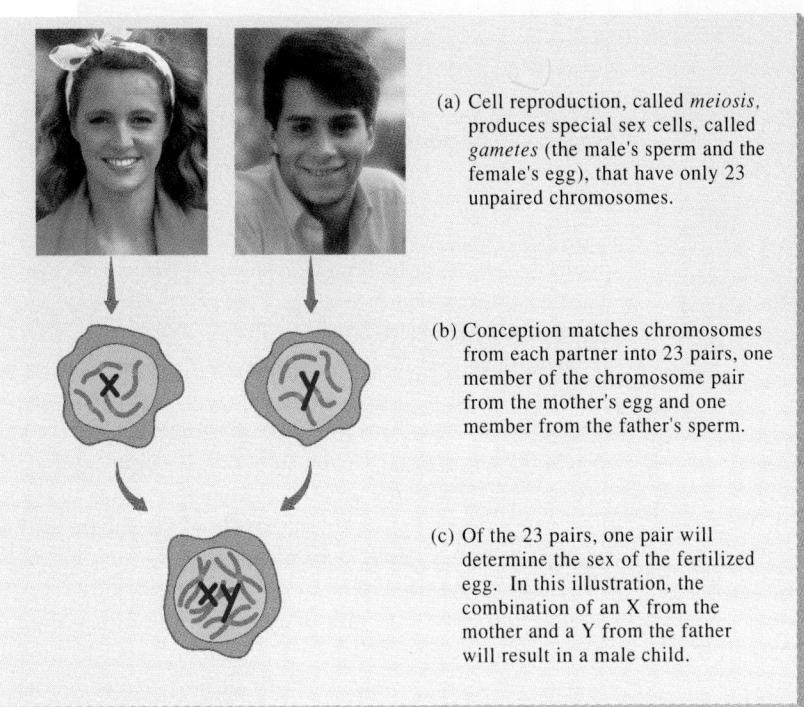

(a) Cell reproduction, called *meiosis,* produces special sex cells, called *gametes* (the male's sperm and the female's egg), that have only 23 unpaired chromosomes.

(b) Conception matches chromosomes from each partner into 23 pairs, one member of the chromosome pair from the mother's egg and one member from the father's sperm.

(c) Of the 23 pairs, one pair will determine the sex of the fertilized egg. In this illustration, the combination of an X from the mother and a Y from the father will result in a male child.

FIGURE 3.3

Genetic Principles of Reproduction

for the stable populations. In the course of this struggle, many of the young must die. Those who survived would be those who had shown better **adaptation,** *behavioral changes to challenges in the environment that enhance the organism's likelihood of survival.* The survivors would reproduce and, in turn, pass on some of their characteristics to the next generation. Over the course of many generations, the organisms with the characteristics most needed for survival (speed and sharp claws in predators or thick fur in Arctic animals, for instance) would make up an increasingly larger percentage of the population.

> *Nature is reckless of the individual. When she has points to carry, she carries them.*
>
> **Ralph Waldo Emerson**

Over many, many generations, this process could modify the entire species through **natural selection,** *the evolutionary process that favors individuals within a species that are best adapted to survive and reproduce in a particular environment.* Also known as "survival of the fittest," natural selection lies at the heart of Charles Darwin's theory of evolution. Fitness has sometimes been interpreted as an attribute of the strongest or most cunning among the

organisms under study. Instead, Darwin proposed **fitness** *as the degree to which an individual can produce viable offspring.* In some instances, fitness can emerge as the result of triumph over other competitors. In other situations, adaptation might promote new behaviors that will reduce competition and promote a different "fit" within the environment to promote reproduction and viability. If environmental conditions were to change, other characteristics might be better suited for survival and the process would move in a different direction.

As astounding as human evolution appears to be, it is important not to regard the human being as the endpoint in a complex continuum in the animal kingdom. Our upright posture, opposable thumbs, and language enhance our ability to adapt to a variety of environments, but we would be ill-suited to the demands of the contexts in which jellyfish live. Of the wide variety of species that inhabit the earth today, each represents the crowning achievement of the evolutionary path of that particular species. In contrast, many species have been lost due to their failure to withstand selective pressures of their environmental contexts.

> *What seest thou else in the dark backward and abysm of time.*
>
> **William Shakespeare,**
> ***The Tempest***

Evolution has been an enduring means of explaining how species interrelate and change over time (Buss, 1995; Daly & Wilson, 1995). Next, we explore a contemporary perspective that has a basis in evolution.

The Sociobiological Perspective

Sociobiology *is a contemporary view that relies on evolutionary biology to explain social behavior.* Sociobiologists believe that psychologists have a restricted understanding of social behavior because they have studied only one mammalian species—*Homo sapiens.* Sociobiology derives its information from the comparison of some of the tens of thousands of animal species that have evolved some form of social life.

According to E. O. Wilson (1985, 1992, 1995), the purpose of sociobiology is not to make crude comparisons

SOCIOCULTURAL WORLDS 3.2

Race and Ethnicity

Race, which originated as a biological concept, is a system for classifying plants and animals into subcategories according to specific physical and structural characteristics. *Race* is one of the most misused and misunderstood words in the English language (Atkinson, Morten, & Sue, 1993; Root, 1992). Loosely, it has come to mean everything from a person's religion to skin color.

Scholars have difficulty even determining how many races the human species comprises. Skin color, head shape, facial features, stature, and the color and texture of body hair are the physical characteristics most widely used to determine race. Racial classifications presumably were created to define and clarify the differences among groups of people; however, they have not been very useful. Many people argue that racial groupings are socially constructed on the basis of physical differences and are not biologically defensible (Van den Berghe, 1978).

One approach to classification specifies three main races: Mongoloid, or Asian; Caucasoid, or European; and Negroid, or African. However, some groups, such as Native Americans, Australians, and Polynesians, do not fit into any of the three main categories. Also, obvious differences *within* groups are not adequately explained. Arabs, Hindus, and Europeans, for instance, are physically different, yet they are all called Caucasian. Although there are some physical characteristics that distinguish "racial" groups, there are, in fact, more similarities than differences among such groups.

Too often we are socialized to accept as facts many myths and stereotypes about people whose skin color, facial features, and hair texture differ from ours. For example, some people still believe that Asians are inscrutable, Jews are acquisitive, and Hispanics are lazy. What people believe about race has profound social consequences. Until recently, for instance, African Americans were denied access to schools, hospitals, churches, and other social institutions attended by Whites.

Although scientists are supposed to be a fair-minded lot, some also have used racial distinctions to further their own biases. Some even claim that one racial group has a biological inheritance that gives it an adaptive advantage over other racial groups. Nineteenth-century biologist Louis Agassiz, for example, asserted that God had created Blacks and Whites as separate species. Also, in Nazi Germany, where science and death made their grisliest alliance, Jews and other "undesirables" were attributed with whatever characteristics were necessary to reinforce the conclusion that "survival of the fittest" demanded their elimination.

Social psychologist James Jones (1990, 1993, 1994) points out that thinking in racial terms has become embedded in cultures as an important factor in human interactions. For example, people often consider what race they will associate with when they decide on such things as where to live, who will make a suitable spouse, where to go to school, and what kind of job they want. Similarly, people often use race to judge whether or not another person is intelligent, competent, responsible, or socially acceptable. Children tend to adopt their parents' attitudes about race as they grow up, often perpetuating stereotypes and prejudice.

Physical and psychological characteristics vary not only across ethnic groups but also within them.

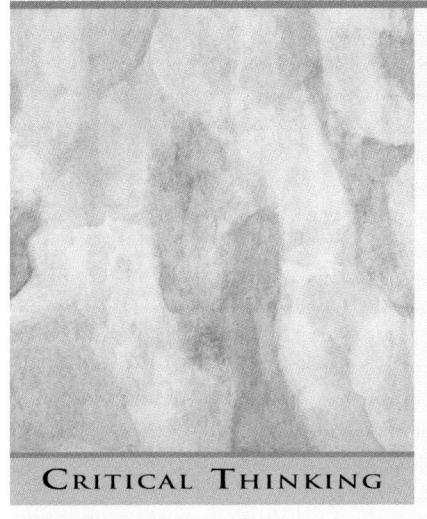

Contrasting Ways of Knowing

Not everyone believes that human beings are the product of evolution. Many religious traditions advocate opposing explanations for the origins of humankind. Science and religion offer different *ways of knowing.*

In this exercise, identify and interview two individuals who represent two different ways of knowing and understanding the origin of humankind. In what ways are their beliefs similar? In what ways are their beliefs different? Based on your interviews, is it possible to believe both scientific and religious explanations? Your completion of the interview process will help you not only *demonstrate appreciation of individual differences,* but also examine how individuals cope with one of life's biggest concerns: Just how did we get here?

between animal species or between animals and humans, such as simply comparing wolf and human aggression. Its purpose is to develop general laws of the evolution and biology of social behavior. The hope also is to be able to extend the principles of sociobiology to assist in the explanation of human behavior.

Sociobiologists believe that an organism is motivated by a desire to dominate the gene pool. Even complex human behaviors such as altruism, aggression, and socialization have been explained as expressing the urge to propagate our own genes. Take altruism, for example. Parents are likely to risk their own lives to save their children from a blazing fire. Although the parents may die, their children's genes survive, increasing the probability that their genes will dominate the gene pool.

Sociobiologists have developed some controversial explanations for the relations between men and women. Since evolution's imperative, according to sociobiologists, is to spread our genes, men and women have evolved different strategies for doing so. Sperm is abundant; men produce billions in a lifetime. However, women have a limited number of eggs, only about 400 in a lifetime. A man has the potential, then, to produce many more offspring than a woman can. To ensure that they spread their genes, it is to a male's advantage to impregnate as many females as possible. Given that women have few eggs and gestation takes a long time, it is to a woman's advantage to choose a mate who will protect her. This, say some sociobiologists, explains why women tend to be monogamous and men do not.

Sociobiologists point to animal models to support their theories. For example, the males of most species initiate sexual behavior more frequently than females do. In some species, such as seals, cattle, and elephants, the male maintains a large harem of females to inseminate and protect. Some human societies incorporate this reproductive strategy into their culture (Hinde, 1984). Sociobiologists also contend that the universality of certain behaviors, such as incest taboos and religious laws, are evidence that such behaviors have a genetic basis.

Despite the evidence and reasoning offered by sociobiologists, many psychologists remain unconvinced (Hinde, 1992; Lerner & von Eye, 1992). Critics argue that sociobiology does not adequately consider human adaptability and experience. They believe that sociobiology reduces human beings to mere automatons in thrall to their genes. They point out that sociobiologists explain things only after the fact, with no evidence of the predictive ability that would characterize a good theory. Male aggression is said to be a sociobiological imperative, but only after sociobiologists have seen that males do indeed behave more aggressively than females. Much of the evidence to support sociobiology is based on animal research. Critics assert that findings from animal research cannot always be generalized to humans. Further, some critics see sociobiology as little more than a justification to discriminate against women and minorities under a scientific umbrella, using genetic determinism as an excuse for ignoring the social injustice and discrimination that contribute to inequality (Paludi, 1995).

There are one hundred and ninety-three living species of monkeys and apes. One-hundred and ninety-two of them are covered with hair. The exception is the naked ape self-named, homo-sapiens.

Desmond Morris,
***The Naked Ape,* 1967**

At this point, we have discussed some important ideas about genetics, evolution, and sociobiology, as well as the interplay of genetics and the environment (nature and nurture) in shaping human behavior. As was mentioned earlier, cultural evolution—our ability to impart vast amounts of knowledge from one generation to the next—sets us apart from other organisms. However, nowhere is our uniqueness more apparent than in the human brain, which we will discuss next.

Perspectives on Nature and Nurture

The interaction of nature and nurture, genes and environment, influences every aspect of mind and behavior. From the genetic perspective, the nucleus of each human cell contains 46 chromosomes, which are composed of DNA. Genes are short segments of DNA and act as blueprints for cells to reproduce and manufacture proteins that maintain life. Most genetic transmission involves combinations of genes.

From the evolutionary perspective, organisms who show better adaptation are more likely to survive; the survivors reproduce and pass on some of their characteristics to the next generation. Over the course of many generations, the organisms with the characteristics most needed for survival make up an increasingly larger percentage of the population. According to the principle of natural selection, over

many generations this process could modify the entire species.

Sociobiology is a contemporary view that relies on evolutionary biology to explain human behavior. Sociobiologists argue that all behavior is motivated by the drive to dominate the gene pool. Critics say that sociobiology ignores the environmental determinants of behavior and is biased against females.

THE NERVOUS SYSTEM

The purpose of the nervous system is to pass messages back and forth among cells. Highly organized, the nervous system is continuously processing information about everything we do—whether we are taking out the garbage, spotting a loved one across a crowded room, or preparing a speech. First we will take a *macro* view of the nervous system and examine how it is organized to execute such complex behaviors. Then we will explore a *micro* view of the nervous system by looking at the function of nerve cells, or **neurons,** *the basic units of the nervous system.*

Elegant Organization

The nervous system is divided into two parts: the central nervous system and the peripheral nervous system. Figure 3.4 displays the hierarchical organization of the nervous

system's major divisions. The **central nervous system (CNS)** *is made up of the brain and spinal cord.* More than 99 percent of all neurons in the body are located in the CNS. The **peripheral nervous system** *is a network of nerves that connects the brain and spinal cord to other parts of the body. The peripheral nervous system takes information to and from the brain and spinal cord and carries out the commands of the CNS to execute various muscular and glandular activities.*

The two major divisions of the peripheral nervous system are the *somatic nervous system* and *autonomic nervous system.* The **somatic nervous system** *consists of sensory nerves, which convey information from the skin and muscles to the CNS about such matters as pain and temperature, and motor nerves, which inform muscles when to act.* The **autonomic nervous system** *takes messages to and from the body's internal organs, monitoring such processes as breathing, heart rate, and digestion. It also is divided into two parts,*

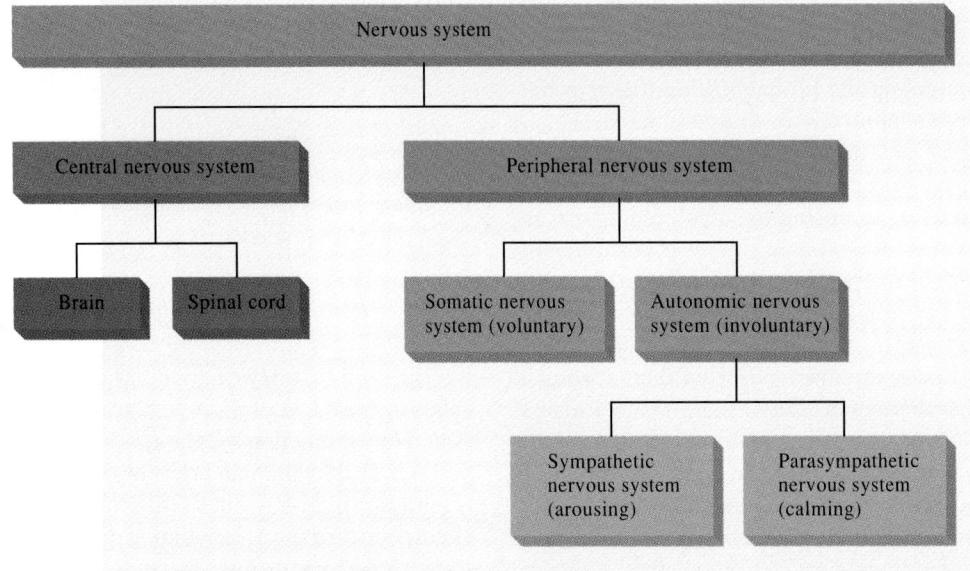

FIGURE 3.4

Major Divisions of the Human Nervous System

Imagine you are preparing to give a speech. Your racing heart, "cotton mouth," and queasy stomach result from sympathetic nervous system activation.

the **sympathetic nervous system,** *the division of the autonomic nervous system that arouses the body,* and the **parasympathetic nervous system,** *the division of the autonomic nervous system that calms the body.* More information about the autonomic nervous system appears toward the end of this chapter.

To get a better feel for how the human nervous system works, imagine that you are preparing to give a speech. As you go over your notes one last time, your peripheral nervous system carries information about the notes to your central nervous system. Your central nervous system processes the marks on the paper, interpreting the words as you memorize key points and plan ways to keep the audience interested. After studying the notes several minutes longer, you scribble a joke midway through them. Your peripheral nervous system is at work again, conveying the information that enables you to make the marks on the paper from your brain to the muscles in your arm and hand. The information transmitted from your eyes to your brain and from your brain to your hand is being handled by the somatic nervous system. Since this is your first speech in a while, you've got the jitters. As you think about getting up in front of the audience, your stomach feels queasy and your heart begins to thump. This is the sympathetic division of the autonomic nervous system functioning as you become aroused. You regain your confidence after reminding yourself that you know the speech. As you relax, 5 minutes into the speech, the parasympathetic division of the autonomic nervous system is working.

Neural Transmission

So far, we have discussed the nervous system's major divisions. However, there is much more to the intriguing story of how the nervous system processes information. Let's go inside the huge nervous system and find out more about the cells, chemicals, and electrical impulses that are the nuts and bolts of this operation.

Neuron Pathways

Information flows to the brain, within the brain, and out of the brain along specialized nerve cells known as *afferent nerves, interneurons,* and *efferent nerves.* **Afferent nerves,** *or sensory nerves, carry information to the brain.* Afferent *comes from the Latin word meaning "bring to."* **Efferent nerves,** *or motor nerves, carry the brain's output. The word* efferent *is derived from the Latin word meaning "bring forth."* To see how afferent and efferent nerves work, let's consider a well-known reflex, the knee jerk. When your knee jerks in response to a tap just below your kneecap, afferent cells transmit information directly to efferent cells; the information processing is quick and simple.

The information involving the knee jerk is processed at the spinal cord. This simple transaction does not require the brain's participation. More complex information processing is accomplished by passing the information through systems of **interneurons,** *central nervous system neurons that mediate sensory input and motor output. Interneurons make up most of the brain.* For example, as you read the notes for your speech, the afferent input from your eye is transmitted to your brain, then is passed through many interneuron systems, which translate (process) the patterns of black and white into neural codes for letters, words, associations, and meanings. Some of the information is stored in the interneuron systems for future associations, and, if you read aloud, some is output as efferent messages to your lips and tongue.

Structure of the Neuron

Neuron is a neuroscientist's label for nerve cell. Neurons handle information processing in the nervous system at the cellular level. There are about 100 billion neurons in the human brain. The average neuron is as complex as a small computer, with as many as 15,000 physical connections with other cells. At times the brain may be "lit up" with as many as a quadrillion connections.

The three basic parts of the neuron are the cell body, the dendrites, and the axon (see figure 3.5). The neuron's **cell body** *contains the nucleus, which directs the manufacture of the substances the neuron uses for its growth and maintenance.* Most neurons are created very early in life and will not be replaced if they are destroyed. Interestingly, though, some types of neurons continue to multiply in adults. Most are capable of changing their shape, size, and connections throughout the life span (Levitan & Kaczmarek, 1991).

The **dendrite** *is the receiving part of the neuron, serving the important function of collecting information and orienting it toward the cell body.* Most nerve cells have a number of dendrites radiating from the cell body of the neuron, but there is only one axon. The **axon** *is the part of the neuron that carries information away from the cell body to other cells.* The axon typically is much thinner and longer than a dendrite and looks like an ultrathin cylindrical tube. The axon of a single neuron may extend all the way from the top of the brain to the base of the spinal cord, a distance of over

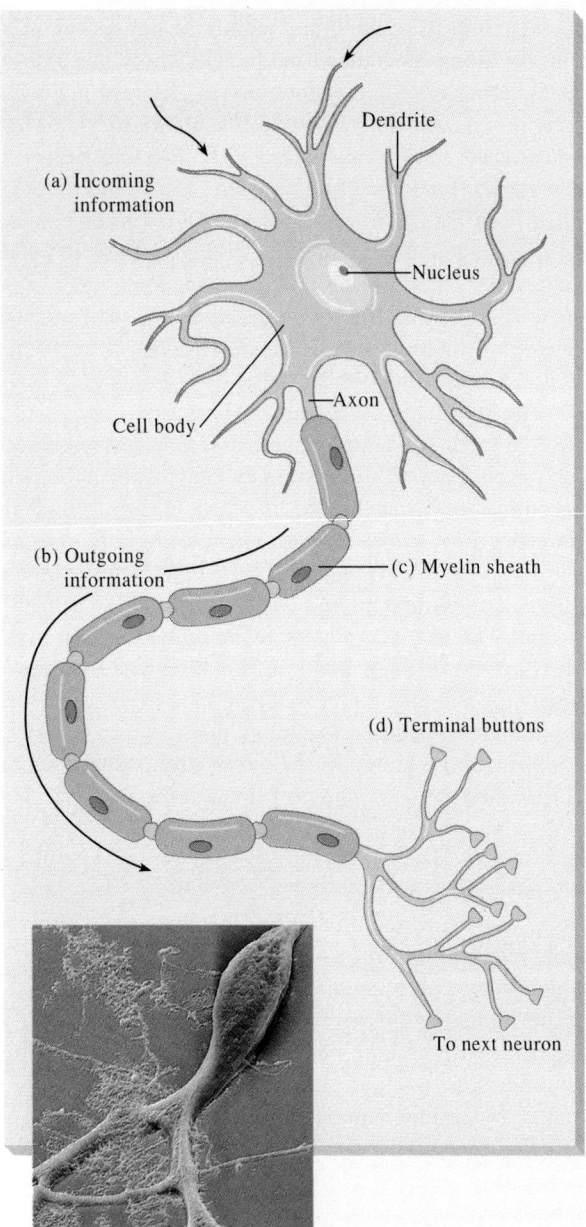

FIGURE 3.5

The Neuron
(a) The dendrites of the cell body receive information from other neurons, muscles, or glands through the axon. *(b)* Axons transmit information away from the cell body. *(c)* A myelin sheath covers most axons and speeds information transmission. *(d)* As it ends, the axon branches out into terminal buttons. Shown in the insert is a photograph of a neuron. Notice the branching dendrites at the bottom and the cell body at the top right.

3 feet. A **myelin sheath,** *a layer of fat cells, encases most axons. Not only does the myelin sheath insulate the nerve cell, it also helps the nerve impulse travel faster.* The myelin sheath developed as the brain evolved and became larger, making it necessary for information to travel over long distances in the nervous system. This is similar to the appearance of freeways and turnpikes as cities grew. The newly developed roadways keep the fast-moving long-distance traffic from getting tangled up with slow-moving traffic. The axon terminates in small synaptic knobs called *terminal buttons,* the storage sites of neurotransmitters, which will be discussed in a later section.

The Nerve Impulse

Neurons send information down the axon as brief impulses, or waves, of electricity. Perhaps in a movie you have seen a telegraph operator sending a series of single clicks down a telegraph wire to the next station. That is what neurons do. To transmit information to other neurons, they send a series of single electrical clicks down their axons. By changing the rate and timing of the clicks, neurons can vary the nature of the message they send. As you reach to turn this page, hundreds of such clicks stream down the axons in your arm to tell your muscles when to flex and how vigorously.

To understand how a neuron, which is a living cell, creates and sends electrical signals, we need to examine this cell and the fluids in which it floats. A neuron is a balloon-like bag filled with one kind of fluid and surrounded by a slightly different kind of fluid. A piece of this balloonlike bag is stretched and pulled to form a long, hollow tube, which is the axon. The axon tube is very thin; a few dozen in a bundle would be about the thickness of a human hair.

To see how this fluid-filled "balloon" creates electrical signals, we must look at two things: the particles that float in the fluids and the actual wall of the cell, the membrane. The important particles in the fluids are **ions,** *electrically charged particles that include sodium (NA^+), chloride (Cl^-), and potassium (K^+). The neuron creates electrical signals by moving these charged ions back and forth through its membrane; the waves of electricity that are created sweep along the membrane.*

How does the neuron move these ions? The membrane, the wall of the neuron, is covered with hundreds of thousands of small doors, or gates, that open and close to let the ions pass in or out to the cell. Normally, when resting, or not sending information, the membrane gates for sodium are closed and those for potassium and chloride are partly open. Therefore, the membrane is in what is called a *semipermeable state,* and the ions separate; sodium is kept outside, lots of potassium ends up inside, and most of the chloride goes outside. Because the ions are separated, a charge is present along the membrane of the cell (figure 3.6 shows the movement of the sodium and potassium ions). **Resting potential** *is the stable, negative charge of an inactive neuron.* That potential is about one-fourteenth of a volt, so fourteen neurons could make a one-volt battery; an electric eel's 8,400 cells could generate 600 volts.

When a neuron gets enough stimulation to cause it to send a message, the sodium gates at the base of the axon open briefly, then shut again. While those gates are open,

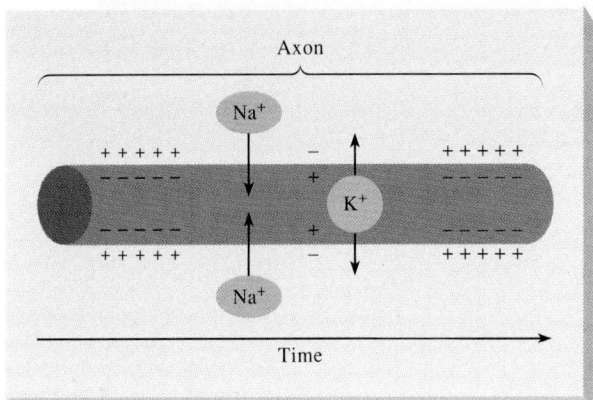

FIGURE 3.6

Movement of Sodium and Potassium Ions Down the Axon and the Action Potential
Electrical/chemical changes in the neuron produce an action potential. The sodium and potassium ions are shown moving down the axon. As the nerve impulse moves down the axon, electrical stimulation of the membrane makes it more permeable to sodium ions (Na$^+$). Sodium rushes into the axon, carrying an electrical charge, and that charge causes the next group of gates on the axon to flip open briefly. So it goes, all the way down the axon. After the sodium gates close, potassium ions (K$^+$) flow out of the cell.

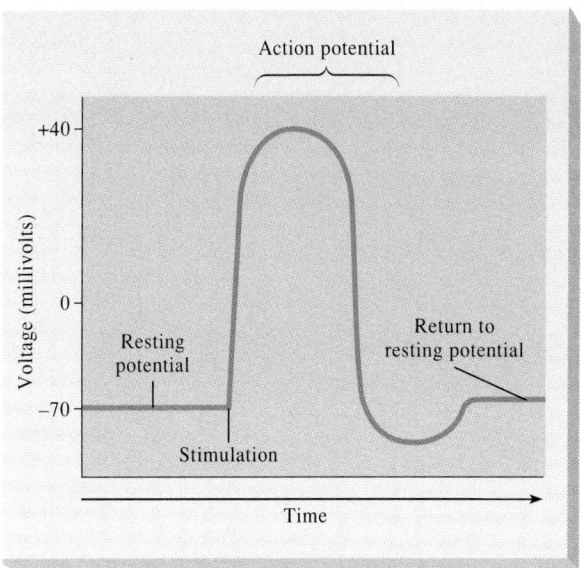

FIGURE 3.7

Action Potential
The action potential is shown on this graph in terms of its electrical voltage. The action potential is the positive charge in the cell generated by the influx of sodium (Na$^+$) ions. In the example shown here, the wave of electrical charge reaches about 40 millivolts. After the sodium gates close, potassium ions (K$^+$) flow out of the cell and bring the voltage back to its resting potential.

sodium rushes into the axon, carrying an electrical charge. That charge causes the next group of gates on the axon to flip open briefly. So it goes, all the way down the axon, like a long row of cabinet doors opening and closing in sequence. After the sodium gates close, potassium ions flow out of the cell and bring the membrane charge back to the resting condition. **Action potential** *is the brief wave of electrical charge that sweeps down the axon* (see figure 3.7).

The wave of electrical charge that sweeps down the axon abides by the **all-or-none principle,** *which means that once the electrical impulse reaches a certain level of intensity, it fires and moves all the way down the axon, remaining at the same strength throughout its travel.* The electrical impulse traveling down an axon is much like a fuse on a firecracker. It doesn't matter whether a match or blowtorch is used to light the fuse; as long as a certain minimal intensity is reached, the spark travels quickly and at the same level of strength down the fuse until it reaches the firecracker. In the same manner, once stimulation exceeds minimum requirements, the neuron fires regardless of the intensity of the stimulation.

Synapses and Neurotransmitters

What happens once the neural impulse reaches the end of the axon? Neurons do not touch each other directly; nevertheless, they manage to communicate. The story of the connection between one neuron and another is one of the most intriguing and highly researched areas of contemporary neuroscience.

Synapses *are tiny gaps between neurons. Most synapses are between the axon of one neuron and the dendrites or cell body of another neuron.* How does information get across this gap to the next neuron? The end of an axon branches out into a number of fibers, which end in structures called terminal buttons. Neurotransmitters are found in the tiny synaptic vesicles (chambers) located in the terminal buttons. **Neurotransmitters** *are chemical substances that carry information across the synaptic gap to the next neuron.* The molecules of these chemical substances wait for a nerve impulse to come down through the axon. Once the nerve impulse reaches the terminal buttons, the electrical signal causes these miniature, springlike molecules to contract, pulling the vesicles out to the edge of the terminal buttons. At the edge, the vesicles burst open, and the neurotransmitter molecules spew forth into the gap between the two neurons. In the synaptic gap, the neurotransmitter molecules bump about in random motion, and some land on receptor sites in the next neuron, where they open a "door," and electrical signals begin to sweep through the next neuron. In effect, a message in the brain is "ferried" across the synapse by a neurotransmitter, which pours out of the end of the cell just as the message approaches the synapse. Synapses and neurotransmitters can be just as mysterious as genes and DNA. Turn to figure 3.8 for an illustration of this.

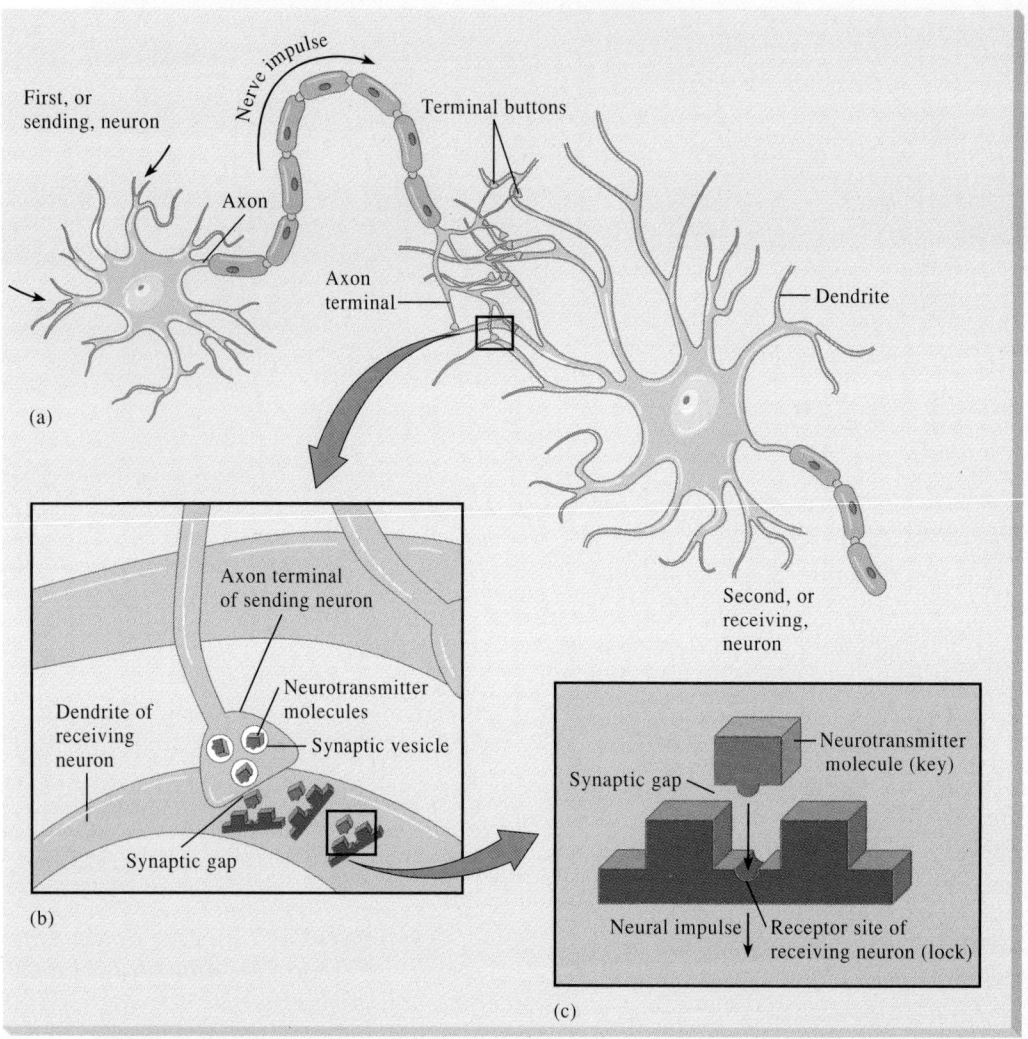

FIGURE 3.8

How Synapses and Neurotransmitters Work

(a) When an axon reaches its destination, it branches out into a number of fibers that end in terminal buttons. There is a tiny gap between these terminal buttons at the tip of the axon terminal and the next neuron. (b) When it reaches the terminal buttons, the neural impulse releases tiny chemical molecules that are stored in synaptic vesicles in the knobs. These chemical substances are called neurotransmitters. They bump around in the synaptic gap between the sending and receiving neurons. Some of them land on receptor sites in the next neuron, where the neural impulse continues its travel. (c) Neurotransmitter molecules fit like small keys in equally small locks, once they reach the receptor site in the receiving neuron. The key in the lock opens the "door," and the neural impulse begins its travel through the second neuron.

More than 50 neurotransmitters, each with a unique chemical makeup, have been discovered, and the list probably will grow to 100 or more in the near future (Barnard & Darlison, 1989). Interestingly, most creatures that have been studied, from snails to whales, use the same type of neurotransmitter molecules that our own brains use. Neurotransmitters are either excitatory or inhibitory; they facilitate or disrupt the transfer of information from one neuron to another. Many animal venoms, such as that of the black widow spider, are neurotransmitter-like substances that disturb neurotransmission. What are some of these neurotransmitters and how are they related to our behavior?

GABA, *gama aminobutyric acid, is a neurotransmitter that inhibits the firing of motor neurons.* It is found throughout the brain and spinal cord and is believed to be the neurotransmitter in as many as one-third of the brain's synaptic connections. GABA is so important in the brain because it keeps many neurons from firing. This inhibition helps control the precision of the signal being carried from one neuron to the next. The degeneration of GABA may be responsible for Huntington's chorea, a deadly disease that includes a loss of muscle control. Without GABA's inhibiting influence, nerve impulses become imprecise and muscles lose their coordination. GABA may also be involved in modulating anxiety (Zorumski & Isenberg, 1991).

Biological and Perceptual Processes

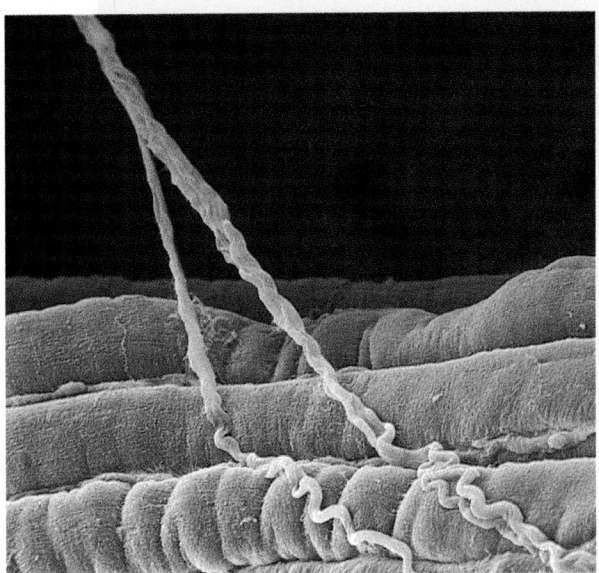

FIGURE 3.9

Nerves, Acetylcholine, and Muscles
The nerve impulse, conducted down a nerve fiber that ends in skeletal muscle, releases a small amount of the chemical acetylcholine. The action of acetylcholine at the motor end-plate initiates the chemical changes that cause the muscle to contract. The photo shows a number of nerve fibers leading to and crossing several striated muscle cells.

Acetylcholine (ACh) *is a neurotransmitter that produces contractions of skeletal muscles by acting on motor nerves* (see figure 3.9). Whereas GABA inhibits neurons from firing, in most instances ACh excites neurons and stimulates them to fire. The venom of the black widow causes ACh to gush through the synapses between the spinal cord and skeletal muscles, producing violent spasms. The drug curare, found on the tips of some South American Indians' poisoned darts, blocks some receptors for ACh. This paralyzes skeletal muscles.

Norepinephrine *is a neurotransmitter that usually inhibits the firing of neurons in the brain and spinal cord but excites the heart muscles, intestines, and urogenital tract.* Too little norepinephrine is associated with depression and too much is linked to highly agitated, manic states.

Dopamine *is an inhibitory neurotransmitter that is related to movement, attention, learning, and mental health; too much dopamine in the brain's synapses is associated with the severe mental disorder called schizophrenia, in which an individual loses contact with reality.* When dopaminergic neurons degenerate, Parkinson's-related behaviors result. **Serotonin** *is an inhibitory neurotransmitter that is involved in the regulation of sleep, mood, arousal, and pain regulation. Like norepinephrine, serotonin seems to play a role in depression* (Marek & Seiden, 1991).

A long-distance runner, a woman giving childbirth, and a person in shock after a car wreck all have elevated

CRITICAL THINKING

Sticks and Stones and Mustard Gas

In the first part of this chapter, you read about how humankind has evolved over the centuries to its present state. Not only have we physically evolved, we have also evolved in our abilities to use weapons. Early humans most likely used clubs and stones during aggressive acts. Metal-working arts moved us into combat with blades. The invention of gunpowder led to the development of an astounding array of methods for penetrating, disabling, and killing the opponent. With the introduction of greater sophistication about how the body works also comes the opportunity to use that knowledge toward aggressive ends. The first appearance of chemical warfare methods appeared in World War I. Like all aggressive methods that came before it, mustard gas rendered the body incompetent. Although we didn't understand the underlying mechanisms at the time, we now understand that chemical warfare methods interfere with the body's normal functioning by disturbing neurotransmitter functions.

Under what circumstances do you believe that chemical methods of aggression or defense are appropriate? Many individuals see no difference between the use of chemicals and the use of bullets, if the end point is to defeat the opponent. Others believe that chemical warfare is a particularly inhumane manner of dealing with opposing forces. Where do you stand on this issue? This exercise encourages you to think about the *standards of ethical treatment of individuals and groups.*

Man, biologically considered, and whatever else he may be in the bargain, is simply the most formidable of all beasts of prey, and, indeed, the only one that preys systematically on its own species.

William James

levels of **endorphins,** *natural opiates that are neurotransmitters. Endorphins are involved in pleasure and the control of pain.* As early as the fourth century B.C., the Greeks used the wild poppy to induce euphoria. However, it wasn't until more than 2,000 years later that the magical formula behind opium's addictive action was discovered. In the early 1970s, scientists found that opium plugs into a sophisticated system of natural opiates lying deep within the brain's pathways (Pert & Snyder, 1973). The system is involved in shielding the body from pain and elevating feelings of pleasure.

As you will see in later chapters, neurotransmitters play a major role in biological explanations of some mental health disorders. See table 3.1 for a summary of the most prominent neurotransmitters.

Next, we will explore the brain, its structure, its functions, and the methods used to conduct research on this remarkable organ.

"Runner's high" may be due to an elevation of endorphins. Many researchers, however, believe the connection between endorphins and runner's high has been exaggerated.

TABLE 3.1

Selected Neurotransmitters and Their Functions

Neurotransmitter	Type	Site of Influence	Function
GABA	Inhibitory	Brain and spinal cord; motor nerves	Improves signal precision; suppresses anxiety
ACh	Excitatory	Spinal cord and skeletal muscles	Facilitates muscle contraction
Norepinephrine	Inhibitory	Brain, spinal cord	Linked to balance between agitation and depression
	Excitatory	Heart, intestines, and urogenital tract	
Dopamine	Inhibitory	Brain stem	Governs motor control; implicated in Parkinson's disease
Serotonin	Inhibitory	Brain stem	Regulates sleep, arousal; involved in depression
Endorphins	Inhibitory	Brain/bloodstream	Pain control

REVIEW

The Brain and Nervous System

The central nervous system consists of the brain and spinal cord; it contains more than 99 percent of all neurons. The peripheral nervous system is a network of nerves that connects the brain and spinal cord to other parts of the body. Two major divisions are the somatic nervous system and the autonomic nervous system. The autonomic nervous system is subdivided into the sympathetic and parasympathetic systems.

Afferent nerves (sensory nerves) carry input to the brain; efferent nerves (motor nerves) carry output away from the brain; interneurons do most of the information processing within the brain. The three basic parts of the neuron are the cell body, dendrite, and axon. The myelin sheath speeds information transmission. Neurons send information in the form of brief impulses, or waves, of electricity. These waves are called the

action potential; they operate according to the all-or-none principle.

The gaps between neurons are called synapses. The neural impulse reaches the axon terminal and stimulates the release of neurotransmitters from tiny vesicles. These carry information to the next neuron, which fits like a key in a lock. Important neurotransmitters are GABA, acetylcholine, norepinephrine, serotonin, and endorphins.

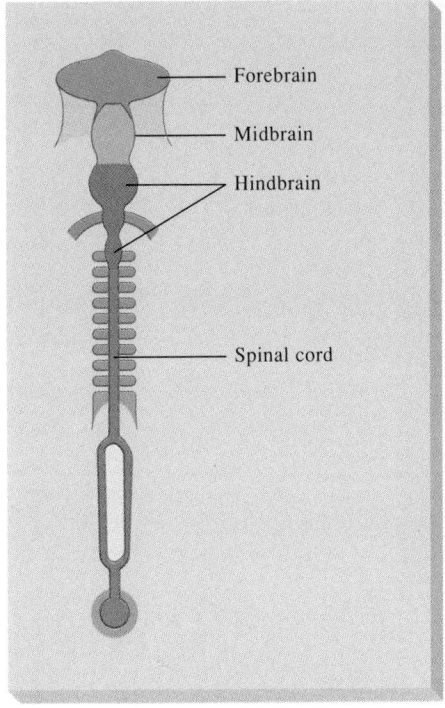

FIGURE 3.10

Embryological Development of the Nervous System
In the photograph on the right, you can see the primitive, tubular appearance of the nervous system at 6 weeks in the human embryo. The drawing shows the major brain regions and spinal cord as they appear early in the development of a human embryo.

THE CENTRAL NERVOUS SYSTEM

Most of the information we have covered about the brain has been about one or two cells. Earlier you learned that about 99 percent of all neurons in the nervous system are located in the brain and the spinal cord; however, neurons do not simply float in the brain. Connected in precise ways, they constitute the various structures of the brain.

As a human embryo develops inside the womb, the central nervous system begins as a long, hollow tube on the embryo's back. At 3 weeks or so after conception, the brain forms into a large mass of neurons and loses its tubular appearance. The elongated tube changes shape and develops into three major divisions: the hindbrain, which is the portion of the brain adjacent to the spinal cord; the midbrain, which is above the hindbrain; and the forebrain, which is at the highest region of the brain (see figure 3.10).

The nervous system's command center, the brain, controls all your thoughts and movements. It weighs about 3 pounds and is slightly larger than a grapefruit. With a crinkled outer layer, it looks like an oversized, shelled walnut. Inside, the brain resembles undercooked custard or a ripe avocado. In this section, we will examine the structure and function of the parts of the brain and spinal cord. We will explore the substantial research that has been generated about hemispheric specialization. Finally, we will examine current methods used to study the central nervous system.

The Hindbrain

The **hindbrain,** *located at the skull's rear, is the lowest portion of the brain. The three main parts of the hindbrain are the medulla, cerebellum, and pons* (figure 3.11 shows the location of these brain structures as well as some of the forebrain's main structures). The **medulla** *begins where the spinal cord enters the skull. It helps control breathing and regulates a portion of the reflexes that allow us to maintain an upright posture.* The **cerebellum** *extends from the rear of the hindbrain and is located just above the medulla. It consists of two rounded structures thought to play important roles in motor control.* Leg and arm movements are coordinated at the cerebellum, for example. When we play golf, practice the piano, or perfect our moves on the dance floor, the cerebellum is hard at work. If a higher portion of the brain commands us to write the number 7, it is the cerebellum that integrates the muscular activities required to do so. If the cerebellum becomes damaged, our movements become uncoordinated and jerky. The **pons** *is a bridge in the hindbrain that contains several clusters of fibers involved in sleep and arousal.*

The Midbrain

The **midbrain,** *located between the hindbrain and forebrain, is an area where many nerve fiber systems ascend and descend to connect the higher and lower portions of the brain. In particular, the midbrain relays information between the brain and the eyes and ears.* The ability to attend to an object visually, for example, is linked to one bundle of neurons in the midbrain. Parkinson's disease, a deterioration of movement that produces rigidity and tremors in the elderly, damages a section near the bottom of the midbrain.

Two systems in the midbrain are of special interest. One is the **reticular formation** (see figure 3.12), *a diffuse collection of neurons involved in stereotyped patterns of behavior such as walking, sleeping, or turning to attend to a sudden noise.* The other system is comprised of small groups of neurons that use the special neurotransmitters serotonin, dopamine, and norepinephrine. These three groups contain relatively few cells, but they send their axons to a remarkable variety of brain regions, perhaps explaining their involvement in high-level, integrative functions.

It is not the hindbrain or midbrain that separates humans from animals, however. In humans, it is the forebrain that becomes enlarged and specialized.

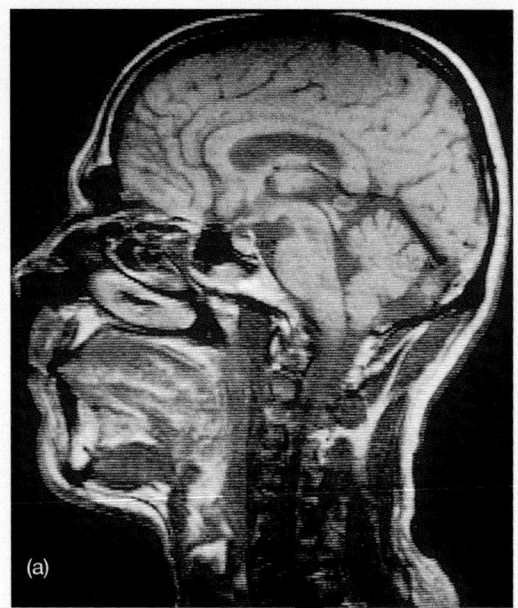

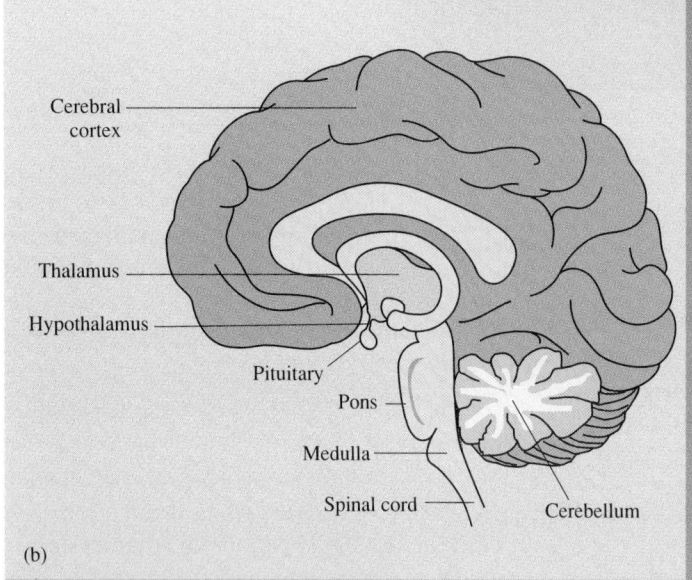

Forebrain structures	
Cerebral cortex	Extensive, wrinkled outer layer of the forebrain governs higher brain functions, such as thinking, learning, and consciousness
Thalamus	Relays information between lower and higher brain centers
Hypothalamus	Governs eating, drinking, and sex; plays a role in emotion and stress
Pituitary	Governs endocrine system

Hindbrain structures	
Pons	Governs sleep and arousal
Medulla	Governs breathing and reflexes
Cerebellum	Rounded structure involved in motor behavior
Spinal cord	Connects the brain with the rest of the body; governs simple reflexes

FIGURE 3.11

Structure and Regions in the Human Brain
(a) This image of a cross-section of the brain includes some of the brain's most important structures, which we will discuss shortly. As we discuss these structures, you might find it helpful to refer to this figure to obtain a visual image of what the structures look like. (b) This drawing reproduces the main structures in the forebrain and the hindbrain and corresponds to the image of the brain shown in (a).

The Forebrain

You try to understand what all of these terms mean and what all of these parts of the brain do. You talk with friends and plan a party for this weekend. You remember that it has been 6 months since you went to the dentist. You are confident that you will do well on the next exam in this course. All of these experiences, and millions more, would not be possible without the **forebrain.** *Among its most important structures are the thalamus, the hypothalamus and endocrine system, the limbic system, and the cerebrum,* each of which we will discuss in turn.

The Thalamus

The **thalamus** *is about the size of a peach pit and sits at the top of the brain stem in the central core of the brain. It serves as a very important relay station, functioning much like a telephone switchboard between the diverse areas of the cortex and the reticular formation.* One area of the thalamus orients information from the sense receptors (hearing, seeing, and so on) and might be involved particularly in the perception of pain. Other regions coordinate sleep and wakefulness as well as motor movements (see figure 3.12 for the location of the thalamus).

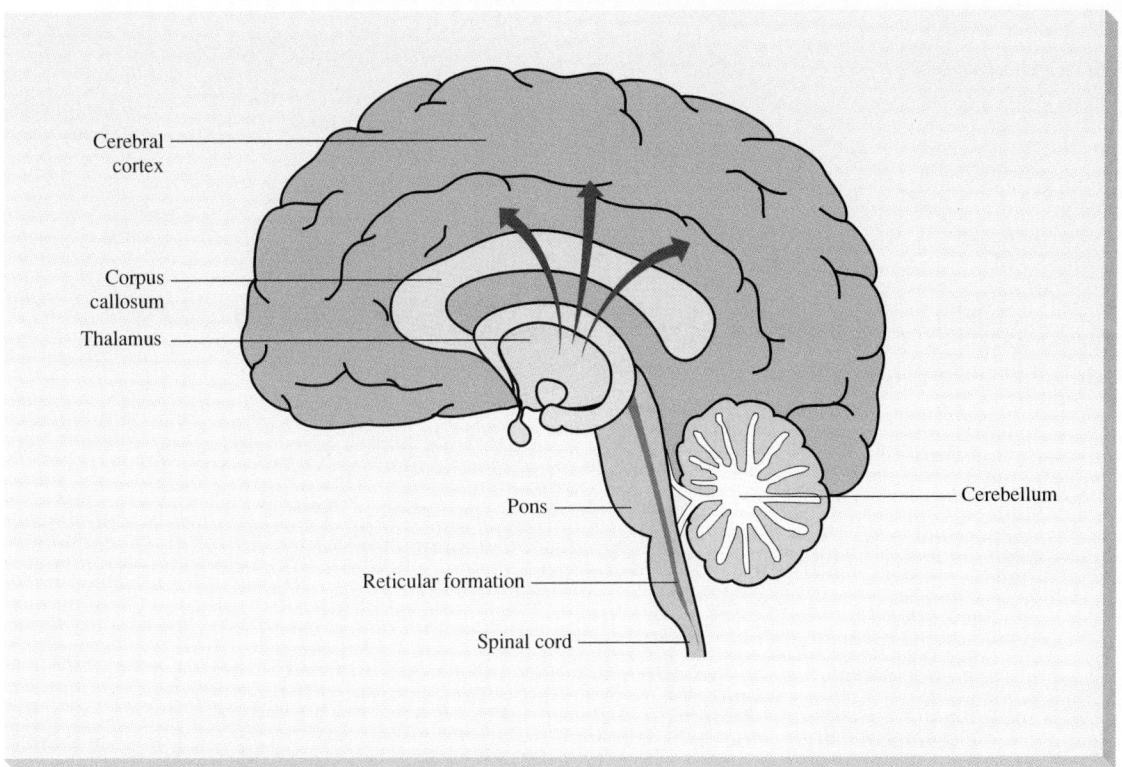

FIGURE 3.12

Connections in the Brain

The midbrain includes the reticular formation, a network of nerve fibers that runs through the brain stem. The reticular formation governs stereotyped patterns, arousal, and attention. The arrows radiating from the brain stem are drawn to show the connections of the reticular formation to the higher portions of the brain in the cerebral cortex. The corpus callosum is the thick band of fibers that connects the hemispheres of the cerebral cortex.

The Hypothalamus and Endocrine System

The **hypothalamus**, *much smaller than the thalamus and about the size of a kidney bean, is located just below the thalamus. The hypothalamus monitors three enjoyable activities—eating, drinking, and sex; it helps direct the endocrine system through the pituitary gland; and it is involved in emotion, stress, and reward.*

Perhaps the best way to describe the hypothalamus is in terms of its being a regulator and motivator. It is sensitive to changes in the blood and neural input, and it responds to these by influencing the secretion of hormones and neural outputs. For example, if the temperature of blood circulating near the hypothalamus is increased by just 1 or 2 degrees, certain cells in the hypothalamus increase their rate of firing. As a result, a chain of events is set into motion. Circulation in the skin and sweat glands increases immediately to release perspiration from the body. The cooled blood circulating to the hypothalamus slows down the activity of some of the neurons there, stopping the process when the temperature is right—37.1 degrees Centigrade. These temperature-sensitive neurons function like a finely tuned thermostat to restore the body to a balanced state.

The hypothalamus acts as an essential coordinator of the central nervous system. It is also involved in emotional states and plays an important role in handling stress. The hypothalamus acts on the pituitary gland, located just below it, to integrate sensory signals such as hunger, aggression, and pleasure. When certain areas of the hypothalamus are electrically stimulated, feelings of pleasure result.

In a classic experiment, James Olds and Peter Milner (1954) implanted an electrode in the hypothalamus of a rat's brain. When the rat ran to a corner of an enclosed area, its hypothalamus received a mild electric shock. The researchers thought the rat would steer clear of the corner to avoid the shock. Much to their surprise, the rat kept returning. Olds and Milner believed they had discovered a pleasure center in the hypothalamus.

In similar experiments, Olds (1958) later found that rats would press bars until they dropped from exhaustion just to feel pleasure. Figure 3.13 shows one rat that pressed a bar more than 2,000 times an hour for 24 hours to receive the pleasurable stimulus to its hypothalamus. Today researchers agree that the hypothalamus is one of the links between the brain and pleasure, but they know that other areas of the brain also are important (Kornetsky, 1986).

Recently an area adjacent to the hypothalamus has been linked with the intense pleasure and craving triggered by cocaine use. This finding has important implications for treating drug addiction. Researchers hope eventually to

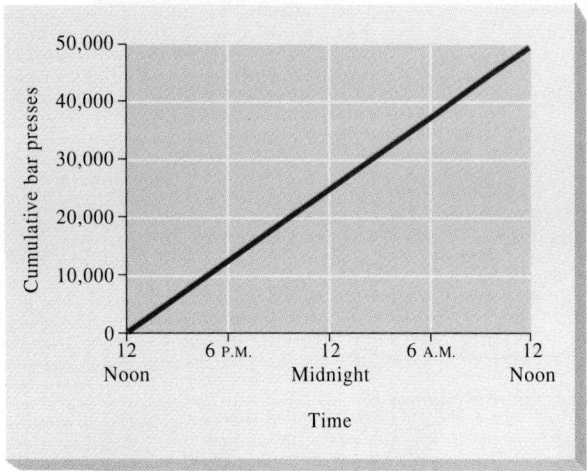

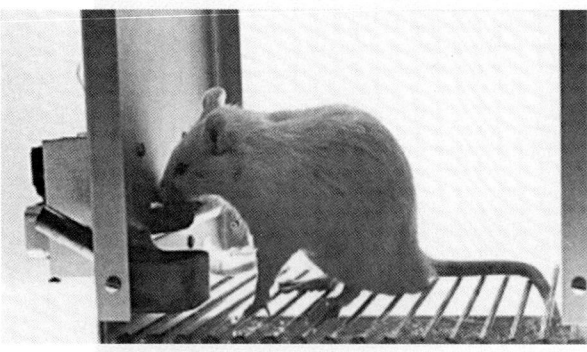

FIGURE 3.13

Results of the Experiment by Olds (1958) on the Role of the Hypothalamus in Pleasure

The graphed results for one rat show that it pressed the bar more than 2,000 times an hour for a period of 24 hours to receive the stimulus to its hypothalamus. One of the rats in Olds and Milner's experiments is shown pressing the bar to receive stimulation to its hypothalamus.

develop drugs that mimic or block an addictive drug's effects on the brain. There also is increasing evidence that the pleasure or reward a drug induces outweighs the fear of pain or suffering that withdrawal produces (Wise & Rompre, 1989). The Olds and Milner experiments illustrate this: when the rats pressed the bar, the pleasure they received overrode the pain from the electric shock. Similarly, when cocaine users talk about the drug, they highlight its ability to heighten pleasure in a variety of activities, including eating and sex. They tend to overlook the discomfort that comes as the drug's effects wear off. The story of addiction is complex; it is not like a bout of pneumonia that goes away with antibiotics. Much more about drug addiction appears in chapter 5.

The **endocrine system** *consists of the hypothalamus and other endocrine glands that release their chemical products directly into the bloodstream.* **Hormones** *are chemical messengers manufactured by the endocrine glands.* The bloodstream conveys hormones to all parts of the body, and the membrane of every cell has receptors for one or more hormones.

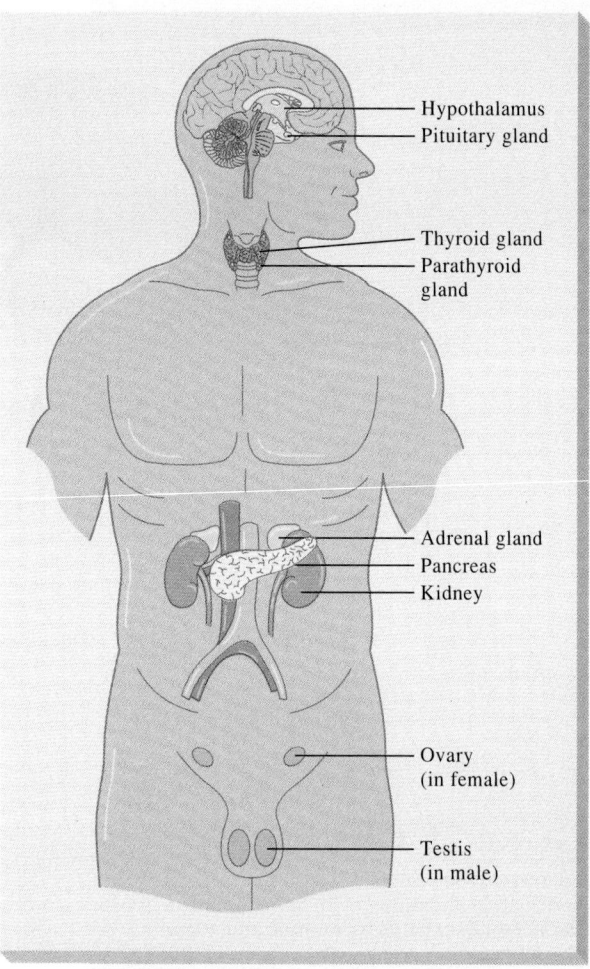

FIGURE 3.14

The Major Endocrine Glands

The pituitary gland releases hormones that regulate the hormone secretions of the other glands. The pituitary gland is itself regulated by the hypothalamus.

The endocrine glands consist of the hypothalamus and the pituitary gland at the base of the brain, the thyroid and parathyroid glands at the front of the neck, the adrenal glands just above the kidneys, the pancreas in the abdomen, the ovaries in the female's pelvis, and the testes in the male's scrotum (see figure 3.14). Other hormones are produced as well, including several that control digestion in the gastrointestinal tract. In much the same way that the brain's control of muscular activity is constantly monitored and altered to suit the information received by the brain, the action of the endocrine glands is continuously monitored and changed by the nervous, hormonal, and chemical information sent to them.

The **pituitary gland** *is an important endocrine gland that sits at the base of the skull and is about the size of a pea; the pituitary gland controls growth and regulates other glands.* The anterior (front) part of the pituitary is known as the master gland because most of its hormones direct the activity

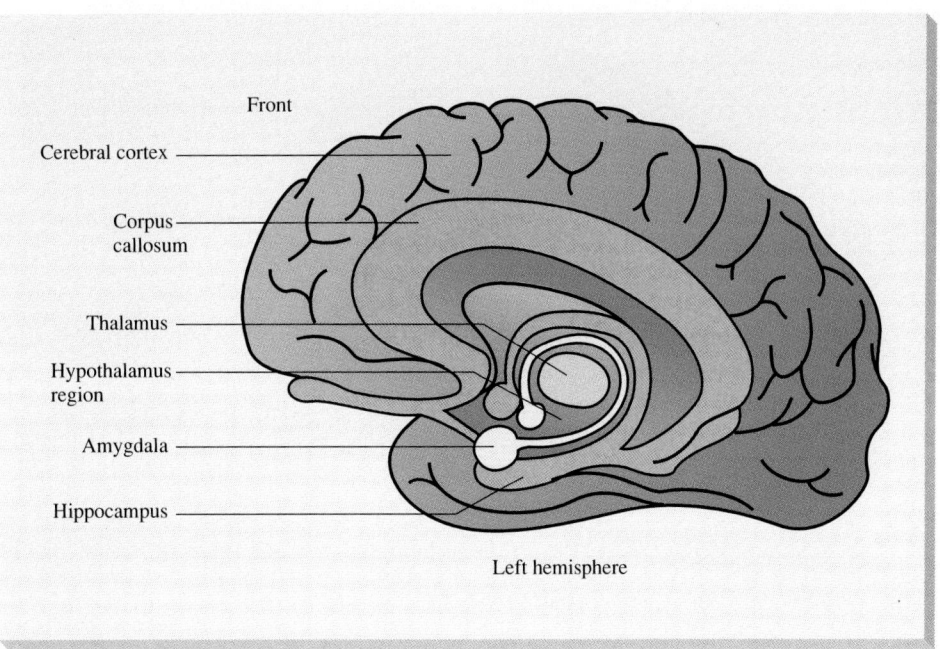

Front

Cerebral cortex

Corpus callosum

Thalamus

Hypothalamus region

Amygdala

Hippocampus

Left hemisphere

Figure 3.15

Limbic System
Considered part of the forebrain, the limbic system governs emotion and memory. The amygdala facilitates object discrimination in skills oriented to survival—eating, aggression, and mating. The hippocampus selects information for memory storage. The limbic system works in conjunction with other forebrain structures—the thalamus, hypothalamus, and pituitary gland.

of target glands elsewhere in the body. For example, follicle-stimulating hormone (FSH) produced by the pituitary monitors the level of sex hormones in the ovaries of females and the testes of males. Although most pituitary hormones influence specific organs, growth hormone (GH) acts on all tissues to produce growth during childhood and adolescence. Dwarfs have too little of this hormone, giants too much.

The **adrenal glands** *play an important role in our moods, our energy level, and our ability to cope with stress. Each adrenal gland secretes epinephrine (also called adrenaline) and norepinephrine (also called noradrenaline).* Although most hormones travel rather slowly, epinephrine and norepinephrine do their work quickly. Epinephrine helps a person get ready for an emergency by acting on the smooth muscles, heart, stomach, intestines, and sweat glands. Epinephrine also stimulates neurons in the midbrain, which in turn arouses the sympathetic nervous system; this system subsequently excites the adrenal glands to produce more epinephrine. Norepinephrine also alerts the individual for emergency situations by interacting with the pituitary and the liver. You may remember that norepinephrine also functions as a neurotransmitter when released by neurons. In the case of the adrenal glands, norepinephrine

is released as a hormone. In both instances, norepinephrine conveys information—in the first instance to neurons, in the second to glands.

Recall that the autonomic nervous system involves connections with internal organs, regulating such processes as respiration, heart rate, and digestion. The autonomic nervous system acts on the endocrine glands to produce a number of important physiological reactions to strong emotions, such as rage and fear.

Limbic System

The **limbic system,** *a loosely connected network of structures under the cerebral cortex, plays important roles in both memory and emotion.* Its two principal structures are the amygdala and hippocampus (see figure 3.15).

The **amygdala** *(named in Latin for its "almond" shape) is a limbic system structure located within the base of the temporal lobe and is involved in the discrimination of objects that are important in the organism's survival, such as appropriate food, mates, and social rivals.* Neurons in the amygdala often fire selectively at the sight of such stimuli, and lesions in the amygdala can cause animals to attempt to eat, fight, or mate, even with inappropriate objects such as chairs.

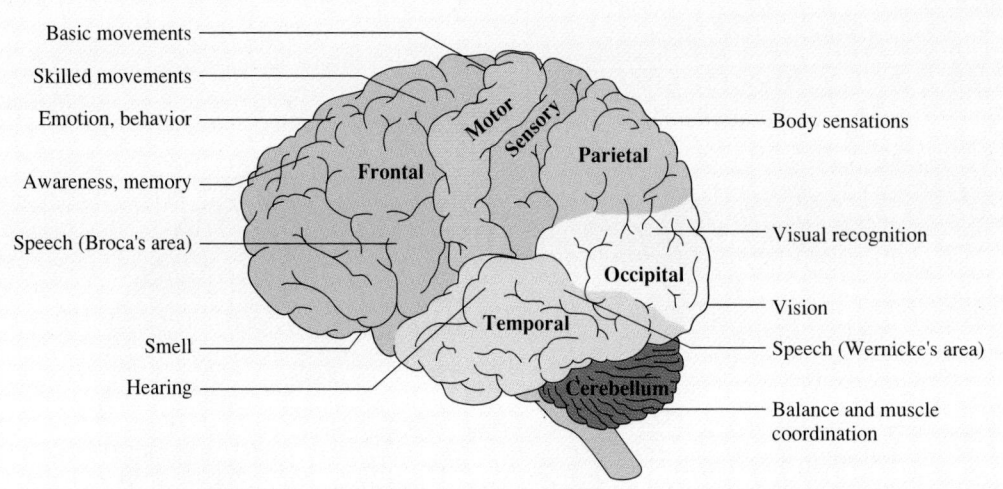

FIGURE 3.16

The Brain's Four Lobes
Shown here are the locations of the brain's four lobes: occipital, temporal, frontal, and parietal.

The **hippocampus** *is a limbic system structure that has a special role in the storage of memories.* Individuals suffering extensive hippocampal damage simply cannot retain any new conscious memories after the damage. It is fairly certain, though, that memories are not stored "in" the limbic system. Instead, the limbic system seems to control what parts of all the information passing through the cortex should be "printed" into durable, lasting neural traces in the cortex.

The Cerebral Cortex (Cerebrum)

The **cerebral cortex** (**cerebrum**) *is a region of the forebrain that is the most recently developed part of the brain in the evolutionary scheme. It is the largest part of the brain in volume (about 80 percent) and covers the lower portions of the brain like a large cap.* Let's look at the cerebral cortex in more detail.

The wrinkled surface of the *cerebral cortex* is divided into halves, called hemispheres. Each hemisphere is divided into four lobes—occipital, temporal, frontal, and parietal—each conveniently named for the main skull bone that covers it (see figure 3.16). These landmarks help us map the surface of the brain, but the lobes are not strictly functional regions. Nonetheless, they are often used in somewhat loose ways to describe the brain's functions. For example, the **occipital lobe,** *the portion of the cerebral cortex at the back of the head, is involved in vision;* the **temporal lobe,** *the portion of the cerebral cortex just above the ears, is involved in hearing;* the **frontal lobe,** *the portion of the cerebral cortex behind the forehead, is involved in the control of voluntary muscles and in intelligence;* and the **parietal lobe,** *the portion of the cerebral cortex at the top of the head and toward the rear, is involved in processing body sensations.*

In the same way that each cerebral cortex lobe is associated with different processes, regions within each lobe have different jobs. Scientists have determined this primarily through topographic mapping. Wilder Penfield (1947), a neurosurgeon at the Montreal Neurological

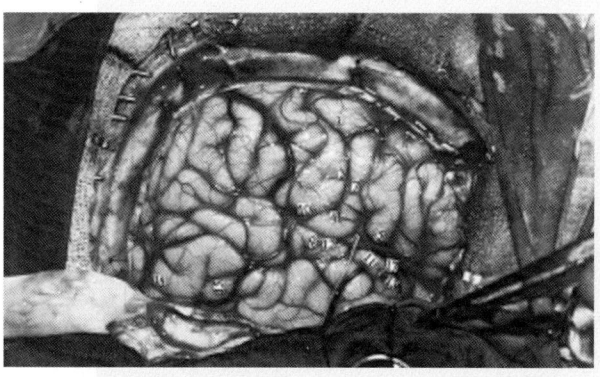

FIGURE 3.17

The Exposed Cortex of One of Penfield's Patients
The numbers identify the locations that Penfield stimulated with a very thin electric probe. When he stimulated the area marked by number 11, for example, the patient opened his mouth, sneezed, and began chewing.

Institute, pioneered mapping the brain. He worked with a number of patients who had very serious forms of epilepsy, a neurological disease that produces a storm of electrical activity across the cortex. Although Penfield sometimes surgically removed portions of the epileptic patients' brains to reduce their symptoms, he was concerned that such surgery might impair some of the patients' ability to function normally. Penfield's solution was to map the cerebral cortex during surgery. Penfield gave the patients a local anesthetic so they would remain awake during the operation. As he stimulated certain sensory and motor areas of the brain, different parts of the patient's body moved (see figure 3.17). For both sensory and motor areas, there is a point-to-point relation between a body part and a location on the cerebral cortex (see figure 3.18).

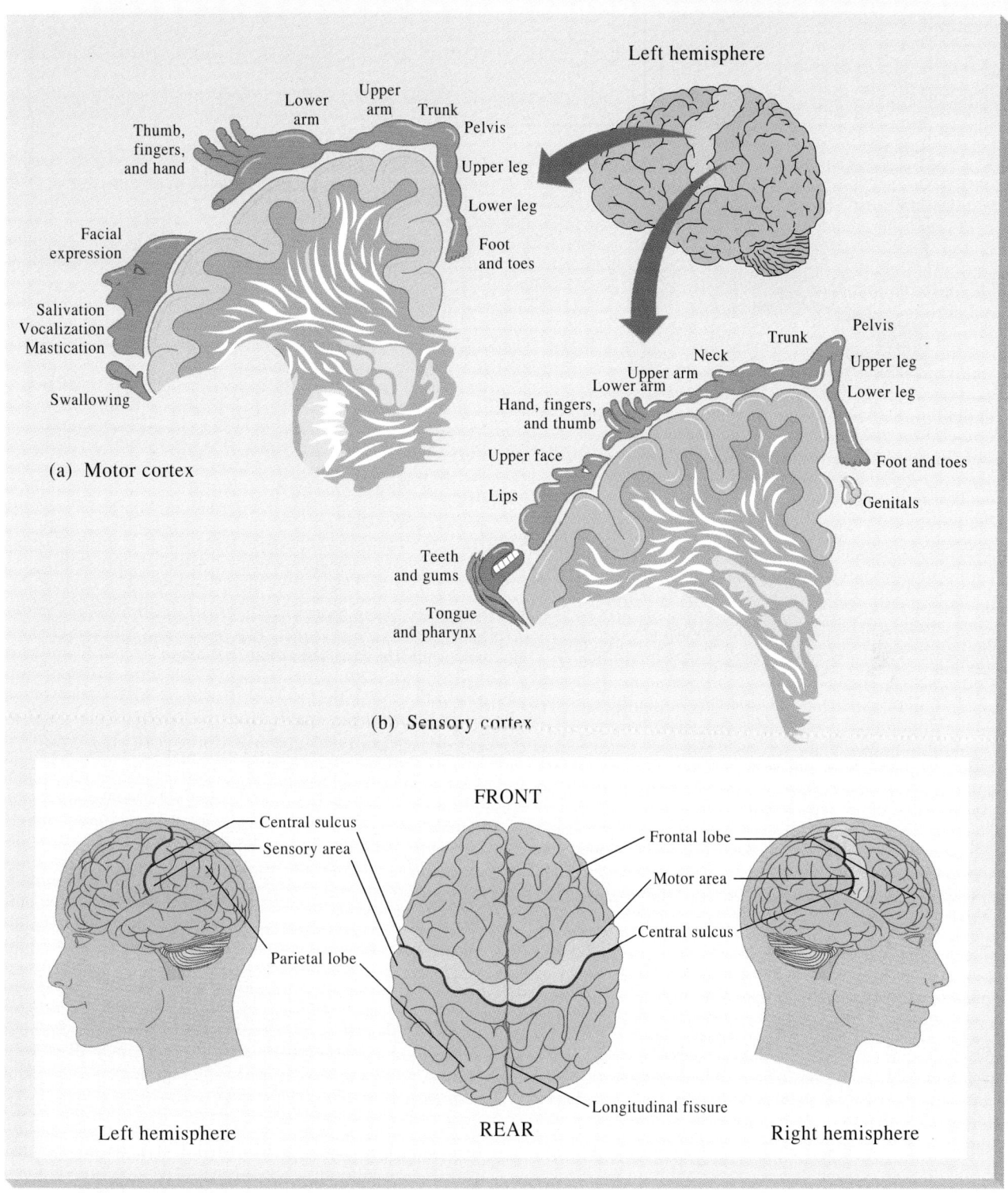

(a) Motor cortex

(b) Sensory cortex

FIGURE 3.18

Locations of the Motor and Sensory Areas on the Cerebral Cortex
This figure shows *(a)* the motor areas involved with the control of voluntary muscles and *(b)* the sensory areas involved with cutaneous and certain other senses. The body is disproportionately represented on the parietal and frontal lobes, with the hands and face receiving the most representation. Organization is inverse—functions represented at the top of the parietal lobe occur in the lower regions of the body, for example.

It's unlikely that Mr. Osborne's student has a good excuse. Experts believe that we use a fraction of the brain's potential.

The face and hands have proportionally more space on the cerebral cortex than other body parts because they are capable of finer perceptions and movements.

My own brain is to me the most unaccountable of machinery—always buzzing, humming, soaring, roaring, diving, and then buried in the mud.

Virginia Woolf

Our ability to perceive the world in an accurate and orderly way depends on this point-to-point mapping of sensory input onto the surface of the cerebral cortex. When something touches your lip, for example, your brain registers pressure on the lip. That's because the nerve pathways from your lips project to a specific part of the cerebral cortex designated to receive only signals from your lips. This arrangement is analogous to the private "hot line" that connects Washington and Moscow. If the red phone rings in the president's office in Washington, the call must be from Moscow, because Moscow is the only city that is connected to the other end of the line. In the sensory cortex, every small region has its own neural hot line bringing in information directly from the corresponding part of the sensory field. In our telephone analogy, it would be as if the president (the cerebral cortex) had hundreds of telephones, each one connected directly to the capital city of a different country. Whichever phone was ringing would indicate which country (sensory field) had a message to convey.

Occasionally these neural hot lines get tangled or connected the wrong way. One familiar example of this is the Siamese cat. Many Siamese cats have a genetic defect that causes the pathways from the eyes to connect to the wrong parts of the visual cortex. The result is that, in an effort to get the visual image to straighten out on their visual cortex, these cats spend their lives looking cross-eyed.

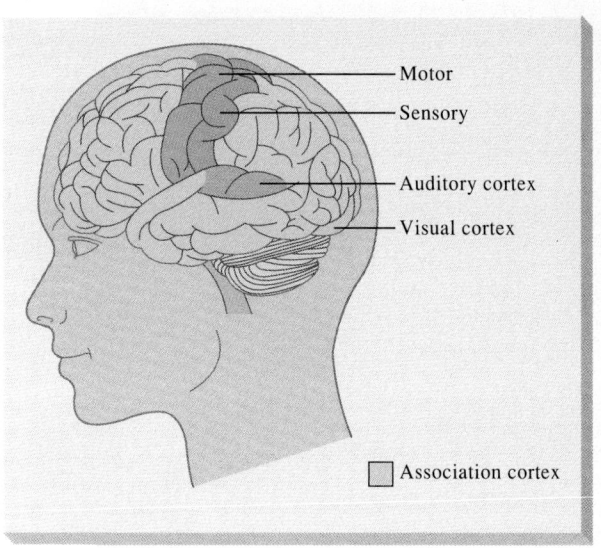

FIGURE 3.19

Association Cortex
The very large areas of the cerebral cortex, called the association cortex or association areas, do not respond when electrically stimulated, unlike the motor and sensory areas. Neurons in the association cortex communicate with neurons in other areas of the association cortex and with sensory and motor areas. Neuroscientists believe that the association areas are involved in thinking and problem solving.

So far our description of the cerebral cortex has focused on sensory and motor areas, but more than 75 percent of the cerebral cortex is made up of areas called the association cortex (see figure 3.19). The **association cortex** *(or association areas) is involved in our highest intellectual functions, such as problem solving and thinking.* The neurons in the association cortex communicate with each other and with neurons in the motor cortex. By observing brain-damaged people and using topographic mapping techniques, scientists have found that the association cortex is involved in linguistic and perceptual processes. Interestingly, damage to a specific part of the association cortex does not necessarily lead to a specific loss of function. With the exception of language areas, which *are* localized, loss of function seems to depend more on the extent of damage to the association areas than to the specific location of the damage. The largest portion of the association cortex is located in the frontal lobe, beneath the forehead. An individual whose frontal lobes have been damaged does not lose sensory or motor control but may become "a different person," leading researchers to believe that the frontal lobes are linked with personality (see figure 3.20). This area may be most directly related to thinking and problem solving. Early experiments suggested that the frontal lobe is the center of intelligence, but more recent research indicates that damage to the frontal lobes may not result in a loss of intelligence. The ability to make plans, think creatively, and make decisions are other mental processes associated with the frontal lobe.

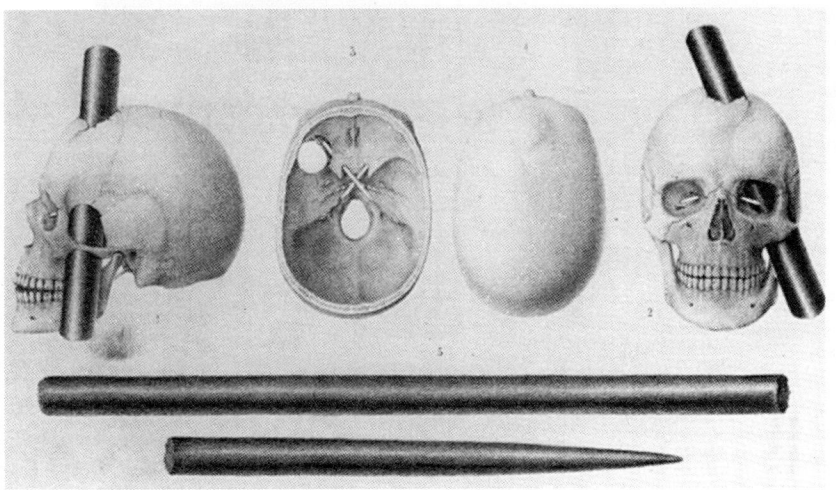

Figure 3.20

The Injury to Phineas T. Gage

Phineas T. Gage, a 25-year-old foreman who worked for the Rutland and Burlington Railroad in Vermont, met with an interesting experience on September 13, 1848. Phineas and several co-workers were using blasting powder to construct a roadbed. The crew drilled holes in the rock and gravel, poured in the blasting powder, and then tamped down the powder with a steel rod. The powder blew up while Phineas was still tamping it down, driving the iron up through the left side of his face and out through the top of his head. Phineas was thrown to the ground, but, amazingly, he was still conscious and able to talk. His co-workers placed him on an ox cart and drove him almost a mile to his hotel. Phineas got out of the cart himself and walked up the flight of stairs to his room. A physician was called, and he discovered he could put the entire length of his index finger through the cylindrical hole in Phineas's skull.

Though the wound in Phineas's skull healed in a matter of weeks, he became a different person. He had been a mild-mannered, hard-working, emotionally calm individual prior to the accident. He was well liked by all who knew him. Afterward, he became obstinate, moody, irresponsible, selfish, and incapable of participating in any planned activities. Phineas's misfortune illustrates the brain's importance in determining the nature of personality.

Split-Brain Research and the Cerebral Hemispheres

The brain is split into two halves, and these two halves have been involved in some fascinating research as well as speculation about what role they play in brain functioning.

Split-Brain Research

For many years, scientists speculated that the **corpus callosum,** *a large bundle of axons that connects the brain's two hemispheres,* had something to do with relaying information between the two sides. Roger Sperry and his colleagues confirmed this in experiments in which they cut the corpus callosum in cats. They also severed certain nerve endings leading from the eyes to the brain. After the operations, Sperry and Myers trained the cats to solve a series of visual problems with one eye blindfolded. After each cat learned the task, with only one eye uncovered, its other eye was covered and the animal was tested again. The split-brain cat behaved as if it had never learned the task. It seems that the memory was stored only in the left hemisphere, which could no longer directly communicate with the right hemisphere.

Further evidence of the corpus callosum's function has come from experiments with patients who have severe, even life-threatening, forms of epilepsy. Epilepsy's electrical storms flash uncontrollably across the corpus callosum. One of the most famous cases is that of "W. J." Neurosurgeons severed the corpus callosum of this epileptic patient in a final attempt to reduce his unbearable seizures. Sperry (1968) examined W. J. and found that the corpus callosum functions the same in humans as in animals—cutting the corpus callosum seems to leave patients with two separate minds that learn and operate independently. The right hemisphere receives information from the left side of the body, and the left hemisphere receives information from the right side of the body. When you hold an object in your left hand, for example, the right hemisphere of your brain detects the object. When you hold an object in your right hand, the left hemisphere of your brain detects the object (see figure 3.21). In a normal corpus callosum, both hemispheres receive this information.

The most extensive and consistent research findings on the brain's hemispheres involve language. In most right-handed individuals in whom the corpus callosum is intact, the left hemisphere controls the ability to use language, whereas the right hemisphere is unable to translate sensations into words. The split-brain patients in Sperry's (1974) experiments, such as W. J., could verbally describe sensations that were received by the left hemisphere—that is, a stimulus in the right visual field, but they could not verbally describe sensations that were received by the right hemisphere—a stimulus in the left visual field. Because the corpus callosum was severed, the information could not be communicated from one hemisphere to the other. More recent investigations of split-brain patients document that language is rarely processed in the right hemisphere (Gazzaniga, 1986).

Hemispheric Specialization

There has been lots of speculation over the past few years about the brain's hemispheric specialization, the notion being that the hemispheres function in different ways and that some psychological processes are restricted to one hemisphere. In fact, Americans commonly use the terms *left-brained* and *right-brained* to describe which hemisphere is dominant. According to the media and popular books, the left hemisphere is rational, logical, and Western, whereas the brain's right hemisphere is creative, intuitive, and Eastern.

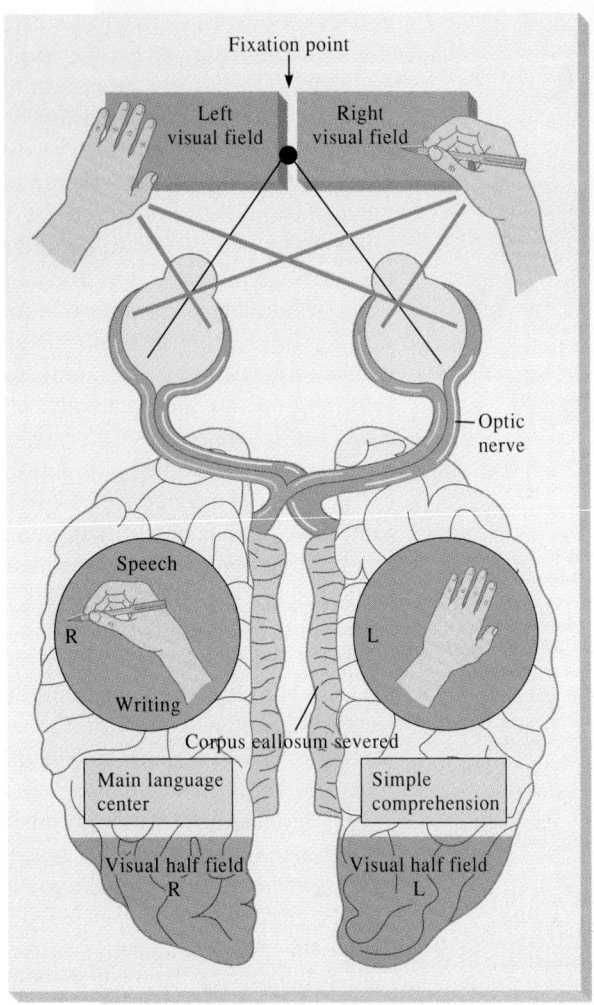

FIGURE 3.21

Visual Information in the Split Brain
Although both eyes take in the full visual field, the organization of the eye and brain are specialized. For example, images in the right visual field (such as the hand holding the pen) fall on the left side of both retinas and then are channeled to the left hemisphere by way of the optic nerves. Images seen in the right visual field reach only the left hemisphere and images seen in the left visual field reach only the right hemisphere in the initial stages of processing. Visual information in both hemispheres is then shared via the corpus callosum. Following split-brain surgery in which the corpus callosum is severed, each hemisphere has access only to the information originally processed from the corresponding visual field for which it is responsible.

Everyone seems to accept this, everyone, that is, except the scientists who have researched left and right hemisphere functions. To them, the concept of the brain as split into tidy halves—one the source of creativity, the other the source of logical thinking—is too simplistic (Dolnick, 1988). Jerre Levy, a neuroscientist at the University of Chicago, points out that no complex function—making music, creating art, reading, and so on—can be assigned to one hemisphere. Complex thinking in normal people involves communication between both sides of the brain (Efron, in press).

Jerre Levy has conducted extensive research on the nature of hemispheric function in the brain.

How did the left-brain/right-brain myth get started? It actually had its origin in Sperry's classic studies of split-brain patients. Remember that Sperry examined people whose corpus callosum had been severed and found that after surgery the two sides of the brain learned and operated independently. As his findings made their way into the media, the complexity of Sperry's research was lost and his findings became oversimplified. Media reports indicated that, when a writer works on a novel, the left hemisphere is busy while the right is silent. In creating an oil painting, the right brain is working while the left is quiet. People appeared either right-brained (artistic) or left-brained (logical). An example of the either/or oversimplification of the brain's left and right hemispheres is shown in the drawing of how the brain divides its work (see figure 3.22).

Roger Sperry discovered that the left hemisphere is superior in the kind of logic used to prove geometric theorems, but, in the logic of everyday life, our problems involve integrating information and drawing conclusions. In these instances, the right brain's functions are crucial. In virtually all activities, there is an interplay between the brain's hemispheres (Hellige, 1990). For example, in reading, the left hemisphere comprehends syntax and grammar, which the right does not. However, the right brain is better at understanding a story's intonation and emotion. The same is true for music and art. Pop psychology assigns both to the right brain. In some musical skills, such as recognizing chords, the right hemisphere is better. In others, such as distinguishing which of two sounds is heard first, the left hemisphere takes over. Enjoying or creating music requires the use of both hemispheres.

There is so much more to understanding brain function and organization than to characterize people as right- or left-brained. After all, we are trying to understand the most complex piece of matter in the known universe. As we will see next, scientists have been ingenious at developing techniques to learn more about this astonishing organ.

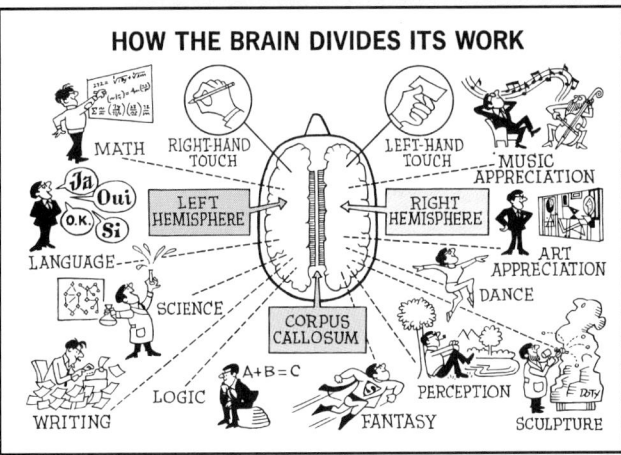

HOW THE BRAIN DIVIDES ITS WORK

MATH
RIGHT-HAND TOUCH
LEFT-HAND TOUCH
MUSIC APPRECIATION
LANGUAGE
LEFT HEMISPHERE
RIGHT HEMISPHERE
ART APPRECIATION
SCIENCE
DANCE
CORPUS CALLOSUM
LOGIC
A+B=C
PERCEPTION
WRITING
FANTASY
SCULPTURE

Is left-brain, right-brain specialization all-or-none,
as this drawing implies? No.

© Roy Doty, *Newsweek.*

FIGURE 3.22

Stereotyped Myths About Left-Brain, Right-Brain
Popular visions of right-brain, left-brain specialization suggest
that artist Andy Warhol's and singer Aretha Franklin's right
brains are responsible for their artistic and music talents, and
that astronaut Guion Stewart Bluford's and physicist Albert
Einstein's left brains are responsible for their gifts. Is this popular
vision overdramatized? Yes, extensively.

His Brain and Her Brain

Do the left and right·hemispheres develop differently in girls
and boys? According to one theory, the male brain is more
"lateralized," that is, its hemispheres are specialized in their
abilities, while females use both hemispheres more symmet-
rically, because in the female brain the corpus callosum supposedly is larger and houses more fibers (Geschwind &
Behan, 1982). In this theory, effects of testosterone (a hormone dominant in males) on the prenatal brain produce
superior right-hemisphere talents, such as artistic, musical,
or math skills. Right-hemisphere dominance is also said to

explain the male's excellence in some tests of visuospatial
ability, such as the ability to visualize three-dimensional objects. Males also have been said to have greater left-brain
specialization as well (which advocates say explains their intellectual advantage). Females' skills, especially those involving language, are said to be more evenly divided between the
left and right hemispheres. One interesting source of support for this view comes from differences in damage after
stroke; males are three times more likely than females to develop **aphasia,** *inability to recognize or express language,* after
left-hemisphere damage.

Gender expert Carol Tavris (1992) believes that talk of a
gender dichotomy regarding brain function has been taken
too far. She says that females and males, on the average, might
differ in the physiology of their brains, but most brain researchers today believe the two hemispheres complement
each other to the extent that one side can sometimes take over
the functions of a side that has been damaged. And specific
skills often involve components from both sides: One side has
the ability to tell a joke, the other side the ability to laugh at
one. Math abilities involve both visuospatial skills and reasoning skills. The right hemisphere is involved in creating art, the
left hemisphere in appreciating and analyzing art.

Tavris also documented that most of the brain studies examining sex differences have been based on animals,
with unknown generalizability to humans. And she commented that perhaps the most damaging blow to attempts
at basing gender differences on brain differences is that the
supposed sex differences that they are trying to account
for—in verbal, spatial, and math abilities—are rapidly fad-
ing. Researchers and the public often err in focusing on
very small differences rather than on the extensive overlap
between females and males. We will have much more to
say about the similarities between females' and males' cognitive abilities, and how such differences have been greatly
exaggerated, in chapter 11.

In summary, there are some anatomical differences
in the brains of females and males. However, there are far
more similarities than differences between female and
male brains, and there is little evidence that the brain differences that do exist cause behavioral differences in females and males. Such behavioral differences, which are
often small, may be due to environmental influences and
social experiences. Similarity rather than dissimilarity was
the rule rather than the exception in a recent study of
metabolic activity in the brains of females and males (Gur
& others, 1985). The exceptions involved emotional expression (more active in females) and physical expression
(more active in females).

TECHNIQUES FOR STUDYING THE BRAIN

Eastern and Western traditions in medicine have regarded
the human body very differently. Many Eastern religions
prohibit invading the body after death as sacrilegious. Their
medical systems evolved through careful observation and
inference. In contrast, Western science grew from knowledge derived from autopsy and other invasive techniques.

*Education for
the Right Brain*

Another offshoot of the left-brain/right-brain hoopla is speculation that more right-brain activities and exercises should be incorporated into our nation's schools (Edwards, 1979). Suppose that you have been asked to serve on a committee for the local school's parent-teacher association. In the middle of a meeting devoted to school budget issues, one enthusiastic parent reports that she has just returned from a workshop on the importance of enhancing the creative side of the brain through special activities designed to stimulate the right hemisphere. Although her enthusiasm is impressive, her evidence might not be. How would you *develop a psychological argument using evidence* to determine whether or not you should lend your support to special programs for enhancing right-brain function?

In schools that rely heavily on rote learning to instruct students, children would probably benefit from exercises in intuitive thought and holistic thinking, but this deficiency in school curriculum is unrelated to the left-brain/right-brain specialization.

Today, neuroscientists no longer have to perform surgery on living patients or cadavers to study the brain. Sophisticated techniques—such as using high-powered microscopes, the electroencephalograph, single-unit recordings, CAT scan, PET scan, and magnetic resonance imaging (MRI)—allow researchers to peer into the brain while it's at work. We will consider each of these techniques in turn.

High-powered microscopes are widely used in neuroscience research. Neurons are stained with the salts of various heavy metals, such as silver and lead. These stains coat only a small portion of any group of neurons, and they allow neuroscientists to view and study every part of a neuron in microscopic detail.

Also widely used, the **electroencephalograph** *records the electrical activity of the brain. Electrodes placed on an individual's scalp record brain-wave activity, which is reproduced on a chart known as an electroencephalogram (or EEG)* (see figure 3.23). This device has been used to assess brain damage, epilepsy, and other problems. In chapter 5, we will see how the EEG has been helpful in charting sleeping and waking patterns.

Not every recording of brain activity is made with electrodes. In single-unit recording—a portrayal of a single neuron's electrical activity—a thin wire or needle is inserted in or near an individual neuron. The wire or needle transmits the neuron's electrical activity to an amplifier.

For years X rays have been used to determine damage inside or outside our bodies, both in the brain and in other locations. However, a single X ray of the brain is hard to interpret because it shows the three-dimensional nature of the brain's interior in a two-dimensional image. **Computer-assisted axial tomography, or CAT scan,** *is a three-dimensional imaging technique obtained by passing X rays through the head; then a computer assembles the individual pictures*

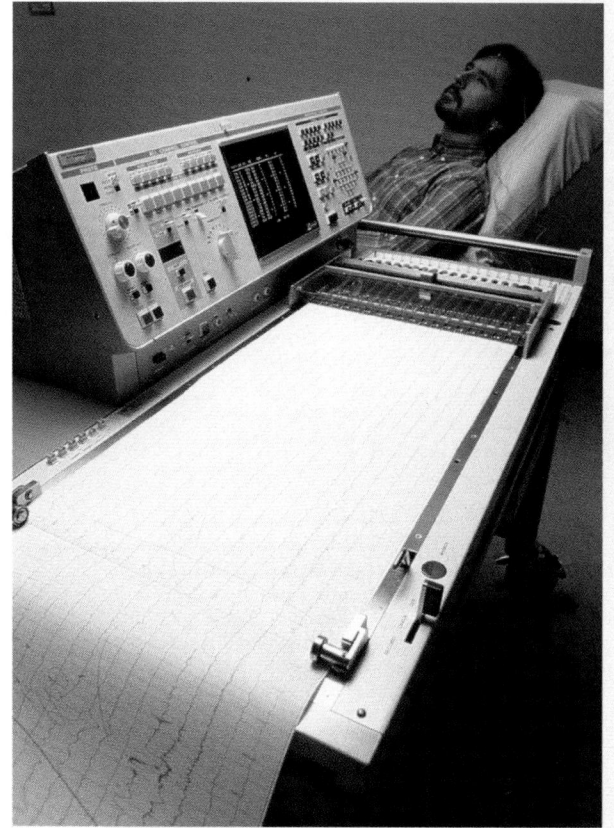

FIGURE 3.23

An Individual Shown During an EEG Recording
The electroencephalogram (EEG) is widely used in sleep research. Its use led to some major breakthroughs in understanding sleep by showing how the brain's electrical activity changes during sleep.

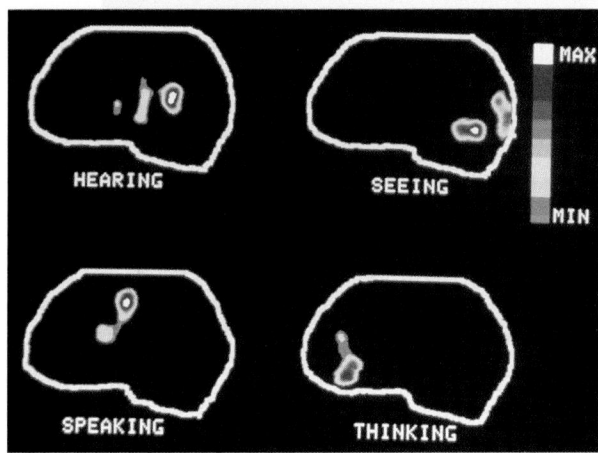

FIGURE 3.24

This PET scan of the left hemisphere of the brain contrasts the areas used in various aspects of language activity: hearing, seeing, speaking, and thinking.

into a composite image. The CAT scan provides valuable information about the location of damage due to a stroke, language disorder, or loss of memory.

Positron-emission tomography, or PET scan, *measures the amount of specially treated glucose in various areas of the brain, then sends this information to a computer.* Because glucose levels vary with the levels of activity throughout the brain, tracing the amounts of glucose generates a picture of activity level in the brain. Several PET scans of a person's brain activity while she was hearing, seeing, speaking, and thinking are shown in figure 3.24.

Another technique for studying the brain is **magnetic resonance imaging (MRI)**, *which involves creating a magnetic field around a person's body and using radio waves to construct images of tissues (such as brain tissues) and biochemical*

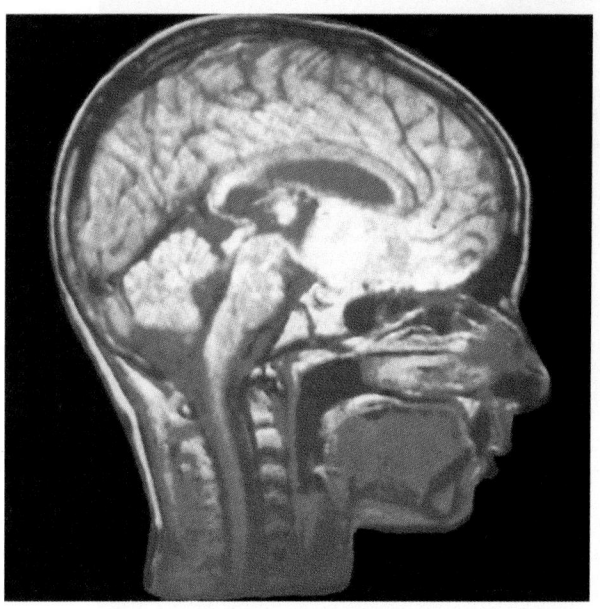

FIGURE 3.25

Magnetic Resonance Imaging (MRI) involves creating a magnetic field around the individual's body and using radio waves to produce images of tissues (such as brain tissues) and biochemical activity. As shown here, MRI gives a vivid picture of the brain's interior.

activity. It provides very clear pictures of the brain's interior, it does not require injecting the brain with a substance, and it does not pose a problem of radiation overexposure. A photograph of MRI is shown in figure 3.25.

In the next chapter, you will learn more about the brain and its afferent systems as we investigate the nature of sensation and perception by examining such fascinating questions as how we see, hear, smell, touch, and feel pain.

REVIEW

Brain Structure and Function

A neural tube develops into the hindbrain (lowest level), midbrain (middle level), and forebrain (highest level). The main structures of the hindbrain are the medulla, cerebellum, and pons. The midbrain is an area where many fiber systems ascend or descend. Among the forebrain's most important structures are the thalamus, hypothalamus and endocrine system, limbic system, and cerebrum. Each is specialized to process certain kinds of information.

The wrinkled surface of the cortex is divided into two hemispheres (left and right) and four lobes (frontal, parietal, temporal, and occipital). Topographic mapping has helped scientists determine the neocortex's role in different behaviors. The neocortex consists of sensory, motor, and association areas. Pioneered by Sperry, split-brain research involves severing the corpus callosum. This led to the conclusion that language is primarily a left-hemisphere function. In normal people, the hemispheres

work together to process information. A number of myths have developed that exaggerate left-brain/right-brain functions. Although there are some anatomical differences in the brains of females and males, there are far more similarities than differences between female and male brains. Among the most widely used tools for studying the brain are high-powered microscopes, the electroencephalograph, single-unit recordings, CAT scan, PET scan, and magnetic resonance imaging (MRI).

Things should be as simple as possible, not simpler.

Albert Einstein

If you are like many introductory students, you may have found the contents of this chapter to be especially challenging. Many terms and processes in the neurobiological arena are difficult to grasp from two-dimensional illustrations or text descriptions. Yet a thorough understanding of the contributions of biology to behavior is an important foundation for the rest of your study in this course. In addition, as the science of psychology continues to grow through research, the neurobiological area will grow in complexity. If you return to this area of study 10 years from now, you likely will be impressed to see how many more details and concepts have been added to come progressively closer to a complete picture of how the body works.

Yearning for less-complex explanations might be a routine part of the human condition. If the brain happened to come with an owner's manual, it would need to contain this warning: "Your brain might interpret things as being simpler than they really are." We can find several examples of this tendency in the history of research in this area.

One of the first attempts to explain brain function was a curious approach called phrenology (see figure 3.A). A German physician named Franz Joseph Gall developed phrenology, in which various bumps and indentations on the skull were interpreted as providing a map of character. A bump corresponded to an excess of the characteristic. An indentation signified a deficiency. A phrenological reading might describe you as generous or stingy, based on whether you had a bump or an indentation at the particular site believed to correspond to this trait. This simplistic system of connecting characteristics of the skull to specialized features had some merit. It anticipated the more extensive brain-localization studies of scientists such as Wilder Penfield, but the content of phrenology was wrong. However, phrenology was widely appealing because it presented such a simple system of explanation.

Identifying specific structures responsible for brain functions has also proved to be a difficult problem. Unlike the helpful color graphics in this book, the brain tends to be a uniform color, so simply differentiating brain structures has not been easy. In addition, most behaviors are complex events that involve many brain functions and structures simultaneously. Isolating causal relationships requires sophisticated medical techniques. As you also studied in this chapter, the distinction between left and right hemispheric function is a simplification that has

been enthusiastically and erroneously adopted by many in our culture. Attributions about race as a cause of behavior are also oversimplifications that are likely to create even more complex problems in our adaptation to an increasingly diverse world.

Simple explanations might be very compelling, but when it comes to behavior, simple explanations are rarely very satisfying. Have you experienced situations in which a simple solution fell short because it underestimated the complexity of the problem? Can you think of behaviors that you interpreted in a simple manner that turned out to be far more complicated? Your awareness of this interpretive bias can help you overcome the tendency to draw premature conclusions. This awareness will also assist you to *pursue alternative explanations to promote comprehensive explanations.*

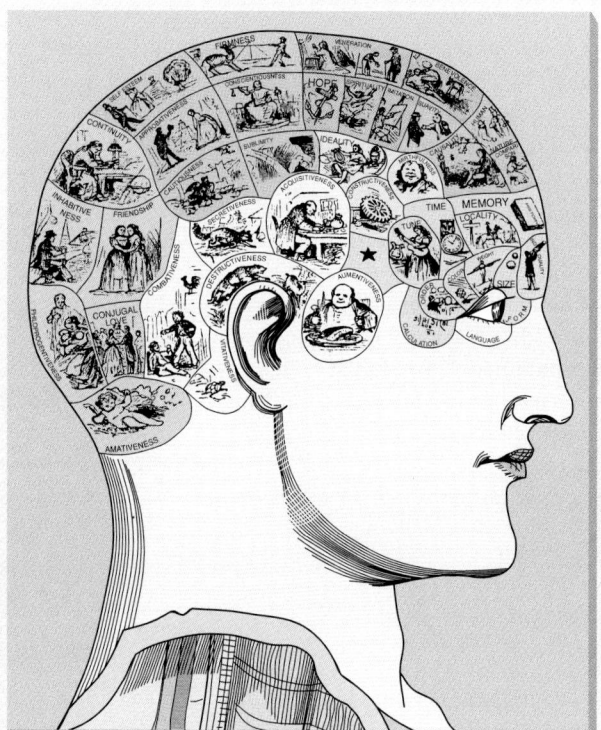

FIGURE 3.A

Phrenology Map Based on Gall's System
Gall was the father of the pseudoscience of phrenology. He believed that the brain was made up of about 30 "organs," each responsible for a single trait. Phrenology swept the United States and Europe, spawning phrenological societies, books, pamphlets, and sideshows. The craze attracted Edgar Allan Poe, Karl Marx, and Queen Victoria, who got a phrenologist to examine the royal children's cranial knobs. One fanatic proclaimed, "Phrenologist after phrenologist may die, but phrenology will never perish"; perish it did, however, under the onslaught of reason and ridicule.

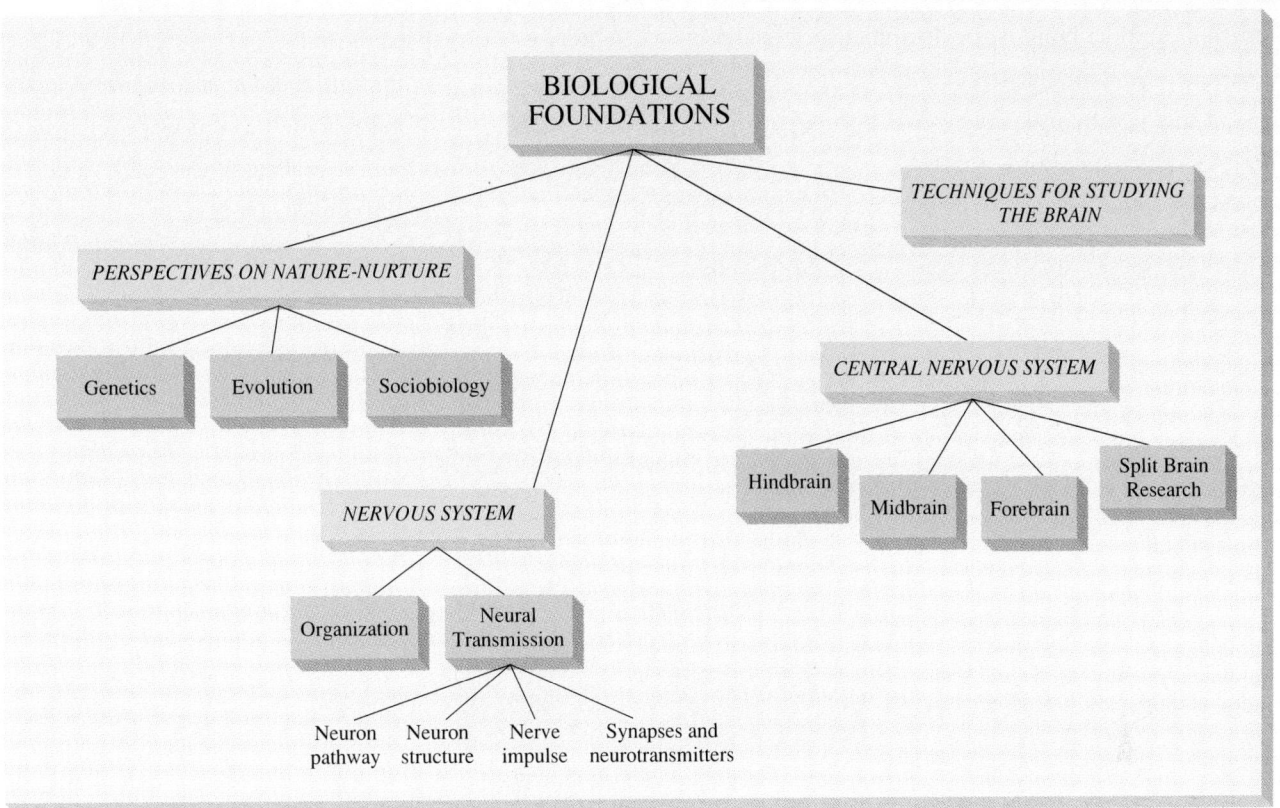

We began this chapter on biological foundations and the brain by studying perspectives on nature versus nurture, evaluating genetics, evolution, and sociobiology. Then we turned our attention to the nervous system, reading about its organization and the nature of neural transmission. We discussed the central nervous system, including its structure and function and split-brain research. We also described techniques for studying the brain. Don't forget that you can obtain an overall summary of the chapter by again reading the in-chapter reviews on pages 66, 72, and 85.

By far the dominant perspective in this chapter on biological foundations and the brain is the neurobiological perspective. Virtually the entire chapter reflects the neurobiological perspective: perspectives on nature and nurture (pp. 59–65), the nervous system (pp. 66–72), the central nervous system (pp. 73–83), and techniques for studying the brain (pp. 83–85). The sociocultural perspective also appeared in the material on the human species' being a culture-making species (p. 60) and race and ethnicity (p. 64).

Neurobiological

Sociocultural

Cognitive

Behavioral

Psychoanalytic

Humanistic

KEY TERMS

environment All of the surrounding conditions and influences that affect the development of living things. 59

nurture A term often used to describe an organism's environmental experiences. 59

nature A term often used to describe an organism's biological inheritance. 59

chromosomes Threadlike structures, located in the nucleus of each human cell, that come in 23 pairs, one member of each pair coming from each parent. 59

deoxyribonucleic acid (DNA) A complex molecule that contains genetic information. 60

genes Short segments of DNA that contain the hereditary information. 60

dominant-recessive genes principle The principle that if one gene of a pair is dominant and the other is recessive, the dominant gene exerts its effect, overriding the potential influence of the recessive gene. A recessive gene exerts its influence only if both genes of the pair are recessive. 60

adaptation Behavioral changes in response to challenges in the environment that enhance the organism's likelihood of survival. 63

natural selection The evolutionary process that favors the individuals within a species that are best adapted to survive and reproduce in their particular environment. 63

fitness In evolutionary theory, the degree to which an individual can produce viable offspring. 63

sociobiology A contemporary view that relies on evolutionary biology to explain social behavior. 63

neurons Nerve cells, the basic units of the nervous system. 66

central nervous system (CNS) The brain and spinal cord. 66

peripheral nervous system A network of nerves that connects the brain and spinal cord to other parts of the body. Takes information to and from the brain and spinal cord and carries out the commands of the CNS to execute various muscular and glandular activities. 66

somatic nervous system A division of the peripheral nervous system consisting of sensory nerves that convey information from the skin and muscles to the central nervous system about such matters as pain and temperature, and motor nerves, which tell muscles when to act. 66

autonomic nervous system The division of the peripheral nervous system that takes messages to and from the body's internal organs, monitoring such processes as breathing, heart rate, and digestion. 66

sympathetic nervous system The division of the autonomic nervous system that arouses the body. 67

parasympathetic nervous system The division of the autonomic nervous system that calms the body. 67

afferent nerves Sensory nerves that carry information to the brain. 67

efferent nerves Motor nerves that carry the brain's output. 67

interneurons Central nervous system neurons that mediate sensory input and motor output. Interneurons make up most of the brain. 67

cell body The part of the neuron that contains the nucleus, which directs the manufacture of the substances the neuron uses for its growth and maintenance. 67

dendrite The receiving part of the neuron, serving the important function of collecting information and orienting it toward the cell body. 67

axon The part of the neuron that carries information away from the cell body to other cells. 67

myelin sheath A layer of fat cells that encases most axons; it not only acts to insulate the axon but also helps nerve impulses travel faster. 68

ions Electrically charged particles that include sodium (NA^+), chloride (Cl^-), and potassium (K^+). The neuron creates electrical signals by moving these charged ions back and forth through its membrane; the waves of electricity that are created sweep along the membrane. 68

resting potential The stable, negative charge of an inactive neuron. 68

action potential The brief wave of electrical charge that sweeps down the axon. 69

all-or-none principle The principle that once the electrical impulse reaches a certain level of intensity, it fires and moves all the way down the axon, remaining at the same strength throughout its travel. 69

synapses Tiny gaps between neurons. Most synapses are between the axon of one neuron and the dendrites or cell body of another neuron. 69

neurotransmitters Chemical substances that carry information across the synaptic gap to the next neuron. 69

GABA Gamma aminobutyric acid, a neurotransmitter that inhibits the firing of motor neurons. 70

acetylcholine (ACh) A neurotransmitter that produces contractions of skeletal muscles by acting on motor nerves. 71

norepinephrine A neurotransmitter that usually inhibits the firing of neurons in the brain and spinal cord but excites the heart muscles, intestines, and urogenital tract. 71

dopamine An inhibitory neurotransmitter that is involved in movement, attention, learning, and mental health. Too much dopamine in the brain's synapses is associated with a severe mental disorder, schizophrenia. 71

serotonin An inhibitory neurotransmitter that is involved in the regulation of sleep as well as depression. 71

endorphins Natural opiates that are neurotransmitters; endorphins are involved in pleasure and the control of pain. 72

hindbrain The lowest portion of the brain, located at the skull's rear. It consists of the spinal cord, the lower brain stem (pons and medulla), and the cerebellum. 73

medulla A part of the brain that begins where the spinal cord enters the skull; it helps to control breathing and regulates a portion of the reflexes that allow us to maintain an upright posture. 73

cerebellum A part of the brain that extends from the rear of the hindbrain and is located above the medulla; it consists of two rounded structures thought to play important roles in motor control. 73

pons A bridge in the hindbrain that contains several clusters of fibers involved in sleep and arousal. 73

midbrain An area between the hindbrain and the forebrain where many nerve fiber systems ascend and descend to connect lower and higher portions of the brain; in particular, the midbrain relays information between the brain and the eyes and ears. 73

reticular formation A diffuse collection of neurons involved in stereotyped patterns of behavior such as walking, sleeping, or turning to attend to a sudden noise. 73

forebrain The region of the brain that governs its highest functions; among its important structures are the thalamus, the hypothalamus and endocrine system, the limbic system, and the cerebral cortex. 74

thalamus An area at the top of the brain stem in the central core of the brain; it serves as an important relay station functioning much like a telephone switchboard between the diverse areas of the cortex and the reticular formation. 74

hypothalamus An area just below the thalamus that monitors three enjoyable activities—eating, drinking, and sex; it also helps to direct the endocrine system through the pituitary gland; and it is involved in emotion, stress, and reward. 75

endocrine system The hypothalamus and other endocrine glands that release their chemical products directly into the bloodstream. 76

hormones Chemical messengers manufactured by the endocrine glands. 76

pituitary gland An important endocrine gland that sits at the base of the skull and is about the size of a pea; this gland controls growth and regulates other glands. 76

adrenal glands Glands whose secretions play an important role in our moods, energy level, and ability to cope with stress; each adrenal gland secretes epinephrine (also called adrenaline) and norepinephrine (also called noradrenaline). 77

limbic system A loosely connected network of structures under the cerebral cortex that plays an important role in both memory and emotion. 77

amygdala A limbic system structure, located within the base of the temporal lobe, that is involved in discrimination of objects that are important for an organism's survival, such as appropriate food, mates, and social rivals. 77

hippocampus A limbic system structure that has a special role in the storage of memories. 78

cerebral cortex (cerebrum) The most recently evolved part of the brain; covering the rest of the brain almost like a cap, it is the largest part of the brain and makes up about 80 percent of its volume. 78

occipital lobe The portion of the cerebral cortex at the back of the head that is involved in vision. 78

temporal lobe The portion of the cerebral cortex that is just above the ears and is involved in hearing. 78

frontal lobe The portion of the cerebral cortex that is behind the forehead and is involved in the control of voluntary muscles and in intelligence. 78

parietal lobe The portion of the cerebral cortex at the top of the head and toward the rear; it is involved in processing bodily sensations. 78

association cortex Areas of the brain that are involved in our highest intellectual functions, such as problem solving and thinking; also called association areas. 80

corpus callosum A large bundle of axons that connects the brain's two hemispheres. 81

aphasia An inability to recognize or express language. 83

electroencephalograph An instrument that records the electrical activity of the brain; electrodes placed on an individual's scalp record brain-wave activity, which is reproduced on a chart known as an electroencephalogram (EEG). 84

computer-assisted axial tomography (CAT scan) A three-dimensional imaging technique in which pictures obtained by passing X rays through the head are assembled by a computer into a composite image. 84

positron-emission tomography (PET scan) An imaging technology that measures the amount of specially treated glucose in various areas of the brain, then sends this information to a computer. 85

magnetic resonance imaging (MRI) An imaging technique that involves creating a magnetic field around a person's body and using radio waves to construct images of the person's tissues (such as brain tissues) and biochemical activity. 85

PRACTICAL KNOWLEDGE ABOUT PSYCHOLOGY

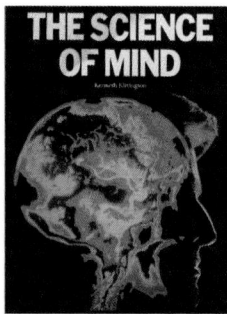

THE SCIENCE OF MIND

(1989) edited by Kenneth Klivington. Cambridge, MA: MIT Press.

This beautifully illustrated book describes how intelligence, love, hate, daily body rhythms, sleep and dreams, schizophrenia, and drug addictions are linked to functions in the brain. Among the other topics covered are the brain's role in Alzheimer's disease, brain implants, sex differences, language, immune responses, depression, and learning. Hundreds of color photographs take you inside the brain to uncover its intricate workings.

THE MIND

(1988) by Robert Restak. New York: Bantam.

This attractive, well-written book provides a broad overview of some of psychology's most fascinating frontiers, especially from a biological perspective. Topics covered include new technologies for mapping the brain, the roles of heredity and environment, the brain's role in depression and alcoholism, the aging brain, what takes place in the brain when a person explodes in a violent rage, the brain's role in addiction, and the nature of pain. The book includes hundreds of well-chosen photographs that illustrate key points made in the book.

***Brain, Mind, and Behavior* (2nd ed.) (1985)**
by F. E. Bloom, A. Lazerson, & L. Hofstader New
York: W. H. Freeman

This book is part of a multimedia teaching package involving the Public Broadcasting System's series "The Brain." The beauty of the brain is captured in both well-written essays and photographs.

**Genetics Society of Canada/Société
de génétique du Canada**
151 Slater Street #907
Ottawa, ON K1P 5H4 CANADA
613–232–9459

The Genetics Society is a professional membership organization for geneticists; they publish their own research journal.

Human Growth Foundation
7777 Leesburg Pike
Falls Church, VA 22043
703–883–1773

This organization seeks to promote better understanding of human growth problems caused by pituitary gland irregularities. Information about hormone-related problems is available, as are recommendations for educational programs.

Huntington's Disease Society of America
140 W. 22nd Street, 6th Floor
New York, NY 10011-2420
800–345–4372

This organization is for individuals and volunteers concerned with Huntington's disease, an inherited and terminal neurological condition that causes progressive brain and nerve deterioration. Audiovisual materials, referral services, and general information are available.

***The Mismeasure of Man* (1981)**
by Stephen J. Gould
New York: Norton

Gould is one of the best contemporary scientist-writers. In this book, he gives fascinating insights into the nature of biological and cultural evolution.

National Genetics Foundation
555 West 57th Street
New York, NY 10019
212–586–5800

This foundation provides information about birth defects, the genetic basis of disorders, and their treatment.

Parkinson Foundation of Canada
710-390 Bay Street
Toronto, ON M5H 2V2 CANADA
416–366–0099
1–800–565–3000

The foundation is dedicated to heightening public awareness, raising funds for research, developing and distributing literature and materials to individuals and organizations across Canada, and providing services to support persons with Parkinson's, their families, and caregivers. Their newsletter, *Network,* is published five times a year.

Parkinson's Educational Program
3900 Birch Street, No. 105
Newport Beach, CA 92660

This program serves as a clearinghouse for information about Parkinson's disease, a neurological disorder. It assists in establishing support groups throughout world. Educational materials are available.

The Twins Foundation
P.O. Box 9487
Providence, RI 02940
401–274–6910

For information about twins and multiple births, contact this organization.

CHAPTER 4

Sensation and Perception

The setting sun, and music at close,
As the last taste of sweets,
is sweetest last,
Writ in remembrance more
than things long past.

William Shakespeare

Imagine the enormous thrill of suddenly regaining your sight after nearly a lifetime of blindness. Colors and shapes, faces of loved ones, images that go with familiar sounds, smells, and feels—you could experience it all. Most of us imagine the restoration of sight would be like a miracle. However, Virgil's experience makes us reconsider.

A patient of renowned neurologist Oliver Sacks (1993), Virgil was born just after the start of World War II. He lost his sight at the age of 3 when he was simultaneously infected with meningitis (inflammation of the brain), polio, and cat-scratch fever. Eventually he recovered his motor function and could have recovered his vision; however, cataracts had formed, leaving him functionally blind by the age of 6. Despite this setback, he went to a school for the blind and learned to read Braille. As an adult he supported himself as a massage therapist at the YMCA, had significant social relationships, and had a passion for baseball, including a comprehensive knowledge of the game's statistics. Most people described him as passive but content with his life and limitations.

In 1991, Virgil became engaged to Amy, a woman he had known for about 20 years. Amy saw Virgil's life as rather dull. She began to encourage him to explore having cataract surgery. Although the possibility of sight was remote because his retinas might have deteriorated, she pushed for the surgery in the hopes that, after 45 years of blindness, he would be able to see for the wedding. Virgil was passive in this situation as well; he agreed to go along with the procedure without being particularly eager for the change.

Amy's diary describes the moment when the bandages were removed as more strange than dramatic. According to Virgil, all was a blur of meaningless lights and colors. Out of the confusion, a voice asked, "Well?" Only at that moment did the shapes and shadows converge into the image of his surgeon's face. Although his visual system was transmitting images, he had no experience with imagery to make sense of what he saw. Although he had sustained some damage to his visual system, he was able to see movement, shapes, and colors. His physicians predicted his vision would be stable.

You might be expecting a happy ending in which Virgil and Amy lived happily ever after. However, Virgil experienced many difficulties in adjusting to his new sensory world. He had trouble recognizing letters and preferred Braille. He seemed unable to integrate details into a meaningful whole. For example, he failed to recognize his own dog when seen from different angles. It took him a long time to understand how trunks and leaves go together to form the visual image of a tree. Faces were especially challenging. It seemed that Virgil couldn't sustain looking at faces to interpret facial expressions. He no longer found his job satisfying. The bodies he knew well by touch now were somewhat repugnant because he could see the skin imperfections that he hadn't noticed when he was blind.

To make matters worse, his health deteriorated. His childhood bout of polio had left him with some lung problems that compromised his breathing. He also gained a substantial amount of weight. Eventually he was stricken with pneumonia and became gravely ill, requiring intensive care and a constant tether to oxygen. During this period Virgil alternated between functional blindness and periods in which he claimed he couldn't see but behaved as though he could. For example, he could reach for objects or avoid them even though he said he couldn't see them.

When he emerged from the hospital, he was sufficiently weakened that he had to leave his job and move out of his home at the YMCA. His rehabilitation specialists reported that he had lost all of the vision the operations had restored. Subsequent tests indicated that he was totally blind; he had lost even the few functions he had had prior to the surgery. Dr. Sacks believed that the loss could be the result of three factors. Perhaps the sensitive retinas at the back of the eyes simply burned out. Perhaps his obesity had led to gradual oxygen starvation of visual tissues. But perhaps psychological factors were also responsible. Virgil was not at home in the sighted world. His brief access to vision also interfered with his competence in the area of touch. His serious illness allowed him to return to the world of touch—but as an unemployed, dependent, chronically ill, and decidedly depressed man.

As has been reported in many case histories of the newly sighted, the euphoria of seeing is soon replaced with a sense of chaos and frustration that makes adaptation challenging. Sacks believed that "one must die as a blind person to be born again as a sighted person."

Each of us has a number of sensory and perceptual systems for detecting, processing, and interpreting our environment. Sensing and perceiving involve a complex and sophisticated visual system, an auditory system that is an elaborate engineering marvel compacted into a space the size of an Oreo cookie, and other processes that inform us about soft caresses and excruciating pain, sweet and sour tastes, floral and peppermint odors, and whether our world is upside down or right side up. Before we tackle each of the senses in greater detail, we need to know more about the nature of sensation and perception, that is, how we detect and perceive the world.

DETECTING AND PERCEIVING THE WORLD

How do you know the color of grass, that a smell is sweet, that a sound is a sigh, that the lights around the shore are dim? You know these things because of your abilities to sense and perceive stimuli in the environment. All outside information comes into us through our senses. Without vision, hearing, touch, taste, smell, and other senses, your brain would be isolated from the world; you would live in a dark silence—a tasteless, colorless, sensationless void. Without the perceptual abilities to organize incoming stimulation, the world would be a chaotic combination of afferent stimulation. Let's examine the concepts of sensation and perception in greater detail.

Defining Sensation and Perception

Sensation *is the process of detecting and encoding stimulus energy in the world.* Stimuli emit physical energy—light, sound, and heat, for example. The sense organs detect this energy and then transform, or transduce, it into a code that can be transmitted to the brain. The first step in "sensing" the world is the work of receptor cells, which respond to certain forms of energy. For example, the retina of the eye is sensitive to light, and special cells in the ear are sensitive to the vibrations that make up sound. The physical energy is transduced into electrical impulses; the information carried by these electrical impulses travels through nerve fibers that connect the sense organs with the central nervous system. Information about the external world then travels to the appropriate area of the cerebral cortex.

Perception *is the brain's process of organizing and interpreting sensory information to give it meaning.* The retinas in our eyes record a fast-moving silver object in the sky, but they do not "see" a passenger jet; our eardrum vibrates in a particular way, but it does not "hear" a Beethoven symphony. Organizing and interpreting what is sensed, that is, "seeing" and "hearing" meaningful patterns in sensory information, is perception.

People only see what they are prepared to see.

Ralph Waldo Emerson

In our everyday lives, the two processes of sensation and perception are virtually inseparable. When the brain receives sensory information through afferent nerves, for example, it automatically interprets the information. Because of this, most contemporary psychologists refer to sensation and perception as a unified information-processing system.

The world is full of meaningful sights, sounds, smells, and touches. To know about the events that cause our sensory experience, we must be able to detect and discriminate stimuli in our environment. In the next section we will look at how psychologists study our abilities to detect and respond to this stimulation.

Sensory Thresholds

How close does an approaching bumble bee have to be before you can hear its buzzing? How far away does a brewing coffeepot have to be for you to detect the smell of coffee? How different does the percentage of fat have to be for you to taste a difference between the "low fat" and "regular" versions of your favorite ice cream?

Absolute Threshold

A basic problem for any sensory system is detecting varying degrees of energy in the environment (Andreassi, 1989). This energy can take the form of light, sound, chemical, or mechanical stimulation. How much of a stimulus is necessary for you to see, hear, taste, smell, or feel something? One way to address these questions is to assume that each of us has an **absolute threshold,** *or minimum amount of energy that we can detect.* When a stimulus has less energy than this absolute threshold, we cannot detect its presence; when the stimulus has more energy than the absolute threshold, we can detect the stimulus. An experiment with a wristwatch or a clock will help you understand the principle of absolute threshold. Find a wristwatch or clock that ticks;

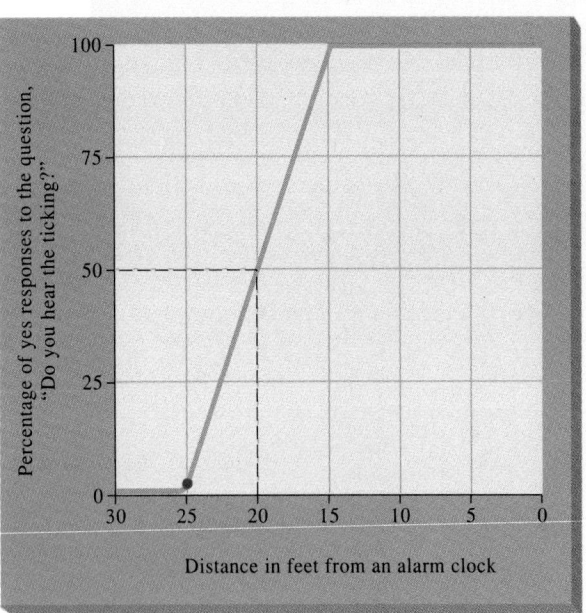

FIGURE 4.1

Determining the Absolute Threshold
Absolute threshold is the stimulus value a person detects 50 percent of the time. Here the individual's absolute threshold for detecting the ticking of a clock is 20 feet. People have different absolute thresholds. Another individual tested with the ticking clock might have an absolute threshold of 22 feet, for example.

put it on a table and walk far enough across the room so that you no longer hear the ticking. Then gradually move toward it again. At some point you will begin to hear the ticking. Hold your position and notice that occasionally the ticking fades and you may have to move forward to reach the threshold; at other times it may become loud and you

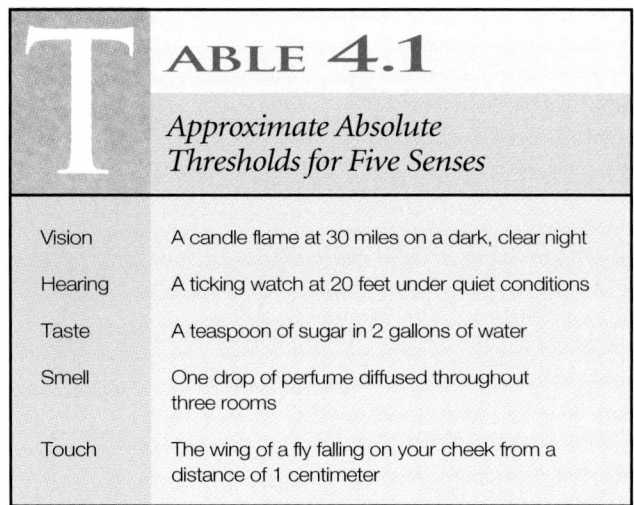

TABLE 4.1

Approximate Absolute Thresholds for Five Senses

Vision	A candle flame at 30 miles on a dark, clear night
Hearing	A ticking watch at 20 feet under quiet conditions
Taste	A teaspoon of sugar in 2 gallons of water
Smell	One drop of perfume diffused throughout three rooms
Touch	The wing of a fly falling on your cheek from a distance of 1 centimeter

Source: Adapted from Galanter, 1962.

can move backward (Coren & Ward, 1989). Because of this variability, researchers define absolute threshold as the stimulus value a person can detect 50 percent of the time.

In this experiment, the absolute threshold was not always what you thought it was. If the experiment had been conducted a number of times, several distances would have been recorded as the absolute threshold. For example, the first time you tried the experiment you may have heard the ticking at 25 feet from the clock. But you probably wouldn't have heard it every time at 25 feet. Maybe you heard it ticking at 25 feet only 38 percent of the time. You might have heard the ticking at 20 feet 50 percent of the time. And you might have heard its ticking at 15 feet 65 percent of the time.

People have different thresholds, because some people have better hearing than others, and some people have better vision than others. Figure 4.1 shows one person's absolute threshold for detecting a clock's ticking sound. Using the same clock, another person might have an absolute threshold of 26 feet, another at 22 feet, yet another at 17 feet. To learn about the approximate absolute thresholds of five senses, see table 4.1

Under ideal circumstances, our senses have very low absolute thresholds, and so, we can be remarkably good at detecting small amounts of stimulus energy. You can demonstrate this to yourself by taking a sharp pencil point and carefully lifting a single hair on your forearm. You will probably be surprised to realize that for most of us, this tiny bit of pressure on the skin is easily detectable. You might also be surprised to learn in table 4.1 that the human eye can see a candle flame at 30 miles on a dark, clear night. But our environment seldom gives us ideal conditions to detect stimuli. If the night is cloudy and the air is polluted, for example, you would have to be much closer to see the flicker of a candle flame. And other lights on the horizon—car or house lights—may hinder your ability to detect the candle's flame. **Noise** *is the term given to irrelevant and competing stimuli.* For example, someone speaks to you from the door

Biological and Perceptual Processes

Most people who watch television have favorite commercials. Identify a commercial that has had particular appeal for you and try to figure out how the commercial hooked you. What about the commercial captured your interest? Was it auditory? Was it visual? Even if you really like a commercial, in most cases you will grow tired of it as habituation sets in, so most advertisers try to remove commercials before stimulus boredom arises. *Applying psychological concepts to enhance personal adaptation* can enrich even the experience of watching commercials on television.

Weber's law *states that the difference threshold is a constant percentage of the magnitude of the comparison stimulus rather than a constant amount. Weber's law generally holds true.* For example, we add one candle to 60 candles and notice a difference in the brightness of the candles; we add one candle to 120 candles and do not notice a difference. We discover, though, that adding two candles to 120 candles does produce a difference in brightness. Adding two candles to 120 candles is the same proportionately as adding one candle to 60 candles. The exact proportion varies with the stimulus involved. For example, a 3 percent change in a tone's pitch can be detected, but a 20 percent change in taste and a 25 percent change in smell are required for a person to detect a difference.

of the room where you are sitting. You might fail to respond because your roommate is talking on the phone and a CD player is blaring out your favorite song. We usually think of noise as being auditory, but in the psychological concept, noise also involves other senses. The pollution, cloudiness, car lights, and house lights are forms of visual noise that hamper your ability to see a candle flame from a great distance.

Difference Threshold

In addition to studying the amount of stimulation required for a stimulus to be detected, psychologists investigate the degree of difference that must exist between two stimuli before this difference is detected. This **difference threshold,** *or just noticeable difference (jnd), is the smallest difference in stimulation required to discriminate one stimulus from another 50 percent of the time.* An artist might detect the difference between two very similar shades of color. A tailor might determine a difference in the texture of two fabrics by feeling them. How different must the colors and textures be for these people to determine the difference? Just as the absolute threshold is determined by a 50 percent detection rate, the difference threshold is the point at which a person reports 50 percent of the time that two stimuli are different.

An important aspect of difference thresholds is that the threshold increases with the magnitude of the stimulus. You may notice when someone living with you turns up the volume on the stereo by even a small amount when the music is playing softly. But if the volume is turned up an equal amount when the music is playing very loudly, you may not notice. More than 150 years ago, E. H. Weber, a German psychologist, noticed that, regardless of their magnitude, two stimuli must differ by a constant proportion to be detected.

Subliminal Perception

What about the possibility that we experience the sensory world at levels below our abilities to consciously detect it? **Subliminal perception** *is the perception of stimuli below the threshold of awareness.* Is this type of perception possible? Some years ago, *Life* magazine reported that 45,000 unknowing movie viewers were exposed to very brief flashes of the words *Drink Coca-Cola* while they were watching movie screens. The article stated that Coke sales soared more than 50 percent because of the subliminal messages (Brean, 1958). Scientists have shown that sensory information too faint to be recognized consciously may be picked up by sensory receptors and transmitted to the brain at a level beneath conscious awareness (Fowler & others, 1981). Advertisers are especially interested in knowing whether or not they can coax us to buy their products by embedding subliminal messages in their advertisements. And in one recent study individuals failed to perceptually detect any information in subliminal self-help auditory tapes (Moore, 1995).

The belief that subliminal messages have been slipped into rock music has stirred considerable controversy. Some rock groups allegedly have inserted Satanic messages played backward into their records and tapes. According to this theory, when the record is played normally (forward), the messages cannot be consciously perceived, but they influence our behavior in a subliminal way. Researchers have been unable to find any evidence of such subliminal messages in these recordings, or any evidence that they can influence our behavior (McIver, 1988). Even if we were to play a very clearly recorded message backward, no one would be able to tell what it said.

Sensory Adaptation

Naked except for capes that hang to their knees, two Ona Indians wade in freezing water as they use a bow and arrow to kill fish for their dinner. Darwin encountered the Ona Indians when he rounded Cape Horn on the southern tip of South America. At night they slept naked on the wet, virtually frozen ground. The ability of these Indians to endure the freezing temperatures, wearing little or no clothing, reflects the principle of **sensory adaptation**, *weakened sensitivity to prolonged stimulation.* You have experienced sensory adaptation countless times in your life—adapting to the temperature of a shower, to the water in a swimming pool, to the taste of jalapenos, to loud sounds of rock music, or to the rank smell of a locker room. Over time we become less responsive and less sensitive to these sensory experiences; this is due to sensory adaptation.

Sensory adaptation, also called *habituation* or *stimulus boredom,* is a mixed blessing. When we are exposed to unpleasant stimuli, such as rotting garbage or sneakers gone bad, habituation rescues us from being preoccupied with unpleasant stimulation. However, the charming smell of roses fades and the superb taste of a gourmet meal also loses its impact all too quickly, due to habituation. On a larger scale, we can gradually get used to conditions that might not be particularly healthy. For example, our senses readily adapt to increasing levels of pollution, and individuals in urban areas might have habituated to the sound of car alarms to such a degree that they no longer pay attention to them.

Let's return to the dilemma of the advertiser. Rather than attempting to influence through subliminal perception, most advertisers try to capture our attention by creating stimuli with louder sound levels, provocative visual images, or creative messages that break through our habituated patterns of processing commercial messages.

REVIEW

Detecting and Perceiving the World

Sensation is the process of detecting and encoding stimulus energy in the world. Perception is the process of organizing and interpreting sensory information. Most contemporary psychologists refer to sensation and perception as a unified information-processing system. A basic problem for any sensory system is to detect varying degrees of energy in the environment.

One way to cope with this problem is to assume that each of us has an absolute threshold, or minimum amount of energy we can detect. Noise is irrelevant competing stimuli. Subliminal perception is the perception of stimuli below the threshold of awareness; this is a controversial topic. Also, the difference threshold, or just noticeable difference (jnd), is the smallest difference in stimulation required to discriminate one stimulus from another 50 percent of the time. Weber's law states that the difference threshold is a constant percentage of the magnitude of the comparison stimulus rather than a constant amount. Sensory adaptation is weakened sensitivity due to prolonged stimulation.

SENSATION

The brain continuously receives a variety of information during our waking hours. Vision, hearing, smell, touch, and taste are obvious sensory channels in which we process input. We also manage upright posture and orientation in space as part of our kinesthetic senses. We will examine each of these sensory abilities in turn.

O for a life of Sensations rather than Thoughts!

John Keats

The Visual System

We see a world of shapes and sizes, some stationary, others moving, some in black and white, others in color. *How do we see this way? What is the machinery that enables us to experience this marvelous landscape?*

The Visual Stimulus and the Eye

Light *is a form of electromagnetic energy that can be described in terms of wavelengths.* Waves of light are much like the waves formed when a pebble is tossed into a lake. The **wavelength** *is the distance from the peak of one wave to the peak of the next.* Visible light's wavelengths range from about 400 to 700 nanometers (a nanometer is one-billionth of a meter and is abbreviated *nm*). The difference between visible light and other forms of electromagnetic energy is its wavelength. Outside the range of visible light are longer radio and infrared radiation waves, and shorter ultraviolet and X rays (see figure 4.2). These other wavelengths can bombard us, but we do not see them. Why do we see only the narrow band of the electromagnetic spectrum between 400 and 700 nanometers? The most likely answer is that our visual system evolved in the sun's light. Thus, our visual system is able to perceive the spectrum of energy emitted by the sun. By the time sunlight reaches the earth's surface, it is strongest in the 400 to 700 nanometer range.

Biological and Perceptual Processes

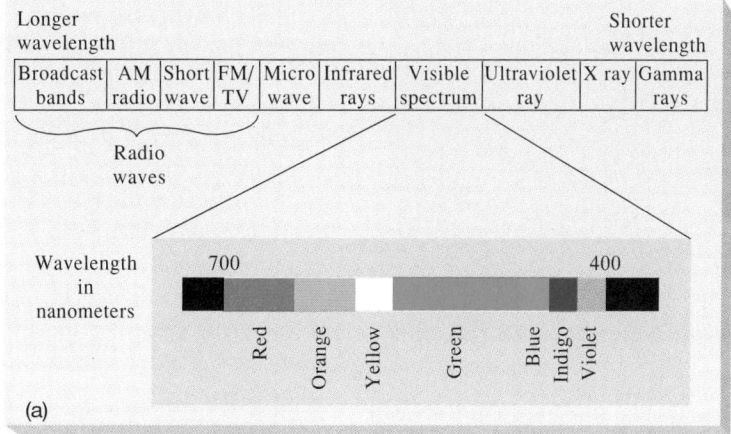

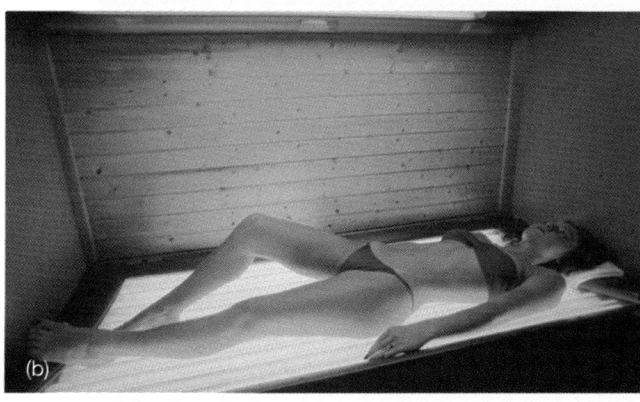

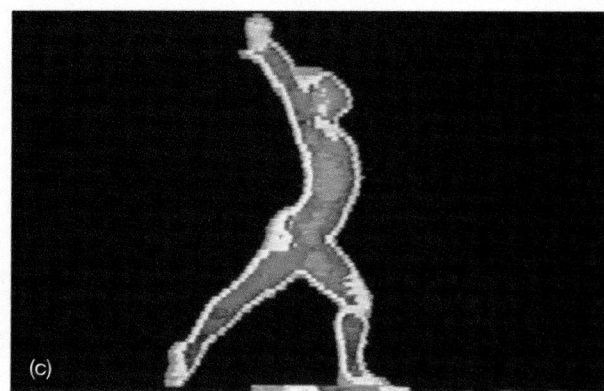

FIGURE 4.2

The Electromagnetic Spectrum and Visible Light

(a) Visible light is only a narrow band in the electromagnetic spectrum. Visible light's wavelengths range from about 400 to 700 nanometers; X rays are much shorter and radio waves are much longer. *(b)* Most ultraviolet rays are absorbed by the ozone in the earth's upper atmosphere. The small fraction that reaches the earth is the ingredient in sunlight that tans the skin (and can cause skin cancer). *(c)* The electromagnetic radiation just beyond red in the spectrum (infrared) is felt as heat by receptors in the skin.

This narrow band of the electromagnetic spectrum strikes our eyes, which have a number of structures to handle the incoming light. By looking closely at your eyes in a mirror, you notice three parts—the sclera, iris, and pupil (figure 4.3 shows the main structures of the eye). The **sclera** *is the white part of the eye, which helps maintain the shape of the eye and protect it from injury.* The **iris** *is a ring of muscles, which range in color from light blue to dark brown.* The **pupil,** *which appears black, is the opening in the center of the iris; its primary function is to reduce glare in high illumination.*

If the eye is to act like a camera, in addition to having the right amount of light, the image has to be in focus at the back of the eye. Two structures serve this purpose: the **cornea,** *which is a clear membrane just in front of the eye,* and the **lens of the eye,** *which is a transparent and somewhat flexible ball-like entity filled with a gelatinous material. The function of both of these structures is to bend the light falling on the surface of the eye just enough to focus it at the back of the eye. The curved surface of the cornea does most of this bending, while the lens fine-tunes the focus as needed.*

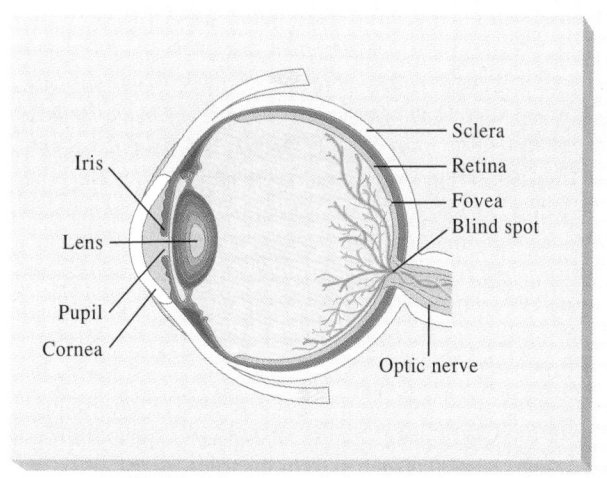

FIGURE 4.3

Main Structures of the Eye

Figure 4.4

The Eye's Blind Spot
There is a normal blind spot in your eye, a small area where the optic nerve leads to the brain. To find your blind spot, hold this book at arm's length, cover your left eye, and stare at the red pepper with your right eye. Move the book slowly toward you until the yellow pepper disappears. To find the blind spot in your left eye, cover your right eye, concentrate on the yellow pepper, and adjust the distance of the book until the red pepper disappears.

When you are looking at far-away objects, the lens has a relatively flat shape. This is because the light reaching the eye from far-away objects is parallel and the bending power of the cornea is sufficient to keep things in focus. The light reaching the eye from objects that are close, however, is more scattered and so more bending of the light is required to achieve focus. This focusing is done by a process called **accommodation,** *which occurs when the lens increases its curvature.* Without this fine-tuning ability, it would be difficult to focus on objects that are close to us, as we do with needlework or reading. As we get older, the lens of our eye begins to lose its flexibility, and hence, its ability to change from its normal flattened shape to the rounder shape needed to bring close objects into focus. This is why many people with normal vision throughout their young adult life require reading glasses when they get older.

The parts of the eye that we have discussed so far work together to get the best possible picture of the world. All of this effort, however, would be for naught without a method for keeping or "recording" the images we take of the world. In a camera, film serves just such a purpose. Film is made of a material that responds to light. Likewise, the **retina** *is the light-sensitive surface in the back of the eye. It consists of light receptors called rods and cones, and different kinds of neurons that you will read about shortly.* Making an analogy between the film of a camera and the retina, however, vastly underestimates the complexity and elegance of the retina's design. Even after decades of intense study, the full marvel of this structure is far from understood.

The most important part of the retina is the **fovea,** *which is a minute area in the center of the retina where vision is at its best. The fovea is able to resolve much finer detail than*

any other part of the retina. The fovea is vitally important to many visual tasks that we take for granted such as reading. (Try reading out of the corner of your eye!) The **blind spot** *is the area of the retina where the optic nerve leaves the eye on its way to the brain.* We cannot see anything that reaches only this part of the retina. To experience your blind spot, follow the directions in figure 4.4.

Because the retina is so important to vision, we need to study its makeup more closely. There are two kinds of receptors in the retina: rods and cones. They serve to turn the electromagnetic energy of light into a form of energy that can be processed by the nervous system. **Rods** *are the receptors in the retina that are exquisitely sensitive to light, but are not very useful for color vision.* Thus, they function well under low illumination; as you might anticipate, they are hard at work at night. **Cones** *are the receptors that we use for color perception.* There are three types of cones, each maximally sensitive to a different range of wavelengths or hues. As we will see shortly, our color perception operates by being able to compare the responses of these three cone systems to a stimulus. Like the rods, cones are light sensitive. However, they require a larger amount of light than the rods do to respond, and, so, operate best in daylight or under high illumination.

The rods and cones in the retina are specialized nerve cells that transduce light into neural impulses by means of a photochemical reaction. The breakdown of the chemicals produces a neural impulse that is first transmitted to the bipolar cells and then moves to the ganglion cells (see figure 4.5). The nerve impulse then passes along the axons of the ganglion cells, which make up the optic nerve.

Rods and cones are involved in different aspects of vision and differ both in their response properties to light and in their distribution on the surface of the retina. As their name suggests, rods are long and cylindrical. Since they require less light to respond than do cones, they work best under conditions of low illumination. Rods are found almost everywhere on the retina except in the fovea. As a consequence, we are actually able to detect fainter spots of light in the peripheral retina than at the fovea. It has been known for centuries that if you want to see a very faint star, you should gaze slightly to the right or left of the star. A more modern example of the peripheral retina's greater light sensitivity is the annoying flicker of a dying fluorescent light that can be detected easily when you are not gazing at the light, but seemingly disappears when you look directly at the light. The rods throughout the peripheral retina are sensitive enough to detect these small fluctuations in the intensity of the dying light, when the less sensitive cones on the fovea fail.

Recall that color perception works by comparing the responses of the three types of cones. Since there is only one type of rod, rods are not very useful for color perception. Combining this fact with the importance of the rod system under conditions of low illumination, it is easy to see why we have difficulty seeing color at night.

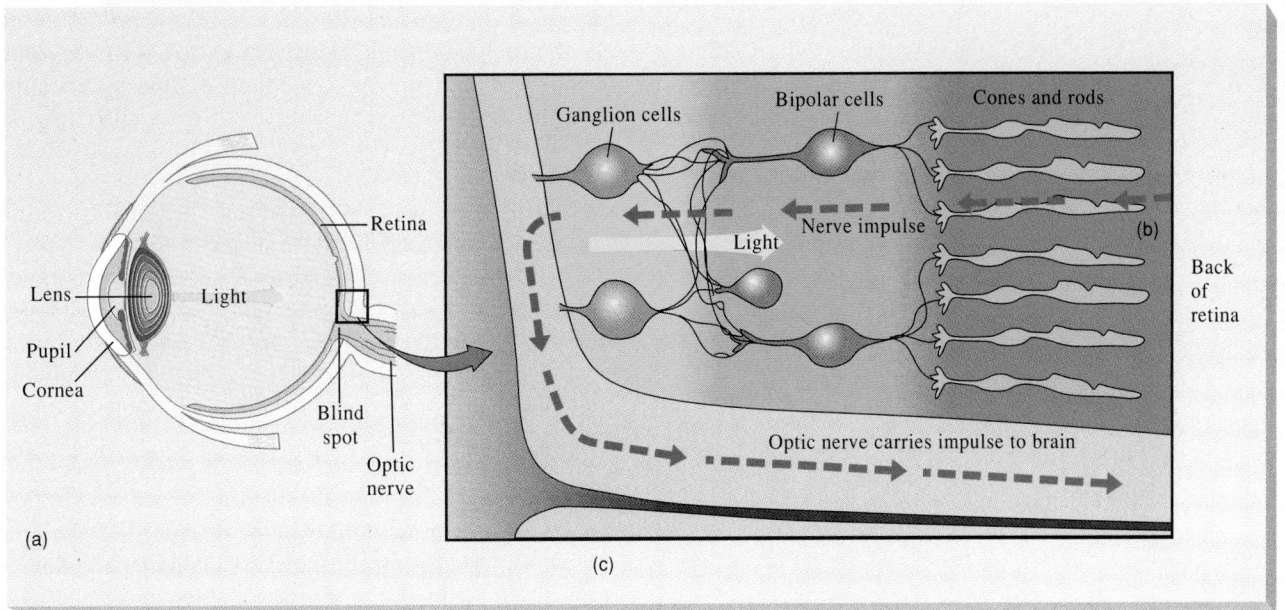

FIGURE 4.5

Three Stages of Transmission of Light Information Through the Eye
(a) In the first stage, light passes (from left to right in this representation) through the cornea, pupil, and lens and then falls on the retina, a light-sensitive surface in the back of the eye. *(b)* Once light triggers a photochemical reaction in the rods and cones at the back of the retina, the direction of light processing reverses to create the second stage. The photochemical reaction of the rods and cones activates the bipolar cells, which in turn activate the ganglion cells at the front of the retina. *(c)* In the final stage, the ganglion cells intersect to become the optic nerve, which carries information to the parts of the brain that process visual information.

Cones are shorter and fatter than rods, and are concentrated at the fovea. Because we know that rods are used in poorly lit conditions and that the fovea has no rods, we can conclude that vision is poor for objects registered on the fovea at night. There are three kinds of cones, each of which is maximally sensitive to different wavelengths, but responds across a range of wavelengths. The three receptor types respond best to colors that correspond roughly to blue (around 435 nm), green (around 535 nm), and red (565 nm). While the three types of receptors respond best to these colors, they also respond to a range of wavelengths around these "best colors." We will discuss the properties of color vision shortly, but for now, know that the color sensitive properties of these three kinds of cones form the basis of our color perception abilities. A summary of some of the main characteristics of rods and cones is presented in table 4.2.

So far we have studied the importance of light and structures of the eyes. The journey of vision now leads us to the brain and how it processes visual information.

From Eye to Brain and Neural-Visual Processing

The optic nerve leads out of the eye toward the brain carrying information about light. The optic chiasm is the point at which approximately half of the optic nerve fibers cross over the midline of the brain. Before reaching the optic chiasm,

TABLE 4.2

Characteristics of Rods and Cones

Characteristics	Rods	Cones
Type of vision	Black and white	Color
Light conditions	Dimly lighted	Well lighted
Shape	Thin and long	Short and fat
Distribution	Not on fovea	On fovea

stimuli in the left visual field were registered in the right half of the retina in both eyes, and stimuli in the right visual field were registered in the left half of the retina in both eyes. At the optic chiasm the optic nerve fibers divide. The visual information originating in the right halves of the two retinae is then transmitted to the left side of the occipital lobe in the back of the brain, and the visual information originating in the left halves of the retinae is transmitted to the right side of the occipital lobe. What all of these crossings mean is that what we see in the left side of our visual field ends up in the right side of our brain, and what we see in the right visual field ends up in the left side of our brain (see figure 4.6).

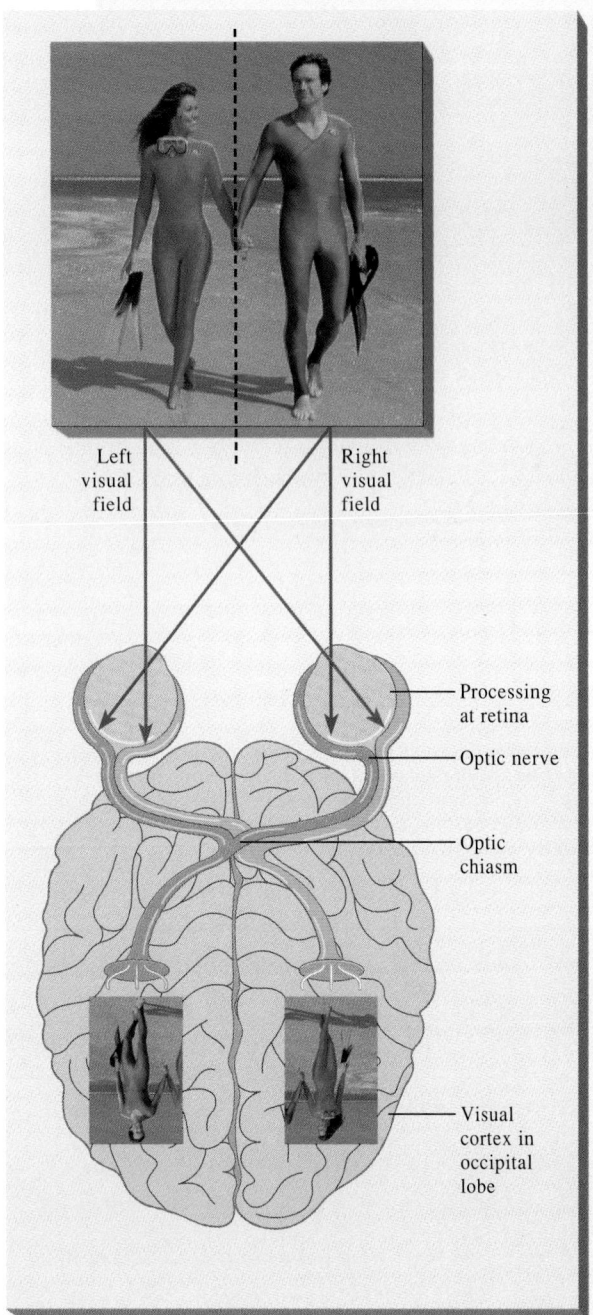

FIGURE 4.6

Visual Pathways to and Through the Brain
Light from each side of the visual field falls on the opposite side
of each eye's retina. Visual information then travels along the
optic nerve to the optic chiasm, where most of the visual
information crosses over to the other side of the brain. From
there visual information goes to the occipital lobe at the rear of
the brain. What all of the crossings mean is that what we see in
the left side of our visual field (in this figure, the woman) ends
up in the right side of our brain, and what we see in the right
visual field (the man) ends up on the left side of our brain.

The visual cortex in the occipital lobe combines information from both eyes and is responsible for higher levels of visual processing. David Hubel and Torsten Wiesel (1965) won a Nobel Prize for their discovery that some neurons detect different features of the visual field. By recording the activity of a *single* neuron in a cat while it looked at patterns that varied in size, shape, color, and movement, the researchers found that the visual cortex has neurons that are individually sensitive to different types of lines and angles. For example, one neuron might show a sudden burst of activity when stimulated by lines of a particular angle; another neuron might fire only when moving stimuli appear; yet another neuron might be stimulated when the object in the visual field has a combination of angles, sizes, and shapes.

Color Vision

We spend a lot of time thinking about color—the color of the car we want to buy, the color we are going to paint the walls of our room, the color of the clothes we wear. We can change our hair color or even the color of our eyes to make us look more attractive.

What Is Color?   The human eye registers light wavelengths between 400 and 700 nm (as you saw in figure 4.2). Light waves themselves have no color. The sensations of color reside in the visual system of the observer, so if we talk about red light, we refer to the wavelengths of light that evoke the sensation of red. Objects appear a certain color to us because they reflect specific wavelengths of light to our eyes. These wavelengths are split apart into a spectrum of colors when the light passes through a prism, as in the formation of a rainbow. We can remember the colors of the light spectrum by thinking of an imaginary man named ROY G. BIV, for the colors red, orange, yellow, green, blue, indigo, and violet.

If you go into a paint store and ask for some red paint, the salesperson will probably ask you what kind of red paint you want—dark or light, pinkish or more crimson, pastel or deep, and so on. A color's **hue** *is based on its wavelength content,* a color's **saturation** *on its purity,* and a color's **brightness** *on its intensity.* As shown in figure 4.2, the longest wavelengths seen by the human eye (about 700 nm) appear as red; the shortest (about 400 nm) appear as violet. Hue is what we commonly think of color to be. To understand a color's saturation, turn to figure 4.7. The purity of a color is determined by the amount of white light added to a single wavelength of color. Colors that are very pure have no white light—they are located on the outside of the color tree. As we move toward the color tree's interior, notice how the saturation of the color changes. The closer we get to the tree's center, the more white light has been added to the single wavelength of a particular color. That is, the deep colors at the edge fade into the more pastel colors toward the center. When saturation is added to hue, we see a much larger range of colors—pink and crimson, as well as a basic red, for example. However, another dimension is involved in color—brightness. White has the most brightness, black the least.

When we mix colors, we get different results, depending on whether we mix light or pigments (see figure 4.8). An **additive mixture** *of color refers to mixing beams of light from different parts of the color spectrum.* Through additive mixing, we can produce virtually the entire color circle by using any three widely spaced colors. Television is an example of additive mixing—only three colors are involved—red, blue, and green. If you look at a color television screen through a magnifying glass, you will notice that a yellow patch of light is actually a combination of tiny red and green dots. Look at the other patches of color on a television screen with a magnifying glass to observe their composition.

In contrast, a **subtractive mixture** *of color refers to mixing pigments rather than beams of light.* An artist's painting is an example of subtractive mixing. When blue and yellow are mixed on the television screen, a gray or white hue appears, but, when an artist mixes a dab of blue paint with a dab of yellow paint, the color green is produced. In a subtractive color mixture, each pigment absorbs (subtracts) some of the light falling on it and reflects the rest of the light. When two pigments are mixed, only the light that is not absorbed or subtracted from either one emerges (Wasserman, 1978).

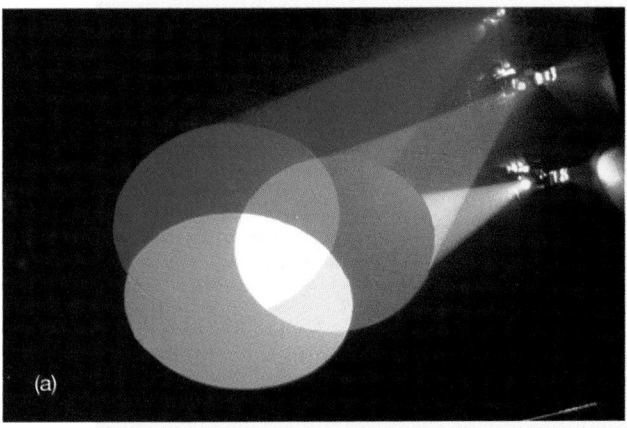

FIGURE 4.7

A Color Tree Showing Color's Three Dimensions: Hue, Saturation, and Brightness

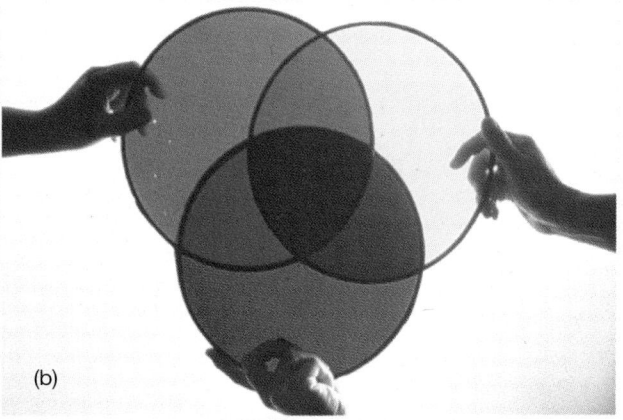

(a) (b)

FIGURE 4.8

Comparing the Mixing of Light with the Mixing of Pigments
(a) Additive color mixtures occur when lights are mixed. For example, red and green lights when combined yield yellow. The three colors together give white. *(b)* Subtractive color mixtures occur when pigments are mixed or light is shown through colored filters placed over one another. Most of the time, a mixture of blue-green and yellow produces green, and a mixture of complementary colors produces black.

Theories of Color Vision For centuries scientists have puzzled over how the human eye sees the infinite variety of color in the world. Though we can discriminate among 319 colors, no one believes that we have 319 kinds of cones in our retinas (Bartley, 1969). Instead, even the earliest theorists assumed that our retinas respond to a few primary colors and then relay the information to the brain, where it is synthesized into the many different hues we perceive. However, early theorists disagreed about which colors the retina was selecting. Two main theories were proposed, and each turned out to be right.

The first color vision theory we discuss is based on what you just learned about the three kinds of cone receptors in the retina. The **trichromatic theory** *states that color perception is based on the existence of three types of receptors, each of which is maximally sensitive to different, but overlapping, ranges of wavelengths.* The trichromatic theory of color vision was proposed by Thomas Young in 1802 and extended by Hermann von Helmholtz in 1952. The theory is based on the results of experiments on human color-matching abilities. These experiments show that a person with normal vision can match any color in the spectrum by combining three other wavelengths. In this type of experiment, individuals are given a light of a single wavelength and are asked to combine three other single-wavelength lights to match the first light. They can do this by changing the relative intensities of three lights until the color of the combination light is indistinguishable from the color of the first light. Young and Helmholtz reasoned that if the combination of any three wavelengths in different intensities is indistinguishable from any single pure wavelength, the visual system must be basing its perception of color on the relative responses of three receptor systems. To understand how this works, imagine that we have one kind of receptor mechanism for each wavelength in the spectrum of visible light and that each receptor responds to only one wavelength. The color represented by a wavelength of 550 nm would be registered in our visual system whenever the receptor type that was sensitive to 550 nm responded. With this system there is no way to match any color perceptually with any other set of colors, since only one type of receptor response could signal that color. By contrast, with three kinds of receptors that respond best to different overlapping ranges of wavelengths, by adjusting the relative intensities of any combination of three wavelengths we can exactly match the response that is produced for any single wavelength.

These color matching experiments were carried out long before anything was known about the physiological properties of receptors in the retina. The existence of three types of color receptors, or cones, with different color-sensitive properties was confirmed in the 1960s, over 100 years after the proposal of the trichromatic theory of color perception (Wald & Brown, 1965)!

Further convincing support for the trichromatic theory is found in the study of defective color vision. The term *color blind* is somewhat misleading because it suggests that a color-blind person cannot see color at all. Complete color blindness is rare; most people who are color blind, the vast majority of whom are men, can see some colors but not others. The nature of color blindness depends on which of the three kinds of cones is inoperative. For example, in the most common form of color blindness, the green cone system malfunctions in some way. Green is indistinguishable from certain combinations of blue and red. Color-matching experiments performed by people with this form of color blindness show that they need only two other colors to match a pure color and hence have dichromatic color perception. **Dichromats** *are people with only two kinds of cones.* **Trichromats** *are people with normal color vision, and have three kinds of functional cone receptors.*

The German physiologist Ewald Hering was not completely satisfied with the trichromatic theory of color vision. Hering observed that some colors cannot exist together whereas others can. For example, it is easy to imagine a greenish-blue or a reddish-yellow, but nearly impossible to imagine a reddish-green or a bluish-yellow. Hering also observed that trichromatic theory could not adequately explain **afterimages,** *sensations that remain after a stimulus is removed.* See figure 4.9 to experience an afterimage. Color afterimages are common and they involve complementary colors. One example of afterimages that many people are familiar with occurs after prolonged exposure to a computer terminal screen with green lettering, such as those used in many businesses. After working with a computer like this all day, it is not unusual for white objects and walls to appear reddish. Conversely, if you look at red long enough, eventually a green afterimage will appear; if you look at yellow long enough, eventually a blue afterimage will appear. Such information led Hering to propose that the visual system treats colors as complementary pairs—red-green and blue-yellow.

THE FAR SIDE By GARY LARSON

" . . . And please let Mom, Dad, Rex, Ginger, Tucker, me and all the rest of the family see color."

Vision researchers believe that dogs see the world only in black and white. Thus, *what kind of* visual receptors *dominate their vision? (Rods)*

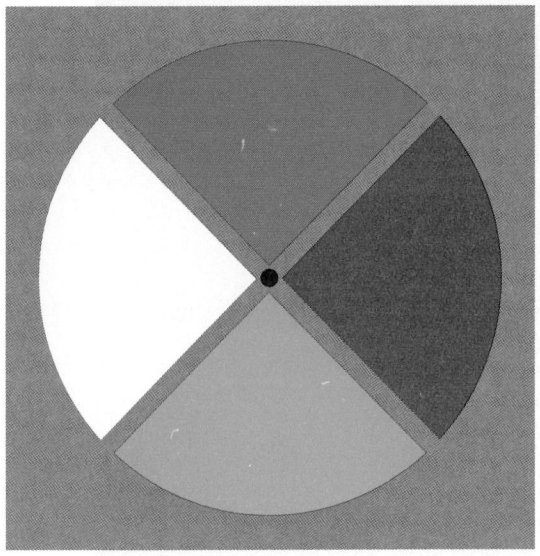

FIGURE 4.9

Negative Afterimage—Complementary Colors
If you gaze steadily at the dot in the colored panel on the left for a few moments, then shift your gaze to the gray box on the right, you will see the original hues change into their complementary colors. The blue appears as yellow, the red as green, the green as red, and the yellow as blue. This pairing of colors has to do with the fact that color receptors in the eye are apparently sensitive as pairs; when one color is turned off (when you stop staring at the panel), the other color in the receptor is briefly "turned on." The afterimage effect is especially noticeable when you spend time painting walls or objects in bright colors.

Hering's view is called **opponent-process theory,** *which states that cells in the visual system respond to red-green and blue-yellow colors; a given cell might be excited by red and inhibited by green, while another cell might be excited by yellow and inhibited by blue.* Researchers have found that opponent-process theory does explain afterimages (Hurvich & Jameson, 1969; Jameson & Hurvich, 1989). If you stare at red, for instance, your red-green system seems to "tire," and when you look away, it rebounds and gives you a green afterimage. Also, if you mix equal amounts of opponent colors, such as blue and yellow, you see gray.

Our tour of the visual system has been an extensive one—you have read about the light spectrum, the structures of the eye, neural visual processing, and the marvels of color vision. Next, you will study the second most researched sensory system, our hearing.

REVIEW

The Visual System

Light is a form of electromagnetic energy that can be described in terms of wavelengths. The receptors in the human eye are sensitive to wavelengths from 400 to 700 nm. Key external parts of the eye are the sclera, iris, pupil, and cornea. The lens focuses light rays on the retina, the light-sensitive mechanism in the eye. Chemicals in the retina break down light into neural impulses. The optic nerve transmits neural impulses to the brain. Because of the crossover of neural fibers, what we see in the left visual field is registered in the right side of the brain and vice versa. Visual information reaches the occipital lobe of the brain, where it is stored and further integrated. Hubel and Wiesel discovered that neurons in the visual cortex can detect features of our visual world, such as line, angle, and size.

Objects appear colored because they reflect certain wavelengths of light between 400 and 700 nm. Important properties of color are hue, saturation, and brightness. Mixing colors of light involves an additive mixture; mixing pigments involves a subtractive mixture. Scientists have found support for two theories of color vision. The Young-Helmholtz theory states that the retina's cones are sensitive to one of three colors—red, green, or blue. The Young-Helmholtz theory explains color blindness but not afterimages. The opponent-process theory does explain afterimages. It states that information is coded into pairs of opposite colors—blue-yellow or red-green.

The Auditory System

Just as light provides us with information about the environment, so does sound. Think about what life would be like without music, the rushing sound of ocean waves, or the gentle voice of someone you love. Sounds in the world tell us about the approach of a person behind us, an approaching car, the force of the wind outside, the mischief of a 2-year-old, and, perhaps most importantly, about the kinds of information that we transmit through language and song.

The Nature of Sound

At a rock concert you may have felt the throbbing pulse of loud sounds or sensed that the air around you was vibrating. Bass instruments are especially effective at creating mechanical pulsations, even causing the floor or a seat to vibrate on occasion. When a bass is played loudly we can sense air molecules being pushed forward in waves from the speaker. **Sounds,** *or sound waves, are vibrations in the air that are processed by our auditory (or hearing) system.*

Remember that we described light waves as being much like the waves fanned when a pebble is tossed into a lake, with concentric circles moving outward from where the pebble entered the water. Sound waves are similar. They vary in wavelength, which determines the **frequency** *of the sound waves or the number of cycles (or full wavelengths) that pass through a point in a given time* (see figure 4.10). **Pitch** *is the perceptual interpretation of the frequency of sound.* High-frequency sounds are perceived as having a high pitch, low-frequency sounds are perceived as having a low pitch. A soprano voice sounds high-pitched, a bass voice sounds low-pitched. As with the wavelengths of light, human sensitivity is limited to a range of sound frequencies. It is common knowledge that dogs, for example, can hear higher frequencies than humans can.

Sound waves vary not only in frequency, but also in amplitude. The sound wave's **amplitude** *is measured in decibels (dB), the amount of pressure produced by a sound wave relative to a standard;* the typical standard is the weakest sound the human ear can detect. Thus, zero decibels would be the softest noise detectable by humans. Noise rated at 80 decibels or higher, if heard for prolonged periods of time, can cause permanent hearing loss. A quiet library is about 40 decibels, a car horn about 90 decibels, a rock band at close range 120 decibels, and a rocket launching 180 decibels. **Loudness** *is the perception of a sound wave's amplitude.* In general, the higher the amplitude of the sound wave, the louder the sound is perceived to be. In the world of amplitude, this means that air is moving rapidly for loud sounds and slowly for soft sounds.

So far we have been describing a single sound wave with just one frequency. This is similar to the single-wavelength, or pure colored, light we just discussed in the context of color matching. Most sounds, however, including those of speech and music, are complex sounds. **Complex sounds** *are those in which numerous frequencies of sound*

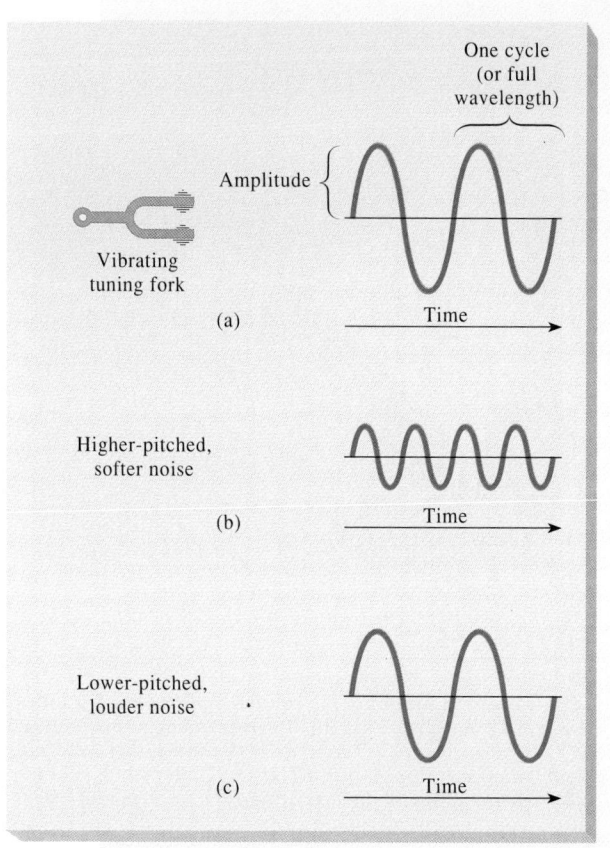

FIGURE 4.10

Frequency and Amplitude of Sound Waves
(a) A tuning fork is an instrument with two prongs that produces a tone when struck. You may have seen one in a music classroom or science laboratory. The vibrations of the tuning fork cause air molecules to vibrate like a musical instrument, producing a sound wave pattern like the one shown. Wavelength determines the frequency of the sound wave, which is the number of cycles, or full wavelengths, that can pass through a point in a given time. In the tuning fork example, two cycles (full wavelengths) have occurred in the time frame shown. *(b)* In the sound wave shown here, four cycles have occurred in this time frame, so this sound wave has a higher frequency than the sound wave with the tuning fork; hence, it has a higher pitch. Its small amplitude is indicative of softer sounds. The amplitude of the sound wave is the change in pressure created by the sound wave and is reflected in the sound wave's height. *(c)* This sound wave has a larger amplitude than the sound wave shown with the tuning fork; thus, it sounds louder. The reduced frequency of the wave indicates a lower pitch.

blend together. **Timbre** *is the tone color or perceptual quality of a sound.* Timbre differences are what make the difference between a trumpet and a trombone playing the same note, and are also responsible for the quality differences we hear between human voices.

A good listener is usually thinking about something else.
Kin Hubbard

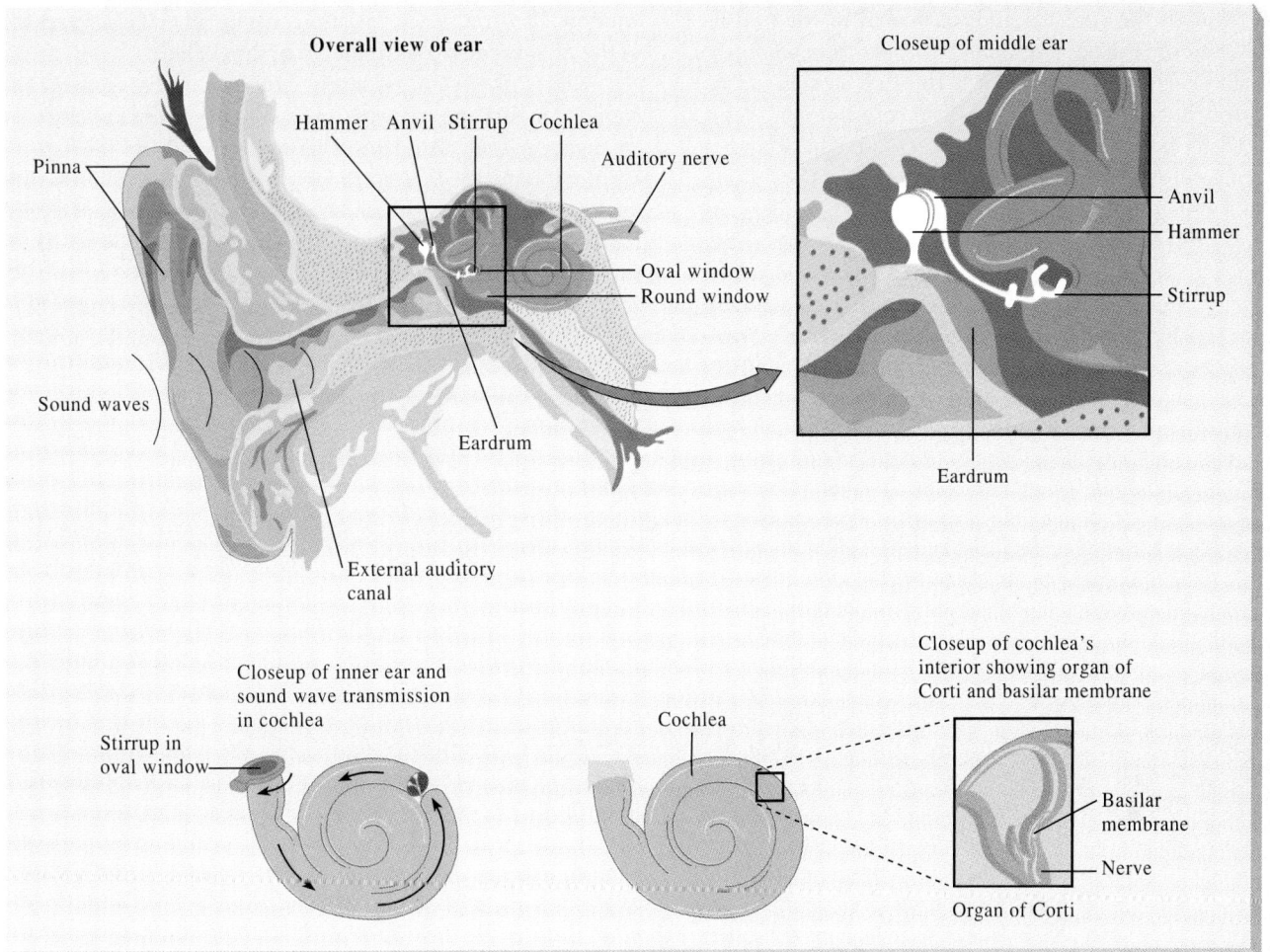

Overall view of ear

Pinna

Sound waves

Hammer Anvil Stirrup Cochlea

Auditory nerve

Oval window
Round window

Eardrum

External auditory
canal

Closeup of middle ear

Anvil
Hammer

Stirrup

Eardrum

Closeup of inner ear and
sound wave transmission
in cochlea

Stirrup in
oval window

Cochlea

Closeup of cochlea's
interior showing organ of
Corti and basilar membrane

Basilar
membrane

Nerve

Organ of Corti

FIGURE 4.11

Major Structures of the Human Ear and the Transmission of Sound Waves
Sound waves are funneled through the external auditory canal to the eardrum in the middle ear. Three bony structures in the middle ear—hammer, anvil, and stirrup—concentrate sound waves so they can be further processed in the inner ear. The stirrup relays the eardrum's vibrations through the oval window to the cochlea, a snail-like, fluid-filled structure, where sound waves are further processed before the auditory information moves on to the auditory nerve to be transmitted to the brain. The organ of Corti runs the entire length of the cochlea and contains the basilar membrane at its base. The movement of sound waves in the cochlear fluid causes the basilar membrane to vibrate and its hair cells to bend. The vibrating hair cells stimulate nearby nerve cells, which join to form the auditory nerve.

Structures and Functions of the Ear

What happens to sound waves once they reach your ear? How do various structures of the ear transform sound waves of expanded and compressed air so they can be understood by the brain as sound? The function of the ear is analogous to the function of the eye. The ear serves the purpose of transmitting a high-fidelity version of sounds in the world to the brain for analysis and interpretation. Just as an image needs to be in focus and sufficiently bright for the brain to interpret it, a sound needs to be transmitted in a way that preserves information about its location (think how confusing life would be if you could hear sounds without being able to determine where they are coming from!);

its frequency, which helps us distinguish the voice of a child from that of an adult; and its timbre, which allows us to identify the voice of a friend on the telephone.

The ear is divided into the *outer ear, middle ear,* and *inner ear* (the major structures of the ear are shown in figure 4.11). The **outer ear** *consists of the pinna and the external auditory canal.* The pinna is the outer visible part of the ear (elephants have very large ones). Its shape helps us to localize sounds by making the sound different in front of us than behind us. The pinnae of many animals such as dogs are movable and serve a more important role in sound localization than do the pinnae of humans. Dogs will prick up their ears toward the direction of a faint and interesting sound.

After passing the pinna, sound waves are then funneled through the external auditory canal to the middle ear. The **middle ear** *has four main parts: eardrum, hammer, anvil, and stirrup.* The *eardrum* is the first structure that sound touches in the middle ear. The *eardrum* is a membrane that vibrates in response to a sound. The sound is then transmitted by the three smallest bones in the human body—the hammer, anvil, and stirrup—to the inner ear. The middle ear bones translate the sound waves in air into sound waves in fluid (lymph) so they can be processed further in the inner ear. Most of us know that sound travels far more easily in air than in fluids. When we are swimming underwater, loud shouts from the side of the pool are barely detectable to us. Sound waves entering the ear travel in air until they reach the inner ear, at which point they begin to be transmitted through body fluids. At this border between air and fluid, sounds meet the same kind of resistance that shouts directed at an underwater swimmer meet when they hit the surface of the water. The hammer, anvil, and stirrup form a connected chain of bones that act like a lever to amplify the sound waves before they reach the liquid-filled inner ear.

The main parts of the **inner ear** *are the oval window, cochlea, and the organ of Corti.* The stirrup is connected to the *oval window,* which is a membrane like the eardrum and transmits the waves to the cochlea. The **cochlea** *is a long tubular fluid-filled structure that is coiled up like a snail.* The **basilar membrane** *is housed inside the cochlea and runs its entire length.* The **organ of Corti,** *also running the length of the cochlea, sits on the basilar membrane and contains the ear's sensory receptors, which change the energy of the sound waves into nerve impulses that can be processed by the brain.* Hairlike sensory receptors in the organ of Corti are stimulated by vibrations of the basilar membrane. Sound waves traveling in the fluid of the inner ear cause these hairlike receptors to move. The movement generates nerve impulses, which vary with the frequency and extent of the membrane's vibrations.

One of the auditory system's mysteries is how the inner ear registers the frequency of sound. Two theories have been proposed to explain this mystery: place theory and frequency theory. **Place theory** *is a theory of hearing that states that each frequency produces vibrations at a particular spot on the basilar membrane.* Georg von Békésy won a Nobel Prize in 1961 for his research on the basilar membrane. Von Békésy (1960) studied the effects of vibration applied at the oval window on the basilar membrane of human cadavers. Through a microscope, he saw that this stimulation produced a traveling wave on the basilar membrane. A traveling wave is like the ripples that appear in a pond when you throw in a stone. However, since the cochlea is a long tube, the ripples can travel only in one direction, from the end of the cochlea, where the oval window is located, to the far tip of the cochlea. High-frequency vibrations create traveling waves that maximally displace (or move) the area of the basilar membrane next to the oval window; low-frequency vibrations maximally displace areas of the membrane closer to the tip of the cochlea.

Place theory adequately explains high-frequency sounds but fares poorly with low-frequency sounds. A high-frequency sound stimulates a very precise area on the basilar membrane. By contrast, a low-frequency sound causes a large part of the basilar membrane to be displaced, so it is hard to localize the "maximal displacement" of the basilar membrane. Because humans can hear low-frequency sounds better than predicted by looking at the precision of the basilar membrane's response to these sounds, some other factors must be involved. **Frequency theory** *states that the perception of a sound's frequency is due to how often the auditory nerve fires.* One problem with frequency theory is that a single neuron has a maximum firing rate of about 1,000 times per second. Because of this limitation, frequency theory cannot be applied to tones with frequencies that would require a neuron to fire more than 1,000 times per second. To deal with this limitation, a modification of place theory called **volley theory** *states that high frequencies can be signaled by teams of neurons that fire at different offset times to create an overall firing rate that could signal a very high frequency.* The term *volley* was used because the neurons fire in a sequence of rhythmic volleys at higher frequencies. The alteration in neural firing makes possible frequencies above 1,000 times per second. Thus, frequency theory can better explain the perception of low-frequency sounds, and place theory can better explain the perception of high-frequency sounds. There is some evidence that the auditory system uses both place and frequency theory (Goldstein, 1994). And so, it is possible that both are correct but that sounds of high and low frequencies might be signaled with different coding schemes.

Neural-Auditory Processing

As we saw in the visual system, once energy from the environment is picked up by our receptors, it must be transmitted to the brain for processing and interpretation. An image on the retina does not a Picasso make—likewise, a pattern of receptor responses in the cochlea does not a symphony make! In the retina, we saw that the responses of the rod and cone receptors feed into ganglion cells in the retina and leave the eye via the optic nerve. In the auditory system, the **auditory nerve** *carries neural impulses to the brain's auditory areas.* Auditory information moves up the auditory pathway in a more complex manner than does visual information in the visual pathway. Many synapses occur in the ascending auditory pathway, with some fibers crossing over the midline and others proceeding directly to the hemisphere on the same side as the ear of reception. The auditory nerve extends from the cochlea to the brain stem, with some fibers crossing over the midline. The cortical destination of most of these fibers is the temporal lobes of the brain (beneath the temples of the head).

Now that we have described the visual and auditory systems in some detail, we turn to a number of other sensory systems—the skin senses, the chemical senses (smell and taste), the kinesthetic senses, and the vestibular sense.

The Haptic System

You are at an amusement park. Your mouth and fingers feel sticky from the cotton candy you just ate. The sun is hot, warming your skin and scalp. A cool breeze softens the effect of the sun. Eager to get in line for the loop-to-loop ride, you grab your partner's hand. It is cold and clammy. As you strap yourself into your seat, you feel the pressure of the special harness as you wonder for just a moment whether this was such a good idea. In just moments, you'll be upside down, feeling the force of gravity and counterforce. At ride's end, you will feel exhilarated or nauseated. All of these sensations involve the touch, kinesthetic, and vestibular senses of the haptic system. According to J. J. Gibson (1966), the haptic system provides information about the body in relation to its environment. Let's explore in turn each of the senses of the haptic system.

Touch

Many of us think of our skin as a canvas rather than a sensory organ. We color it with cosmetics, dyes, and tattoos. We modify it with face lifts, hair transplants, and fake fingernails. The skin is an efficient container for our internal organs; it is "waterproof, dustproof, and miraculously—until we grow old—always the right size" (Montague, 1971, p. 5). The skin is actually our largest sensory system, draping over the body, with receptors for pressure, temperature, and pain.

Pressure

With a rubber band, lightly touch the following parts of your body: the bottom of your foot, your leg, your nose, and your forefinger. You should be able to sense that these different parts of your body do not have the same sensitivity to touch. The body's most sensitive areas are in the head region (nose and upper lip, for example), and the least sensitive areas are in the foot region (sole of the foot, for example) (Weinstein, 1968). Women are more sensitive to touch over most of their bodies than men are.

Temperature   Do you feel too hot or too cold right now, or do you feel about right? Our bodies have a regulatory system that keeps the body's temperature at about 98.6 degrees Fahrenheit, and the skin plays an important role in this regulatory system. Some years ago, it was found that we have separate locations on our skin that sense warmth and cold (Dallenbach, 1927). The forehead is especially sensitive to heat, the arm is less sensitive, and the calf is the least sensitive.

Pain   For all living things, avoiding harm is critical for a strategy of survival, and pain is part of that strategy. Pain is information that warns us, protects us, and instructs us about what is harmful in the world. The importance of pain for humans is clearly illustrated by 7-year-old Sarah, who was born with an insensitivity to pain. She constantly hurts herself but does not realize it. A wound on her knee is protected from further harm by a cast on her leg. Her arm is bandaged to heal a bruise on her elbow. Sarah has something wrong with the nerve pathways that normally transmit signals to the brain that it interprets as pain.

Aside from a few people like Sarah, we all experience pain. Even so, we can never be sure whether another person is experiencing pain. You might infer from her expression or behavior that your friend is in pain, but you cannot directly experience her pain.

Many stimuli can cause pain. Intense stimulation of any one of our senses can produce pain—too much light, very loud sounds, extreme temperatures, strong pressure on the skin, for example. However, like other perceptions, our perception of pain reflects our subjective judgments. Among other factors, our expectations, moods, and body's makeup influence how we perceive pain. If we expect something to hurt us, we are more likely to perceive pain, and if our body has a weak spot, we are more likely to experience pain there. **Pain threshold** *is the stimulation level at which pain is first perceived.* Because our perception of pain reflects subjective judgments, pain thresholds vary considerably from one person to another, from one point in time to another, and from one cultural group to another. Information about cultural and ethnic variations in reactions to pain appears in Sociocultural Worlds 4.1.

How is pain transmitted to the brain? Consider the situation when you miss a nail with a hammer and smash your thumb—it almost hurts just to think about it. The pain message begins with the release of chemicals usually found in or near the nerve endings in the skin (among these are chemicals known as substance P and bradykinin). These chemicals sensitize the nerve endings and help transmit the pain message from your thumb to your brain. The pain signal is converted into a series of electrochemical impulses that travel through the peripheral nervous system to the central nervous system and up the spinal cord. From there the pain signal becomes a cascade of chemical messages as it relays through the brain to the thalamus. Then, the pain message is routed to the cerebral cortex, where the pain's intensity and specific location is identified. It is also in the cerebral cortex that the pain is symbolically interpreted. In the case of martyrs and patriots, the pain may even be welcome (Restak, 1988). In our case of hitting the thumb with

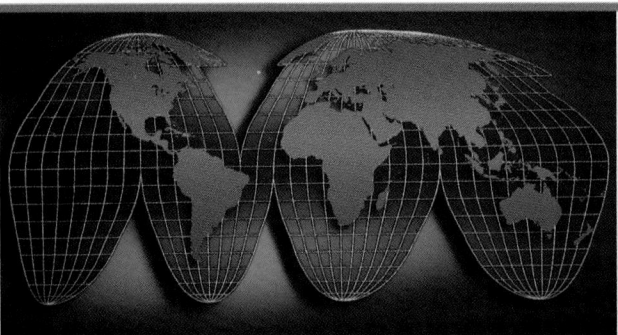

Cultural and Ethnic Differences in Reactions to Pain

In a remote village, a cart slowly wends its way along a dusty road. A man swings from a pole in the cart; ropes from two large steel hooks embedded in the man's back attach him to the pole. The man is not being punished or tortured; he is blessing the children and crops in a centuries-old ritual practiced in certain parts of India. His role is an honor. The man does not seem to be suffering; instead, he appears to be in a state of exaltation. What's more, his wounds heal rapidly after the hooks are removed, even with little medical treatment.

How does the man unflinchingly withstand such pain? Experiences such as these have been described as hypnotic, inducing an altered state of consciousness (which is discussed extensively in chapter 5). Aside from culturally variant religious roles, studies of several ethnic and cultural groups have shown differences in how people in more usual states of mind react to pain. In one investigation, Jewish patients tended to postpone taking an analgesic until after the determination of their diagnosis and future prognosis, whereas Italian patients were more likely to request immediate pain relief (Weisenberg, 1982).

Another example of cultural differences regarding pain is how Haitian Americans react to both familiar and unfamiliar symptoms. Any symptom that resembles an illness a relative died from, for instance, is a red flag for Haitian Americans to seek medical attention immediately. Conversely, they are likely to dismiss any sign of illness if there is no family history of that particular symptom. For example, Joseph, a Haitian American teacher from Port-au-Prince who migrated to New York, had no family history of diabetes; his diabetic condition remained undiagnosed until he fell into a coma and was hospitalized (Laguerre, 1981).

Stoicism may also have cultural roots. Both Navajo and Chinese American patients have been described as "stoic." Navajos and Chinese Americans may be reluctant to breach the barriers between their culture and Western medical practices. This reluctance may keep them from seeking medical assistance and may increase their psychological tolerance of pain. Their impassive demeanor may be learned; as they observe how others react, they adopt the culturally appropriate response to pain. Verbal expressions of pain may also be learned. If you were Navajo or Chinese, for example, you might give out a 50- or 60-decibel moan after pounding your thumb with a hammer, but a 90-decibel shriek might be a typical response if you're from a middle-class White background.

Social class may be another factor that influences a person's ideas about illness and wellness. People from poor neighborhoods might not have access to adequate health care through an HMO or good health insurance. As a result, they might use a higher threshold to define unbearable pain. For example, a person who must take a day off from work without pay, find a physician or clinic, and pay immediately for medical services might wait until a symptom becomes severe before seeking treatment.

Although cross-cultural research on the perception of pain may yield some intriguing findings, several caveats are warranted. First, even when differences among groups are found, as in the comparison between Jewish and Italian patients, there are differences within groups as well. Not all of the Italian patients in the study moaned, groaned, and wanted immediate medication—many did, but some did not. Second, many studies on cultural and ethnic variations in reactions to pain are based on findings from a small number of people who are not always carefully selected to be truly comparable on all dimensions except the one difference the researcher is studying. Third, researchers in this area have not attended to the effects of mixing cultures. For instance, are Italians who live in the Little Italy section of an urban area more likely to show a desire for early medication than Italians who live in more integrated areas?

a hammer, it is undoubtedly not welcome. One other important fact about afferent information processing is that sound is processed faster than touch is. The crunch of the thumb beneath the hammer will be heard before the pain is felt.

Further understanding of how we experience pain involves a closer look at the spinal cord. Ronald Melzack and Patrick Wall (1965, 1983) pointed out that the nervous system can process only a limited amount of sensory information of any kind—pain, touch, or anything else—at a given moment. They discovered that, when too much information moves through the nervous system, certain neural cells in the spinal column stop the signal. **Gate-control theory** *is Melzack and Wall's theory that the spinal column contains a neural "gate" that can be opened (allowing the perception of pain) or closed (blocking the perception of pain).* In the case of the throbbing thumb you hammered,

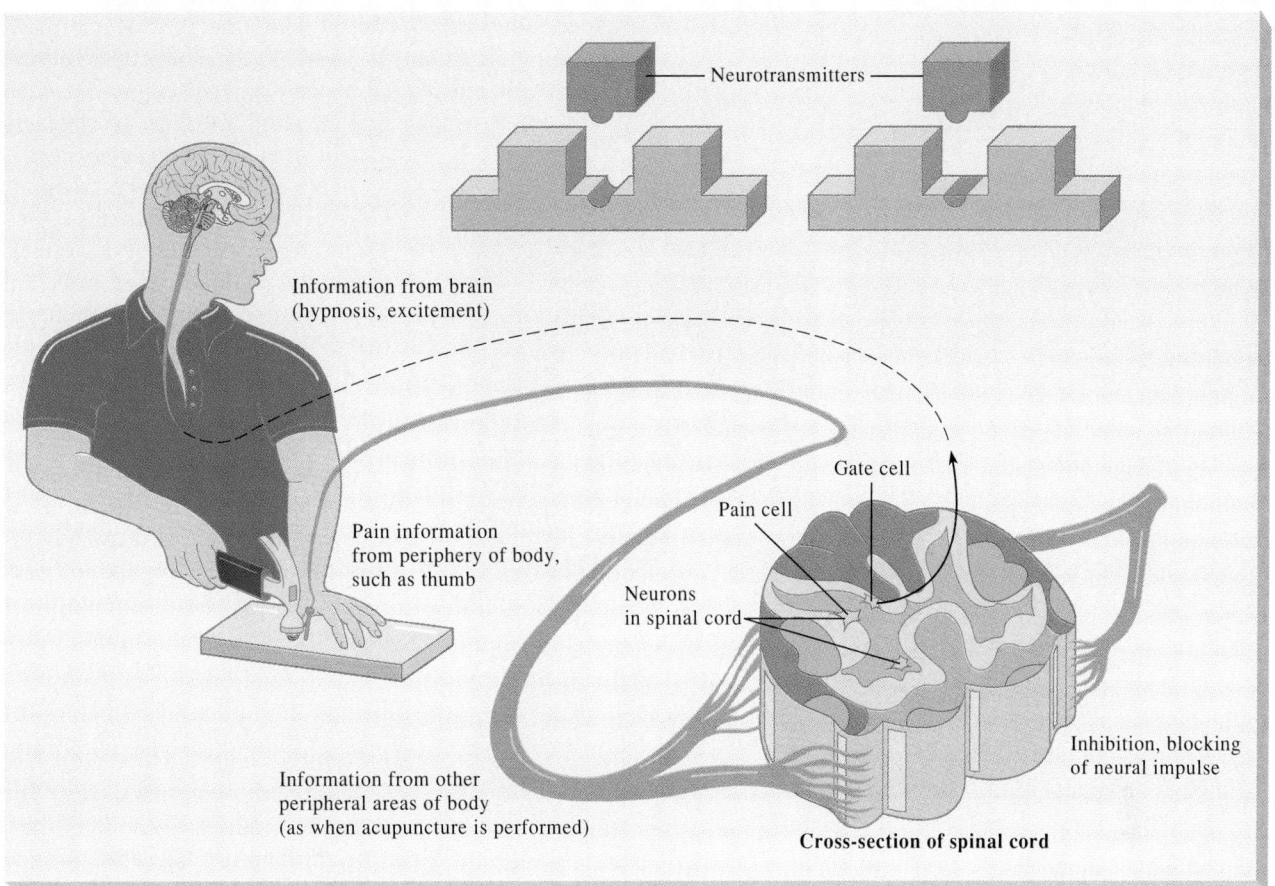

FIGURE 4.12

Gate-Control Theory of Pain

In the case of hitting your thumb with a hammer, pain signals initially go through the spinal cord and then to the brain. Gate-control theory states that pain information can be blocked in the spinal cord. Pain pathways from the periphery of the body (thumb, foot, etc.) make a synaptic connection in the spinal cord and then ascend to the brain. Interneurons can inhibit transmission through these pathways, as shown in the drawing on the right. When a strong peripheral stimulus (as applied during acupuncture) comes into the spinal cord, this can turn on the interneuron and close the gate in the pain pathway. Also, when a signal comes down from the brain (during hypnosis or the excitement of athletic competition), it, too, can turn on the interneuron and close the gate. The gate is not a physical structure that actually opens and shuts; rather, the gate is the inhibition of neural impulses. Neurotransmitters (the tiny circles in the synapse between the pain cell and the gate cell) are involved in gate control, but much is yet to be known about their identity.

you quickly grab a bunch of ice cubes and press them against your thumb. The pain lessens. According to gate-control theory (see figure 4.12), the ice sent signals to the spinal cord and slammed the gate in the face of competing pain signals. The brain also, in turn, can send information down the spinal cord and influence whether a gate is open or closed. In this way, emotions, attitudes, hypnosis, and neurotransmitters can influence how much pain we sense. The gate in gate-control theory is not a physical gate that opens and shuts; rather, the gate is the inhibition of neural impulses.

When the spinal cord receives a strong peripheral signal, such as the prick of an acupuncture needle, it, too, can turn on the interneuron and close the gate. **Acupuncture** *is a technique in which thin needles are inserted at specific points in the body to relieve specific symptoms* (see figure 4.13).

Interestingly, the point of stimulation may be some distance from the symptom being treated. For example, when acupuncture is used as an anesthetic in abdominal surgery, four acupuncture needles are placed in the pinna of each ear. Although acupuncture is still considered somewhat unorthodox in the United States, the technique is used widely in China in dentistry and occasionally in abdominal surgery. How does acupuncture reduce the sensation of pain? The gate-control mechanisms may be partly responsible, and neurotransmitters, such as endorphins (see chapter 3), may also play a role.

Our ability to interpret a specific sensation as pain hinges on complex neurochemical reactions. Researchers are investigating this cascade of events, not only to understand better the mechanism of pain but also to find ways to reduce human suffering.

The Kinesthetic and Vestibular Senses

Your body has two kinds of senses that provide information to your brain about your movement and orientation in space: **kinesthetic senses** *provide information about movement, posture, and orientation,* and the **vestibular sense** *provides information about balance and movement.*

No specific organ contains the kinesthetic senses. Instead, these senses are located in the cells of our muscles, joints, and tendons. For example, suppose you decide to strengthen your body. You begin a weight-lifting regimen and are at the point where you can bench-press 150 pounds. You decide to go for it and put the key in the Nautilus machine at 200 pounds. After several deep breaths, you thrust the 200 pounds upward; it quickly falls back to the bar holding the rest of the weights. Your body's ability to sense that it was not ready to press the 200 pounds was due to your kinesthetic senses. However, it doesn't take 200 pounds of weights to set off your kinesthetic senses. Move your hand forward and touch this page. Wiggle your toes. Smile. Frown.

The vestibular sense tells you whether your body is tilted, moving, slowing down, or speeding up. It works in concert with the kinesthetic senses to coordinate your proprioceptive

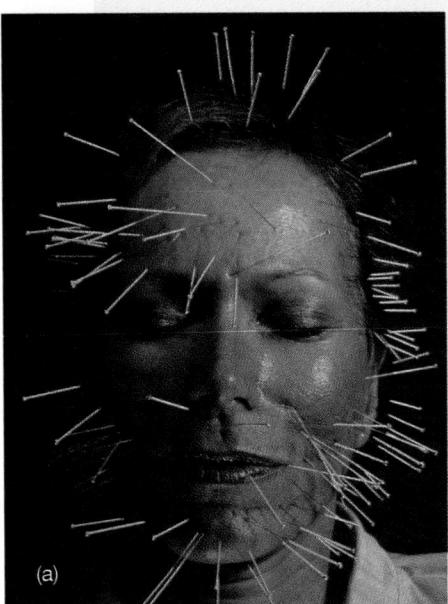
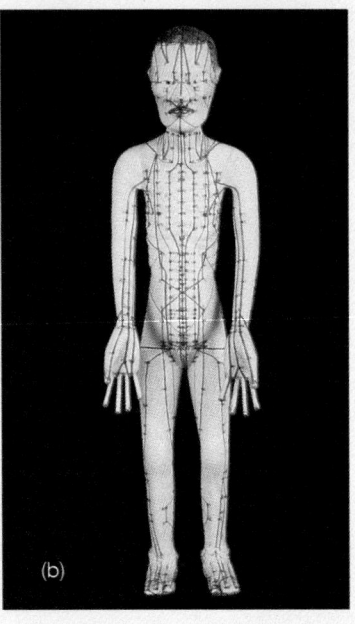

FIGURE 4.13

Acupuncture

(a) A woman is being treated for pain by an acupuncturist. *(b)* Acupuncture points are carefully noted on this nineteenth-century Japanese papier-mâché figure. In their adaptation of the Chinese methodology, the Japanese identified 660 points.

CRITICAL THINKING

Mixing Medicines

Western physicians have been slow to accept acupuncture as a valid method of reducing pain, despite the fact that its use has continued to grow in America. Imagine that you are part of a research team that has just been given a grant to test the effectiveness of acupuncture compared to traditional methods of pain control, such as the use of aspirin. How would you design a research study that would allow us to determine its effectiveness? This exercise encourages you to *evaluate the validity of conclusions about behavior* by using psychological research as evidence.

The key to a well-designed outcome study would hinge on your use of three groups and good control procedures.

First, we would randomly assign subjects suffering the same kind of pain-inducing problem to one of three groups; one group would receive aspirin or some other traditional pain management approach, one group would receive acupuncture, and one group would be placed on a waiting list as a control group. The assignment would constitute the independent variable. We would need to measure subjective experiences of pain, the dependent variable, after a specific period of time. Other aspects of control would also enhance the final conclusion. What do you predict the results would be?

Reprinted with special permission of King Features Syndicate, Inc.

FIGURE 4.14

The Semicircular Canals and Vestibular Sense
(a) This is a photograph of the semicircular canals located in the ear. The semicircular canals play an important role in the vestibular sense. The three canals are roughly perpendicular to each other in three planes of space. Any angle of head rotation is registered by hair cells in one or more semicircular canals in both ears. *(b)* The semicircular canals provide feedback to this gymnast's brain as her body and head tilt in different directions.

feedback, which is the information about the position of your limbs and body parts in relation to other body parts. The **semicircular canals,** *located in the inner ear, contain sensory receptors that detect body motion, such as tilting of the*

head or body (see figure 4.14). These canals consist of three circular tubes that lie in three planes of the body—left-right, up-down, and front-back. The tubes provide feedback to the brain when the body or head tilts in one of these three directions.

Because the semicircular canals and the vestibular sense inform us about our equilibrium, this sense is sometimes called the *equilibratory sense.* The most accepted view of why we are able to maintain our equilibrium and orientation is that the brain is constantly receiving information about the body's motion and position from three sources: the inner ear, the eyes, and other sensors in various parts of the body. Information from these sources is fed into the brain, which compares it with stored information about motion and position. There are occasions when we might wish our equilibratory sense were not so sensitive. When motion sickness occurs, these various sources send contradictory messages. For example, passengers on a ship's deck can see the rail of the ship rising and falling as they watch the waves. The roll of the deck makes them feel like they are riding a roller coaster. The brain is not accustomed to all of this contradictory information. Over time, though, the brain recognizes that stored information is no longer relevant to the current discordant input. Two to three days usually is long enough to adjust to sensory conflict, but it can take longer.

The Chemical System

In the spring of 1985, a group of chemists practically turned American society upside down simply by shifting a few carbon, hydrogen, and oxygen atoms, or so it seemed when the Coca-Cola Company changed the formula for Coke. The uproar forced the company to bring back the original flavor that summer—even after spending millions of dollars advertising the virtues of the new Coke. The chemists at the Coca-Cola Company were dealing with the savor system, comprised of taste (gustation) and smell (olfaction). Both taste and smell differ from other senses—seeing, hearing, and the skin senses, for example—because they react to *chemicals,* whereas other senses react to *energy.* Together, smell and taste determine the flavors we experience when we ingest food and drink.

Taste

It won't be the prettiest sight you've ever seen, but try this anyway. Take a drink of milk and allow it to coat your tongue. Then go to a mirror, stick out your tongue, and look carefully at its surface. You should be able to see rounded bumps above the surface of your tongue (Matlin, 1983). Those bumps, called **papillae,** *contain your taste buds, the receptors for the taste sense.* Although the quantities of taste buds vary, taste buds are distributed on your tongue, around your mouth, and even in your throat.

Taste buds respond to four main qualities: sweet, bitter, salty, and sour. All areas of the tongue can detect each of these four tastes. Although many researchers have attempted to map zones of sensitivity on the tongue, clinical cases suggest that such concentrated areas do not exist. For example, individuals who have lost their tongues to cancer surgery still report taste sensitivity, which would not be possible if the tongue were more specialized in its transduction of the characteristics of food (Bartoshuk, 1994).

The efficiency of taste buds seems to vary according to genetic inheritance. For example, some individuals cannot tolerate diet sodas because of a heightened sensitivity to a bitter aftertaste. Others might happily guzzle the soda with no experience of an aftertaste. Research on these sensitivities has identified three categories of response to bitter tastes: nontasters, tasters, and supertasters, who show heightened responsiveness to bitter stimuli.

Babies are born with an innate preference for sweet tastes and a dislike of bitter substances. In addition, women appear to have greater sensitivity to sweet and bitter substances when they are pregnant or menstruating, suggesting that estrogen may be implicated in this gender-linked sensitivity. This causal relation is supported by initial observations that elderly women seem to have fewer papillae, reducing their effectiveness in sensing food characteristics (Bartoshuk, 1994). Older individuals' loss of interest in food could be the natural consequence of deteriorating taste bud responsiveness. This developmental outcome might explain why older individuals season their foods more heavily—as compensation for their diminished ability to taste.

From supper to bedtime is twice as long as from breakfast to supper.

Edna Ferber

The perception of taste in a food is a complex event that goes far beyond the sensory signals of the papillae on the tongue. For example, you have probably noticed that a good head cold substantially diminishes your ability to taste food. The influence of the head cold is not on the tongue but on the sense of smell. Flavor in food results from a combination of sensations from taste and **retronasal olfaction,** *the portion of the olfaction system involved in processing food-related smells.* We will explore the sense of smell next.

Smell

Smell is an important but mysterious sense. We take the time to see a sunset or a play, to hear a symphony or a rock concert, and to feel the tension leave our muscles during a massage. However, many of us do not take the time to indulge our sense of smell (Matlin, 1988). Smell can kindle pleasure or trigger discomfort—when we inhale the aroma of a fresh flower or when we encounter a skunk, for example. The nose actually serves two purposes. We sample the air from the outside world when we smell the scent of a fresh flower or the distinctly unpleasant aroma of the skunk. But we also sample the air from the inside of the mouth to enhance the taste of wine or the goodness of chocolate.

We detect the scent of a fresh flower or a skunk when airborne molecules of an odor reach tiny receptor cells in the roof of the nasal cavity (see figure 4.15). The **olfactory epithelium,** *located at the top of the nasal cavity, is the sheet of receptor cells for smell.* These receptor sites are covered with millions of minute, hairlike antennae that project through mucus in the nasal cavity and make contact with air on its way to the throat and lungs. Ordinarily only a small part of the air you inhale passes the smell receptors. That is why we sometimes have to sniff deeply to get the full odor of an interesting or alarming smell—the bouquet of a fine wine or the odor of escaping gas, for example. Doing so changes the normal flow of air so that more air, with its odorous molecules, contacts the receptors.

You just read about how taste can be classified into four main categories: sweet, sour, salty, and bitter. Are there agreed-upon main categories of odors too? Some researchers argue that there are seven primary odors—floral, peppermint, ethereal (as in the gas ether), musky, camphoraceous (such as the odor of mothballs), pungent, and putrid (Amoore, 1970). However, the consensus is that olfactory researchers have yet to demonstrate that different categories of smell have distinct chemical makeups and receptor sites on the olfactory epithelium.

Unlike the sense of taste, in which infants show immediate preferences at birth and even in utero, babies do not show innate preferences for smell. Preferences for smell must be learned from consequences or by modeling (Bartoshuk, 1994).

Smell is the potent wizard that transports us across thousands of miles and all the years we have lived.

Helen Keller

How good are you at recognizing smells? Without practice, most people do a rather poor job of identifying odors; however, the human olfactory sense can be improved. Perfumers, as perfume testers are called, can distinguish between 100 and 200 fragrances. If you have or have had a dog, though, you probably know that canines have a keener sense of smell than humans do. One reason is that a dog's smell receptors are located along the main airflow route and its smell-receptor sites are 100 times larger than a human's.

We have examined all the sensory systems that bring stimulation from the environment to the brain for further processing. Next, we will explore the nature of perception.

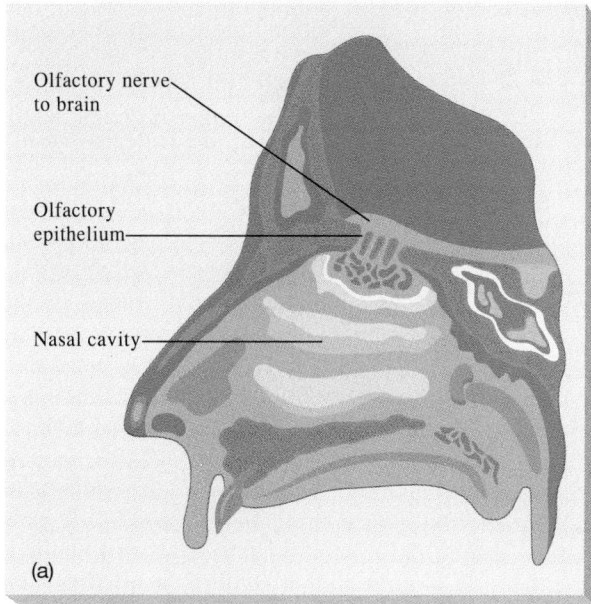

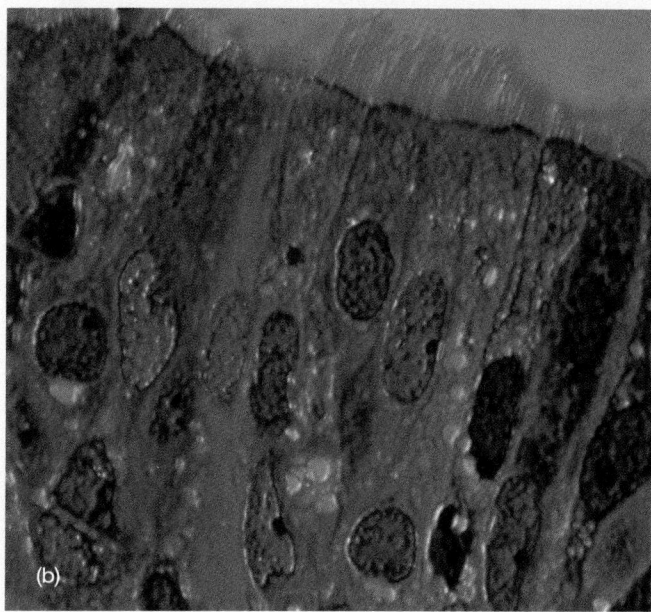

FIGURE 4.15

The Olfactory Sense
(a) Airborne molecules of an odor reach tiny receptor cells in the roof of our nasal cavity. The receptor cells form a mucus-covered membrane called the olfactory epithelium. Then the olfactory nerve carries information about the odor to the brain for further processing. (b) Shown here is a microphotograph of the olfactory epithelium with the minute hairlike antennae.

REVIEW

The Auditory System, the Haptic System, and the Chemical System

Sound waves vary in frequency, amplitude, and complexity; the perceptions are pitch, loudness, and timbre, respectively. The ear comprises the outer ear, the middle ear, and the inner ear. The basilar membrane, located inside the cochlea in the inner ear, is where vibrations are changed into nerve impulses. There are three main theories of hearing. Place theory emphasizes a particular place on the basilar membrane; frequency theory stresses the frequency of auditory nerve firing; and volley theory is a modification and expansion of frequency theory to handle high-frequency sounds. Frequency theory is better for explaining lower-frequency sounds, volley and place theories for higher-frequency sounds.

The haptic system involves touch, the kinesthetic senses, and the vestibular sense. Skin contains three important senses: pressure, temperature (warmth, cold), and pain. Pain has the important adaptive function of informing us when something is wrong with our body. No theory of pain is completely accepted. Gate-control theory has been given considerable weight. The kinesthetic senses provide information about movement, posture, and orientation. The vestibular sense provides information about balance and movement. The chemical senses—taste and smell—differ from other senses in that they react to chemicals rather than energy.

Computer Science, Engineering, and Psychology

Computer scientists and engineers have been making their presence felt in the study of perception for nearly two decades (O'Toole, 1994). In attempting to build machines/robots with simple perceptual abilities, computer scientists and engineers ask questions about perception that psychologists and scientists from other biologically based domains had not previously considered. Consider the following dilemma. A nuclear reactor accident makes a large area of a power plant unsafe for human beings. A simple mechanical adjustment needs to be performed on a machine in an unsafe area. Wouldn't it be nice to be able to send a robot to make such an adjustment? The robot might have to get on an elevator—push a few buttons, navigate to the correct room (watching out for furniture and walls), unscrew a screw and replace a part, and verify that it is secure. This requires a great deal more than a sensory system—it requires an ability to perceive the positions and shapes of objects. It requires the ability not only to discern shapes but also to identify objects of interest.

As computers become more sophisticated and the workplace becomes more mechanized, computer scientists and engineers are faced with more and more design problems of this sort. These researchers have made many discoveries about the nature of perception as a computational problem. One of the most important of these discoveries is that the problem is *much harder* than anyone with a functioning perceptual system would imagine. Perception seems so effortless for us that it is hard to believe that getting a computer to perceive is difficult. *Why is it difficult to get a computer to perceive?* By expanding the scope of inquiry across several domains, scientists who have addressed this question quickly realized that, despite a few surface commonalities (such as an input and output mechanism, and some internal computational abilities), the standard digital computer is nothing like a brain.

In contrast to the simple logical structure of a digital computer, the human brain is an immense conglomeration of approximately 100 billion neurons hooked up in various combinations via synapses. Even though the standard digital computer can transmit information at far greater speeds than neurons can, the brain manages to use neurons to compute the answers to perceptual problems at speeds that leave even the fastest of digital computers in the dust. One reason for the brain's ability to operate at speeds in excess of the average computer is that the brain inherently uses parallel processing, which means that neurons are organized in a way that makes it possible for many neurons to work on a problem at the same time. The average digital computer is forced to process events in a serial fashion, working on the parts of a problem one at a time. A simple example of the parallel nature of information processing in the brain can be seen by looking at the wonderful human ability to perform many perceptual and cognitive processes at the same time. We can listen to and appreciate music while we read; we can change a baby's diaper while listening intently to a friend on the telephone; we can knit while watching television.

PERCEPTION

Earlier in this chapter, you learned that perception is the brain's process of organizing and interpreting sensory information to give it meaning. When perception goes to work, sensory receptors have received energy from stimuli in the external world and sensory organs have processed and transformed the information so it can be transmitted to the brain. Perception is a creation of the brain; it is based on input from sensory organs, such as the eye, ear, and nose. However, perception goes beyond this input. The brain uses previous information as a basis for making educated guesses, or interpretations, about the state of the outside world. Usually the interpretations are correct and useful. For example, on the basis of a perceived change in color or texture, we can conclude that a dog is on the rug. On the basis of a continuous increase in size, we can conclude that a train is coming toward us. Sometimes, though, the interpretations or inferences are wrong; the result is an illusion—we see something that is not there. Our exploration of perceptual worlds evaluates the following questions: How do we perceive shape, depth, motion, and constancy? What are perceptual illusions and why do we see these illusions? Is perception innate or learned? What is extrasensory perception? Is it real? To read about ways that computer science and engineering are involved in the study of perception, turn to Applications in Psychology 4.1.

FIGURE 4.16

A Demonstration of the Automatic and Selective Qualities of Perception
Are you certain you read the contents accurately? How many words are in the triangle?

FIGURE 4.17

Reversible Figure-Ground Pattern
Either a goblet or a pair of silhouetted faces in profile can be seen.

Blessed is he who expects nothing, for he shall never be disappointed.

Jonathan Swift

Perceptual Processes

Whether we are organizing the diverse sounds of the instruments of an orchestra to appreciate a movement in a symphony or interpreting the complex visual action of a soccer game, perception determines how we will experience the environment. Perceptual processes, regardless of the sensory mode in which they operate, have four characteristics; they are *automatic, selective, contextual,* and *creative.* We do not have to be purposeful in organizing our sensory input. It happens *automatically.* Quickly read aloud the phrase in the triangle in figure 4.16 for an illustration of this characteristic. Perceptual preferences tend to influence what we experience, leading to perceptual *selectivity.* Leaving out a portion of the message within the triangle demonstrates how selective we can be. For another example, if you develop a crush on a film star, you might focus on the actor rather than on the action in the movie. Perception is *contextual;* our expectations about being scared in a haunted house enhance our fearful reactions to the sights and sounds within. Finally, our perceptual systems are *creative;* they help us fill in incomplete information, whether this information prevents us from having a visual blind spot or completes an unresolved chord in our auditory imagination. In total, these characteristics contribute to the development of a **perceptual set,** *expectations that influence how perceptual elements will be interpreted.* Perceptual sets act as filters in how we process information about the environment.

Next, we will look at shape perception, depth perception, and perceptual constancy as examples of perceptual processes in vision.

Shape Perception

Think about the world you see and its shapes—buildings against the sky, boats on the horizon, letters on this page. We see these shapes because they are marked off from the rest of what we see by **contour,** *a location at which a sudden change of brightness occurs.* Think about the letters on this page again. As you look at the page, you see letters, which are shapes, in a field or background, the white page. The **figure-ground relationship** *is the principle by which we organize the perceptual field into stimuli that stand out (figure) and those that are left over (ground).* Some figure-ground relationships, though, are highly ambiguous, and it is difficult to tell what is figure and what is ground. A well-known ambiguous figure-ground relationship is shown in figure 4.17. As you look at the figure, your perception is likely to shift between seeing two faces or a single goblet. Another example of figure-ground ambiguity is found in the work of artist M. C. Escher, which keeps us from favoring one figure over another, seemingly because spatial location and depth cues are not provided (see figure 4.18).

One group of psychologists has been especially intrigued by how we perceive shapes in our world—the Gestalt psychologists. **Gestalt psychology** *is an approach that states that people naturally organize their perceptions*

FIGURE 4.18

Sophisticated Use of Figure-Ground Relationship in Escher's Woodcut *Relativity* (1938)

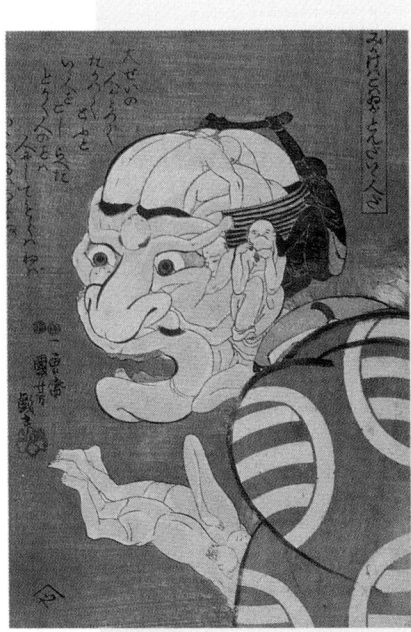

FIGURE 4.19

Example of the Gestalt Principle That the Whole Does Not Equal the Sum of the Parts
In *A Kindly Man of Fearful Aspect* by Kuniyoshi Ichiyusai, the configuration of the whole is clearly qualitatively different than the sum of its parts.

according to certain patterns; Gestalt is a German word that means "configuration" or "form." One of Gestalt psychology's main principles is that *the whole is not equal to the sum of its parts.* For example, when you watch a movie, the motion you see in the film cannot be found in the film itself; if you examine the film, you see only separate frames—but you see many of them per second. When you watch the film, you perceive a whole that is very different from the individual pictures that are its parts. Figure 4.19 also illustrates this fundamental principle of Gestalt psychology.

The figure-ground relationship just described is another Gestalt principle. Three other Gestalt principles are closure, proximity, and similarity. The principle of *closure* states that, when individuals see a disconnected or incomplete figure, they fill in the spaces and see it as a complete figure (see figure 4.20a). The principle of *proximity* states that, when individuals see objects close to each other, they tend to group them together (see figure 4.20b). The principle of *similarity* states that, the more similar objects are, the more likely we are to group them together (see figure 4.20c). By turning to figure 4.21, you can observe some of the basic principles of Gestalt psychology in a famous artist's work.

Depth Perception

The images we see of the world appear on our retinas in two-dimensional form, yet we see a three-dimensional world. **Depth perception** *is the ability to perceive objects three-dimensionally.* Look at the setting you are in. You don't see it as flat. You see some objects farther away, some closer. Some objects overlap. The scene you are looking at and the objects in it have depth. How do we see depth? We use both binocular and monocular cues. **Binocular cues** *are depth cues that are based on both eyes working together.* **Monocular cues** *are depth cues based on each eye working independently.*

People with vision in only one eye do not have binocular cues for depth perception available to them, but they still see a world of depth. They can still see depth because of monocular cues that can be perceived by one eye only. Following are four monocular cues:

1. *Linear perspective.* The farther an object is from the viewer, the less space it takes up in the visual field. As an object recedes in the distance, parallel lines in the object converge.

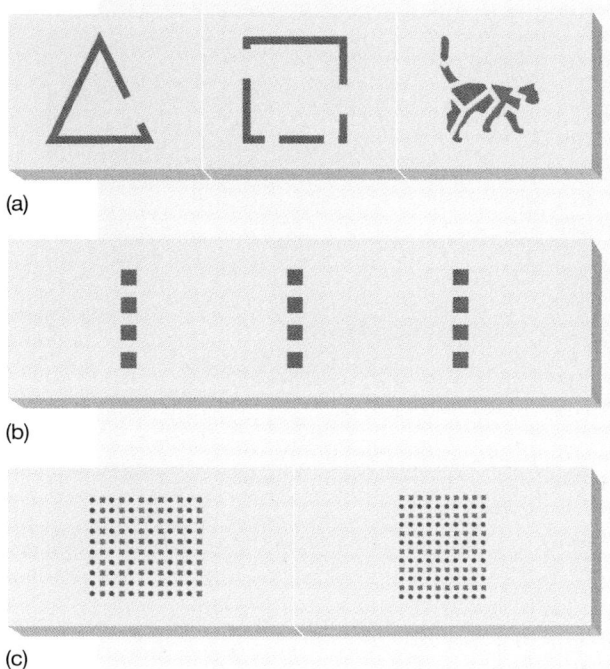

(a)

(b)

(c)

FIGURE 4.20

Gestalt Principles of Closure, Proximity, and Similarity
(a) Closure: when we see disconnected or incomplete figures, we fill in the spaces and see them as complete figures. *(b)* Proximity: when we see objects that are near each other, they tend to be seen as a unit. You are likely to perceive the grouping as 3 columns of 4 squares, not 1 set of 12 squares. *(c)* Similarity: when we see objects that are similar to each other, they tend to be seen as a unit. In this display, you are likely to see vertical columns of circles and squares in the left box but horizontal rows of circles and squares in the right box.

2. *Texture gradient.* Texture becomes denser the farther away it is from the viewer.
3. *Relative size.* Objects farther away create a smaller retinal image than those nearby.
4. *Interposition.* An object that partially conceals or overlaps another object is perceived as closer.

Located several inches apart above your nose, your two eyes see the world from slightly different locations. **Retinal or binocular disparity** *is the perception in which an individual sees a single scene, even though the images on the eyes are slightly different.* The brain blends the two sets of overlapping information it receives from the retinas into a single image that gives the proper impression of depth and distance. Retinal disparity is one binocular cue that helps us see depth. **Convergence** *is a binocular cue for depth perception in which the eyes turn more inward as an object gets closer. When the eyes converge or diverge, information is sent to the brain, which interprets the information about the inward (object is closer) or outward (object is farther away) eye movement.* To experience convergence, hold your finger at

FIGURE 4.21

Gestalt Principles of Closure, Proximity, and Similarity in Picasso's *The Nude Woman*, 1910
Look at the painting and think about some of the Gestalt principles of perception that are incorporated. The nude is an incomplete figure. You have to fill in the spaces to make it a complete figure (principle of closure). Both the principles of proximity and similarity cause you to see the two objects toward the bottom of the painting as feet.

arm's length and then slowly move it to a point between your eyes. As you move your finger closer, you have to turn your eyes inward to follow it.

Depth perception is especially intriguing to artists. Their challenge is to depict the three-dimensional world on a two-dimensional canvas. As shown in figure 4.22, artists often use monocular cues to give the feeling of depth to their paintings. Indeed, monocular cues have become so widely used by artists that they have also been called *pictorial cues.*

FIGURE 4.22

An Artist's Use of the Monocular Cue of Linear Perspective
Famous landscape artist J. M. W. Turner used linear perspective to give the perception of depth to his painting *Rain, Steam, and Speed.*

Perceptual Constancy

Retinal images are constantly changing as we experience our world. Even though the stimuli that fall on the retinas of our eyes change as we move closer to or farther away from objects, or as we look at objects from different orientations and in light or dark settings, we perceive objects as unchanging. We experience three types of perceptual constancies: size constancy, shape constancy, and brightness constancy. **Size constancy** *is the recognition that an object remains the same size even though the retinal image of the object changes* (see figure 4.23). **Shape constancy** *is the recognition that an object remains the same shape even though its orientation to us changes.* Look around the room in which you are reading this book. You probably see objects of various shapes—chairs and tables, for example. If you walk around the room, you will see these objects from different sides and angles. Even though the retinal image of the object changes as you walk, you still perceive the objects as being the same shape (see figure 4.24).

FIGURE 4.23

Size Constancy
Why do these hot air balloons look as if they are different sizes, yet when asked, people would say they are all about the same size?

Figure 4.24

Shape Constancy
The various projected images from an opening door are quite different, yet you perceive a rectangular door.

Brightness constancy *is the recognition that an object retains the same degree of brightness even when different amounts of light fall on it.* For example, regardless of whether you are reading this book indoors or outdoors, the white pages and the black print do not look any different to you in terms of their whiteness or blackness.

How are we able to resolve the discrepancy between a retinal image of an object and its actual size, shape, and brightness? Experience is important. For example, no matter how far away you are from your car, you know how large it is. Not only is familiarity important in size constancy, but so are binocular and monocular distance cues. Even if we have never previously seen an object, these cues provide us with information about an object's size. Many visual illusions are influenced by our perception of size constancy.

Illusions

A **visual illusion** *occurs when two objects produce exactly the same retinal image but are perceived as different images.* Illusions are incorrect, but they are not abnormal. They can provide insight into how our perceptual processes work. More than 200 types of illusions have been discovered; we will study five.

One of the most famous is the Müller-Lyer illusion, shown in figure 4.25. The two lines are exactly the same length, although *b* looks longer than *a*. Another illusion is the horizontal-vertical illusion (see figure 4.26), in which the vertical line looks longer than the horizontal line, even though the two are equal. The Ponzo illusion is another line illusion in which the top line looks much longer than the bottom line (see figure 4.27).

Why do these line illusions trick us? One reason is that we mistakenly use certain cues for maintaining size constancy. For example, in the Ponzo illusion, we see the upper line as being farther away (remember that objects higher in a picture are perceived as being farther away).

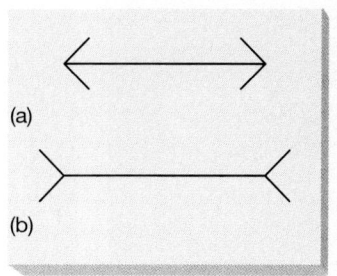

Figure 4.25

Müller-Lyer Illusion
The two lines are exactly the same length, although *(b)* looks longer than *(a)*.

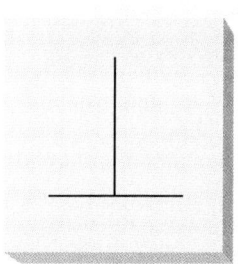

Figure 4.26

The Horizontal-Vertical Illusion
The vertical line looks longer than the horizontal line, but they are the same length.

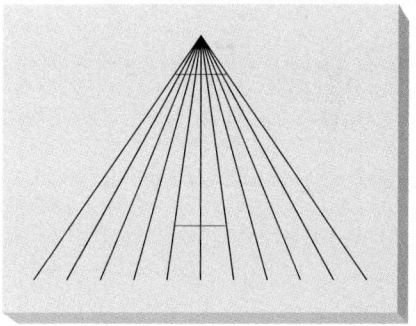

Figure 4.27

Ponzo Illusion
The top line looks much longer than the bottom line, but they are equal in length.

The Müller-Lyer illusion, though, is not as easily explained. We may make our judgments about the lines by comparing incorrect parts of the figures. For example, when people were shown the Müller-Lyer illusion with the wings painted a different color than the horizontal lines,

FIGURE 4.28

The Moon Illusion
The moon illusion is that when the moon is on the horizon *(a)*, it looks much larger than when it is high in the sky, directly above us *(b)*. *Why does the moon look so much larger on the horizon?*

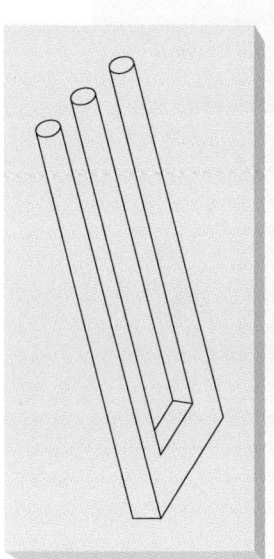

FIGURE 4.29

Devil's Tuning Fork

the illusion was greatly reduced (Coren & Girus, 1972). Shortly we also will discuss how cultural experiences influence an individual's perception of the Müller-Lyer illusion.

Another well-known illusion is the moon illusion (see figure 4.28). The moon is 2,000 miles in diameter and 289,000 miles away. Since both the moon's size and its distance from us are beyond our own experience, we have difficulty judging how far away it really is. When the moon is high in the sky, directly above us, little information is present to help us judge its distance—no texture gradients or stereoscopic cues exist, for example. However, when the moon is on the horizon, we can judge its distance in relation to familiar objects—trees and buildings, for example—which make it appear farther away. The result is that we estimate the size of the moon as much larger when it is on the horizon than when it is overhead (Hershenson, 1989).

The devil's tuning fork is another fascinating illusion. Look at figure 4.29 for about 30 seconds, then close the book. Now try to draw the tuning fork. You undoubtedly found this a difficult, if not impossible, task. Why? Since the figure's depth cues are ambiguous, you had problems interpreting it correctly.

Is Perception Innate or Learned?

One long-standing question in psychology is whether or not perception is innate (inborn, unlearned) or learned. Researchers have tried to unravel this nature-nurture question on depth perception in a number of ways: through experiments with infants, studies of individuals (like Virgil, whom you read about at the beginning of the chapter) who recover from blindness, and cross-cultural studies about how people perceive their world.

The Visual Cliff

An experiment by Eleanor Gibson and Richard Walk (1960) indicates that, by at least 6 months of age, infants have an understanding of depth. Gibson and Walk constructed a miniature cliff with a shallow side and a drop-off that was covered by firm glass (see figure 4.30). This structure is known as a *visual cliff*. Infants old enough to crawl (6 months and older) were placed on the shallow side. The infants stayed in place and did not venture out onto the glass-covered drop-off, indicating that they perceived depth. However, infants at 6 months are old enough to have encountered many situations where they could have *learned* to perceive depth, so the visual cliff experiment failed to provide convincing evidence that depth perception is innate. Whether or not infants younger than 6 months perceive depth is controversial.

Other studies have shown that, during the first month of life, human infants turn away to avoid objects that move

B. C.   by Johnny hart

By permission of Johnny Hart and Creators Syndicate, Inc.

directly toward them but do not turn away when objects move toward them at angles at which they would not collide with them (Ball & Tronick, 1971). Also, animals with little visual experience—including day-old goats and just-hatched chicks—respond just as 6-month-old infants do; they remain on the visual cliff's shallow side and do not venture out onto the glass-covered drop-off. These studies suggest that some of the ability to perceive depth is innate.

FIGURE 4.30

Visual Cliff
The visual cliff was developed by Eleanor Gibson and Richard Walk (1960). The infant shown here hesitates as he moves onto the glass-covered drop-off, the deep side of the visual cliff. In the study, even when coaxed by their mothers, the infants were still reluctant to venture out onto the deep drop-off, indicating they could perceive depth.

Recovery from Blindness

In further attempts to determine whether or not depth perception is innate, psychologists have also studied people who were born blind, or became blind shortly after birth, and whose sight later was restored by medical procedures. If the ability to interpret sensory information is innate, such people should be able to see their world clearly after they recover from the operation. Consider S. B., blind since birth, who had a successful corneal transplant at the age of 52 (Gregory, 1978). Soon after his bandages were removed, S. B. was able to recognize common objects, identify the letters of the alphabet, and tell time from a clock. However, S. B. had some perceptual deficiencies. Although his eyes functioned effectively, S. B. had difficulty perceiving objects he had not previously touched (see figure 4.31).

The findings for formerly blind persons also do not answer the question of whether perception is innate or learned. Some people recognize objects soon after their bandages are removed; others require weeks of training before they recognize such simple shapes as a triangle. Neural connections, such as those between the eyes and the brain, can deteriorate from disuse, so a person whose sight has been restored after a lifetime of blindness may have an impaired ability to perceive visual information. Further, previously blind adults, unlike infants, have already experienced the world through their nonvisual senses, such as touch and hearing, and those perceptual systems may continue to contribute to their perception after they regain their vision.

Culture and Perception

Whereas our biological inheritance equips us with some elegant perceptual capabilities, our experiences also contribute to how we perceive the world. Some cross-cultural psychologists have proposed that the demands of various cultures lead to a greater emphasis on certain senses (Wober, 1966). For example, hunters who have to stalk small game animals might develop their kinesthetic senses more than office workers in highly industrialized nations do.

Cross-cultural psychologists have been especially interested in how people from different cultures perceive visual illusions (Segall & others, 1990). The **carpentered-world hypothesis** *states that people who live in cultures in which straight lines, right angles, and rectangles predominate (in which rooms and buildings are usually rectangular, and many objects, such as city streets, have square corners) should be more susceptible to illusions involving straight lines, right angles, and rectangles (such as the Müller-Lyer illusion) than people who live in noncarpentered cultures are.* These people have learned to interpret nonrectangular figures as

FIGURE 4.31

S. B.'s Drawings of a Bus After His Recovery from Blindness
S. B. drew the bus at the top 48 days after a corneal transplant restored his vision, and he drew the bus at the bottom a year after the operation. Both drawings reflect more detail for the parts of the bus S. B. used or touched while he was blind than the parts he did not use or touch. In the bottom drawing, notice the absence of the front of the bus, which S. B. never touched.

The Zulu live in isolated regions of southeastern Africa in a world of open spaces and curves. Their huts are round with round doors, and they even plow their fields in curved, rather than straight, furrows. As the carpentered-world hypothesis would predict, the Zulu are not very susceptible to the Müller-Lyer illusion.

rectangular, to perceive figures in perspective, and to interpret them as two-dimensional representations of three-dimensional objects. This tendency enhances the Müller-Lyer illusion (see figure 4.25). For example, the Zulu in isolated regions of southeastern Africa live in a world of open spaces and curves. Their huts are round with round doors, and they even plow their fields in curved, rather than straight, furrows. According to the carpentered-world hypothesis, the Zulu would not be very susceptible to the Müller-Lyer illusion. Cross-cultural psychologists have found this to be the case (Segall, Campbell, & Herskovits, 1963).

Another example in which culture shapes perception is found in Pygmies who live in the dense rain forests of the African Congo. Because of the thick vegetation, the Pygmies rarely see objects at long distances. Anthropologist Colin Turnbull (1961) observed that, when the Pygmies traveled to the African plains and saw buffalo on the horizon, they thought the animals were tiny insects and not huge buffalo. The Pygmies' lack of experience with distant objects probably accounts for their inability to perceive size constancy. More information about cultural influences on perception is presented in Sociocultural Worlds 4.2, where you will read about the role of experience with three-dimensional objects.

It seems that both nature and nurture are responsible for the way we perceive the world. One view of how the two influences interact to shape perception is that all people, regardless of culture, have the same perceptual processes and the same potential for perceptual development, but cultural factors determine what is learned and at what age (Kagitcibasi & Berry, 1989; Irvine & Berry, 1988). So far we have discussed perception in terms of shape, depth, constancy, illusion, and whether or not perception is innate or learned. However, we will also briefly discuss another, curious realm of perceptual phenomena—extrasensory perception.

Extrasensory Perception

Our eyes, ears, mouth, nose, and skin provide us with sensory information about the external world. Our perceptions are based on our interpretation of this sensory information. Some people, though, claim they can perceive the world through something other than normal sensory pathways. Literally, **extrasensory perception (ESP)** *is perception that occurs without the use of known sensory processes.* The majority of psychologists do not believe in ESP; however, a small number of psychologists do investigate it (Persinger & Krippner, in press).

Extrasensory experiences fall into three main categories. The first is **telepathy,** *which involves the transfer of*

Perceiving Three-Dimensionality in Two-Dimensional Drawings in Different Cultures

You probably had difficulty drawing the Devil's tuning fork in figure 4.29. The world you live in bombards you with visual representations of three-dimensional objects in two-dimensional form—such as billboards, travel posters, and artwork in magazines. Your eyes are constantly taking in information in a two-dimensional format, which your brain then perceives as three-dimensional, so even though the tuning fork had ambiguous depth cues, your brain interpreted it as a three-dimensional object. Africans who have no formal education easily reproduce the Devil's tuning fork. Why? Because they don't interpret the form as three-dimensional. We see a "Devil's tuning fork"; they simply see a pattern of flat lines they can easily reproduce.

Researchers have also investigated people from isolated tribes to determine if they have difficulty perceiving depth in two-dimensional drawings or photographs (Deregowski, 1980; Hudson, 1960). For example, look at figure 4.A, a drawing used to test the ability to respond to pictorial depth cues. A person responding to pictorial depth would say that the hunter is trying to spear the antelope (which would appear nearer to the hunter than the elephant is).

Conversely, a person responding only to the two-dimensional cues would say that the hunter is trying to spear the elephant, which is actually closer to the spear's tip in the picture. This interpretation would indicate that the observer had not responded to the depth cues (such as the fact that the antelope partially conceals the hill, meaning it is closer to the hunter) that place the elephant at a greater distance from the hunter.

In Hudson's examination of cultures, although education and intellectual endowment were related to depth perception in Western cultures, this was not the case with the African Bantu tribe. Hudson hypothesized that it was exposure to pictures at a preschool age that influenced performance, since the Bantu live in environments that do not include many pictorial materials. Perception, as with most complex human abilities, is influenced by several factors in both Western and non-Western cultures. No matter how smart you are or how much you have achieved in school spelling and arithmetic, if you have not seen many pictures, it is unlikely that you would immediately be able to perceive depth cues.

FIGURE 4.A

Drawing Used to Assess the Perception of Pictorial Cues for Depth in Different Cultures

Adapted from "Pictorial Perception and Culture" by Jean B. Dergowski. Copyright © 1992 by Scientific American, Inc. All rights reserved.

thought from one person to another. For example, this skill is supposedly possessed by people who can "read" another person's mind. If two people are playing cards and one person can tell what cards the other person picks up, telepathy is taking place (see figure 4.32). **Precognition** *involves "knowing" events before they happen.* For example, a fortune teller might claim to see into the future and tell you what will happen to you in the coming year. **Clairvoyance** *involves the ability to perceive remote events that are not in sight.* For example, a person at a movie theater "sees" a burglar breaking into his house at that moment. **Psychokinesis,** *closely associated with ESP, is the mind-over-matter*

phenomenon of being able to move objects without touching them, such as mentally getting a chair to rise off the floor or shattering a glass merely by concentrating on doing so.

One of the most famous claims of ESP involved Uri Geller, a psychic who supposedly performed mind-boggling feats. Observers saw Geller correctly predict the number on a die rolled in a closed box eight out of eight times, reproduce drawings that were hidden in sealed envelopes, bend forks without touching them, and start broken watches. Although he had worked as a magician, Geller claimed his supernatural powers were created by energy sent from another universe. Careful investigation of Geller's feats revealed they were nothing more than a magician's tricks. For example, in the case of the die, Geller was allowed to shake the box and open it himself, giving him an opportunity to manipulate the die (Randi, 1980).

> A psychic is an actor playing the role of a psychic.
>
> **Daryl Bem**

Through their astonishing stage performances, many psychics are very convincing. They seemingly are able to levitate tables, communicate with spirits, and read an audience member's mind. Many psychics, such as Uri Geller, are also magicians, who have the ability to perform sleight-of-hand maneuvers and dramatic manipulations that go unnoticed by most human eyes. One magician's personal goal, though, is to expose the hoaxes of such psychics. James Randi (1980) has investigated a number of psychics' claims and publicized their failures (see figure 4.33).

Not only have magicians, such as Randi, investigated some psychics' claims, but scientists have also examined ESP in experimental contexts. Some ESP enthusiasts believe that the phenomenon is more likely to occur when a subject is totally relaxed and deprived of sensory input. In this kind of ESP experiment, the subject lies down, and half a Ping-Pong ball is affixed over each eye with cotton and tape. An experimenter watches through a one-way mirror from an adjacent room, listening to and recording the subject's statements. At an agreed-upon time, someone from another location concentrates on the message to be sent mind-to-mind.

Carl Sargent (1987) has used this procedure in a number of telepathy experiments and reported a great deal of success. In one experiment, Sargent had a "sender" mentally transmit an image of one of four pictures selected from 1 of 27 randomly selected sets of four pictures. Immediately afterward, the experimenter and the subject examined a duplicate set of four pictures and together judged and ranked their degree of correspondence with the subject's recorded impression. Experimental psychologist Susan Blackmore (1987) was skeptical about Sargent's success in ESP experiments, so she visited his laboratory at Cambridge University in England and observed a number of his telepathy sessions. With the subject shown four pictures, the success rate expected by chance was 25 percent (one of four pictures). In the experimental sessions Blackmore observed, the subjects' hit rate was 50 percent, far exceeding chance.

Sargent supposedly invokes a number of elaborate procedures to protect randomization, experimenter bias,

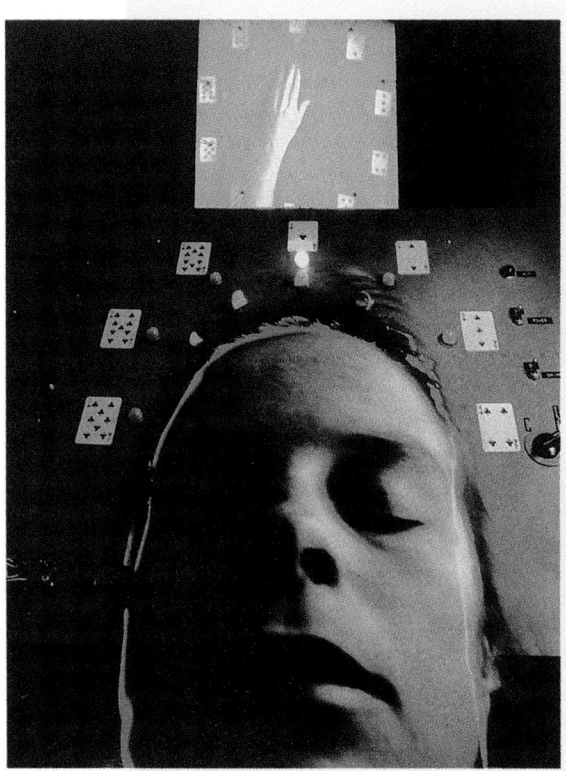

FIGURE 4.32

An Experimental Situation Involving an Attempt to Demonstrate Telepathy
At the top (blue insert), a person in one room tries to "send" a message through thought to a person (the subject) in another room. The sender selects a card and then attempts to relay the information mentally to the subject. The subject then selects a card, and it is compared to the one previously chosen by the sender to see if the cards match. If the mind-to-mind communication occurs beyond chance, then it would be argued that telepathy has taken place.

FIGURE 4.33

Magician James Randi
Randi has a standing offer of $10,000 to anyone whose psychic claims can withstand his analysis. No one has yet claimed Randi's $10,000 prize.

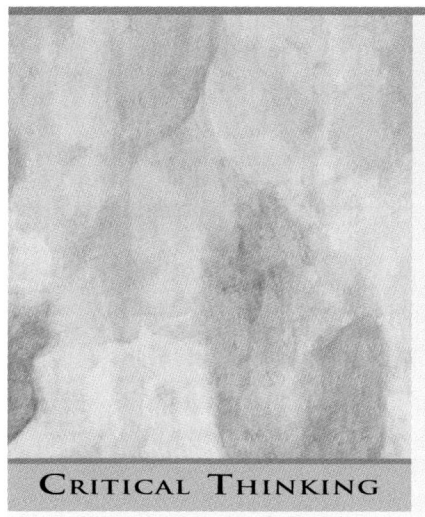

ESP Versus Science

Psychologists pride themselves on being open-minded, yet when it comes to extrasensory perception, they are almost uniformly skeptical. Why would they take such a hard line on discouraging belief in ESP? There are three main reasons. First, there is no known physical mechanism of sensation and perception that could account for the transduction of others' thoughts. Second, there has been no objective, controlled evidence, to date, that reliably demonstrates ESP. Illusionist Randi has offered an enormous sum to anyone who can demonstrate extrasensory abilities in any way that he cannot explain away as an illusion. So far, he has been able to keep his money in the bank. Third, psychologists have an underlying concern for the harm that could be done to unsuspecting believers.

Where do you stand on the existence of ESP? What values do you hold that support your belief? Do you require objective evidence to support your belief regarding the existence of ESP, or has subjective experience been more persuasive to you? Your position will reflect your *awareness of the underlying values that motivate behavior.*

---

unbiased selection by the subject, and so on. Blackmore was still skeptical, finding some disturbing flaws in the way Sargent's experiments were conducted. In some sessions, he randomized the pictures himself, putting himself where he could manipulate the order of the pictures. In other sessions, he came in while the subject was judging the pictures and "pushed" the subject toward the picture that had been "transmitted by the sender."

No one has been able to replicate the high hit rates in Sargent's experiments. Proponents of ESP, such as Sargent, claim they have demonstrated the existence of ESP, but critics, like Blackmore, demand to see or experience the same phenomena themselves. Replication is one of the hallmarks of scientific investigation, yet replication has been a major thorn in the side of ESP researchers. ESP phenomena have not been reproducible when rigorous experimental standards have been applied (Hines, 1988).

In the next chapter, we will explore many other aspects of our awareness, both of the external world and the internal world. Sleep, dreams, altered states of consciousness, and the influence of drugs on mental processes and behavior are discussed in chapter 5.

REVIEW

Perception

Shape is perceived because it is marked off by contour. An important aspect is figure-ground relationship. Gestalt psychologists have developed a number of principles of perceptual organization, a fundamental one being that the whole is not equal to the sum of its parts. Depth perception is our ability to perceive objects as three-dimensional. To see a world of depth, we use binocular cues, such as retinal disparity and convergence, and monocular cues (also called pictorial cues), such as linear perspective, texture gradient, relative size, and interposition. Perceptual constancy includes size, shape, and brightness. Experience with objects and with distance cues helps us see objects as unchanging.

Illusions occur when two objects produce exactly the same retinal image but are perceived as different images. Among the more than 200 visual illusions are the Müller-Lyer illusion and the moon illusion. Perceptual constancies and cultural experiences are among the factors responsible for illusions.

Is perception innate or learned? Experiments using the visual cliff with young infants and animals indicate that some of the ability to perceive depth is innate. Investigations of formerly blind adults are inconclusive with regard to whether perception is innate or learned.

Our experiences contribute to how we perceive the world. People in different cultures do not always perceive the world in the same way. The carpentered-world hypothesis and varying abilities to respond to depth cues in two-dimensional drawings across cultures reveal how experiences influence perception.

Extrasensory perception is perception that does not occur through normal sensory channels. Three main forms are telepathy, precognition, and clairvoyance. Psychokinesis is a closely related phenomenon. The claims of ESP enthusiasts have not held up to scientific scrutiny.

The Creative Brain

In chapters 2 and 3 you have studied the impressive abilities of the brain, the command center of the central nervous system. There is much we can marvel at about the brain. It weighs only 3 pounds. It never rests. It seems to have an unlimited capacity for performance. We use only a portion of its potential.

One of the most interesting features of the brain and the perceptual systems within it is our capacity to fill in missing information. The simplest example of this phenomenon is the blind spot. You have two holes in your visual field, corresponding to where the optic nerve attaches to the back of the retina, yet you do not see these holes. You see a unified field of vision because the brain creatively fills in the holes to be consistent with the surrounding information.

However, the same creative ability that assists our adaptation can also make life more complicated. For example, many of us commonly experience a perceptual illusion that is most annoying, due to the brain's capacity to create explanations. Have you ever heard the phone ringing after you have stepped into the shower, only to find that it stopped as soon as you left the shower? Someone might have been trying to get in touch with you; however, it is more likely that you suffered a hallucination. The phone-ringing hallucination is a compelling one that illustrates the extent to which the brain automatically processes information and creates text to explain perceptions.

Let's examine a second example. You are home alone. You begin to hear odd noises. The floorboards of the house creak. The wind howls. You begin to consider all the possibilities that would explain this set of disturbances. It gets worse. You feel a cold wind across your cheek. You might hear your name spoken. The curtain moves suddenly. Is it an intruder? Is it a ghost? Your active imagination creates an explanatory text that gives you a sense of control over the environment and may prompt you to take some self-protective action even if the explanation isn't valid.

A final example of the brain's creativity involves grief. A surprising number of people report that when a loved one dies, they experience some unsettling perceptions. Mourning individuals sometimes report that they hear the voice of the loved one. Some see the loved one. These hallucinations appear to be a normal part of grieving, enhanced by a brain and its perceptual systems eager to make comforting interpretations.

How might our brain's creativity be related to convictions about extrasensory perception? If we are convinced that extrasensory phenomena are real, then we are more likely to experience events that support the beliefs. In contrast, if we are disbelievers, our perceptual set is likely to encourage different interpretations of the same perceptual cues.

How many of these circumstances have you experienced? You might have thought yourself a bit mad at the time, but these experiences simply attest to the brain's power to interpret perceptual experiences creatively. Psychologists believe that maintaining a skeptical outlook is probably one of the best ways to overcome our tendencies to arrive at inappropriate conclusions about our own experiences. Practicing skepticism encourages *making accurate observations, descriptions, and inferences.*

Imagination frames events unknown,
In wild, fantastic shapes of hideous ruin,
And what it fears, creates.

Hannah More

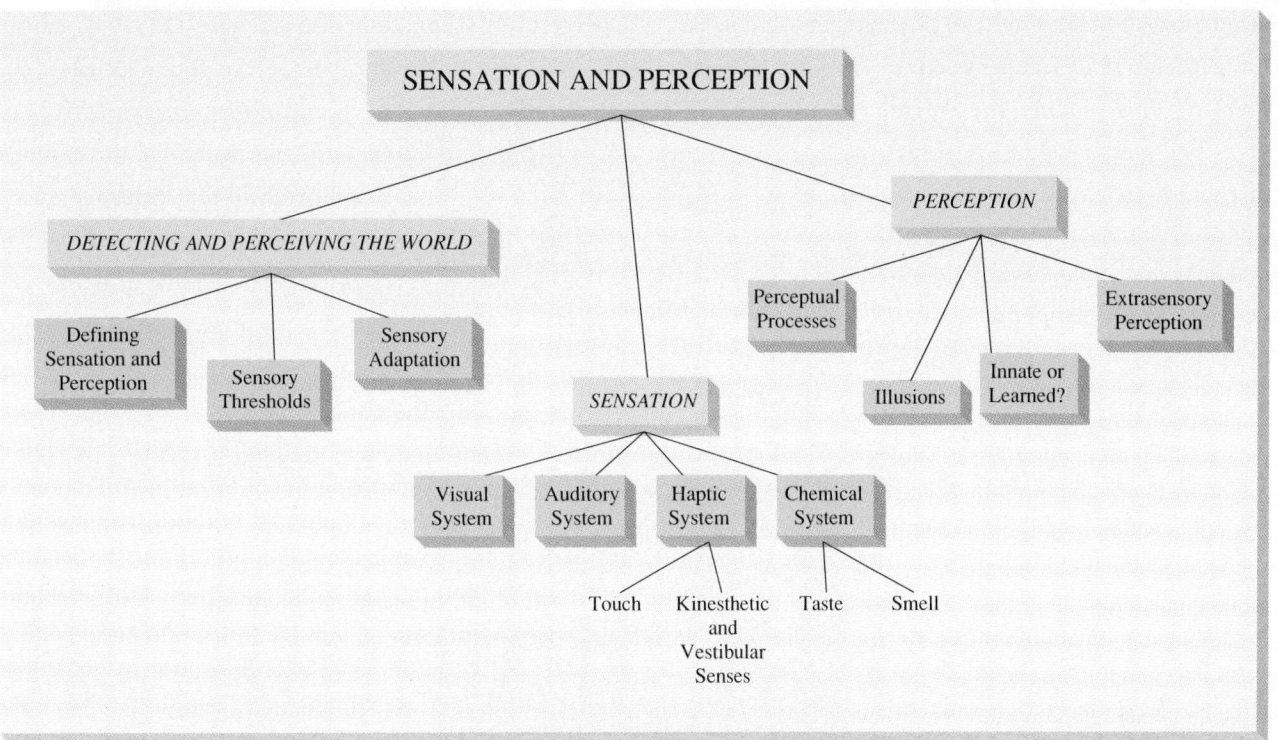

We began this chapter by studying how we sense and interpret the environment, defining sensation and perception, and also reading about sensory thresholds and sensory adaptation. Our coverage of sensation focused on the following sensory systems: visual, auditory, haptic (touch, as well as the kinesthetic and vestibular senses), and chemical (taste and smell). To learn about the nature of perception, we discussed perceptual processes, illusions, whether perception is innate or learned, and extrasensory perception. Remember that you can obtain an overall summary of the chapter by again reading the in-chapter reviews on pages 98, 105, 115, and 127.

The main perspective emphasized in this chapter is the neurobiological perspective. All of the main sections reflect the neurobiological perspective: Detecting and sensing the world (pp. 95–97), sensation (the visual system (pp. 98–105), the auditory system (pp. 106–109), the haptic system (pp. 109–113), the chemical system (pp. 113–115), and perception (pp. 116–127). The sociocultural

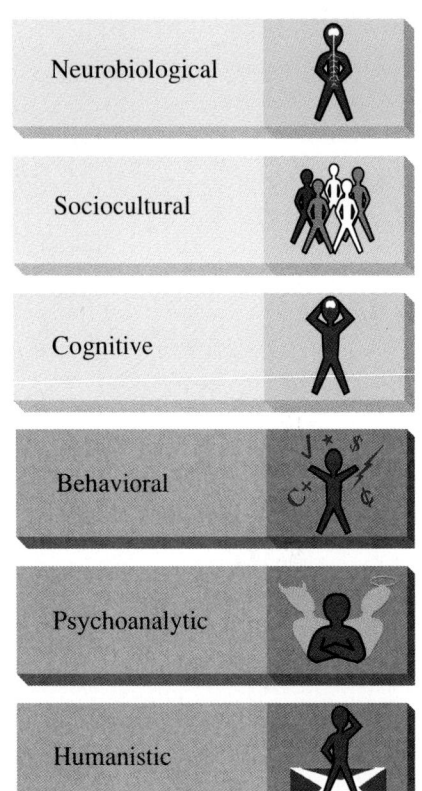

perspective appeared in the material on whether perception is innate or learned (pp. 122–124), culture and perception (pp. 123–124), cultural and ethnic reactions to pain (p. 110), and perceiving three-dimensionality in two-dimensional drawings in different cultures (p. 125). The cognitive perspective also was presented in the discussion of perception (pp. 116–127).

sensation The process of detecting and encoding stimulus energy in the world. 95

perception The brain's process of organizing and interpreting sensory information to give it meaning. 95

absolute threshold The minimum amount of energy that we can detect. 95

noise The term given to irrelevant and competing stimuli. 96

difference threshold Also called the just noticeable difference (jnd); the smallest difference in stimulation required to discriminate one stimulus from another 50 percent of the time. 97

Weber's law The principle that the difference threshold is a constant percentage of the magnitude of the comparison stimulus rather than a constant amount. Weber's law generally holds true. 97

subliminal perception Perception of stimuli below the threshold of awareness. 97

sensory adaptation Weakened sensitivity due to prolonged exposure to a stimulus. 98

light A form of electromagnetic energy that can be described in terms of wavelengths. 98

wavelength The distance from the peak of one wave to the peak of the next. 98

sclera The white outer part of the eye, which helps to maintain the shape of the eye and to protect it from injury. 99

iris The colored part of the eye, which can range from light blue to dark brown. 99

pupil The opening, which appears black, in the center of the iris. 99

cornea A clear membrane just in front of the eye; its function is to bend the light falling on the surface of the eye just enough to focus it at the back of the eye. 99

lens of the eye The transparent and somewhat flexible ball-like entity filled with a gelatinous material; its function is to bend the light falling on the surface of the eye just enough to focus it at the back of the eye. 99

accommodation The action of the lens of the eye to increase its curvature. 100

retina The light-sensitive surface in the back of the eye that houses light receptors called rods and cones. 100

fovea A minute area in the center of the retina where vision is at its best. 100

blind spot The area of the retina where the optic nerve leaves the eye on its way to the brain. 100

rods Receptors in the retina that are exquisitely sensitive to light but are not very useful for color vision. 100

cones Receptors for color perception. 100

hue A characteristic of color based on its wavelength content. 102

saturation A characteristic of color based on its purity. 102

brightness A characteristic of color based on its intensity. 102

additive mixture The mixing of light beams from different parts of the color spectrum. 103

subtractive mixture The mixing of pigments rather than of beams of light. 103

trichromatic theory The theory that color perception is based on the existence of three types of receptors, each of which is maximally sensitive to different, but overlapping, ranges of wavelengths. 104

dichromats People with only two kinds of cones. 104

trichromats People with normal color vision; they have three kinds of cone receptors. 104

afterimages Sensations that remain after a stimulus is removed. 104

opponent-process theory The theory that cells in the visual system respond to red-green and blue-yellow colors; a given cell might be excited by red and inhibited by green, while another cell might be excited by yellow and inhibited by blue. 105

sounds Vibrations of air that are processed by the auditory (hearing) system; also called sound waves. 106

frequency With respect to sound waves, the number of cycles (full wavelengths) that pass through a point in a given time. 106

pitch The perceptual interpretation of sound's frequency. 106

amplitude Measured in decibels (dB), the amount of pressure produced by a sound wave relative to a standard. 106

loudness The perception of a sound wave's amplitude. 106

complex sounds Sounds in which numerous frequencies of sound blend together. 106

timbre The tone color or perceptual quality of a sound. 106

outer ear The pinna and the external auditory canal 107

middle ear An area of the ear with these four main parts: eardrum, hammer, anvil, and stirrup. 108

inner ear The oval window, cochlea, and organ of Corti. 108

cochlea A long tubular fluid-filled structure in the inner ear that is coiled up like a snail. 108

basilar membrane A membrane that is housed inside the cochlea and runs its entire length. 108

organ of Corti A part of the ear that runs the length of the cochlea and sits on the basilar membrane. It contains the ear's sensory receptors, which change the energy of sound waves into nerve impulses that can be processed by the brain. 108

place theory The theory of hearing that states that each frequency produces vibrations at a particular spot on the basilar membrane. 108

frequency theory The theory of hearing that states that the perception of a sound's frequency is due to how often the auditory nerve fires.   108

volley theory The theory of hearing that states that high frequencies can be signaled by teams of neurons that fire at different offset times to create an overall firing rate that could signal a very high frequency.   108

auditory nerve The nerve that carries neural impulses to the brain's auditory areas.   108

pain threshold The stimulation level at which pain is first perceived.   109

gate-control theory The theory that the spinal column contains a neural gate that can be opened (allowing the perception of pain) or closed (blocking the perception of pain).   110

acupuncture A technique in which thin needles are inserted at specific points in the body to produce effects such as local anesthesia.   111

kinesthetic senses Senses that provide information about movement, posture, and orientation.   112

vestibular sense The sense that provides information about balance and movement.   112

semicircular canals Canals in the inner ear that contain the sensory receptors that detect body motion such as tilting of the head or body.   113

papillae Bumps on the surface of the tongue that contain taste buds, which are the receptors for taste.   114

retronasal olfaction The portion of the olfaction system involved in processing food-related smells.   114

olfactory epithelium Tissue located at the top of the nasal cavity that contains a sheet of receptor cells for smell.   114

perceptual set Expectations that influence how perceptual elements will be interpreted.   117

contour A location at which a sudden change of brightness occurs.   117

figure-ground relationship The principle by which we organize the perceptual field into stimuli that stand out (figure) and those that are left over (ground).   117

Gestalt psychology An approach that states that people naturally organize their perceptions according to certain patterns. *Gestalt* is a German word that means "configuration" or "form." One of Gestalt psychology's main principles is that the whole is not equal to the sum of its parts.   117

depth perception The ability to perceive objects three-dimensionally.   118

binocular cues Depth cues that are based on both eyes working together.   118

monocular cues Depth cues based on each eye working independently.   118

retinal or binocular disparity Perception in which the individual sees a single scene even though the images on the eyes are slightly different.   119

convergence A binocular cue for depth perception in which the eyes turn inward as an object gets closer. When the eyes converge or diverge, information is sent to the brain, which interprets the information about the inward (object is closer) or outward (object is further away) eye movement.   119

size constancy Recognition that an object remains the same size even though the retinal image of the object changes.   120

shape constancy Recognition that an object remains the same shape even though its orientation to us changes.   120

brightness constancy Recognition that an object retains the same degree of brightness even when different amounts of light fall on it.   121

visual illusion An illusion that occurs when two objects produce exactly the same retinal image but are perceived as different images.   121

carpentered-world hypothesis The hypothesis that people who live in cultures in which straight lines, right angles, and rectangles predominate (in the West, rooms and buildings are usually rectangular, and many environmental features, such as city streets, have right-angle corners) should be more susceptible to illusions, such as the Müller-Lyer illusion, involving straight lines, right angles, and rectangles than are people who live in noncarpentered cultures.   123

extrasensory perception Perception that occurs without the use of any known sensory processes.   124

telepathy The transfer of thought from one person to another.   124

precognition "Knowing" events before they occur.   125

clairvoyance The ability to perceive remote events that are not in sight.   125

psychokinesis Closely associated with ESP; the mind-over-matter phenomenon of being able to move objects without touching them, such as mentally getting a chair to rise off the floor or shattering a glass merely by staring at it.   125

PSEUDOSCIENCE AND THE PARANORMAL

(1988) by Terence Hines. Buffalo, NY: Prometheus Books.

This very comprehensive book examines the empirical evidence behind virtually all forms of paranormal and pseudoscientific claims, from biorhythms to graphology, from plant perception to subliminal perception, from the "Hollow Earth" theory to recent claims of UFO abductions. Author Hines analyzes the puzzling question of why people continue to believe in the supernatural despite overwhelming evidence against it. Among the other topics covered are faith healing, astrology, the lunar effect, health and nutrition quackery, psychics, firewalking, and the Bermuda Triangle.

RESOURCES FOR PSYCHOLOGY AND IMPROVING HUMANKIND

Canadian Association of the Deaf/ Association des sourds du Canada

2435 Holly Lane #205
Ottawa, ON K1V 7P2 CANADA
613–526–4785

The Association protects and promotes the rights, needs, and concerns of deaf Canadians.

The Canadian Council of the Blind/Le conseil canadien des aveugles

396 Cooper Street #405
Ottawa, ON K2P 2H7 CANADA
613–567–0311

The Council is a non-profit, nationally based center for advocacy, consumerism, peer support, and social and recreational activities for blind Canadians. They maintain contact with divisional offices across Canada.

Human Behavior in Global Perspective (1990)

by Marshall Segall, Pierre Dasen, John Berry, and Ype Poortinga.
New York: Pergamon

Segall's research has made important contributions to an understanding of cultural influences on perception. An entire chapter of this book is devoted to how culture affects our perception of visual illusions.

National Alliance of Blind Students

1115 15th Street NW, Suite 720
Washington, DC 20005
800–424–8666

This is an organization for postsecondary blind students that seeks to improve their educational opportunities and protect their rights.

National Association of the Deaf

814 Thayer Avenue
Silver Spring, MD 20910
301–587–1788

This association serves adult deaf persons, parents of deaf children, professionals, students, and others interested in deafness. The group publishes *Deaf American* and provides information about various books on American Sign Language.

National Federation of the Blind

1320 Johnston Street
Baltimore, MD 21230
410–659–9314

This organization seeks to establish the complete equality and integration of the blind into society. It publishes *Braille Monitor,* a monthly magazine, and a number of educational brochures. Job opportunities for the blind are listed.

Seeing: Illusion, Brain, and Mind (1980)

by J. P. Frisby
New York: Oxford University Press

This fascinating book presents many different illusions and describes attempts to explain them.

The Story of My Life (1970)

by Helen Keller
New York: Airmont

This fascinating account of Helen Keller's life as a blind person provides insights into blind people's perception of the world and how they use other senses.

5

States of Consciousness

*The ultimate gift of conscious life
is a sense of the mystery that
encompasses it.*

Lewis Mumford

THE STORY OF COLIN KEMP: A FATAL NIGHT TERROR

I t was August 1985, and Colin Kemp, a 33-year-old salesman in Caterham, England, went to sleep as usual. About 2 hours later, two Japanese soldiers appeared in his bedroom. They started to chase him. One soldier had a knife; the other a gun. Kemp ran away from them as fast as he could, but he wasn't fast enough. Kemp wrestled with the knife-wielding soldier. The other soldier aimed his gun at Kemp's head. Kemp tripped him, gripped his neck, and began choking him, but he slipped away. He turned, aimed the gun at Kemp, and fired. Kemp awoke in a state of panic, sweat pouring down his head. In a frenzy of terror, he turned to his wife, who was lying next to him in bed. She was dead. Kemp had strangled her, not a Japanese soldier.

At his trial 9 months later, Kemp said he was asleep when he killed his wife. He pleaded not guilty to the murder charge because he had intended to kill a Japanese soldier, not his wife. Psychiatrists testified on Kemp's behalf, instructing the jury that Kemp was having a night terror at the time he killed his wife. A **night terror** *is characterized by sudden arousal from sleep and intense fear, usually accompanied by a number of physiological reactions, such as rapid heart rate and breathing, loud screams, heavy perspiration, and physical movement.* In most instances, individuals have little or no memory of what happens during a night terror.

Kemp experienced night terrors on two occasions prior to the fatal event. Both times intruders chased him during his sleep. In one of the night terrors, he punched at his wife. She awakened and asked what was happening. The second time, he kicked her in the back. Strangling someone to death is a much more elaborate and sustained activity than kicking an individual in the back. Is it possible that an action like Kemp's— strangling someone to death—could actually take place during sleep? The jury apparently thought so, because they acquitted Kemp. They saw his act as an *automatic* one. That is, although Kemp was capable of the action, the jury concluded that he was not *conscious* of what he was doing (Restak, 1988).

PREVIEW

Most of us take for granted this nightly sojourn into the realm of sleep; however, Kemp's experiences make us wonder about the nature of sleep and states of consciousness. What is consciousness? What happens when we sleep? Why do we dream? In this chapter, we'll explore those questions, as well as the fascinating subjects of hypnosis and how psychoactive drugs alter states of consciousness.

THE NATURE OF CONSCIOUSNESS

For much of the twentieth century, psychologists shunned the slippery, subjective trappings of consciousness that intrigued their predecessors in the late nineteenth century. Instead, they focused on overt behaviors of individuals and the rewards and punishments that determined those behaviors (Skinner, 1938; Watson, 1913). However, recently psychologists have granted respectability to the study of consciousness in cognitive science. For the first time in many decades psychologists from many different fields are interested in consciousness, including its relation to unconsciousness (Bowers, 1992).

Consciousness

Psychologists do not always agree on what the nature of conscious thought is or how it works in concert with or apart from unconscious thought. Although there is still disagreement about the nature of consciousness, we will define **consciousness** *as awareness of both external and internal stimuli or events.* External events include what you attend to as you go through your day—the comment your best friend makes about your new hairstyle, the car in front of you that swerves to miss a dog, the music you are listening to on your cassette player, and so on. Internal events include your awareness of your sensations—your headache has returned, you are breathing too fast, your stomach is rumbling—as well as your thoughts and feelings—you're having trouble in biology this semester, you are anxious about the exam next week, you are happy that your friends are going with you to the game tonight.

The contents of our awareness may change from one moment to the next, since information can move rapidly in and out of consciousness. Many years ago, William James (1890) described the mind as a **stream of consciousness**—*a continuous flow of changing sensations, images, thoughts, and feelings.* Your mind races from one topic to the next, from thinking about the person who is approaching you, to how well you feel, to what you are going to do tomorrow, to where you are going for lunch.

William James was interested in charting the shifting nature of our stream of consciousness. In contrast, Sigmund Freud (1900/1953) believed that unconscious thoughts exert more powerful influences on our behavior. **Unconscious thought** *is Freud's concept of a reservoir of unacceptable wishes, feelings, and thoughts that are beyond conscious awareness.* Unconscious thought in the Freudian sense has nothing to do with being unconscious after being knocked out by a blow on the head in a boxing match, being anesthetized, or falling into a coma.

According to Freud, unconscious thoughts are too laden with sexual and aggressive meaning for consciousness to admit them. For example, a young man who is nervous around women breaks into a cold sweat as a woman approaches him. He is unconscious that his fear of women springs from the cold, punitive way his mother treated him when he was a child. Freud believed that one of psychotherapy's main goals is to bring unconscious thoughts into conscious awareness so their disruptive influence can be modified.

Freud accurately recognized the complexity of consciousness. It is not simply a matter of being aware or unaware. Consciousness comes in different forms and levels. Sometimes consciousness is highly focused and alert; at other times it is more passive (Baars, 1989). Even sleep, once thought to be completely passive and unconscious, has active and at least minimally conscious properties.

Controlled processes *represent the most alert state of consciousness in which individuals actively focus their effort toward a goal.* Controlled processes require focused attention and interfere with other ongoing activities. Consider Anne, who is learning how to use her new personal computer. She is completely absorbed in reading the tutorial manual that accompanies the computer—she doesn't hear her roommate humming to herself or the song on the radio. This state of focused awareness is what is meant by controlled processes.

In contrast, **automatic processes** *are a form of consciousness that requires minimal attention and does not interfere with other ongoing activities.* Once Anne learns how to use the software, maneuvers on the computer keyboard become almost automatic; that is, she doesn't have to

concentrate so hard on how to perform each of the steps required to get the computer to do something. Two weeks ago she had to stop and concentrate on which keys to press to move a paragraph from one page to another. Now her fingers fly across the computer keyboard when she needs to move a block of material. This kind of consciousness involves automatic processes. Automatic processes require less conscious effort than controlled processes do. Our automatic behaviors when we are awake should be thought of as lower in awareness than controlled processes, rather than not conscious at all. Since Anne pushed the right keys at the right time on her computer keyboard, she apparently was aware at a certain level of what she was doing.

Daydreaming *is another form of consciousness that involves a low level of conscious effort.* It is a little like dreaming when we are awake. Daydreams usually start spontaneously when what we are doing requires less than our full attention. Mind wandering is probably the most obvious type of daydreaming. We regularly take brief side trips into our own private realms of imagery and memory even as we read, listen, or work. When we daydream, we drift off into a world of fantasy. We imagine ourselves on dates, at parties, on television, at faraway places, at another time in our lives. Sometimes our daydreams are about ordinary, everyday events, such as paying the rent, getting a new hairstyle, or dealing with someone at work. This semiautomatic thought flow can be useful. As you daydream while you brush your teeth, iron your clothes, or walk to the store, you might be making plans or solving a problem. Daydreams can remind us of important things ahead. Daydreaming keeps our minds active while helping us to cope, to create, and to fantasize.

Altered States of Consciousness

The states of consciousness we have described so far are normal, everyday occurrences in our lives. In contrast, an **altered state of consciousness** *occurs when a person is in a mental state that noticeably differs from normal awareness. Drugs, meditation, traumas, fatigue, hypnosis, and sensory deprivation produce altered states of consciousness.* Whether a state of consciousness is described as normal or altered depends on how the word *normal* is defined. Someone who has drunk a caffeinated soda to increase alertness, for instance, is considered to be in a normal state of consciousness. However, someone who takes a drug that induces hallucinations, such as LSD, is considered to be in an altered state of consciousness. In Sociocultural Worlds 5.1, we will discuss the role that altered states of consciousness played in the origin of some of the world's great religions.

Western cultures tend to regard altered states of consciousness with some suspicion. Our strong bias toward rational and logical processes encourages us to view many kinds of exotic states as pathological. However, exotic altered states of consciousness involving trance states or possession appear to be a natural occurrence in about

Altered States of Consciousness and the World's Religions

- Yemenite Jews in a Jerusalem synagogue—wrapped in their prayer shawls, barefoot, sitting cross-legged, and swaying back and forth—recite the Torah.
- Dar Jo and Lai Sarr, Zen monks, explore the Buddha-nature at the center of their beings through zazen meditation, meditative walking, and chanting sutras.
- Coptic Christians in Cairo, Egypt, emit an eerie and spine-tingling cry of spiritual fervor.
- Muslims in Pakistan fast from dawn to dusk during the month of Ramadan, consistent with the fourth pillar of Islam.

Today billions of people around the world guide their lives by the tenets of Judaism, Christianity, Islam, and Buddhism (Hood, 1995). Most religions involve the practice of altered states of consciousness as expected parts of religious ritual, whether the altered state is derived through meditation, prayer, fasting, or substance use.

Many of the world's great religions began with a moment of revelation, an ecstatic moment infused with such mystery, power, and beauty that it forever altered the founding prophet's consciousness (Paloutzian, 1996). God called Abraham, bidding him to leave his homeland in Mesopotamia to seek a promised land known as Canaan. There he founded a religious faith, Judaism, whose followers were to enjoy a special relationship with the creator of heaven and earth. In the Christian religion, death could not vanquish Jesus in A.D. 29; following his death, Jesus appeared in a revelation to Paul, who then became a believer in Christ's resurrection and traveled widely to preach Christianity. In the Islamic religion, Mohammed saw a vision and heard a voice in the year 610 B.C. that would alter his life; the angel Gabriel came to Mohammed and said, "Mohammed, thou art a messenger of God."

Mystical revelation did not play a role in the creation of Buddhism. In the late sixth century A.D., Siddhartha Gautama (Buddha) developed enlightenment without assistance from any teachers or divine revelation. The Buddhist path to enlightenment involves meditating—turning inward to discover that within oneself is the origin of the world, the end of the world, and the way to all goals.

Regardless of whether you believe in the teachings of one or more of the world's religions, you can recognize the importance of altered states of consciousness as a critical component in the foundation or practice of the religions of the world. *Can you identify how altered states of consciousness might play a role in your own religious tradition?*

Among those who practice altered states of consciousness in the world's religions are *(a)* Zen monks who explore the Buddha-nature at the center of their beings and *(b)* Moslems in Pakistan who fast from dawn to dusk during the month of Ramadan as the fourth pillar of Islam.

An extraordinary ritual practiced by the Hindu of Malaysia, described by Colleen Ward (1994), informs us of how different life can be in other cultures. After a devotee goes into trance, assisted by the noise and encouragement of other believers, the priest skewers the devotee's mouth from cheek to cheek with a sharp metal shaft. The devotee seems unaffected; he doesn't bleed or flinch. When the priest finishes piercing his flesh with other hooks dictated by the ritual, the devotee and his group of believers begin a pilgrimage to a special temple to make offerings. If the devotee can complete the pilgrimage without bleeding or complaints of pain, he has proven his purity of heart.

Initially this practice might seem harsh to us; it might even be hard to read about it. However, this religious ritual permits individuals to demonstrate their strength of character and the depth of their religious convictions. Are there similar rituals in our own culture that serve as evidence of our own higher development? Is there a means by which we can prove our purity? Comparing these approaches in different cultures *demonstrates appreciation for individual differences* that are magnified when we study other cultures.

90 percent of all societies (Bourguignon & Evascu, 1977). The bias against such phenomena has discouraged psychology from vigorously examining them, except when they could be simulated in the lab. Disconnecting an altered state from its cultural context might substantially alter its impact and significance (Ward, 1994)

Ritual possession appears to be widely practiced all over the globe. In our own culture, charismatic Christian churches believe that the Holy Spirit takes possession of the believer. Similarly, voodoo proponents in the Caribbean, Sasale dancers in Niger, and devil dancers in Sri Lanka all demonstrate the characteristics of ritual possession, including uncontrollable body movements, unusual eye movements, and personality transformation consistent with the expectations of the religion. Most ritual transformation is induced by "sensory bombardment—repetitive clapping, singing, and chanting" (Ward, 1994, p. 62).

Rejecting ritual possession as a legitimate area of study overlooks the adaptive features of this form of altered consciousness (Ward, 1989). Participating in such rituals offers psychological and biological benefits. Participants report feelings of rejuvenation and contentment upon the ritual's completion. The sudden emotional release involved in the ritual compares favorably to the release clients pursue in psychotherapy. Socially by completing the ritual a participant may gain prestige as well as be liberated from the normal expectations that typically govern behavior. Sharing the experience of ritualized possession encourages social cohesion in the group.

As you can see, our states of consciousness are many, varied, and complex. A summary of some of the main forms of consciousness is presented in figure 5.1. Now we will turn our attention to the fascinating world of sleep and dreams.

SLEEP AND DREAMS

Each night something lures us from work, from play, and from our loved ones into a solitary state. Sleep claims about one-third of the time in our lives, more than any other pursuit. This alluring realm of mental escapades we enter each night has intrigued philosophers and scientists for centuries. Those who first investigated sleep were primarily interested in its role as a springboard for dreams. We no longer regard sleep as the complete absence of consciousness. Now we know that sleep involves much more.

Cycles of Sleep and Wakefulness

We are unaware of most of our body's rhythms—for example, the rise and fall of hormones in the bloodstream, accelerated and decelerated cycles of brain activity, highs and lows in body temperature (Monk, 1989). Both wakefulness and sleep exhibit reliable cycles of activity. We will explore both types of cycles in turn.

Wakefulness Cycles

Some rhythms are *circadian,* from the Latin words *circa* meaning "about" and *dies* meaning "day." A **circadian rhythm** *is a daily behavioral or physiological cycle; an example is the 24-hour sleep/wake cycle.*

High level awareness	Controlled processes	High level of awareness, focused attention required		This student is using controlled processes that require focused concentration.
Lower-level awareness	Automatic processes	Awareness, but minimal attention required	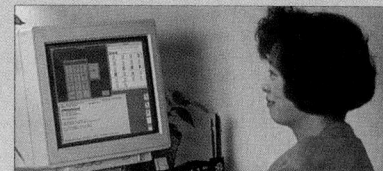	This woman is an experienced computer operator. Her maneuvers with the keyboard are automatic, requiring minimal awareness.
	Daydreaming	Low level of awareness and conscious effort, somewhere between active consciousness and dreaming while asleep		Our daydreams often start spontaneously when what we are doing requires less than our full attention.
	Altered states of consciousness	A mental state noticeably different from normal awareness; produced by drugs, trauma, fatigue, hypnosis, meditation, and sensory deprivation		Shown here is a woman being hypnotized.
	Sleep and dreams	No longer thought of as the absence of consciousness, but they are at very low levels of consciousness	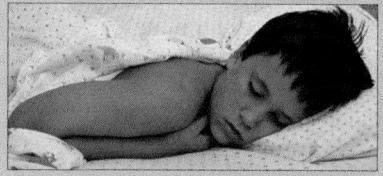	All of us dream while we sleep, but some of us dream more than others.
No awareness	Unconscious mind (Freudian)	Reservoir of unacceptable wishes, feelings, and memories, often with sexual and aggressive overtones, that are too anxiety provoking to be admitted to consciousness		The woman shown lying on the couch is undergoing psychoanalytic therapy to reveal her unconscious thoughts.
	Unconscious (non-Freudian)	Being knocked unconscious by a blow or when we are anesthetized; deep prolonged unconciousness characterizes individuals who go into a coma as the result of injury, disease, or poison		Unconsciousness can result from an injury, such as a blow to the head.

FIGURE 5.1

Forms of Consciousness and Levels of Awareness and Unawareness

Biological and Perceptual Processes

FIGURE 5.2

Michel Siffre, in Midnight Cave Near Del Rio, Texas
Because Siffre could not see or sense the sun rising and setting in the cave, he began to live by biological cycles instead of by days. When Siffre wanted to go to sleep, he called the support crew outside and told them to turn off the lights in the cave. When he woke up, he called the support crew and asked them to turn on the cave's lights. Siffre's days closely resembled a 24-hour pattern through most of the 6 months in the cave, but toward the end they were slightly longer and more varied. In the last month of his cave stay, his days averaged about 28 hours.

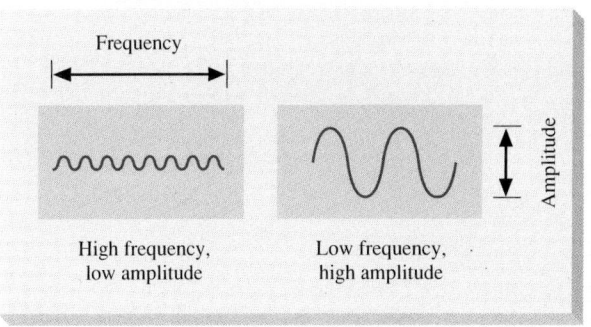

FIGURE 5.3

A Comparison Between Two EEG Patterns
Two examples of electrical activity in the brain (measured by EEG) that demonstrate the characteristics of amplitude (height of curve) and frequency (cycles per second).

The natural circadian rhythm of most animals, including humans, is 25 to 26 hours, but our internal clocks easily adapt to the 24-hour rhythms (light, sounds, warmth) of the turning earth. When we are isolated from environmental cues, our sleep/wake cycles continue to be rather constant but slightly longer than 24 hours. For example, in 1972 French scientist Michel Siffre isolated himself in Midnight Cave near Del Rio, Texas, for 6 months (see figure 5.2). What were Siffre's days and nights like when he was completely isolated from clocks, calendars, the moon, the sun, and all the normal markers of time? Siffre's (1975) days closely resembled a 24-hour cycle, but they were slightly longer and more varied toward the end of his 6-month stay in the cave.

Our own circadian rhythms can become desynchronized when we take a cross-country or transoceanic flight. If you fly from Los Angeles to New York and then go to bed at 11 P.M. Eastern Standard Time, you may have trouble falling asleep because your body is still on West Coast time. Even if you sleep for 8 hours that night, you may find it hard to wake up at 7 A.M. (which would be 4 A.M. in Los Angeles).

Sleep Cycles

The invention of the electroencephalograph (described in chapter 2) led to some major breakthroughs in understanding the nature of sleep, including the important fact that the brain is active, rather than inactive, during sleep. The brain's electrical activity shows specific patterns throughout the period of sleep. The EEG patterns vary in **amplitude,** *the height of the wave,* and **frequency,** *the number of cycles per second.* See figure 5.3 for a depiction of these characteristics. Brain waves show gradual changes from one stage to the next; sleep researchers designated five phases of sleep to correspond to the dominant patterns observed in each of these phases. Figure 5.4 describes the EEGs typical of these phases.

"MY PROBLEM HAS ALWAYS BEEN AN OVERABUNDANCE OF ALPHA WAVES"

© 1990 by Sidney Harris.

Imagine that you are a volunteer in research to study sleep patterns in college students. You have EEG monitors attached in various locations on your head to measure the electrical activity of your brain as you drift off to sleep. As you read your final homework assignment, your EEG measurements will probably reflect **beta waves,** *high-frequency electrical activity in the brain characteristic of periods of concentration.* When you shut off the lights, yawn, and stretch, your EEG patterns are likely to change slowly to **alpha waves,** *the EEG pattern of individuals who are in a relaxed or drowsy state.* Both of these patterns occur in awake individuals.

As you fall asleep, you begin the first of several cycles of sleep stages that will occur over the course of sleeping.

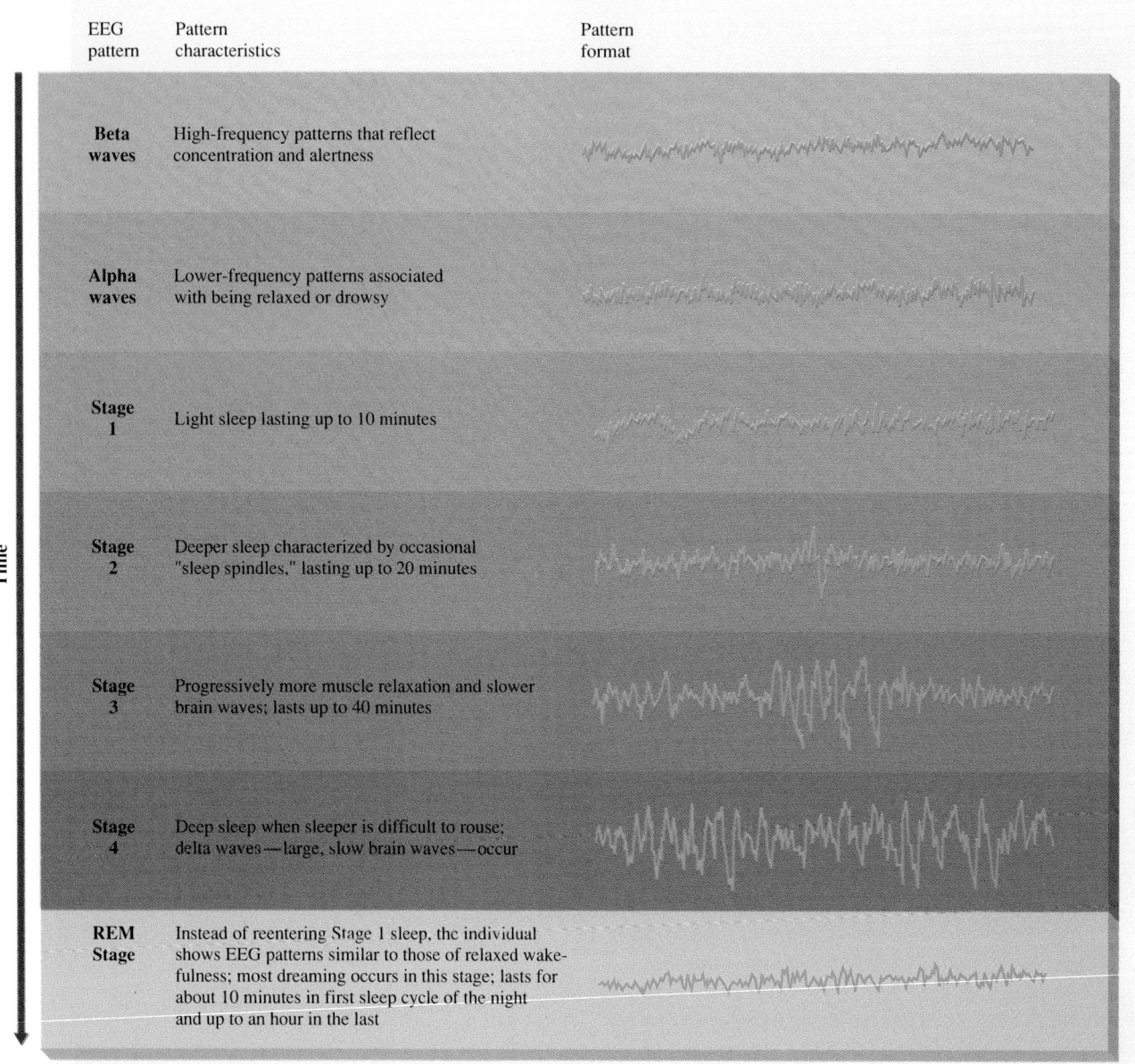

EEG pattern	Pattern characteristics	Pattern format
Beta waves	High-frequency patterns that reflect concentration and alertness	
Alpha waves	Lower-frequency patterns associated with being relaxed or drowsy	
Stage 1	Light sleep lasting up to 10 minutes	
Stage 2	Deeper sleep characterized by occasional "sleep spindles," lasting up to 20 minutes	
Stage 3	Progressively more muscle relaxation and slower brain waves; lasts up to 40 minutes	
Stage 4	Deep sleep when sleeper is difficult to rouse; delta waves—large, slow brain waves—occur	
REM Stage	Instead of reentering Stage 1 sleep, the individual shows EEG patterns similar to those of relaxed wakefulness; most dreaming occurs in this stage; lasts for about 10 minutes in first sleep cycle of the night and up to an hour in the last	

Time (vertical axis label on left side)

FIGURE 5.4

Characteristics and Format of EEG Recordings During Stages of Wakefulness and Sleep

Slower brain waves called **delta waves,** *characteristic of deepening sleep and progressive muscle relaxation,* begin to emerge and intensify throughout the four stages of sleep. These waves exhibit larger amplitude and greater irregularity as sleep deepens.

During light sleep in stage 1, which lasts up to 10 minutes, slower brain waves begin to emerge; **theta waves,** *low-frequency and low-amplitude EEG patterns,* characterize stage 1 sleep. In this stage people can awaken us fairly easily.

In stage 2 sleep, which lasts up to 20 minutes, the EEG pattern reflects the presence of **sleep spindles,** *brief bursts of higher-frequency waves.* During this stage, EEG patterns may show responsiveness to external stimulation or internal sensation. Otherwise, electrical activity continues to slow down in stage 2.

In stage 3, which lasts up to 40 minutes, delta-wave activity becomes prominent. Delta-wave patterns dominate the deep sleep that occurs in stage 4. A sleeper who awakens during this stage often appears confused. Sleepwalking, sleeptalking, and bedwetting are most likely to occur in this deep state of sleep.

During the first 70 minutes of sleep, the sleeper spends most of the time in stages 3 and 4 in delta-wave activity. After stage 4, the patterns of electrical activity change again. The sleeper drifts up through the sleep stages toward wakefulness. Instead of reentering stage 1, however, the sleeper enters a form of sleep called "rapid eye movement" (REM) sleep. **REM sleep** *is a periodic stage of sleep during which dreaming occurs.* During REM sleep, the EEG pattern shows fast, high-intensity waves similar to those of the alpha waves of relaxed wakefulness. During REM sleep, the eyeballs move up and down and from left to right (Benbadis & others, 1995) (see figure 5.5).

Sleep that knits up the ravelled sleave of care . . .
Balm of hurt minds, nature's second course,
Chief nourisher in life's feast.

William Shakespeare

Sleepers awakened during REM sleep are more likely to report having dreamed than are sleepers awakened at any other stage. Even people who claim that they rarely dream frequently report dreaming when they are awakened during REM sleep (McCarley, 1989). The longer the period of REM, the more likely a person will report dreaming. Dreams do occur during slow-wave or non-REM sleep, but the frequency of dreams in the other stages is relatively low (Webb, 1978).

The REM period is distinctive in other ways as well. While dreaming in REM, the body is severely limited in its capacity to execute voluntary behavior. Psychologists presume that this paralysis acts as a safeguard by allowing fairly vivid dreaming without the challenges associated with acting out the action in the dream. In contrast, dreams that occur during stage 4 deep sleep do not have the motor paralysis protection. Many sleep researchers believe such dreams prompt sleepwalking and talking because these motor safeguards are not in place.

So far we have described a normal cycle of sleep, consisting of four stages plus REM sleep. As we move into later sleep cycles during the period, there are several important points to remember about the nature of these cycles (see figure 5.6). One cycle lasts about 90 minutes, and cycles recur several times during the night. The amount of deep sleep (stage 4) is much greater in the first half of a night's sleep than in the second half. Later cycles of sleep might not even include stages 3 or 4. The majority of REM sleep takes place during the latter part of a night's sleep when the REM period becomes progressively longer. The night's first REM period might last for only 10

minutes; the final REM period can last as long as an hour. Finally, REM patterns change over the course of the lifetime. As infants, we spend significantly more time in REM. As we grow older, we spend proportionately more time in lighter sleep stages rather than in deep sleep.

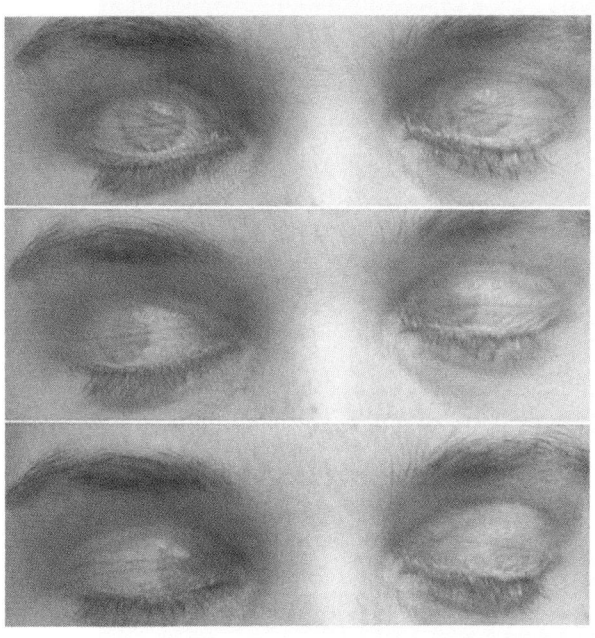

FIGURE 5.5

REM Sleep
During REM sleep, our eyes move rapidly as if we were observing the images we see moving in our dreams.

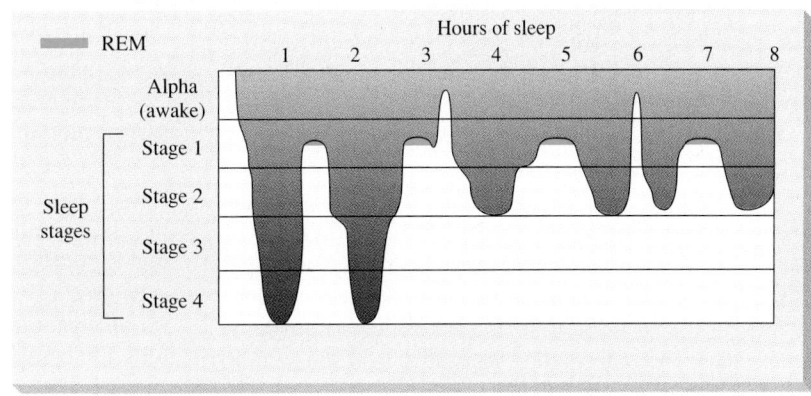

FIGURE 5.6

Normal Sleep Patterns of Young Adults
This graph illustrates six sleep cycles as they might occur over an 8-hour period of sleep in the young adult. The graph reflects that the sleeper descends from a relaxed, wakeful state into sleep, moving into stage 1 (light sleep) through stage 4 (deep sleep) during the first hour. The first cycle is complete when the sleeper reenters stage 1, during which the first of several REM sleep experiences occurs. Notice that slow-wave sleep, especially in stage 4, is less frequent during the latter part of the sleep period. Notice that REM sleep also increases during this period. In this example, the sleeper wakes up briefly after 3 hours and again just before the end of the sixth hour.

Why We Sleep and Sleep Deprivation

Why do we sleep? How long can we go without sleep?

Why We Sleep

For many years, researchers thought sleep occurred in the absence of enough sensory stimulation to keep the brain awake. They believed that without stimulation the brain just slowed down, producing sleep. However, researchers realized that sleep comes and goes without any obvious change in the amount of environmental stimulation. Theorists suggested we might have an internal "activating system" in the reticular formation that keeps the brain activated, or awake, all day. According to this theory, fatigue of the so-called activating system, or an accumulation of "sleep toxin" that chemically depresses the activating system, might induce sleep (Monnier & Hosli, 1965).

The contemporary view of sleep is radically different. As you have learned, the brain does not stop during sleep but instead carries out complex processes that produce both REM and non-REM sleep behaviors. In fact, at the cellular level, many neurons fire faster during sleep than in a waking state (Jones, 1989).

The puzzle is not completely solved, but some of the major pieces of the brain's machinery involved in sleep have been identified. Non-REM sleep, for example, requires the participation of neurons in both the forebrain and medulla. REM sleep is a period of especially intense brain activity, also requiring the cooperation of a number of brain systems (Hobson, 1992).

There are two theories about why we sleep—repair theory and ecological theory. **Repair theory** *states that sleep restores, replenishes, and rebuilds our brains and bodies, which somehow are worn out or used up by the day's waking activities.* This idea fits with the feeling of being "worn out" before we sleep and "restored" when we wake. Aristotle proposed a repair theory of sleep centuries ago, and most experts today believe in a version of repair.

Ecological theory *is a relatively recent view of why we sleep. This evolution-based approach argues that the main purpose of sleep is to prevent animals from wasting their energy and harming themselves during the parts of the day or night to which they have not adapted.* For example, it was not adaptive for our ancestors to fumble around in the dark, risking accidents or attack by large predators, such as lions and tigers, so, like chimpanzees that slept safely in treetops, our ancestors presumably hid and slept through the night.

Both repair theory and ecological theory have some merit. Perhaps sleep was originally most important for keeping us out of trouble but has since evolved to allow for certain repair processes.

Sleep Deprivation

How long can people go without sleep and still function? The effects of profound sleep loss are difficult to study, because preventing a person from sleeping causes stress. After 2 or 3 days without sleep, people tend to become irritable, lose concentration, and show other signs of stress (Webb, 1978). In one recent study, individuals' performance of physical work tasks declined substantially after 48 hours of sleep deprivation (Rodgers & others, 1995).

How much sleep do we need each night? Some sleep researchers, such as William Dement (1993) and Mary Carskadon (1993), believe that Americans do not get enough sleep. Two dramatic examples illustrate the impact of sleep deprivation:

- The 1989 Exxon *Valdez* oil spill in Alaska, in which the third mate, who was piloting the ship, fell asleep
- The 1979 Three Mile Island nuclear plant accident, in which fatigued workers at 4 A.M. did not respond to a mechanical failure warning

Carskadon (1993) says that the human brain has an inherent daily rhythm of sleepiness that for most people consists of two time periods: a main one between 2 A.M. and 6 A.M. and another during mid-afternoon. Many cultures acknowledge the afternoon period with culturally endorsed napping or siesta during which businesses close and social activities diminish.

Sleep experts say that sleep deficits have gradually developed in this century in response to the flexibility in lifestyle that followed the introduction of electric lights. In 1910, adolescents 13 through 17 years old averaged 9½ hours of sleep a night; today they average 7½ to 8 hours a night. We do not know all of the consequences of chronic sleep loss, but 25 percent of adolescents report that they fall asleep in school at least once a week, and more than 10 percent say they are late for school at least once a week because they overslept. Surveys indicate that less than half of American adults get 8 hours of sleep each day and that one-fourth get less than 7 hours.

The exact amount of sleep a person needs does vary from individual to individual, but Carskadon (1993) argues that almost all adults need to get at least 7 hours of sleep a night to avoid accumulating a sleep debt. She believes that most adults need 8 hours. So, although some highly motivated individuals can function reasonably well even after no sleep for several days, the vast majority of us should get at least 7 to 8 hours of sleep on a regular basis to function competently.

So far we have discussed normal aspects of sleep. Next we'll see that sleep is not always predictable. There are many ways sleep can go awry.

Sleep Disorders

Most people go to bed, fall asleep, and have a restful night. However, some people have fitful nights and want to sleep much of the day. Others sleepwalk, sleeptalk, have nightmares or night terrors, or have breathing problems while they sleep.

CRITICAL THINKING

Managing Your Need to Sleep

How much sleep do you need? Are you one of the sleepers who turn foul if they do not get at least 8 hours? Are you able to function on less than the average sleep requirement? If you are sleep-deprived, what would have to happen in your life for you to develop more appropriate sleep patterns? What are the probable costs to you if you do not adjust your sleep patterns to suit your real sleep needs?

Answering these questions demonstrates the manner in which you can *apply psychological concepts to enhance personal adaptation.* The next section will offer some suggestions for persons whose sleep deprivation warrants the diagnosis of insomnia. Is this an area in which you should take some action?

effectiveness, requiring ever greater dosages to achieve the same effect (Syvalahti, 1985). Sedatives and non-prescription sleeping pills should be used with caution and only for short-term sleep problems.

What can you do if you spend too many sleepless nights tossing and turning in bed? Rather than turning to sleeping pills, an alternative is the chemical compound *tryptophan,* which is found in milk and milk products. Although it's not a surefire cure for insomnia, it does seem to help some people sleep better. Next time you have trouble falling asleep, a glass of milk may do the trick.

Caffeine and nicotine may be the culprits in some cases of insomnia. Experts recommend decreasing their use if you are having sleep problems (Zarcone, 1989). Avoid large quantities of alcohol before going to bed. Drinking before going to bed may initially help you fall asleep, but after the sedative effects wear off, you probably will have difficulty staying asleep.

Other suggested remedies for insomniacs emphasize changing bedtime routines. Adopt a regular schedule so that you go to sleep and wake up at approximately the same time each day. Do something relaxing before you go to bed, such as listening to soft music. Avoid discussion of highly stressful issues, such as money or intimacy problems, right before you go to bed. Do not use your bed for activities that would compete with sleeping, such as studying or watching television. Adopt a regular exercise program (but don't exercise just before going to bed; that would increase your energy and alertness).

Sleepwalking and Sleeptalking

Somnambulism *is the formal term for sleepwalking; somnambulism occurs during the deepest stages of sleep.* For many years, experts believed that somnambulists were acting out their dreams. However, somnambulism occurs during stages 3 and 4 of sleep, the time when a person usually does not dream. Although some adults sleepwalk, sleepwalking is most common in children. Most children outgrow the problem without having to seek professional help. Except for the danger of accidents while wandering about in the dark, there is nothing abnormal about sleepwalking. Contrary to popular belief, it is not only safe but wise to awaken sleepwalkers, because they might harm themselves as they roam through the night.

Another quirky night behavior is sleeptalking. Most sleeptalkers are young adults, but sleeptalkers come in all ages. If you were to interrogate a sleeptalker, could you find out what he did last Thursday night? Probably not.

© 1991 by Sidney Harris—"You Want Proof? . . ." W. H. Freeman and Company.

Insomnia

Insomnia *is a common sleep problem; put simply, it is the inability to sleep.* Insomnia may involve a problem in falling asleep, waking up during the night, or waking up too early. As many as one in five Americans has insomnia (Zorick, 1989). It is more common among women, older adults, thin people, depressed or stressed people, and people who are poor.

We spend large sums of money, especially on drugs, trying to sleep better. Many sleep experts now believe that physicians have been too quick to prescribe sedatives for insomniacs (Nicholson, Bradley, & Pasco, 1989). Sedatives reduce the amount of time a person spends in stage 4 and REM sleep and may disrupt the restfulness of sleep. There is a danger of overdose, and over time sedatives lose their

Although he may speak to you and make fairly coherent statements, the sleeptalker is soundly asleep. Most likely, the sleeptalker will mumble a response to your question, but don't count on its accuracy.

Nightmares and Night Terrors

A **nightmare** *is a frightening dream that awakens the sleeper from REM sleep.* A nightmare's content invariably involves some danger—the dreamer is chased, robbed, raped, murdered, or thrown off a cliff. Nightmares are common. Most of us have had them, especially when we were children. Even most adults experience a nightmare occasionally. Nightmares are usually so vivid that we can remember them if someone awakens us, although they account for only a small portion of our dream world.

Recall from the opening of the chapter that night terrors are characterized by sudden arousal from sleep and intense fear, usually accompanied by a number of physiological reactions, such as rapid heart rate and breathing, loud screams, heavy perspiration, and physical movement. Night terrors are less common than nightmares, and the person usually has little or no recall of an accompanying dream. Also unlike nightmares, night terrors occur in slow-wave, non-REM sleep.

Narcolepsy

Narcolepsy *is the overpowering urge to fall asleep.* The urge is so strong that the person may fall asleep while talking or standing up. Narcoleptics immediately enter REM sleep rather than moving through the first four sleep stages. Researchers suspect it is an inherited disorder, since narcolepsy runs in families.

Sleep Apnea

Sleep apnea *is a sleep disorder in which individuals stop breathing while they are asleep because their windpipe fails to open or brain processes involved in respiration fail to work properly.* They wake up periodically during the night so they can breathe better, although they are not usually aware of their awakened state. During the day, these people may feel sleepy because they were deprived of sleep at night. This disorder is most common among infants and people over the age of 65.

In our tour of sleep, we have seen that dreams usually occur during REM sleep. Let's now explore the fascinating world of dreams in greater detail.

REVIEW
Consciousness and Sleep

Consciousness is awareness of both external and internal stimuli and events. Consciousness is a rich, complex landscape of the mind, consisting of processes at varying levels of awareness. Among the many forms of consciousness are controlled processes, automatic processes, daydreaming, altered states of consciousness, sleep and dreams, unconscious thought (Freudian), and unconsciousness (non-Freudian, such as in an anesthetized state).

Important dimensions of sleep include the kinds of sleep, circadian rhythms, why we sleep, the neural basis of sleep, and sleep disorders. Various kinds of sleep can be measured by an electroencephalograph (EEG), which measures the brain's electrical activity. Alpha waves occur when we are in a relaxed state. The transition from waking to sleep is

called a hypnagogic state. When we sleep, we move from light sleep in Stage 1 to deep sleep in Stage 4 (delta waves). Then we go directly into REM sleep, where dreams occur. Each night we go through a number of these sleep cycles.

A circadian rhythm refers to cycles that are about 24 hours long. The human sleep/wake cycle is an important circadian rhythm. This cycle can become desynchronized. In some experiments, people have isolated themselves in caves for months; these people continue to have an approximate 24-hour cycle, although at times the cycle is slightly longer. There is no set amount of sleep we need each night.

We sleep mainly for two reasons—for restoration and repair (repair theory) and to keep us from wasting energy and harming ourselves during the times of the day or night to

which we are not adapted (ecological theory). Although some highly motivated individuals can go several days without sleep and function reasonably well, most people need at least 7 or 8 hours of sleep a day on a regular basis to function competently. A contemporary concern is that people have increasingly gotten less sleep as the twentieth century has progressed. Early views of sleep emphasized the role of environmental stimulation and subsequently an internal activating system in the reticular formation. The contemporary view is radically different: the brain is actively engaged in producing sleep behaviors and different neurotransmitters are involved. Among the most prominent sleep disorders are insomnia, sleepwalking and sleeptalking, nightmares and night terrors, narcolepsy, and sleep apnea.

Dreams

Ever since the dawn of language, dreams have been imbued with historical, personal, and religious significance (Dement, 1976). As early as 5000 B.C., Babylonians recorded and interpreted their dreams on clay tablets. Egyptians built temples in honor of Serapis, the god of dreams. People occasionally slept there, hoping Serapis would make their dreams more enjoyable. Dreams are described at length in more than seventy passages in the Bible, and in many less-developed cultures dreams are an extension of reality. For example, there is an account of an African chief who dreamed that he had visited England. On awakening, he ordered a wardrobe of European clothes. As he walked through the village in his new wardrobe, he was congratulated for having made the trip. Similarly Cherokee Indians who dreamed of being bitten by a snake were treated for the snake bite.

Sleep has its own world
And a wide realm of wild reality,
And dreams in their development have breath,
And tears, and tortures, and the touch of joy.

Byron, *The Dream*, 1816

Today we still try to figure out what dreams mean. Much of the interest stems from psychoanalysts who have probed the unconscious mind to understand the symbolic content of dreams. Although there is concrete information regarding sleep stages, there is very little scientific data to explain why we dream or what dreams mean.

The Interpretation of Dreams

Many of us dismiss the nightly excursion into the world of dreams as a second-rate mental activity, unworthy of our rational selves. By focusing only on the less mysterious waking world, we deny ourselves the opportunity of chance encounters with distant friends, remote places, dead relatives, gods, and demons. Four approaches have been developed to explain dreams.

Dreams as Wish Fulfillment In Freud's (1900/1953) theory, the reason we dream is *wish fulfillment*. After analyzing clients' dreams in therapy, Freud concluded that dreams are unconscious attempts to fulfill needs, especially those involving sex and aggression, that cannot be expressed, or that go ungratified, during waking hours. For example, people who are sexually inhibited while awake would likely have dreams with erotic content; those who have strong aggressive tendencies and hold in anger while awake would likely have dreams filled with violence and hostility. Freud also stressed that dreams often contain memories of infancy and childhood experiences, and especially of events associated with parents. He said our dreams frequently contain information from the day or two preceding the dream. In his view, many of our dreams consist of combinations of these distant, early experiences with our parents and more recent daily events. He emphasized that the task of dream interpretation is complicated because we successfully disguise our wish fulfillment in dreams.

Our unconscious is like a vast subterranean factory
with intricate machinery that is never idle, where work
goes on day and night from the time we are born until
the moment of our death.

Milton Saperstein,
***Paradoxes of Everyday Life*, 1955**

Freud believed that, in disguising our wish fulfillment, our dreams create a great deal of symbolism. Do you dream about elongated objects—sticks, tree trunks, umbrellas, neckties, and snakes? If so, Freud would have said, you are dreaming about male genitals. Do you dream about small boxes, ovens, cavities, ships, and rooms? Freud would have claimed your dreams were about female genitals. Freud thought that, once a therapist understood a client's symbolism, the nature of a dream could then be interpreted.

Dreams as Problem Solving Whether or not dreams are an arena in which we can play out our ungratified needs, they are a mental realm where we can solve problems and think creatively. Scottish author Robert Louis Stevenson (1850–1894), for example, claimed he got the idea for *Dr. Jekyll and Mr. Hyde* in a dream. Elias Howe, attempting to invent a machine that sewed, reportedly dreamed he was captured by savages carrying spears with holes in their tips. On waking, Howe realized he should place the hole for the thread at the end of the needle, not the middle. Dreams might spark such gifts of inspiration because they weave together, in unique and creative ways, current experiences with the past.

Rosalind Cartwright (1978, 1989) studied the role of dreaming in problem solving. Participants in her study were awakened just after they had completed a period of REM sleep and then were questioned about their dreams. The first dream of the night, it turns out, often reflects a realistic view of a problem. The second dream usually deals with a similar experience in the recent past. Frequently the third dream goes back to an earlier point in the dreamer's life. The next several dreams often take place in the future. It is at this point, Cartwright says, that problem solving begins. However, many sleepers never get this far in a night's dreaming, and others just keep repeating the problem.

Dreams as Entertainment Can we banish evil, fly high and fast, or create a happy ending for our dreams at will? According to Stanford researcher Stephen LaBerge (1992), in the landscape of "lucid dreams," you can actually learn to take control of your dreams. **Lucid dreams** *are a class of dreams in which a person "wakes up" mentally but remains in the sensory landscape of the dream world.* During

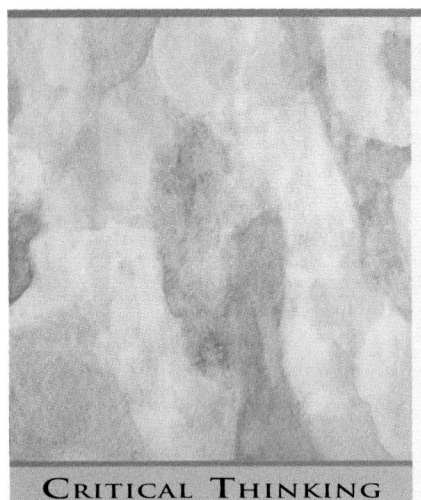

Conducting Research on Lucid Dreaming

You have read about some strategies to promote lucid dreaming. You might have experienced some dreams in which you experienced having greater control over the action in the dream than you did in other dreams. One example is when you wake up in the middle of a dream and then, when you resume sleeping, pick up the dream right where you left off. At other times, especially during nightmares, your dreams might seem intractable and threatening; if you could direct your dreams, you'd certainly interrupt this dream process or redesign the content to be more comforting.

Speculate about the kinds of difficulties dream researchers would have when conducting research on lucid dreaming. What kinds of challenges would arise if you were conducting dream research in a laboratory, particularly research that explores the amount of control the dreamer can exert over experience? This exercise will assist you to *evaluate the quality of conclusions about behavior* using psychological research.

Several questions may have occurred to you as you analyzed the difficulties involved in dream research:

- How would you reliably identify when a dreamer is dreaming?
- What if the phenomenon works only some of the time?
- How long would you have to track and analyze one dreamer's experience in order to establish the usefulness of the approach?
- What if the dreamer has dreams, but simply can't remember the detail or action of the dream?
- What if participation in a dream research laboratory sets up competing processes that interfere with the processes you wish to study?
- Were there other variables that influence the quality of research?

---

a lucid dream, the sleeper is consciously aware that the dream is taking place and can gain some control over dream content.

LaBerge describes a number of techniques to increase lucid dreaming. If you awaken from a dream in the middle of the night, immediately return to the dream in your imagination. Then envision yourself recognizing the dream. Tell yourself that the next time you dream you want to recognize that you are dreaming. If your intention is strong and clear enough, when you return to sleep you might discover that you are in a lucid dream.

Dreams as Meaningless   The **activation-synthesis view** *states that dreams have no inherent meaning. Rather, they reflect the brain's efforts to make sense out of or find meaning in the neural activity that takes place during REM sleep.* In this view, the brain's activity involves a great deal of random activity during REM sleep, and dreams are an attempt to synthesize this chaos (McCarley, 1989).

The Nature of Dreams

The world of dreams raises some intriguing questions. Do we dream in color? Why can't we remember all of our dreams? Do animals dream?

Some people say they dream only in black and white, but virtually everyone's dreams contain color. However, we often forget the color by the time we awaken and recall the dream. Some people claim that certain colors have fixed meanings in their dreams—white for purity, red for passion, green for vitality, black for evil or death, for example. However, no evidence has been found to support this belief. Red may stand for passion in one dream, danger in another, and anger in yet another dream.

Everyone dreams, but some of us remember our dreams better than others do. It's not surprising that we don't remember all of our dreams, since dreaming occurs at such a low level of consciousness. Psychoanalytic theory suggests we forget most of our dreams because they are threatening, but there is no evidence to support this belief. We remember our dreams best when we are awakened during or just after a dream. Similarly the dreams we have just before we awaken are the ones we are most likely to remember. People whose sleep cycles have long periods between their last REM stage and awakening are more likely to report that they don't dream at all or rarely remember their dreams.

It is impossible to say for certain whether or not animals dream; we know they have periods of REM sleep, so it

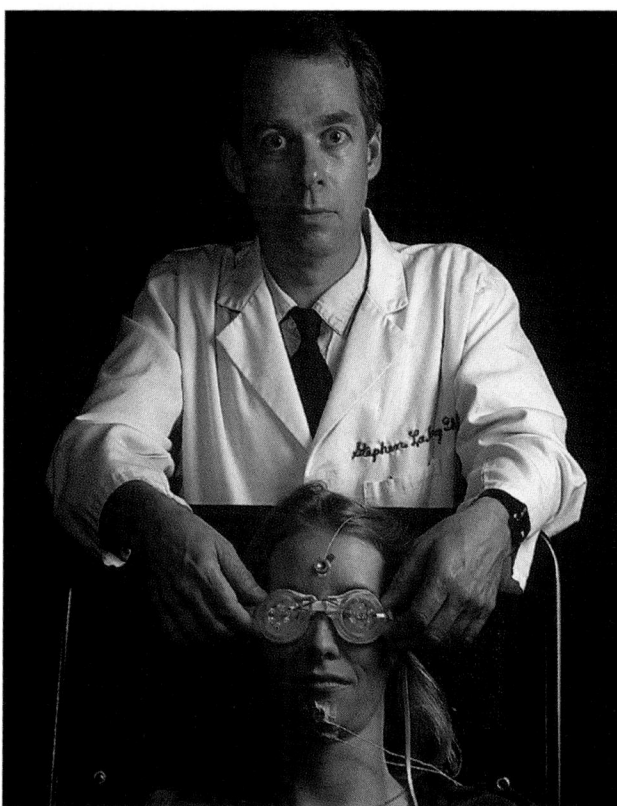

One of Stephen LaBerge's strategies for studying lucid dreaming is to ask volunteers to wear a sleep mask with sensors that turn on a red flashing light when REM sleep appears. The drowsy individual detects the flashing red light, then usually goes back to sleep after the light is turned off. The red light alerts dreamers that they were dreaming.

is possible that they do. However, dogs' twitching and howling during sleep, for instance, should not be taken as evidence that they are dreaming.

Dreams and Culture

Although dreams are a private world, reflecting our unique hopes, fears, and circumstances, they also reflect the environment around us. For example, Americans may dream about being naked in front of strangers and feeling deeply embarrassed about their predicament, but it's unlikely that someone from an African culture who wears little or no clothing would have such a dream. Similarly, few urban Americans dream of being chased by cows, but this is a common nightmare for the inhabitants of Ghana in western Africa (Barnouw, 1963).

In one study, the dreams of Mexican American and Anglo-American college students were analyzed for images of death, such as cadavers and graveyards (Roll, Hinton, & Glazer, 1974). Predictably, the theme of death figured considerably more in the dreams of Mexican American students than in Anglo-American students' dreams. One explanation for the difference is that the Mexican American students probably had more experience in caring for sick or dying relatives at home.

Although dreams are used in psychotherapy to gain insight and self-awareness, they do not play much of a role in our everyday lives. Some cultures, however, regard dreams as supernatural visions that guide personal behavior. Sociocultural Worlds 5.2 describes the role of dreams in a remote Malaysian culture.

REVIEW

Dreams

Understanding dreams requires knowledge of how dreams are interpreted, the role of culture in dreams, whether we dream in color, whether animals dream, why we can't remember all of our dreams, and whether we can influence what we dream about. Freud's psychoanalytic view states that dreams are wish fulfillment of unmet needs in our waking state. Freud believed that dreams often involve a combination of daily residue and early childhood experiences. He stressed that dreams have rich symbolic content. A second view of dreams states that dreams are thinking activities and attempts to solve problems. A third view, the activation-synthesis view, states that dreams are the brain's way of trying to make sense out of neural activity during REM sleep. The content of dreams is often influenced by cultural experiences. Dreams play a more salient role in many cultures other than Western cultures. We usually dream in color but don't remember. We don't know whether or not animals dream, but they may, since they experience REM sleep. Some people can influence their dreams through lucid dreaming.

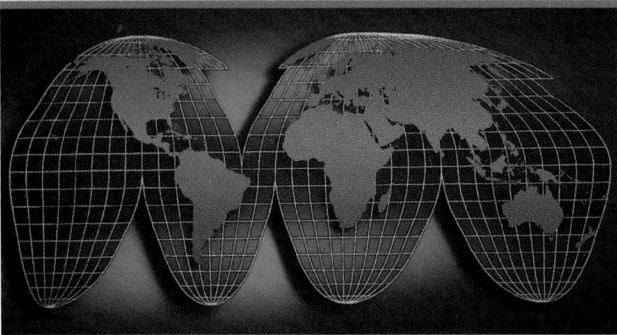

The Role of Dreams in the Senoi Tribe of Malaysia

The Senoi, numbering between 20,000 and 30,000, are an easygoing and nonviolent people who inhabit the jungle highlands of West Malaysia in Southeast Asia. They hunt small game with blowpipes, gather fruit and berries, and fish with traps and baskets when they are not tending their fields. They are said to be among the happiest and healthiest people in the world. Their happiness and health have been attributed to their ability to control their dreams and to use dreams as an integral part of their culture.

According to Kilton Stewart (1953, 1972), who studied the Senoi culture in the 1930s, Senoi life is a veritable dream clinic. Not only do the Senoi share and interpret their dreams, more importantly, they shape and control them. They dream the dreams they desire, free of fearful chases and frightening falls and full of sensuality and creativity. Senoi parents discuss their children's dreams every day at breakfast. They ask their children what they dreamed, praise them for dreaming, and talk about the dreams' significance.

When a Senoi child recounted a dream about falling, Stewart reported that the parent answered, "This is a wonderful dream, one of the best dreams a person can have. Where did you fall to, and what did you discover?" According to Stewart, the adult further encouraged the child by saying, "Everything you do in a dream has a purpose, beyond your understanding while you are asleep. You must relax and enjoy yourself when you fall in a dream. Falling is the quickest way to get in contact with the powers of the spirit world, the powers laid open to you through your dreams." Stewart claimed that instructions such as these brought about changes in the child's dreams.

Recently Stewart's claims have been questioned by anthropologists who spent considerable time observing the Senoi culture throughout the 1960s and 1970s (Denton, 1988). In keeping with Stewart's conclusions, the anthropologists found that dreams are far more important in the Senoi culture than in any Western culture. Dreams are essential for contacting the supernatural world and play a role in Senoi healing ceremonies. However, the anthropologists found that dreams do not dominate the Senoi culture the way Stewart described, and they also could find no evidence that the Senoi conduct morning dream clinics with their children. In fact, there was no evidence that parents instruct their children about dreaming in any way. In addition, the anthropologists found that violent acts did occur and that the Senoi were not as healthy as Stewart had claimed.

According to his critics, Stewart was a well-meaning charmer and storyteller, but he was not a careful, data-gathering scientist. He misunderstood how dreams are used in the Senoi culture and he let his imagination work overtime. The saga of Stewart reminds us of one of science's most important caveats, mentioned in chapter 1: be skeptical of anything that claims access to wondrous powers and supernatural forces.

HYPNOSIS

A young cancer patient is about to undergo a painful bone marrow transplant procedure. A doctor directs the boy's attention, asking him to breathe with him and listen carefully. The boy becomes absorbed in a pleasant fantasy—he is riding a motorcycle over a huge pizza, dodging anchovies and maneuvering around chunks of mozzarella. Minutes later the procedure is over. The boy is relaxed and feels good about his self-control (Long, 1986). The doctor successfully used hypnosis as a technique to help the young cancer patient control pain.

Hypnosis *is a psychological state of altered attention and awareness in which the individual is unusually receptive to suggestions.* Hypnosis has been used since the beginning of recorded history. It has been associated with religious ceremonies, magic, the supernatural, and many erroneous theories. Today hypnosis is recognized as a legitimate process in psychology and medicine, although much is yet to be learned about how it works.

In the eighteenth century, Austrian physician Anton Mesmer cured his patients by passing magnets over their bodies. Mesmer said the problems were cured by "animal magnetism," an intangible force that passes from therapist to patient. In reality, the cures were due to a form of hypnotic suggestion. Mesmer's claims were investigated by a committee appointed by the French Academy of Science. The committee agreed that Mesmer's treatment was effective. However, they disputed his theoretical claims about animal magnetism and prohibited him from practicing in Paris. Mesmer's theory of animal magnetism was called mesmerism, and even today we use the term *mesmerized* to mean hypnotized or enthralled.

Features of the Hypnotic State

There are four steps used to induce hypnosis. First, the hypnotist minimizes distraction and makes the subject comfortable. Second, the hypnotist tells the subject to concentrate on something specific, such as an imagined scene or the ticking of a watch. Third, the hypnotist describes what to expect in the hypnotic state (for example, relaxation or a pleasant floating sensation). Fourth, the hypnotist suggests certain events or feelings he or she knows will occur or observes occurring (for instance, "your eyes are getting tired"). When the suggested effects occur, the subject interprets them as being caused by the hypnotist's suggestions and accepts them as an indication that something is happening. This increases the subject's expectations that the hypnotism will make things happen in the future and makes the subject even more suggestible.

An important characteristic of the hypnotic state is the subject's suggestibility. When individuals are hypnotized, they readily accept and respond to ideas offered by the hypnotist. **Posthypnotic suggestion** *is a suggestion, made by the hypnotist while the subject is in a hypnotic state, that the subject carries out after emerging from the hypnotic state.* **Posthypnotic amnesia,** *induced by the hypnotist's suggestion, is the subject's inability to remember what took place during hypnosis.*

Individual Differences in Hypnosis

Do you think you could be hypnotized? What about your friends—are they more likely or less likely to be influenced by hypnosis than you are? For as long as hypnosis has been studied, about 200 years, some people have appeared to be more easily hypnotized than others. In fact, about 10 to 20 percent of the population are very susceptible to hypnosis, 10 percent or less cannot be hypnotized at all, and the remainder fall somewhere in between (Hilgard, 1965). There is no simple way to tell whether you can be hypnotized, but if you have the capacity to immerse yourself in imaginative activities—listening to a favorite piece of music or reading a novel, for example—you are a likely candidate. People who are susceptible to hypnosis become completely absorbed in what they are doing, removing the boundaries between themselves and what they are experiencing in their environment.

Theories of Hypnosis

Ever since Anton Mesmer proposed his theory of "animal magnetism," psychologists have been trying to figure out why hypnosis works. Contemporary theorists are divided. Does hypnosis produce a special cognitive process, or is it simply a form of learned social behavior?

In the **special process theory,** *hypnotic behavior is different from nonhypnotic behavior. Hypnotic responses elicited by suggestions are involuntary, rather than voluntary, reactions. Dissociations in cognitive systems take place and amnesic barriers are formed.* **Hidden observer** *is the term used by Ernest Hilgard to describe how part of a hypnotized individual's mind is completely aware of what is happening. The individual remains a passive, or hidden, observer until called on to comment.* Hilgard (1977) discovered this double train of thought in hypnosis during a class demonstration with a blind student. Hilgard, the hypnotist, induced deafness in the blind student and demonstrated that the subject was completely unresponsive to what was going on around him.

A student asked whether the subject really was an unresponsive as he seemed. Hilgard, being a flexible teacher, asked the subject if there was a part of him that could hear. If so, he was told to raise a finger. Surprisingly, the finger rose. Hilgard asked the subject to report from the part that was listening and made his finger rise; at the same time, he told the subject that he would not be able to hear what this part of himself said. The second part of the individual's awareness had heard all that went on and reported it. Further inquiry by Hilgard revealed that approximately half of a group of highly hypnotizable subjects had a hidden observer but were unaware of it until they went through a procedure similar to the blind individual's.

A conflicting perspective, the **nonstate view,** *says that hypnotic behavior is similar to other forms of social behavior and can be explained without resorting to special processes. According to this perspective, hypnotic behavior is purposeful, goal-directed action that is best understood by the way subjects interpret their situation and how they try to present themselves.* The nonstate view recognizes that "good" hypnotic subjects often act as if they have lost control over their behavior, but these aspects of behavior are interpreted as voluntary rather than automatic (Spanos & others, 1992).

Applications of Hypnosis

Hypnosis is widely used in psychotherapy, medicine and dentistry, criminal investigation, and sports. Hypnosis has been used in psychotherapy to treat alcoholism, somnambulism, suicidal tendencies, overeating, and smoking. One of hypnosis's least effective, yet most often used, applications is to help people stop overeating and quit smoking. Hypnotists direct their patients to stop these behaviors, but dramatic results rarely are achieved unless the patient is already highly motivated to change. The most effective use of hypnosis is as an adjunct to various forms of psychotherapy, which we will discuss in chapter 17.

In our discussion of hypnosis, we have seen that, in the special process view, hypnosis alters a person's state of consciousness. Next we will see that ever since the dawn of human history people have used drugs to alter consciousness, to "get high."

"You certainly may <u>not</u> try to hypnotize me."

Drawing by Frascino; © 1983 The New Yorker Magazine, Inc.

Hypnosis

Hypnosis is a psychological state of altered attention in which the subject is unusually receptive to suggestion. The history of hypnosis began with Austrian physician Anton Mesmer and his belief in animal magnetism; a present view is the hidden-observer view. Regardless of how hypnosis is induced, it includes these features: the subject is made comfortable and distracting stimuli are reduced; the individual is told to concentrate on something that takes him or her away from the immediate environment; and suggestions are made about what the subject is expected to experience in the hypnotic state. About 10 to 20 percent of the population are highly susceptible to hypnosis, about 10 percent cannot be hypnotized at all, and the remainder fall in between.

There are two broad, competing theories about hypnosis. In the special process view, hypnotic behavior is qualitatively different from normal behavior. It is involuntary and dissociation between cognitive systems and amnesic barriers is believed to be involved. Hilgard's hidden observer theory is an important perspective. The alternative, nonstate view argues that hypnotic behavior is similar to other forms of social behavior and can be explained without special processes. From this perspective, goal-directed action is purposeful and understood by the way subjects interpret their role and how they try to present themselves. Hypnosis has been widely applied, with mixed results, to a variety of circumstances, including psychotherapy, medicine and dentistry, criminal investigation, and sports.

PSYCHOACTIVE DRUGS AND ADDICTION

When Sigmund Freud began to experiment with cocaine, he was searching for possible medical applications, such as a painkiller for eye surgery. He soon found that the drug induced ecstasy. He even wrote to his fiancée and told her how just a small dose of cocaine produced lofty, wonderful sensations. As it became apparent that some people become psychologically addicted to cocaine, and after several died from overdoses, Freud quit using the drug. Just what are psychoactive drugs?

Psychoactive Drugs

Psychoactive drugs *act on the nervous system to alter our state of consciousness, modify our perceptions, and change our moods.* Ever since our ancient ancestors first sat entranced in front of a communal fire, humans have searched for substances that would produce pleasurable sensations and alter their states of consciousness. Among the substances that alter consciousness are alcohol, hemp and cactus plants, mushrooms, poppies, and tobacco, an herb that has been smoked and sniffed for more than 400 centuries.

Human beings are attracted to psychoactive substances because they help them adapt to or escape from an ever-changing environment. Smoking, drinking, and taking drugs reduce tension and frustration, relieve boredom and fatigue, and in some cases help us to escape from the harsh realities of the world. Psychoactive drugs provide us with pleasure by giving us tranquility, joy, relaxation, kaleidoscopic perceptions, surges of exhilaration, and prolonged heightened sensation. They sometimes have practical uses, like the use of amphetamines to stay awake all night to study for an exam. We might also take drugs because we are curious about their effects, in some cases because of sensational accounts in the media. We may wonder if drugs can provide us with unique, profound experiences. We also take drugs for social reasons, hoping they will make us feel more at ease and happier in our interactions and relationships with others.

In our culture, however, the use of psychoactive drugs for such personal gratification and temporary adaptation carries a high price tag: drug dependence, personal and social disorganization, and a predisposition to serious and sometimes fatal diseases. What might initially have been intended as enjoyment and adaptation can eventually turn into sorrow and maladaptation. For example, drinking might initially help people relax and forget about their worries. But then they might begin to drink more and more, until the drinking becomes an addiction that destroys relationships and careers and leads to physical and psychological damage, including permanent liver damage and major depression.

Addiction

What is addiction? Are addictions diseases?

The Nature of Addiction

As a person continues to take a psychoactive drug, the body develops a **tolerance,** *which means that a greater amount of the drug is needed to produce the same effect.* The first time someone takes 5 milligrams of Valium, for example, the drug will make them feel very relaxed. But after taking the pill every day for 6 months, the person might need to take 10 milligrams to achieve the same calming effect.

Addiction *is a physical dependence on a drug.* **Withdrawal** *is the undesirable intense pain and craving that an addicted person feels when the addicting drug is withdrawn.* **Psychological dependence** *is the need to take a drug to cope with problems and stress.* In both physical addiction and psychological dependence, the psychoactive drug plays a powerful role in the user's life.

Are Addictions Diseases?

Controversy swirls about whether addictions are diseases. The **disease model of addiction** *describes addictions as biologically based, lifelong diseases that involve a loss of control over behavior and require medical and/or spiritual treatment for recovery.* According to the disease model, addiction is either inherited or taught to a person early in life. As such, alcohol might have more far-reaching and damaging effects on the addiction-prone individual whose genetic vulnerabilities induce severe reactions to addicting substances. Current or recent problems or relationships do not cause the disease. Addiction is a progressive, irreversible disease from which there is never complete recovery. People with the disease cannot control their addiction themselves; they require help from others and from a higher power or spiritual redemption. Denial characterizes addicted people—they resist perceiving that they have an addiction. And relapse is viewed as a reemergence of the disease. The disease model has been strongly promoted and supported by the medical profession and Alcoholics Anonymous.

Critics of the disease approach offer several arguments against it (Magid, 1995). The biological mechanisms that might account for addictive behavior have not been identified. Addiction is not necessarily a lifelong process. The disease model discourages people from developing self-control and stigmatizes people with labels like *addict* and *alcoholic,* in some cases for life. The disease approach prescribes a rigid program of therapy rather than advocating more flexible approaches.

Two critics of the disease model, Stanton Peele and Archie Brodsky (1991), believe that addiction is a habitual response and a source of gratification or security. They say that an addiction can involve *any* attachment or desire for sensations that grows to such proportions that it impairs the person's life; such attachments can include attachments to drugs, food, gambling, shopping, love, and sex. In this view, the "hook" of the addiction—what keeps people coming back to it—is that it provides people with feelings and gratifying sensations that they are not able to get in other ways. Peele and Brodsky believe that understanding addiction requires placing it in the proper context, as part of people's lives, their personalities, their relationships, their environments, and their perspectives. They call their model the "life-process" model. In sum, the **life-process model** *argues that addiction is not a disease but rather a habitual response and a source of gratification or security that can be understood only in the context of social relationships and experiences.* Each of these views of addiction—the disease model and the nondisease, life-process model—has its supporters. To read further about these two contrasting views of treating alcoholism, turn to Applications in Psychology 5.1.

Alcohol is an extremely powerful drug that acts on the body primarily as a depressant and slows down the brain's activities.

Alcohol

We do not always think of alcohol as a drug, but it is an extremely powerful one. Alcohol acts upon the body primarily as a depressant and slows down the brain's activities. This might seem surprising, since people who normally tend to be inhibited might begin to talk, dance, or socialize after a few drinks, but people "loosen up" after one or two drinks because the areas in the brain involved in controlling inhibition and judgment *slow down.* As people drink more, their inhibitions become even further reduced and their judgments become increasingly impaired. Activities requiring intellectual functioning and skill, such as driving, become impaired as more alcohol is consumed. Eventually the drinker becomes drowsy and falls asleep. With extreme intoxication, a person may even lapse into a coma and die. Each of these effects varies with how the person's body metabolizes alcohol, body weight, the amount of alcohol consumed, and whether previous drinking has led to tolerance.

Alcohol is the most widely used drug in our society. A 1992 Gallup poll revealed that 64 percent of American adults drank beer, wine, or liquor at least occasionally—

Contrasting Views on Treating Alcoholism

Alcoholism exacts a horrible toll on the drinker and the drinker's family, but the damage doesn't stop there. Drunk driving, workplace losses, and overburdened health care systems are only some of the larger-scale loss issues related to alcohol abuse. The search for effective methods of intervention has never been more intense. Among the treatments for alcoholism are twelve-step programs, cognitive therapy, and life-skills training programs. *Twelve-step programs,* such as Alcoholics Anonymous (AA), emphasize the importance of confession, group support, and spiritual commitment to God to help individuals cope with alcoholism. The twelve steps represent the heart of AA's principles, providing a precise guide for members to use in their recovery. AA's list of the twelve steps is presented in table 5.A.

Alcoholics Anonymous groups are open and free to anyone, alcoholics as well as nonalcoholics. The AA organization reports that 29 percent of AA members stay sober for more than 5 years. The age range of members is from teenagers to the elderly. The principles of AA have been revised and adopted by a number of other self-help groups, such as Narcotics Anonymous, Gamblers Anonymous, and Al-Anon. AA meetings often include extensive personal testimonies by AA members.

In a recent book (Ellis & Velton, 1992), cognitive therapist Albert Ellis, with his colleague Emmett Velton, tailored rational emotive therapy to the treatment of alcoholics. They believe that the way to treat alcoholism is by replacing maladaptive thought patterns with adaptive ones. In contrast to AA's emphasis on spiritual commitment and powerlessness, they argue that self-control and personal responsibility rather than control by a higher power will help alcoholics increase their sobriety.

Rational Recovery (RR), one of the many nonreligious self-help groups for recovering alcoholics and their relatives that have been formed in recent years, traces its roots directly to Ellis. RR teaches that problem drinking results from people's beliefs that they are powerless and incompetent. Using Ellis's approach, a moderator (usually an RR member who has recovered from alcoholism) helps guide group discussion and get members to think more rationally and act more responsibly. While AA stresses that alcoholics can never become recovered but are always in some phase of recovery, RR tells members that recovery is not only possible but that their methods help members kick their drinking problem in a year or so. Two other self-help groups (unrelated to Ellis's approach) that have sprung up in recent years as alternatives to AA are the Secular Organization for Sobriety (SOS) and Women for Sobriety (WFS). Turned off by AA's religious emphasis, the new groups rely more on willpower and self-control than on a higher power.

Stanton Peele and Archie Brodsky (1991) developed a life-skills training program for combating alcoholism. They train people to develop skills for taking control of their lives. Like Ellis, they believe that an approach emphasizing responsibility and self-control is better than AA's emphasis on helplessness and abdication of power. In the life-skills training approach, people learn how to assess their values and what is really important to them, how to carry out plans for change, and how to establish community ties.

TABLE 5.A

AA's Twelve-Step Recovery Program

Following are the twelve steps as they were originally presented in the *Big Book, Alcoholics Anonymous.*

1. We admitted we were powerless over alcohol, that our lives had become unmanageable.
2. Came to believe that a Power greater than ourselves could restore us to sanity.
3. Made a decision to turn our will and our lives over to the care of God *as we understood Him.*
4. Made a searching and fearless moral inventory of ourselves.
5. Admitted to God, to ourselves, and to another human being the exact nature of our wrongs.
6. Were entirely ready to have God remove all these defects of character.
7. Humbly asked Him to remove our shortcomings.
8. Made a list of all persons we had harmed, and became willing to make amends to them all.
9. Made direct amends to such people wherever possible, except when to do so would injure them or others.
10. Continued to take personal inventory and when we were wrong promptly admitted it.
11. Sought through prayer and meditation to improve our conscious contact with God *as we understood Him,* praying only for knowledge of His will for us and the power to carry that out.
12. Having had a spiritual awakening as the result of these steps, we tried to carry this message to alcoholics, and to practice these principles in all our affairs.

down from 71 percent in the late 1970s. More than 13 million people in the United States call themselves alcoholics. Alcoholism is the third leading killer in the United States. Each year approximately 25,000 people are killed, and 1.5 million injured, by drunk drivers. More than 60 percent of homicides involve the use of alcohol by either the offender or the victim, while 65 percent of aggressive sexual acts against women involve the use of alcohol by the offender. Alcohol costs the United States more than $40 billion each year in health costs, lost productivity, accidents, and crimes.

Alcohol is a good preservative for everything but brains.
Mary Pettibone Poole,
***A Glass Eye at a Keyhole,* 1938**

A special concern is the high rate of alcohol use and abuse by adolescents and college students. Alcohol is the substance most abused by adolescents and college students. According to national surveys of more than 15,000 high school seniors taken every year since 1975, approximately one-third have consumed 5 or more drinks in a row in the past 2-week interval (Johnston, O'Malley, & Bachman, 1994). Alcohol use by high school students has gradually declined since the early 1980s; for example, the percentage of high school seniors who use alcohol monthly has declined from 72 percent in the early 1980s to 50 percent in 1994. However, the drinking habits of college students have shown little drop—almost half of all college students say they drink heavily (Johnston, O'Malley, & Bachman, 1992).

The assumption among many college students that "everyone" is getting drunk, or wishes they were, might increase alcohol abuse. In one recent series of studies, students systematically overestimated their fellow students' support for heavy drinking (Prentice & Miller, 1993). Thus, many college students are under the false impression that everyone else approves of heavy drinking, and they don't want to appear "uncool." See table 5.1 for some questions that often identify young adult substance abusers.

A special concern that has surfaced recently is an increase in drug use, including alcohol consumption, by young adolescents (Gullotta, Adams, & Montemayor, 1995). While the gradual decline in drinking by high school seniors continued, the decline did not occur for eighth-graders; in fact, they showed a slight increase in drinking (Johnston, O'Malley, & Bachman, 1994).

People in many other countries actually drink more than Americans do. More than 90 percent of the adults in Belgium, England, the Czech Republic, and Hungary drink, and more than 85 percent of the adults in Australia, Norway, and Spain drink (compared to 64 percent of adults in the United States). Some ethnic groups have higher rates of alcoholism than others. Irish and Native Americans, as well as people in many European countries, such as France, have high rates of alcoholism. Jews, Greeks, and Chinese have low rates of alcoholism. To read further about ethnic and sociocultural influences on alcohol abuse, turn to Sociocultural Worlds 5.3.

Some conclude that heredity plays an important role in certain forms of alcoholism (Goodwin, 1988). However, the

TABLE 5.1

Items on the Rutgers Collegiate Substance Abuse Screening Test That Were Most Likely to Identify Young Adult Substance Abusers

1. Have you gotten into financial difficulties as a result of drinking or using other drugs?
2. Is alcohol or other drug use making your college life unhappy?
3. Has drinking alcohol or using other drugs ever been behind your losing a job?
4. Has alcohol ever interfered with your preparation for exams?
5. Has your efficiency decreased since drinking &/or using other drugs?
6. Is your drinking &/or drug use jeopardizing your academic performance?
7. Has your ambition decreased since drinking &/or drug using?
8. Does drinking or using other drugs cause you to have difficulty sleeping?
9. Have you ever felt remorse after drinking &/or using other drugs?
10. Do you crave a drink or other drug at a definite time daily?
11. Do you want a drink or other drug the next morning?
12. Have you ever had a complete or partial loss of memory as a result of drinking or using other drugs?
13. Is drinking or using other drugs affecting your reputation?
14. Does drinking &/or using other drugs make you careless of your family's welfare?
15. Have you ever been to a hospital or institution on account of drinking or other drug use?

Note: Young adults who answered yes to these questions were more likely to be substance abusers than were those who answered no.

The RCSAST is to be used only as part of a complete assessment battery since more research needs to be done with this instrument.

From Bennett, et al., "Identifying Young Adult Substance Abusers: The Rutgers Collegiate Substance Abuse Screening Test" in *Journal of Studies on Alcohol,* 54:522–527. Copyright © 1993 Alcohol Research Documentation, Inc., Piscataway, NJ. Reprinted by permission.

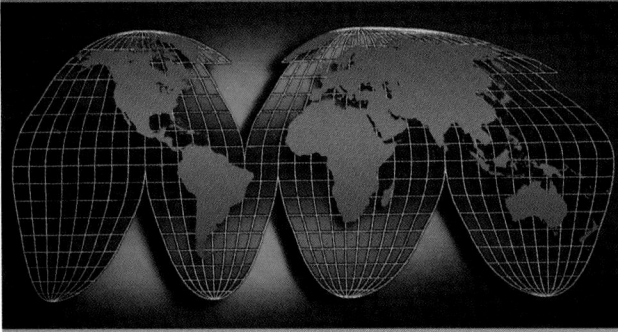

SOCIOCULTURAL WORLDS 5.3

Sociocultural Influences on Alcohol Abuse

Cultural attitudes about drinking are related to alcohol abuse. For example, Muslims and Mormons, whose religious views prohibit drinking alcohol, as well as Orthodox Jews, who traditionally have limited drinking alcohol for religious purposes, have low incidences of alcoholism. In contrast, alcoholism is high among Europeans, who make up less than 15 percent of the world's population but consume approximately half the alcohol. The French have the highest rate of alcoholism in the world—approximately 15 percent are alcoholics, and 30 percent have impaired health as a result of alcohol consumption.

Various Asian populations (Chinese, Japanese, and Koreans) have a genetic protective mechanism against alcohol abuse. The enzyme that metabolizes alcohol is inactive in their bodies, causing a flushed face after they ingest even a small amount of alcohol. Nonetheless, when Asian youth immigrate to the United States, they tend to drink more than their peers who remain in Asian countries, suggesting a cultural influence on their drinking.

Anxiety and stress may help explain the increase in alcohol abuse in other ethnic and cultural subgroups. People who must make the transition from one cultural tradition to another often experience conflict and alienation. These stresses may lead to excessive drinking. For example, the Agringados in southern Texas, who face the challenge of shifting from the Latin to the Anglo culture, have a high incidence of alcohol abuse (Madsen, 1964). Higher rates of cirrhosis of the liver also have been found among Hopi Indians who moved into cities than among those who remained on the reservation (Kunitz & others, 1971). Alcoholism occurs in significant numbers among the Tarahumara Indians of northern Mexico only when they come into frequent contact with other cultures, such as through intermarriage with *mestizos* (persons with mixed Indian and European ancestry) (West, 1972). Another study has shown that most of the Muslims who violate the religious prohibition against drinking live in a predominately Christian neighborhood and are not active in their mosques (Midgely, 1971).

Strategies to help people navigate the stressful transition between cultures also help reduce alcohol abuse. Some of the more promising strategies include education programs that encourage the whole community to support their members who are at risk for alcohol abuse, economic development programs for Native Americans, who have an especially high rate of alcoholism (Watts & Lewis, 1988), and training programs to teach alternative ways of coping with stress (Lorion & Allen, 1989).

Three cultures in which there is a low incidence of alcohol abuse are the *(a)* Muslim, *(b)* Mormon, and *(c)* Orthodox Jewish cultures.

precise mechanism for inheritance has not yet been identified. Family studies consistently find a high frequency of alcoholism in the first-degree relatives of alcoholics (Cotton, 1979). In one review of research on family alcoholism, when the father was an alcoholic, both sons and daughters had increased rates of alcoholism; when the mother was an alcoholic, increased rates of alcoholism occurred only for daughters (Pollock & others, 1987). Twin studies of alcoholism have revealed a modest influence of heredity (Sher, 1991), while adoption studies document the contribution of biological relatives' alcoholism to alcoholism in male adoptees (Sher, 1993).

Although the family, twin, and adoption studies reveal a genetic influence on alcoholism, they also indicate that environmental factors play an important role. For example, family studies indicate that many alcoholics do not have close relatives who are alcoholics (Sher, 1993). Adoption studies suggest that heredity and environment interact for at least one form of alcoholism (environmentally dependent susceptibility), and some alcoholics do not have alcoholic biological parents. The large cultural variations in alcohol use also underscore that the environment plays an important role in alcoholism. Like other behaviors and problems, alcoholism is multiply determined, has multiple pathways, and can be effectively treated in multiple ways (Sobell & Sobell, 1992, in press).

Other Psychoactive Drugs

Now that we have discussed alcohol, let's explore the nature of a number of other psychoactive drugs.

Barbiturates and Tranquilizers

Barbiturates, *such as Nebutal and Seconal, are depressant drugs that induce sleep or reduce anxiety.* In heavy dosages, they can lead to impaired memory and decision making. When combined with alcohol (for instance, sleeping pills taken after a night of binge drinking), the result can be lethal. Barbiturates by themselves also can produce death in heavy dosages, which makes them the drug most often chosen in suicide attempts. Abrupt withdrawal from barbiturates can produce seizures.

Tranquilizers, *such as Valium and Xanax, are depressant drugs that reduce anxiety and induce relaxation.* They are among the most widely used drugs in the United States and can produce withdrawal symptoms when a person stops taking them.

Opiates

Opiates, *which consist of opium and its derivatives, depress the central nervous system's activity.* The most common opiate drugs—morphine and heroin—affect synapses in the brain that use endorphins as their neurotransmitter. When these drugs leave the brain, the affected synapses become understimulated. For several hours after taking

"Just tell me where you kids get the idea to take so many drugs."

© 1990 by Sidney Harris.

an opiate, a person feels euphoric and relieved of pain and has an increased appetite for food and sex. But the opiates are among the most physically addictive drugs, leading to craving and painful withdrawal when the drug becomes unavailable. Morphine is sometimes used medically as a painkiller.

Recently, another hazardous consequence of opiate addiction has surfaced: AIDS. Most heroin addicts inject the drug intravenously. When they share their needles, blood from the needles can be passed on. When this blood comes from someone with AIDS, the virus can spread from the infected user to the uninfected user.

Stimulants

Stimulants *are psychoactive drugs that increase the central nervous system's activity.* The most widely used stimulants are caffeine, nicotine (in cigarettes), amphetamines, and cocaine. Coffee, tea, and caffeinated soft drinks are mild stimulants. Amphetamines and cocaine are much stronger stimulants.

Amphetamines are widely prescribed, often in the form of diet pills. They are also called "pep pills" and "uppers." Amphetamines increase the release of the neurotransmitter dopamine, which increases the user's activity level and pleasurable feelings.

Cocaine comes from the coca plant, native to Bolivia and Peru. For centuries Bolivians and Peruvians have chewed on the plant to increase their stamina. Today cocaine is either snorted or injected in the form of crystals or powder. The effect is a rush of euphoria, which eventually wears off, followed by depression, lethargy, insomnia, and irritability. Cocaine can even trigger a heart attack, stroke, or brain seizure.

When animals and humans chew coca leaves, small amounts of cocaine gradually enter the bloodstream, without any apparent adverse effects. However, when extracted cocaine is sniffed, smoked, or injected, it enters the bloodstream very rapidly, producing a rush of euphoric feelings that lasts for about 15 to 30 minutes. Because the rush depletes the supply of the neurotransmitters dopamine and norepinephrine in the brain, an agitated, depressed mood usually follows as the drug's euphoric effects decline.

Crack *is an intensified form of cocaine, consisting of chips of pure cocaine that are usually smoked.* Crack is believed to be one of the most addictive substances known, being much more addictive than heroin, barbiturates, and alcohol (Carroll & Miller, 1994). Emergency-room admissions related to crack have soared from less than 600 cases in 1985 to more than 15,000 cases a year in the early 1990s.

Treatments for cocaine addiction have not been very successful. Cocaine's addictive properties are so strong that 6 months after treatment, more than 50 percent of cocaine abusers return to the drug. Experts on drug abuse believe the best approach to reduce cocaine addiction is through prevention programs.

Marijuana

Marijuana is the dried leaves and flowers of the hemp plant, *Cannibas sativa,* which originated in central Asia but is now grown in most parts of the world. The plant's dried resin is known as hashish. The active ingredient in marijuana is THC, which stands for the chemical delta-9-tetrahydrocannabinol. This ingredient does not resemble the chemicals of other psychoactive drugs and does not affect a specific neurotransmitter. Rather, marijuana disrupts the membranes of neurons and affects the functioning of a variety of neurotransmitters and hormones.

The physical effects of marijuana include increases in pulse rate and blood pressure, reddening of the eyes, coughing, and dryness of the mouth. Psychological effects include a mixture of excitatory, depressive, and mildly hallucinatory characteristics, making it difficult to classify the drug. Marijuana can trigger spontaneous unrelated ideas, distorted perceptions of time and place, increased sensitivity to sounds and colors, and erratic verbal behavior. Marijuana can also impair attention and memory. When used daily in large amounts, marijuana can also alter sperm count and change hormonal cycles; it might be involved in some birth defects. Marijuana use declined during the 1980s, but an upsurge in its use has occurred in the 1990s (Johnston, O'Malley, & Bachman, 1994).

Hallucinogens

Hallucinogens *are psychoactive drugs that modify a person's perceptual experiences and produce visual images that are not real. Hallucinogens are also called psychedelic drugs, which means "mind altering."* LSD, PCP, and mescaline are examples of hallucinogens.

LSD (lysergic acid diethylamide) is a hallucinogen that even in low doses produces striking perceptual changes. Objects change their shape and glow. Colors become kaleidoscopic, fabulous images unfold as users close their eyes. Designs swirl, colors shimmer, bizarre scenes

FIGURE 5.7

LSD-Induced Hallucination
Under the influence of hallucinogenic drugs, such as LSD, several users have reported seeing images that have a tunnel effect like the one shown here.

appear. Sometimes the images are pleasurable; sometimes they are grotesque. Figure 5.7 shows one kind of perceptual experience that a number of LSD users have reported. LSD can influence the user's perception of time as well. Time often seems to slow down dramatically, so that brief glances at objects are experienced as deep, penetrating, and lengthy examinations, and minutes often seem to be hours or days.

LSD's effects on the body can include dizziness, nausea, and tremors. LSD acts primarily on the neurotransmitter serotonin in the brain, though it can affect dopamine as well. Emotional and cognitive effects can include rapid mood swings and impaired attention and memory. LSD was popular in the late 1960s and early 1970s, but its popularity dropped after its unpredictable effects became well publicized. However, a recent increase in LSD use by high school and college students has been reported (Johnston, O'Malley, & Bachman, 1994). LSD may be a prime example of generational forgetting. Today's youth don't hear what an earlier generation heard—that LSD can cause bad trips and undesirable flashbacks.

At this point we have discussed a number of drugs and their effects. A summary of the main types of drugs we have studied is presented in figure 5.8.

This chapter on states of consciousness completes Section Two, "Biological and Perceptual Processes." In the next section we will explore the nature of learning and cognition, beginning with chapter 6, "Learning."

Psychoactive Drugs and Addictions

Psychoactive drugs act on the central nervous system to alter states of consciousness, modify perceptions, and alter mood. Psychoactive substances have been used since the beginning of recorded history for pleasure, utility, curiosity, and social reasons. Tolerance for a psychoactive drug develops when a greater amount of the drug is needed to produce the same effect. Physical withdrawal is the intense pain and craving that arise when an addicted person stops taking the addictive drug. Psychological dependence is the need to take a drug to cope with problems and stress.

The disease model of addiction describes addictions as biologically based, lifelong diseases that involve a loss of control over behavior and require medical and/or spiritual treatment for recovery. Critics of the disease model argue that the biological mechanisms of alcoholism have not been identified, that alcoholism is not necessarily lifelong, that the disease model stigmatizes people with labels like *addict* and *alcoholic,* and that it advocates a rigid program of therapy.

In the life-process model, addiction is not a disease but rather a habitual response and a source of gratification or security that can be understood and treated only in the context of social relationships and experience.

Alcohol is an extremely powerful drug that acts on the body primarily as a depressant. Drinking makes people less inhibited and impairs their judgment, motor skills, and intellectual functioning. With extreme intoxication, the drinker may lapse into a coma and even die. Effects of alcohol vary according to a number of factors. Alcohol is the most widely used drug in America and the third leading killer. A special concern is the high rate of alcohol consumption by high school and college students. People in many countries drink more than people in the United States do.

Barbiturates are depressant drugs that induce sleep or reduce anxiety. Tranquilizers are depressant drugs that reduce anxiety and induce relaxation. Opiates (opium and its derivatives) depress the central nervous system's activity. Stimulants are psychoactive drugs that increase central nervous system activity. The most widely used stimulants are caffeine, nicotine, amphetamines, and cocaine. Cocaine provides a euphoric rush that is followed by depression, lethargy, insomnia, and irritability. Cocaine can trigger a heart attack, stroke, or brain seizure. Crack is an intensified form of cocaine and is believed to be one of the most addictive drugs. Treatments for cocaine addiction have not been very successful. Marijuana's psychological effects include a mixture of excitatory, depressive, and mildly hallucinatory characteristics, making the drug difficult to classify. Marijuana affects a number of neurotransmitters and hormones, and can impair attention and memory. Hallucinogens are psychoactive drugs that modify a person's perceptual experiences and produce visual images that are not real. Hallucinogens are also called psychedelic ("mind altering") drugs. LSD, PCP, and mescaline are examples of hallucinogens. There has been a recent increase in use of LSD.

Drug classification	Medical uses	Duration of effects	Short-term effects
Depressants			
Alcohol	Pain relief	3–6 hours	Relaxation, depressed brain activity, slowed behavior, reduced inhibitions
Barbiturates	Sleeping pill	1–16 hours	Relaxation, sleep
Tranquilizers	Anxiety reduction	4–8 hours	Relaxation, slowed behavior
Opiates (narcotics)	Pain relief	3–6 hours	Euphoric feelings, drowsiness, nausea
Stimulants			
Amphetamines	Weight control	2–4 hours	Increased alertness, excitability; decreased fatigue, irritability
Cocaine	Local anesthetic	1–2 hours	Increased alertness, excitability, euphoric feelings; decreased fatigue, irritability
Hallucinogens			
LSD	None	1–12 hours	Strong hallucinations, distorted time perception
Marijuana	Treatment of the eye disorder glaucoma	2–4 hours	Euphoric feelings, relaxation, mild hallucinations, time distortion, attention and memory impairment

One glass of wine equals one can of beer in alcoholic content.

Cocaine is extracted from coca plants.

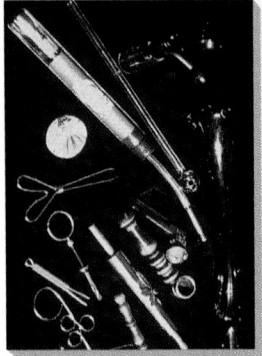

Cannabis paraphernalia, drug equipment or gadgets, is usually sold in "head shops" for use in smoking marijuana.

FIGURE 5.8

Drugs—Their Use, Effects, and Addictive Characteristics

Biological and Perceptual Processes

Overdose	Health risks	Risk of physical addiction	Risk of psychological dependence
Disorientation, loss of consciousness, even death at high blood-alcohol levels	Accidents, brain damage, liver disease, heart disease, ulcers, birth defects	Moderate	Moderate
Breathing difficulty, coma, possible death	Accidents, coma, possible death	High	High
Breathing difficulty, coma, possible death	Accidents, coma, possible death	Low	Low–moderate
Convulsions, coma, possible death	Accidents, infectious diseases such as AIDS	Very high	Very high
Extreme irritability, feelings of persecution, convulsions	Insomnia, hypertension, malnutrition, possible death	Moderate	High
Extreme irritability, feelings of persecution, convulsions, cardiac arrest, possible death	Insomnia, hypertension, malnutrition, possible death	Moderate–high	High
Severe mental disturbance, loss of contact with reality	Accidents	None	Very low
Fatigue, disoriented behavior	Accidents, respiratory disease	None	Low–moderate

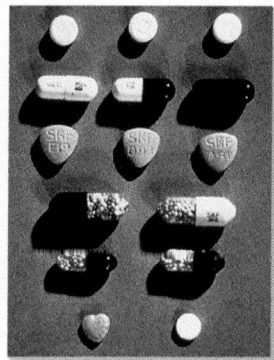

Tranquilizers are used for reducing anxiety and inducing relaxation.

Amphetamines are stimulants used to increase alertness and energy.

Shown here is a private, illegal laboratory for manufacturing LSD.

CRITICAL THINKING ABOUT BEHAVIOR
Critical Thinking as a Controlled Process

To be uncertain is to be uncomfortable, but to be certain is to be ridiculous.

Chinese proverb

As you have gathered by now, critical thinking can be a complex activity. How does the topic of consciousness relate to critical thinking? You learned in this chapter that human abilities allow us to function consciously at different levels of attention. The first distinction we discussed in this chapter emphasized the difference between automatic and controlled processes. In the early stages of learning an activity, we focus our attention. We concentrate hard to master the skills involved. As we become experienced and skilled in the activity, our actions become more automatic and we can reduce the conscious attention we pay to it. This process is much like being on "automatic pilot." We are free to direct our conscious attention elsewhere and still do a reasonable job at the task at hand.

Critical-thinking processes may be similar. We might struggle at first to learn the component skills, but then we can ease up. Or can we? It is fairly easy to be a lazy or uncritical thinker—one who engages in experience without analyzing it very much. We can invest very little energy in thinking and still "get by." We can stop paying attention in such concentrated ways and function on automatic pilot as a thinker. We can formulate opinions, express ideas, and even advocate action without necessarily demonstrating critical-thinking skills. We can give in to the forces that encourage us to think of our environment as unchallenging, stable, and certain.

How can we ward off these automatizing influences and maximize our critical-thinking skills? We can promote critical thinking as a controlled and purposeful process by adopting the following attitudes or skills:

- *Observe carefully.*
  Scrutinize the phenomenon or argument carefully so you understand it as completely as possible. Careful observation can help you identify some new features that eluded you at first glance.

- *Look for discrepancies.*
  It sometimes helps to ask, "What's missing from this picture?" Are there elements that should be present? How well do all the pieces fit together?

- *Expect that criticism will be appropriate.*
  Almost any argument will have a flaw or a special advantage.
  Almost any work of art or thought will have aspects to criticize.
  Almost any product or creation could be improved or refined.

- *Examine assumptions that underlie any position.*
  What would you have to believe in order to endorse the position?
  Are the values consistent with or discrepant from your own?

- *Adopt a skeptical stance.*
  If you are skeptical, it will be easier to ask meaningful questions about any phenomenon. Question even the obvious.

- *Tolerate uncertainty.*
  We might not be able to explain any behavior completely; but this doesn't justify withdrawing from critical analysis. Grappling with complex, incomplete ideas can be a very rewarding and adaptive activity.

If you notice that your critical-thinking experiences start to become easy or less frequent, be on your guard. Automatizing forces can rob you of some meaningful critical-thinking activities.

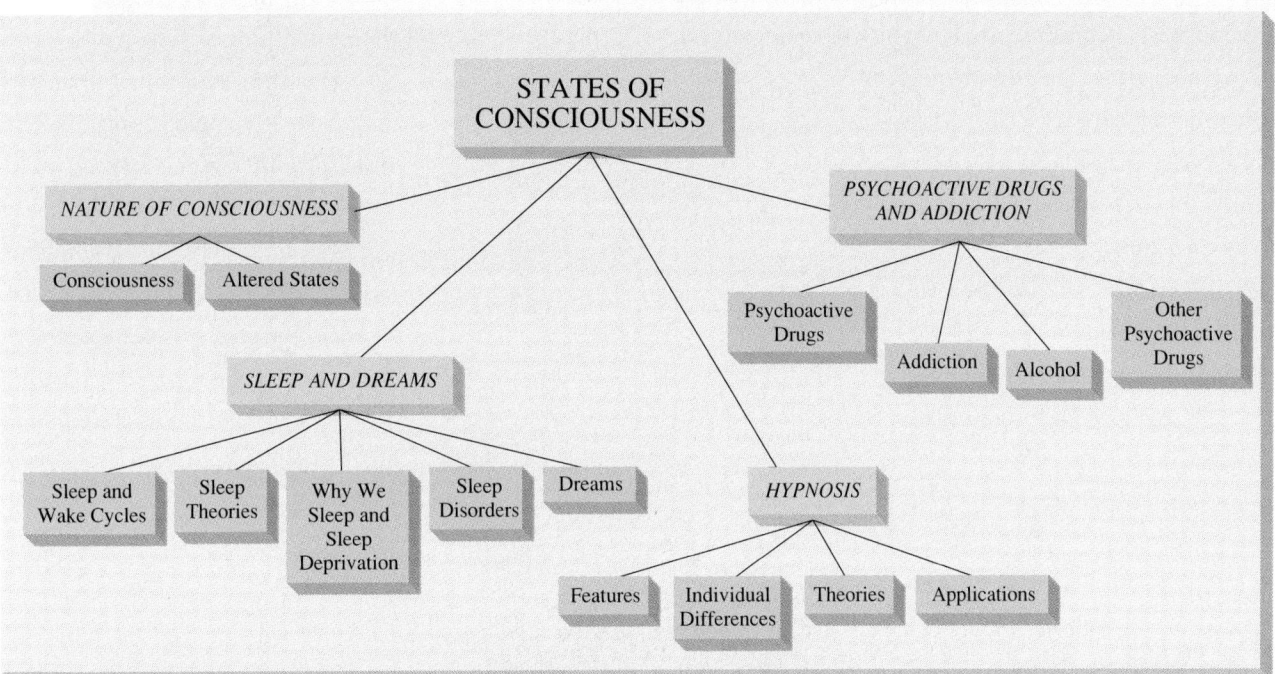

STATES OF CONSCIOUSNESS

NATURE OF CONSCIOUSNESS

Consciousness   Altered States

SLEEP AND DREAMS

Sleep and Wake Cycles   Sleep Theories   Why We Sleep and Sleep Deprivation   Sleep Disorders   Dreams

PSYCHOACTIVE DRUGS AND ADDICTION

Psychoactive Drugs   Addiction   Alcohol   Other Psychoactive Drugs

HYPNOSIS

Features   Individual Differences   Theories   Applications

W e began this chapter by exploring the nature of consciousness, and then studied about sleep and dreams— sleep and wake cycles, sleep theories, sleep deprivation, sleep disorders, and dreams. Next, we examined hypnosis, evaluating its features, individual differences, theories, and applications. In the final section of the chapter we read about psychoactive drugs and addiction. Don't forget that you can obtain an overall summary of the chapter by again reading the in-chapter reviews on pages 146, 149, 152, and 159.

Four perspectives are highlighted in this chapter on states of consciousness: neurobiological, cognitive, sociocultural, and psychoanalytic. The neurobiological perspective appears in the discussion of cycles of sleep and wakefulness (pp. 139–143), the activation-synthesis theory of dreams (p. 148), psychoactive drugs (p. 152), addiction (pp. 152–153), alcohol (pp. 153–157), and other psychoactive drugs (pp. 157–161). The cognitive perspective is represented in the discussion of the nature of consciousness (pp. 136–139), lucid dreams (pp. 147–148), and the special process theory of hypnosis (p. 151). The sociocultural perspective is present in the discussion of altered states of consciousness and the world's religions (p. 138), dreams and culture (p. 149), and sociocultural influences on alcohol abuse (p. 156). The psychoanalytic perspective is evaluated in the discussion of the nature of consciousness (p. 136) and the wish fulfillment theory of dreams (p. 147).

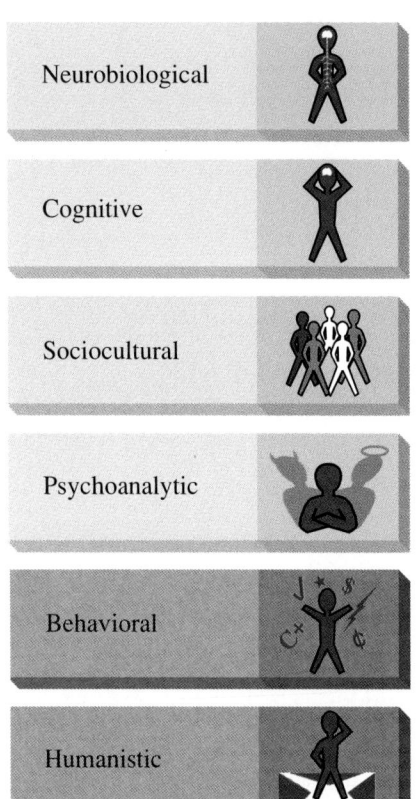

Neurobiological

Cognitive

Sociocultural

Psychoanalytic

Behavioral

Humanistic

night terror A state characterized by sudden arousal from sleep and intense fear, usually accompanied by a number of physiological reactions. 136

consciousness Awareness of external and internal stimuli or events. 136

stream of consciousness A continuous flow of changing sensations, images, thoughts, and feelings. 137

unconscious thought Freud's concept of a reservoir of unacceptable wishes, feelings, and thoughts that are beyond conscious awareness. 137

controlled processes The most alert states of consciousness, in which individuals actively focus their efforts toward a goal. 137

automatic processes A form of consciousness that requires minimal attention and does not interfere with other ongoing activities. 137

daydreaming A form of consciousness that involves a low level of conscious effort. 137

altered state of consciousness A mental state that is noticeably different from normal awareness. Drugs, meditation, traumas, fatigue, hypnosis, and sensory deprivation produce altered states of consciousness. 137

circadian rhythm A daily behavioral or physiological cycle, such as the 24-hour sleep/wake cycle. 139

amplitude The height of a wave. 141

frequency The number of wave cycles per second. 141

beta waves The EEG pattern for high-frequency electrical activity in the brain, characteristic of periods of concentration. 141

alpha waves The EEG pattern of individuals who are in a relaxed or drowsy state. 141

delta waves The EEG pattern characteristic of deepening sleep and progressive muscle relaxation. 142

theta waves Low-frequency and low-amplitude EEG patterns that characterize stage 1 sleep. 142

sleep spindles Brief bursts of higher-frequency brain waves during sleep 142

REM sleep A periodic stage of sleep during which dreaming occurs. 143

repair theory The theory that sleep restores, replenishes, and rebuilds our brains and bodies, which are somehow worn out by the day's waking activities. 144

ecological theory A relatively recent view of sleep that is based on the theory of evolution. It argues that the main purpose of sleep is to prevent animals from wasting their energy and harming themselves during the parts of the day or night to which they have not adapted. 144

insomnia A common sleep problem; the inability to sleep. 145

somnambulism Sleepwalking; it occurs during the deepest stages of sleep. 145

nightmare A frightening dream that awakens the sleeper from REM sleep. 146

narcolepsy The overpowering urge to fall asleep. 146

sleep apnea A sleep disorder in which individuals stop breathing because their windpipe fails to open or brain processes involved in respiration fail to work properly. 146

lucid dreams A class of dreams in which a person "wakes up" mentally but remains in the sensory landscape of the dream world. 147

activation-synthesis view The view that dreams have no inherent meaning but, rather, reflect the brain's efforts to make sense out of or find meaning in the neural activity that takes place during REM sleep. In this view, the brain has considerable random activity during REM sleep, and dreams are an attempt to synthesize the chaos. 148

hypnosis A psychological state of altered attention and awareness in which the individual is unusually receptive to suggestions. 150

posthypnotic suggestion A suggestion, made by the hypnotist while the subject is in a hypnotic state, that the subject carries out after emerging from the hypnotic state. 151

posthypnotic amnesia The subject's inability to remember what took place during hypnosis, induced by the hypnotist's suggestion. 151

special process theory The view that hypnotic behavior is different from nonhypnotic behavior. Hypnotic responses are elicited by suggestion rather than being voluntary reactions. 151

hidden observer The term used by Hilgard for the part of a hypnotized individual's mind that is completely aware of what is happening. This part of the individual remains a passive, or hidden, observer until called upon to comment. 151

nonstate view The view that hypnotic behavior is similar to other forms of social behavior and can be explained without appealing to special processes. Hypnotic behavior is purposeful, goal-directed action that is best understood by the way subjects interpret their situation and how they try to present themselves. 151

psychoactive drugs Substances that act on the nervous system to alter our states of consciousness, modify our perceptions, and change our moods. 152

tolerance The state in which a greater amount of a drug is needed to produce the same effect. 152

addiction Physical dependence on a drug. 152

withdrawal An addict's undesirable intense pain and craving for an addictive drug when the drug is withdrawn. 152

psychological dependence The need to take a drug to cope with problems and stress. 152

disease model of addiction The view that addictions are biologically based, lifelong diseases that involve a loss of control over behavior and require medical and/or spiritual treatment for recovery. 153

life-process model of addiction The view that addiction is not a disease but rather a habitual response and source of gratification or security that can be understood only in the context of social relationships and experiences. 153

barbiturates Depressant drugs, such as Nebutal and Seconal, that induce sleep or reduce anxiety. 157

tranquilizers Depressant drugs, such as Valium and Xanax, that reduce anxiety and induce relaxation. 157

opiates Opium and its derivatives, which depress the central nervous system's activity. 157

stimulants Psychoactive drugs that increase the central nervous system's activity. 157

crack An intensified form of cocaine that consists of chips of pure cocaine that are usually smoked. 158

hallucinogens Psychoactive drugs that modify a person's perceptual experiences and produce hallucinatory visual images. Hallucinogens are also called psychedelic ("mind altering") drugs. 158

One of the Ten Best Books of 1991—New York Times
CONSCIOUSNESS EXPLAINED

DANIEL C. DENNETT
Author of Brainstorms and coauthor of The Mind's I

CONSCIOUSNESS EXPLAINED
(1991) by Daniel Dennett.
Boston: Little, Brown.

This witty, intellectual book provides an in-depth look at contemporary thinking about the nature of consciousness. The author draws on the fields of psychology, philosophy, neuroscience, and artificial intelligence to portray how consciousness works. Dennett criticizes a number of simpleminded commonsense views of consciousness and explains how we feel sensations and have conscious experiences. He tackles such difficult topics as how the brain represents time, how human beings develop a self, how we use imagination, how we experience the external world, and how we experience our internal worlds.

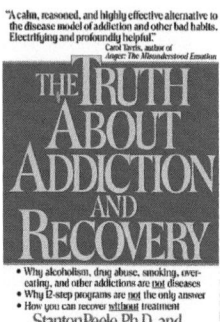

"A calm, reasoned, and highly effective alternative to the disease model of addiction and other bad habits. Electrifying and profoundly helpful."
Carol Tavris, author of
Anger: The Misunderstood Emotion

THE TRUTH ABOUT ADDICTION AND RECOVERY

• Why alcoholism, drug abuse, smoking, over-eating, and other addictions are not diseases
• Why 12-step programs are not the only answer
• How you can recover without treatment

Stanton Peele, Ph.D., and Archie Brodsky
Authors of Love and Addiction • with MARY ARNOLD

THE TRUTH ABOUT ADDICTION AND RECOVERY
(1991) by Stanton Peele and Archie Brodsky. New York: Simon & Schuster.

Drawing on recent research and detailed case studies, the authors conclude that addictions—whether to food, cigarettes, alcohol, or drugs—are not diseases and are not necessarily lifelong problems. Instead of twelve-step treatment programs like AA, Peele and Brodsky recommend their "life process program" that emphasizes coping with stress and achieving one's goals. Separate chapters deal with alcoholism, different drugs, smoking, obesity, gambling, and love and sex. You learn how to assess your values and what is really important to you, how to carry out plans of change, and how to develop life skills. Information is presented about how to prevent addiction in children, how to establish community ties, how to understand the struggles you have endured, and how to prepare and maintain an addiction-free future.

THE MAKING OF A
DRUG-FREE AMERICA
PROGRAMS THAT WORK

THE MAKING OF A DRUG-FREE AMERICA
(1992) by Mathea Falco.
New York: Times Books.

The author makes the point that the way Americans think about illegal drugs contrasts dramatically with the way they think about many legal addictive drugs. The millions of Americans who abuse alcohol, tobacco, and prescription drugs like Valium are thought to need help, not punishment. Falco argues that early prevention efforts have often failed because they rely too heavily on scare tactics and moral exhortations, and that this results in a loss of credibility with youth. She describes programs that are tailored to children's and adolescents' interests and concerns.

Addiction Research Foundation/Fondation de la recherche sur la toxomanie

> 33 Russell St.
> Toronto ON M5S 2S1 CANADA
> 416–595–6111
> 1–800–387–2916 (in Canada)

The Foundation's information line offers a tape on drug and alcohol abuse. The staff will discuss substance abuse issues. They maintain a reference library, an audiovisual desk, and a pharmacy, and they provide educational materials. They also provide information on treatment programs. Information is available in English, French, Cantonese, Greek, Hindi, Italian, Mandarin, Polish, Portuguese, Punjabi, Spanish, and Urdu.

Alcoholics Anonymous World Services

> 475 Riverside Drive
> New York, NY
> 212–870–3400

Alcoholics Anonymous (AA) provides support groups for individuals with drinking problems or other addictive behaviors. Most communities have local chapters of AA.

Alliance for a Drug-Free Canada/Alliance pour un canada sans drogues

> P.O. Box 355 Station A
> Toronto, ON M5W 1C5
> 416–730–4217
> 1–800–563–5000 (in Canada)

American Narcolepsy Association

> 425 California Street
> San Francisco, CA 94104
> 800–222–6085

This organization is devoted to improving the quality of life of individuals who suffer from narcolepsy or sleep apnea. The association maintains a library and publishes the quarterly newsletter *Eye Opener.*

Association for the Study of Dreams

> P.O. Box 1600
> Vienna, VA 22183
> 703–242–8889

This association provides an international, interdisciplinary forum for furthering knowledge about dreams. Medical professionals, psychologists, educators, and students are welcomed as members. The group publishes a quarterly newsletter.

***Hypnosis: Questions and Answers* (1986)**

> by B. Zilbergeld, M. Edlestein, and D. Araoz
> New York: Norton

A number of experts answer questions about a wide range of topics pertaining to hypnosis.

***Lucid Dreaming* (1988)**

> by Stephen LaBerge
> Los Angeles: Tarcher

If you want to try to increase your lucid dreaming, this book will tell you how. Easy-to-follow instructions are included, along with an examination of the nature of dreaming.

National Clearinghouse for Alcohol Information

> P.O. Box 2345
> 1776 East Jefferson Street
> Rockville, MD 20852

This clearinghouse provides information about a wide variety of issues related to drinking problems.

Rational Recovery Systems

> P.O. Box 800
> Lotus, CA 95651
> 916–621–4374

This organization uses the techniques of Albert Ellis's rational emotive therapy to teach individuals how to eliminate their addictive behavior. An increasing number of cities have Rational Recovery programs.

Sleep/Wake Disorders Canada/ Affections du sommeil/eveil Canada

> 3089 Bathurst St. Suite 304
> Toronto, ON M6A 2A4 CANADA
> 416–787–5374
> 1–800–387–9253

Sleep/Wake Disorders Canada is a national, self-help registered charity dedicated to helping the thousands of Canadians suffering from sleep/wake disorders. They have chapters across the country, and members work to improve the quality of life, altertness, and productivity of persons with sleep/wake disorders. SWDC offers information brochures, articles, booklets, and videos and publishes a quarterly newsletter, *Good/Night Good/Day.*

Learning and Cognition

*Learning is an ornament in prosperity,
a refuge in adversity.*

Aristotle

Our learning, memory, thinking, language, and
intelligence are remarkable and enchanting gifts.
We thirst to know, to understand, and to create.
In this third section of *Psychology: The Contexts of
Behavior,* you will read three chapters:
"Learning" (chapter 6), "Memory" (chapter 7),
and "Thinking, Language, and Intelligence"
(chapter 8).

SEURAT
Invitation to the Sideshow, detail

CHAPTER

6

Learning

> *Experience is the only teacher.*
> **Ralph Waldo Emerson**

H e is over 8 feet tall, has big orange feet, and is covered with yellow feathers. He has spent years practicing basic skills, such as counting and rehearsing the letters in the alphabet, and asking questions of the other inhabitants of "Sesame Street." He definitely prefers the company of little people to adults. And he is a surprisingly effective teacher.

Television is a powerful vehicle for *observational learning* (learning by watching what other people do and say). Observational learning has changed drastically in the twentieth century because of television, which has touched the life of virtually every person in the United States. Television has been called a lot of names, not all of them good— *the one-eyed monster* or *the boob tube,* for example. Television has also been accused of interfering with children's academic growth, luring them away from schoolwork and books and making them passive learners. It has also been criticized for promoting violence. However, many psychologists believe that the influence is not entirely negative.

Big Bird's success demonstrated that television can contribute to children's learning. Television can introduce children to worlds that are different from the ones in which they live. "Sesame Street" was designed to improve children's cognitive and social skills (Green, 1995). Almost half of America's 2- to 5-year-olds watch it regularly (Liebert & Sprafkin, 1988). "Sesame Street" uses fast-paced action, sound effects, music, and humorous characters to grab the attention of its young audience. With their eyes glued to the screen, young children learn basic academic skills. Studies have shown that regular "Sesame Street" viewers from low-income families, when they enter first grade, are rated by their teachers as better prepared for school than their counterparts who don't watch "Sesame Street" regularly (Bogatz & Ball, 1972; Wright, 1995).

Joan Ganz Cooney had no idea when her company, the Children's Television Workshop, created a home for Big Bird and his companions that they would become an influential force in learning for children, not just in the United States but in locations as distant as Kuwait, Israel, Latin America, and the Philippines. Since "Sesame Street" first aired in the United States in 1969, the show has been televised in eighty-four countries and has been adapted in thirteen foreign-language versions of the show. "Plaza Seesamo," shown in seventeen South and Central American countries as well as Puerto Rico, emphasizes diversity in cultures and lifestyles. Israel's "Rechove Sumsum" encourages children to learn how people from different ethnic and religious backgrounds can live in harmony. In the Netherlands, "Sesamstraat" teaches children about the concept of school from a 7-foot-tall blue bird named Pino. Whatever his color, Big Bird may be our best ambassador.

(*Left*) Big Bird, a surprisingly effective teacher; (*right*) Don Pimpon of Spain's "Barrio Sesamo" is a shaggy old codger who has traveled extensively and entertains with stories of his adventures. "Barrio Sesamo" helps young children in Spain learn social and cognitive skills.

PREVIEW

Psychologists explain our many experiences in terms of a few basic learning processes. We respond to things that happen to us, we act and then experience the consequences of our behavior, and we observe what others say and do. These aspects of experience form the three main types of learning we will study in this chapter: classical conditioning (responding), operant conditioning (acting), and observational learning (observing). As we study the nature of learning, you will discover that early approaches investigated the way experience and behavior are connected without referring to cognitive, or mental, processes. In recent years, cognitive processes have assumed a more important role in learning. We will discuss cognitive approaches to learning later in the chapter, but first we will further explore what learning is.

DEFINING LEARNING

When you think of learning, you might imagine yourself seated at a desk, poring over books, trying hard to absorb facts so that you can do well on an examination. Studying does help you learn about and remember new ideas, but the concept of learning in this chapter emphasizes acquiring new behaviors, skills, and knowledge. Let's look at some examples to clarify this distinction.

In learning how to use a computer, you might make some mistakes along the way, but at a certain point you will get the knack of the behaviors that make the computer work efficiently. You will *change* from someone who could not operate a computer into one who can. Usually, once you have learned to use a computer, your skills remain stable. (This is like learning to drive a car—once you have learned how, you do not have to repeat the process again.) Learning involves a *relatively permanent* influence on behavior. Through *experience* you also learned that you need to study in order to do well on a test or that you need to allow extra time when traveling during rush hour traffic. Putting these pieces together, we arrive at a definition: **Learning** *is a relatively permanent change in behavior that occurs through experience.*

To learn is a natural pleasure.

Artistotle

We need to draw one other distinction between behaviors that are learned versus behaviors that are unlearned. The capacities for some behaviors are inborn, or innate. For example, we do not have to be taught to swallow, to flinch at loud noises, or to blink when an object comes too close to our eyes. These behaviors are reflexes and do not have to be learned. However, most complex human behaviors cannot be considered innate. Learning is an important, complex process that promotes our adaptation to the challenges of our environment (Howard, 1995).

Psychologists argue about what is the best way to describe learning. Some believe that learning is a single but complex process. Others believe that we can distinguish different types of learning. We will begin by exploring the form of learning that psychologists call classical conditioning.

CLASSICAL CONDITIONING

It is a nice spring day. A father takes his baby out for a walk. The baby reaches over to touch a pink flower and is stung by a bumblebee sitting on the petals. The next day, the baby's mother brings home some pink flowers. She removes a flower from the arrangement and takes it over for her baby to smell. The baby cries loudly as soon as she sees the pink flower. The baby's panic at the sight of the pink flower illustrates the learning process of **classical conditioning,** *in which a neutral stimulus becomes associated with a meaningful stimulus and acquires the capacity to elicit a similar response.*

How Classical Conditioning Works

In the early 1900s, Russian physiologist Ivan Pavlov investigated the way the body digests food. As part of his experiments, he routinely placed meat powder in a dog's mouth, causing the dog to salivate. Pavlov began to notice that the meat powder was not the only stimulus that caused the dog to salivate. The dog also salivated in response to a number of stimuli associated with the food, such as the sight of the food dish, the sight of the individual who brought the food into the room, and the sound of the door closing when the food arrived. Pavlov recognized that the dog's association of these sights and sounds with the food was an important type of learning (which came to be called classical conditioning).

Pavlov wanted to know *why* the dog salivated to various sights and sounds before eating the meat powder. Pavlov observed that the dog's behavior included both learned and unlearned components. The unlearned part of classical conditioning is based on the fact that some stimuli automatically produce certain responses apart from any

If a bee stings this young girl while she is holding a pink flower, how would classical conditioning explain her panic at the sight of pink flowers in the future?

Cartoon by John Chase.

prior learning; in other words, the responses are inborn, or innate. **Reflexes** *are automatic stimulus-response connections that are "hard-wired" into the brain.* They include salivation in response to food, nausea in response to bad food, shivering in response to low temperature, coughing in response to the throat's being clogged, pupil constriction in response to light, and withdrawal in response to a blow, burns, or pain, among others. An **unconditioned stimulus (US)** *is a stimulus that produces a response without prior learning;* food was the US in Pavlov's experiments. An **unconditioned response (UR)** *is an unlearned response that is automatically associated with the US.* In Pavlov's experiments, the saliva that flowed from the dog's mouth was the UR in response to the food, which was the US. In the case of the baby and her pink flower, the baby did not have to learn to cry when the bee stung her. Pain reactions are reflexive, or unlearned; a child's crying occurs automatically in response to the pain of a bee sting. In this example, the bee's sting is the US and the crying is the UR.

In classical conditioning, the **conditioned stimulus (CS)** *is a previously neutral stimulus that elicits the conditioned response after being associated with the unconditioned*

stimulus. The **conditioned response (CR)** *is the learned response to the conditioned stimulus that occurs after CS-US association* (Pavlov, 1927). While he was conducting studies on digestive processes in dogs, Pavlov observed that ringing a bell before giving meat powder to a dog stimulated the dog's saliva flow. Prior to its association with food, the bell had no particular effect on the dog; the bell was a neutral stimulus. Once the dog began to associate the sound of the bell with the arrival of the food, the dog salivated when it heard the bell. The bell became a conditioned (learned) stimulus (CS) and the salivation a conditioned response (CR). Before conditioning (or learning), the bell and the food were not related. After the association, the conditioned stimulus (the bell) elicited a conditioned response (salivation). For the unhappy baby, the flower was the CS and the crying was the CR after the baby associated the flower with the sting (US). Figure 6.1 shows Pavlov's laboratory setting for studying classical conditioning and Pavlov demonstrating the procedure. A summary of how classical conditioning works is shown in figure 6.2.

Classical Conditioning Phenomena

Pavlov became intrigued with the associations dogs would make through conditioning. He began systematic study of classical conditioning phenomena and established many principles that are still accepted today. We will examine generalization, discrimination, extinction, and spontaneous recovery.

Generalization

After many conditioning trials, Pavlov found that the dog not only responded to the bell with salivation but also salivated in response to other sounds, such as a whistle. Pavlov did not pair these sounds with the unconditioned stimulus of the food. He discovered that the more similar the noise

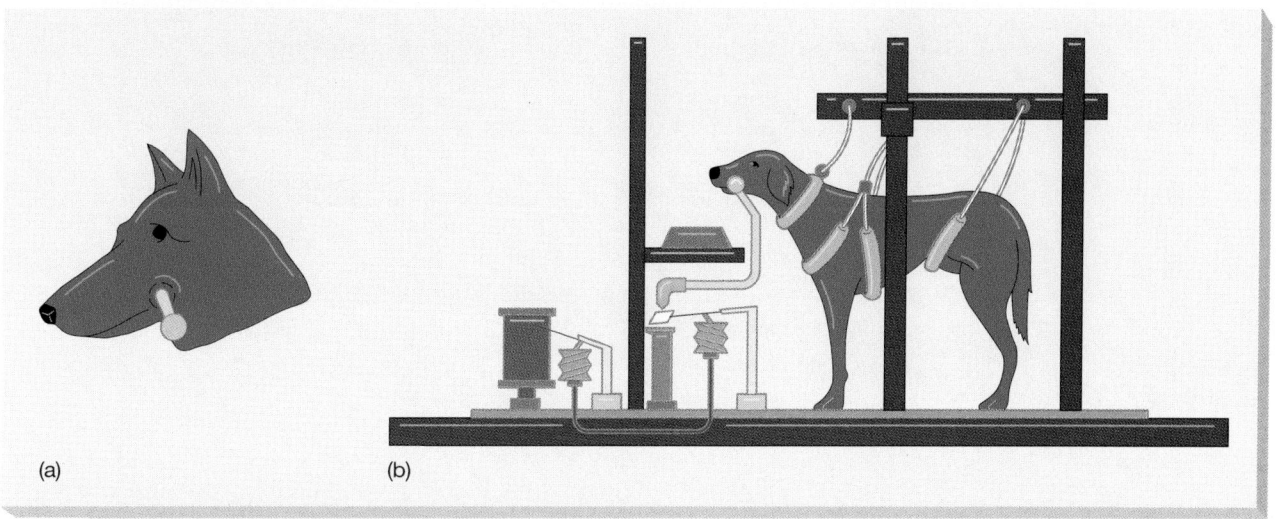

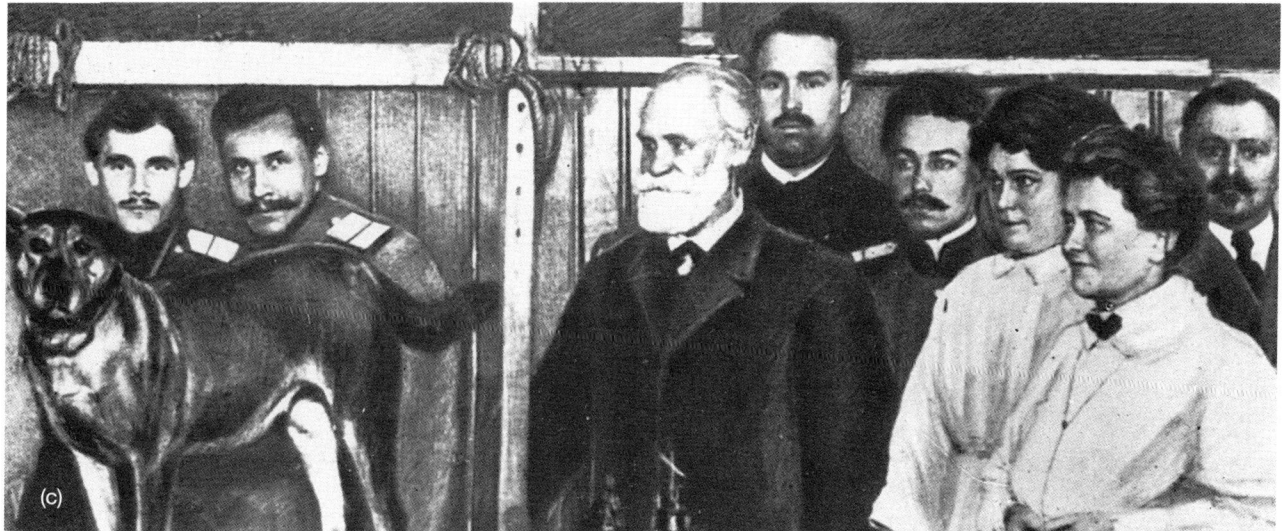

FIGURE 6.1

Pavlov's Experimentation
(*a*) Surgical preparation for studying the salivary reflex: when the dog salivated, the saliva collected in a glass funnel attached to the dog's cheek. This way the strength of the salivary response could be measured precisely. (*b*) Shown here is Pavlov's experimental apparatus used to examine classical conditioning. (*c*) Pavlov (the white-bearded gentleman in the center) is shown demonstrating the nature of classical conditioning to students at the Military Medical Academy in the Soviet Union.

was to the original sound of the bell, the stronger the dog's salivary flow. In the example of conditioned fear of pink flowers, the baby not only cried at the sight of pink flowers, but she also learned to cry at the sight of red and orange flowers. **Generalization** *in classical conditioning is the tendency of a new stimulus that is similar to the original conditioned stimulus to elicit a response that is similar to the conditioned response.*

Discrimination

Generalizing from one stimulus to another is not always beneficial. For example, a cat who generalizes from a minnow to a piranha has a major problem: In the one situation, the cat might retrieve dinner; in the other, the cat might become dinner. Therefore, in many situations it can be important to discriminate between stimuli. **Discrimination** *in classical conditioning is the process of learning to respond to*

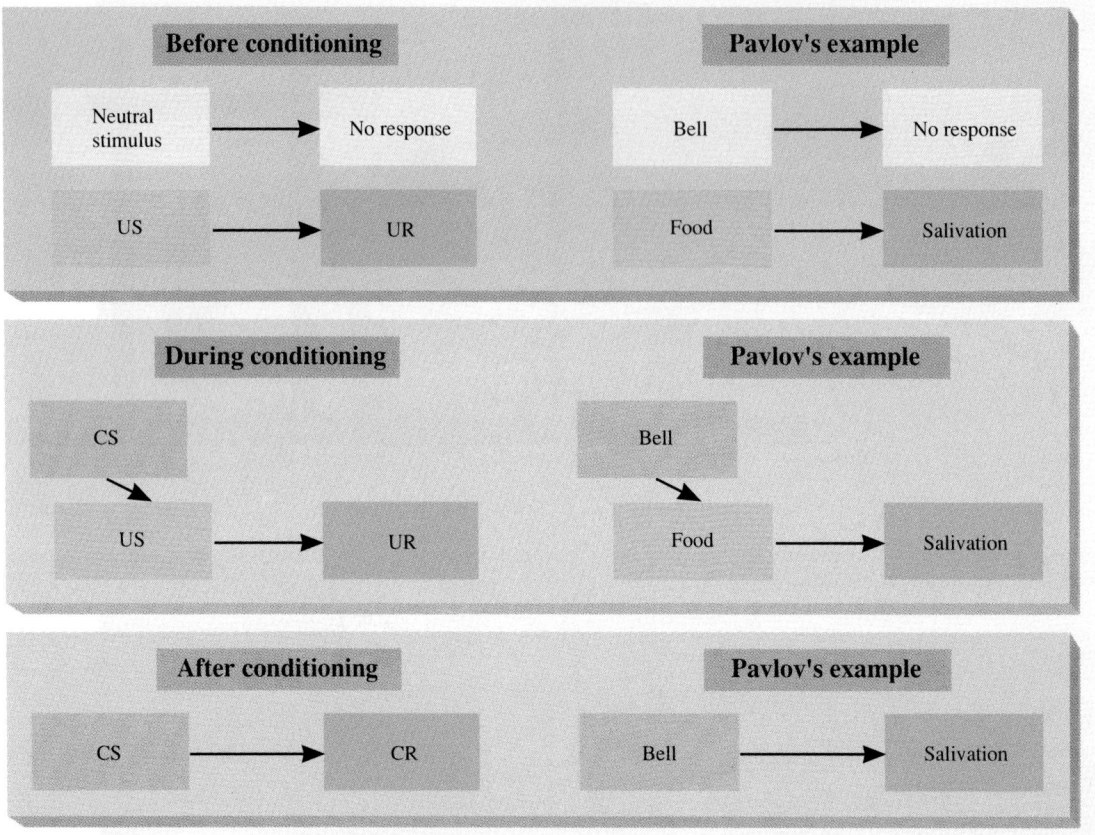

FIGURE 6.2

Classical Conditioning Procedure
At the start of conditioning, the US (food) will evoke the UR (salivation), but the bell, initially a neutral stimulus, does not. During conditioning, the bell becomes a CS through pairing with the US; the bell precedes the food presentation, which reliably elicits salivation. With repeated pairings, conditioning is achieved; the CS eventually elicits the CR (salivation) when presented alone.

certain stimuli and not to respond to others. To produce discrimination among different stimuli, Pavlov gave food to the dog only after ringing the bell and not after any other sounds. In this way the dog learned to distinguish between the bell and other sounds. Similarly, the baby did not cry at the sight of blue flowers, thus discriminating between blue and pink flowers.

Extinction

When Pavlov rang the bell repeatedly in a single session and did not give the dog any food, eventually the dog stopped salivating. This result is **extinction,** *which in classical conditioning is the weakening of the conditioned response in the absence of the unconditioned stimulus.* Without continued association with the unconditioned stimulus (US), the conditioned stimulus (CS) loses its power to elicit the conditioned response (CR). Over time the baby encountered many pink flowers and was not stung by a bee. Consequently, her fear of pink flowers subsided and eventually disappeared. The pink flower (CS) lost its capacity to generate fear (CR) when the flower was no longer associated with bee stings (US) and the pain and fear they cause (UR).

Spontaneous Recovery

Extinction is not always the end of the conditioned response. The day after Pavlov extinguished the conditioned salivation at the sound of a bell, he took the dog to the laboratory and rang the bell, still not giving the dog any meat powder. The dog salivated, indicating that an extinguished response can spontaneously appear again. **Spontaneous recovery** *is the process in classical conditioning by which a conditioned response can appear again without further conditioning.* In the case of the baby, even though she saw many pink flowers after her first painful encounter and was not "stung" by them, she showed some signs of fear of pink flowers from time to time. Over time, her conditioned fear (CR) of pink flowers (CS) diminished; she showed less tendency to recover her fear of pink flowers spontaneously, particularly because she didn't experience further painful stings (US). Figure 6.3 shows the sequence of extinction and spontaneous recovery. Spontaneous recovery can occur several times; however, as long as the conditioned stimulus is presented without the unconditioned stimulus, spontaneous recovery becomes weaker over time and eventually ceases to occur.

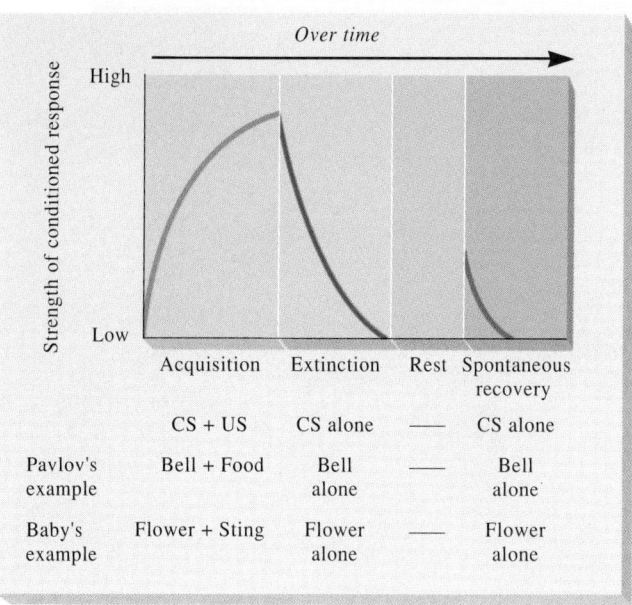

FIGURE 6.3

The Strength of a Classically Conditioned Response During Acquisition, Extinction, and Spontaneous Recovery
During acquisition, the experimenter pairs the conditioned stimulus and the unconditioned stimulus. As seen in the graph, when this occurs over time, the strength of the conditioned response increases. During extinction, the experimenter presents the conditioned stimulus alone. This results in a decrease of the conditioned response. After a rest period, spontaneous recovery appears, although the strength of the conditioned response is not nearly as great at this point as it was after a number of CS-US pairings. When the experimenter presents the CS alone again after spontaneous recovery, the response extinguishes rapidly.

Applications—Classical Conditioning in Humans

Since Pavlov's accidental discovery, individuals have been conditioned to an impressive array of stimuli in the laboratory and in life. Because of classical conditioning, we jerk our hands away before they are burned by fire. We move out of the way of a rapidly approaching truck before it hits us. We escape if someone yells, "Fire!" Our capacity for making associations has a great deal of survival value.

Classical conditioning also explains some pleasant emotions. The sight of a rainbow, a sunny day, or a favorite song might produce special pleasure due to classical conditioning. If you have had a romantic experience, the location where that experience took place can become a conditioned stimulus. This is the result of the pairing of a neutral place (CS) with a pleasurable event (US). In the same vein, a pleasant interaction with someone who is quite different from other people you have known (for instance, who comes from another country or who is physically different) can also, through classical conditioning, lead you to have positive expectations about others who are similar to that person.

Psychologists have also shown that classical conditioning can enhance the quality of life. For example, by imagining a tranquil scene—such as an abandoned beach with waves lapping onto the sand—a harried executive might relax as if she were actually lying on that beach. This result is due to her ability to make associations. Psychotherapists often recommend mental imagery about positive scenes to promote relaxation.

However, sometimes classical conditioning can make life miserable, as when **phobias,** or *irrational fears,* develop. Classical conditioning provides an explanation of how we acquire irrational fears of pink flowers and other harmless objects. Behaviorist John Watson conducted an investigation to demonstrate classical conditioning's role in phobias. He showed a little boy named Albert a white laboratory rat to see if Albert was afraid of it. He was not. As Albert played with the rat, Watson crashed together two garbage can lids behind Albert's head to make a loud noise. As you might imagine, the noise caused little Albert to startle and cry. After only seven pairings of the loud noise with the white rat, Albert began to fear the rat even when the noise was not sounded. Albert's fear was generalized to a rabbit, a dog, and a sealskin coat (see figure 6.4). Today we could not ethically conduct such an experiment because research review boards would have determined that the experiment lacked appropriate protection for little Albert. Especially noteworthy is the fact that Watson and his associate (Watson & Rayner, 1920) did not later remove Albert's fear of rats, so presumably this phobia remained with him after the experiment. Many of our fears—fear of the dentist after painful dental work, fear of driving after being in an automobile accident, and fear of dogs after being bitten, for example—can be learned through classical conditioning.

There is perhaps nothing so bad and so dangerous in life as fear.

Jawaharlal Nehru

If we can produce fears by classical conditioning, we should be able to eliminate them using conditioning procedures. **Counterconditioning** *is a classical conditioning procedure for weakening a conditioned response of fear by*

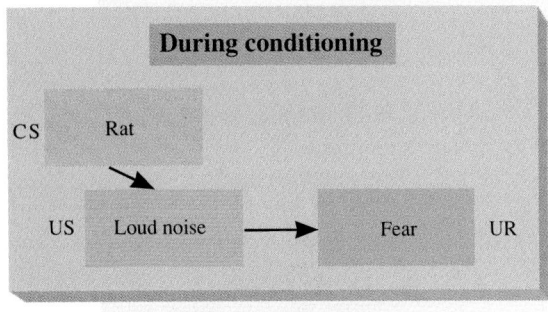

During conditioning

CS Rat

US Loud noise → Fear UR

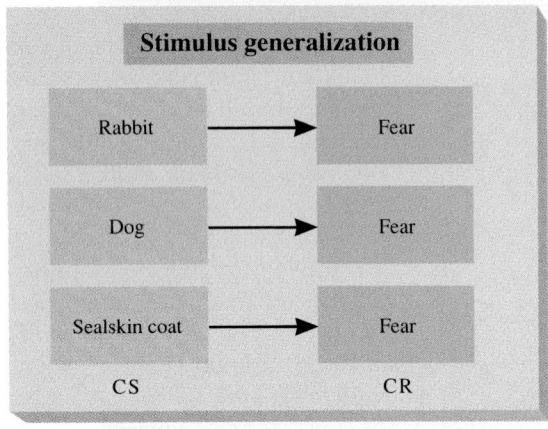

Stimulus generalization

Rabbit → Fear

Dog → Fear

Sealskin coat → Fear

CS   CR

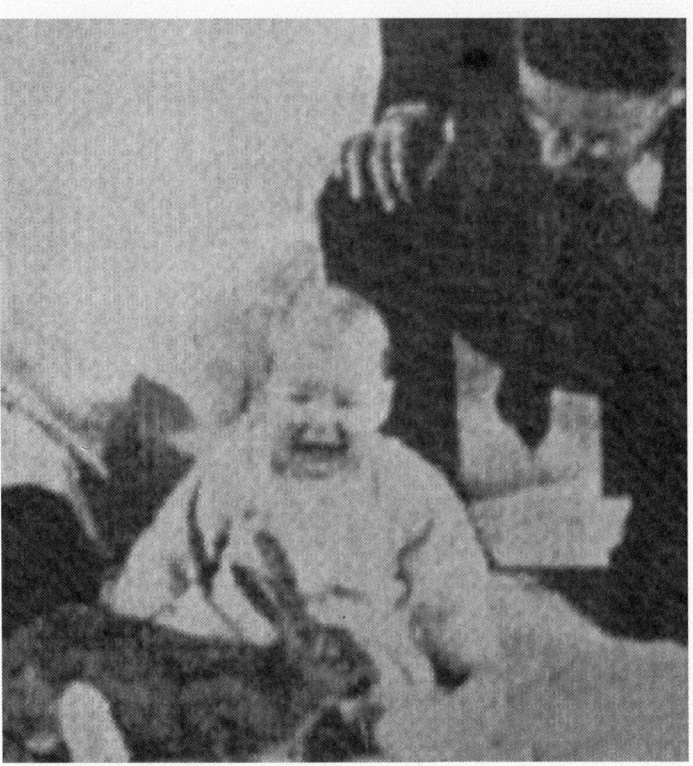

FIGURE 6.4

Little Albert's Generalized Fear

In 1920, Watson and Rayner conditioned 9-month-old little Albert to fear a white rat by pairing the rat with a loud noise. When little Albert was subsequently placed with other stimuli similar to the white rat, such as the rabbit shown here with little Albert, he was afraid of them, too. This illustrates the principle of stimulus generalization in classical conditioning.

associating the fear-producing stimulus with a new response that is incompatible with the fear. Though Watson did not eliminate little Albert's fear of white rats, an associate of Watson's, Mary Cover Jones (1924), did eliminate the fears of a 3-year-old boy named Peter. Peter had many of the same fears as Albert; however, Peter's fears were not produced by Jones. Among Peter's fears were white rats, fur coats, frogs, fish, and mechanical toys. To eliminate these fears, a rabbit was brought into Peter's view but kept far enough away that it would not upset him. At the same time the rabbit was brought into view, Peter was fed crackers and milk. On each successive day, the rabbit was moved closer to Peter as he ate crackers and milk. Eventually Peter reached the point where he could eat the food with one hand and pet the rabbit with the other.

Some of the behaviors we associate with certain health problems or mental disorders can involve classical conditioning. Classical conditioning can play a role in stress-related physical complaints, such as asthma, headaches, ulcers, and high blood pressure. We usually say that such health problems are caused by stress, but they are more properly said to be aggravated by stress. Often certain stimuli, such as a boss's critical attitude or a

spouse's threat of divorce, become conditioned stimuli for physiological responses. Over time the frequent presence of the physiological responses may produce a health problem or disorder. A boss's persistent criticism may cause an employee to develop muscle tension, headaches, or high blood pressure. Anything associated with the boss, such as work itself, can then trigger stress responses in the employee (see figure 6.5).

Classical conditioning also explains how prejudices develop and spread. For example, young children might regularly hear bigoted adults use negative nouns or adjectives—such as *stingy, lazy, alcoholic,* or *stupid*—to describe particular groups (such as Native Americans, Whites, or Jews). Eventually the child might associate those negative connotations with the groups themselves, and these negative evaluations of the groups might remain with the child into adulthood.

Evaluation of Classical Conditioning

Several of Pavlov's principles have been challenged by more recent research in classical or Pavlovian conditioning (Rescorla, 1988). Pavlov proposed that repeated pairing of the CS and US would *eventually* produce a conditioned

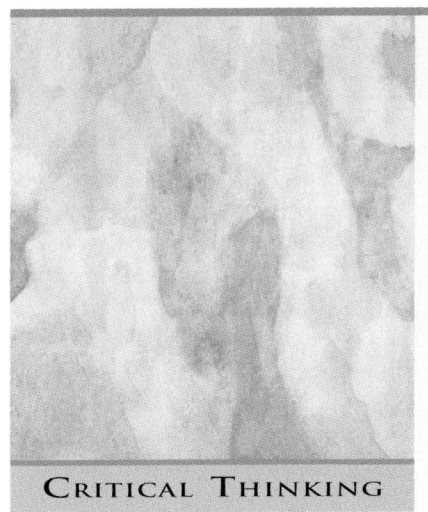

When Dogs Aren't Man's Best Friend

Mike had been afraid of dogs all of his life. He didn't know why it was so hard to be in the company of dogs, but his new girlfriend had a large black Labrador retriever and he knew he would have to stop being afraid of dogs in order for the relationship to thrive. What three things could you recommend to *solve this problem* using classical conditioning principles?

1. Mike could extinguish the problem. This would require exposing Mike to a friendly dog and waiting for his anxious reactions to fade.
2. Mike could actively countercondition the anxious reaction. His girlfriend could hug him as the dog is brought closer and closer to him. Pleasant reactions replace anxious feelings.
3. Mike could exercise some stimulus discrimination and date only women who do not own dogs.

These alternatives suggest the power of *using the psychological concepts of classical conditioning to enhance personal adaptation.*

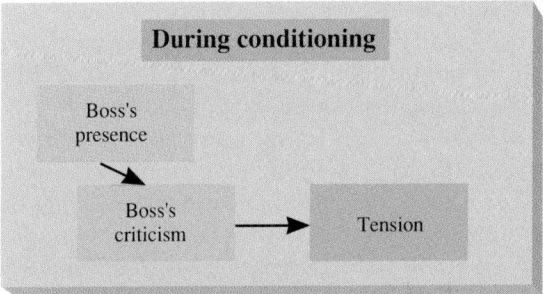

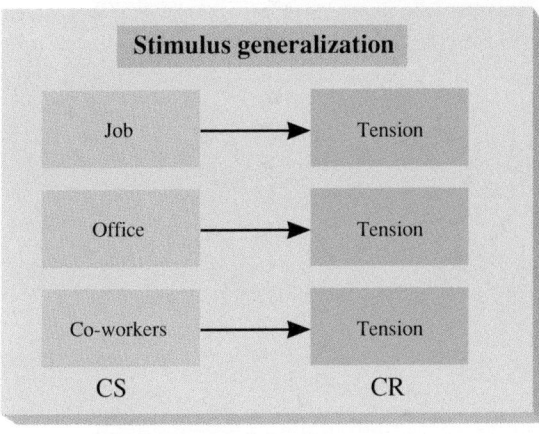

FIGURE 6.5

Classical Conditioning at Work
An unpleasant feedback session with the boss can contribute to chronic stress-related problems. The punishing session with the boss (US) elicits frustration and tension. Stimulus generalization can promote similar tense responses to other elements of the situation. *Have you ever experienced a similar problem in a work-related or interpersonal situation?*

response. He believed that the interval between the CS and the US is one of the most important aspects of classical conditioning. The interval between the CS and the US defines the strength of association, or *contiguity*, of the stimuli. In many instances, optimal spacing between the CS presentation and the onset of the US is very short, a matter of seconds or even a fraction of a second (Kimble, 1961).

Some examples of classical conditioning contradict the need for repeated pairings of CS and US, or the importance of contiguity. For example, you might have had the unfortunate experience of eating chicken salad that gave you food poisoning. When you were exposed to chicken salad in the future, you may have been somewhat surprised to find not only that it didn't appeal to you, but that the sight of the food literally made you sick. This common example of classical conditioning is called **conditioned taste aversion,** *classically conditioned avoidance reactions to food.* The bad chicken salad (US) produces nausea (UR) as an unlearned process. Future exposures to harmless chicken salad (CS) can also elicit nausea (CR), due to the power of the one-trial learning in this form of classical conditioning, even though several minutes elapsed between exposure to the tainted salad and the nausea that followed.

Pavlov also believed that neutral stimuli must be linked to a reflex in order for conditioning to be effective. He thought that the conditioned response would be physically similar to the unconditioned response. In some forms of conditioning, these observations hold. However, contrary to Pavlov's predictions, higher-order conditioning can produce new associations by pairing two conditioned stimuli without directly involving reflexive responding.

One of the most important differences between the contemporary view of classical conditioning and Pavlov's view involves the issue of how classical conditioning works. **Stimulus substitution** *was Pavlov's theory of how classical conditioning works; it states that the nervous system is structured in such a way that the CS and US bond together and eventually the CS substitutes for the US.* However, if the CS substitutes for the US, the two stimuli should produce similar responses. This does not always happen. Using a shock as a US often elicits flinching and jumping, whereas a light (CS) paired with a shock may cause the organism to be immobile, for example.

Information theory *is the contemporary explanation of how classical conditioning works; the key to understanding classical conditioning is in the information the organism obtains from the situation* (Rescorla & Wagner, 1972). Some years ago, E. C. Tolman (1932) said the information value of the CS is important in telling the organism what will follow. In Tolman's words, the organism uses the CS as a sign or expectation that a US will follow. Tolman's belief that the information the CS provides is the key to understanding classical conditioning was a forerunner of contemporary thinking.

The contemporary view of classical conditioning sees the organism as an information seeker using logical and perceptual relations among events, along with preconceptions, to form a representation of the world (Rescorla, 1988). The contemporary view still recognizes contiguity between the CS and the US as important in classical conditioning, but it emphasizes that what is important about the CS-US connection is the information the stimuli give the organism. A classic experiment conducted by Leon Kamin (1968) illustrates the importance of an organism's history and the information provided by a conditioned stimulus in classical conditioning. A rat was conditioned by repeatedly pairing a tone (CS) and a shock (US), until the tone alone produced a strong conditioned response (fear). The tone continued to be paired with the shock, but a light (a second CS) was turned on each time the tone was sounded. Even though the light (a CS) and the shock (US) were repeatedly paired, the rat showed no conditioning to the light. The light by itself produced no CR. Conditioning to the light was blocked, almost as if the rat had not attended to it. The rat apparently used the tone as a signal to predict that a shock would be forthcoming; it did not need to learn information about the light's pairing with the shock, because that information was redundant with the information already learned in the pairing of the tone and the shock. In this experiment, conditioning was governed not by the contiguity of the CS and US but, rather, by the rat's history and the information it received (see figure 6.6 for an illustration). Contemporary classical conditioning researchers are exploring further the role of information in an organism's learning (Fanselow, DeCola, & Young, 1993).

Pavlov emphasized learning processes in terms of classical conditioning. Although classical conditioning helps us learn about our environment, we learn about our world in other ways, too. Classical conditioning emphasizes the organism's responding to the environment, a view that originally failed to capture the active nature of the organism and its influence on the environment. Next we will study a major explanation of learning that places more emphasis on the organism's *activity* in the environment— operant conditioning.

You will note that their ability to comprehend, assess and process information increases dramatically when Professor Podhertz throws in the cat.

© Leo Cullum. 1995.

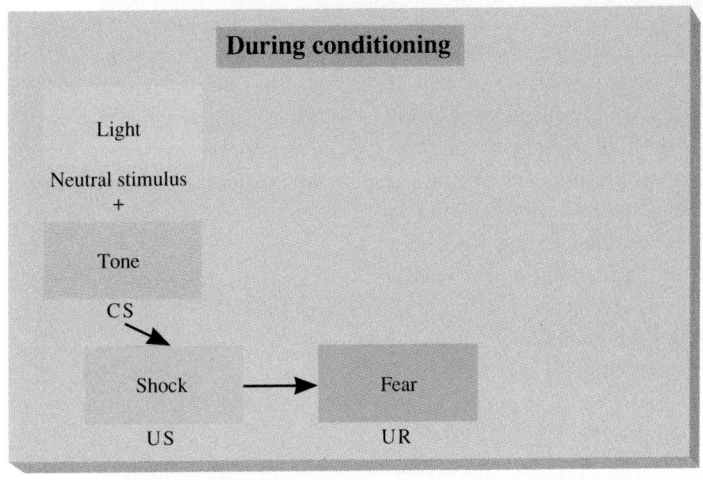

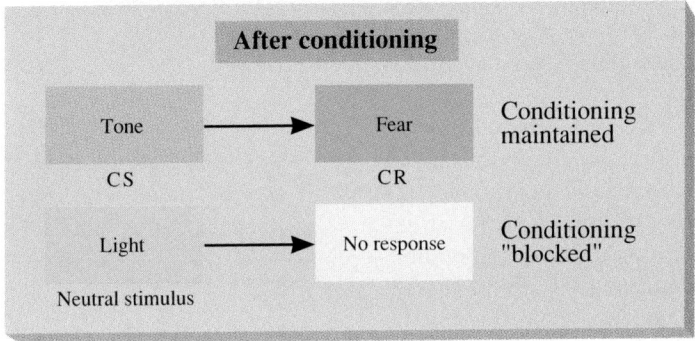

FIGURE 6.6

Kamin's Blocking Effect
Kamin paired a light with a tone (CS) that had already been classically conditioned with shock (US) to produce fear (CR). He discovered that he was unable to produce conditioned fear to the light alone. He argued that the rat had already learned the signal system for shock with the tone so that exposure to the light offered no new information. Kamin suggested that the conditioned effect was blocked.

REVIEW

The Nature of Learning and Classical Conditioning

Learning is a relatively permanent change in behavior due to experiences. How we respond to the environment (classical conditioning), how we act in the environment (operant conditioning), and how we observe the environment (observational learning) are the most important ways in which we experience. Early approaches emphasized connections between environment and behavior; many contemporary approaches stress that cognitive factors mediate environment-behavior connections.

Pavlov discovered that an organism learns the association between an unconditioned stimulus (US) and a conditioned stimulus (CS). The US automatically produces the UR (unconditioned response). After conditioning (CS-US pairing), the CS elicits the CR (conditioned response) by itself. Generalization, discrimination, and extinction also are involved. Classical conditioning has survival value for humans, as when we develop fear of hazardous conditions. Irrational fears often are explained by classical conditioning. Counterconditioning has been used to eliminate fears. Pavlov explained classical conditioning in terms of stimulus substitution, but the modern explanation is based on information theory. Classical conditioning is important in explaining the way learning occurs in animals. It is not the only way we learn and misses the active nature of organisms in the environment.

Operant Conditioning

Classical conditioning excels at explaining how we learn some kinds of behavior that seem involuntary, but it might not be as effective in explaining voluntary behaviors, such as studying hard for a test, playing slot machines in Las Vegas, or teaching a dog to roll over. Operant conditioning is usually better than classical conditioning at explaining *voluntary* behavior. American psychologist B. F. Skinner (1938) developed the concept of **operant conditioning (instrumental conditioning),** *a form of learning in which the consequences of a behavior produce changes in the probability of the behavior's occurrence.* In operant conditioning, an organism acts, or *operates,* on the environment to produce a change in the probability of the behavior's occurrence. The consequences of the behavior are *contingent* (dependent) on the organism's behavior. For example, a simple operant involves pressing a lever that leads to the delivery of food; the delivery of food is contingent on pressing the lever.

We have mentioned one difference between classical and operant conditioning—classical conditioning is better at explaining learning that results from involuntary responding, whereas operant conditioning is better at explaining learning that results from voluntary responding. The emphasis in each form of learning is different as well. In classical conditioning, the emphasis is on the relation between the stimulus and the response. In operant conditioning, the emphasis is on the relation between the behavior (response) and its consequence. For example, suppose that we wanted to teach a dog to roll over. In operant conditioning, we would focus on the relation of the dog's trick behavior to the consequence (or rewarding stimulus), such as a pat on the head or a dog treat; the stimuli that govern behavior in operant conditioning *follow* the behavior. In classical conditioning, we are more likely to attend to the stimuli that *precede* the behavior. We might focus on developing discrimination between the cue for rolling over and the cue for sitting up if we were trying to apply classical conditioning procedures to dog training.

Thorndike's Law of Effect

Although B. F. Skinner has emerged as the primary figure in operant conditioning, E. L. Thorndike's experiments established the power of consequences in determining voluntary behavior. At about the same time as Ivan Pavlov was conducting classical conditioning experiments with salivating dogs, Thorndike (1898) studied the behavior of cats in puzzle boxes (see figure 6.7).

Thorndike put a hungry cat inside a box and a piece of fish outside. To escape from the box, the cat had to learn how to open the latch inside the box. At first the cat made a number of ineffective responses. It clawed and bit at the bars or thrust its paw through the openings. Eventually the cat accidentally stepped on the treadle that released the door bolt. When the cat returned to the box, it went through the same random activity until it stepped on the treadle once more. On subsequent trials, the cat made fewer and fewer random movements until it learned to claw the treadle immediately to open the door (see figure 6.8). The **law of effect,** *developed by Thorndike, states that behaviors followed by positive outcomes are strengthened, whereas behaviors followed by negative outcomes are weakened.*

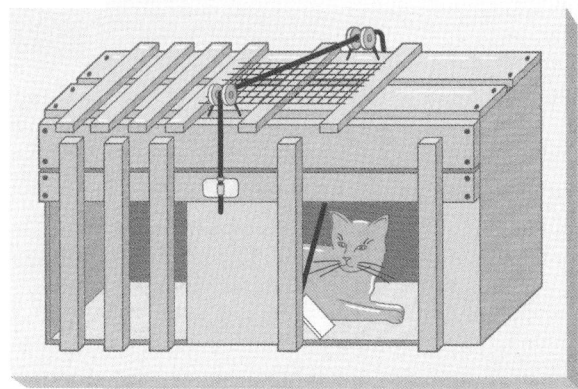

Figure 6.7

Thorndike Puzzle Box
This box is typical of the puzzle boxes Thorndike used in his experiments with cats to study the law of effect. Stepping on the treadle released the door bolt. A weight attached to the door then pulled the door open and allowed the cat to escape.

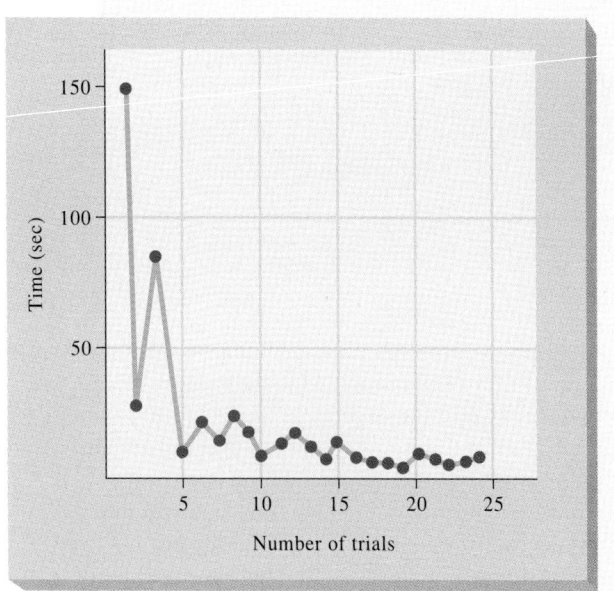

Figure 6.8

Learning Curve of One Cat's Escape Time
This learning curve shows the time required by one cat to escape from the puzzle box on 24 separate trials. Notice how the cat learned to escape much more quickly after about 5 trials.

The key question for Thorndike was how the correct stimulus-response (S-R) bond strengthens and eventually dominates incorrect stimulus-response bonds. According to Thorndike, the correct S-R association strengthens, and the incorrect association weakens, because of the *consequences* of the organism's actions. Thorndike's view is called *S-R theory* because the organism's behavior is due to a connection between a stimulus and a response. As we will see next, Skinner's operant conditioning approach expanded Thorndike's basic ideas.

Skinner's Operant Conditioning

Earlier you learned that Skinner described operant conditioning as a form of learning in which the consequences of behavior lead to changes in the probability of that behavior's occurrence. The consequences—rewards or punishments—are contingent on the organism's behavior. **Reinforcement (reward)** *is a consequence that increases the probability a behavior will occur.* In contrast, **punishment** *is a consequence that decreases the probability a behavior will occur.* For example, if someone you meet smiles at you and the two of you continue talking for some time, the smile has reinforced your talking. However, if someone you meet frowns at you and you quickly leave the situation, then the frown has punished you for talking with the individual.

Who has conditioned whom?

Drawing by Bernard Schoenbaum; © 1987 The New Yorker Magazine, Inc.

Positive Reinforcement

Reinforcement can be complex. Usually we think of reinforcement as positive, but it can be positive or negative. In **positive reinforcement,** *the frequency of a response increases because it is followed by a pleasant stimulus,* as in our example of the smile's increasing talking. Similarly, complimenting someone you are attracted to may make that person more receptive to your advances and increase the probability you will get to know the person better (see figure 6.9). The same principle of positive reinforcement is at work when an animal trainer teaches a dog to "shake hands" by giving it a piece of food when it lifts its paw.

Negative Reinforcement

Conversely, in **negative reinforcement,** *the frequency of a response increases because the response either removes a negative circumstance, an unpleasant stimulus or lets an individual avoid the stimulus altogether.* For example, your father

FIGURE 6.9

Positive Reinforcement
In positive reinforcement, the frequency of a behavior increases because it is followed by a pleasant consequence. For example, in this stimulus situation, a man's flattering comments have positive consequences, increasing his chances of getting to know his new friend better and increasing the likelihood that he will flatter her in the future.

Negative reinforcement

Behavior	Consequence	Future behavior
Taking aspirin	Pain removed	Taking aspirin increases

FIGURE 6.10

Negative Reinforcement
In negative reinforcement, the frequency of a behavior increases because the consequence of the behavior removes unpleasant stimuli or avoids the stimulus altogether. For example, aspirin removes or lessens pain, increasing the likelihood that one will take aspirin in the future at the first sign of a headache.

nags at you to clean the garage. He keeps nagging. Finally you get tired of the nagging and clean the garage. Your response (cleaning the garage) removed the negative circumstance (nagging). Torture works the same way. An interrogator might say, "Tell me what I want to know and I will stop dripping water on your forehead." Taking aspirin is the same process: taking aspirin is reinforced when this behavior is followed by a reduction of pain (see figure 6.10).

Another way to remember the distinction between positive and negative reinforcement is to understand that in positive reinforcement something positive is added, or obtained; in negative reinforcement, something negative is avoided or escaped. For example, if you receive a sweater as a graduation present, something has been added to increase your achievement behavior. However, consider the situation in which your parents criticize you for not studying hard enough. As you study harder, they stop criticizing you—something has been escaped, in this case their criticism. In both circumstances the outcome is favorable to you, and you are likely to repeat your behavior.

Punishment

Earlier we defined punishment as a consequence that decreases the probability that a behavior will occur. Richard Solomon (1964) stressed that punishment can be effective under certain conditions. He emphasized that to be effective, punishment needs to be immediate, consistent, and severe enough to alter the targeted behavior. He added that punishment is often misused because these principles are not followed.

What are some of the circumstances when punishment might effectively be used? Punishment can be considered when positive reinforcement has not been found to work. Also, when the behavior that is being punished is viewed as more destructive than the punishment itself, then punishment might be justified. For example, some children engage in a behavior that is dangerous to their well-being, such as head banging. Punishment might reduce the destructive behavior. Nonetheless, as punishment is reduced, it is always wise to reinforce an alternative behavior so that undesirable behavior does not replace the punished response (Santrock, 1996).

Less-severe forms of punishment create a negative consequence by removing opportunities for reward. *Time out* involves physically removing a child from a rewarding circumstance, such as play, for a specified period of time, say 5 or 10 minutes. Time-out procedures need to be adjusted according to the child's attention span and the severity of the behavior. *Response cost* is another punishment method. For example, an English professor might require students to complete one additional essay for each day they delay in turning in an assignment. When the response is inadequate (lateness), the penalty is the cost attached due to the additional writing.

Skinner believed that punishment is not especially effective in reducing the frequency of behavior and recommended positive reinforcement techniques as preferable. Punished individuals might learn to suppress the undesirable behavior rather than replace it with something more positive. When punishment is used, desirable as well as undesirable behaviors might be eliminated. For example, a child might stop interacting with other children altogether if he is slapped for biting another child. Punishment also can increase aggression. For example, a person who administers punishment is serving as an aggressive model, possibly inadvertently modeling how to behave in an aggressive, punitive way. Punishment can also lead to escape or avoidance. Punishment used with children is of special concern, because a significant proportion of child abuse evolves from excessive punishment used as an attempt to control children.

Negative reinforcement and punishment are easily confused because they both involve aversive or unpleasant stimuli, such as an electric shock or a slap in the face. To keep them straight, remember that negative reinforcement increases the probability a response will occur, whereas punishment decreases the probability a response will occur. When an alcoholic consumes liquor to alleviate uncomfortable withdrawal symptoms, the probability of future alcohol use is increased. Avoiding withdrawal symptoms negatively reinforces drinking. However, if an inebriated alcoholic is seriously injured in a car wreck in which his drinking was a factor and he subsequently stops drinking, then punishment is involved because a behavior—drinking—was decreased.

Extinction

One final principle of operant conditioning that Skinner articulated will sound familiar. In our discussion of classical conditioning we discovered that extinction is the weakening of the CS's tendency over time to elicit the CR when the CS is presented without the US. **Extinction** *in operant conditioning is a decrease in the tendency to perform a behavior that results in neither a positive nor a negative consequence.* For example, suppose you want to ask a question in your history class, but your history professor fails to notice your raised hand and continues with what she thinks is a fascinating lecture. Eventually your arm fatigues and you abandon your question. Your question-asking behavior weakens and disappears in this context. In the absence of a reinforcing or punishing consequence, an operant response will become extinguished.

Table 6.1 provides an overview of the distinctions among positive reinforcement, negative reinforcement, and punishment.

Further Dimensions of Operant Conditioning

Now that you know the basic concepts of operant conditioning, several additional points will help you understand how behaviorists study operant conditioning. One of Skinner's basic beliefs was that the mechanisms of learning are the same for all species. This belief led him to an extensive study of animals in the hope that the basic mechanisms of learning could be understood with organisms more simple than humans.

For example, during World War II, Skinner constructed a rather strange project—a pigeon-guided missile. A pigeon in the warhead of a missile operated the flaps on the missile and guided it home by pecking at an image of a target. How could this possibly work? When the missile was in flight, the pigeon pecked the moving image on a screen.

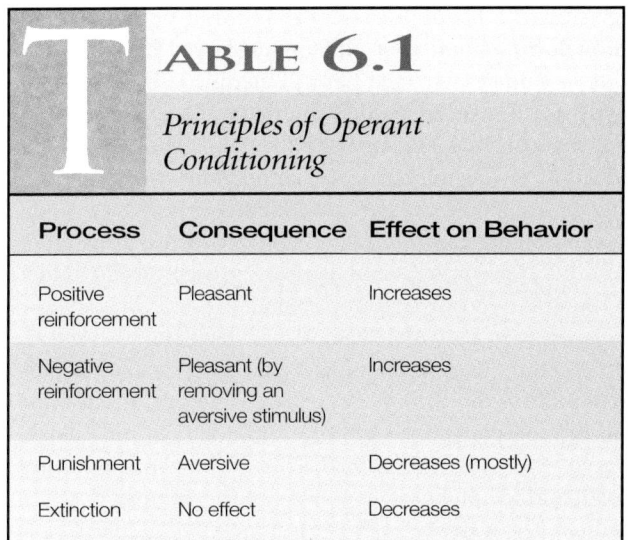

Process	Consequence	Effect on Behavior
Positive reinforcement	Pleasant	Increases
Negative reinforcement	Pleasant (by removing an aversive stimulus)	Increases
Punishment	Aversive	Decreases (mostly)
Extinction	No effect	Decreases

TABLE 6.1

Principles of Operant Conditioning

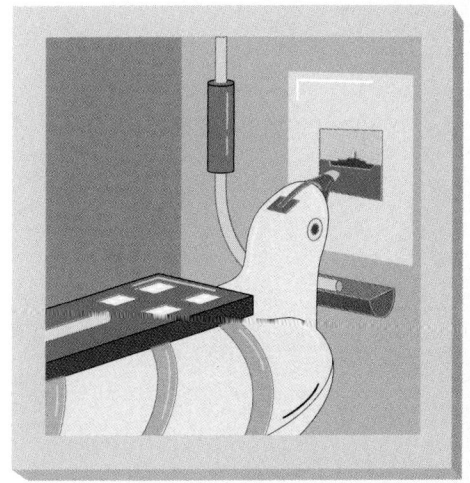

FIGURE 6.11

Skinner's Pigeon-Guided Missile
Skinner wanted to assist the military by using pigeons' tracking behavior. A gold electrode covered the tip of the pigeons' beaks. Contact with the screen on which the image of the target was projected sent a signal informing the missile's control mechanism of the target's location. A few grains of food occasionally given to the pigeons maintained their tracking behavior. Despite the pigeons' high degree of accuracy, the military declined to employ the pigeons. *How comfortable would you have been with supporting this military strategy?*

This produced corrective signals to keep the missile on its course. The pigeons did their job well in trial runs, but top Navy officials could not accept pigeons piloting their missiles in a war. Skinner, however, congratulated himself on the degree of control he was able to exercise over the pigeons (see figure 6.11).

Following the pigeon experiment, Skinner (1948) wrote *Walden Two*, a novel in which he presented his ideas about building a scientifically managed society. Skinner envisioned a utopian society that could be engineered through behavioral control. Skinner viewed existing societies as poorly managed because people believe in such myths as free will. He pointed out that humans are no more free than pigeons are; denying that our behavior is controlled by environmental forces is to ignore science and reality, he argued. In the long run, Skinner believed we would be much happier when we recognized such truths, especially his concept that we could live a prosperous life under the control of positive reinforcement.

Skinner and other behaviorists have made every effort to study organisms under precisely controlled conditions so that the connection between the operant and the specific consequences could be examined in minute detail. One of the ways in which Skinner achieved such control was his development in the 1930s of the Skinner box (see figure 6.12). A device in the box delivered food pellets into a tray at random. After a rat became accustomed to the box, Skinner installed a lever and observed the rat's behavior. As the hungry rat explored the box, it occasionally pressed the lever and a food pellet was dispensed. Soon after, the rat learned that the consequences of pressing the lever were positive—it would be fed. Further control was achieved by soundproofing the box to ensure that the experimenter was the only influence on the rat. In many experiments, the responses were mechanically recorded by a cumulative recorder, and the food (the stimulus) was dispensed automatically. Such precautions were designed to avoid human error.

Skinner's search for a more precise analysis of behavior and its controlling conditions led to the development of a number of concepts. He identified the time intervals and procedures that would produce the most efficient conditioning. He examined how different kinds of reinforcers vary in their power to strengthen behavior, and explored what would happen to the strength of the behavior when reinforcement wasn't consistent. Skinner also examined how behavior could be generalized and discriminated. We will explore each of these problems in turn.

Time Interval   As with classical conditioning, in most situations learning is more efficient in operant conditioning when the interval is more likely on the order of seconds rather than minutes or hours. An especially important distinction to remember is that learning is more efficient under *immediate* rather than delayed consequences. To read further about the importance of time interval in learning, turn to Applications in Psychology 6.1.

Shaping and Chaining   When a behavior takes time to occur, the learning process in operant conditioning may be shortened if an *approximation* of the desired behavior is rewarded. **Shaping** *is the process of rewarding approximations of desired behavior.* In one situation, parents used shaping to toilet train their 2-year-old son. The parents knew all too well that the child's grunting sound signaled he was about to fill his diaper. In the first week, they gave him candy if the boy made the sound within 20 feet of the bathroom. The second week he was given candy only if he grunted within 10 feet of the bathroom, the third week only if he was in the bathroom, and the fourth week he had to use the toilet to get the candy. It worked (Fischer & Gochros, 1975).

Chaining *is an operant conditioning technique used to teach a complex sequence, or chain, of behaviors. The procedure begins by shaping the final response in the sequence, then working backward until a chain of behaviors is learned.* For example, after the final response is learned, the next-to-last response is reinforced, and so on. Both shaping and chaining are used extensively by animal trainers to teach complex or unusual sequences of behavior. A dolphin who does three back flips, throws a ball through a hoop, places a hat on its head, and finally applauds itself learned the sequence of tricks in reverse order if its trainer used chaining. Figure 6.13 shows a sequence of behaviors a rat learned through the process of chaining.

Primary and Secondary Reinforcement   Positive reinforcement can be classified as primary reinforcement or secondary reinforcement. These classifications focus on a

FIGURE 6.12

Operant Conditioning in a Behavioral Laboratory
Shown here is a rat being conditioned in a Skinner box. Notice the elaborate machinery used to deliver food pellets as reinforcers and to keep track of the rat's behavior.

How Immediate and Delayed Consequences Influence Your Self-control

- "That double-dutch chocolate dessert is just too good to pass up."
- "I know I should start exercising more but I guess I'm just too lazy to get started."
- "I've got an important paper due tomorrow morning. Why am I here at this party? Why aren't I home writing the paper?"

If you are like most people, self-control problems like these crop up in your life, unfortunately all too frequently. We often describe ourselves as not having enough willpower to handle these situations. Actually, many of these situations reflect a conflict between immediate and delayed consequences of behavior involving various combinations of reinforcers and punishers (Martin & Pear, 1988).

Immediate Small Reinforcers Versus Delayed Strong Punishers

One reason obesity is a major health problem is that eating is a behavior with immediate positive consequences—food tastes very good and quickly provides a pleasurable feeling. Although the potential delayed consequences of overeating (obesity and other possible health risks) are negative, immediate consequences are difficult to override. When the delayed consequences of behavior are punishing and the immediate consequences are reinforcing, the immediate consequences usually win, even when the immediate consequences are small reinforcers and the delayed consequences are major punishers. Smoking and drinking follow a similar pattern. The immediate consequences of smoking (the powerful combination of positive reinforcement—tension relief, energy boost—and negative reinforcement—removal of craving, "nicotine fit") are reinforcing for most smokers. The punishing aspects of smoking are primarily long-term,

including shortness of breath, a sore throat, coughing, emphysema, heart disease, lung cancer, and other cancers. The immediate pleasurable consequences of drinking override the delayed consequences of a hangover or even alcoholism.

Immediate Small Reinforcers Versus Delayed Stronger Reinforcers

Self-control problems also are brought about by the choice we face when we can obtain a small immediate reinforcer or wait for a delayed but much-higher-valued reinforcer. For example, you can spend your money now on clothes, trinkets, parties, and the like or save your money and buy a house or car later. In another circumstance, you can play around now and enjoy yourself, which produces immediate small reinforcers, or you can study hard over a long period of time, which can produce delayed stronger reinforcers such as good grades, scholarships to graduate school, and better jobs.

Immediate Punishers Versus Delayed Reinforcers

Why are some of us so reluctant to take up a new sport? To try a new dance step? To go to a social gathering? To do something different? One reason is that learning new skills often involves minor punishing consequences, such as initially looking stupid, not knowing what to do, having to put up with sarcastic comments from onlookers, and so on. In these circumstances, reinforcing consequences are often delayed. For example, it takes us a long time to become a good golfer or a good dancer and enjoy ourselves in these activities.

Immediate Weak Punishers Versus Strong Delayed Punishers

Why do so many of us postpone such activities as going to the dentist, scheduling minor surgery, or paying campus parking fines? In this kind of self-control problem, if we act immediately we experience a weak punisher—it hurts to get our teeth drilled, it is painful to have minor surgery, and it is not very pleasurable to pay a campus parking fine. However, the delayed consequences can be more punishing—our teeth can fall out, we might need major surgery, and our car might get towed away or we might get thrown in jail. All too often, though, immediate consequences win out in these self-control situations.

In these examples of different combinations of immediate and delayed consequences of our behavior, we have seen that immediate consequences often interfere with our ability to control our behavior. Later in the chapter, we offer some suggestions for ways to improve self-control through behavioral strategies.

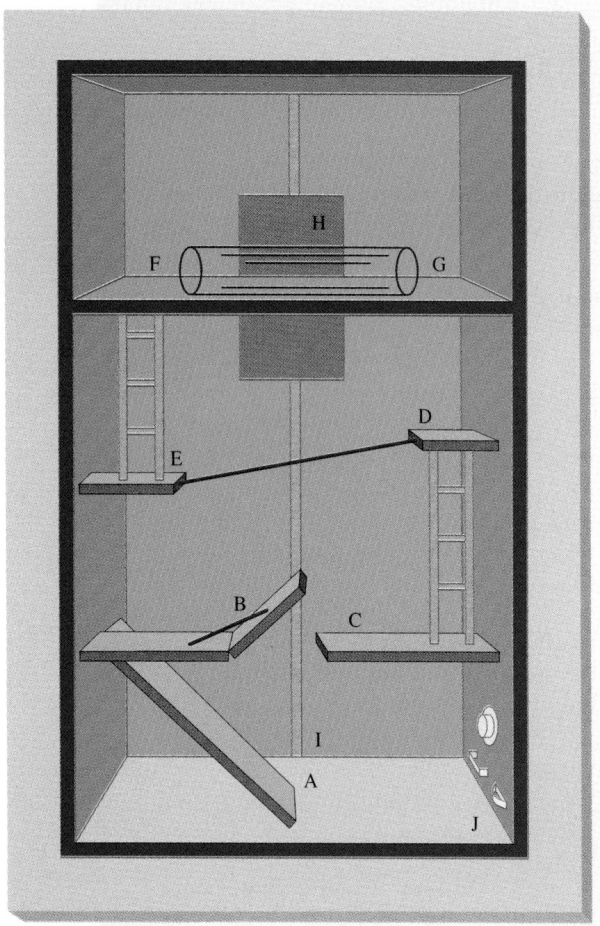

FIGURE 6.13

An Example of Chaining
Starting at A, the rat climbs the ramp to B, crosses the drawbridge to C, climbs the ladder to D, crosses the tightrope to E, climbs the ladder to F, crawls through the tunnel to G, enters the elevator at H, descends to I, presses the lever in the lower right hand corner at J, and then receives food. In chaining, the experimenter would reinforce lever pressing at J first, then movement from I to J, and so forth.

distinction between inborn (unlearned) and learned aspects of behavior. **Primary reinforcement** *involves the use of reinforcers that are innately satisfying; that is, it does not take any learning on an organism's part to make them pleasurable.* Food, water, and sexual satisfaction are primary reinforcers.

Secondary reinforcement *acquires its positive value through experience; secondary reinforcers are learned, or conditional, reinforcers.* Hundreds of secondary reinforcers characterize our lives. For example, secondary reinforcers include such social situations as getting praise and making eye contact. One popular story in psychology focuses on the use of eye contact as a secondary reinforcer to shape the behavior of a famous university professor, an expert on operant conditioning. Some students decided to train the

professor to lecture from one corner of the classroom. They used eye contact as a reinforcer and begin reinforcing successive approximations of the desired response. Each time the professor moved toward the appropriate corner, the students looked at him. If he moved in another direction, they looked away. By gradually rewarding successive approximations to the desired response, the students were able to get the professor to deliver his lecture from one corner of the classroom. The well-known operant conditioning expert denies that this shaping ever took place. Whether it did or not, the story provides an excellent example of how secondary reinforcers can be used to shape behavior in real-life circumstances (Chance, 1979).

> *The deepest principle of Human Nature is the craving to be appreciated.*
>
> **William James**

Another example may also help you understand the importance of secondary reinforcement in our everyday lives. When a student is given $25 for an A on her report card, the $25 is a secondary reinforcer. It is not innate, and it increases the likelihood that the student will work to get another A in the future. (The A grade is also a secondary reinforcer.) Money is often referred to as a *token reinforcer.* When an object can be exchanged for another reinforcer, the object may have reinforcing value itself, so it is called a token reinforcer. Gift certificates and poker chips are token reinforcers.

Schedules of Reinforcement   In most of life's experiences, we are not reinforced every time we make a response. A golfer does not win every tournament she enters; a chess whiz does not win every match he plays; a student is not patted on the back each time she solves a problem. **Partial reinforcement** *(intermittent reinforcement) simply means that responses are not reinforced each time they occur.* **Schedules of reinforcement** *are timetables that determine when a response will be reinforced.* Four schedules of reinforcement are fixed-ratio, variable-ratio, fixed-interval, and variable-interval.

A **fixed-ratio schedule** *reinforces a behavior after a set number of responses.* For example, if you are playing the slot machines in Atlantic City and they are on a fixed-ratio schedule, you might get $5 back every 20 times you put money in the machine. It wouldn't take long to figure out that, if you watched someone else play the machine 18 or 19 times, not get any money back, and then walk away, you should step up, insert your coin, and collect $5.

Consequently, slot machines are on a **variable-ratio schedule,** *a timetable in which responses are rewarded an average number of times, but on an unpredictable basis.* For example, a slot machine might pay off every twentieth time, on the average, but, unlike with the fixed-ratio schedule, the gambler does not know when this payoff will be. The slot machine might pay off twice in a row and then not again until after 58 coins have been inserted, which averages out to a reward for every 20 responses, but when the reward is given is unpredictable.

The remaining two reinforcement schedules are determined by *time elapsed* since the last behavior was rewarded. A **fixed-interval schedule** *reinforces the first appropriate response after a fixed amount of time has elapsed.* For example, you might get a reward the first time you put money in a slot machine after every 10-minute period has elapsed. A **variable-interval schedule** *reinforces a response after a variable amount of time has elapsed.* On this schedule, the slot machines might reward you after 10 minutes, then after 2 minutes, then after 18 minutes, and so forth.

Which of these schedules is the most effective? The closer a schedule is to continuous reinforcement, the faster an individual learns. However, once behavior is learned, the intermittent schedules can be effective in maintaining behavior. As shown in figure 6.14, the rate of behavior varies from one schedule to the next (Skinner, 1961). The fixed-ratio schedule produces a high rate of behavior, with a pause occurring between the reinforcer and the behavior. This type of schedule is used widely in our lives. For example, if an individual is paid $100 for every 10 lawns he mows, then he is on a fixed-ratio schedule. The variable-ratio schedule also elicits a high rate of behavior, and the pause after the reinforcement is eliminated. This schedule usually elicits the highest response rate of all four schedules.

The interval schedules produce behavior at a lower rate than the ratio schedules do. The fixed-interval schedule stimulates a low rate of behavior at the start of an interval and a somewhat faster rate toward the end. This happens because the organism apparently recognizes that the behavior early in the interval will not be rewarded but that later behavior will be rewarded. A scallop-shaped curve characterizes the behavior pattern of an organism on a fixed-interval schedule. The variable-interval schedule produces a slow, consistent rate of behavior.

Generalization In classical conditioning, generalization is the tendency of a stimulus similar to the conditioned stimulus to produce a response similar to the conditioned response. **Generalization** *in operant conditioning means giving the same response to similar stimuli.* For example, in one study, pigeons were reinforced for pecking at a disc of a particular color (Guttman & Kalish, 1956). Stimulus generalization was tested by presenting the pigeons with discs of varying colors. As shown in figure 6.15, the pigeons were most likely to peck at the disc closest in color to the

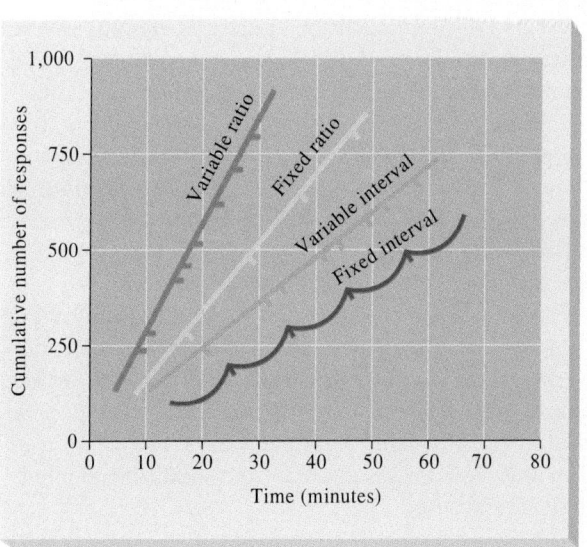

FIGURE 6.14

Performance Curves Produced by Four Schedules of Reinforcement
The steeper the slope of the curve, the faster the response. Each pause indicated by a hash mark indicates the point at which reinforcement was given. Notice that the fixed-interval schedule reveals a scalloped effect rather than a straight line because the organism stops responding for a while after each reinforcement but quickly responds as the next reinforcement approaches.

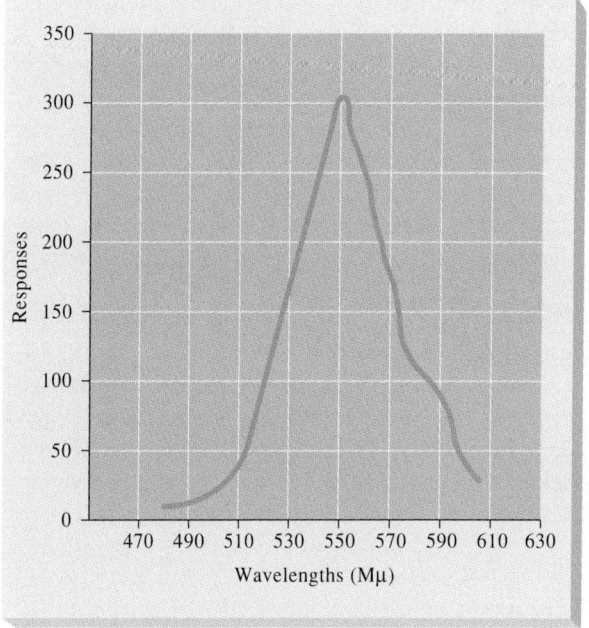

FIGURE 6.15

Stimulus Generalization
In the experiment by Guttman and Kalish (1956), pigeons initially pecked a disc of a particular color (in this graph, a color with a wavelength of 550 Mμ) after they had been reinforced for this wavelength. Subsequently, when the pigeons were presented discs of colors with varying wavelengths, they were more likely to peck discs that were similar to the original disc.

original. An example of stimulus generalization in everyday life that is familiar to many parents involves an infant's learning to say "Doggie" to a hairy, four-legged creature with floppy ears and a friendly bark (Martin & Pear, 1988). Later the infant sees a different kind of dog and says, "Doggie." This is an example of stimulus generalization because a previously reinforced response ("Doggie") appeared in the presence of a new stimulus (a new kind of dog). Later the infant sees a horse and says, "Doggie." This is another example of stimulus generalization, even though the infant's labeling is incorrect, which indicates that not all instances of stimulus generalization are favorable and illustrates why discriminations need to be taught.

Discrimination   In classical conditioning, discrimination is the process of learning to respond to certain stimuli and not to others. **Discrimination** *in operant conditioning is the process of responding in the presence of another stimulus that is not reinforced.* For example, you might look at two street signs, both made of metal, both the same color, and both with words on them. However, one sign says "Enter at your own risk" and the other reads "Please walk this way." The words serve as discriminative stimuli because the sign that says "Please walk this way" indicates that you will be rewarded for doing so, whereas the sign that says "Enter at your own risk" suggests that the consequences may not be positive. **Discriminative stimuli** *signal that a response will be reinforced.* Discrimination is one of the techniques used to teach animals to perform tricks. When Kent Burgess (1968) wanted to teach a killer whale tricks, he used a whistle as the discriminative stimulus (S^D). Whenever the whistle sounded, the killer whale got fed. Burgess blew the whistle immediately after a correct response and the killer whale approached the feeding platform, where it was fed. Using this tactic, Burgess taught the killer whale to spout water, leap in the air, and so on (see figure 6.16).

Applications of Operant Conditioning

A preschool child repeatedly throws his glasses and breaks them. A high school student and her parents have intense arguments. A college student is deeply depressed. An elderly woman is incontinent. Operant conditioning procedures have helped such people adapt more successfully to their environment and cope more effectively with their problems.

Behavior Modification

Behavior modification *is the application of operant conditioning principles to changing human behavior; its main goal is to replace unacceptable responses with acceptable, adaptive ones.* Psychologists establish consequences for behavior to ensure that acceptable actions are reinforced and unacceptable ones are not. Advocates of behavior modification believe that many emotional and behavioral problems are caused by inadequate (or inappropriate) response consequences. A child who throws down his glasses and breaks

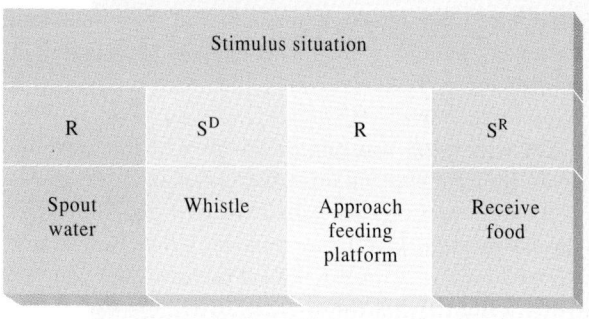

FIGURE 6.16

Teaching Behavior to a Killer Whale
When spouting water was followed by a whistle, it reinforced spouting and provided the signal for approaching the feeding platform to receive the reinforcing stimulus (S^R) of food (Chance, 1979).

them may be receiving too much attention from his teacher and peers for his behavior; they unwittingly reinforce an unacceptable behavior. In this instance, the parents and teachers would be instructed to divert their attention from the destructive behavior and transfer it to a more constructive behavior, such as working quietly or playing cooperatively with peers (Harris, Wolf, & Baer, 1964).

Consider another circumstance in which behavior modification can help people solve problems. Barbara and her parents were on a collision course. Things got so bad that her parents decided to see a clinical psychologist. The psychologist, who had a behavioral orientation for addressing clinical problems, talked with each family member, trying to get them to pinpoint the problem. The psychologist convinced the family to sign a behavioral contract that spelled out what everyone needed to do to reduce the conflict. Barbara agreed to (1) be home before 11 P.M. on weeknights, (2) look for a part-time job so she could begin to pay for some of her activities, and (3) refrain from calling her parents insulting names. Her parents agreed to (1) talk to Barbara in a low tone of voice rather than yell if they were angry; (2) refrain from criticizing teenagers, especially Barbara's friends; and (3) give Barbara a small sum of money each week for gas, makeup, and socializing, but only until she found a job.

Also consider Sam, a 19-year-old college student, who has been deeply depressed lately. His girlfriend broke off their relationship of 2 years, and his grades have been dropping. He decides to go to a psychologist who has a behavioral orientation. The psychologist enrolls him in the Coping with Depression course developed by Peter Lewinsohn (1987). Sam learns to monitor his daily moods and increase his ratio of positive to negative life events. The psychologist trains Sam to develop more efficient coping skills and gets Sam to agree to a behavioral contract, just as the psychologist did with Barbara and her parents.

Mary is an elderly woman who lives in a nursing home. In recent months, she has become incontinent and is increasingly dependent on the staff for help with her daily activities. The behavioral treatment designed for Mary's problem involves teaching her to monitor her behavior and schedule going to the toilet. She is also required to do pelvic exercises. The program for decreasing Mary's dependence requires that the nursing home staff attend more to her independent behavior when it occurs and remove attention from dependent behavior whenever possible. Such strategies with the elderly have been effective in reducing problems with incontinence and dependence (Burgio & Burgio, 1986).

Psychologists use behavior modification to teach couples to communicate more effectively, to encourage fathers to engage in more competent caregiving with their infants, to train autistic children's interpersonal skills, to help individuals lose weight, and to reduce individuals' fear of social situations.

Self-control Techniques

Another effective use of behavior modification is to improve a person's self-control. Chances are that each of us could stand to change something about our lives. What would you like to change? What would you like to be able to control more effectively in your life? To answer these questions, you first have to specify your problem in a concrete way. This is easy for Bob—he wants to lose 30 pounds. Even more precisely, he wants to consume about 1,000 fewer calories per day than he uses, to give him a weight loss of about 2 pounds per week. Some problems are more difficult to specify, such as "wasting time," "having a bad attitude toward school," "having a poor relationship with _____," or "being too nervous and worrying a lot." These types of problems have been called "fuzzies" because of their vague, abstract nature (Mager, 1972). It is important to "unfuzzify" these abstract problems and make them more specific and concrete. You can make your problems more precise by writing out your goal and by listing the things that would give you clear evidence you have reached your goal.

A second important step in a self-control program is to make a *commitment* to change (Martin & Pear, 1988). Both a commitment to change and a knowledge of change techniques have been shown to help college students become more effective self-managers of their smoking, eating, studying, and relationship problems. Building a commitment to change requires you to do things that increase the likelihood you will stick to your project. Tell others about your commitment to change—they will remind you to stick to your program. Rearrange your environment to provide frequent reminders of your goal, making sure the reminders are associated with the positive benefits of reaching your goal. Put a lot of time and energy into planning your project. Make a list of statements about your projects, such as

"I've put a lot of time into this project; I certainly am not going to waste all of this effort now." Because you will undoubtedly face temptations to backslide or quit your project, plan ahead for ways you can deal with temptation, tailoring these plans to your specific problem.

A third major step in developing a self-control program is to collect data about your behavior. This is especially important in decreasing such excessive behaviors as overeating and frequent smoking. One of the reasons for tracking your behavior is that it provides a reference point for evaluating your progress. When recording the frequency of a problem during initial observations, you should examine the immediate consequences that could be maintaining the problem (Martin & Pear, 1988). Consider Bob's situation. When first asked why he eats so much, Bob said, "Because I like the taste, and eating makes me feel comfortable." However, when Bob began evaluating the circumstances in which he usually snacks, he noticed that, most of the time, when he eats, his behavior is reinforced: a candy bar and then he meets his girlfriend; potato chips and then his favorite basketball star scores another basket; a beer and then his fraternity brothers laugh at his jokes. Bob eats while getting ready to meet his girlfriend, while watching television, while socializing with his fraternity brothers, and in many other social situations, during which he comes into contact with a variety of reinforcing events in the environment. No wonder Bob has trouble with his weight.

A fourth important step in improving your self-control is to design a program. There are many strategies you can follow. Virtually every self-control program incorporates self-instruction or self-talk (Meichenbaum, 1986). Consider the self-instruction program followed by a Canadian psychologist to improve his running (Martin & Pear, 1988). During the winter, he started an exercise program that consisted of running 2 miles (14 laps) at a university's indoor track. He often found that, after 9 or 10 laps, fatiguing thoughts set in and he talked himself out of completing the last few laps, saying, "I've done pretty well today by running 9 laps." He decided to start a self-reinforcement program to increase his antifatigue thoughts in the last few laps of his running regimen. Specifically, during the tenth to fourteenth laps, he came up with an antifatigue thought and followed it with a pleasurable one. The antifatigue thought he chose was a TV commercial for fitness that claimed that the average 60-year-old Swede is in the same physical condition as the average 30-year-old Canadian (the claim is actually false, but this is not important to this example). Each time the psychologist got to a certain place on the track, he thought about a healthy Swede jogging smoothly along the track. At the next turn, he thought about something enjoyable, such as going to the beach or a party where others complimented him on his healthy appearance. After practicing this sequence of thoughts for about 2 weeks as he ran, he was able to eliminate his fatiguing thoughts and complete his 2-mile runs.

Behavioral strategies for improving self-control have been effectively applied to college students' *(a)* smoking, *(b)* eating, *(c)* relationships, and *(d)* studying. For ways to tailor a self-control program to your specific needs, you might want to contact the counseling center at your college or university.

A fifth important step in improving your self-control is to make it last. One strategy is to establish specific dates for postchecks and to plan a course of action if your postchecks are not favorable. For instance, if your self-control program involves weight reduction, you might want to weigh yourself once a week. If your weight increases to a certain level, then you immediately go back on your self-control program. Another strategy is to establish a buddy system by finding a friend or someone with a similar problem. The two of you set mutual maintenance goals. Once a

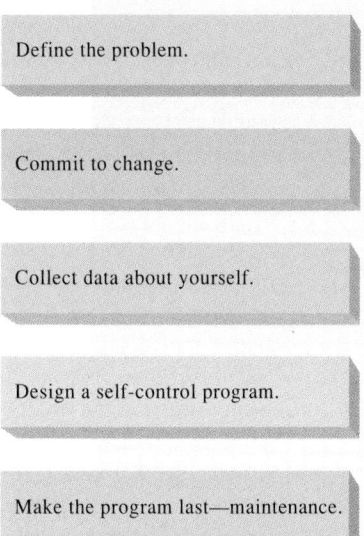

FIGURE 6.17

Five Important Steps in Developing a Program of Self-control

The five steps shown in the figure are:

Define the problem.

Commit to change.

Collect data about yourself.

Design a self-control program.

Make the program last—maintenance.

month, get together and check each other's behavior. If your goals have been maintained, get together and celebrate. Figure 6.17 summarizes the main steps in the self-control program just described.

For other ideas on how to establish an effective self-control program tailored to your specific needs, you might want to contact the counseling center at your college or university. A good book on behavior modification or self-control also can be helpful: one is by Brian Yates (1985).

Evaluation of Operant Conditioning

Operant conditioning has been used in a variety of contexts to change human and animal behavior. Many clinical applications have produced dramatic changes in behavior that might not have been easily accomplished using other methods. Operant psychologists have been praised for their reliance on observable and measurable behavior, which enables them to provide clear documentation for the changes they report.

Yet operant conditioning is not without its critics, particularly in relation to many of the positions taken by B. F. Skinner. Skinner believed that behavior is determined solely by its consequences. His critics argue that his adherence to operant explanations is reductionistic and that operant conditioning reduces human experience to connections between behavior and consequences, disparaging matters of spirit and will. Among Skinner's

more controversial stands was his insistence that humans have no free will (Skinner, 1971), that what appears to be freely chosen can, in fact, be predicted from the distinctive reinforcement history the organism has experienced.

Many psychologists believe that operant conditioning is effective only in explaining simple behaviors. Complex behaviors are likely to require other kinds of cognitive mediation in order to be sustained (Chance, 1988). However, Skinner proposed that operant theory had no room for cognitive processes and believed that the contemporary shifts toward cognitive psychology would be ruinous to psychology (Skinner, 1990).

Some critics believe that operant explanations contain an unfortunate circularity. For example, suppose that a teacher wished to increase question asking among her students. She designs a behavior modification protocol in which questions will be reinforced on an intermittent schedule with chocolate candy. The plan works just fine for most of the students, but several seem to disengage from class discussion rather than increase their responsiveness. Later we discover a variety of reasons why their participation decreased, including having an allergy to chocolate, being on a sweet-restricted diet, and being embarrassed. The positive reinforcer in these cases was not truly a positive reinforcer. We can be certain a stimulus is a positive reinforcer if, and only if, it strengthens or increases the response that it follows. Therefore, sometimes we may be forced to identify operant components after the fact.

Just as in classical conditioning, the vocabulary of operant conditioning is challenging to learn. Most students who are new to learning processes struggle with distinguishing the terms. Skinner himself regretted that the terminology was not as distinctive as it could be (Skinner, 1992).

Operant techniques and those who use them have been criticized for manipulating behavior. Nowhere in psychology is the issue of control more pronounced. Skinner received national attention when he placed his daughter Deborah in a crib-sized "Skinner box" that responded to her infant needs. The "air-crib," as Skinner called it, was completely enclosed, soundproofed, and temperature controlled. It not only allowed Skinner greater control over his daughter's behavior, but also allowed Deborah to exercise some control over the amount of stimulation she received. Despite Skinner's reports that his daughter was not adversely affected by the crib, many individuals were outraged. Critics suggest that the degree of control offered in operant conditioning techniques may challenge our sense of professional ethics as well as the protection of individual rights.

Self-control and the Happy Life

Take a few moments and think about your own life. Is there one aspect of your life that you would like to improve? How could you define this problem so that your target behavior could be the focus of the self-control procedure? What five steps would be appropriate in addressing this problem so that you could live a happier life?

Using self-control techniques is a good example of how to *apply psychological concepts and skills to enhance personal adaptation. If self-control techniques offer some promise of creating a happier life, what is stopping you?*

A final criticism has to do with the fuzzy boundaries between operant and classical conditioning. For example, some psychologists believe that learning is really a unified process rather than two separate systems. Consider the acquisition of a fear of dogs. Being bitten by a dog is a punishing consequence that reduces future approaches to dogs (operant principle of punishment leading to avoidance) but also might cause the heart to pound with fear when dogs are in view (classical conditioning of fear). This challenge led Paul Chance (1988, p. 124) to suggest that classical and operant procedures are "so intertwined that it is hard to say where one begins and the other ends."

REVIEW

Operant Conditioning

Operant conditioning (instrumental conditioning) is a form of learning in which the consequences of a behavior produce changes in the probability of the behavior's occurrence. Operant conditioning focuses on what happens after a response is made, whereas classical conditioning emphasizes what occurs before a response is made. The key connection in classical conditioning is between two stimuli; in operant conditioning, it is between an organism's response and its consequences. Operant conditioning is often better at explaining voluntary behavior. Classical conditioning is often better at explaining involuntary behavior. Although Skinner has emerged as the primary figure in operant conditioning, E. L. Thorndike's experiments established the power of consequences in determining voluntary behavior. His view is referred to as S-R theory and involves the law of effect.

In operant conditioning, reinforcement (reward) is a consequence that increases the probability a behavior will occur. Operant conditioning can involve positive reinforcement and negative reinforcement. Also, punishment is a consequence that decreases the probability a behavior will recur. Punishment involves the use of noxious stimuli or aversive consequences to reduce responding. Extinction in operant conditioning is a decrease in the tendency to perform a behavior that receives neither a positive nor a negative consequence.

Immediate consequences are more effective than delayed consequences. Shaping is the process of rewarding approximations of a desired behavior. Chaining involves establishing a complex chain of responses. The final response in the sequence is learned first, then the next to the last, and so on. Primary reinforcement refers to innate reinforcers (such as food, water, and sex); secondary reinforcement refers to reinforcers that acquire positive value through experience (such as money and smiles). In schedules of reinforcement, a response will be reinforced on a fixed-ratio, variable-ratio,

fixed-interval, or variable-interval schedule. These schedules have various degrees of effectiveness. Generalization means giving the same response to similar stimuli. Discrimination is the process of responding in the presence of one stimulus that is reinforced but not responding in the presence of another stimulus that is not reinforced.

Behavior modification is the use of learning principles to change maladaptive or abnormal behavior. It focuses on changing behavior by following the behavior with reinforcement. Behavior modification is widely used to reduce maladaptive behavior.

Operant conditioning methods have been praised for their broad effectiveness in changing behavior and for promoting more rigorous methods for documenting behavior change. Critics describe operant approaches as reductionistic, manipulative, and overreliant on explanation after the fact. Many psychologists do not believe in separating operant and classical conditioning into discrete processes. In practice, it is often difficult to distinguish between the two approaches.

OBSERVATIONAL LEARNING

Humans show a remarkable capacity to imitate others' behavior. Babies as young as 3 days old show the capacity to stick out their tongues in response to adult models (Meltzoff & Moore, 1988). Children also acquire fine motor skills (such as tying a shoelace) and gross motor skills (such as riding a bicycle) largely as a result of effective modeling.

We are in truth, more than half what we are by imitation.

Lord Chesterfield

Bandura's Contributions

Albert Bandura (1971, 1986, 1994) believes that if our learning occurred only in a trial-and-error fashion, it would be exceedingly tedious and at times hazardous. Instead, many of our complex behaviors are the result of exposure to competent models who display appropriate behavior in solving problems and coping with their world. **Observational learning,** *also called imitation or modeling, is learning that occurs when a person observes and imitates someone else's behavior.* The capacity to learn behavior patterns by observation eliminates tedious trial-and-error learning. The only requirement for learning is that the individual must be connected in time and space with the model.

In chapter 2, we discussed an experiment by Bandura on the nature of observational learning. An equal number of boys and girls of nursery school age watched one of three films in which someone beat up an adult-sized plastic toy called a Bobo doll. In the first film, the experimenter rewarded the aggressor with candy, soft drinks, and praise for aggressive behavior; in the second film, the experimenter criticized and spanked the aggressor for the aggressive behavior; and in the third film, there were no consequences to the aggressor for the behavior. Subsequently, each child was left alone in a room filled with toys, including a Bobo doll. The child's behavior was observed through a one-way mirror. As shown in figure 6.18, children who watched the film in which the aggressive behavior was rewarded or went unpunished imitated the behavior more than did the children who saw aggressive behavior punished. As might be expected, boys were more aggressive than girls were. However, when children were given positive incentives to display the aggression they had seen, the differences among the groups virtually disappeared. Most children were able to demonstrate the aggressive behavior they had seen performed by the model, whether or not the behavior had been rewarded.

Since his early experiments, Bandura (1986, 1994) has focused on some of the processes that influence an

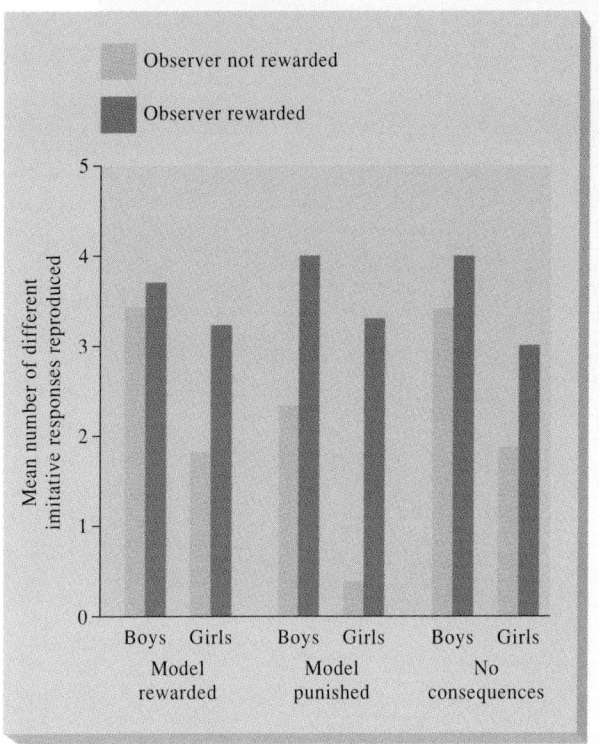

FIGURE 6.18

Results of Bandura's Experiment on Observational Learning and Aggression
Children who watched an aggressor be reinforced or experience no consequences for aggressive behavior imitated the aggressive behavior more than did children who watched the aggressor be punished. Boys were more aggressive than girls. When children were offered rewards for imitating the aggressive model's behavior, even those children who had seen the model punished demonstrated they had learned the model's behavior by behaving aggressively.

observer's behavior following exposure to a model. One of these is *attention*. Before a person can reproduce a model's actions, she must attend to what the model is doing or saying. You might not hear what a friend says if the stereo is blaring, or you might miss the teacher's analysis of a problem if you are admiring someone sitting in the next row. Attention to the model is influenced by a host of characteristics. For example, warm, powerful, atypical people command more attention than do cold, weak, typical people.

Retention is also important. To reproduce a model's actions, you must encode the information and keep it in memory so that it can be retrieved. A simple verbal description or a vivid image of what the model did assists retention. Memory is such an important cognitive process that most of the next chapter is devoted to it.

*The Role of
Role Models*

Who have been the most important role models in your life? What life lessons did you acquire through observational learning? Some research indicates that your selection of your major area of study will depend upon your identification of a professional for whom you have great admiration who is a success in the field that you are considering. Have you identified your major? Your consideration of the influence of role models on your future demonstrates another opportunity to *apply psychological concepts and skills to enhance personal adaptation.*

A final process in Bandura's conception of observational learning involves *reinforcement,* or incentive conditions. On many occasions, we attend to what a model says or does, retain the information in memory, and possess the motor capabilities to perform the action, but we fail to repeat the behavior because of inadequate reinforcement. This was demonstrated in Bandura's (1965) study when the children who had seen a model punished for aggression reproduced the model's aggression only when they were offered an incentive to do so. A summary of Bandura's model of observational learning is shown in figure 6.19.

Children need models more than they need critics.

Joseph Joubert

Another process involved in observational learning is *motor reproduction.* A person may attend to a model and encode in memory what he has seen, but because of limitations in motor development he may not be able to reproduce the model's action. A 13-year-old may see Monica Seles hit a great two-handed backhand or Shaquille O'Neal do a reverse two-handed dunk but be unable to reproduce the pro's actions.

At the beginning of this chapter, we discussed the powerful role of television in children's lives and how observational learning is the basic way people learn information from television. To find out about the types of models children observe on television and in schools, turn to Sociocultural Worlds 6.1.

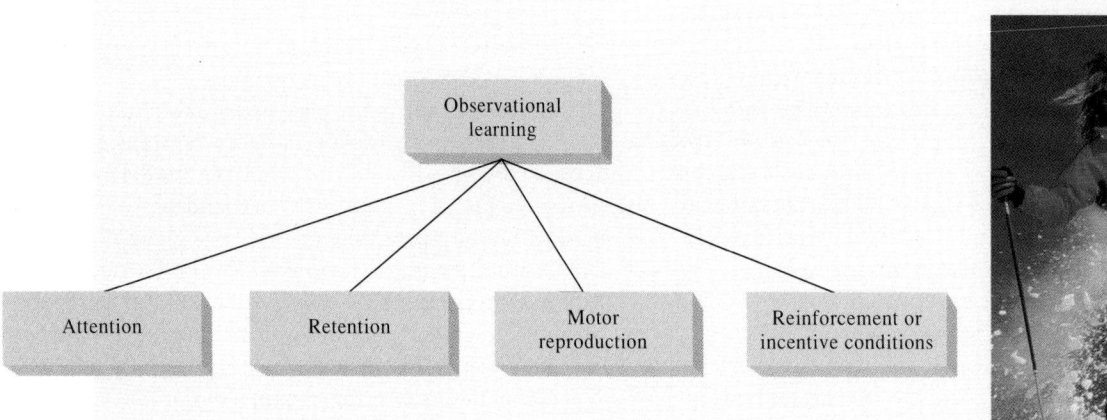

FIGURE 6.19

Bandura's Model of Observational Learning
Bandura argues that observational learning consists of four main processes: attention, retention, motor reproduction, and reinforcement or incentive conditions. Consider a circumstance involving learning to ski. You need to attend to the instructor's words and demonstrations. You need to remember what the instructor did and her tips for avoiding disasters. You also need the motor abilities to reproduce what the instructor has shown you, and praise from the instructor after you have completed a few moves on the slopes should improve your motivation to continue skiing.

Ethnicity and Role Models

Many children from ethnic minority groups may be hard-pressed to observe competent role models with whom they can identify and from whom they can learn. A number of educators believe that the exposure of children and adolescents to competent role models is one way to reduce the high school dropout problem. Role models stimulate alternative ways of thinking about the future.

Television is one source of exposure to role models. However, historically television has underrepresented and misrepresented ethnic minorities (Pouissant, 1972). One study looked at portrayals of ethnic minorities in programs broadcast during children's heavy viewing hours (weekdays from 4 to 6 P.M. and from 7 to 11 P.M.) (Williams & Condry, 1989). The percentage of White characters in the programs far exceeded the percentage of Whites in the United States population. African Americans, Asian Americans, and Latinos were especially underrepresented. For example, only 0.6 percent of the characters were Latino, although the Latino population was 6.4 percent of the total U.S. population in 1989. Television usually presents less positive and less dignified portrayals of African American, Asian American, Latino, and Native American characters than of White characters (Condry, 1989). In their depictions on television, ethnic minorities tended to hold lower-status jobs and were more likely than Whites to be cast as criminals or victims.

Live role models, or *mentors,* can be even more influential examples for ethnic minorities. A mentor is an older, more experienced person who helps a younger person in a one-to-one relationship that goes beyond the formal obligations of a teaching or supervisory role. Mentors who are competent and caring provide young people with concrete images of who they can become and lend guidance and support to help enable them to fulfill their aspirations.

In the Each One/Reach One Program in Milwaukee, Wisconsin, African American professional women are recruited and trained to serve as role models. Each mentor spends a minimum of 10 hours a month with the adolescent girl she is paired with, visiting each other's homes and attending cultural events. The adolescent might also visit her mentor where she works. Because the program hopes to expose not only the girl but her whole family to an alternative lifestyle, the mother and siblings of the adolescent are included whenever possible. One study of mentoring, an adopt-a-student program in Atlanta, Georgia, paired 200 underachieving juniors and seniors with mentors from the business community, who helped students plan their futures and counseled them about achieving goals. The participating students were much more likely to be employed or to continue their education than were similar students who did not take part (Anson, 1988).

A special concern is that children and adolescents from ethnic minority groups be exposed to competent role models with whom they can identify and from whom they can learn. One way this is being accomplished is through mentoring.

Bandura views observational learning as an information-processing activity. As a person observes, information about the world is transformed into cognitive representations that serve as guides for action. As we will see in the next section, interest in the cognitive factors of learning has increased dramatically in recent years.

Applications of Observational Learning

Observational learning plays a substantial role in human behavior, although many other species function very well without developing this process. For example, dogs and cats show some capacity for observational learning, but not to the same extent as humans and other primates. Species lower on the evolutionary ladder have no capacity for observational learning (Chance, 1988). Bandura explained this difference as being due to lower species' inability to represent the observed behavior symbolically and to rehearse the new behavior covertly before performing it.

The effectiveness of observational learning depends on many factors. For example, a sailor described how he learned to tie a bowline when he was assigned to an aircraft carrier. The instructor had informed his new crew that he would demonstrate the knot once and that anyone unable to imitate the process would be thrown overboard. The focused attention and negative incentive resulted in rapid learning. Other influences involve the competence and attractiveness of the model (Berger, 1971) and the arousal level of the learner (Warden & Jackson, 1935).

Evaluation of Observational Learning

Anyone who has struggled to acquire a new skill by watching a master, whether the goal is to become a better golfer, a better driver, or a better writer, recognizes that observing does not always translate into learning. Simple behaviors may be more easily explained and copied by observation than complex behaviors are. Teachers recognize the importance of breaking down complex performances into smaller units in order to achieve mastery of the whole through modeling.

When imitation fails, it might not be clear what the problem is. Is it insufficient exposure to the model? Is it that the model is insufficiently engaging? Is it that the rewards of performance are unclear? Ironically, we might know far less about the influences that promote or hinder observational learning than we know about classical and operant procedures (Chance, 1988).

Some critics suggest that observational learning merely represents variants of classical and operant conditioning. The learner watches the model undergo either form of conditioning and learns from the model's experiences. Therefore, the same factors that influence classical and operant conditioning will influence observational learning.

REVIEW

Observational Learning

Observational learning occurs when an individual observes someone else's behavior. Observational learning is also called imitation or modeling. Observational learning accounts for much of human behavior and little of the behavior of lower species. Factors that influence its effectiveness include attention, incentive conditions, model characteristics, and learner characteristics. Less is known about observational learning than about conditioning processes. However, modeling tends to be more effective with simpler behaviors or complex behaviors broken into simpler units.

COGNITIVE, BIOLOGICAL, AND CULTURAL INFLUENCES ON LEARNING

So far, we have focused on explanations of learning from the behavioral perspective. However, three other perspectives have also contributed to our current understanding of how organisms learn. The cognitive perspective has become more accepted over the last several decades. The neurobiological perspective stresses the limitations imposed on learning by biological factors. Finally, cultural contexts can inhibit learning or cause it to flourish.

Cognitive Influences

When we learn, we often cognitively represent or transform our experiences. In our excursion through learning, we avoided saying much about these cognitive processes, except in our description of observational learning. In the operant conditioning view of Skinner and the classical conditioning view of Pavlov, no room is given to the possibility that cognitive factors, such as memory, thinking, planning, or expectations, might be important in the learning process. Skinnerians do not deny the existence of thinking processes;

---

however, they say that attempts to study thought processes can divert attention away from discovering the true causes of behavior—environmental conditions.

Many contemporary psychologists, including behavioral revisionists who recognize that cognition should not have been ignored in classical and operant conditioning, believe that learning involves much more than stimulus-response connections. The **S-O-R model** *is a model of learning that gives some importance to cognitive factors. S stands for stimulus, O for organism, and R for response. (The O sometimes is referred to as the* black box, *because the mental activities of the organism cannot be seen and, therefore, must be inferred.)*

Bandura (1986, 1989) described another model of learning that involves behavior, person, and environment. As shown in figure 6.20, behavior, person and cognitive factors, and environmental influences interact. Behavior influences cognition, and vice versa; a person's cognitive activities influence the environment; environmental experiences change the person's thought; and so on.

Let's consider how Bandura's model might work in the case of a college student's achievement behavior. As the student studies diligently and gets good grades, her behavior produces in her positive thoughts about her abilities. As part of her effort to make good grades, she plans and develops a number of strategies to make her studying more efficient. In these ways, her behavior has influenced her thought, and her thought has influenced her behavior. At the beginning of the semester, her college made a special effort to involve students in a study skills program. She decided to join. Her success, along with that of other students who attended the program, has led the college to expand the program next semester. In these ways, environment influenced behavior, and behavior changed the environment. The expectations of the college administrators that the study skills program would work made it possible in the first place. The program's success has spurred expectations that this type of program could work in other colleges. In these ways, cognition changed environment, and the environment changed cognition. Expectations are an important variable in Bandura's model. How might expectations be further involved in understanding learning?

Expectations and Cognitive Maps

E. C. Tolman says that, when classical and operant conditioning occur, the organism acquires certain expectations. In classical conditioning, a young boy fears a rabbit because he expects it to hurt him. In operant conditioning, a woman works hard all week because she expects to be paid on Friday.

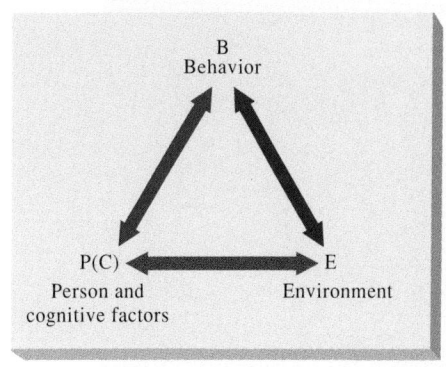

FIGURE 6.20

Bandura's Model of Reciprocal Influences of Behavior (B), Personal and Cognitive Factors (P[C]), and Environment (E). The arrows reflect how relations between these factors are reciprocal rather than unidirectional. Examples of personal factors include intelligence, skills, and self-control.

In 1946 Tolman and his colleagues (Tolman, Ritchie, & Kalish, 1946) conducted a classic experiment to demonstrate the power of expectations in learning. Initially rats ran on an elevated maze, shown in figure 6.21a. The rats started at *A* and then ran across the circular table at *B*, through an alley at *CD*, then along the path to the food box at *G*. *H* represents a light that illuminated the path from *F* to *G*. This maze was replaced by one with several false runways, shown in figure 6.21b. The rats ran down what had been the correct path before but found that it was blocked. Which of the remaining paths would the rats choose? We might anticipate that they would choose paths 9 and 10 because those were nearest the path that led to success. Instead, the rats explored several paths, running along one for a short distance, returning to the table, then trying out another one, and so on. Eventually the rats ran along one path all the way to the end. This path was number 6, not 9 or 10. Path 6 ran to a point about 4 inches short of where the food box had been located previously. According to Tolman, the rats had learned not only how to run the original maze, but also to expect food on reaching a specific place.

In his paper "Cognitive Maps in Rats and Men," Tolman (1948) articulated his belief that organisms select information from the environment and construct a cognitive map of their experiences. A **cognitive map** *is an organism's mental representation of the structure of physical space.* In Tolman's maze experiment just described, the rats had developed a mental awareness of physical space and the elements in it. The rats used this cognitive map to find where the food was located.

Drawing by S. Gross; © 1978 The New Yorker Magazine, Inc.

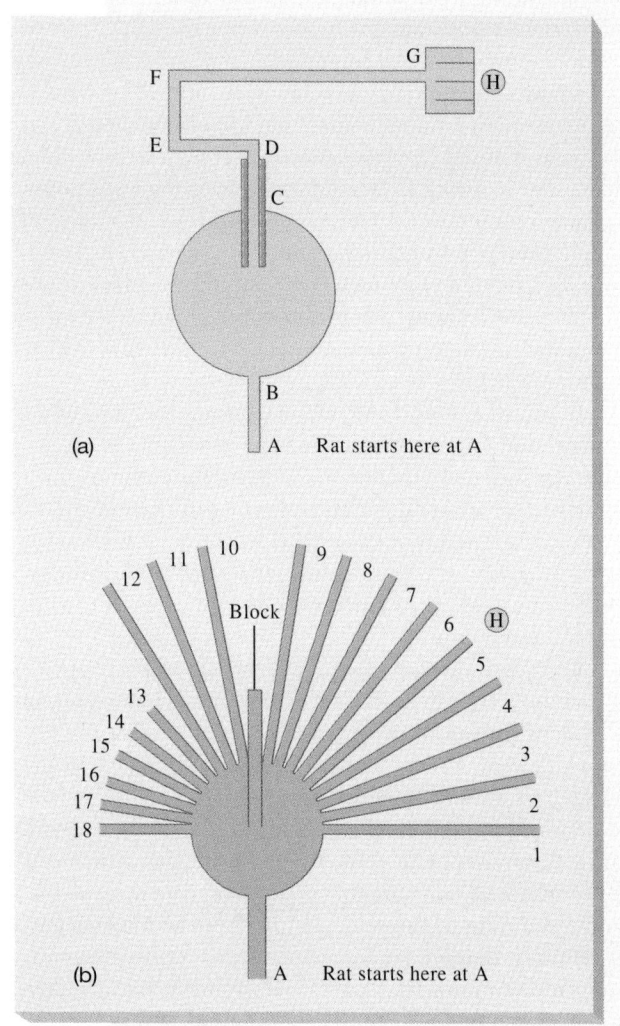

FIGURE 6.21

Tolman's Experiment on Expectations in Learning
In Tolman's classic experiment on the role of expectations in learning, initially rats ran on this elevated maze from A through G, with H representing a light that illuminated the path from F to G. After the rats ran the maze in (a), they were placed in the maze shown in (b). What path did the rats follow in (b)? Why?

Tolman's idea of cognitive maps is alive and well today. When we move around in our environment, we develop a cognitive map of where things are located, on both small and large scales. We have a cognitive map of where rooms are located in our house or apartment, and we have a cognitive map of where we are located in the United States, for example. A popular tradition is to draw a cognitive map reflecting our perception of the city or state in which we live, relative to the rest of the United States. In Texas, for example, the state of Texas is usually drawn about three-fourths the size of the entire United States. In Manhattan, "The City" is often drawn about nine-tenths the size of the United States. Of course, such cognitive maps deliberately distort the physical world, reflecting the perceivers' egocentric interest in their city or state.

Tolman was not the only psychologist who was dissatisfied with the S-R view of learning. Gestalt psychologist Wolfgang Kohler thought that the cognitive process of insight learning was also an important form of learning.

Insight Learning
During World War I, Wolfgang Kohler, a German psychologist, spent 4 months in the Canary Islands, observing the behavior of apes. While there he conducted two fascinating experiments. One is called the "stick problem," the other the "box problem." Though these two experiments are basically the same, the solutions to the problems are different. In both situations, an ape discovers that it cannot reach an alluring piece of fruit, either because the fruit is too high or because it is outside of the ape's cage and beyond its reach. To solve the stick problem, the ape has to insert a small stick inside a larger stick to reach the fruit. To master the box problem, the ape must stack several boxes to reach the fruit (see figure 6.22).

According to Kohler (1925), solving these problems does not involve trial and error or mere connections between stimuli and responses. Rather, when the ape realizes that its customary actions are not going to get the fruit, it sits for a period of time and appears to ponder how to solve the problem. Then it quickly gets up, as if it had a sudden flash of insight, piles the boxes on top of one another, and gets the fruit. **Insight learning** *is a form of problem solving in which an organism develops a sudden understanding of how to solve a problem.*

FIGURE 6.22

Kohler's Box Problem Involving Insight Learning
Sultan, one of Kohler's brightest chimps, is faced with the problem of reaching a cluster of bananas overhead. Suddenly he solves the problem by stacking boxes on top of one another to reach the bananas. Kohler called this type of problem solving "insight learning."

Biological Influences

We can't breathe under water, fish can't play Ping-Pong, and cows can't solve math problems. The structure of an organism's body permits certain kinds of learning and prohibits others. For example, chimpanzees cannot learn to speak English because they lack the necessary vocal equipment. Some of us cannot solve difficult calculus problems; others of us can. The differences do not all seem to be the result of experiences.

Albert Einstein serves as a good example. He combined enormous creativity with great analytic ability to develop some of this century's most important insights about the nature of matter and the universe. Einstein's extraordinary intellectual skills encouraged him to think and reason on a very high plane. His genetic endowment for intelligence was impressive; however, he also experienced intellectual limitations as well. Many scholars believed Einstein experienced a learning difference or disability that made him struggle with mathematics. This example demonstrates both the potential and the constraints imposed by biological factors on learning.

Preparedness

Biological preparedness is an enhanced capacity to learn due to biological factors. Some animals learn readily in one situation but show difficulty learning in slightly different circumstances. The difficulty might result not from an aspect of the learning situation but from the organism's predisposition (Selgiman, 1970). **Preparedness** *is the species-specific biological predisposition to learn in certain ways but not in others.*

Instinctive Drift

Another example of biological influences on learning is **instinctive drift,** *the tendency of animals to revert to instinctive behavior that interferes with learning.* Consider the situation of two students of B. F. Skinner, Keller and Marion Breland (Breland & Breland, 1961), who used operant conditioning to train animals to perform at fairs, at conventions, and in television commercials. They used Skinner's techniques of shaping, chaining, and discrimination to teach pigs to cart large wooden nickels to a piggy bank and deposit them. They also trained raccoons to pick up a coin and place it in a metal tray. Although the pigs, raccoons, and other animals, such as chickens, performed well at most of the tasks (raccoons became adept basketball players, for example—see figure 6.23), some of the animals began acting strangely. Instead of picking up the large wooden nickel and carrying it to the piggy bank, the pigs dropped the nickel on the ground, shoved it with their snouts, tossed it in the air, and then repeated these actions. The raccoons began to hold on to their coin rather than drop it into the metal container. When two coins were introduced, the raccoons rubbed them together in a miserly fashion. Somehow these behaviors overwhelmed the strength of the reinforcement that was given. Why were the pigs and raccoons misbehaving? The pigs were rooting, an

FIGURE 6.23

Instinctive Drift
This raccoon's skill in using its hands made it an excellent basketball player, but the raccoon had a much more difficult time taking money to the bank. *What factors explain why one behavior would be relatively easy to learn while the other would be more challenging?*

instinct used to uncover edible roots. The raccoons engaged in an instinctive food-washing response. Their instinctive drift interfered with their learning.

Now that we have examined biological factors in learning, let's turn our attention to the role that culture plays in learning.

Cultural Influences

Although Albert Einstein was impressively endowed by his genes to be intelligent, his abilities were also shaped by his culture. He received an excellent, rigorous European education. Later in the United States he had the freedom and support that are believed to be important in creative exploration. It is unlikely that Einstein would have been able to develop his intellectual skills fully and have such brilliant insights if he had grown up in the less technologically developed cultures of his time or even in a Third World country today.

> *Experience is the comb that Nature gives us when we are bald.*
>
> **Belgian proverb**

In traditional views of learning, psychologists have given little or no attention to such concepts as those of culture

and ethnicity. The behavioral orientation that dominated American psychology for much of the twentieth century focused on the contexts of learning, but the organisms in those contexts have often been animals. When humans have been the subjects, there has been no interest in the cultural context. Esteemed psychologist Robert Guthrie (1976) once wrote a book entitled *Even the Rat Was White*—a comment on psychology's heavy reliance on animal research and the failure to consider cultural and ethnic factors in behavioral research.

How does culture influence learning? Most psychologists agree that the principles of classical conditioning, operant conditioning, and observational learning are universal and are powerful learning processes in every culture. However, culture can influence the *degree* to which these learning processes are used, and it often determines the *content* of learning. For example, punishment is a universal learning process, but, as we will see next, there is considerable sociocultural variation in its use and type.

When behaviorism was dominant in the United States between 1910 and 1930, child-rearing experts regarded an infant as capable of being shaped into almost any kind of child. Desirable social behavior could be achieved if the child's antisocial behaviors were always punished and never indulged and if positive behaviors were carefully conditioned and rewarded in a highly controlled and structured child-rearing regime. Behaviorist John Watson (1928) authored the publication *Psychological Care of the Infant and Child,* which was the official government booklet for parents. This booklet advocated never letting children suck their thumbs and, if necessary, restraining children by tying their hands to the crib at night and painting their fingers with foul-tasting liquids. Parents were advised to let infants "cry themselves out" rather than reinforce this unacceptable behavior by picking them up to rock and soothe them.

However, from the 1930s to 1960s, a more permissive attitude prevailed, and parents were advised to be concerned with the feelings and capacities of the child. Since the 1960s, there has been a continued emphasis on the role of parental love in children's socialization, but experts now advise parents to play a less permissive and more active role in shaping children's behavior. Experts stress that parents should set limits and make authoritative decisions in areas where the child is not capable of reasonable judgment. However, they should listen and adapt to the child's point of view. They should explain their restrictions and discipline, but they should not discipline the child in a hostile, punitive manner.

Most child-rearing experts in the United States today do not advocate the physical punishment of children, but this country does not have a law that prohibits parents from spanking their children. In 1979 Sweden passed a law forbidding parents from using physical punishment, including spanking and slapping, when disciplining their children (Ziegert, 1983). Physical punishment of children is treated as a punishable offense, just like any other attack on a person. The law is especially designed to curb child abuse. Sweden is the only industrial country in the world to have passed such a law.

The United States probably could not pass this type of law. Many Americans would view such a law as totalitarian, and the law would likely stimulate protest from civil libertarians and others. An important factor in Sweden's "antispanking" law is its attitude toward rule of law. The United States enforces laws through punishment, but Sweden takes a softer approach, encouraging respect for law through education designed to change attitudes and behavior. When people, often teachers or doctors, suspect that a parent has spanked a child, they often will report the incident because they know that the state will try to provide the parent with emotional and educational support rather than assess a fine or send the parent to jail. Accompanying the antispanking law was a parenting guide—*Can One Manage to Raise Children Without Spanking or Slapping?*—that was widely available at day-care centers, preschool programs, physicians' offices, and other similar locations. The publication includes advice about why physical punishment is not a good strategy for disciplining children, along with specific information about better ways to handle children's problems.

It is not the whip that makes men, but the lure of things that are worthy to be loved.

Woodrow Wilson

The content of learning is also influenced by culture. We cannot learn about something we do not experience. A 4-year-old who has grown up among the Bushmen of the Kalahari Desert is unlikely to learn about taking baths or pouring water from one glass into another. Similarly a child growing up in Chicago is unlikely to be skilled at tracking animals or finding water-bearing roots in the desert. Learning usually requires practice, and certain behaviors are practiced much more often in some cultures than in others. In Bali many children are skilled dancers by the age of 6, whereas Norwegian children are much more likely to be good skiers and skaters by that age. Children growing up in a Mexican village famous for its pottery may work with clay day after day, whereas children in a nearby village famous for its woven rugs and sweaters rarely become experts at making clay pots (Price-Williams, Gordon, & Ramirez, 1969). More about a culture's role in learning is presented in Sociocultural Worlds 6.2, where you will read about cultural influences on the learning of mathematics.

In this chapter, we have seen that learning is a pervasive aspect of life and has a great deal of adaptive significance for organisms. We have studied many forms of learning and have seen how cognitive, biological, and cultural factors influence learning. In the next chapter, we will become absorbed more deeply in the world of cognition as we explore the nature of memory.

REVIEW

Cognitive, Biological, and Cultural Factors in Learning

Many psychologists recognize the importance of studying how cognitive factors mediate environment-behavior connections. The S-O-R model reflects this, as does Bandura's contemporary model, which emphasizes reciprocal connections between behavior, person (cognition), and environment. Tolman reinterpreted classical and operant conditioning in terms of expectations. We construct cognitive maps of our experiences that guide our behavior; psychologists still study the nature of cognitive maps. Kohler, like Tolman, was dissatisfied with the S-R view of learning. He believed that organisms reflect and suddenly gain insight into how a problem should be solved.

Biological factors restrict what an organism can learn from experience. These constraints include physical characteristics, preparedness, and instinctive drift. Although most psychologists would agree that the principles of classical conditioning, operant conditioning, and observational learning are universal, cultural customs can influence the degree to which these learning processes are used, and culture often determines the content of learning.

SOCIOCULTURAL WORLDS 6.2

Learning Math in New Guinea, Brazil, Japan, China, and the United States

Children's math learning depends not only on their innate ability to handle abstractions and adult efforts to teach math concepts, but also on the adults' own knowledge about numbers, which in turn depends on culture's heritage (Cole & Cole, 1989). Children growing up among the Oksapmin of New Guinea seem to have the same ability to grasp basic number concepts as children growing up in Tokyo or Los Angeles. However, the counting system used in the Oksapmin culture—counting by body parts—does not support the more sophisticated development of algebraic thinking (Saxe, 1981). The Oksapmin use 29 body

parts in their system of counting (see figure 6.A). In the United States it is not unusual for children to use their fingers to keep track of numbers early in their math learning, but because of schooling they go far beyond Oksapmin children in learning math.

Although schooling often helps with learning math, in some cultures children who do not attend school learn math as part of their everyday experience. For example, whereas most Brazilian children attend school, Brazilian market children do not, yet they learn remarkable math skills in the context of everyday buying and selling. However, when presented with the same math problems in a schoollike format, they have difficulty (Carraher & Carraher, 1981). For another example, many high school students in the United States can solve certain physics problems, which they consider elementary, that baffled the brilliant Greek philosopher Aristotle in ancient times. In each of these instances, culture has shaped the course of learning.

In the last decade, the poor performance of American children in math and science has become well publicized (Stevenson, 1995). For example, in one recent cross-national comparison of the math and science achievement of 9- to 13-year-old students, the United States finished 13th (out of 15) in science and 15th (out of 16) in math achievement (Educational Testing Service, 1992). In this study, Korean and Taiwanese students placed first and second, respectively.

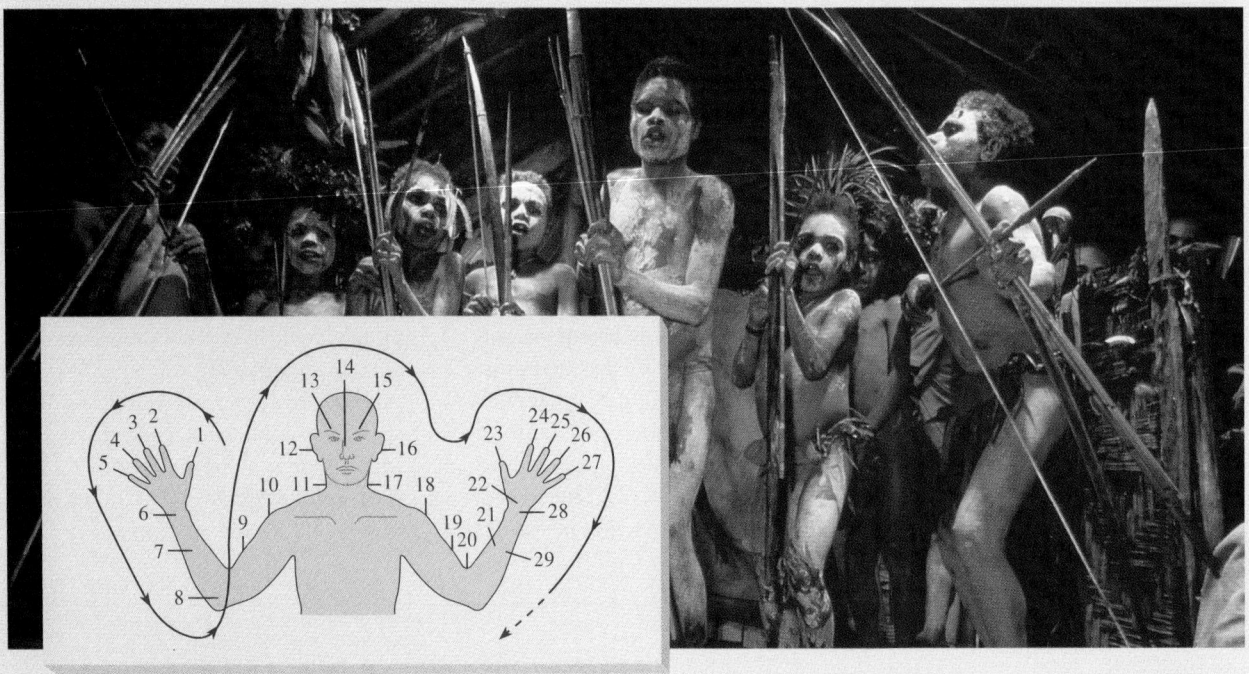

FIGURE 6.A

The Counting System of the Oksapmin of New Guinea
The arithmetic counting of the Oksapmin of New Guinea is based on 29 numbers that correspond to a sequence of body parts.

Harold Stevenson and his colleagues (Stevenson, 1995; Stevenson, Chen, & Lee, 1993) have conducted a series of cross-national studies of children's learning and achievement in various Asian countries and the United States over a period of about 15 years. Rather than just describe the deficiencies of the American children's achievement in comparison to children from other nations, Stevenson has sought to answer the all important question, Why? He has found that, contrary to popular stereotypes, Asian children's high level of achievement does not result from rote learning and repeated drilling in tension-filled schools. Rather, children are motivated to learn and teaching is innovative and interesting in many Asian schools. Knowledge is not force-fed to children, but rather children are encouraged to construct their own ways of representing the knowledge. Long school days in Asia are punctuated by extended recess periods. Asian schools embrace many of the ideals Americans have for their own schools, but are more successful in implementing them in interesting and productive ways that make learning more enjoyable for children.

These conclusions were reached by Stevenson and his colleagues following five different cross-national studies of children in the United States, China, Taiwan, and Japan. In these studies, Asian children consistently outperformed U.S. children in math. And the longer the children were in school, the wider the gap between the Asian and American children's math scores became, with the lowest differential in the first grade, the biggest in the eleventh grade.

To learn more about the reasons for these large cross-cultural differences in achievement, the researchers spent hundreds of hours observing classrooms; interviewing teachers, children, and mothers; and giving questionnaires to the fathers. They found that parental satisfaction with American children's achievement and education is high but their standards are low in comparison with their Asian counterparts. And while American parents emphasize that their children's math achievement is primarily determined by innate ability, Asian parents believe their children's math achievement is mainly the result of effort and training.

In 1990, former President Bush and the nation's governors adopted a well-publicized goal: to change American education in ways that will help students to lead the world in math achievement by the year 2000. Stevenson (1992, 1995) says that is unlikely to happen because American standards and expectations for children's math achievement are too low by international standards.

While Asian students are doing so well in math achievement, might there be a dark underside of too much stress and tension in the students and their schools? Stevenson and his colleagues (1995; Stevenson, Chen, & Lee, 1993) have not found that to be the case. They asked eleventh-grade students in Japan and the United States how often in the past month they had experienced feelings of stress, depression, aggression, and other problems, such as not being able to sleep well. They also asked the students about how often they felt nervous when they took tests. On all of these characteristics, the Japanese students expressed less distress and fewer problems than the American students did. Such findings do not support the Western stereotype that Asian students are tense, wired individuals driven by relentless pressures for academic excellence. The lower stress reported by Japanese students also could be interpreted as a reluctance to report stress, because making disclosures about one's problems, especially to a stranger, is not common in Eastern cultures. For example, in one recent study Chinese students were less likely to engage in self-disclosure than American students (Chen, 1995).

Critics of cross-national studies say that such comparisons are flawed because the percentage of children who go to school and the curricula vary widely within each country. Even in the face of such criticisms, there is a growing consensus based on information collected by different research teams that American children's achievement is very low, that American educators' and parents' expectations for children's math achievement are too low, and that American schools are long overdue for an extensive overhaul.

Asian grade schools intersperse studying with frequent periods of activities. This approach helps children maintain their attention and likely makes learning more enjoyable. Shown here are Japanese fourth-graders making wearable masks.

Behavior modification has become a popular resource for parents who find themselves struggling with misbehaving children in grocery stores. If you think about it, children in grocery stores are at the mercy of an environment that is not particularly conducive to good behavior. The store is filled with all kinds of stimulating sights, smells, and sounds. Advertisers have gone to great lengths to encourage consumers to reach out and pluck their product from the shelves. Why shouldn't such inducements also appeal to children? They do.

Unfortunately, it is very easy to teach children to misbehave in this setting. As the shopper in charge, you probably have a keen sense of the amount of time you wish to spend in the store, and it might be far longer than your child's attention span. How to fix this problem? Some shoppers offer candy as a diversionary tactic when the child gets fussy or feisty. An operant perspective shows how foolhardy this practice can be. In the short run, the child might be quieted for as long as the candy lasts. In the long run, the shopper has taught the child that the way to get candy is to be fussy, whiny, or obnoxious.

What suggestions from the principles of behavior modification would help reduce the stress involved in a trip to the grocery story? Which principle of operant behavior would be most effective in curbing children's misbehavior and in helping the beleaguered shopper—positive reinforcement, negative reinforcement, punishment, or extinction?

If you answered punishment, guess again. Skinner and other behavior modification theorists believe that punishment may be ineffective in the long run in reducing the frequency of an undesirable behavior. Punishment has many side effects that make its use unattractive. It might be too easy for the punisher to overuse punishment to get the intended effect; the punisher risks becoming abusive. The child might learn to behave in the presence of the punisher but continue the behavior when the punisher is not around. Children dislike the punisher, and punishers might not like themselves too much, either. Most of all, punishment discourages undesirable behavior but doesn't teach appropriate behavior in its place. However, many parents have found some success in managing children with time-out consequences (removing the child from the environment for short periods of time as a consequence to each onset of inappropriate behavior).

If you guessed extinction, you are on target. The parent would identify the specific kind of misbehavior to be suppressed. For instance, suppose the child whines. Rather than pay attention to or punish the child, the parent ignores the child, waiting for more appropriate behavior before attending to the child again. As you can easily imagine, there are some problems with this technique. Because extinction can take a long time, it is sometimes tempting to return to old methods out of fatigue. These lapses have the additional danger of intermittently reinforcing the behavior that preceded. We know from reading about schedules of reinforcement earlier in the chapter that intermittent reinforcement can encourage resistance to extinction. Therefore, once you begin operant conditioning by extinction, you must stay with the plan in order for the child to learn the inappropriateness of acting out in the grocery store.

If you guessed positive reinforcement, you could be right. However, you would need to positively reinforce the appropriate behavior of nonwhining rather than reinforce whining. Behavior modification theorists point out that the longer the period in which children manage themselves well, the less time available to be spent in misbehavior. Yet it can feel awkward to compliment children on controlling their behavior.

What about negative reinforcement? Most whining children are not really in real distress; they have learned to whine because it so often pays off in candy and attention from the caregiver. Therefore, negative reinforcement doesn't really apply to the child's situation. However, negative reinforcement explains well how the caregiver's behavior of doling out candy developed originally in response to the child's distress. The noise and embarrassment caused by an acting-out child is hard to bear. When a child embarks on this strategy, the parent might offer candy as a way to escape or avoid the problem.

Can you see how *applying operant conditioning principles enhances your personal adaptation* and can enhance the well-being of others?

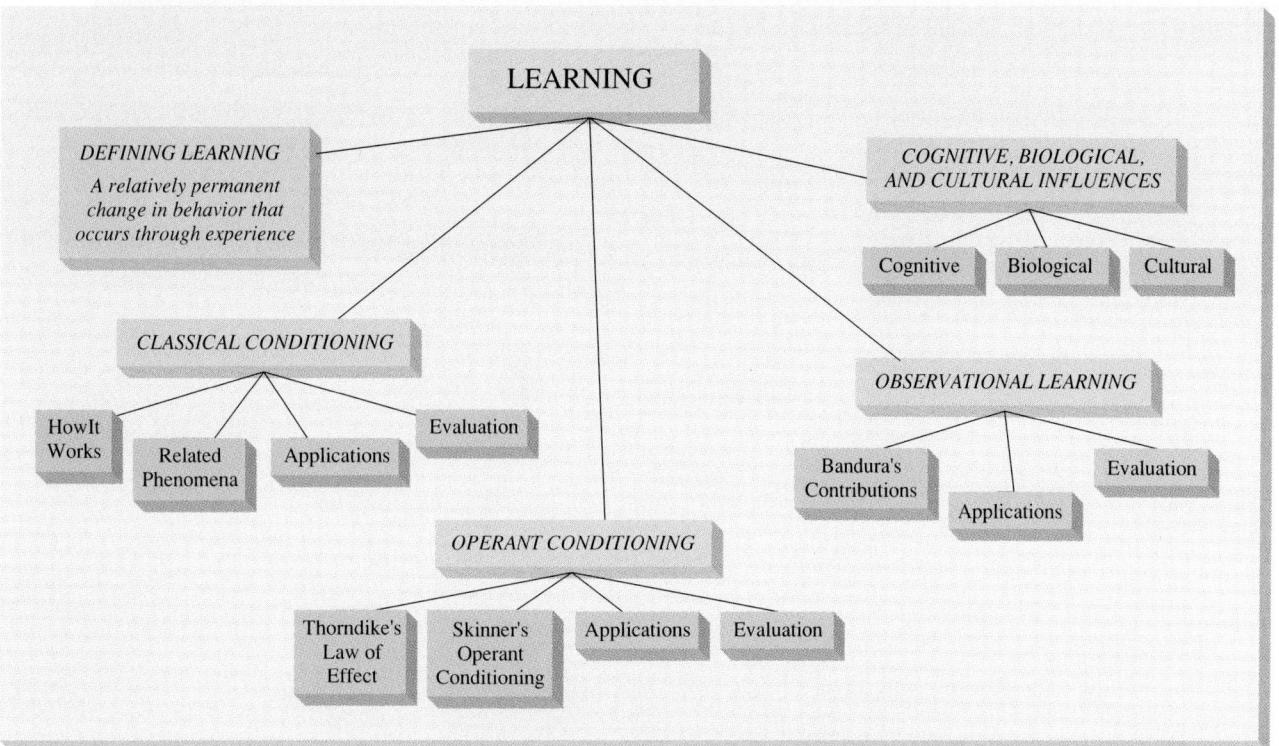

We began this chapter by defining learning and then turned our attention to three main forms of learning—classical conditioning, operant conditioning, and observational learning. Our coverage of classical conditioning focused on how it works, related classical conditioning phenomena, applications to human behavior, and an evaluation of classical conditioning. Our discussion of operant conditioning emphasized Thorndike's S-R theory and the law of effect, how operant conditioning works, its applications, and an evaluation. Our overview of observational learning stressed Bandura's contributions, applications, and an evaluation. We concluded the main part of the chapter by describing cognitive, biological, and cultural influences on learning. Don't forget that you can obtain an overall summary of the chapter by again reading the in-chapter reviews on pages 181, 194, 198, and 203.

PERSPECTIVES

The behavioral perspective was the main perspective emphasized in this chapter. The entire sections of the chapter on classical conditioning (pp. 173–181), operant conditioning (pp. 182–194), and observational learning (pp. 195–198) reflect the behavioral perspective. The cognitive perspective was reflected in the discussion of cognitive influences on learning (pp. 198–201), the neurobiological perspective in biological influences (pp. 201–202), and the sociocultural perspective in cultural influences (pp. 202–203), international Big Bird (p. 172), ethnicity and role models (p. 197), and learning math in different cultures (pp. 204–205).

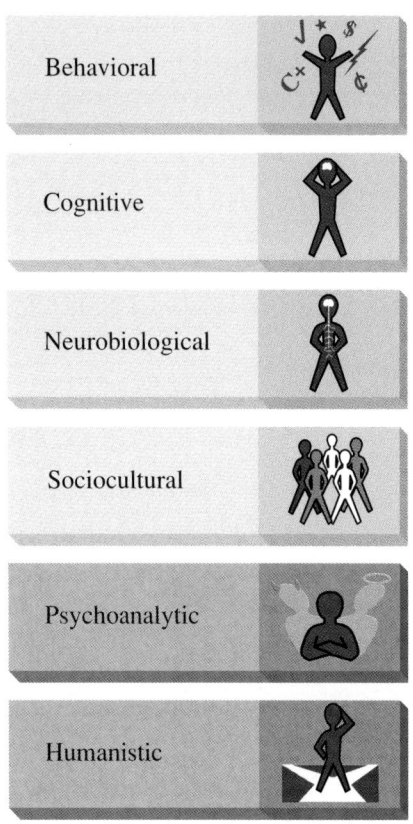

Behavioral

Cognitive

Neurobiological

Sociocultural

Psychoanalytic

Humanistic

KEY TERMS

learning A relatively permanent change in behavior that occurs through experience.   173

classical conditioning A form of learning in which a neutral stimulus becomes associated with a meaningful stimulus and acquires the capacity to elicit a similar response.   173

reflexes Automatic stimulus-response connections that are "hardwired" into the brain.   174

unconditioned stimulus (US) A stimulus that produces a response without prior learning.   174

unconditioned response (UR) An unlearned response that is automatically associated with the unconditioned stimulus.   174

conditioned stimulus (CS) A previously neutral stimulus that elicits the conditioned response after being paired with the unconditioned stimulus.   174

conditioned response (CR) The learned response to the conditioned stimulus that occurs after CS-US association.   174

generalization In classical conditioning, the tendency of a new stimulus that is similar to the original conditioned stimulus to elicit a response that is similar to the conditioned response.   175

discrimination In classical conditioning, the process of learning to respond to certain stimuli and not to others.   175

extinction In classical conditioning, the weakening of the conditioned response in the absence of the unconditioned stimulus.   176

spontaneous recovery The process in classical conditioning by which a conditioned response can reappear without further conditioning.   176

phobias Irrational fears.   177

counterconditioning A classical conditioning procedure for weakening a conditioned response of fear by associating the fear-provoking stimulus with a new response that is incompatible with the fear.   177

conditioned taste aversions Classically conditioned avoidance reactions to food.   180

stimulus substitution Pavlov's theory of how classical conditioning works; the nervous system is structured in such a way that the CS and US bond together and eventually the CS substitutes for the US.   180

information theory The contemporary explanation of how classical conditioning works; the key to understanding classical conditioning is the information the organism obtains from the situation.   180

operant conditioning (instrumental conditioning) A form of learning in which the consequences of behavior produce changes in the probability of the behavior's occurrence.   182

law of effect The hypothesis, developed by E. L. Thorndike, that behaviors followed by positive outcomes are strengthened, whereas behaviors followed by negative outcomes are weakened.   182

reinforcement (reward) A consequence that increases the probability that a behavior will occur.   183

punishment A consequence that decreases the probability that a behavior will occur.   183

positive reinforcement The relationship in which the frequency of a response increases because it is followed by a pleasant stimulus.   183

negative reinforcement The relationship in which the frequency of a response increases because the response either removes a negative circumstance/stimulus or lets the individual avoid the negative stimulus altogether.   183

extinction In operant conditioning, a decrease in the tendency to perform a behavior that receives neither a positive nor a negative consequence.   185

shaping The process of rewarding approximations of desired behavior.   186

chaining An operant conditioning technique used to teach a complex sequence, or chain, of behaviors. The procedure begins by shaping the final response in the sequence, then works backward until a chain of behaviors is learned.   186

primary reinforcement The use of reinforcers that are innately satisfying; that is, no learning is required on the organism's part to make them pleasurable.   188

secondary reinforcement Reinforcement that acquires its positive value through experience; secondary reinforcers are learned, or conditional, reinforcers.   188

partial reinforcement Intermittent reinforcement; responses are not reinforced every time they occur.   188

schedules of reinforcement Timetables that determine when a response will be reinforced.   188

fixed-ratio schedule Reinforcement of a behavior after a set number of responses.   188

variable-ratio schedule Reinforcement of responses at an average rate but on an unpredictable basis.   188

fixed-interval schedule Reinforcement of the first appropriate response after a fixed amount of time has elapsed.   189

variable-interval schedule Reinforcement of a response after variable amounts of time have elapsed.   189

generalization In operant conditioning, giving the same response to similar stimuli.   189

discrimination In operant conditioning, the process of responding in the presence of another stimulus that is not reinforced.   190

discriminative stimuli A signal that a response will be reinforced.   190

behavior modification The application of operant conditioning principles to changing behavior; its main goal is to replace unacceptable responses with acceptable, adaptive ones.   190

observational learning Learning that occurs when a person observes and imitates someone else's behavior; also called imitation or modeling.   195

S-O-R model A model of learning that gives some importance to cognitive factors. S stands for stimulus, O for organism, and R for response.   199

cognitive map An organism's mental representation of the structure of physical space.   199

insight learning A form of problem solving in which an organism develops a sudden understanding of how to solve a problem.   200

preparedness The species-specific biological predisposition to learn in certain ways but not in others.   201

instinctive drift The tendency of animals to revert to instinctive behavior that interferes with learning.   201

FAMILIES

(1975) by Gerald Patterson. Champaign, IL: Research Press.

Families presents behavior modification techniques that parents can use to correct children's problem behaviors. Patterson begins by discussing some important behavioral concepts, such as social reinforcers, aversive stimuli, and accidental training. Time-out procedures and behavioral contracts are integrated into a step-by-step reinforcement management program for parents to implement with their own children. Behavioral management strategies are also tailored to children with specific problems. This book is especially helpful in modifying the behavior of aggressive boys who are engaging in out-of-control behavior.

MENTORS

(1992) by Thomas Evans. Princeton, NJ: Peterson's Guides.

This book describes the enriching experiences of dozens of motivated individuals—from eye-to-the-future executives to conscientious parents—whose passion for education, especially the education of poor children and youth, has carried them to the classroom and beyond. Author Evans describes how to make a difference in a child's life. The difference consists in becoming involved as a mentor for a child and developing a role as a tutor for students in a one-to-one situation. Evans gives explicit instructions on how to become an effective mentor. Mentoring has helped many children and adolescents become more competent, and Evans's book is an excellent overview of the topic.

Behavior Modification: What It Is and How to Do It **(1992, 4th ed.)**
> by G. Martin and J. Pear
> Englewood Cliffs, NJ: Prentice Hall

This excellent, easy-to-read book provides guidelines for using behavior modification to change behavior.

Don't Shoot the Dog! How to Improve Yourself and Others Through Behavioral Training **(1991)**
> by K. Pryor
> New York: Simon & Schuster

This is a practical guide for applying the principles of reinforcement to everyday life. Topics include how to train animals, manage employees, cope with intrusive roommates, and improve self-control.

Games for Learning **(1991)**
> by Peggy Kane
> New York: Noonday Press

This book is filled with ingenious learning games that parents can adopt for use with their children.

Learning Disabilities Association of America
> 4156 Library Road
> Pittsburgh, PA 15234
> 412–341–1515

This organization provides education and support for parents of children with learning disabilities and interested professionals and others. More than 500 chapters are in operation nationwide. Information services, pamphlets, and book recommendations are available.

Learning Disabilities Association of Canada/Troubles d'apprent issage-association canadienne
> 323 Chapel Street Suite 200
> Ottawa, ON K1N 7Z2
> 613–238–5721

The Association works to advance the education, employment, social development, legal rights, and general well-being of people with learning disabilities. They publish many handbooks for parents, children, and adults with learning disabilities, including *Together for Success: A Road Map for Secondary Students with Learning Disabilities* as well as their quarterly newsletter, *National.*

National Center for the Study of Corporal Punishment
> Temple University
> 253 Ritter Annex
> Philadelphia, PA 19122
> 215–787–6091

This center provides information about the psychological and educational aspects of school discipline. It also provides legal advocacy to protest the use of corporal punishment and psychological abuse in schools. Consultation service for parents and teachers is available.

Social Foundations of Thought **(1986)**
> by Albert Bandura
> Englewood Cliffs, NJ: Prentice Hall

This book presents Bandura's cognitive social learning theory, which emphasizes reciprocal connections among behavior, environment, and person (cognition). Extensive coverage of observational learning is included.

Through Mentors
> 202–393–0512

Mentors are recruited from corporations, government agencies, universities, and professional firms. The goal of the organization is to provide every youth in the District of Columbia with a mentor through high school. To learn how to become involved in a mentoring program or to start such a program, call the number listed above. Also, the National One-to-One Partnership Kit guides businesses in establishing mentoring programs (call 202–338–3844).

Walden Two **(1948)**
> by B. F. Skinner
> New York: Macmillan

Skinner once considered a career as a writer. In this interesting and provocative book, he outlines his ideas on how a more complete understanding of the principles of instrumental conditioning can produce a happier life. Critics argue that his approach is far too manipulative.

CHAPTER

7

Memory

I come into the fields and spacious palaces of my memory, where are treasures of countless images of things of every manner.

St. Augustine

THE STORIES OF M. K. AND MARCEL PROUST: CONTRASTS IN MEMORY

onsider the unfortunate case of M. K., a high school teacher who at the age of 43 was stricken with an acute episode of encephalitis. Within hours the viral agent robbed him of most of the memories he had formed during the previous 5 years. Worse still, he was rendered incapable of forming new memories. Since his illness began, M. K. has learned a few names and a few major events, and he can get around the hospital. However, he is doomed to an existence in which every moment vanishes behind him as soon as he lives it. M. K.'s tragic circumstance conveys the emptiness of a life without memory.

In contrast, consider the wealth of images stored in the mind of the narrator in a monumental work by Marcel Proust (1928). In the first of its seven volumes, *Remembrance of Things Past,* the narrator sips a spoonful of tea in which a crumb of cake is soaked and immediately experiences a flood of memories:

> The taste was that of the little crumb of "madeleine" which on Sunday mornings at Combray . . . my Aunt Leonie used to give me. . . . Immediately the old grey house upon the street rose up like the scenery of a theatre . . . and just as the Japanese amuse themselves by filling a porcelain bowl with water and steeping in it little crumbs of paper which . . . stretch and bend, take on color and distinctive shapes, so in that moment all the flowers in our garden . . . , and the water lilies

on the Vivonne and the good folk of the village and their little dwellings and the parish church and the whole of Combray and of its surroundings, taking their proper shapes and growing solid, sprang into being, town and gardens alike, from my cup of tea. (p. 65)

Proust was an invalid who rarely ventured from his bedroom, yet both he and his characters enjoyed lives filled with vivid imagery born out of his powerful ability to create and store memories, then retrieve them, either at will or when prompted by a cue from the past.

Proust's tea cake has nothing on one hour in a college dorm.

Gloria Steinem, *Outrageous Acts and Everyday Rebellions,* **1983**

PREVIEW

As playwright Tennessee Williams once commented, *"Life is all memory, except for the one present moment that goes by so quick you can hardly catch it going."* Indeed, there are few moments when we are not steeped in memory. Memory can quietly stir, or spin off, with each step we take, each thought we think, each word we utter. Memory is the skein of private images that weaves the past into the present. It anchors the self in continuity. In this chapter, we will explore many different facets of memory: the nature of memory, the processes of memory, the biological and cultural contexts of memory, and strategies for improving memory.

THE NATURE OF MEMORY

Memory *is the retention of information over time. Psychologists study how information is initially placed, or* encoded, *into memory; how it is retained, or* stored, *after being encoded; and how it is found, or* retrieved, *for a specific purpose later.* To explore the nature of memory, we will study memory's time frames and contents.

Time Frames of Memory

We remember some information for less than a second, some for half a minute, and other information for minutes, hours, years, even a lifetime. Since memory often functions differently across these varied time intervals, we can distinguish among different types of memory partly on the basis of their differing time frames. The three types of memory that vary according to their time frames are *sensory memory,*

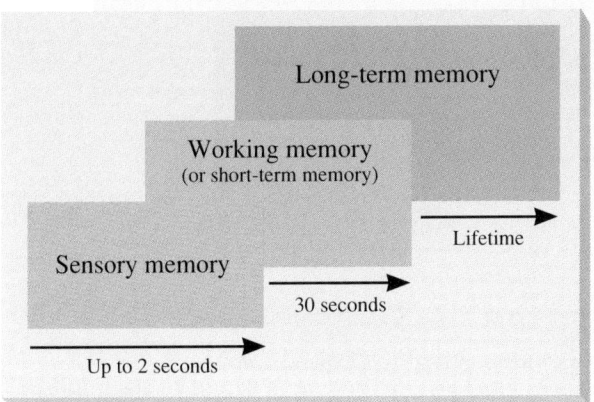

FIGURE 7.1

The Time Frames of Memory

time frames of a fraction of a second to several seconds; *working memory* (also often called short-term memory), time frames of up to 30 seconds; and *long-term memory*, time frames of up to a lifetime (see figure 7.1).

Sensory Memory

Sensory memory *holds information from the world in its original sensory form for only an instant, not much longer than the brief time for which one is exposed to the visual, auditory, and other sensations.* Sensory memory is very rich and detailed, but the information in it is very quickly lost unless certain processes are engaged in that transfer it into working or long-term memory.

Think about all the sights and sounds you encounter as you walk to class on a typical morning. Literally thousands of stimuli come into your fields of vision and hearing—cracks in the sidewalk, chirping birds, a noisy motorcycle, the blue sky, faces of hundreds of people. We do not process all of these stimuli, but we do process a number of them. In general, you process many more stimuli at the sensory level than you consciously notice. The sensory registers retain this information from your senses, including a large portion of what you think you ignore. But the sensory registers do not retain the information for very long.

Psychologists believe that sensory memory exists for all of the senses, but sensory memories for two senses—visual and auditory—have the strongest research base. Sensory memory for other senses, such as smell and touch, have received little attention. **Echoic memory** *(from the word* echo*) is the name given to the auditory sensory registers in which information is retained for up to several seconds.* **Iconic memory** *(from the word* icon, *which means "image") is the name given to the visual sensory registers, in which information is retained only for about ¼ second* (see figure 7.2).

Though the way sensory memory functions is difficult to research, several common experiences reveal its existence. Consider the "What-did-you-say-Oh-never-mind"

Type of sensory register	
Auditory	Visual
Up to several seconds	About 1/4 second

FIGURE 7.2

Auditory and Visual Sensory Registers
Imagine that you are walking near a lake when you encounter a heron. You hear the bird call. *Which sensory register would hold the impression of the bird longer—the iconic or the echoic?* Visual images last about ¼ of a second in the iconic sensory register. Auditory impressions last longer (about 2 seconds) in the echoic sensory register.

phenomenon that can occur when you are reading. You are engrossed in a book when someone walks into the room and asks you a question. You notice they are speaking, but since your attention is focused on your book, you do not comprehend the message. You experience the *sound* but not the *sense.* Looking up, you ask, "What did you say?" Before the person can answer, though, you somehow just "know." Then you say, "Oh, never mind," and respond to their question because you now understand. The sensory features of the spoken message made it to your echoic sensory memory, but initially they made it no further. Looking up, you switched your attention, retrieving the information from echoic memory and sending it "upstream" for higher-level analysis (comprehension).

The "What-did-you-say-Oh-never-mind" phenomenon involves echoic memory. The first scientific research on sensory memory, however, focused on iconic memory. In his classic study in 1960, George Sperling presented his subjects with patterns of stimuli like those in figure 7.3. As you look at the letters, you have no trouble recognizing them. But Sperling flashed the letters on a screen for only very brief intervals, about $1/20$th of a second. After a pattern was flashed on the screen, the subjects could report only four or five letters. With such short exposure, reporting all nine letters was impossible.

But some of the participants in Sperling's study reported feeling that, for an instant, they could *see* all nine letters within a briefly flashed pattern. But they ran into trouble when they tried to *name* all the letters they had initially *seen*. One hypothesis to explain this experience is that all nine letters were initially processed by iconic sensory memory. This is why all nine letters were *seen*. However, forgetting was so rapid that the subjects could name only a handful of letters before they were lost from sensory memory.

Sperling decided to test this hypothesis. He reasoned that if all nine letters were actually processed in sensory memory, they should all be available for a brief time. To test this possibility, Sperling sounded a low, medium, or high tone just after a pattern of letters was shown. The subjects were told that the tone was a signal to report only the letters from the bottom, middle, or top row, respectively. Under these conditions, the subjects performed much better, suggesting a brief memory for most or all of the letters.

Working Memory

Working memory, *also sometimes called short-term memory, is a limited-capacity memory system in which information is retained for as long as 30 seconds, unless the information is rehearsed, in which case it can be retained longer.* Compared to sensory memory, working memory is limited in capacity, but is relatively longer in duration. Its limited capacity was examined by George Miller (1956) in a classic paper with a catchy title, "The Magical Number Seven, Plus or Minus Two." Miller pointed out that on many tasks individuals are limited in how much information they can keep track of without external aids. Usually the limit is in the range of 7 ± 2 items. The most widely cited example of the 7 ± 2 phenomenon involves **memory span,** *which is the number of digits an individual can report back in order after a single presentation.* Most college students can handle lists of 8 or 9 digits without making any errors. Longer lists, however, pose problems because they exceed your working memory capacity. If you rely on simple working memory to retain longer lists of items, you probably will make errors.

Of course, there are many examples where working memory seems to hold for much more than 5 or 6 units. For instance, consider a simple list of words: *hot, city, book, time, forget, tomorrow,* and *smile.* Try to hold these words in memory for a moment, then write them down. If you

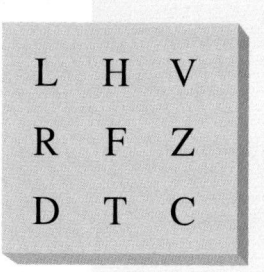

FIGURE 7.3

Sperling's Sensory Registers Experiment
This array of stimuli is similar to those flashed for about $1/20$th of a second to subjects in Sperling's experiment. Trained subjects could reliably report any row, suggesting that iconic memory could hold as many as nine "bits" of information despite the subject's inability to name all nine.

recalled all seven words, you succeeded in holding 34 letters in your working memory. Does this make you a genius with outrageous working memory skills? Or does it disprove the idea of limited capacity? The answer is neither. **Chunking** *is the grouping or "packing" of information into higher-order units that can be remembered as single units. Chunking expands working memory by making large amounts of information more manageable.* In demonstrating working memory for 34 letters, you "chunked" the letters into seven meaningful words. Since your working memory can handle seven chunks, you were successful in remembering 34 letters. Although working memory has limited capacity, chunking lets you make the most of it.

Maintenance rehearsal *is the conscious repetition of information that increases the length of time it stays in working memory* (Craik & Lockhart, 1972). To understand what we mean by maintenance rehearsal, imagine you are looking up a telephone number. If you can directly reach for the telephone, you will probably have no trouble dialing the number, because the entire combined action of looking up the number and dialing it can take place in the 30-second time frame of your working memory. But what if the telephone is not right by the phone book? Perhaps the phone book is in the kitchen and you want to talk privately on the extension in the den. You will probably *rehearse* the number as you walk from the kitchen to the den. Most of us experience a kind of "inner voice" that repeats the number again and again until we finally dial it. If someone or something interrupts our maintenance rehearsal, we may lose the information from short-term memory.

Working memory without maintenance rehearsal lasts half a minute or less, but if rehearsal is not interrupted, information can be retained indefinitely. Our rehearsal is often verbal, giving the impression of an inner voice, but it can also be visual or spatial, giving the impression of an inner eye. One way to use your visualization skills is to maintain the appearance of an object or scene for a period of time after you have viewed it. **Eidetic**

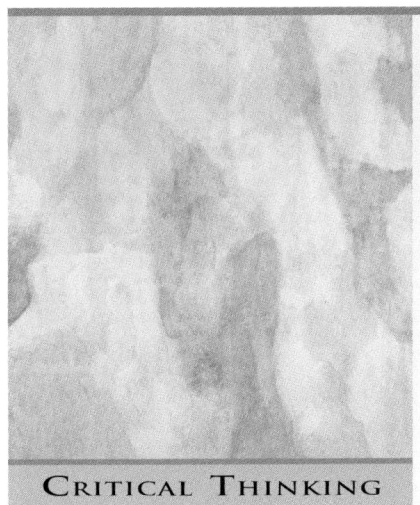

You Can Get There from Here

To gain a better grasp of the working memory system, imagine that a friend is telling you the complex route you should take to get to a party and you have nothing to write on. You will try to rehearse the directions, but your method will depend on the organization of your working memory. Do you hold the names of the streets in your working memory involving the phonological loop? Or do you try to picture the route using your visuo-spatial scratchpad? You might picture the route following a zigzag pattern going generally northeast until the last turn, which goes west. In this case, although you still want to remember the sequence of street names, you no longer have to worry about the left and right turn—your imagery captured this information. The phonological loop and the visuo-spatial scratchpad often work in concert like this to help us process information more efficiently. This analysis of working memory serves as another example of *applying psychological concepts and skills to enhance personal adaptation.*

FRANK & ERNEST reprinted by permission of UFS, Inc.

memory, *also called photographic memory, involves especially vivid images. The small number of individuals who have eidetic memory can recall significantly more details of visual information than most people can.* Individuals with eidetic memory say they literally "see" the page of a textbook as they attempt to remember information during a test. However, eidetic memory is so rare that it has been difficult to study; some psychologists even doubt that it exists (Gray & Gummerman, 1975).

Rehearsal is an important aspect of working memory, but there is much more we need to know about this type of memory. Working memory is a kind of mental "workbench" that lets us manipulate and assemble information when we make decisions, solve problems, and comprehend written and spoken language. For example, in one study young children who were accurate readers had trouble comprehending what they had read (Yuill, Oakhill, & Parkin, 1989). Why couldn't this group of children comprehend what they read? Examination of their cognitive skills revealed that their poor working memory—their 30-second processing tool—was responsible for their poor comprehension.

One model of working memory is shown in figure 7.4 (Baddeley, 1990, 1993). In this model, working memory consists of a general "executive" and two "slave" systems that help the executive do its job. One of the slave systems is the phonological loop, which is specialized to process language information. This is where maintenance rehearsal occurs. The other slave system is the visuo-spatial scratch pad, which underlines some of our spatial imagery skills, such as visualizing an object or a scene. We will soon see that such visualization has powerful effects when we learn new information.

Working memory has a wide range of functions that affect many aspects of our lives. For example, we all admire people with elaborate vocabularies, and many individuals spend considerable time trying to increase their vocabulary. Some persons seem to learn new words with little effort; for others, increasing their vocabulary is extremely hard work. In one investigation, the talent some individuals have in easily improving their vocabulary was located in the phonological loop (Gathercole & Baddeley, 1989). In this study, 4- to 5-year-old children were tested for their ability to repeat back nonsense words, which

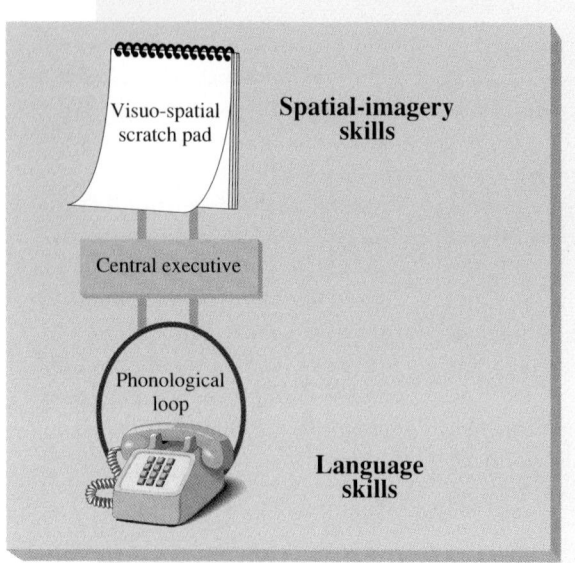

FIGURE 7.4

A Model of Working Memory
In the model, the two slave systems—visuospatial scratchpad and phonological loop—help the executive do its job. The visuo-spatial scratchpad involves our spatial imagery skills; the phonological loop involves our language skills (Baddeley, 1986, 1990).

Working memory deficits are involved in Alzheimer's disease. The central executive of the working memory model may be the culprit, because Alzheimers' patients have considerable difficulty coordinating different mental activities—one of the central executive's functions.

reflects the functioning of the phonological loop. The children's performance on this task was a good predictor of their vocabulary 1 year later.

Working memory can also help us understand how brain damage influences cognitive skills. For example, some types of amnesiacs perform well on working memory tasks but show gross deficits in learning new information in long-term memory tasks. Another group of patients have normal long-term memory abilities, yet do very poorly on working memory tasks. One such patient had good long-term memory despite having a memory span of only 2 digits (Baddeley, 1992)! Working memory deficits also are involved in Alzheimer's disease—a progressive, irreversible brain disorder in older adults. Baddeley and his colleagues (in press) believe the central executive of the working memory model is the culprit, because Alzheimer's patients have great difficulty coordinating different mental activities, one of the central executive's functions.

Long-Term Memory

Long-term memory *is a type of memory that holds huge amounts of information for a long period of time, relatively permanently.* In one study, people remembered the names and faces of their high school classmates with considerable accuracy for at least 25 years (Bahrick, Bahrick, & Wittlinger, 1975). The storehouse of long-term memory

is indeed staggering. John von Neumann, a distinguished computer scientist, put the size at 2.8×10^{20} (280 quintillion) bits, which in practical terms means that our storage capacity is virtually unlimited. Von Neumann assumed we never forget anything; but even considering that we do forget things, we can hold several billion times more information than a large computer can. Even more impressive is the efficiency with which we retrieve information. It usually takes only a moment to search through this vast storehouse to find the information we want. Who discovered America? What was the name of your first date? When were you born? Who developed the first psychology laboratory? You can, of course, answer these questions instantly.

Contents of Memory

Just as different types of memory can be distinguished by how long they last—time frames of memory—memories within each time frame can be distinguished by their *content*. As we discussed earlier, the contents of sensory memory consist of memory for audition (echoic memory) and vision (iconic memory). Similarly, we learned that the contents of working memory vary according to at least two kinds of content—the articulatory loop, which holds information about speech, and the visuo-spatial scratch pad, which holds mental images. Therefore, it should be no surprise that the contents of

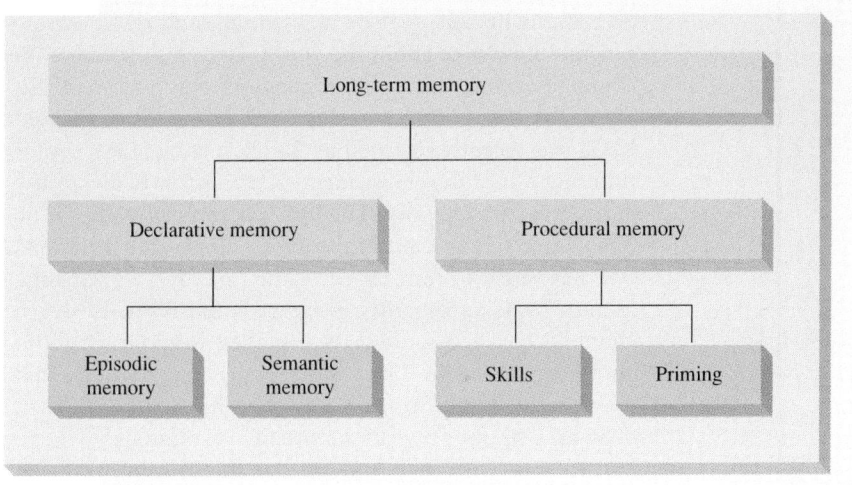

FIGURE 7.5

The Hierarchical Organization of Long-Term Memory's Contents

Imagine you are at Wimbledon: Steffi Graf moves gracefully for a wide forehand, finishes her follow-through, skips quickly back to the center of the court, pushes off for a short ball, and volleys the ball for a winner. *What kind of knowledge is involved when Steffi Graf hits a tennis ball?*

If we asked her to describe this rapid sequence of movements (using procedural or implicit memory), she probably would have difficulty explaining each move. If we asked her who is her toughest opponent (using declarative or explicit memory), she would quickly respond, "Seles."

long-term memory can also be differentiated. Indeed, many psychologists today accept the three-level hierarchy of long-term memory contents shown in figure 7.5 (Squire, 1987). In this hierarchical organization of long-term memory's contents, long-term memory is divided into the subtypes of declarative and procedural memory. Declarative memory is subdivided into episodic memory and semantic memory, while procedural memory is subdivided into skills and priming.

Declarative and Procedural Memory

Declarative memory *is the conscious recollection of information, such as specific facts or events, and, at least in humans, information that can be verbally communicated.* Declarative memory has been called "knowing that," and, more recently, it has been called "explicit memory." Examples of declarative (or explicit) memory include recounting the events of a movie you have seen and describing a basic principle of psychology to someone. However, you do not need to be talking to be using declarative memory. Simply sitting and consciously reflecting about Einstein's theory of relativity, or the date you had last weekend, involves declarative memory.

Procedural memory *refers to knowledge in the form of skills and cognitive operations about how to do something. Procedural memory cannot be consciously recollected, at least not in the form of specific events or facts; and this makes procedural memory difficult, if not impossible, to communicate verbally.* Procedural memory has been called "knowing how" and, more recently, "implicit memory" (Masson & Graf, 1993; Schacter, Chiu, & Ochsner, 1993). Examples of procedural (implicit) memory include the skills of playing tennis, riding a bicycle, and typing. They also include purely perceptual skills such as finding a product on a grocery store shelf. The first time you purchase a certain kind of product, it often takes a while to find it on the shelf, even if you know what aisle to walk down. But, with practice, the product "pops out" perceptually as you scan along an aisle. This sort of perceptual learning is a type of procedural memory.

Episodic and Semantic Memory

Canadian cognitive psychologist Endel Tulving (1972) has been the foremost advocate of distinguishing between two subtypes of declarative memory: episodic and semantic. **Episodic memory** *is the retention of information about the where and when of life's happenings—what it was like when*

Which kind of memory system—declarative
or procedural—is at fault here?

THE FAR SIDE cartoon by Gary Larson is reprinted by permission of
Chronicle Features, San Francisco, CA.

your younger brother or sister was born, what happened to
you on your first date, what you were doing when you
heard that the Gulf war had begun, and what you had for
breakfast this morning. Episodic memory is like an autobiographical filing system, organized in a manner that reflects
each person's uniqueness.

> *How we remember, what we remember, and why we
> remember form the most personal map of our individuality.*
> **Christina Baldwin, *One to One*, 1977**

Semantic memory *is a person's general knowledge
about the world. It includes a person's fields of expertise* (such
as knowledge of chess, for a skilled chess player); *general
academic knowledge of the sort learned in school* (such as
knowledge of geometry); *and "everyday" knowledge about
meanings of words, famous individuals, important places, and
common things* (such as who Nelson Mandela and Mahatma
Gandhi are). *Semantic memory knowledge appears to be independent of the individual's personal identity with the past.*
For example, you can access a fact—such as "Lima is the
capital of Peru"—and not have the foggiest notion of when
and where you learned it.

Several examples help to clarify the distinction between episodic and semantic memory. In a certain type of
amnesiac state, a person might forget entirely who she is—

her name, family, career, and all other personal information about herself—yet be able to talk and demonstrate
general knowledge about the world. Her episodic memory
is impaired, but her semantic memory is functioning. An
especially dramatic case of this type, a young man named
K. C., was recently reported by Endel Tulving (1989). After
suffering a motorcycle accident, K. C. lost virtually all use
of his episodic memory. The loss was so profound that he
was unable to consciously recollect a single thing that had
ever happened to him. At the same time, K. C.'s semantic
memory was sufficiently preserved that he could learn
about his past as a set of facts, just as he would learn about
another person's life. He could report, for example, that
the saddest day of his life was when his brother died of
drowning about 10 years before. This sounds as if K. C.
had episodic memory, but further questioning revealed
that he had no conscious memory of the drowning event.
He simply knew about the drowning because he was able
to recall—apparently through use of his semantic memory—what he had been told about his brother by other
members of his family.

Priming

Priming *is the facilitation in responding to a stimulus that
immediately follows a related stimulus.* For example, priming occurs when an individual says the word *doctor* faster
after just having said the word *nurse* rather than some unrelated word such as *box*. Priming is conceived of as a facil-
itative effect that is typically automatic and a product of a
representational system, such as spread of activation,
which we will discuss later in the chapter. Some memory
experts believe that priming is a fourth type of memory (in
addition to episodic, semantic, and procedural) (Tulving &
Schacter, 1990).

To see how priming works, try to complete the following word fragments to make English words:

    __SS__SS__N
    A__PI__N
    Y__G__R__
    R__I__I__
    R__M__UN__TI__US

If you had some difficulty completing the words, you
are not alone. But what if, before doing the fragment completion, you had seen the following words: *assassin, aspirin,
yogurt, raisin,* and *rambunctious?* You might suspect that
your performance in completing the fragments would have
been much better. Memory researchers have found that
such prior exposure to stimuli often improves people's performance on fragment completion tasks (Tulving, Schacter,
& Stark, 1982).

The Nature of Memory, Time Frames of Memory, Contents of Memory, and Interactions Between Types of Memory

Memory is the retention of information over time. Psychologists study how information is encoded into memory, how it is stored, and how it is retrieved for some purpose later. Two important features of memory are its time frame and its contents. Time frames of memory include sensory memory, working memory, and long-term memory. Sensory memory holds information from the world in its original sensory form only for an instant, not much longer than the brief time for which it is exposed to the visual, auditory, and other senses. Visual sensory memory (iconic memory) retains information for about ¼ of a second, auditory sensory memory (echoic memory) for several seconds. Working memory, also called short-term memory, is a limited-capacity memory system in which information is retained for as long as 30 seconds, unless the information is rehearsed, in which case it can be retained longer. Compared to sensory memory, working memory is limited in capacity but has a relatively long duration. According to George Miller, the limitation of working memory is 7 ± 2 units of information. Chunking can expand working memory, and maintenance rehearsal keeps information in working memory longer. In one model of working memory, an executive plus two slave systems—the phonological loop (which holds speech information) and the visuo-spatial scratchpad (which holds mental images)—are involved. Long-term memory is a relatively permanent type of memory that holds huge amounts of information for a long period of time.

Many psychologists today accept the model of a three-level hierarchical organization of memory in which long-term memory is subdivided into declarative and procedural memory. Declarative memory is subdivided into episodic and semantic memory, and procedural memory is subdivided into skills and priming. Declarative memory is the conscious recollection of information, such as specific facts or events, and, at least in humans, information that can be verbally communicated. Declarative memory has been called "knowing that" and, more recently, "explicit memory." Procedural memory refers to knowledge in the form of skills and cognitive operations, of how to do something. Procedural memory cannot be consciously recollected, at least not in the form of specific events or facts, and this makes procedural memory difficult, if not impossible, to communicate verbally. Procedural memory has been called "knowing how" and, more recently, "implicit memory." Episodic memory is the retention of information about the where and when of life's happenings. Semantic memory is a person's general knowledge about the world. Priming is the facilitation in responding to a stimulus that immediately follows a related stimulus.

THE PROCESSES OF MEMORY

Psychologists who study memory are especially interested in **memory processes:** *the encoding of new information into memory, the representation of information, and the retrieval of what was previously stored.*

Encoding

Encoding *is the transformation and/or transfer of information into a memory system.* Information can be encoded into sensory memory and short-term or working memory, but here our main focus is on encoding information into long-term memory. In everyday language, encoding has much in common with learning. When you are listening to a lecture, watching a movie, listening to music, or talking to a friend, you are encoding information into your long-term memory. It is unlikely, though, that you are encoding all the information you receive. Psychologists are interested not only in how much encoding takes place, but also in the types of processes involved and their operating principles. Among the processes believed to be extremely important in encoding are attention, automatic and effortful processing, depth of processing and elaboration of information, organization, and imagery.

Attention

Pay attention is a phrase we hear all of the time. Just what is attention? When you take an exam, you attend to it. This implies that you have the ability to focus your mental effort on certain stimuli (the test questions) while excluding other stimuli. Thus, an important aspect of attention is selectivity. **Selective attention** *is the focusing of attention on a narrow band of information.* Sometimes we have difficulty ignoring information that is irrelevant to our interests or goals. For example, if a television set or stereo is blaring while you are studying, you may have trouble concentrating.

Not only is attention selective, it also is shiftable. If a professor asks you to pay attention to a certain question and you do so, your behavior indicates that you can shift the focus of your mental effort from one stimulus to another. If the telephone rings while you are studying, you shift your attention from studying to the telephone. However, an external stimulus is not necessary to elicit an attention shift. At this moment you can shift your attention from one topic to another virtually at will. You might think about the last time you ate at a Chinese restaurant, then think about yesterday's soccer game, then think about your date tonight.

As we have seen, attention is concentrated and focused mental effort, a focus that is both selective and shifting. Effort plays an important role in the two ways of encoding information—automatic and effortful processing.

Automatic and Effortful Processing

Research on attention sparked interest in the role of effort in encoding information. Encoding processes differ in how much effort they require. For example, imagine you are driving down the street and chatting with a friend. You're fine as long as the driving is easy and the concentration involves an everyday topic, such as gossip about a mutual acquaintance. But what if the streets are icy, or if the conversation turns serious and you find yourself in an intense argument? Something probably has to give—the driving or talking. If two or more activities are somewhat difficult, it is almost impossible to perform them simultaneously without overloading your focus of attention. In explaining the potential for overload, many cognitive psychologists believe that what is being focused in attention is a kind of mental energy for doing mental work. They believe the amount of this energy is limited, and because it is limited, overload can occur. This mental energy is defined as *capacity, cognitive resources,* or simply *effort.* Psychologists make a distinction between effortful processing and automatic processing. **Effortful processing** *requires capacity or resources to encode information in memory.* **Automatic processing** *does not require capacity, resources, or effort to encode information in memory.* Automatic processing occurs regardless of how people focus their attention (Hasher & Zacks, 1979).

Information about spatial aspects of the environment or frequency of events can be encoded automatically. For example, many students who are taking a test remember reading a certain piece of information on a specific page of the text. Such memory for location of written information is based not on conscious memorization strategies, but rather on automatic memory processes. However, many activities that are important for memory—organization, rehearsal, visualization, and elaboration, for example—do require mental effort. In a number of studies, this allocation of capacity, or effort, was related to having a good memory (Ellis, Thomas, & Rodriguez, 1984).

Now we consider some of the most important effortful processes—depth of processing and elaboration, organization, and imagery.

Depth of Processing and Elaboration

Following the discovery that maintenance rehearsal was not an efficient way to improve long-term memory, Fergus Craik and Robert Lockhart (1972) developed a new model of memory. **Levels of processing theory** *is Craik and Lockhart's theory that memory is on a continuum from shallow to deep; in this theory, deeper processing produces better memory.* The sensory or physical features of stimuli are analyzed first at a *shallow* level. This might involve detecting the lines, angles, and contours of a printed word's letters, or a spoken word's frequency, duration, and loudness. At an *intermediate* level of processing, the stimulus is recognized and given a label. For example, a four-legged, barking object is identified as a dog. Then, at the *deepest* level, information is processed semantically, in terms of its meaning. For example, if you saw the word *boat,* at the shallow level you might notice the shapes of the letters, at the intermediate level you might think of characteristics of the word (such as that it rhymes with *coat*), and at deepest level you might think about the kind of boat you would like to own and the last time you went fishing. Figure 7.6 depicts the levels of processing theory of memory. A number of studies have shown that people's memories improve when they make semantic associations to stimuli, as opposed to attending just to their physical aspects. In other words, you're more likely to remember something when you process information at a deep, rather than a shallow, level.

However, cognitive psychologists soon recognized that there was more to a good memory than "depth." Within deep, semantic processing, psychologists discovered, the more extensive the processing, the better the memory (Craik & Tulving, 1975). **Elaboration** *is the term used to describe the extensiveness of processing at any given depth in memory.* For instance, rather than memorizing the definition of *memory,* you would do better to learn the concept of memory by coming up with examples of how information enters your mind, how it is stored, and how you can retrieve it. Thinking of examples of a concept is a good way

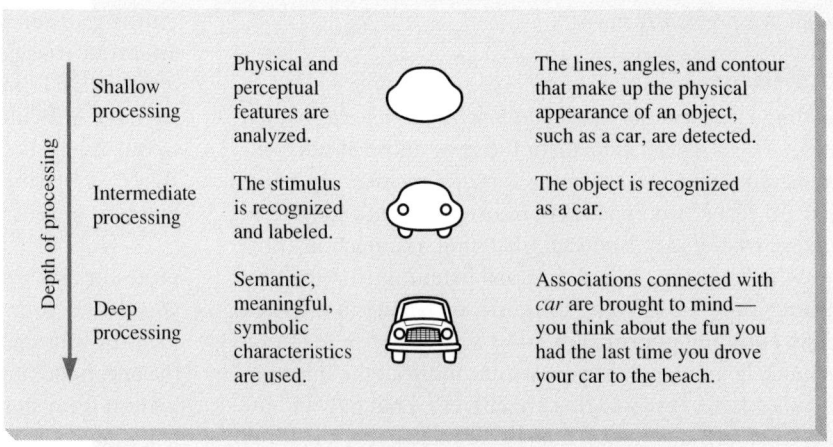

FIGURE 7.6

An Example of Craik and Lockhart's Levels of Processing

The more that you elaborate about an event, the better your memory of the event will be. For example, if you were at Woodstock II and you encoded information about how large the crowd was, who accompanied you, which songs you heard, how powerful the performances were, what the weather was like, and other vivid sights, sounds, and smells, you probably will remember the concert more clearly.

robbery and observe that the getaway car is a red 1987 or 1988 Pontiac with tinted windows and spinners on the wheels, your memory of the car is more distinctive than that of a person who notices only that the getaway car is red.

Organization

Recall the 12 months of the year as quickly as you can. How long did it take you? What was the order of your recall? The answers to these questions probably are "4 to 6 seconds" and "natural order" (January, February, March, etc.). Now try to remember the months in alphabetical order. Did you make any errors? How long did it take you? There is a clear distinction between recalling the months naturally and recalling them alphabetically. This demonstration makes it easy to see that your memory for the months of the year is organized. Indeed, one of memory's most distinctive features is its organization.

An important feature of memory's organization is that sometimes it is hierarchical. A *hierarchy* is a system in which items are organized from general classes to more specific classes. An example of a hierarchy for the general category of minerals is shown in figure 7.7. In an experiment using conceptual hierarchies of words, such as those in figure 7.7, Gordon Bower and his colleagues (1969) showed the importance of organization in memory. Subjects who were presented the words in hierarchies remembered the words much better than did subjects who were given the words in random groupings. Other investigations have revealed that if people are simply encouraged to organize material, their memory of the material improves, even if no warning is given that memory will be tested (Mandler, 1980). This simple finding has implications for how you can better design your study activities (even for this course).

Imagery

How many windows are in your apartment or house? If you live in a dorm room with only one or two windows, this question may be too easy. If so, how many windows were in the last home you lived in? Few of us have ever memorized this information, but many of us believe we can come up with a good answer, especially if we use imagery to "reconstruct" each room. We take a mental walk through the house, counting windows as we go.

to understand it. Self-reference is another effective way to elaborate information. For example, if the word *win* is on a list of words to remember, you might think of the last time you won a bicycle race, or if the word *cook* appears, you might imagine the last time you cooked dinner. In general, deep elaboration—elaborate processing of meaningful information—is an excellent way to remember.

One reason that elaboration produces good memory is that it adds to the *distinctiveness* of the "memory codes" (Ellis, 1987). To remember a piece of information, such as a name, an experience, or a fact about geography, you need to search for the code that contains this information among the mass of codes contained in long-term memory. The search process is easier if the memory code is somehow unique. The situation is not unlike searching for a friend at a crowded airport. If your friend is 6 feet tall and has flaming red hair, it will be easier to find him or her in the crowd. Similarly, highly distinctive memory codes can be more easily differentiated. Also, as encoding becomes more elaborate, more information is stored. And as more information is stored, the more likely it is that this highly distinctive code will be easy to differentiate from other memory codes. For example, if you witness a bank

For many years psychologists ignored the role of imagery in memory because it was believed to be too mentalistic by behaviorists. But studies by Allan Paivio (1971, 1986) documented how imagery can improve memory. Paivio argued that there are two ways a memory can be stored: as a verbal code or as an image code. For example, a picture can be remembered by a label (a verbal code) or a mental image. Paivio thinks that the image code, which is highly detailed and distinctive, produces better memory. Although imagery is widely accepted as an important aspect of memory, there is controversy over whether we have separate codes for words and images (Pylyshyn, 1973). More about imagery appears later in the chapter when we discuss strategies for improving memory. For now, just keep in mind that if you need to remember a list of things, forming mental images will help you out (Cornoldi & Logie, 1995).

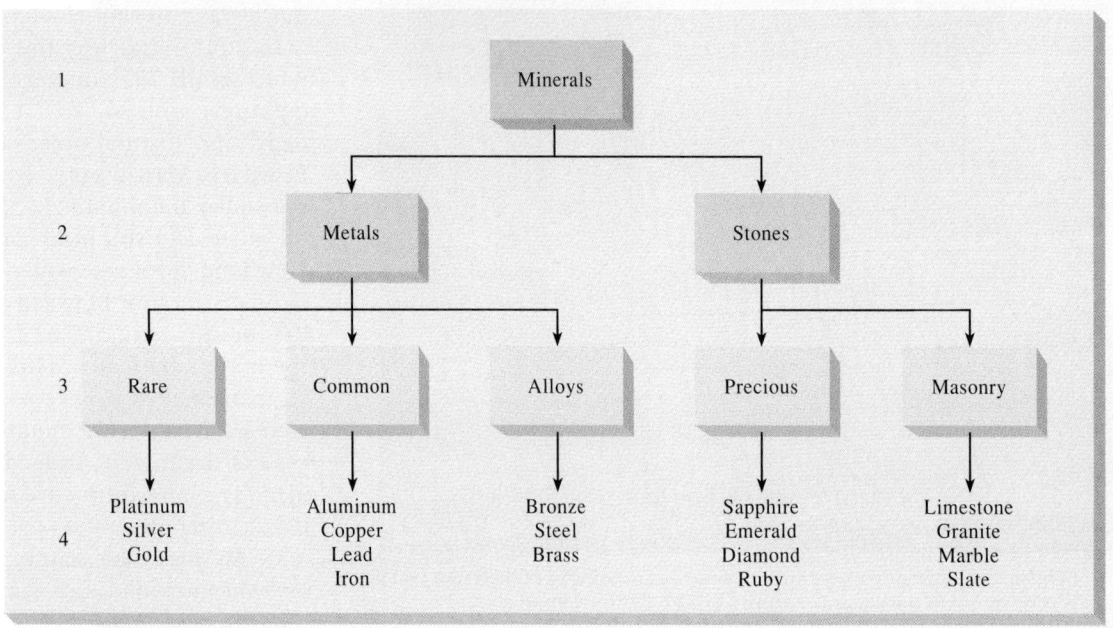

FIGURE 7.7

Example of a Hierarchical Organization

REVIEW

Encoding

Encoding is the transformation and/or transfer of information into a memory system. Information can be encoded into sensory memory and short-term memory, but the main focus is on encoding information into long-term memory. Among the important aspects of encoding are attention, automatic and effortful processing, depth of processing and elaboration, imagery, and organization.

Attention is the ability to focus on certain stimuli. Attention is both selective (the ability to focus and concentrate on a narrow band of information) and shifting. Automatic processes do not require capacity or resources; conversely, effortful processes require capacity or resources. Effortful processing includes depth of processing and elaboration, imagery, and organization. Craik and Lockhart developed the levels of processing view of memory, which stresses that memory is on a continuum from shallow to deep. In this view, deeper processing produces better memory. Elaboration refers to the extensiveness of processing at any depth and it leads to improved memory, making encoding more distinctive. Imagery involves sensations without an external stimulus present. One of the most pervasive aspects of memory is organization, which involves grouping or combining items. Information is often organized hierarchically. Paivio argued that we have two separate verbal and imaginal codes, but this is controversial. Imagery often improves memory.

We have seen that semantic elaboration, organization, and imagery are effective ways to encode information for long-term memory storage but that maintenance rehearsal is not. Now we turn our attention to the ways we can represent information in memory storage.

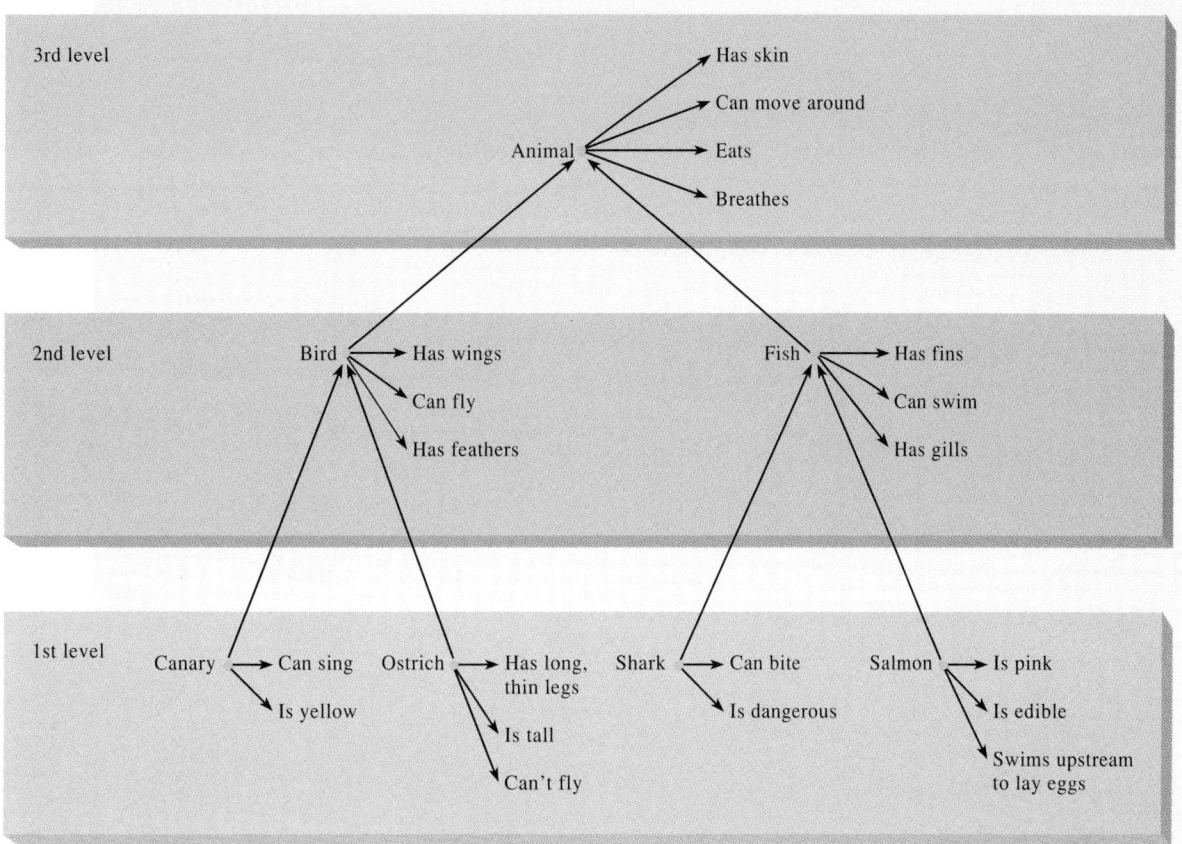

FIGURE 7.8

The Hierarchical Organization of Memory with Nodes (Branching Points) at Three Levels in the Hierarchy
Notice how the information becomes more detailed and specific as you move through the levels of the hierarchy in this model. Some psychologists have challenged this representation as too "clean" to portray the true complexity of our representation processes.

Representation

Although we have talked about the time frames and content of memory, as well as the processes of encoding and retrieval, we have not tackled the question of how knowledge is represented in memory. Two approaches that have addressed this issue are network theories and schema theories.

Network Theories

One of the first network theories claimed that our memories consist of a complex network of nodes that stand for labels or concepts (see figure 7.8). The network was assumed to be hierarchically arranged with more-concrete concepts (canary, for example) nestled under more-abstract concepts (bird). More recently, cognitive psychologists realized that such hierarchical networks were too neat to fit the way human cognition actually works (Shanks, 1991). For example, people take longer to answer the true-or-false statement "An ostrich is a bird" than they do to answer the statement "A canary is a bird." Memory researchers now envision the network as more irregular and distorted: a *typical* bird, such as a canary, is closer to the node or center of the category *bird* than is the atypical ostrich.

Figure 7.9 shows an example of the revised model, which allows for the typicality of information while retaining the original notion of node and network.

We add new material to this network by placing it in the middle of the appropriate region. The new material is gradually tied in—by meaningful connections—to the appropriate nodes in the surrounding network. That is why if you cram for a test, you will not remember the information over the long term. The new material is not knit into the long-term web. In contrast, discussing the material or incorporating it into a research paper interweaves it and connects it to other knowledge you have. These multiple connections increase the probability that you will be able to retrieve the information many months or even years later.

Schema Theories

Long-term memory has been compared to a library. Your memory stores information just as a library stores books. We retrieve information in a fashion similar to the process we use to locate and check out a book. But the process of retrieving information from long-term memory is not as precise as the library analogy suggests. When we search

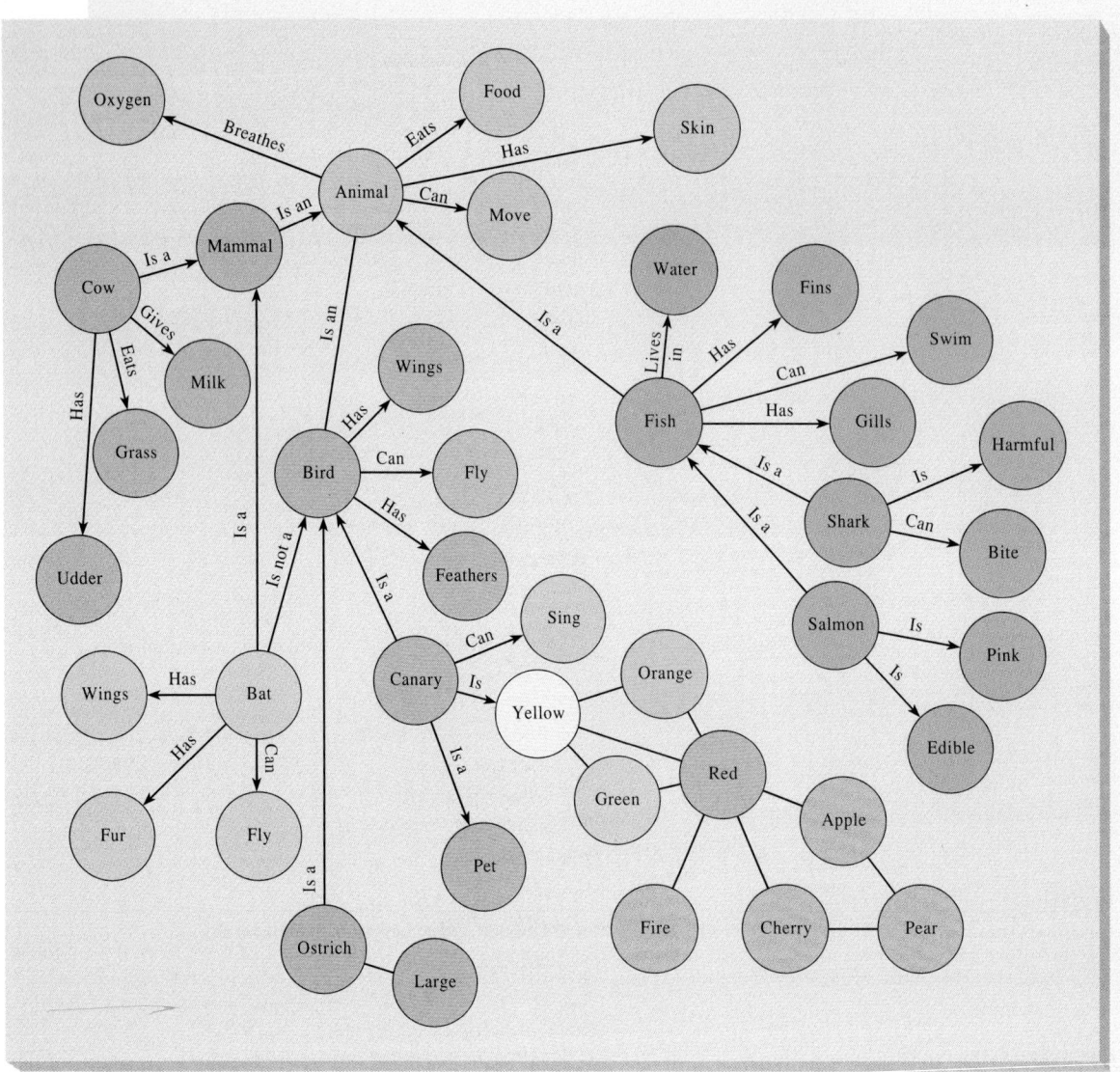

FIGURE 7.9

Revision of the Hierarchical Network View of How Information Is Organized in Long-Term Memory

through our long-term memory storehouse we don't always find the *exact* "book" we want, or we might find the book we want but discover that only several pages are intact. We have to *reconstruct* the rest.

When we reconstruct information, we often fit it into information that already exists in our mind. A **schema** *is information—concepts, events, and knowledge—that already exists in a person's mind.* Schemas from prior encounters with the environment influence the way we encode, make inferences about, and retrieve information. Unlike network theories, which assume that retrieval involves specific facts, schema theory claims that long-term memory searches are not very exact. We seldom find precisely what we want, or at least not all of what we want; hence, we have to reconstruct the rest. Our schemas support this reconstruction process, helping us fill in the gaps between our fragmented memories.

The schema theory of memory began with Sir Frederick Bartlett's (1932) studies of how people remember stories. Bartlett was concerned about how people's backgrounds determine what they encode and remember about stories. Bartlett chose stories that sounded strange and were difficult to understand. He reasoned that a person's background, which is encoded in schemas, would reveal itself in the person's reconstruction (modification and distortion) of the story's content. For example, one of Bartlett's stories was called "War of the Ghosts," an English translation of an American Indian folktale. The story contained events that were completely foreign to the experiences of the middle-class British research participants.

Summarized, the story goes like this: An Indian joins a war party that turns out to consist entirely of ghosts. They go off to fight some other Indians, and the main character

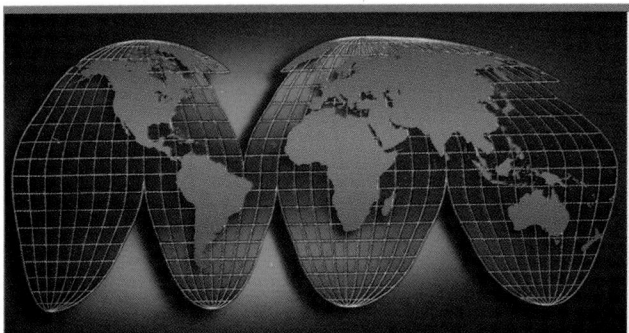

Eyewitness Testimony

At times, one person's memories can take on national importance. This was true for John Dean in the Watergate cover-up in the early 1970s. It is in the legal arena, especially, that one person's memory of events given as testimony can be crucial in determining a defendant's, or a nation's, future. Much of the interest in eyewitness testimony has focused on distortion, bias, and inaccuracy in memory (Loftus, 1993a; Wells, 1993).

Memory fades over time. That's why the amount of time that has passed between an incident and a person's recollection of it is a critical factor in eyewitness testimony. In one study, people were able to identify pictures with 100 percent accuracy after a 2-hour time lapse. However, 4 months later they achieved an accuracy of only 57 percent; chance alone accounts for 50 percent accuracy (Shepard, 1967).

Unlike a videotape, memory can be altered by new information. In one study, students were shown a film of an automobile accident (Loftus, 1975). Some of the students were asked how fast the white sports car was going when it passed a barn. Other students were asked the same question without any mention of a barn. In fact, there was no barn in the film. However, 17 percent of the students who heard the question that included the barn mentioned it in their answer; only 3 percent of those whose question did not include

the barn mentioned that they saw it. New information, then, can add or even replace existing information in memory.

Studies have shown that people of one ethnic group are less likely to recognize individual differences among people of another ethnic group. Latino eyewitnesses, for example, may have trouble distinguishing among several Asian suspects. This makes identifying individuals from a police lineup or photographs an unreliable tool. In one investigation, clerks in small stores were asked to identify photographs of customers who had shopped there 2 hours earlier (Brigham & others, 1982). Only 33 percent of the customers were correctly identified. In another experiment, a mugging was shown on a television news program. Immediately after, a lineup of six suspects was broadcast and viewers were asked to phone in and identify which of the six individuals they thought committed the robbery. Of the 2,000 callers, more than 1,800 identified the wrong person. In addition, even though the robber was White, one-third of the viewers identified an African American or Latino suspect as the criminal.

Identification of individuals from police lineups or photographs is not always reliable. People from one ethnic group often have difficulty recognizing differences among people of another ethnic group.

gets hit but feels no pain. He returns to his people, describes his adventure, and goes to sleep. But in the morning he dies as something black comes out of his mouth.

What interested Bartlett was how differently the participants might reconstruct this and other stories from the original versions. The British participants used both their general schemas for daily experiences and their schemas for adventurous ghost stories in particular to reconstruct "War of the Ghosts." Familiar details from the story that "fit into" the participant's schemas were successfully recalled. But

details that departed from the person's schemas were often extensively distorted. For example, the "something black" that came out of the Indian's mouth became blood in one reconstruction and condensed air in another.

There has been a flurry of interest in reconstructive memory, especially in the way people recall stories, give eyewitness testimony, remember their past, and recall conversations (Fivush, 1995; Howe, 1995). To learn more about the nature of reconstructive memory in eyewitness testimony turn to Sociocultural Worlds 7.1.

FIGURE 7.10

Eating Scripts

All people are made alike.
They are made of bone, flesh, and dinners.
Only the dinners are different.

Gertrude Louise Cheney

And we would add, so are their scripts. Shown above are representative scripts from a Japanese tea ceremony, an extravagant Western dinner, and an Ethiopian meal. *With which script do you feel most comfortable? least comfortable?*

In memory each of us is an artist: each of us creates.
Patricia Hampl, *A Romantic Education*, 1981

We have schemas not only for stories but also for scenes or spatial layouts (a beach or a bathroom), as well as for common events (going to a restaurant, playing football, writing a term paper). The term **script** *is given to a schema for an event* (Schank & Abelson, 1977). Consider a restaurant script. This script has information about physical features, people, and typical occurrences in restaurants. This kind of information is helpful when people need to figure out what is happening around them. For example, if you are enjoying your after-dinner coffee in a restaurant and a man in a tuxedo comes over and puts a piece of paper on the table, your script tells you that the man probably is a waiter who has just given you the check. Figure 7.10 shows some eating scripts in different cultures.

In one study, individuals in the United States and Mexico remembered according to script-based knowledge, consistent with common and familiar United States and Mexican cultural scripts (Harris, Schoen, & Hensley, 1992). For example, individuals in the United States remembered information about a dating script better when no chaperone was present on the date, while individuals in Mexico remembered the information better when a chaperone was present.

After information has been encoded and represented in memory, it also can be retrieved. Next we explore the nature of retrieval and forgetting in memory.

"Why? You cross the road because it's in the script—that's why!"

Drawing by Bernard Schoenbaum; © 1988 The New Yorker Magazine, Inc.

Retrieval and Forgetting

Have you ever forgotten where you parked your car, your mother's birthday, or to meet a friend to study? Have you ever sat in a class taking an exam, unable to remember the answer to a question but remembering where the elusive concept was on the page? Psychologists have developed a number of theories about why we forget information and how we retrieve it.

Memory is more delible than ink.

Anita Loos

Retrieval from Long-Term Memory

To retrieve something from our mental "data bank," we search our store of memory to find the relevant information. Just as with encoding, this search can be virtually automatic or it can require effort. For example, if someone asks you what your mother's first name is, the answer immediately springs to your lips; that is, retrieval is automatic. But if someone asks you the name of your first-grade teacher, it may take some time to dredge up the answer; that is, retrieval requires more effort. As appropriate information is found, it is pulled together to guide and direct a person's verbal and motor responses. Let's explore several concepts related to retrieval.

One glitch in retrieving information that we're all familiar with is the **tip-of-the-tongue phenomenon, or TOT state.** *It is a type of "effortful retrieval" that occurs when people are confident they know something but just can't quite seem to pull it out of memory.* In one study on the TOT state, participants were shown photographs of famous people and asked to say their names (Yarmey, 1973). The researcher found that people tended to use two strategies to try to retrieve the name of a person they thought they knew. One strategy was to pinpoint the person's profession. For example, one participant correctly identified the famous person as an artist but the artist's name, Picasso, remained elusive. Another retrieval strategy was to repeat initial letters or syllables—such as *Monetti, Mona, Magett, Spaghetti,* and *Bogette*—in the attempt to identify Liza Minelli. The tip-of-the-tongue phenomenon suggests that without good retrieval cues, information encoded in memory may be difficult to find.

Understanding how retrieval works also requires knowledge of the **serial position effect:** *the effect of an item's position in a list on our recall of it; in particular, recall is superior for items at the beginning and at the end of a list.* If someone gave you the directions "Left on Mockingbird, right on Central, right on Stemmons, left on Balboa, and right on Parkside," you probably would remember "Left on Mockingbird" and "right on Parkside" more easily than the turns and streets in the middle. The **primacy effect** *refers to superior recall for items at the beginning of a list.* The **recency effect** *refers to superior recall for items at the end of the list.* Together with the relatively low recall of items from the middle of the list, this pattern makes up the serial position effect. See figure 7.11 for a typical serial position effect that shows a weaker primacy effect and a stronger recency effect.

How can primacy and recency effects be explained? The first few items in the list are easily remembered because they are rehearsed more often than later items are (Atkinson

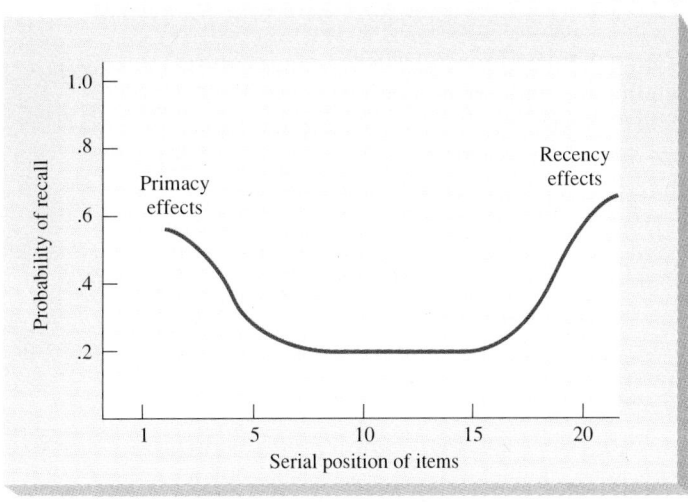

FIGURE 7.11

Serial Position Effect
When a person is asked to memorize a list of words, the words memorized last usually are recalled best, those at the beginning next best, and those in the middle least efficiently.

& Shiffrin, 1968). Working memory is relatively empty when they enter, so there is little competition for rehearsal time. And since they get more rehearsal, they stay in working memory longer and are more likely to be successfully encoded into long-term memory. In contrast, many items from the middle of the list drop out of working memory before being encoded into long-term memory. The last several items are remembered for different reasons. First, at the time these items are recalled, they may still be in working memory. Second, even if these items are not in working memory, their relative recency, compared to other list items, makes them easier to recall. For example, if you are a sports fan, try remembering, at the end of the football season, what football games you saw that year, or, at the end of the baseball season, what baseball games you saw. You probably will find that the more recent games are easier to remember than less recent games. This represents a recency effect that extends far beyond the time span of working memory.

Two other factors involved in retrieval are (a) the nature of the cues that can prompt your memory, and (b) the retrieval task that you set for yourself. If effective cues for what you are trying to remember do not seem to be available, you need to create them—a process that takes place in working memory. For example, if you have a "block" about remembering a new friend's name, you might go through the alphabet, generating names that begin with each letter. If you manage to stumble across the right name, you'll probably recognize it.

While cues help, your success in retrieving information also depends on the task you set for yourself. For instance, if you're simply trying to decide if something seems familiar, retrieval is probably a snap. Let's say you see a short, dark-haired woman walking toward you. You quickly decide she's someone who lives in the next dorm. But remembering her name or a precise detail, such as when you met her, can be harder (Brown, Deffenbacher, & Sturgill, 1977). Such findings have implications for police investigations: A witness might be certain she has previously seen a face, yet she might have a hard time deciding if it was at the scene of the crime or in a mug shot.

The two factors just discussed—the presence or absence of good cues, and the retrieval task required—are involved in an important memory distinction: recall versus recognition memory. **Recall** *is a memory measure in which the individual must retrieve previously learned information, as on an essay test.* **Recognition** *is a memory measure in which the individual only has to identify ("recognize") learned items, as on a multiple-choice test.* Most college students prefer multiple-choice tests because they're easier than essay tests or fill-in-the-blank tests. Recall tests, such as fill-in-the-blank tests, have poor retrieval cues. You are told to try to recall a certain class of information ("Discuss the factors that caused World War II."). In multiple-choice "recognition" tests, you merely judge whether a stimulus is familiar or not (does it match something you experienced in the past?).

You have probably heard people say they are terrible at remembering names but they "never forget a face." If you have made that claim yourself, try to actually *recall* a face. It's not so easy. Police officers know that witnesses can be terrible at describing a suspect, so they often bring in an artist to reconstruct the suspect's face. Recalling faces is difficult. If you think you are better at remembering faces rather than names, it is probably because you are better at recognition than recall.

Researchers have found that when people are faced with a recall task—a merciless professor gives a lengthy essay exam, for example—their memory improves when retrieval cues correspond to the situation when the information was encoded (Eich, 1990). For example, you'll probably recall information more easily when you take a test in the same room you heard the lecture and took notes in—that is, where the information was originally encoded. The strongest evidence for this conclusion is based on a study in which scuba divers learned information both on land and under water (Godden & Baddeley, 1975). They were then asked to recall the information. The scuba divers' recall was much better when the encoding and retrieval locations were constant (both on land or under water) (see figure 7.12). Although changing from land to under water or vice versa adversely affects one's memory, less dramatic changes in environmental context, such as moving to a new room to take an exam, show weaker effects.

Cue-dependent forgetting *is a form of forgetting information because of failure to use effective retrieval cues.* Cue-dependent forgetting can explain why we sometimes fail to retrieve a needed fact on an exam even when we "know" that piece of information. These failures to retrieve what is stored in memory occur because we do not use the right cues. For example, you might forget the point of

FIGURE 7.12

Relative Efficiency in Godden and Baddeley's Experiment on Encoding and Retrieval Cues
Divers recalled information better when encoding and retrieval locations were constant (both on land, both under water).

Sperling's experiment, described earlier, if "Sperling's experiment" is your only cue. But if you also use the cue "sensory memory" or "iconic memory," you might suddenly recollect what Sperling did and what he discovered.

Some important retrieval processes are clearly revealed in the study of autobiographical memory—a person's memory for events in his or her personal life. In one investigation of autobiographical memory, students were asked to think out loud as they remembered a specific event, such as going to the zoo, feeling sad, or being turned down for a date (Reiser, Black, & Abelson, 1985). The students called on several strategies to remember such events. They often used the particular activity, person, or time period they thought was involved to establish the general context of memory, as well

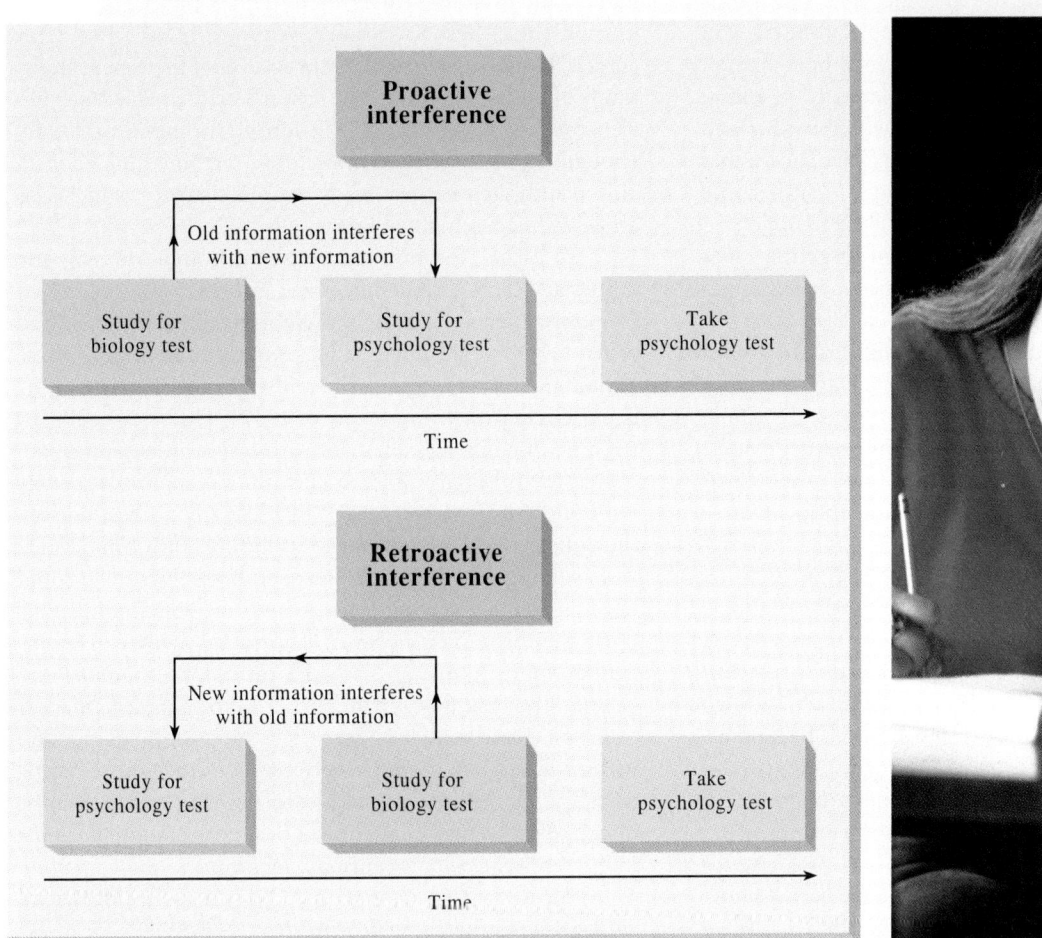

FIGURE 7.13

Proactive and Retroactive Interference
Pro means forward, so in proactive interference old information has a forward influence by getting in the way of new material learned. *Retro* means backward, so in retroactive interference new information has a backward influence by getting in the way of material learned earlier. *How would this information help you organize your study period more effectively over the next few weeks?*

as to limit their search process. When asked about the circumstances that made them sad, for example, they searched for activities in which they felt sad. In another study, both emotional reactions to an event and many rehearsals of the event were required to maintain details of the event over a long period of time (Bohannon, 1988). A common strategy for remembering certain information is to think about events in a given time period. We tend to remember something that happened about the same time as, before, or after a particular event (Conway & Rubin, 1993).

Interference and Decay

The principle of cue-dependent forgetting is consistent with a previously developed view of forgetting—**interference theory,** *which states that we forget not because memories are actually lost from storage, but because other information gets in the way of retrieving what we want to remember.* There are two kinds of interference: proactive and retroactive.

Proactive interference *occurs when material that was learned earlier disrupts the recall of material learned later.* In this usage, *pro-* means "forward in time." For example, suppose you had a good friend 10 years ago named *Mary*, and last night you met someone at a party named *Marie*. You might find yourself calling your new friend *Mary* because the old information (*Mary*) interferes with retrieval of new information (*Marie*). **Retroactive interference** *occurs when material learned later disrupts retrieval of information learned earlier.* Remember that *retro-* means "backward in time." Suppose you have become friends with *Marie* (and finally have gotten her name straight). If you find yourself sending a letter to your old friend *Mary*, you might address it to *Marie* because the new information (*Marie*) interferes with the old information (*Mary*) (see figure 7.13).

Proactive and retroactive interference *both* can be explained by cue-dependent forgetting. The reason that *Mary* interferes with *Marie*, and *Marie* interferes with *Mary* might be that the cue you are using to remember does not distinguish between the two memories. For example, if the cue you are using is "my good friend," it might evoke both names. This could result in retrieving the wrong name, or in a kind of blocking in which each name interferes with the other and neither comes to mind. Memory researchers have shown that retrieval cues (like "friend" in our example) can become overloaded, and when that happens we are likely to forget.

Although interference is involved in forgetting, it is not the whole story. **Decay theory** *states that when something new is learned a neurochemical "memory trace" is formed, but over time this trace tends to disintegrate.* Decay theory suggests that the passage of time always increases forgetting. However, there is one circumstance in which older memories can be stronger than more recent ones: Older memories are sometimes more resistant to shocks or physical assaults on the brain than recent memories are.

Amnesia

Consider the case of H. M. At the age of 10, H. M. underwent surgery to stop his epileptic seizures and emerged with his intelligence and most of his mental abilities intact, but the part of his brain that was responsible for laying down new memories (the hippocampus) was damaged beyond repair. **Amnesia** *is the loss of memory.* Although some types of amnesia clear up over time, H. M.'s amnesia endured. In the years following surgery, H. M.'s memory showed no improvement. The amnesia suffered by H. M. was anterograde in nature. **Anterograde amnesia** *is a memory disorder that affects the retention of new information or events. What was learned before the onset of the condition is not affected.* For example, H. M. could identify his friends, recall their

names, and even tell stories about them—but only if he had known them before surgery. Anyone H. M. met after surgery remained a virtual stranger, even if they spent thousands of hours with him. The vast majority of H. M.'s experiences were never encoded in long-term memory. Oddly enough, H. M.'s short-term memory remained unchanged, and as indicated earlier, his overall intelligence, which was above average, remained intact.

Contrary to common sense, although anterograde amnesiacs cannot remember new information, this deficit primarily affects declarative memory (that is, episodic and semantic memory) rather than procedural memory. These patients can learn new skills, and in many instances they show normal priming (Squire, 1987). One especially intriguing case involves a patient with severe amnesia who acquired the necessary skills to perform a complex data entry job (Glisky & Schacter, 1987). Just like any normal person, the patient became more adept at her job with time. But it was as though each day was her first day, because she could never remember having learned her job. This finding supports the distinction between declarative memory (for information, or knowing that) and procedural memory (for skill, or knowing how) made earlier in the chapter. In addition, some case studies of amnesiacs support the distinction within declarative memory between episodic and semantic memory. One amnesic could learn new facts and semantic information (semantic memory) despite gross impairments in remembering events (episodic memory).

Amnesia also occurs in a second form, known as **retrograde amnesia,** *which involves memory loss for a segment of the past but not for new events.* It is much more common than anterograde amnesia, and frequently occurs when the brain is assaulted by an electrical shock or a physical blow—such as a head injury to a football player. The key difference from anterograde amnesia is that the forgotten information is *old* (prior to the event that caused the amnesia), and the person's ability to acquire new memories is not affected.

Repression and Memory

Repression is one of psychology's most controversial concepts. Long the province of clinical psychology, repression of threatening, anxiety-laden unconscious thoughts has caught the eye of memory researchers in cognitive psychology. Repression takes place when something shocking happens and the mind pushes the occurrence into some inaccessible part of the unconscious mind. At some later point in time, the memory might emerge in consciousness. Repression is one of the foundations on which the field of psychoanalysis rests. To read further about the nature of repressed memories, turn to Applications in Psychology 7.1.

APPLICATIONS IN PSYCHOLOGY 7.1

Repressed Memories, Child Abuse, and Reality

Recently there has been a dramatic increase in reported memories of childhood sexual abuse that were allegedly repressed for many years. With recent changes in legislation, people with recently discovered memories are suing alleged perpetrators for events that occurred 20, 30, even 40 or more years earlier. Memory researcher Elizabeth Loftus (1993b) recently analyzed the nature of repressed memories, child abuse, and reality.

In 1991, popular actress Roseanne's story was on the cover of *People* magazine. She reported that her mother had

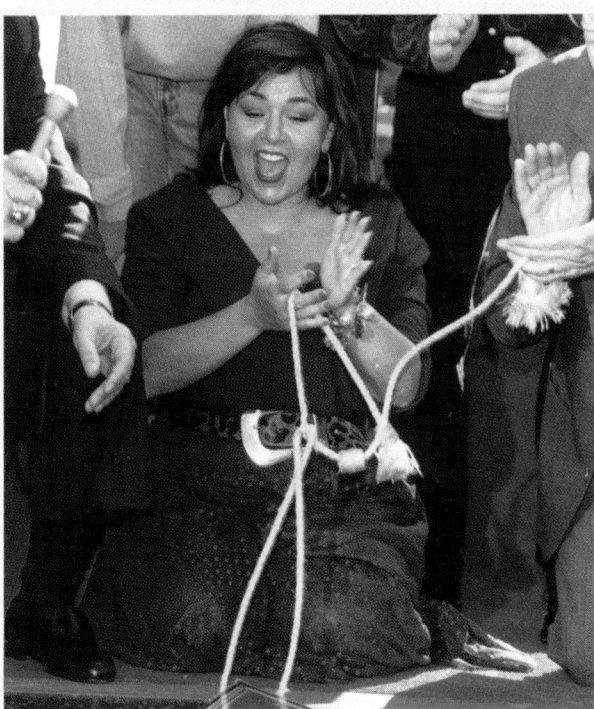

Roseanne said that her mother abused her from the time she was an infant until she was 6–7 years old. *Why have many psychologists questioned some of the reports of activation of repressed memories, such as Roseanne's?*

abused her from the time she was an infant until she was 6 or 7 years of age, only becoming aware of the abuse recently during therapy. Other highly publicized cases of repressed memories of child abuse coming into awareness during therapy dot the pages of large numbers of popular magazines, and many self-help books encourage readers to uncover repressed memories of childhood abuse.

There is little doubt that actual childhood abuse is tragically common. Loftus (1993b) and others (Kutchinsky, 1992) don't dispute that child abuse is a serious social problem. What Loftus does take issue with is how the abuse is recalled in the minds of adults. Despite the belief on the part of many in the therapeutic community that childhood repression of abuse is very common, few research studies provide evidence about the extent to which repression occurs. At present, there aren't any completely satisfying methods for discovering the answer to how common repressed abuse is. Repression researchers are in the unenviable position of asking people about a memory for a forgotten memory. In the studies that have been conducted, from 18 to 59 percent of therapists' clients have reported having repressed memories of child abuse and then becoming aware of the incidents as an adult. As Loftus (1993b) points out, this is a large range and hardly suggestive of an accurate, agreed-upon incidence of repressed memories of child abuse.

Repressed memories of abuse often return in therapy, in some cases after suggestive probing by the therapist. The media (television, self-help books, magazines) are full of reports that also can be the source of suggestion. The result is memories that often are detailed and confidently held. Despite an absence of corroboration, some of the recollections could be authentic, while others might not be.

According to Loftus (1993b), psychotherapists, counselors, social service agencies, and law enforcement personnel need to be careful about probing for horrors on the other side of some amnesiac barrier. They should be cautious in their interpretation of uncorroborated repressed memories that return. Clarification, compassion, and gentle confrontation along with a demonstration of empathy are techniques that can be used to help individuals in their painful struggle to come to grips with their personal truths.

One final tragic risk of suggestive probing and uncritical acceptance of all allegations made by clients is that these activities lead to an increased likelihood that society in general will disbelieve the actual cases of child abuse that deserve extensive attention and evaluation. In general, any careless or uncritical acceptance of unreplicated findings in psychology, especially when they have a colorful element that attracts media attention, harms public attitudes toward the contributions of psychological research (Howe, 1995; Ornskin, 1995).

Two theories of how knowledge is represented in memory are network and schema. Early network theories stressed that memories consist of a complex network of nodes that are hierarchically arranged. More recent network theories stress the role of meaningful nodes in the surrounding network. The concept of schema refers to information we have about various concepts, events, and knowledge. Schema theory claims that long-term memory is not very exact and that we reconstruct our past. Schemas for events are called scripts.

Retrieval involves getting information out of long-term memory. The search can be automatic or effortful. An interesting aspect is the tip-of-the-tongue phenomenon (TOT state), which occurs when we just can't quite pull something out of memory. The implication of TOT is

that, without good retrieval cues, stored information is difficult to find. The serial position effect influences retrieval—retrieval is superior for items at the beginning of a list (primacy effect) and at the end of a list (recency effect). One key factor that makes retrieval effortful is the absence of effective cues. A second factor is the nature of the retrieval task, which, along with the presence or absence of retrieval cues, distinguishes recall from recognition memory. Failure to use effective retrieval cues is one reason we forget, a phenomenon known as cue-dependent forgetting.

The principle of cue-dependent forgetting is consistent with a previously developed view of forgetting—interference theory, the belief that we forget, not because memories are actually lost from storage, but because other information

gets in the way of what we want to remember. Proactive interference occurs when material that was learned earlier disrupts the recall of material learned later. Retroactive interference occurs when material learned later disrupts the retrieval of information learned earlier. Decay theory argues that, when something new is learned, a memory trace is formed, but as time passes this trace begins to disintegrate.

Amnesia involves extreme memory deficits. There are two forms of amnesia. Anterograde amnesia is a memory disorder that affects the retention of new information and events. Retrograde amnesia is a memory disorder that involves memory loss for a segment of the past but not for new events. Memory researchers have recently become interested in repression, long a province of clinical psychology.

THE BIOLOGICAL AND CULTURAL CONTEXTS OF MEMORY

The forces of nature and nurture, of biology and experience, make us who we are and shape us as individuals. Memory is no exception. In this section, we explore the neurobiological basis of memory and memory's cultural dimensions.

The Neurobiological Origins of Memory

Karl Lashley (1950) spent a lifetime looking for a location in the brain where memories are stored. He trained rats to discover the correct pathway in a maze and then cut out a portion of the animals' brains and retested their memory of the maze pathway. After experimenting with thousands of rats, Lashley found that the loss of various cortical areas did not affect rats' ability to remember the maze's path. Lashley concluded that memories are not stored in a specific location in the brain.

Neural Circuits

Many neuroscientists today believe that memory is located in discrete sets or circuits of neurons. Brain researcher Larry Squire (1990; Squire, Knowlton, & Musen, 1993), for example, says that most memories are probably clustered in groups of about 1,000 neurons. He points out that memory is distributed throughout the brain, in the sense that no specific memory center exists. Many parts of the brain and nervous system participate in the memory of a particular

event. Yet memory is localized, in the sense that a limited number of brain systems and pathways are involved, and each probably contributes in different ways (Lynch, 1990).

Single neurons, of course, are at work in memory. Researchers who measure the electrical activity of single cells have found that some respond to faces, others to eye or hair color, for example. But for you to recognize your Uncle Albert, individual neurons that provide information about hair color, size, and other characteristics must act together.

Ironically, some of the answers to the complex questions about the neural mechanics of memory come from studies on a very simple experimental animal—the inelegant sea slug. Eric Kandel and James Schwartz (1982) chose this large snail-without-a-shell because of the simple architecture of its nervous system, which consists of only about 10,000 neurons.

The sea slug can hardly be called a quick learner or an animal with a good memory, but it is equipped with a reliable reflex. When anything touches the gill on its back, it quickly withdraws it. First the researchers repeatedly prodded the sea slug's gill. After awhile, it ignored the prodding and stopped withdrawing its gill. Next the researchers applied an electric shock to its tail when they touched the gill. After many rounds of the shock-accompanied prodding, the sea slug violently withdrew its gill at the slightest touch. The researchers found that the sea slug remembered this message for hours or even weeks.

More important than the discovery that sea slugs had memories was the finding that memory seems to be written in chemicals. Shocking the sea slug's gill releases the neurotransmitter serotonin at the synapses, and this chemical release basically provides a reminder that the gill was shocked. This "memory" informs the nerve cell to send out chemical commands to retract the gill the next time it is touched. If nature builds complexity out of simplicity, then the mechanism used by the sea slug might work in the human brain as well. Chemicals, then, might be the ink with which memories are written.

The inelegant sea slug with its elegant memory. *How do neurobiologists study the sea slug to learn about memory?*

Broad-Scale Architecture

While some neuroscientists are unveiling the cellular basis of memory, others are examining the broad-scale architecture of memory in the brain. In a series of studies, Mortimer Mishkin and his colleagues (Mishkin & Appenzellar, 1987) examined the role of brain structures in the memories of monkeys. They assume that the same brain structures that are responsible for memory in monkeys are also responsible for memory in humans, an assumption that generates spirited debate.

In a typical experiment, Mishkin and his colleagues compare the memory of monkeys who have an intact brain with the memory of monkeys who have undergone surgery that has impaired some part of their brain. Impairment at any point in the "memory circuit" can produce deficits in memory. Damage to the amygdala and the hippocampus, two brain regions deep inside the brain at the tip of the brain stem, cause the most serious deficits in memory. However, damage to the thalamus and the mammillary body causes deficits as well, as does damage to the basal forebrain and the prefrontal cortex. Figure 7.14 shows the location of all six of these brain structures that are involved in the memory of monkeys.

Is there any evidence that these brain structures are responsible for memory in humans? Researchers have found that evidence from humans who have brain damage due to strokes, Alzheimer's disease, Korsakoff's syndrome, and operations intended to cure epilepsy implicates the same brain structures in human memory. Recall the case of H. M., who was virtually unable to recall events that had occurred since his operation for epilepsy. H. M.'s hippocampus had been destroyed.

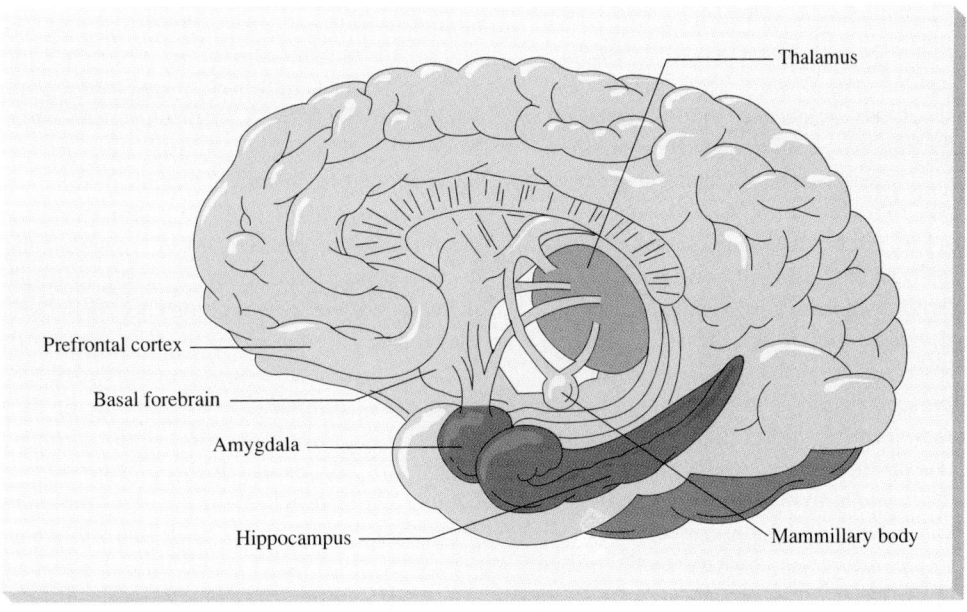

Figure 7.14

Memory Circuit Involved in Declarative Memory
Mortimer Mishkin and his colleagues have demonstrated that the amygdala, hippocampus, thalamus, mammillary body, basal forebrain, and prefrontal cortex are involved in declarative memory. Neuroscientists call the combination of brain structures involved in memory a "memory circuit."

The "memory circuit" outlined by Mishkin and his colleagues appears to be involved in declarative memory only, not being responsible for procedural memory. The procedural memory of human amnesiacs such as H. M. also is preserved, which means that procedural memory likely has a memory circuit somewhere else in the brain. As yet, neuroscientists have yet to discover this circuit. Ultimately, researchers may be able to link each type and subtype of memory we have discussed (episodic, semantic, priming, sensory memory, and working memory) to discrete brain circuits.

As neuroscientists discover the identity of memory circuits in the brain, might we reach a point at which the psychological study of memory becomes unimportant? That's unlikely. First, we are far from working out all of the complexities of the neurochemical underpinnings in human memory. And second, even if we were successful in unraveling the neurochemical mystery of memory, each person's private kingdom of memories will remain intact.

Cultural Influences on Memory

A culture sensitizes its members to certain objects and events in the environment, which in turn can influence the nature of memory (Mistry & Rogoff, 1994). Remember from our discussion of schema theory that Sir Frederick Bartlett believed that a person's background, which is encoded in schemas, is revealed in the way the person reconstructs a story. This effect of background on memory is called the **culture specificity hypothesis,** *which states that cultural experiences determine what is socially relevant in a person's life and, therefore, what the person is most likely to remember.*

Cross-cultural studies have often treated memory as a context-free skill rather than an activity that is embedded in a cultural context. Ignoring the degree to which memory is intertwined with culture has led researchers into some interesting mistakes that reveal a strong Western bias. For example, Western individuals routinely outperform non-Western individuals on skills that involve recalling words or pictures. Critics of this procedure suggest that performance differences should not be attributed to some natural Western superiority in memory functions, but, rather, that using objects more familiar to Western culture in the testing procedure confers an advantage on Westerners. In addition, formal schooling practices in the West, which emphasize rehearsal strategies, prepare Western students better for the specific type of recall required in tasks of this kind (Mistry & Rogoff, 1994).

In contrast, cross-cultural studies that respect cross-cultural specificity try to examine memory processes in contexts that incorporate meaningful materials and organization. For example, Bartlett (1932) described the social meaningfulness in a case study of a cowherd in the Swazi tribe of southeastern Africa. In this agrarian culture, the cowherd remembered, a year after the events, identifying marks and prices from cow sales in which he had been only peripherally involved. Cattle herding is the primary economic resource of the Swazi, so any aspect of cattle care takes on social significance. Another example of the cultural specificity of meaningfulness can be found in the enormous

amounts of information that can be transmitted in oral traditions. In certain communities, storytellers can repeat complex narratives that not only demonstrate impressive memory but also help to maintain traditions within the community (Cole & Scribner, 1977).

We might hypothesize that cultural specificity explains why basketball fans can rattle off NBA statistics long after nonfans have heard more than they care to. Perhaps you know people who have excellent memories for their preferred content areas.

Research in Other Cultures

In an experiment conducted among the Tumbuka tribe in Zambia, researchers investigated the culture specificity of time (Deregowski, 1970). The investigator reasoned that memory for time concepts would be greater among groups for whom time was culturally valued. He selected two contrasting groups: students living in town, whose daily experiences usually meant adhering to strict time schedules, and people living in a rural village, whose lives did not depend on clocks. The subjects were given a short story containing eight numerical details, four of which dealt with time. After the participants heard the story, they were asked questions designed to elicit how much numerical information they had retained. Predictably the rural inhabitants recalled less information relating to time than did the students, but they recalled just as many nontemporal numerical details. Research such as this suggests that cultural experiences influence *what* we remember.

In another study, two dimensions of memory and cultural contexts were studied: structural features of memory, such as echoic memory and short-term memory, which develop early in life, and control processes, such as retrieval strategies, which are more likely to be influenced by cultural and environmental experiences, such as schooling (Wagner, 1980). The participants were males from 7 years of age through adulthood who lived in the northwest African country of Morocco. The groups were from rural or urban areas and were either educated or illiterate. Their short-term memory for seven drawings was assessed. The researcher found that all the groups of Moroccans tended to remember the last (most recent) drawing. The recency effect is a structural dimension of memory (see the serial position effect in figure 7.11). However, the tendency to remember the first drawing (the primacy effect) was much more pronounced among the educated Moroccans and, to a lesser extent, among the uneducated urban Moroccans. The primacy effect is more strongly influenced by the control process of rehearsal. This study showed that the cultural factors of education and urbanization influence an important aspect of memory, the primacy effect.

Educational Implications

Because we do not have comparable information from students in diverse schools within a single culture, we cannot say precisely what it is about education that influences memory skills. Schools train students to use specialized memory strategies—such as committing large amounts of information to memory in a short time and

Cultural Literacy

In his provocative book, *Cultural Literacy*, University of Virginia English Professor E. D. Hirsch (1987) argued that every literate adult should learn certain things in school to function well in contemporary society. To get a feel for the kinds of information Hirsch regarded as important, look at the following terms and see if you can identify the significance of each one:

1066	burgher
Zurich	golden rule
mainspring	nicotine
golden fleece	probate court

These words were randomly selected from a glossary of several thousand that Hirsch believes should define every literate person's "memory knowledge." The glossary includes terms drawn from history, literature, government, science, math, art, geography, and other areas of knowledge.

Simply, the following are Hirsch's bold claims.

1. To be a full participant in our modern democratic culture, it is necessary to be literate.
2. Adult literacy is built on a broad and wide-ranging base of knowledge.
3. This knowledge is *schematic*. It doesn't have to be detailed or complete. For example, it's sufficient to know that nicotine is an ingredient in cigarettes or that Zurich is a city in Switzerland.
4. American schools used to make students commit more schematic knowledge to memory. The curriculum had substance and factual content. Recently it has slipped into faddish concerns such as critical thinking, process, and developmental curricula.
5. We need to overhaul the American educational curriculum, beginning during the earliest years of elementary school, to incorporate more memorization of facts, specifically of the sort outlined in Hirsch's glossary.
6. To guarantee that recommendation 5 is taken seriously, school systems should immediately begin creating tests to determine whether the base of children's knowledge is improving.

What do you think of Hirsch's ideas? Do they make sense to you? Do you accept his arguments? If you haven't already done so, you might want to read his book and think about it further. Few educators could, or would want to, argue against the notion that a broad base of knowledge is important. A child's general knowledge is an important factor in learning and probably is related to success as an adult in our literate culture. However, Hirsch's approach raises several questions: Should we be content with the kind of "shallow" knowledge that would be encouraged by a test like Hirsch's? Should everyone be expected to be a Renaissance collector and memorizer of information? More important, how will we solve the perpetually thorny issue of who defines what is on the test and what constitutes contemporary cultural literacy? Shouldn't we also be concerned about improving children's memory skills, not just their memory knowledge? Are the contributions of people from a wide variety of cultural groups adequately recognized in the creation of these tests?

---

using logical organization and categories to remember information—that have few analogies in societies without formal schooling.

In some cultures, children are required to memorize huge amounts of information. For example, in Iran children must memorize large blocks of cultural and religious texts. Iranians are often surprised at how little Americans seem to know. Some educational reformists in the United States are also concerned about Americans' general lack of cultural literacy. To read more about this issue, turn to Sociocultural Worlds 7.2.

IMPROVING MEMORY

In the fifth century B.C., the Greek poet Simonides attended a banquet. After he left, the building collapsed, crushing the guests and maiming their bodies beyond recognition. Simonides was able to identify the bodies by using a memory technique. He generated vivid images of each individual and mentally pictured where they had sat at the banquet table. Specific techniques such as this, many of which involve imagery, have been used to improve memory. **Mnemonics** *is the term used for techniques designed to make memory more efficient.*

Imagery

The memory technique Simonides used is called the *method of loci*. It is an imagery technique you can apply to memory problems of your own. Suppose you have a list of chores to do. To ensure that you remember them all, first associate a concrete object with each chore. A trip to the store becomes a dollar bill, a telephone call to a friend becomes a telephone, cleanup duty becomes a broom, and so on. Then produce an image of each object so you can imagine it in a particular location in a familiar building, such as your house. You might imagine the dollar bill in the kitchen, the telephone in the dining room, and so on. The vividness of the image and the unusual placement virtually guarantee

Developing Cross-Cultural Precaution

When memory experts attempted to compare the memory skills of 9-year-olds from different cultures, they took great pains to make the contexts as comparable as possible. Rogoff and Waddell (as reported in Rogoff & Mistry, 1985) compared the quality of story recall of children from the United States to that of Mayan children living in Guatemala. When they tested the Mayan children, the researchers selected stories from the Mayan oral traditions and adapted them for research purposes. They ensured that the Mayan children would hear the stories in their own dialect from a familiar young adult in familiar surroundings. The researchers tested the children by having them repeat the story to another familiar person, this time an older woman that the children already knew. The researchers were shocked to discover that the Mayan children's recall was very poor in comparison to that of children in the United States. Since the researchers had taken so many precautions to enhance the Mayan children's comfort level, should they conclude that Mayan children have poorer memories than children from the United States?

The answer is no. The researchers neglected to take into account an important social tradition that enhanced the children's difficulty. Mayan culture discourages children from giving information to an elder, because the Mayans believe it demonstrates lack of respect. For example, when Mayan children are asked to give a message to an elder, they conclude the message by saying "Cha" ("so I have been told") so they do not seem impertinent. When the researchers included telling a story to an elder in the test conditions in order to test story recall, they virtually guaranteed that Mayan children would render a diminished performance out of politeness.

This wonderful error in an otherwise careful design illustrates the difficulty of *making accurate inferences from observations* when the data are incomplete.

recollection. It also helps if you mentally move logically through the house as you place the images.

A second imagery strategy is the *peg method,* in which a set of mental pegs, such as numbers, have items attached to them. For instance, you might begin with something like: "One is a bun, two is a shoe, three is a tree," and so forth up to as many as ten to twenty numbers. Once you can readily reproduce these rhymes, you can use them as mental pegs. For example, if you were required to remember a list of items in a specific order—such as the directions to someone's house—you could use the following mental pegs: one-bun-left on Market; two-shoe-right on Sandstone; three-tree-right on Balboa, and so on. Then develop an image for each direction: I left the bun at the market; my right shoe got caught in the sand and stone; there's a tree right on Balboa. When you have to retrieve the directions, you select the appropriate cue word, such as *bun* or *shoe,* and this should stimulate the production of the compound image with the correct response. Researchers have been encouraged by the effectiveness of such strategies in improving memory (McDaniel & Pressley, 1987).

Creating images to enhance memory can be an effective study tool. For example, you can illustrate elements of whatever will be stored in and retrieved from memory. This technique is also recommended as a means of remembering names. For instance, if you can visualize the face of someone whose name you have yet to learn, select some image that might remind you of the person's name. By putting the two together, the name might be easier to retrieve at some future social moment.

To read further about putting names and faces together, turn to Applications in Psychology 7.2.

Another example of the use of imagery to enhance memory can be found at the end of each chapter of this text. As you have probably noticed, cognitive "maps" are provided as a way of visualizing the main sections of the chapter.

Techniques Using Words

Some mnemonics involve word play rather than imagery. A simple mnemonic strategy for memorizing lists involves creating a memorable word using the first letter of each word in the list. You saw one example of this approach in the chapter on perception. *ROY G. BIV* represents the colors of the visible portion of the light-wave spectrum: red, orange, yellow, green, blue, indigo, and violet.

Another example of this strategy—ARESIDORI—denotes the components of memory: (1) Attention, (2) Rehearsal, (3) Elaboration, (4) Semantic processing, (5) Imagery, (6) Distinctiveness, (7) Organization, (8) Retrieval, (9) Interest (Ellis, 1987). *Interest* refers to motivation. Intrinsic interest in the ideas you are studying will make their encoding and retrieval much easier. It is helpful to determine which of the principles of ARESIDORI you already use effectively and which you could use more often in order to improve your study habits.

In this chapter, we have studied many different aspects of memory. In the next chapter, we will continue our discussion of learning and cognition by focusing on thinking, language, and intelligence.

I'll Never Forget What's-His-Name

Have you ever had trouble remembering someone's name? Probably so. A face might look familiar, but the name escapes you. This problem can be helped with the use of mnemonics.

Remembering someone's name can be broken down into three subproblems: remembering the face, remembering the name, and remembering the connection between the two. To remember the face, look at it closely while focusing on a distinctive feature, such as a large nose. To remember the name, try to find a meaning in it, and assign this a key word. As with a foreign language, you might think about a part of the name that sounds like an English word.

Finally, to remember the connection between the face and the name, think of an image that links the key word and the distinctive feature in the face. If you have just been introduced to Mr. Clausen, a man with the large nose, you might think of the English word *claws* as a key word for *Clausen*. Now imagine a large lobster claw tearing away at Clausen's large nose. When you see Mr. Clausen the next time, recall this image and the name *Clausen* should come to mind.

Another technique for remembering someone's name involves an expanded pattern of rehearsal. When you are introduced to someone, repeat the person's name immediately. You might say, "Tom Naylor? Hello, Tom." About 10 to 15 seconds later, look at the individual and rehearse his name silently. Do it again after 1 minute and then again after 3 minutes. The name will have a good chance of being retained in your long-term memory. One reason this spacing strategy works is that most forgetting occurs within a very short time after you first learn a fact (Loftus, 1980).

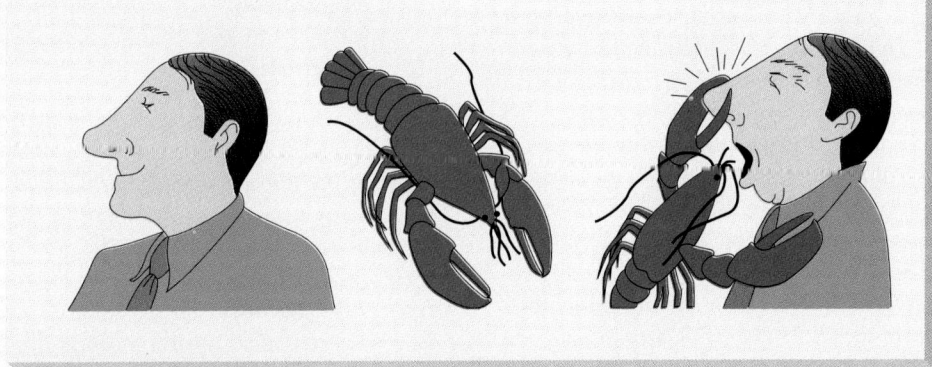

How might you effectively remember someone's name, such as Mr. Clausen?

REVIEW

The Nature and Nurture of Memory, and Mnemonics and Memory Strategies

The nature and nurture of memory involve the neurobiological basis of memory (nature) and the cultural dimensions of memory (nurture). In the study of the neurobiological basis of memory, a major issue is the extent to which memory is localized or distributed. Single neurons are involved in memory, but some neuroscientists believe that most memories are stored in circuits of about 1,000 neurons. There is no specific memory center in the brain; many parts of the brain participate in the memory of an event.

A culture sensitizes its members to certain objects and events in the environment, and these cultural experiences can influence the nature of memory. Bartlett's schema theory and Hirsch's ideas about cultural literacy reflect the role of culture in memory.

Mnemonics are techniques that improve memory. Many of these involve imagery, including the method of loci and the peg method. Systems based on a number of aspects of our knowledge about memory have been developed, including ARESIDORI, to improve memory.

"Are You Sure About That?": Declarative Memory and Confidence

Think back to the last time you had an argument with someone whom you cared about, an argument that centered on whose memory was most accurate. Your serious disagreement probably reflected different "realities" constructed out of the same experience. Let's explore systematically many of the ways in which two individuals can disagree about what constitutes the "truth" of any situation. In how many ways can individual differences affect common understanding?

1. *Differences in attention at the level of the sensory register and working memory.* Just because two people share the same physical space doesn't mean they "take in" the same sensory data. Whether the stimulus is visual or auditory, two people might extract different elements of the experience for further processing in working memory.

2. *Differences in the quality of working memory.* Individuals differ in the efficiency and effectiveness of their working memory. Some people seem to process information quickly; others labor harder to convert working memory contents into long-term memory.

3. *Differences in the strength of semantic long-term memory.* People differ in the kinds of ready access they have to different ideas in long-term memory. For example, some people readily learn a variety of facts about art or gardening or sports. Some have a big investment in developing expertise in specific areas; others find such endeavors boring or foolish. These areas of specialty in semantic memory can be a source of differences in different people's memories.

4. *Differences in schemas as a basis for attention and reconstruction.* We enter into situations with different schemas in different stages of development that shape our expectations about how things will work. Schemas filter out what we do not find to be important and can influence what we recall through reconstruction. We might believe our memories to be accurate not because they are accurate but because they seem to fit best with our general expectations about how things *should have been.*

5. *Differences in the quality (and quantity) of episodic recall.* Some people seem to have a knack for describing details of interpersonal discussions. Others seem to extract only larger details. These differences in ability show up in partners with maddening frequency.

Reexamine your own position in your argument with your friend. What elements were produced by your own episodic memory? Do any of these elements explain how your disagreement with your friend might have arisen?

- Did you both process the same elements of the situation?
- Did you both process working memory efficiently?
- Did differences in semantic memory affect your position?
- Could different scripts influence attention?
- Could aspects of the problem have been reconstructed?
- Did you both pay attention to the same details of the episode?

So who was wrong and who was right? Regardless of how convinced we are that we have a handle on the truth and that our friend is wrong (deluded, stupid, misguided, or mentally unbalanced), we have to conclude that there might be other interpretations. The number of points in the memory process that are vulnerable to error should temper our convictions about the accuracy of our own recall and help us have a more open-minded stance toward resolving differences of opinion. The analysis also supports the importance of *actively taking the perspective of others in solving problems,* even when we run the risk of demonstrating our own fallibility.

It isn't so astonishing the number of things that I can remember, as the number of things I remember that aren't so.

Mark Twain

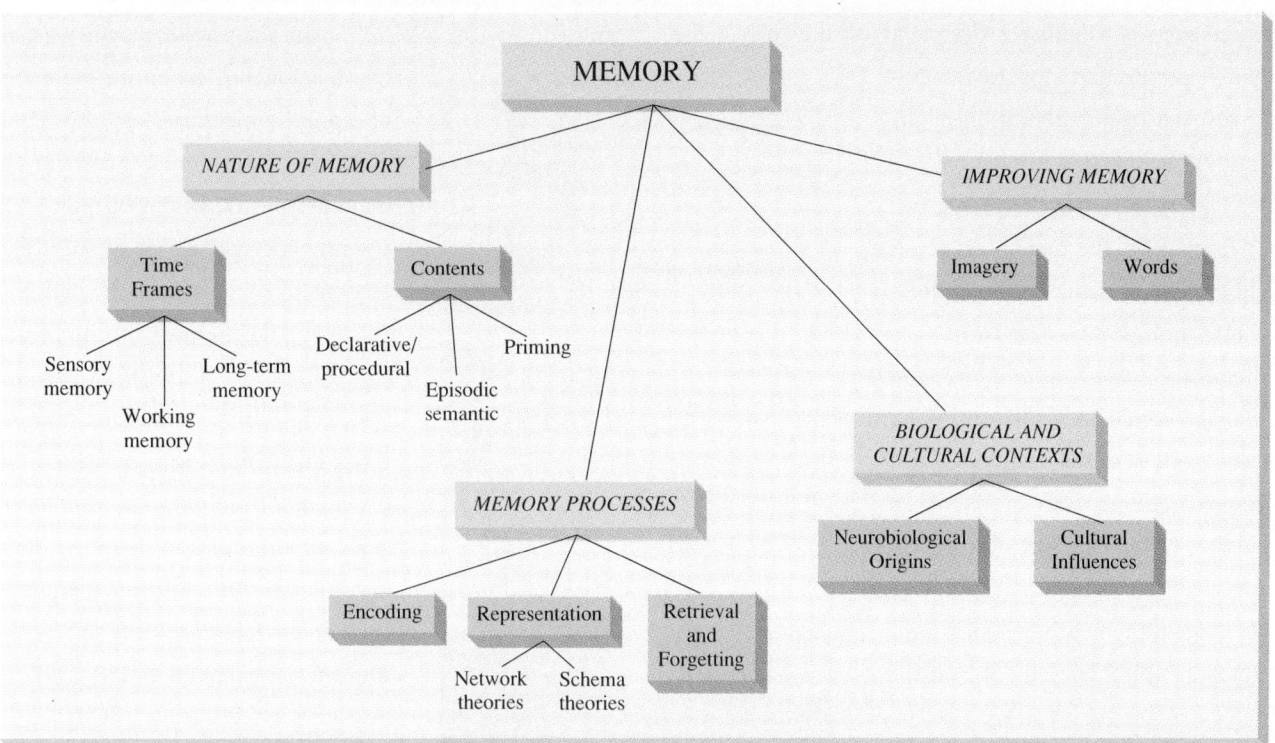

We began our exploration of memory by studying the nature of memory and memory's time frames— sensory memory, working memory, and long-term memory. Then we evaluated the contents of memory—declarative and procedural memory, episodic and semantic memory, and priming. Next, we turned our attention to memory processes—encoding, representation, retrieval, and forgetting. We also studied the biological and cultural foundations of memory as well as improving memory (through imagery and techniques using words). Don't forget that you can obtain a more detailed overall summary of the entire chapter by rereading the reviews on pages 221, 224, 234, and 239.

By far the dominant perspective in this chapter is the cognitive perspective. Memory processes are at the core of the cognitive perspective. How we remember was part of our definition of the cognitive perspective in chapter 1—where we defined it as the perspective that emphasizes the mental processes involved in knowing: how we direct our attention, how we perceive, *how we remember,* and how we think and solve problems. In addition to the memory part of this definition, we also discussed the process of attention (pp. 221–222). The neurobiological perspective was also represented in our evaluation of the neurobiological basis of memory (pp. 234–236). So was the sociocultural perspective, in our coverage of cultural factors in memory (pp. 236–237). And the psychoanalytic perspective was touched on in our evaluation of repressed memories (p. 233). However, we underscore that by far the main perspective in this chapter is the cognitive perspective. It permeates all sections of the chapter—the nature of memory and memory's time frames (pp. 214–220), contents of memory (pp. 218–220), interactions between types of memory (pp. 219–220), the processes of memory (pp. 221–233), representation of knowledge in memory (pp. 225–228), the nature and nurture of memory (pp. 234–237), and improving memory (pp. 237–239).

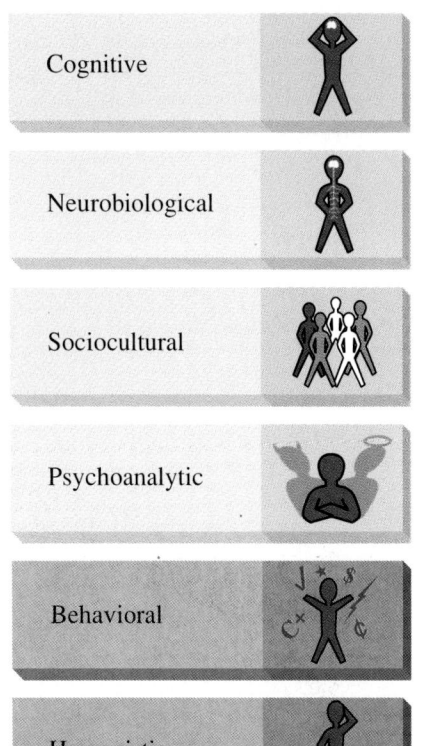

Cognitive

Neurobiological

Sociocultural

Psychoanalytic

Behavioral

Humanistic

KEY TERMS

memory The retention of information over time. Psychologists study how information is initially placed, or encoded, into memory; how it is retained, or stored, after being encoded; and how it is found, or retrieved, for a certain purpose later. 214

sensory memory Memory that holds information from the world in its original sensory form for only an instant, not much longer than the brief time for which one is exposed to the visual, auditory, and other sensations. 215

echoic memory The auditory sensory registers in which information is retained for up to several seconds. 215

iconic memory The visual sensory registers, in which information is retained for about ¼ second. 215

working memory Also sometimes called short-term memory, this is a limited-capacity memory system in which information is retained for as long as 30 seconds, unless the information is rehearsed, in which case it can be retained longer. 216

memory span The number of digits an individual can report back in order following a single presentation of them. 216

chunking The grouping, or "packing," of information into higher-order units that can be remembered as single units. Chunking expands working memory by making large amounts of information more manageable. 216

maintenance rehearsal The conscious repetition of information that increases the length of time the information stays in working memory. 216

eidetic memory Also called photographic memory; a form of memory involving especially vivid details. The small number of individuals who have eidetic memory can recall significantly more details of visual information than most of us can. 216

long-term memory A type of memory that holds huge amounts of information for a long period of time, relatively permanently. 218

declarative memory The conscious recollection of information, such as specific facts or events, and, at least in humans, information that can be verbally communicated. Declarative memory has been called "knowing that" and, more recently, "explicit memory." 219

procedural memory Knowledge in the form of skills and cognitive operations about how to do something. Procedural memory cannot be consciously recollected, at least not in the form of specific events or facts; this makes procedural memory difficult, if not impossible, to communicate verbally. Procedural memory has been called "knowing how" and, more recently, "implicit memory." 219

episodic memory The retention of information about the where and when of life's happenings. 219

semantic memory A person's general knowledge about the world. It includes knowledge about a person's fields of expertise, general academic knowledge of the sort learned in school, and "everyday" knowledge about meanings of words, famous individuals, important places, and common things. Semantic memory knowledge appears to be independent of the individual's personal identity with the past. 220

PRACTICAL KNOWLEDGE ABOUT PSYCHOLOGY

TOTAL RECALL

(1984) by Joan Minninger.
New York: Pocket Books.

This book is filled with helpful techniques for improving your memory. The author has given seminars on improving memory to a number of corporations, including IBM and General Electric.

Tips on how to improve your memory draw on such important dimensions of memory as retrieval cues, depth of processing, linkages between short-term and long-term memory, episodic memory, and semantic memory. You also learn how to remember what you read, how to remember names and faces, how to remember dates and numbers, how to remember what you hear, and effective study strategies.

RESOURCES FOR PSYCHOLOGY AND IMPROVING HUMANKIND

Human Memory (1990)
by A. Baddeley
Boston: Allyn & Bacon

The chapter you have just read highlighted Baddeley's working memory model, a contemporary view. In his book, Baddeley extensively reviews research on memory to support the development of his memory model.

The 36-Hour Day (1981)
by Nancy Mace and Peter Rabins
Baltimore: Johns Hopkins University Press

Alzheimer's disease is a widespread disorder in aging individuals. Among its characteristics is memory loss. This book is a family guide to caring for persons with Alzheimer's.

Witness for the Defense (1991)
by E. Loftus and K. Ketcham
New York: St. Martin's Press

This excellent book provides insight about ways in which the reconstructive nature of memory can generate extensive but error-filled reports of the past.

Your Memory: How It Works and How to Improve It (1988)
by K. L. Higbee
Englewood Cliffs, NJ: Prentice Hall

This practical book outlines strategies for using the principles of memory to remember all sorts of things in your personal life.

Thinking, Language, and Intelligence

The mind is an enchanting thing.

Marianne Moore

The Story of Jay Leno: Intelligence with a Difference

Jay Leno became the talk of the entertainment world a few years ago when he was named the new permanent host of "The Tonight Show." He had served as a substitute host for the show for many years on Tuesday nights when Johnny Carson, legendary host for 30 years, was off. Leno polished his comedy skills on the road, sometimes playing as many as three hundred gigs per year. Admirers like his clean humor, political expertise, and affable nature. However, most people do not realize that Jay Leno rose to prominence despite a learning difference that influences his ability to use language.

Born James Douglas Muir Leno in Andover, Massachusetts, Leno had a blissful childhood (Stengel, 1992). His father, Angelo, was a successful insurance salesman whom Leno describes as "the funniest guy at the office." His mother, Catherine, worked in the home. He credits his parents with nurturing his sense of humor. He also describes his own humor as rising from his "female" side. He takes special pleasure in making women laugh, attested to by his strict avoidance of wife jokes.

School, however, was not much to his liking. He was the classroom cutup and prided himself on being able to make his teachers laugh. His fifth-grade teacher speculated that if Jay "used the effort toward his studies that he uses to be humorous, he would be an A student." In retrospect, Jay's humor might have served to cover up some insecurities he had about his academic skills.

He began experimenting with stand-up comedy when he was enrolled at Emerson College in Boston. He graduated and became a salesman for a Rolls-Royce dealership but left the job to try his hand at comedy full-time after seeing a terrible comedian on "The Tonight Show." He knew he could do better. After a few appearances, Leno launched a career that ultimately led him into the spotlight as the permanent host of "The Tonight Show."

On rare occasions, Leno demonstrates the impact of his learning difference, dyslexia. People with dyslexia

Jay Leno has succeeded in the field of entertainment despite his learning difference.

sometimes have difficulty with the order of letters in words. Refreshingly, Leno is open about his dyslexia. He tosses off verbal misfires with statements such as, "The things a dyslexic can do to language. . . ." His ownership of the difficulties associated with dyslexia has inspired children and their families who struggle with the impact of learning differences on school performance. Like many other successful adults, Jay Leno demonstrates that a learning difference does not automatically produce failure or social stigma.

PREVIEW

The story of Jay Leno illustrates many aspects of psychology that we will examine in this chapter. We will explore the nature of thinking, including how we form concepts, how we solve problems and reason, and how we think critically. We will evaluate how language and thought influence each other. We will also look at intelligence—how it is conceptualized, how it is measured, and its variations. We begin by exploring the positive impact of the cognitive revolution in psychology.

The Cognitive Revolution in Psychology

Behaviorism was a dominant force in psychology until the late 1950s and 1960s, when many psychologists began to realize that they could not understand or explain human behavior without making reference to mental processes (Gardner, 1985). The term *cognitive psychology* became a label for approaches that sought to explain observable behavior by investigating mental processes and structures that cannot be directly observed.

Although behaviorists like John B. Watson had argued that psychology could not be a legitimate "scientific" discipline unless it restricted itself to the study and description of directly observable events, proponents of the cognitive revolution argued that scientific explanations usually explain the observable using terms or concepts that cannot be directly observed (Weimer, 1974). For example, Isaac Newton explained the behavior of falling objects using the concept of gravitational force, a force that could not be directly observed.

Although the term *introspection* is seldom seen in contemporary psychological research, cognitive psychologists still use subjective descriptions of thinking as one source of information about thought processes. These subjective descriptions are sometimes referred to as *problem-solving protocols*. Unlike earlier research that was based primarily on subjective reports, cognitive psychologists realize the limitations of subjective reports and use a variety of other measures to explore thinking and mental processes. For example, cognitive psychologists might examine the precise time taken to make decisions, the accuracy of decisions, the type of information used by a person to make a decision, or even the ability to transfer thinking skills from one context to another. Indeed, most current investigations of thinking use a combination of measures to explore thinking and mental processes. While a variety of factors stimulated the growth of cognitive psychology, perhaps one of the more important was the development of computers (Johnson-Laird, 1989; Stillings & others, 1995).

The first modern computer, developed by John von Neumann in the late 1940s, showed that inanimate machines could perform logical operations. This indicated that some mental operations might be modeled by computers, possibly telling us something about the way cognition works. Cognitive psychologists often use the computer as an analogy to help explain the relation between cognition and the brain. The physical brain is described as the computer's hardware and cognition as its software (see figure 8.1).

While the development of computers played an important role in psychology's cognitive revolution, it is important to realize that inanimate computers and human brains function quite differently in some respects (Restak, 1988). For example, each brain cell, or neuron, is alive and can be altered in its functioning by many types of events in its biological environment. Current attempts to simulate neural networks greatly simplify the behavior of neurons. The brain derives information about the world through a rich system of visual, auditory, olfactory, gustatory, tactile, and vestibular sensory receptors that operate on analog signals. Most computers receive information from a human who has already digitally coded the information and represented it in a way that removes much of the ambiguity in the natural world. Attempts to use computers to process visual information or spoken language have achieved only limited success in highly constrained situations where much of the natural ambiguity is removed. The human brain also has an incredible ability to learn new rules, relationships, concepts, and patterns that it can generalize to novel situations. In comparison, current approaches to artificial intelligence are quite limited in their ability to learn and generalize.

The differences between computers and brains are reflected in the fact that computers can do some things better than humans, and humans can do some things better than computers. Computers can perform complex numerical calculations much faster and more accurately than humans could ever hope to. Computers can also apply and follow rules more consistently and with fewer errors than humans can and represent complex mathematical patterns better than humans can. Although a computer can simulate

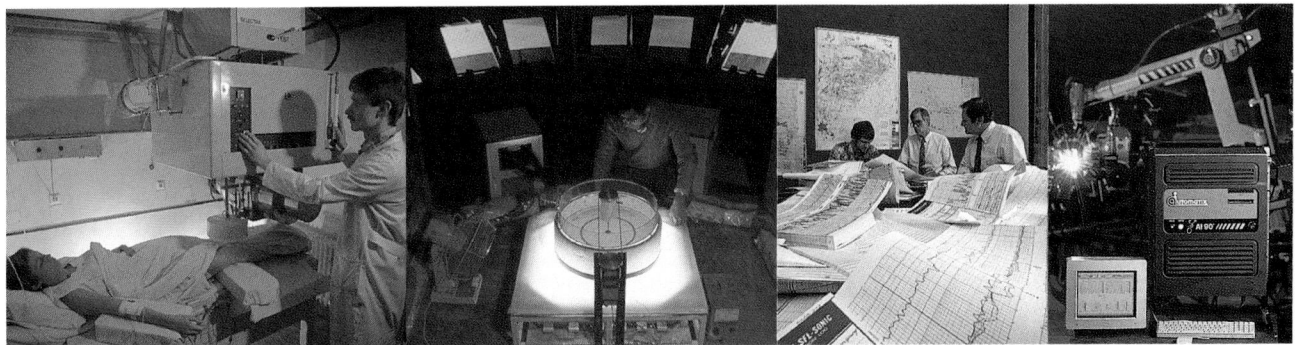

Expert systems are used for advances in medical diagnosis and treatment, weather prediction, analysis of geological formations, and automobile construction.

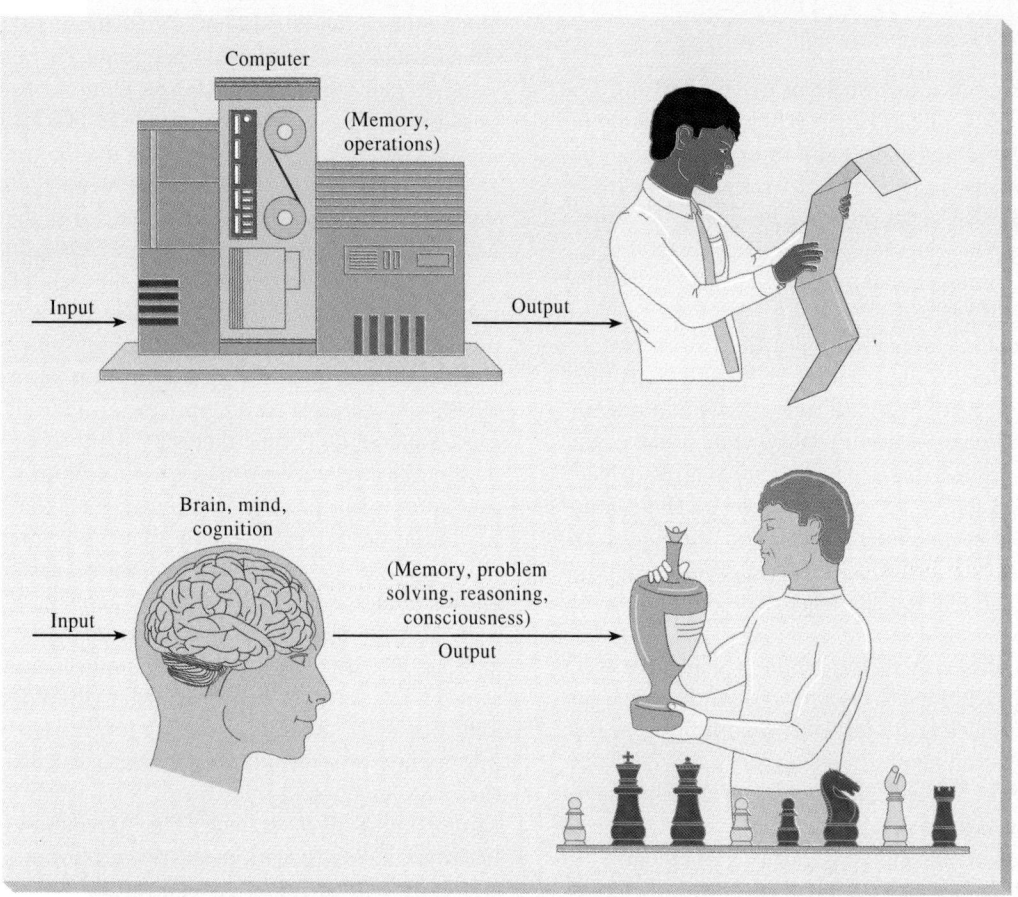

FIGURE 8.1

Computers and Cognition: An Analogy
The physical brain is described by cognitive psychologists as analogous to a computer's hardware; cognition is described as analogous to a computer's software.

certain types of learning that may improve its ability to recognize patterns or use rules of thumb to make decisions, it does not have the means to develop new learning goals. Furthermore, the human mind is aware of itself; the computer is not. Indeed, no computer is likely to approach the richness of human consciousness. In short, the brain's extraordinary capabilities will probably not be mimicked in a comprehensive manner by computers anytime in the near future.

The computer's role in cognitive psychology continues to increase, giving rise in recent years to a field called **artificial intelligence (AI),** *the science of creating machines capable of performing activities that require intelligence when they are done by people.* AI is especially helpful in tasks requiring speed, persistence, and a vast memory (Wagman, 1995). For example, today we have chess-playing programs that can beat everyone but the best players our species has to offer.

These so-called **expert systems,** *computer-based systems for assessing knowledge and making decisions in advanced skill areas,* not only have been applied to playing chess, but have been designed to assist in the diagnosis of medical illnesses,

diagnosing equipment failures, developing integrated circuits, evaluating loan applicants, advising students about what courses to take, and a broad range of other problems. These programs are especially beneficial when human experts are in short supply or are not available in the locations where they are needed. Expert systems also might help to preserve the expertise of talented individuals when they retire or die.

THINKING

Information in memory is manipulated and transformed through thinking. We can think about the concrete, such as boats and beaches, and the abstract, such as freedom and independence. We can think about the past (life in the 1940s, 1960s, 1980s) and the future (life in the year 2000). We can think about reality (how to do better on the next test in this course) and fantasy (what it would be like to meet Catherine the Great or land a spacecraft on Jupiter). When we think, we often use concepts. What characterizes these basic units of thinking, and how are they formed?

Concept Formation

We have a special ability for categorizing things. We know that apples and oranges are fruits but have different tastes and colors. We know that Porsches and Yugos are both automobiles, but we also know that they differ in cost, speed, and prestige. How do we know that apples and oranges are fruits and that Porsches and Yugos are automobiles, despite their differences? The answer lies in our ability to ignore their different forms and group them on the basis of their features. For example, all Porsches and Yugos have four wheels and a steering wheel and provide transportation. In other words, we have a concept of what an automobile is. A **concept** *is a category used to group objects, events, and characteristics on the basis of common properties.*

Why are concepts important? Without concepts, each object and event in our world would seem unique to us. Any kind of generalization would be impossible. Concepts allow us to relate experiences and objects. Weimaraners, cocker spaniels, and labrador retrievers are all called sporting dogs by the American Kennel Club. The concept of sporting dogs gives us a way to compare dogs.

Concepts grease the wheels of memory, making it more efficient. When we group objects to form a concept, we remember the characteristics of the concept rather than each object or experience. When one stockbroker tells another stockbroker that the Dow Jones Industrial Average went up today, the second broker knows that there is a good chance that IBM, Exxon, and General Motors, whose stocks contribute to the average, increased in value. The concept of the Dow Jones Industrial Average makes communication more efficient and probably jogs memory as well.

Concepts also keep us from "reinventing the wheel" each time we come across a piece of information. For example, we don't have to relearn what the Dow Jones Industrial Average is each time we pick up a newspaper. We already know what the concept means. Concepts also provide clues about how to react to an object or experience. For example, if we see a bowl of pretzels, our concept of food lets us know it is okay to eat them. Concepts allow us to associate classes of objects or events. Some classes of objects are associated in structured patterns. For example, the Indigo Girls won a Grammy Award; Grammies are given for achievements in the music recording industry; music recording is a performing art.

Because concepts are so critical to our ability to make sense of the world around us, researchers have spent a lot of time studying the process of concept formation. In doing so, they have investigated our ability to discover a rule for why some objects fall within a concept whereas others do not. These rules are based on features or combinations of features. A common methodology uses geometric forms. For example, a rule for a concept might be "all stimuli that are triangles (but not circles or squares)," "all stimuli that are circles," "all stimuli that are colored red," or "stimuli that are both circles and red" ("all that are circles and red").

Drawing by Koren; © 1986 The New Yorker Magazine, Inc.

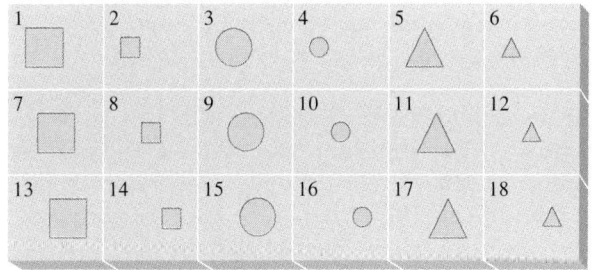

FIGURE 8.2

Typical Concept Formation Task
This array of cards might be presented to a number of subjects. The experimenter arbitrarily chooses the correct concept, such as "large circles," and then the subject tries to discover the rule that defines the concept by trial and error selection of cards that fit the rule.

To get a better sense of cognition, let's examine more closely how an experiment on concept formation might proceed. Figure 8.2 displays a number of cards shown to a person in a typical concept formation study (Moates & Schumacher, 1980). The shapes (square, circle, or triangle), sizes (small or large), and position (left, middle, or right) of the figures on the cards vary. The experimenter arbitrarily chooses a concept, such as "large circles," and asks the subjects to discover what concept she or he has chosen. They are shown an example of the concept (such as card 3) and asked to choose other cards until they discover the nature of the concept. After each choice, subjects are told whether or not the chosen card is an example of the concept.

An important process in concept formation is to develop hypotheses about what defines the concept and to test these hypotheses in new examples. Suppose you are an avid tennis player but think you are losing too many matches because your serve is weak. Despite hours of practice, your serve just isn't getting any better. Your problem might be that you have only a vague concept of what a "killer" serve is really like. To get a feel for the concept and to see how the best players serve, you head for the tennis courts. Based on your observations, you develop a hypothesis about the mechanics of an excellent serve. For example, after hours of watching the "weekend pros" ace their opponents, you decide that the ball must be tossed high, so that the server has to stretch to reach it, and that the server needs to swing the racket like a baseball pitcher throws a ball. You might want to scrutinize the serves of more-skilled players to see if they confirm your hypothesis. You'll also want to test the hypothesis in your own game to see if the two aspects of the hypothesis—that good servers toss the ball high and that they swing the racket like a baseball player throws a ball—improve your serve.

Even though your concept formation is on track and your tennis serve improves, chances are you'll still be somewhat dissatisfied. With a difficult concept (such as the mechanics of a good serve), you may need an expert—a professional tennis coach—to help you. The pro's concept is likely to include many more features than the ones you discovered, as well as complex rules related to those features. For example, the pro might tell you that tossing the ball high helps, but that it works much better if you rotate the grip on your racket counterclockwise. In general, concepts with more features and more complicated rules are more difficult to learn. Part of being an expert in any field is grasping the complicated rules of difficult concepts.

In any type of cognitive testing, it is important to keep in mind that cultural experience affects concept formation. For example, inner-city children might be at a disadvantage when reading textbooks that focus on suburban experiences rather than urban apartment life. Around the world, people perform better when asked questions that are consistent with their cultural experiences (Segall & others, 1990).

Although psychologists have learned much about concept formation, some believe that most of the research has been too artificial. Eleanor Rosch (1973) argues that real-life concepts are less precise than those used in many psychological experiments, such as the earlier example of "large circles." Real-life concepts, she says, often have "fuzzy boundaries"; that is, it often is unclear exactly which features are critical to a concept. Consider the concept "cup." A little thought might suggest five properties of cups: They (1) are concrete objects, (2) are concave, (3) can hold liquids and solids, (4) have handles, and (5) can be used to drink hot liquids. However, what about the cups in Chinese restaurants that do not have handles? What about the poor-quality paper cups that conduct too much heat to be used for hot drinks? Although such objects lack certain "critical features" of cups, we still call them cups.

Rosch also contends that our everyday concepts have "internal structure"; that is, some members of concepts are more typical of the concept than others are. Think of your concept of a football player: perhaps very muscular, big, and stressed out by the pressure of combining athletics and academics. Football players who match this description are said to be *prototypical*—they fit our prototype of a football player. However, some football players are large and do well in academic pursuits; others are skinny and fail every subject. They are not prototypical, but they are still football players. Thus, members of a conceptual category can vary greatly and still have the qualities that make them members of the category.

Problem Solving

It would be impossible to solve problems without using concepts. Think about driving, something most of us do every day. Signs and traffic signals every few blocks tell us to stop, yield, or proceed apace. Usually we don't think of these signs and signals as solutions to problems, but they are (Bransford & Stein, 1984). Most of the symbols that keep traffic moving so smoothly are the brainchild of William Eno, the "father

In the nineteenth century, New York City began to experience traffic jams. The horse-drawn vehicles were making street traffic dangerous. *How did William Eno solve this problem?*

of traffic safety." Eno, born in New York City in 1858, became concerned about the horrendous traffic jams in the city. Horse-drawn vehicles were making street traffic dangerous. Eno published a paper about the urgency of street traffic reform. His concept proposed solutions to the problem—stop signs, one-way streets, and pedestrian safety islands—ideas that affect our behavior today.

What is problem solving? **Problem solving** *is an attempt to find an appropriate way of attaining a goal when the goal is not readily available.* We face many problems in the course of our everyday lives—trying to figure out why our car won't start, planning how to get enough money to buy a stereo, working a jigsaw puzzle, or estimating our chances of winning at blackjack. Whatever the problem is, we want to come up with the best and fastest solution possible. John Bransford and Barry Stein (1984) developed an effective method of problem solving with a catchy title, IDEAL: Identify the problem, Define and represent the problem, Explore possible strategies, Act on the strategies, and Look back and evaluate the effects of your activities. Let's run through this problem-solving strategy step by step.

Identifying Problems

Before a problem can be solved, it first needs to be recognized and identified. Consider the problem two brothers faced. Ladislao and George Biro were proofreaders who spent a lot of their time correcting spelling mistakes and typographical errors in the days before computers. Even though fountain pens were messy, they recorded the errors they found in ink because pencil marks faded. The Biro brothers recognized they had a problem, so they came up with a solution—they invented the ballpoint pen. Their original company is now part of a corporation known as Bic.

The next time you receive a mail-order catalog, sit down and peruse it. Depending on the catalog, you'll find everything from continuous-feed pet food bowls to inflatable bathtub pillows. Most of the gadgets are good examples of clever solutions to common problems (see figure 8.3). The first step the inventors of these objects took was to identify a problem.

Defining Problems

The second step is to define the problem as carefully as possible. For example, a doctor recognizes her patient's symptoms as high blood pressure. The doctor knows that different sources, or definitions, of the problem call for different treatments. Both hardening of the arteries and everyday stress can produce high blood pressure; however, hardening of the arteries may require surgery, whereas reducing stress may require a change in lifestyle.

A problem well stated is a problem half-solved.

Charles Kettering

Defining the problem may sound simple. Sometimes it is, as in the case of studying before a big test or fixing a leaky faucet. However, many of life's most interesting problems are ill-defined. How can you write a book that will become a best-seller? What does it take before you can call yourself a success? What is happiness?

Exploring Alternative Approaches

The next step is to explore alternative strategies for solving the problem. To do this, analyze how you are reacting to the problem and then consider the options or strategies you might use. You might try dividing a problem into subproblems, attacking it piece by piece, or you might work a problem backward. Imagine that you need to meet someone for lunch across town and you don't want to be late. If you want to arrive at noon and know that it takes 30 minutes of travel time, the problem can easily be worked backward in time (noon – 30 minutes = 11:30 departure). Working backward is a good strategy when the goal is clear but the original intention is not.

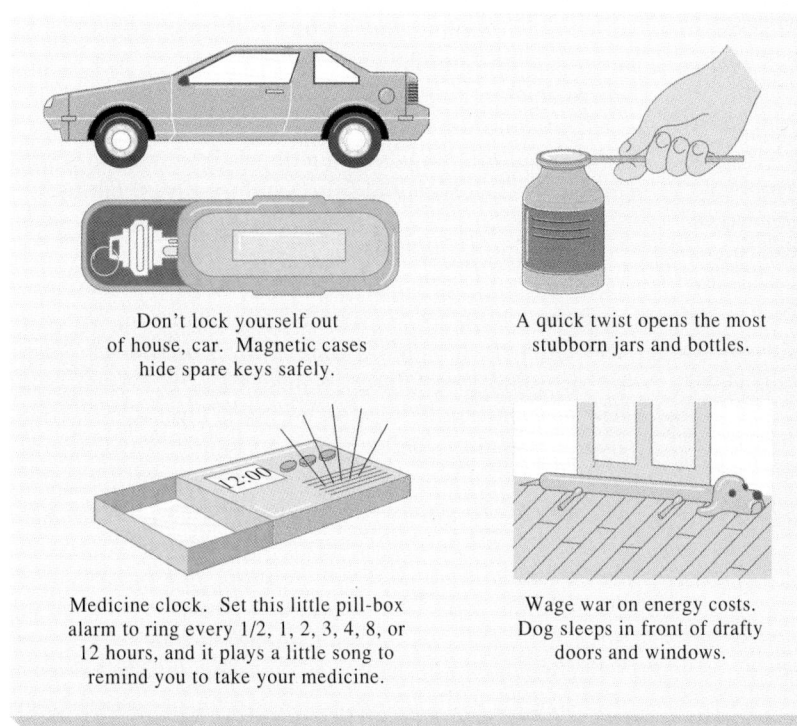

Don't lock yourself out of house, car. Magnetic cases hide spare keys safely.

A quick twist opens the most stubborn jars and bottles.

Medicine clock. Set this little pill-box alarm to ring every 1/2, 1, 2, 3, 4, 8, or 12 hours, and it plays a little song to remind you to take your medicine.

Wage war on energy costs. Dog sleeps in front of drafty doors and windows.

FIGURE 8.3

Inventions Designed to Solve Some Common Problems

Two strategies for problem solving are using algorithms and heuristics. **Algorithms** *are procedures that guarantee an answer to a problem.* When you solve a multiplication problem, you are using an algorithm—you learned this algorithm as part of your schooling. When you follow the directions for putting together a lawn chair, you are using an algorithm. In contrast to algorithms, **heuristics** *are rules of thumb that can suggest a solution to a problem but do not ensure that it will work.* Let's say you're heading to a friend's house and you've never been there before. You are driving around in an unfamiliar part of town, and after a while you realize you're lost. If you know your destination is north, you might use the heuristic of turning onto a road that heads in that direction. This procedure might work, but it also might fail—the road might end or turn off to the east.

Although we can solve some problems by using algorithms, we are usually forced to rely on heuristics. Working backward and dividing into subproblems are both heuristics. They do not guarantee a solution to the problem, but they often help.

Each of us occasionally gets into the mental rut of solving problems by using a particular strategy. A **learning set** *is a strategy an individual tends to use to solve problems.* Learning sets often serve us efficiently. Without them, we would waste time looking for the solution to a problem we already know. You may have encountered a problem with learning sets in your college classes. Let's say several of your professors base their exams primarily on lecture materials. You pore over your lecture notes and ace the exams, so you follow the same strategy for your psychology class and spend very little time studying the textbook. When you see the first exam in this class, you learn that the strategy is inappropriate—this exam has a number of questions based only on the text.

The following puzzle is often used to demonstrate the concept of a learning set. It's called the nine-dot problem. Take out a piece of paper and copy the arrangement of the dots:

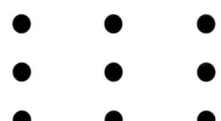

Without lifting your pencil, connect the dots using only four or three straight lines. Most people have difficulty— and lots just give up on—finding a solution to the nine-dot

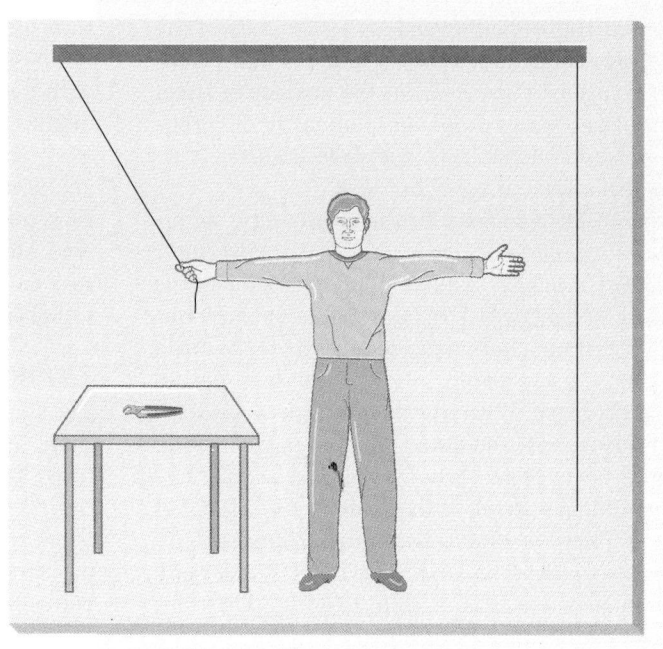

FIGURE 8.4

Maier String Problem
How can you tie the two strings together if you cannot reach them both at the same time?

problem. Part of the difficulty is that we have a learning set that tells us to think of the nine-dot configuration as a square. We consider the outer dots as the boundary and do not extend the lines beyond them, yet the solutions to the nine-dot problem, shown at the end of the chapter, require going outside the square.

If you've ever used a shoe to hammer a nail, you've overcome what's called "functional fixedness" to solve a problem. The concept of **functional fixedness,** *the inability to solve a problem because it is viewed only in terms of usual functions,* is similar to the concept of learning set. If the problem to be solved involves usual functions, then it can easily be solved, but, if the problem involves something new and different, solving the problem will be trickier. An example of functional fixedness involves pliers (Maier, 1931). The problem is to figure out how to tie together two strings that are hanging from a ceiling (see figure 8.4). If you hold one and then move toward the other, you cannot reach the second one. It seems as though you're stuck, but there is a pair of pliers on a table. Can you solve the problem?

The solution is to use the pliers as a weight and tie them to the end of one string (see figure 8.5). Swing this string back and forth like a pendulum. Then let go of the "weight" and grasp the stationary string. Finally, reach out and grab the swinging string. Your past experience with pliers makes this a difficult problem to solve. To solve the problem, you need to find a unique use for the pliers, in this case as a weight to create a pendulum.

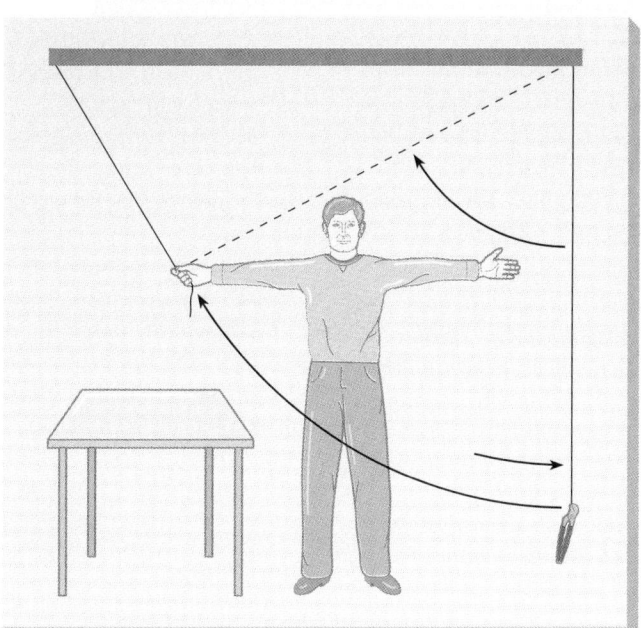

FIGURE 8.5

Solution to the Maier String Problem
Use the pliers as a weight to create a pendulum motion that brings the second string closer.

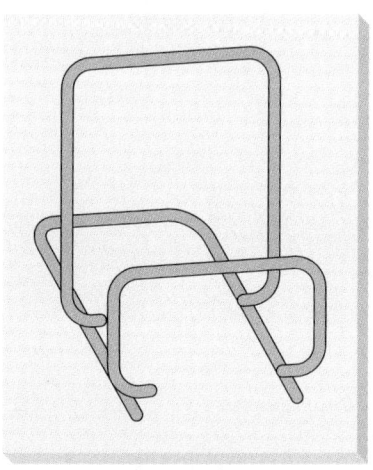

FIGURE 8.6

Book Holder

Acting on a Plan and Looking at the Effects

We can't know if we have correctly identified a problem, defined it, and explored strategies for solving it until we act on our strategies to see if they really work. These final two steps (acting on and looking at the effects of a strategy) are closely related. Figure 8.6 illustrates the importance of acting on the strategies and looking at the effects. This item was invented to solve the problem of following a recipe in a cookbook while your hands are busy chopping vegetables and measuring spices. Let's say you invented this apparatus. You probably would want to try it out to see if it works. As you use it, you would soon see that there's a problem—the cookbook is not protected from spilled or splattered food. Looking at these effects, you might revise the apparatus to look like the holder shown in figure 8.7. Without acting on your plan and evaluating the effects, you might not have improved your invention.

A summary of the steps in the IDEAL problem solver is shown in figure 8.8.

Reasoning

"Elementary, my dear Watson," Sherlock Holmes, the master detective, would say to his baffled companion. Holmes would then go on to explain how he had solved a particularly difficult case. No matter how tough the problem, Holmes always came up with the right solution. Dr. Watson would listen in amazement at how Holmes had spotted all the clues and made sense of them, whereas he had either missed them or misinterpreted them. Holmes's adventures, written by Sir Arthur Conan Doyle, all involve intricate problems that Holmes solves with amazing powers of reasoning.

FIGURE 8.7

Book Holder That Guards Against Stains

CRITICAL THINKING

Personal Problem Solving

You have just learned a five-stage process proposed by Bransford and Stein for solving problems. Think about a problem that you recently confronted in your family, school, or work life. Compare how you went about solving your problem to the IDEAL method.

- Which steps of the IDEAL process did you use?
- Were there steps in the IDEAL process that you probably should have used but did not?
- Which steps in the IDEAL process may have been inappropriate to use in your situation?
- How would you evaluate the five-step IDEAL process?

- Are there some situations for which the IDEAL process is less suited? more suited?
- Are there other processes that you have found to be effective in solving personal problems?

Your discussion of the Bransford and Stein IDEAL model reflects your ability to *evaluate the validity of conclusions about behavior,* in this case using the process specified by Bransford and Stein for solving problems.

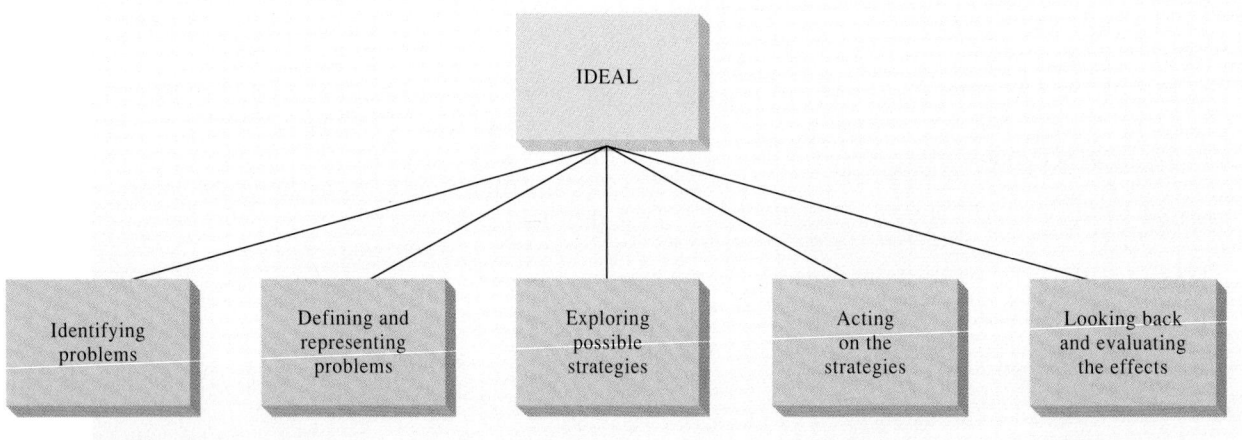

FIGURE 8.8

IDEAL Problem Solver
According to Bransford and Stein's model of the IDEAL problem solver, problem solving can be divided into five steps.

What exactly is reasoning? **Reasoning** *is the mental activity of transforming information to reach conclusions.* Examples of this transformation of information to reach conclusions are found in inductive reasoning and deductive reasoning, as well as other forms of reasoning we will discuss.

I think, therefore I am.

René Descartes

Inductive Versus Deductive Reasoning

Inductive reasoning *is reasoning from the specific to the general—that is, drawing conclusions about all members of a category based on observing only some of the members.* Any time a psychologist studies a small number of individuals (say, twenty college freshmen) and draws conclusions about a larger number of individuals (say, all college students), inductive reasoning is taking place.

In contrast, **deductive reasoning** *is reasoning from the general to the specific. Deductive reasoning involves working* with abstract statements, usually called "premises," and deriving a conclusion. When a psychologist makes a prediction from a theory, deductive reasoning is taking place.

Working out any complex problem often requires both inductive and deductive reasoning. For example, a psychologist might use her theory of how children develop to predict that 6-year-olds will succeed in a task but 4-year-olds will fail. To test this prediction, the psychologist conducts an experiment on a sample of twenty 4-year-olds. Making a prediction is an example of deductive reasoning, but conducting a study and applying the findings to children in general is an example of inductive reasoning.

Formal Reasoning Tasks

Four kinds of formal reasoning tasks have been studied more than any others: one is the inductive task of making analogies; three others are the deductive tasks of ordering ideas, judging relations between conditions, and understanding syllogisms. We will consider each in turn.

He who will not reason is a bigot; he who cannot is a fool; and he who dares not is a slave.

Sir William Drummond

Making Analogies   An **analogy** *is a type of formal reasoning that is always made up of four parts, and the relation between the first two parts is the same as the relation between the last two.* Consider the following example: "Beethoven is to music as Picasso is to _____." To answer correctly (fill in the word *art*), you must make an induction. You must induce the relation between Beethoven and music (the former created the latter) and apply this to Picasso (what did Picasso create?). When you took the SAT or ACT test, you probably were asked to supply correct words in analogies.

Analogies can be very helpful in solving problems, especially when they are visually represented. Benjamin Franklin noticed that a pointed object drew a stronger spark than a blunt object when both were in the vicinity of an electrified body. Originally he believed that this was an unimportant observation. It was not until he recognized that clouds did not draw a strong spark in the vicinity of an electrified body that he realized that pointed rods of iron could be used to protect buildings and ships from lightning. The pointed rod attracted the lightning, thus deflecting it from buildings and ships. Wilhelm Kekulé discovered the ringlike structure of the benzene molecule in organic chemistry only after he visualized its structure using the analogy of a snake biting its tail (see figure 8.9). In many ways, analogies make the strange familiar and the familiar strange.

Ordering Ideas and Judging Relations   Deductive reasoning can also facilitate problem solving. Perhaps the simplest form of deduction involves the ordering of ideas, such as the problem that follows:

> If you like Jean better than Julie,
> and you like Jane less than Julie,
> whom do you like the least?

A second deductive reasoning task involves judging relationships between conditions, which requires processing if/then statements. For example, is the following reasoning valid?

> If it's raining, the streets are wet.
> The streets are wet.
> Therefore, it is raining.

The reasoning is not valid. The streets could be wet for a variety of reasons—it may have snowed, someone may have washed her car, or a fire hydrant may have been opened. The fact that the streets are wet will not support the inference that it is raining.

Understanding Syllogisms   A **syllogism** *is a deductive reasoning task that consists of a major premise, a minor premise, and a conclusion.* A premise is a general assumption. This kind of problem invariably involves a reference to quantity, such as some, all, or none. Consider the following statements:

> All elephants are fond of dry martinis.
> All those who are fond of dry martinis are bankers.
> Therefore, all elephants are bankers.

The first sentence is the major premise, and the second is the minor premise. In this kind of reasoning, if the premises are true, the conclusion will be true, due to the structure of the syllogism (Matlin, 1983). In the syllogism above, the conclusion follows logically from the premises, but the absurdity of the conclusion is due to the fact that the premises are false.

There is a mighty big difference between good, sound reasons and reasons that sound good.

Burton Hillis

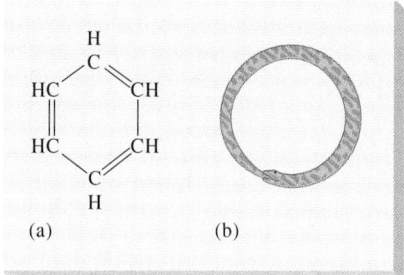

FIGURE 8.9

Use of Analogy in Problem Solving
The benzene ring *(a)* is one of the most important structures in organic chemistry. It was discovered by Wilhelm Kekulé after he imagined how its structure might be analogous to a snake biting its tail *(b)*.

How Logical Is Everyday Reasoning?

The Greeks sometimes referred to humans as featherless bipeds. However, they also gave us another lofty distinction: rational beings. How rational are we? If we look at ourselves objectively, we can come up with countless examples of failures in rational thinking. Many people do not do very well on formal reasoning problems, such as analogies and syllogisms. In our everyday lives, we are not as systematic and logical as formal logicians are.

What are some of the differences between formal reasoning and everyday reasoning? The differences are sufficient to make some theorists wonder if the two kinds of reasoning have any relation to each other at all. Consider the reasoning involved in deciding where to go to college or deciding whether to marry someone. There is no clear set of premises with which to begin your reasoning. It often is unclear exactly what information you should use even to start reasoning at all. The problem you face also is not self-contained. Your decision about marriage might influence your decision about where to go to school and even the career you pursue. Also, although some of your friends might offer strong opinions, they are likely to disagree—there is no one correct answer to most everyday reasoning dilemmas that you face. Similarly a textbook on logic is of doubtful use in teaching you the best methods for answering your everyday reasoning problems. It may not even be clear when you have solved or completed work on this problem about getting married. Three years after marriage, you may begin to wonder if this was, after all, the appropriate decision. Finally, everyday reasoning tasks are too important to you personally for you to simply work on them "for their own sake." Your work on these problems is directed at your larger life goals. In all of these ways, everyday reasoning differs from formal reasoning as examined by logicians and from formal reasoning studied in laboratories by psychologists.

Although there are fundamental differences between formal reasoning and the reasoning we use everyday to get along in the world, there are many circumstances when it helps to have the power of reasoning on our side. In almost every scientific investigation, reasoning is used to set up the basic hypothesis to be studied and to understand the findings. When we perform analytical and computational tasks, such as working out a family budget or filing an income tax report, we use reasoning. When we play chess, bridge, or even tick-tacktoe, we reason. When we are a juror, plaintiff, or defendant, we reason about the law. When we talk, plead, or argue with another or grapple with some of life's knotty problems, much of our reasoning consists of logical inferences—whether valid or not—from what we already know or think we know. In short, our reasoning is both rational and irrational, not always perfect, but usually functional.

Critical Thinking

Currently there is considerable interest in critical thinking among both psychologists and educators (Ennis, 1991; Halonen, 1995), although it is not a completely new idea.

Educator John Dewey (1933) was working with a similar idea when he contrasted "reflective thinking" with "nonreflective thinking in the use of formulas or rules to achieve goals." Although today's definitions of **critical thinking** vary, *they have in common the notions of grasping the deeper meaning of problems, of keeping an open mind about different approaches and perspectives, and of deciding for oneself what to believe or do.* Another, often implicit, assumption is that critical thinking is a very important aspect of everyday reasoning. Critical thinking can and should be used, not just in the classroom but outside it as well.

The thirst to know and understand . . . these are the goods in life's rich hand.

Sir William Watson, 1905

Critical-thinking skills are being taught in many schools. Robert J. Sternberg (1985a, 1985b) believes that most school programs that teach critical thinking are basically flawed. He thinks that schools focus too much on formal reasoning tasks and not enough on the critical-thinking skills needed in everyday life. Sternberg believes that students should get more practice in identifying and defining problems precisely as well as coping with ill-defined problems and problems with ambiguous criteria for solution. He cites four additional critical-thinking skills on which, to date, there has been little research: obtaining information, using informal knowledge, thinking in groups, and developing long-term approaches to long-term problems.

One goal of this book is to teach critical thinking about psychology. In the section at the front of the book entitled "Learning to Learn in Psychology," we described the ability to think critically in the context of psychology. You might want to review the section entitled "Your Critical Thinking Skills" at this time. Table 8.1 summarizes these abilities.

Creativity

Most of us would like to be both gifted and creative. Why was Thomas Edison able to invent so many things? Was he simply more intelligent than most people? Did he spend long hours toiling away in private? Surprisingly, when Edison was a young boy, his teacher told him he was too dumb to learn anything. Other famous people experienced unpleasantness in their lives despite their creativity, including Katharine Hepburn, whose genius for acting failed to protect her from criticism about her nonconformist behavior; Walt Disney, who was fired from a newspaper job because he did not have any good ideas; Enrico Caruso, whose music teacher told him that his voice was terrible; and Winston Churchill, who failed a year of secondary school.

Hepburn, Disney, Edison, Caruso, and Churchill were intelligent and creative people; however, experts on creativity believe that intelligence is not the same as

---

Four problem-solving skills needed in life that are not effectively taught by our schools are *(a)* getting the proper data, as when a student needs to do a research paper; *(b)* using informal knowledge ("on-the-job" knowledge); *(c)* thinking with others in a group; and *(d)* coping with long-term problems. Too often government, just like many individuals, looks for quick-fix solutions rather than long-term approaches that ultimately might be much better.

TABLE 8.1

Critical Thinking Skills in Psychology

Make accurate observations, descriptions, and inferences about behavior

Pursue alternative explanations to explain behavior comprehensively

Demonstrate appreciation for individual differences

Develop psychological arguments using evidence

Evaluate the validity of conclusions about behavior

Demonstrate awareness of underlying values that motivate behavior

Actively take the perspective of others in solving problems

Practice standards of ethical treatment toward individuals and groups

Apply psychological concepts and skills to enhance personal adaptation

Use psychological knowledge to promote human welfare

creativity. One common distinction is between **convergent thinking,** *which produces one correct answer and is characteristic of the kind of thinking tested on standardized intelligence tests,* and **divergent thinking,** *which produces many answers to the same question and is more characteristic of creativity* (Guilford, 1967). For example, the following is a typical problem on an intelligence test that requires convergent thinking: "How many quarters will you get in return for 60 dimes?" The following question, though, has many possible answers: "What image comes to mind when you hear the phrase 'sitting alone in a dark room'?" (Barron, 1989). Such responses as "the sound of a violin with no strings" and "patience" are considered creative answers. Conversely, answers like "a person in a crowd" or "insomnia" are not very creative, because they are common answers.

Creativity *is the ability to think in novel ways and to come up with unique solutions to problems.* When creative people, such as artists and scientists, describe what enables them to solve problems in novel ways, they say that the ability to find affinities between seemingly unrelated elements plays a key role. They also say they have the time and independence in an enjoyable setting to entertain a wide range of possible solutions to a problem. How strongly is creativity related to intelligence? Although most creative people are quite intelligent, the reverse is not necessarily true. Many highly intelligent people (as measured by IQ tests) are not very creative.

Some experts remain skeptical that we will ever fully understand the creative process. Others believe that a psychology of creativity is in reach. Most experts agree, however, that the concept of creativity as spontaneously bubbling up from a magical well is a myth. Momentary flashes of insight, accompanied by images, make up only a small part of the creative process. At the heart of the creative process are ability and experience that shape an individual's intentional and sustained effort, often over the course of a lifetime (Baer, 1993). As Edison supposedly put it, "Genius is one-tenth inspiration and nine-tenths perspiration." Further thoughts about the nature of creativity are presented in Applications in Psychology 8.1.

Our next topic, language, is, like thinking, an important dimension of our cognitive world. Language helps us think, make inferences, tackle tough decisions, and solve problems. Thinking influences language, too. For example, because of the ways we think, we choose certain words to name objects. Let's now examine the nature of language.

REVIEW

The Cognitive Revolution and Thinking

The cognitive revolution occurred in the last half-century. The computer has played an important role, stimulating the model of the mind as an information-processing system. Artificial intelligence (AI) is the science of creating machines capable of performing activities that require intelligence when they are done by people. Expert systems, computer-based systems for assessing knowledge and making decisions in advanced-skill areas, have been applied to many domains.

A concept is used to group objects, events, or characteristics. Concepts help us generalize, improve our memory, keep us from constantly needing to learn, have informational value, and improve our association skills. Psychologists have often investigated a person's ability to detect why an object is included in a particular concept. Developing hypotheses about concepts is important in thinking. Natural concepts have fuzzy boundaries (unclear which features are critical to the concept) and internal structure (some members are better examples than others).

Problem solving is an attempt to find an appropriate way of attaining a goal when the goal is not readily available. Bransford and Stein described a valuable model, IDEAL, to illustrate the steps in problem solving: *I* = identifying problems, *D* = defining problems, *E* = exploring alternative approaches, *A* = acting on a plan, and *L* = looking at the effects. Algorithms, heuristics, learning sets, and functional fixedness are involved in exploring alternative approaches.

Reasoning is the mental activity of transforming information to reach a conclusion. Inductive reasoning is drawing conclusions from the specific to the general; deductive reasoning is drawing conclusions from the general to the specific. Four kinds of formal reasoning tasks have been studied more than others: one is an inductive task (analogies); three are deductive tasks (ordering ideas, judging relations between conditions, and using syllogisms). Much of our everyday reasoning does not follow formal logic, but there are many instances when it helps to have the power of logic on our side. Much interest has recently developed in the concept of critical thinking, which involves grasping the deeper meaning of problems, keeping an open mind about different approaches, and deciding for oneself what to believe or do. Sternberg believes that when schools teach critical thinking, they rely too much on formal logic; instead, they should spend more time teaching critical thinking skills needed in everyday life. Creativity is the ability to think about something in novel ways and to come up with unique solutions to problems.

The Snowflake Model of Creativity

Daniel Perkins (1984) describes his view as the *snowflake model of creativity*. Like the six sides of a snowflake, each with its own complex structure, Perkins's model consists of six characteristics common to highly creative individuals (see figure 8.A). Children and adults who are creative may not have all six characteristics, but the more they have, the more creative they tend to be, says Perkins.

First, creative thinking involves aesthetics as much as practical standards. Aesthetics involves beauty. Outside of literature and the arts, conventional schooling pays little attention to the aesthetics of human inquiry. For example, the beauty of scientific theories, mathematical systems, and historical syntheses teachers rarely address, and how often do teachers comment on the aesthetics of students' work in math and science?

Second, creative thinking involves an ability to excel in finding problems. Creative individuals spend an unusual amount of time thinking about problems. They also explore a number of options in solving a particular problem before choosing a solution to pursue. Creative individuals value good questions because they can produce discoveries and creative answers. A student once asked Nobel laureate Linus Pauling how he came up with good ideas. Pauling said he developed a lot of ideas and threw away the bad ones. Most assignments in school are so narrow that students have little opportunity to generate or even select among different ideas, according to Perkins.

Third, creative thinking involves mental mobility, which allows individuals to find new perspectives and approaches to problems. One example of mental mobility is being able to think in terms of opposites and contraries while seeking a new solution. According to Perkins, most problems students work on in school are convergent, not divergent. For the most part, the learning problems students face in school lack the elbow room for exercising mental mobility.

Fourth, creative thinking involves the willingness to take risks. Accompanying risk is the acceptance of failure as part of the creative quest and the ability to learn from failures. Creative geniuses don't always produce masterpieces. For example, Picasso produced more than 20,000 works of art, but much of it was mediocre. The more children produce, the better is their chance of creating something unique. According to Perkins, most schools do not challenge students to take the risk necessary to think creatively and to produce creative work.

Fifth, creative thinking involves objectivity. The popular image of creative individuals usually highlights their subjective, personal insights and commitments; however, without some objectivity and feedback from others, they would create a private world that is distant from reality and could not be shared or appreciated by others. Creative individuals not only criticize their own work but they also seek criticism from others. Schools typically do highlight objectivity, although usually not in the arts.

Sixth, creative thinking involves inner motivation. Creative individuals are motivated to produce something for its own sake, not for school grades or for money. Their catalyst is the challenge, enjoyment, and satisfaction of the work itself. Researchers have found that individuals ranging from preschool children through adults are more creative when they are internally rather than externally motivated. Work evaluation, competition for prizes, and supervision tend to undermine internal motivation and diminish creativity (Amabile & Hennessey, 1988).

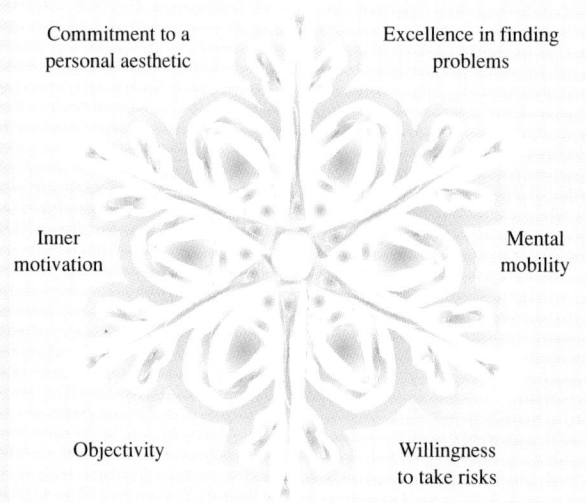

Commitment to a personal aesthetic

Excellence in finding problems

Inner motivation

Mental mobility

Objectivity

Willingness to take risks

FIGURE 8.A

Snowflake Model of Creativity
Like a snowflake, Perkins's model of creativity has six parts: commitment to a personal aesthetic, excellence in finding problems, mental mobility, willingness to take risks, objectivity, and inner motivation.

In 1799 a nude boy was observed running through the woods in France. The boy was captured when he was approximately 11 years old, and it was believed he had lived in the wild for at least 6 years. He was called the Wild Boy of Aveyron (Lane, 1976). When the boy was found, he made no effort to communicate. Even after a number of years, he never learned to communicate effectively. The Wild Boy of Aveyron raises an important issue in language: What are the biological, environmental, and cultural underpinnings of language? Later in the chapter, we will describe a modern-day wild child named Genie, who will shed some light on this issue. The contributions of biology, environment, and culture figure prominently in our discussion of language.

The Nature of Language

Language is a form of communication, both spoken and written, that sets humans apart from all other animals. We speak to others, listen to others, and write something that others will read, all as part of using language to communicate. Our language enables us to describe past events in detail and to plan for the future in carefully considered steps. Language gives us the opportunity to pass along knowledge from generation to generation and to create a rich cultural heritage.

Every culture depends on language. Human languages number in the thousands, differing so much on the surface that many of us despair of learning even more than one. However, all human languages have some common characteristics. **Language** *is a system of symbols used to communicate with others. In humans, language is characterized by organizational rules and infinite generativity.* **Infinite generativity** *is a person's ability to produce an endless number of meaningful sentences using a finite set of words and rules,* which makes language a highly creative enterprise. Studies on the structure and mechanics of language include phonology, morphology, syntax, and semantics, each of which we will now discuss.

Children pick up words as pigeons pick up peas.

John Ray

Language is made up of basic sounds, or phonemes. **Phonology** *is the study of language's sound system.* Phonological rules ensure that certain sound sequences occur (for example, *sp, ba,* or *ar*) and others do not (for example, *zx,* or *qp*). A good example of a phoneme in the English language is /k/, the sound represented by the letter *k* in the word *ski* and the letter *c* in the word *cat.* Although the /k/ sound is slightly different in these two words, the variation is not distinguished, and the /k/ sound is described as a single phoneme. In some languages, such as Arabic, this kind of variation represents separate phonemes.

"If you don't mind my asking, how much does a sentence diagrammer pull down a year?"

© Bob Thaves.

Morphology *refers to the rules for combining morphemes, which are meaningful strings of sounds that contain no smaller meaningful parts.* Every word in the English language is made up of one or more morphemes. Some words consist of a single morpheme (for example, *help*), whereas others are made up of more than one morpheme (for example, *helper,* which has two morphemes, *help* + *-er,* with the morpheme *-er* meaning "one who," in this case "one who helps"). However, not all morphemes are words (for example, *pre-, -tion,* and *-ing*). Just as the rules that govern phonemes ensure that certain sound sequences occur, the rules that govern morphemes ensure that certain strings of sounds occur in particular sequences. For example, we would not re-order *helper* to *erhelp.*

Syntax *involves the way words are combined to form acceptable phrases and sentences.* If someone says to you, "Bob slugged Tom," and "Bob was slugged by Tom," you know who did the slugging and who was slugged in each case because you share the same syntactic understanding of sentence structure. You also understand that the sentence "You didn't stay, did you?" is a grammatical sentence but that "You didn't stay, didn't you?" is unacceptable and ambiguous.

Semantics *refers to the meaning of words and sentences.* Every word has a set of semantic features. *Girl* and *woman,* for example, share many of the same semantic features as the word *female,* but differ semantically in regard to age. Words have semantic restrictions on how they can be used in sentences. The sentence *The bicycle talked the boy into buying a candy bar* is syntactically correct but semantically incorrect. The sentence violates our semantic knowledge that bicycles do not talk.

How Language Develops

Most individuals in the United States acquire a vocabulary of nearly 10,000 words in a complex language by the time they are adults. How does this development take place?

Early Development

Before babies ever say their first words, at the age of 10 to 13 months, they babble. Babbling—endlessly repeating sounds and syllables such as *goo-goo* and *ga-ga*—begins at about the age of 3 to 6 months and is determined by biological readiness, not reinforcement or the ability to hear (Locke & others, 1991). Even deaf babies babble for a time (Lenneberg, Rebelsky, & Nichols, 1965). Babbling probably allows the baby to exercise its vocal chords and helps develop articulation.

A child's first words name important people (*dada*), familiar animals (*kitty*), vehicles (*car*), toys (*ball*), food (*milk*), body parts (*eye*), clothes (*hat*), household items (*clock*), or greetings (*bye*). These were babies' first words 50 years ago and they are babies' first words today (Clark, 1983). The **holophrase hypothesis** *is the concept that single words can be used to imply complete sentences, and that infants' first words characteristically are holophrastic.* For example, the demand "Milk!" might mean "I'm hungry and want to eat *now*."

By the time children reach the age of 18 to 24 months, they usually utter two-word statements. They quickly grasp the importance of expressing concepts and the role that language plays in communicating with others. To convey meaning in two-word statements, the child relies heavily on gesture, tone, and context. The wealth of meaning children can communicate with two words includes the following:

Identification: See doggie.
Location: Book there.
Repetition: More milk.
Nonexistence: Allgone thing.
Negation: Not wolf.
Possession: My candy.
Attribution: Big car.
Agent-action: Mama walk.
Action-direct-object: Hit you.
Action-indirect-object: Give papa.
Action-instrument: Cut knife.
Question: Where ball? (Slobin, 1972)

These examples are from children whose first languages were English, German, Russian, Finnish, Turkish, and Samoan. Although these two-word sentences omit many parts of speech, they are remarkably succinct in conveying many messages. In fact, a child's first combination of words has this economical quality in every language. **Telegraphic speech** *is the use of short and precise words to communicate; it is characteristic of young children's two- or three-word combinations.* When we send a telegram, we try to be short and precise, excluding any unnecessary words. As a result, articles, auxiliary verbs, and other connectives usually are omitted. Of course telegraphic speech is not limited to two-word phrases. "Mommy give ice cream" and "Mommy give

"What's the big surprise? All the latest theories of linguistics say we're born with the innate capacity for generating sentences."

© 1991 by Sidney Harris—"You Want Proof? . . ." W. H. Freeman and Company.

Tommy ice cream" also are examples of telegraphic speech. As children leave the two-word stage, they move rather quickly into three-, four-, and five-word combinations.

As we have just seen, language unfolds in a sequence. At every point in development, the child's linguistic interaction with parents and others obeys certain principles (Budwig, 1995; Tomasello & Merriman, 1995). Not only is this development strongly influenced by the child's biological wiring, but the language environment is more complex than behaviorists such as Skinner imagined.

Is There a Critical Period for Learning Language?

Almost all children learn one or more languages during their early years of development, so it is difficult to determine whether there is a critical period for language development. In the 1960s, Erik Lenneberg (1967) proposed a biological theory of language acquisition. He said that language is a maturational process and that there is a critical period, between about 18 months of age and puberty, during which a first language must be acquired. Central to Lenneberg's thesis is the idea that language develops rapidly and with ease during the preschool years as a result of maturation. Lenneberg provided support for the critical-period concept from studies of several atypical populations, including children with left-hemisphere brain damage, deaf children, and children with mental retardation (Tager-Flusberg, 1994). The children's brains had plasticity, and the children recovered their language skills but the adults did not. Lenneberg believed that adults had already passed the critical period during which plasticity of brain functioning allows reassignment and relearning of language skills.

The stunted language development of a modern "wild child" also supports the idea of a critical period for language acquisition. In 1970 a California social worker made a routine visit to the home of a partially blind woman who had applied for public assistance. The social worker discovered that the woman and her husband had kept their 13-year-old daughter Genie locked away from the world. Kept in almost total isolation during childhood, Genie could not speak or stand erect. She was forced to sit naked all day on a child's potty seat, restrained by a harness her father had made—she could move only her hands and feet. At night she was placed in a kind of straitjacket and caged in a crib with wire mesh sides and a cover. Whenever Genie made a noise, her father beat her. He never communicated with her in words but growled and barked at her.

Genie spent a number of years in extensive rehabilitation programs, such as speech and physical therapy (Curtiss, 1977; Rymer, 1993). She eventually learned to walk upright with a jerky motion and to use the toilet. Genie also learned to recognize many words and to speak in rudimentary sentences. At first she spoke in one-word utterances. Later she was able to string together two-word combinations, such as "big teeth," "little marble," and "two hand." Consistent with the language development of most children, three-word combinations followed—for example, "small two cup." Unlike normal children, however, Genie did not learn how to ask questions and she doesn't understand grammar. Genie is not able to distinguish between pronouns or passive and active verbs. Four years after she began stringing words together, her speech still sounded like a garbled telegram. As an adult she speaks in short, mangled sentences, such as "Father hit leg," "Big wood," and "Genie hurt."

Second-language acquisition represents another independent source of evidence for the critical-period concept. Young children who are exposed to more than one language have little difficulty acquiring both languages and eventually speaking each with little or no interference from the other. By late childhood, children exposed to a new language have more difficulty learning it. At some point in late childhood or adolescence (as yet not pinpointed), there is a critical-period cutoff for speaking a new language without an accent (Obler, 1993).

Biological, Environmental, and Cultural Influences

Is the ability to generate rules for language, and then use them to create an infinite number of words, learned and influenced by the environment and cultural factors, or is it the product of biological factors and biological evolution?

Biological Influences

Estimates vary as to how long ago humans acquired language—from about 20,000 to 70,000 years ago. In evolutionary time, then, language is a very recent acquisition. A number of experts believe that biological evolution undeniably shaped humans into linguistic creatures (Chomsky,

1957; Howe, 1993). The brain, nervous system, and vocal apparatus of our predecessors changed over hundreds of thousands of years. Physically equipped to do so, *Homo sapiens* went beyond grunting and shrieking to develop abstract speech. However, the development of language has to be explained in terms of both biological and cultural evolution.

Anthropologists speculate about the social conditions that led to the development of language. Social forces may have pushed humans to develop abstract reasoning and to create an efficient system for communicating with others (Crick, 1977). For example, early humans probably developed complex plans and strategies for hunting. If the hunters could verbally signal one another about changes in strategies for hunting big game, the hunt much more likely would be successful. Language clearly gave humans an enormous edge over other animals and increased the chances of survival.

The strongest evidence for the biological basis of language is that children all over the world acquire language milestones at about the same time developmentally and in about the same order, despite vast variations in the language input they receive. For example, in some cultures adults never talk to infants under 1 year of age, yet these infants still acquire language. Also, there is no other convincing way to explain how quickly children learn language than through biological foundations.

Environmental Influences

We do not learn language in a social vacuum. Most children are steeped in language at a very early age (Snow, 1989). And children's earliest exposures to language are usually through their parents. Roger Brown (1973) wondered how parents might help their children learn language. He was especially interested in whether parents reinforce their children for speaking in grammatical ways, as behavioral theories would predict. After spending many hours observing parents and their young children, he found that parents sometimes smiled and praised their children for correct sentences, but they also reinforced many ungrammatical sentences. Brown concluded that learning grammar is not based on reinforcement.

What are some of the ways in which environment does contribute to language development? Imitation is one important candidate. A child who is slow to develop her language ability can be helped if her parents speak to her carefully in grammatically correct sentences. Recent evidence also suggests that parents provide more corrective feedback for children's ungrammatical utterances than Brown originally thought (Penner, 1987). Even so, a number of experts believe that imitation and reinforcement facilitate language but are not absolutely necessary for language acquisition.

In every culture, individuals are bathed in language from a very early age.

One intriguing environmental factor that contributes to a young child's language acquisition is called **motherese**, *the way parents and other adults often talk to babies in a higher-pitched voice than normal and with simple words and sentences.* Most people automatically shift into motherese as soon as they start talking to a baby—usually without being aware they're doing so. We speak in motherese, it seems, to capture the infant's attention and maintain communication.

Motherese was documented as early as the first century B.C., and it's virtually universal (Ferguson, 1977). However, the particular format motherese may take varies somewhat from culture to culture. For example, a study of American English and Spanish speakers in Texas showed that English speakers favored altering the volume and pitch of speech, or altering the sounds of words, such as shortening vowels or consonants. In contrast, Spanish speakers tended to substitute and repeat words, strategies designed to promote interaction between the speaker and the child (Blount, 1982).

Today, most language acquisition researchers believe that children from a wide variety of cultural contexts acquire their native language without explicit teaching, in some cases without apparent encouragement. Thus, the necessary aspects of learning a language seem to be quite minimal. However, enhanced language learning usually requires more support and involvement from caregivers and teachers. Of special concern are children who grow up in poverty-infested areas and are not exposed to guided participation in language. In Sociocultural Worlds 8.1, you can read about how the rich language traditions of African Americans are dying out in such poverty conditions.

It is important to recognize that children differ in their ability to acquire language and that this variation cannot be readily explained by differences in environmental input alone. For children who are slow in developing language skills, opportunities to talk and be talked with are important; but remember that encouragement of language development is the key, not drill and practice. Language development is not a simple matter of imitation and reinforcement, a fact acknowledged even by most behaviorists today.

Recently, John Locke (1993) argued that one reason why social interactionist aspects have been underplayed recently in explaining language development is the fact that linguists concentrate on language's complex structural properties, especially the acquisition of grammar. The emphasis on grammar acquisition has resulted in inadequate attention to the communicative aspects of language, in Locke's view. Locke reminds us that language learning occurs in the very real context of physical and social maturation, and that children are neither exclusively little biological linguists (whose sophisticated language abilities are innate) nor exclusively social beings (who learn language by interacting with others) (Ratner, 1993). In sum, an interactionist view emphasizes the contributions of both biology and experience in language: that is, children are already biologically prepared to learn language when they and their caregivers interact.

Cultural Influences

It's a beautiful thing, the destruction of words. . . . If you have a word like "good," what need is there for a word like "bad"? "Ungood" will do just as well. . . . It was B. B.'s (Big Brother's) idea originally, of course. . . . Do you know that Newspeak is the only language in the world whose vocabulary gets smaller every year? . . . Don't you see that the whole aim of Newspeak is to narrow the range of thought? In the end we shall make thought crime literally impossible, because there will be no words in which to express it. . . . Every year fewer and fewer words, and the range of consciousness always a little smaller.

So says a colleague at the Ministry of Truth to Winston Smith in George Orwell's novel *Nineteen Eighty-four,* published in 1949. The novel is about the life of an intelligent man who lives under absolute totalitarian control. The government regulates every facet of life and, above all, corrupts

SOCIOCULTURAL WORLDS 8.1

The Rich Language Traditions of African Americans and the Effects of Urban Poverty

Shirley Heath (1989) recently examined the language traditions of African Americans from low-income backgrounds. She traced some aspects of African American English to the time of slavery. Heath also examined how those speech patterns have carried over into African American English today. She found that agricultural areas in the southern United States have an especially rich oral tradition.

Specifically she found that adults do not simplify or edit their talk for children, in essence challenging the children to be highly active listeners. Also, adults ask only "real questions" of children—that is, questions for which the adult does not already know the answer. Adults engage in a type of teasing with children, encouraging them to use their wits in communication. For example, a grandmother might pretend that she wants to take a child's hat and then starts a lively exchange in which the child must understand many subtleties of argument, mood, and humor—Does Grandma really want my hat? Is she mad at me? Is she making a joke? Can I persuade her to give it back to me? Finally, there is an appreciation of wit and flexibility in how language is used,

as well as an acknowledgment of individual differences—one person might be respected for recounting stories, another for negotiating and peacemaking skills.

Heath argues that the language tradition she describes is richly varied, cognitively demanding, and well suited to many real-life situations. She says that the oral and literary traditions among poor African Americans in the cities are well suited for many job situations. Years ago many inner-city jobs required only that a person follow directions in order to perform repetitive tasks. Today many positions require continuous interactions involving considerable flexibility in language, such as the ability to persuade co-workers or to express dissatisfaction, in a subtle way, for example.

Despite its utility in many job situations, the rich language tradition possessed by low-income African Americans does not meet with the educational priorities of our nation's schools. Too often schools stress rote memorization, minimizing group interaction and discouraging individual variations in communicative style. Also, the language tradition of African American culture is rapidly dying in the face of current life among poor African Americans, where the structure of low-income, frequently single-parent families often provides little verbal stimulation for children.

One mother agreed to let researcher Shirley Heath (in press) tape-record her interactions with her children over a 2-year period and to write notes about her activities with them. Within 500 hours of tape and more than 1,000 lines of notes, the mother initiated talk with her three preschool children on only 18 occasions (other than giving them a brief directive or asking a quick question). Few of the mother's conversations involved either planning or executing actions with or for her children.

Heath (1989) points out that the lack of family and community supports is widespread in urban housing projects, especially among African Americans. The deteriorating, impoverished conditions of these inner-city areas severely impede the ability of young children to develop the cognitive and social skills they need to function competently.

Children who grow up in low-income, poverty-ridden neighborhoods of large cities often experience a lack of family and community support, which can seriously undermine the development of their language skills.

Many African Americans have a rich language tradition that is varied, cognitively demanding, and well suited to many real-life situations. *How has this tradition recently been abandoned?*

The linguistic relativity hypothesis states that our cultural experiences for a particular concept shape a catalog of names that can be either rich or poor. Consider how different your mental library of names for *camel* might be if you had extensive experience with camels in a desert world and how different your mental library of names for *snow* might be if you lived in an arctic world of ice and cold. Despite its intriguing appeal, the linguistic relativity concept is controversial and many psychologists do not believe it plays a pivotal role in shaping thought.

language in its pursuit of power. The purpose of Newspeak was not only to provide a means of expressing "appropriate" thoughts, but to make all other modes of thought impossible. This bleak picture of the influence of culture on language might feel far removed from your own rich experiences with language.

Take a moment and reflect on these questions: How did the culture in which you grew up influence your language? What role does language play in academic achievement? Would the range of thought diminish if language were cut down to the bone as Smith's colleague at the Ministry of Truth predicted?

The Linguistic Relativity Hypothesis

Linguist Benjamin Whorf claimed that language determines the way we think. Whorf's (1956) **linguistic relativity hypothesis** *states that culture shapes language, which further determines the structure of thinking and shapes our basic ideas.* The Inuit in Alaska, for instance, have a dozen or more words to describe the various textures, colors, and physical states of snow; the Hopi Indians have no words for past and future; and Arabs have 6,000 words for camels.

Our cultural experiences for a particular concept shape a catalog of names that can be either rich or poor. For example, if the "camel" part of your mental library of names is the product of years of experience with camels, you probably see and think about this desert animal in finer gradations than does someone who has no experience with camels. In this way, language acts like a window that filters the amount and nature of information passed on for further processing.

Critics of Whorf's theory say that words merely reflect, rather than cause, the way we think. The Inuits' adaptability and livelihood in Alaska depend on their capacity to recognize various conditions of snow and ice. Recent criticism of the linguistic relativity hypothesis argues that the Inuits have no more words for snow and ice than do people living in the United States. On the other hand, a

What are the arguments for and against bilingual education?

professional football player's vocabulary contains a number of unique words; for instance, a player might know thirty terms for a defensive alignment and seven terms for rushing the passer. All the same, even though you don't know the words for the different defensive alignments in football, just like you don't have words for all the different conditions of snow and ice, you might still be able to perceive these differences.

Rosch (1973) found just that. She studied the effect of language on color perception among the Dani in New Guinea. The Dani have only two words for color—one that approximates white and one that approximates black. If the linguistic relativity hypothesis were correct, the Dani would lack the ability to tell the difference among such colors as green, blue, red, yellow, and purple. However, Rosch found that the Dani perceive colors just as we perceive them. As we know from chapter 3, color perception is biologically determined by receptors in the retinas in the eyes. Whorf's linguistic relativity hypothesis missed the mark, but researchers agree that although language does not determine thought, it can influence it.

Language's Role in Achievement and School

Octavio's Mexican parents moved to the United States a year before Octavio was born. They do not speak English fluently and have always spoken to Octavio in Spanish. At 6 years of age, Octavio has just entered the first grade at an elementary school in San Antonio, Texas, and he speaks no English. What is the best way to teach Octavio? How much easier would elementary school be for Octavio if his parents had been able to speak to him in Spanish *and* English when he was an infant?

Well over 6 million children in the United States come from homes in which English is not the primary language. Often, like Octavio, they live in a community in which a language other than English is the main means of communication. These children face a more difficult task than most of us: They must master the native tongue of their family to communicate effectively at home and they must also master English to make their way in the larger society. The number of bilingual children is expanding at such a rapid rate in our country (some experts predict a tripling of their number early in the twenty-first century) that they constitute an important subgroup of language learners that society must deal with. Although the education of such children in the public schools has a long history, only recently has a national policy evolved to guarantee high-quality language experience for them.

Bilingual education *refers to programs for students with limited proficiency in English that instruct students in their own language part of the time while they learn English.* The rationale for bilingual education was provided by the United States Commission on Civil Rights (1975): Lack of English proficiency is the main reason language minority students do poorly in school; bilingual education should keep students from falling far behind in a subject while they are learning English. Bilingual programs vary extensively in content and quality. At a minimum, they include instruction in English as a second language for students with limited English proficiency. Bilingual programs often include some instruction in Spanish as well. The largest number of bilingual programs in the United States are in Spanish, so our examples refer to Spanish, although the principles also apply to bilingual programs in other languages. Bilingual programs differ in the extent to which Latino culture is taught to all students. Some bilingual programs teach Spanish to all students, regardless of whether their primary language is Spanish.

Most bilingual education programs are simply transitional programs developed to support students in Spanish until they can understand English well enough to function in the regular classroom, which is taught in English. A typical bilingual program begins teaching students with limited English proficiency in their primary language in kindergarten and then changes to English-only classes at the end of the first or second grade (Slavin, 1988).

Research evaluation of bilingualism has led to the conclusion that bilingualism does not interfere with performance in either language (Hakuta & Garcia, 1989). There is no evidence that the native language should be eliminated as early as possible because it might interfere with learning a

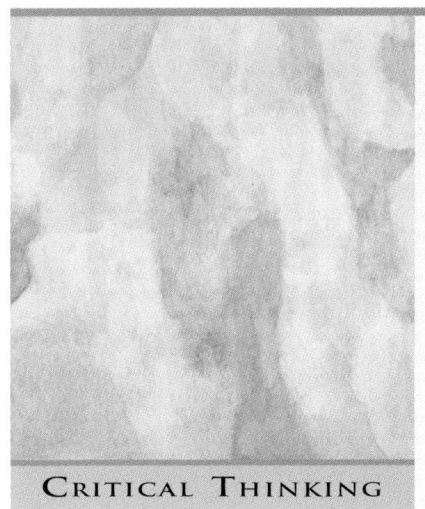

*Language and
Educational Policy*

You have read a great deal about the nature of bilingual education and its impact on the language development of ethnic minority children. Assume that you have been asked to provide your evaluation of the value of bilingual education to a board of education that is currently considering adopting a bilingual approach in its elementary school. What arguments would you construct to support your position from the psychological evidence? What arguments do you think the opposing side would use to counter your position? Your consideration of this issue is a good example of how to *develop psychological arguments using evidence*.

One final point about bilingualism deserves attention. The United States is one of the few countries in the world in which most students graduate from high school knowing only their own language. For example, in Russia, schools have ten grades, called forms, which correspond roughly to the twelve grades in American schools. Children begin school at age 7. In the third form, Russian students begin learning English. Because of the emphasis on teaching English in their schools, most Russian citizens today under the age of 35 speak at least some English (Cameron, 1988).

Do Animals Have Language?

Many animal species do have complex and ingenious ways to signal danger and to communicate about basic needs such as food and sex. For example, in one species of firefly the female has

second language. Instead, higher degrees of bilingualism are associated with cognitive flexibility and improved concept formation (Diaz, 1983). These findings are based primarily on research in additive bilingual settings—that is, in settings where the second language is added as an enrichment to the native language and not at its expense. Causal relations between bilingualism and cognitive or language competence are difficult to establish, but, in general, positive outcomes are often noted in communities where bilingualism is not socially stigmatized.

Increasingly, researchers are recognizing the complexity of bilingualism's effects (Brislin, 1993; Oller, 1995; Yeni-Komshian, 1995). For example, as indicated earlier, bilingualism programs vary enormously. Some are of excellent quality; others are of poor quality. Some teachers in bilingual education programs are completely bilingual; others are not. Some programs begin in kindergarten, others in elementary school. Some programs end in the first or second grade; others continue through the fifth or sixth grade. Some include instruction in Latino culture; others focus only on language instruction. Some researchers select outcome measures that include only proficiency in English; others focus on cognitive variables such as cognitive flexibility and concept formation; and still others include more social variables such as integration into the school, self-esteem, and attitude toward school. In sum, there is more to understanding the effects of bilingual education than simple language proficiency.

learned to imitate the flashing signal of another species to lure the aliens into her territory. Then she eats them. But is this language in the human sense? And what about higher animals, such as apes? Is ape language similar to human language? Can we teach language to apes?

Some researchers believe that apes can learn language. One celebrity in this field is a chimp named Washoe, who was adopted when she was about 10 months old (Gardner & Gardner, 1971). Since apes do not have the vocal apparatus to speak, the researchers tried to teach Washoe the American Sign Language, which is one of the sign languages of the deaf. Washoe used sign language during everyday activities, such as meals, play, and car rides. In 2 years, Washoe learned 38 different signs, and by the age of 5 she had a vocabulary of 160 signs. Washoe learned how to put signs together in novel ways, such as "You drink" and "You me tickle." A number of other efforts to teach language to chimps have had similar results (Premack, 1986).

The debate about chimpanzees' ability to use language focuses on two key issues: Can apes understand the meaning of symbols; that is, can they comprehend that one thing stands for another? And can apes learn syntax; that is, can they learn the mechanics and rules that give human language its creative productivity? The first of these issues may have been settled recently by Sue Savage-Rumbaugh and her colleagues (1993). The researchers found strong evidence that two chimps named Sherman and Austin can understand symbols (see figure 8.10). For example, if

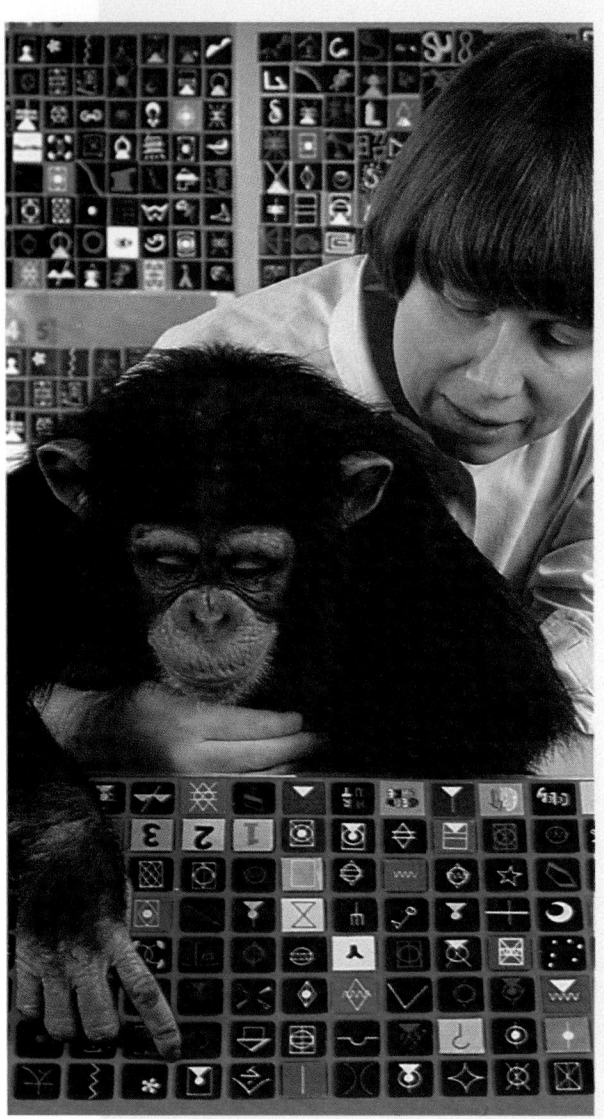

FIGURE 8.10

Sue Savage-Rumbaugh with a Chimp in Front of a Board with Languagelike Symbols
The Rumbaughs (Sue and Duane) of the Yerkes Primate Center and Georgia State University have studied the basic question of whether chimps understand symbols. Their research evidence suggests chimps can understand symbols.

Sherman or Austin is sitting in a room, and a symbol for an object is displayed on a screen, he will go into another room, find the object, and bring it back. If the object is not there, he will come back empty-handed (Cowley, 1988). The two chimps can play a game in which one chimp points

"I hope we get to communicate with them—I'd just like to tell them we have no interest in communicating with them."

© 1991 by Sidney Harris—"You Want Proof? . . ." W. H. Freeman and Company.

to a symbol for food (M & Ms), and the other chimp selects the food from a tray, then they both eat it. These observations are clear evidence that chimps can understand symbols (Rumbaugh & others, 1991).

However, there still is no strong evidence that chimps can learn syntax. Perhaps other animals can. Ron Schusterman has worked with a sea lion named Rocky, teaching him to follow commands such as "Ball fetch" and "Disc ball fetch." The first command means that Rocky should take a disc to a ball in his tank. The second command means that Rocky should take the ball to the disc. Although Rocky and other sea lions make some errors in decoding these complex commands, they perform at levels much better than chance, indicating that they have learned rules that link the ordering of symbols to abstract meanings. Such rules are either syntax or something close to it.

The debate over whether or not animals can use language to express thoughts is far from resolved. Researchers do agree that animals can communicate with each other and that some can be trained to manipulate language-like symbols. While such accomplishments may be remarkable, they fall far short of human language with its infinite number of novel phrases to convey the richness and subtleties of meaning that are the foundation of human relationships.

Our thinking and language skills set us apart from other life forms on this planet. Through our thinking and language, we have mastered our world and adapted effectively to its challenges. We will continue our investigation of thinking and language as we explore individual differences in mental functioning by studying the nature of intelligence.

Language

Language involves a system of symbols we use to communicate with each other. The system is governed by rules yet allows infinite generativity. Some of the mechanics of language include phonology, morphology, syntax, and semantics.

One-word utterances occur at about 10 – 13 months of age; the holophrase hypothesis has been applied to this. By 18 – 24 months, most infants use two-word combinations. This is often referred to as telegraphic speech. Based on the effects of brain injury on language at different points in development, Lenneberg argued that a critical period for language acquisition ends at puberty. The experiences of Genie and other such children also suggest that the early childhood years are a critical period in language development. And the facts about second-language acquisition, especially the timetable for learning to speak a second language without an accent, provides evidence for a critical period.

Biological evolution shaped humans into linguistic creatures. The strongest evidence for the biological basis of language is that children all over the world reach language milestones at about the same age and in about the same order, despite vast differences in the language input they receive. Cultural evolution spurred the need to communicate as humans worked together for survival.

Reinforcement and imitation probably facilitate language development but might not play a critical role. Adults universally seem to adopt motherese when speaking to children. An interactionist view emphasizes the contributions of both biology and experience in language—that is, children are already biologically prepared to learn language when they and their caregivers interact.

Whorf's controversial linguistic relativity hypothesis states that language determines the structure of thinking. Thoughts and ideas are associated with words, and different languages promote different ways of thinking. Language does not determine thought, but it does influence it. One critical variable in understanding language's role in achievement and school is whether the child speaks the language in which the classes are taught and, if so, how well. National debate rages about the best way to teach children whose native language is not English. There is great diversity in bilingual programs.

Although animals can communicate about basic drives, it is unclear whether animals have all the properties of human language. Chimpanzees, however, can be taught to use symbols.

INTELLIGENCE

The primary components of intelligence are close to the mental processes we have already discussed in this chapter—thinking and language. The difference between how we discussed thinking and language and how we will discuss intelligence lies in the concept of individual differences in assessment. **Individual differences** *are the consistent, stable ways people are different from each other.* We can talk about individual differences in personality (which we will do in chapter 15) or in any other domain of psychology, but it is in the area of intelligence that psychologists give the most attention to individual differences. For example, an intelligence test informs you whether you can logically reason better than most others who have taken the test. Before we discuss intelligence tests, though, we need to examine what intelligence is and how tests are constructed.

The Nature of Intelligence

Intelligence is one of our most highly prized possessions, yet its concept is something that even the most intelligent people have failed to agree on. Unlike such characteristics as height, weight, and age, intelligence cannot be directly measured. It's a bit like size, which is a more abstract notion than height or weight. We can only estimate size from a set of empirical measures of height and weight. Similarly, we can only estimate a person's intelligence. We cannot peel back a scalp and observe intellectual processes in action. The only way we can study these processes is indirectly, by evaluating a person's intelligent acts (Kail & Pellegrino, 1985). For the most part, psychologists rely on intelligence tests to provide an estimate of these mental abilities.

Many psychologists and laypeople equate intelligence with verbal ability and problem-solving skills. Others prefer to define it as a person's ability to learn from and adapt to the experiences of everyday life. Let's combine the two and settle on the following definition of **intelligence:** *verbal ability, problem-solving skills, and the ability to learn from and adapt to the experiences of everyday life* (see figure 8.11).

Although we have just defined general intelligence, keep in mind that the way intelligence is expressed in behavior may vary from culture to culture (Lonner, 1990). For example, in most Western cultures, people are considered intelligent if they are both smart (have considerable

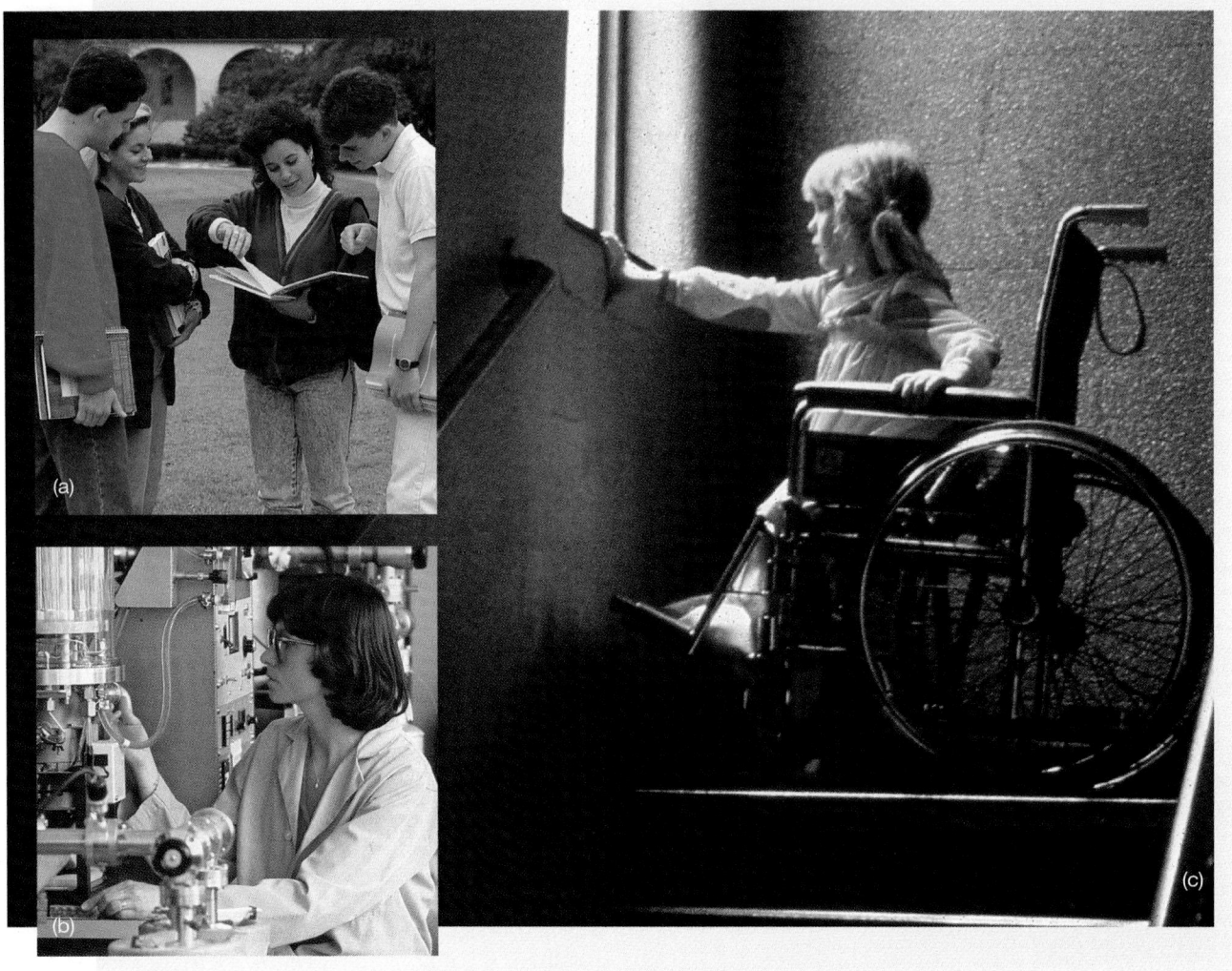

FIGURE 8.11

Defining Intelligence

Intelligence is an abstract concept that has been defined in various ways. The three most commonly agreed-upon aspects of intelligence are the following: *(a)* verbal ability, as reflected in the verbal skills of these college students faced with the task of writing a paper for tomorrow morning's class; *(b)* problem-solving skills, as reflected in this scientist's search for an AIDS cure; and *(c)* the ability to learn from and adapt to experiences of everyday life, as reflected in this handicapped child's adaptation to her inability to walk.

knowledge and can solve verbal problems) and fast (can process information quickly). On the other hand, in the Buganda culture in Uganda, people who are wise, slow in thought, and say the socially correct thing are considered intelligent (Wober, 1974).

Does Intelligence Have a Single Nature?

Is it more appropriate to think of intelligence as something general in terms of which people can be adjudged "smart" or "dumb"? Or is it a number of specific abilities? Long before Wechsler analyzed intelligence in terms of general and specific abilities (giving an individual an overall IQ but also providing information about specific subcomponents of intelligence), Charles Spearman (1927) proposed that intelligence has two factors. **Two-factor theory** *is Spearman's theory that individuals have both general intelligence, which*

he called g, *and a number of specific intelligences, which he called* s. Spearman believed that these two factors accounted for a person's performance on an intelligence test.

Theories of Multiple Intelligences

Some researchers abandoned the idea of a general intelligence and searched for specific factors only. **Multiple-factor theory** *is L. L. Thurstone's (1938) theory that intelligence consists of seven primary mental abilities: verbal comprehension, number ability, word fluency, spatial visualization, associative memory, reasoning, and perceptual speed.*

Sternberg's Triarchic Theory Two psychologists have proposed popular contemporary theories of multiple intelligences. Robert J. Sternberg (1986) believes that intelligence has three factors. **Triarchic theory** *is Sternberg's theory* *that intelligence consists of componential intelligence, experiential intelligence, and contextual intelligence.* Consider Ann, who scores high on traditional intelligence tests, such as the Stanford-Binet, and is a star analytical thinker. Consider Juan, who does not have the best test scores but has an insightful and creative mind. Consider also Art, a street-smart person who has learned to deal in practical ways with his world, although his scores on traditional IQ tests are low.

Sternberg calls Ann's analytical thinking and abstract reasoning componential intelligence; it is the closest to what we call intelligence in this chapter and what is commonly measured by intelligence tests. Juan's insightful and creative thinking is called experiential intelligence by Sternberg. Art's street smarts and practical knowledge are called contextual intelligence by Sternberg (see figure 8.12).

In Sternberg's view of componential intelligence, the basic unit in intelligence is a component, simply defined as a basic unit of information processing. Sternberg believes that such components include the ability to acquire or store information, to retain or retrieve information, to transfer information, to plan, to make decisions, to solve problems, and to translate thoughts into performance. Notice the similarity of these components to the description of memory in chapter 7 and the description of thinking earlier in this chapter.

The second part of Sternberg's model focuses on experience. According to Sternberg, intellectual people have the ability to solve new problems quickly, but they also learn how to solve familiar problems in an automatic, rote way so their minds are free to handle other problems that require insight and creativity.

The third part of the model involves practical intelligence—such as how to get out of trouble, how to replace a fuse, and how to get along with people. Sternberg describes this practical, or contextual, intelligence as all of the important information about getting along in the real world that we are not taught in school. He believes that contextual intelligence is sometimes more important than "book knowledge."

Gardner's Frames of Intelligence Howard Gardner (1983) also objected to the notion of a unitary IQ score. However, Gardner's approach to intelligence was based on studying case histories in which either substantial deficits or impressive abilities existed. He was able to define seven frames of intelligence that corresponded to these case studies. Gardner identified *spatial skills, bodily awareness (movement skills), mathematics, artistic abilities, verbal abilities, interpersonal abilities, and intrapersonal abilities (insightful skills for analyzing oneself)* as frames in which we can have strengths or weaknesses.

Everyone is ignorant, only on different subjects.

Will Rogers

Let's explore one frame of intelligence proposed by Gardner. He suggested that many individuals demonstrate

(a)

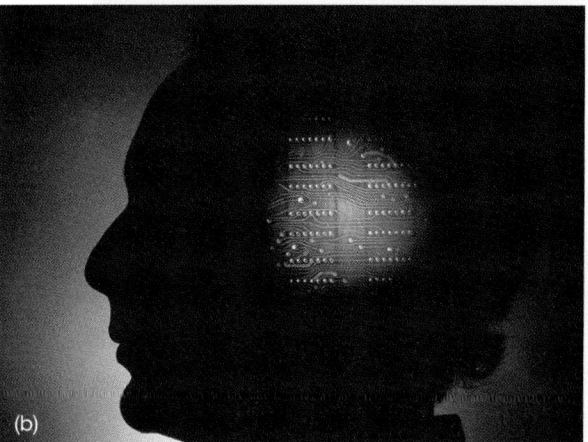

(b)

(c)

FIGURE 8.12

Sternberg's Triarchic Model of Intelligence
(a) Componential intelligence is the closest to what is commonly measured on intelligence tests and is reflected in the ability to process information as we read. *(b)* Photographer Mieke Maas showed experiential intelligence in creating this unique image of a printed circuit board inside an individual's head. Experiential intelligence involves creativity and insight. *(c)* Contextual intelligence refers to practical knowledge, especially "street smarts."

"You're wise, but you lack tree smarts."

Drawing by D. Reilly; © 1988 The New Yorker Magazine, Inc.

Dustin Hoffman's portrayal in *Rain Man* depicted how a man with autism and cognitive deficits could accomplish remarkable feats of counting and mathematics. Such skills are described as *savant skills*. They support the idea that intelligence can be expressed in multiple abilities.

deficits in arithmetic skills. Although they are far more rare, there are also individuals who show extraordinary calculation skills. For example, some individuals can identify, as a function of their calculation skills on what day of the week a specific day well in the future will fall. Others can perform complex calculations without pencil or paper. Gardner argued that some individuals who measure in the mentally retarded range might show a contrasting splinter skill in the area of calculation. This outcome was the focus of the fascinating film *Rain Man,* in which the autistic main character was able to do a variety of calculations, including card counting in Las Vegas.

Measuring Intelligence

The first evidence of formal tests comes from China. In 2200 B.C. the emperor Ta Ўu conducted a series of three oral "competency tests" for government officials; based on the results, they were either promoted or fired. Numerous variations on those early exams have been causing anxiety for employees and students ever since.

Robert J. Sternberg recalls being terrified of taking IQ tests as a child. He literally froze, he says, when the time came to take such tests. Even as an adult, Sternberg stings with humiliation when he recalls being in sixth grade and taking an IQ test with the fifth graders. Sternberg finally overcame his anxieties about IQ tests and not only performed much better on them, but at age 13 he even devised his own IQ test and began assessing his classmates—until the school psychologist found out and scolded him. In fact, Sternberg became so fascinated with the topic that he's made it a lifelong pursuit.

No man is smart, except by comparison with others who know less.

Edgar Watson Howe

Criteria for Test Design

Any good test must meet three criteria—it must be reliable, it must be valid, and it must be standardized. With a reliable test, scores should not fluctuate significantly as a result of chance factors, such as how much sleep the test taker got the night before, who the examiner is, or the temperature in the testing room. **Reliability** *is how consistently a person performs on a test.* One method of assessing reliability is **test-retest reliability,** *the consistency of results when the same person is given the same test on two different occasions.* For example, a reliable test would be one on which the same college students who score high one day also score high 6 months later. One drawback of test-retest reliability is that people sometimes do better the second time they take the test because they are familiar with it.

Another way that consistency can be deceptive is that a test might or might not measure the attribute we seek. For example, let's say we want to measure intelligence but the test design is flawed and we actually measure something else, such as anxiety. The test might consistently measure how anxious the subjects are and, thus, have high reliability but fail to measure intelligence. **Validity** *is the extent to which a test measures what it is intended to measure.* Two important forms of validity are content validity and criterion validity.

Content validity *is the extent to which the test covers broadly the content it purports to cover.* For example, if your instructor for this class plans a comprehensive final exam, it will probably cover topics from each of the chapters rather than just two or three chapters. If an intelligence test purports to measure both verbal ability and problem-solving ability, the test should include a liberal sampling of each.

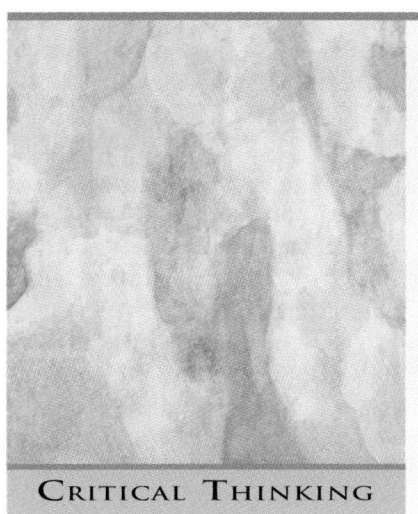

Both Sternberg and Gardner have proposed interesting theories to explain human intelligence. If you adopt Sternberg's triarchic model, which aspect of the triangle would you consider to be your relative strength—the componential (analytic and abstract reasoning), the experiential (insightful and creative thinking), or the contextual (practical intelligence or street smarts)? Which would be your relative weakness?

If you adopt Gardner's approach, in which of the seven frames of intelligence do your intellectual strengths mostly clearly lie?

- Are you mathematically inclined?
- Do you seem to have special gifts in understanding spatial relations?
- Do you show comfort and confidence in moving your body through space?

- Do you have special artistic talents?
- Are words and languages your forte?
- Do you have special abilities in relating to other people?
- Do you show unusual insights into what makes people tick?

Which of these frames is least comfortable for you?

Now that you have applied two theoretical frameworks to your own abilities, which framework do you prefer? Why does this framework appeal more to you? Your ability to *apply these psychological concepts to enhance personal adaptation* may have some implications for the course of study you select and the future career path you choose.

The test would not have high content validity if it asked you to define several vocabulary items (one measure of verbal ability) and did not require you to use reason in solving a number of problems.

Criterion validity *is a test's ability to predict other measures, or criteria, of an attribute.* For example, rather than relying solely on the results of one intelligence test to assess a person's intelligence, a psychologist might also ask that person's employer how he or she performs at work. The employer's perceptions would be another criterion for assessing intelligence. Using more than one measure—such as administering a different intelligence test, soliciting an employer's perception of intelligence, or observing a person's problem-solving ability—is a good strategy for establishing criterion validity.

Good tests are not only reliable and valid, but they also are standardized. **Standardization** *involves developing uniform procedures for administering and scoring a test, and it also involves developing norms for the test.* Uniform testing procedures require that the testing environment be as similar as possible for everyone who takes the test. For example, the test directions and the amount of time allowed to complete the test should be uniform. **Norms** *are established standards of performance for a test. Norms are developed by giving the test to a large group of people who represent the target population. This allows the researcher to determine the distribution of test scores. Norms inform us which scores are considered high, low, or average.* For example, a score of 120 on an intelligence test has little meaning alone. The score takes on meaning when we compare it with other scores. If only 20 percent of the standardized group scores above 120, then we can interpret that score as high, rather than average or low.

Although there has been some effort in recent years to standardize intelligence tests for African Americans and Latinos, little has been done to standardize tests for people from other ethnic minorities. Psychologists need to ensure that the tests are standardized for a person's particular ethnic group and to put the test results in an appropriate cultural context (Sue, 1990). Otherwise they must use caution interpreting the test's results (Saklofske & Zeidner, 1995).

Intelligence Tests

Psychologists have several options to choose from for measuring intelligence. Two of the most popular choices are the Binet tests and the Wechsler scales.

The Binet Tests In 1904 the French Ministry of Education asked psychologist Alfred Binet to devise a method of identifying children who were unable to learn in school. School officials wanted to reduce overcrowding by placing those who did not benefit from regular classroom teaching into special schools. Binet and his student Theophile Simon developed an intelligence test to meet this request. The test is referred to as the 1905 Scale and consisted of 30 questions ranging from the ability to touch one's nose or ear when asked to the ability to draw designs from memory and define abstract concepts.

Binet developed the concept of **mental age (MA)**, *which is an individual's level of mental development relative to others.* Binet reasoned that a mentally retarded child would perform like a normal child of a younger age. He developed averages for intelligence by testing 50 normal children from 3 to 11 years of age. Children who were thought to be mentally retarded also were tested. Their scores were then compared with the scores of normal children of the same chronological age. Average mental-age scores (MA) correspond to chronological age (CA), which is age from birth. A bright child has an MA above CA; a dull child has an MA below CA.

The term **intelligence quotient (IQ)** *was devised in 1912 by William Stern. IQ consists of a person's mental age divided by chronological age, multiplied by 100:*

$$IQ = MA/CA \times 100$$

If mental age is the same as chronological age, then the person's IQ is 100; if mental age is above chronological age, then IQ is more than 100; if mental age is below chronological age, then IQ is less than 100. Scores noticeably above 100 are considered above average, and scores noticeably below 100 are considered below average. For example, a 6-year-old child with a mental age of 8 would have an IQ of 133, whereas a 6-year-old child with a mental age of 5 would have an IQ of 83.

The Binet test has been revised many times to incorporate advances in the understanding of intelligence and intelligence testing. These revisions are called the Stanford-Binet tests (Stanford University is where the revisions were done). Many of the revisions were carried out by Lewis Terman, who applied Stern's IQ concept to the test, developed extensive norms, and provided detailed, clear instructions for each problem on the test.

In an extensive effort to standardize the Stanford-Binet test, it has been given to thousands of children and adults of different ages, selected at random from various parts of the United States. By administering the test to large numbers of people and recording the results, researchers have found that intelligence measured by the Stanford-Binet approximates a normal distribution (see figure 8.13). A **normal distribution** *is symmetrical, with a majority of cases falling in the middle of the possible range of scores and few scores appearing toward the extremes of the range.*

The Wechsler Scales   Besides the Stanford-Binet, the other widely used intelligence tests are the Wechsler scales, developed by David Wechsler. They include the Wechsler Adult Intelligence Scale–Revised (WAIS-R); the Wechsler Intelligence Scale for Children–Revised (WISC-R), to test children between the ages of 6 and 16; and the Wechsler Preschool and Primary Scale of Intelligence (WPPSI), to test children from the ages of 4 to 6½ (Wechsler, 1949, 1955, 1967, 1974, 1981).

Not only do the Wechsler scales provide an overall IQ score, but the items are grouped according to 11 subscales, 6 of which are verbal and 5 nonverbal. This allows an examiner to obtain separate verbal and nonverbal IQ

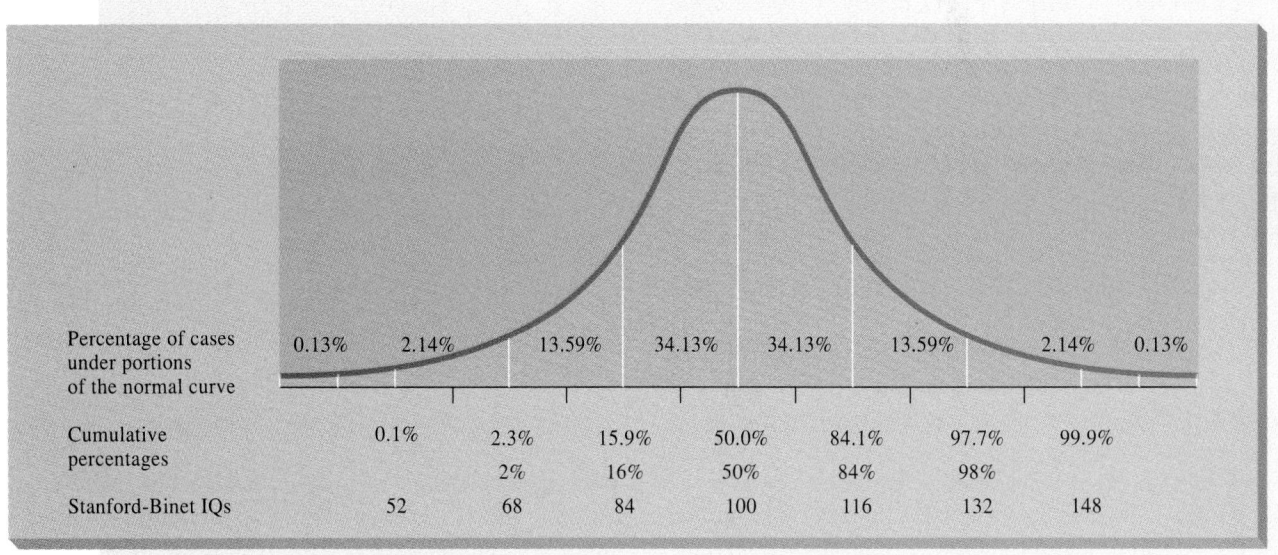

FIGURE 8.13

The Normal Curve and Stanford-Binet IQ Scores
The distribution of IQ scores approximates a normal curve. Most of the population falls in the middle range of scores. Notice that extremely high and extremely low scores are very rare. Slightly more than two-thirds of the scores fall between 84 and 116. Only about 1 in 50 individuals has an IQ of more than 132 and only about 1 in 50 individuals has an IQ of less than 68.

Learning and Cognition

VERBAL SUBSCALES

SIMILARITIES

An individual must think logically and abstractly to answer a number of questions about how things might be similar.

For example, "In what ways are boats and trains the same?"

COMPREHENSION

This subscale is designed to measure an individual's judgment and common sense.

For example, "Why do individuals buy automobile insurance?"

PERFORMANCE SUBSCALES

PICTURE ARRANGEMENT

A series of pictures out of sequence is shown to an individual, who is asked to place them in their proper order to tell an appropriate story. This subscale evaluates how individuals integrate information to make it logical and meaningful.

For example, "The pictures below need to be placed in an appropriate order to tell a story."

BLOCK DESIGN

An individual must assemble a set of multicolored blocks to match designs that the examiner shows. Visual-motor coordination, perceptual organization, and the ability to visualize spatially are assessed.

For example, "Use the four blocks on the left to make the pattern at the right."

Remember that the Wechsler includes 11 subscales, 6 verbal and 5 nonverbal. Four of the subscales are shown here.

FIGURE 8.14

Sample Subscales of the Wechsler Adult Intelligence Scale–Revised
Simulated items similar to those in the Wechsler Intelligence Scales for Adults and Children. Copyright 1949, 1955, 1974, 1981, 1991 by The Psychological Corporation. Reproduced by permission. All rights reserved.

scores and to see quickly the areas of mental performance in which a tested individual is below average, average, or above average. The inclusion of a number of nonverbal subscales makes the Wechsler test more representative of verbal and nonverbal intelligence; the Stanford-Binet test includes some nonverbal items but not as many as the Wechsler scales. Several of the Wechsler subscales are shown in figure 8.14.

Variations in Cognitive Ability

Intelligence tests have been used to discover indications of mental retardation or intellectual giftedness, the extremes of intelligence. At times intelligence tests have been misused for this purpose. Keep in mind the theme that an intelligence test should not be used as the sole indicator of mental retardation or giftedness as we explore the nature of these intellectual extremes.

Mental Retardation

The most distinctive feature of mental retardation is inadequate intellectual functioning. Long before formal tests were developed to assess intelligence, the mentally retarded were identified by a lack of age-appropriate skills in learning and caring for themselves. Once intelligence tests were developed, numbers were assigned to indicate degree of mental retardation. It is not unusual to find that of two retarded people with the same low IQ, one is married, employed, and involved in the community and the other requires constant supervision in an institution. These differences in social competence led psychologists to include

FIGURE 8.15

A Mother Caring for Her Down Syndrome Child
What causes a child to develop Down syndrome? In what major classification of mental retardation does this condition fall?

deficits in adaptive behavior in their definition of mental retardation. **Mental retardation** *is a condition of limited mental ability in which an individual has a low IQ, usually below 70 on a traditional intelligence test, and has difficulty adapting to everyday life.* About 5 million Americans fit this definition of mental retardation.

There are several classifications of mental retardation. About 89 percent of the mentally retarded fall into the mild category, with IQs of 55 to 70. About 6 percent are classified as moderately retarded, with IQs of 40 to 54; these people can attain a second-grade level of skills and may be able to support themselves as adults through some types of labor. About 3.5 percent of the mentally retarded are in the severe category, with IQs of 25 to 39; these individuals learn to talk and engage in very simple tasks but require extensive supervision. Less than 1 percent have IQs below 25; they fall into the profoundly mentally retarded classification and are in constant need of supervision.

Mental retardation can have an organic cause, or it can be social and cultural in origin. **Organic retardation** *is mental retardation caused by a genetic disorder or by brain damage;* organic *refers to the tissues or organs of the body, so there is some physical damage in organic retardation.* Down syndrome, one form of mental retardation, occurs when an extra chromosome is present in an individual's genetic makeup (see figure 8.15). It is not known why the extra chromosome is present, but it may involve the health or age of the female ovum or male sperm. Most people who suffer from organic retardation have IQs that range between 0 and 50.

Cultural-familial retardation *is a mental deficit in which no evidence of organic brain damage can be found; individuals' IQs range from 50 to 70. Psychologists suspect that such mental deficits result from the normal variation that distributes people along the range of intelligence scores above 50, combined with growing up in a below-average intellectual environment.* As children those who are familially retarded can be detected in schools, where they often fail, need tangible rewards (candy rather than praise), and are highly sensitive to what others—both peers and adults—want from them. However, as adults the familially retarded are usually invisible, perhaps because adult settings don't tax their cognitive skills as sorely. It may also be that the familially retarded increase their intelligence as they move toward adulthood.

Learning Differences

Perhaps as many as one in ten of all Americans suffers academically from a **learning difference,** *a problematic development in specific academic skills that does not reflect overall intellectual ability.* Learning differences are distinct from intelligence. Some individuals who have a learning difference even have IQ scores in the genius range. The famous Americans who have gone public with their learning differences include actors Tom Cruise and Tracy Gold.

TABLE 8.2

Do You Have a Learning Difference?

Despite the fact that your intelligence test results register in the average or above-average range for intellectual ability, you may have a learning difference or disability if you show a significant degree of the following performance problems:

- Difficulties in reading comprehension (processing and retaining the meaning of written words)
- Difficulties with math, including basic mathematics and quantitative reasoning
- Problems in written and oral expression, including spelling, written composition, listening, speaking, vocabulary skills, and related abilities
- Underdeveloped or uneven cognitive learning strategies
- Difficulties in concentrating, which might include distractibility, hyperactivity, or attention disorder
- Poor spatial orientation and difficulties in ideas related to directions (e.g., discerning right vs. left; north vs. south)
- Inadequate time concepts (including chronic lateness and confusion about personal responsibility related to time)
- Difficulties in making relationships and comparisons (e.g., discerning light vs. heavy)
- Poor gross or fine motor coordination
- Problems in interpreting subtleties in social interaction
- Difficulties in following directions as well as in following the flow of class discussion
- Perceptual disturbance (e.g., letter reversals)
- Diminished auditory or visual memory
- Experience of accusations from teachers that you are "being lazy," despite working hard and putting in lots of time in your studies

Source: Derived from Gearheart and Gearheart, 1989.

There are many kinds of learning differences. **Dyslexia** *is a learning difference that negatively influences the ability to read.* People with dyslexia, such as Jay Leno, describe frustration from strings of letters (words and sentences) that are hard to decipher. These individuals might perform poorly in school, especially when called on by teachers. Because of their anxieties about poor performance and their slower learning rate, students with dyslexia often have wounded self-esteem. They are sometimes accused of "not trying" or "being lazy" by those who fail to understand their struggles. Other learning differences involve deficits in performing arithmetic calculations (dyscalculia), problematic writing skills, and difficulties in articulating or expressing speech. Turn to table 8.2 to see whether you might have a learning difference that could be impeding your success in college.

The field of learning disabilities is relatively new. However, some tests have been developed to determine whether an individual has a learning difference. Historically, psychologists interpreted a large difference between performance and verbal subscales on the Wechsler scales as possibly indicating a learning disability. More-recent testing techniques address the specific forms of learning differences. Individuals who have a verified learning difference as determined by a qualified examiner might be entitled to special support through the Education for All Handicapped Children Act of 1975.

Learning differences do not automatically predict academic failure. Successful students with learning differences often use compensating strategies to assist them in areas that are influenced by their differences. For example, students with dyslexia might find it easier to learn concepts by listening to audiotape versions of text than by reading

text. They might also find classes easier to cope with if they audiotape professors' lectures rather than rely on written notes. Switching to auditory learning circumvents the need to rely on skills in which they routinely fare poorly. Students with expressive problems can invest in spell-checking devices or recruit proofreaders to compensate for their limitations in recognizing misspelled words.

Giftedness

There have always been people whose abilities and accomplishments outshine others'—the whiz kid in class, the star athlete, the natural musician. People who are **gifted** *have above-average intelligence (an IQ of 120 or higher) and/or superior talent for something.* When it comes to programs for the gifted, most school systems select children who have intellectual superiority and academic aptitude. Children who are talented in the visual and performing arts (arts, drama, dance), athletics, or other special aptitudes tend to be overlooked.

Never to be cast away are the gifts of the gods, magnificent.
Homer, *The Iliad*, 9th century B.C.

Until recently giftedness and emotional distress were thought to go hand in hand. English novelist Virginia Woolf suffered from severe depression, for example, and eventually committed suicide. Sir Isaac Newton, Vincent van Gogh, Ann Sexton, Socrates, and Sylvia Plath all had emotional problems. However, these are the exception rather than the rule; in general, no relation between giftedness and mental disorder has been found. A number of recent studies support the conclusion that gifted people tend to be more mature, have fewer emotional problems than others, and grow up in a positive family climate (Draper & others, 1993; Feldman & Piirto, 1995).

Lewis Terman (1925) has followed the lives of approximately 1,500 children whose Stanford-Binet IQs averaged 150 into adulthood; the study will not be complete until the year 2010. Terman has found that this remarkable group is an accomplished lot: Of the 800 males, 78 have obtained doctorates (they include two past presidents of the American Psychological Association), 48 have earned M.D.'s, and 85 have been granted law degrees. Most of these figures are 10 to 30 times higher than those found among the 800 men of the same age chosen randomly as a comparison group. These findings challenge the commonly held belief that the intellectually gifted are emotionally disturbed or socially maladjusted.

The 672 gifted women studied by Terman (Terman & Oden, 1959) underscore the importance of relationships and intimacy in women's lives. Two-thirds of these exceptional women graduated from college in the 1930s, and one-fourth attended graduate school. Despite their impressive educational achievements, when asked to order their life's priorities, the gifted women placed families first, friendships second, and careers last. For these women, having a career often meant not having children. Of the 30 most successful women, 25 did not have any children. Such undivided commitments to the family are less true of women today. Many of the highly gifted women in Terman's study questioned their intelligence and concluded that their cognitive skills had waned in adulthood. Studies of gifted women today reveal that they have a stronger confidence in their cognitive skills and intellectual abilities than the gifted women in Terman's study had (Tomlinson-Keasey, 1990). Terman's gifted women represented a cohort who reached midlife prior to the women's movement and the pervasiveness of the dual-career couple and the single-parent family (Tomlinson-Keasey, 1993).

Gift, like genius, I often think only means an infinite capacity for taking pains.

Jane Ellice Hopkins

There is a special concern about gifted disadvantaged children. When gifted disadvantaged children learn to adapt their behavior to the values and demands of school, they begin to accomplish required tasks successfully, their achievements start to attract teachers' attention, and more opportunities are made available to them. This "snowball effect" has crucial implications for the child's personal and motivational development (Arroyo & Sternberg, 1993).

Parents in low-income families can help their children develop the self-management skills required to function well in a school setting, but in many instances they do not. For gifted disadvantaged children, teachers and other influential persons within the school can compensate for the lack of appropriate direction these children have received at home. Alternative socialization agents can expose gifted disadvantaged children to a wide range of experiences that can influence their emerging view of themselves and their future.

It is especially important to develop measures to identify gifted disadvantaged children. Traditionally, giftedness has been assessed in one dimension—intellectual exceptionality. However, to adequately identify gifted disadvantaged children, it is necessary to widen the assessment procedure to include not only intellectual abilities but also behavior, motivation, and personality attributes. Researchers have found that high-achieving disadvantaged children are self-confident, industrious, tough-minded, individualistic, and raceless (Comer, 1988). These same characteristics often appear in children high in creativity that come from advantaged backgrounds.

The behaviors of the gifted disadvantaged are often motivated by the desire to transform their social and economic conditions. Because this goal requires long-range planning and self-management, giftedness among disadvantaged children needs to be assessed over time (Arroyo & Sternberg, 1993).

Culture and Ethnicity

Are there cultural and ethnic differences in intelligence? How does adaptation affect the role culture plays in understanding intelligence? Are standard intelligence tests biased? If so, can we develop tests that are fair?

The Heredity-Environment Controversy

Arthur Jensen (1969) sparked lively and at times hostile debate when he stated his theory that intelligence is primarily inherited and that environment and culture play only a minimal role in intelligence. In one of his most provocative statements, Jensen claimed that genetics account for clear-cut differences in the average intelligence among races, nationalities, and social classes. When Jensen published an article in the *Harvard Educational Review* stating that lower intelligence probably is the reason why African Americans do not perform as well in school as Whites, he was called naive and racist. He received hate mail by the bushel, and police had to escort him to his classes at the University of California at Berkeley.

Jensen reviewed the research on intelligence, much of which involved comparisons of identical and fraternal twins. Remember that identical twins have exactly the same genetic makeup. If intelligence is genetically determined, Jensen reasoned, identical twins' IQs should be similar. Fraternal twins and ordinary siblings are less similar genetically, so their IQs should be less similar. Jensen found support for his argument. The studies on intelligence in identical twins that Jensen examined showed an average correlation between their IQs of .82, a very high positive association. Investigations of fraternal twins, however, produced an average correlation of .50, a moderately high positive correlation. Note

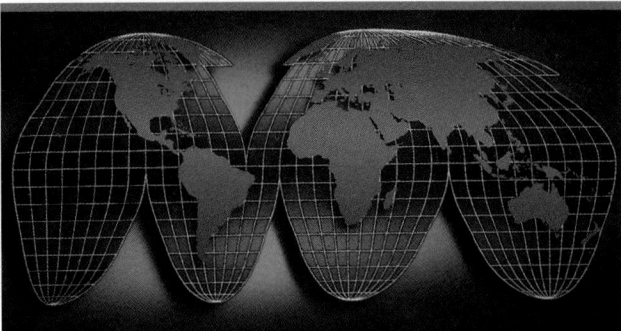

The Bell-Curve Controversy

The most recent controversy about heredity and intelligence focuses on the book *The Bell Curve: Intelligence and Class Structure in Modern Life* (Hernstein & Murray, 1994), in which Richard Hernstein and Charles Murray argued that America is rapidly evolving a huge underclass that consists of intellectually deprived individuals whose cognitive abilities will never match the future needs of most employers. The authors predicted that this underclass, a large proportion of which is African American, may be doomed by their shortcomings to welfare dependency, poverty, crime, and lives devoid of any hope of ever reaching the American dream.

Hernstein and Murray believe that intelligence can be quantitatively measured, as IQ, and that IQ test scores vary in systematic ways across ethnic groups. They pointed out that, in the United States, the average Asian American score is several points higher than the average White score, while the average African American score is about 15 points lower than the average White score. They also argued that these IQ differences are at least partly due to heredity. The authors stated that government money spent on education programs such as Project Head Start is wasted, helping only the government's bloated bureaucracy.

Why did Hernstein and Murray entitle their book *The Bell Curve*? Because a normal distribution graph (review figure 8.13) has a bell-shaped curve: it looks like a bell, bulging in the middle and thinning out at the edges. The normal distribution graph is used to represent large numbers of people who are sorted according to some shared characteristic, such as weight, exposure to asbestos, taste in clothing, or IQ.

Hernstein and Murray often referred to bell curves to make a point: that predictions about any individual based exclusively on the person's IQ are virtually useless. Weak correlations between, say, intelligence and job success, have predictive value only when they are applied to large groups of people. Within such large groups, say Hernstein and Murray, the pervasive influence of IQ on human society becomes apparent (Browne, 1994).

Many psychologists believe that a unitary IQ score is an inadequate evaluation of anything as multifaceted as intelligence. For example, a "street-smart" person might adapt well, even creatively, to the intellectual challenge of life on the street but fare poorly in the structured setting of a psychologist's office. No test has been devised to measure the special abilities involved in adapting to street life, but few would say that these skills are unrelated to intelligence.

Significant criticisms have been leveled at Jensen's work as well as at *The Bell Curve* (Fraser, 1995). Experts on intelligence generally agree that the average IQ score for African Americans is lower than the average IQ score for Whites. However, many of these experts raise serious questions about the ability of IQ tests to measure a person's intelligence accurately. Among the criticisms of IQ tests is that the tests are culturally biased against African Americans and Latinos. In 1971, the Supreme Court endorsed such criticisms and ruled that tests of general intelligence, in contrast to tests that solely measure fitness for a particular job, are discriminatory and cannot be administered as a condition of employment.

A final criticism is that most investigations of heredity and environment do not include environments that differ radically. Thus, it is not surprising that many genetic studies show environment to be a fairly weak influ-

the substantial difference of .32. To show that genetic factors are more important than environmental factors, Jensen compared the intelligence of identical twins reared together with that of those reared apart. The correlation for those reared together was .89 and for those reared apart it was .78, a difference of .11. Jensen argued that if environmental factors are more important than genetic factors, siblings reared apart, who experience different environments, should have IQs that differ by more than .11. Jensen places heredity's influence on intelligence at about 80 percent. To read about the most recent controversy about heredity and intelligence, turn to Sociocultural Worlds 8.2.

Today most researchers agree that genetics do not determine intelligence to the extent Jensen envisioned.

Their estimates fall more in the 50/50 range—50 percent genetic makeup, 50 percent environmental factors (Plomin, DeFries & McClearn, 1990). For most people, this means that modifying their environment can change their IQ scores considerably (Weinberg, 1989). It also means that programs designed to enrich a person's environment can have a considerable impact, improving school achievement and the acquisition of skills needed for employability. Although genetic endowment may always influence a person's intellectual ability, the environmental influences and opportunities we provide children and adults make a difference.

Keep in mind, though, that environmental influences are complex. Growing up with "all the advantages," for

Exploring IQ and Inheritance

Consider Jensen's controversial conclusion that intelligence is largely a matter of inheritance. What are various reasons children from different cultural backgrounds might score poorly on standardized tests? In what way do the specific aspects of the testing context contribute to relatively poorer performance? What could be some explanations of why such children do poorly in school? Your full consideration of the array of factors that influence intellectual performance demonstrates your ability to *consider alternative explanations to explain behavior comprehensively.*

example, does not necessarily guarantee success. Children from wealthy families may have easy access to excellent schools, books, travel, and tutoring, but they may take such opportunities for granted and fail to develop the motivation to learn and achieve. In the same way, being "poor" or "disadvantaged" does not automatically mean that one is "doomed,"

Some years ago, one of the authors of this book (John Santrock) knocked on the door of a house in a low-income area of a large city. The father came to the door and invited the author into the living room. Even though it was getting dark outside, no lights were on inside the house. The father excused himself, then returned with a light bulb, which he screwed into a lamp socket. He said he could barely pay his monthly mortgage and the electric company had threatened to turn off the electricity, so he was carefully monitoring how much electricity his family used. There were seven children in the family, ranging in age from 2 to 16 years old. Neither parent had completed high school. The father worked as a bricklayer when he could find a job, and the mother ironed clothes in a laundry. The parents wanted their children to pursue education and to have more opportunities in life than they had had. The children from the inner-city family were exposed to both positive and negative influences. On the one hand, they were growing up in an intact family in which education was encouraged, and their parents provided a model of the work ethic. On the other hand, they were being shortchanged because they had few opportunities to develop their intellectual abilities.

Researchers increasingly are interested in manipulating the early environment of children who are at risk for impoverished intelligence. The emphasis is on prevention rather than remediation. Many low-income parents have difficulty providing an intellectually stimulating environment for their children. Programs that educate parents to be more sensitive caregivers and that train them to be better teachers, as well as support services such as Head Start, can make a difference in a child's intellectual development (Ramey, 1989).

Cultural and Ethnic Comparisons

In the United States, children from African American and Latino families score below children from White families on standardized intelligence tests. On the average, African American schoolchildren score 10 to 15 points lower on standardized intelligence tests than White schoolchildren do (Anastasi, 1988). We are talking about average scores, though. Estimates also indicate that 15 to 25 percent of all African American schoolchildren score higher than half of all White schoolchildren, and many Whites score lower than most African Americans do. This is because the distributions of the scores for African Americans and Whites overlap.

How extensively are ethnic differences in intelligence influenced by heredity and environment? The evidence in support of a genetic interpretation is suspect. For example, as African Americans have gained social, economic, and educational opportunities, the gap between African American and White children on standardized intelligence tests has begun to narrow, and when children from disadvantaged African American families are adopted into more-advantaged middle-class families, their scores on intelligence tests more closely resemble national averages for middle-class children than averages for lower-class children (Scarr, 1991). This comparison also presumes the acceptance of the definition of intelligence used for standardized intelligence tests. If intelligence is measured in a manner inconsistent with a child's own culture, the child is likely to have a lower score.

Culture, Intelligence, and Adaptation

People adapt to their environment, and what's appropriate in one environment might not be appropriate in another. As mentioned earlier in the chapter, intelligence is expressed differently in different cultures (Berry & Bennett, 1992; Berry & others, 1992; Irvine & Berry, 1988; Kagitcibasi & Berry, 1989; Sternberg, 1988). In one study, the researcher asked members of the Kpelle in Liberia (located on the western coast of Africa) to sort twenty objects (Glick,

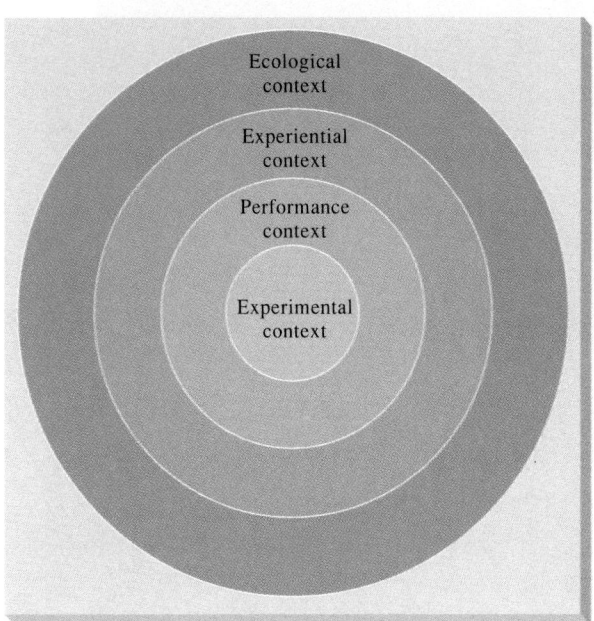

FIGURE 8.16

Berry's Model of the Contexts of Intelligence
In this model of the intelligence, there is much more to consider than the actual context in which a test is being administered (the experimental context). In addition, it is also important to consider three other contextual levels—the performance context, experiential context, and ecological context.

"You can't build a hut, you don't know how to find edible roots and you know nothing about predicting the weather. In other words, you do terribly on our IQ test."

1975). Rather than sort the objects into the "appropriate" categories the researcher had predicted, the Kpelle sorted the objects into functional groups—such as a knife with an apple and a potato with a hoe. Surprised by the answers, the researcher asked the Kpelle to explain their reasoning. The Kpelle responded that that was the way a wise person would group things. When the researchers asked how a fool would classify the objects, the Kpelle answered that four neat piles of food in one category, four tools in another category, and so on was the fool's way. The Kpelle were not lacking in intelligence; the researcher lacked an understanding of the Kpelle culture. The Kpelle sorted the items in ways that were adaptive for their culture.

Another example of human adaptability involves spatial ability. One study showed that people who live in hunter-gatherer societies score higher on spatial ability tests than do people from industrialized societies (Berry, 1971). People who must hunt to eat depend on the spatial skills for survival.

Few of us will ever have firsthand experience with hunter-gatherer societies, but many of us know people who are adaptable, savvy, and successful yet do not score correspondingly high on intelligence tests. Canadian cross-cultural psychologist John Berry (1983) has an explanation for this gap between intelligence exhibited in one's own culture and intelligence displayed in a

formal testing situation. He describes people as being embedded in four levels of environmental contexts. Level 1, the ecological context, is an individual's natural habitat. Level 2, the experiential context, is the pattern of recurring experiences from which the individual regularly learns. Level 3, the performance context, is the limited set of circumstances in which the individual's natural behavior is observed. Level 4, the experimental context, is the set of environmental circumstances under which test scores are actually generated (Berry's model is presented in figure 8.16).

When the experimental context differs considerably from the ecological or experiential context, Berry says, the individuals being tested are at a disadvantage. Presumably, the greater the difference, the greater the disadvantage. However, relations among contexts change. If an individual has been given the same test previously, some of the gap between the experiential and experimental contexts closes, resulting in higher test scores.

Cultural Bias and Culture-Fair Tests

Many of the early intelligence tests were culturally biased, favoring people from urban rather than rural environments, middle-class rather than lower-class people, and Whites rather than African Americans (Miller-Jones, 1989). For example, a question on an early test asked what should be done if you find a 3-year-old child in the street. The correct answer was "call the police"; however, children from inner-city families who perceive the police as adversaries are unlikely to choose this answer. Similarly, children from rural areas might not choose this answer if there is no police force nearby. Such questions clearly do not measure the knowledge necessary to adapt to one's environment or to be "intelligent" in an inner-city neighborhood or in rural America (Scarr,

---

FIGURE 8.17

Iatmul and Caroline Islander Intelligence
(a) The intelligence of the Iatmul people of Papua, New Guinea, involves the ability to remember the names of many clans. *(b)* The Caroline Islands number 680 in the Pacific Ocean east of the Philippines. The intelligence of their inhabitants includes the ability to navigate by the stars.

1984). Also, members of minority groups often do not speak English or might speak nonstandard English. Consequently, they may be at a disadvantage in trying to understand verbal questions framed in standard English, even if the content of the test is appropriate.

Cultures also vary in the way they define intelligence. Most European Americans, for example, think of intelligence in terms of technical skills, but people in Kenya consider responsible participation in family and social life an integral part of intelligence. Similarly, an intelligent person in Uganda is someone who knows what to do and then follows through with appropriate action. Intelligence to the Iatmul people of Papua, New Guinea, involves the ability to remember the names of 10,000 to 20,000 clans, and the islanders in the widely dispersed Caroline Islands incorporate the talent of navigating by the stars into their definition of intelligence (see figure 8.17).

An example of possible cultural bias in intelligence tests can be seen in the case study of Gregory Ochoa. When

Gregory was a high school student, he and his classmates took an IQ test. When Gregory looked at the test questions, he understood only a few words, since he did not speak English very well and spoke Spanish at home. Several weeks later, Gregory was placed in a special class for mentally retarded students. Many of the students in the class, it turns out, had last names such as Ramirez and Gonzales. Gregory lost interest in school, dropped out, and eventually joined the Navy. In the Navy, Gregory took high school courses and earned enough credits to attend college later. He graduated from San Jose City College as an honors student, continued his education, and became a professor of social work at the University of Washington in Seattle.

As a result of such cases, researchers have tried to develop tests that accurately reflect a person's intelligence. **Culture-fair tests** *are intelligence tests that are intended not to be culturally biased.* Two types of culture-fair tests have been devised. The first includes questions that are familiar to people from all socioeconomic and ethnic backgrounds.

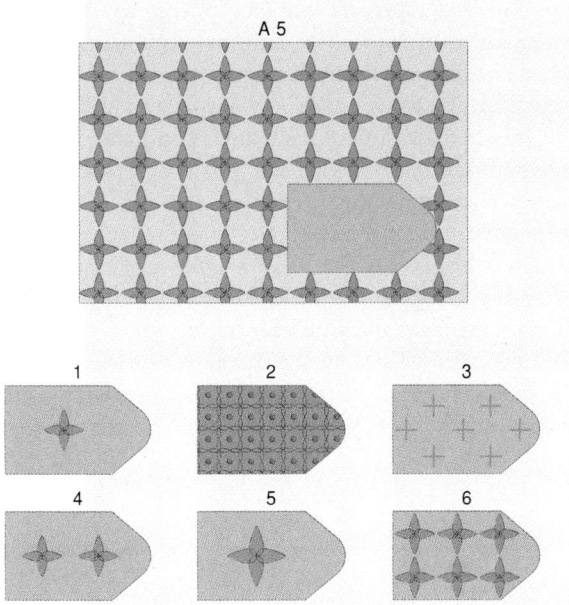

A 5

1 2 3

4 5 6

FIGURE 8.18

Sample Item from the Raven Progressive Matrices Test
Psychologists present a matrix arrangement of symbols, such as
the one at the top of this figure, and ask the person to be tested
to complete the matrix by selecting the appropriate missing
symbol from a group of symbols.

Figure A5 from the Raven Standard Progressive Matrices. Copyright © J. C. Raven Limited.
Reprinted by permission.

For example, a child might be asked how a bird and a dog
are different, on the assumption that virtually all children
are familiar with birds and dogs. The second type of culture-fair test excludes all verbal questions. Figure 8.18
shows a sample question from the Raven Progressive Matrices Test. Even though such tests are designed to be culture-
fair, people with more education still score higher on them
than those with less education do.

One test that takes into account the socioeconomic
background of children is the SOMPA, which stands for
System of Multicultural Pluralistic Assessment (Mercer &
Lewis, 1978). This test can be given to children from 5 to
11 years of age and was especially designed for children
from low-income families. Instead of relying on a single
test, SOMPA is based on information from four areas of a
child's life: (1) verbal and nonverbal intelligence, assessed
by the WISC-R; (2) social and economic background,
obtained through a 1-hour parent interview; (3) social
adjustment to school, determined through a questionnaire
that parents complete; and (4) physical health, assessed by
a medical examination.

The Kaufman Assessment Battery for Children (K-
ABC) has been trumpeted as an improvement over other
culture-fair tests (Kaufman & Kaufman, 1983). The test is
based on a more representative sample, which includes a
greater number of minority and handicapped children. The
intelligence portion focuses less on language than the

Stanford-Binet does, and the K-ABC includes an achievement section, with subtests for arithmetic and reading.
However, the K-ABC, like other culture-fair tests, has its
detractors. Based on the three main criteria for evaluating
tests, the K-ABC fares well on reliability and standardization, but not as well on validity (Sax, 1989).

Most researchers agree that traditional intelligence
tests are probably culturally biased. However, efforts to develop culture-fair tests so far have yielded unsatisfactory results. The construction of culture-fair tests does not
guarantee culture-fairness, but it does attempt to minimize
errors derived from differences in cultural contexts.

The Use and Misuse
of Intelligence Tests

Psychological tests are tools. Like all tools, their effectiveness depends on the knowledge, skill, and integrity of the
user. A hammer can be used to build a beautiful kitchen
cabinet or it can be used as a weapon of assault. Like a hammer, psychological tests can be used for positive purposes
or they can be badly abused. It is important for both the test
constructor and the test examiner to be familiar with the
current state of scientific knowledge about intelligence and
intelligence tests.

Even though they have limitations, tests of intelligence are among psychology's most widely used tools. To
be effective, though, intelligence tests must be viewed realistically. They should not be thought of as unchanging indicators of intelligence. They should be used in conjunction
with other information about an individual, not relied on as
the sole indicator of intelligence. For example, an intelligence test should not solely determine whether a child is
placed in a special education or gifted class. The child's developmental history, medical background, performance in
school, social competencies, and family experiences should
be taken into account too.

The single number provided by many IQ tests can
easily lead to stereotypes and expectations about an individual. Many people do not know how to interpret the results
of intelligence tests, and sweeping generalizations are too
often made on the basis of an IQ score. For example, imagine that you are a teacher in the teacher's lounge the day
after school has started in the fall. You mention a student—
Johnny Jones—and a fellow teacher remarks that she had
Johnny in class last year; she comments that he was a real
dunce and points out that his IQ is 78. You cannot help but
remember this information, and it might lead you to think
that Johnny Jones is not very bright so it is useless to spend
much time teaching him. In this way, IQ scores are misused
and stereotypes are formed (Rosenthal & Jacobsen, 1968).

Ability tests can help a teacher divide children into homogeneous groups of children who function at roughly the
same level in math or reading so they can be taught the same
concepts together. However, when children are placed in
tracks, such as "advanced," "intermediate," and "low," extreme caution needs to be taken. Periodic assessment of the

"How are her scores?"

Drawing by Koren; © 1987 The New Yorker Magazine, Inc.

groups is needed, especially with the "low" group. Ability tests measure *current* performance, and maturational changes or enriched environmental experiences may advance a child's intelligence, requiring that he or she be moved to a higher group.

Despite their limitations, when used judiciously by a competent examiner, intelligence tests provide valuable information about individuals. There are not many alternatives to these tests. Subjective judgments about individuals simply reintroduce the bias the tests were designed to eliminate.

In this chapter, we have discussed many facets of thinking, language, and intelligence, including some ideas about how children's language develops and the nature of children's intelligence. In the next chapter, we will turn our attention exclusively to how we develop as human beings.

REVIEW

Intelligence

Intelligence is verbal ability, problem-solving skills, and the ability to learn from and adapt to the experiences of everyday life. In the study of intelligence, extensive attention is given to individual differences and the assessment of intelligence. The way intelligence is expressed in behavior may vary from one culture to another.

Psychologists debate whether intelligence is a general ability or a number of specific abilities. Spearman's two-factor theory and Thurstone's multiple-factor theory state that a number of specific factors are involved. Sternberg's triarchic theory states that intelligence consists of three factors: componential, experiential, and contextual. Gardner proposed that there are seven factors in intelligence.

Three important criteria for tests are reliability, validity, and standardization. Reliability is how consistently an individual performs on a test; one type is test-retest reliability. Validity is the extent to which a test measures what it is intended to measure. Two kinds of validity are content and criterion. Standardization involves uniform procedures for administering and scoring a test, as well as norms.

Binet developed the first intelligence test, known as the 1905 Scale.

He developed the concept of mental age, whereas Stern developed the concept of IQ. The Binet has been standardized and revised a number of times. The many revisions are called the Stanford-Binet tests. The test approximates a normal distribution. Besides the Stanford-Binet, the most widely used intelligence tests are the Wechsler scales. They include the WAIS-R, WISC-R, and WPPSI. These tests provide an overall IQ, verbal and performance IQs, and information about 11 subscales.

A mentally retarded individual has a low IQ, usually below 70 on a traditional IQ test, and has difficulty adapting to everyday life. There are several classifications of mental retardation. The two main types of retardation are organic and cultural-familial. A learning difference is a learning difference that negatively influences the development of specific academic skills that does not reflect overall intellectual ability. Dyslexia is one kind of learning difference. A gifted individual has above-average intelligence (an IQ of 120 or more) and/or superior talent for something. Gifted disadvantaged children are of special concern.

In the late 1960s, Jensen argued that intelligence is approximately 80

percent hereditary and that genetic differences exist in the average intelligence of ethnic groups and social classes. Intelligence is influenced by heredity, but not as strongly as Jensen believed. The environments we provide children and adults make a difference. There are cultural and ethnic differences on intelligence tests, but the evidence suggests they are not genetically based. In recent decades, the gap between African Americans and Whites on intelligence test scores has diminished as African Americans have experienced more socioeconomic opportunities. To understand intelligence within a given culture, the adaptive requirements of the culture must be known. Early intelligence tests favored White, middle-class, urban individuals. Current tests try to reduce this bias. Culture-fair tests are an alternative to traditional tests; most psychologists believe they cannot completely replace the traditional tests.

Despite their limitations, when used by a judicious examiner, intelligence tests are valuable tools for determining individual differences in intelligence. The tests should be used in conjunction with other information about the individual. IQ scores can produce unfortunate stereotypes and expectations about intelligence.

CRITICAL THINKING ABOUT BEHAVIOR

What's in a Name?

What's in a name?
that which we call a rose by any other name
would smell as sweet.

Juliet, in *Romeo and Juliet,* act 2, scene 2

Not many people in today's heated sociopolitical climate are as nonchalant about the process of labeling as Juliet indicated in the famous balcony scene from *Romeo and Juliet.* It seems as though controversy attaches to nearly every reference that labels some aspect of our identity. For example, if you are in your first year of college, are you a freshman? A freshperson? A first-year student? Some individuals believe the choice of term may reflect the value system of the user. The term *freshman* might disenfranchise the majority of students, who are women. Although the term *freshperson* might be more "politically correct," many people believe that the term is awkward. Using the term *first-year student* might avoid the dilemmas associated with the other terms.

A similar evolution in language has taken place in relation to describing people who perform poorly in intelligence testing. Alfred Binet's early diagnostic efforts distinguished "imbeciles" and "morons" from people of normal intelligence. Eventually these terms became popularly used as insults, to such a degree that psychologists developed a different labeling system, referring to "retardates" who experienced varying degrees of "retardation." A more recent refinement in educational systems now labels such individuals as "cognitively different." Similarly, learning-disabled children are now referred to as children with a "learning difference."

The evolution of language has also complicated matters among ethnic groups. For example, African Americans appear to be divided on a preferred designation for themselves. Some prefer to be referred to as African Americans. Some prefer to be referred to as Black

Americans. Some find the argument profound. Some find it silly. Some find it overwhelming to consider the possibility of hyphenating references to identity, particularly when the identity may be unknown.

Why do language and labeling have the power to create such strong feelings? The answer lies in the distinction between connotation and denotation. Language is very flexible. It can be used to refer to specific qualities (denotation), or it can be used to imply other characteristics (connotation), sometimes favorable and sometimes unfavorable. Labels can make it easier to identify some important characteristics. They can also be used to disparage others. People can be offended by a label they regard as inappropriate, whether or not offense was intended.

Let's take the example of the use of the term *girl* to denote women. One of the major accomplishments of the women's movement was to develop some general sensitivity in society to the connotations of the term *girl.* For instance, must a female have children before she "earns" the designation *woman*? Does it make sense to refer to the "girls" in the office when most of them are over 40? Why is there no comparable confusion in the distinction between boys and men?

How do we minimize the problems associated with inappropriate or offensive use of language? One way is to determine whether the label you have in mind is truly necessary to get your communication across. Another is to pay specific attention to the evolution of language use. Popular usage is often reflected in the media. A final method is to embark on a frank discussion with people of different backgrounds (for instance, persons of different gender or ethnicity) whose opinions matter to you, to see if you have been using language that has negative connotations to them. Your own sensitivity to the power of language will demonstrate your ability to *use psychological knowledge to promote human welfare.*

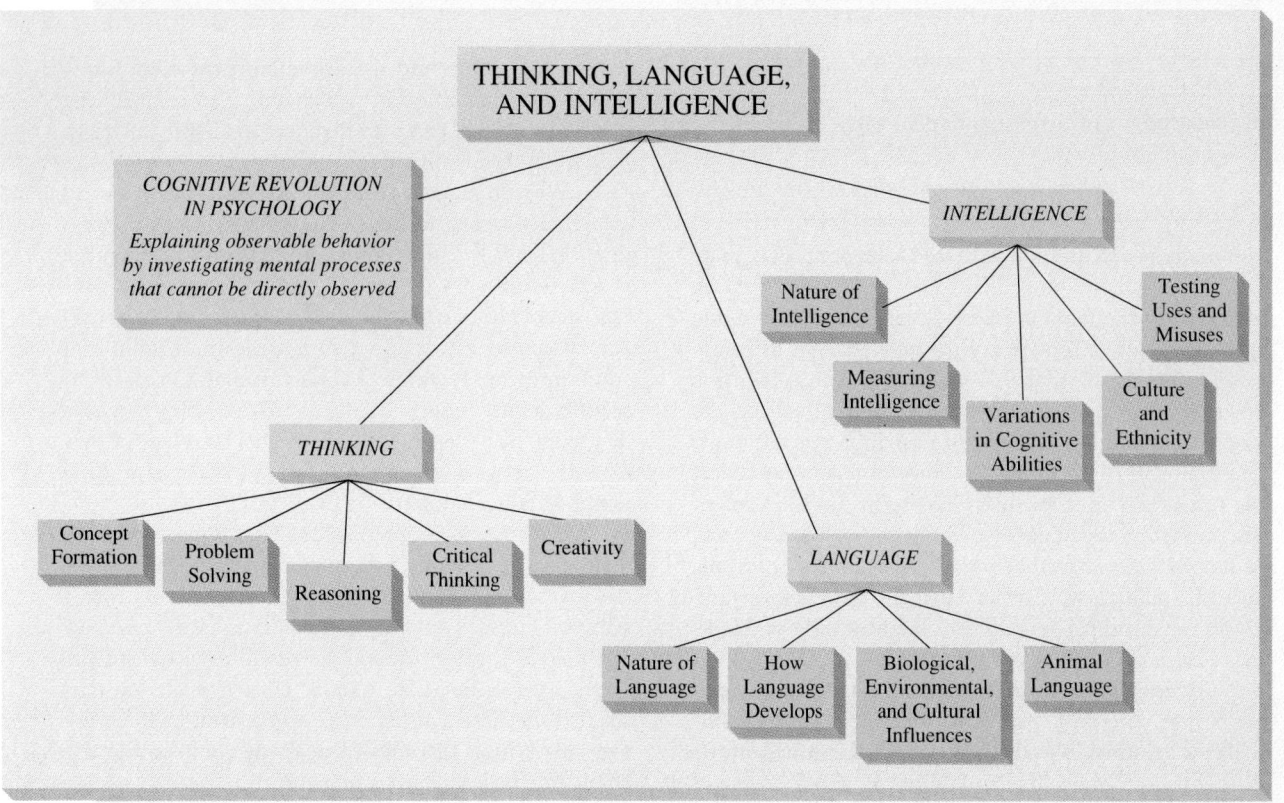

THINKING, LANGUAGE, AND INTELLIGENCE

COGNITIVE REVOLUTION IN PSYCHOLOGY
Explaining observable behavior by investigating mental processes that cannot be directly observed

INTELLIGENCE

Nature of Intelligence

Measuring Intelligence

Variations in Cognitive Abilities

Culture and Ethnicity

Testing Uses and Misuses

THINKING

Concept Formation

Problem Solving

Reasoning

Critical Thinking

Creativity

LANGUAGE

Nature of Language

How Language Develops

Biological, Environmental, and Cultural Influences

Animal Language

We began this chapter by learning about the cognitive revolution in psychology. Then we turned our attention to thinking, evaluating the nature of concept formation, problem solving, reasoning, critical thinking, and creativity.

Next, we studied language, including its nature, how it develops, biological, environmental, and cultural influences, and animal language. In the last part of the chapter we explored intelligence, its nature, how it is measured, variations in cognitive abilities, cultural and ethnic influences, and the use and misuse of intelligence tests. Remember that you can obtain an overall summary of the chapter by again reading the reviews on pages 258, 269, and 284.

PERSPECTIVES

By far the main perspective emphasized in this chapter is the cognitive perspective. Each of the chapter's four main topics reflects this perspective—the cognitive revolution in psychology (pp. 247–248), thinking (pp. 248–259), language (pp. 260–268), and intelligence (pp. 269–284). Three other perspectives also appeared: sociocultural, neurobiological, and behavioral. Material reflecting the sociocultural perspective appeared in the discussion of the language traditions of African Americans and the effects of urban poverty (p. 264), cultural influences on language (pp. 263–265), bilingual education (pp. 266–267), gifted disadvantaged children (p. 278), culture, ethnicity, and intelligence (pp. 278–283), and the bell-curve controversy (p. 279). Information about the neurobiological perspective was presented in the description of critical periods of learning language (pp. 261–262), biological influences on language (p. 262), whether animals have language (pp. 267–268), and the heredity-environment controversy in intelligence (pp. 278–280). Ideas related to the behavioral perspective were presented in the material on environmental influences on language (pp. 262–263) and the heredity-environment controversy in intelligence (pp. 278–280).

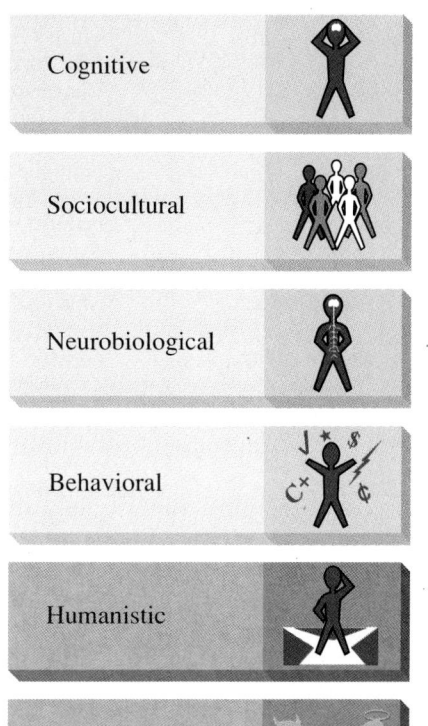

Cognitive

Sociocultural

Neurobiological

Behavioral

Humanistic

Psychoanalytic

KEY TERMS

artificial intelligence (AI) The science of creating machines capable of performing activities that require intelligence when they are done by people. 248

expert systems Computer-based systems for assessing knowledge and making decisions in advanced skill areas. 248

concept A category used to group objects, events, and characteristics on the basis of common properties. 249

problem solving An attempt to find an appropriate way of attaining a goal when the goal is not readily available. 251

algorithms Procedures that guarantee an answer to a problem. 252

heuristics Rules of thumb that can suggest a solution to a problem but do not ensure that it will work. 252

learning set A strategy that an individual tends to use to solve problems. 252

functional fixedness The inability to solve a problem because it is viewed only in terms of usual functions. 252

reasoning The mental activity of transforming information to reach conclusions. 254

inductive reasoning Reasoning from the specific to the general; drawing conclusions about all members of a category based on observing only some of the members. 254

deductive reasoning Reasoning from the general to the specific; working with abstract statements (premises) and deriving a conclusion. 254

analogy A type of formal reasoning that always has four parts, in which the relation between the first two parts is the same as the relation between the last two. 255

syllogism A deductive reasoning task that consists of a major premise, a minor premise, and a conclusion. 255

critical thinking Grasping the deeper meaning of problems, keeping an open mind about different approaches and perspectives, and deciding for oneself what to believe or do. 256

convergent thinking Thinking that produces one correct answer and is characteristic of the kind of thinking on standardized intelligence tests. 258

divergent thinking Thinking that produces many answers to the same question and is characteristic of creativity. 258

creativity The ability to think in novel ways and to come up with unique solutions to problems. 258

language A system of symbols used to communicate with others; in humans, characterized by organizational rules and infinite generativity. 260

infinite generativity A person's ability to produce an endless number of meaningful sentences using a finite set of words and rules, which makes language a highly creative enterprise. 260

phonology The study of language's sound system. 260

morphology The rules for combining morphemes, which are the smallest meaningful strings of sounds that contain no smaller meaningful parts. 260

syntax The ways words are combined to form acceptable phrases and sentences. 260

semantics The meanings of words and sentences. 260

holophrase hypothesis The concept that a single word can be used to imply a complete sentence, and that infants' first words characteristically are holophrastic. 261

telegraphic speech The use of short and precise words to communicate; characteristic of young children's two- and three-word utterances. 261

motherese Talking to babies in a higher-pitched voice than normal and with simple words and sentences. 263

linguistic relativity hypothesis The view that culture shapes language, which further determines the structure of thinking and shapes our basic ideas. 265

bilingual education Programs for students with limited proficiency in English that instruct students in their own language part of the time while they learn English. 266

individual differences The consistent, stable ways people differ from each other. 269

intelligence Verbal ability, problem-solving skills, and the ability to learn from and adapt to the experiences of everyday life. 269

two-factor theory Spearman's theory that individuals have both general intelligence, which he called *g*, and a number of specific intelligences, which he called *s*. 270

multiple-factor theory L. L. Thurstone's theory that intelligence consists of seven primary mental abilities: verbal comprehension, number ability, word fluency, spatial visualization, associative memory, reasoning, and perceptual speed. 270

triarchic theory Sternberg's theory that intelligence consists of componential intelligence, experiential intelligence, and contextual intelligence. 270

reliability How consistently a person performs on a test. 272

test-retest reliability Consistency of results when a person is given the same test on two different occasions. 272

validity The extent to which a test measures what it is purported to measure. 272

content validity The extent to which a test covers broadly the content it is purported to cover. 272

criterion validity A test's ability to predict other measures, or criteria, of an attribute. 273

standardization The development of uniform procedures for administering and scoring a test; also the development of norms for the test. 273

norms Established standards of performance for a test. Norms are established by giving the test to a large group of people who represent the target population. This allows the researcher to determine the distribution of test scores. Norms tell us which scores are high, low, or average. 273

mental age (MA) An individual's level of mental development relative to others. 274

intelligence quotient (IQ) Devised in 1912 by William Stern; a person's mental age divided by chronological age, multiplied by 100. 274

normal distribution A symmetrical distribution in which a majority of cases fall in the middle of the possible range of scores and few scores fall in the extremes of the range. 274

mental retardation A condition of limited mental ability in which an individual has a low IQ, usually below 70 on a traditional intelligence test, and has difficulty adapting to everyday life. 276

organic retardation Mental retardation caused by a genetic disorder or by brain damage. *Organic* refers to the tissues or organs of the body, so there is some physical damage in organic retardation. 276

cultural-familial retardation A mental deficit in which no evidence of organic brain damage can be found; these individuals' IQs range from 50 to 70. Psychologists suspect that such mental deficits result from the normal variation that distributes people along the range of intelligence scores above 50, combined with growing up in a below-average intellectual environment. 276

learning difference Problematic development in specific academic skills that does not reflect overall intellectual ability. 276

dyslexia A learning difference that negatively influences the quality and rate of reading. 277

gifted Having above-average intelligence (an IQ of 120 or higher) and/or superior talent for something. 277

culture-fair tests Intelligence tests that are intended to not be culturally biased. 282

GENIE

(1993) by Russ Rymer. New York: HarperCollins

In this book, Russ Rymer tells the poignant story of Genie, a child who grew up without language or any form of social training. Rymer skillfully weaves the tale of Genie's hesitant progress toward adulthood with the bitter ethical debates over her treatment by psychologists and other professionals after she was discovered and rescued from her parents' home. Rymer also explores how theories of language development can be used to address Genie's case. This eye-opening biography reveals how personal squabbles and the research bureaucracy may have impeded Genie's development.

GROWING UP WITH LANGUAGE

(1992) by Naomi Baron. Reading, MA: Addison-Wesley.

Dr. Naomi Baron is a professor of linguistics at American University in Washington, D.C. In this book, she does an excellent job of conveying the appropriate role of parents in children's language development. Baron focuses on three representative children and their families, exploring how children put their first words together, how they struggle to understand meaning, and how they come to use language as a creative tool. She shows parents how their own attitudes about language are extremely important in the child's language development. Baron especially advocates that parents instill an enduring love of language in children by asking them interactive questions, using humor in conversation, and engaging with them through books, computers, and even television. Concerns about gender differences, birth order, raising bilingual children, and adults' use of "baby talk" are evaluated. Katherine Nelson, an expert in language development, commented that Baron's book provides an insightful analysis of how children become skilled language users.

CREATING MINDS

(1993) by Howard Gardner. New York: Basic Books.

Building on his framework of seven intelligences, ranging from artistic intelligence to intelligence involved in understanding oneself, Gardner explores the lives of seven extraordinary individuals—Sigmund Freud, Albert Einstein, Pablo Picasso, Igor Stravinsky, T. S. Eliot, Martha Graham, and Mahatma Gandhi—each an outstanding exemplar of one kind of intelligence. In analyzing their lives, Gardner describes patterns crucial to understanding how people can become more creative. He believes it takes at least 10 years to make the initial creative breakthrough and another 10 years for subsequent breakthroughs. Gardner argues that an essential element in the creative process is the support of caring individuals who believe in the revolutionary ideas of their creators.

Association for Children and Adults with Learning Disabilities (ACLD)

4156 Library Road
Pittsburgh, PA 15234
412–341–1515

This organization provides free information and referrals to anyone. It publishes a newsletter, *ACLD Newsbriefs,* and also distributes books.

Canadian Down Syndrome Society/Société canadienne de syndrome de Down

12837 76 Ave. #206
Surrey, BC V3W 2V3
604–599–6009

The Society works to improve the lives of Canadians with Down syndrome and to educate the public about Down syndrome.

***Choosing Books for Kids* (1986)**

by Joanne Oppenheim, Barbara Brenner, and Betty Boegehold
New York: Ballantine

This is an excellent book on how to choose the right book for the right child at the right time.

Council of Canadians with Disabilities

294 Portage Ave. #926
Winnipeg, MB R3C 0B9
204–947–0303

This national advocacy organization for people with disabilities publishes the newsletter *A Voice of Our Own.*

***The Ideal Problem Solver* (1984)**

by John Bransford and Barry Stein
New York: W. H. Freeman

This book discusses hundreds of fascinating problems and ways to solve them effectively.

Literacy Volunteers of America

5795 Widewaters Parkway
Syracuse, NY 13214
315–445–8000

This group trains and aids individuals and organizations to tutor adults in basic literacy and conversational English. Training materials and services are available.

National Association for Gifted Children

1155 15th Street
Washington, DC 20005
202–785–4268

This is an association of academicians, educators, and librarians. The organization's goal is to improve the education of gifted children. They provide periodic reports on the education of gifted children and publish the journal *Gifted Children Quarterly.*

National Down Syndrome Congress

1800 Dempster Street
Park Ridge, IL 60068-1146
800–232–NDSC

This organization promotes the well-being of individuals with Down syndrome. They publish a newsletter and maintain a library of books about mental retardation.

National Organization on Disability

910 Sixteenth Street, NW
Washington, DC 20006
202–293–5960

This organization acts as a clearinghouse for information about many forms of disability, including mental retardation.

***The New York Times Parents' Guide to the Best Books for Children* (1991)**

by Eden Lipson
New York: Random House

This revised and updated edition includes book recommendations for children of all ages. More than 1,700 titles are evaluated. The six sections are organized according to reading level: Wordless, picture, story, early reading, middle reading, and young adult. Each entry provides the essential information needed to become acquainted with the book's content and find it in a local library or bookstore. More than 55 indexes make it easy to match the right book to the right child. This is an extensive, thorough, competent guide to selecting children's books.

***Odyssey: A Curriculum for Thinking* (1986)**

by M. J. Adams (Coordinator)
Watertown, MA: Mastery Education Corporation

This comprehensive program attempts to improve adolescent decision making in a number of circumstances. The program consists of about a hundred 45-minute lessons, and a teacher's manual describes topics such as verbal reasoning, problem solving, decision making, and inventive thinking.

Special Olympics International

13150 New York Ave, NW, Suite 500
Washington, DC 20005

This international organization is dedicated to sponsoring year-round sports training and athletic competition in a variety of Olympic-type events for mentally retarded children and adults.

***Testing and Your Child* (1992)**

by Virginia McCullough
New York: Plume

Written for parents, this comprehensive guide provides details about 150 of the most common educational, psychological, and medical tests, focusing on everything from intelligence to giftedness to achievement to personality.

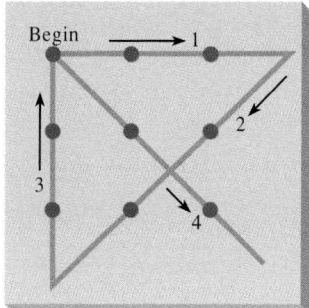

Life-Span Development

*All the world's a stage,
And all the men and women merely players;
They have their exits and their entrances,
And one man in his time plays many parts . . .*

William Shakespeare

We live our lives as part of the life cycle of the species *Homo sapiens*. This section is a window on our journey through the human life cycle. Life's examination in the context of the human life cycle gives rhythm and meaning to our personal lives. Understanding this rhythm and meaning gives us wisdom. Section Four consists of two chapters. In chapter 9, "Child Development," you will read about development from conception through the elementary school years. In chapter 10, "Adolescence, Adult Development, and Aging," you will read about our continuing development as adolescents and adults.

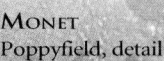

MONET
Poppyfield, detail

C H A P T E R

9

Child Development

A child is to be treated very carefully.

Luganda proverb

THE STORY OF BECKY AND KEITH DILLEY (AND COMPANY): A SCIENTIFIC SIX-PACK

After years of trying, Becky and Keith Dilley had grown weary of letting nature take its course. Eager to have a child, they turned to a new procedure, the use of Perganol, a drug that stimulates the ovaries to release eggs, in an effort to improve their prospects for fertilization. When successful, this technique sometimes also produces multiple conceptions. When they reported for an ultrasound assessment early in the pregnancy, they were surprised at the doctor's appraisal. Not just one heartbeat but *five* were apparent on the monitor. This news heralded the start of a harrowing adventure for the young couple. Their physician advised them to undergo "selective reduction," a procedure in which the multiple fetuses observed on ultrasound are reduced to just two, the number of babies that can be comfortably carried by the mother. The physician predicted that carrying all the babies to term would have been life threatening to the babies as well as to Becky. The couple rejected that option.

Becky endured 6 weeks in the hospital, a weight gain of over 125 pounds, surgery to tie off her uterus, paralysis of her facial muscles, and the intense scrutiny of the medical community until their babies were delivered by cesarean section by a team of thirty doctors. But there were even more surprises ahead. A sixth baby had escaped ultrasound detection, hidden behind the spleen. All six children were healthy, making the Dilleys the parents of the only surviving sextuplets born in America in this century. The parents face extraordinary hardship and exhilaration, as their challenges of parenting are multiplied by six. To date, the Dilley babies continue to thrive; not all families experiencing multiple births are so lucky. Sometimes babies born in multiple births show birth defects, and some do not survive. Thus, technological developments in childbirth have been the source of great hope and heartbreak.

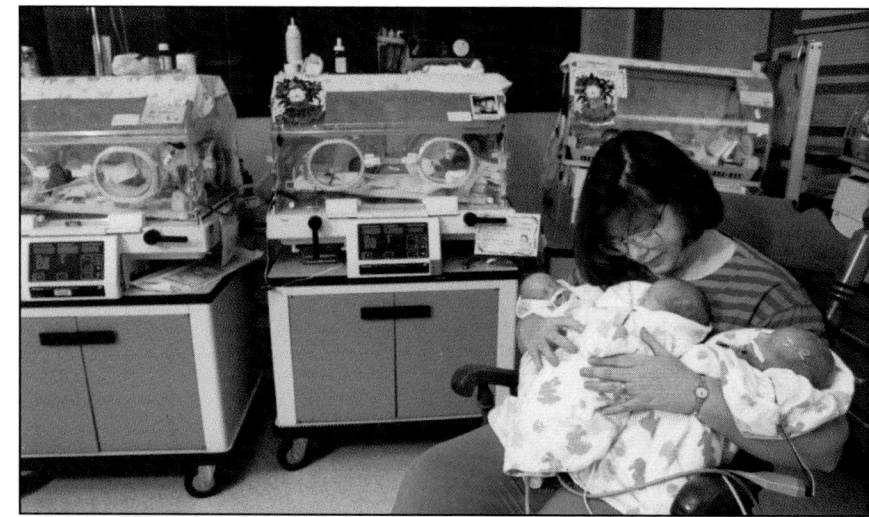

The arrival of six healthy babies—with the assistance of fertility technology—dramatically transformed the lives of Becky and Keith Dilley.

PREVIEW

The story of the Dilley family introduces the miracle of human development. Examining the shape and dimensions of childhood allows us to understand human development better. Every childhood is distinct, the first chapter in a new biography in the world. This chapter explores development's themes and issues, and its universal features and individual variations. Physical, cognitive, and socioemotional dimensions of childhood blend into a portrait of who each of us was as a child.

THEMES AND ISSUES IN DEVELOPMENT

One New Orleans first-grader shaves a piece of chalk and passes the dust around the classroom, acting as if it is cocaine. Another New Orleans first-grader, who has never heard of cocaine, ignores the pretending and listens attentively to the teacher's instruction. What factors contributed to the differences in these children's development?

The Nature of Development

Each of us—from Leonardo da Vinci, Joan of Arc, Mother Teresa, and Martin Luther King, Jr., to you—unfolded as a human being in some predictable ways. We all start as infants, become children, mature into adults, and grow old, yet we are unique. No one else in the world, for example, has the same set of fingerprints as you. Researchers who study child development are intrigued by children's universal characteristics, as well as by their idiosyncracies.

When we speak of a child's **development,** we mean *a pattern of movement or change that begins at conception and continues throughout the life cycle.* Most development involves growth, although it also consists of decay (and death). The pattern of change is complex because it is the product of several processes—biological, cognitive, and socioemotional.

Developmental Processes

Development unfolds as a result of three main kinds of processes—biological, cognitive, and socioemotional. **Biological processes** *involve changes in an individual's physical nature.* Genes inherited from parents, the development of the brain, height and weight gains, motor skills, and the hormonal changes of puberty all reflect the role of biological processes in development.

Cognitive processes *involve changes in an individual's thought, intelligence, and language.* Watching a colorful mobile swinging above a crib, putting together a two-word sentence, memorizing a poem, solving a math problem, and imagining what it would be like to be a movie star all reflect the role of cognitive processes in children's development.

Socioemotional processes *involve changes in an individual's relationships with other people, changes in emotions, and changes in personality.* An infant's smile in response to her mother's touch, a young boy's aggressive attack on a playmate, a girl's development of assertiveness, and an adolescent's joy at the senior prom all reflect the role of social processes in children's development.

Developmental Issues

Three important developmental issues involve maturation and experience, continuity and discontinuity, and early and later experience.

Maturation and Experience   In addition to biological, cognitive, and socioemotional processes, the interplay between maturation and experience shapes human development.

Maturation *is the orderly sequence of changes dictated by the genetic code.* We all grow rapidly in infancy and less so in early childhood, experience a rush of sexual hormones in puberty after a lull in childhood, reach the peak of our physical strength in late adolescence and early adulthood, and then decline. Psychologists who emphasize the role of maturation argue that, despite the vast range of environments humans inhabit, the genetic code determines a common path for human growth and development. They do, however, acknowledge that psychologically barren or hostile environments can depress development.

In contrast, other psychologists emphasize the importance of experience in shaping human development. Our individual experiences spring from our environment, whether biological (such as nutrition, medical care, and physical accidents) or social (such as family, peers, and culture).

The debate about whether development is influenced primarily by maturation or by experience is yet another version of the nature-nurture controversy, discussed in chapter 3.

Continuity and Discontinuity   Think for a moment about who you are. Did you become this person gradually, in the slow, cumulative way a seedling grows into a giant oak, or did you experience sudden, distinct changes in your development, like the way a caterpillar changes into a butterfly (see figure 9.1)? For the most part, developmental psychologists who emphasize experience have described development as a gradual, continuous process; those who emphasize maturation have described development as a series of distinct stages (Bornstein & Krasnegor, 1989).

Continuity of development *is gradual, cumulative change from conception to death.* Theories that view human development as continuous emphasize that, for example, a child's utterance of its first word, although seemingly an abrupt, discrete event, is actually the result of weeks and months of growth and practice. Similarly, although the onset of puberty may seem to erupt overnight, it is actually a gradual process that occurs over several years.

Discontinuity of development *is development involving distinct stages in the life span.* In theories that view human development as discontinuous, each of us is described as passing through a sequence of stages of qualitative rather than quantitative change. This is like the caterpillar as it changes into a butterfly: It does not become *more* caterpillar, it changes into a different kind of organism; its development is discontinuous. For example, a child who earlier could think only in concrete terms becomes capable of thinking abstractly about the world. This is a qualitative, discontinuous change in development, not a quantitative, continuous change.

Early and Later Experience   Another important developmental topic is the **early-later experience issue,** *which focuses on the degree to which early experiences (especially in infancy) or later experiences are the key determinants of the child's development.* That is, if infants experience negative,

FIGURE 9.1

Continuity and Discontinuity in Development
Is human development more like a seedling's gradually growing into a giant oak or a caterpillar's suddenly becoming a butterfly?

of early experience rests on the belief that each life is an unbroken trail on which a psychological quality can be traced back to its origin (Kagan, 1992).

The early-experience doctrine, which implies statue-like permanence after infancy, contrasts with the later-experience view that development continues like the ebb and flow of a river. Those who advocate the significance of later experience argue that children are malleable throughout development and that later sensitive caregiving is just as important as earlier sensitive caregiving. A number of life-span developmentalists, who focus on the entire life span rather than only on child development, stress that too little attention has been given to later experiences in development (Baltes, 1987). They argue that early experiences are important contributors to development but no more important than later experiences.

Jerome Kagan (1992) points out that even children who show the qualities of an inhibited temperament, which is linked to heredity, have the capacity to change their behavior. In Kagan's research, almost one-third of a group of children who had an inhibited temperament at 2 years of age were not unusually shy or fearful when they were 4 years of age.

People in Western cultures have tended to support the idea that early experiences are more important than later experiences (Lamb & Sternberg, 1992). This stance reflects an enduring reliance on the Freudian belief that children's key developmental experiences occur with their parents in their first 5 years of life. But most people in the world do not share this belief. For example, people in many Asian countries believe that experiences occurring after about 6 or 7 years of age are more important influences on development than earlier experiences are. This stance stems from the long-standing Eastern belief that children's reasoning skills begin to develop in important ways in the middle childhood years.

Social Policy and Children's Development

Social policy *is a national government's course of action designed to influence the welfare of its citizens.* A current trend in psychology is to conduct child development research that produces knowledge that will lead to wise and effective decision making in the area of social policy (Duncan, 1993; McLoyd, 1993). More than 20 percent of all children and more than half of all ethnic minority children are being raised in poverty. Between 40 and 50 percent of all children can expect to spend at least 5 years in a single-parent home. Children and young adolescents are giving birth. The use and abuse of drugs is widespread. AIDS is spreading. Many people believe that our nation needs revised social policy related to children (Bloom, 1995; Garbarino & Kostelny, 1995). Figure 9.2 vividly portrays one day in the lives of children in the United States.

stressful circumstances in their lives, can those experiences be overcome by later, more positive experiences? Or are the early experiences so critical, possibly because they are the infant's first, prototypical experiences, that they cannot be overridden by a later, more enriched environment?

The early-later experience issue has a long history and continues to be hotly debated by developmentalists. Some believe that unless infants experience warm, nurturant caregiving in the first year or so of life, their development will never be optimal (Bowlby, 1989; Sroufe, in press). Plato was sure that infants who were rocked frequently became better athletes. Nineteenth-century New England ministers told parents in Sunday sermons that the way they handled their infants would determine their children's future character. The emphasis on the importance

17,051	women get pregnant.	6	teenagers commit suicide.
2,795	of them are teenagers.	135,000	children bring a gun to school.
1,106	teenagers have abortions.	7,742	teens become sexually active.
372	teenagers miscarry.	623	teenagers get syphilis or gonorrhea.
1,295	teenagers give birth.	211	children are arrested for drug abuse.
689	babies are born to women who have had inadequate prenatal care.	437	children are arrested for drinking or drunken driving.
719	babies are born at low birthweight.	1,512	teenagers drop out of school.
129	babies are born at very low birthweight.	1,849	children are abused or neglected.
67	babies die before one month of life.	3,288	children run away from home.
105	babies die before their first birthday.	1,629	children are in adult jails.
27	children die from poverty.	2,556	children are born out of wedlock.
10	children die from guns.	2,989	see their parents divorced.
30	children are wounded by guns.	34,285	people lose jobs.

FIGURE 9.2

One Day in the Lives of Children in the United States

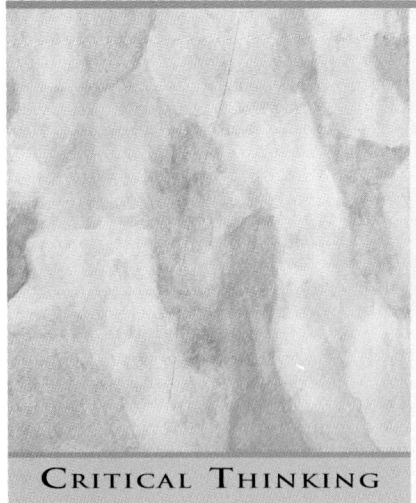

*Examining Early and
Later Experience*

Which do you believe has a more important influence on development—early experience or later experience? What kinds of evidence would you cite to support your position? Is your evidence persuasive or debatable? How could you strengthen your position against opposing points of view? What implications does your belief have for the manner in which our country funds the well-being of children? Your ability to *develop a psychological argument based on evidence* is one of the key abilities of critical thinking in psychology.

The shape and scope of social policy related to children is heavily influenced by our political system, which is based on negotiation and compromise (Garwood & others, 1989). The values held by individual lawmakers, the nation's economic strengths and weaknesses, and partisan politics all influence the policy agenda and the likelihood that children's welfare will be improved. Periods of comprehensive social policy are often the outgrowth of concern over broad social issues. For example, child labor laws protected not only children but also jobs for adults. Federal day-care funding during World War II was justified by the need for women laborers in factories. Head Start and the other War on Poverty programs in the 1960s were implemented to decrease intergenerational poverty (Zigler & Muenchow, 1992).

Among the groups that have worked to improve the lives of the world's children are UNICEF in New York and the Children's Defense Fund in Washington, D.C. Marian Wright Edelman, president of the Children's Defense Fund, has been a tireless advocate of children's rights. Especially troubling to Edelman (1992, 1995) are the indicators of societal neglect that place the United States at or near the bottom of industrialized nations in the treatment of children. Edelman says that parenting and nurturing the next generation of children is our society's most important function and that we need to take it more seriously than we have in the past. Sociocultural Worlds 9.1 provides some rather stunning comparisons of American children with children in other countries, underscoring the need for improved social policy for children.

As the twenty-first century approaches, the well-being of children is one of America's foremost concerns. Children are the future of any society. Those who do not reach their potential, who are destined to make fewer contributions to society than society needs, and who do not take their place as productive adults diminish the power of that society's future (Horowitz & O'Brien, 1989).

There is a special concern about children in poverty (Huston, 1995; Jarrett, 1995). More than one of every five children in the United States lives in poverty; this figure is twice as high as for other industrialized nations. For example, the child poverty rates in Canada and Sweden are about 9 percent and 2 percent, respectively (Danzinger & Danzinger, 1993).

Why are poverty rates for American children so high? Three reasons are apparent (Huston, McLoyd, & Coll, 1994): Economic changes have eliminated many blue-collar jobs that paid reasonably well; the percentage of children living in single-mother families has increased; and government benefits declined during the 1970s and 1980s.

When poverty is persistent and long-standing, it can have especially damaging effects on children (Zigler, 1995). In one recent study, the more time children lived in families with income below the poverty line, the lower was the quality of their home environments (Garrett, Ng'andu, & Ferron, 1994).

The United States currently lags behind many other countries in developing adequate policies for children and families (Edelman, 1995). For instance, the United States is the only industrialized country in the world that does not have a policy guaranteeing women paid leave for childbirth and the care of young infants. In the United States, many employed mothers must use their own sick leave time or take leave without pay in the weeks before and after the baby's birth. By contrast, many European countries give one parent 6 to 12 months leave, and they usually allow parents to stay home when a child is ill in the early years of the child's life.

Some government-sponsored programs do provide support for children and families in the United States. However, most of these programs—income assistance, medical care, food programs, job training, and day care, for example—are directed at only the neediest families. Most of these programs have come into being in a piecemeal fashion over many years. Also, most are crisis-oriented interventions; few are aimed at preventing family problems before they occur. Funding for these various government programs

Caring for Children Around the World

According to a report by the Children's Defense Fund (1990), the United States does not fare well in caring for children when compared with other nations. In this report, the Children's Defense Fund gave the United States an A for capacity to care for children but an F for performance on many key markers of children's well-being. Consider the following cross-cultural comparisons:

- United States 1-year-olds have lower immunization rates against polio than 1-year-olds in 14 other countries. Polio immunization rates for non-White infants in the United States rank behind 48 other countries, including Albania, Colombia, and Jamaica.
- The United States' overall infant mortality rate lags behind 18 other countries. Our non-White infant mortality rate ranks 13th compared to other nations' overall rates. An African American child born in inner-city Boston has less chance of surviving the first year of life than does a child born in Panama, North or South Korea, or Uruguay.
- In a study of 8 industrialized nations (the United States, Switzerland, Sweden, Norway, former West Germany, Canada, England, and Australia), the United States had the highest poverty rate.
- The United States has the highest adolescent pregnancy rate of any industrialized Western nation.
- The United States and South Africa are the only industrialized countries that do not provide child care and universal health coverage to families.
- American schoolchildren know less geography than schoolchildren in Iran, less math than schoolchildren in Japan, and less science information than schoolchildren in Spain.
- The United States invests a smaller portion of its gross national product (GNP) in child health than do 18 other industrialized nations. It invests a smaller portion of its GNP in education than do 6 other industrialized countries.

In sum, the current picture is bleak. The United States needs to devote more attention to caring for its children. Too many American children from every socioeconomic and ethnic group are neglected and are not given the opportunity to reach their full potential.

The United States does not fare well in caring for children, compared to other nations. The United States' overall infant mortality rate lags behind that of eighteen other countries. An African American child born in inner-city Boston has less chance of surviving the first year of life than a child born in Panama, North or South Korea, or Uruguay. American schoolchildren know less science information than their counterparts in Spain do.

to support families has been inconsistent. To an extent, the American tradition of individualism, self-sufficiency, and family privacy has made government decision makers unwilling to become involved in family matters, except when extreme problems surface. As child development expert Edward Zigler (1989) commented, it is difficult to find any overarching or consistent goals for the support of children and families in America.

PRENATAL DEVELOPMENT AND BIRTH

Within a matter of hours after fertilization, a human egg divides, becomes a system of cells, and continues this mapping of cells at an astonishing rate until, in a mere 9 months, there is a squalling bundle of energy that has its grandmother's nose, its father's eyes, and its mother's abundant hair.

The Course of Prenatal Development

Conception, *also called fertilization, occurs when a single sperm cell from the male penetrates the female's ovum (egg).* A **zygote** *is a fertilized egg.* It receives one-half of its chromosomes from the mother, the other half from the father. The zygote begins as a single cell. The **germinal period** *is the first 2 weeks after conception.* After 1 week and many cell divisions, the zygote is made up of 100 to 150 cells. At the end of 2 weeks, the mass of cells attaches to the uterine wall.

During the **embryonic period,** *2 to 8 weeks after conception,* some remarkable developments unfold (see figure 9.3). Before most women even know they are pregnant, the rate of cell differentiation intensifies, support systems for the cells form, and organs appear. In the third week, the neural tube that eventually becomes the spinal cord is forming. At about 21 days, eyes begin to appear, and by 24 days, the cells of the heart begin to differentiate. During the fourth week, arm and leg buds emerge. At 5 to 8 weeks, arms and legs become more differentiated, the face starts to form, and the intestinal tract appears. All of this is happening in an organism that, by 8 weeks, weighs only 1/30 ounce and is just over 1.5 inches long (see figure 9.4).

The **fetal period** *begins 2 months after conception and lasts, on the average, for 7 months.* Growth and development continue their dramatic course, and organs mature to the point where life can be sustained outside the womb. At 4 months after conception, the fetus is about 6 inches long and weighs 4 to 7 ounces. Prenatal reflexes become more apparent, and the mother feels the fetus move for the first time (see figure 9.5). At 6 months after conception, the eyes and eyelids are completely formed, a fine layer of hair covers the fetus, the grasping reflex appears, and irregular breathing begins. By 7 to 9 months, the fetus is much longer and weighs considerably more. In addition, the functioning of various organs steps up.

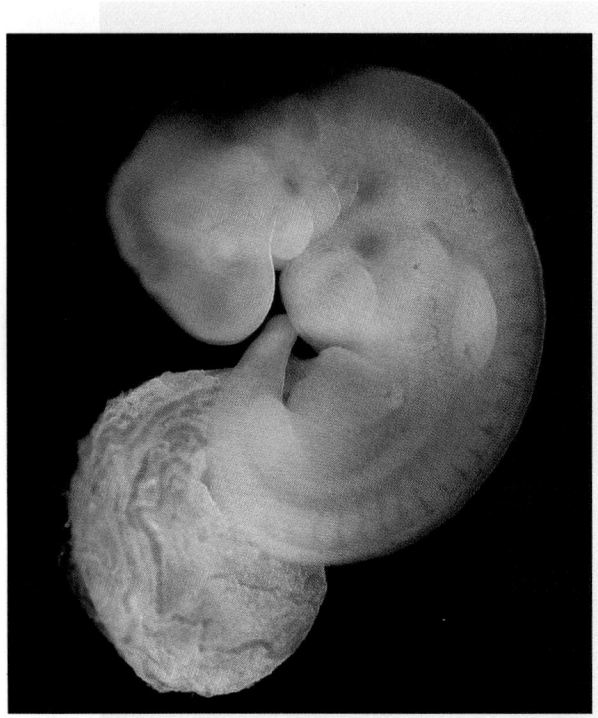

FIGURE 9.3

Embryo at 4 Weeks
At about 4 weeks, an embryo is about 0.2 inch in length. The head, eyes, and ears begin to show. The head and neck are half the body length; the shoulders will be located where the whitish arm buds are attached.

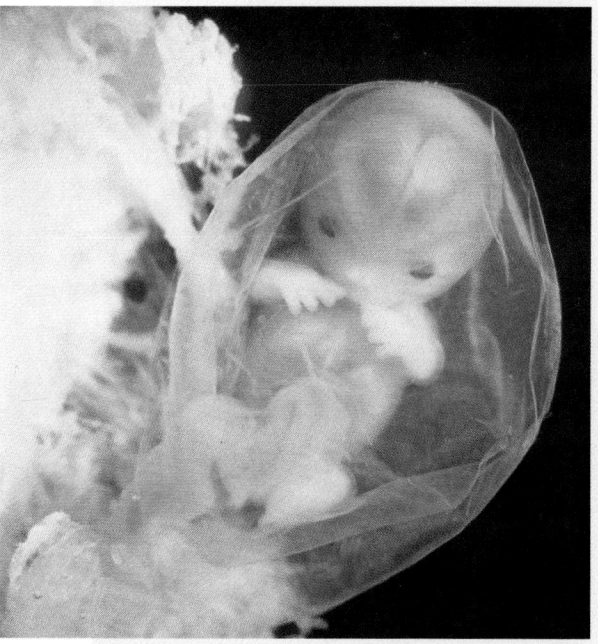

FIGURE 9.4

Embryo at 8 Weeks
At 8 weeks and 4 centimeters (1.6 inches), the developing individual is no longer an embryo, but a fetus. Everything that will be found in the fully developed human being has now been differentiated. The fetal stage is a period of growth and perfection of detail. The heart has been beating for a month, and the muscles have just begun their first exercises. Two of the mother-to-be's menstrual periods have now been skipped. Ideally, at about this time, the mother-to-be goes to a doctor or clinic for prenatal care.

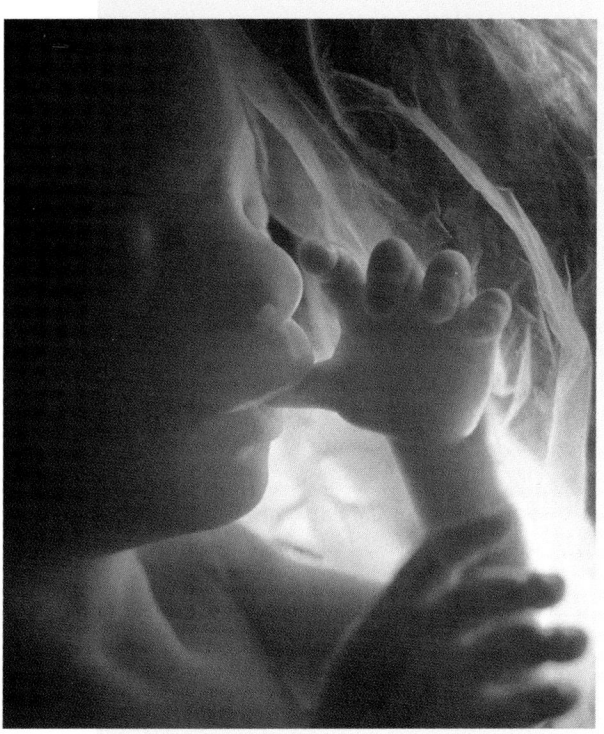

FIGURE 9.5

Fetus at 4½ Months
At 4½ months, the fetus is about 18 cm (just over 7 inches).
When the thumb comes close to the mouth, the head may
turn, and lips and tongue begin their sucking motions—
a reflex for survival.

Challenges to Prenatal Development

As these massive changes take place during prenatal development, some pregnant women tiptoe about in the belief that
everything they do has a direct effect on the unborn child.
Others behave more casually, assuming their experiences
have little impact. The truth lies somewhere between these
extremes. Although it floats in a comfortable, well-protected
environment, the fetus is not totally immune to the larger environment surrounding the mother (Kopp & Kaler, 1989).

A **teratogen** *(from the Greek word tera, meaning
"monster") is any agent that causes a birth defect.* Rarely do
specific teratogens, such as drugs, link up with specific birth
defects, such as leg malformation. One example of this linkage is the drug *thalidomide.* During the late 1950s, several
hundred women took thalidomide early in pregnancy to
prevent morning sickness and insomnia. Tragically, babies
born to these mothers had arms and legs that had not developed beyond stumps.

Heavy drinking by pregnant women can also be
devastating to offspring. **Fetal alcohol syndrome (FAS)** *is
a cluster of abnormalities that appear in the offspring of
mothers who drink alcohol heavily during pregnancy.* The
abnormalities include facial deformities and defective
limbs, face, and heart. Most of these children are below
average in intelligence, and some are mentally retarded.

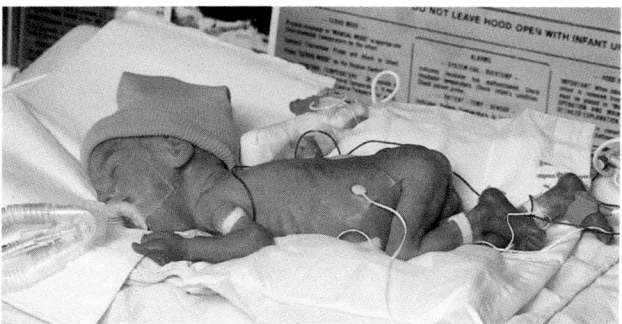

This baby was born addicted to cocaine because its mother was a
cocaine addict. Researchers have found that the offspring of
women who use cocaine during pregnancy often have
hypertension and heart damage. Many of these infants face a
childhood full of medical problems.

Even moderate drinking during pregnancy is associated
with developmental deficits. In one study, infants whose
mothers drank moderately during pregnancy (for example, one to two drinks a day) were less attentive and alert,
with the effects still present at 4 years of age (Streissguth
& others, 1984).

With the increased use of cocaine in the United
States, there is growing concern about its effects on the embryos, fetuses, and infants of pregnant cocaine users (Dow-
Edwards, 1995; Field, 1995; Lester, Freier, & LaGasse,
1995). The most consistent finding is that infants born to
cocaine abusers have reduced birthweight and length
(Chasnoff & others, 1989). There are increased frequencies
of congenital abnormalities in the offspring of cocaine users
during pregnancy, but other factors in the drug addict's
lifestyle, such as malnutrition and other substance abuse,
may be responsible for the congenital abnormalities (Eyler,
Behnke, & Stewart, 1990). For example, cocaine users are
more likely to smoke cigarettes and marijuana, drink alcohol, and take amphetamines than are cocaine nonusers. Researchers struggle to distinguish these potential influences
from the effects of cocaine itself. Obtaining valid information about the frequency and type of drug use by mothers is
also complicated, since many mothers fear prosecution or
loss of custody because of their drug use.

The importance of women's health to the health of
their offspring is nowhere better exemplified than when the
mother has acquired immune deficiency syndrome (AIDS).
As the number of women with HIV grows, more children
are born exposed and infected with AIDS (*The Health of
America's Children,* 1992).

AIDS was the eighth leading cause of death among
children ages 1 to 4 in 1989. Through the end of 1991, 3,123
children younger than 13 had been diagnosed with AIDS.
The number of pediatric AIDS cases does not include as
many as 10,000 children infected with HIV who have not
yet suffered the full effects of AIDS. African American and
Latino children make up 83 percent of all pediatric AIDS
cases. The majority of mothers who transmit HIV to their
offspring were infected through intravenous drug use or
heterosexual contact with injecting drug users.

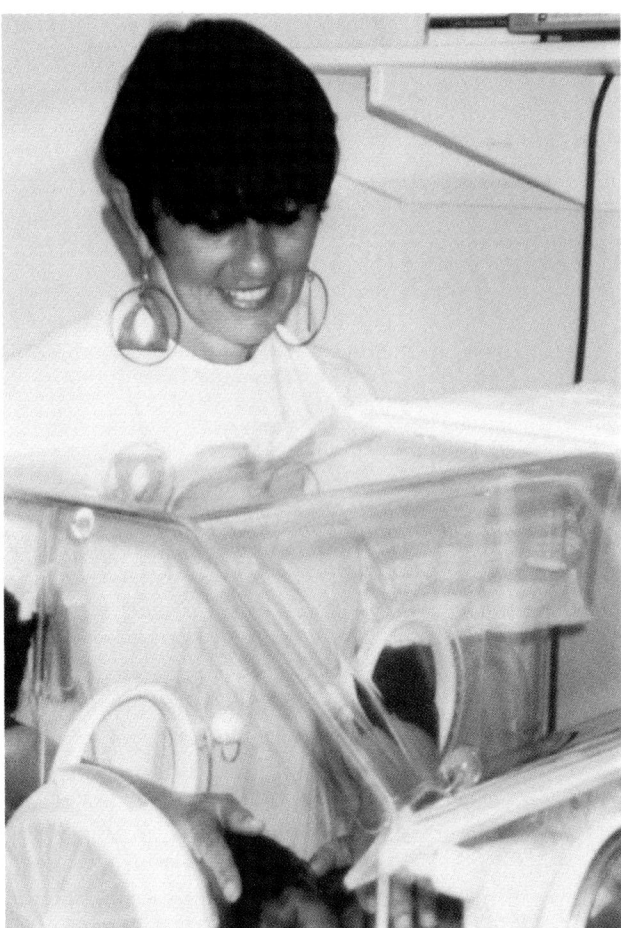

Shown here is Dr. Tiffany Field massaging a newborn infant. Dr. Field's research has clearly demonstrated the power of massage in improving the developmental outcome of at-risk infants. Under her direction the Touch Research Institute in Miami, Florida, was recently developed to investigate the role of touch in a number of domains of health and well-being.

Birth and the Newborn

The newborn is on a threshold between two worlds. In the womb, the fetus exists in a dark, free-floating, low-gravity environment at a relatively warm, constant temperature. At birth the newborn must quickly adapt to light, gravity, cold—a buzzing array of changing stimuli.

Whereas a full-term infant has grown in the womb for the full 38 to 42 weeks between conception and delivery, a **preterm infant** *(also called a premature infant) is an infant born prior to 38 weeks after conception.* Whether a preterm infant will have developmental problems is a complex issue. Very small preterm infants are more likely to have developmental problems than are their larger counterparts. Also, preterm infants who grow up in conditions of poverty are more likely to have developmental problems than are those who live in middle-class surroundings. Indeed, many larger preterm infants from middle-class families do not have developmental problems. Nonetheless, overall, more preterm infants than full-term babies have learning disorders (Kopp, 1994).

DIMENSIONS OF CHILD DEVELOPMENT

Change is a constant in childhood. Children develop their abilities for movement and physical interaction with their environment, for processing information, and for connecting meaningfully with others in patterns that grow richer and more complicated as they age. We will discuss each of these areas systematically, focusing on the changes that characterize physical, cognitive development, and socio-emotional development in childhood.

Physical Development

At no other time in a person's life will there be so many changes occurring so fast as during the first few years. During infancy we change from being virtually immobile, helpless beings to being insatiably curious, talking creatures who toddle as fast as our legs can carry us.

Infancy

An old French proverb says, "A baby is an angel whose wings decrease as its legs increase." Learning to walk, though, is only one of infancy's physical milestones. We will find out how infants respond to their world, what an infant's nutritional needs are, and whether or not a newborn can see and hear.

Reflexes A newborn is not an empty-headed organism. It comes into the world already equipped with several genetically "wired" reflexes. For example, a newborn has no fear of water, naturally holding its breath and contracting its throat to keep water out. Some of the reflexes we possess as newborns persist throughout our lives—coughing, blinking, and yawning, for example. Others disappear in the months following birth as higher brain functions mature and we develop voluntary control over many behaviors. One of the most dramatic reflexes of a newborn is the Moro reflex. When a newborn is roughly handled, hears a loud noise, sees a bright light, or feels a sudden change of position, it becomes startled, arches its back, and throws back its head. At the same time, the newborn flings its arms and legs out and then rapidly closes them to the center of its body as if falling. The Moro reflex disappears by 3 to 4 months of age.

Gross Motor Development An infant's physical development in the first 2 years of life is dramatic. At birth a newborn (neonate) has a gigantic head (relative to the rest of the body), which flops around uncontrollably. In the span of 12 months, the infant becomes capable of sitting anywhere, standing, stooping, climbing, and often walking. During the second year, growth decelerates, but rapid increases in such activities as running and climbing take place.

Rates of infant motor development vary among some ethnic groups, largely for environmental reasons (Super, 1981). In many Black African cultures, infants have

You may have wondered how researchers are able to estimate infants' visual acuity. After all, infants are not able to report what they see on an eye chart. Can you imagine a simple method by which we might be able to establish visual acuity in infants? By thinking of such a method, you demonstrate the ability to *make accurate inferences about behavior.*

One method is to move a large object toward newborns, then observe whether they turn their heads away, as if to avoid a collision. Newborns do turn away from oncoming objects, indicating that they can see them.

Sensation and Perception William James (1890) described a newborn's world as "a great, blooming, buzzing confusion." A century later, we know James was wrong. A newborn's ability to perceive visual information is far more advanced than previously thought. We now know that newborns can see; they're just terribly near-sighted, registering at about $^{20}/_{600}$ on the well-known Snellen chart used by optometrists. By 6 months of age, this improves to $^{20}/_{100}$.

We also know that infants can hear. In fact, the fetus responds to sounds 2 weeks before birth (Spence & DeCasper, 1982). Shortly after birth, infants also can smell, taste, touch, and sense pain.

Brain Development An infant's brain develops dramatically. Remember that you began as a single cell, and just 9 months later your brain and nervous system alone contained 10 to 20 billion neurons. This means that, at a point during prenatal development, neurons were reproducing at a rate of 25,000 per minute. Babies are born with all the neurons they will ever have. At birth and during early infancy the networks connecting neurons are sparse. In figure 9.6 you can see the substantial

precocious motor skills. Black African infants ride on their caregivers' hips or backs—which strengthens the muscles used for sitting and walking—much more often than Anglo-American infants do. In addition, Black African infants are actually taught to sit and to walk, so they tend to reach these motor milestones much sooner than infants from other cultures do.

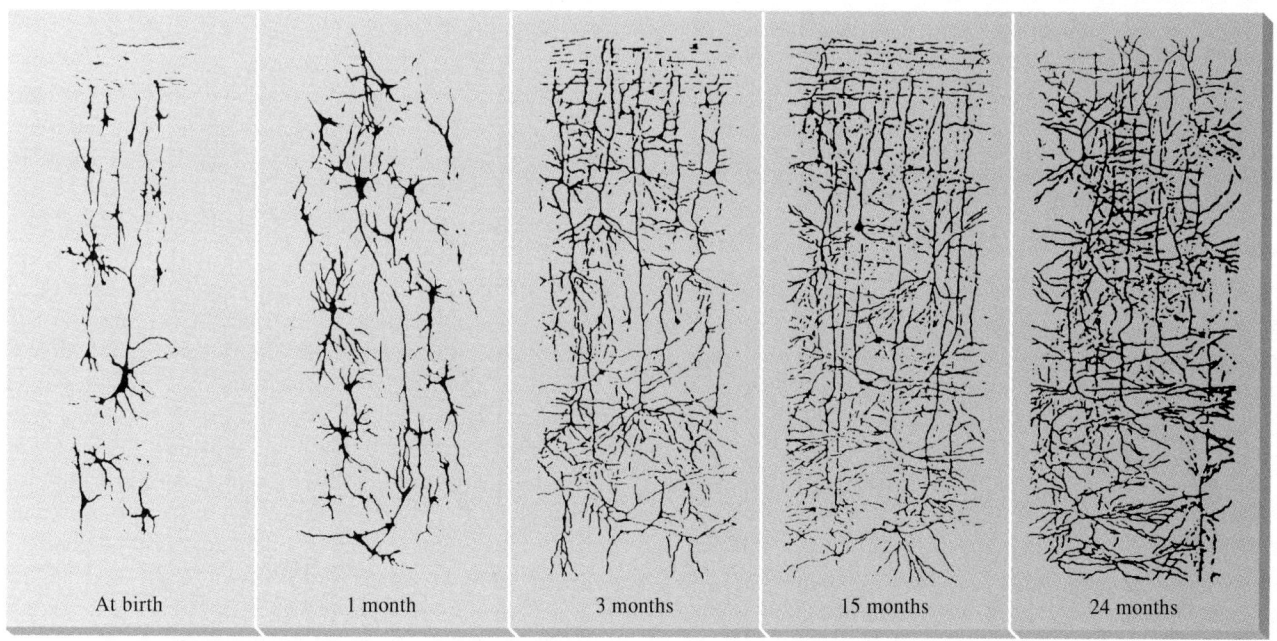

| At birth | 1 month | 3 months | 15 months | 24 months |

FIGURE 9.6

Increased Dendritic Branching from Birth to 2 Years of Age
The branching of dendrites spreads dramatically during the course of life's first 2 years, allowing for more extensive connections among neurons. Notice how many more connections exist between dendrites at 2 years of age than at birth. Some developmentalists and neuroscientists believe the increased dendritic spreading plays an important role in the infant's advances in information processing.

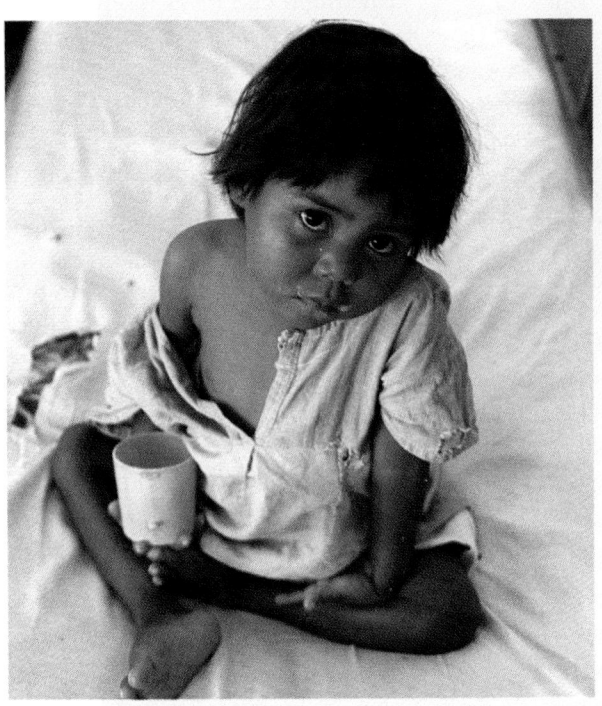

FIGURE 9.7

Malnutrition in Impoverished Countries
Malnutrition is common among children in many parts of
the world (Grant, 1994). In an infant's first year of life, severe
protein-calorie deficiency can lead to a wasting away of the
infant's body tissues. One of the main causes of this wasting
away is early weaning from breast milk to inadequate nutrients,
such as unsuitable and unsanitary cow's milk formula. In many
third world countries, mothers used to breast-feed their infants
for at least 2 years. To become more modern, they stopped
breast-feeding much earlier and replaced it with bottle-feeding.
In impoverished countries, such as Afghanistan, Haiti, Ghana,
and Chile, comparisons of bottle-fed and breast-fed infants
reveal a death rate that is at times 500 percent higher for bottle-
fed infants. *What would we have to know to determine if method
of feeding alone is responsible for the dramatic increase in mortality
among bottle-fed babies in impoverished countries?*

increase in dendritic growth, which allows greater communication between neurons, from birth to 2 years of age.

Nutrition Babies need adequate nutrition if they are to
grow into healthy adults. The importance of this factor cannot be overstated. Infants depend on human milk or "formula" for the first 4 to 6 months. One debate that has raged
for years is the "breast or bottle" issue. Those who favor
breast-feeding assert that it provides clean, digestible milk
and helps immunize newborns from diseases (see figure
9.7). Breast-fed babies also gain weight more rapidly than
bottle-fed babies. Only about one-half of all mothers nurse
their newborns and even fewer continue to nurse after several months.

This may be, in part, because many mothers who work
outside the home find it impossible to breast-feed their

infants. Proponents of bottle-feeding argue that there is no
long-term evidence of physiological or psychological harm to
American infants when they are bottle-fed (Ferguson, Harwood, & Shannon, 1987). Even so, the American Academy of
Pediatrics, the majority of physicians and nurses, and two
leading publications for parents—the *Infant Care* manual
and *Parents* magazine—endorse breast-feeding for its physiological and psychological benefits over bottle-feeding
(Young, 1990). In addition, experts agree that breast-feeding
is the preferred practice in developing countries where
poverty and inadequate nutrition are common. Although the
issue of breast- versus bottle-feeding continues to be hotly
debated, the growing consensus is that breast-feeding is better for a baby's health.

Childhood

By age 3, children are full of new tricks, such as climbing,
skipping, and jumping. They are beginning to be able to
make their body do what they want it to do, giving them a
greater sense of self-control.

Catching, throwing, kicking, balancing, rolling, cutting, stacking, snapping, pushing, dancing, and swimming—
preschool children perform these physical feats and many,
many more. As poet Dylan Thomas put it, "All the sun long
they were running." The growth rate slows down in early
childhood. Otherwise, we would be a species of giants. The
growth and development of the brain underlie a young
child's improvement in motor skills, reflected in such activities as the ability to hold a pencil and make increasingly efficient marks with it. A child's brain is closer to full growth
than is the rest of its body, attaining 75 percent of the brain's
adult weight by the age of 3 and 90 percent by age 5.

In middle and late childhood, motor development is
much smoother and more coordinated than in early childhood. Whereas a preschool child can zip, cut, latch, and
dance, an elementary school child can zip, cut, latch, and
dance more efficiently and with more flair. Physical activities are essential for children to refine their developing
skills. Child development experts in the United States believe that children should be active rather than passive and
that they should be able to plan and select many of their
own activities (Katz & Chard, 1989). An ideal elementary
school, for example, would include the following: a gym
and a safe, elaborate outdoor play area, where students can
participate in a variety of games and sports; a classroom
with a fully equipped publishing center, complete with materials for writing, typing, illustrating, and binding student-
made books; and a science area with animals and plants for
observation and books to study. Children also need to "just
play." Education experts recognize that spontaneous play
provides additional opportunities for children to learn.

Schools that offer children many opportunities to engage in a wide range of self-initiated activities, such as the
ideal school just described, greatly enhance their students'
physical and cognitive development.

What Development Is, Prenatal Development and Birth, and Children's Physical Development

Development is a pattern of movement or change that occurs throughout the life span. Development involves the interplay of biological, cognitive, and social processes. Development is influenced by the interaction of maturation and experience. The debate over the role of maturation and experience is another version of the nature-nurture controversy. Development may be described as either continuous (gradual, cumulative change) or discontinuous (an abrupt sequence of stages). Whether development is determined more by earlier experiences or more by later experiences is a hotly debated issue. Social policy is a national government's course of action designed to influence the welfare of its citizens. Improved social policy related to children is needed to help all children reach their potential.

Conception occurs when a sperm unites with an ovum. The fertilized egg is a zygote. The first 2 weeks after conception is the germinal period, 2 to 8 weeks is the embryonic period, and 2 to 9 months is the fetal period. Teratogens are agents that cause birth defects. Drugs and maternal diseases are examples of teratogens. Birth marks a dramatic transition for the fetus. Special interest focuses on preterm infants. Social class and ethnic differences characterize the preterm infant's development.

An infant comes into the world equipped with a number of reflexes. At birth infants can see, but their vision is about $20/600$. Shortly after birth, infants also can smell, taste, touch, and sense pain. Brain development is dramatic during prenatal development and the first 2 years of life. Nutrition is important in an infant's growth. Breast-feeding is healthier for babies than bottle-feeding, but the merits of breast-feeding over bottle-feeding continue to be debated. Physical development slows during the childhood years, although motor development becomes smoother and more coordinated.

Cognitive Development

Matthew is 1 year old. He has seen over 1,000 flash cards, each containing a picture of objects—shells, flowers, insects, flags, countries, or words, for example. His mother, Billie, has made close to 10,000 such cards for Matthew and his 4-year-old brother Mark. Billie is following the regimen recommended by Glenn Doman, director of the Philadelphia Institute for Human Potential. Using Doman's methods, Billie expects Matthew to be reading and mastering simple math problems by the age of 2. She is also teaching Matthew Japanese.

Although some parents may believe that such strategies give their child an academic edge in a competitive world, many developmental psychologists believe that Doman's institute is a money-making scheme and that something is fundamentally wrong with his methods. They argue that intense tutoring stifles curiosity, creativity, and the ability to learn. It might even keep children from discovering the world on their own.

Swiss developmental psychologist Jean Piaget was so often asked by American audiences "What should we do to foster a child's cognitive development?" that he called it the American question. As we will see next, Piaget's theory suggests that Doman's approach is not the best way to help children learn about their world.

Piaget's Theory of Cognitive Development

Piaget (1896–1980) stressed that children do not just passively receive information from their environment; they actively construct their own cognitive world. Two processes underlie a child's mental construction of the world—organization and adaptation. To make sense of our world, we organize our experiences. For example, we separate important ideas from less important ones. We connect one idea to another. However, not only do we organize our observations and experiences, but we also *adapt* our thinking to include those new ideas. Piaget (1960) believed we adapt in two ways: through assimilation and accommodation.

Assimilation *occurs when individuals incorporate new information into their existing knowledge.* **Accommodation** *occurs when individuals adjust to new information.* Imagine giving a hammer and some nails to a 5-year-old and then asking her to hang a picture on the wall. She has never used a hammer, but from experience and observation she realizes that a hammer is an object to be held, that to hit the nail she must swing the hammer by the handle, and that she probably will need to swing it a number of times. Recognizing each of these things, she fits her behavior into information she already has (assimilation). However, the hammer is heavy, so she holds it near the top. She swings too hard and the nail bends, so she adjusts the pressure of her strikes. These adjustments reveal her ability to alter slightly her conception of the world (accommodation).

Piaget thought that even young infants are capable of assimilation and accommodation. Newborns reflexively suck everything that touches their lips (assimilation), but after several months they come to a new understanding of their world. Some objects, such as fingers and the mother's breast, can be sucked but others, such as fuzzy blankets, won't work as well (accommodation).

TABLE 9.1

Piaget's Stages of Cognitive Development

Stage	Description	Age Range
Sensorimotor	An infant progresses from reflexive, instinctual action at birth to the beginning of symbolic thought. The infant constructs an understanding of the world by coordinating sensory experiences with physical actions.	Birth to 2 years
Preoperational	The child begins to represent the world with words and images; these words and images reflect increased symbolic thinking and go beyond the connection of sensory information and physical action.	2 to 7 years
Concrete operational	The child can now reason logically about concrete events and classify objects into different sets.	7 to 11 years
Formal operational	The adolescent reasons in more abstract and logical ways. Thought is more idealistic.	11 to 15 years

Jean Piaget, the famous Swiss developmental psychologist, changed the way we think about the development of children's minds. For Piaget, a child's mental development is a continuous creation of increasingly complex forms.

Piaget also believed that we go through four stages in understanding the world. Each of the stages is age related and consists of distinct ways of thinking. Remember, it is the *different* way of understanding the world that makes one stage more advanced than another; knowing *more* information does not make a child's thinking more advanced, in Piaget's view. This is what Piaget meant when he said that a child's cognition is *qualitatively* different in one stage compared to another. A brief overview of Piaget's four stages of cognitive development is shown in table 9.1. We will discuss preoperational and concrete operational thought later in this chapter and formal operational thought, which characterizes adolescents, in the next chapter. For now, let's find out more about an infant's cognitive world.

Sensorimotor Thought

Sensorimotor thought *is Piaget's name for the stage of development that lasts from birth to about 2 years of age, corresponding to the period of infancy. An infant constructs an understanding of the world by coordinating sensory experiences (such as seeing and hearing) with physical (motor) actions*—hence the term *sensorimotor*. At the beginning of this stage, a newborn engages with its environment with little more than reflexive patterns; at the end of the stage, however, the 2-year-old has complex sensorimotor patterns and is beginning to use primitive symbols in thinking.

We live in a world of objects. Imagine yourself as a 5-month-old infant and how you might experience the world. You are in a playpen filled with toys. One of the toys, a monkey, falls out of your grasp and rolls behind a larger toy, a hippopotamus. Would you know the monkey is behind the hippopotamus, or would you think it is completely gone? Piaget believed that "out of sight" literally was "out of mind" for young infants; at 5 months of age, then, you would not have reached for the monkey when it fell behind the hippopotamus. By 8 months of age, though, an infant begins to understand that out of sight is not out of mind; at this age you probably would have reached behind the hippopotamus to search for the monkey, coordinating your senses with your movements.

Object permanence *is Piaget's term for one of an infant's most important accomplishments: understanding that objects and events continue to exist even when they cannot directly be seen, heard, or touched.* The most common way to study object permanence is to show an infant an interesting toy and then cover the toy with a sheet or blanket. If infants understand that the toy still exists, they try to uncover it (see figure 9.8). Object permanence continues to develop throughout the sensorimotor period. For example, when infants initially understand that objects exist even when out of sight, they look for them only briefly. By the end of the sensorimotor period, infants engage in a more prolonged and sophisticated search for hidden objects (Flavell, 1985).

Object permanence is also important in an infant's social world. Infants develop a sense that people are permanent, just as they come to understand that toys are permanent. Five-month-old infants do not sense that caregivers exist beyond moment-to-moment encounters, but they do by 8 months of age. Infants' cognitive accomplishments, then, not only tell us how infants understand a

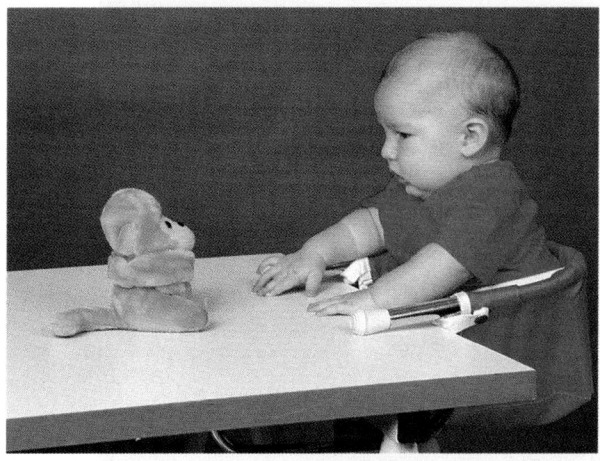

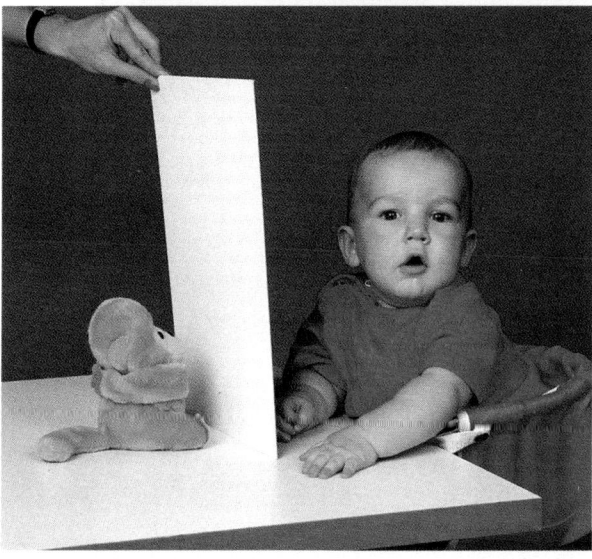

FIGURE 9.8

Object Permanence
Piaget thought that object permanence was one of infancy's
landmark cognitive accomplishments. For this 5-month-old
boy, "out-of-sight" is literally out of mind. The infant looks at
the toy monkey *(top)*, but, when his view of the toy is blocked
(bottom), he does not search for it. Eventually, he will search
for the hidden toy monkey, reflecting the presence of
object permanence.

world of blocks, toys, and playpens but also how they construct a world of relationships with people. A summary of
the main characteristics of sensorimotor thought is presented in figure 9.9.

Preoperational Thought

Possibly because young children are not very concerned
about reality, their drawings are fanciful and inventive.
Suns are blue, skies are yellow, and cars float on clouds in
their symbolic, imaginative world. One 3½-year-old looked

Ability to
organize and
coordinate
sensations
with physical
movements

Inability to use
symbols through
most of its duration

Consists of
six substages
of cognitive
development

Object
permanence
develops

FIGURE 9.9

**Piaget's Description of the Main Characteristics of
Sensorimotor Thought**

at a scribble he had just drawn and described it as a pelican
kissing a seal (see figure 9.10a). The symbolism is simple
but strong, like the abstractions found in some modern art.
As Picasso commented, "I used to draw like Raphael but it
has taken me a lifetime to draw like young children." In the
elementary school years, a child's drawings become more
realistic, neat, and precise (see figure 9.10b). Suns are yellow, skies are blue, and cars travel on roads (Winner, 1986).

Preschool children represent their world with words,
images, and drawings. Symbolic thoughts go beyond simple
connections of sensorimotor information and physical action. Although preschool children can symbolically represent the world, they still cannot perform operations.
Operations, *in Piaget's theory, are mental representations
that are reversible.* Preschool children have difficulty understanding that reversing an action brings about the original
conditions from which the action began. This sounds rather
complicated; however, the following two examples will help
you understand Piaget's concept of reversibility. A

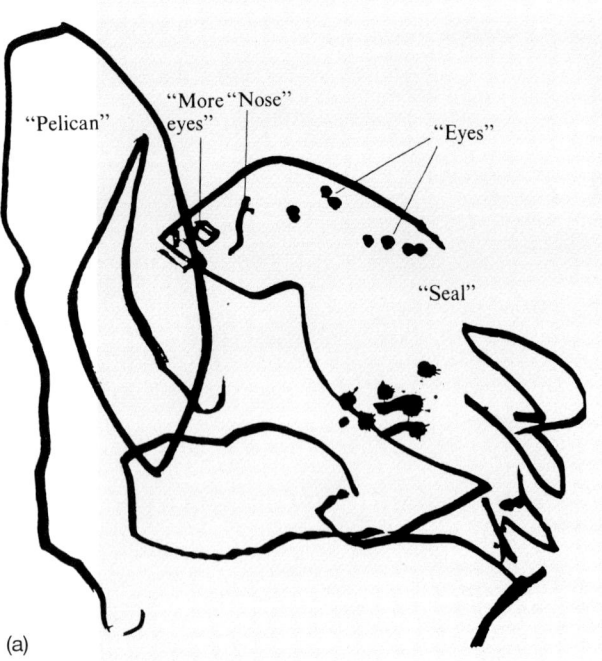

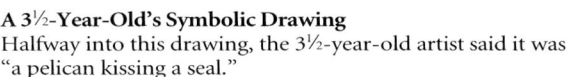

(a)

(b)

A 3½-Year-Old's Symbolic Drawing
Halfway into this drawing, the 3½-year-old artist said it was "a pelican kissing a seal."

An 11-Year-Old's Drawing
An 11-year-old's drawing is neater and more realistic but also less inventive.

FIGURE 9.10

preschool child may know that 4 + 2 = 6 but not understand that the reverse, 6 − 2 = 4, is true. Let's say a preschooler walks to her friend's house each day but always gets a ride home. If you were to ask her to walk home one day, she would probably reply that she doesn't know the way, since she has never walked home before. **Preoperational thought** *is the term Piaget gave to a 2- to 7-year-old child's understanding of the world. Children at this stage of reasoning cannot understand such logical operations as the reversibility of mental representations.*

A well-known test of whether a child can think "operationally" is to present a child with two identical beakers, A and B, filled with liquid to the same height (see figure 9.11). Next to them is a third beaker, C. Beaker C is tall and thin, whereas beakers A and B are wide and short. The liquid is poured from B into C, and the child is asked whether the amounts in A and C are the same. A 4-year-old child invariably says that the amount of liquid in the tall, thin beaker (C) is greater than that in the short, fat beaker (A). Eight-year-old children consistently say the amounts are the same. The 4-year-old child, a preoperational thinker, cannot mentally reverse the pouring action; that is, she cannot imagine the liquid going back from container C to container B. Piaget said that children like this 4-year-old have not grasped the concept of **conservation,** *the principle that a substance's quantity stays the same even though its shape changes.*

In the preoperational stage, a child's thought is also egocentric. By **egocentrism** *Piaget meant the inability to distinguish between one's own perspective and someone else's.* The following telephone conversation between 4-year-old Mark, who is at home, and his father, who is at work, illustrates Mark's egocentric thought:

Father: Mark, is Mommy there?
Mark: (silently nods)
Father: Mark, may I speak to Mommy?
Mark: (nods again silently)

Piaget also called preoperational thought *intuitive,* because, when he asked children why they knew something, they often did not give logical answers but offered personal insights or guesses instead. However, as Piaget observed, young children seem sure they know something, even though they do not use logical reasoning to arrive at the answer. Young children also have an insatiable desire to know their world, and they ask a trillion questions:

"Who was the mother when everybody was the baby?"
"Why do leaves fall?"
"Why does the sun shine?"

At this point, we have discussed four main characteristics of preoperational thought. A summary of these is presented in figure 9.12.

Concrete Operational Thought

Concrete operational thought *is Piaget's term for the 7- to 11-year-old child's understanding of the world. At this stage of thought, children can use operations—they can mentally reverse the liquid from one beaker to another and understand that the volume is the same even though the beakers are different in height and width. Logical reasoning replaces intuitive thought as long as the principles are applied to concrete examples.* For instance, a concrete operational thinker cannot imagine the steps necessary to complete an algebraic equation, which is too abstract at this stage of children's development.

Earlier you read about a beaker task that was too difficult for a child who had not yet reached the stage of operational thought. Another well-known conservation task used to demonstrate concrete operational thought involves two equal amounts of clay (see figure 9.13). An experimenter shows a child two identical balls of clay and then rolls one ball

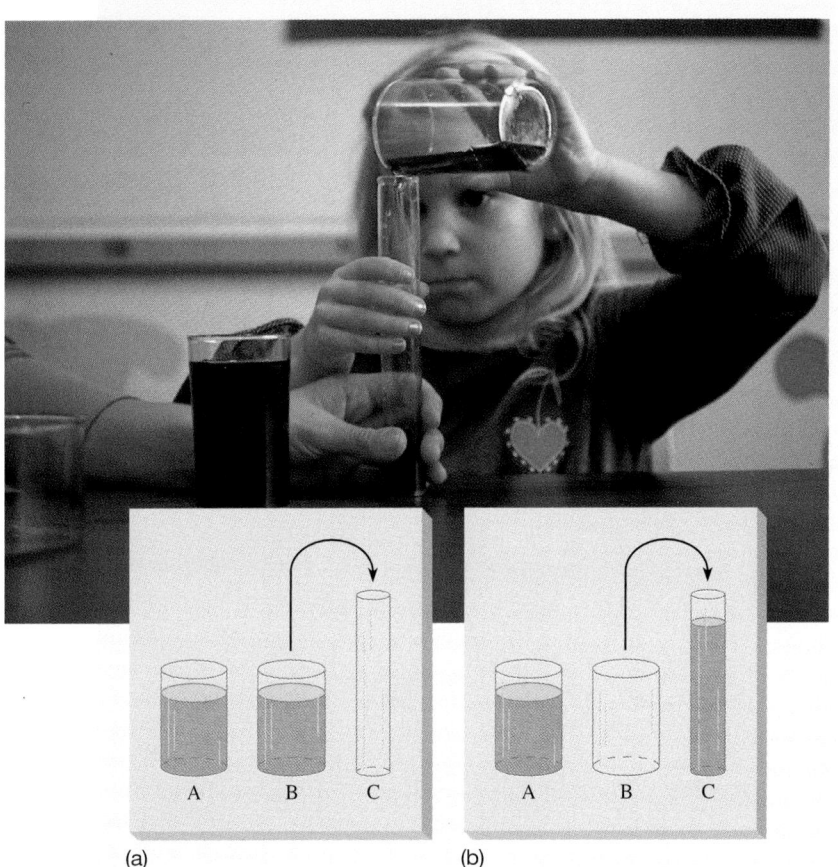

(a)   (b)

Figure 9.11

Piaget's Conservation Task
The beaker test is a well-known Piagetian test to determine whether a child can think operationally—that is, can mentally reverse actions and show conservation of the substance. *(a)* Two identical beakers are presented to the child. Then, the experimenter pours the liquid from B into C, which is taller and thinner than A or B. *(b)* The child is asked if these beakers (A and C) have the same amount of liquid. The preoperational child says no. When asked to point to the beaker that has more liquid, the preoperational child points to the tall, thin beaker. *What inferences do you think the preoperational child makes when observing the liquid being poured from beaker to beaker?*

More symbolic than sensorimotor thought

Inability to engage in operations; can't mentally reverse actions: lacks conservation skills

Egocentric (inability to distinguish between own perspective and someone else's)

Intuitive rather than logical

Figure 9.12

Preoperational Thought's Characteristics

Type of conservation	Initial presentation	Manipulation	Preoperational child's answer	Concrete operational child's answer
Matter	Two identical balls of clay are shown to the child. The child agrees that they are equal.	The experimenter changes the shape of one of the balls and asks the child whether they still contain equal amounts of clay.	"No, the longer one has more."	"Yes, the same amount."

FIGURE 9.13

Preoperational and Concrete Operational Children's Views on the Conservation of Matter

"I still don't have all the answers, but I'm beginning to ask the right questions."

Drawing by Lorenz: © 1989 The New Yorker Magazine, Inc.

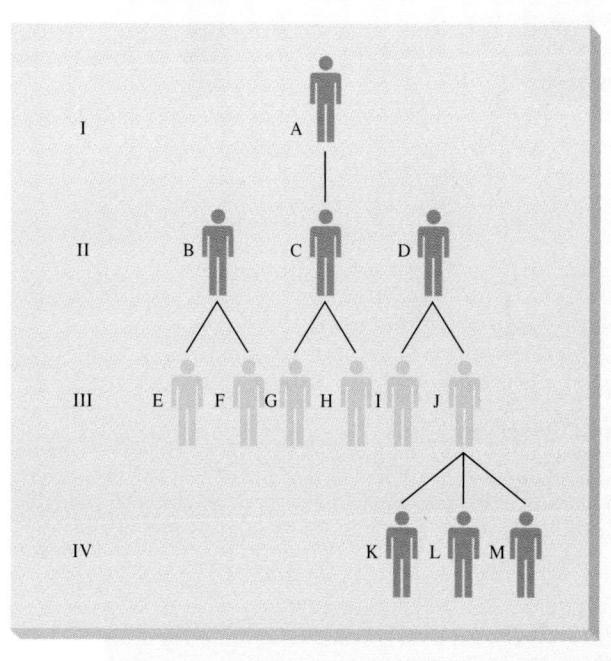

FIGURE 9.14

Classification: An Important Ability in Concrete Operational Thought
A family tree of four generations (I to IV): The preoperational child has trouble seeing the relationships among the members of the four generations. Concrete operational children can classify the members vertically, horizontally, and obliquely (up and down and across). For example, they can report a family member to be a son, a brother, and a grandfather, all at the same time.

into a long, thin shape. The experimenter retains the other in its original ball shape. The experimenter asks the child if there is more clay in the ball or in the long, thin piece of clay. By the time children reach 7 to 8 years of age, most answer that the amount of clay is the same. To solve this problem correctly, children have to imagine that the clay ball is rolled out into a long, thin strip and then returned to its original round shape—imagination that involves a reversible mental action. Concrete operations allow the child to coordinate several characteristics rather than focusing on a single property of an object. In the clay example, the preoperational child is likely to focus on height *or* width. The child who has reached the stage of concrete operational thought coordinates information about both dimensions. Piaget articulated how the child develops conservation skills in other dimensions of the physical environment in addition to mass (the clay ball demonstrations) and volume (the beaker demonstration).

All of the concrete operations Piaget identified focus on the way children think about the properties of objects. One important skill at this stage of reasoning is the ability to classify, or divide, things into different sets or subsets and to consider their interrelations. One way to see if children possess this ability is to see if they can understand a family tree of four generations (see figure 9.14) (Furth & Wachs, 1975). This family tree suggests that the grandfather (A) has three sons (B, C, and D), each of whom has two sons (E through J), and that one of these sons (J) has three

FIGURE 9.15

Characteristics of Concrete Operational Thought

sons (K, L, and M). A child who comprehends the classification system can move up and down a level (vertically), across a level (horizontally), and up and down and across a level (obliquely) within the system. A child who grasps concrete operational thought understands that person J can, at the same time, be father, brother, and grandson, for example. A preoperational child cannot perform this classification and says that a father cannot fulfill these other roles.

We have discussed four main characteristics of concrete operational thought. A summary of these characteristics is presented in figure 9.15. In the next chapter, we will discuss Piaget's fourth stage, formal operational thought—the way, he believed, adolescents think.

Piagetian Contributions and Criticisms

We have spent considerable time outlining Piaget's theory of cognitive development. Let's briefly summarize some of Piaget's main contributions, and then enumerate criticisms of his theory.

Contributions Piaget's contributions established the field of cognitive development. He offered a long list of masterful concepts of enduring power and fascination, such as object permanence, conservation, assimilation, and accommodation. Piaget also proposed the currently accepted vision of children as active, constructive thinkers who, through their commerce with the environment, make them manufacturers of their own development (Flavell, 1992).

Piaget was a genius when it came to observing children; his astute observations showed us inventive ways to discover how children, and even infants, act on and adapt to their world. Piaget showed us some important things to look for in children's cognitive development, including the shift from preoperational to concrete operational thought. He also showed us how we must make experiences fit our cognitive framework yet simultaneously adapt our cognitive orientation to experience. Piaget also revealed how cognitive change is likely to occur if the situation is structured to allow gradual movement to the next higher level.

Criticisms Piaget's theory has not gone unchallenged, however. Critics have raised questions about the following areas: estimates of the child's competence at different developmental levels; stages; training of children to reason at higher levels; and culture and education.

Some cognitive abilities emerge earlier than Piaget thought, and their subsequent development is more prolonged than he believed. As we saw earlier in the chapter,

Piaget was especially intrigued with the points of transition that children make as they improve in their ability to understand principles in the physical world. For example, when on a trip with the family and crossing the "state line," preoperational children will literally expect a line to be observable on the ground. They discover that the line is an abstract concept rather than a real physical descriptor. Can you think of examples from your past or from your interactions with children that could also illustrate a shift from preoperational to concrete operational stages? Hint: Any superstitions held by children or cultural rituals involving magical or mystical forces will be good phenomena to examine. For example,

many Americans practice the ritual of the "tooth fairy." When children lose their baby teeth, the parent coaches the child to leave the tooth under the pillow and then later replaces the tooth with a coin. What kinds of experiences and insights might make belief in the tooth fairy break down? Gathering these examples from your own life shows your ability to _apply psychological concepts and skills to enhance personal adaptation_ as well as appreciation of your own development.

some aspects of object permanence emerge much earlier in infancy than Piaget believed. Even 2-year-olds are nonegocentric in some contexts—when they realize that another person will not see an object they see if the person is blindfolded or is looking in a different direction (Lempers, Flavell, & Flavell, 1977). Some conservation skills have been demonstrated in children as young as 3 years of age, although Piaget did not think it came about until 7 years of age. Young children are not as "pre" this and "pre" that (precausal, preoperational) as Piaget thought. Some aspects of formal operational thinking that involve abstract reasoning do not consistently emerge in early adolescence as Piaget envisioned. And adults often reason in far more irrational ways than Piaget believed (Siegler, 1995). In sum, recent trends highlight the cognitive competencies of infants and young children and the cognitive shortcomings of adolescents and adults (Flavell, 1992).

Piaget conceived of cognitive stages as unitary structures of thought, so his theory assumes synchrony in development. That is, various aspects of a stage should emerge at about the same time. However, several concrete operational concepts do not appear in synchrony. For example, children do not learn to conserve at the same time they learn to cross-classify.

Most contemporary developmentalists agree that children's cognitive development is not a grand stage as Piaget thought. **Neo-Piagetians** _are developmentalists who have elaborated on Piaget's theory, believing children's cognitive development is more specific in many respects than he_

thought. Neo-Piagetians don't believe all of Piaget's ideas should be abandoned. However, they argue that a more accurate vision of the child's cognitive development involves fewer references to grand stages and more emphasis on the roles of strategies, skills, how fast and automatically children can process information, the task-specific nature of children's cognition, and the importance of dividing cognitive problems into smaller, more precise steps (Case, 1993).

Neo-Piagetians still believe that children's cognitive development contains some general properties (Flavell, 1992). They stress that there is a regular, maturation-based increase with age in some aspects of the child's information-processing capacity, such as how fast or efficient the child processes information. As the child's information-processing capacity increases with increasing age, new and more complex forms of cognition in all content domains are possible because the child can now hold in mind and think about more things at once. For example, Canadian developmentalist Robbie Case (1985) argues that adolescents have increasingly more available cognitive resources than they did as children because they can process information more automatically, they have more information-processing capacity, and they are more familiar with a range of content knowledge.

Children who are at one cognitive stage, such as preoperational thought, can be trained to reason at a higher cognitive stage, such as concrete operational thought. This poses a problem for Piaget, who argued that such training works only on a superficial level and is ineffective unless the child is at a transitional point from one stage to the next.

Culture and education exert stronger influences on children's development than Piaget believed. Earlier in the chapter, we studied how the age at which individuals acquire conservation skills is associated to some extent with the degree to which their culture provides relevant practice. And in many developing countries, formal operational thought is a rare occurrence. And as you will learn shortly, there has been a wave of interest in how children's cognitive development progresses through interaction with skilled adults and peers, and how the children's embeddedness in a culture influences their cognitive growth. Such views stand in stark contrast to Piaget's view of the child as a solitary little scientist.

Vygotsky's Theory of Cognitive Development

Children's cognitive development does not occur in a social vacuum. Lev Vygotsky (1896–1934), a Russian psychologist, recognized this important point about children's minds more than half a century ago. Vygotsky's theory is increasingly receiving attention as we move toward the close of the twentieth century (Rogoff, 1993; Steward, 1995).

One of Vygotsky's (1962) most important concepts is that of the **zone of proximal development (ZPD),** *which refers to tasks that are too difficult for children to master alone but that can be mastered with the guidance and assistance of adults or more-skilled children.* Thus, the lower limit of the ZPD is the level of problem solving reached by a child working independently. The upper limit is the level of additional responsibility the child can accept with the assistance of an able instructor (see figure 9.16). Vygotsky's emphasis on the ZPD underscored his belief in the importance of social influences on cognitive development. The practical teaching involved in ZPD begins toward the zone's upper limit, where the child is able to reach the goal only through close collaboration with an instructor. With continued instruction and practice, the child depends less and less on explanations, hints, and demonstrations, until she masters the skills necessary to perform the task alone. Once the goal is achieved, it may become the foundation for a new ZPD.

Many researchers who work in the field of culture and development find themselves comfortable with Vygotsky's theory, which focuses on sociocultural contexts. Vygotsky emphasized how the development of higher mental processes, such as reasoning, involve learning to use the inventions of society, such as language and mathematical systems. He also stressed the importance of teachers and role models in children's mental development. Vygotsky's emphasis on the importance of social interaction and culture

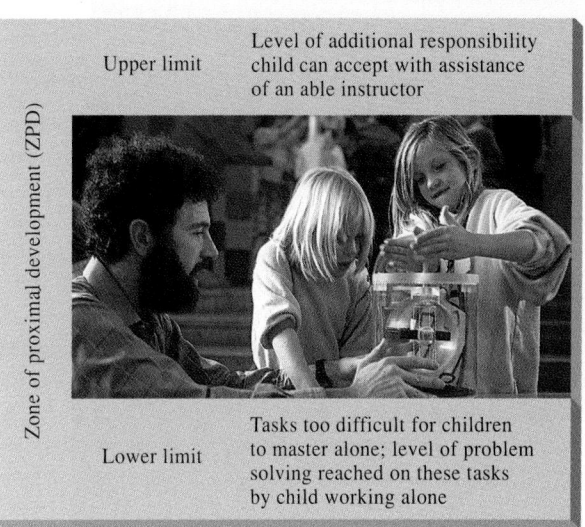

FIGURE 9.16

Vygotsky's Zone of Proximal Development
Vygotsky's zone of proximal development has a lower limit and an upper limit. Tasks in the ZPD are too difficult for the child to perform alone. They require assistance from an adult or a skilled child. As children experience the verbal instruction or demonstration, they organize the information in their existing mental structures so they can eventually perform the skill or task alone. *What implications does the ZPD have for school design?*

in children's cognitive development contrasts with Piaget's description of the child as a solitary young scientist.

American developmental psychologist Barbara Rogoff (1990) also believes that social interaction and culture play important roles in children's cognitive development. She argues that a child's cognitive development should involve an "apprenticeship" with companions who will strengthen the child's written and oral language skills, math skills, and memory strategies to preserve information over time. In mastering these skills, a child would use all sorts of tools—everything from notches on sticks to calculators and computers—that would be consistent with the culture in which the tools were developed and used.

Piaget once observed that children's cognitive development is a continuous creation of increasingly complex forms. As we will see next, this observation applies to children's social development as well.

If a child is to keep alive his inborn sense of wonder without any such gift from the fairies, he needs the companionship of at least one adult who can share it, rediscovering with him the joy, excitement and mystery of the world we live in.

Rachel Carson

Children's Cognitive Development

Piaget, a famous Swiss psychologist, developed an important theory of children's minds. A child constructs an understanding of the world through organization and adaptation. Adaptation consists of assimilation and accommodation. Piaget identified four stages of cognitive development: sensorimotor, preoperational, concrete operational, and formal operational. Sensorimotor thought lasts from birth to about 2 years of age and involves the coordination of sensorimotor action. Object permanence is an important accomplishment in the sensorimotor stage. A key aspect of cognitive development is being able to perform operations, mental representations that are

reversible. The preoperational child (2 to 7 years) cannot do this. Preoperational thought is more symbolic than sensorimotor thought, it lacks conservation skills, it is egocentric, and it is intuitive rather than logical. A concrete operational child (7 to 11 years) can engage in operations, shows conservation skills, reasons logically but only in concrete circumstances, does not think abstractly, and has classification skills.

Piaget was a genius at observing children. He showed us some important things to look for and mapped out some general cognitive changes that occur during children's development. Criticisms of Piaget's views focus on such matters as

estimates of children's competence, stages (neo-Piagetians offer more-precise views and information-processing explanations), training children to reason at higher levels, and culture and education.

In Vygotsky's view, cognitive skills develop through social interaction embedded in a cultural backdrop. Vygotsky emphasized the importance of the zone of proximal development (ZPD), which refers to tasks too difficult for children to master alone but that can be mastered with the guidance and assistance of adults or more highly skilled children. Vygotsky's view is receiving increased attention.

Socioemotional Development

As children grow and develop, they socialize and are socialized by others—parents, siblings, peers, and teachers. Their small world widens as they discover new refuges and new challenges. We will examine Erikson's masterpiece on how we develop socially; it is a grand perspective of our complex journey through life.

Erikson's Theory of Social Development

Erik Erikson (1902–1994) spent his childhood and adolescence in Europe. After working as a psychoanalyst under Freud's direction, Erikson came to the United States in 1933. He became a U.S. citizen and taught at Harvard University.

Erikson recognized Freud's contributions to our understanding of human development, but he broke rank with some of Freud's basic tenets. In contrast to Freud's psychosexual stages, for instance, Erikson (1950, 1968) argues that we develop in *psychosocial stages*. In addition, Freud believed that the first 5 years of life shape our basic personality, but Erikson emphasizes developmental change throughout the life span. The **epigenetic principle** *is Erikson's term for the process that guides development through the life cycle. The epigenetic principle states that human beings unfold according to a blueprint, with each stage of development coming at a predictable time.* In Erikson's view, everyone must pass through eight stages of development on the way to maturity and wisdom. The first four of these stages occur in childhood (see figure 9.17). Each stage is precipitated by a "crisis" that requires a person to grapple with a unique developmental task. According to Erikson, this crisis

is not a catastrophe but a turning point of increased vulnerability and enhanced potential. The more successfully a person resolves the crises, the more complete a human being he or she will become.

In the end the power behind development is life.

Erik Erikson

Trust versus mistrust, *which occurs during an infant's first year, is Erikson's first psychosocial stage. Trust is built when an infant's basic needs—such as comfort, food, and warmth—are met.* Trust in infancy sets the stage for a lifelong expectation that the world will be a good and pleasant place to live.

Erikson's second stage of development, **autonomy versus shame and doubt,** *occurs from approximately 1 to 3 years of age. After developing trust, infants begin to discover that their behavior is their own. They start to assert their sense of independence, or autonomy; they realize their will. If infants are restrained too severely or punished too harshly, they are likely to develop a sense of shame and doubt.*

Initiative versus guilt, *Erikson's third stage of development, occurs during the preschool years. As preschool children encounter a widening social world, they are challenged more than they were as infants. Active, purposeful behavior is needed to cope with these challenges. Children are asked to assume responsibility for their body, their behavior, their toys, and their pets. Developing a sense of responsibility increases initiative. Uncomfortable guilt feelings may arise,*

Erikson's stages	Developmental period	Characteristics
Trust versus mistrust	Infancy (first year)	A sense of trust requires a feeling of physical comfort and a minimal amount of fear about the future. Infants' basic needs are met by responsive, sensitive caregivers.
Autonomy versus shame and doubt	Infancy (second year)	After gaining trust in caregivers, infants start to discover that they have a will of their own. They assert their sense of autonomy, or independence. They realize their will. If infants are restrained too much or punished too harshly, they are likely to develop a sense of shame and doubt.
Initiative versus guilt	Early childhood (preschool years, ages 3–5)	As preschool children encounter a widening social world, they are challenged more and need to develop more purposeful behavior to cope with these challenges. Children are now asked to assume more responsibility. Uncomfortable guilt feelings may arise, though, if the children are irresponsible and are made to feel too anxious.
Industry versus inferiority	Middle and late childhood (elementary school years, 6 years–puberty)	At no other time are children more enthusiastic than at the end of early childhood's period of expansive imagination. As children move into the elementary school years, they direct their energy toward mastering knowledge and intellectual skills. The danger at this stage involves feeling incompetent and unproductive.

FIGURE 9.17

Erikson's Stages of Childhood
The first four stages of Erikson's eight stages are presented here. We will explore the final four stages in chapter 10.

though, if the child is irresponsible or made to feel too anxious. Erikson has a positive outlook on this stage. He believes most guilt can be quickly compensated for by a sense of accomplishment.

Sometime during the elementary school years, children go through Erikson's fourth developmental stage, **industry versus inferiority.** *Children's initiative brings them into contact with a wealth of new experiences. As they move into middle and late childhood, they direct their energy toward mastering knowledge and intellectual skills.* With their expansive imaginations, children at this stage are eager to learn. The danger in the elementary school years is a sense of inferiority—feeling incompetent and inadequate. Erikson believes that teachers have a responsibility to help children develop a sense of competence and achievement. They should "mildly but firmly coerce children into the adventure of finding out that one can learn to accomplish things which one would never have thought of by oneself" (Erikson, 1968, p. 127).

In chapter 10 we will discuss Erikson's last four developmental stages: identity versus identity confusion, in adolescence; intimacy versus isolation, in early adulthood; generativity versus stagnation, in middle adulthood; and integrity versus despair, in late adulthood.

Attachment

Erikson (1968) believes that caregivers' responsive and sensitive behavior toward infants during their first year provides an important foundation for later development. So do a number of contemporary developmental psychologists who study the process of "attachment" during infancy. Attachment usually refers to a strong relationship between two people, in which each person does a number of things to continue the relationship. Many types of people are attached: relatives, lovers, a teacher and student. In the language of developmental psychology, **attachment** *is primarily the close emotional bond between an infant and its caregiver.*

Theories of Attachment   Theories about infant attachment abound. Freud believed that an infant becomes attached to the person or object that provides oral satisfaction. For most infants, this is the mother, since she is most likely to feed the infant. However, researchers have questioned the importance of feeding in attachment. In a classic study, Harry Harlow and Robert Zimmerman (1959) evaluated whether feeding or contact comfort was more important to infant attachment. The researchers separated infant monkeys from their mothers at birth and placed them in cages, where they had access to two artificial "mothers." One of the mothers was made of wire, the other of cloth (see figure 9.18). Half of the infant monkeys were fed by the wire mother, half by the cloth mother. The infant monkeys nestled close to the cloth mother and spent little time on the wire one, even when it was the wire mother that gave milk. This study clearly demonstrated that contact comfort, not feeding, is the crucial element in the attachment process.

FIGURE 9.18

Harlow's Classic "Contact Comfort" Study
Regardless of whether they were fed by a wire mother or by a cloth mother, the infant monkeys overwhelmingly preferred to be in contact with the cloth mother, demonstrating the importance of contact comfort in attachment. *What implications does this research have for child-care practices?*

The importance of contact over feeding has also been demonstrated among humans. Hausa infants in Nigeria, for example, have several caregivers, but they show the strongest attachment to the person with whom they have the most physical contact, not the person who feeds them (Super, 1980).

In another classic study, Konrad Lorenz (1965) examined attachment behavior in geese. Lorenz separated the eggs laid by one goose into two groups. He returned one group to the goose to be hatched; the other group was hatched in an incubator. The goslings in the first group performed as predicted; they followed their mother as soon as they hatched. However, those in the second group, which first saw Lorenz after hatching, followed him everywhere, as if he were their mother. Lorenz marked the goslings and then placed both groups under a box. Mother goose and "mother" Lorenz stood aside as the box was lifted. Each group of goslings went directly to its "mother" (see figure 9.19). Lorenz called this process **imprinting,** *the tendency of an infant animal to form an attachment to the first moving object it sees and/or hears.*

For goslings the critical period for imprinting is the first 36 hours after birth. There appears to be a longer, more

FIGURE 9.19

Imprinting
Konrad Lorenz, a pioneering student of animal behavior, is followed through the water by three imprinted greylag geese. Lorenz described imprinting as rapid, innate learning within a critical period that involves attachment to the first moving object seen. For goslings the critical period is the first 36 hours after birth.

flexible critical period for attachment in human infants. Many developmental psychologists believe that human attachment to a caregiver during the *first year* provides an important foundation for later development. This view has been especially emphasized by John Bowlby (1969, 1989) and Mary Ainsworth (1979). Bowlby believes that an infant and its mother instinctively form an attachment. He believes that a newborn is innately equipped to elicit its mother's attachment behavior; it cries, clings, smiles, and coos. Later the infant crawls, walks, and follows the mother. The infant's goal is to keep the mother nearby. Research on attachment supports Bowlby's view that the infant's attachment to its caregiver intensifies at about 6 to 7 months (Ainsworth, 1967).

Individual Differences in Attachment Some babies seem to have a more positive attachment experience than others. Ainsworth (1979) believes that the difference depends on how sensitive a caregiver is to an infant's signals. Ainsworth says that, in **secure attachment,** *infants use the caregiver, usually the mother, as a secure base from which to explore the environment.* Infants who are securely attached are more likely to have mothers who are more sensitive, accepting, and expressive of affection toward them than those who are insecurely attached (Waters, 1991).

A securely attached infant moves freely away from its mother but also keeps tabs on her location by periodically glancing at her. The infant responds positively to being picked up by others and, when put back down, happily moves away to play. In contrast, an insecurely attached infant avoids its mother or is ambivalent toward her. Such an infant fears strangers and is upset by minor, everyday separations.

If early attachment to a caregiver is important, it should relate to a child's social behavior later in development. Research by Alan Sroufe (1985; Hiester, Carlson, & Sroufe, 1993; Ostoja & others, 1995) documents this connection. In one investigation, infants who were securely attached to their mothers early in infancy were less frustrated and happier at 2 years of age than their insecurely attached counterparts (Matas, Arend, & Sroufe, 1978). Linkages between secure attachment and many other aspects of children's competence have been found (Gruys, 1993; Posada, Lord, & Waters, 1995).

Attachment Criticisms Not all developmentalists believe that a secure attachment in infancy is the only path to competence in life. Indeed, some developmentalists believe that too much emphasis is placed on the importance of the attachment bond in infancy. Jerome Kagan (1987, 1992), for example, believes that infants are highly resilient and adaptive; he argues that they are evolutionarily equipped to stay on a positive developmental course even in the face of wide

In the Hausa culture in Nigeria, Africa, older siblings provide a significant amount of caregiving to their younger siblings. In such cultures, younger siblings often form strong attachments to older siblings.

variations in parenting. Kagan and others stress that genetic and temperament characteristics play more important roles in a child's social competence than the attachment theorists, such as Bowlby, Ainsworth, and Sroufe, are willing to acknowledge (Calkins & Fox, 1992; DiBiase, 1993). For example, infants may have inherited a low tolerance for stress; this, rather than an insecure attachment bond, may be responsible for their inability to get along with peers.

Another criticism of attachment theory is that it ignores the diversity of socializing agents and contexts that exist in an infant's world (Thompson, 1991). In some cultures, infants show attachments to many people. In the Hausa culture in Nigeria, both grandmothers and siblings provide a significant amount of care to infants (Super, 1980). Infants in agricultural societies tend to form attachments to older siblings, who are assigned a major responsibility for

younger siblings' care. The attachments formed by infants in group care in Israeli kibbutzim provide another challenge to the singular attachment thesis.

Researchers recognize the importance of competent, nurturant caregivers in an infant's development—at issue, though, is whether or not secure attachment, especially to a single caregiver, is critical.

Parent-Child Relationships

Although many children spend a great deal of time in child-care situations away from the home, parents are still the main caregivers for the vast majority of the world's children. Parents have always wondered what is the best way to rear their children, and cultures develop many adages about child rearing (such as "Spare the rod, spoil the child" and "Children should be seen and not heard"). There was a time when parents took those adages seriously. However, our attitudes toward children—and parenting techniques—have changed. In this section, we'll discuss various parenting styles; the role of culture, social class, and ethnicity in parenting; as well as changes within the structure of the American family itself (Marsiglio, 1995).

Parenting is a very important profession, but no test of fitness for it is ever imposed in the interest of children.

George Bernard Shaw, 1944

Parenting Styles Diana Baumrind (1971, 1991) believes that parents interact with their children in one of three basic ways. She classifies these parenting styles as authoritarian, authoritative, and permissive.

Authoritarian parenting *is a restrictive, punitive style that exhorts a child to follow the parent's directions and to respect work and effort. An authoritarian parent firmly limits and controls the child, allowing little verbal exchange. Authoritarian parenting is associated with children's social incompetence.* In a difference of opinion about how to do something, for example, an authoritarian parent might say, "You do it my way or else. There will be no discussion!" Children of authoritarian parents often are anxious about social comparison, they fail to initiate activity, and they have poor communication skills.

Authoritative parenting *encourages children to be independent but still places limits and controls on their behavior. Parents allow extensive verbal give-and-take and are warm and nurturant toward the child. Authoritative parenting is associated with children's social competence.* An authoritative parent might put his arm around the child in a comforting way and say, "You know you should not have done that; let's talk about how you can handle the situation better next time." Children whose parents are authoritative tend to be socially competent, self-reliant, and socially responsible.

The Latino family reunion of the Limon family in Austin, Texas. Latino American children often grow up in families with a network of relatives that runs into scores of individuals.

Permissive parenting comes in two forms: permissive-indifferent and permissive-indulgent (Maccoby & Martin, 1983). **Permissive-indifferent parenting** *is a style in which parents interact very little with their children. This style is associated with children's social incompetence, especially a lack of self-control.* This parent cannot give an affirmative answer to the question, "It is 10 P.M. Do you know where your child is?" Children have a strong need for their parents to care about them; children whose parents are permissive-indifferent may develop the sense that other aspects of the parents' lives are more important than they are. Children whose parents are permissive-indifferent tend to show poor self-control and do not handle independence well.

Permissive-indulgent parenting *is a style in which parents are involved with their children but place few demands or controls on them. Permissive-indulgent parenting is associated with children's social incompetence, especially a lack of self-control.* Such parents let their children do what they want, with the result that children never learn to control their own behavior and always expect to get their way. Some parents deliberately rear their children this way because they believe the combination of warm involvement with few restraints will produce a creative, confident child. One boy whose parents deliberately reared him in a permissive-indulgent manner moved his parents out of their bedroom suite and took it over for himself. He is almost 18 years old and still has not learned to control his behavior; when he can't get something he wants, he throws temper tantrums. As you might expect, he is not very popular with his peers. Children whose parents are permissive-indulgent never learn respect for others and have difficulty controlling their behavior.

"Are you going to believe me, your own flesh and blood, or some stranger you married?"

Reprinted by permission of Jerry Marcus.

I looked on child rearing not only as a work of love and duty but as a profession that was fully as interesting and challenging as any honorable profession in the world and one that demanded the best that I could bring to it.

Rose Kennedy

Cultural, Social Class, and Ethnic Variations Among Families In the broadest sense, good parents everywhere seem to share a common approach to child rearing. One study examined the behavior of parents in

A Pyramid Model for Serving Families

Children's health and well-being are enhanced when their parents have reasonable jobs, housing, and health care. Many families, especially those in low-income circumstances, need access to family services and support that will help them cope with challenges and stress that invade their lives. One model that was recently proposed emphasizes that communities need to offer a pyramid of services with a range of provisions for families (Allen, Brown, & Finlay, 1992). Some families need only minimal assistance, while other families do not have sufficient resources to protect or treat children at home (see figure 9.A). In between are families needing some extra support, families needing special assistance, and families in crisis. Programs should be tailored to address the needs identified at each level of the pyramid.

Two overall types of programs help families do a better job of nurturing and protecting their children. The first consists of programs that are variously called *family support programs, family resource programs,* or *parent education programs.* These programs offer low-intensity preventive services designed to strengthen family functioning early on, to avert crises. Programs of the second, more intensive type, *family preservation services,* are intended to help families already in crisis change their behavior to remove the immediate risk to the children and, if possible, avert the need to remove the children from the home.

As services become more family focused, the families served by many intervention programs are becoming increasingly diverse. Many families are characterized by attitudes, beliefs, values, customs, languages, and behaviors that are unfamiliar to interventionists. It is not uncommon for interventionists in some locations to work with families from as many as ten or more different cultures. In a large school district, as many as fifty languages might be spoken.

186 cultures around the world and found that most parents use a warm and controlling style, one that is neither permissive nor restrictive, in dealing with their children (Rohner & Rohner, 1981). Good parents seem to know instinctively that children do best when they are guided by love and at least some moderate parental control.

Despite such commonalities, researchers have also found telling differences in parenting across social classes and cultures (Harkness & Super, 1995). For example, there is wide variation in some child-rearing practices among social classes in the United States and most Western cultures (Hoff-Ginsberg & Tardif, 1995). Working-class and low-income parents, for instance, often place a high value on "external characteristics," such as obedience and neatness. Middle-class families, on the other hand, seem to prize "internal characteristics," such as self-control and the ability to delay gratification. Middle-class parents also are more likely to explain things, to use reasoning to accompany their discipline, to ask their children questions, and to praise them. In contrast, parents in low-income and working-class households are more likely to discipline their children with physical punishment and to criticize their children (Kohn, 1977).

Children in low-income families benefit when family support and services are available. To read about a pyramid of services for families, turn to Applications in Psychology 9.1.

Ethnic minority families differ from White American families in their size, structure and composition, reliance on kinship networks, and level of income and education (Garcia & others, 1995). Large and extended families are more common among ethnic minority groups than among White Americans (Wilson, 1989). For example, more than 30 percent of Latino American families consist of five or more individuals (Keefe & Padilla, 1987). African American and Latino American children interact more with grandparents, aunts, uncles, cousins, and more distant relatives than do White American children (Zambrana, 1995). Single-parent families are more common among African Americans and Latino Americans than among White Americans (Marín & Marín, 1991). In comparison with two-parent households, single parents often have more limited resources of time, money, and energy. This shortage of resources may prompt them to encourage early autonomy among their children and adolescents (Spencer & Dornbusch, 1990). Also, ethnic minority parents are less well educated

Residential treatment centers
Therapeutic group homes
Foster family homes

Families Whose Children Cannot Be
Protected or Treated at Home

• Intensive family
preservation
services
• Child protective
services

• Comprehensive
substance abuse
treatment
• Respite
(temporary) child
care
• Family-based
services
• Special health &
education services

Families in Crisis

• Home visiting
programs
• Family support
centers
• Parent education
programs

Families Needing Special Assistance

• Adequate
income, housing,
health care, child
care, education,
and recreational
services

Families Needing Some Extra Support

All Families

FIGURE 9.A

A Pyramid of Services to Improve Family Health and Well-Being
When communities are able to offer a pyramid of assistance that matches the pyramid of family needs, problems are likely to be solved or alleviated at earlier stages, when they are easier and less costly to address. As family needs grow in intensity, so do services to meet those needs.

(a)

(b)

(a) Is the play of today's children different from the play of children in collective village life, as shown in *Children's Games* by Pieter Breughel? *(b)* American children's play once took place in the rural fields and city streets. Today play is often confined to backyards, basements, playrooms, and bedrooms. The content of children's play today is often derived from video games, television dramas, and Saturday-morning cartoons.

Some aspects of home life can help protect ethnic minority children from social patterns of injustice (Spencer & Dornbusch, 1990). The community and family can filter out destructive racist messages, parents can provide alternate frames of reference than those presented by the majority, and parents can also provide competent role models and encouragement (Jones, 1990, 1994). The extended family system in many ethnic minority families also provides an important buffer against stress.

Many Native Americans value autonomy and, thus, encourage their children to become independent at an early age (LaFromboise & Low, 1989). Conversely, Puerto Rican parents living in the United States are more likely to promote nonassertive and compliant behavior in their children (Inclan & Herron, 1989). Japanese American families value the family over the individual, stress duty and obligation over love, and encourage social conformity. Mainstream American families, however, emphasize the individual, promote social control through love and punishment, and praise independent behavior (Nagata, 1989). In addition, African American parents are less likely than White American parents to socialize their children along strict gender lines. African American parents are also more likely to share child care and decision making about child rearing and to value a child's social competence over an ability to deal with objects (Allen & Majidi-Ahi, 1989).

and engage in less joint decision making than do White American parents, and ethnic minority children are more likely to come from low-income families than are White American children (Committee for Economic Development, 1987). Although impoverished families often raise competent children, poor parents may have a diminished capacity for supportive and involved parenting (McLoyd, 1993).

Peers and Play

If you think back to your childhood, some of the first memories that spring to mind may be of the times you spent hanging out with friends. You learned all sorts of things from your peers about the world outside your family. All children do. By talking to a friend, a child may learn that another child's parents argue all the time, make him go to bed early, or give him an allowance. Many children get their first information (much of it wrong) about sex from friends. Children frequently compare themselves with their peers: are they better than, about the same as, or worse than their peers at skateboarding, math, or making friends?

Most children want to have friends and be popular. Children who are happy and enthusiastic, show concern for others, and have good conversational skills tend to be popular and make friends easily (Hartup, 1995). In fact, peer relations have been found to be important predictors of children's adjustment and future competence. For example, children who are rejected by their peers tend to have more problems than children who are popular (Coie, 1993).

It is largely through play that children forge the bonds of friendship. The word *play* is a conspicuous part of children's conversations: "What can we play now?" "Let's play hide-and-seek." "Let's play outside." Most young children spend a good deal of their day playing.

Children learn to cooperate with their peers, set and follow rules, work off frustrations, and explore the world around them through play. By the age of 5 or 6, however, children in most societies face an important transition— they can no longer spend their day at play; they must devote most of their day to school.

You are troubled at seeing him spend his early years in doing nothing. What! Is it nothing to be happy? Is it nothing to skip, to play, to run about all day long? Never in his life will he be so busy as now.

Jean-Jacques Rousseau

Development does not end with childhood. We also develop as adolescents and adults, as we will discuss in the next chapter.

REVIEW

*Erikson's Theory of Social Development,
Attachment, Families, Peers and Play*

Erikson's theory emphasizes development throughout the human life span. Erikson says that individuals go through eight psychosocial stages, guided by the epigenetic principle. Erikson's four childhood stages are trust versus mistrust (first year), autonomy versus shame and doubt (second year), initiative versus guilt (3–5 years), and industry versus inferiority (6 years–puberty).

Attachment is a close bond between an infant and a caregiver. A number of attachment theories exist. Feeding does not seem to be critical in attachment, but contact comfort,

familiarity, and the caregiver's sensitivity and responsiveness are. Many developmental psychologists, especially Bowlby and Ainsworth, believe that attachment in the first year provides an important foundation for later development. Ainsworth argues that secure attachment is critical for competent social development; others do not.

Baumrind's parenting strategies—authoritarian, authoritative, and permissive—are widely used classifications. Socially competent children are more likely to have authoritative parents. Although there

are cross-cultural variations in families, authoritative parenting is the most common childrearing style around the world. Working-class and low-income parents place a higher value on "external characteristics," middle-class parents a higher value on "internal characteristics." However, there are variations in any social class, especially among ethnic groups. Chinese American, African American, and Mexican American families all have a strong tradition of the extended family. Peers and play are also important contexts in the child's development.

This chapter began with the poignant and inspiring story of the Dilley family, who, with successful drug therapy, traded in their childless state for an existence few of us could imagine. The delivery of six infants transformed their lifestyle in a whirlwind of high technology and a barrage of diapers and formula.

Technological advances have moved ahead rapidly to provide new hopes and alternatives for people who want to have children. However, many scientists are concerned that our technological abilities have outpaced our moral capacity to make sound judgments about the very technologies being developed. A few examples from contemporary news stories illustrate this complexity:

- Parents die in an airliner crash, leaving a fertilized embryo as heir.
- New methods may allow fertilization to occur using two eggs, rather than a sperm and an egg.
- It might be possible to clone (make exact genetic copies of) smaller organisms. What would the effect be of human cloning?
- Unused eggs extracted for fertility procedures may be donated for scientific research purposes.
- A grandmother gives birth to her own grandchildren on behalf of her daughter, who is unable to conceive and bear her own babies.
- Genetic engineering might encourage "selection" of child characteristics most desired by parents.

Each circumstance offers a challenging opportunity for critical thinkers to exercise some analysis about what effects these challenges might produce in our technologically oriented culture.

However, the challenge of this example is based on the values that undergird decisions about reproduction that is facilitated through technology. Our culture is based on the pursuit of individual rights. In contrast with collectivist cultures, in which group members tend to act in accordance with the best interests of the group, individualist cultures show greater allegiance to the interests of the individual. How does this relate to technology-assisted birth? A couple with difficulties in conceiving has the right to pursue whatever means are available (such as in vitro fertilization, egg donors, and surrogate mothers). Many people invest significant sums in procedures that do not produce the desired conception. Some contend that the original medical condition of either parent that prevents natural fertilization should be regarded as a medical problem; treatment of the condition should be sponsored by health insurance plans. In such cases, the cost of high technology fertilization is passed on to other insurance holders.

Where do you stand with regard to access to technological advances in reproductive interventions? Should these techniques be available only to those who can pay for it? Should any woman with childbearing intentions gain access to sophisticated technology, regardless of her age? As newer and more unusual methods are developed, how will we make appropriate determinations about access? How do such investments compare to the challenge of caring for children who are already here? In times of rising taxes and health insurance costs, how much of the cost should be borne by persons not directly involved in raising the child?

Obviously these are messy ethical questions indeed. However, your pattern of responses to these questions may reveal something about your underlying values system. Are you more inclined to champion an *individual rights* stance or a *collectivist* position? Are you more likely to favor the value of *scientific progress* in support of new technologies or a *naturalistic* perspective in which any artificial methods are likely to be condemned? Does being able to *identify these values and the role they play in decisions* make your choices about these and other ethical dilemmas easier to predict?

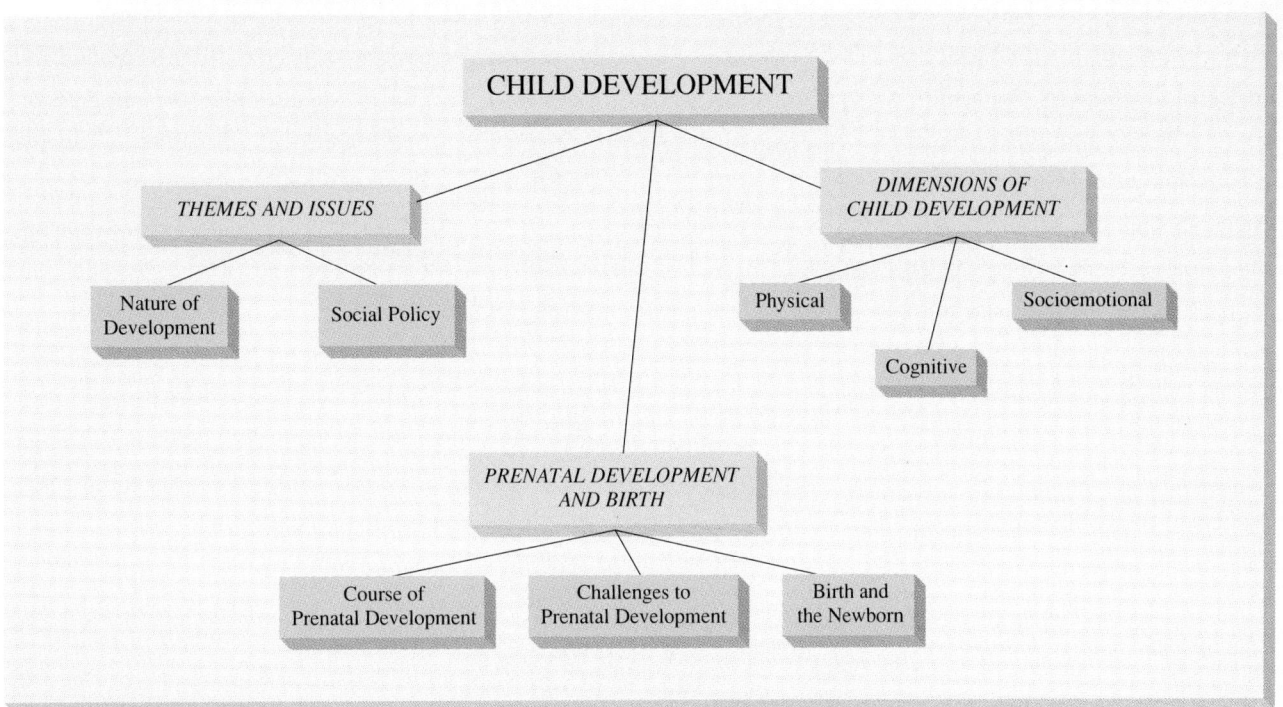

Our coverage of child development began with an exploration of themes and issues in development. We evaluated what development is, developmental processes, developmental issues, and social policy. Then we studied prenatal development and birth, examining the course of prenatal development, challenges to prenatal development, and birth and the newborn. We concluded the chapter by reading about the three main dimensions of child development: physical, cognitive, and socioemotional. Don't forget that you can obtain an overall summary of the chapter by again reading the in-chapter reviews on pages 307, 316, and 325.

Children's development takes place because of biological, cognitive, and socioemotional processes. These processes are intricately interwoven. Socioemotional processes shape cognitive processes, cognitive processes promote or restrict socioemotional processes, and biological processes influence cognitive processes. Although it is helpful to study various processes in separate sections, like we did in this chapter, remember that development unfolds in an integrated human being.

The main psychological perspectives represented in this chapter were neurobiological, cognitive, sociocultural, and psychoanalytic. Our discussions of prenatal development and birth (pp. 301–304) and physical development (pp. 304–306) reflect the neurobiological perspective. Our coverage of children's cognitive development (pp. 307–315) reflects the cognitive perspective. Our exploration of socioemotional development (pp. 316–325) reflects the sociocultural perspective. Erikson's theory (pp. 316–318) represents the psychoanalytic perspective.

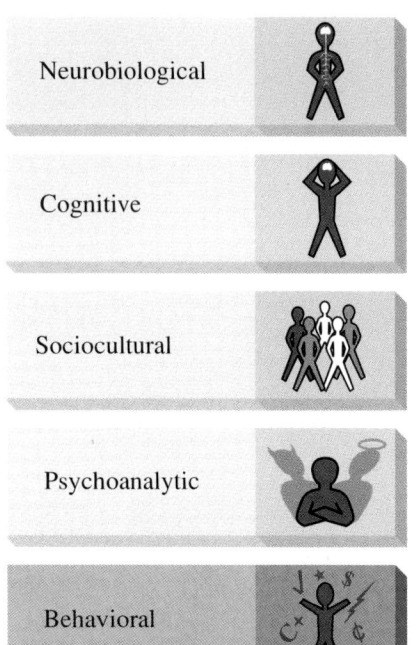

Neurobiological

Cognitive

Sociocultural

Psychoanalytic

Behavioral

Humanistic

KEY TERMS

development A pattern of movement or change that begins at conception and continues through the life cycle.   297

biological processes Processes that involve changes in an individual's physical nature.   297

cognitive processes Processes that involve changes in an individual's thought, intelligence, and language skills.   297

socioemotional processes Processes that involve changes in an individual's relationships with people, changes in emotion, and changes in personality.   297

maturation The orderly sequence of changes dictated by the genetic code.   297

continuity of development Gradual, cumulative change from conception to death.   297

discontinuity of development Development involving qualitatively distinct stages in the life span.   297

early-later experience issue An issue that focuses on the degree to which early experiences (especially in infancy) or later experiences are the key determinants of a child's development.   297

social policy A national government's course of action designed to influence the welfare of its citizens.   298

conception The penetration of an ovum (egg) by a sperm; also called fertilization.   302

zygote A fertilized egg.   302

germinal period The first 2 weeks after conception.   302

embryonic period The second through eighth weeks after conception.   302

fetal period The third through ninth months after conception.   302

teratogen Any agent that causes a birth defect. (*Teratogen* comes from the Greek word *tera*, meaning "monster.")   303

fetal alcohol syndrome (FAS) A cluster of abnormalities that appear in the offspring of mothers who drink alcohol heavily during pregnancy.   303

preterm infant An infant born prior to 38 weeks after conception; also called a premature infant.   304

assimilation The incorporation of new information into one's existing knowledge.   307

accommodation An individual's adjustment to new information.   307

sensorimotor thought In Piaget's theory, the stage of development that lasts from birth to about 2 years of age, corresponding to the period of infancy. An infant constructs an understanding of the world by coordinating sensory experiences (such as seeing and hearing) with physical (motor) actions.   308

object permanence Piaget's term for one of the infant's most important accomplishments: understanding that objects and events continue to exist even when they cannot directly be seen, heard, or touched.   308

operations In Piaget's theory, mental representations that are reversible.   309   .

preoperational thought The term Piaget gave to the 2- to 7-year-old's understanding of the world. Children at this stage of reasoning cannot understand such logical operations as the reversibility of mental representations.   310

conservation The principle that a substance's quantity stays the same even though its shape changes.   310

egocentrism Piaget's term for the inability to distinguish between one's own perspective and someone else's.   310

concrete operational thought Piaget's term for the 7- to 11-year-old child's understanding of the world. At this stage of thought, children can use operations—for instance, they can mentally reverse the pouring of liquid from one beaker to another and understand that the volume is the same even though the beakers are different in height and weight. Logical reasoning replaces intuitive thought as long as the principles are applied to concrete examples.   313

neo-Piagetians Developmentalists who have elaborated on Piaget's theory, believing that children's cognitive development is more specific in many respects than he thought.   314

zone of proximal development (ZPD) Vygotsky's term for tasks too difficult for children to master alone, but that can be mastered with the guidance and assistance of adults or more-skilled children.   315

epigenetic principle Erikson's term for the process that guides development through the life cycle. The epigenetic principle states that human beings unfold according to a blueprint, with each stage of development coming at a predictable time. Ultimately, all stages contribute to a complete identity.   316

trust versus mistrust Erikson's first psychosocial stage, which is experienced in the first year of life. A sense of trust requires a feeling of physical comfort and a minimal amount of fear and apprehension about the future.   316

autonomy versus shame and doubt Erikson's second stage of development, occurring in late infancy and toddlerhood (1–3 years).   316

initiative versus guilt Erikson's third stage of development, occurring during the preschool years.   316

industry versus inferiority Erikson's fourth developmental stage, occurring approximately in the elementary school years.   318

attachment A close emotional bond between the infant and the caregiver.   318

imprinting The tendency of an infant animal to form an attachment to the first moving object it sees or hears.   318

secure attachment Attachment in which infants use the caregiver, usually the mother, as a secure base from which to explore the environment. Ainsworth believes that secure attachment in the first year of life provides an important foundation for psychological development later in life.   319

authoritarian parenting A restrictive, punitive style that exhorts the child to follow the parent's directions and to respect work and effort. The authoritarian parent places firm limits and controls on the child, with little verbal exchange allowed. Authoritarian parenting is associated with children's social incompetence.   320

authoritative parenting A parenting style that encourages children to be independent but still places limits and controls on their actions. Extensive verbal give-and-take is allowed, and parents are warm and nurturant toward the child. Authoritative parenting is associated with children's social competence.   320

permissive-indifferent parenting A style of parenting in which the parents interact very little with their children; it is associated with children's social incompetence, especially a lack of self-control.   321

permissive-indulgent parenting A style of parenting in which parents are highly involved with their children but place few demands or controls on them. Permissive-indulgent parenting is associated with children's social incompetence, especially lack of self-control.   321

THE MEASURE OF OUR SUCCESS: A LETTER TO MY CHILDREN AND YOURS

(1992) by Marian Wright Edelman. Boston: Beacon Press.

Marian Wright Edelman founded the Children's Defense Fund in 1973 and for more than two decades has been working to advance the health and well-being of America's children and parents. This slim volume begins with a message to her oldest son, Joshua, 22. In that message and throughout the book, Edelman conveys her belief that parenting and nurturing the next generation are the most important functions of a society and that we need to take them more seriously than we have in the past. Edelman suggests that there is no free lunch. She believes that you should not feel entitled to anything you don't sweat and struggle for. She also warns against working only for money or for power, because they won't save your soul, build a decent family, or help you sleep at night. She tells her sons, Remember that your wife is not your mother or your maid. Edelman also admonishes our society for not developing better safety nets for children and not being the caring community that children and parents need.

Edelman's book stimulates thought about what kind of nation we want to be, what kind of values mean the most to us, and what we can do to improve the health and well-being of our nation's children and parents.

WHAT TO EXPECT WHEN YOU'RE EXPECTING

(1988, 2nd ed.) by Arlene Eisenberg, Heidi Murkoff, and Sandee Hathaway. New York: Workman.

What to Expect When You're Expecting is a month-by-month, step-by-step guide to pregnancy and childbirth. This is an excellent book for expectant parents. It is reassuring, thorough, and filled with charts and lists that make understanding pregnancy an easier task.

TOUCHPOINTS

(1992) by T. Berry Brazelton. Reading, MA: Addison-Wesley.

Touchpoints is highly respected pediatrician T. Berry Brazelton's most recent book. Brazelton focuses on the concerns and questions that parents have about their child's feelings, behavior, and development from pregnancy to first grade. The title derives from Brazelton's belief that there are universal spurts of development and trying times of adaptation that accompany them throughout childhood. Section 1 discusses development from pregnancy through 3 years; section 2 describes a number of challenges to development, from allergies to toilet training; and section 3 focuses on important figures in the child's development, such as fathers, mothers, grandparents, friends, caregivers, and the child's doctor.

RAISING BLACK CHILDREN

(1992) by James P. Comer and Alvin F. Poussaint. New York: Plume.

Raising Black Children is written by two of the most highly respected experts on African American children—James Comer and Alvin Poussaint, professors of psychiatry at Yale and Harvard, respectively. Comer and Poussaint argue that African American parents face additional difficulties in raising emotionally healthy African American children because of race and income problems. Comer and Poussaint's guide contains almost a thousand child-rearing questions they have repeatedly heard from African American parents across the income spectrum. They give advice to parents on how to improve the African American child's self-esteem and identity, how to confront racism, how to teach their children to handle anger, conflict, and frustration, and how to deal with the mainstream culture and retain an African American identity. This is an excellent book for African American parents and includes wise suggestions that are not in most child-rearing books (almost all others are written for middle-class White parents and do not deal with special problems faced by ethnic minority parents or parents from low-income backgrounds).

RESOURCES FOR PSYCHOLOGY AND IMPROVING HUMANKIND

Beyond Rhetoric: A New American Agenda for Children and Families (1991)

> by the National Commission on Children
> 111 Eighteenth Street NW, Suite 810
> Washington, DC 20036

The National Commission on Children is composed of a 34-member bipartisan group appointed by the president and 34 congressional leaders. This report describes families as the cornerstone of children's development and urges the nation to adopt policies and legislation aimed at strengthening and supporting families in their child-rearing role. The commission also publishes other reports on children and families.

Child Poverty Action Group

> 22 Wellesley St. East
> Toronto, ON M4Y 1G3 CANADA
> 416–922–3126

Among other advocacy initiatives, they sponsor a toll-free help line for children in trouble.

Children's Defense Fund

> 25 E Street
> Washington, DC 20001
> 800–424–9602

The Children's Defense Fund exists to provide a strong and effective voice for children and adolescents who cannot vote, lobby, or speak for themselves. The Children's Defense Fund is especially interested in the needs of poor, minority, and handicapped children and adolescents. The fund provides information, technical assistance, and support to a network of state and local child and youth advocates. The Children's Defense Fund publishes a number of excellent books and pamphlets related to children's needs.

How to Save the Children (1992)

> by Amy Hatkoff and Karen Klopp
> New York: Simon & Schuster

This is an innovative resource filled with practical ideas about how volunteerism can help to counter the effects of poverty and neglect on America's children. The book has more than two hundred specific suggestions for things you can do to help children. The book is a clearinghouse of ideas, addresses, and phone numbers for individuals who want to become involved in volunteering their time and talent.

National Black Child Development Institute

> 1463 Rhode Island Avenue NW
> Washington, DC 20005
> 202–387–1281

This nonprofit organization is dedicated to improving the quality of life for African American children. Issues and services related to health, child welfare, education, and child care are the foci of the institute. The organization publishes *Child Health Talk*, which addresses a variety of issues involving children's health.

National Information Center for Children and Youth with Handicaps

> P.O. Box 1492
> Washington, DC 20013
> 703–893–6061
> 800–999–5599

This organization provides useful publications and other materials to parents, educators, caregivers, advocates, and others who want to help children with disabilities.

CHAPTER

10

Adolescence, Adult Development, and Aging

CHAPTER OUTLINE

CRITICAL THINKING ABOUT BEHAVIOR

CHAPTER BOXES

The generations of living things pass in a short while, and like runners, pass on the torch of life.

Lucretius

J onathan Swift said, "No wise man ever wished to be younger." Without a doubt, a 70-year-old body does not work as well as it once did. It is also true that an individual's fear of aging is often greater than need be. As more individuals live to a ripe *and* active old age, our image of aging is changing. While on the average a 75-year-old's joints should be stiffening, people can practice not to be average. For example, a 75-year-old man may *choose* to train for and run a marathon; an 80-year-old woman whose capacity for work is undiminished may *choose* to continue making and selling children's toys.

Consider 85-year-old Sadie Halperin, who has been working out for 11 months at a rehabilitation center for the aged in Boston, lifting

Eighty-five-year-old Sadie Halperin doubled her strength in exercise after just 11 months. Before developing an exercise routine, she felt wobbly and often had to hold on to a wall when she walked. Now she walks down the middle of hallways and says she feels wonderful.

weights and riding a stationary bike. She says that before she started working out, about everything she did— shopping, cooking, walking—was a major struggle. Initially she could lift only 15 pounds with both legs; now she lifts 30 pounds. At first she could bench-press only 20 pounds; now she bench-presses 50 pounds. Sadie's exercise routine has increased her muscle strength and helps her to battle osteoporosis by slowing the calcium loss from her bones, which can lead to deadly fractures (Ubell, 1992).

PREVIEW

The experiences of 85-year-old Sadie Halperin raise some truly interesting questions about development, among them how much people can continue to change even when they are old. In the 1990s, psychologists have increasingly stressed the importance of successful aging rather than stereotyping older adults as always in decline. Later in this chapter we will explore many different facets of development in older adults, but we will begin our coverage in this chapter with adolescence and then move on to the early and middle adulthood years.

ADOLESCENCE

Twentieth-century poet and essayist Roger Allen remarked, "In case you are worried about what's going to become of the younger generation, it's going to grow up and start worrying about the younger generation." Virtually, every society has worried about its younger generations, but it was not until the beginning of the twentieth century that the scientific study of adolescence began.

The Nature of Adolescence

Adolescence *is the transition from childhood to adulthood, which involves physical, cognitive, and socioemotional changes. In most cultures, adolescence begins at approximately 10 to 13 years of age and ends at approximately 18 to 21 years.* In 1904 psychologist G. Stanley Hall wrote the first scientific book on the nature of adolescence. Hall referred to the teen years as a period of "storm and stress." The **storm-and-stress view** is *G. Stanley Hall's concept that adolescence is a turbulent time charged with conflict and mood swings.* Thoughts, feelings, and actions oscillate between conceit and humility, goodness and temptation, happiness and sadness. An adolescent may be nasty to a peer one moment and kind the next moment. At one time the adolescent may want to be alone but seconds later seek companionship.

Anthropologist Margaret Mead (1928) studied adolescents in the Samoan Islands in the South Pacific. She observed that Samoan adolescents make a smooth, gradual transition from childhood to adulthood, rather than experiencing the storm and stress Hall envisioned in all cultures. Mead argued that in a culture that allows children to observe sexual activity, engage in sex play, do important work, be assertive, and know precisely what adult roles will encompass, adolescence is relatively free of stress. One controversial critique of Mead's work, however, suggested that Samoan adolescents experience considerably more stress than Mead believed (Freeman, 1983), leaving the cultural prescription for stress-free adolescents still debatable. However, Mead did establish that cross-cultural research can reveal variations among different cultural contexts, contrary to theories that propose universal patterns.

During most of the twentieth century, American adolescents have been described as abnormal and deviant. In addition to Hall, Freud described adolescents as sexually driven and conflicted, and some media portrayals of adolescents—like the movies *Rebel Without a Cause* in the late 1950s and *Easy Rider* in the 1960s—portrayed adolescents as rebellious, conflicted, faddish, delinquent, and self-centered. Consider also the images of adolescents as stressed and disturbed in the movies *The Breakfast Club* in the 1980s to *Boyz in the Hood* in the 1990s.

Adults probably forget their own adolescence. With a little effort, though, most adults can recall things they did that stretched—even broke—the patience of their own parents. In matters of taste and manners, young people of every generation have seemed radical, unnerving, and different to adults—in how they look, how they behave, and the music they enjoy. However, it is an enormous error to confuse adolescent enthusiasm for trying on new identities and for enjoying moderate amounts of outrageous behavior with hostility toward parental and societal standards. Acting out and boundary testing are time-honored ways in which adolescents move toward accepting, rather than rejecting, parental values (Santrock, 1996).

Adults often have short memories about their adolescence. With a little effort, though, most adults can remember behavior that stretched, or even broke, the patience of their elders. Acting out and boundary testing are time-honored methods that move adolescents toward identities of their own. Adolescence should not be viewed as a time of crisis, rebellion, pathology, and deviation. Far more accurate is a vision of adolescence as a time of evaluation, decision making, and commitment as adolescents seek to find out who they are and carve out a place for themselves in the world.

It does little good, and can do considerable disservice, to think of adolescence as a time of rebellion, crisis, pathology, and deviation. It's far more accurate to view adolescence as a time of evaluation, decision making, and commitment as young people carve out their place in the world. How competent they will become often depends on their access to a range of legitimate opportunities and long-term support from adults who deeply care about them (William T. Grant Foundation Commission, 1988).

As we move toward the close of the twentieth century, experts on adolescence are trying to dispel the myth that adolescents are a sorry lot (Brooks-Gunn, 1992). That stereotype is usually based on a small group of highly visible adolescents. Daniel Offer and his colleagues (1988) showed that the vast majority of adolescents are competent human beings who are not experiencing deep emotional turmoil. They sampled the self-images of adolescents around the world—in the United States, Australia, Bangladesh, Hungary, Israel, Japan, Taiwan, Turkey, and Germany—and found that three out of four had a positive self-image. The adolescents were moving toward adulthood in generally healthy ways—happy most of the time, enjoying life, valuing work and school, having positive feelings about their family and friends, expressing confidence in their sexual selves, and believing they have the ability to cope with life's stresses—not exactly in the throes of storm and stress.

At the same time, adolescents have not experienced an improvement in health over the past 30 years, largely as a result of a new group of dangers called the "new morbidity" (Roghmann, 1981). These include such problems as accidents, suicide, homicide, substance abuse, sexual diseases (including AIDS), delinquency, and emotional difficulties.

Poverty exacerbates the problems of adolescence. In 1988, 16.3 percent of all adolescents were poor, with ethnic minorities vastly overrepresented in this figure: 38 percent of all African American teenagers and 32.2 percent of all Latinos, compared to 11.6 percent of all White teenagers, lived in poverty. Poverty increases the chance that an adolescent will fall prey to the physical, emotional, and social problems of the new morbidity.

Our discussion underscores an important point about adolescents: They do not make up a homogeneous group. The majority of adolescents negotiate the lengthy path to adult maturity successfully, but a large number of them do not. Ethnic, cultural, gender, socioeconomic, age, and lifestyle differences influence the actual life trajectory of every adolescent. Different portrayals of adolescence emerge. As we will see, some of the problems faced by today's adolescents involve adults' idealized images of what adolescents should be and society's ambivalent messages to adolescents.

In no order of things is adolescence the time of simple life,
Janet Erskine Stewart

Dimensions of Development

The complex relationships among physical, cognitive, socioemotional, and moral development that influence rates of health and emotional problems make it important for us to understand these aspects of adolescent development. Let's examine physical development first.

Physical Development

Imagine a toddler displaying all the features of puberty—a 3-year-old girl with fully developed breasts or a boy just slightly older with a deep male voice. We would see this by the year 2250 if the age of puberty were to continue to decrease at its present pace. Menarche (first menstruation) has declined from 14.2 years of age in 1900 to about 12.45 years of age today. Age of menarche has been declining an average of about 4 months a decade for the past century (see figure 10.1). We are unlikely, though, to see pubescent

From *Penguin Dreams and Stranger Things* by Berke Breathed. Copyright © 1985 by The Washington Post Company. By permission of Little, Brown and Company.

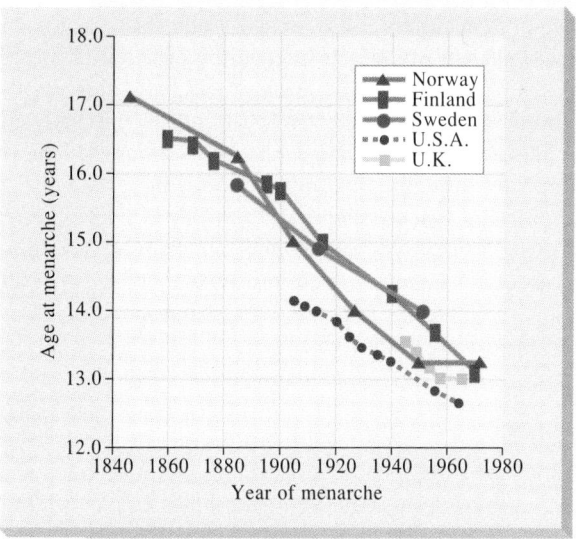

FIGURE 10.1

Median Ages at Menarche in Selected Northern European Countries and the United States from 1845 to 1969
Notice the steep decline in the age at which girls experienced menarche in five different countries. Recently the age at which girls experience menarche has been leveling off.

toddlers in the future, because what happened in the last century is special. That something special is the acquisition of a higher level of nutrition and health (Brooks-Gunn, 1991). A lower age of menarche is associated with higher standards of living (Petersen, 1979).

Menarche is one event that characterizes puberty, but there are others as well. **Puberty** *is a period of rapid skeletal and sexual maturation that occurs mainly in early adolescence.* However, it is not a single, sudden event. We know when a young person is going through puberty, but pinpointing its beginning and its end is difficult. Menarche occurs rather late in puberty. For boys, the first whisker or first change of voice could mark its appearance, but both may go unnoticed.

Hormonal changes characterize pubertal development (Dorn & Lucas, 1995). Remember from chapter 3 that hormones are powerful chemical substances excreted by the endocrine glands and carried through the body in the bloodstream. The concentrations of certain hormones increase dramatically during puberty. **Testosterone** *is a hormone associated with the development of genitals, an increase in height, and a change in voice in boys.* **Estradiol** *is a hormone associated with breast, uterine, and skeletal development in girls.* In one study, testosterone levels only doubled in the girls but increased eighteenfold in the boys during puberty; similarly, estradiol doubled in the boys but increased eightfold in the girls (Nottelmann & others, 1987). These hormonal and bodily changes occur, on the average, about 2 years earlier in girls (10½ years) than in boys (12½ years) (see figure 10.2).

Some children enter puberty early, others late, and those who are "off schedule" one way or the other often think of themselves as "different." Some years ago, in the California Longitudinal Study, the early-maturing boys perceived themselves more positively and had more successful peer relations than did their late-maturing counterparts (Jones, 1965). The findings for the early-maturing girls were similar but not as strong. When the late-maturing boys were studied in their thirties, however, they had developed a stronger sense of identity than the early-maturing boys had (Peskin, 1967).

More-recent research conducted in the United States confirms, though, that at least during adolescence it is advantageous to be an early-maturing rather than a late-maturing boy (Simmons & Blyth, 1987). More-recent findings for girls suggest that early maturation is a mixed blessing: Early-maturing girls experience more problems in school but also more independence and popularity with boys. Grade level also makes a difference. In the sixth grade, the early-maturing girls were more satisfied with their figures than the late-maturing girls were, but by the tenth grade the late-maturing girls were more satisfied. The explanation is

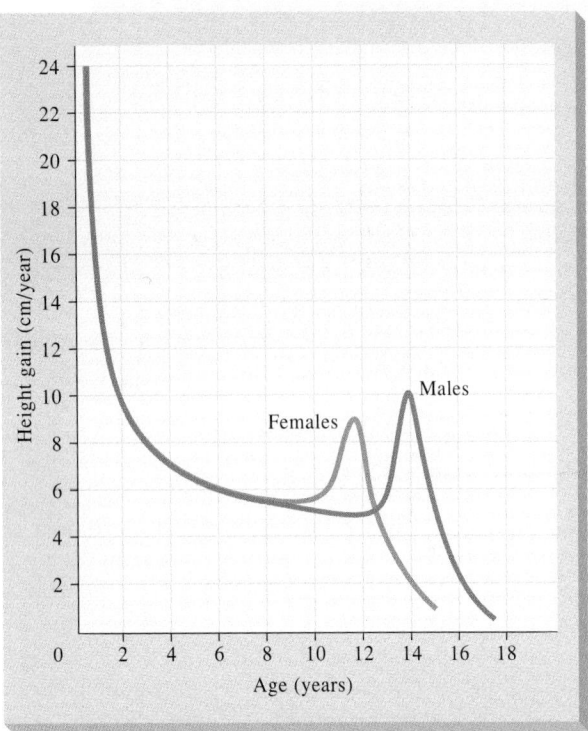

FIGURE 10.2

Pubertal Growth Spurt
On the average, the growth spurt that characterizes pubertal change occurs 2 years earlier for girls (age 10½) than for boys (age 12½).

that, by late adolescence, early-maturing girls tend to be shorter and stockier, late-maturing girls taller and thinner; late-maturing girls in late adolescence have bodies that more closely resemble today's media idea of feminine beauty—tall and thin.

Some researchers now question whether the effects of puberty are as strong as once believed (Lerner, Petersen, & Brooks-Gunn, 1991). Puberty affects some adolescents

more strongly than others, and some behaviors more strongly than others. Body image, interest in dating, and sexual behavior are clearly affected by pubertal change. If we were to look at overall development and adjustment in the human life cycle, pubertal variations (such as early and late maturation) would appear to be less dramatic than is commonly thought. In thinking about puberty's effects, keep in mind that an adolescent's world involves cognitive and social changes, as well as physical changes. As with all periods of development, these processes work in concert to produce who we are in adolescence. Now we will turn our attention to the cognitive changes that occur in adolescence.

Cognitive Development

Aristotle remarked that adolescents think they know everything and are quite sure about it. Their overconfidence might be a natural outgrowth of their expanded cognitive capabilities. **Formal operational thought** *is Piaget's name for the fourth stage of cognitive development, which appears between 11 and 15 years of age. Formal operational thought is abstract, idealistic, and logical.* Unlike an elementary school child, an adolescent is no longer limited to concrete experience as the anchor of thought. Adolescents can conceive make-believe situations, hypothetical possibilities, or purely abstract propositions.

At the same time that adolescents think more abstractly, they also think more logically. Adolescents begin to think more as a scientist thinks, devising plans to solve problems and systematically testing solutions. This type of problem solving has an imposing name. **Hypothetical-deductive reasoning** *is Piaget's name for adolescents' cognitive ability to develop hypotheses, or best guesses, about ways to solve problems, such as an algebraic equation. They then systematically deduce, or conclude, which is the best path to follow to solve the equation.* By contrast, children are more likely to solve problems in a trial-and-error fashion.

In adolescence, thought also becomes more idealistic. Adolescents often compare themselves and others to ideal standards. They think about what an ideal world would be like, wondering if they couldn't carve out a better world than the one the adult generation has handed to them.

Adolescent thought, especially in early adolescence, is also egocentric. **Adolescent egocentrism** *involves the belief that others are as preoccupied with the adolescent as she herself is, the belief that one is unique, and the belief that one is indestructible* (Elkind, 1978). Attention-getting behavior, so common in adolescence, reflects egocentrism and the desire to be on stage, noticed, and visible. Imagine an eighth-grade boy who feels as if all eyes are riveted on his tiny facial blemish. Imagine also the sense of uniqueness felt by the following adolescent girl: "My mother has no idea about how much pain I'm going through. She has never been hurt like I have. Why did Bob break up with me?" Also imagine

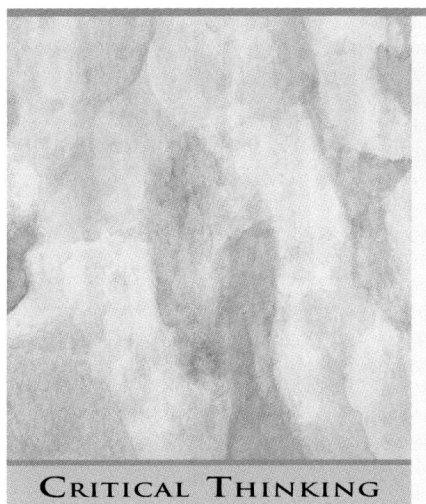

CRITICAL THINKING

*The Advantage of
Blooming Late*

Harvey Peskin's (1967) study on late-versus early-maturing boys established that early maturity was negatively related to strength of identity measured around age 30. Can you propose some explanations that might account for the advantage of having been a late-bloomer in adolescence? How many hypotheses or alternative explanations can you generate for this finding?

Late-maturing boys may have had more time to explore a wide variety of options. They may have focused on career development and achievement that would serve them better in life than their early-maturing counterparts' emphasis on physical status.

These differences have important implications for surviving the sometimes turbulent social aspects of high school. Late bloomers often report feeling harassed by those who are popular and physically well developed in high school. High school reunions later in life can sometimes feel like sweet revenge for the successful late bloomer.

Can you think of other explanations? The speculations that you develop demonstrate your *pursuit of alternative explanations to understand behavior comprehensively.*

the sense of indestructibility of two adolescent males drag racing down a city street. This sense of indestructibility may lead to drug use and suicide attempts. Figure 10.3 summarizes the main features of formal operational thought.

In youth, we clothe ourselves with rainbows, and go brave as the zodiac.
Ralph Waldo Emerson, *The Conduct of Life,* 1860

Some researchers have begun to challenge Piaget's ideas on formal operational thought (Overton & Byrnes, 1991). Much more individual variation exists in formal operational thought than Piaget envisioned. For example, only about one in three young adolescents is a formal operational thinker. As many as half of all adults never reach the stage of formal operational thinking (Muuss, 1988).

Many adults in other cultures don't either. Consider the following conversation between a researcher and an illiterate Kpelle farmer in the West African country of Liberia (Scribner, 1977):

Researcher: All Kpelle men are rice farmers. Mr. Smith is not a rice farmer. Is he a Kpelle man?

Kpelle farmer: I don't know the man. I have not laid eyes on the man myself.

Formal operational thinkers recognize that the identity of Mr. Smith can be solved with the clues provided. Since all Kpelle men farm rice and Mr. Smith does not, then he is not a Kpelle farmer. The more concrete response of the Kpelle farmer implies that the puzzle couldn't be solved without knowing the man. In contrast to the Kpelle farmer, members of the Kpelle culture who had experienced formal schooling were able to deal with the abstract example and answered the researcher using formal operational thinking.

It is difficult to assess formal operational thinking in nonliterate adults because the usual tests for this kind of thinking are all from the math and science curriculum of Western schools. These tests are inappropriate for use in other cultures and perhaps for many adults in the United States.

Adults in other cultures do demonstrate formal thinking when queried about situations with which they are more familiar (Jahoda, 1980). As with concrete operational thought, cultural experiences influence whether individuals reach a Piagetian stage of thought. Education in the logic of science and mathematics is an important cultural experience that promotes the development of formal operational thinking.

So far we have discussed a number of physical and cognitive changes in adolescence. Next, we will study the equally impressive social changes in adolescence.

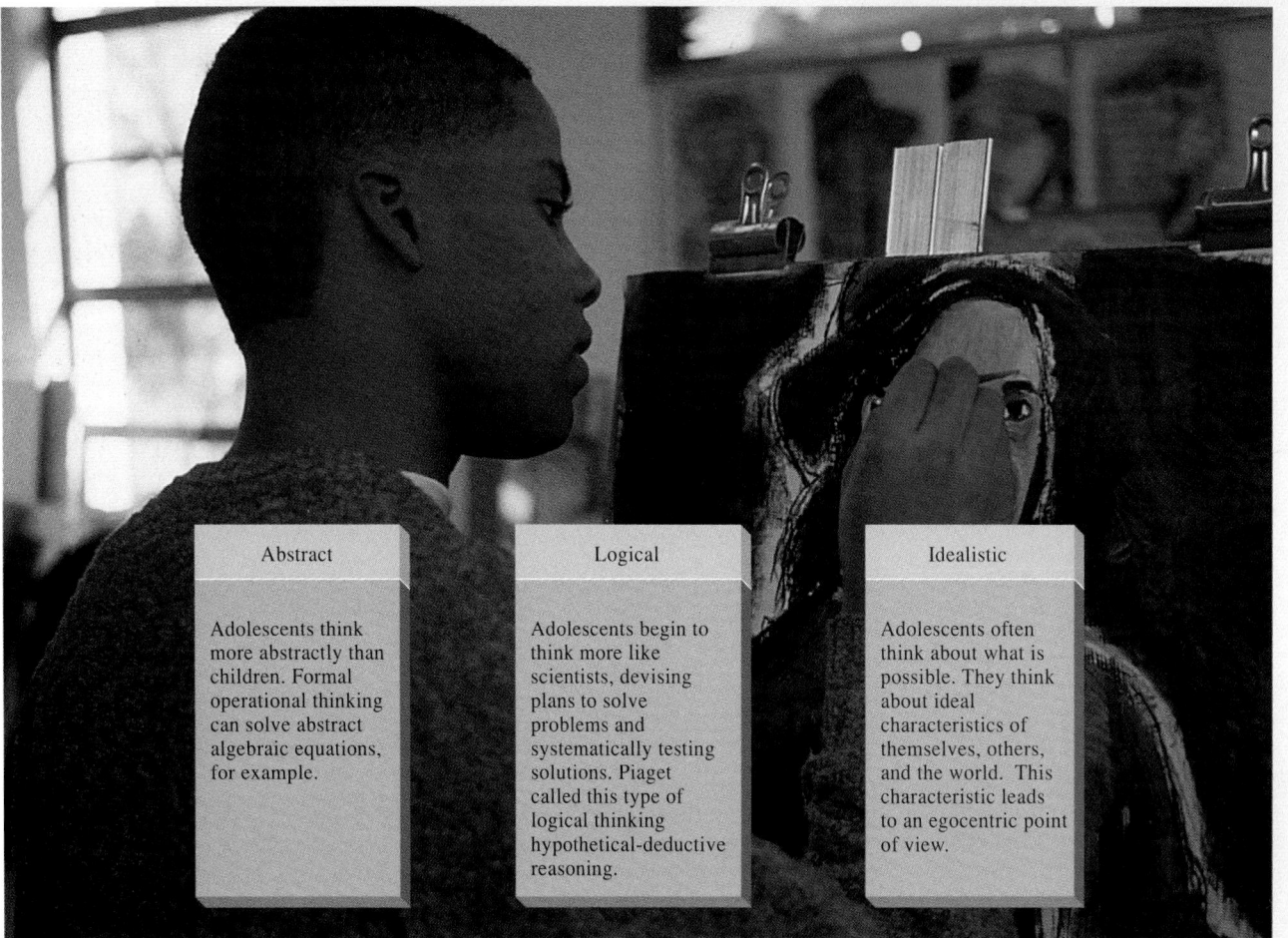

Abstract

Adolescents think more abstractly than children. Formal operational thinking can solve abstract algebraic equations, for example.

Logical

Adolescents begin to think more like scientists, devising plans to solve problems and systematically testing solutions. Piaget called this type of logical thinking hypothetical-deductive reasoning.

Idealistic

Adolescents often think about what is possible. They think about ideal characteristics of themselves, others, and the world. This characteristic leads to an egocentric point of view.

FIGURE 10.3

Characteristics of Formal Operational Thought
Adolescents begin to think more as scientists think, devising plans to solve problems and systematically testing solutions. Piaget gave this type of thinking the imposing name of hypothetical-deductive reasoning.

REVIEW

The Nature of Adolescence, Physical Development, and Cognitive Development

G. Stanley Hall is the father of the scientific study of adolescence. In the early 1900s, he proposed the storm-and-stress view. Adolescence is a transition between childhood and adulthood that involves biological, cognitive, and social development. In most cultures, adolescence begins at approximately 10 to 13 years of age and ends at approximately 18 to 21 years of age. Adolescence is more appropriately viewed as a time of decision making and commitment rather than a time of rebellion, crisis, and disturbance. Different portrayals of adolescence emerge.

Puberty is a rapid change in maturation that occurs during early adolescence. Its onset has begun earlier in recent years. Hormonal changes are prominent. Puberty occurs roughly 2 years earlier for girls than boys, although its normal range is large. Early maturation generally favors boys and often has mixed effects for girls. Some experts believe that puberty's effects are overstated.

Piaget stated that formal operational thought begins between 11 and 15 years of age. Formal operational thought is abstract and idealistic, but includes planning and logical analysis. Some of Piaget's ideas on formal operational thought are being challenged. Egocentrism also characterizes adolescent thought.

Socioemotional Development

Mark Twain, reflecting on his youth, commented, "When I was a boy of 14 my father was so ignorant I could hardly stand to have the man around. But when I got to be 21, I was astonished how much he learnt in seven years." Let's explore the world of parent-adolescent relationships that Twain spoke about.

Parent-Adolescent Relationships   In the United States there are many myths about parent-adolescent relationships, including these: (1) adolescents detach themselves from parents and move into an isolated world of peers and (2) throughout adolescence, parent-adolescent relationships are intense, filled with conflict, and highly stressful.

Adolescents do not simply move away from parental influence into a decision-making world all their own. As adolescents move toward becoming more autonomous, it is healthy for them to continue to be attached to their parents (Holmbeck, Paikoff, & Brooks-Gunn, 1995; Kobak & Frenz-Gilles, 1993). Just as they did in infancy and childhood, parents continue to provide an important support system that helps an adolescent explore a wider, more complex social world full of uncertainties, challenges, and stresses (Hill & Holmbeck, 1986). Although adolescents show a strong desire to spend more time with their peers, they do not necessarily isolate themselves (Ladd & LeSieur, 1995). In one investigation, adolescents who were securely attached to their parents were also securely attached to their peers; those who were insecurely attached to their parents were also insecurely attached to their peers (Armsden & Greenberg, 1984). Of course, there are times when adolescents reject this closeness, connection, and attachment as they pursue a more autonomous life. For the most part, however, an adolescent's worlds of parents and peers are coordinated and connected, not uncoordinated and disconnected. For example, parents' choices of neighborhoods, churches, schools, and their own friends influence the pool from which their adolescents select possible friends (Cooper & Ayers-Lopez, 1985).

Adolescence is a period of development when individuals push for autonomy, but the development of mature autonomy is a lengthy process, taking place over 10 to 15 years. As adolescents pursue a more autonomous life, many parents perceive them as changing from compliant children to noncompliant adolescents. Parents tend to adopt one of two strategies to handle the noncompliance: They either clamp down and put more pressure on the adolescents to conform to parental standards, or they become more permissive and let the adolescents do as they please. Neither is a wise overall strategy; rather, a more flexible, adaptive approach is called for. At the onset of adolescence, the average boy or girl does not have the knowledge to make appropriate decisions in all areas of life. As adolescents push for autonomy, a wise parent relinquishes control in areas where adolescents can make mature decisions. A wise parent also calmly communicates with an adolescent and tries to help the adolescent make reasonable decisions in areas where he or she shows less mature behavior (Santrock, 1996).

Oh, to be only half as wonderful as my child thought I was when he was small, and only half as stupid as my teenager now thinks I am.

Rebecca Richards

Conflict with parents does increase in adolescence, but it does not usually reach the tumultuous proportions described by G. Stanley Hall, and it is not uniformly intense throughout adolescence (Steinberg, 1993). Rather, much of the conflict involves the everyday events of family life, such as keeping a bedroom clean, dressing neatly, getting home by a certain hour, not talking on the phone so long, and so on. Such conflicts with parents are more common in early adolescence, especially during the apex of pubertal change, than in late adolescence, and the conflicts usually do not involve major dilemmas, such as drugs and delinquency (Montemayor & Flannery, 1991). The everyday negotiations and conflicts that characterize parent-adolescent relationships can even serve a positive developmental function (Cooper & Grotevant, 1989). These minor disputes and negotiations facilitate an adolescent's transition from being dependent on parents to being more autonomous. For example, in one investigation, the adolescents who disagreed with their parents also explored identity issues more actively than did the adolescents who consistently agreed with their parents (Cooper & others, 1982).

In sum, the old model of parent-adolescent relationships suggested that as adolescents mature, they detach themselves from parents and move into a world of autonomy apart from parents through intense and stressful conflicts throughout adolescence. The new model emphasizes that parents serve as important attachment figures and support systems as adolescents explore a wider, more complex social world; parent-adolescent conflict is usually moderate rather than severe (see figure 10.4).

The developmental trajectories of both parents and adolescents are changing (Parke, 1988). In the past 2 decades, the timing of parenthood has undergone some dramatic shifts. Parenthood is taking place earlier for some, later for others. On the one hand, there has been a substantial increase in the number of adolescent pregnancies. On the other hand, the number of women who postpone childbearing until their thirties or forties has simultaneously increased. When childbearing is delayed, education usually has been completed and career development is well established. Researchers have found that older fathers are warmer and communicate better with their children. However, they are less likely to place demands on them and enforce rules (MacDonald, 1987).

Rites of Passage   Aunts, uncles, and cousins from all over come to celebrate Josh Maisel's bar mitzvah. That morning Josh entered the temple as a child. According to

---

CRITICAL THINKING

Predicting Parent-Adolescent Trends

The parents of adolescents will be increasingly older in the future because of delays in marriage and childbearing. How do you think this will influence the nature of parent-adolescent relationships? Are there good reasons to believe that these relationships will be more stormy and stressful? Why might such relationships be even more harmonious than they are today? Which scenario do you think will be true for the majority of older parents and their adolescent children? By answering these questions, you will get practice in *creating psychological arguments based on evidence.*

people unsure whether or not they have reached adult status. Perhaps high school graduation ceremonies come closest to being a rite of passage for adolescents in today's industrialized world (Fasick, 1988). Even so, many high school graduates continue to live with their parents, are economically dependent on them, and are undecided about their career and lifestyle.

Peers Imagine that you are back in junior or senior high school: friends, cliques, parties, and clubs probably come to mind. During adolescence, especially early adolescence, we conform more than we did in childhood. Conformity to peers, especially to their antisocial standards, often peaks around the eighth or ninth grade, a time when teenagers might join a peer in stealing hubcaps from a car, drawing graffiti on a wall, or harassing a teacher (Berndt & Perry, 1990).

his faith, he emerged as a man. Josh's bar mitzvah represents one of the few American **rites of passage**—*ceremonies or rituals that mark an individual's transition from one status to another.*

In some cultures, rites of passage mark a clear distinction between childhood and adulthood. Their absence in many industrialized cultures tends to leave many young

Remember that as a teenager you are at the last stage in your life when you will be happy to hear that the phone is for you.

Fran Lebowitz

Old model of parent-adolescent relationships

- Autonomy, detachment from parents; parent and peer worlds isolated

- Intense conflict throughout adolescence; stormy and stressful on a daily basis

New model of parent-adolescent relationships

- Autonomy, but attachment to parents; adolescent-parent and adolescent-peer worlds interconnected

- Moderate conflict promotes growth; conflict greater in early adolescence

FIGURE 10.4

Old and New Models of Parent-Adolescent Relationships

These Congolese Kota boys painted their faces as part of a rite of passage to adulthood. *What kinds of rites of passage do American adolescents have?*

During adolescence, individuals enter what Erikson calls a "psychological moratorium"—a gap between the security of childhood and the autonomy of adulthood. In their search for identity, adolescents experiment with various roles. Those who successfully explore a number of alternatives emerge with a new sense of self that is both refreshing and acceptable; those who do not successfully resolve the identity crisis are troubled, suffering what Erikson calls identity confusion. This confusion takes one of two courses: Individuals either withdraw, isolating themselves from peers and family, or lose themselves in the crowd. Adolescents want to decide freely for themselves such matters as what careers they will pursue, whether they will go to college, and whether they will marry. In other words, they want to free themselves from the shackles of their parents and other adults and make their own choices. At the same time, many adolescents have a deep fear of making the wrong decision and of failing. However, as adolescents pursue their identity and their thoughts become more abstract and logical, they reason in more sophisticated ways. They are better able to judge what is morally right and wrong and become capable decision makers (Garrod & others, 1995; Suls, 1989).

Adolescent peer relations take place in diverse settings—at school, in the neighborhood, and in the community. Ethnic minority adolescents often have two sets of peer relationships, one at school, the other in the community. Community peers are more likely to be from their own ethnic group in their immediate neighborhood. Sometimes, they go to the same church and participate in activities together, such as Black History Week, Chinese New Year, or the Cinco de Mayo Festival. As a result, researchers should focus their questions on relationships both at school and in the community when they ask about adolescents' peers and friends. Ethnic minority adolescents who are social isolates at school may be very popular in their more segregated ethnic community (Gibbs & Huang, 1989).

Identity Development **Identity versus identity confusion** *is the fifth of Erik Erikson's (1968) stages of human development, occurring primarily during the adolescent years. The development of identity involves finding out who we are, what we are all about, and where we are headed in life.* Seeking an identity is about trying on one face after another, looking for one's own.

"Who are you?" Said the caterpillar. Alice replied rather shyly, "I—I hardly know, sir, just at present—at least I know who I was when I got up this morning, but I must have changed several times since then."

Lewis Carroll, *Alice in Wonderland*, 1865

Erikson is especially sensitive to the role of culture in identity development. He points out that, throughout the world, ethnic minority groups have struggled to maintain their cultural identities while blending into the dominant culture (Erikson, 1968). Erikson says that this struggle for an inclusive identity, or identity within the larger culture, has been the driving force in the founding of churches, empires, and revolutions throughout history.

For ethnic minority individuals, adolescence is often a special juncture in their development (Burton, Allison, & Obeidallah, 1995; McHale, 1995; Phinney & Rosenthal, 1992; Spencer & Dornbusch, 1990). Although children are aware of some ethnic and cultural differences, most ethnic

Margaret Beale Spencer, shown here talking with adolescents, believes that adolescence is often a critical juncture in the identity development of ethnic minority individuals. Most ethnic minority individuals consciously confront their ethnicity for the first time in adolescence.

minority individuals consciously confront their ethnicity for the first time in adolescence. Compared with children, adolescents are more able to interpret ethnic and cultural information, to reflect on the past, and to speculate about the future (Harter, 1990). As they cognitively mature, ethnic minority adolescents become acutely aware of the evaluations of their ethnic group by the majority White culture (Comer, 1988; Ogbu, 1989). As one researcher commented, the young African American child may learn that Black is beautiful, but conclude as an adolescent that White is powerful (Semaj, 1985).

Ethnic minority youths' awareness of negative appraisals, conflicting values, and restricted occupational opportunities can influence life choices and plans for the future (Spencer & Dornbusch, 1990). As one ethnic minority youth stated, "The future seems shut off, closed. Why dream? You can't reach your dreams. Why set goals? At least if you don't set any goals, you don't fail."

For many ethnic minority youth, a lack of successful ethnic minority role models with whom to identify is a special concern (Blash & Unger, 1992). The problem is especially acute for inner-city ethnic minority youth. Because of the lack of adult ethnic minority role models, some ethnic minority youth may conform to middle-class White values and identify with successful White role models. However, for many adolescents, their ethnicity and skin color limit their acceptance by the White culture. Thus, many ethnic minority adolescents have the difficult task of negotiating two value systems—that of their own ethnic group and that of the White society. Some adolescents reject the mainstream, foregoing the rewards that might be accessible through that path; others adopt the values and standards of the majority White culture; and yet others take the difficult path of biculturalism (Hiraga & others, 1993).

In one investigation, ethnic identity exploration was higher among ethnic minority than among White college students (Phinney & Alipura, 1990). In this same investigation, ethnic minority college students who had thought about and resolved issues involving their ethnicity had higher self-esteem than did their ethnic minority counterparts who had not. Another investigation studied the ethnic identity development of Asian American, African American, Latino, and White American tenth-grade students in Los Angeles (Phinney, 1989). Adolescents from each of the three ethnic minority groups faced a similar need to deal with their ethnic-group identification in a predominately White American culture. In some instances, the adolescents from the three ethnic minority groups perceived different issues to be important in their resolution of ethnic identity. Asian American adolescents were concerned about pressures to achieve academically and quotas that make it difficult to get into good colleges. Many African American adolescent females discussed their realization that White American standards of beauty (especially hair and skin color) did not apply to them; African American adolescent males were concerned with possible job discrimination and the need to distinguish themselves from a negative societal image of African American male adolescents. For Latino adolescents, prejudice was a recurrent theme, as was the conflict in values between their Latino cultural heritage and the majority culture. To read further about identity development in ethnic minority youth, turn to Sociocultural Worlds 10.1.

Finding out who you are, what you are all about, and where you are going—the search for identity—is an important developmental task for every human being. As we will see next, another important developmental task involves developing a system of moral standards. The emergence of changes in moral reasoning parallels learning complex social roles and changes in abstract problem solving.

Moral Development

In Europe a woman was near death from a rare form of cancer. There was one drug that the doctors thought might save her: a form of radium that a druggist in the same town had recently discovered. The drug was expensive to make, but the druggist was charging ten times what the drug cost him to make it. He paid $200 for the radium and charged $2,000 for a small dose of the drug. The sick woman's husband, Heinz, went to everyone he knew to borrow the money, but he could get together only $1,000. He told the druggist that his wife was dying and asked him to sell it cheaper or let him pay later. However, the druggist said, "No. I discovered the drug, and I am going to make money from it." Desperate, Heinz broke into the man's store to steal the drug for his wife (Kohlberg, 1969, p. 379).

This story is one of eleven devised by Lawrence Kohlberg (1976, 1986) to investigate the nature of moral thought. After reading the story, interviewees answer a series of questions about the moral dilemma. Should Heinz have done that? Was it right or wrong? Why? Is it a husband's duty to steal the drug for his wife if he can get it in

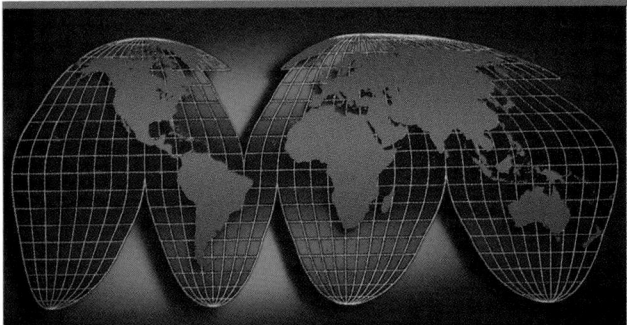

The Development of Identity in Native American Adolescents

Substandard living conditions, poverty, and chronic unemployment place many Native American youths at risk for school failure and poor health, which can contribute to problems in developing a positive identity (LaFromboise & Low, 1989). A special concern is the negative image of Native Americans that has been perpetuated for centuries in the majority White American culture. To consider further the development of identity in Native American youth, we will examine the experiences of a 12-year-old Hopi Indian boy.

The Hopi Indians are a quiet, thoughtful people who go to great lengths not to offend anyone. In a pueblo north of Albuquerque, a 12-year-old boy speaks: "I've been living in Albuquerque for a year. The Anglos I've met, they're different. I don't know why. In school, I drew a picture of my father's horse. One of the other kids wouldn't believe that it was ours. He said, 'You don't really own that horse.' I said, 'It's a horse my father rides, and I feed it every morning.' He said, 'How come?' I said, 'My uncle and my father are good riders, and I'm pretty good.' He said, 'I can ride a horse better than you, and I'd rather be a pilot.' I told him I never thought of being a pilot."

The Hopi boy continues, "Anglo kids, they won't let you get away with anything. Tell them something, and fast as lightning and loud as thunder, they'll say, 'I'm better than you, so there!' My father says it's always been like that."

Psychiatrist Robert Coles (1986) concluded that the Indian adolescent is not really angry or envious of the White adolescent. Maybe he is in awe of his future power; maybe he fears it, and the White adolescent can't keep from wondering somehow that he has missed out on something and may end up "losing."

The following poetry of another American Indian vividly captures some important ingredients of a Hopi adolescent's interest in a peaceful identity:

River flow.	A small pebble
The sea sings.	On a giant shore;
Oceans roar.	Who am I
Tides rise.	To ask who I am?
Who am I?	Isn't it enough to be?

The Native American adolescent's quest for identity involves a cultural meshing of tribal customs and the technological, educational demands of modern society.

no other way? Would a good husband do it? Did the druggist have the right to charge that much when there was no law setting a limit on the price? Why?

Based on the answers that individuals have given to questions about this and other moral dilemmas, Kohlberg believed that three levels of moral development exist, each of which is characterized by two stages. A key concept in understanding moral development, especially Kohlberg's theory, is **internalization**, *the developmental change from behavior that is externally controlled to behavior that is controlled by internal, self-generated standards and principles.*

1. The **preconventional level** *is Kohlberg's lowest level of moral thinking, in which an individual shows no internalization of moral values—moral thinking is based on punishments (stage 1) or rewards (stage 2) that come from the external world.* In regard to the

story about Heinz and the druggist, at stage 1 an individual might say that Heinz should not steal the drug because it is a big crime; at stage 2, an individual might say he shouldn't steal the drug because the druggist needs to make a profit.

2. The **conventional level** *is Kohlberg's second level of moral thinking, in which an individual has an intermediate level of internalization. The individual abides by certain standards (internal), but they are the standards of others (external), such as the standards of parents (stage 3) or the laws of society (stage 4).* At stage 3, an individual might say that Heinz should steal the drug for his wife because that is what a good husband would do; at stage 4, an individual might say that it is natural to want to save his wife but that it is always wrong to steal.

3. The **postconventional level** *is Kohlberg's highest level of moral thinking; moral development is completely internalized and not based on others' standards. An individual recognizes alternative moral courses, explores the options, and then develops a personal moral code. The code is among the principles generally accepted by the community (stage 5) or it is more individualized (stage 6).* At stage 5, an individual might say that the law was not set up for these circumstances so Heinz can steal the drug; it is not really right, but he is justified in doing it. At stage 6, the individual is faced with the decision of whether to consider the other people who need the drug just as badly as Heinz's wife. Heinz should consider the value of all lives involved.

Kohlberg believed that these levels and stages occur in a sequence and are age-related. Some evidence of Kohlberg's theory has been found, although few people reach stages 5 and 6 (Colby & others, 1983). Kohlberg stated that moral development occurs through maturation of thought, the mutual give-and-take of peer relations, and opportunities for role taking. Parent-child relationships contribute very little to moral thought, in Kohlberg's view, because they are too dominated by parents' moral values, with little opportunity for the youths to experiment with alternative moral choices.

Kohlberg's provocative view continues to generate considerable research on moral development. However, critics challenge his theory (Killen & Hart, 1995). One criticism of Kohlberg's view is that moral reasons are often a shelter for immoral behavior. When bank embezzlers and presidents are asked about their moral reasoning, they may be at an advanced level, even at Kohlberg's postconventional level, but when their behavior is examined it may be filled with cheating, lying, and stealing. The cheaters, liars, and thieves may know what is right and what is wrong but still do what is wrong.

A second major criticism of Kohlberg's view is that it does not adequately reflect relationships and concerns for others. The **justice perspective** *is a theory of moral development that focuses on the rights of the individual; individuals independently make moral decisions. Kohlberg's theory is a justice perspective.* By contrast, the **care perspective**

Carol Gilligan (*center*) is shown with some of the students she has interviewed about the importance of relationships in a female's development. According to Gilligan, the sense of relationships and connectedness is at the heart of female development.

is Carol Gilligan's theory of moral development, which sees people in terms of their connectedness with others and focuses on interpersonal communication, relationships with others, and concern for others. According to Gilligan (1982), Kohlberg greatly underplayed the care perspective in moral development. She believes that this may have happened because he was a male, most of his research was with males rather than females, and he used male responses as a model for his theory.

Gilligan conducted extensive interviews with girls from 6 to 18 years of age (Gilligan, 1990, 1992). She and her colleagues found that girls consistently reveal reported, detailed knowledge about human relationships, based on listening and watching what happens between people. According to Gilligan, girls have the ability to pick up different rhythms in relationships and are often able to follow the pathways of feelings.

Gilligan also believes that girls reach a critical juncture in their development when they reach adolescence. Gilligan says that at the beginning of adolescence, at about 11 to 12 years of age, girls become aware that their intense interest in intimacy is not prized by the male-dominated culture, even though society values females as caring and altruistic. The dilemma, says Gilligan, is that girls are presented with a choice that makes them appear either selfish (if they become independent and self-sufficient) or selfless (if they remain responsive to others). Gilligan states that, as young adolescent girls experience this dilemma, they increasingly "silence" their own distinctive voices. They become less confident and more tentative in offering their opinions, and this often persists into adulthood. Some researchers believe that this self-doubt and ambivalence too often translates into depression and eating disorders among adolescent girls.

Some critics argue that Gilligan and her colleagues overemphasize differences between genders. One of those critics is developmentalist Eleanor Maccoby, who says that Gilligan exaggerates the differences in intimacy and connectedness between males and females. Other critics fault Gilligan's research strategy, which rarely involves a comparison group of boys and rarely includes statistical analysis. Instead, Gilligan conducts extensive interviews with girls and then provides excerpts from the girls' narratives to buttress her ideas. Other critics fear that Gilligan's findings reinforce stereotypes—females as nurturing and sacrificing, for example—that might undermine females' struggle for equality. These critics say that Gilligan's different voice should perhaps be called "the voice of the victim."

In reply, revisionists, such as Gilligan, say that their work provides a way to liberate females and transform a society that has far too long discriminated against females. If females' approach to life is acknowledged as authentic, they will no longer have to act like males. The revisionists state that females' sensitivity in relationships is a special gift in our culture. Influenced by Gilligan's and other feminists' thinking, some schools are beginning to incorporate the feminine voice into their curriculum. For example, at the Emma Willard School in Troy, New York, the entire curriculum has been revamped to emphasize cooperation rather than competition and to encourage girls to analyze and express ideas from their own perspectives rather than responding in stereotyped or conformist ways.

A third criticism of Kohlberg's view is that it is culturally biased (Bronstein & Paludi, 1988; Jensen, 1995; Miller, 1995). Kohlberg's scoring system was strongly influenced by the individualistic biases of his own culture. Therefore his stage theory might fit his own cultural context better than it fits other cultures. One review of research on moral development in 27 countries found that moral reasoning appears to be more culture-specific than Kohlberg envisioned and that Kohlberg's scoring system does not recognize higher-level moral reasoning in certain cultural groups (Snarey, 1987). Kohlberg did not recognize such values as communal equity and collective happiness in Israel, the unity and sacredness of all life forms in India, or the relation of an individual to the community in New Guinea as examples of higher-level moral reasoning. Kohlberg's system would not score these values at the highest level of moral reasoning because they do not emphasize an individual's rights and abstract principles of justice. In summary, moral reasoning is shaped more by the values and beliefs of a culture than Kohlberg acknowledged.

The Challenges of Adolescence

In many instances, adolescents have more than one problem. Researchers are increasingly finding that problem behaviors in adolescence are interrelated. For example, heavy substance abuse is related to early sexual activity, lower grades, dropping out of school, and delinquency. Early initiation of sexual activity is associated with the use of cigarettes and alcohol, use of marijuana and other illicit drugs, lower grades, dropping out of school and delinquency. Delinquency is related to early sexual activity, early pregnancy, substance abuse, and dropping out of school. As many as 10 percent of the adolescent population in the United States have serious multiple-problem behaviors (such as dropping out of school or being behind in their grade level, using heavy drugs, regularly using cigarettes and marijuana, and being sexually active but not using contraception). Many, but not all, of these very high-risk youth "do it all." Another 15 percent of adolescents participate in many of these same behaviors but with slightly lower frequency and less deleterious consequences. These high-risk youth often engage in two- or three-problem behaviors (Dryfoos, 1992). Let's explore several of these challenges in greater detail.

High School Dropouts

Dropouts are a serious educational and societal problem. By leaving high school before graduating, many dropouts take with them educational delinquencies that severely curtail their economic and social well-being throughout their adult lives. We will study the scope of the problem, the causes of dropping out, and ways to reduce dropout rates.

Although dropping out of high school often has negative consequences for young people, the picture is not entirely bleak (William T. Grant Foundation Commission, 1988). Over the past 40 years, the number of adolescents who have not finished high school has decreased considerably. In 1940 more than 60 percent of all 25- to 29-year-olds had not completed high school. By 1986 this proportion had dropped to less than 14 percent. From 1973 to 1983, the annual dropout rate nationwide fell by almost 20 percent, from 6.3 to 5.2 percent.

Despite the decline in overall high-school dropout rates, the higher dropout rate of minority group and low-income students, especially in large cities, remains a major concern. Although the dropout rates of most minority grade students have been declining, they remain substantially above those of White students. Latinos made up a disproportionate percentage of high school dropouts in 1986. More than one-third of Latino students, about 17 percent of African American students, and 13.5 percent of White students had dropped out (William T. Grant Foundation, 1989). Dropout rates are staggeringly high for Native Americans: Fewer than 10 percent graduate from high school. In some inner-city areas, the dropout rate for ethnic minority students is especially high, reaching more than 50 percent in Chicago, for example (Hahn, 1987).

TABLE 10.1

A Comparison of Adolescent Pregnancy and Birth Rates per 1,000 Women, Ages 15 to 19

Country	Pregnancies	Births
Netherlands	15.0	7.7
Sweden	33.2	11.7
Denmark	34.0	12.0
Finland	37.4	15.7
Canada	45.4	24.8
Norway	45.8	19.6
New Zealand	52.8	32.4
England and Wales	53.4	27.5
Czechoslovakia	79.3	53.7
Hungary	93.3	54.2
United States	109.9	51.7

Source: Alan Guttmacher Institute, 1991.

Students drop out of school for many reasons (Evans & others, 1995). In one study, almost 50 percent of the dropouts cited school-related reasons for leaving school, such as simply not liking school or being expelled or suspended (Rumberger, 1983). Twenty percent of the dropouts (but 40 percent of the Latino students) cited economic reasons for leaving school. One-third of the female students dropped out for personal reasons, such as pregnancy or marriage.

To help reduce the dropout rate, community institutions, especially schools, need to break down the barriers between work and school. Many young people leave school long before reaching the level of a professional career, often left to their own devices to search for work. They need more assistance than they are now receiving. The following are among the approaches worth considering (William T. Grant Foundation Commission, 1988):

- Monitored work experiences, through cooperative education, apprenticeships, internships, preemployment training, and youth-operated enterprises
- Community and neighborhood services, including voluntary service and youth-guided services
- Redirected vocational education, the principal thrust of which should not be preparation for specific jobs but acquisition of basic skills needed for a wide range of jobs
- Guarantees of continuing education, employment, or training, especially in conjunction with mentor programs
- Career information and counseling to expose young people to job opportunities and career options as well as to successful role models
- School volunteer programs, not only for tutoring but to provide access to adult friends and mentors

Adolescent Pregnancy

In the United States, another rite of passage, the initiation of sexual intercourse, occurs earlier each decade (Kilpatrick, 1992). Approximately 5 million adolescent females and 7 million adolescent males are sexually active. As a result of early sexuality, the rate of adolescent pregnancy has soared. For example, 14-year-old girls become pregnant at the rate of more than 5 per 1,000, and the rate for young women between the ages of 15 and 17 jumped to 62 per 1,000. What's more, one of every eight births to young women under the age of 18 is not a first birth.

The problem of adolescent pregnancy in the United States becomes even more dramatic when compared with teen pregnancy rates in other industrialized countries (see table 10.1). Among mothers aged 15 to 19, the United States has the highest pregnancy rate; for every 1,000 adolescent women, there are nearly 110 pregnancies and over 50 births.

The long-range consequences of teenage births are bleak. Young mothers tend to drop out of school. With little education, they have limited job opportunities. In addition, there are significant increases in maternal mortality and nonfatal maternal complication rates—especially among young, poor, and African American adolescents. The offspring of adolescent mothers also are adversely affected. For example, they often have low birthweights and other medical and psychological complications (Brooks-Gunn & Chase-Lansdale, 1995).

In addition to the lives put on hold or potentials never reached, teen pregnancies represent significant costs to society. Many of these young women and their children may need social service supports, such as Aid to Families with Dependent Children, Medicaid, or educational and job-training programs. The best use of tax dollars, say many experts, is to prevent adolescent pregnancies in the first place.

Meeting the Challenge of Multiple-Problem Behavior

In addition to understanding that many adolescents engage in multiple-problem behaviors, it also is important to develop programs that reduce adolescent problems. In a recent review of the programs that have been successful in preventing or reducing adolescent problems, adolescent researcher Joy Dryfoos (1990, 1992) described the common components of these successful programs. The two most successful common components were these:

1. *Intensive individualized attention.* In successful programs, each high-risk child is attached to a

responsible adult who gives the child attention and deals with the child's specific needs. This theme occurred in a number of different programs. In a successful substance-abuse program, a student assistance counselor was available full-time for individual counseling and referral for treatment.

2. *Communitywide multiagency collaborative approaches.* The basic philosophy of communitywide programs is that a number of different programs and services have to be in place. In one successful substance abuse program a communitywide health promotion campaign was implemented that used local media and community education in concert with a substance-abuse curriculum in the schools. Information about one successful program appears in Sociocultural Worlds 10.2.

Although many of today's adolescents are privileged, wielding unprecedented economic power, many have little access to resources or opportunity. They simultaneously move through what seems like an endless preparation for life. Each generation of adolescents is the fragile cable by which the best and worst of their parents' generation is transmitted to the present. In the end, there are only two lasting gifts adults can leave youth—one being roots, the other wings.

REVIEW

Adolescent Socioemotional Development

The old model of parent-adolescent relationships emphasized autonomy and detachment from parents, as well as intense, stressful conflict throughout adolescence. The new model emphasizes both attachment and autonomy, with parents acting as important support systems and attachment figures for adolescents; the new model also emphasizes that moderate, rather than severe, conflict is common and that it can serve a positive developmental function. Conflict with parents is greater in early adolescence, especially during the apex of puberty, than in late adolescence. The developmental trajectories of parent-adolescent relationships are changing. Adolescents spend increased time with peers. Conformity to antisocial behavior peaks at about the eighth or ninth grade. A special concern is the peer relations of ethnic minority adolescents.

The function of secondary schools continues to be debated. Some maintain that the function should be to promote intellectual development; others argue for a much more comprehensive scope. Successful schools take individual differences in development seriously, show a deep concern for what is known about early adolescence, and emphasize social and emotional development as much as intellectual development. Dropping out of school has been a serious problem for decades. Many dropouts have educational deficiencies that curtail their economic and social well-being for much of their adult lives. Some progress has been made; dropout rates for most ethnic minority groups have declined in recent decades, although dropout rates for inner-city, low-income minorities are still precariously high. Students drop out of school for school-related, economic, and personal reasons. To reduce the dropout rate, community institutions, especially schools, need to break down the barrier between work and school.

Erikson believes that identity versus identity confusion, the fifth stage of the human life cycle, characterizes adolescence. Adolescents enter a psychological moratorium between childhood dependency and adult independence, seeking to discover who they are and where they are going in life. Erikson shows a special concern for the role of culture and ethnicity in identity development. Adolescence is often a special juncture in the identity development of ethnic minority adolescents because, for the first time, they consciously confront their ethnic identity. Kohlberg proposed three levels (each with two stages) of moral development: preconventional, conventional, and postconventional. The three levels vary in the degree to which moral development is internalized. Among his critics is Gilligan, who believes that Kohlberg underrepresents the care perspective.

Rites of passage are ceremonies that mark an individual's transition from one status to another, especially from childhood to adulthood. In some primitive cultures, rites of passage are well defined. In contemporary America, rites of passage are ill defined. The dropout rate for ethnic minority adolescents is disproportionately high. Many American adolescents are experiencing one rite of passage, sexual intercourse, earlier than adolescents in the past. One untoward consequence is adolescent pregnancy.

Many at-risk adolescents have more than one problem. The two most successful prevention or intervention strategies, according to Dryfoos's review, are intensive individualized attention and communitywide multiagency collaboration.

SOCIOCULTURAL WORLDS 10.2

The Midnight Basketball League

The dark side of peer relations is nowhere more present than in the increasing number of youth gangs. Beginning in 1990, the Chicago Housing Authority began offering young gang members an alternative to crime—the Midnight Basketball League (MBL) (Simons, Finlay, & Yang, 1991). Most crimes were being committed between 10 P.M. and 2 A.M. by males in their late teens and early twenties. The MBL offers these males a positive diversion during the time they are most likely to get into trouble. There are eight teams in the housing projects and 160 players in all. The year-round program provides top-quality basketball shoes, uniforms, championship rings, all-star games, and awards banquets.

Attitude is considered more important than ability, so most teams consist of one or two stars and eight or nine enthusiastic, mediocre-to-poor players. Different gang factions are represented on each team.

Basketball, however, is only one component of the MBL. To stay in the league, players must follow rules that prohibit fighting, unsportsmanlike behavior, profanity, drugs, alcohol, radios, and tape players. If they break the rules, they don't play basketball. Practices are mandatory, and so are workshops after each game. During the workshops, the youths are encouraged to seek drug-abuse counseling, vocational counseling and training, life skills advising, basic health care, adult education and GED services, and various social services. The program is funded by the Chicago Housing Authority and private donations.

In a recent year, not one of the MBL players had been in trouble, and 54 of the 160 participants registered for adult education classes once the season had ended. The program has been replicated in Hartford, Connecticut, Louisville, Kentucky, and Washington, DC. For more information about the MBL, contact Gil Walker, MBL Commissioner, Chicago Housing Authority, 534 East 37th Street, Chicago, IL 60653, 312–791–4768.

Players in a recent Midnight Basketball League in Chicago. Gil Walker, MBL commissioner, is the first person on the left in the front row.

EARLY AND MIDDLE ADULTHOOD

Just as the years from conception to adulthood are characterized by certain stages, so, too, are the adult years. **Early adulthood** *begins in the late teens or early twenties and ends in the late thirties to early forties. It is a time when individuals establish personal and economic independence, intensely pursue a career, and seek intimacy with one or more individuals.* **Middle adulthood** *begins at about 35 to 45 years of age and ends at 55 to 65 years of age. It is a time of expanding personal and social involvement, increased responsibility, adjustment to physical decline, and career satisfaction.*

Age is a high price to pay for maturity.

Tom Stoppard

Notice that approximate age bands identify the periods of adult development and that the age bands overlap. Psychologists are more certain about the periods of childhood than the periods of adulthood—most of us would agree that a 1-year-old child is in the period of infancy and that a 4-year-old child is in the period of early childhood. However, the periods of adulthood are much broader; there is less agreement on whether or not a 41-year-old is in middle adulthood. Not only are the criteria and age bands for adult periods less clear-cut than for childhood, but as prominent life-span theorist Bernice Neugarten (1986) argues, we are rapidly becoming an age-irrelevant society. She points out that we are already familiar with the 28-year-old mayor, the 30-year-old college president, the 35-year-old grandmother, and the 65-year-old father of a preschooler.

Neugarten believes that most adult themes appear and reappear throughout the adult years. Issues of intimacy and freedom that haunt a couple throughout a relationship in early adulthood may be just as salient in later adulthood. The pressure of time, reformulating goals, and coping with success and failure are not the exclusive properties of adults at any particular age. Keeping in mind that the age bands of adult periods are fuzzy, let's now see what physical, cognitive, and social changes take place during the adult years.

Dimensions of Adulthood

Changes continue in adulthood in the physical, cognitive, and socioemotional dimensions. To begin with, we will explore the physical changes that occur in early and middle adulthood.

Physical Development

Athletes keep getting better. Today's athletes run faster, jump higher, lift more weight than athletes did in earlier years. Despite this steady improvement, the age which athletes are at their best has stayed virtually the same. Richard Schultz and Christine Curnow (1988) analyzed records from track and field, swimming, baseball, and golf to learn at what age athletes truly hit their stride. They found that most athletes reach their peak performance under the age of 30, often between the ages of 19 and 26. Athletes who specialize in strength and speed events peak relatively early. Golf stars peak around the age of 31. In recent years, though, the "biological window" of peak performance has widened, even in the strength and speed events. Weight training, once unthinkable for women, has become standard procedure for star athletes like Florence Griffith Joyner. At age 28, her ability to lift 320 pounds helped build the strength behind her explosive start and leg drive that won world records in the 100 and 200 meters in the 1988 Olympics.

Not only do we reach our peak performance during early adulthood, but we also are the healthiest then. Few young adults have chronic health problems. They have fewer colds and respiratory problems than they had as children. However, young adults rarely recognize that bad eating habits, heavy drinking, and smoking in early adulthood can impair their health as they age. Despite warnings on packages and in advertisements that cigarettes are hazardous to health, individuals increase their use of cigarettes as they enter early adulthood (Johnston, Bachman, & O'Malley, 1989). They also increase their use of alcohol, marijuana, amphetamines, barbiturates, and hallucinogens.

As we enter middle adulthood, we are more acutely concerned about our health status. We experience a general decline in physical fitness throughout middle adulthood and some deterioration in health. The three greatest health concerns at this age are heart disease, cancer, and weight. Cancer related to smoking often surfaces for the first time in middle adulthood.

The *Harvard Medical School Newsletter* reports that about 20 million Americans are on a "serious" diet at any particular moment. Being overweight is a critical health problem, especially in middle adulthood. For individuals who are 30 percent or more overweight, the probability of dying in middle adulthood increases by 40 percent. Obesity also increases the probability an individual will suffer other ailments, including hypertension and digestive disorders.

Because U.S. culture stresses a youthful appearance, physical deterioration—graying hair, wrinkling skin, and a sagging body—in middle adulthood is difficult to handle. Many middle-aged adults dye their hair and join weight reduction programs; some even undergo cosmetic surgery to look young. In one study, the middle-aged women focused more attention on their facial attractiveness than did the older or younger women. Middle-aged women also perceived that the signs of aging had a more detrimental effect on their appearance (Novak, 1977).

For women, middle age also means that menopause will occur. **Menopause** *is the time in middle age, usually in the late forties or early fifties, when a woman's menstrual periods cease completely.* The average age at which women have their last period is 52. A small percentage of women—10 percent—undergo menopause before 40. There is a dramatic decline in the production of estrogen by the ovaries. Estrogen decline produces some uncomfortable symptoms in some menopausal women—"hot flashes," nausea, fatigue, and rapid heartbeat, for example. Some menopausal women report depression and irritability, but in some instances these feelings are related to other circumstances in the women's life, such as becoming divorced, losing a job, caring for a sick parent, and so on (Dickson, 1990).

Research investigations reveal that menopause does not produce psychological problems or physical problems for the majority of women. For example, in a large survey of more than 8,000 randomly selected women, the majority judged menopause to be a positive experience (feeling relief that they no longer had to worry about becoming pregnant or having periods or a neutral experience with no particular feelings at all (McKinlay & McKinlay, 1984). Only 3 percent said they regretted reaching menopause. Except for some temporary bothersome symptoms, such as hot flashes, sweating, and menstrual irregularity, most women simply said that menopause was not nearly so negative and painful as a lot of people make it out to be.

Why, then, do so many individuals have the idea that menopause is so negative and painful? Why do we have so many erroneous assumptions—that menopausal women will lose their sexuality and femininity, that they will become deeply depressed, and that they will experience extensive physical pain? Much of the research on menopause is based on small, selective samples of women who go to physicians or therapists because they are having problems associated with menopause. These women are unrepresentative of the large population of women in the United States.

The problem of using a small, selective sample was recently reflected in the popular author Gail Sheehy's book *The Silent Passage* (1991). Sheehy writes about her own difficult experiences and reports the frustrations of a few women she chose to interview. Although Sheehy dramatically overstates the percentage of women who have serious problems with menopause, she does not overstate the stigma attached to menopause or the inadequate attention accorded it by the medical community.

For the minority of menopausal women whose experiences are physically painful and psychologically difficult, estrogen replacement therapy may be beneficial. The painful symptoms are usually related either to low estrogen levels or to hormonal imbalance. Estrogen replacement therapy has been successful in relieving low-estrogen menopausal symptoms like hot flashes and sweating. Medical experts increasingly recommend that, prior to menopause, women have their level of estrogen monitored. In this way, once menopause occurs and estrogen level declines, the physician knows how much estrogen to replace to maintain a woman's normal level.

While estrogen replacement therapy has a lot going for it, some worries about its use have surfaced. According to Veronica Ravnikar (1992), head of the menopause unit at Massachusetts General Hospital, the biggest worry about estrogen replacement is that it might increase the risk of breast cancer. The results of studies usually show no increased risk of breast cancer, but in a few investigations the risk of the disease has increased from 1 case per 1,000 women to 1.2 cases per 1,000 in women taking estrogen. One negative health consequence of estrogen replacement is undisputed: Given by itself, estrogen can increase the risk of cancer of the uterine lining. To combat this effect, most women also take a synthetic form of a second female hormone, progesterone. This second hormone, though, may lessen estrogen's protection against heart attacks, and in about 25 percent of women it causes PMS-like bloating and irritability.

Our portrayal of menopause has been much more positive than its usual portrayals in the past. While menopause overall is not the negative experience for most women it was once thought to be, the loss of fertility is an important marker for women—it means that they have to make final decisions about having children. Women in their thirties who have never had children sometimes speak about being "up against the biological clock" because they cannot much longer postpone questions about having children (Blechman & Brownell, 1987).

Cognitive Development

Piaget believed that adults and adolescents think in the same way; however, some developmental psychologists believe it is not until adulthood that individuals consolidate their formal operational thinking. That is, they may begin to plan and hypothesize about problems as adolescents, but as adults they become more systematic in approaching problems. Although some adults are more proficient at developing hypotheses and deducing solutions to problems than adolescents are, many adults do not think in formal operational ways at all (Keating, in press).

Some psychologists believe that the absolute nature of adolescent logic and youth's buoyant optimism diminish in early adulthood (Labouvie-Vief, 1986). They argue that competent young adults are less caught up in idealism than they were in childhood. They tend to think logically and to adapt to life as circumstances demand. Less clear is whether our mental skills, especially memory, decline with age.

Long-term memory appears to decline more than short-term memory. For example, middle-aged individuals can remember a phone number they heard 30 seconds ago, but they probably won't remember the number as efficiently the next day. Memory is also more likely to decline when organization and imagery are not used. In addition, memory tends to decline when the information to be recalled is recently acquired or when the information is not used often. For example, middle-aged adults probably won't remember the rules to a new card game after only a lesson or two, and they are unlikely to know the new fall television schedule after its first week. Finally, memory tends to decline if recall rather than recognition is required. Middle-aged individuals can more efficiently select a phone number they heard yesterday if they are shown a list of phone numbers (recognition) rather than simply recalling the number off the top of their head. Memory in middle adulthood also declines if the individual's health is poor (Rybash, Roodin, & Santrock, 1991).

Socioemotional Development

As both Sigmund Freud and Russian novelist Leo Tolstoy observed, adulthood is a time for work and a time for love. For some of us, though, finding our place in society and committing ourselves to a stable relationship take longer than we would have imagined. Among the changes in social development during early and middle adulthood are those involving careers and work, lifestyles, marriage, and other life-events.

Careers and Work   At age 21, Thomas Smith graduated from college and accepted a job as a science teacher at a high school in Boston. At age 26, Sally Caruthers graduated from medical school and took a job as an intern at a hospital in Los Angeles. At age 20, Barbara Breck finished her training at a vocational school and went to work as a computer programmer for an engineering firm in Chicago. Earning a living, choosing an occupation, establishing a career, and developing a career—these are important themes of adulthood.

By the end of adolescence or the beginning of early adulthood, most people have an occupation. A few people seem to have known what they wanted to be ever since they were children, but for many people "getting there" may seem more like a time of foundering, ambiguity, and stress. Career counselors widely recommend exploring a variety of career options.

Among the most important social changes in the past few decades is the increased number of women in the workforce. Women have made great strides into careers that were once male bastions. For example, slightly more than half of all law students are women. However, some experts believe that many women restrict their career choices to nurturant, traditionally feminine occupations, such as nursing and teaching, overlooking other fields, such as mathematics and engineering (Diamond, 1988).

In today's economic climate, one wage is often no longer adequate to support a family. When married women with children decide to become paid employees, both men and women are more likely to share the roles and responsibilities of both work and family life (Gustafson & Magnusson, 1991). Fortunately, despite some role strain, multiple roles are healthy for both women and men. That is, the more roles (such as spouse, parent, worker) women and men have, the higher their levels of psychological well-being and physical health (Crosby, 1991).

A popular notion about midlife is that it is a time when people carefully examine their career, evaluate what they have accomplished, and seriously consider a change. However, only about 10 percent of Americans change careers in midlife. Some do so because they seek greater fulfillment; others do so because they get laid off or fired.

> By working faithfully eight hours a day, you may eventually get to be a boss and work twelve hours a day.
>
> **Robert Frost**

> The trouble with the rat race is that even if you win, you're still a rat.
>
> **Lily Tomlin**

Marriage   Until about 1930, the goal of having a stable marriage was accepted as a legitimate end point of adult development. In the past 50 years, however, we have seen the emergence of the desire for personal fulfillment—both inside and outside a marriage—as a force that can compete with marriage's stability. The changing norm of male-female equality in marriage has produced relationships that are more fragile and intense than they were earlier in the twentieth century. More adults are remaining single longer in the 1990s, and the average duration of a marriage in the United States is just over 9 years. The divorce rate, which increased astronomically in the 1970s, has finally begun to slow down, although it still remains alarmingly high. Even with adults remaining single for longer and divorce a frequent occurrence, Americans still show a strong predilection for marriage—the proportion of women who never marry has remained at about 7 percent throughout the twentieth century, for example (Hernandez, 1988).

The age at which men and women marry, their expectations about what the marriage will be like, and how the marriage unfolds are aspects of marriage that vary both over time within a given culture and across cultures. For example, you might remember from chapter 1 that a marriage law that sets a minimum age for marriage—22 years for males, 20 years for females—took effect in China in 1981. Late marriage and late childbirth are critical to China's efforts to control population growth.

> Married couples who love each other tell each other a thousand things without talking.
>
> **Chinese proverb**

Americans often have idealistic expectations of marriage, which helps explain our nation's high divorce rate and dissatisfaction in marriage. We expect our spouse to be simultaneously a lover, a friend, a confidant, a counselor, a career person, and a parent. Many myths about marriage contribute to these unrealistic expectations. Jeffrey Larson (1988) developed a marriage quiz to measure college students' knowledge about marriage and compared their responses with what social scientists know about marriage in the research literature. The college students responded incorrectly to almost half of the questions. Female students

TABLE 10.2

The Marriage Quiz

On a sheet of paper, number from 1 to 15. Answer each of the following items true or false. After completing the quiz, turn to the end of this chapter for the correct answers.

1. A husband's marital satisfaction is usually lower if his wife is employed full time than if she is a full-time homemaker.
2. Today most young, single, never-married people will eventually get married.
3. In most marriages, having a child improves marital satisfaction for both spouses.
4. The best single predictor of overall marital satisfaction is the quality of a couple's sex life.
5. The divorce rate in America increased from 1960 to 1980.
6. A greater percentage of wives are in the work force today than in 1970.
7. Marital satisfaction for a wife is usually lower if she is employed full time than if she is a full-time homemaker.
8. If my spouse loves me, he/she should instinctively know what I want and need to be happy.
9. In a marriage in which the wife is employed full time, the husband usually assumes an equal share of the housekeeping.
10. For most couples, marital satisfaction gradually increases from the first year of marriage through the childbearing years, the teen years, the empty nest period, and retirement.
11. No matter how I behave, my spouse should love me simply because he/she is my spouse.
12. One of the most frequent marital problems is poor communication.
13. Husbands usually make more lifestyle adjustments in marriage than wives.
14. Couples who cohabited before marriage usually report greater marital satisfaction than couples who did not.
15. I can change my spouse by pointing out his/her inadequacies, errors, etc.

From J. Larson, "The Marriage Quiz: College Students' Beliefs in Selected Myths About Marriage" in *Family Relations*, 37:4. Copyrighted © 1988 by the National Council on Family Relations, 3989 Central Ave., NE, Suite 550, Minneapolis, MN 55421. Reprinted by permission.

"Career track or mommy track?"

Drawing by D. Reilly; © 1990 The New Yorker Magazine, Inc.

missed fewer items than male students did, and students with a less romantic perception of marriage missed fewer items than more romantic students did. See table 10.2 to take the marriage quiz yourself.

As growing numbers of women pursue careers, they are faced with questions involving career and family (Gottfried, Gottfried, & Bathurst, 1995; Wilson & Gottman, 1995). Should they delay marriage and childbearing and establish their career first, or should they combine their career, marriage, and childbearing in their twenties? Some females continue to embrace the domestic patterns of an earlier historical period. They have married, borne children, and committed themselves to full-time mothering. These "traditional" women have worked outside the home only intermittently, if at all, and have subordinated the work role to the family role. Many other women, though, have veered from this time-honored path. They have postponed motherhood, or in some cases chosen not to have children. They have developed committed, permanent ties to the workplace

that resemble the pattern once reserved only for men. When they have had children, they have strived to combine a career and motherhood. Although there have always been "career" women, their numbers are growing at an unprecedented rate.

Dual-career marriages can have both advantages and disadvantages (Thompson & Walker, 1989). One of the main advantages is financial. One of every three wives earns 30 to 50 percent of the family's total income, which helps explain why most first-time home buyers are dual-career couples. Other than financial benefits, dual-career marriages can contribute to a more equal relationship between husband and wife and enhanced feelings of self-esteem for women. Among the possible disadvantages of dual-career marriages are added time and energy demands, conflict between work and family roles, competitive rivalry between husband and wife, and, if the family includes children, concerns of whether the children's needs are being met adequately.

Many men, especially those with low earnings, have a difficult time accepting their wives' employment. For example, in one investigation, married men who opposed their wives' employment were more depressed when their own earnings were low rather than high (Ulbrich, 1988). These men apparently experience a double insult to themselves as providers. Many husbands whose wives work report that they would like to have a wife who is a full-time homemaker. For example, in one study, although husbands appreciated their wives' earnings, they felt they had lost the services of a full-time homemaker—someone who is there when they get home, someone who cooks all their meals, and someone who irons all their clothes (Ratcliff & Bogdan, 1988). Some husbands, of course, encourage their wives' employment, or support their decision to pursue a career. In one investigation of high-achieving women, many of their husbands took pride in their wives' accomplishments and did not feel competitive with them (Epstein, 1987).

Gender, Intimacy, and Family Work The experiences and implications of marriage for a wife may differ from those for her husband (Thompson & Walker, 1989). This is especially true in the expression of intimacy and in family work. In one study, only one-third of the married African American women said they would go to their husbands first for support if they had a serious problem, such as being depressed or anxious (Brown & Gary, 1985). Only one-third of these women named their husbands as one of the three people closest to them. More of the men than the women viewed their spouses as best friends (Rubin, 1984).

Wives consistently disclose more to their partners than husbands do (Peplau & Gordon, 1985). Women also tend to express more tenderness, fear, and sadness than their male partners do. Many women complain that their husbands do not care about their emotional lives and do not express their own feelings and thoughts, whereas men feel that they are open or they do not understand what their wives want from them (Rubin, 1984). Men often say that, no matter how much they talk, it is not enough for their wives; women say they want more warmth and openness from their husbands. For example, women are more likely than men to give their partners a spontaneous kiss or hug when something positive happens (Blumstein & Schwartz, 1983). Overall, women are more expressive and affectionate than men are in marriage, and this difference bothers many women.

Not only are there gender differences in terms of marital intimacy, but there also are strong gender differences in family work (Thompson & Walker, 1989). Most women and men agree that women should be responsible for family work and that men should "help out," and wives typically do much more family work than husbands do (Warner, 1986). Even though most wives do two to three times more family work than their husbands, most wives report they are satisfied with the small amount their husbands do (Kamo, 1988). In one study, 10 percent of the husbands did as much family work as their wives (Berk, 1985); most of these "exceptional" men had many, usually young, children and wives who worked full-time.

Women's involvement in family work is often different in nature from men's. Besides the fact that women do more, women's family work differs from men's in the kind of work women do and how they experience it. The family work most women do is unrelenting, repetitive, and routine, often involving cleaning, cooking, child care, shopping, laundry, and straightening up. The family work most men do is infrequent, irregular, and nonroutine, often involving household repairs, taking out the garbage, and yard work. Women often report having to do several tasks at once, which may explain why they find domestic work less relaxing and more stressful than men do.

I hate housework! You make the beds, you do the dishes—
and six months later you have to start all over again.

Joan Rivers

Because family work is intertwined with love and embedded in family relations, it has complex and contradictory meanings. Most women feel that family tasks are mindless but essential. They usually enjoy tending to the needs of their loved ones and keeping the family going, even if they do not find the activities themselves enjoyable and fulfilling. Family work is both positive and negative for women. They are unsupervised and rarely criticized, they plan and control their own work, and they have only their own standards to meet. However, women's family work is often worrisome, tiresome, menial, repetitive, isolating, unfinished, inescapable, and often unappreciated. It is not surprising that men report that they are more satisfied with their marriage than women do.

Divorce The stress of separation and divorce places both men and women at risk for psychological and physical difficulties (Hetherington, 1995; Hetherington & Stanley-Hagan, 1995). Separated and divorced men and women have higher rates of psychiatric disturbance, admission to psychiatric hospitals, clinical depression, alcoholism, and psychosomatic problems, such as sleep disturbances, than do married adults. There is increasing evidence that stressful events of many types—including marital separation—reduce the immune system's capabilities, rendering separated and divorced men and women vulnerable to disease and infection. In one recent study, the most recently separated women (1 year or less) were more likely to show impaired immunological functioning than were women whose separations had occurred 1 to 6 years earlier (Kiecolt-Glaser & Glaser, 1988). In addition, the unhappily married individuals had poorer immune function than the happily married individuals.

Single Adults Many myths are associated with being single, ranging from "the swinging single" to the "desperately lonely, suicidal single." Most singles are somewhere between these two extremes. The pluses of being single include time to make decisions about one's life, time to develop personal resources to meet goals, freedom to make autonomous decisions and pursue one's own schedule and interests, opportunities to explore new places and try new things, and privacy. Some common problems of single adults include a lack of intimate relationships with others, loneliness, and trouble finding a niche in a marriage-oriented society. Some single adults would rather remain single; others would rather be married.

Theories of Adult Personality Development

Psychologists have proposed several theories about adult development. Most theories address the themes of work and love, career and intimacy. One set of theories proposes that adult development unfolds in stages.

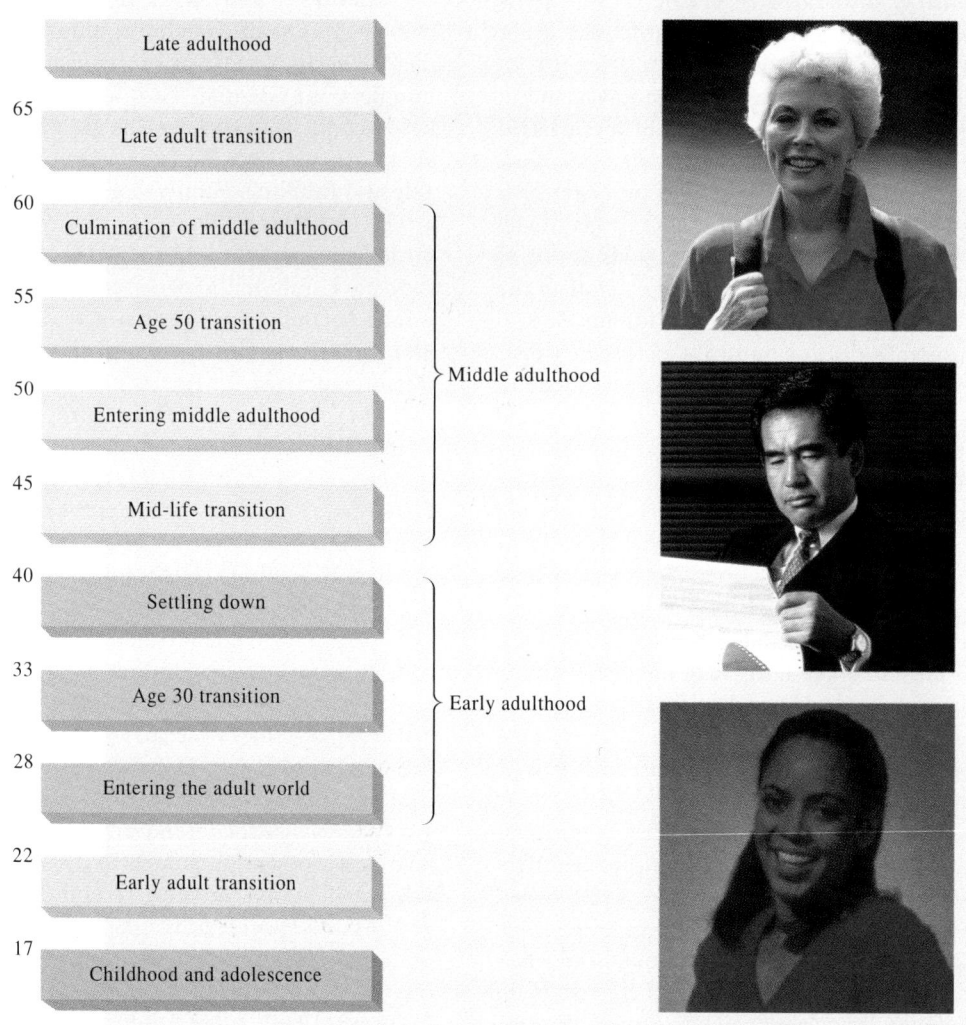

	Late adulthood	
65	Late adult transition	
60	Culmination of middle adulthood	
55	Age 50 transition	
50	Entering middle adulthood	Middle adulthood
45	Mid-life transition	
40	Settling down	
33	Age 30 transition	Early adulthood
28	Entering the adult world	
22	Early adult transition	
17	Childhood and adolescence	

FIGURE 10.5

Levinson's Periods of Adult Development

Erik Erikson's Life-Span Theory

Erikson's eight stages of the life cycle include one stage for early adulthood and one stage for middle adulthood. Erikson believes that only after identity has been well developed can true intimacy occur. **Intimacy versus isolation** *is Erikson's sixth stage of development, occurring mainly in early adulthood. Intimacy is the ability to develop close, loving relationships.* Intimacy helps us form our identity because, in Erikson's words, "We are what we love." If intimacy does not develop, Erikson argues, a deep sense of isolation and impersonal feelings overcome the individual. **Generativity versus stagnation** *is Erikson's seventh stage of development, occurring mainly in middle adulthood. Middle-aged adults need to assist the younger generation in leading useful lives as well as the older generation of elderly, often frail, parents.* Competent child rearing is one way to achieve generativity.

However, adults can also satisfy this need through guardianship or a close relationship with the children of friends and relatives. The positive side of this stage—generativity—reflects an ability to positively shape the next generation. The negative side—stagnation—leaves the individual with a feeling of having done nothing for the next generation. As Erikson (1968) put it, "Generations will depend on the ability of all procreating individuals to face their children."

Daniel Levinson's "Seasons" Theory

In *Seasons of a Man's Life* (1978), Daniel Levinson also described adult development as a series of stages. He extensively interviewed middle-aged male hourly workers, academic biologists, business executives, and novelists, and concluded that developmental tasks must be mastered at a number of points in adulthood (see figure 10.5).

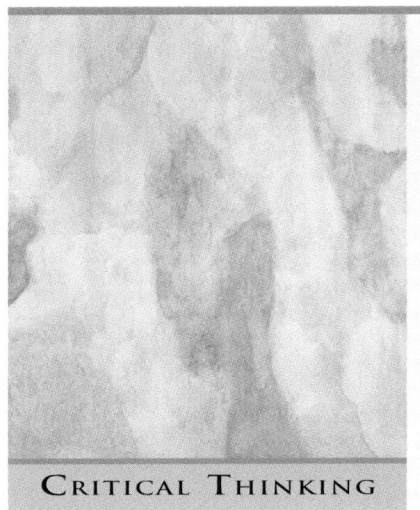

Levinson argues that his adult stages are basically the same for women as for men. Do you agree or disagree? What kind of evidence would you need to support your position? Thinking about these questions offers an opportunity for you to *develop psychological arguments based on evidence* by examining whether the results of research are generalizable from one population to another. If the stages are not the same, in what ways do you think development for women would be different from development for men?

Seasons of a Woman's Life

In early adulthood, the two major tasks are exploring the possibilities for adult living and developing a stable life structure. The twenties represent the novice phase of adult development. By the end of a boy's teens, according to Levinson, a transition from dependence to independence should occur. This transition is marked by a dream—an image of the kind of life the young man wants, especially in terms of marriage and a career. The novice phase is a time of experimenting and testing the dream in the real world.

Men usually determine their goals by the age of 28 to 33. During his thirties, a man usually works to develop his family life and career. In the late thirties, he enters a phase of becoming his own man (or BOOM, "becoming one's own man," as Levinson calls it). By age 40, he reaches a stable point in his career, outgrows his earlier, more tenuous status as an adult, and looks forward to the kind of life he will lead as a middle-aged adult.

In Levinson's view, the change to middle adulthood lasts about 5 years and requires that men come to grips with four major conflicts that have existed since adolescence: (1) being young versus being old, (2) being destructive versus being constructive, (3) being masculine versus being feminine, and (4) being attached to others versus being separated from them. The success of the midlife transition depends on how effectively they can reduce these polarities and accept each of them as a part of their being. Levinson's original subjects were all males, but more recently he reported that these midlife issues hold for females as well (Levinson, 1987).

Erikson and Levinson emphasize that we go through a number of adult stages of development. In evaluating these stage theories, several points need to be kept in mind. First, the research on which they are based is not empirically sound—much of it involves clinical observations rather than rigorous, controlled observations. Second, the perspectives tend to describe the stages as crises, especially in the case of the midlife stage. Research on middle-aged adults reveals that few adults experience midlife in the tumultuous way described by the stage-crisis views: Individuals vary extensively in how they cope with and perceive midlife (Vaillant, 1977).

Most middle-aged adults experience not a midlife crisis but a midlife consciousness (Santrock, 1995). This midlife consciousness is characterized by an increased concern about time (How much time do I have left to do what I want in life, and how well have I done with the time I have had?), about being young versus being old (What is the best way to cope with my aging? How can I optimize my life, and what kind of compensations do I have to make?), about generativity (What have I done and what can I do to contribute to the next generation? What kind of legacy will I leave?), and about the meaning of life (What is the purpose of life? What is the personal meaning of my life?).

Middle age is such a foggy place.

Roger Rosenblatt, 1987

"Goodbye, Alice, I've got to get this California thing out of my system."

Drawing by Leo Cullum; © 1984 The New Yorker Magazine, Inc.

Activity/event	Appropriate age range	% who agree (late '50s study)		% who agree (late '70s study)	
		Men	Women	Men	Women
Best age for a man to marry	20–25	80	90	42	42
Best age for a woman to marry	19–24	85	90	44	36
When most people should become grandparents	45–50	84	79	64	57
Best age for most people to finish school and go to work	20–22	86	82	36	38
When most men should be settled on a career	24–26	74	64	24	26
When most men hold their top jobs	45–50	71	58	38	31
When most people should be ready to retire	60–65	83	86	66	41
When a man has the most responsibilities	35–50	79	75	49	50
When a man accomplishes most	40–50	82	71	46	41
The prime of life for a man	35–50	86	80	59	66
When a woman has the most responsibilities	25–40	93	91	59	53
When a woman accomplishes most	30–45	94	92	57	48

FIGURE 10.6

Individuals' Conceptions of the Right Age for Major Life Events and Achievements: Late 1950s and Late 1970s

Life Events, Cohort Effects, and Social Clocks

Life events rather than stages may be responsible for changes in our adult lives. Such events as marriage, divorce, the death of a spouse, a job promotion, and being fired from a job involve varying degrees of stress and influence our development as adults (Holmes & Rahe, 1967). However, we also need to know about the many factors that mediate the influence of life events on adult development—for example, physical health, intelligence, personality, family support, and income (Hansell, 1991). In addition, we need to know how people perceive the life events and how they cope with the stress involved. For instance, one person may perceive a divorce as highly stressful, whereas another person may perceive the same life event as a challenge. We also need to consider the person's life stage and circumstances. Divorce may be more stressful for an individual in his fifties who has been married for many years, for example, than for someone in her twenties who has been married only a few years (Chiriboga, 1982). Similarly, people may cope with divorce more effectively in the 1990s than in the 1890s because divorce is more commonplace and accepted today.

An increasing number of developmental psychologists believe that changing social expectations influence how different cohorts—groups of individuals born in the same year or time period—move through the life cycle. For example, people born during the Depression may have a different outlook on life than those born during the optimistic 1950s (Rossi, 1989).

Bernice Neugarten (1986) believes that the social environment of a particular age group can alter its "social clock"—the timetable according to which individuals are expected to accomplish life's tasks, such as getting married, having children, and establishing themselves in a career. Social clocks act as guides for our lives. People who are somehow out of sync with these social clocks find their lives more stressful than do those who are on schedule, says Neugarten. One study found that, between the late 1950s and the late 1970s, there was a dramatic decline in adults' beliefs that there is a "right age" for major life events and achievements (Passuth, Maines, & Neugarten, 1984) (see figure 10.6).

The Nature of Middle Age

For $8 each, about 2.5 to 3 million Americans who turn 50 each year become members of the American Association for Retired Persons (AARP). There is something incongruous about 50-year-olds joining a retirement group when hardly any of them are retired. Indeed, many of today's 50-year-olds are in better shape, more alert, and more productive than were their 40-year-old counterparts of a generation or two earlier. As more people lead healthier lifestyles and medical discoveries help to stave off the aging process, the boundaries of middle age are being pushed upward. It looks like middle age is starting later and lasting longer for increasing numbers of active, healthy, and productive people. June Reinisch (1992), highly respected researcher and director of the Kinsey Institute for Research in Sex, Gender, and Reproduction at Indiana University, recently said, "I'm 49 this year. I wear clothes that my mother would never have thought of wearing when she was this age. When skirts went up, my skirts went up" (p. 52).

Sigmund Freud and Carl Jung studied midlife transitions around the turn of the twentieth century, but "midlife" came much earlier then. In 1900, the average life expectancy was only 47 years of age; only 3 percent of the population lived past 65. Today, the average life expectancy is 75; 12 percent of the U.S. population is older than 65. As a much greater percentage of the population lives to an older age, the midpoint of life and what constitutes middle age or middle adulthood are becoming harder to pin down. In only one century, we have added 30 years to the average life expectancy. Statistically, the middle of life today is about 37 years of age—hardly any 37-year-olds, though, wish to be called middle-aged! What we think of as middle age comes later—anywhere from 40 to about 60 to 65 years of age. And as more people live longer, the upper boundary of 60 to 65 years will likely be nudged upward. When the American Board of Family Practice asked a random sample of 1,200 Americans when middle age begins, 41 percent said it was when you worry about having enough money for health-care concerns, 42 percent said it was when your last child moves out, and 46 percent said it was when you don't recognize the names of music groups on the radio anymore (Beck, 1992).

In sum, middle adulthood is not a crisis for most people. As life-span expert Gilbert Brim (1992) commented recently, middle adulthood is full changes, twists, and turns; the path is not fixed. People move in and out of states of success and failure.

Gender, Culture, and Middle Age

Stage theorists have tried to chart how our lives generally unfold over the years. Critics say that, when it comes to the middle years, these blueprints focus on career choice and work achievement, issues that traditionally have dominated men's lives more than women's (Deutsch, 1991). They also assert that stage theories do not adequately address women's concerns about relationships, interdependence, and caring and that they give short shrift to the importance of childbearing and child rearing (Gilligan, 1982). As mentioned earlier, women bear the burden of family work; men seldom experience the same demands of balancing career and family roles that women do.

One problem of comparing men and women according to stage theory is the assumption that most people encounter a given developmental stage—graduating from high school and college, starting a family, and retiring, for example—at more or less the same time. As Neugarten points out, however, today people adhere less to social clocks. Many women return to college and begin careers, for example, after spending a number of years starting a family. Many other women delay marriage and childbearing until after they have successfully established a career. As a result of women's increasingly complex and varied roles, defining *what* women should be doing *when* has become difficult, if not impossible.

Although middle age may be a time of fewer options for many women in Western cultures, it carries many advantages in some nonindustrialized societies. Anthropologist Judith Brown (1985) argues that as women in many nonindustrialized societies reach middle age, three changes take place that improve their status. First, they are often freed from cumbersome restrictions that were placed on them as younger women. For example, in middle age they are freer to travel. Middle-aged women can visit distant relatives, go on religious pilgrimages, and venture from their villages to seek money-making opportunities. The second major change is that their work tends to be administrative; they can delegate tasks to younger women. Middle-aged women also make some important family decisions, such as what a grandchild is to be named, who is ready to be initiated, and who is eligible to marry whom. The third major change for middle-aged women is the opportunity to step into venerated functions, such as midwife, curer, holy woman, and matchmaker, roles that bring recognition beyond the household.

We have already seen that midlife crises are less pervasive in the United States than is commonly believed. There has been little cross-cultural research on middle adulthood; adult stage theories, such as Levinson's, have not been tested in other cultures. In some cultures, especially those in nonindustrialized countries, the concept of middle age is ambiguous or absent. For example, a person may be described as young or old, but not as middle-aged (Foner, 1984). Some cultures have no words for *adolescent*, *young adult*, or *middle-aged adult*.

Gender is such a powerful perceptual organizer in the Gusii culture of Kenya in Africa that the flow of life is described differently for females than for males (LeVine, 1979):

Females	Males
1. Infant	1. Infant
2. Uncircumcised girl	2. Uncircumcised boy
3. Circumcised girl	3. Circumcised boy warrior
4. Married woman	4. Male elder
5. Female elder	

Life events, not age, determine a person's status in the Gusii culture. Although the Gusii do not clearly label midlife, around the age of 40 some individuals reassess their lives and examine the limited time that remains. Recognizing that their physical strength is decreasing and that they cannot farm their land forever, some Gusii become spiritual practitioners or healers. As is true for Americans, a midlife crisis among the Gusii is the exception rather than the rule.

The concept of a midlife crisis implies that middle adulthood involves considerable change. Let's explore further the issue of change in adult development.

Continuity and Discontinuity

Richard Alpert, an achievement-oriented, hard-working college professor in the 1960s became Ram Dass, a free-spirited guru in search of an expanded state of consciousness in the 1970s. It would seem as though Richard Alpert and Ram Dass were two very different people. However, Harvard psychologist David McClelland, who knows Ram Dass well, says that he is the same old Richard—still charming, still concerned with inner experience, and still power hungry. Jerry Rubin viewed his own transformation from yippie to Wall Street businessman in a way that underscores continuity in personality. Rubin said that he discovered his identity in a typical Jerry Rubin fashion—trying out anything and everything, behaving in a wild and crazy manner. Whether yippie or Wall Street yuppie, Rubin approached life with enthusiasm and curiosity.

William James (1890) said that our basic personality is like plaster, set by the time we are 30. James believed that our bodies and attitudes may change through the adult years—as did Richard Alpert's and Jerry Rubin's—but the basic core of our personality remains the same. Some modern researchers, such as Paul Costa, also believe that such traits as how extraverted we are, how well-adjusted we are, and how open we are to new experiences do not change much during our adult lives (Costa, 1988; Costa & McRae, 1995). Costa says that a person who is shy and quiet at age 25 will be basically that same shy, quiet person at age 50. Still other psychologists are enthusiastic about our capacity for change as adults, arguing that too much importance is attached to personality change in childhood and not enough to change in adulthood.

A more moderate view on the issue of stability versus change comes from the architects of the California Longitudinal Study, which now spans more than 50 years (Eichorn & others, 1981). These researchers believe that some stability exists over the long course of adult development but that adults are more capable of changing than Costa thinks. For example, a person who is shy and introverted at age 25 may not be completely extraverted at age 50, but she may be less introverted than at 25. This person might have married someone who encouraged her to be more outgoing and supported her efforts to socialize; perhaps she changed jobs at age 30 and became a salesperson, placing her in a situation in which she was required to develop her social skills.

Humans are adaptive beings. We are resilient throughout our adult lives, but we do not acquire entirely new personalities. In a sense, we change but remain the same—underlying the change is coherence and stability.

How much does personality change, and how much does it stay the same, through adulthood? In the early 1970s, Jerry Rubin was (a) a yippie demonstrator, but in the 1980s Rubin became (b) a Wall Street businessman. Rubin said that his transformation underscored continuity in personality: Whether yippie or Wall Street yuppie, he approached life with curiosity and enthusiasm until his death in 1994.

Early and Middle Adulthood

The peak of our physical skills and health usually comes in early adulthood, a time when it is easy to develop bad health habits. In middle adulthood, most individuals experience a decline in physical fitness, and they start to take an interest in health as they notice signs that their health begins to deteriorate. Menopause is a marker that signals the cessation of childbearing capability, arriving usually in the late forties and early fifties. The vast majority of women do not have substantial problems with menopause, although the public perception of menopause has often been negative. Estrogen replacement therapy is effective in reducing the physical pain of menopause.

Some psychologists argue that cognition is more pragmatic in early adulthood. Cognitive skills are strong in early adulthood. In middle adulthood, memory may decline, although such strategies as organization can reduce the decline.

Special concerns in early and middle adulthood are careers and work, lifestyles, theories of adult personality development, cohort effects, gender, culture, and the issue of continuity-discontinuity. Among the important aspects of careers and work are the increasing number of females in the workforce. Adults must choose the lifestyle they want to follow—single, married, or divorced, for example. One set of adult personality development theories proposes that adult development unfolds in stages (Erikson, Levinson). Other theories emphasize life events, social clocks, and cohort effects. The stage theorists have exaggerated the prevalence of a midlife crisis. Today midlife comes later and lasts longer. Critics say the adult stage theories have a male bias by emphasizing career choice and achievement. The stage theories do not adequately address women's concerns about relationships. The stage theories assume a normative sequence, but, as women's roles have become more varied and complex, determining what is normative is difficult. In many nonindustrialized societies, a woman's status often improves in middle age. In many cultures, the concept of middle age is not clear, although most cultures distinguish between young and old adults. There is both continuity and discontinuity in adult personality development.

LATE ADULTHOOD AND AGING

In the words of twentieth-century Italian poet Salvatore Quasimodo, "Each of us stands alone at the heart of the earth pierced through by a ray of sunlight: And suddenly it is evening." Although we may be in the evening of our lives in late adulthood, we are not meant to live out passively our remaining years. **Late adulthood** *begins around the age of 60 to 70 and ends when the individual dies. It is a time of adjustment to decreased strength and health, retirement, reduced income, new social roles, and learning how to age successfully.*

The Nature of Late Adulthood

We are no longer a youthful society. The concept of a late adulthood period is a recent one. Until the twentieth century, most people died before age 65. In 1900 only 1 American in 25 was over 65. Today the figure is 1 in 9. By the middle of the twenty-first century, 1 in 4 Americans will be 65 years of age or older (see figure 10.7).

FIGURE 10.7

Millions of Americans over Age 65 in 1900, 1940, 1980, and Projected for the Year 2040

All we know about older adults indicates that they are healthier and happier the more active they are. Several decades ago, it was believed that older adults should be more passive and inactive to be well adjusted and satisfied with life. In today's world, we believe that while older adults may be in the evening of life's human cycle, they were not meant to live out their remaining years passively.

require the everyday help of other persons. However, as we discussed earlier in this chapter, the oldest old are a heterogeneous group and until recently this diversity has not been adequately recognized. Although almost one-fourth of the oldest old are institutionalized, the majority live in the community and remain independent (Suzman & others, 1992).

Because so much attention has been given to the chronic disability of the oldest old, those who have aged successfully have gone virtually unnoticed and unstudied. An increased interest in successful aging is giving a more optimistic portrayal of the oldest old than was painted in the past (Rowe & Kahn, 1987). Health service researchers are discovering that a relatively large portion of people in old age are low-cost users of medical services; a small percentage account for a large fraction of expenditures, usually in the last year of life, a period that is expensive at any age (Scitovsky, 1988). A surprisingly large portion of the oldest old do not require personal assistance on a daily basis and are physically robust (Garfein & Herzog, 1995).

In sum, earlier portraits of the oldest old have been stereotypical. There exists a substantial subgroup of the oldest old who are robust and active, and there is cause for optimism in the development of new regimens of prevention and intervention (Suzman & others, 1992). Strategies for successful aging are discussed later in this chapter. But first let's explore the developmental dimensions of late adulthood.

Dimensions of Late Adulthood

Although we tend to view the period of late adulthood as a period of decline, not all aspects of development deteriorate. Let's begin by looking at physical changes in late adulthood.

Physical Development

Virtually all biological theories of aging and the life span assign an important role to genes. Research demonstrates that the body's cells can divide only a limited number of times; cells from embryonic tissue can divide about 50 times, for example (Hayflick, 1977). Cells extracted from older adults divide fewer times than those taken from younger adults. Although the cells of elderly people are still able to divide,

The life span—the upper boundary of life, the maximum number of years an individual can live—has remained virtually unchanged since the beginning of recorded history. What has changed is life expectancy—the number of years that will probably be lived by the average person born in a particular year. Even though improvements in medicine, nutrition, exercise, and lifestyle have given us, on the average, 22 additional years of life since 1900, few of us will live to be 100. In Sociocultural Worlds 10.3, you will read about three areas of the world purported to have large numbers of inhabitants who live to be more than 100 years old.

Our image of the oldest old (eighties and older) is predominantly of being disabled and frail. The implications of the projected rapid growth of the oldest-old population have often been unremittingly pessimistic—an expensive burden of chronic disability in which the oldest old often

SOCIOCULTURAL WORLDS 10.3

Aging in Russia, Ecuador, and Kashmir

Imagine that you are 120 years old. Would you still be able to write your name? Could you think clearly? What would your body look like? Would you be able to walk? To run? Could you still have sex? Would you have an interest in sex? Would your eyes and ears still function? Could you work?

Has anyone ever lived to be 120 years old? Supposedly. In three areas of the world, not just a single person but many people have reportedly lived more than 130 years. These areas are the Republic of Georgia in Russia, the Vilcabamba valley in Ecuador, and the province of Hunza in Kashmir (in northern India). Three people over 100 years old (centenarians) per 100,000 people is considered normal. But in the Russian region where the Abkhasian people live, approximately 400 centenarians per 100,000 people have been reported. Some of the Abkhasians are said to be 120 to 170 years old (Benet, 1976).

However, there is reason to believe that some of these claims are false (Medvedev, 1974). Indeed, we really do not have sound documentation of anyone living more than 120 years. In the case of the Abkhasians, birth registrations and other documents, such as marriage certificates and military registrations, are not available. In most instances, the ages of the Abkhasians have been based on the individuals' recall of important historical events and interviews with other members of the village (Benet, 1976). In the Russian villages where people have been reported to live a long life, the elderly experience unparalleled esteem and honor. Centenarians are often given special positions in the community,

such as the leader of social celebrations. Thus there is a strong motivation to give one's age as older than one really is. One individual who claimed to be 130 years of age was found to have used his father's birth certificate during World War I to escape army duty. Later it was discovered that he only was 78 years old (Hayflick, 1975).

(a) Selakh Butka, who says he is 113 years old, is shown with his wife, who says she is 101. The Butkas live in the Georgian Republic of Russia, where reports of unusual longevity have surfaced. (b) Eighty-seven-year-old José Maria Roa is from the Vilcambamba region of Ecuador, which also is renowned for the longevity of its inhabitants. *Why are scientists skeptical about their age estimates?*

we rarely live to the end of our life-span potential. Based on the rate at which human cells divide, biologists place the upper limit of the human life cycle at 115 to 120 years.

In old age, arteries become more resistant to the flow of blood, and heart output—about 5 quarts a minute at age 50—drops about 1 percent a year after age 50. The increased resistance of the blood vessels results in elevated heart rate and blood pressure, which are related to heart disease. Even in a healthy older person, blood pressure that was 100/75 at age 25 will probably be 160/90 at age 70.

As we age in late adulthood, the probability that we will have a disease or become seriously ill increases. For example, a majority of individuals who are alive at age 80 have some physical impairment. Alzheimer's disease is of special concern (Butters, Delis, & Lucas, 1995). **Alzheimer's disease** *is a degenerative, irreversible brain disorder that impairs memory and social behavior.* More than 2 million people over the age of 65 have Alzheimer's disease. To read about the elderly and the health-care system, turn to Applications in Psychology 10.1.

The Elderly and the Health-Care System

The elderly should seek out doctors who will fully answer their questions, from the implications of physical and mental symptoms to medications and their side effects. The elderly should not be afraid to find a new doctor if they don't like the one they have, even though it might be inconvenient. Robert Butler, former head of the National Institute of Aging, says that some doctors put off Medicare and Medicaid patients by offering them appointments weeks or months away. Not much can be done about that, because doctors are not required to take Medicare patients. Some doctors who do see the elderly say that their complaints come from being old ("You should just take it easy"); an elderly patient who is told this should seek another doctor. Being told to take it easy is one of the worst prescriptions a doctor can give to an elderly person, because remaining active is the best medicine for older people, says Butler.

There are good and caring doctors for the elderly. Once elderly people find one, the following rules of thumb can help them cope effectively with their health problems (Podolsky & Silberner, 1993):

Speak up. If the elderly want more-aggressive care, they need to speak up, ask their doctor to give them alternatives for treatment and explanations for things they don't understand. They can help their doctor by bringing to their office visits all of the drugs they are taking.

Question assertions based solely on age. Often such statements are based on limited information and subjective expectations. The elderly need to bear in mind that their physiological age—how well their body works—is often more relevant to their treatment than their chronological age is.

Get the family involved. Doctors and nurses who care for the elderly say that frustrated families, battling to stave off the death of a loved one who is going to die no matter what, often push medical professionals into giving heroic care that can't help. Both family and doctor need a clear idea of the care patients want if they are unable to speak for themselves. Guessing can be tragic. In a survey of seventy patients, the patients predicted that doctors and loved ones would know what they wanted if they became senile and then had a heart attack. But the physicians were wrong half the time and the patients' families were not much better in their predictions.

Decide now. The Patient Self-Determination Act, which became effective in December 1991, requires hospitals to inform patients on admission that they can refuse life-sustaining treatment. However, only people who are alert and conscious are offered the directives. Filling out a living will while an elderly person is feeling fine may upset the elderly person's family, but it is better than becoming a headline. Once the elderly person is incapacitated, it is too late for her or his wishes to be carried out.

Ira Baldwin, age 97, was told he would die, but he chose to fight instead. In 1990, after physicians told him that his rare form of liver cancer was incurable, he searched for a doctor who would help seek a cure. The drug alpha interferon initially kept the cancer in check, but when the tumor started to grow again, Baldwin was switched to a platinum-based drug. Baldwin says he feels fine after the switch (Podolsky & Silberner, 1993).

Cognitive Development

At age 70, Dr. John Rock developed the birth-control pill. At age 89, Arthur Rubinstein gave one of his best performances at New York's Carnegie Hall. From 85 to 90 years of age, Pablo Picasso completed three sets of drawings, and at age 76 Anna Mary Robertson Moses took up painting. As Grandma Moses, she became internationally famous and staged fifteen one-woman shows throughout Europe. Are the feats of Grandma Moses and others rare exceptions? As Aeschylus said in the fifth century B.C., "It is always in season for the old to learn."

We have seen that the further we go through the late adulthood years, the more likely it is that we will be physically impaired. Controversy continues about whether our cognitive abilities, such as memory and intelligence, decline as we become older. Intelligence test maker David Wechsler (1972) concluded that intellectual decline is simply part of the general aging process we all go through. The issue seems more complex, however. Although it is true that older adults do not score as high on intelligence tests as young adults do, this is probably because older adults just don't think as fast as young adults. When we consider general knowledge and wisdom, however, older adults often outperform younger adults (Perlmutter, 1994).

Socioemotional Development

Enduring loss is an inevitable part of growing older. Losses can encourage retreat, which might be responsible for the image of older adults as sitting in rocking chairs watching the world go by. Now we know that the most well-adjusted and satisfied older adults are active, not passive, in the face of their challenges.

I have everything now I had twenty years ago—except it's all lower.

Gypsy Rose Lee

Activity Theory Activity theory *states that the more active and involved older people are, the more satisfied they are and the more likely it is that they will stay healthy.* Researchers have found that older people who go to church, attend meetings, take trips, and exercise are happier than those who simply sit at home. Predictably, the better the health and the higher the income, the more likely it is that an older person will be satisfied with life as well.

Ageism The elderly often face painful discrimination. A new word in our vocabulary is **ageism,** *which is prejudice against people based on their age.* Older adults might be branded by a number of stereotypes—such as being feebleminded, boring, ugly, parasitic. As a result, they might be treated like children and described as cute and adorable. Far worse, they often are not hired for new jobs or are forced out of existing ones, they might be shunned, or they might even be edged out of their own families. The elderly who are poor or from ethnic minority backgrounds face special hardships.

Ethnicity and Gender Of special concern are the ethnic minority elderly, especially African Americans and Latinos, who are overrepresented in the elderly poor in the United States (Hernandez, 1991; Markides, 1995). Nearly one-third of all elderly African Americans live on less than $5,300 per year. Among African American women living alone, the figure is 55 percent. Almost one-fourth of all elderly Latinos are below the poverty line. Only 10 percent of elderly White Americans fall below the poverty line.

Comparative information about African Americans, Latinos, and White Americans indicates a possible double jeopardy for elderly ethnic minority individuals, who face problems related to *both* ageism and racism (Tran, Wright, & Chatters, 1991). Both wealth and health decrease more rapidly for the ethnic minority elderly than for elderly White Americans. The ethnic minority elderly are more likely to become ill but less likely to receive treatment. They

Because of ageism, older adults might be shunned socially because they are perceived as senile or boring. Their children might edge them out of their lives. In these circumstances, a social network of friendships becomes an important support system for older adults. Researchers have found that close attachment to one or more individuals, whether friends or family, is associated with greater life satisfaction.

---

are also more likely to have a history of less education, unemployment, worse housing conditions, and shorter life expectancies than their elderly White American counterparts. Many ethnic minority workers never enjoy the Social Security and Medicare benefits to which their earnings contribute, because they die before reaching the age of eligibility for benefits.

A possible double jeopardy also faces many women—the burden of *both* ageism and sexism (Harrison, 1991; Lopata, 1995). The poverty rate for elderly women is almost double that of elderly men. According to Congresswoman Mary Rose Oakar, the number one priority for midlife and older women should be economic security. She predicts that 25 percent of all women working today can expect to be poor in old age. Only recently has scientific and political interest in aging women developed. For many years, aging women were virtually invisible in aging research and in protests involving rights for the elderly. An important research and political agenda for the 1990s is increased interest in the aging and rights of elderly women (Markson, 1995).

Not only is it important to be concerned about the double jeopardy of ageism and sexism involving older women, but special attention also needs to be devoted to the elderly who are female ethnic minority individuals. They face what could be described as triple jeopardy—ageism, sexism, and racism (Stoller & Gibson, 1994). Income is a special problem for these women. For example, more than one-third of all older Black American women have incomes below the poverty level (compared to less than one-fourth of all older African American men and approximately 13 percent of older White American women). One-fourth of all older Latino women have incomes below the poverty level (compared to 19 percent of Latino men) (U.S. Bureau of the Census, 1990). More information about being female, ethnic, and old appears in Sociocultural Worlds 10.4.

Cultural Comparisons   For many generations, the elderly in China and Japan experienced higher status than did the elderly in the United States (Ikels, 1989). In Japan the elderly are more integrated into their families than are the elderly in most industrialized countries. More than 75 percent live with their children; few single older adults live alone. Respect for the elderly surfaces in many circumstances: the best seats may be reserved for the elderly, cooking caters to their tastes, and individuals bow to them.

However, the image of elderly Japanese who are spared the heartbreak associated with aging in the United States by the respect and devotion they receive from children, grandchildren, and society is probably idealized and exaggerated (Tobin, 1987). Americans' images of the elderly in other cultures may be inaccurate, too—we imagine elderly Eskimos adrift on blocks of ice and 120-year-old Russian yogurt eaters, in addition to the honored elders of

As Japan has become more urbanized and Westernized, fewer elderly adults have lived with their children and more elderly adults have returned to work. Today respect for the elderly in Japan is greater than in the United States but not as strong as the idealized images we sometimes have.

Japan. For example, Japan has become more urbanized and Westernized; fewer elderly live with their children, and more elderly adults return to work, usually in a lower-status job with lower pay, a loss of fringe benefits, and a loss of union membership. The Japanese culture has acted as a powerful brake in slowing the decline in the respect for the elderly—today respect for the elderly is greater in Japan than in the United States, but not as strong as the idealized images we sometimes have.

Seven factors are most likely to predict high status for the elderly in a culture (Sangree, 1989):

1. Older persons have valuable knowledge.
2. Older persons control key family/community resources.
3. Older persons are permitted to engage in useful and valued functions as long as possible.
4. There is role continuity throughout the life span.
5. Age-related role changes involve greater responsibility, authority, and advisory capacity.
6. The extended family is a common family arrangement in the culture, and the older person is integrated into the extended family.
7. The culture is more collectivistic than individualistic.

Life Review and Integrity   "Life is lived forward, but understood backwards," said Danish philosopher Soren Kierkegaard. This is truer of late adulthood than of any other life period. Kierkegaard's words reflect Erikson's final stage of development through the life span. Erikson called this eighth stage **integrity versus despair;** *occurring mainly in late adulthood, it is a time of looking back at what we have done with our lives.* If an older person has developed a positive outlook in each of the preceding periods of development, the

SOCIOCULTURAL WORLDS 10.4

Being Female, Ethnic, and Old

Part of the unfortunate history of ethnic minority groups in the United States has been the negative stereotypes against members of their groups. Many have also been hampered by their immigrant origins in that they are not fluent or literate in English, might not be aware of the values and norms involved in American social interaction, and might have lifestyles that differ from the mainstream. Often included in these cultural differences is the role of women in the family and in society. Many, but not all, immigrant ethnic groups traditionally have relegated the woman's role to family maintenance. Many important decisions may be made by a woman's husband or parents, and she if often not expected to seek an independent career or enter the workforce except in the case of dire financial need.

Some ethnic minority groups may define an older woman's role as unimportant, especially if she is unable to contribute financially. However, in some ethnic minority groups, an older woman's social status improves. For

example, older African American women can express their own needs and can be given status and power in the community. Despite their positive status in the African American family and the African American culture, African American women over the age of 70 are the poorest population group in the United States. Three of five elderly African American women live alone; most of them are widowed. The low incomes of elderly African American women translate into less than adequate access to health care. Substantially lower incomes for African American elderly women are related to the kinds of jobs they hold, which either are not covered by Social Security or, in the case of domestic service, are not reported even when legally required.

A portrayal of older African American women in cities reveals some of their survival strategies. They highly value the family as a system of mutual support and aid, adhere to the American work ethic, and view religion as a source of strength. The use of religion as a way

of coping with stress has a long history in the African American culture, with roots in the slave experience. The African American church came to fulfill needs and functions once met by religious-based tribal and community organizations that African Americans brought from Africa (McAdoo, 1979). In one investigation, the elderly African American women valued church organizations more than their male counterparts did, especially valuing the church's group activities and organizations (Taylor, 1982).

In sum, African American elderly women have faced a considerable stress in their lives (Edmonds, 1990). In the face of this stress, they have shown remarkable adaptiveness, resilience, responsibility, and coping skills.

A special concern is the stress faced by elderly African American women, many of whom view religion as a source of strength to help them cope with stress.

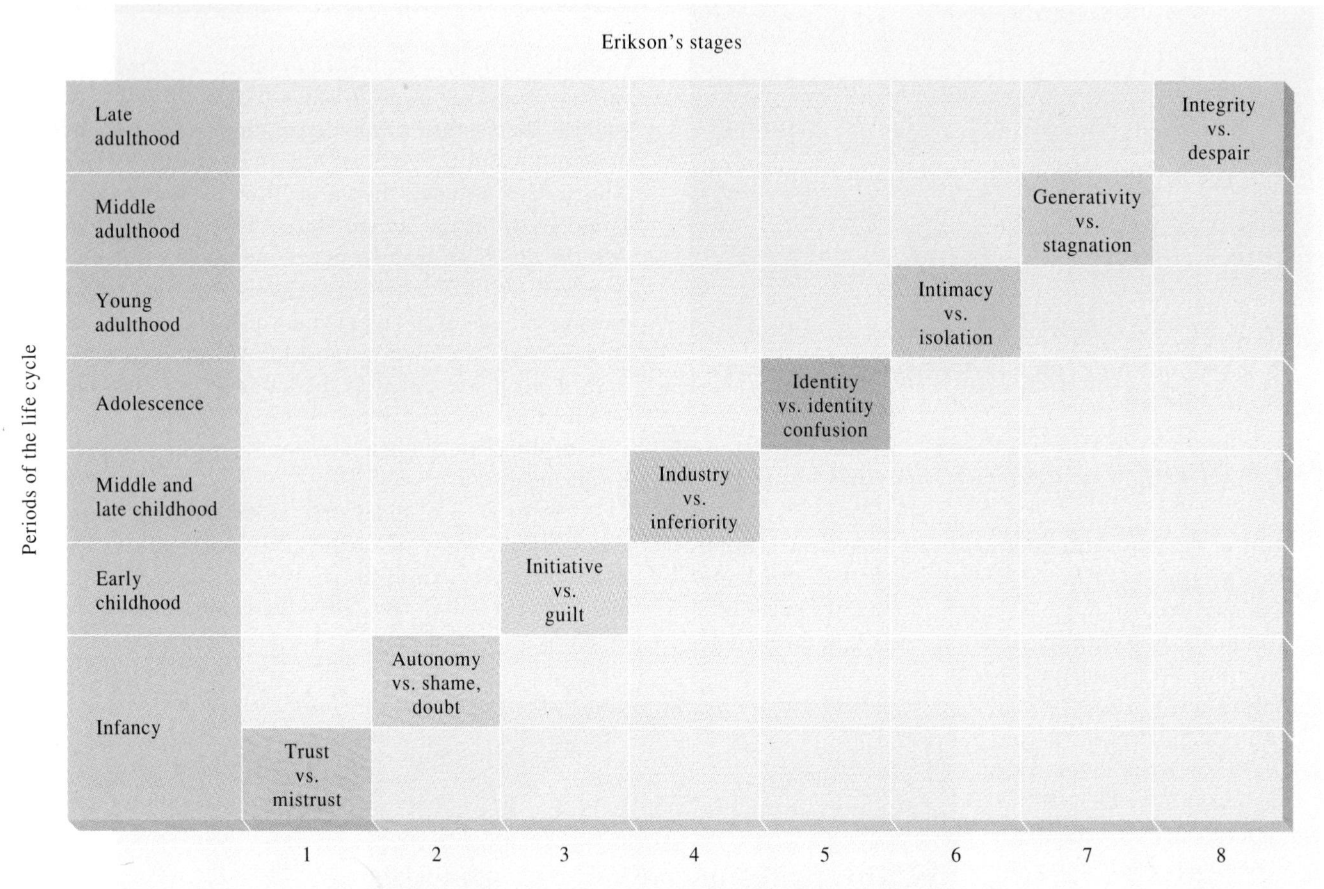

Erikson's stages

Periods of the life cycle	1	2	3	4	5	6	7	8
Late adulthood								Integrity vs. despair
Middle adulthood							Generativity vs. stagnation	
Young adulthood						Intimacy vs. isolation		
Adolescence					Identity vs. identity confusion			
Middle and late childhood				Industry vs. inferiority				
Early childhood			Initiative vs. guilt					
Infancy		Autonomy vs. shame, doubt						
	Trust vs. mistrust							

FIGURE 10.8

Erikson's Eight Stages of the Human Life Span

retrospective glances and reminiscences will reveal a life well spent, and the individual will feel satisfied (integrity). However, if the older adult has a negative outlook on life, the retrospective glances may produce doubt, gloom, and despair about the value of one's life. (For an overview of Erikson's eight stages of development, see figure 10.8.) As Erikson (1968) put it, "To whatever abyss ultimate concerns may lead individual men, man as a psychosocial creature will face, toward the end of his life, a new edition of the identity crisis, which we may state in the words, 'I am what survives me.'"

Successful Aging

The good news about aging is that, barring disease, many of our capabilities decline very slowly. Proper diet, exercise, mental stimulation, and good social relationships and support all play a role in making aging an optimal experience. Throughout our discussion of late adulthood, we have underscored that leading an active rather than passive life will reap physical and psychological benefits. However, successful aging does require effort and coping skills.

Adopting these strategies for successful aging can be especially difficult in late adulthood because of declining strength and energy. Nonetheless, older adults who develop a commitment to an active life and who believe that developing coping skills can produce greater life satisfaction are more likely to age successfully than are older adults who don't make this commitment. Let's explore some specific strategies in more detail.

Exercise and Healthful Practices

John Pianfetti, age 70, and Madge Sharples, age 65, recently completed the New York Marathon. Older adults don't have to run marathons to be healthy and happy; even moderate exercise benefits their health. One investigation over an 11-year period of more than 13,000 men and women at the Aerobics Institute in Dallas, Texas, found that the sedentary participants were more than twice as likely to die during that period than were those who were moderately fit (Blair & Kohl, 1988).

In yet another recent study, cigarette smoking and changes in level of physical activity were associated with risk

Life-Span Development

*Engaging in
a Life Review*

A life review can benefit you when you identify several areas of your life and then write down your perspectives about the past, present, and future prospects of each. Consider the areas listed in the sample life review chart, as well as others that may hold more personal meaning to you. The end result of this process can be a broader view on life that is put together in a meaningful, whole picture (Simons, Kalichman, & Santrock, 1994).

An alternative means of life review would be to take a more chronological approach. For example, a person might construct what could be called a "lifeline." Rather than examine specific aspects of your life one at a time, you could evaluate your life one period or phase at a time. Construct a time line, starting as far back as you like—with your birth, say, or even with where your family came from before your birth. Then, looking at your infancy, childhood, adolescence, and adulthood, list all of the major events of your life and where they brought you. The result would again be a clearer depiction of your life that could have all of the benefits discussed above.

Other strategies you can follow include discussing your life with elder family members, constructing a family tree, and keeping an extensive diary. Regardless of the exact method you use, engaging in a personal life review illustrates *applying psychological concepts to enhance personal adaptation.*

Example of a Life Review Chart			
	Past	**Present**	**Future**
Family			
Friends			
Education			
Career			
Travel			
Financial security			
Religious/spiritual			

of death during the middle and late adulthood years (Paffenbarger & others, 1993). Beginning moderate vigorous sports activity from the forties through the eighties was associated with a 23 percent lower risk of death; quitting cigarette smoking was associated with a 41 percent lower death risk. Gerontologists are increasingly recommending strength training, in addition to stretching, for older adults (Butler, 1993).

Jogging hogs have even shown the dramatic effects of exercise on health. Colin Bloor and Frank White (1983) trained a group of hogs to run approximately 100 miles per week. Then they narrowed the arteries that supplied blood to the hogs' hearts. The hearts of these jogging hogs developed extensive alternate pathways for the blood supply, and the researchers salvaged 42 percent of the threatened heart tissue, compared to only 17 percent in a control group of hogs (see figure 10.9).

Exercise is an excellent way to maintain health in late adulthood and possibly increase our longevity. However, coping strategies will also enhance our satisfaction in living longer.

Coping Strategies

Life-span developmentalist Paul Baltes and his colleagues (Baltes & Baltes, 1990; Marsisker & others, 1995) believe that successful aging is related to three main factors: selection, optimization, and compensation. *Selection* is based on the concept that in old age there is a reduced capacity and loss of functioning, which mandates a reduction of performance in most domains of life. *Optimization* suggests that it is possible to maintain performance in some areas by practice and the use of new technologies. *Compensation* becomes relevant when life tasks require a level of capacity

FIGURE 10.9

The Experimental Setup in Bloor and White's Study of Exercise and Health

Hogs, such as the one shown here, were trained to run approximately 100 miles per week. Then the experimenters narrowed the arteries that supplied blood to the hogs' hearts. The jogging hogs' hearts developed alternative pathways for the blood supply, whereas a group of nonjogging hogs were less likely to recover.

beyond the current level of the older adult's performance potential. Older adults especially need to compensate in circumstances with high mental or physical demands, such as when thinking about and memorizing new material, reacting quickly when driving a car, or when running fast. Illness in old age makes the need for compensation obvious.

Consider the late Arthur Rubinstein, who was interviewed when he was 80 years old. Rubinstein said that three factors were responsible for his ability to maintain his status as an admired concert pianist into old age. First, he mastered the weaknesses of old age by reducing the scope of his repertoire and playing fewer pieces (an example of selection). Second, he spent more time at practice than earlier in his life (an example of optimization). And third, he used special strategies such as slowing down before fast segments, thus creating the image of faster playing than was objectively true (an example of compensation) (Baltes, Smith, & Staudinger, in press).

There is an increasing interest in the roles of selective optimization with compensation as a model for successful aging (Carstensen, Hanson, & Feund, 1995; Dixon & Backman, 1995). The process of selective optimization with compensation is likely to be effective whenever loss is an important component of a person's life. Loss is a common dimension of old age, although there are wide variations in the nature of the losses involved. Thus, while all aging persons are likely to engage in some form of selection, optimization, and compensation, the specific form of adaptation will vary depending on each individual's life history, pattern of interests, values, health, skills, and resources (Abraham & Hansson, 1995).

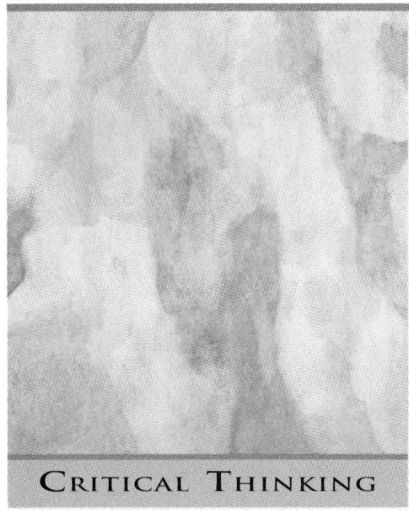

CRITICAL THINKING

Older Adults in Shopping Malls

Shopping malls serve as community centers for urban cities in the United States. Many adults in the later stages of their lives tend to gather in malls to participate in the hectic atmosphere, to keep themselves stimulated, or simply to exercise in the broad walkways provided in the malls. For this exercise, go to a mall and watch the activity levels of ten "senior citizens." By *observing their behavior and making accurate inferences about their behavior,* you should be able to

- speculate about the variation in energy levels observed,
- note any gender differences that seem systematic in the population,
- examine any systematic differences that might be attributed to ethnicity or religious tradition,
- record any obvious physical impairments associated with aging,
- identify any compensating strategies, and
- observe what kind of treatment older adults get from younger mall citizens.

Were there other interesting dimensions of behavior that you discovered through observation and inference?

DEATH AND DYING

"I'd like to know what this show is all about before it's out," wrote the twentieth-century Dutch poet and inventor Piet Hein. Death may come at any time, but it is during late adulthood that we realize that our days are literally numbered. This concluding section of the chapter addresses cultural variations in response to death, Kübler-Ross's theory that describes typical Western responses to death, and the challenges of surviving a life partner.

Cultural Perspectives

Societies throughout history have had philosophical or religious beliefs about death, and most have rituals to mark the passing from life to death. Some cultures hold a ceremonial meal accompanied by festivities. In others, mourners wear a black arm band. The variations in ways of celebrating and mourning death show the importance of cultural context in understanding grief. Figure 10.10 shows rituals that deal with death.

In most cultures, death is not viewed as the end of existence—although the biological body dies, the spirit lives on. This belief is held by many Americans. Reincarnation, the belief that the soul is reborn in a new human body, is an important aspect of Hindu and Buddhist religions. Cultures often differ in their perception of and reaction to death. In the Gond culture of India, death is believed to be caused by magic and demons; Gonds react to death with anger. In the Tanala culture of Madagascar, death is thought to be caused by natural forces. The members of the Tanala culture react peacefully to death. This reaction contrasts distinctly with the intense reactions described by Elisabeth Kübler-Ross, which we explore in the next section.

Reactions to Dying

Elisabeth Kübler-Ross (1974) says that we go through five stages in facing death: denial and isolation, anger, bargaining, depression, and acceptance. Initially a dying individual responds, "No, it can't be me. It's not possible." However, denial is only a temporary defense. When the individual recognizes that denial can no longer be maintained, she often becomes angry and resentful; the individual's question becomes, "Why me?" Anger often is displaced onto physicians, nurses, family members, and even God. In the third stage, the dying person develops the hope that death can somehow be postponed or delayed. The individual says, "Yes, me, but . . ." The dying person bargains and negotiates, often with God, offering a reformed life dedicated to God and the service of others for a few more months of life.

As a dying individual comes to accept the certainty of her death, she often enters a period of preparatory grief, becoming silent, refusing visitors, and spending much of the time crying or grieving. This behavior is a normal effort to disconnect the self from all love objects. Kübler-Ross describes the final stage, characterized by peace and acceptance of one's fate, as the end of the struggle, the final resting stage before death. Not everyone goes through the stages in the

FIGURE 10.10

Cultural Variations in Death
(a) A New Orleans street funeral is in progress. *(b)* A deceased person's belongings are left on a mountainside in Tibet.

sequence Kübler-Ross proposed. Indeed, Kübler-Ross says she has been misread, pointing out that she never believed every individual copes with death in a specific sequence. She does maintain, however, that the optimal way to cope with death is through the stages she has outlined.

> *Death is simply a shedding of the physical body, like the butterfly coming out of a cocoon. . . . It's like putting away your winter coat when spring comes.*
>
> **Elisabeth Kübler-Ross**

Some individuals struggle until the very end, angrily hanging onto their lives. They follow the encouragement of Dylan Thomas: "Do not go gentle into that good night. Old age should burn and rave at close of day. . . . rage, rage against the dying of the light." In these instances, acceptance of death never comes. People die in different ways and experience different feelings and emotions in the process: hope, fear, curiosity, envy, apathy, relief, even anticipation. They often move rapidly from one mood to another and, in some instances, two moods may be present simultaneously.

Man is the only animal that finds his own existence a problem he has to solve and from which he cannot escape. In the same sense man is the only animal who knows he must die.

Erich Fromm

Losing a Life Partner

Those left behind after the death of an intimate partner suffer profound grief and often endure financial loss, loneliness, increased physical illness, and psychological disorders, including depression. How they cope with the crisis varies considerably. Widows outnumber widowers by the ratio of 5 to 1, because women live longer than men, because women tend to marry men older than themselves, and because a widowed man is more likely to remarry. Widowed women are probably the poorest group in America, despite the myth of huge insurance settlements. Many are also lonely. The poorer and less educated they are, the lonelier they tend to be. The bereaved are also at increased risk for many health problems, including death (Fredman, Daly, & Lazur, 1995).

Optimal adjustment after a death depends on several factors. Women do better than men largely because, in our society, women are responsible for the emotional life of a couple, whereas men usually manage the finances and material goods. Thus, women have better networks of friends, closer relationships with relatives, and experience in taking care of themselves psychologically. Older widows do better than younger widows, perhaps because the death of a partner is more expected for older women. For their part, widowers usually have more money than widows do, and they are much more likely to remarry (DiGiulio, 1989).

For either widows or widowers, social support helps them adjust to the death of a spouse (Hughes, 1995; Kastenbaum, 1995). Such programs as Widow-to-Widow, begun in the 1960s, provide support for newly widowed people. Its objective is to prevent the potentially negative effects of the loss. Volunteer widows reach out to other widows, introducing them to others who may have similar problems, leading group discussions, and organizing social activities. The program has been adopted by the American Association of Retired Persons and disseminated throughout the United States as the Widowed Person's Service. The model has since been adopted by numerous community organizations to provide support for those going through a difficult life transition that will confront the vast majority of us.

By now you can appreciate that much development takes place in adolescence and adulthood, just as in infancy and childhood. In Section Five, you will read about the nature of gender roles and sexuality, a discussion that includes information about how our gender roles develop and issues of sexuality at various points in the life cycle.

REVIEW

Late Adulthood and Death and Dying

Everything we know about older adults suggests that, the more physically active they are, the healthier and happier they are, and they live longer. Life expectancy has increased dramatically, but the life span has remained virtually stable for centuries. Longevity is influenced by such factors as heredity, family, health, education, personality, and lifestyle. Virtually all biological theories of aging assign an important role to genes. Based on the rate at which cells divide, biologists place the upper limit on the human life cycle at 115 to 120 years. As we grow old, our chances of becoming seriously ill increase. Alzheimer's disease is a degenerative brain disorder that impairs memory and social behavior.

Whether or not intelligence actually declines in late adulthood is unclear. Remember that we have many forms of intelligence and the overall question of intellectual decline is a global one. As we age, some of our mental skills slow down, but wisdom often increases.

Everything we know about late adulthood suggests that an active older life is preferred to disengagement. Special concerns are ageism and the ethnic minority elderly. Cross-cultural comparisons reveal greater respect for the elderly in some cultures, such as Japan, than in the United States. Erikson believes that the final issue in the life cycle is integrity versus despair, which involves a life review.

Successful aging occurs when older adults follow a proper diet, exercise, seek mental stimulation, and have good social relationships and support. Successful aging requires effort and coping skills. There is increasing interest in a model of successful aging that involves selective optimization with compensation. This model involves the three factors of selection, optimization, and compensation. It is especially applicable when loss is present.

Death may come at any point in the life cycle but in late adulthood we know it is near. Most societies have rituals that deal with death, although cultures vary in their orientation toward it. Kübler-Ross proposed five stages of coping with death. A special concern is the coping skills of widows and widowers.

It is a good thing that we don't regularly have to face decisions as difficult as Heinz's about whether or not to steal a drug to save his wife's life. However, decisions about right and wrong regularly confront us on a much smaller scale. Examine the everyday moral dilemmas described below, decide on your likely course of action, and think about the reasons why you would act in that manner.

- Do you tell the waitress who has charged you an insufficient amount about her error, or do you pocket the difference?
- Do you comment to Don that his new hairstyle which you find unflattering, is "different" or "awful"?
- Have you ever found your eyes wandering to your neighbor's test paper to compare your answer, when the teacher is out of the room?
- At tax time are you scrupulous about reporting to the Internal Revenue Service every earned penny, or do you look for opportunities to misrepresent your income?
- Do you invite people to parties because you wish to be in their company or do you sometimes ask people you don't like because you might lose some social status?
- When you sell a car, do you identify every aspect of the car that will need repair?

Kohlberg was less interested in establishing moral absolutes in relation to the dilemmas he created than he was in the justifications or reasons that his interviewees provided to justify their actions. As you examine your responses to the small moral dilemmas described above, do any patterns emerge in your answers? Would you have been scrupulously honest in those circumstances? Or would you have acted according to self-protection or personal gain? Was there any variation in your responses?

Let's examine just one moral dilemma from Kohlberg's point of view to sort out the levels of moral reasoning that apply to the situation. This exercise will encourage *the practice of ethical treatment toward individuals and groups.* Suppose we examine the moral challenge of properly paying income taxes. Are you ever tempted to cheat or do you consistently pay what the government says you owe? What is your justification?

You could pay your taxes out of fear of getting caught, or you could decide to take some inappropriate write-offs because you'd be willing to pay the penalty if you get caught. Both of these answers reflect a *preconventional* level of reasoning because a concern with the rewards and punishments is at the heart of your decision. At the *conventional* level, you might pay your taxes because everyone else does. You would not like to risk the disapproval of other good citizens. On the other hand, you might decide to misrepresent your tax debt, justifying your actions with your belief that most taxpayers engage in the same sort of tactics. You might even believe that you would lose others' approval by paying your appropriate amount. Finally, *postconventional* reasoning can also be present in justifying either course of action. You might choose fair payment because you believe democratic governments need to be well funded to function well and serve the citizenry effectively. You might even be proud to pay your fair share. On the other hand, the postconventional reasoner might justify nonpayment as withholding support from government activities that aren't humane. As you can see, the specific decision does not dictate whether an act is evaluated as moral or immoral. The complexity of the justification is what determines the level of reasoning, according to Kohlberg.

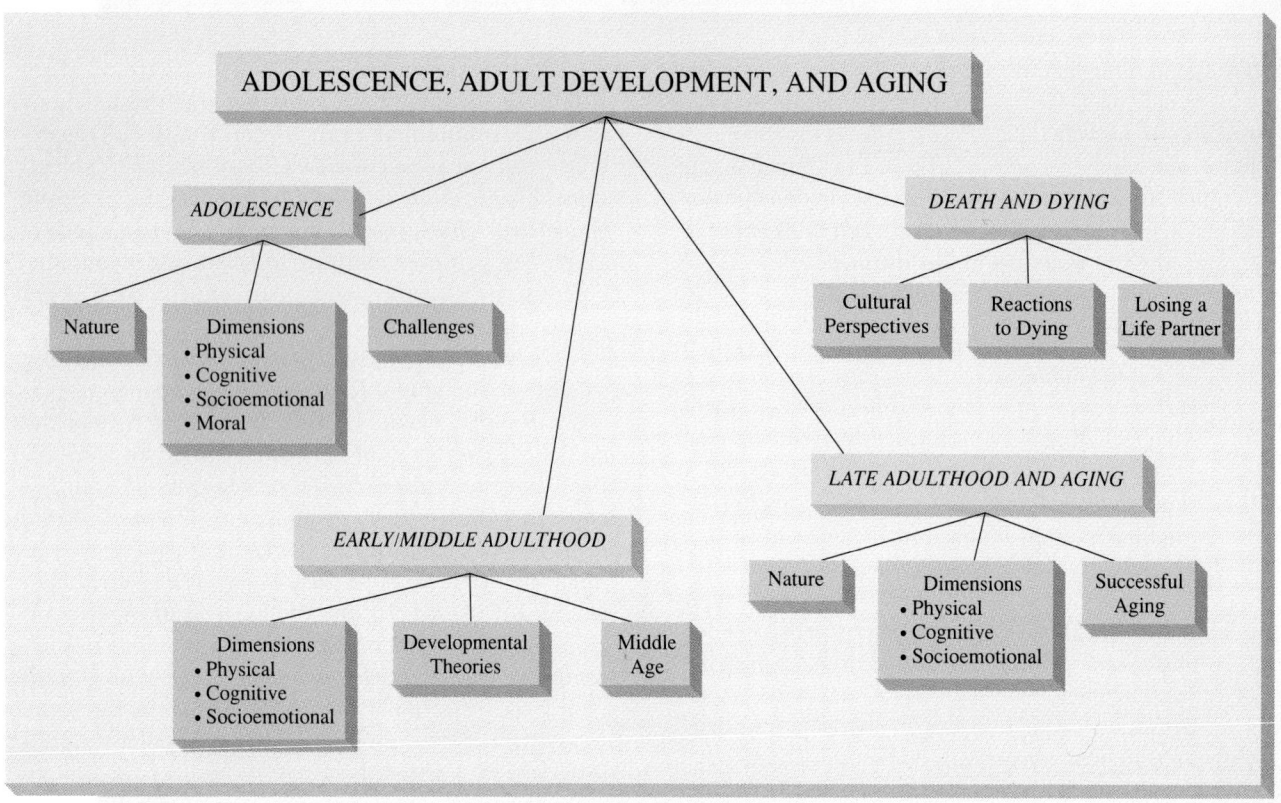

ADOLESCENCE, ADULT DEVELOPMENT, AND AGING

ADOLESCENCE

Nature

Dimensions
• Physical
• Cognitive
• Socioemotional
• Moral

Challenges

DEATH AND DYING

Cultural Perspectives

Reactions to Dying

Losing a Life Partner

EARLY/MIDDLE ADULTHOOD

Dimensions
• Physical
• Cognitive
• Socioemotional

Developmental Theories

Middle Age

LATE ADULTHOOD AND AGING

Nature

Dimensions
• Physical
• Cognitive
• Socioemotional

Successful Aging

I n this chapter we learned that development continues throughout the human life span. We began the chapter by studying adolescence—its nature, dimensions (physical, cognitive, socioemotional, and moral), and challenges. Then we explored development in early and middle adulthood by examining the physical, cognitive, and socioemotional dimensions of development, developmental theories (Erikson's, Levinson's life events, and the social clock theory). Then we continued our journey through development by studying late adulthood and aging—their nature, their dimensions, and successful aging. The chapter concluded with discussion of death and dying—cultural perspectives, Kübler-Ross's theory, and losing a life partner. Don't forget that you can obtain an overall summary of the chapter by again reading the in-chapter reviews on pages 340, 349, 361, and 372.

Three main perspectives were emphasized in this chapter: neurobiological, cognitive, and sociocultural. The neurobiological perspective was reflected in the exploration of puberty and physical development in adolescence (pp. 336–338), as well as physical development in early adulthood (pp. 336–338), middle adulthood (pp. 351–352), and late adulthood and aging (pp. 362–364). Coverage of the cognitive perspectives appeared in the material on adolescence, including moral development (pp. 344–347), as well as early adulthood (p. 351), middle adulthood (p. 351), and late adulthood (p. 365). The sociocultural perspective was present in the discussion of socioemotional development in adolescence (pp. 335–349), as well as socioemotional development in early adulthood (pp. 351–361), middle adulthood (pp. 351–361), and late adulthood (pp. 365–368). The sociocultural perspective also was described in the section on death and dying (pp. 371–372).

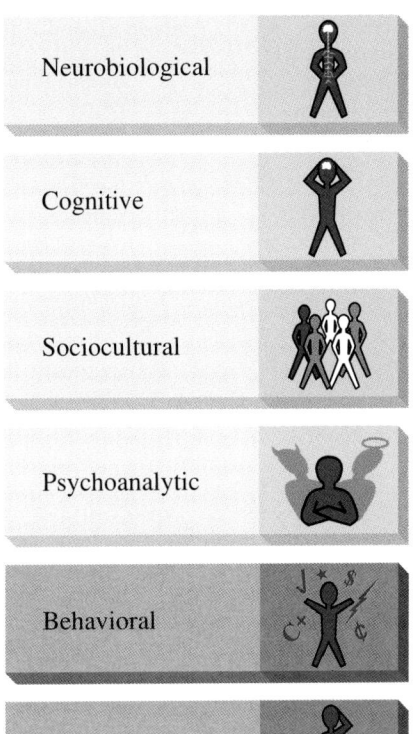

Neurobiological

Cognitive

Sociocultural

Psychoanalytic

Behavioral

Humanistic

adolescence The transition from childhood to adulthood, which involves physical, cognitive, and socioemotional changes. In most cultures adolescence begins at about 10 to 13 years of age and ends at about 18 to 21 years of age. 335

storm-and-stress view G. Stanley Hall's view that adolescence is a turbulent time charged with conflict and mood swings. 335

puberty A period of rapid skeletal and sexual maturation that occurs in early adolescence. 337

testosterone A hormone associated, in boys, with the development of genitals, an increase in height, and a change of voice. 337

estradiol A hormone associated, in girls, with breast, uterine, and skeletal development. 337

formal operational thought Piaget's fourth stage of cognitive development, which appears between 11 and 15 years of age. Formal operational thought is abstract, idealistic, and logical. 338

hypothetical-deductive reasoning Piaget's name for adolescents' cognitive ability to develop hypotheses, or best guesses, about how to solve problems, such as algebraic equations. 338

adolescent egocentrism The adolescent's belief that others are as preoccupied with the adolescent as she herself is, the belief that one is unique, and the belief that one is indestructible. 338

rites of passage A ceremony or ritual that marks an individual's transition from one status to another. 342

identity versus identity confusion The fifth of Erikson's stages of human development, occurring primarily during the adolescent years. The development of identity involves finding out who we are, what we are all about, and where we are going in life. 343

internalization The developmental change from behavior that is externally controlled to behavior that is controlled by internal, self-generated standards and principles. 345

preconventional level Kohlberg's lowest level of moral thinking, in which an individual shows no internalization of moral values—moral thinking is based on expectations of punishments (stage 1) or rewards (stage 2) that come from the external world. 345

conventional level Kohlberg's second level of moral thinking, in which an individual shows an intermediate level of internalization. The individual abides by certain standards (internal), but they are the standards of others (external), such as parents' standards (stage 3) or society's laws (stage 4). 346

postconventional level Kohlberg's highest level of moral thinking; moral development is completely internalized and not based on others' standards. An individual recognizes alternative moral courses, explores the options, and then develops a personal moral code. The code is among the principles generally accepted by the community (stage 5) or it is more individualized (stage 6). 346

justice perspective A theory of moral development that focuses on the rights of the individual; individuals independently make moral decisions. Kohlberg's theory is a justice perspective. 346

care perspective Carol Gilligan's theory of moral development, which sees people in terms of their connectedness with others and focuses on interpersonal communication, relationships with others, and concern for others. 346

early adulthood A developmental period that begins in the late teens or early twenties and ends in the late thirties to early forties. It is a time when individuals establish personal and economic independence, intensely pursue a career, and seek intimacy with one or more individuals. 351

middle adulthood A developmental period that begins at about 35 to 45 years of age and ends at about 55 to 65 years of age. It is a time of expanding personal and social involvement, increased responsibility, adjustment to physical decline, and career satisfaction. 351

menopause The time in middle age, usually in the late forties or early fifties, when a woman's menstrual periods cease completely. 351

intimacy versus isolation Erikson's sixth stage of development, occurring mainly in early adulthood. Intimacy is the ability to develop close, loving relationships. 356

generativity versus stagnation Erikson's seventh stage of development, occurring mainly in middle adulthood. Middle-aged adults need to assist the younger generation in leading useful lives. 356

late adulthood A developmental period that begins around 60 to 70 years of age and ends when the individual dies. It is a time of adjustment to decreased strength and health, retirement, reduced income, new social roles, and learning how to age successfully. 361

Alzheimer's disease A degenerative, irreversible brain disorder that impairs memory and social behavior. 363

activity theory The theory that the more active and involved older people are, the more satisfied they will be with their lives and the more likely it is that they will stay healthy. 365

ageism Prejudice against people based on their age. 365

integrity versus despair Erikson's eighth and final stage of human development, which occurs mainly in late adulthood; it is a time of looking back at what we have done with our lives. 366

PRACTICAL KNOWLEDGE ABOUT PSYCHOLOGY

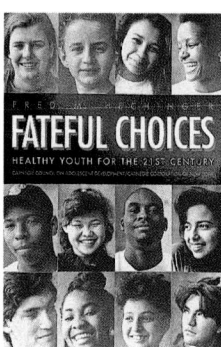

FATEFUL CHOICES

(1992) by Fred Hechinger. New York: Hill & Wang.

This excellent book is based on the findings of the Carnegie Council on Adolescent Development and clearly sounds one of the council's main themes: linking health and education in adolescent development. The author's valuable recommendations can improve the health and well-being of all adolescents, especially those at risk for problems. Various chapters focus on adolescents at risk, adolescent pregnancy, drug abuse, nutrition and exercise, and youth organizations.

YOU AND YOUR ADOLESCENT

(1990) by Laurence Steinberg and Ann Levine. New York: Harper Perennial.

You and Your Adolescent provides a broad, developmental overview of adolescence, with parental advice mixed in along the way. Author Laurence Steinberg is a professor of psychology at Temple University and a highly respected researcher in adolescent development. The book is divided into the preteens (ages 10 to 13), the teens (ages 11 to 17), and toward adulthood (ages 18 to 20). In the approach presented here, knowing how adolescents develop keeps parents from making a lot of mistakes. This is an excellent book for parents of adolescents. It serves the dual purpose of educating parents about adolescent development and giving them valuable parenting strategies for coping with teenagers.

THE ROAD LESS TRAVELED

(1978) by M. Scott Peck. New York: Simon & Schuster.

The Road Less Traveled presents an approach to self-fulfillment based on spirituality and emotion. Peck begins by stating that life is difficult and that we all suffer pain and disappointment. He believes we should face up to life's difficulties and not be lazy. Indeed, Peck equates laziness with the original sin, going on to say that people's tendency to avoid problems and emotional suffering is the root of mental disorders. Peck also believes that people are thirsting for integrity in their lives. They are not happy with a country that has "In God we trust" as one of its main emblems and at the same time still leads the world's arms race. They also can't tolerate being just Sunday-morning Christians, he says. To achieve integrity, Peck believes, people need to move spirituality into all phases of their lives.

Peck speaks of four important tools to use in life's journey: delaying gratification, accepting responsibility, dedication to the truth, and balancing. After a thorough analysis of each, Peck explores the will to use them, which he calls love. Then he probes further and analyzes the relation between growth and religion, which leads him to examine the final step of "the road less traveled": grace. By grace, Peck means the whole range of human activities that support the human spirit. Grace operates at the interface between persons and God and at the frontier between unconscious and conscious thought, in Peck's view.

The Road Less Traveled has been an immensely popular book, on the *New York Times* best-sellers list for more than a year. Peck has developed a cultlike following, especially among young people. The book's enthusiasts say that Peck recognized some important voids in people's lives, especially the need for an integrated, spiritually based existence. Some critics say that Peck's ideas are not new and that his thoughts are occasionally fuzzy, especially when he arrives at the meeting point between God and persons, and unconscious and conscious selves.

WHAT COLOR IS YOUR PARACHUTE?

(1995) by Richard Bolles. Berkeley, CA: Ten Speed Press.

What Color Is Your Parachute? is an extremely popular book on job hunting. Author Richard Bolles is an Episcopal priest who changed from pastoral counseling to career counseling. *What Color Is Your Parachute?* was first published in 1970. Since 1975, an annual edition has appeared. This book has become the career seeker's bible. Bolles tries to answer concerns about the job-hunting process and refers readers to many sources that provide valuable information. Unlike many self-help books on job hunting, *What Color Is Your Parachute?* does not necessarily assume that you are a recent college graduate seeking your first job. He also spends considerable time discussing job hunting for people who seek to change careers. Bolles describes many myths about job hunting and successfully combats them. He also provides invaluable advice about where jobs are, what to do to get yourself hired, and how to cut through all of the red tape and confusing hierarchies of the business world to meet with the key people who are the most likely to make the decision about whether to hire you or not. The book has remained appreciably the same over the years with updates where appropriate. More recent editions have added material on job hunting for handicapped workers, how to effectively use career counselors to your benefit, and how to find a mission in life.

What Color Is Your Parachute? was one of the top 25 self-help books in a recent national survey of clinical and counseling psychologists. This is an excellent self-help book on job hunting and career change. Bolles writes in a warm, engaging, and personal tone. His chatty comments are often entertaining, and the book is attractively packaged with cartoons, drawings, and many self-administered exercises. One of Bolles's gifts is to convince you that job hunting does not have to be a dull, arduous, overwhelming task.

MAN'S SEARCH FOR MEANING

(1984) by Viktor Frankl. New York: Pocket.

Man's Search for Meaning presents an existentialist approach to the pursuit of self-fulfillment. The word *existentialist* refers to attempts to explain human beings' existence and an emphasis on each person's uniqueness, freedom of choice, and responsibility. After Victor Frankl survived the German concentration camp at Auschwitz, he founded a school of psychotherapy known as logotherapy, which maintains that the desire to find a meaning in life is the primary human motive. Frankl's mother, father, brother, and wife died in the concentration camps or gas chambers. Frankl emphasizes each person's uniqueness and finiteness of life. He thinks that examining the finiteness of your existence and certainty of your death adds meaning to the remaining days of your life. If life were not finite, says Frankl, you could spend your time doing just about whatever you please because time would last forever for you.

HOW TO SURVIVE THE LOSS OF A LOVE

(1991) by Melba Colgrove, Harold Bloomfield, and Peter McWilliams. Los Angeles, CA: Prelude Press.

This book provides messages about how to cope with the loss of a loved one. The authors address loss through death as well as other types of loss, such as divorce, rape, loss of long-term goals, and loss through aging. The presentation is unusual. Poetry, common sense, and psychologically based advice are interwoven throughout the more than one hundred briefly discussed topics. Understanding loss, surviving, healing, and growing are overriding themes. The chapter headings include:

- It's Okay to Feel
- Tomorrow Will Come
- Seek the Comfort of Others
- Touching and Hugging
- Do the Mourning Now
- When You Might Want Counseling or Therapy
- Nutrition
- Pray
- Meditate
- Contemplate
- Keep a Journal
- Your Happiness Is Up to You

RESOURCES FOR PSYCHOLOGY AND IMPROVING HUMANKIND

American Association for Adult and Continuing Education

    1112 Sixteenth Street NW, Suite 140
    Washington, DC 20036
    202–463–6333

This organization provides information about and support for continuing education for adults and education as a life-long pursuit.

American Association of Retired Persons Womens Initiative Network

    1909 K Street NW
    Washington, DC 20049
    202–434–2642

Advocates and supports policies, programs, and legislation that improve the status of midlife and older women. Publishes a newsletter, *AARP WIN.*

Boys Town

    Father Flanagan's Boys' Home
    Boys Town, NE 68010
    800–448–3000

Boys Town has been a resource for abused and neglected boys and girls since 1917. Information about residential homes, hospital care, shelters, family crisis intervention, alternative education, foster care services, and parenting training is available. The hot-line number listed above is available free to any parent or adolescent in the United States. Adolescents and parents can call with any problem or serious concern, including physical and sexual abuse, drug abuse, parenting problems, suicide, running away, school problems, and so on. The hot line is staffed by highly trained professionals and includes Spanish-speaking operators. The hot line has a computer database of 50,000 local agencies and services around the country.

The Carnegie Council on Adolescent Development

2400 N Street NW
Washington, DC 20037
202–429–7979

The Carnegie Council on Adolescent Development, headed by David Hamburg, is an operating program of the Carnegie Foundation of New York. Its goal is to improve the health and well-being of adolescents. The council has generated a number of task forces to improve education, reduce adolescent pregnancy, and reduce alcohol and drug use among adolescents.

Center for Early Adolescence

University of North Carolina
D-2 Carr Mill Town Center
Carrboro, NC 27510
919–966–1148

The Center for Early Adolescence was founded in 1978 to promote healthy growth and development of young adolescents. The center provides information services, research training, and leadership development for people who can have an impact on 10- to 15-year-olds. The center can be contacted for information services, research knowledge, training/leadership development, and consultation. A number of excellent brochures and books on a wide range of early adolescent topics are available, including school improvement, adolescent literacy, parent education, program planning, adolescent health, and resource lists.

Foster Grandparent Program

ACTION, The National Volunteer Association
Washington, DC
202–634–9108

This program matches older Americans with special-needs children. Older adult volunteers work in many different settings, ranging from Head Start programs to foster care homes. ACTION also runs the Senior Companion Program, which matches older adults with frail elderly persons. A special goal of this program is to help the homebound elderly gain the confidence needed for independent living.

Grandparents Request Access and Dignity Society

670 Albert St. Rm. 225
Ottawa ON K1R 6L2 CANADA
613–234–7263

A support/action group that helps grandparents to access to their grandchildren.

National Advisory Council on Aging/Conseil consultatif national sur la troisieme age

473 Albert St. 3rd floor
Ottawa, ON K1A OK9 CANADA
613–957–1968

The council advises the government and informs the public on issues that affect Canada's aging population and recommends remedial action.

The National Council on Aging

1331 F Street NW
Washington, DC 20005
202–347–8800

This organization is dedicated to increasing the well-being of older Americans. The council publishes a number of materials about aging and services available to older Americans.

Starserve

701 Santa Monica Boulevard, Suite 220
Santa Monica, CA 90401
800–888–8232

This organization has sent a kit of materials to every school in the United States to encourage teachers to motivate students to become involved in community service. For further information, call the toll-free number listed above.

Youth Information Services (1987)

By Marda Woodbury
New York: Greenwood Press

This book is an annotated guide for parents, professionals, students, researchers, and concerned citizens. It is intended to provide useful resources for anyone working with adolescents and lists a wide array of information resources. Especially beneficial are the chapters on directories and on youth-related clearinghouses and organizations. Many libraries have this book in their reference collection.

ANSWERS TO THE MARRIAGE QUIZ

1.	False	6.	True	11.	False
2.	True	7.	False	12.	True
3.	False	8.	False	13.	False
4.	False	9.	False	14.	False
5.	True	10.	False	15.	False

Gender and Sexuality

We are born twice over; the first time for existence, the second time for life; Once as human beings and later as men or as women.

Jean-Jacques Rousseau

As female and male, human beings are involved in the enterprise and continuation of human life. As female and male, we are different, yet similar, sometimes each other's best friend, sometimes each other's worst enemy. Psychologists are increasingly recognizing that gender and sexuality are important aspects of behavior. Section Five contains two chapters: "Gender" (chapter 11) and "Human Sexuality" (chapter 12).

KLIMIT
The Kiss, detail

Gender

> We are all androgynous,
> not only because we are all born of a
> woman impregnated by the seed
> of a man but because each of us,
> helplessly and forever, contains
> the other—male in female, female in
> male, white in black and black in
> white. We are a part
> of each other.
>
> **James Baldwin**

THE STORY OF TITA DE LA GARZA: BOUND BY TRADITION

In her novel *Like Water for Chocolate*, Laura Esquivel shows us the scene of young Tita steeling herself before her mother, Mama Elena. Tita had told her mother that Pedro Muzquiz intended to come and speak with her, and her mother responded vigorously:

> "If he intends to ask for your hand, tell him not to bother. He'll be wasting his time and mine, too. You know perfectly well that being the youngest daughter means you have to take care of me until the day I die."
>
> "But in my opinion . . ."
>
> "You don't have an opinion, and that's all I want to hear about it. For generations, not a single person in my family has ever questioned this tradition, and no daughter of mine is going to be the one to start."

Tita lowered her head, and the realization of her fate struck her as forcibly as her tears struck the table. . . . Still Tita did not submit. Doubts and anxieties sprang to her mind. For one thing, she wanted to know who started this family tradition. It would be nice if she could let that genius know about one little flaw in this perfect plan for taking care of women in their old age. If Tita couldn't marry and have children, who would take care of her when she got old? . . . Or are daughters who stay home and take care of their mothers not expected to survive too long after the parent's death? And what about women who marry and can't have children, who will take care of them? And besides, she'd like to know what kind of studies had established that the youngest daughter and not the eldest is best suited to care for their mother. Had the opinion of the daughter affected by the plan ever been taken into account? If she couldn't marry, was she at least allowed to experience love? Or not even that? Tita knew perfectly well that all these questions would have to be buried forever in the archive of questions that have no answers.

PREVIEW

Laura Esquivel's charming tale about Tita in *Like Water for Chocolate* reveals how culture can be a context in which gender and destiny are intertwined. In well-born Mexican families, the youngest daughter was expected to become the careprovider for her aging parents. Tita's reflections and questions reveal a great deal about the role of gender in human development. In some cultures, privilege, responsibility, sacrifice, and restriction are clearly delineated along gender lines; in other cultures, they are less so. In this chapter we will explore the following topics: Defining gender, gender comparisons, gender identity, and sociocultural variations.

DEFINING GENDER

Gender *refers to the sociocultural dimension of being female or male.* In her 1993 Senate confirmation hearings for the position of Supreme Court Justice, Ruth Bader Ginsberg distinguished gender as *related to* but *distinct from* sex. She suggested that the term *sex* can be a distraction because it pertains more specifically to biological matters. Use of the term *gender* maintains the focus on the social constructions that distinguish women and men. Her own path through Harvard Law School provided many examples of sex discrimination that fueled her interest in gender differences. Ultimately, her expertise in equal opportunity influenced her successful appointment as the second woman Supreme Court Justice (Thomas, 1993).

Ruth Bader Ginsberg's appointment as the second female Supreme Court Justice was a personal triumph for her. She experienced discrimination throughout law school and in her legal career, based on her being "a female, a mother, and a Jew." This spurred her to develop her expertise in equal-opportunity law, which in turn was an influential factor in her appointment.

See It Go

"Look," said Dick.

"See it go.

See it go up."

Jane said, "Oh, look!

See it go.

See it go up."

"Up, up," said Sally.

"Go up, up, up."

Some social critics have identified subtle sexist influences in unusual places. This example from the *Fun with Dick and Jane* readers illustrates boys as active in the environment and girls as passive onlookers. Many contemporary readers strive not to perpetuate these stereotypes.

Following are two terms that we will use throughout this chapter. **Gender roles** *are sets of expectations that prescribe how females and males should think, act, and feel.* We will explore how gender roles have been changing in the United States. **Gender identity** *is the sense of being male or female, a part of the self-concept that most children begin to acquire by the age of 2 or 3 years.* Several theories based on different psychological perspectives have been proposed to explain the process of the development of gender identity.

The Changing American Landscape

Until not too long ago, it was accepted that boys should grow up to be masculine and that girls should grow up to be feminine; boys were said to be made of "frogs and snails and puppy dogs' tails," and girls of "sugar and spice and everything nice." In children's literature, boys were depicted as active and exploring, girls as passive admirers. The well-adjusted adult male was expected to be independent, aggressive, and power-oriented. The well-adjusted adult female was expected to be dependent, nurturant, and uninterested in power. Further, masculine characteristics were considered to be healthy and good by society; female characteristics were deemed undesirable.

These beliefs and stereotypes have led to *sexism,* the negative treatment of females because of their sex. Females receive less attention in schools. They are less visible in leading roles on television and continue to rarely be depicted as competent, dominant characters in children's books. They are paid less than males even when they have more education. They are underrepresented in decision-making roles throughout society, from corporate suites to Congress.

Controversy swirls around the question of what are appropriate roles for today's women and men. Although women have gained greater influence in a variety of professional spheres, many continue to find themselves confronted by invisible ceilings that limit access to many of the most powerful positions. Women electing more-traditional roles sometimes feel criticized by other women for "selling out." Men report confusion about the chronic anger they experience from women. Best-sellers emphasize the differences between women and men, persuading us that there is little likelihood that the genders can reasonably coexist. Social critic Naomi Wolff coined the term *gender-quake* to describe the specific gender-based problems that face individuals in our culture.

Women and men. Men and women. It'll never work.
Erica Jong

As is true in many cultures, well-defined and well-practiced gender roles take the ambiguity out of how women and men relate to each other. However, even where such definitive roles exist, there is likely to be some strain. Anthropologist Florence Kluckhohn (1969) showed that cultures encompass a broad range of experiences, and that very different lives can be lived within one culture. With respect to gender, it is likely that not all members of a culture are content with the gender roles practiced in their culture.

On the other hand, the turmoil currently characterizing gender relations in America offers opportunity to both genders. A girl's mother might promote femininity, the girl might be close friends with a tomboy, and the girl's teachers at school might encourage her assertiveness. Boys might experience fewer restrictions in the goals they set for themselves. For example, Wall Street star Peter Lynch, who headed Fidelity Investment's leading mutual fund, resigned to have more time with his family and to pursue humanitarian projects (Gibbs, 1990). And as you might guess, many individuals in this culture are not pleased with the expanded opportunities for women, because they believe this expansion requires undesirable and unwarranted sacrifices by men.

Many contemporary students say they want it all—good careers, good marriages, and two or three children who are not raised by "strangers" (Spade & Reese, 1991). Idealistic? Perhaps. Some women will reach these goals, but others will have to make other choices as they move through their adult years. Some women will choose to remain single as they pursue their career goals, others will become married but not have children, some will have children and not marry, and others will somehow balance the demands of both family and work. In a word, not all women have the same goals; neither do all men.

The History of Psychological Research on Gender

Many feminist scholars believe that, historically, psychology has portrayed human behavior with a "male-dominant theme" (Denmark & Paludi, 1993; Paludi, 1995). Psychologists believed that research with males could be generalized to explain how women would behave. In addition, conducting males-only research permitted experimenters to avoid issues like the variations in behavior that might be caused by menstruation, so they continued these practices in the name of promoting better control procedures in their research. However, such practices did not encourage the examination of the role of gender in human development.

Many psychologists believe that the lack of research on women was also related to how few women were psychologists. You may recall from chapter 1 that women had a difficult time entering the field of psychology. For example, even though Mary

Calkins completed her doctoral work in psychology at Harvard University, that university refused to grant her a degree because she was a woman. Even so, Calkins was able to embark on a career of remarkable achievements. Among her other accomplishments, she was the first woman to be elected president of the American Psychological Association. She also became the president of the American Philosophical Association.

Another outstanding woman in early psychology, Leta Stetter Hollingworth, is instructive not just for her achievement but for her selection of gender-specific research topics (Miller, 1990). For example, Hollingworth (1914) correlated the quality of task performance with menstruation and found no empirical support for the view that women become incapacitated by the onset of menses, a phenomenon that had been referred to as "functional periodicity."

Another prominent viewpoint about gender early in this century was the "hypothesis of greater male variability." The hypothesis was based on the belief that males had a broader intellectual range than females; they excelled in public, professional activities and were also more often institutionalized for being feebleminded than women were. Strongly influenced by Darwin's theory of evolution, this doctrine proposed that males were superior because their wider variability had greater adaptive value. Hollingworth (1918) dismissed the supposition that there were many sex differences in mental traits and roundly criticized the psychological research community for reaching subjective conclusions about gender differences without appropriate empirical evidence.

Contemporary feminist scholars are putting greater emphasis on women's life experiences and development,

CRITICAL THINKING

Gender Roles and the Future

In the last two decades, considerable change in gender roles has taken place in the United States. How much change have you personally experienced? What changes do you think will occur in gender roles in the twenty-first century? Or do you believe that gender roles will stay about the way they are now? By formulating your position based on research findings, you are *developing psychological arguments based on evidence.* Finally, how would you defend your predictions against those who disagree with them?

including girls and women as authorities about their own experiences, or, as Harvard psychologist Carol Gilligan (1992) advocates, listening to women's voices; on women's ways of knowing (Belenky & others, 1986); on women's career and family roles (Baruch, Biener, & Barnett, 1987); on the abuse of women and rape (McBride, 1990); and women's experiences of connectedness and self-determination (Chodorow, 1978; Lerner, 1989).

As more women made their way into the field of psychology, gender-related issues became a substantial focus of research. Division 35 of the American Psychological Association supports female and male psychologists in their gender-related research interests.

The Feminist Perspective

Feminism emerged as a strong force in psychology as the culmination of several forces. First, feminism is humanistic; it supports minimizing the barriers that prevent individuals from achieving their full potential (Costello & Stone, 1994; Frieze, 1995; Russo, 1995). Second, both the formal research literature and critiques of existing research have underscored the lack of attention to women and to gender issues. Finally, feminist scholars recognize the power of sociocultural factors in creating contexts that define experience—and therefore they continue to be concerned about the degree to which sexism is still rampant in our society and in others worldwide. See Sociocultural Worlds 11.1 for a brief feminist interpretation of the effects of sexism internationally. Jean Baker Miller (1986), a leading feminist scholar wrote in *Toward a New Psychology of Women,*

> In the last decade it has become clearer that if women are trying to define and create a full personhood, we are engaged in a huge undertaking. We see that this attempt means building a new way of living which encompasses all realms of life, from global economic, social and political levels to the most intimate personal relationships. (p. xi)

Miller (1976, 1986) has been an important voice in stimulating the examination of psychological issues from a female perspective. She believes that the study of women's psychological development opens up paths to a better understanding of all psychological development, female or male. She also concludes that, when researchers examine what women have been doing in life, they find that a large part of it is active participation in the development of others. In Miller's view, women often try to interact with others in ways that foster the others' development along many dimensions—emotionally, intellectually, and socially.

Many feminist thinkers believe that it is important for women not only to maintain their competence in relationships but to be self-motivated too. Miller be-

Harriet Lerner had provided insightful analyses about the way females and males have been socialized to handle anger differently. She also has contributed to our understanding of gender differences in intimacy.

lieves that, through increased self-determination and already developed relationship skills, many women will gain greater power in the American culture. As feminist scholar Harriet Lerner (1989) concludes in her book *The Dance of Intimacy,* it is important for women to bring to their relationships nothing less than a strong, assertive, independent, and authentic self. She believes that competent relationships are those in which the separate "I-ness" of both persons can be appreciated and enhanced while the persons stay emotionally connected to each other.

Not only is a distinct female voice an important dimension of the feminist perspective on gender; so is the effort to reduce and eventually end prejudice and discrimination against women (Paludi, 1995; Yentsch & Sindermann, 1992). Although women have broken through many male bastions in the past several decades, feminists argue that much work is left to be done. Feminists today believe that too many people passively accept traditional gender roles and believe that discrimination no longer exists in politics, work, the family, and education. They encourage individuals to question these assumptions,

SOCIOCULTURAL WORLDS 11.1

Women's Struggle for Equality: An International Journey

What are the political, economic, educational, and psychosocial conditions of women around the world? Frances Culbertson (1991), as president of the section of the American Psychological Association on the Clinical Psychology of Women, summarized these conditions.

Women and Politics

In politics, women too often are treated as burdens rather than assets. Especially in developing countries, women marry early and have many children quickly, in many cases before their undernourished bodies have an opportunity to mature. These women have little access to education, work, health care, and family planning. Some experts on women's issues believe these needs would have a better chance of being met if women were more strongly represented at the decision-making and managerial levels of governments and international organizations. For example, in 1990, less than 10 percent of the members of national legislatures were women, and for every 100 ministerial level positions around the world, only 5 were filled by women (Sadik, 1991).

Women and Employment

Women's work around the world is more limiting and narrower than that of men (Monagle, 1990). Bank tellers and secretaries are most often women. Domestic workers in North America and in Central and South America are most often women. Around the world, jobs defined as women's work carry low pay, low status, and little security. Two authors described many or these circumstances as "job ghettos" (Seager & Olson, 1986). In 1990, the only countries in the world that had

maternity leave and guaranteed jobs on the basis of national law were Brazil, Chile, Mexico, Finland, Sweden, Switzerland, Germany, Italy, Egypt, Syria, and Russia. Among the major countries without these provisions was the United States.

Women and Education

Canada, the United States, and Russia have the highest percentages of educated women (Seager & Olson, 1986). The countries with the fewest women being educated are in Africa, where in some areas women are given no education at all. In developing countries, 67 percent of women and 50 percent of men over the age of 25 have never been to school. In 1985, 80 million more boys than girls were in primary and secondary educational settings around the world.

Women and Psychosocial Issues

Women around the world experience violence, often from someone close to them. In Canada, 10 percent of women reported they had been beaten by the man they lived with in their home. In the United States almost 2 million women are beaten in their homes each year (Seager & Olson, 1986). In a recent survey, "The New Woman Ethics Report," wife abuse was listed number one among the 15 most pressing concerns facing society today (Johnson, 1990). Beating women continues to be accepted and expected in too many countries. While

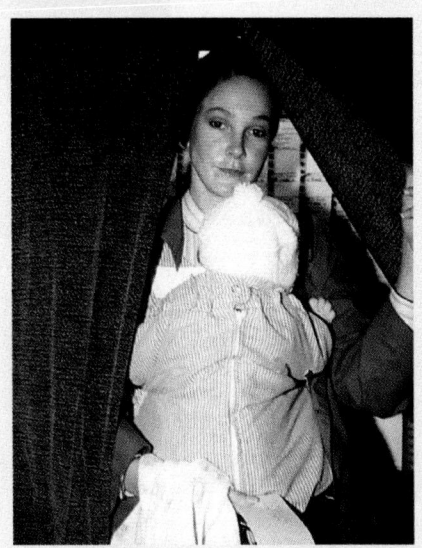

Around the world women too often are treated as burdens rather than assets in the political process. Few women have leadership positions in government. Some experts on women's issues believe that if women are to gain more access to work, education, health care, and family planning, they need to be more strongly represented at the decision-making and managerial levels of government and business.

most countries around the world now have battered women's shelters, the remedy is still usually too little, too late.

In an investigation of depression in high-income countries, women were twice as likely as men to be diagnosed as being depressed (Nolen-Hoeksema, 1990). In the United States, from adolescence through adulthood, females are more likely than males to be depressed (McGrath & others, 1990). Many sociocultural inequities and experiences contribute to the greater incidence of depression in females than in males. We will discuss the nature of depression in women in greater detail in chapter 16, "Abnormal Psychology."

Further inequities that women experience are discussed in chapter 8—"Human Sexuality." In many cultures, sex is not supposed to be pleasurable for women. For example, in the Near East and Africa, a sizable number of women are given clitorectomies, the surgical removal of the clitoris, to reduce their sexual pleasure. Many women are the victims of date rape and stranger rape. Many people—both men and women—expect women to assume total responsibility for contraception.

TABLE 11.1

Misogyny Throughout History

There is a good principle which created order, light, and man, and an evil principle which created chaos, darkness, and women.

Attributed to Pythagoras
6th century B.C.E.

Neither earth nor ocean produces a creature as savage and monstrous as woman.

Euripides
Hecuba, c. 425 B.C.E.

As regards the individual nature, woman is defective and misbegotten.

St. Thomas Aquinas
Summa Theologica, c. 1265–74

Woman is the very root of wickedness, the cause of the bitterest pain, a mine of suffering.

Tulsi Das
Ramayan, 1574

Woman is a pair of ovaries with a human being attached, whereas man is a human being furnished with a pair of testes.

Rudolf Virchow, M.D. (1821–1902)

The most winning woman I ever knew was hanged for poisoning three little children for their insurance money.

Sir Arthur Conan Doyle
The Sign of Four, 1890

Wicked women bother one. Good women bore one. That is the only difference between them.

Oscar Wilde
Lady Windermere's Fan, 1892

You needn't groan when a girl is born—she may in time be the mother of a man!

D. H. Lawrence Letter to Blanche Jennings May 13, 1908

The female of the species is more deadly than the male.

Rudyard Kipling
The Female of the Species, 1911

Woman is at once apple and serpent.

Henrich Heine (1797–1856)

I hate women because they always know where things are.

Attributed to James Thurber (1894–1961)

and especially strive to get females to evaluate the gender circumstances of their lives. For example, if you are a female, you may remember situations in which you were discriminated against because of your sex. If derogatory comments are made to you because you are a female, you may ask yourself why you have allowed these comments to go unchallenged or why they made you so angry. Feminists hope that, if you are a male, you will become more conscious of gender issues, of female and male roles, and of fairness and sensitivity in female-male interactions and relationships.

It may be easy to forget how much progress has been made in fostering equality and egalitarianism in this culture. The quotations in table 11.1 from influential males throughout history and representing many different cultures illustrate the degree to which **misogyny,** *hatred of women,* may have contributed to some ways of thinking that continue to be perpetuated among some men and women even today.

REVIEW

Defining Gender

Gender is the sociocultural dimension of being female or male. Gender roles are sets of expectations that prescribe how females and males should act, think, and feel. Gender-role identification is the sense of being female or male, a part of self-concept that most children begin to acquire by 2 or 3 years of age. Historically, because of their sex females have often been treated more negatively than males; this is sexism. There is much controversy about what are appropriate roles for today's women and men. Many feminist scholars believe that, historically, psychology has portrayed human behavior with a male-dominant theme. They also believe that sexism is still rampant in society and that women are still discriminated against in the workplace, in politics, and at home, and they argue that too many women have low self-esteem because of these inequities. Jean Baker Miller has been an important voice in stimulating examination of psychological issues from a female perspective. She believes that society should place a stronger emphasis on the importance of connectedness and relationships, which women know how to do. She also argues that women need to increase their self-determination while maintaining their competence at relationship skills.

Shown here are women attending an International Women's Conference in Mexico City. Although many cultures around the world remain male-dominant, the feminist viewpoint is becoming an important voice.

Gender Comparisons

We will now turn to several topics involving gender comparisons. First we examine the research on gender roles and gender-role stereotyping. Next we explore the similarities and differences that exist between females and males.

Gender Roles

A classic study in the early 1970s summarized the traits and behaviors that college students believed were characteristic of males and those they believed were characteristic of females (Broverman & others, 1972). The traits clustered into two groups that were labeled "instrumental" and "expressive." The instrumental traits paralleled the male's purposeful, competent entry into the outside world to gain goods for his family; the expressive traits paralleled the female's responsibility to be warm and emotional in the home. Such stereotypes were evaluated by the researchers as more harmful to females than to males because the characteristics assigned to males were more valued than those assigned to females.

In the 1970s, many females and males began to evaluate the constraints imposed by strict gender stereotypes and

to become dissatisfied. Alternatives to masculinity and femininity were explored. Instead of thinking of masculinity and femininity as a continuum, with more of one meaning less of the other, it was proposed that individuals could show both expressive *and* instrumental traits. This thinking led to the development of the concept of **androgyny,** *the presence of desirable masculine and feminine characteristics in the same individual* (Bem, 1977; Spence & Helmreich, 1978). The androgynous individual might be a male who is assertive (masculine) and nurturant (feminine), or a female who is dominant (masculine) and sensitive to others' feelings (feminine).

To be meek, patient, tactful, modest, honorable, brave, is not to be either manly or womanly; it is to be humane.

Jane Harrison

Measures have been developed to assess androgyny. One of the most widely used gender measures, the Bem sex-role inventory, was constructed by a leading early proponent of androgyny, Sandra Bem. To see what the items on Bem's measure are like, see table 11.2. Based on their responses to

TABLE 11.2

The Bem Sex-Role Inventory: Are You Androgynous?

The following items are from the Bem Sex-Role Inventory. To find out whether you score as androgynous, first rate yourself on each item, on a scale from 1 (never or almost never true) to 7 (always or almost always true).

1. self-reliant	17. loyal	32. compassionate	47. gullible
2. yielding	18. unpredictable	33. sincere	48. inefficient
3. helpful	19. forceful	34. self-sufficient	49. acts as a leader
4. defends own beliefs	20. feminine	35. eager to soothe hurt	50. childlike
5. cheerful	21. reliable	feelings	51. adaptable
6. moody	22. analytical	36. conceited	52. individualistic
7. independent	23. sympathetic	37. dominant	53. does not use harsh
8. shy	24. jealous	38. soft-spoken	language
9. conscientious	25. has leadership abilities	39. likable	54. unsystematic
10. athletic	26. sensitive to the needs of	40. masculine	55. competitive
11. affectionate	others	41. warm	56. loves children
12. theatrical	27. truthful	42. solemn	57. tactful
13. assertive	28. willing to take risks	43. willing to take a stand	58. ambitious
14. flatterable	29. understanding	44. tender	59. gentle
15. happy	30. secretive	45. friendly	60. conventional
16. strong personality	31. makes decisions easily	46. aggressive	

From Janet S. Hyde, *Half the Human Experience: The Psychology of Women*, 3d ed. Copyright © 1985 D. C. Heath and Company, Lexington, MA. Reprinted by permission.

SCORING
(a) Add up your ratings for items, 1, 4, 7, 10, 13, 16, 19, 22, 25, 28, 31, 34, 37, 40, 43, 46, 49, 55, and 58. Divide the total by 20. That is your masculinity score.
(b) Add up your ratings for items 2, 5, 8, 11, 14, 17, 20, 23, 26, 29, 32, 35, 38, 41, 44, 47, 50, 53, 56, and 59. Divide the total by 20. That is your femininity score.
(c) If your masculinity score is above 4.9 (the approximate median for the masculinity scale) and your femininity score is above 4.9 (the approximate femininity median) then you would be classified as androgynous on Bem's scale.

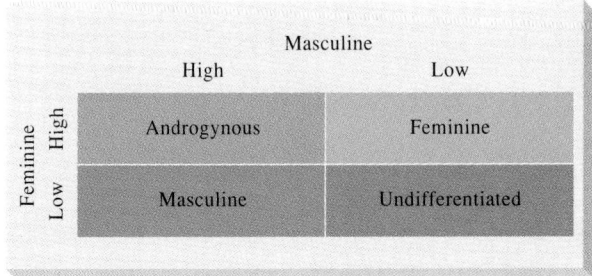

FIGURE 11.1

Gender-Role Classification

the items in the Bem sex-role inventory, individuals are classified as having one of four gender-role orientations: masculine, feminine, androgynous, or undifferentiated (see figure 11.1). The androgynous individual is simply a female or a male who has a high degree of both feminine (expressive) and masculine (instrumental) traits. Bem invokes no new characteristics to describe the androgynous individual. A feminine individual is high on feminine (expressive) traits and low on masculine (instrumental) traits; a masculine individual shows the reverse of these traits. An undifferentiated person is not high on feminine or masculine traits.

Bem speculated that androgynous individuals are more flexible and mentally healthy than either masculine or feminine individuals. She believes that individuals who are undifferentiated are the least competent. To some degree, though, the context influences which gender role is most adaptive (Moskowitz, Suhi, & Desaulniers, 1995). In close relationships, a feminine or androgynous gender role may be more desirable because of the expressive nature of close relationships. However, a masculine or androgynous gender role may be more desirable in academic and work settings because of the instrumental nature of these settings. The culture in which individuals live also plays an important role in determining what is adaptive. On the one hand, increasing numbers of parents in the United Sates and other modernized countries such as Sweden are raising their children to behave in androgynous ways. On the other hand, traditional gender roles continue to dominate the cultures of many countries around the world. We will explore more examples of traditional gender roles in other cultures toward the end of this chapter.

Gender-Role Transcendence

Although the concept of androgyny was an improvement over exclusive notions of femininity and masculinity, it has turned out to be less of a panacea than many of its early proponents envisioned. Some theorists, such as Pleck (1981), believe that the idea of androgyny should be replaced with **gender-role transcendence,** *the belief that an individual's*

The Cost of the Masculine Adolescent

An increasing number of gender theorists and researchers believe that there may be a negative side to traditional masculinity, especially among adolescents. Joseph Pleck and his colleagues (Pleck, 1983; Pleck, Sonnenstein, & Ku, 1994) believe that Western culture encourages certain behaviors as validating masculinity even though they are socially disapproved of. That is, in the male adolescent culture, males perceive that they are more masculine if they engage in premarital sex, drink alcohol, take drugs, and participate in delinquent

activities. In one recent investigation, the gender-role orientation and problem behaviors of 1,680 15- to-19-year-old males were assessed (Pleck, Sonnenstein, & Ku, 1994). In this study—referred to as the National Survey of Adolescent Males—there was strong evidence that problem behaviors in adolescent males are associated with their attitudes toward masculinity. The adolescent males who reported traditional beliefs about masculinity (for example, endorsing such items as "A young man should be tough, even if he's

not big," "It is essential for a guy to get respect from others," and "Men are always ready for sex") also were likely to say that they had school difficulties, engaged in alcohol and drug use, participated in delinquent activities, and were sexually active.

Can you think of any ways of intervening in the process of exaggerated masculine behaviors in adolescence and the social damage that it can cause? Your answer will demonstrate *using psychological knowledge to promote human welfare.*

Joseph Pleck and his colleagues have found that heightened masculinity in adolescence is associated with a number of problems and disorders.

competence should be conceptualized not on the basis of masculinity, femininity, or androgyny, but rather on the basis of the person. Thus, rather than merging gender roles or stereotyping people as "masculine" or "feminine," Pleck believes we should begin to think about people as people. However, both concepts—androgyny and gender-role transcendence—draw attention away from women's unique needs and the power imbalance between women and men in most cultures.

Gender-Role Stereotyping

Gender-role stereotypes *are broad categories that reflect our impressions and beliefs about females and males.* All stereotypes, whether they are based on gender, ethnicity, or something else, are images of the typical member of a particular social category. The world is extremely complex, and using stereotypes is one way individuals simplify complexity so that they are not overwhelmed in their processing of the world. However, simplifications can lead to wrong assumptions and invalid conclusions; they often interfere with seeing other people as the unique individuals that they are. If we simply assign a label, such as *soft,* to someone, we might have much less to consider when we think about that person. However, once labels are assigned, they are remarkably difficult to abandon—even in the face of contradictory evidence.

Inge Broverman and her colleagues (1970) found that professional counselors were also influenced by their attitudes toward men and women. In this study, 33 female and 46 male mental health practitioners were given a list of traits and asked to check off the traits that best describe a mature, healthy, and socially competent adult, adult woman, or adult man. The descriptions they selected of mature and competent adults and adult men were consistent and included characteristics such as being direct, logical, achieving, and active. However, the description they selected of mature and competent adult women was different and included the characteristics of being excitable in minor crises, influenceable, illogical, sneaky, less adventurous, and dependent. For these counselors, a consistent portrait was painted for competent adults and adult men, but competent adult women could not be simultaneously described as competent adults. Although these differences in perceptions are likely to have diminished since 1970, some counselors might still inappropriately hold different standards for their female and male clients.

If you are going to generalize about women, you will find yourself up to here in exceptions.
Dolores Hitches, *In a House Unknown* (1973)

Stereotypes involve diverse behaviors and characteristics. For example, scoring a touchdown and growing facial hair are considered "masculine" behaviors, and playing with dolls and wearing lipstick are considered "feminine" behaviors. Stereotypes often differ in different cultures and historical contexts. During the reign of Louis XIV, for example, French noblemen wore satin breeches, cosmetics, and high heels; in contrast, rugged pioneer American males of that time wore dirty, leather clothing. Stereotypes of "femininity" and "masculinity" also vary across the socioeconomic spectrum. For example, lower socioeconomic groups are the most likely to include "rough and tough" as part of the masculine stereotype.

In a study of college students in thirty countries, stereotyping of females and males was pervasive and far-ranging (Williams & Best, 1982). Across the various cultures, the college students described men as dominant, independent, aggressive, achievement-oriented, and enduring, while women were viewed as nurturant, affiliative, less confident, and more helpful in times of distress. Often such beliefs influence our attitudes toward both women and men.

In one investigation, women and men in developed countries perceived themselves as more similar to one another than did women and men who lived in less-developed countries (Williams & Best, 1989). This makes sense. In the highly developed countries, women are more likely to attend college and have careers. As sexual equality increases,

stereotypes of women and men probably diminish. Women are more likely than men to perceive similarity between the sexes (Williams & Best, 1989).

Gender Similarities and Differences

Some gender researchers believe that differences between the sexes have often been exaggerated (Hyde, 1981; Linn & Hyde, 1991). For instance, some analyses of research findings use language that magnifies apparent differences. A researcher might summarize findings by saying that "only 32 percent of women, versus fully 37 percent of men, were. . . ." This difference of 5 percent might, or might not, be statistically significant. The researcher's language, however, implies that the difference is important (Denmark & others, 1988).

There is more difference within the sexes than between them.
Ivy Compton-Burnett

Similarly, general statements comparing females and males, as in "Males outperform females in math," do not apply to all females versus all males (as in "All males are better than all females at math"). Rather, they usually mean that the average score for males is higher than the average score for females (for instance, that the average math achievement score for males at a certain age is higher than the average math achievement score for females at that age). Indeed (to continue our math achievement score example), the math achievement scores of females and males overlap considerably, and although an average difference might favor males, many females have higher math achievement than most males. See figure 11.2 for an illustration of the overlapping distribution in mathematical scores of females and males.

A further error is the tendency to think of differences between females and males as always being biologically based. Remember that when differences occur, they might be due mainly to societal or cultural factors. The best assumption to make is that human behavior is always due to a combination of biological and environmental factors (Unger, 1992).

Sometimes animal research studies are considered in hopes that they might shed light on human behavior, including patterns of relationships between females and males. It is important to realize that there is great variation among animal species in male and female behaviors—we can select findings at will from various species to back up or discredit various (even incompatible) theories about human behavior. For instance, although in many species males are more aggressive than females, in some species (such as hyenas) the females are much more aggressive than the males.

FIGURE 11.2

Mathematics Performance of Males and Females
Notice that, although the average male mathematics score is higher than the average female score, the overlap between the sexes is substantial. Not all males have better mathematics performance than all females—the substantial overlap indicates that, although the average score of males is higher, many females outperform most males on such tasks.

Let's now examine some of the differences between the sexes, keeping in mind the following: (a) The differences are averages; (b) even when differences are reported, there is considerable overlap between the sexes; (c) differences are due to an interaction between biological and environmental factors; (d) research conducted with other species provides limited, even misleading, information about human males and females. First we will examine physical and biological differences, then we will turn to cognitive and social differences.

Physical and Biological Differences
On the average, females live longer than males. Females are also less likely than males to develop physical disorders. A primary reason for this female advantage is estrogen, which strengthens the immune system, making females more

resistant to infection. Also, female hormones signal the liver to produce more "good" cholesterol, which makes their blood vessels more "elastic." In males, testosterone triggers the production of low-density lipoproteins, which clogs blood vessels. As a result, males have twice the risk of coronary disease as females have. Males also have higher levels of stress hormones, resulting in faster clotting in males but also in higher blood pressure.

Other physical differences are more visible. Adult females have about twice the body fat of their male counterparts. In females, body fat is mostly concentrated around the breasts and hips; in males, fat is more likely to go to the abdomen. Males grow about 10 percent taller than females, on the average, because male hormones promote the growth of long bones while female hormones inhibit such growth at puberty. In short, there are physical differences between females and males. Are there many cognitive differences?

Cognitive Differences
In a 1974 classic review of gender differences, Eleanor Maccoby and Carol Jacklin concluded that males have better math skills and better visual and spatial ability (the kind of skills an architect would need to design a building's angles and dimensions), while females have better verbal abilities (Maccoby & Jacklin, 1974). Recently, Maccoby (1987) revised her conclusions about gender differences. She now states that verbal differences between the sexes have virtually disappeared, though the math and spatial differences still exist. Another recent analysis also found that the spatial difference between females and males does exist (Voyer, Voyer, & Bryden, 1995).

Many researchers believe that there are more cognitive similarities than cognitive differences between females and males (Hyde & Plant, 1995). Moreover, when differences do exist, as with math and visuo-spatial differences, they have been exaggerated. For example, males do outperform females in math, but only for a certain portion of the population—the gifted (Hyde, 1993). Furthermore, males do not outperform females on all visuospatial tasks; consistent differences are found only in the ability to rotate objects mentally (Linn & Petersen, 1986) and in performance on tasks of disembedding figures. Combined with the fact that females

How Good Are Girls at Wudgemaking If the Wudgemaker Is He?

In one investigation, the following description of a fictitious gender-neutral occupation—wudgemaker—was read to third- and fifth-grade children, with repeated references to *he, they, he or she,* or *she* (Hyde, 1984):

> Few people have heard of a job in factories, being a wudgemaker. Wudges are made of oddly shaped plastic and are an important part of video games. The wudgemaker works from a plan or pattern posted at eye level as *he or she* puts together the pieces at a table while *he or she* is sitting down. Eleven plastic pieces must be snapped together. Some of the pieces are tiny, so that *he or she* must have good coordination in *his or her* fingers. Once all eleven pieces are put together, *he or she* must test out the wudge to make sure that all of the moving pieces move properly. The wudgemaker is well paid, and must be a high school graduate, but *he or she* does not have to have gone to college to get the job. (Hyde, 1984, p. 702)

One-fourth of the children were read the story with *he* as the pronoun, one-fourth with *they,* one-fourth with *he or she* (as shown), and one-fourth with *she.* The children were asked to rate how well women could do the job of wudgemaking and also how well they thought men could perform the job. As shown in figure 11.A, ratings of how well women could make wudges were influenced by the pronoun used; women's competence was rated lowest when *he* was used, intermediate when *they* and *he or she* were used, and highest when *she* was used. This suggests that the use of *he,* compared with other pronouns, influences children's conceptions of how competent males and females are in our society.

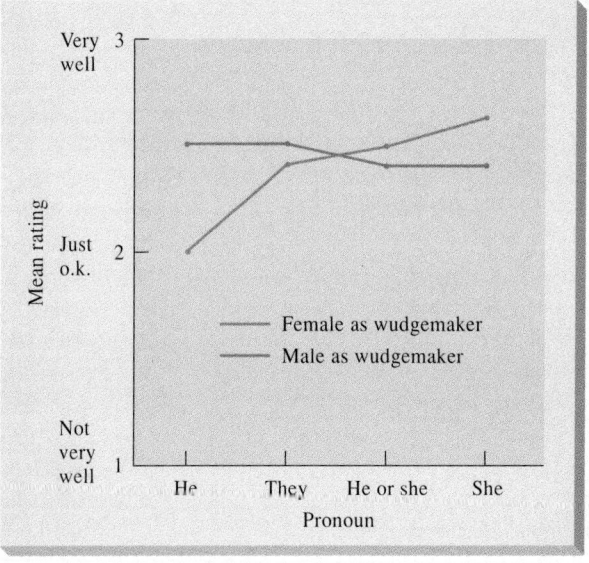

FIGURE 11.A

Children's Mean Ratings of Women and Men as Wudgemakers
Elementary school children's ratings of women's competence were lowest when the pronoun *he* was used, intermediate when *they* or *he or she* was used, and highest when *she* was used.

"So according to the stereotype, you can put two and two together, but I can read the handwriting on the wall."

no longer have higher average scores on the verbal section of the SAT, we can conclude that cognitive differences between females and males exist in only a few areas and are small. Applications in Psychology 11.1 explores how one cognitive area—language—might still include considerable bias.

Social Differences

Although males and females do not experience different emotions, they frequently differ in the behaviors they feel free to engage in publicly (Paludi, 1995). For example, males are more active and aggressive than females (Maccoby, 1987; Maccoby & Jacklin, 1974), a difference that is apparent by the age of 2 years.

With regard to helping behavior, social psychologists Alice Eagly and Maureen Crowley (1986) argue that the female gender role fosters helping that is nurturant and

Sex Differences in Dependency— How Real?

Sex differences that appear at one point in development might not appear at other points. Consider the following evaluation of research by Paula Caplan and Jeremy Caplan (1994).

In 1969, Susan Goldberg and Michael Lewis concluded that their research revealed that girls are dependent and boys are independent. They studied 16 children of each sex who were 6 months old and another 16 of each sex who were 13 months old. Each mother held her child on her lap in a room filled with toys and then placed the child on the floor. After 15 minutes, a mesh barrier in a wooden frame with a latch was placed in the middle of the room, with the mother on one side and the child on the other. They were observed for 30 minutes. When the children were first put on the floor, girls returned more immediately to their mothers, returned more frequently, vocalized more to their mothers, and stayed closer to their mothers. After the barrier was put in place, the girls cried and motioned for help more often than the boys did. Based on these results, Goldberg and Lewis claimed that girls are more dependent and boys are more independent.

For a decade after the Goldberg and Lewis study was conducted, their conclusions were widely cited as evidence of females' greater emotional dependency and males' greater independence and problem-solving ability. Many people also concluded that because this difference appeared so early in development, it must be innate (genetically based). Some people even claimed it would be wrong to try to change these behaviors in girls and boys because they are innate and natural. Can you think of another way to interpret the difference in their behavior?

In 1979, Candice Feiring and Michael Lewis reported their observations from a longitudinal study of the same children in the Goldberg and Lewis study in which the children had been observed in the same context at 25 months of age. The researchers found that, at 25 months of age, the girls spent more time manipulating the latch and vocalizing to their mothers. The boys spent more time fretting and looking at their mothers. Seven of the girls, but only two of the boys, undid the latch and were able to get out from behind the barrier. Overall, at 25 months of age the girls spent more time in problem-solving behavior than boys did and the boys showed more emotional upset.

This pair of research investigations reveals how risky it is to draw conclusions about sex differences in behavior based on one study conducted at one point in children's development (Caplan & Caplan, 1994). Researchers must exercise caution in *making inferences about behavior*. The studies also reveal how unwise it is to assume that just because behaviors occur early in development, they are biologically based.

Furthermore, in the 1990s the term *dependency*, which has had negative connotations for females (that females can't take care of themselves and males can), is being replaced by the term *relational abilities*. Researchers are now demonstrating that females, rather than being dependent, are skilled in forming and maintaining relationships.

caring, while the male gender role promotes helping that is heroic and chivalrous. Each sex is more likely to help in situations that are consistent with their gender role and in which they feel competent. For example, males are more likely than females to help when a person is standing by the roadside with a flat tire, a situation involving some danger as well as involving male competence with automobile problems. In contrast, volunteering time to help a disturbed child is more typical of females than of males; this situation involves little danger and also taps female competence in nurturance (Hyde, 1990). In the American culture, girls exhibit more caregiving behavior than boys do (Zahn-Waxler, 1990). For example, one recent study found that preschool girls spent more time with babies and gave more nurturing attention to babies than preschool boys did (Blakemore, 1993). However, in sibling-care cultures, where both boys and girls are engaged in caring for younger siblings, boys and girls are more similar in their nurturant behaviors (Whiting, 1989).

Some psychologists believe that our culture has not adequately valued women's skills in caring about and taking interest in the emotional well-being of others. One prominent psychologist, Carol Gilligan (1992) believes adolescence may be a critical juncture in female development in which girls incorporate strong societal expectations about females' providing service to others. Although this expectation promotes females' nurturing behavior toward others, it might also encourage suppression of their own feelings, a process Gilligan describes as "silencing their own voices."

In the past the well-adjusted male was supposed to show instrumental traits, the well-adjusted female expressive traits. Masculine traits were more valued by society. Sexism was widespread. In the 1970s, alternatives to traditional masculinity and femininity were explored. It was proposed that individuals could show both expressive and instrumental traits. This thinking led to the development of the concept of androgyny—the presence of desirable feminine and masculine traits in the same individual. Gender-role measures often categorize individuals as masculine, feminine, androgynous, or undifferentiated. Androgynous individuals are often more flexible and mentally healthy, although the particular context and the individual's culture also determine the adaptiveness of a gender-role orientation. Gender-role transcendence is the belief that an individual's competence should be conceptualized not on the basis of masculinity, femininity, or androgyny, but rather on the basis of the person.

Gender-role stereotypes are broad categories that reflect our impressions and beliefs about males and females. These stereotypes are widespread around the world, especially emphasizing the male's power and the woman's nurturance. In more highly developed countries, however, females and males are more likely to be perceived as more similar.

Many gender researchers believe that differences between females and males have been exaggerated. In considering differences, it is important to recognize that differences are averages, there is considerable overlap between the sexes, and the differences may be due primarily to biological factors, sociocultural factors, or both. There are several physical differences between the sexes, but cognitive differences are either small or nonexistent. At the level of the gifted, the average male does outperform the average female in math achievement. In terms of social behavior, males are more aggressive and active than females, but females are usually more adept at "reading" emotions and show more nurturant helping behavior than males. Overall, though, there are more similarities than differences between females and males.

GENDER IDENTITY

Many different perspectives can be linked to contemporary discussions about gender identity. Some perspectives have produced formal theories explaining how gender identity develops. In this section we will emphasize explanations derived from the neurobiological, psychoanalytic, behavioral, and cognitive perspectives.

The Neurobiological Perspective

Gender identity is fundamentally linked to anatomy and physiology. In order to understand biological contributions, we will look at the influence of genetics and hormones. It was not until the 1920s that researchers confirmed the existence of human sex chromosomes, the genetic material that determines our sex. Humans normally have 46 chromosomes, arranged in pairs. Usually the 23rd pair has either two X-shaped chromosomes, which produces a female, or one X-shaped and one Y-shaped chromosome, which produces a male (see figure 11.3). One gene (called the TDF, or testes determining factor) on the sex chromosomes determines biological sex. In other words, the genetic difference between women and men is in 1 of 150,000 genes.

In the first few weeks of gestation, female and male embryos look alike and are identical in development. Male sex organs start to be differentiated from female sex organs when the TDF gene triggers the secretion of **androgens,** *the main class of male sex hormones,* in the male embryo. Low levels of androgens in female embryos allow the normal development of female sex organs.

Although rare, an imbalance in this system of hormone secretion can occur during fetal development. Insufficient androgens in the male embryo or excessive androgens in the female embryo results in an individual with ambiguous genitals—that is, the sex organs appear to be a mix of male and female genitals. This condition is called *pseudohermaphroditism.*

When genetically female infants (with XX chromosomes) are born with masculine-looking genitals, surgery can achieve female-appearing genitals. At puberty, the production of **estrogens,** *the main class of female sex hormones,* influences the physical and behavioral development of these masculinized girls, but prior to puberty they tend to behave more aggressively than other females. Their prepubertal play patterns and clothing preferences are similar to those of boys (Ehrhardt, 1987).

In animal experiments, when male hormones are injected into female embryos, the female animals develop masculine physical traits and behave aggressively (Hines, 1982). However, humans seem to be less controlled by their hormones than other species are. Socializing experiences might exert significant influence. For example, masculinized girls might be more aggressive because they are treated like boys and encouraged to adopt male preferences and behaviors.

Genetic males (with XY chromosomes) with ambiguous genitals pose more-complicated problems than their female counterparts do. Because reconstructive surgery of an infant penis is not possible, most of these infants are reassigned to the female sex. That is, their genitals are surgically reconstructed to be a vagina, clitoris, and labia (the external female genital

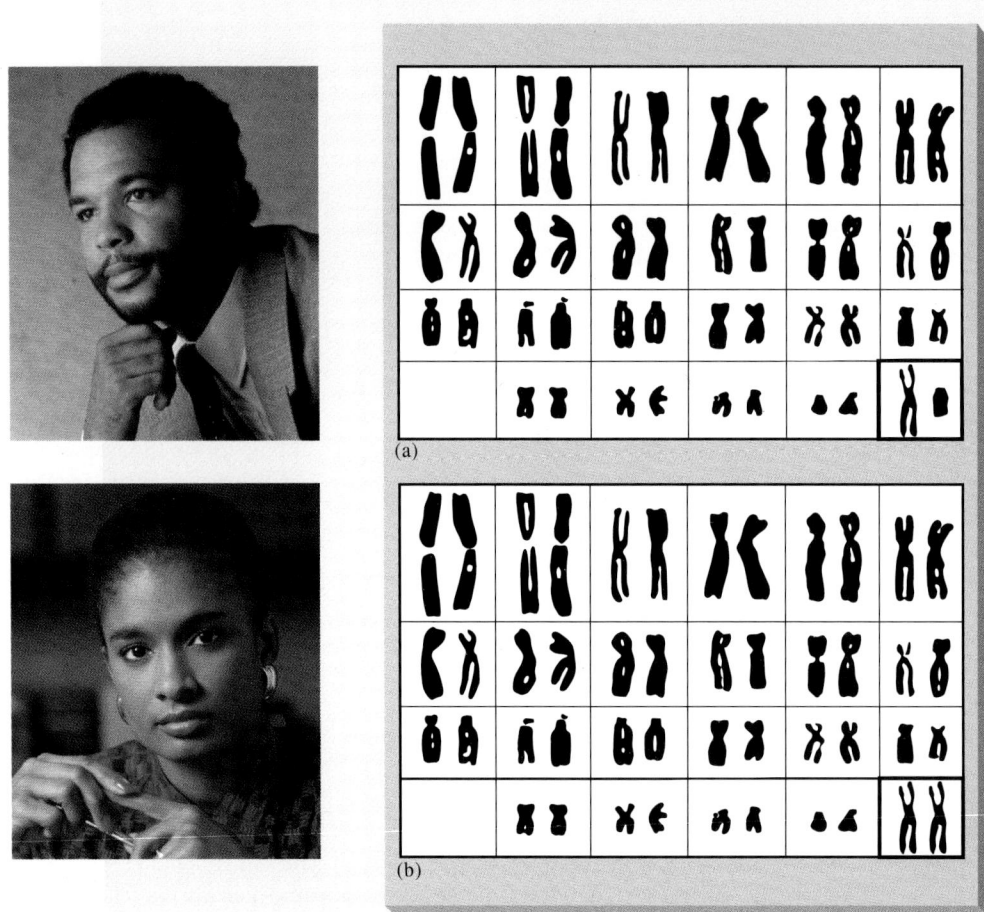

FIGURE 11.3

The Genetic Difference Between Males and Females
In (*a*) is the chromosome structure of a male, and in (*b*) is the chromosome structure of a female. The 23rd pair is shown in the bottom right box of each figure; notice that the Y chromosome of the male is smaller. To obtain this chromosomal picture, a cell is removed from the individual's body, usually from the inside of the mouth. The chromosomes are magnified extensively and then photographed.

structures). At puberty, when hormones are normally released, it is necessary to give estrogens and progesterones to these reassigned females so that they can develop the feminizing effects seen at puberty, such as changes in fatty tissues around the hips and breast development. Despite the complicated procedures involved, these reassigned girls grow up surprisingly well adapted. They look like average females, but they are unable to reproduce.

The Psychoanalytic Perspective

While prenatal hormones might or might not influence gender behavior, psychoanalytic theorists, such as Sigmund Freud and Erik Erikson, have argued that an individual's genitals do play a pivotal role. Freud argued that human behavior and history are directly influenced by sexual drives. He suggested that gender and sexual behavior are essentially unlearned and instinctual.

Anatomy is destiny.

Sigmund Freud

Freud was the first to develop a theory to explain the mechanism by which children acquire masculine and feminine attitudes and behaviors. Freud's **identification theory** *proposed that the preschool child develops a sexual attraction to the opposite-sex parent. By approximately 5 or 6 years of age, the child renounces this attraction because it generates too much anxiety. The child subsequently identifies with the same-sex parent, unconsciously adopting the same-sex parent's characteristics.* Today many experts do not believe gender development proceeds on the basis of parental identification, at least not on the basis of Freud's hypothesized childhood sexual attraction. Critics suggest that children become gender typed much earlier than 5 years old and that they become attuned to gender roles regardless of the presence of a same-sex parent in the family.

Another controversial psychoanalytic figure who addressed the development of gender identification was Erik Erikson. Erikson argued that genital differences contributed

to males' being more intrusive and aggressive and to females' being more inclusive and passive. Critics of Erikson's
central ideas contended that he failed to give enough credit
to the role of experience in personality development and
that women and men are freer to choose their behavior
than Erikson allows. In fact, Erikson later modified his original views. He observed that females in today's world are
transcending their biological heritage and making contributions to society that go beyond childbearing.

Though researchers acknowledge that biology is an
important influence on gender, most believe that social and
cultural expectations have a greater influence on gender
identity than hormones and sexual anatomy do.

The Behavioral Perspective

In our culture, adults discriminate between the sexes from the
moment infants are born. While still in the hospital, many babies are dressed in pink and blue, according to their sex, and
this differentiation often continues in obvious differences between male and female hairstyles, clothing, and toys. Both
adults and peers reward gendered behavior throughout childhood and adolescence. Moreover, boys and girls also learn
gender roles through imitation or observational learning—that
is, by watching what others say and do and doing likewise.

The view that parents are the critical agents in gender-role development has come under fire (Huston, 1983),
because culture, schools, peers, the media, and other family
members have been shown to also influence gender behavior. However, it is important not to disregard parental influence; especially in the early developmental years parents
play important roles in gender-role socialization.

The **social learning theory of gender** *emphasizes that
children's gender development occurs through observation and
imitation of gender-related behaviors, and through rewards
and punishments children experience for gender-appropriate
and gender-inappropriate behavior.* Unlike identification theory, social learning theory does not emphasize sexual attraction as the major factor in gender development (see figure
11.4). Instead, behavioral consequences shape gender-based
behaviors, according to this theory. For example, parents
might reward their daughter's feminine behavior with a
compliment (such as "Karen, you are being a good girl when
you play gently with your doll!") or punish their son's non-
masculine behavior with a reproach (such as "Keith, a big
boy like you is not supposed to cry"). Moreover, parents
provide boys with few, if any, dolls while giving them eighteen times as many toy vehicles as they give girls (Unger,
1992).

While parents are important models of gender roles,
young children also learn gender roles from observing other
adults in their neighborhood and characters on television,
even Saturday-morning cartoons. As children get older,
peers become increasingly important influences. For example, when children play in ways that our culture says are
gender-appropriate, they tend to be rewarded by their
peers. Those who engage in activities that are considered

Theory	Processes	Outcome
Freud's identification theory	Sexual attraction to opposite-sex parent at 3–5 years of age; anxiety about sexual attraction and subsequent identification with same-sex parent at 5–6 years of age	Gender behavior similar to same-sex parent
Social learning theory	Rewards and punishments of gender-appropriate and -inappropriate behavior by adults and peers; observation and imitation of models' masculine and feminine behavior	Gender behavior

FIGURE 11.4

**A Comparison of Identification Theory and Social Learning
Theory Regarding Gender Development**

gender-inappropriate tend to be criticized or even abandoned by their peers. Young Ben loved his Cabbage Patch
boy doll, but when boys a year older than him laughed at
him for bringing it to his preschool's show-and-tell, Ben

As reflected in this tug-of-war battle between boys and girls, the playground in elementary school is like going to "gender school." Elementary school children show a clear preference for being with and liking same-sex peers. Eleanor Maccoby *(at left)* has studied children's gender development for many years. She believes peers play especially strong roles in socializing each other about gender roles.

immediately stopped playing with the doll. His same-sex peers had quickly taught him that even a male doll is not an appropriate toy for a boy.

Children show a clear preference for same-sex peers (Maccoby, 1993). The segregation of the sexes during play is so evident that researchers who have observed elementary school children playing in all-boy and all-girl groups have characterized playgrounds as "gender school" (Luria & Herzog, 1985). Even when engaging in similar activities, such as riding tricycles and bicycles, these same-sex groups play differently. For example, boys, but not girls for the most part, often ride their vehicles deliberately into each other.

The social learning view is sometimes criticized for its emphasis on the passive acquisition of gender roles via modeling and rewards and punishments. Other approaches regard children as more actively constructing their gender worlds. We will discuss those approaches in the next section.

The Cognitive Perspective

The role of cognitive influence on gender has been addressed by two prominent theories: cognitive developmental theory and gender schema theory.

Cognitive Developmental Theory

According to the **cognitive developmental theory of gender,** *children's gender typing occurs after they have developed a concept of gender constancy. Once children consistently conceive of themselves as male or female, they often organize their world on the basis of gender.* Initially developed by psychologist Lawrence Kohlberg (1966), this theory summarizes typical gender development progression in the following way: "I am a girl, I want to do girl things; therefore, the opportunity to do girl things is rewarding." Kohlberg based his ideas on Piaget's cognitive developmental theory, which emphasizes that once they have acquired the ability to categorize things, children strive toward consistency in their use of categories and behavior. Therefore, as children's cognitive development matures, so does their understanding of gender. Two-year-olds can apply the labels *boy* and *girl* correctly to themselves and others; their concept of gender is simple and concrete. Preschool children rely on physical features such as dress and hairstyle to decide who falls into each gender category. Girls are people with long hair; boys are people who never wear dresses. Some preschool children believe that people can change their gender by getting a haircut or a new outfit. Obviously they do not yet have the cognitive machinery to think of gender as adults do. According to Kohlberg, all the reinforcement in the world won't modify that fact.

However, by the concrete operational stage (Piaget's third stage, which begins around the age of 6 or 7 years), children understand gender constancy. They know, for example, that a male is still a male regardless of whether he is wearing pants or a skirt or an earring, or whether his hair is short or long (Tavris & Wade, 1984). Now that their concept

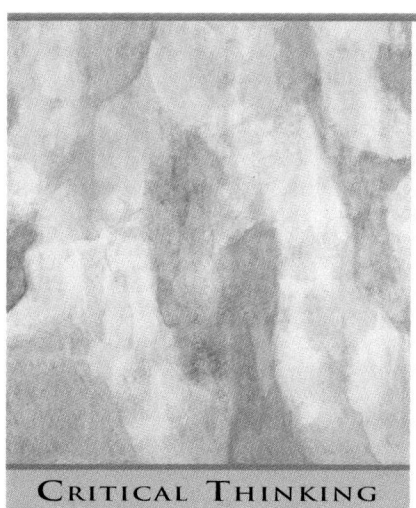

Tita's Plight and How It Evolved

At the beginning of this chapter you were introduced to a young Mexican woman whose mother refused to speak with the man she wished to marry. Depending on your own traditions, you may have struggled to comprehend how Tita could comply with her mother's wishes or how she could consider defying them. Tita not only complied; she watched her older sister marry her beloved and she embarked on a life of service to the family. As we try to comprehend such adherence to role expectations, the frameworks we have studied might help clarify how she reached her decision.

How would the psychoanalytic, neurobiological, behavioral, and cognitive perspectives explain Tita's loyalty? How would the feminist perspective regard Tita's choice? Exploring these points of view underscores the importance of *pursuing alternative explanations to understand complex behavior.*

activities rewarding and imitates the behavior of same-sex models.

Gender Schema Theory

A **schema** *is a cognitive structure, a network of associations that organizes and guides an individual's perceptions.* A **gender schema** *organizes the world in terms of female and male.* **Gender schema theory** *states that an individual's attention and behavior are guided by an internal motivation to conform to gender-based sociocultural standards and stereotypes.* Gender schema theory suggests that "gender-typing" occurs when individuals are ready to encode and organize information along the lines of what is considered appropriate or typical for males and females in a society (Martin, 1993). Whereas Kohlberg's cognitive developmental theory argues that a particular cognitive prerequisite— gender constancy— is necessary for gender-typing, gender schema theory states that a general readiness to respond to and categorize information on the basis of culturally

of gender constancy is clearly established, school-age children become motivated to become a competent, or "proper," boy or girl. Consequently, the child finds same sex defined gender roles fuels children's gender-typing activities. A comparison of the cognitive developmental and gender schema theories is presented in figure 11.5.

REVIEW

Gender Identity—Neurobiological, Psychoanalytic, Behavioral, and Cognitive Perspectives

The 23rd pair of chromosomes determines our sex. Ordinarily females have two X chromosomes; males have an X and a Y. Chromosomes determine anatomical sex differences, but gender behavior is strongly influenced by society and culture. Freud's and Erikson's theories promote the thesis that anatomy determines behavior. Hormones from the testes (androgen) determine whether an organism will have male genitals (if androgen is secreted) or female genitals (if no androgen is secreted). Androgen in males and estrogen in females are the dominant sexual hormones. Hermaphrodites are

individuals whose genitals become intermediate between male and female because of a hormonal imbalance.

Adults and peers reward and model gender-appropriate behavior. Parents—as well as culture, schools, peers, the media, and other family members—influence the development of children's gender behavior. Two prominent theories address the way children acquire masculine and feminine attitudes and behavior from their parents—identification theory and social learning theory.

Two theories address cognitive influences on gender—cognitive developmental theory and gender

schema theory. In the cognitive developmental theory, children's gender typing occurs after children have developed a concept of gender, which is achieved in concert with the development of conservation skills at about 6 or 7 years of age. Gender schema theory states that an individual's attention and behavior are guided by an internal motivation to conform to gender-based, sociocultural standards, and stereotypes. Gender schema theorists point out that very young children have more gender role knowledge than cognitive developmental theory predicts.

Theory	Processes	Emphasis
Cognitive developmental theory	Development of gender constancy, especially around 6–7 years of age, when conservation skills develop; after children develop ability to consistently conceive of themselves as male or female, children often organize their world on the basis of gender, such as selecting same-sex models to imitate	Cognitive readiness facilitates gender-typing.
Gender schema theory	Sociocultural emphasis on gender-based standards and stereotypes; children's attention and behavior are guided by an internal motivation to conform to these gender-based standards and stereotypes, allowing children to interpret the world through a network of gender-organized thoughts	Gender schemas reinforce gender-typing.

FIGURE 11.5

The Development of Gender-Typed Behavior According to the Cognitive Developmental and Gender Schema Theories of Gender Development

SOCIOCULTURAL VARIATIONS

A wide variety of examples reinforce the importance of context in understanding gender. First, we will explore men's issues. Second, we will explore the link between gender and ethnicity. We will conclude by looking at how diverse cultures deal with gender.

Men's Issues

The male of the species—what is he really like? What does he really want? As a result of the women's movement and its attack on society's male bias and discrimination against women, some men have developed their own movement. The men's movement has not been as political or as activist as the women's movement. Rather, it has been more an emotional, spiritual movement that reasserts the importance of masculinity and urges men to resist women's efforts to turn them into "soft" males. Or it has been a psychological movement that recognizes men's need to be less violent and more nurturant but still retain much of their masculine identity. Many of the men's movement disciples argue that society's changing gender arena has led many men to question what being a man really means.

Herbert Goldberg became a central figure in the early development of the men's movement in the 1970s and early 1980s, mainly as a result of his writings about men's rights in *The Hazards of Being Male* and *The New Male*. Goldberg argues that a critical difference between men and women creates a precipitous gulf between them. That difference: Women can sense and articulate their feelings and problems; men, because of their masculine conditioning, can't. The result is an armor of masculinity that is defensive and powerful in maintaining self-destructive patterns. Goldberg says that most men have been effective work machines and performers but most else in their lives suffers. Men live about 8 years less than women, on the average, have higher hospitalization rates, and show more behavioral problems. In a word, Goldberg believes millions of men are killing themselves by striving to be "true" men, a heavy price to pay for masculine "privilege" and power.

How can men solve their dilemma and live lives that are healthier physically and psychologically? Goldberg argues that men need to get in touch with their emotions and their bodies. They can't do this by just piggybacking on the changes that are occurring in women's attitudes, he says. Rather, men need to develop their own realization of what is critical for their survival and well-being. Goldberg especially encourages men to

- Recognize the suicidal "success" syndrome and avoid it
- Understand that occasional impotence is nothing serious
- Become aware of their real needs and desires and get in touch with their own bodies

Once a year, the giant wooden phallus made during one of Robert Bly's male retreats is raised and used as a centerpiece for a naming ceremony at the Mendocino Men's Conference in California.

- Elude the binds of masculine role-playing
- Relate to liberated women as their equals rather than serving as their guilty servants or hostile enemies
- Develop male friendships

Goldberg's messages to men that they need to become more attuned to their inner self and emotional makeup and work on developing more positive close relationships are important ones (Levant, 1995; Pleck, 1995; Pollack, 1995, White, 1995).

One author who helped usher in a renewed interest in the men's movement in the 1990s is Robert Bly, a poet, storyteller, translator, and best-selling author who is a disciple of Carl Jung's ideas. In *Iron John* (1990), Bly says we live in a society that hasn't had fathers around since the Industrial Revolution. With no viable rituals for introducing young boys to manhood, Bly believes, today's men are left confused. Bly thinks that too many of today's males are "soft," having bonded with their mothers because their fathers were unavailable. These "soft" males know how to follow instead of lead, how to be vulnerable, and how to go with the flow, says Bly. He believes that they don't know what it's like to have a deep masculine identity. Iron John, a hairy mythological creature, has a deep masculine identity. He is, he says, spontaneous and sexual, an action taker, a boundary definer, and an earth preserver. He has untamed impulses and thoughtful self-discipline.

The only way women could have equal rights nowadays would be to surrender some.

Burton Hillis

Bly's views have been criticized heavily by feminists and others. Bly dramatically overstates the separateness of the sexes. Regression to the traditional macho model of masculinity, which excludes sensitivity to others in relationships, is not an orientation that most psychologists believe is wise.

Ethnicity and Gender

Are gender-related attitudes and behavior similar across ethnic groups? All ethnic minority females experience gender expectations for women, just as all ethnic minority males experience gender expectations for men. There are many similarities in the gender-related attitudes of females across ethnic minority groups and of males across ethnic minority groups. Nevertheless, the different experiences of African American, Latino, Asian American, and Native American females and males need to be considered in understanding their gender-related attitudes and behavior. Nonetheless, a number of men today report that they experience conflict about just what the male gender role is (Cournoyer & Mahalik, 1995; Good & others, 1995; Heppner, 1995; Landrine, 1995). In some instances even small differences can be important. For example, the socialization of males and females in other cultures who subsequently migrate to America often reflects a stronger gap between the status of males and females than is experienced in America. Keeping in mind that there are many similarities between females in all ethnic minority groups and between males in all ethnic minority groups, we examine, first, information about females from specific ethnic minority groups, followed by a discussion of males from specific ethnic minority groups.

Ethnic Minority Females

Let's now consider the behavior and psychological orientations of females from some ethnic minority groups: specifically, African American, Asian American, Latina, and Native American females.

Researchers in psychology have only begun to focus on the behavior of African American females. For too long, African American females were considered only as a comparison group for White females on selected psychological dimensions, or they were the subjects in studies in which the primary research interest related to poverty, unwed motherhood, and such (Hall, Evans, & Selice, 1989). This narrow research approach could be viewed as attributing no personal characteristics to African American females beyond the labels given to them by society.

The nature and focus of psychological research on African American females has begun to change—to some extent paralleling societal changes (Hall, Evans, & Selice, 1989). In the 1980s, psychological studies of African American females began to shift away from studies focused only on the problems of African American females and toward research on the positive aspects of African American females in a pluralistic society. In the last decade, psychologists have been studying the more individualized, positive dimensions of African American females, such as self-esteem, achievement, motivation, and self-control.

Fortunately, in the past decade, psychologists have begun to study the positive traits of African American females, such as self-esteem, achievement, motivation, and self-control. As with White women, connectedness in close relationships is an important concern of African American women.

African American females, like other ethnic minority females, have experienced the double jeopardy of racism and sexism. The ingenuity and perseverance shown by ethnic minority females as they have survived and grown against the odds is remarkable. For example, 499 African American women earned doctoral degrees in 1986. They represented only 2 percent of the Ph.D.'s awarded (in comparison, 6.4 percent of the U.S. population are African American females). However, the positive side of these figures is that the Ph.D.'s earned by African American women in 1986 represented an almost 16 percent increase over the number earned in 1977. Despite such gains, our society needs to make a strong commitment to providing African American females with the opportunities they deserve (Young, 1993).

Of my two "handicaps," being female puts many more obstacles in my path than being black.

Shirley Chisholm

Asian American women find significant role changes from the gender traditions of their ancestors. Asian females are often expected to carry on domestic duties, to marry, to become obedient helpers of their mothers-in-law, and to bear children, especially males (Nishio & Bilmes, 1993). In China, the mother's responsibility for the emotional nurturance and well-being of the family, and for raising children, derives from Confucian ethics (Huang & Ying, 1989). However, as China has become modernized, these roles have become less rigid. Similarly, in acculturated Chinese families in the United States, only derivatives of these

rigidly defined roles remain. For example, Chinese American females are not entirely relegated to subservient roles. Author Amy Tan, in works like *The Joy Luck Club* (1989), has eloquently described how Chinese Americans manage bicultural gender expectations.

In traditional Mexican families, women assume the expressive role of homemaker and caretaker of children. This continues to be the norm, although less so than in the past (Comas-Diaz, 1993). Historically, the Mexican female's role has been one of self-denial. Her needs were subordinated to those of other family members. Joint decision making and greater equality of males' and females' roles are becoming more characteristic of Mexican American families (Ramirez & Arce, 1981). Of special significance is the increased frequency of Mexican American women's employment outside the home, which in many instances has enhanced a wife's status in the family and in decision making (Espin, 1993).

For Native Americans, roles and family configurations involving women and men depend on the tribe (LaFromboise, 1993). For example, in the traditional matriarchal Navajo family, an older woman might live with her husband, her unmarried children, her married daughter, and the daughter's husband and children. In patriarchal tribes, women function as the central "core" of the family, maintaining primary responsibility for the welfare of children. Grandmothers and aunts often provide child care. As with other ethnic minority females, Native American females who have moved to urban areas experience the cultural conflict of traditional ethnic values and the values of mainstream American society.

Ethnic Minority Males

Just as ethnic minority females have experienced considerable discrimination and have had to develop coping strategies in the face of adversity, so have ethnic minority males. As with ethnic minority females, our order of discussion will be African American males, Asian American males, Latino males, and Native American males.

Statistics indicate the difficulties many African American males have faced (Parham & McDavis, 1993). African American males of all ages are three times as likely as White males to live in poverty. Of males aged 20 to 44, African Americans are twice as likely to die as Whites. African American male heads of households earn 70 percent of the income of their White male counterparts. Although they make up only 6.3 percent of the U.S. population, African American males constitute 42 percent of jail inmates and more than 50 percent of men executed for any reason in the last 50 years. Murder by gun is the leading cause of death among African American males aged 15 through 19, and rates are getting worse. From 1979 to 1989, the death rate by guns among this age group of African American males increased 71 percent. One study found that a lack of male role models in African American boys' development was a contributing factor (Browne & others, 1993).

Statistics sometimes do not tell the complete story (Evans & Whitfield, 1988). The sociocultural aspects of historical discrimination against an ethnic minority group must be taken into account to understand these statistics. Just as with African American females, researchers are beginning to focus on some of the more positive dimensions of African American males. For example, researchers are finding that African American males are especially efficient at the use of body language in communication, decoding nonverbal cues, multilingual/multicultural expression, and improvised problem solving.

Asian cultural values are reflected in traditional patriarchal Chinese and Japanese families (Sue & Sue, 1993). The father's behavior in relation to other family members is generally dignified, authoritative, remote, and aloof. Sons are generally valued over daughters. Firstborn sons have an especially high status. As with Asian American females, the acculturation experienced by Asian American males has eroded some of the rigid gender roles that characterized Asian families in the past. Fathers still are often the figurative heads of families, especially when dealing with the public, but in private they have relinquished some of their decision-making powers to their wives (Root, 1993).

In Mexican families, men traditionally assume the instrumental role of provider and protector of the family (Ramirez, 1989). The concept of machismo continues to influence the role of the male and the patriarchal orientation of Mexican families, though less than in the past. Traditionally, this orientation required men to be forceful and strong, and also to withhold affectionate emotions. Ideally, it involved a strong sense of personal honor, family, loyalty, and care for children. However, it also has involved exaggerated masculinity and aggression. The concepts of machismo and absolute patriarchy are currently diminishing in influence, but adolescent males are still given much more freedom than adolescent females in Mexican American families.

Some Native American tribes are also patriarchal, with the male being the head of the family and primary decision maker. In some tribes, though, child care is shared by men. For example, Mescalero Apache men take responsibility for children when not working away from the family (Ryan, 1980). Autonomy is highly valued among the male children in many Native American tribes, with the males operating semi-independently at an early age (LaFromboise & Low, 1989). As with Native American females, increased movement to urban areas has led to modifications in the values and traditions of some Native American males.

Culture and Gender

Anthropology studies have provided rich resources for studying the social construction of gender. We will examine examples of cultures that narrowly prescribe gender roles, sometimes in a manner that is alien to our own practices.

We will explore examples of cultures that provide unusual gender roles and those that treat gender as a lifelong process rather than a status. We will also examine how gender roles change within culture over time. These examples will illustrate the arbitrary quality of the social construction of gender across and within cultures.

Prescribed Gender Roles

Margaret Mead (1935/1968) identified three different gender constructions in her studies of the people of New Guinea that illustrate narrow, but divergent definitions of gendered behavior. The Arapesh—both men and women—display cooperative, peaceful, and nurturant behavior, characteristics that we have traditionally associated with women in this culture. Mundugumor women and men display aggressive and competitive behavior, qualities that we have traditionally attributed to men. The Tchambuli demonstrate behavior opposite to the dominant expectations we have for gender in this culture. Women have dominance in this culture from political power to sexual conquest. Men behave in a delicate manner and invest their time making themselves attractive to women. The various social systems of New Guinea underscore the degree to which gender roles are influenced by socialization but can still lead to narrow prescriptions within a culture.

Gender Crossing

Some cultures recognize more than two gender categories (Renzetti & Curran, 1992). In such cultures, individuals who have cross-gender characteristics may achieve special status. For example, traditional Navajo societies have a third category—nadle—that is assigned to those with ambiguous genitals at birth or claimed by some males later in life. Nadles, treated as women, perform both masculine and feminine tasks, mediate problems between women and men, and marry either sex.

The Mohave also offer unusual gender roles that are enacted with the full endorsement of the culture. Mohave women may choose to become hwame; they dress like and conduct themselves like men even if they have had children, but they are restricted from leadership or warrior activities. Boys may become alyha by marrying men and doing female tasks. They may even simulate menstruation, pregnancy, and childbirth without stigma in their culture.

Gender as Process

The Hua of Papua New Guinea believe that gender changes over the lifetime (Gilmore, 1990). Feminine people are seen as invincible, but they have low status because they are "polluted." Women gradually lose their femininity—and their status as polluted—by bearing children. They are no longer polluted after bearing three babies, but they are also no longer invincible. At this point they may share in the higher-status activities of men. As men age, they gradually lose their masculinity to young boys through Hua rituals.

In the culture of the Wodaabe, a nomadic group in Niger, Africa, men—not women—compete in beauty contests to enhance their appeal as potential mates. They apply makeup to enhance their features, adopt colorful and appealing attire, and even have talent competitions. The mating rituals involve dancing and eyeball-rolling. The Wodaabe place great value on being able to roll the eyes in and out independently because they link strength of the eye muscles to the ability to make strong marriages. Such contests might sound familiar even if the gender and context are different.

They lose authority and status because the loss of masculinity renders them polluted, but in exchange they earn invincibility. For the Hua, gender is not a stable category, but a dynamic process that confers status and stigma.

Gender Redefinition

Gender expectations may change within a culture over time as the cultural context evolves (Wood, 1994). Masculine and feminine attributes are usually defined in relation to each other and the predominant values of the context in which gender differences will be played out. Anthropologists emphasize that economic arrangements and technology have an impact on the degree to which female and male roles become differentiated (Kottak, 1991). Cultures oriented to gathering or producing food stress cooperation and may promote fewer differences between women and men. Following the Industrial Revolution, task specialization placed

greater value on physical power and endurance as an attribute of masculinity. In contrast, femininity involved physical weakness and dependence. As technology becomes more sophisticated, the importance of physical strength diminishes. Economic competence and intelligence become more highly valued than physical strength. These examples illustrate how social constructions of masculine and feminine behavior can change within a culture over time. For a discussion of gender roles in Egypt and China, see Sociocultural Worlds 11.2.

I asked a Burmese why women, after centuries of following their men, now walk ahead. He said there were many unexploded land mines since the war.

Robert Mueller

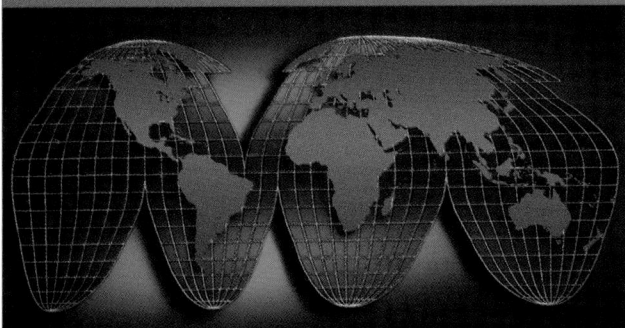

Gender Roles in Egypt and China

In recent decades, roles assumed by males and females in the United States have become increasingly similar—that is, androgynous. In many countries, though, gender roles have remained more gender-specific. For example, in Egypt, the division of labor between Egyptian males and females is dramatic: Egyptian males are socialized to work in the public sphere, females in the private world of home and child rearing. The Islamic religion dictates that the man's duty is to provide for his family, the woman's to care for her family and household (Dickersheid & others, 1988). Any deviations from this traditional gender-role orientation are severely disapproved of.

Egypt is not the only country in which males and females are socialized to behave, think, and feel in strongly gender-specific ways. Kenya and Nepal are two other cultures in which children are brought up under very strict gender-specific guidelines (Munroe, Himmin, & Munroe, 1984). In the People's Republic of China, the female's status has historically been lower than the male's. The teachings of the fifth century B.C. Chinese philosopher Confucius were used to reinforce the concept of the female as an inferior being. Beginning with the 1949 revolution in China, women began to achieve more economic freedom and more equal status in marital relationships. However, even with the sanctions of a socialist government, the old patriarchal traditions of male supremacy in China have not been completely uprooted. Chinese women still make considerably less money than Chinese men in comparable positions, and in rural China, a tradition of male supremacy still governs many women's lives.

Thus, in China, although females have made considerable strides, complete equality remains a distant objective. And in many cultures, such as Egypt and other countries where Islam predominates, gender-specific behavior is pronounced, and females are not given access to high-status positions.

In China, females and males are usually socialized to behave, feel, and think differently. The old patriarchal traditions of male supremacy have not been completely uprooted. Chinese women still make considerably less money than Chinese men, and, in rural China (such as here in the Lixian village of Sichuan), male supremacy still governs many women's lives.

In Egypt near the Aswan Dam, women are returning from the Nile River, where they have filled their water jugs. *How might gender-role socialization for girls in Egypt compare to that in the United States?*

REVIEW

Sociocultural Variations

As a result of the women's movement, men have developed their own movement. Herb Goldberg was a central figure in the men's movement in the 1970s and 1980s. He believes that because of their masculine conditioning men have developed a number of self-destructive behavior patterns. He argues that men need to become more attuned to their inner self and emotional makeup, and work on developing more positive close relationships. A new men's movement in the 1990s, led by Robert Bly, stresses that men are too soft today and that men need to get back to being what a true man really is—deeply masculine. Critics say Bly dramatically overstates the separateness of the sexes, and they don't like his regression to the macho model of masculinity.

There are many similarities between women in different ethnic minority groups and between men in different ethnic minority groups, but even small differences can sometimes be important. The term *women of color* has gained considerable popularity in recent years, but it is important to recognize the diversity that exists among women of color. Women who adopt the label *women of color* believe it underscores their pride and power as women and as people of color. Researchers in psychology have only begun to focus on female behavior in specific ethnic groups in a positive way. Many ethnic minority females have experienced the double jeopardy of racism and sexism. In many instances, Asian American, Latina, and Native American females have lived in patriarchal, male-dominated families, although gender roles have become less rigid in these ethnic groups in recent years. Just as ethnic minority females have experienced considerable discrimination and have had to develop coping strategies in the face of adversity, so have ethnic minority males. Researchers are beginning to focus more on the positive dimensions of African American females and males. A patriarchal, male-dominant orientation has characterized many ethnic minority groups, such as Asian Americans, Latinos, and Native Americans, although women are gaining greater decision making in these cultures, especially women who develop careers and work outside of the home.

CRITICAL THINKING ABOUT BEHAVIOR

Gender Equality and Imbalance

You have been exposed to many stories about the limitations and opportunities linked to gender. Many might have surprised you, perhaps even shocked you. You may have questioned whether you could have thrived under conditions very different from those in which you were raised. Or you might have wondered whether our own culture would be better off with more clearly delineated expectations on gender.

One challenge cross-cultural researchers face is the need to remain objective in their observations and analyses, especially regarding practices that appear contrary to their own sense of values. For example, feminist scholars find it difficult to study cultures with gender systems based on inequity, especially those that deny women full participation in the culture or cause them physical harm. We may struggle to understand practices that involve mutilation of the female genitalia, that restrict freedom of choice and mobility, and that deprive women of any economic or political influence. The temptation is strong to make judgments about the progressiveness—or lack of it—in such a culture.

As much progress as we have made with regard to equal opportunity in our own culture, systems of privilege—subtle and not so subtle—are still operative in the United States. Any socialization that deprives people of one gender the opportunities that are open to people of the other can be suspected of not promoting equality. Reflect on these examples:

- Who is socialized about proper leg position (e.g., knees together)?
- Who pays for the check?
- Can a woman ask a man for a date without enduring suspicion?
- Whose name changes as a result of the wedding ceremony?
- Who drives?
- Who cleans up during major holiday gatherings?
- Who holds back in some skill so as not to embarrass the partner?
- Who initiates sex?
- Who interrupts and who yields?

If we prize equality, we must recognize that social systems take a long time to change. Such understanding can help us *appreciate individual differences* and avoid being judgmental about the adequacy of other cultures. We need to take precautions not to assume that ours is the only or best way of life.

There are very few jobs that actually require a penis or vagina. All other jobs should be open to everybody.

Florynce R. Kennedy

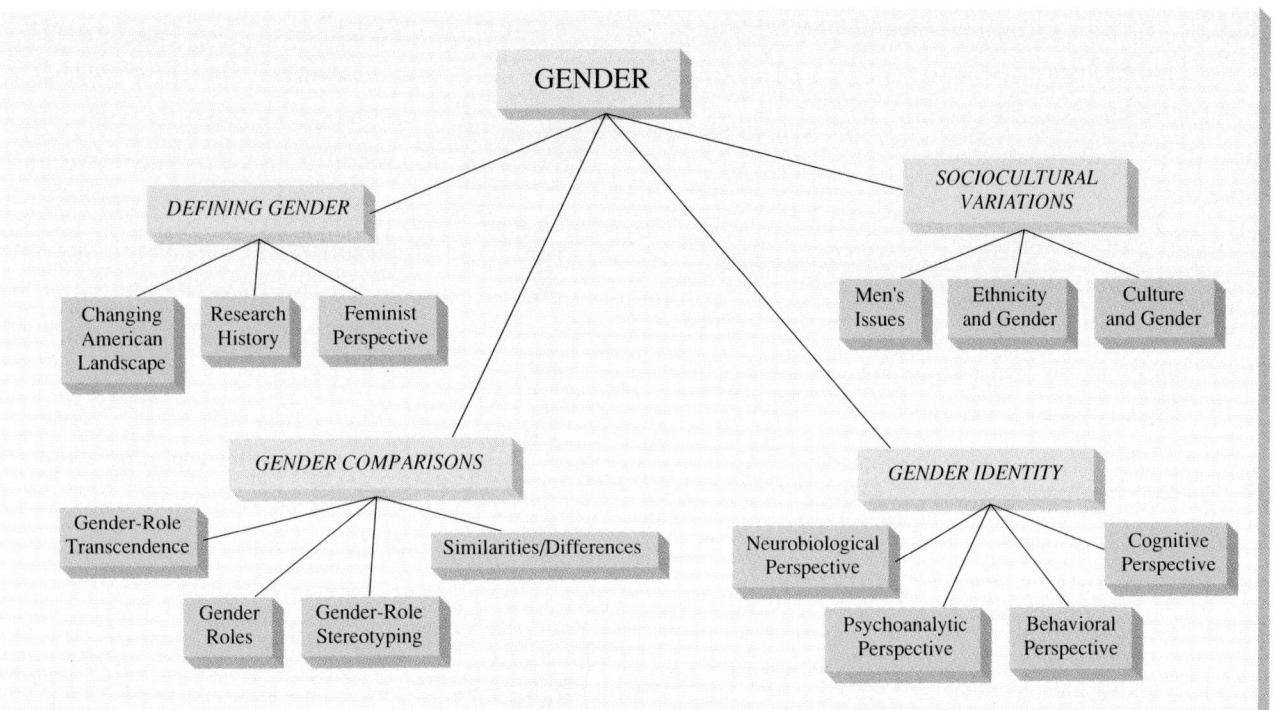

We began this chapter by defining gender, including ideas about the changing American landscape of gender, the history of research on gender, and the feminist perspective. Next we turned our attention to gender comparisons, evaluating the nature of gender roles, gender-role stereotyping, and similarities and differences between women and men. Our coverage of gender identity focused on four main perspectives: the neurobiological, psychoanalytic, behavioral, and cognitive. Then we studied sociocultural variations involving gender—men's issues, ethnicity and gender, and culture and gender. Don't forget that you can obtain an overall summary of the chapter by again reading the in-chapter reviews on pages 389, 397, 401, and 408.

PERSPECTIVES

All six main perspectives were emphasized in this chapter: sociocultural, behavioral, cognitive, neurobiological, psychoanalytic, and humanistic. The sociocultural perspective was reflected in the discussion of defining gender (pp. 384–389), sociocultural variations (pp. 402–406), women's struggle for equality as an international journey (p. 388), and gender roles in China and Egypt (p. 407). The behavioral perspective appeared in the material on the behavioral perspective of gender identity (pp. 399–400) and social differences in gender comparisons (pp. 395–396). The cognitive perspective was present in the description of

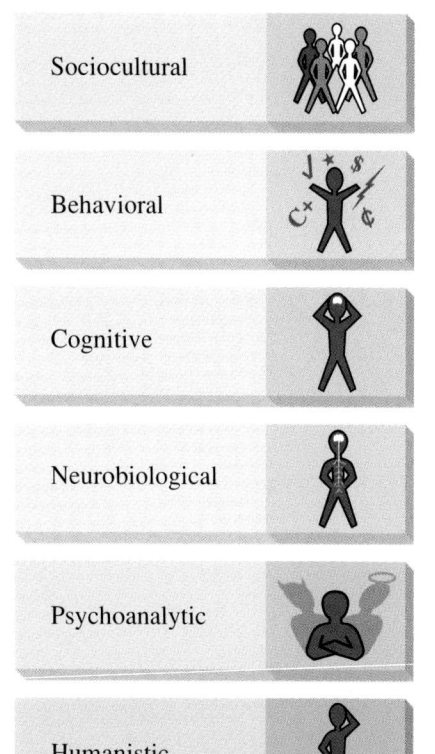

Sociocultural

Behavioral

Cognitive

Neurobiological

Psychoanalytic

Humanistic

the cognitive perspective on gender identity (pp. 400–401), gender-role stereotypes (pp. 392–393), and cognitive differences in gender comparisons (pp. 394–395). The neurobiological perspective appeared in the discussion of the neurobiological perspective on gender identity (pp. 397–398) and physical and biological differences in gender comparisons (p. 394). The psychoanalytic perspective was reflected in the psychoanalytic perspective on gender identity. The humanistic perspective appeared in the discussion of the feminist movement (pp. 387–389).

KEY TERMS

gender The sociocultural dimension of being male or female. 384

gender roles Sets of expectations that prescribe how females or males should think, act, or feel. 385

gender identity The sense of being male or female, which most children begin to acquire by the time they are 2 or 3 years old. 385

misogyny Hatred of women. 389

androgyny The presence of desirable masculine and feminine characteristics in one individual. 390

gender-role transcendence The belief that an individual's competence should be conceptualized not on the basis of masculinity, femininity, or androgyny but, rather, on the basis of the person. 391

gender-role stereotypes Broad categories that reflect our impressions and beliefs about females and males. 392

androgens The main class of male sex hormones. 397

estrogens The main class of female sex hormones. 397

identification theory A theory that stems from Freud's view that preschool children develop a sexual attraction to the opposite-sex parent, then, at 5 to 6 years of age, renounce the attraction, due to anxiety, subsequently identifying with the same-sex parent and unconsciously adopting the same-sex parent's characteristics. 398

social learning theory of gender The theory that children's gender development occurs through observation and imitation of gender-related behavior, as well as through the rewards and punishments children experience for gender-appropriate and gender-inappropriate behaviors. 399

cognitive developmental theory of gender The view that children's gender typing occurs after they have developed a concept of gender. Once they begin to consistently conceive themselves as male or female, children often organize their world on the basis of gender. 400

schema A cognitive structure, or network of associations, that organizes and guides an individual's perception. 401

gender schema A cognitive structure that organizes the world in terms of female and male. 401

gender schema theory The theory that children's attention and behavior are guided by an internal motivation to conform to gender-based sociocultural standards and stereotypes. 401

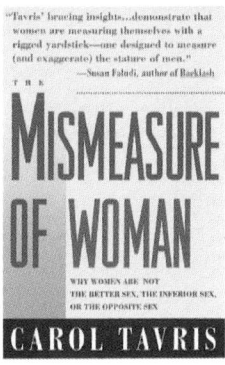

THE MISMEASURE OF WOMAN

(1992) by Carol Tavris. New York: Touchstone.

The Mismeasure of Woman explores the stereotyping of women and similarities and differences between women and men. *The Mismeasure of Woman* explores eight main issues, summarized in her chapter subtitles as follows:

- Why women are not inferior to men
- Why women are not superior to men
- Premenstrual syndrome, postmenstrual syndrome, and other normal "diseases"
- Why women are "sick" but men have problems
- Fables of female sexuality
- How women cornered the love market
- Speaking of gender—the darkened eye restored

Tavris believes that no matter how hard women try, they can't measure up. They are criticized for being too female or not female enough, but they are always judged and mismeasured by how well they fit into a male world. *The Mismeasure of Woman* contains a thorough review of research studies that document how women are ignored, misrepresented, or even harmed by the still male-dominated health professions, which base their standards of normalcy on male anatomy, physiology, and psychology. Whether in the study of heart disease, where the effect of female hormones on cholesterol is ignored, or in the study of brain structure, where unsubstantiated research is used to explain the supposed inferiority of female spatial and reasoning skills, Tavris argues, women are continually evaluated from a male vantage point.

Tavris believes that more evidence exists for similarities between the sexes than for differences between them. She does not accept male superiority or female superiority. The author refutes feminists who say that women are more empathic than men, and she rejects the notion the women are less sexual. Tavris explores how society "pathologizes" women through psychiatric diagnoses, sexist divorce rulings, and images of women as moody, self-defeating, and unstable.

This is an excellent self-help book on gender stereotyping, similarities and differences between the sexes, and how women should be measured by their own standards, not men's. It is well documented and captivating in presenting a witty portrayal of women's issues and dilemmas, and what can be done about them.

YOU JUST DON'T UNDERSTAND

(1990) by Deborah Tannen. New York: Ballantine.

The subtitle of this book is "Women and Men in Conversation." This is a book about how women and men communicate—or all too often miscommunicate—with each other. *You Just Don't Understand* reached the status of number one on best-sellers lists, and as we write this book continues to be on the *New York Times* best-sellers list. Tannen shows that friction between women and men in conversation often develops because boys and girls were brought up in two virtually distinct cultures. As we indicated earlier in the chapter in our presentation of Tannen's ideas, she believes that the two distinct gender cultures are rapport talk (women's) and report talk (men's).

Tannen's book has especially connected with women, many of whom, after reading the book, want their husband or male partner to read it. Prior to Tannen's analysis, the common way to explain communication problems between women and men was to resort to blaming men's desire to dominate women. Tannen presents a more balanced approach to female-male communication problems by focusing on different ways females and males communicate, and a more positive approach, by emphasizing that women and men can get along better by understanding each other's different styles.

THE DANCE OF INTIMACY

(1990) by Harriet Lerner. New York: Harper Perennial.

The Dance of Intimacy is written for women and is about women's intimate relationships. The book is subtitled "A Woman's Guide to Courageous Acts of Change in Key Relationships." Drawing on a combination of psychoanalytic and family systems theories, Lerner weaves together a portrait of a woman's current self and relationships that she believes is derived from long-standing relationships with mothers, fathers, and siblings. Lerner tells women that if they are having problems in intimate relationships with a partner or their family of origin, they need to explore the nature of their family upbringing to produce clues to the current difficulties. Women learn how to distance themselves from their family of origin and how not to overreact to problems. Lerner gives women insights about how to define themselves, how to understand their needs and limits, and how to

positively change. Positive change involves moving from being stuck in relationships that are going nowhere or are destructive to intimate connectedness with others and a solid sense of self. Lerner intelligently tells women that they should balance the "I" and the "We" in their lives, neither becoming too self-absorbed nor too other-oriented. To explore unhealthy patterns of close relationships that have been passed down from one generation to the next in their family, the author helps women create what she calls a *genogram,* a family diagram that goes back to their grandparents or earlier.

This is an outstanding self-help book for understanding why close relationships are problematic and how to change them in positive ways. It does not give simple, quick-fix solutions. Lerner accurately tells women that change is difficult, but possible. Her warm, personal tone helps women to gain the self-confidence necessary to make the changes she recommends.

THE NEW MALE

(1980) by Herb Goldberg. New York: Signet.

This book is subtitled "From Macho to Sensitive but Still Male." Goldberg's purpose in writing *The New Male* was to explore what the world of the traditional male has been like in the past, including his relationship with females; what the male's world is like in today's era of changing gender roles; and what the future could hold for males if they examine, reshape, and expand their gender-role behavior and self-awareness. Goldberg argues that the way the traditional male role has been defined has made it virtually impossible for males to explore their inner selves, examine their feelings, and show sensitivity toward others.

The New Male is divided into four parts: (I) "He," which evaluates the traditional male role and its entrapments, (II) "He and She," which explores the traditional relationship between males and females, (III) "He and Her Changes," which analyzes how the changes in roles of females brought about by the women's movement has affected males, and (IV) "He and His Changes," which provides hope for males by elaborating on how males can combine some of the strengths of traditional masculinity—such as assertiveness and independence—with increased exploration of the inner self, greater awareness of emotions, and more healthy close relationships with others to become more complete, better adjusted males.

American Association of University Women

    1111 Sixteenth Street

    Washington, DC 20036

This organization promotes education and equity for girls and women. It provides sabbaticals for public school teachers to learn how to more effectively teach girls and supports community projects to foster equal opportunities for females.

Boston Women's Health Book Collective

    6 Nichols Street

    Watertown, MA 02172

    617–423–0650

This collective is a widely respected resource for support and information about women's issues. They publish a number of books on gender-related issues, especially women's health concerns.

The Male Experience (1991, 2nd ed.)

    by James Doyle

    Dubuque, IA: Brown & Benchmark

This book covers a number of topics about male issues, including elements of the male role, values, men of color, and gay men.

Meeting at the Crossroads (1992)

    by Lyn Brown and Carol Gilligan

    Cambridge, MA: Harvard University Press

This book presents the view that adolescence is a critical juncture in the development of girls and women.

National Action Committee on the Status of Women/Comite canadien d'action sur le statut de la femme

    234 Eglinton Ave. East #203

    Toronto, ON M4P 1K5 CANADA

    416–932–1718

    1–800–665–5124 (in Canada)

This group sponsors numerous publications dealing with the status and improvement of life of women in Canada.

National Center for Computer Equity

    99 Hudson Street

    New York, NY 10013

    212–925–6635

This organization tries to improve girls' opportunities in computer education, hoping to provide them with equal access to computer learning. The center is sponsored by the National Organization of Women (NOW).

The Psychology of Women (1992)

    by Michelle Paludi

    Dubuque, IA: Brown & Benchmark

This excellent book on women's issues covers many topics, including mental health and well-being, women's communication, career development, and social policy applications.

YMCA of/du Canada

    2160 Yonge St. #200

    Toronto, ON M4S 2A9

    416–485–9447

YMCA of the USA

    101 N. Wacker Drive

    Chicago, IL 60606

The YMCA provides programs for teenage boys in various areas, including personal health and sports.

YWCA of/du Canada

    80 Gerrard Street East

    Toronto, ON M5B 1G6

    416–593–9886

YWCA of the USA

    726 Broadway

    New York, NY 10003

The YWCA promotes health, sports participation, and fitness for women and girls. Its programs include health instruction, teen pregnancy prevention, family life education, self-esteem enhancement, parenting, and nutrition.

CHAPTER

12

Human Sexuality

CHAPTER BOXES

*The sexual embrace can only be
compared with music and with prayer.*

Havelock Ellis, *On Life and Sex*, 1937

THE STORY OF CLELIA MOSHER: SEX RESEARCHER IN THE VICTORIAN ERA

Sexual repression reigned in England and in the United States in the late 1800s during Queen Victoria's rule in England. In this Victorian era, women were not supposed to possess any sexual desires.

A remarkable woman, Dr. Clelia Mosher, emerged in the Victorian context. She attended Wellesley, Stanford, and Johns Hopkins, receiving her M.D. degree at Hopkins in the 1890s. Over a period of three decades, beginning when she was an undergraduate student, Mosher conducted a sex survey of Victorian women, administering her nine-page questionnaire to 47 women. Admittedly, the sample was small and nonrandom—many of the women were faculty wives at universities or women from Mosher's medical practice. Of the sample, more than 4 out of 5 had attended college, a high level of education for women in the 1800s (Jacob, 1981).

Nonetheless, the survey is extremely enlightening because, despite well-known views about Victorian women, Mosher's is the only actual survey about these women known to exist. Following are some intriguing findings from the survey (Hyde, 1994):

- The stereotype about Victorian women is that they experienced no sexual desire. However, in Mosher's survey, 80 percent of the women said they felt a desire for sexual intercourse.
- The Victorian stereotype also includes the belief that Victorian women should not have orgasms. Yet in Mosher's survey, 72 percent of the Victorian women said that they experienced orgasms.
- Some of the women in Mosher's survey reported that women's longer time to reach orgasm might be a source of marital conflict. One woman said that she achieved orgasm if time is taken. Another complained that men have not been properly trained.
- Almost two-thirds of the women used some form of birth control. Douching was the most popular method, followed by withdrawal and "timing." Several women's husbands used a "male sheath," and two women used a "rubber cap over their uterus."

In sum, Clelia Mosher's survey revealed that many Victorian women managed to enjoy sex despite the sexually repressive Victorian attitudes of the time.

PREVIEW

Clelia Mosher's Victorian sex survey calls attention to the extensive role that stereotypes, myths, and sociohistorical contexts play in human sexuality. Sex is a powerful human motive. Philip Wylie, in *Generation of the Vipers* (1942), labeled sex "one of the three or four prime movers of all we do and are and dream." We will explore many different dimensions of human sexuality in this chapter, including sexual arousal and the human sexual response, sexual knowledge, attitudes, and behavior, psychosexual disorders, and sexuality and harm.

SEXUAL AROUSAL AND THE HUMAN SEXUAL RESPONSE CYCLE

The first time you experienced a tingling sensation in your genital area, you may have been reading a book, thinking about a person to whom you were really attracted, or sleeping and having a pleasurable sensuous dream. If you wondered what that tingling sensation was about, you were not alone. Most of us become sexual beings before we have any idea what sex is all about. What causes us to get sexually aroused?

Sexual Arousal

Both biological and psychological factors are involved in our sexual arousal. Human sexual behavior is influenced by the presence of hormones in the blood stream. Hormones are among the most powerful, yet subtle, chemicals in nature. All of the hormones are controlled by the pituitary gland, which is located in the brain. Estrogens are the main class of sex hormones in females, while androgens (of which testosterone is the most important) are the main class in males.

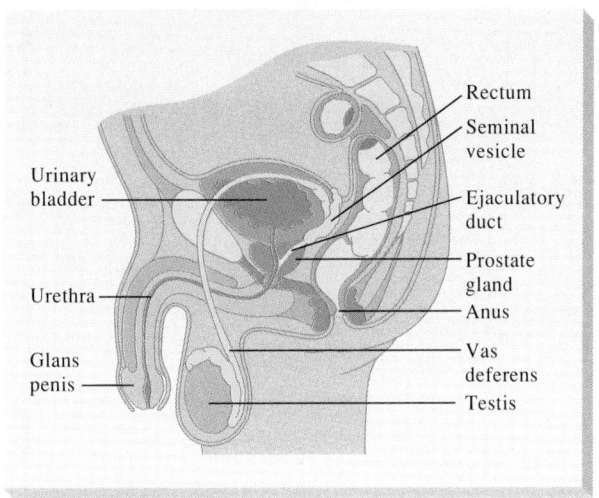

FIGURE 12.1

Male Reproductive Organs
The testes are the male gonads that produce sperm cells and manufacture the male androgen called testosterone. The glans penis is the head of the penis. The vas deferens is the duct through which stored sperm is passed. It is the vas deferens that is cut or blocked in a vasectomy. The seminal vesicles are the two sacs of the male internal genitalia, which secrete nutrients to help sperm become motile. The prostate gland is a structure of the internal male genitalia that secretes a fluid into the semen prior to ejaculation to aid sperm motility and elongate sperm life. The urethra is the tube through which the bladder empties urine outside the body and through which the male sperm exits.

At puberty, males experience a dramatic increase in testosterone levels, with a resultant increase in sexual thoughts and fantasies, masturbation, and nocturnal emissions. Indeed, in male adolescents, the higher the blood levels of testosterone, the more the adolescent is preoccupied with sexual thoughts and engages in sexual activities. Throughout the year, the male's testes secrete androgens in fairly consistent amounts (see figure 12.1 for a diagram of the male reproductive system, including the testes). Because of the consistent levels, males are hormonally ready to be stimulated to engage in sexual behavior at any time. As a man ages, his testosterone level gradually declines; this is usually accompanied by a decline in sexual interest and activity.

At puberty, females' ovaries begin to produce the female sex hormones called estrogen (see figure 12.2 for a diagram of the female reproductive system). Unlike androgen, estrogen is not constantly produced. Rather, estrogen levels vary over an approximately month-long cycle. Estrogen levels are highest when the female is ovulating (releasing an egg from one of her ovaries), which is midway through the menstrual cycle. It is at this time that a female is most likely to become pregnant. In many nonhuman animals, this high-estrogen period is the only time that females are receptive to male initiatives to mate. Although the strength of sexual interest in females varies with estrogen levels, human females are capable of being interested in

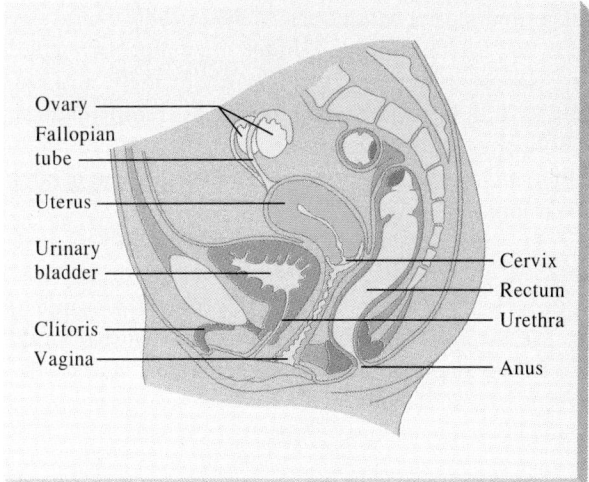

FIGURE 12.2

Female Reproductive Organs
The uterus is a pear-shaped, hollow structure of the female genitalia, in which the embryo and fetus develop prior to birth. The thick, muscular wall of the uterus expands and contracts during pregnancy. The cervix is the mouth of the uterus, through which the vagina extends. The vagina is the hollow, tunneled structure of the female internal genitalia; its reproductive functions are to receive the penis and its ejaculate, to be a route of exit for the newborn, and to provide an exit for menstrual flow. The clitoris is a part of the female genitalia that is very sensitive to stimulation. The ovaries, adjacent to both sides of the uterus, house ova prior to their maturation and discharge; they also produce estrogen. The fallopian tubes are the routes through which eggs leave the ovaries on their way to the uterus. Fertilization usually takes place in the fallopian tubes.

sexual involvement throughout the menstrual cycle. Indeed, only a minimal level of estrogen seems to be required to sustain sexual desire in women. Thus, as we move from the lower to the higher animals, hormonal control over behavior is less dominant, although still important, in sexual arousal; for humans, both sociocultural and cognitive factors play more-important roles. Still, estrogen does have some influence on women's sexuality. Although postmenopausal women have a significant drop in estrogen, they are still sexually active; if given estrogen, they experience an increased interest in sex and report that sexual activity is more pleasurable.

Cultural Contexts and Arousal

What "turns people on" is influenced by their sociocultural background, their individual preferences, and their cognitive interpretations. The range in cultural sexual values is considerable. Some cultures consider sexual pleasures as "normal" or "desirable" while other cultures view sexual pleasures as "weird" or "abnormal." Consider the people who live on the small island of Ines Beag off the coast of Ireland. They are among the most sexually repressed people in the world. They know nothing about tongue kissing or hand stimulation of the penis, and nudity is detested. For both females and males, premarital sex is out of the question. Men avoid most sexual experiences because they believe that sexual intercourse reduces their energy level and is bad for their health. Under these repressive conditions, sexual intercourse occurs only at night and takes place as quickly as possible as the husband opens his nightclothes under the covers and the wife raises her nightgown. As you might suspect, female orgasm is rare in this culture (Messinger, 1971).

By contrast, consider the Mangaian culture in the South Pacific. In Mangaia, young boys are taught about masturbation and are encouraged to engage in it as much as they like. At age 13, the boys undergo a ritual that initiates them into sexual manhood. First their elders instruct them about sexual strategies, including how to aid their female partner in having orgasms. Then, 2 weeks later, the boy has intercourse with an experienced woman who helps him hold back ejaculation until she can achieve orgasm with him. By the end of adolescence, Mangaians have sex virtually every day. Mangaian women report a high frequency of orgasm.

Sexuality is the great field of battle between biology and society.

Nancy Friday, *My Mother/My Self*, 1977

Our culture is more liberal than that of the Ines Beag but less tolerant and more conservative than that of the Mangaians. The cultural diversity in sexual behavior around the world is testimony to the importance of environmental experiences in determining sexual arousal. In complex organisms, experience plays a more powerful role in sexuality than hormones do.

Arousal Cues

We cannot mate in midair like bees or give magnificent displays of plumage like peacocks do, but we can talk about sex with each other, read about it in magazines, and watch it on television or at the movies. Touch, visual cues, certain words written or heard, and smells can all be sexually arousing. However, there are individual differences in what turns people on. One woman might thrill to having her ears nibbled; another might find it annoying. Most of us think of kissing as highly stimulating, but in a vast majority of tribal societies kissing is either unheard of or thought to be disgusting.

Whoever named it necking was a poor judge of anatomy.

Groucho Marx

Men and women differ in the role that visual stimulation plays in sexual arousal. Men are more aroused by what they see; perhaps this fact helps to explain why erotic magazines and X-rated movies are more directed toward males than toward females (Money, 1986). More than through visual stimulation, women become sexually aroused through tender, loving touches that are coupled with verbal

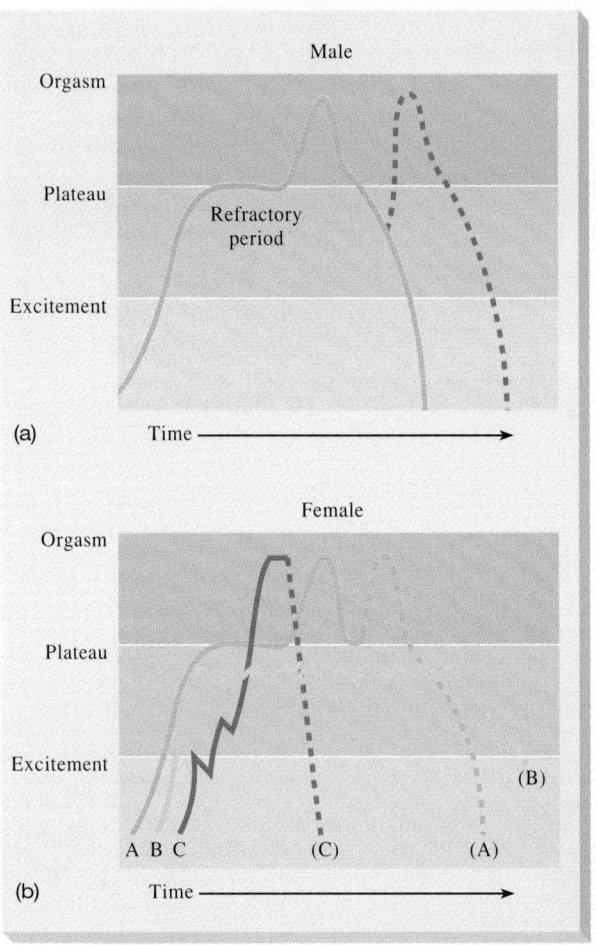

FIGURE 12.3

Male and Female Human Sexual Response Patterns
(*a*) This diagram shows the excitement, plateau, orgasm, and resolution phases of the human male sexual response pattern. Notice that males enter a refractory period, which lasts from several minutes up to a day, in which they cannot have another orgasm. (*b*) This diagram shows the excitement, plateau, orgasm, and resolution phases of the human female sexual response pattern. Notice that female sexual responses follow one of three basic patterns. Pattern *A* somewhat resembles the male pattern, except that pattern *A* includes the possibility of multiple orgasm (the second peak in pattern *A*) without falling below the plateau level. Pattern *B* represents nonorgasmic arousal. Pattern *C* represents intense female orgasm, which resembles the male pattern in its intensity and rapid resolution.

expressions of love. Moreover, men can become aroused quickly, while women's arousal typically builds gradually.

The Human Sexual Response Cycle

How do humans respond physiologically during sexual activity? To answer this question, gynecologist William Masters and his colleague Virginia Johnson (1966) carefully observed and measured the physiological responses of 382 female and 312 male volunteers as they masturbated or had sexual intercourse. The **human sexual response cycle** *consists of four phases—excitement, plateau, orgasm, and resolution—as identified by Masters and Johnson* (see figure 12.3).

Sexual behavior has its magnificent moments throughout the animal kingdom. Insects mate in midair, peacocks display their plumage, and male elephant seals have prolific sex lives. Socioemotional experiences and cognitive interpretation play a more important role in human sexual behavior. We can talk about sex with each other, read about it in magazines, and watch it on television and the movie screen.

The second phase of the human sexual response, called the *plateau phase,* is a continuation and heightening of the arousal begun in the excitement phase. The increases in breathing, pulse rate, and blood pressure that occurred during the excitement phase become more intense, penile erection and vaginal lubrication are more complete, and orgasm is closer.

The third phase of the human sexual response cycle is *orgasm.* How long does orgasm last? Some individuals sense that time is standing still when it takes place, but orgasm lasts for only about 3 to 15 seconds. Orgasm involves an explosive discharge of neuromuscular tension and an intense pleasurable feeling. However, not all orgasms are exactly alike. For example, females show three different patterns in the orgasm phase, as shown in figure 12.3: (a) multiple orgasms, (b) no orgasm, and (c) excitement rapidly leading to orgasm, bypassing the plateau phase; the third

The *excitement phase* begins erotic responsiveness; it lasts from several minutes to several hours, depending on the nature of the sex play involved. Engorgement of blood vessels and increased blood flow in genital areas and muscle tension characterize the excitement phase. The most obvious signs of response in this phase are lubrication of the vagina and partial erection of the penis.

pattern most clearly corresponds to the male pattern in intensity and resolution.

Following orgasm, the individual enters the *resolution phase,* in which blood vessels return to their normal state. One difference between males and females in this phase is that females may be stimulated to orgasm again without delay. Males enter a refractory period, lasting anywhere from several minutes to an entire day, in which they cannot have another orgasm. The length of the refractory period increases as men age.

We have examined some of the biological aspects of human sexual behavior. Next we will explore how individuals in the United States learn about sexuality and how this influences attitudes about sexual expression.

Whatever else can be said about sex, it cannot be called a dignified performance.

Helen Laurenson

REVIEW

Sexual Arousal and the Human Sexual Response

Both biological and psychological factors are involved in sexual arousal. Hormones are important biological factors, with estrogens being the dominant sex hormone in females, androgens in males. From puberty on, the level of male androgens does not vary over short periods of time like the production of estrogens does in females. As we move from the lower to the higher animals, hormonal control over sexual behavior is less dominant, although hormones still play an important role in sexual arousal. In humans, sexual arousal is also influenced by sociocultural standards, individual preferences, and cognitive interpretation. Masters and Johnson mapped out the nature of the human sexual response cycle, which consists of four phases—excitement, plateau, orgasm, and resolution.

SEXUAL KNOWLEDGE, ATTITUDES, AND BEHAVIOR

According to sexuality expert Bernie Zilbergeld (1992), our culture has experienced dramatic changes in the sexual landscape in the last decade—from changing expectations of and about women to new definitions of masculinity, from the fear of disease to renewed focus on long-term relationships. Even though scientific knowledge about sexuality has grown substantially, we are unlikely to acquire sexual knowledge in a scientific or systematic fashion. It is not that American adolescents and adults are sheltered from sexual messages; sexual information and imagery are abundant in this culture. However, much that passes for information is misinformation. Our attitudes about sexuality are shaped by education, experience, media, and mythology.

Sexual Knowledge, Myths, and Education

How widespread are sexual myths? What is the nature of sex education?

Sexual Knowledge

How much do we really know about sex? According to June Reinisch (1990), director of the Kinsey Institute for Sex, Gender, and Reproduction, the United States is a nation whose citizens know more about how their automobiles function than about how their bodies function sexually. Reinisch directed a national assessment of basic sexual knowledge that was given to 1,974 adults. For example, 65 percent did not know that most erection difficulties begin with physical problems. Fifty percent did not know that oil-based lubricants should not be used with condoms or diaphragms because some can produce holes in them in less than 60 seconds. There is a great deal that we might not know, but what might be even more problematic are the unfounded myths about sexuality that we believe.

Sexual Myths

Sexuality's many myths have led to unrealistic expectations for our lives. One man commented that he had learned so much misinformation about sex as a child that it was taking him the rest of his life to unlearn it. In middle age, he still can't believe how much stress he caused himself when he was younger and wishes he could apologize to the women who knew him in his earlier years.

Adolescents in the United States believe in a distressing amount of misinformation and mythology. In one investigation, a majority of adolescents believed that pregnancy risk is greatest during menstruation (Zelnick & Kantner, 1977). Additional examples of the myths that complicate sexual understanding are explored in the critical thinking exercise at the end of this chapter. These examples underscore the serious need for improving our sexual awareness and knowledge; this can help reduce unwanted pregnancies and promote self-protection.

GLENN BERNHARDT

"I don't like this A in sex education."

© Glenn Bernhardt.

Sex Education

We get very little sex education from our parents. A large majority of American adolescents say they cannot talk freely about sex with their parents (Thornburg, 1981). Because many parents so inadequately handle sex education, it is not surprising that most of them prefer to let the schools do the job. In a national poll conducted by *Time* magazine, 78 percent of parents wanted schools to teach sex education, including information about birth control (Wallis, 1985).

Despite the majority opinion, sex education remains controversial. On one side are groups like Planned Parenthood who argue that sex education should be more open and birth control more available, like they are in European countries (see Sociocultural Worlds 12.1 to read about the sex education and attitudes of youth in Holland and Sweden). On the other side are individuals who believe sex education should be provided solely by parents. These persons usually believe that teaching adolescents about birth control is simply giving them a license to have sex and be promiscuous. The controversy has led to clashes at school board meetings throughout the nation. For instance, to combat its runaway adolescent pregnancy problem, New York City initiated a program, among other things, to distribute condoms to students. Religious groups showed up at a school board meeting with a list of over fifty objections. In San Juan Capistrano, California, conservatives appeared at a school board meeting dressed in Revolutionary War clothes to protest liberal sex education practices.

Sex education programs in schools might not by themselves prevent adolescent pregnancy and sexually transmitted diseases. Researchers have found that sex education classes do improve adolescents' knowledge about human sexuality but do not always change their sexual behavior. When sex education classes are combined with readily available contraceptives, teen pregnancy rates are more likely to drop (Wallis, 1985). Such findings have led

Sex Education and Attitudes Among Youth in Holland and Sweden

In Holland and Sweden, sex does not carry the mystery and conflict it does in American society. Holland does not have a mandated sex education program, but adolescents can obtain contraceptive counseling at government-sponsored clinics for a small fee. The Dutch media also have played an important role in educating the public about sex through frequent broadcasts focused on birth control, abortion, and related matters. Most Dutch adolescents do not consider having sex without birth control.

Swedish adolescents are sexually active at an earlier age than are American adolescents, and they are exposed to even more explicit sex on television. However, the Swedish National Board of Education has developed a curriculum that ensures that every child in the country, beginning at age 7, will experience a thorough grounding in reproductive biology and, by the age of 10 or 12, will have been introduced

to information about various forms of contraception. Teachers are expected to handle the subject of sex whenever it becomes relevant, regardless of the subject they are teaching. The idea is to take some of the drama and mystery out of sex so that familiarity will make students less vulnerable to unwanted pregnancy and sexually transmitted diseases (Wallis, 1985). American society is not nearly so open about sex education.

Sex is much more demystified and less dramatized in Sweden than in the United States, and adolescent pregnancy rates are much lower in Sweden than in the United States.

to the development of *school-linked* rather than *school-based* approaches to sex education and pregnancy prevention. In one program pioneered by some Baltimore public schools in cooperation with Johns Hopkins University, family-planning clinics are located adjacent to the schools (Zabin, 1986). These clinics send a nurse and a social worker into the schools to make formal presentations about sexuality and the services available from the clinics. They also make themselves available to the students for counseling several hours each day. The same personnel conduct after-school sessions at the clinic, consisting of further counseling, films, and family-planning information. The results have been very positive. Students who participated in the school-linked programs delayed their first intercourse longer than students in a control group did. After 28 months, the pregnancy rate had declined to 30 percent in the school-linked programs, while it rose to 60 percent in the control group. Thus, the support services provided by the community-based, school-linked family-planning clinic were effective in reducing adolescent pregnancy.

Contraception

Most couples in the United States want to be able to control whether and when they will conceive a child. For them it is important to have accurate knowledge about contraception.

Inadequate knowledge about contraception, coupled with inconsistent use of effective contraceptive methods, has resulted in this country's having the dubious distinction of having the highest adolescent pregnancy rate in the industrialized world (Coleman, 1995). Although the rate of use among teenagers is improving, many still do not use contraception. Moreover, a majority of adolescents do not use contraception during their first sexual intercourse experience (Hofferth, 1990). Seventy percent of females who become sexually active before the age of 15 have unprotected first intercourse; the percentage drops to about 50 percent for those who become active around the age of 18 or 19.

Age also influences the choice of contraceptive method. Older adolescents and young adults are more likely to rely on the pill or diaphragm; younger adolescents are

Adolescents are increasing their use of contraceptives, although large numbers of sexually active adolescents still do not use contraceptives, especially at first intercourse.

more likely to use a condom or withdrawal (Hofferth, 1990). Even adults in stable relationships sometimes do not use adequate contraception, perhaps feeling that some contraceptives, such as condoms, interrupt the spontaneity of sex, or they might overestimate the effectiveness of some of the unreliable methods.

No method of contraception is best for everyone. When choosing a method of contraception, couples need to consider such factors as their physical and emotional concerns, the method's effectiveness, the nature of their relationship, their values and beliefs, and the method's convenience. Calculations of the effectiveness of a contraceptive method often are based on the failure rates during the first year of use. It is estimated that if no contraceptive method were used, about 90 percent of women would become pregnant in their first year of being (heterosexually) sexually active (Hatcher & others, 1988). Table 12.1 shows the typical failure rate of different contraceptive methods.

Women who miscalculate are called "mothers."

Abigail Van Buren

The knowledge we acquire serves as the foundation of our attitudes about sexuality as well as the behaviors we engage in. In the next section we will explore how knowledge, attitudes, and sexual behavior are interrelated.

Heterosexuality and Homosexuality

Gathering accurate information about sexual attitudes and behavior is a difficult task. Consider how you would respond if someone asked you the following questions: How often do you have sex? How many different sexual partners have you had? How often do you masturbate? The people most likely to respond to surveys about sexual behavior are those with liberal sexual attitudes who engage in liberal sexual behaviors. Thus, what we know is limited by the reluctance of some individuals to candidly answer questions about extremely personal matters, and by our inability to get any answer, candid or otherwise, from individuals who believe that they should not talk about sex with strangers. Researchers refer to this as a "volunteer bias." Imagine how challenging this problem would be with the additional complication of studying sexual practices in other cultures. With these cautions in mind, let's now turn to a discussion of sexual attitudes and behavior, primarily in the United States, beginning with heterosexual relations and then turning to homosexual relations.

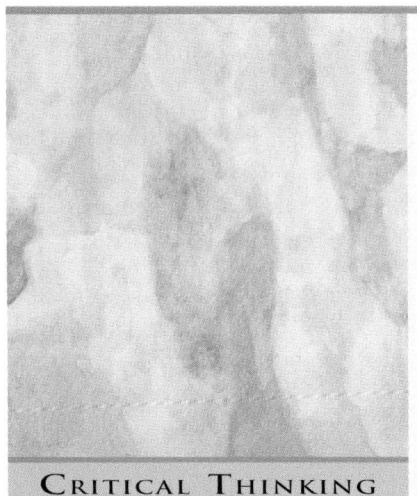

CRITICAL THINKING

Applying Psychology Concepts to Your Own Sexual History

Think about how you learned the "facts of life." Did most of your information come from well-informed sources? Were you able to talk freely and openly with your own parents about what to expect sexually? Did you acquire some false beliefs through your trial-and-error efforts? As you grew older, did you discover any aspects of your sexual knowledge that had to be revised because it was in error? Based on your experience in learning about sexuality, how do you think sex education should be addressed as a larger health issue in society? How would you *develop your psychological argument based on the evidence?*

TABLE 12.1

Failure Rates of Birth Control Methods

Method	Typical Failure Rate (%)	Cost*	Advantages	Disadvantages
1. Abstinence	0.0	0	No chance of pregnancy	May require much motivation
2. Abortion	0.0	$175–$300	Can terminate a pregnancy after positive tests	Surgical risk; possible medical complications; may reduce cervical competence
3. Tubal ligation	0.4	$800–$1500	Permanent relief from pregnancy worries	Low success of surgical reversal; possible surgical/medical/psychological complications
4. Vasectomy	0.15	$300	Permanent relief from pregnancy worries	Low success of surgical reversal; possible surgical/medical/psychological complications
5. Injectable progestin	0.3	$30 per injection/ 3 mo. coverage	No day-to-day attention required; long-lasting protection	Some risk in regaining fertility; side effects
6. Combined birth control pills	3.0	$14/mo ±	Highly effective, easy to use	Daily use required; continuing cost; slight medical risk; side effects
7. Progestin-only minipill	2.5	$15/mo ±	Highly effective; easy to use	Irregular menses; daily use required
8. IUD	6.0	$80–$90	Needs little attention; no expense after insertion	Side effects; possible expulsion; may perforate uterine wall; some incidence of PID
9. Male condom	12.0	$0.50–$1.50/condom	No side effects; easy to use; easy to obtain; helps prevent disease	Continuing expense; must use every time; may interrupt continuity of lovemaking
10. Female condom	13.0–26.0	$7	No side effects; helps prevent disease	Incorrect use
11. Cervical cap	18.0	$160	Can be left in place for several days; uses no hormones; no side effects	May be dislodged by intercourse; requires skill in insertion; may cause vaginal or cervical trauma
12. Diaphragm (with spermicide)	18.0	$15–$18	Easy to obtain and use; uses no hormones; no side effects; helps prevent disease; no prescription required	Continuing expense; requires high motivation to use correctly and consistently with each intercourse
13. Spermicidal agents (foams, creams, jellies and vaginal suppositories)	21.0	$5–$10/container	Easy to obtain and use; no prescription required	Continuing expense; requires high motivation to use correctly and consistently with each intercourse
14. Sponge (with spermicide)	21.0	No longer available		
15. Natural family planning (calendar, basal body temperature, cervical mucus, sympto-thermal methods)	20.0	0	No preparation or cost; no hormones or chemicals	May be frustrating to full enjoyment of intercourse; low effectiveness
16. Withdrawal (coitus interruptus)	18.0	0	No hormones or chemicals; acceptable to those who object to devices or hormones/chemicals	Requires much motivation and cooperation between partners
17. Chance (no protection)	89.0	0	No preparation; no hormones/chemicals	High risk of pregnancy; provides little peace of mind

From Robert H. Hatcher, et al., *Contraceptive Technology 1988–1989*, 14th ed. Copyright © Irvington Publishers, Manchester, NH. Reprinted by permission.

*An approximation, will vary with location; may be less in public clinics.

The graph shows:
- Y-axis: Percent reporting sexual intercourse (10 to 90)
- Range reported for men
- Range reported for women
- X-axis: 1900 1910 1920 1930 1940 1950 1960 1970 1980

Figure 12.4

Percentage of College Women and Men Who Reported Having Sexual Intercourse—a Summary of Data from Studies Conducted from 1900 to 1980

Heterosexual Attitudes and Behavior

To explore heterosexual relations, we examine a number of surveys of sexual attitudes and behavior at different points in the twentieth century, the frequency of sexual intercourse, and sexual scripts.

Trends in Heterosexual Attitudes and Behavior in the Twentieth Century Had you been a college student in 1940, you probably would have had a very different attitude toward many aspects of sexuality than you do today, especially if you are a female. A review of college students' sexual practices and attitudes from 1900 through the 1990s reveals two important trends (Darling, Kallon, &

Van Duesen, 1984; Robinson & others, 1991) (see figure 12.4). First, more young people today are reporting having had sexual intercourse. Second, the gap between the proportion of sexually active males and sexually active females is narrowing. Prior to the 1970s, about twice as many college males as college females reported they had engaged in sexual intercourse, but since 1970 the proportion of males and females has become nearly equal. These changes suggest a major shift away from a double standard of sexual behavior, which held that it was more acceptable for unmarried males than for unmarried females to have sexual intercourse.

Two surveys that included wider age ranges of adults verified this shift in trends. In 1974 Morton Hunt surveyed more than 2,000 adult readers of *Playboy*. Although the magazine readership's bias might have led to an overestimation of sexual permissiveness, the results suggested movement toward increased sexual permissiveness when compared to the results of Alfred Kinsey's inquiries during the 1940s (Hunt, 1974; Kinsey, Pomeroy, & Martin, 1948). Kinsey's earlier survey found that foreplay consisted of a kiss or two, but by the 1970s Hunt had discovered that foreplay had lengthened, averaging 15 minutes. Hunt also found that individuals in the 1970s were using more varied sexual techniques in their lovemaking. For example, oral-genital sex, virtually taboo at the time of Kinsey's survey, was more accepted in the 1970s.

More than 40 years after Kinsey's famous study, Robert Michael and his colleagues (1994) conducted a comprehensive survey of American sexual patterns. The findings are based on face-to-face interviews with nearly 3,500 individuals from 18 to 50 years of age. The sample generated by Michael and his colleagues was randomly selected, unlike the flawed samples of Kinsey, Hunt, and others, which were based on unrepresentative groups of volunteers.

Among the key findings from the 1994 survey:

- Americans tend to fall into three categories: One-third have sex twice a week or more, one-third a few times a month, and one-third a few times a year or not at all.

- Married couples have sex the most and also are the most likely to have orgasms when they do.
- Most Americans do not engage in kinky sexual acts. When asked about their favorite sexual acts, the vast majority (96 percent) said that vaginal sex was "very" or "somewhat" appealing. Oral sex was in third place, after an activity that many have not labeled a sexual act—watching a partner undress.
- Adultery is clearly the exception rather than the rule. Nearly 75 percent of the married men and 85 percent of the married women indicated that they have never been unfaithful.
- Men think about sex far more than women do—54 percent of the men said they think about it every day or several times a day, whereas 67 percent of the women said they think about it only a few times a week or a few times a month.

The findings in the 1994 Sex in America survey contrast sharply with some magazine polls that portray Americans as engaging in virtually unending copulation. The magazine polls are inflated from the start by the individuals who fill them out, such as *Playboy* subscribers who want to brag about their sexual exploits. Even the famous Kinsey studies, which caused such a scandal in the 1940s and 1950s by indicating that half of American men had extramarital affairs, were flawed. Kinsey obtained his subjects where he could find them—in boarding houses, college fraternities, and even mental hospitals. He also quizzed hitchhikers who passed through town. Clearly, Kinsey's subjects were not even close to being a random sample of the population.

In sum, one of the most powerful messages in the 1994 survey was that Americans' sexual lives are more conservative than previously believed. Although 17 percent of the men and 3 percent of the women said they have had sex with at least 21 partners, the overall impression from the survey was that sexual behavior is ruled by marriage and monogamy for most Americans.

Sexual Scripts As we explore our sexual identities, we often follow sexual scripts. A **sexual script** *is a stereotyped pattern of role prescriptions for how individuals should behave sexually.* Two well-known sexual scripts in the United States are the traditional religious script and the romantic script (Nass, Libby, & Fisher, 1981).

In the **traditional religious script**, *sex is accepted only within marriage. Both premarital and extramarital sex are taboo, especially for women.* In some forms of the religious script, sex is viewed positively only in terms of its reproductive value, and sexual ideas and behaviors are often seen as sin. This religious sexual script was more conservative in earlier times than it is in the twentieth century. Early Christian churches proposed that sexual behavior must accord with "natural law," meaning that the only purpose for sex was procreation; all romantic passion, lust, and masturbation were viewed as sinful. The ideal sexual standard was that intercourse was quick, quiet, and infrequent. Marital sex was to be performed only with the man on top, and it was forbidden on Sundays, Wednesdays, Fridays, 40 days before and after Easter, and 40 days before and after Christmas (Money, 1986). Although the current religious sexual script is still comparatively conservative, it is much more liberal now than in previous centuries.

In the **romantic script,** *sex is synonymous with love. If we develop a relationship with someone and fall in love, it is acceptable to have sex with that person, whether or not we are married.* In the twentieth-century United States, the romantic sexual script has become increasingly influential. However, many people regard the traditional religious sexual script as the ideal. As a result, many individuals find themselves struggling to resolve ethical dilemmas created by the conflicting expectations of these two divergent sexual scripts (Wilkinson & Kitzinger, 1993).

Differences in female and male sexual scripts can cause problems for individuals as they work out their sexual identities and seek sexual fulfillment. Females learn to link sexual intercourse with love more than males do (Cassell, 1984). Therefore females are more likely than males to justify their sexual behavior by telling themselves that they were swept away by love. A number of investigators have

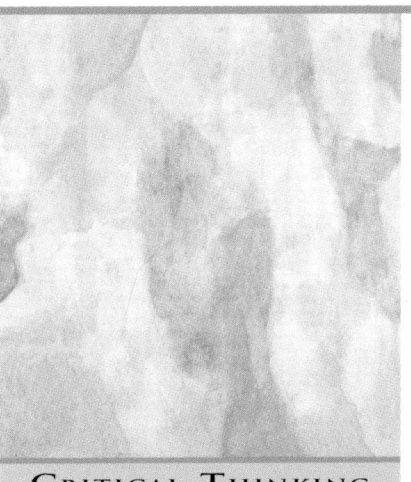

CRITICAL THINKING

Predicting the Future of the Double Standard

Gender roles have loosened considerably in the past few decades. Along with this liberalization of roles, the double standard for sexual behavior has diminished as well. Can you predict the status of the sexual double standard in the twenty-first century? What circumstances would make it fade away, so that men and women would experience equal expectations about their sexual choices? What circumstances might reinvigorate the sexual double standard? By making predictions about gender-role change over time, you demonstrate your ability to *make accurate observations, descriptions, and inferences about behavior.*

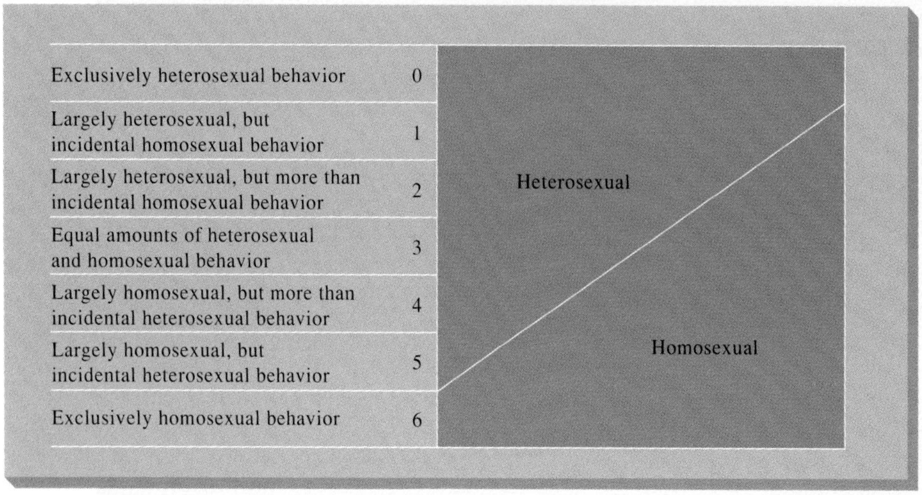

FIGURE 12.5

Continuum of Sexual Orientation

The continuum ranges from exclusive heterosexuality, which Kinsey and associates (1948) rated as 0, to exclusive homosexuality (6). People who are about equally attracted to both sexes (ratings 2 to 4) are bisexual.

found that females, more than males, cite being in love as the main reason for being sexually active. Far more females than males have intercourse only with partners they love and would like to marry. Other reasons females offer for having sexual intercourse include giving in to the male's desire for pleasure, gambling that sex is a way to get a boyfriend or husband, curiosity, and sexual desire unrelated to loving and caring. The male sexual script emphasizes sexual conquest; higher status tends to accrue to males who can claim substantial sexual activity. For males, sex and love might not be as intertwined as they are for females.

Although it has recently become acceptable for females to engage in premarital sex, there is still a **double standard,** *a belief that many sexual activities are acceptable for males but not for females.* The double standard can be hazardous because it encourages women to deny their sexuality and do minimal planning to ensure that their sexual encounters are safe. It can also lead females to think that males are more sexual than females, that males are less in control of their sexual behaviors, and that females must justify their sexual activity by claiming that they were swept away by the passion of the moment.

The double standard encourages males to dismiss or devalue their female partner's values and feelings, and it puts considerable pressure on males to be as sexually active as possible. As one male adolescent remarked, "I feel a lot of pressure from my buddies to go for the score." Further evidence of physical and emotional exploitation of females was found in a survey of 432 adolescents from 14 to 18 years old (Goodchilds & Zellman, 1984). Of the adolescents surveyed, both females and males accepted the view that the

male adolescent had a right to be sexually aggressive and assigned to females the task of setting limits for the male's behavior. Males who accept the double standard might believe that touch and contact are not "manly," and sex with a woman might be the only experience of touch and bodily comfort acceptable to these "real men." The seemingly cold and uncaring concept of "scoring" might be the only option some males think they have to reduce their loneliness, have warmth with another person, and "let their guard down."

He was one of those men who come in a door and make any woman with them look guilty.

F. Scott Fitzgerald

Homosexual Attitudes and Behavior

Until the end of the nineteenth century, it was generally believed that people were either heterosexual or homosexual. Today, many experts in the field of human sexuality view sexual orientation as a continuum ranging from exclusive heterosexuality to exclusive homosexuality. Pioneering this view were Alfred Kinsey and his associates (Kinsey, Pomeroy, & Martin, 1948), who described sexual orientation as a continuum of a six-point scale, with 0 signifying exclusive heterosexuality and 6 signifying exclusive homosexuality (see figure 12.5). Some individuals are *bisexual*, being sexually attracted to people of both sexes. In Kinsey's research, approximately 1 percent of individuals reported being bisexual (1.2 percent of males and 0.7 percent of females) and from 2 to 5 percent reported being homosexual

(4.7 percent of males and 1.8 percent of females). The actual incidence of exclusive homosexuality continues to be debated; estimates range from approximately 1 percent (in a recent national survey, only 1.1 percent said they are exclusively gay) to 10 percent (Billy & others, 1993). In the 1994 Sex in America study, 2.7 percent of men and 1.3 percent of women reported that they had had homosexual sex in the past year (Michael & others, 1994).

Although many people think of heterosexual and homosexual behavior as distinct patterns of behavior that are easy to define and composed of fixed decisions, orientation toward a sexual partner of the same or the opposite sex is not necessarily a fixed decision that is made once in life and adhered to forever. For example, it is not unusual for an individual, especially a male, to engage in homosexual experimentation in adolescence but not as an adult. Homosexual behavior is common among prisoners and others with no alternatives for intimate, enduring relationships. Kinsey's 1948 findings revealed that 37 percent of men and 13 percent of women had participated in some homosexual acts to orgasm between adolescence and old age.

Male and female homosexual experiences reflect different behavioral choices, too. Sexual researchers report that lesbians are more likely to be involved in intimate, enduring relationships, have fewer sexual partners, and have fewer "one-night stands" than homosexual men (Bell & Weinberg, 1978). Also, just like cohabiting and married heterosexual couples, homosexual couples have sex more frequently in their first 2 years of being together than when they have been together for 2 to 10 years (Blumstein & Schwartz, 1983).

For the last few decades, attitudes toward homosexuality have been becoming more permissive, at least until recently. Beginning in 1986, Gallup polls began to detect a shift in attitudes brought about by increasingly conservative views and by public awareness of acquired immunodeficiency syndrome (AIDS). For example, in 1985 slightly more than 40 percent of Americans believed that "homosexual relations between consenting adults should be legal"; by 1986 the figure had dropped to about 30 percent (Gallup Report, 1987). On the other hand, this increase in "hard-line" attitudes against homosexuals might have been only temporary; a 1989 Gallup poll once again showed increased acceptance of homosexuality and increased support for civil rights for gays.

Individuals who have negative attitudes toward homosexuality also are likely to favor severe controls for AIDS, such as excluding AIDS carriers from the workplace and schools. Irrational and negative feelings against homosexuals produce a variety of hostile responses. Typically hostility is associated with avoidance of homosexuals, false beliefs about homosexuals (such as believing that child molesters are homosexuals), and subtle or overt discrimination in housing, employment, and other areas of life. In extreme

What are some similarities and differences between heterosexual and homosexual couples?

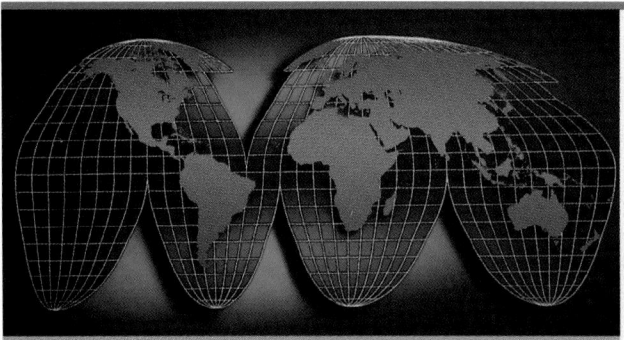

Homosexual Couples

In the United States, most Judeo-Christian religions approve only of sexual acts that can lead to conception within marriage, making homosexual relations unacceptable in their church doctrine. Although some churches have begun to perform marriage ceremonies for homosexual couples, no state legally recognizes marriage between partners of the same sex.

In most aspects of relationships, homosexual couples are similar to heterosexual couples. A significant difference, however, is that homosexual couples often do not receive the social sanctions extended to heterosexual couples, including legal recognition of their relationship, joint property rights, support from family and the community, and rituals such as a marriage ceremony. In addition, homosexual couples face most of the problems heterosexual couples face, including coping with differences, having difficulty communicating, not adequately controlling negative emotions such as anger and jealousy, and dealing with power and control in the relationship. However, because homosexual relationships receive little social support, they might be less stable than heterosexual marriages (Farley, 1990). Nevertheless, many homosexuals do remain with the same partner for many years, and many have the same partner for life.

cases, hostility toward homosexuals can result in ridicule, assault, and even murder.

Why are some individuals homosexual and others heterosexual? Speculation about this question has been extensive, but no firm answers are available. Homosexuals and heterosexuals have similar physiological responses during sexual arousal and seem to be aroused by the same types of tactile stimulation. Investigators find no differences between homosexuals and heterosexuals for a wide range of attitudes, behaviors, and adjustments (Bell, Weinberg, & Mammersmith, 1981). In the 1970s, recognizing that homosexuality is not a form of mental illness, both the American Psychiatric Association and the American Psychological Association discontinued their classification of homosexuality as a mental disorder.

Recently researchers have explored the possible biological basis of homosexuality by examining genetic factors, hormone levels, and differences in anatomical structures (Gladue, 1994). In one study of pairs of identical twins of which one of the twins was homosexual, over 50 percent of the other twins in the pairs were also homosexual. In contrast, only one-fourth of the fraternal twins of homosexuals were homosexual (Bailey & Pillard, 1991). (Fraternal twins are genetically no more similar than ordinary siblings, because they come from different eggs and sperm; identical twins develop from the same fertilized egg.) The results of hormone studies have been inconsistent. If male homosexuals are given male sex hormones (androgens), their sexual orientation does not change; their sexual desire simply increases (Meyer-Bahlburg, 1977). A critical period in fetal development might influence sexual orientation. In the sec-

ond to fifth months after conception, exposure of the fetus to hormone levels characteristic of females might cause the individual (female or male) to become attracted to males (Ellis & Ames, 1987). If this critical-period hypothesis turns out to be correct, it would explain why clinicians have found that sexual orientation is difficult, if not impossible, to modify.

With regard to anatomical structures, neuroscientist Simon LeVay (1991) proposed, based on autopsy evidence, that an area of the hypothalamus that governs sexual behavior is twice as large (about the size of a grain of sand) in heterosexual men as it is in homosexual men. In homosexual men, this part of the hypothalamus is about the same size as in heterosexual females. Critics of LeVay's work point out that many of the homosexuals in the study had AIDS and suggest that their brains could have been altered by the disease.

An individual's sexual orientation—homosexual, heterosexual, or bisexual—is most likely determined by a combination of genetic, hormonal, cognitive, and environmental factors (Whitman, Diamond, & Martin, 1993). Most experts on homosexuality believe that no one factor alone causes homosexuality and that the relative weight of each factor can vary from one individual to the next. In effect, no one knows exactly what causes an individual to be homosexual. Scientists have a clearer picture of what does not cause homosexuality. For example, children raised by gay or lesbian parents or couples are no more likely to be homosexual than are children raised by heterosexual parents (Patterson, 1995). There also is no evidence that male homosexuality is caused by a

TABLE 12.2

Level of Sexual Satisfaction

Instructions

This questionnaire is designed to measure your degree of sexual satisfaction with a partner. Answer each item as carefully and as accurately as you can. Place the number that represents your response in the space provided.

Ratings and Items

1 = Rarely or none of the time
2 = A little of the time
3 = Some of the time
4 = A good part of the time
5 = Most of the time

_____ 1. I think that my partner enjoys our sex life.

_____ 2. My sex life is very exciting.

_____ 3. Sex is fun for my partner and me.

_____ 4. I think that my partner sees little in me except for the sex I can give.

_____ 5. I think that sex is dirty and disgusting.

_____ 6. My sex life is monotonous.

_____ 7. When we have sex, it is too rushed and hurriedly completed.

_____ 8. I think my sex life is lacking in quality.

_____ 9. My partner is sexually very exciting.

_____ 10. I enjoy the sex techniques that my partner likes or uses.

_____ 11. I think that my partner wants too much sex from me.

_____ 12. I think that sex is wonderful.

_____ 13. My partner dwells on sex too much.

_____ 14. I think that sex is something that has to be endured in our relationship.

_____ 15. My partner is too rough or brutal when we have sex.

_____ 16. My partner observes good personal hygiene.

_____ 17. I think that sex is a normal function of our relationship.

_____ 18. My partner does not want sex when I do.

_____ 19. I think that our sex life really adds a lot to our relationship.

_____ 20. I would like to have sexual contact with someone other than my partner.

_____ 21. It is easy for me to get sexually excited by my partner.

_____ 22. I think that my partner is sexually pleased with me.

_____ 23. I think that I should have sex more often.

_____ 24. I think that my sex life is boring.

Please turn to the end of the chapter to interpret your responses.

Although most of us manage to develop a mature sexuality, most of us also have some periods of vulnerability, confusion, and even dysfunction along the way. Many individuals have an almost insatiable curiosity about sexuality. Many people wonder and worry about their sexual attractiveness and their ability to satisfy their sexual partner. Often our worries about our sexuality are fueled by media stereotypes about sexual potency and superhuman sexual exploits. The next section explores how we evaluate sexual satisfaction.

Sexual Satisfaction

Too often people think of sex as a performance skill like race car driving or swimming. However, sex is best conceptualized as a form of communication within a relationship. Indeed, caring couples with good communication skills can usually survive most sexual problems, but uncaring couples with poor communication skills often do not have lasting relationships even if their sex is adequate or even good. Each of us seeks sexual satisfaction, whether we have a heterosexual, homosexual, or bisexual orientation. To learn about your own personal level of sexual satisfaction, turn to table 12.2

> *Sex ought to be a wholly satisfying link between two affectionate people from which they emerge unanxious, rewarded, and ready for more.*
>
> **Alex Comfort**

Myths about males and females would have us believe that many women are "frigid" and uninterested in sexual pleasure, while most men can hardly get enough. Both myths are challenged by the accumulated observations of sex researchers and sex therapists. Women and men have similar desires for sexual pleasure, but individuals of both sexes can experience psychological problems that interfere with their attaining pleasure. We explore these difficulties in the next section.

dominant mother or a weak father, or that female homosexuality is caused by girls' choosing male role models. Sociocultural Worlds 12.2 provides information about homosexual couples.

Sexual Knowledge, Attitudes, and Behavior

According to a recent national survey, Americans are not very knowledgeable about sex. Many American adults and adolescents have misconceptions about sex. A majority of parents favor letting schools handle sex education, although school-based sex education has been controversial. School-linked, community-based family-planning clinics have reduced adolescent pregnancy rates. In many European countries such as Holland and Sweden, sex does not carry the mystery and conflict it does in America. Most couples want to be able to control when they will conceive a child, and for them, it is important to be knowledgeable about contraception. In choosing a method of contraception, such factors as physical and emotional effects, effectiveness, and convenience need to be considered.

Although heterosexual attitudes and behavior have become more liberal in the twentieth century, the 1994 Sex in America survey portrayed Americans' sex lives as more conservative than previously believed. The sample of subjects for the 1994 survey was more random than those of previous studies. Sexual scripts are stereotyped patterns of role prescriptions about how individuals should behave sexually. Two well-known sexual scripts are the traditional religious script and the romantic script. Females and males have often been socialized to follow different sexual scripts. Sexual scripts often involve a double standard.

Today, it is generally accepted to view sexual orientation along a continuum from exclusively heterosexual to exclusively homosexual rather than as an either-or proposition. Some individuals (approximately 1 percent) are bisexual. About 2 to 5 percent of individuals report being exclusively homosexual. Preference for a sexual partner of the same sex is not always a fixed decision. Until recently, acceptance of homosexuality had been increasing, but in concert with the AIDS epidemic, acceptance of homosexuality temporarily decreased. Acceptance of lesbian and gay lifestyles seems to be increasing again. An individual's sexual orientation—heterosexual, homosexual, or bisexual—is likely determined by a combination of genetic, hormonal, cognitive, and environmental factors. A special concern is sexual satisfaction regardless of a person's sexual orientation.

PSYCHOSEXUAL AND GENDER IDENTITY DISORDERS

Psychosexual disorders *are sexual problems caused mainly by psychological factors.* Some psychosexual disorders we will discuss are psychosexual dysfunctions and paraphilias. Transsexualism is a disorder of gender identity.

Psychosexual Dysfunctions

Psychosexual dysfunctions *are disorders that involve impairments in the sexual response cycle, either in the desire for gratification or in the ability to achieve it* (Kaplan, 1974). In disorders associated with the desire phase, individuals show little or no sexual drive or interest. For women, a common problem in the excitement phase is inhibited orgasm. Many women do not routinely experience orgasm during sex; this pattern is so common that it can hardly be called dysfunctional. Although inhibited male orgasm does occur, it is much less common. Men with excitement-phase disorders are more likely to experience difficulties in achieving or maintaining an erection. In the orgasmic phase, men may experience premature ejaculation, or rapid orgasm, when the time between the beginning of sexual stimulation and ejaculation is unsatisfactorily brief.

> *Some nights he said that he was tired, and some nights she said that she wanted to read, and other nights no one said anything.*
>
> **Joan Didion**

The treatment of psychosexual dysfunctions has undergone nothing short of a revolution in recent years. Once thought of as an extremely difficult therapeutic challenge, most cases of psychosexual dysfunction now yield to techniques tailored to improve sexual functioning.

Attempts to treat psychosexual dysfunctions through traditional forms of psychotherapy, as if the dysfunctions were personality disorders, have not been successful; however, new treatments that focus directly on each sexual dysfunction have reached success rates of 90 percent or more (McConaghy, 1993). For example, the success rate of a treatment that encourages women to enjoy their bodies and engage in self-stimulation to orgasm, with a vibrator if necessary, approaches 100 percent (Anderson, 1983). Many of these women subsequently transfer their newly developed sexual responsiveness to interactions with partners. Success rates also approach 100 percent in the treatment of premature ejaculation, but considerably lower success rates occur in the treatment of males who cannot maintain an erection.

Over the past two decades, sex researchers and therapists have developed a broad technology for treating sexual problems (Masters, 1993; Simons, Kalichman, & Santrock, 1994). Since the turn of the century, sex researchers have recognized that many sexual problems are caused by psychological factors. This insight led to attempts to use psychological techniques to treat sexual dysfunctions. Most early psychological interventions resulted in only limited success. More recent work, however, has been highly successful. A major breakthrough occurred in the pioneering work of Masters and Johnson. After detailing the sexual response of human beings, and all of the physical changes that occur in sexual functioning, Masters and Johnson proposed a method of sex therapy. The techniques they suggested formed the basis for modern psychological treatments of sexual problems.

Masters and Johnson based their therapy on several principles. First, they stated that therapy should be focused on the actual problem the person is experiencing, rather than on things that might be unrelated or irrelevant to the problem. They also said that therapy should occur in the context of a sexual relationship. Whenever possible, the therapist should include the partner of the person who is having sexual difficulties in the therapy. Masters and Johnson believed that heterosexual therapy should be conducted by two therapists, a female and a male. They believed that most issues can be dealt with better when the therapists present the perspectives of both sexes and when both partners are present. Finally, they suggested that therapy be kept as brief as possible and include "homework" for couples to try corrective measures on their own and report back to the therapists about their progress.

Following the lead of Masters and Johnson, psychiatrist Helen Kaplan (1974) proposed "the new sex therapy." While accepting and building on Masters and Johnson's work, Kaplan focused even more on relationship issues that might be related to sexual difficulties. She also emphasized the importance of an individual's sexual desires, pointing out that often sexual difficulties are directly related to inhibitions in sexual desires.

Keep in mind that sex therapy is a very specialized field. Not all professional helpers can legitimately call themselves sex therapists. To be qualified as a competent sex therapist, a mental health professional should receive very specific training. Unlike general counseling or psychotherapy, sex therapy is a specialization. This training usually occurs in very specific workshops, professional training seminars, or postgraduate training.

How can you tell if a sex therapist is qualified to be conducting sex therapy? One way is to find out whether she or he has been certified as a sex therapist. The American Association of Sex Educators, Counselors, and Therapists (AASECT) certifies sex therapists to ensure that the professional has received very specific training, has been supervised by qualified professionals, and has satisfied rather strict criteria. These are minimum standards for professionals to be qualified to practice sex therapy. Given the great deal of success seen with today's sex therapy techniques and the availability of qualified sex therapists, people who suffer from sexual difficulties should be encouraged to seek help.

Paraphilias

Paraphilias *are psychosexual disorders in which the source of an individual's sexual satisfaction is an unusual object, ritual, or situation.* Many sexual patterns deviate from what we consider to be "normal." These abnormal patterns of sexual arousal from unusual sources include fetishism, transvestism, exhibitionism, voyeurism, sadism, masochism, and pedophilia.

Fetishism *is a psychosexual disorder in which an individual relies on inanimate objects or a specific body part for sexual gratification.* Even though an individual might have a similar preference—for example, a man's preference for women with long legs or a woman's preference for men with beards—most of us are attracted to another person because of a wide range of personal factors. Some fetishists become obsessed with certain objects—fur, women's underpants, stockings—that arouse them. The objects take on greater importance than the arousing qualities of any one partner. Most fetishists are male.

Transvestism *is a psychosexual disorder in which an individual obtains sexual gratification by dressing up as a member of the opposite sex.* Most transvestites view themselves as heterosexual and lead quiet, conventional lives, cross dressing only in the privacy of their homes. One pattern of transvestites is to cross-dress only during sexual relations with their partners.

Exhibitionism and voyeurism are the two sex practices that most often come to the attention of the police. **Exhibitionism** *is a psychosexual disorder in which individuals expose their sexual anatomy to others to obtain sexual gratification.* **Voyeurism** *is a psychosexual disorder in which individuals derive sexual gratification from observing the sex organs or sex acts of others, often from a secret vantage point.* Both exhibitionism and voyeurism provide substitute gratification and a sense of power to otherwise sexually anxious individuals, especially males. In many instances, voyeurs are sexually inhibited.

Sadism *is a psychosexual disorder in which individuals derive sexual gratification from inflicting pain on others.* The word *sadism* comes from the novels of the Marquis de Sade (1740–1814), who wrote about erotic scenes in which women were whipped. **Masochism** *is a psychosexual disorder in which individuals derive sexual gratification from being subjected to physical pain, inflicted by others or themselves.* The word *masochism* comes from the novels of Austrian writer Leopold von Sacher-Masoch (1836–1895), whose male characters became sexually excited and gratified when they were physically abused by women. It is not unusual for

(*Left*) Dr. Richard Raskin is shown playing tennis before he underwent a transsexual operation that transformed him into a woman. (*Right*) Raskin changed his name to Renée Richards following the transsexual operation. Richards caused quite a stir by entering women's professional tennis tournaments. After considerable controversy, Richards was allowed to play on the women's professional tennis tour.

a sadist and a masochist to pair up to satisfy each other's sexual wishes; such relationships are called sadomasochistic. However, it is rare for a sadist and masochist to match each other's needs and have a stable and lasting relationship.

Pedophilia *is a psychosexual disorder in which the sex object is a child and the intimacy involves manipulation of the child's genitals.* A pedophile covertly or overtly masturbates while talking to children, manipulates the child's sex organs, or engages the child in sexual behavior. Most pedophiles are men, usually in their thirties or forties. Like exhibitionists,

pedophiles often have puritanical ideas about sex and see sex with children as being purer, safer, or less embarrassing. Often the target of a male pedophile is a child he knows, such as a child of a relative, neighbor, or family friend.

Gender Identity Disorder

Transsexualism *is a disorder of gender identity in which an individual has an overwhelming desire to become a member of the opposite sex.* The individual's gender identity is at odds with his or her genetic makeup and anatomical features. A transsexual might eventually decide to undergo surgery to change sex. Transsexuals often say that, as far back as they can remember, they have felt uncomfortable in their own bodies. They believe that they were born in a body of the wrong sex. Psychologists are uncertain why people are transsexual.

Can transsexuals lead full sex lives? In the female-to-male transsexual transformation, the surgically constructed male sex organs are cosmetic and the clitoris retains its orgasmic sensations; male sex hormones are given to intensify orgasm. Male-to-female transsexuals describe their sexual sensations as diffuse and intense. They report that they enjoy functioning as females, especially in terms of physical closeness, skin responsiveness, and breast sensations.

Next we will explore other behaviors related to sex that have been clearly linked to causing harm, including sexual harassment, sexual assault, incest, pornography, and sexually transmitted diseases.

REVIEW

Psychosexual Disorders

Psychosexual dysfunctions involve impairments in the sexual response cycle, either in the desire for sexual gratification or in the ability to achieve it. Significant advances in the treatment of psychosexual dysfunctions have been made in recent years. Paraphilias are psychosexual disorders in which the source of an individual's sexual satisfaction is an unusual object, ritual, or situation. Many sexual patterns deviate from what we consider to be normal. These abnormal patterns of sexual arousal from unusual sources include fetishism, transvestism, exhibitionism, voyeurism, sadism, masochism, and pedophilia. Gender identity disorder or transsexualism is a psychosexual disorder in which the person's gender identity is discordant with his or her anatomical sex and genetic makeup.

SEXUALITY AND HARM

Sexuality can be a context in which the participants are harmed. From the psychological harm that results from sexual harassment through the physical and emotional harm that results from rape and incest, we will examine some harsh realities associated with sex. We will also explore the effects of pornography on sexual behavior. We will conclude this chapter with a discussion of the harm engendered by sexually transmitted diseases.

Sexual Harassment

Women encounter sexual harassment in many different forms—from sexist remarks and covert physical contact (patting, brushing against their bodies) to blatant propositions and sexual assaults (DeFour & Paludi, 1991; Gidycz, Hanson, & Layman, 1995). Literally millions of women experience such sexual harassment each year in work and educational settings. In one investigation of the behavior of Harvard University faculty, 17 percent of women students said they had been the recipients of inappropriate verbal sexual advances, 14 percent experienced improper sexual invitations, 6 percent had been subjected to indecent physical advances, and 2 percent received direct sexual bribes (Adams, Kottke, & Padgitt, 1983). In this same study, 13 percent of the women students said they had avoided taking a class or working with certain professors because of the risk of being subjected to sexual advances. Sexual harassment, a manifestation of power and domination of one person over another, can result in serious psychological consequences for the victim (Koss, 1993). The elimination of such exploitation requires the development of work and academic environments that are compatible with the needs of women workers and students, providing them with equal opportunities to develop a career and obtain an education in a climate free of sexual harassment. In addition, social intolerance of sexual harassment will help decrease this pervasive problem (Lee & others, 1995).

Forcible Sexual Behavior

Most people choose to engage in sexual intercourse or other sexual activities, but, unfortunately, some people force others to engage in sex. **Rape** *is forcible sex with a person who does not give consent.* Legal definitions of rape differ from state to state. For example, in some states husbands are not prohibited from forcing their wives to have intercourse, because the wife is considered the husband's property. States that still have this antiquated law are being challenged in the courts.

It is difficult to determine the actual incidence of rape because many rape victims do not tell anyone that they have been raped and because disagreement exists about what behaviors and circumstances constitute rape. Rape is more common in large cities. However, rape does exist in every type of community across the nation. Nearly 200,000 rapes are reported annually in the United States. Experts believe the actual number of rapes might be as high as ten times this number (Lott, 1994).

Why is rape so pervasive in the American culture? Feminist writers believe males are socialized to be sexually aggressive, to regard women as inferior beings, and to view their own pleasure as the most important goal. Rapists share some common characteristics: Rapists use aggression to enhance their sense of power or masculinity; rapists are generally angry at women; and rapists almost always want to hurt their victims.

A recently acknowledged significant problem is **date or acquaintance rape,** *which is coercive sex forced by someone with whom the victim is at least casually acquainted.* Date rape is an increasing problem on college campuses (Himelein, 1995; Rosen & Stith, 1995). Almost two-thirds of college men admit that they fondle women against their will, and one-half admit to having forced sexual activity. Men who coerce women into sexual activity tend to endorse a wide range of cultural myths about rape, such as that women want to be raped and that men are unable to control their sexual behavior (Bohmer & Parrot, 1993).

Rape is a traumatic experience for the victim and those close to her. The rape victim initially feels shock and numbness and often is acutely disorganized. Many choose not to report rape because they fear criticism, stigma, and shame. Some women show their distress through words and tears, others show more internalized suffering. As victims strive to get their lives back to normal, they may experience depression, fear, and anxiety for months or years. Sexual dysfunctions, such as reduced sexual desire and the inability to reach orgasm, occur in 50 percent of rape victims (Sprei & Courtois, 1988). Many rape victims make changes in their lifestyle, such as moving to a new apartment or refusing to go out at night. About one-fifth of rape victims have attempted suicide; this rate is eight times higher than that of women who have not been raped.

A woman's recovery after a rape depends on both her coping abilities and her psychological adjustment prior to the assault. Social support from parents, partner, and others close to her are important factors in recovery, as is the availability of professional counseling, which sometimes is obtained through a rape crisis center (Koss, 1990, 1993). Many rape victims become empowered by reporting the rape to the police and assisting in the prosecution of the rapist if he is caught. Women who prosecute rapists should be sure they have the aid of supportive counselors throughout the legal ordeal. Because prosecution can magnify feelings of victimization, each woman must be allowed to make her own, individual decision about whether to report the rape or not.

Although most victims of rape are women, male rape does occur. A review of the victims treated at a sexual assault treatment center found that 6 percent were men (Lipscomb & others, 1992). Of those, 20 percent were assaults in the community and 80 percent were assaults in prison.

Feminists organized campaigns against pornography in the late 1970s. When sexual content is combined with violence, increased male aggression toward females may occur. However, there is no evidence that sexual content without violence stimulates aggression against women.

Men in prisons are especially vulnerable to rape, usually by heterosexuals who are using rape to establish their domination and power within the prison. Though it might seem impossible for a man to be raped by a woman, a man's erection is not completely under his voluntary control; some cases of male rape by women have been reported (Sarrel & Masters, 1982). Although male victims account for fewer than 5 percent of all rapes, the trauma that males suffer is just as great as that experienced by females.

Incest

Incest *is sex between people who are close relatives; it is virtually universally taboo.* By far the most common form of incest in the United States is brother-sister incest; father-daughter incest is the second most common. Mother-son incest and same-sex incest (usually father-son) are not as common incestuous patterns. Incest is psychologically harmful, not only for immediate family relationships, but also for the future relationships of a child involved in incest. Another misfortune associated with incest is that any resulting offspring have higher than average risks for genetic disorders and mental retardation.

Taboos against incest have developed in virtually all human societies, although a few exceptions have been noted, such as the Incan society and the societies of ancient Iran and ancient Egypt (Murdock, 1949). Possibly the taboos arose because of the harmful physical, psychological, and social effects that incest carries with it.

Pornography and Violence Against Women

Contemporary campaigns against pornography began in the late 1970s. Initial feminist arguments against pornography were of two main sorts: (1) Pornography demeans women (for

instance, by depicting them as sex slaves in male fantasies); and (2) much of pornography glorifies violence against women, perpetuating the cultural myth that women who say no to sex really want to be overpowered and raped.

Sex researchers have found that the visual cues in erotic films and pictures influence sexual behavior, but only for a brief period of time. Both men and women show increased sexual activity within 24 hours of exposure to sexually explicit material. Viewing sexual violence and reading sexually violent material increase male acceptance of sexual and other forms of aggression against females. However, sex researcher Edward Donnerstein (1987) argues that it is the violence against women, not the erotic material, that causes negative attitudes toward women.

In one investigation, Donnerstein (1980) studied college males in a three-part experiment. First the subjects were either provoked or treated neutrally by a male or female accomplice of the experimenter. Next they were shown one of three types of films—neutral, erotic, or aggressive-erotic depicting rape. Third, the subjects were led to believe that they could administer a shock to the accomplice of any intensity they chose. Men who had been provoked by the accomplice and had seen the aggressive-erotic film showed the highest levels of aggression (chose the highest intensity of shock to administer to the accomplice). Other studies by Donnerstein and his colleagues also pinpoint aggression and violence, rather than erotic content, as a contributor to males' aggressive attitudes toward women.

Rapists themselves report less exposure to erotic magazines and movies during their adolescent years than do those who are not sex offenders. Indeed, when Denmark ended its censorship of pornographic materials in the 1960s, sex-related crimes there decreased. In short, it appears that sexual content combined with violence can increase male aggression against females (Malamuth & Donnerstein, 1983), but there is no evidence that sexual content that is not paired with violence stimulates aggression against women.

Erotica is about sexuality, but pornography is about power and sex-as-weapon.

Gloria Steinem

Sexually Transmitted Diseases

Sexually transmitted diseases (STDs) *are diseases that are contracted primarily through sex—intercourse as well as oral-genital and anal-genital sex.* You may be more familiar with

the term *venereal disease,* or *VD,* an older term that has been increasingly replaced with the term STD. STDs are an increasing health problem in the United States, especially for adults in their late teens and early twenties (Leukefeld & Haverkos, 1993; Nevid & Gottfried, 1995). For example, in 1988, 720,000 new cases of gonorrhea were reported by the National Center for Health Statistics. At greatest risk are 20-to-24-year-olds (32 percent of cases, compared with their being 8 percent of the population). Those who are 15 to 19 years old have the second highest level of risk (27 percent of reported cases, for 7 percent of the population). We hope the information presented in this section will encourage you to protect yourself and your sexual partner(s) from these highly contagious sexually transmitted diseases. We begin with three STDs caused by bacterial infections—gonorrhea, syphilis, and chlamydia. Each of these STDs is a serious disease, but, fortunately, detected cases can be successfully treated.

Except for the few years between the invention of the Pill and the discovery of herpes, sex has always been dangerous.

Vogue magazine

Gonorrhea

Gonorrhea, *a sexually transmitted disease that is commonly called the "drip" or the "clap," is a common STD in the United States.* It is caused by a bacterium from the gonococcus family, which thrives in the moist mucous membranes lining the mouth, throat, vagina, cervix, urethra, and anal tract. The bacterium is spread by contact between the infected moist membranes of one individual and the membranes of another. Thus, virtually all forms of sexual contact can spread the gonococcus, although transfer does not necessarily occur with every contact. Males have a 10 percent chance of becoming infected with each exposure to gonococcus. Females have more than a 40 percent chance of infection with each exposure, because of the large surface area of the vaginal mucous membrane.

Symptoms of gonorrhea appear in males within 3 days to a month after contact. The symptoms include discharge from the penis, burning during urination, blood in the urine, aching pain or pressure in the genitals, and swollen and tender lymph glands in the groin. Unfortunately, 80 percent of infected females show no symptoms in the early stages of the disease, although pelvic inflammation is common at this early point. Untreated, the disease causes infection in the reproductive area and the pelvic region within 2 months. Scarring of the fallopian tubes and infertility can result. Gonorrhea can be successfully treated in its early stages with penicillin or other antibiotics. Despite reporting laws, many gonorrhea cases go unreported. The incidence of reported gonorrhea cases in 1990 was 690,000, down from 1 million in 1975 but still well above the number of reported cases in other industrialized countries (Billy & others, 1993).

Syphilis

Syphilis *is a sexually transmitted disease caused by the bacterium* Treponema pallidum, *a member of the spirochete family.* The spirochete needs a warm, moist environment to survive. It is transmitted by penile-vaginal, oral-genital, or anal contact. Syphilis can also be transmitted from a pregnant woman to her fetus after the fourth month of pregnancy. If the mother is treated before this time with penicillin, the syphilis will not be transmitted to the fetus.

Syphilis occurs in four stages: primary, secondary, latent, and tertiary. In the primary stage, a sore, or chancre, appears at the site of the infection. The sore heals after 4 to 6 weeks, giving the impression that the problem has gone away, but, untreated, it moves into the secondary stage. A number of symptoms occur at this stage, including a rash, fever, sore throat, headache, swollen glands, joint pain, poor appetite, and hair loss. Treatment with penicillin can be successful if begun at this stage or earlier.

Without treatment, symptoms of the secondary stage go away after 6 weeks, and the disease enters a latent stage. The spirochetes spread throughout the body, and, in 50 to 70 percent of those affected, remain there for years in the same stage. After the first 2 years, the disease can no longer be transmitted through sexual contact, but it can still be passed from a pregnant woman to her fetus. For 30 to 50 percent of those who reach the latent stage, a final, tertiary stage follows. In this advanced stage, syphilis can cause paralysis, insanity, and death. In 1988, the Public Health Service received 103,000 reports of syphilis, and in many areas of the United States syphilis is on the rise.

Chlamydia

Chlamydia, *the most common of all sexually transmitted diseases, is named for* Chlamydia trachomatis, *an organism that spreads by sexual contact and infects the genital organs of both males and females.* Although fewer individuals have heard of chlamydia than of gonorrhea and syphilis, its incidence is much higher. About 4 million Americans are infected with chlamydia each year. In fact, about 10 percent of all college students have chlamydia. This STD is highly infectious; women run a 70 percent risk of contracting it in a single sexual encounter, and the male risk is estimated as being between 25 and 50 percent.

The main symptoms of chlamydia are a thin, usually clear genital discharge and mild discomfort while urinating. The symptoms are somewhat similar to those of gonorrhea in the male, but gonorrhea produces more-painful urination and a more profuse, puslike discharge. Chlamydia is treated with tetracycline or erythromycin; it does not respond to penicillin. Poorly treated or undiagnosed cases can lead to a number of complications, such as urethral damage in females and males and pelvic inflammatory disease in females (Hyde, 1994).

Next we will study two STDs that are caused by viruses—herpes genitalis and acquired immunodeficiency syndrome (AIDS). Neither of these is curable.

Genital Herpes

Genital herpes *is a sexually transmitted disease in which the symptoms are small, painful bumps or blisters on the genitals.* These sores are caused by the herpes simplex virus type II in about 85 percent of the cases; the rest are caused by the type I virus. Type I is usually characterized by cold sores and fever blisters in nongenital parts of the body. Genital herpes is transmitted by sexual intercourse, and type I can be transmitted to the genitals during oral-genital sex.

Three to 5 days after sexual contact, itching and tingling can occur, followed by an eruption of sores and blisters—on the vaginal lips (labia) in women and on the penis in men. The blisters heal on their own in about 3 weeks in the first episode of infection. The virus continues to live in the body, sometimes remaining dormant for the rest of the person's life. However, the symptoms can recur unpredictably so that the person repeatedly experiences 7-to 14-day periods of sores. On the average, individuals with herpes have four recurrences per year; they are most infectious when they are having an active outbreak, although it is not clear that there is any entirely safe period (Hyde, 1994). The disease also can be trans-

mitted from a pregnant woman to her fetus, which can lead to brain damage or even death for the infant. A cesarean section can prevent infection, because infection occurs as the baby moves through the birth canal. Women with herpes are eight times more likely to develop cervical cancer than are unaffected women (*Harvard Medical School Newsletter,* 1981).

With an estimated 600,000 new cases of herpes per year in the United States, genital herpes approaches gonorrhea and chlamydia in frequency. These figures don't count recurrent cases, which may number 5 to 10 million. In one investigation, 16 percent of individuals in the United States between the ages of 15 and 74 reported that they were infected with genital herpes (Johnson & others, 1989).

There is no known cure for genital herpes. Researchers are pursuing two solutions—drugs that would cure symptoms in a person who is already infected, and vaccinations that would prevent contracting herpes. The drug acyclovir can prevent or reduce recurring symptoms, but it does not cure the disease.

AIDS

No single STD has had a greater impact on sexual behavior, or created more public fear in the last decade, than AIDS. **AIDS** *is a sexually transmitted disease that is caused by the human immunodeficiency virus (HIV), which destroys the body's immune system.* A person who is infected with HIV is vulnerable to germs that a normal immune system could destroy. In 1981, when AIDS was formally recognized in the United States, there were fewer than 60 reported cases. Beginning in 1990, we started losing as many Americans each year to AIDS as the total number of Americans killed in the Vietnam War—almost 60,000. According to federal health officials, from 1 to 1.5 million Americans are now asymptomatic carriers of AIDS—they are infected with the virus and capable of infecting others, but they show no clinical symptoms of AIDS.

The incidence of AIDS is especially high among Latinos and African Americans in the United States (Jemmott

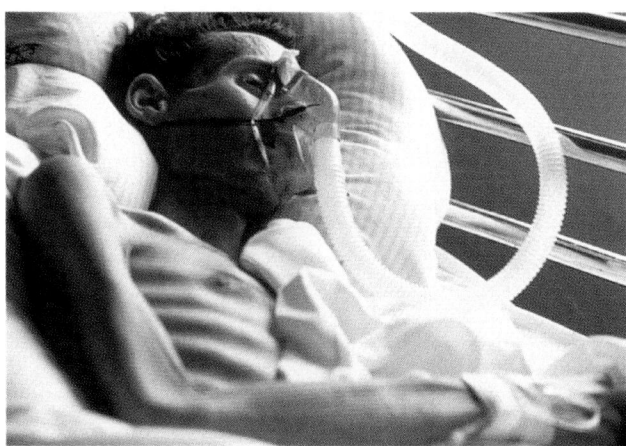

The AIDS virus destroys the body's immune system. The individual with AIDS shown here is one of more than 60,000 Americans who die every year from AIDS.

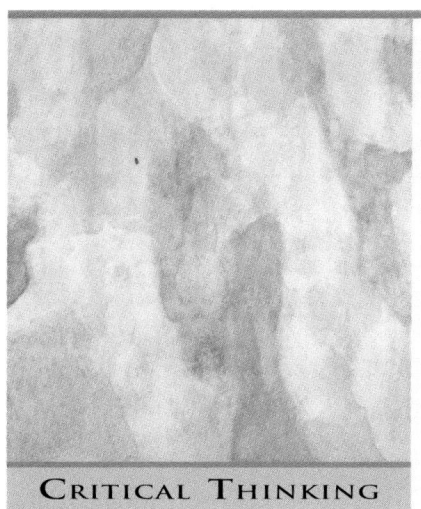

Caroline contracted genital herpes from her boyfriend, whom she had been dating for the past 3 years. After breaking off that relationship and spending some time on her own, Caroline began dating Charles. Before becoming sexually involved with him, Caroline told Charles about her herpes infection, thinking that it was the right thing to do. Charles seemed accepting of the news, but soon after the discussion he began treating Caroline differently. He became distant and cold toward her, and eventually broke off their relationships saying that it "just wasn't working." Caroline firmly believed it was because she had told him about the herpes.

Caroline later met Jeff, whom she really liked and wanted to start dating. As they became closer to developing a sexual relationship, Caroline felt that she should tell Jeff about the herpes, but she was afraid that he also would abandon her. She thought that if she arranged it so that they never had sexual contact when she had herpes blisters (the time when infecting someone else is most likely to occur), she could protect him. She also thought that if they used latex condoms for protection, he would be safe, even though condoms can break.

Would Caroline's not telling Jeff be acceptable to you, even if she acted to protect him? If Jeff should know, in what ways would it be best to tell him? If Caroline did tell Jeff, and he did end their relationship, would telling him have been a mistake? Does Jeff have a right to know? Does Caroline have a right to privacy? Your consideration of these questions encourages you to *identify the values that influence behavior* and to *practice standards of ethical treatment of individuals.*

& Jones, 1993; Mays, 1991, 1993). Latino men are three times more likely to have contracted AIDS than are non-Latino White male adults, for example (Richwald, Schneider-Munoz, & Valdez, 1989). Much of the AIDS prevention literature, as well as the instructions included with condoms, requires a high school reading proficiency. About 40 percent of adult Latinos lack this proficiency.

In 1989 researchers made the first attempt to assess the rate of AIDS infection in American college students. Tests of 16,861 students found 30 infected with the virus (American College Health Association, 1989). If the 12.5 million students attending college that year were infected in the same proportion, 25,000 students had the AIDS virus.

Experts say that AIDS can be transmitted only by sexual contact, the sharing of needles, contaminated blood transfusions (which intensified testing in the last few years has made very unlikely), or other contact with an infected person's blood, semen, or vaginal fluids through cuts in the skin or mucous membranes (Kalichman, 1995). Although it continues to be the case that 90 percent of AIDS cases in the United States occur among homosexual males and intravenous drug users, researchers have reported a disproportionate increase among females who are heterosexual partners of bisexual males or intravenous drug users (Squire, 1993). In 1994, 18 percent of AIDS patients were female, nearly triple the rate in 1984 (Centers for Disease Control, 1995). This increase suggests that in the United States the risk of AIDS might be increasing among heterosexuals who have multiple sex partners (Dolcin & others, 1995).

Remember that it is not who you are, but what you do, that puts you at risk for getting HIV. *Anyone* who is sexually active or takes drugs intravenously is at risk. No one is immune. Once an individual is infected, the prognosis is likely illness and death. The only *safe* sexual behavior is abstinence from sex, which is not perceived as an option by most individuals. Beyond abstinence, there is only *safer* behavior, such as sex that does not involve the exchange of semen, vaginal fluids, or blood; the use of condoms during sexual intercourse and all other forms of penetration; or sex restricted to a healthy partner.

Just asking a date about his or her sexual behavior does not guarantee protection from AIDS and other sexually transmitted diseases (Szapoznik, 1995). For example, in one investigation, 655 college students were asked to answer questions about lying and sexual behavior (Cochran & Mays, 1990). Of the 422 respondents who said they were sexually active, 34 percent of the men and 10 percent of the women said they had lied so their partner would have sex with them. Much higher percentages—47 percent of the men and 60 percent of the women—said they had been lied to by a potential sexual partner. When asked what aspects of their past they would be most likely to lie about, more than 40 percent of the men and women said they would understate the number of their sexual partners. Twenty percent of the men, but only 4 percent of the women, said they would lie about their results from an AIDS blood test.

Having discussed AIDS transmission, let's now examine the course of AIDS. In the first stage of the disease,

APPLICATIONS IN PSYCHOLOGY 12.1

Improving Your Communication Skills in Discussing Sexually Transmitted Diseases

Sensitive issues arise in relationships when sharing information in an open, honest way can have a negative effect on the relationship. People often must decide how best to be honest and how to sensitively share information. In our earlier example, Caroline had a bad experience after being honest with one boyfriend about her herpes, but should she have assumed that other boyfriends would respond in the same way? What are some ways she could have started a discussion of her infection and conveyed her care and concern for the other person?

Similar sensitive situations arise in relationships when one of the persons is concerned about contracting HIV, the virus that causes AIDS. The only method with a fairly good chance of preventing the spread of HIV during sex that involves penetration or the exchange of bodily fluids is proper and consistent use of latex condoms, particularly when they are treated with the spermicide nonoxynol-9. Asking a sexual partner about using condoms can present some of the same types of problems that Caroline faced about her herpes infection. Raising the topic of condoms can imply to your partner that you have an "undesirable past" or that you do not trust your partner. On the other hand, starting a discussion about using condoms can be taken as showing concern for your partner's health and well-being, as well as respect and care for yourself. How can people discuss the use of condoms, as well as other sensitive issues revolving around disease prevention and contraception?

One way to think about these issues is to consider the *way* things are said rather than *what* is said. Too often people approach such topics with great hesitation because they are worried about what the other person will think of them. Their own uncomfortableness is conveyed even before the conversation starts. So, the place to start might be to evaluate your own feelings and beliefs before even considering how to approach another person. Once you are clear on your own values and views, then you can plan how to best initiate the conversation. Where and how such a discussion occurs may be most important. Carefully consider privacy and comfort. Also, the mood should be right. For example, would it be wise to begin discussing the use of condoms or one's sexual past in the middle of an argument, or after watching a comedy act? The mood of this conversation should be serious, though it could also be somewhat light.

How best to start such a sensitive discussion depends on many aspects of yourself, your partner, and your relationship. At the heart of any such discussion is usually a concern over your own welfare, the health of your partner, and doing what is best for your relationship. Perhaps it would be best to express these feelings at the start. In addition, as is true in many situations that require you to be assertive, it is best to express your own needs and to acknowledge the other person's feelings. Through such mutual concern, it is likely that you and your partner can find ways to protect each other and liberate yourselves from the fears and worries you would suffer if you stayed in silence and doubt (Simons, Kalichman, & Santrock, 1994).

referred to as being HIV-positive (HIV+) and asymptomatic, infected individuals do not show the symptoms of AIDS but can transmit the disease to others. Researchers estimate that 20 to 30 percent of those in stage 1 will develop AIDS within 5 years. In stage 2—HIV+ and symptomatic—the infected individual develops symptoms, including swelling of the lymph glands, fatigue, weight loss, diarrhea, fever, and sweats. Many who are HIV+ and symptomatic continue to the final stage—AIDS. With AIDS, a person has the symptoms just mentioned plus at least one disease, such as pneumonia, which is fatal to AIDS patients because of their vulnerable immune systems. Although there is no known cure for AIDS, scientists are testing several drugs, including AZT

(zidovudine), which was approved by the FDA for treatment of the symptoms of AIDS in 1987.

Because it is possible, and even probable among high-risk groups, to have more than one STD at a time, efforts to prevent one disease help reduce the prevalence of other diseases (Tafoya, 1993). Efforts to prevent AIDS can also help prevent adolescent pregnancy and other sex-related problems. Given the high rate of sexually transmitted diseases, it's crucial that both teenagers and adults understand these diseases and act in accordance with standards of safety. It is also crucial to be able to communicate effectively about sexually transmitted diseases. To read about ways to improve your skills in communicating about sexually transmitted diseases, turn to Applications in Psychology 12.1.

REVIEW

Sexuality and Harm

Unfortunately, some individuals force others to engage in a sexual activity. Rape is forcible sex with a person who does not give consent. Legal definitions of rape sometimes vary from state to state. An increasing concern is date or acquaintance rape. Rape is a traumatic experience, and a woman's recovery depends on her coping resources as well as how well she was adjusted psychologically prior to the assault. Male rape constitutes about 5 percent of all rape cases. Sexual harassment is an expression of one person's power over another. Incest is sex between two close relatives, which is virtually universally taboo. The most common form is brother-sister, followed by father-daughter. Incest can cause extensive psychological harm to children.

Feminists and others organized the first campaigns against pornography in the late 1970s. When sexual content is combined with violence, increased male aggression toward females may occur. However, there is no evidence that sexual content without violence stimulates aggression against women.

Sexually transmitted diseases (STDs) are contracted primarily through sexual contact. Gonorrhea, commonly called the "drip" or the "clap," is one of the most common STDs in the United States. Gonorrhea is caused by a tiny gonococcus bacterium. It can be treated with penicillin and other antibiotics. Syphilis is caused by the bacterium *Treponema pallidum,* also called a spirochete. Syphilis occurs in four phases—primary, secondary, latent,

and tertiary. If detected in the first two phases, it can be successfully treated with penicillin. Chlamydia is the most common of all sexually transmitted diseases. Herpes is caused by a family of viruses with different strains. Herpes simplex has two variations. Type 1 is characterized by cold sores and fever blisters. Type 2 includes sores on the lower body—genitals, thighs, and buttocks. There is no known cure for herpes. AIDS is caused by a virus, HIV (human immunodeficiency virus), that destroys the body's immune system. AIDS can be transmitted only through sexual contact, the sharing of needles, blood transfusions, or other contact with an infected person's blood, semen, or vaginal fluids through cuts in the skin or mucous membranes. There is no known cure for AIDS.

One of the most important skills of good critical thinkers in psychology is *being able to evaluate the validity of behavioral claims.* Because misinformation about sex is so widespread, it is especially important to adopt a skeptical attitude about many claims about sex until evidence confirms or disconfirms them.

Here is a sample of the myths that some psychology students have claimed to believe until they encountered disconfirming evidence:

- You can get pregnant most easily if you make love in water.
- If women don't achieve an orgasm during sex, then they won't get pregnant.
- A woman can prevent pregnancy by jumping up and down after sex.
- You can't get pregnant the first time you have intercourse.
- Women can't achieve orgasm without direct stimulation of the G-spot.
- The size of a man's penis determines how satisfying sex will be.
- The size of a man's penis corresponds to the size of his nose (foot, thumb).
- Simultaneous orgasm is the only acceptable form of satisfaction.
- Breast-feeding prevents pregnancy.
- If men can't ejaculate after a certain threshold of stimulation has been reached, they'll become sick.

Some of these myths are abandoned after experience provides (sometimes painful) disconfirmation. How can adolescents and adults learn to navigate the precarious waters of sexuality with a minimum of misinformation to make informed choices about their behavior? The following specific strategies can help protect you.

1. *Regard cause-and-effect claims about sexuality with suspicion.* Nature encourages behavior that will help living organisms reproduce. Pregnancy requires contact of an egg and sperm. Measures that don't directly prevent that contact are not likely to be effective against pregnancy.

2. *Remember your own mortality.* It is relatively easy, especially in moments of passion, to abandon good judgment about self-protection. In such moments we tend to think of ourselves as immune to the laws of nature ("It won't happen to me"; "Just this once and never again"). Many carefree lovers end up very care-ridden by the biological consequences of impulsive unprotected sex.

3. *Evaluate the risk if the claim appears to be untrue.* Taking risks is part of life. However, sexual risk-taking in the absence of knowledge can result in dramatic life-changing outcomes. Where the risk is too great, restraint is the wiser course.

4. *Assess whether the source of the claims is trustworthy and astute.* Sometimes people promote myths as a strategy for getting a sexual relationship. Claims made by a person in the hopes of achieving intimacy could be manipulative; you need to establish whether you can trust a person you are considering becoming intimate with. People also sometimes pass along misguided sexual lore, with an intention not to take advantage but only to inform—but end up only misinforming. You need to establish whether the person you are discussing sexual lore with is likely to be well informed.

5. *Ask for evidence to support claims that are risk-promoting.* Always require evidence in support of any claim about a cause-and-effect relationship in behavior. This is imperative regarding claims that are relevant to the risks you might be taking by engaging in sexual activity. Questions to keep in mind include the following: *How did you learn about that? How much confidence do you have in the claim? What if you are wrong?*

Remembering the specific aspects of practicing sexual skepticism can help you make more responsible and reasonable sexual choices in an increasingly challenging world. Developing a skeptical attitude can assist you in *evaluating the validity of claims about behavior.*

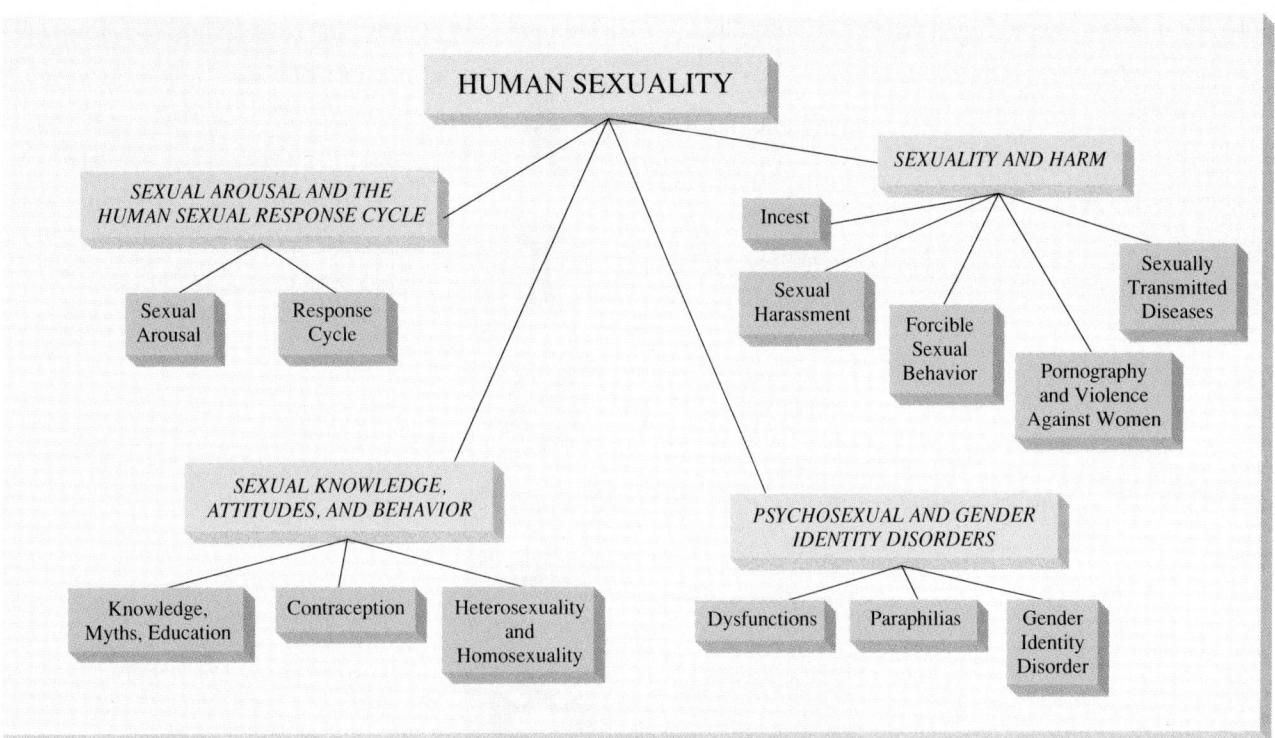

ur coverage of human sexuality began with consideration of sexual arousal and the human sexual response cycle. Then we evaluated sexual knowledge, attitudes, and behavior, focusing on heterosexuality and homosexuality. Next, we studied psychosexual disorders, including sexual dysfunctions, paraphilias, and gender identity disorder. We concluded the chapter by exploring sexuality and harm—sexual harassment, forcible sexual behavior, incest, pornography, and sexually transmitted diseases. Don't forget that you can obtain an overall summary of the chapter by again reading the in-chapter reviews on pages 419, 430, 432, and 439.

Three perspectives were represented in this chapter on human sexuality: the neurobiological, cognitive, and sociocultural. The neurobiological perspective appeared in the discussion of sexual arousal (pp. 416–418), the human sexual response cycle (pp. 418–419), and homosexuality (pp. 426–429). The cognitive perspective was represented in the material on sexual knowledge and myths (p. 420), heterosexual attitudes (pp. 424–426), and sexual scripts (pp. 425–426).

The sociocultural perspective was discussed in the sections on cultural contexts and arousal (pp. 417–418), sex education in the United States and Holland (p. 421), homosexuality (pp. 426–429), and incest (p. 434).

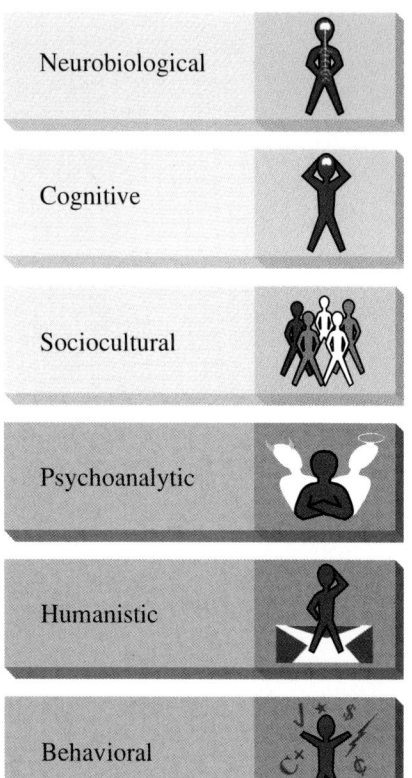

Neurobiological

Cognitive

Sociocultural

Psychoanalytic

Humanistic

Behavioral

KEY TERMS

human sexual response cycle The four phases of human sexual response—excitement, plateau, orgasm, and resolution—identified by Masters and Johnson. 418

sexual script A stereotyped pattern of role prescriptions for how individuals should behave sexually. 425

traditional religious script The behavioral script according to which sex is acceptable only within marriage; both premarital and extramarital sex are taboo, especially for women. 425

romantic script The behavioral script according to which sex is synonymous with love; in this script, it is acceptable to have sex with a person, whether we are married or not, if we are in love with that person. 425

double standard The belief that many sexual activities are acceptable for males but not for females. 426

psychosexual disorders Sexual problems caused mainly by psychological factors. 430

psychosexual dysfunctions Disorders that involve impairments in the sexual response cycle, either in the desire for gratification or in the ability to achieve it. 430

paraphilias Psychosexual disorders in which the source of an individual's sexual satisfaction is an unusual object, ritual, or situation. 431

fetishism A psychosexual disorder in which an individual relies on inanimate objects or a specific part of the body for sexual gratification. 431

transvestism A psychosexual disorder in which an individual obtains sexual gratification by dressing as a member of the opposite sex. 431

exhibitionism A psychosexual disorder in which individuals expose their sexual anatomy to others to obtain sexual gratification. 431

voyeurism A psychosexual disorder in which individuals derive sexual gratification by observing the sex organs or sex acts of others. 431

sadism A psychosexual disorder in which an individual derives sexual gratification from inflicting pain on others.   431

masochism A psychosexual disorder in which individuals derive sexual gratification from being subjected to physical pain, inflicted by others or themselves.   431

pedophilia A psychosexual disorder in which the sex object is a child and the intimacy usually involves manipulation of a child's genitals.   432

transsexualism A gender identity disorder in which an individual has an overwhelming desire to become a member of the opposite sex.   432

rape Forcible sex with a person who does not give consent.   433

date or acquaintance rape Coercive sex forced by someone with whom the victim is at least casually acquainted.   433

incest Sex between two close relatives; virtually universally taboo.   434

sexually transmitted diseases (STDs) Diseases that are contracted primarily through sex—intercourse as well as oral-genital and anal-genital sex.   434

gonorrhea A sexually transmitted disease that is commonly called the "drip" or the "clap"; one of the most common STDs in the United States, it is caused by a bacterium from the gonococcus family, which thrives in the moist mucous membranes lining the mouth, throat, vagina, cervix, urethra, and anal tract.   435

syphilis A sexually transmitted disease caused by the bacterium *Treponema pallidum*, a member of the spirochete family.   435

chlamydia The most common of all sexually transmitted diseases, named for *Chlamydia trachomatis*, an organism that spreads by sexual contact and infects the genital organs of both males and females.   436

genital herpes A sexually transmitted disease in which the symptoms are small, painful bumps or blisters on the genitals.   436

AIDS A sexually transmitted disease that is caused by the human immunodeficiency virus (HIV), which destroys the body's immune system.   436

PRACTICAL KNOWLEDGE ABOUT PSYCHOLOGY

FOR YOURSELF
(1975) by Lonnie Barbach.
New York: Signet.

For Yourself provides advice for women about how to achieve sexual fulfillment. Barbach addresses the worries that often distress nonorgasmic women and tells them how to achieve orgasm. Barbach attacks the negative cultural attitudes that say women should not enjoy sex. Several exercises that will enable women to achieve orgasm are presented—each exercise that is given is accompanied by an explanation of why it can be effective and potential pitfalls to avoid. The book also includes many examples of the sexual lives of women Barbach has counseled in her sex therapy groups. How to achieve an orgasm through masturbation and the eventual transference of orgasms from masturbation to orgasms with a partner are covered. This book does a good job of taking women step-by-step through the pleasurable sensations that society has unfortunately told them they should not experience. A second book by Barbach, *For Each Other*, is also a good choice; it devotes more time to achieving an orgasm with a sexual partner (especially the communication aspects of sexuality with a partner), women who rarely desire sex, and women who find sex painful.

The New Male Sexuality

(1992) by Bernie Zilbergeld.
New York: Bantam.

The New Male Sexuality is a very up-to-date, comprehensive book about male sexuality. (Zilbergeld's *Male Sexuality* is also a very good book, first published in 1978.) Why did Zilbergeld write *The New Male Sexuality*? Because, he says, in the last decade we have seen dramatic changes in the sexual landscape, from the changing expectations of women to new definitions of masculinity, and from the fear of disease to the renewed focus on long-term relationships.

An introductory section in *The New Male Sexuality* tackles male sexual myths and unrealistic expectations, and then the author turns to sexual reality and gives men a brief course in sexual knowledge. The next section explores better sex through topics such as how to be a good lover with your partner, how to be a better listener, touching, arousal, and how to keep the spark alive in long-standing relationships. A final section is devoted to resolving problems and includes discussion of ejaculatory control, erection difficulties, problems of sexual desire, and even advice for fathers on how to communicate more effectively about sex with their sons.

This is an excellent, easy-to-read, well-organized, authoritative guide to male sexuality. It is a giant step above the crass, how-to sex books that have populated the sex self-help sections of many book stores in recent years. *The New Male Sexuality* is a sensitive and thoughtful map to better and more fulfilling sexual lives for men.

Permanent Partners

(1988) by Betty Berzon.
New York: Plume.

Permanent Partners presents the knowledge and understanding that will help gay and lesbian couples make their relationship work and last. Berzon examines the obstacles that same-sex couples face as they try to create a new life together. The author is a lesbian who has counseled same-sex couples for many years. Among the obstacles she explores are the lack of visible long-term couples as role models; the absence of support from society—from employers to landlords to insurers—and too often from a gay or lesbian couple's families of origin; a tradition of failure; and the guidance gap that has not provided adequate advice for how to effectively build a life with another man or woman.

This is an excellent book on gay and lesbian relationships, both for gays and lesbians who are thinking about becoming coupled or are perplexed about their current relationship, and for anyone who wants to improve their understanding of gay and lesbian couples. Two other good books on gay and lesbian relationships are *The New Loving Someone Gay,* by Don Clark, and *Lesbian Couples,* by D. Merilee Clunis and G. Dorsey Green.

RESOURCES FOR PSYCHOLOGY AND IMPROVING HUMANKIND

AIDS Hotline
National AIDS Information Clearinghouse
P.O. Box 6003
Rockville, MD 20850
800–342–AIDS
800–344–SIDA (Spanish)
800–AIDS–TTY (Deaf)

The people answering the hotline will respond to any questions children, youth, or adults have about HIV infection or AIDS. Pamphlets and other materials on AIDS are available.

Alan Guttmacher Institute
111 Fifth Avenue
New York, NY 10003
212–254–5656

The Alan Guttmacher Institute is an especially good resource for information about sexuality. The Institute publishes a well-respected journal, *Family Planning Perspectives,* which includes articles on many dimensions of sexuality, such as adolescent pregnancy, statistics on sexual behavior and attitudes, and sexually transmitted diseases.

Canadian AIDS Society/Société canadienne du sida

100 Sparks Street #400
Ottawa, ON K1P 5B7 CANADA
613–230–3580

Coalition on Sexuality and Disability, Inc.

380 Second Avenue, 4th Floor
New York, NY 10010
212–242–3900

This organization provides education and advocacy related to sexuality and socialization of individuals with disabilities.

Division of STD/HIV Prevention

National Center for Prevention Services
Centers for Disease Control
Atlanta, GA 30333
404–639–2564

This organization offers very up-to-date information about prevention-related issues involving sexually transmitted diseases; this division administers a number of government programs for the prevention of STDs and HIV infection.

***Early Adolescent Sexuality: Resources for Professionals, Parents, and Young Adolescents* (1989)**

Center for Early Adolescence
University of North Carolina
D-2 Carr Mill Town Center
Carrboro, NC 27510
919–966–1148

This resource lists books, films and videos, journals, curricula, pamphlets, and organizations for people seeking information on specific topics or a general treatment of early adolescent sexuality. Among the topics covered are AIDS, decision making, homosexuality, parent-adolescent communication, and pregnancy prevention.

Herpes Resource Center

P.O. Box 13827
Research Triangle Park, NC 27709

This organization provides information and support for individuals with recurrent genital herpes infections. Ninety-eight local groups are located throughout the United States.

***International Directory of Gay and Lesbian Periodicals* (1987)**

by H. R. Malinowsky
Phoenix: Oryx Press

This directory profiles a large number of gay, lesbian, and related journals, newsletters, and other periodicals that are currently being published throughout the world.

National Gay and Lesbian Task Force (NGLTF)

1734 14th Street, N.W.
Washington, DC 20009-3409
202–332–6483

This is the oldest national gay and lesbian civil rights advocacy organization. NGLTF lobbies, provides grassroots organizing, publishes materials, and offers referrals.

Sex Information and Education Council of the United States (SIECUS)

130 West 42nd Street
New York, NY 10036
212–819–9770

This organization serves as an information clearinghouse about sex education. The group's objective is to promote the concept of human sexuality as an integration of physical, intellectual, emotional, and social dimensions.

LEVEL OF SEXUAL SATISFACTION

First, be sure you have responded to all the items. *Second,* you have to rescore some of the items because they are worded in a different direction than the others. Change the scores for items 1, 2, 3, 9, 10, 12, 17, 19, 21, 22, 23 as follows:

An answer of 5 is changed to a 1
4 is changed to a 2
3 remains a 3
2 is changed to a 4
1 is changed to a 5

Third, after rescoring, add your scores for all 24 items and from the total subtract 20. This is your **total score:**
_____.

INTERPRETATION

Fourth, the possible range of scores is from 0 to 100. This exercise, of course is not absolute, but only an indication of the magnitude of sexual satisfaction in a two-person relationship. A low score would indicate a very small problem or no sexual problem existing in your relationship with this person, and a high score would indicate the presence of a sexual problem to some degree. Keep in mind that a "sexual problem" will be relative to the personality dynamics of the individuals involved in the relationship. It could be helpful to go back over your responses and look for ways to improve the sexual aspect of your relationship with your partner.

Motivation, Emotion, Health, and Personality

*The passions and desires, like the two twists of
a rope, mutually mix with the other, and
twine inextricably round the heart; producing
good, if moderately indulged; but certain
destruction if suffered to become inordinate.*

Robert Burton

Why do we do what we do? What do we feel?
How can we live healthy lives and cope effectively
with stress? Who are we? These questions deal
with motivation, emotion, health, and
personality, which mix to direct our behavior,
color our lives, and give meaning to our identity
as human beings. Motivation, emotion, health,
and personality are the topics of the three
chapters you will read in this section:
"Motivation and Emotion" (chapter 13),
"Health, Stress, and Coping" (chapter 14), and
"Personality" (chapter 15).

BILL RANE
The Effect of the Moon on Historic Certainty, detail

CHAPTER

13

Motivation and Emotion

*The passions are at once temptors
and chastisers. As temptors, they come
with garlands of flowers on brows of
youth; as chastisers, they appear with
wreaths of snakes on the forehead of
deformity. They are angels of light in
their delusion; they are fiends of
torment in their inflictions.*

Henry Giles

THE STORY OF GERARD D'ABOVILLE: DRIVEN TO THE SEA

On July 11, 1991, a 45-year-old former French paratrooper cast off in his rowboat from Choshi, a small fishing village nestled on a peninsula east of Tokyo, and began rowing toward the United States. Gerard d'Aboville had made a name for himself 11 years earlier when he became the first person to row solo across the Atlantic Ocean from the mainland of the United States to the mainland of Europe. Afterward, he swore to his friends that he would never try such a challenge again. He wrote a book, designed motorboats for a race down the river Niger in Africa, and pursued catamaran and off-road racing as other accomplishments. Then, in spite of past vows, d'Aboville decided to try the trans-Pacific crossing.

He created a specially designed half-ton rowboat, which he called the *Sector*. It was equipped with a ham radio, dehydrated food, a gas stove, and a desalination pump, activated by the motion of the boat oars, that could turn sea water into drinking water. The *Sector* also had a watertight cabin for sleeping and eating that was positioned behind the open cockpit. Although d'Aboville had hoped to leave in June, typhoons in the Pacific forced him to delay his launch until July, even though Japanese oceanographers warned him that further storms were likely. "Once I believed that maybe it was possible," d'Aboville said, "it was all over." He planned to row 12 hours per day and progress slowly across the ocean, but a typhoon blew him back toward the Japanese coast just 5 days after he'd started, and another held him in place for over a week despite back-breaking rowing. He suffered numerous capsizings; one of these gave him a broken rib. Still, he rowed on and on and on, for 6,300 miles, until he finally reached the shore near Portland, Oregon, over 4 months after he had started.

Overcoming wind, rain, unspeakable loneliness, physical exhaustion, and fears of dying at sea, d'Aboville overcame impossible odds to complete something that no one else had ever accomplished. He described his accomplishment by saying, "Whenever I felt that I could not go further, I just did something."

Gerard d'Aboville overcame wind, rain, unspeakable loneliness, physical exhaustion, and fears of dying at sea to accomplish something no one else ever had—crossing the Pacific Ocean from Japan to the United States in a rowboat. What motivates people like d'Aboville to overcome great odds to achieve something?

Like Gerard d'Aboville, we all know people who have overcome great odds to accomplish something. What motivates great achievements, and what motivates each of us to get out of bed each morning and work toward our own goals (like completing an introductory psychology course)? Why do some people succeed while others fail or even give up on life altogether? The psychology of motivation tries to answer these and many other such questions.

PREVIEW

Most of us do not have the motivation to cross the Pacific Ocean in a rowboat. Yet the example of Gerard d'Aboville prompts us to consider why some people behave the way they do. In this chapter, we explore much more about the whys of behavior. We also examine the fascinating world of emotions.

PERSPECTIVES ON MOTIVATION

"Every why hath a wherefore," said Shakespeare. Why are you so hungry? Why are you so interested in having sex? Why do you want to get an A in this class? Why do you want a change in your life? The answer is because you are motivated. **Motivation** *involves the question of why people behave, think, and feel the way they do. Motivated behavior is energized and directed.*

If you are hungry, you will probably put this book down and go to the refrigerator. If you are sexually motivated, you may go to a party and flirt with someone you think is attractive. If you are motivated to achieve, you may study in the library until midnight. When you are motivated, you go to the refrigerator, to a party, to the library.

Motivations differ not only in kind, such as an individual's being motivated to eat rather than have sex, but also in intensity. We can speak of an individual's being more or less hungry or more or less motivated to have sex. We can also speak of one person's being more motivated to achieve than another is.

Most psychologists today recognize that behavior is energized and directed by a complex mix of factors. These factors tend to be associated with specific perspectives, in psychology, each contributing to our overall understanding of the principles of motivation.

The Neurobiological Perspective

The role of biological factors in motivation is the focus of the neurobiological perspective. We will explore four traditions in this perspective: instinct theory, drive reduction theory, ethology, and physiology.

Instinct Theory

The late Sam Walton, entrepreneur and founder of Wal-Mart, made $6 billion in 1988. Did Sam Walton have an instinct for acquisitiveness? Early in this century, psychologists were interested in explanations of motivation based on **instinct,** *an innate, biological determinant of behavior.* Influenced by Darwin's evolutionary theory, American psychologist William McDougall (1908) argued that all behavior is determined by instincts. He said we have instincts for acquisitiveness, curiosity, gregariousness, pugnacity, and self-assertion, among others.

It was not long before a number of psychologists had created copious lists of instincts. Psychologists thought that perhaps we have one instinct for physical aggression, one for assertive behavior, and yet another for competitive behavior. Instinct theory, though, did not really explain anything; the wherefore behind Shakespeare's why was not adequately explored. An instinct was invariably inferred from the behavior it was intended to explain. For example, if a person was aggressive, it was inferred that he had an instinct for aggression. If another person was sociable, it was inferred that she had an instinct for sociability. However, instinct theory did call attention to the idea that some of our motivation is unlearned and involves physiological factors. This idea is important in our understanding of motivation today, but instinct theory itself landed in psychology's dustheap many years ago.

Drive Reduction Theory

If you do not have an instinct for sex, maybe you have a need or a drive for it. A **drive** *is an aroused state that occurs because of a physiological need.* A **need** *is a deprivation that energizes the drive to eliminate or reduce the deprivation.* You might have a need for water, for food, or for sex. The need for food, for example, arouses your hunger drive. This motivates you to do something—to go to McDonald's for a Big Mac, for example—to reduce the drive and satisfy the need. As a drive becomes stronger, we are motivated to reduce it. This explanation is known as **drive reduction theory,** *which states that a physiological need creates an aroused state (drive) that motivates the organism to satisfy the need.*

Usually needs and drives are closely associated in time. For example, when your body needs food, your hunger drive will probably be aroused. An hour after you have eaten a Big Mac, you might still be hungry (thus, you need food), but your hunger drive might have subsided. From this example, you can sense that *drive* pertains to a psychological state, *need* pertains to a physiological state.

The goal of drive reduction is **homeostasis,** *the body's tendency to maintain an equilibrium, or steady state.* Hundreds of biological states in the body must be maintained within a certain range: temperature, blood sugar level, potassium and sodium levels, oxygen level, and so on. When you dive into an icy swimming pool, your body heats up. When you walk out of an air-conditioned room into the heat of a summer day, your body cools down. These changes occur automatically in an attempt to restore your body to its optimal state of functioning.

Homeostasis is achieved in the body much like a thermostat in a house keeps the temperature constant. For example, assume the thermostat in your house is set at 68 degrees. The furnace heats the house until a temperature of 68 degrees is reached, then the furnace shuts off. Without a source of heat, the temperature in the house eventually falls below 68 degrees. The thermostat detects this and turns the furnace back on again. The cycle is repeated so that the temperature is maintained within narrow limits.

Ethology

Although psychologists rejected the biological concept of instinct many years ago, biology's role in motivation continues to be strong. You might remember our discussion of Konrad Lorenz's classic study of imprinting in chapter 9.

Recall how the goslings became attached to Lorenz because he was the first moving object they saw shortly after they were born. Lorenz interpreted the goslings' behavior as evidence of rapid, innate learning within a critical time period. Lorenz's field is **ethology,** *the study of the biological basis of behavior in natural habitats.* Ethology is sometimes referred to as modern instinct theory, although Lorenz and other ethologists have carefully avoided using the term *instinct* because of the tainted name it got earlier in psychology's history. Ethology emerged as an important field because of the work of European zoologists, such as Lorenz, in the 1930s, who argued that behaviorism had gone too far in promoting the role of environmental experiences in motivation.

Like behaviorists, ethologists are careful observers of behavior. Unlike many behaviorists, though, ethologists believe that laboratories are not good settings for observing behavior. They observe behavior in its natural surroundings instead, believing that behavior cannot be completely understood unless it is examined in the context in which it evolved. For example, ethologists have observed many species of animals in the wild, discovering their powerful motivation to stake out their own territory and band together to fight off any intruders (Lorenz, 1966).

Ethological theory reminds us of our biological origins and raises the issue of how strongly we are motivated by our biological makeup versus our experiences in life. Are we motivated to hurt someone else because we were born that way or because of our interactions with people who hit and yell, for example? As you can see, even though classical instinct theory bit the dust, the issue regarding whether motivation is innate or learned, biologically or experientially based, is still alive.

Physiology

The body's physiological makeup—reflexes, brain structures, body organs, and hormones—also plays an important role in contemporary views of motivation. Later in this chapter we will discuss these physiological mechanisms in our discussion of hunger, which is just one of many physiological drives that govern our behavior.

The Behavioral Perspective

"If a man runs after money, he's money mad; if he keeps it, he is a capitalist; if he spends it, he is a playboy; if he doesn't try to get it, he lacks ambition; and if he accumulated it after a lifetime of hard work, people call him a fool who never got anything out of life." These words of Vic Oliver suggest that something more than internal drives can motivate our behavior—something more external. Money is an example of an external stimulus that is a powerful motivator of behavior.

In the behavioral perspective, external factors play a key role in determining a person's motivation. **Incentives** *are positive or negative stimuli or events that motivate an individual's behavior.* For example, a yearly income of more than $100,000 is a positive incentive for becoming a physician; the threat of an intruder is a negative incentive for purchasing a security system for your home. By identifying the concept of incentive, psychologists expanded their definition of the why of behavior to include both internal factors (physiological needs and psychological drives) and external factors (incentives).

In recent years, some behaviorally oriented psychologists have expanded their conceptualization of motivation to include cognitive factors. For example, Albert Bandura (1991, 1994) believes that cognitive factors such as plans and self-efficacy (the belief that one can master a situation and produce positive outcomes) play powerful roles in motivation. If individuals have low self-efficacy, they might not even try to pursue a goal. A plan can motivate a person's behavior for days, weeks, months, and even years. For instance, if a college student decides she wants to become a marine biologist, she might map out an educational plan that encompasses the next decade of her life.

In sum, behaviorists believe external factors and environmental contexts strongly influence a person's motivation. More recently, cognitively oriented behaviorists have introduced concepts such as those of self-efficacy and plans to explain motivation.

The Psychoanalytic Perspective

William McDougall, in his advocacy for instinct theory, found an intellectual ally in Sigmund Freud (1917), who proposed that behavior is instinctually based. Freud believed that sex and aggression are especially powerful in motivating behavior, and he based his theories about personality development on this motivational construct.

One major legacy of Freud's theorizing about motivation is the belief that we are largely unaware of why we behave the way we do. Psychoanalytic theorists argue that few of us know why we love someone, why we eat so much, why we are so aggressive, or why we are so shy. Although Freud's perspective is no longer as powerful a paradigm as it once was, psychologists continue to debate the role of conscious versus unconscious thought in understanding motivation. (Much more detail about psychoanalytic theory appears in chapter 15.)

The Cognitive Perspective

The contemporary view of motivation also emphasizes the importance of cognitive factors. Consider your motivation to do well in this class. Your confidence in your ability to do well and your expectation for success may help you relax, concentrate better, and study more effectively. If you think too much about not doing well in the class and fear that you will fail, you may become too anxious and not perform as well. Your ability to consciously control your behavior and resist the temptation to party too much and to avoid studying will improve your achievement, too. So will your ability to use your information-processing abilities of attention, memory, and problem solving as you study for and take tests.

One of the most important recent trends in motivation is the increased interest in conscious, *self-generated goals.* The belief is that these goals influence a person's ongoing thought, behavior, and emotional reactions (Emmons, in press). Examples of self-generated goals include "current concerns" (Klinger, 1987) and "personal projects" (Little, 1989). A **current concern** *is a state a person occupies between becoming committed to pursuing a goal and either attaining it or abandoning it.* Current concerns can be broad (such as "Be a positive influence in my world") or narrow (such as "Pick up my dry cleaning"). Their time frames may be transient or lifelong. **Personal projects** *are sequences of personally relevant actions, similar to current concerns, but focused more on actual behavioral enactment than on thought.* Personal projects may include "trivial pursuits," such as letting a bad haircut grow out, or life goals such as becoming a good parent.

Unlike psychoanalytic theorists, who believe that people are unaware of what motivates them, cognitive psychologists argue that people are rational and aware of what motivates them. The cognitive approach is explored in greater detail later in this chapter.

The Humanistic Perspective

Is getting an A in this class more important to you than eating? If the person of your dreams were to tell you that you are marvelous, would that motivate you to throw yourself in front of a car for that person's safety? According to humanist Abraham Maslow (1954, 1971), our "basic" needs must be satisfied before our "higher" needs can be. The **hierarchy of motives** *is Maslow's concept that all individuals have five main needs that must be satisfied in the following sequence: physiological, safety, love and belongingness, self-esteem, and self-actualization* (see figure 13.1). According to Maslow's hierarchy of motives, people need to eat before they can achieve, and they must satisfy their needs for safety before they can satisfy their needs for love.

CRITICAL THINKING

The Best of Times and the Worst of Times

For this exercise, identify two dramatically different periods in your life. One should be a time when things were far from satisfactory. The other should be a time when things were going very well for you. Now, compare these two periods in terms of the hierarchy of needs proposed by Maslow. For the rockier time, at what level were your needs not being met? For the more satisfying time, Maslow would predict that if all your needs were met, this period might qualify as a self-actualizing experience. Does that fit? If not, what do you think would have to have been improved in order for you to have had a peak experience? Understanding life's ups and downs from Maslow's point of view demonstrates your ability to *apply psychological concepts to enhance personal adaptation.*

"Well, I've had my coffee, so I guess it's on to the rest of Maslow's list."

Courtesy of Mark Litzler.

It is the need for self-actualization that Maslow has described in the greatest detail. **Self-actualization,** *the highest and most elusive of Maslow's needs, is the motivation to develop one's full potential as a human being.* According

FIGURE 13.1

Maslow's Hierarchy of Motives

Abraham Maslow developed the hierarchy of human motives to show how we have to satisfy certain basic needs before we can satisfy higher needs. The diagram shows lower-level needs toward the base of the pyramid, higher-level needs toward the peak. The lowest needs (those that must be satisfied first) are physiological—hunger, thirst, and sleep, for example. The next needs that must be satisfied are safety needs, which ensure our survival—we have to protect ourselves from crime and war, for example. Then we must satisfy love and belongingness needs—we need the security, affection, and attention of others, for example. Near the top of Maslow's hierarchy are self-esteem needs—we need to feel good about ourselves as we learn skills, pursue a profession, and deal with people, for example. Finally, at the top of the pyramid and the highest needs are self-actualization needs—reaching our full potential as human beings. Included among self-actualization needs are the motivations for truth, goodness, beauty, wholeness, and justice.

Chinese needs hierarchy

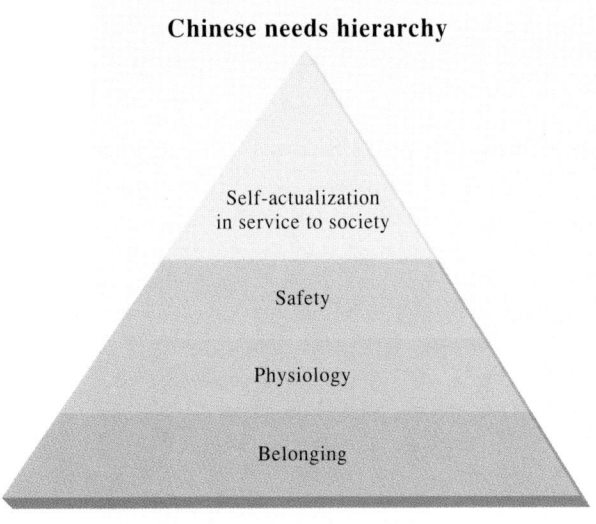

- Self-actualization in service to society
- Safety
- Physiology
- Belonging

American needs hierarchy

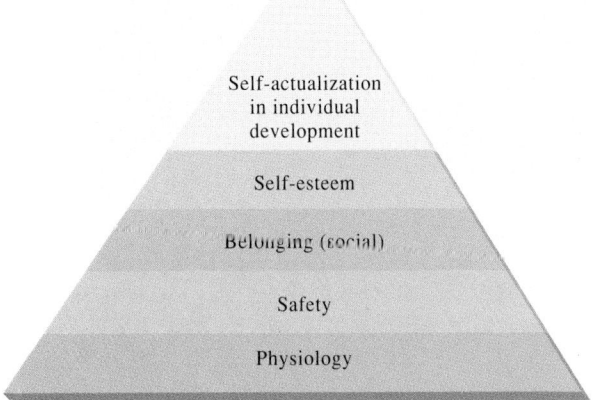

- Self-actualization in individual development
- Self-esteem
- Belonging (social)
- Safety
- Physiology

FIGURE 13.2

Chinese Needs Hierarchy and American Needs Hierarchy

to Maslow, self-actualization is possible only after the other needs in the hierarchy are met. Maslow cautions that most people stop maturing after they have developed a high level of self-esteem and, thus, do not become self-actualized. Many of Maslow's writings focus on how people can reach the elusive motivational state of self-actualization. We will discuss much more about Maslow's theory in chapter 15, "Personality."

The idea that human motives are hierarchically arranged is an appealing one. Maslow's theory stimulates us to think about the ordering of motives in our own lives. However, the ordering of needs is somewhat subjective. Some people seek greatness in a career in order to achieve self-esteem, for example, while putting their needs for love and belongingness on hold.

The Sociocultural Perspective

As is true of so much human behavior, environmental and sociocultural influences play an important role in motivation (D'Andrade & Strauss, 1992). For example, Maslow's hierarchy seems to be a comprehensive explanation and ordering of the motives that influence behavior. How well would this description fit the motivational patterns observed in other cultures? A different sequence of needs exists in Chinese culture (Nevis, 1983). The emphasis in the Chinese hierarchy involves the promotion of connectedness to others in the culture, in contrast to the emphasis on self-development in Maslow's version (see figure 13.2). We must always exercise caution in applying Western frameworks to non-Western cultures.

Even "biological" motives have environmental and sociocultural underpinnings. Why does the same meal—say, steak, baked potato, and salad—satisfy our hunger so much more when we are seated near someone we love in a candlelit room than in a noisy school cafeteria, for example? Consider also the social motive of achievement. To fully understand achievement, we need to examine how parents and children interact, how peers compare one another, and which people we look up to as models of success, along with the standards for achievement in various cultures.

The role of sociocultural and environmental factors raises another important issue regarding motivation: Are we internally motivated or externally motivated? Do we study hard because we have an internal standard that motivates us to do well or because of external factors, such as wanting to get good grades so we can get into a doctoral program in psychology or medical school? As a rule, the study of biological and cognitive factors stresses the role of internal motivation, and the study of sociocultural and environmental factors stresses the role of external motivation. We'll get back to the internal-external issue in motivation later in the chapter in our discussion of achievement motivation.

Some Important Issues in Motivation

In our description of motivation's complex underpinnings, we have encountered three important questions: (1) To what degree are we motivated by innate, unlearned, biological factors as opposed to learned, sociocultural, experientially based factors? (2) To what degree are we aware of what motivates us—that is, to what extent is our motivation conscious? (3) To what degree are we internally or externally motivated? These are issues that researchers continue to wrangle with and debate. Not only will these issues reappear in this chapter, but they also will resurface in our discussion of personality in chapter 15. Now we will turn our attention to a discussion of specific motives that influence our behavior.

REVIEW

Perspectives on Motivation

Motivation involves the question of why people behave, think, and feel the way they do. Most psychologists today believe that behavior is energized and directed by a complex mix of factors. The role of biological factors is the focus of the neurobiological perspective. Four traditions in this perspective are instinct theory, drive theory, ethology, and physiology. Instinct theory flourished early in the twentieth century, but instincts do not entirely explain motivation. According to drive reduction theory, a physiological need creates an aroused state (drive) that motivates the organism to satisfy the need. Homeostasis is an important motivational process promoted by drive reduction theory.

Ethology is the study of the biological basis of behavior in natural habitats. The body's physiological makeup—including reflexes, brain structures, organs, and hormones—also plays an important role in contemporary theories of motivation.

In the behavioral perspective, external factors and environmental contexts play powerful roles in motivation. Incentives are positive or negative stimuli or events that motivate an individual's behavior. More recently, cognitively oriented behaviorists have introduced concepts such as those of self-efficacy and plans to explain a person's motivation. According to Freud's psychoanalytic theory, instincts (especially sex and aggression) are the motivational forces underlying human behavior. In Freud's theory, individuals are largely unaware of what motivates them. The

contemporary view of motivation also emphasizes the importance of cognitive factors. In the cognitive perspective, people are aware and rational. Maslow's hierarchy of motives reflects the humanistic perspective. Maslow believed that some motives need to be satisfied before others; self-actualization is the highest motive in Maslow's hierarchy. And as is true of so much human behavior, environmental and sociocultural factors play an important role in motivation.

Three important issues in motivation are the degree to which motivation is innate versus learned, conscious versus unconscious, and internal versus external.

Selected Motives

In this portion of the chapter, we will explore different types of motives. First, we will study hunger, which is strongly based in the physiological dimension emphasized by the neurobiological perspective. Other drives with important physiological underpinnings include drives to satisfy our thirst and our sleep, breathing, sex, and safety needs. Second, we will read about the aspect of motivation that involves the development of competence in the environment. And third, we will examine motives that are primarily social, such as the need for affiliation and the need for power.

Hunger

Imagine that you live in the Bayambang area of the Philippines. You are very poor and have little food to eat. Hunger continuously gnaws at everyone in your village. Now imagine yourself as the typical American, eating not only breakfast, lunch, and dinner, but snacking along the way—and maybe even raiding the refrigerator at midnight.

Food is an important aspect of life in any culture. Whether we have very little or large amounts of food available to us, hunger influences our behavior. What mechanisms explain why we get hungry?

Physiological Factors

You are sitting in class and it is 2 P.M. You were so busy today that you skipped lunch. As the professor lectures, your stomach starts to growl. For many of us, a growling stomach is one of the main signs that we are hungry. Psychologists have wondered for many years about the role of peripheral factors—such as the stomach, liver, and blood chemistry—in hunger.

Peripheral Factors

In 1912 Walter Cannon and A. L. Washburn conducted an experiment that revealed a close association between stomach contractions and hunger (see figure 13.3). As part of the procedure, a partially inflated balloon was passed through a tube inserted in Washburn's mouth and pushed down into his stomach. A machine that measures air pressure was connected to the balloon to monitor Washburn's stomach contractions. Every time Washburn reported hunger pangs, his stomach was also contracting. This finding, which was confirmed in subsequent experiments with other volunteers, led the two to believe that gastric activity is *the* basis for hunger.

Stomach signals are not the only factors that affect hunger, however. People who have had their stomachs surgically removed still get hunger pangs. Stomach contractions can be a signal for hunger, but the stomach also can send signals that stop hunger. We all know that a full stomach can decrease our appetite. In fact, the stomach actually tells the brain not only how full it is, but also how much

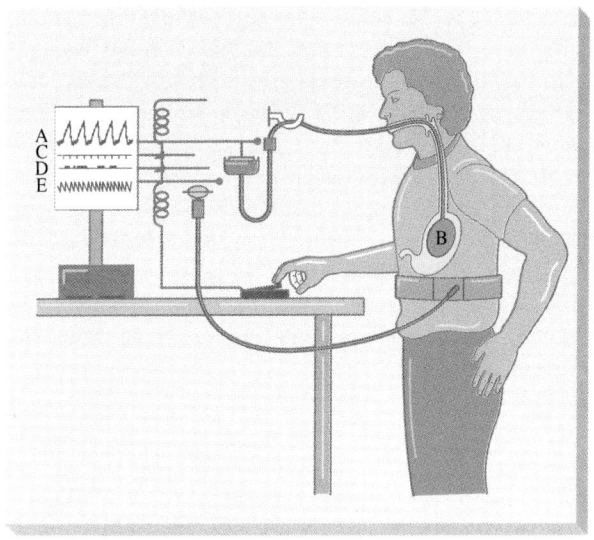

Figure 13.3

Cannon and Washburn's Classic Experiment on Hunger
Notice the letters *A, B, C, D,* and *E* in the drawing. *A* is the record of the increases and decreases in the volume of the balloon in the subject's stomach, *B*. Number of minutes elapsed is shown in *C*. The subject's indication of feeling hungry is recorded at *D*. *E* is a reading of the movements of the abdominal wall to ensure that such movements are not the cause of changes in stomach volume.

nutrient is in the stomach load. That is why a stomach full of rich food stops your hunger faster than a stomach full of water (Deutsch & Gonzales, 1980). The same stomach hormone (called cholecystokinin, or CCK) that helps start the digestion of food reaches your brain through the bloodstream and signals you to stop eating.

Blood sugar (or glucose) is an important factor in hunger, probably because the brain is critically dependent on sugar for energy. One set of sugar receptors is located in the brain itself, and these receptors trigger hunger when sugar levels get too low. Another set of sugar receptors is in the liver, which is the organ that stores excess sugar and releases it into the blood when needed. The sugar receptors in the liver signal the brain via the vagus nerve; this signal can also make you hungry (Novlin & others, 1983). Another important factor in blood sugar control is the hormone insulin, which causes excess sugar in the blood to be stored in the cells as fats and carbohydrates. Insulin injections cause profound hunger because they drastically lower blood sugar.

Psychologist Judith Rodin (1984) has further clarified the role of insulin and glucose in understanding hunger and eating behavior. She points out that when we eat complex carbohydrates, such as cereals, bread, and pasta, insulin levels go up but then fall off gradually. When we consume simple sugars, such as candy bars and soft drinks, insulin levels rise and then fall off sharply—the familiar "sugar low." Glucose levels in the blood are affected by these complex carbohydrates and simple sugars in similar ways. The consequence is that we are more likely to eat again within several hours if we have just eaten simple sugars than we are if we have just eaten complex carbohydrates. Also, the food we eat at one meal often influences how much we will eat at our next meal. Thus, consuming doughnuts and candy bars, in addition to providing no nutritional value, sets up an ongoing sequence of what and how much we probably will crave the next time we eat.

Brain Processes

So far we have been talking about peripheral factors in hunger. However, the brain is also involved in hunger. The brain's **ventromedial hypothalamus (VMH)** *is a region of the hypothalamus that plays an important role in controlling hunger.* When a rat's VMH is surgically destroyed, it immediately becomes hyperphagic (that is, it eats too much) and rapidly becomes obese (Brobeck, Tepperman, & Long, 1943). Researchers thought that the VMH was a "satiety center" and its destruction left animals unable to fully satisfy their hunger. The picture now emerging, however, suggests that the destruction causes a hormonal disorder (remember that the hypothalamus is the master control center for many hormones). After the VMH is destroyed, a rat's body cells act as if they are starving, constantly converting all nutrients from the blood into fat and never releasing them. That is the main reason the animals become obese (see figure 13.4). One of the fascinating aspects of this condition is that the animals stop gaining weight once they reach a certain weight, suggesting that hormones and body cells control the body's overall "set point" for body weight. **Set point** *refers to the weight maintained when no effort is made to gain or lose weight.*

To summarize, the brain monitors both blood sugar levels and the condition of the stomach, then integrates this information (and probably other information as well) in the process of regulating hunger. Hypothalamic regions, especially the VMH, are involved in integrating information about hunger.

Your internal physiological world is very much involved in your feelings of hunger. In addition to the physiological processes, some external and cognitive factors are involved.

External Cues

Psychologists are interested in how environmental cues might stimulate hunger. You may know someone who seems incapable of walking past an ice cream shop without stopping to eat a huge hot fudge sundae.

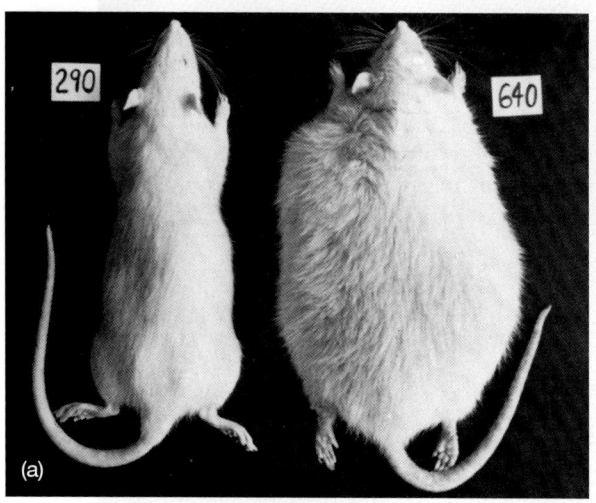

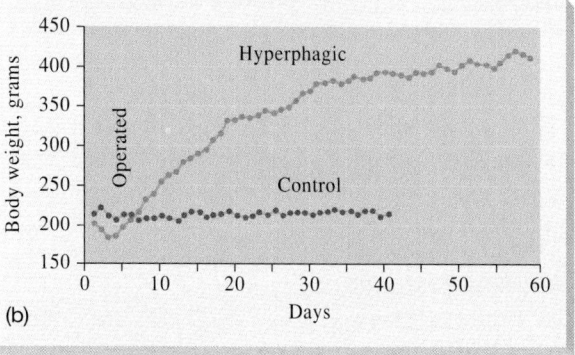

FIGURE 13.4

The Role of the Ventromedial Hypothalamus (VMH) in the Obesity of Rats
(*a*) A hyperphagic rat gained three times its body weight after a lesion (surgical destruction) had been made in its VMH.
(*b*) This graph displays the weight gain by a group of rats in which lesions had been made in the VMH (hyperphagic) and by a group of rats in which no lesions had been made (control). *Examine the graph. At what point does it look like the set point kicks in for the hyperphagic rat?* It is at about 1 month—notice the leveling off of the weight gain in the graph.

Stanley Schachter (1971) believes that one of the main differences between obese and normal-weight individuals is their attention to environmental cues. From his perspective, people of normal weight attend to internal cues for signals of when to eat—for example, when blood sugar level is low or hunger pangs are sensed in the stomach. In contrast, an obese person responds to such external cues as signals of when to eat—how food tastes, looks, and smells, for example.

Self-control and Exercise

Rodin (1984) points out that, not too long ago, we believed that obesity was caused by such factors as unhappiness or responses to external food cues. According to Rodin, a number of biological, cognitive, and social factors are more

"Let's just go in and see what happens."

Drawing by Booth; © 1986 The New Yorker Magazine, Inc.

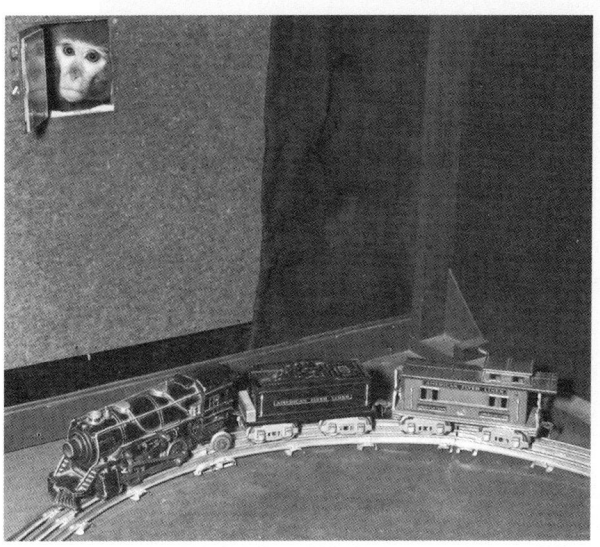

FIGURE 13.5

Motivation for Novel Stimulation
This monkey showed a motivation for novel stimulation and was willing to work just so he could unlock the window and watch a toy train go around in a circle.

important. We already discussed the important biological factors, including the roles of complex carbohydrates and simple sugars in insulin and glucose levels. In regard to external cues, Rodin says that, although obese persons are more responsive to external food cues than normal-weight persons are, there are individuals at all weight levels who respond more to external than to internal stimuli. Many persons who respond to external cues also have the conscious ability to control their behavior and keep environmental food cues from externally controlling their eating patterns (Stunkard, 1989).

Rodin believes that, not only is conscious self-control of eating patterns important in weight control, but so is exercise. No matter what your genetic background, aerobic exercise increases your metabolic rate, which helps you burn calories. Much more information about dieting, eating behavior, and exercise appears in our discussion of health in chapter 14.

I've been on a constant diet for the last two decades. I've lost a total of 789 pounds. By all accounts, I should be hanging from a charm bracelet.

Erma Bombeck

At this point, we have discussed a number of ideas about the overall nature of motivation and about hunger. Next, we will consider the motivation involved in adapting to and mastering our environment.

Competence Motivation

We are a species motivated to gain mastery over our world, to explore unknown environments with enthusiasm and curiosity, and to achieve. In the 1950s, psychologists recognized

that motivation involves much more than the reduction of biological needs. **Competence motivation** *is the motivation to deal effectively with the environment, to be adept at what we attempt, to process information efficiently, and to make the world a better place.* R. W. White (1959) said we do these things not because they serve biological needs, but because we have an internal motivation to interact effectively with our environment.

Among the research White used to support his concept of competence motivation were experiments that showed that organisms are motivated to seek stimulation rather than to reduce a need. For example, monkeys solved simple problems just for the opportunity to watch a toy train (Butler, 1953) (see figure 13.5). Rats consistently chose a complex maze with a number of pathways over a simple maze with few pathways. A series of experiments suggested that college students could not tolerate sensory deprivation for more than 2 to 3 days (Bexton, Heron, & Scott, 1954). These students developed a strong motivation to quit the experiment, even though they were getting paid to participate in it. They became bored, restless, and irritable (figure 13.6 shows the isolation chamber of the sensory deprivation experiment).

Psychologists have investigated how shorter periods of sensory deprivation—such as spending time in a water immersion tank—can reduce stress (Suedfeld & Coren, 1989). Imagine that you have just stepped into a shallow pool of densely salted water. You close the hatch, then lie

---

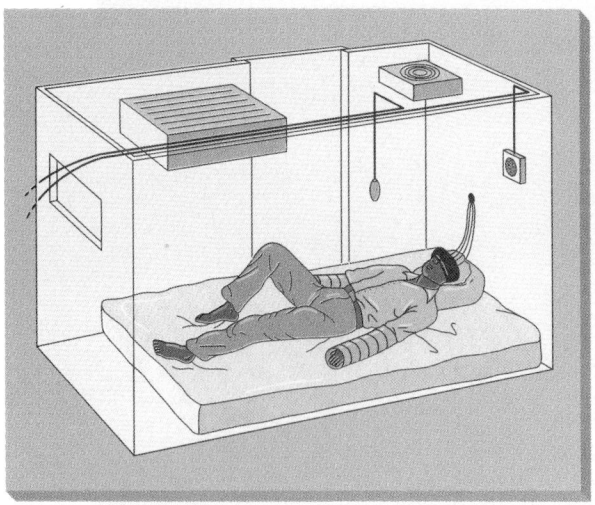

FIGURE 13.6

Isolation Chamber Used in Heron's Sensory Deprivation Study
College students were paid $20 a day to remain in this isolation chamber ($20 was a reasonably good sum of money in the 1950s, especially since the students were getting paid to do as little as possible). Their sensory input was drastically reduced. Outside noises were masked by fans, the subjects wore goggles that kept them from seeing, and they were prevented from touching objects by having their arms wrapped in cotton. How did the students react to this situation? Initially they slept most of the time. After 2 to 3 days, though, they quit the experiment, which they were free to do at any time. The students said they became very bored and restless, and, after several days, they felt so uncomfortable they couldn't wait to get out of the situation, even though it meant losing $20 a day.

Adapted from "The Pathology of Boredom" by Woodburn Heron. Copyright © 1957 by Scientific American, Inc. All rights reserved.

on your back and float (see figure 13.7). The tank is totally dark. The only sound is your own breathing, which is barely audible. Feeling suspended, you have no sense of temperature and little sense of time. Gradually your muscles relax. After 55 minutes, music is piped into the tank to signal the end of the session. The flotation tank experience is called Restricted Environmental Stimulation Therapy (REST). Researchers have documented that a series of about twenty REST sessions can significantly lower the blood pressure of many individuals with hypertension (Fine & Turner, 1987). REST also has been found to improve athletic performance and creative thinking and to reduce chronic pain. Researchers suspect that REST is effective because our fast-paced lives have become overstimulating and demanding. REST allows us to "get away from it all" in a dramatic way. In summary, sensory deprivation can both harm and help. It's harmful when we are deprived of sensory input for too long; it's helpful in short spurts.

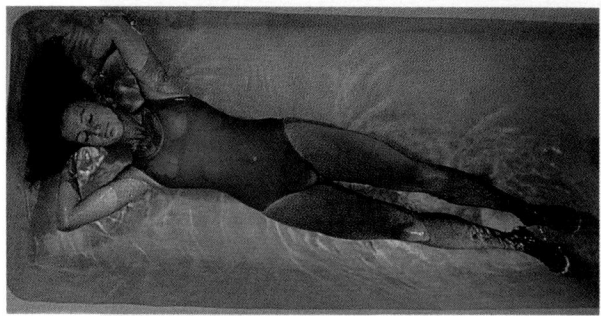

FIGURE 13.7

Restricted Environmental Stimulation Therapy (REST)
The woman shown here is lying in a water immersion tank during a Restricted Environmental Stimulation Therapy (REST) session. This virtual absence of environmental stimuli for approximately 1 hour at a time during the "float" has been effective in improving such conditions as hypertension.

Achievement Motivation

"Winning isn't everything, it is the *only* thing," exhorted Vince Lombardi, the former coach of the Green Bay Packers. We live in an achievement-oriented world with standards that tell us success is important (Boggiano & Pittman, 1993). Some psychologists believe our world is too achievement oriented. David Elkind (1981) said we are a nation of hurried, wired people who are too uptight about success and failure, and far too worried about what we accomplish in comparison to others.

Some people are highly motivated to succeed and expend a lot of effort striving to excel. Other people are not as motivated to succeed and don't work as hard to achieve. These two types of individuals vary in their **achievement motivation, or need for achievement,** *the desire to accomplish something, to reach a standard of excellence, and to expend effort to excel.* Borrowing from Henry Murray's (1938) theory and measurement of personality, psychologist David McClelland (1955) assessed achievement by showing individuals ambiguous pictures that were likely to stimulate achievement-related responses. The individuals were asked to tell a story about the picture, and their comments were scored according to how strongly they reflected achievement. Researchers have found that individuals whose stories reflect high achievement motivation have a stronger hope for success than fear of failure, are moderate rather than high or low risk takers, and persist with effort when tasks become difficult (Atkinson & Raynor, 1974).

Whatever you can do, or dream you can, begin it. Boldness has genius, power and magic in it.

Johann Wolfgang von Goethe

Motivation, Emotion, Health, and Personality

McClelland (1978) also wondered if you could boost achievement behavior by increasing achievement motivation. To find out, he trained the businessmen in a village in India to become more achievement oriented, encouraging them to increase their hope for success, reduce their fear of failure, take moderate risks, and persist with a great deal of effort when tasks become difficult. Compared to village businessmen in a nearby town, the village businessmen who were trained by McClelland started more new businesses and employed more new people in the 2 years after the training.

Even if you are on the right track, you'll get run over if you just sit there.

Will Rogers

Cognitive Factors in Achievement

In the contemporary view of achievement, cognitive factors play an important role. Cognitive factors in achievement are highlighted in attribution theory, in the concepts of intrinsic and extrinsic motivation, and in the concepts of mastery and helpless orientations.

Attribution Theory **Attribution theory** *states that individuals are motivated to discover the underlying causes of behavior as part of the effort to make sense out of the behavior.* In a way, attribution theorists say, people are like intuitive scientists, seeking the cause behind what happens.

The reasons individuals behave the way they do can be classified in a number of ways, but one basic distinction stands out above all others—the distinction between internal causes, such as the actor's personality traits or motives, and external causes, which are environmental, situational factors such as rewards or task difficulty (Heider, 1958). If college students do not do well on a test, do they attribute it to the teacher's plotting against them and making the test too difficult (external cause) or to their not studying hard enough (internal cause)? The answer to such a question influences how people feel about themselves. If students believe that their performance is the teacher's fault, they will not feel as bad as when they do poorly because they do not spend enough time studying.

An extremely important aspect of internal causes for achievement is *effort*. Unlike many causes of success, effort is under a person's control and amenable to change (Jagacinski & Nicholls, 1990). The importance of effort in achievement is recognized even by children. In one study, third- to sixth-grade students felt that effort was the most effective strategy for good school performance (Skinner, Wellborn, & Connell, 1990).

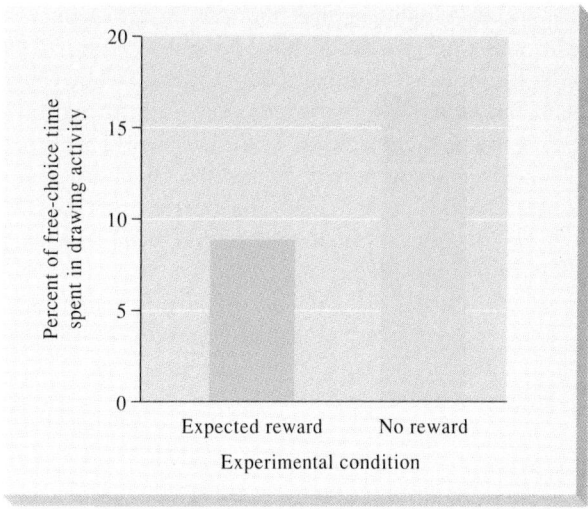

FIGURE 13.8

Intrinsic Motivation and Drawing Activity
Students spent more time in art activity when no reward was mentioned than when a reward was expected for their participation (Lepper, Greene, & Nisbett, 1973).

Lord, grant that I always desire more than I can accomplish.

Michelangelo

Intrinsic and Extrinsic Motivation Closely related to the concept of internal and external causes of behavior is the concept of intrinsic and extrinsic motivation. Achievement motivation—whether in school, at work, or in sports—can be divided into two main types: **intrinsic motivation,** *the internal desire to be competent and to do something for its own sake;* and **extrinsic motivation,** *the influence of external rewards and punishments.* If you work hard in college because a personal standard is important to you, intrinsic motivation is involved. But if you work hard in college because you know it will bring you a higher-paying job when you graduate, extrinsic motivation is at work.

Almost every boss, parent, or teacher has wondered whether or not to offer a reward to someone who does well (extrinsic motivation), or whether to let the individual's internal, self-determined motivation operate (intrinsic motivation). If someone is producing shoddy work, seems bored, or has a negative attitude, offering incentives may improve his or her motivation. But there are times when external rewards can diminish achievement motivation. One study showed that, of students who already had a strong interest in art, those who did not expect a reward spent more time drawing than did their counterparts who knew they would be rewarded for drawing (Lepper, Greene, & Nisbett, 1973) (see figure 13.8).

Some of the most achievement-oriented people are those who have a high personal standard for achievement (internal) and who also are highly competitive (external). In one study, students who had poor math skills but who set their own goals (internal) and received information about their peers' achievement (external) worked more math problems and got more of them correct than did their counterparts who experienced either situation alone (Schunk, 1983). Other research suggests that social comparison by itself is not a wise strategy (Ames & Ames, 1989). The argument is that social comparison puts the individual in an ego-involved, threatening, self-focused state rather than a task-involved, effortful, strategy-focused state.

One of psychology's newest and most rapidly growing fields is sport psychology. Whether Little League baseball or Olympic competition, sports have become an integral part of our society. Do athletes become stars because they are internally motivated or because they are externally motivated? Just as with other areas of life, both internal and external factors are involved. Star athletes experience a remarkable set of teachers, parents, and other external supports throughout their careers. Many are motivated by a desire for fame and fortune or by a competitive spirit; however, most top athletes also have a deep, burning desire to do their best, to reach a personal standard of excellence (McAuley & Duncan, 1991). To read more about the area of sport psychology and motivation, see Applications in Psychology 13.1.

Mastery Versus Helpless and Performance Orientations   Closely related to an emphasis on intrinsic motivation, attributions of internal causes of behavior, and the importance of effort in achievement is a mastery orientation. Valanne Henderson and Carol Dweck (1990) have found that children and adolescents show two distinct responses to difficult or challenging circumstances. The **helpless orientation** *describes individuals who seem trapped by the experience of difficulty. They attribute their difficulty to lack of ability.* They frequently say things like, "I'm not very good at this," even though they may have earlier demonstrated their ability through numerous successes. And once they view their behavior as failure, they often feel anxious about the situation, and their performance worsens even further. People who have the **mastery orientation** *are task oriented. Instead of focusing on their ability and winning at all costs, they are concerned about their learning strategies and the process of achievement, rather than outcomes.* Mastery-oriented individuals often instruct themselves to pay attention, to think carefully, and to remember strategies that have worked for them in previous situations. They frequently report feeling challenged and excited by difficult tasks, rather than being threatened by them.

Another issue in motivation involves whether to adopt a mastery or a performance orientation. We have already described what a mastery orientation is like. A **performance orientation** *involves being concerned with the achievement outcome, whereas a mastery focuses on the process of achievement. In the performance orientation, winning is what matters and happiness is thought to result from winning.*

What sustains mastery-oriented individuals is the self-efficacy and self-satisfaction they feel from effectively dealing with the world in which they live. By contrast, what sustains performance-oriented individuals is winning. Although skills can and often are involved in winning, performance-oriented individuals often do not view themselves as necessarily having skills. Rather, they see themselves as using tactics, such as undermining others, to get what they want.

Does all of this mean that mastery-oriented individuals do not like to win and that performance-oriented individuals are not motivated to experience the self-efficacy that comes from being able to take credit for one's behavior? No it does not. A matter of emphasis or degree is involved, though. For mastery-oriented individuals, winning isn't everything, but winning is everything for their performance counterparts. And for performance-oriented individuals, skill development and self-efficacy take a back seat to winning, whereas for their mastery counterparts they do not.

Goal-Setting and Self-efficacy

The current position in the motivation field is that the self produces thoughts and images but not actions (Franken, 1994). It is goal-setting that produces action (Locke & Latham, 1990). Goals help us reach our dreams, provide the focus needed for success, provide the basis for self-discipline, and maintain our interest (Lecci, Okuni, & Karoly, 1994).

It is often helpful to have both long-term and more immediate goals. Albert Bandura (1986) argues that having immediate (also called proximal or subgoals) goals can generate self-satisfaction based on personal accomplishment. Such immediate subgoals can provide a continuing source of motivation apart from loftier superordinate goals that often take a long time to accomplish. For example, an undergraduate student may have a superordinate goal of getting into a graduate program. The student can also set more immediate goals such as getting good grades this semester, on the next test, and so on.

Bandura (1991, 1994) also stresses that **self-efficacy,** *belief in mastery over a situation and the ability to produce positive outcomes,* is an important dimension of achievement. Self-efficacy can help people adhere to behavior change programs, such as quitting smoking, and engage in competent decision-making (Bandura & Jourden, 1991). As a part of self-efficacy, individuals learn the skills they need to deal with specific situations. For example, if people fear public speaking, they need to develop the skills to engage in effective public speaking. Such skills often increase individuals' sense of mastery over the situation.

APPLICATIONS IN PSYCHOLOGY 13.1

Sport Psychology and Motivation

Nancy Lopez is tied for the lead in the Ladies' Professional Golf Championship. On the eighteenth hole of the final round, she sinks a birdie putt to win the championship. What psychological and motivational characteristics allow athletes like Lopez to perform so well under pressure?

One study showed that elite athletes—the stars in 23 sports—differed from lesser athletes in several important ways (Mahoney, Gabriel, & Perkins, 1987). Although all professional athletes have innate physical gifts, the way elite athletes handle psychological matters—self-confidence, anxiety, concentration, and motivation—is what tips the balance and makes them great.

Self-confidence is a tricky area to study, partly because it is not simply the absence of self-doubt. And while it is a uniquely personal experience, there are also some characteristics common to all self-confident athletes (Mahoney, 1989). They show a willingness, sometimes even an eagerness, to be under pressure, and the ability to remain focused on immediate demands. In sudden-death play with hundreds watching, a few special, gifted athletes, such as Lopez, confidently sink a 25-foot putt.

Star athletes generally report that they have set reasonable and personally meaningful goals in training, but that sometimes pushing themselves too hard can harm their performance or lead to "burnout." Athletes who seek a balanced life, for example, tend to do better than those who spend all their time in training.

Top athletes also have the ability to control their emotions. In particular, they are able to control their anxiety. For many years sport psychologists thought that very low and very high levels of anxiety produced lower performances. That view is now seen as too simplistic. Top athletes say that what is more important is what anxiety means to them and what they do with it (Mahoney, 1989). Many get the jitters at some time before a game—maybe a week before, maybe just minutes before. Sometimes their anxiety even spills over into the first few minutes of the game. But once they are into the heat of competition, they are able to get past their anxiety and become totally absorbed in the moment. When athletes let their anxiety get the upper hand, however, their muscles tense, their minds race, and they can "choke."

Self-esteem

Self-esteem *involves the evaluative and affective dimensions of self-concept. Self-esteem is also referred to as self-worth or self-image.* What are the consequences of having low self-esteem? Self-esteem has been implicated in low achievement, depression and many other adjustment problems (Harter & Marold, 1992). Also, individuals with high self-esteem tend to focus on their strengths whereas their low self-esteem counterparts are more likely to dwell on their negative qualities or weaknesses (Showers, 1992).

How can an individual's self-esteem be improved? Four ways are: 1) identifying the causes of low esteem, 2) emotional support and approval, 3) achievement, and 4) coping (Bednar & Peterson, 1995). Emphasis on achievement

UCLA psychologist Sandra Graham is shown here talking with a group of young boys about motivation. Dr. Graham has conducted important research showing that middle-class African American children—like their White counterparts—have high achievement expectations and understand that their failure is often due to lack of effort rather than to lack of luck.

fits with Bandura's concept of self-efficacy. The straightforward teaching of real skills often results in increased achievement, and thus, in enhanced self-esteem. Individuals develop higher self-esteem because they know what tasks are important for achieving goals.

Self-esteem is also increased when individuals face a problem and try to cope with it rather than avoid it (Lazarus, 1991). If coping rather than avoidance prevails, individuals are more likely to face problems realistically, honestly, and nondefensively. The converse is true of low self-esteem. Unfavorable self-evaluations trigger denial, deception, and avoidance in an attempt to disavow that which has already been glimpsed as true. This process leads to self-generated disapproval as a form of feedback to the self about personal adequacy.

Cultural, Ethnic, and Social-Class Variations in Achievement

People in the United States are often more achievement oriented than people in many other countries. One study of 104 societies revealed that the parents in nonindustrialized countries placed a lower value on their children's achievement and independence and a higher value on obedience and cooperation than did the parents in industrialized countries (Barry, Child, & Bacon, 1959). In comparisons between Anglo-American children and Mexican and Latino children, the Anglo-American children were more competitive and less cooperative. For example, one study found that Anglo-American children are more likely to keep other children from gaining when they could not realize those gains themselves (Kagan & Madsen, 1972). Another study

showed that Mexican children are more family oriented, whereas Anglo-American children tend to be more concerned about themselves (Holtzmann, 1982).

Until recently, researchers studying achievement focused almost exclusively on White males, and when achievement in ethnic minority groups has been studied, the cultural differences have too often been viewed against standards of achievements for White males. As a result, many researchers have reached the conclusion that ethnic minorities are somehow deficient when it comes to achievement (Gibbs & Huang, 1989).

In addition, most studies on ethnic minorities do not take into account socioeconomic status. Socioeconomic status (also called SES) is determined by a combination of occupation, education, and income. When both ethnicity and social class are taken into account in the same study, social class tends to be a far better predictor of achievement than is ethnicity (Graham, 1986). For example, middle-class individuals, regardless of their ethnic background, have higher aspirations and expectations for success, and they recognize the importance of effort more than their lower-class counterparts do (Gibbs, 1989).

Psychologist Sandra Graham (1986, 1987, 1990), for example, has found that middle-class African American children do not fit the stereotypes of either deviant or special populations. They, like their middle-class White counterparts, have high expectations for their own achievement and understand that failure is often due to lack of effort rather than to lack of luck.

It's also an indisputable fact that many people from ethnic minority backgrounds face educational, career, and social barriers (Huang & Gibbs, 1989; Huston, McLoyd, & Coll, 1994; Swanson, 1995). The Civil Rights Acts of 1964 and 1991 have made some progress in chipping away at these barriers, but much more needs to be done. We do not have all of the answers to the problems of poverty and racism in this country, but, as the Reverend Jesse Jackson commented, perhaps we have begun to ask some of the right questions.

Achievement and Gender

The motivation for work and achievement is the same for both sexes; however, women and men often make different career choices because of the way they have been socialized and the opportunities available to them. Because women have been socialized to adopt nurturing roles rather than career or achieving roles, traditionally they have not seriously planned careers, have not extensively explored career options, and have restricted their choices to gender-stereotyped careers (Baumrind, 1989).

For some areas of achievement, gender differences are so large they can best be described as nonoverlapping. For example, no major league baseball players are female, and 96 percent of all registered nurses are female. In contrast, many

Some of the brightest and most gifted girls do not have achievement and career aspirations that match their talents. Gender researchers hope that gender-role stereotypes that prevent girls from developing a more positive orientation toward math and science can be eliminated.

Such differences reflect the American culture's value-laden definition of achievement (Paludi, 1995). The areas that are perceived as successful often have a masculine bias—prestigious occupations, academic excellence, and other accomplishments that are associated with masculine values. Accomplishments associated with traditional feminine values are given less attention. Many women manage a household and children, yet this accomplishment is rarely categorized as achievement motivation and work.

Parents play an important role in their sons' and daughters' career development. In one recent study, 1,500 mothers and their young adolescent sons and daughters were studied to determine the role of maternal expectations, advice, and the provision of opportunities in their daughters' and sons' occupational aspirations (Harold & Eccles, 1990). Mothers were more likely to encourage their sons to consider the military, to expect their sons to go into the military right after high school, and to discuss with their sons the education needed for and likely income of various jobs. Expecting marriage right after high school and discussing the problems of combining work and family were more common to daughters. Also, mothers were more worried that their daughters would not have a happy marriage, and they were more likely to want their sons to have a job that would support a family. This study also indicated that the mothers worked more with the boys on computers; they also more often provided the boys with computers, software, and programs. The mothers also bought more math or science books and games for the boys and more often enrolled the boys in computer classes. The boys had more sports opportunities, whereas the girls had more opportunities in music, art, and dance. The mothers said the boys had more talent in math and were better suited for careers involving math, although they believed that the girls had more talent in English and were better suited for English-related careers. In sum, there were differences in the kinds of advice and opportunities the mothers provided and in their expectations.

Social Motives

Social motives *are the needs and desires of people that are learned through experience with the social world. Such motives are not derived from basic biological factors like hunger, thirst, sleep, and to some degree sexuality are. People who are high in a particular social motive will keep trying to reach goal states related to the motive.*

When psychologists began extensively studying social needs, they used the term *social motives* interchangeably with *social needs.* Maslow's hierarchy of needs includes both biological and social needs (or motives). The social motive tradition in psychology was stimulated by American psychologist Henry Murray (1938), who conceptualized human motivation as a long catalog of

measures of achievement-related behaviors do not reveal gender differences. For example, girls show just as much persistence at tasks as boys do. The question of whether males and females differ in their expectations for success at various achievement tasks is not yet settled (Eccles, 1987).

Gender roles produce different expectations of success depending on the gender stereotyping of the activity. Both educational programs and vocational options are gender stereotyped in our culture (Sadker & Sadker, 1994). Many high-level professions, especially those that are math-related and scientific/technical, are thought to be male activities. In contrast, teaching below the college level, working in clerical and related support jobs, and excelling in language-related courses are thought to be female activities by both children and adults (Eccles, 1987).

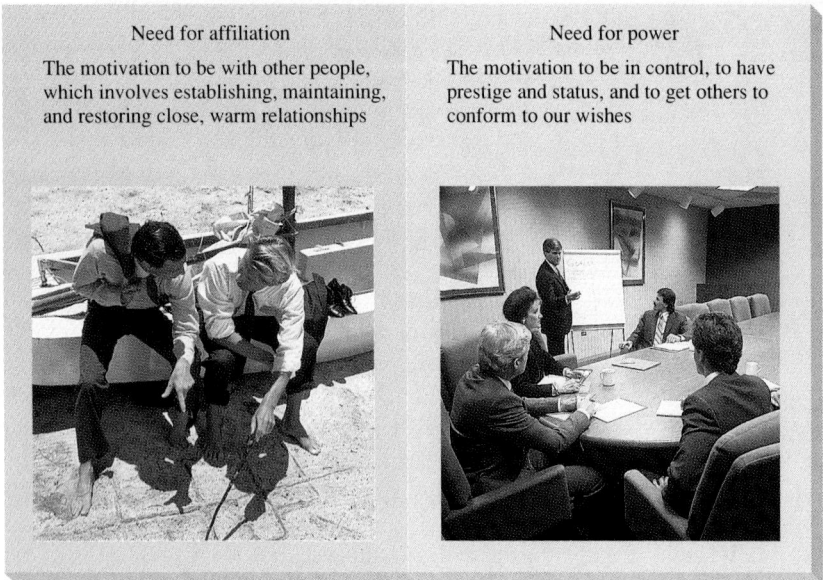

Need for affiliation	Need for power
The motivation to be with other people, which involves establishing, maintaining, and restoring close, warm relationships	The motivation to be in control, to have prestige and status, and to get others to conform to our wishes

FIGURE 13.9

Social Motives: The Need for Affiliation and Need for Power

needs that include the need for achievement, the need for affiliation, the need for aggression, the need for defendance, the need for dominance, the need for nurturance, the need for play, and even the need for embarrassment. Murray believed that our needs are largely unconscious—we don't know what it is that drives us, and we would have a difficult time telling other people about this. Two important social motives are the need for affiliation and the need for power (see figure 13.9).

Need for Affiliation

Are you the kind of person who likes to be around people a lot? Or would you rather stay home and read a book? The **need for affiliation** *is the motive to be with other people, which involves establishing, maintaining, and restoring warm, close, personal relationships.* Our need for affiliation is reflected in the importance of caregiving by parents during children's development, the intimate moments of sharing private thoughts in friendship, the uncomfortable feelings we have when we are lonely, and the powerful attraction we have for someone else when we are in love. While each of us has a need for affiliation, some people have a stronger need than others. Some of us like to be surrounded by lots of friends and feel like something is drastically missing from our lives if we are not in love with someone and they with us. Others of us don't have such a

strong need for affiliation. We don't fall apart if we don't have several close friends around all the time and we don't sit around all day in an anxious state because we don't have someone in love with us.

Cultures also vary in how strongly they promote the need for affiliation. Many Western cultures—such as the United States, Canada, and Western European countries like England and France—emphasize individual achievement, independence, and self-reliance. Many Eastern cultures—such as China, Japan, and India—emphasize affiliation, cooperation, and interdependence.

Another aspect of lives that has important implications for our need for affiliation is our gender. The master stereotype is that females have a stronger need for affiliation than males do. Carol Gilligan (1982) argues that men often view close attachment as threatening, while women frequently perceive it as very welcome. In one investigation, men inserted bizarre imagery in their TAT protocols in response to "intimacy"-related pictures, while females inserted bizarre violent imagery in response to "achievement or power" pictures (Pollack & Gilligan, 1985). A flurry of counterstudies followed, contradicting the stereotype of men feeling extremely uncomfortable with affiliation and intimacy and women feeling extremely uncomfortable with achievement and power (Helgeson & Sharpsteen, 1987).

As with other areas of gender similarities and differences, it is important to go beyond the master stereotype and consider the specific affiliation experiences involved and the context in which affiliation is displayed. It's just not the case that women have a need for affiliation and men don't. All of us—men and women—need to affiliate with others in our lives. And both sexes depend on each other. Further, when differences in affiliation are found, they often are small differences, or in some instances they don't exist at all (Benton & others, 1983).

Need for Power

The **need for power** *involves the motivation to be in control, to have prestige and status, and to get others to conform to our wishes.* The motivation for power can be expressed in a number of ways, with the manner of expression somewhat dependent on the person's sex and socioeconomic status.

Following are some of the ways that individuals with a strong need for power express themselves (Hoyenga & Hoyenga, 1984):

- Acting impulsively and aggressively (this might be especially true of men in lower socioeconomic categories)
- Participating in competitive sports, such as football, hockey, baseball, tennis, and basketball
- Joining organizations and becoming officers in these organizations
- For males, drinking and dominating women

- Obtaining and accumulating possessions, such as sports cars, guns, jewelry, and expensive clothes
- Choosing occupations that provide an opportunity to exercise considerable control over people, such as becoming a police officer, a lawyer, or a business executive

Power has a negative connotation for some people, but it is important to remember that power is part of the personality of many effective leaders. By trying to understand the role that power plays in an individual's personality, we can understand the person better.

REVIEW

Selected Motives—Hunger, Competence Motivation, and Social Motives

In hunger the brain monitors both blood sugar level and the condition of the stomach (interest in the stomach was stimulated by Cannon's research), then integrates this information. Hypothalamic regions are important in hunger, especially VMH. Schachter stressed that environmental cues are involved in the control of eating, but Rodin argues that conscious self-control and exercise are more important than external cues in understanding hunger and eating behavior.

Competence motivation is the motivation to deal effectively with the environment, to be adept at what one attempts, to process information efficiently, and to make the world a better place. This concept recognizes that motivation is much more than simply reducing physiological needs. We studied two aspects of competence motivation—stimulus-seeking motives and achievement motivation.

Achievement motivation (need for achievement) is the desire to accomplish something, to reach a standard of excellence, to expend effort to excel. Cognitive factors in achievement are highlighted in attribution theory, intrinsic and extrinsic motivation, and mastery versus helpless achievement orientations. Intrinsic motivation is the desire to be competent and to do something for its own sake. Extrinsic

motivation is externally determined by rewards and punishments. In many instances, individuals' achievement motivation is influenced by both internal and external factors. The helpless orientation describes individuals who seeem trapped by the experience of difficulty. They attribute their difficulty to lack of ability. The mastery orientation describes individuals who remain extremely task oriented. Instead of focusing on their ability, they are concerned about their learning strategies, often instructing themselves to pay attention, to think carefully, and to remember strategies that have worked in previous situations. They frequently report feeling challenged and excited by difficult tasks, rather than being threatened by them. Performance-oriented individuals are concerned with the outcome, whereas mastery-oriented individuals are concerned with the process. In the performance orientation, winning is what matters most and happiness is thought to result from winning. Goal-setting is the action-producing dimension of achievement. Individuals should set goals; more immediate, proximal goals are especially helpful. Bandura stresses the importance of self-efficacy—belief in mastery over a situation and the ability to produce positive outcomes— in achievement. Self-esteem is the evaluative and affective dimension of

self-concept; it is also called self-worth or self-image. Four ways to improve self-worth are (1) identify the causes of low self-esteem; (2) emotional support and approval, (3) achievement; and (4) coping. Individuals in the United States are more achievement oriented than individuals in most other cultures are. A special concern is the achievement of individuals from various ethnic groups. Too often ethnic differences are interpreted as "deficits" by middle-class, White standards. When researchers examine both ethnicity and social class in the same study, social class is often a much better predictor of achievement. Middle-class individuals fare better than their lower-class counterparts in a variety of achievement situations. The motivation for achievement and work is the same for both sexes; however, females and males often make different career choices because of the way they have been socialized and the opportunities available to them.

Social motives are the needs and desires of people that are learned through experience with the social world. People who are high in a particular motive will keep trying to reach goal states related to the motive. Two important social motives are the need for affiliation (the motive to be with other people) and the need for power (the motivation to be in control).

EMOTION

Motivation and emotion are closely linked. Think about sex, which often is associated with joy; about aggression, which usually is associated with anger; and about achievement, which is associated with pride, joy, and anxiety. The terms *motivation* and *emotion* both come from the Latin word *movere*, which means "to move." Both motivation and emotion spur us into action.

Defining Emotion

Just as with motivation, there are different kinds and intensities of emotions. A person can be not only motivated to eat rather than have sex, but more or less hungry, or more or less interested in having sex. Similarly, a person can be happy or angry, and can be fairly happy or ecstatic, annoyed or fuming.

Defining emotion is difficult because it is not easy to tell when a person is in an emotional state. Are you in an emotional state when your heart beats fast, your palms sweat, and your stomach churns? when you think about how much you are in love with someone? when you smile or grimace? The body, the mind, and the face play important roles in understanding emotion. Psychologists debate how critical each is in determining whether we are in an emotional state (Evans, 1989). For our purposes, we will define **emotion** *as feeling, or affect, that involves a mixture of physiological arousal (fast heart beat, for example), conscious experience (thinking about being in love with someone, for example), and overt behavior (smiling and grimacing, for example).*

Blossoms are scattered by the wind and the wind cares nothing, but the blossoms of the heart no wind can touch.

Yoshida Kenko, *The Harvest of Leisure*, 1930

Classifying Emotion

When we think about emotions, a few dramatic feelings, such as rage, fear, and glorious joy, usually spring to mind. But emotions can be subtle as well—the anticipation of seeing good friends, the mild irritation of boredom, the uneasiness of living in the nuclear age. And the kinds of emotions we can experience are legion. There are more than two hundred words for emotions in the English language. How have psychologists handled the complex task of classifying emotions?

Wheel Models

A number of psychologists use wheel diagrams to classify the emotions we experience. One such model was proposed by Robert Plutchik (1980), who believes that emotions have four dimensions: (1) they are positive or negative; (2) they are primary or mixed; (3) many are polar opposites; and

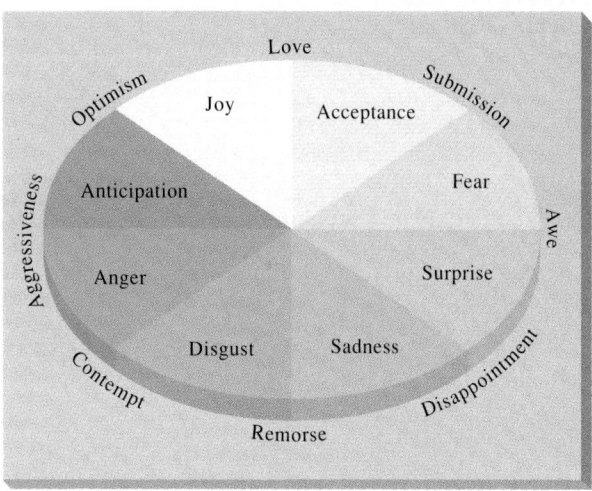

FIGURE 13.10

Plutchik's Wheel of Emotions
This diagram shows the eight primary emotions and "dyads" that result from mixtures of adjacent primaries. For example, a combination of the primary emotions of fear and surprise produces awe. Joy mixed with acceptance leads to love.

(4) they vary in intensity. Ecstasy and enthusiasm are positive emotions; grief and anger are negative emotions. For example, think about your ecstasy when you get an unexpected *A* on a test, or your enthusiasm about the football game this weekend—these are positive emotions. In contrast, think about negative emotions, such as your grief when someone close to you dies or your anger when someone verbally attacks you. Positive emotions enhance our self-esteem; negative emotions lower our self-esteem. Positive emotions improve our relationships with others; negative emotions depress the quality of those relationships.

Plutchik also believes that emotions are like colors. Every color of the spectrum can be produced by mixing the primary colors. Possibly some emotions are primary, and, if mixed together, they combine to form all other emotions. Happiness, disgust, surprise, sadness, anger, and fear are candidates for primary emotions. For example, combining sadness and surprise gives disappointment. Jealousy is composed of love and anger. Plutchik developed the emotion wheel (shown in figure 13.10) to show how primary emotions work. Mixtures of primary emotions adjacent to each other combine to produce other emotions. Some emotions are opposites—love and remorse, optimism and disappointment. Plutchik believes we cannot experience emotions that are polar opposites simultaneously. You cannot feel sad at the same time you feel happy, he says. Imagine just getting a test back in this class. As you scan the paper for the grade, your emotional response is happy or sad, not both.

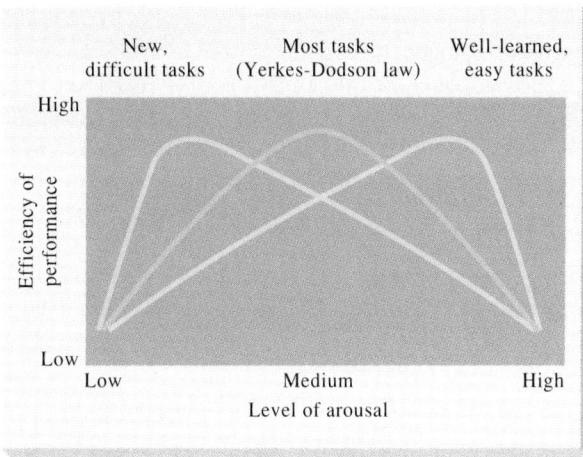

Figure 13.11

Arousal and Performance: The Yerkes-Dodson Law
The Yerkes-Dodson law states that optimal performance occurs under moderate arousal. However, for new or difficult tasks, low arousal may be best; for well-learned, easy tasks, high arousal can facilitate performance.

"My life is O.K., but it's no jeans ad."
Drawing by Cline; © 1988 The New Yorker Magazine, Inc.

Two-Dimensional Approach

The two-dimensional approach to classifying emotions argues that there are two broad dimensions of emotional experience; positive affectivity and negative affectivity. **Positive affectivity (PA)** *refers to the range of positive emotion, from high energy, enthusiasm, and excitement to being calm, quiet, and withdrawn. Joy or happiness involves positive affectivity.* **Negative affectivity (NA)** *refers to emotions that are negatively toned, such as anxiety, anger, guilt, and sadness.* PA and NA are independent dimensions, in that a person can be high along both dimensions at the same time (for example, in a high energy state and enthusiastic, yet angry).

Positive Affectivity: Happiness Our positive affectivity is influenced by how aroused we are. Early in this century, two psychologists described the role of arousal in performance. What is now known as the **Yerkes-Dodson law** *states that performance is best under conditions of moderate rather than low or high arousal.* At the low end of arousal, you might be too lethargic to perform tasks well; at the high end, you may not be able to concentrate. Think about how aroused you were the last time you took a test. If your arousal was too high, your performance probably suffered.

Moderate arousal often serves us best in tackling life's tasks, but there are times when low or high arousal produces optimal performance. For well-learned or simple tasks (signing your name, pushing a button on request), optimal arousal can be quite high. By contrast, when learning a task (such as how to play tennis) or doing something complex (such as solving an algebraic equation), much lower arousal is preferred. Figure 13.11 projects how

arousal might influence easy, moderate, and difficult tasks. As tasks become more difficult, the ability to be alert and attentive, but relaxed, is critical to optimal performance.

In addition to arousal level, an important dimension of positive affectivity is happiness. Happiness is one of the most elusive emotions we seek. Like other emotions, its intensity varies. Sometimes we are incredibly happy, at other times only a little happy. You might be overwhelmed with happiness if you get the highest grade on the next test in this class but only slightly happy if you get a B or a low A.

It was not until 1973 that *Psychological Abstracts*, the major source of psychological research summaries, included *happiness* as an index term. The recent interest in happiness focuses on positive ways we experience our lives, including cognitive judgments of our well-being. That is, psychologists want to know what makes you happy and how you perceive your happiness. Many years ago, French philosopher Jean-Jacques Rousseau described the subjective nature of happiness this way: "Happiness is a good bank account, a good cook, and a good digestion."

In a recent review of research on happiness, being a good cook and good digestion were not on the list of factors that contribute to our happiness, but these four factors were (Myers, 1992):

- Self-esteem—happy people like themselves
- Optimism—happy people are hope-filled
- Extroversion—happy people are outgoing
- Personal control—happy people believe that they choose their own destinies

Some factors that many people believe are involved in happiness, such as age and gender, actually are not.

But what about Rousseau's "good bank account"? Can we buy happiness? One study tried to find out if lottery winners are happier than people who have not received a windfall of money (Brickman, Coates, & Janoff-Bulman, 1978). Twenty-two major lottery winners were compared with twenty-two people living in the same area of the city. The general happiness of the two groups did not differ when they were asked about the past, present, and the future. The people who hadn't won a lottery actually were happier doing life's mundane things such as watching television, buying clothes, and talking with a friend.

Winning a lottery does not appear to be the key to happiness. What is important, though, is having enough money to buy life's necessities. Extremely wealthy people are not happier than people who can purchase the necessities. People in wealthy countries are not happier than people in poor countries. The message is clear: If you believe money buys happiness, think again (Diener, 1984).

Happiness is not a state to arrive at, but a manner of traveling.
Margaret Lee Runbeck

Psychologist Ed Diener (1984) agrees that intense positive emotions—such as we would feel at winning a lottery or getting a date with the person of our dreams—do not add much to a person's general sense of well-being, in part because they are rare, and in part because they can decrease the positive emotion and increase the negative emotion we feel in other circumstances. According to Diener, happiness boils down to the frequency of positive emotions and the infrequency of negative emotions. Diener's view flies in the face of common sense; you would think that frequent, intense positive emotions and minimal nonintense negative emotions produce the most happiness. But the commonsense view fails to consider that intense positive moments can diminish the sensation of future positive events. For example, you will be overwhelmed with happiness the first time you shoot par in a round of golf, but if you play golf a week later and do well but not great, the previous emotional high can diminish your positive experience. It is the rare, if nonexistent, human being who experiences intense positive emotions and infrequent negative emotions week after week after week.

Negative Affectivity: Anger
Remember that negative affectivity includes all moods or emotions that are negatively toned, such as anger, anxiety, guilt, and sadness. To illustrate the nature of negative affectivity, we will focus on one emotion—anger.

Anger is a powerful emotion. It has a strong impact not only on our social relationships, but also on the person experiencing the emotion (Lazarus, 1991). We can easily recount obvious examples of anger that often harm not only others but the angry individual as well—unrestrained and recurrent violence toward others, verbal and physical abuse of children, perpetual bitterness, the tendency to carry a "chip on the shoulder" in which a person overinterprets others' actions as demeaning, and the inability to inhibit the expression of anger.

What makes people angry? People often get angry when they feel they are not being treated fairly or when their expectations are violated. One researcher asked people to remember or keep records of their anger experiences (Averill, 1983). Most of the people said they became at least mildly angry several times a week; some said they became mildly angry several times a day. In many instances, the people said they got angry because they perceived that a friend or a loved one performed a misdeed. They especially got angry when they perceived the other person's behavior as unjustified, avoidable, and willful.

Doesn't getting angry sometimes make us feel better and possibly help us cope better with our challenging lives? Just as catharsis (releasing anger or aggressive energy by directly or vicariously engaging in anger) doesn't reduce aggression over the long term, but rather usually increases it, so it also is with anger. As psychologist Carol Tavris (1989) commented in her book *Anger: The Misunderstood Emotion*, one of the main results of the ventilation approach to anger is to raise the noise level of our society, not to reduce anger or solve our problems.

Every person gets angry at one time or another. How can we control our anger so it does not become destructive? Tavris (1989) makes the following recommendations:

1. When your anger starts to boil and your body is getting aroused, work on lowering the arousal by waiting. Emotional arousal will usually simmer down if you just wait long enough.
2. Cope with the anger in ways that involve neither being chronically angry over every little bothersome annoyance nor passively sulking, which simply rehearses your reasons for being angry.
3. Form a self-help group with others who have been through similar experiences with anger. The other people will likely know what you are feeling and together you might come up with some good solutions to anger problems.
4. Take action to help others, which can put your own miseries in perspective, as exemplified in the actions of the women who organized Mothers Against Drunk Drivers, or any number of people who work to change conditions so that others will not suffer what they did.
5. Seek ways of breaking out of your usual perspective. Some people have been rehearsing their "story" for years, repeating over and over the reasons for their anger. Retelling the story from other participants' points of view often helps individuals to find routes to empathy.

Let not the sun go down on your wrath.
Ephesians 4:26

Motivation, Emotion, Health, and Personality

The Nature of Emotion and the Range and Classification of Emotions

Emotions are feelings, or affect, that involves a mixture of physiological arousal, conscious experience, and overt behavior. A number of psychologists have classified emotions by placing them on a wheel. One such model was proposed by Plutchik, who believes that emotions are positive or negative, are primary or mixed, are bipolar opposites, and vary in intensity. The two-dimensional approach argues there are two broad dimensions of emotional experience: Positive affectivity and negative affectivity. Positive affectivity refers to the range of positive emotion from high energy, enthusiasm, and excitement to calm, quiet, and withdrawn. Joy or happiness involves positive affectivity. Negative affectivity refers to emotions that are negatively toned such as anxiety, anger, guilt, and sadness.

Our positive affectivity is influenced by how aroused we are. The Yerkes-Dodson law addressed the issue of arousal and performance, emphasizing maximum performance under moderate arousal. However, task difficulty needs to be considered when determining optimal arousal. Happiness is an important dimension of positive affectivity. Self-esteem, a good marriage or love relationship, social contacts, regular exercise, the ability to sleep well, and religious faith are all related to happiness. Positive emotions such as happiness are more likely to increase generosity, eagerness, expansiveness, and free-flowing use of one's resources than negative emotions like sadness. People are the happiest when they develop a sense of mastery over their lives.

We examined anger as a representative of negative affectivity. Anger is a powerful emotion that not only has a strong influence on social relationships, but also on the person experiencing anger. Most psychologists consider catharsis to be an ineffective way of coping with anger. Strategies for reducing anger include: waiting, not being chronically angry over every little annoyance or passively sulking, forming a self-help group with others who have been through similar experiences with anger, taking action to help others, and seeking ways of breaking out of a usual perspective.

Theories of Emotion

As you drive down a highway, the fog thickens. Suddenly you see a pile of cars in front of you. Your mind temporarily freezes, your muscles tighten, your stomach becomes queasy, and your heart feels like it is going to pound out of your chest. You immediately slam on the brakes and try to veer away from the pile of cars. Tires screech, windshield glass flies, metal smashes, then all is quiet. After a few seconds, you realize you are alive. You find that you can walk out of the car. Your fear turns to relief, as you sense your luck in not being hurt. In a couple of seconds, the relief turns to anger. You loudly ask who caused the accident. In this situation, what triggered your emotion? Was it your body? Your mind? Extensive debate characterizes whether the mind or the body is primarily responsible for our experience of emotion.

We will begin our investigation of the mind-body debate in emotion by examining the dominant theories.

The James-Lange Theory

In the automobile crash, common sense tells you that you are trembling because of your fear and anxiety. But William James (1890/1950) and Carl Lange (1922) said emotion works in the opposite way. The **James-Lange theory** *states that emotion results from physiological states triggered by stimuli in the environment.* That is, according to the James-Lange theory, you saw the pile of cars, tried to avoid it, then crashed. Subsequently, you noticed your heart was almost beating out of your body and your hands were trembling. Now your feelings of anxiety and fear follow your body's reactions. In sum, you perceive a stimulus in the environment, your body responds, and then you interpret the body's reaction as emotion. In one of James's own examples, you perceive you have lost your fortune, you cry, and then interpret the crying as feeling sad. This goes against the commonsense sequence of losing your fortune, feeling sorry, and then crying.

The Cannon-Bard Theory

Walter Cannon (1927) objected to the James-Lange theory. To understand his objection, consider the car crash once again. Seeing the pileup of cars causes the hypothalamus of your brain to do two things simultaneously: First it stimulates your autonomic nervous system to produce the physiological changes involved in emotion (increased heart rate, rapid breathing, for example); second, it sends messages to your cerebral cortex, where the experience of emotion is perceived. Philip Bard (1934) supported this theory, and so it became known as the **Cannon-Bard theory,** *the theory that emotion and physiological reactions occur simultaneously.* Figure 13.12 shows how the James-Lange and Cannon-Bard theories differ. A pivotal difference between these theories

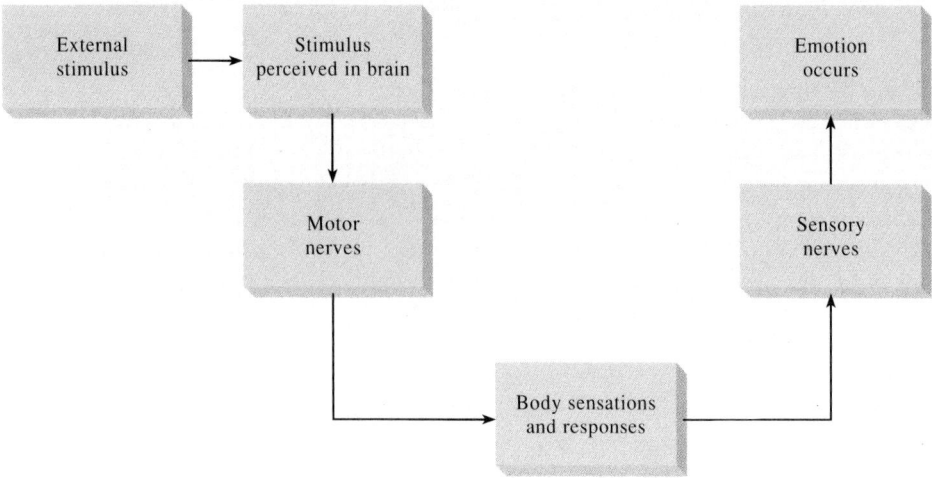

James-Lange theory

External stimulus → Stimulus perceived in brain

Stimulus perceived in brain → Motor nerves

Motor nerves → Body sensations and responses

Body sensations and responses → Sensory nerves

Sensory nerves → Emotion occurs

Emotion takes place after physiological reactions.

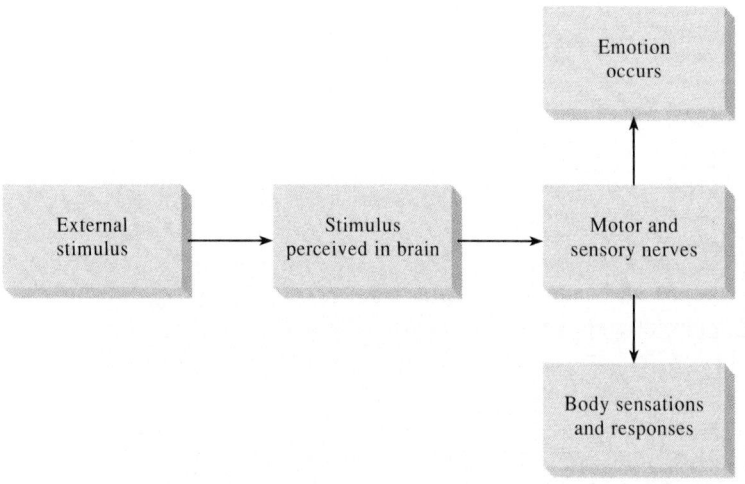

Cannon-Bard theory

External stimulus → Stimulus perceived in brain → Motor and sensory nerves → Emotion occurs

Motor and sensory nerves → Body sensations and responses

Emotions and physiological reactions occur simultaneously.

FIGURE 13.12

James-Lange and Cannon-Bard Theories of Emotion

concerns the nature of physiological changes associated with emotion. Whereas the James-Lange camp emphasized biological activity throughout the body (such as a racing heart, a tightening of the stomach, and trembling muscles), the Cannon-Bard camp focused more on what was happening in the brain. Since the original formulations of the theories, psychological and medical researchers have found evidence that the components of both theories are true.

Cognitive Theories of Emotion

Does emotion depend on the tides of the mind? Are we happy only when we think we are happy? Cognitive theories of emotion share an important point: Emotion always has a cognitive component. Thinking is said to be responsible for feelings of love and hate, joy and sadness. While giving cognitive processes the main credit for emotion, the cognitive theories also recognize the role of the brain and body in emotion (Mandler, 1984). That is, the hypothalamus and autonomic nervous system make connections with the peripheral areas of the body when emotion is experienced. According to cognitive theorists, body and thought are involved in emotion.

Schachter and Singer's View: The Cognitive Interpretation of Arousal

Stanley Schachter and Jerome Singer (1962) developed a theory of emotion that gives cognition a strong role. They agree that emotional events produce internal, physiological arousal. As we sense the arousal, we look to the external world for an explanation of why we are aroused. We interpret the external cues present and then label the emotion. For example, if you feel good after someone has made a pleasant comment to you, you might label the emotion "happy." If you feel bad after you have done something wrong, you may label the feeling "guilty." Schachter and Singer believe much of our arousal is diffuse and not tied to specific emotions. Because the arousal is not instinctive, its meaning is easily misinterpreted.

FIGURE 13.13

Capilano River Bridge Experiment: Misinterpreted Arousal Intensifies Emotional Experiences
The precarious Capilano River Bridge in British Columbia is shown at left; the experiment is shown in progress at right. An attractive woman approached men while they were crossing the 200-foot-high bridge; she asked them to make up a story to help her out. She also made the same request on a lower, much safer bridge. The men on the Capilano River Bridge told sexier stories, probably because they were aroused by the fear or excitement of being up so high on a swaying bridge. Apparently they interpreted their arousal as sexual attraction for the female interviewer.

To test their theory of emotion, Schachter and Singer (1962) injected subjects with epinephrine, a drug that produces high arousal. After volunteer subjects were given the drug, they observed someone else behave in either a euphoric way (shooting crumpled paper at a wastebasket) or an angry way (stomping out of the room). As predicted, the euphoric and angry behavior influenced the subjects' cognitive interpretation of their own arousal. When they were with a happy person, they rated themselves as happy; when they were with an angry person, they said they were angry. But this effect was found only when the subjects were not told about the true effects of the injection. When subjects were told that the drug would increase their heart rate and make them jittery, they said the reason for their own arousal was the drug, not the other person's behavior.

Psychologists have had difficulty replicating the Schachter and Singer experiment but, in general, research supports the belief that misinterpreted arousal intensifies emotional experiences (Leventhal & Tomarken, 1986). An intriguing study substantiates this belief. It went like this: An attractive woman approached men while they were crossing the Capilano River Bridge in

British Columbia. Only those without a female companion were approached. The woman asked the men to make up a brief story for a project she was doing on creativity (Dutton & Aron, 1974). By the way, the Capilano River Bridge sways precariously more than 200 feet above rapids and rocks (see figure 13.13). The female interviewer made the same request of other men crossing a much safer, lower bridge. The men on the Capilano River Bridge told more sexually oriented stories and rated the female interviewer more attractive than men on the lower, less frightening bridge did.

The Primacy Debate: Cognition or Emotion?

Richard Lazarus (1984, 1991) believes cognitive activity is a precondition for emotion. He says we cognitively appraise ourselves and our social circumstances. These appraisals, which include values, goals, commitments, beliefs, and expectations, determine our emotions. People may feel happy because they have a deep religious commitment, angry because they did not get the raise they anticipated, or fearful because they expect to fail an exam.

Robert Zajonc (1984; Murphy & Zajonc, 1993) disagrees with Lazarus. Emotions are primary, he says, and our thoughts are a result of them. Who is right? Both likely are correct. Lazarus refers mainly to a cluster of related events that occur over a period of time, whereas Zajonc describes single events or a simple preference for one stimulus over another. Lazarus speaks about love over the course of months and years, a sense of value to the community, and plans for retirement; Zajonc talks about a car accident, an encounter with a snake, and liking ice cream better than spinach. Some of our emotional reactions, such as a shriek on detecting a snake, are virtually instantaneous and probably don't involve cognitive appraisal. Other emotional circumstances, especially those that occur over a long period of time, such as a depressed mood or anger toward a friend, are more likely to involve cognitive appraisal.

Distinguishing Emotions

Is there a difference in the way our bodies respond when we are feeling angry, compared to when we are feeling nervous? In other words, are there specific physiological reactions for each emotion we experience? To answer these questions, we need to understand the basic nature of the autonomic nervous system.

The Physiology of Emotion

Is it possible to distinguish anger and fear on a physiological level? In a classic study, Albert Ax (1953) brought unsuspecting college students into his laboratory to measure their autonomic nervous system levels. After they were hooked up to physiological monitoring equipment, a surly experimenter (who worked for Ax—such a person is called a confederate of the experimenter) entered the room and began insulting the unsuspecting student. After the student became visibly angry, the experimenter "checked" on the equipment and nervously told the student that there was a potentially dangerous electrical malfunction. The student was told to sit quietly while the experimenter went for help. All of this was a cruel hoax to pull on the student, and rigorous ethical safeguards exist to prevent such excesses in contemporary research. Nonetheless, Ax learned that the emotional states of anger and fear were, in fact, different. Apparently, during anger the sympathetic nervous system prompts an increase in heart rate and blood pressure and causes a person's hands to become warm. Fear also resulted in faster heartbeats but was linked to much cooler hands and feet. In more recent studies focused on facial expressions and autonomic nervous system activity, researchers have found support for these general findings (Ekman, Levenson, and Friesen, 1983).

Although fear and anger can sometimes be distinguished using a sophisticated monitoring apparatus, most day-to-day moods cannot be distinguished by autonomic nervous system (ANS) activity (see chapter 3 for a portrayal of the autonomic nervous system). Recently researchers have begun to focus on the role of different types of brain activity as a function of mood. For example, Richard Davidson and his colleagues (1990) have found that sad moods are related to brain-wave activity in the left frontal region of the brain, while positive moods provoke right frontal region activity. Also, emotional states associated with fear and anxiety result in increased neurotransmitter activity in the temporal lobes of the cortex.

Different types of drugs that selectively alter specific neurotransmitters in the brain are effective in exaggerating or modulating many mood states. For example, certain antidepressant medications reduce the massive fear associated with some panic attacks. Other drugs, such as alcohol, also can elevate a person's mood.

In sum, emotions affect our physiological states, and vice versa. William James was partially correct in arguing that different emotions occasionally produce unique patterns of autonomic nervous system activity. He probably overestimated the effects of the specific changes, however. Walter Cannon was partially correct in noting that the brain plays a pivotal role in dictating emotional experiences. However, Cannon failed to appreciate that different emotions can trigger completely different brain regions, which, by themselves, might or might not influence autonomic nervous system activity.

The Polygraph and Lie Detection

You have been asked to think about your emotional states in the face of an automobile crash. Now put yourself in the situation of lying to someone. Because body changes predictably accompany emotional states, scientists reasoned that a machine might be able to determine if a person is lying. The **polygraph** *is a machine that is used to try to determine if someone is lying by monitoring changes in the body— heart rate, breathing, and electrodermal response (an index that detects skin resistance to passage of a weak electric current)—thought to be influenced by emotional states.* In a typical polygraph test, an individual is asked a number of neutral questions and several key, not so neutral, questions. If the individual's heart rate, breathing, and electrodermal response increase substantially when the key questions are asked, the individual is assumed to be lying. (Figure 13.14 shows a polygraph testing situation.)

The polygraph has been widely used, especially in business, to screen new employees for honesty and to reveal employee theft. Following President Reagan's directive in 1983, the government increased its use of the polygraph to discover which individuals were leaking information to the media. Congressional hearings followed, and psychologists were called to testify about the polygraph's effectiveness (Saxe, Dougherty, & Cross, 1985). Testimony focused on countermeasures to avoid detection. Drugs, such as tranquilizers that have a calming effect on the individual, are difficult to detect unless a test is conducted to reveal their use. Sometimes, though, the mere presence of the polygraph and the subject's belief that it is accurate at detecting deception triggers confession. Police might use the polygraph in this way to get a criminal to confess. In such cases, the polygraph has served a positive purpose, but in too many instances it has been misused and misrepresented. Experts argue that the polygraph errs about one-third of the time, especially because it cannot distinguish between such feelings as anxiety and guilt (Lykken, 1985). The testimony of psychologists that lie detectors are not always accurate led to the Employee Polygraph Protection Act of 1988, which restricts most nongovernment polygraph testing.

> *A lie can travel half way around the world while the truth is putting on its shoes.*
>
> **Mark Twain**

Paul Ekman and Wallace Frieson (1974) argued that people often attend more to what they are saying than to what they are doing with their bodies. They believe nonverbal leakage permeates our communication. **Nonverbal leakage** *involves the communication of true emotions through nonverbal channels even when the person verbally tries to conceal the truth.* For example, a student may say that he is not nervous about an upcoming test but as he speaks his voice becomes high pitched and has occasional cracks, he blinks more than usual, and he bites his lower lip.

How accurately can people tell if someone is being deceptive in their communication? Not very, unless they are trained to detect deceiving expressions (Costanzo, 1992; DePaulo, 1994). In one study, Paul Ekman and Maureen O'Sullivan (1991) videotaped college students as they watched either an enjoyable film about nature or an emotion-laden gory film. Regardless of which film they saw, the students were asked to describe the film as pleasant and enjoyable. The researchers were able to correctly detect in more than 4 of 5 cases which students were lying and which were telling the truth by focusing on such cues as a raised voice. Could you or I do as well as the trained researchers? Probably not. Ekman and Sullivan asked college students, psychiatrists, court judges, police officers, and polygraph experts if they could detect which students were lying and which were telling the truth. Each of these groups scored at about chance (50 percent). One additional group—secret service agents—did perform above chance, detecting the lies about two-thirds of the time.

How might you become better at detecting the nonverbal cues that determine whether someone is trying to

FIGURE 13.14

The Polygraph
The polygraph tries to tell whether someone is lying by monitoring changes in the body believed to be influenced by emotional states. Controversy has swirled about the polygraph's use. Because of the polygraph's inaccuracy, Congress passed the Employee Polygraph Protection Act of 1988, virtually prohibiting the use of the polygraph in nongovernment settings.

how a standard lie detector situation does not exist. Inferring truth or deception based on physiological assessment of emotions requires a number of strategies. The complexity of the lie detector situation was brought out in testimony. Although the degree of arousal in response to a series of questions is measured through simple physiological changes, no unique physiological response to deception has been revealed (Lykken, 1987). Heart rate and breathing can increase for reasons other than lying, making interpretation of the physiological indicators of arousal complex.

Accurately identifying truth or deception rests on the skill of the examiner and the skill of the individual being examined. Individuals intent on lying can take

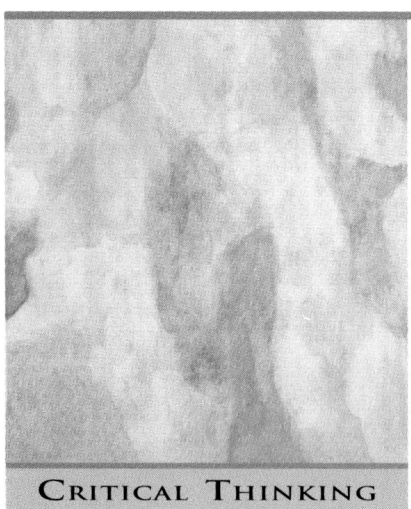

Suppose you find yourself in the suspicious situation of confronting a lie detector test. Even though such tests have been ruled virtually illegal in most contexts, occasionally they are still used by employers or officials who haven't learned of the polygraph's limitations. What kinds of countermeasures do you think you could employ to make the readings unreliable?

There are simple things people can do to confuse the polygraph results. You will recall that the polygraph records general arousal and changes in arousal levels. Countermeasures during questioning that influence polygraph reliability include subtle body movements (tensing your muscles, biting your tongue, squeezing your toes, shifting your position in the chair), relaxation or biofeedback techniques, thinking arousing thoughts while answering bland questions, and even taking calming drugs. Were you able to think up any of these or other countermeasures? Recognizing the relationships between arousal and inaccurate polygraph readings demonstrates your ability to *make accurate observations, descriptions, and inferences about behavior*. The ease with which interpretation can be confused supports the growing skepticism about the use of the polygraph.

deceive you? One possibility is to become more knowledgeable about the kinds of behaviors that really do distinguish truths from lies. Researchers have found that compared to people telling the truth, liars (DePaulo, 1994):

- Blink more and have more dilated pupils
- Show more self-manipulating gestures, such as rubbing and scratching
- Give shorter responses that are more negative, more irrelevant, and more generalized
- Speak in a more distancing way, as if they do not want to commit themselves to what they are saying
- Speak in a higher pitch
- Take more time to plan what they are about to say but the resulting statements tend to be more internally discrepant and more marred by hestitations, repetitions, grammatical errors, and slips of the tongue

Sociocultural Influences on Emotion

The complete experience of emotion depends not only on the body's responses and the mind's perceptions but also on the nature of social relationships and society's customs (Roseman & others, 1995). How do social factors influence our emotional experiences? How does culture affect emotions? How is gender related to emotion?

Social Factors

Emotions often involve someone else: your enthusiasm for going to the beach or skiing with *friends,* your love for the *person* of your dreams, your surprise when your *parents* tell you that your younger *brother* is coming to your college next year, your fear of giving a speech in front of your *classmates* and *professor,* and your sadness when you discover that your *roommate* lost her job (Bronstein & Paludi, 1988; Magai & McFadden, 1995).

The Universality of Emotional Expressions

In *The Expression of the Emotions in Man and Animals,* Charles Darwin (1872/1965) argued that the facial expressions of human beings are innate, are the same in all cultures around the world, and evolved from the emotions of animals. Darwin compared the similarity of human snarls of anger with the growls of dogs and the hisses of cats. He compared the giggling of chimpanzees, when they are tickled under their arms, with human laughter.

Today psychologists still believe that emotions, especially facial expressions of emotion, have strong biological ties (Sherer & Wallbott, 1994). For example, children who are blind from birth and have never observed the smile or frown on another person's face, still smile or frown in the same way that children with normal vision do.

The universality of facial expressions and the ability of people from different cultures to label accurately the emotion that lies behind a facial expression has been extensively researched (Matsumoto, 1989). Psychologist Paul Ekman's (1980, 1985, 1993) careful observations revealed that our many faces of emotion do not vary significantly from one culture to another. For example, Ekman and his colleague photographed people expressing such emotions as happiness, fear, surprise, disgust, and grief. When they showed the photographs to people from the United States,

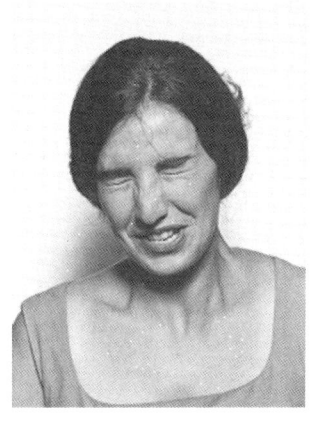   

FIGURE 13.15

Emotional Expressions in the United States and New Guinea
At left is a woman from the United States and, on the right, two men from the Fore tribe in New Guinea. Notice the similarity in the expression of disgust and happiness. Psychologists believe that the facial expression of emotion is virtually the same in all cultures.

Chile, Japan, Brazil, and Borneo (an Indonesian island in the western Pacific Ocean), each person tended to label the faces with the same emotions (Ekman & Friesen, 1968). Another study focused on the way the Fore tribe, an isolated, Stone Age culture in New Guinea, matched descriptions of emotions with facial expressions (Ekman & Friesen, 1971). Before Ekman's visit, most of the Fore had never seen a Caucasian face. Ekman showed them photographs of American faces expressing such emotions as fear, happiness, anger, and surprise. Then he read stories about people in emotional situations. The Fore were able to match the descriptions of emotions to the facial expressions in the photographs. The similarity of facial expressions of emotions between people in New Guinea and people in the United States is shown in figure 13.15.

Variations in Emotional Expression

Whereas facial expressions of basic emotions appear to be universal across cultures, display rules for emotion are not culturally universal. **Display rules** *are sociocultural standards that determine when, where, and how emotions should be expressed.* For example, although happiness is a

Our emotional reactions are influenced by the culture in which we live. The Utku Eskimos, for example, discourage anger by cultivating acceptance and by dissociating themselves from any expression of anger.

In the Middle Eastern country of Yemen, male-male mouth-to-mouth kissing is commonplace. In Western European countries, cheek-to-cheek kissing is a commonplace practice for males, but in the United States it is very uncommon.

unexpected snowstorm, the Utku do not become frustrated but accept the presence of the snowstorm and build an igloo. Most of us would not act as mildly in the face of subzero weather and barriers to our travel.

Many nonverbal signals of emotion, though, vary from one culture to another. For example, male-to-male kissing is commonplace in some cultures, such as Yemen (in the Middle East), but uncommon in other cultures, such as the United States. The "thumb up" sign, which means either everything is "OK" or the desire to hitch a ride in most cultures, is an insult in Greece, similar to a raised third finger in the United States (Morris & others, 1979). More information about cultural determinants of emotion appears in Sociocultural Worlds 13.1, where we will discuss the nature of emotional experiences in Japan, Europe, and the United States.

universally expressed emotion, when, where, and how it is displayed may vary from one culture to another. The same is true for other emotions, such as fear, sadness, and anger. For example, members of the Utku culture in Alaska discourage anger by cultivating acceptance and by dissociating themselves from any display of anger (Briggs, 1970). If a trip is hampered by an

Think for a moment about how display rules for emotion influence your own behavior. Can you think of a time when you felt an emotion strongly but did not show this to others who were around you at the time? Why did you not show the emotion? How did you hide your emotion?

REVIEW

Theories of Emotion

In the James-Lange theory, we initially perceive a stimulus, our body responds, and then we experience the emotion. In the Cannon-Bard theory, emotion and physiological reactions occur simultaneously. Whereas the James-Lange theory emphasizes biological activity throughout the body, the Cannon-Bard theory focuses more on what is happening in the brain.

Cognitive theories argue that emotion always has a cognitive component and that, in most instances, cognition directs emotion. In Schachter and Singer's view, people cognitively interpret their arousal. Emotional events produce emotional arousal. Arousal is often diffuse, so we look to the external world to interpret

it. We label the emotion based on environmental cues. Lazarus believes that cognition always directs emotion; Zajonc says emotion is dominant. Both are probably right.

Can emotions be distinguished on the basis of their physiological nature? Emotions affect our physiological states, and vice versa. James was partially correct in arguing that different emotions occasionally produce unique patterns of autonomic nervous system (ANS) activity. He probably overestimated the effects of specific changes. Cannon was partially correct in noting that the brain plays a pivotal role in dictating emotional experiences. However, Cannon failed to appreciate that different emotions can trigger different brain regions,

which in themselves might not influence ANS activity. Polygraphs are based on the principle of arousal in emotion. The polygraph situation is complex, and psychologists are skeptical about its validity. One of the polygraph's most beneficial functions is to induce confession. Nonverbal leakage can occur when we communicate with others.

Emotions often involve social contexts and relationships. Most psychologists believe that facial expressions of basic emotions are universal across all cultures. However, display rules for emotion often vary from one culture to another. Display rules include rules for nonverbal signals in body movements, posture, and gesture.

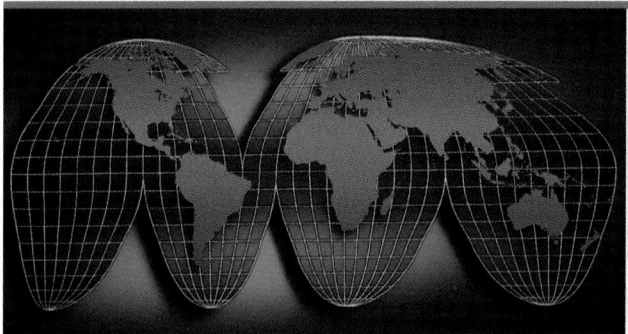

SOCIOCULTURAL WORLDS 13.1

Culture and Emotion: Comparison of Japan, Europe, and the United States

One cross-cultural study examined the cultural differences in *when* people express emotions and *how* they do it. The researchers found that university students in Europe and the United States tend to express emotions similarly, but differently from Japanese students (Scherer & others, 1988). The researchers asked the students questions about situations or events that led them to feel joy/happiness, sadness/grief, fear/anxiety, or anger/rage. The Japanese students showed fewer physical signs of joy, gave fewer sad responses to separation and death, were fearful of but quicker to get angry at strangers, and were less likely to get angry in the face of injustice than their American and European counterparts. These differences in the expression of emotion probably are the result of cultural differences in values, customs, and the way people interact.

The researchers also found that the way these students, especially the Japanese and American students, expressed their emotions differed. The Americans reported a high intensity of emotional expressiveness and a frequent use of nonverbal expressions to show emotion—that is, the Americans were more likely to literally jump for joy, whereas the Japanese were much more circumspect. One reason for these differences may be that the Japanese culture values physical restraint—which may be interpreted as stoicism—as an essential part of everyday decorum. In the study, the American and Japanese students attempted to control their emotions more than their European counterparts did.

Some cross-cultural psychologists caution about the difficulty of interpreting nonverbal behaviors across cultures. For example, the Japanese may have very subtle nonverbal behaviors that they learn to interpret within their own culture—such as a slight blankness of the face to indicate disinterest, pauses between sentences, and subtle movements of the eyes. When asked to describe these nonverbal behaviors, they may not have these in mind but, rather, report about the larger, less subtle body movements they see among Americans (either face-to-face or on American television shows they watch).

Also, despite the differences revealed in the cross-cultural study involving Americans, Japanese, and Europeans, the researchers also found the following similarities in emotion across the cultures:

- People tend to recall situations that elicit anger and joy more readily than ones that elicited sadness and fear.
- There were clear differences in the average duration of different emotions: fear < anger < joy < sadness.
- People try to control the three negative emotions (fear, anger, and sadness) more than joy.

Motivation and Emotion 479

Unless you've been isolated on a mountaintop, away from people, television, magazines, and newspapers, you probably know the dominant stereotype about gender and emotion: She is emotional, he is not. This stereotype is a powerful and pervasive image in our culture (Shields, 1991a). Critical thinkers are able to transcend common beliefs and stereotypes by *evaluating the validity of conclusions about behavior* to determine if there is objective support for this way of thinking.

Is this emotional stereotype supported when researchers study female and male experiences? Researchers have found that females and males are often more alike in the way they experience emotion than the dominant stereotype would lead us to believe. Females and males often use the same facial expressions, adopt the same language, and describe their emotional experiences similarly when they keep diaries about their life experiences. Thus, the stereotype—that females are emotional and males are not—is simply that—a stereotype. Given the complexity and vast territory of emotion, we should not be surprised that this stereotype is not supported when actual emotional experiences are examined. Both sexes are equally likely to experience love, jealousy, anxiety in new social situations, anger when insulted, grief when close relationships end, and embarrassment when they make mistakes in public (Tavris & Wade, 1984).

Gender does matter in understanding emotion when we consider specific emotional experiences, the contexts in which emotion is displayed, and certain beliefs about emotion (Shields, 1991a, 1991b). Consider anger. Men are more likely to show anger toward strangers, especially other men, when they feel they have been challenged, and men are more likely than women to turn their anger into aggressive action (Tavris, 1989). Can you think of other specific emotions that might demonstrate gender differences?

Female-male differences in emotion are more likely to occur in contexts that highlight social roles and relationships. For example, females are more likely than males to give accounts of emotion that include interpersonal relationships (Saarni, 1988). And females are more likely than males to express fear and sadness, especially when communicating with their friends and family.

Beliefs about emotion play an important role in understanding how gender and emotion work in our culture. We often use beliefs about emotion to define the difference between what is masculine and feminine, male and female (Shields, 1991a). For example, in one study, men were more likely than women to agree with the belief that men should conceal their feelings, but when reporting their own behavior, women more than men reported greater inhibition of emotional expression. Sex differences in self-reports tend to be consistent with emotion stereotypes, as if individuals compare themselves to a cultural standard when generating a response—"I must be emotional. After all, I'm a woman" or "I must not show my emotions. After all, I'm a man" (Shields, 1991b).

Before we leave this topic, it is important to consider why we are so prone to stereotyping females as emotional and males as not. What could be the advantages (and disadvantages) of being expected to behave more emotionally? What could be the advantages (and disadvantages) of being expected to behave with more controlled emotions? Is it a relatively harmless stereotype or one that contributes to serious strain in communications? Knowing that this stereotype is generally untrue, what can you do to avoid this and other kinds of inaccurate stereotyping?

What is the nature of female-male differences in emotion?

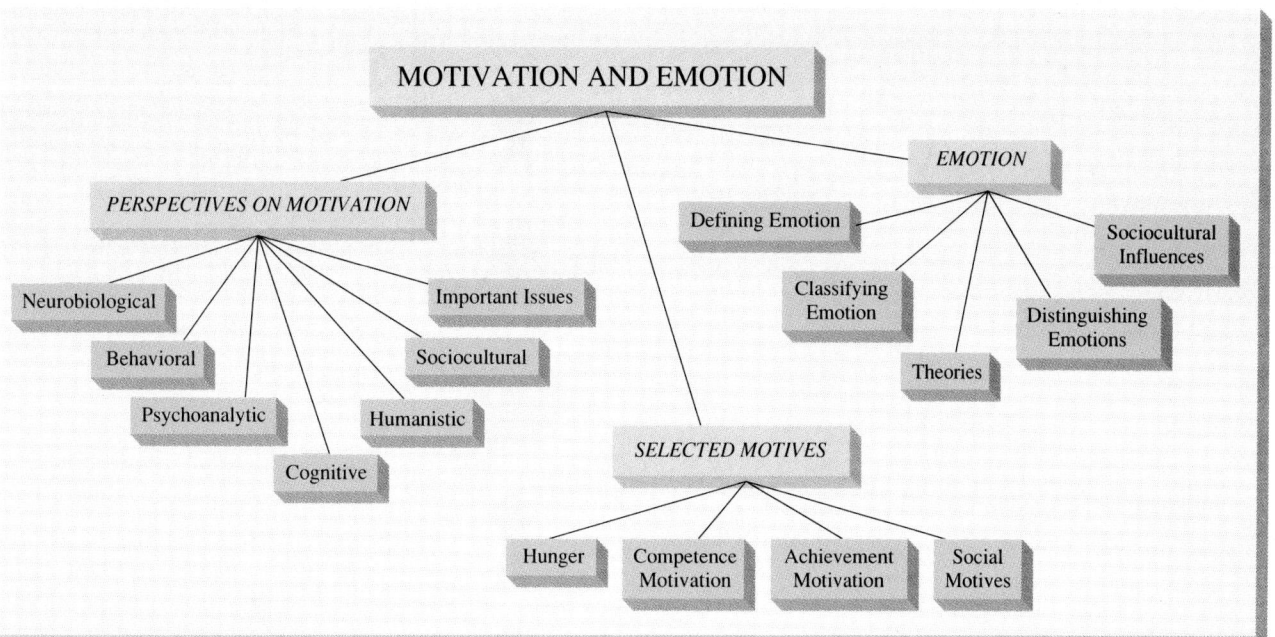

We began our coverage of motivation and emotion by discussing these perspectives on motivation: the neurobiological, behavioral, psychoanalytic, cognitive, humanistic, and sociocultural. We also described some important issues in motivation. Next, we studied the following selected motives: hunger, competence motivation, achievement motivation, and social motives. In the final section of the chapter we evaluated the nature of emotion by defining emotion, classifying emotion, studying theories of emotion, distinguishing emotions, and reading about sociocultural influences on emotion.

Don't forget that you can obtain an overall summary of the chapter by again reading the in-chapter reviews on pages 456, 467, 471, and 478.

Understanding motivation and emotion is complex, and so no single theoretical perspective can be adequate. Each of the main psychological perspectives was represented in this chapter. The neurobiological perspective was emphasized in the discussion of perspectives on motivation (pp. 451–452), hunger (pp. 457–459), defining emotion (p. 468), the physiology of emotion (p. 474), and the polygraph and lie detector (pp. 474–476). The behavioral perspective was discussed in perspectives on motivation (p. 452), and defining emotion (p. 468). The psychoanalytic perspective was stressed in perspectives on motivation (p. 452)

and issues in motivation (p. 456). The cognitive perspective was emphasized in perspectives on motivation (pp. 452–453), achievement motivation (pp. 460–465), defining emotion (p. 468), and cognitive theories of emotion (pp. 472–474). The humanistic perspective was presented in perspectives on motivation (pp. 453–455). The sociocultural perspective was stressed in perspectives on motivation (pp. 455–456), cultural, gender, ethnic, and social class variations in achievement (p. 464), and sociocultural influences on emotion (pp. 476–478).

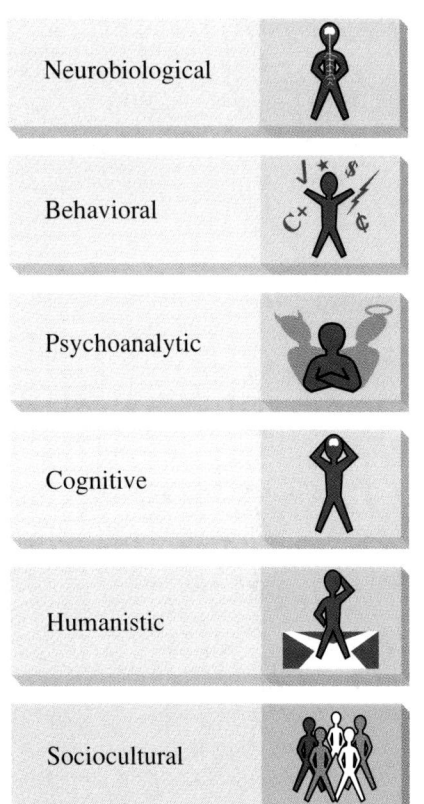

Neurobiological

Behavioral

Psychoanalytic

Cognitive

Humanistic

Sociocultural

KEY TERMS

motivation Why people behave, think, and feel the way they do. Motivated behavior is energized and directed. 451

instinct An innate, biological determinant of behavior. 451

drive An aroused state that occurs because of a physiological need. 451

need A deprivation that energizes the drive to eliminate or reduce the deprivation. 451

drive reduction theory The theory that a physiological need creates an aroused state (drive) that motivates the organism to satisfy the need. 451

homeostasis The body's tendency to maintain an equilibrium or steady state. 451

ethology The study of the biological basis of behavior in natural habitats. 452

incentives Positive or negative stimuli or events that motivate a person's behavior. 452

current concern A state the person occupies between becoming committed to pursuing a goal and either attaining it or abandoning it. 453

personal projects Sequences of personally relevant actions, similar to current concerns, but focusing on behavioral enactment more than on thought. 453

hierarchy of motives Maslow's concept that all individuals have five main needs that must be satisfied, in the following sequence: physiological, safety, love and belongingness, self-esteem, and self-actualization. 453

self-actualization The highest and most elusive of Maslow's needs; the motivation to develop to one's full potential as a human being. 453

ventromedial hypothalamus (VMH) A region of the hypothalamus that plays an important role in controlling hunger. 458

set point The weight maintained when no effort is made to gain or lose weight. 458

competence motivation The motivation to deal effectively with the environment, to be adept at what we attempt, and to make the world a better place. 459

achievement motivation (need for achievement) The desire to accomplish something, to reach a standard of excellence, and to expend effort to excel. 460

attribution theory The theory that individuals are motivated to discover the underlying causes of behavior as part of their effort to make sense out of the behavior. 461

intrinsic motivation The internal desire to be competent and to do something for its own sake. 461

extrinsic motivation The influence of external rewards and punishments. 461

helpless orientation The orientation of individuals who seem trapped by the experience of difficulty. They attribute their difficulty to a lack of ability. 462

mastery orientation The orientation of individuals who are task oriented. Instead of focusing on their ability and winning at all costs, they are concerned about learning strategies and the process of achievement rather than outcomes. 462

performance orientation Involves being concerned with the outcome in achievement, whereas a mastery orientation focuses on the process of achievement. In the performance orientation, winning is what matters and happiness is thought to result from winning. 462

self-efficacy Belief in mastery over a situation and the ability to produce positive outcomes. 462

self-esteem Involves the evaluative and affective dimensions of self-concept; self-esteem is also referred to as self-worth or self-image. 463

social motives The needs and desires of people that are learned through experience with the social world. Such motives are not derived from basic biological factors, the way hunger, thirst, sleep, and to some degree sexuality are. People who are high in a particular social motive will keep trying to reach goal states related to that motive. 465

need for affiliation The social motive to be with other people, which involves establishing, maintaining, and restoring warm, close, personal relationships. 466

need for power The motivation to be in control, to have prestige and status, and to get others to conform to our wishes. 466

emotion Feeling, or affect, that involves a mixture of arousal (fast heartbeat, for example), conscious experience (thinking about being in love with someone, for example), and overt behavior (smiling or grimacing, for example). 468

positive affectivity (PA) The range of positive emotion, from high energy, enthusiasm, and excitement to being calm, quiet, and withdrawn. Joy and happiness involve positive affectivity. 469

negative affectivity (NA) Emotions that are negatively toned, such as anxiety, anger, guilt, and sadness. 469

Yerkes-Dodson law The generalization that performance is best under conditions of moderate, rather than low or high, arousal. 469

James-Lange theory The theory that emotion results from physiological states triggered by stimuli in the environment. 471

Cannon-Bard theory The theory that emotion and physiological states occur simultaneously. 471

polygraph A machine that is used to try to determine if someone is lying, by monitoring changes in the body—heart rate, breathing, and electrodermal response (an index that detects skin resistance to passage of a weak electric current)—thought to be influenced by emotional states. 474

nonverbal leakage Involves the communication of true emotions through nonverbal channels even when the person tries to verbally conceal the truth. 475

display rules Sociocultural standards that determine when, where, and how emotions should be expressed. 477

PRACTICAL KNOWLEDGE ABOUT PSYCHOLOGY

FLOW

(1990) by Mihaly Csikszentmihalyi. New York: Harper & Row.

Flow is about the optimal experiencing of life. Csikszentmihalyi (pronounced "chik-*sent*-me-high-yee") has been investigating the concept of flow for more than two decades. In the author's view, flow is a deep happiness people feel when they have a sense of mastering something. Flow is a state of concentration in which a person becomes absorbed while engaging in an activity. We can develop flow by setting challenges for ourselves, by stretching ourselves to the limits to achieve something worthwhile, by developing competent coping skills, and by combining life's many experiences into a meaningful pattern. Flow is the antidote of the twin evils of boredom and anxiety, says Csikszentmihalyi.

The famous humanistic psychologist Abraham Maslow described a similar sense of euphoria. What especially distinguishes Csikszentmihalyi's concept of flow from Maslow's peak experiences is the frequency of flow experiences. Maslow thought people were fortunate if they caught a peak experience several times in their entire life. By contrast, Csikszentmihalyi says that if you cultivate flow experiences you can have them several times a day. One of *Flow*'s most important messages is its reminder that the path to happiness does not lie in mindless hedonism but rather in mindful challenge.

THE PURSUIT OF HAPPINESS

(1992) by David Myers. New York: William Morrow.

The Pursuit of Happiness describes who is happy and why. After conducting an extensive review of the research on happiness, Myers concluded that happy people have four main characteristics: self-esteem, optimism, extroversion, and personal control. He also elaborates on what won't get you happiness, concluding that money can't buy happiness, age is not related to happiness, and men are not happier than women. The book is filled with other valuable information about happiness, including what makes a happy marriage, the value of spirituality, the importance of attitude, love, friendships, meaningful work, and more.

ANGER: THE MISUNDERSTOOD EMOTION

(1989) by Carol Tavris. New York: Touchstone Books.

While Lerner's *The Dance of Anger* (following) was written primarily for women, *Anger: The Misunderstood Emotion* covers a wider terrain of anger. Indeed, it is hard to think of any facet of anger—from wrecked friendships to wars—that Tavris does not tackle. In addition to extensive coverage of anger between marital partners, she addresses highway anger, violence in sports, and young women's anger. Tavris debunks myths about anger, attacks the catharsis, ventilationist approach to anger, describes the toll of anger on the body, and tells readers how to rethink anger and make more-adaptive choices. Anyone wanting to cope more effectively with the anger in their lives will find this book a welcome tonic.

THE DANCE OF ANGER

(1985) by Harriet Lerner. New York: Harper Perennial.

The Dance of Anger was written mainly for women about the anger in their lives, both theirs and the people they live with, especially men. Lerner believes that women have more difficulty coping with anger than men do. She says that expressions of anger are not only encouraged more in boys and men, but may be glorified to maladaptive extremes. In contrast, girls and women have been denied even the healthy and realistic expression of anger. Lerner argues that to express anger—especially openly, directly, or loudly—makes a woman unladylike, unfeminine, unmaternal, and sexually unattractive. Society has taught women to be passive and quiet, not angry. Many women fear that if they express anger they will rock the relationship boat. Lerner explains not only the difficulties women have in getting angry, but how to use their anger to gain a stronger, more independent sense of self. Insights into numerous patterns of anger in intimate relationships are woven throughout *The Dance of Anger*.

Rooted in both family systems and psychoanalytic theory, *The Dance of Anger* discusses styles of managing anger that don't work for women in the long run—silent submission, ineffective fighting and blaming, and emotional distancing. She also paints the cultural context of an American society that has created these ineffective styles in women, and she motivates women to develop the courage to change these old, protective ways.

Advocates For Women

414 Mason St.

San Francisco, CA 94102

415–391–4870

An economic development center devoted to improving the economic status of women. They publish a semi-annual newsletter.

Job Corps

Employment Training Administration

200 Constitution Avenue, NW

Washington, DC 20210

202–535–0550

This national, federally funded training program provides education, vocational training, and work experience for disadvantaged youth 16 to 21 years of age.

***The Psychology of Eating and Drinking* (1991, 2nd ed.)**

by A. W. Logue

New York: W. H. Freeman

This book is an authoritative review of the determinants of food preferences, hunger and thirst, and the major eating and drinking disorders.

***Telling Lies: Clues to Deceit in the Marketplace, Politics, and Marriage* (1985)**

by Paul Ekman

New York: W. W. Norton

Ekman describes how to read facial expressions and gestures to determine whether people are lying.

United States Women of Today

Rte. 2, Box 152

Walnut Grove, MN 56180

507–629–3532

A community-service organization that promotes the personal development of members through such programs as Focus On Women, Success Through Enthusiastic Participation. Publishes a monthly newletter.

14

Health, Stress, and Coping

> *Look to your health and if you have it
> value it next to a good conscience. . . .
> Health is a blessing we mortals
> can achieve.*
>
> **Izaak Walton**

M ort, age 52, has worked as an air traffic controller for the past 15 years. An excitable person, he compares the job to being in a cage. During peak air traffic, the tension is almost unbearable. In these frenzied moments, Mort's emotions are a mixture of rage, fear, and anxiety. Unfortunately, the tension also spills over into his family life. In his own words, "When I go home, my nerves are hopping. I take it out on the nearest person." Two years ago, Mort's wife, Sally, told him that if he could not calm his emotions and handle stress more effectively, she would leave him. She suggested that he change to a less upsetting job, but he ignored her advice. His intense emotional behavior continued, and she left him. Last Sunday evening the roof fell in on Mort—the computer that monitors air traffic temporarily went down, and Mort had a heart attack. Quadruple bypass surgery saved his life.

Yesterday his doctor talked with him about the stress in his life and what could be done to reduce it. Mort rarely gets enough sleep, weighs too much but frequently skips meals, never exercises, smokes two packs of cigarettes a day, and drinks two or three scotches every evening (more on weekends). He professes no religious interests. He rarely dates since his divorce and has no relatives within 50 miles. He has only one friend and does not feel very close to him. Mort says that he never has enough time to do the things he wants to do and rarely has quiet

time to himself during the day. He has fun only about once every 2 weeks.

The doctor gave Mort a test, shown in table 14.1, to reveal his vulnerability to stress. Mort's score of 68 on the stress test indicates that he is seriously vulnerable to stress and close to the extremely vulnerable range. Stress is inevitable in our lives, so it is important to understand what factors are involved in managing stress and in maintaining a healthy lifestyle. How do *you* fare on the stress test?

Stress is inevitable in our lives, so it is important to understand it and cope with it effectively.

TABLE 14.1

Stress Test

Rate yourself on each item, using this scale:

      1 = almost always
      2 = often
      3 = sometimes
      4 = seldom
      5 = never

1. I eat at least one hot, balanced meal a day.
2. I get 7 to 8 hours of sleep at least four nights a week.
3. I give and receive affection regularly.
4. I have at least one relative within 50 miles whom I can rely on.
5. I exercise to the point of perspiration at least twice a week.
6. I smoke less than half a pack of cigarettes a day.
7. I take fewer than five alcoholic drinks a week.
8. I am the appropriate weight for my height.
9. I have an income adequate to meet my basic expenses.
10. I get strength from my religious beliefs.
11. I regularly attend church.
12. I have a network of friends and acquaintances.
13. I have one or more friends to confide in about personal matters.
14. I am in good health (including eyesight, hearing, teeth).
15. I am able to speak openly about my feelings when angry or worried.
16. I have regular conversations with the people I live with about domestic problems (e.g., chores, money, and daily living issues).
17. I do something for fun at least once a week.
18. I am able to organize my time effectively.
19. I drink fewer than three cups of coffee (or tea or cola drinks) a day.
20. I take quiet time for myself during the day.

Total:

"Vulnerability Scale" from the Stress Audit, developed by Lyle H. Miller and Alma Dell Smith. Copyright 1987, Biobehavioral Associates, Brookline, MA, reprinted with permission.

To get your total score, add up the figures and subtract 20. Any number over 30 indicates a vulnerability to stress. You are seriously vulnerable if your score is between 50 and 75 and extremely vulnerable if it is over 75.

There are too many Morts in the world who haven't figured out how to live a healthy lifestyle. This chapter is about the role psychology plays in understanding health, stress, and coping. We will examine how people like Mort can cope more effectively with stress and live healthier lives. You will learn about both effective and ineffective coping strategies. Before we tackle health, stress, and coping, we will examine the historical and contemporary approaches to understanding health concerns.

RELATING HEALTH AND PSYCHOLOGY

The link between health and psychological factors is easy to make. You may have noticed in your own life that when you are feeling healthy, life is great. When you are "under the weather" from illness or "under the gun" from stress, other aspects of your life—the quality of your work, the smoothness of your relationships, your ability to study—are all likely to suffer. This connection was first observed many centuries ago.

The body never lies.

Martha Graham

Historical Background

Good health requires good habits. This was recognized as early as 2600 B.C. by Asian physicians and around 500 B.C. by Greek physicians. Unlike other early cultures, these cultures did not blame the gods for illness. Nor did they think that magic would cure illness. Instead, they realized that people have some control over their health. In these two cultures, the physician's role was to guide and assist the patient in restoring a natural and emotional balance in life.

Despite the wisdom of this integrated viewpoint, this belief did not persist during much of the history that followed. Later ideas about health and illness were based more on superstition and folklore, and old treatment methods seem primitive and foolish by today's standards. For example, it used to be common to apply leeches for a variety of illnesses—a treatment that might have hastened many a sick person's demise.

As we approach the twenty-first century, once again we recognize the power of lifestyles and psychological states in promoting health. We are returning to the ancient view that the ultimate responsibility for influencing health rests with the individuals themselves. Without negating the importance of our genetic predispositions and the power of viruses and bacteria, we have come to believe that our daily behavioral choices and our general attitude about life play a significant role in the quality of our health. In addition, we affirm this belief using extensive research strategies in a variety of contexts. Psychologists and other health-related scientists generate evidence to support many of the relationships that the ancient Asians and early Greeks originally suspected.

Contemporary Approaches

Several specialized fields have emerged, primarily in the disciplines of psychology and biology, to explore how health and psychology relate. We will examine each specialty area in turn.

Health psychology *is a multidimensional approach to health that emphasizes psychological factors, lifestyle, and the nature of the health-care delivery system.* To underscore the increasing interest in health, the American Psychological Association created a new division, Health Psychology, in 1978. **Behavioral medicine,** *a field closely related to health psychology, attempts to combine medical and behavioral knowledge to reduce illness and promote health.* The interests of health psychologists and behavioral medicine researchers are broad: They include examining decisions about adherence to medical recommendations, evaluating the effectiveness of media campaigns in reducing smoking, identifying the psychological factors that affect weight loss, and exploring the role of exercise in reducing stress.

Psychoneuroimmunology *is the field that explores connections among psychological factors (such as attitudes and emotions), the nervous system, and the immune system.* The immune system keeps us healthy by recognizing and destroying foreign materials such as bacteria, viruses, and tumors. The machinery of the immune system consists of billions of white blood cells located in the lymph system. Stress levels appear to influence the efficiency of the white blood cells in keeping the system clean of foreign viruses or bacteria.

Researchers are beginning to uncover connections between psychological factors and the immune system (Anderson, Kiecolt, & Glaser, 1994). For example, Sandra Levy (1985) explored the immune system's activity when cancer spread to the lymph nodes of women treated for breast cancer. Levy found that women who became angry

The pursuit of healthy habits varies greatly across and within different cultures. (*a*) Members of the Masai tribe in Kenya, Africa, can stay on a treadmill for a long time because of their very active life. Heart disease is extremely low in the Masai tribe, which also can be attributed to the energetic lifestyle of the members of the tribe. In contrast, (*b*) Americans show a greater incidence of heart disease. Unfortunately, many Americans are inactive. However, many Americans are increasingly recognizing the health benefits of exercise and an active lifestyle and are working hard to make these habitual. The role of exercise in health is one of health psychology's many interests.

and agitated about their disease had stronger immune systems than women who passively accepted the disease and adjusted to their condition. Levy believes that accepting the disease reflects a feeling of helplessness; in contrast, anger indicates that patients believe they can fight the disease. Beliefs about control, she says, might affect the immune system. Psychologists increasingly believe that directly confronting problems, seeking solutions, getting answers, sharing concerns, and taking an active role in treatment are wise strategies that help cancer patients cope more effectively and might have physical benefits (Weisman, 1989).

The scientific study of psychoneuroimmunology is relatively young. Many of our findings need to be clarified, explained, and confirmed. Researchers hope to tease apart the precise links between psychological factors, the brain, and the immune system (Redd, 1995). Some preliminary

hypotheses about the interactions that cause vulnerability to disease include the following: (1) Stressful experiences lower the efficiency of immune systems, making individuals more susceptible to disease; (2) stress directly promotes disease-producing processes; and (3) stressful experiences might cause the activation of dormant viruses that diminish the individual's ability to cope with disease. These hypotheses may lead to clues for more successful treatments for some of the most baffling diseases—cancer and AIDS among them. To increase your understanding of AIDS, turn to Applications in Psychology 14.1.

In summary, the specialty areas of health psychology, behavioral medicine, and psychoneuroimmunology provide scientific evidence that psychological factors play a role in health and illness. Before we examine the effects of stress and illness in greater detail, let's explore the challenges of promoting health.

PROMOTING HEALTH

We can do a great deal to promote better health by establishing healthy habits and evaluating and changing our behaviors that interfere with good health. Regular exercise and good nutrition are essential ingredients to a healthier lifestyle. Avoiding overeating and smoking are also important in improving the quality of health.

Little with health is better than much with sickness.

Berber proverb

Regular Exercise

In 1961, President John F. Kennedy offered the following message: "We are underexercised as a nation. We look instead of play. We ride instead of walk. Our existence deprives us of the minimum of physical activity essential for healthy living." Without question, people are jogging, cycling, and aerobically exercising more today than in 1961, but far too many of us are still couch potatoes. **Aerobic exercise** *is sustained exercise—jogging, swimming, or cycling, for example—that stimulates heart and lung activity* (Cooper, 1970).

This exhausted runner at the end of a grueling marathon endorses the "no pain, no gain" philosophy of exercise's role in health. An alternative philosophy is that, for most individuals, moderate exercise is more pleasurable and easier to participate in over the long term. For some of us, intense exercise may be best, for others moderate exercise is best, but a sedentary life with little exercise at all should be avoided.

Preventing Heart Disease

The main focus of research on the effects of exercise on health has involved preventing heart disease. Most health experts recommend that you should try to raise your heart rate to 60 percent of your maximum heart rate. Your maximum heart rate is calculated as 220 minus your age divided by 0.6, so if you are 20, you should aim for an exercise heart rate of 120 (220 − 20 = 200 × 0.6 = 120). If you are 45, you should aim for an exercise heart rate of 105 (220 − 45 = 175 × 0.6 = 105).

People in some occupations get more vigorous exercise than those in others. For example, longshoremen have about half the risk of fatal heart attacks as co-workers like crane drivers and clerks who have physically less demanding jobs. Further, elaborate studies of 17,000 male alumni of Harvard University found that those who exercised strenuously on a regular basis had a lower risk of heart disease and were more likely to still be alive in their middle adulthood years (Lee, Hsieh, & Paffenbarger, 1995; Paffenbarger & others, 1986). Based on such findings, some health experts conclude that, regardless of

other risk factors (smoking, high blood pressure, overweight, heredity), if you exercise enough to burn more than 2,000 calories a week, you can cut your risk of heart attack by an impressive two-thirds (Sherwood, Light, & Blumenthal, 1989). Burning up 2,000 calories a week through exercise requires a lot of effort, far more than most of us are willing to expend. To burn 300 calories a day, through exercise, you would have to do one of the following: swim or run for about 25 minutes, walk for 45 minutes at about 4 miles an hour, or participate in aerobic dancing for 30 minutes.

The risk of heart attack can also be cut by as much as one-third over a 7-year period with such moderate exercise as rapid walking and gardening. The catch is that you have to spend an hour a day in these activities to get them to pay off. Going against the popular "no pain, no gain" philosophy, Robert Ornstein and David Sobel (1989) believe that exercise should be pleasurable, not painful. They point out that 20 percent of joggers running 10 miles a week suffer significant injuries, such as torn knee cartilage and pulled hamstring muscles. Ornstein and Sobel argue that most people can stay healthy by participating in exercise that

Increasing Your Understanding of AIDS

Valerie and Tom had been dating for about 3 years. They mutually decided to think about a few things, including their level of sexual intimacy and where marriage fit in their plans. As they discussed these matters, Tom brought up the issue of birth control and wondered about the relative effectiveness of the different methods. Valerie and Tom knew little about this and wanted more information. Together, they visited the health department in their community and picked up a number of brochures and pamphlets, including pamphlets about AIDS. After reading them they realized that condoms are the only birth control method that is protective against diseases. They also started to talk more about their past relationships, something they really had never done before. Sharing this information relieved them of many concerns and raised others. Together, though, they were able to work out many of the issues they were thinking about and were able to make several important informed decisions about their relationship that could have a dramatic impact on their health.

The most rapidly emerging threat to public health is infection from human immunodeficiency virus (HIV) which results in acquired immunodeficiency syndrome (AIDS). In fact, no disease has ever become such a major public health threat so soon after being recognized. As of early 1992, more than 200,000 persons had AIDS in the United States, with the last 100,000 cases occurring since 1989. HIV, the virus that causes AIDS, is transmitted from one person to another in only a few specific ways. A person can get infected with HIV from engaging in sexual intercourse with an infected partner or sharing syringes and other injection equipment when shooting up drugs. Some people have been infected after receiving blood transfu-

sions; however, this is rare today because blood banks routinely test blood before using it in transfusions. The primary way that people are getting infected with HIV today is through sexual contact and injecting drugs. To evaluate your own knowledge of AIDS, turn to table 14.A.

Recently in the United States, many people thought that gay men were the only people who needed to be concerned about HIV and AIDS. This could not be further from the truth. Although in the United States gay men were hit hardest early in the AIDS epidemic, there are no boundaries to AIDS. People of all sexual orientations, ethnic backgrounds, incomes, and geographical locations can be at risk for HIV infection. The things a person *does*, not the person that they *are*, put people at risk. The general public came to realize this most vividly when basketball star Earvin "Magic" Johnson announced that he was infected with HIV. Magic Johnson's message was that anyone could get HIV if they engaged in behaviors that put them at risk, such as having sex without using a condom. Although condoms can break and are effective only when used properly, they do substantially decrease the chances of HIV infection. Condoms offer the best protection against the virus during sexual intercourse.

Although the greatest risk for HIV infection comes from sexual behaviors, not all sexual behavior is risky with regard to HIV infection. Some sexual behaviors are high-risk, while others are lower in risk, and still other sexual behaviors have absolutely no risk of infection at all. Those that are highest in risk are those that allow for the exchange of blood (even if in microscopic amounts), semen (the fluid men release that carries sperm), and vaginal fluids. These body fluids can contain HIV and cause infection. Thus, using a condom during sexual intercourse decreases the chance of infection because it prevents the fluids from entering sexual partners' bodies. Also, behaviors like hugging, and caressing, which do not allow for the exchange of body fluids, do not pose any risk for HIV infection. Today, scientists also state that kissing is safe with respect to HIV, as there is no evidence that people can get infected from kissing (Kalichman, 1994). The illustration in this section depicts the relative risks of various sexual behaviors.

Changing sexual behaviors, perhaps even more so than other habits and behaviors, is very difficult. Sex and drug-use behaviors involve personal and private acts between people. What steps can people take to reduce their risk for HIV infection? Start to talk to your friends about AIDS. Discussions about AIDS can lead to a greater awareness and may raise

burns up only 500 calories a week. They believe it is overkill to run 8-minute miles, 3 miles at a time, 5 days a week, for example. Not only are fast walking and gardening on their recommended list of exercises, so are 20 minutes of sex (110 calories), 20 minutes of playing with children (106

calories), and 45 minutes of dancing (324 calories). Remember, regardless of your ultimate exercise program, health experts uniformly recommend that if you are unaccustomed to exercise, always start any exercise program slowly (Morgan & Goldson, 1987).

TABLE 14.A

Knowledge of AIDS Risk Behavior

Instructions

This is a true/false test. Please do not skip any questions. Because this is a test, some of the statements are true and accurate, others are false and inaccurate.

Items

1. Most people who transmit the AIDS virus look unhealthy.
2. Anal intercourse is a high-risk behavior for transmitting the AIDS virus.
3. Oral sex carries risk for AIDS virus transmission.
4. A person can be exposed to the AIDS virus in one sexual contact.
5. Keeping in good physical condition is the best way to prevent exposure to the AIDS virus.
6. It is unwise to touch a person with AIDS.
7. Condoms make intercourse completely safe.
8. Showering after sex greatly reduces the transmission of AIDS.
9. When people become sexually exclusive with one another, they no longer need to follow "safe sex" guidelines.
10. Oral sex is safe if the partners "don't swallow."
11. Most people who have been exposed to the AIDS virus quickly show symptoms of serious illness.
12. By reducing the number of different sexual partners, you are effectively protected from AIDS.
13. The AIDS virus does not penetrate unbroken skin.
14. Female-to-male transmission of the AIDS virus has not been documented.
15. Sharing toothbrushes and razors can transmit the AIDS virus.
16. Pre-ejaculatory fluids carry the AIDS virus.
17. Intravenous drug users are at risk for AIDS when they share needles.
18. A person must have many different sexual partners to be at risk from AIDS.
19. People carrying the AIDS virus generally feel quite ill.
20. Vaginal intercourse carries high risk for AIDS virus transmission.
21. Withdrawal immediately before orgasm makes intercourse safe.
22. Persons who are exclusively heterosexual are not at risk from AIDS.
23. Healthy persons in AIDS risk groups should not donate blood.
24. Sharing kitchen utensils or a bathroom with a person with AIDS poses no risk.
25. Intravenous drug users become exposed to the AIDS virus because the virus is often contained in heroin, amphetamines, and the injected drugs.
26. A wholesome diet and plenty of sleep will keep a person from becoming exposed to the AIDS virus.
27. A cure of AIDS is expected within the next 2 years.
28. It is more important to take precautions against AIDS in large cities than in small cities.
29. A negative result on the AIDS virus antibody test can occur even for people who carry the virus.
30. A positive result on the AIDS virus antibody test can occur even for people who do not carry the virus.
31. Coughing does not spread AIDS.
32. Only receptive (passive) anal intercourse transmits AIDS.
33. Most present cases of AIDS are due to blood transfusions that took place before 1984.
34. Most persons who have been exposed to the AIDS virus know they have been exposed.
35. A great deal is now known about how the AIDS virus is transmitted.
36. Donating blood carries no AIDS risk for the donor.
37. No cases of AIDS have ever been linked to social (dry) kissing.
38. Mutual masturbation and body rubbing are low in risk unless the partners have cuts or scratches.
39. People who become exposed to the AIDS virus through needle sharing can transmit the virus to others during sexual activities.
40. The AIDS virus can be transmitted by mosquitoes and cockroaches.

Reprinted with permission from "An Objective Test of AIDS Risk Behavior Knowledge: Scale Development, Validation, and Norms" in *Journal of Behavior Therapy and Experimental Psychiatry*, 20:227–234, by J. Kelly, et al. Copyright © 1989 Elsevier Science Ltd., Pergamon Imprint, Oxford, England.

Please turn to the end of the chapter to score and interpret your responses.

Improving Mental Health

Researchers have found that exercise benefits not only physical health, but mental health as well. In particular, exercise improves self-concept and reduces anxiety and depression (Ossip-Klein & others, 1989). In one study,

109 nonexercising volunteers were randomly assigned to one of four conditions: high-intensity aerobic training, moderate-intensity aerobic training, low-intensity non-aerobic training, and waiting list (Moser & others, 1989). In the high-intensity aerobic group, participants engaged

continued

some questions that you or your friends will want to get answers to. Questions about HIV and AIDS can be answered through the national AIDS information hotline, which is a toll free number, 1–800–HIV–INFO. Calling this number is one of the best ways to get fast and accurate information about AIDS.

But what about talking with dates and sexual partners about AIDS? How can people raise the topic of AIDS with an intimate partner without their thinking that their past is being questioned? One way to raise such an issue is to think about it in terms of care and concern for your own as well as the other person's health and welfare. Emphasizing the need to be concerned about AIDS in the 1990s, and that AIDS is everybody's problem, assures that the reason for talking about AIDS is concern. Once a discussion is started, the couple can openly discuss the use of condoms and engaging in sexual behavior that does not have any risk for the spread of HIV. Taking actions that protect each other can have very positive benefits for couples. They can learn to trust discussing such difficult things together, they can feel more safe and secure in their relationship, and they can know that they do not have to worry about AIDS or other sexually transmitted diseases in their relationship. Today, it is important for each person to recognize the impact of HIV and AIDS and to take responsibility for their own protection as well as the protection of people that they care about.

HIGH RISK
Activities that exchange body fluids:
• Unprotected oral, anal, or vaginal sex
• Sharing needles and syringes

LOW RISK
Latex barrier-protected activities,
as long as the barrier remains intact and
in place and is used properly:
• Oral, anal, or vaginal sex WITH a condom
• Oral sex without fluid exchange

NO RISK
No exchange of blood, semen,
vaginal secretions:
• Mutual masturbation
• Abstinence
• Hugging
• Cuddling
• Kissing
• Fantasies

Levels of Risk Behavior: The Stoplight as a Metaphor for Sexual Risk-Taking Related to AIDS

in a continuous walk-jog program that elevated their heart rate to 70 to 75 percent of maximum. In the moderate-intensity aerobic group, participants engaged in walking or jogging that elevated their heart rate to 60 percent of maximum. In the low-intensity nonaerobic group, participants engaged in strength, mobility, and flexibility exercises in a slow, discontinuous manner for approximately 30 minutes. Those who were assigned to exercise programs worked out 3 to 5 times a week. Those who were on the waiting list did not exercise.

The programs lasted for 10 weeks. As expected, the group assigned to the high-intensity aerobic program showed the greatest aerobic fitness on a 12-minute walk-run. Fitness also improved for those assigned to moderate- and low-exercise programs; however, only the people assigned to the moderate-intensity aerobic training programs showed psychological benefits. These benefits appeared immediately in the form of reduced tension and anxiety. And after 3 months, the moderate-intensity group showed improved aerobic conditioning. The superiority of the moderate aerobic training program over the nonaerobic low-exercise program suggests that a minimum level of aerobic conditioning may be required to obtain important psychological benefits.

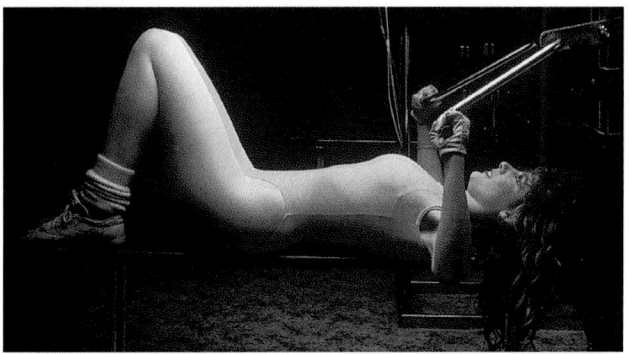

In one experiment, the self-concept of depressed women was improved by either weight lifting or running (Ossip-Klein & others, 1989).

Research on the benefits of exercise suggests that both moderate and intense activities produce important physical and psychological gains. Some people enjoy rigorous, intense exercise. Others enjoy more moderate exercise routines. The enjoyment and pleasure we derive from exercise cooperate with its aerobic benefits to make exercise one of life's most important activities.

Proper Nutrition

We are a nation obsessed with food, spending an extraordinary amount of time thinking about, gobbling up, and avoiding food. In chapter 13, "Motivation and Emotion," we discussed the nature of hunger. In this chapter, we will focus on the problem of obesity, weight-loss programs, and eating disorders, and on the cultural factors in nutrition.

Obesity

Understanding obesity is complex because body weight involves a number of factors—genetic inheritance, physiological mechanisms, cognitive factors, and environmental influences (Brownell, 1993; Brownell & Fairburn, 1995; Friedman & Brownell).

Heredity Until recently, the genetic component in obesity had been underestimated by scientists. Some individuals do inherit a tendency to be overweight. Only 10 percent of children who do not have obese parents become obese themselves, whereas 40 percent of children who become obese have one obese parent and 70 percent of children who become obese have two obese parents. The actual extent to which this is due to genes rather than experience cannot be determined in research with humans, but research documents that animals can be inbred to develop a propensity for obesity (Blundell, 1984). Further, identical human twins have similar weights, even when they are reared apart (Stunkard & others, 1990). Estimates of variance in body mass that can be explained by heredity range from 25 percent to 70 percent (Bouchard & others, 1990).

Set Point and BMR The amount of stored fat in your body is an important factor in your **set point,** *the weight maintained when no effort is made to gain or lose weight.* Fat is stored in adipose cells. When these cells are filled, you do not get hungry. When people gain weight—because of genetic predisposition, early childhood eating patterns, or adult overeating the number of fat cells increases, and they might not be able to get rid of them. A normal-weight individual has 30 to 40 billion fat cells. An obese individual has 80 to 120 billion fat cells. When individuals go on a diet, their fat cells might shrink but they do not go away.

Another factor in weight is **basal metabolism rate (BMR),** *the minimal amount of energy an individual uses in a resting state.* BMR varies with age and sex. Rates decline precipitously during adolescence and then more gradually during adulthood; they also are slightly higher for males than for females. Many individuals gradually increase their weight over a period of many years. To some degree the weight gain may be due to a declining basal metabolism rate. The declining BMR underscores the importance of reducing our food intake as we grow older if we want to maintain our weight.

Sociocultural Factors In addition to hereditary and biological factors, environmental factors are involved in weight and shape in important ways. The human gustatory system and taste preferences developed at a time when reliable sources of food were scarce. Our earliest ancestors probably developed a preference for sweets, since ripe fruit, which is a concentrated source of sugar (and thus calories), was so accessible. Today many people still have a "sweet tooth," but unlike our ancestors' ripe fruit, which contained sugar *plus* vitamins and minerals, the soft drinks and candy bars we snack on today too often fill us with empty calories.

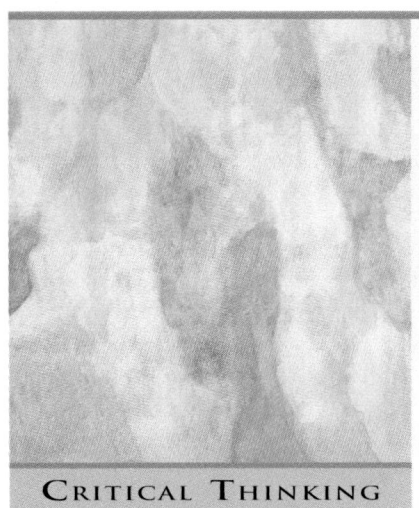

Explaining Counterintuitive Results

The results of the research study by Moser and others (1989) were somewhat surprising. It would be easy to assume that the group that became the most fit would also be the most psychologically satisfied with their experience. Yet the researchers discovered that only the moderate exercisers demonstrated psychological benefits. Can you provide some explanations for this counterintuitive finding?

It helps to remember that all of the individuals in the study were nonexercisers at the outset. Therefore, the high-intensity training program might have been quite taxing, and the subjects in that group, although they became more fit, might have found the new demands more stressful. This explanation highlights the importance of *identifying underlying values that influence behavior.*

health professionals and a growing minority of the press and the public who, although recognizing the alarmingly high incidence of obesity, are frustrated by high relapse rates and are increasingly concerned that chronic dieting may have negative effects on health and well-being (Brownell & Rodin, 1994).

Eat, drink, and be merry, for tomorrow ye shall diet.

Lewis C. Henry

Dieting is a pervasive concern of many individuals in the United States. Two large-scale national surveys revealed that approximately 40 percent of women and 24 percent of men are currently dieting (Horm & Anderson, 1993; Serdula & others, 1993). In one of these surveys, 52 percent of women and 37 percent of men believed that they were overweight (Horm & Anderson, 1993).

Following are some fundamental issues in the dieting debate and the current status of their empirical evaluation (Brownell & Rodin, 1994).

Strong evidence of the environment's influence is the doubling of the rate of obesity in the United States since 1900, likely due to greater availability of food (especially food high in fat), energy-saving devices, and declining physical activity. The obesity rate also increased more than 50 percent from the 1960s to 1980 (Dietz, 1986). Obesity is six times more frequent among low-income women than among upper-income women, and more common among Americans than Europeans. To read about the nutritional health of ethnic minorities in the United States, turn to Sociocultural Worlds 14.1.

Obesity and Its Costs   Estimates indicate that 31 percent of men and 24 percent of women in the United States are overweight, with 12 percent of both sexes severely overweight (National Academy of Sciences Research Council, 1989). The economic costs of obesity are estimated at $39 billion per year, or more than 5 percent of all health costs. The staggering cost figures stem from obesity's association with diabetes, hypertension, cardiovascular diseases, and some cancers.

Dieting

Many divergent interests are involved in the topic of dieting—the public, health professionals, policy makers, the media, and the powerful diet and food industries. On the one side are societal norms that promote a very lean, aesthetic ideal, supported by an industry valued at more than $30 billion per year that provides diet books, programs, videos, foods, pills, and the like. On the other side are

Does Weight Loss Reduce or Increase Health Risks?
Few studies have explored the effects of weight loss on disease and death. The most common type of data comes from population studies in which some individuals lose weight and others do not, and then their mortality is compared. However, the subjects who lose weight are self-selected; possible mediating factors such as body fat distribution and dieting history are not considered. Subjects might be gaining or losing weight because of factors that are related to disease, such as starting and stopping smoking. The type of study required to directly address the relation between dieting and mortality—a longitudinal study with random assignment to weight-loss and no-weight-loss groups, and with a sufficient sample size to evaluate mortality—has not been conducted. Such a study would be costly and difficult to undertake. Possibly because of such limitations, studies on weight loss and mortality are striking in the inconsistency of their results. In sum, the available data present a mixed picture of whether weight loss is related to mortality.

Do Diets Work?   Some critics argue that all diets fail (Wooley & Garner, 1991). Although there are reports of poor long-term results (Wilson, 1994), some recent studies revealed that programs that combine very-low-calorie diets with intensive education and behavior modification produce good long-term results. In one such

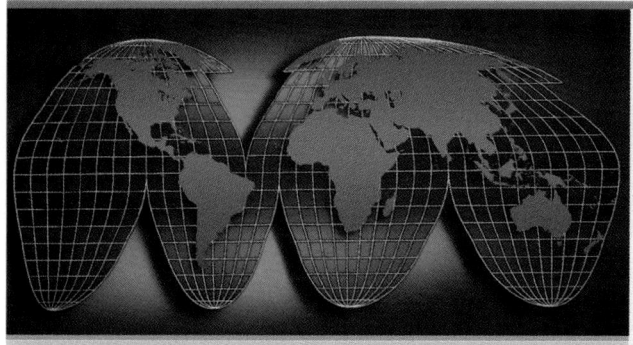

SOCIOCULTURAL WORLDS 14.1

Ethnicity and Nutrition

In the late 1960s, and again in the 1980s, national attention focused on the relationship between poverty and malnutrition for millions of Americans, a disproportionate percentage of whom are members of ethnic minority groups. In response to grim evidence from a ten-state survey of more than 40,000 individuals, Congress expanded the existing food assistance programs and created new ones, such as the special Supplemental Food Program for Women, Infants, and Children (WIC). Despite these programs, which largely survived the budget-cutting fever of the 1980s, malnutrition, obesity, and other dietary problems remain a national problem (Allen & Mitchell, in press).

African American women are much less likely than White women to develop eating disorders that reflect an obsession with thinness; African American women seem more comfortable with larger body sizes. However, African American women who do become anorexic, like their White counterparts, are usually members of the middle class. A high rate of obesity among African American women is often due to both low rates of exercise and diets high in fat and sodium, a legacy of the southern roots of most African Americans. Haitian Americans believe that a fat person is healthy and happy but a thin person is the opposite (Laguerre, 1981).

Both economic and cultural factors affect the nutritional intake of Native Americans (Walter, 1974). Many Navajo Indians have a lactose intolerance, making it difficult for them to consume dairy products. Further, because they have strong ethnic food preferences, surplus foods supplied by the Department of Agriculture are often discarded, even when their normal supply of food is disrupted (Kunitz & Levy, 1981). Mexican Americans also have high rates of lactose intolerance, contributing to high rates of malnutrition among pregnant, lactating Mexican American women and their children under the age of 6 (Schrieber & Homiack, 1981).

Chinese Americans have an elaborate system of classifying foods and herbs into *hot* and *cold,* which must be balanced to achieve health. Chinese Americans consume a wide variety of foods, so, unless they are poor, they usually eat nutritionally balanced meals. The elderly Chinese American poor tend to eat a lot of salt despite their high rates of hypertension. Salt is present in soy sauce, which is used liberally by most Chinese Americans (Gould-Martin & Ngin, 1981).

In short, ethnic background is related to a person's preferences for certain foods and to his or her nutritional health.

study, participants lost an average of 55 pounds, with more than half of this weight kept off 2½ years later (Nunn, Newton, & Faucher, 1992). Thus, it appears that some individuals do lose weight and maintain the loss. How often this occurs and whether some programs produce this outcome better than others are open questions.

Are Diets Harmful?   One main concern about diets being harmful focuses on weight cycling ("yo-yo dieting" involving a recurring cycle of dieting and regaining the weight). The empirical evidence does suggest a link between frequent changes in weight and chronic disease (Brownell & Rodin, in press). Another important concern about dieting is that it might lead to eating disorders. Dieting often does precede the development of eating disorders, but no causal link has been documented (Wilson, 1993). Also, overweight individuals who diet and then maintain their weight do become less depressed and reduce their risk for a number of health-impairing disorders.

Does Exercise Benefit Individuals Who Want to Lose Weight?   Exercise not only burns up calories but continues to raise the metabolic rate for several hours *after* the exercise. Exercise actually lowers your body's set point for weight, making it much easier to maintain a lower weight (Bennett & Gurin, 1982). Nonetheless, it is difficult to convince obese individuals to exercise. One problem is that moderate exercise does not reduce calorie consumption, and in many cases individuals who exercise take in more calories than their sedentary counterparts (Stern, 1984). Still, exercise combined with conscious self-control of eating habits can produce a viable weight-loss program (Stotland & Zuroff, 1991). When exercise is a component of weight-loss programs, individuals keep weight off longer than when calorie reduction alone is followed.

Who Should Diet?   The population is not uniform, and clearly not everyone should go on a diet. A 10 percent reduction in body weight may produce striking benefits in

Everything we know about weight loss suggests that a combination of eating healthy foods and exercising works best.

an older, obese, hypertensive man but be unhealthy in an adolescent female who is not overweight. The pressure to be thin, and thus diet, is greatest among young women, yet they are not the group in which the greatest risk of obesity exists or in which the benefits of dieting outweigh the risks.

Researchers have not adequately investigated the question of who should lose weight. This question will likely be best answered by consideration of the medical and psychosocial consequences of weight loss, which may be a highly individualized matter.

Eating Disorders

Eighteen-year-old Jane gradually eliminated foods from her diet to the point at which she subsisted by eating *only* applesauce and eggnog. She spent hours observing her body, wrapping her fingers around her waist to see if it was getting any thinner. She fantasized about becoming a beautiful fashion model and wearing designer bathing suits. However, even when she dropped to 85 pounds, Jane still felt fat. She continued to lose weight, eventually emaciating herself. She was hospitalized and treated for **anorexia nervosa,** *an eating disorder that involves the relentless pursuit of thinness through starvation.* Anorexia nervosa can eventually lead to death, as it did for popular singer Karen Carpenter (Casper, 1989).

Anorexia nervosa primarily afflicts females during adolescence and the early adulthood years (only about 5 percent of all anorexics are male). Most adolescents with this disorder are White and from well-educated, middle- and upper-income families. Although anorexics avoid eating, they have an intense interest in food. They cook for others, they talk about food, and they insist on watching others eat. Anorexics have a distorted body image, perceiving themselves as overweight even when they become skeletal. As self-starvation continues and the fat content of their body drops to a bare minimum, menstruation usually stops and their behavior often becomes hyperactive.

Numerous causes of anorexia nervosa have been proposed, including societal, psychological, and physiological factors (Mizes, 1995; Striegel-Moore & others, 1993). The societal factor most often held responsible is the current fashion image of thinness, reflected in the saying "You can't be too rich or too thin." Psychological factors include motivation for attention, desire for individuality, denial of sexuality, and a need to cope with overcontrolling parents. Some anorexics have parents that place high demands for achievement on them. Unable to meet their parents' high standards, they feel unable to control their own lives. By limiting their food intake, anorexics gain some sense of self-control. Physiological causes involve the hypothalamus, which becomes abnormal in a number of ways when an adolescent becomes anorexic. Unfortunately, we are uncertain of the exact causes of anorexia at this time.

Bulimia *is an eating disorder in which the individual consistently follows a binge-and-purge eating pattern.* The bulimic goes on an eating binge and then purges by self-induced vomiting or using a laxative. Sometimes the binges alternate with fasting, at other times with normal eating. Like anorexia nervosa, bulimia is primarily a female disorder. Bulimia has become prevalent among traditional-age college women. Some estimates suggest that one in every two college women binges and purges at least some of the time. Recent estimates, however, suggest that true bulimics—those who binge and purge on a regular basis—make up less than 2 percent of the college female population (Stunkard, 1987). Another survey of 1,500 high school and university students found that 4 percent of the high school students and 5 percent of the university students were bulimic (Howat & Saxton, 1988). Anorexics can control their eating, but bulimics cannot. Depression is a common characteristic of bulimics. Bulimia can produce gastric and chemical imbalance in the body. Many of the causes proposed for anorexia nervosa are also offered for bulimia (Fairburn, 1995).

Eating disorders are especially common among female gymnasts, who have the lowest body-fat percentage of all women athletes. Perhaps one of every four gymnasts is bulimic in order to control weight. In a study of college gymnasts, about three in four had some bulimic behaviors (such as vomiting more than twice a week; using laxatives, diuretics, and diet pills; starving themselves). Other female sports with high rates of bulimia include field hockey, distance track, and skating, while low rates are found in basketball, golf, and swimming. In addition, some male wrestlers are bulimic.

Cultural Factors in Nutrition

Current food preferences in the United States reflect problematic relationships with food. Many people eat too much fast food, which increases fat and cholesterol intake, both of which are implicated in heart disease and high blood pressure. Some individuals have adopted more rigorous nutritional habits to limit or avoid foods associated with poor health. For example, vegetarians exclude meat but plan their diets carefully to ensure that they get the proper amounts and kinds of proteins. Proper nutrition is ensured not just by limiting calorie intake but by carefully selecting foods that provide plenty of nutrients with their calories. Researchers have found that mice fed a high-fat diet are more likely to develop breast cancer than mice fed on a low-fat diet, and a cross-national study involving women also found a strong positive correlation between fat consumption and death rates from breast cancer (Cohen, 1987) (see figure 14.1).

One of the most telling comparisons to link fat intake and cancer is between the United States and Japan. Both countries have similar levels of industrialization and education, as well as high medical standards. Although the overall cancer rates of the two countries are similar, cancers of the breast, colon, and prostate are common in the United States but rare in Japan. By contrast, cancer of the stomach is common in Japan but rare in the United States. Within two generations, Japanese immigrants to Hawaii and California

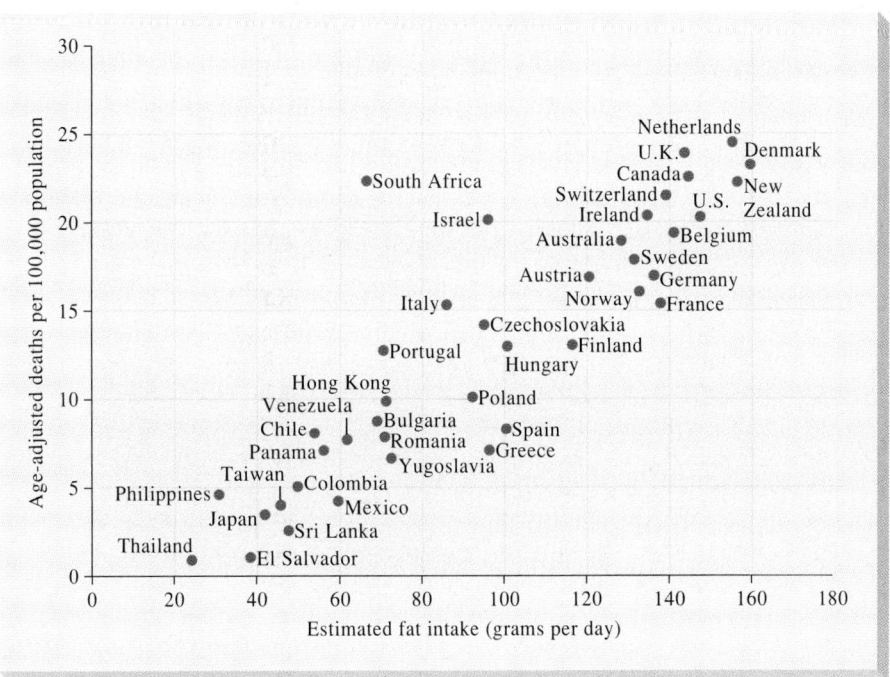

FIGURE 14.1

Cross-Cultural Comparisons of Diet and Cancer
In countries in which individuals have a low daily intake of fat, the rate of breast cancer is low (in Thailand, for example). In countries in which individuals have a high daily intake of fat, the rate of breast cancer is high (in the Netherlands, for example).

have breast cancer rates that are significantly higher than those in Japan and that approach those of Americans. Many researchers believe that the high fat intake of Americans and the low fat intake of the Japanese are implicated in the countries' different cancer rates.

The general good health, low cancer rates, and longevity of Seventh-Day Adventists, an evangelical Protestant faith, further support the link between cultural factors, especially diet, and cancer. Strict Seventh-Day Adventists adhere to biblical precepts that determine diet and other lifestyle behaviors. Their well-balanced diet includes generous portions of unrefined foods, grains, vegetable protein, fruits, and vegetables. Smoking is prohibited. As a result, there is a very low incidence of lung cancer among Seventh-Day Adventists. In addition, Seventh-Day Adventists have less cancer of any type—including breast, pancreas, and colorectal cancer—than other cultural groups in the United States.

As is the case with any cultural group, some Seventh-Day Adventists adhere more strictly to the sect's lifestyle than do others. In one study of religiously inactive Norwegian Seventh-Day Adventists, their risk of disease was similar to that of Norwegians who were not Seventh-Day Adventists (Fonnebo, 1985). Similarly, Seventh-Day Adventists in the United States who marginally adhere to the sect's guidelines for physical, mental, and spiritual health have an increased risk of disease (Phillips & others, 1980).

Freedom from Smoking

The year 1988 marked the 75th anniversary of the introduction of Camel cigarettes. Some magazines surprised readers with elaborate pop-up advertisements for Camels. Camel's ad theme was "75 years and still smokin'." Coincidentally 1988 was also the 75th anniversary of the American Cancer Society.

In 1989 the surgeon general and his advisory committee issued a report, *Reducing the Health Consequences of Smoking: 25 Years of Progress.* It was released 25 years after the original warnings that cigarettes are responsible for major health problems, especially lung cancer. New evidence was presented to show that smoking is even more harmful than previously thought. For example, the report indicated that in 1985 cigarette smoking accounted for more than one-fifth of all deaths in the United States—20 percent more than previously believed. Thirty percent of all cancer deaths were attributed to smoking, as were 21 percent of all coronary heart disease deaths and 82 percent of chronic pulmonary disease deaths.

Researchers are also increasingly finding that passive smoke (environmental smoke inhaled by nonsmokers who live or work around smokers) carries health risks (Sandler & others, 1989). Passive smoke is estimated to be the culprit in as many as 8,000 lung cancer deaths a year in the United States. Children of smokers are at special risk for respiratory and middle-ear diseases. For children under the age of 5, the risk of upper respiratory tract infection is doubled if their mothers smoke. And in one recent study, the greater the number of cigarettes the infant was passively exposed to after birth from all adults, the higher was the infant's risk of sudden infant death syndrome, a condition that occurs when the infant stops breathing and suddenly dies (Klonoff-Cohen & others, 1995).

The surgeon general's 1989 report contains some good news, however. Fewer people smoke today, and almost half of all living adults who ever smoked have quit. In particular the prevalence of smoking among men fell from over 50 percent in 1965 to about 30 percent in 1989. Current estimates place smoking prevalence at just over 25 percent (National Institutes of Health, 1994). As a consequence, a half-century's uninterrupted escalation in the rate of death due to lung cancer among males has ceased, and the incidence of lung cancer among White males has fallen. Although approximately 56 million Americans 15 to 84 years of age were smokers in 1985, the surgeon general's report estimates that 91 million would have been smoking had there been no changes in smoking and health knowledge, norms, and policy over the past quarter century (Warner, 1989).

However, the bad news is that over 50 million Americans *continue* to smoke, most having failed at attempts to quit. No single voluntary behavior would do more to prevent death than stopping smoking. Why, in the face of the damaging figure that more than one-fifth of all deaths are due to smoking, do so many people still smoke?

Smoking as an Addiction

Most adult smokers would like to quit, but their addiction to nicotine often turns their efforts into dismal failure. Nicotine, the active drug in cigarettes, is a stimulant that increases a smoker's energy and alertness, a pleasurable experience that is positively reinforcing. Nicotine also causes the release of acetylcholine and endorphin neurotransmitters, which have a calming and pain-reducing effect. However, smoking not only works as a positive reinforcer; it also works as a negative reinforcer by ending a smoker's painful craving for nicotine. A smoker gets relief from this painful aversive state simply by smoking another cigarette.

Smoking is costly in more ways than physical health. A two-packs-per-day habit costs $1,300 per year (U.S. Department of Labor, Bureau of Labor Statistics, 1991).

We are rational cognitive beings. Can't we develop enough self-control to overcome the pleasurable, immediate, reinforcing circumstances by thinking about the delayed, long-term, damaging consequences of smoking? As indicated earlier, many adults have quit smoking because they recognize that it is "suicide in slow motion," but the immediate pleasurable effects of smoking are extremely difficult to overcome. In chapter 6, "Learning," we described self-control programs that are effective in helping individuals quit smoking.

Smoking Is Preventable

Smoking usually begins during childhood and adolescence. A 1992 survey of eighth-graders in Michigan found that 45 percent had already tried cigarettes (Institute for Health

Policy, 1993). Adolescent smoking reached its peak in the mid-1970s, when 29 percent of high school seniors smoked on a daily basis. In 1992, the rate had dropped to 17 percent (Johnston, O'Malley, & Bachman, 1993). Among adolescents, females are now more likely to be smokers than males are. The smoking rate is still at a level that will cut short the lives of many adolescents. Despite the growing awareness that it is important to keep children from starting to smoke, there are fewer restrictions on children's access to cigarettes today than there were in 1964, and the existing restrictions are rarely enforced (United States Department of Health and Human Services, 1989).

Traditional school health programs appear to have succeeded in educating adolescents about the long-term health consequences of smoking but have had little effect on adolescent smoking *behavior*. That is, adolescents who smoke know the facts about the health risks, such as their chances of getting lung cancer and emphysema, but they go ahead and smoke just as much anyway (Miller & Slap, 1989). Few teenagers think that the serious unpleasant effects of smoking will affect their own lives, because rationalizations such as "Yes, but it won't happen to me" are typical of the adolescent thinking style called the *personal fable*.

As a result of this gap between what teens *know* and what they *do* in regard to smoking, researchers are focusing on the factors that place teens at high risk for future smoking, especially social pressures from peers, family members, and the media (Urberg, Shyu, & Liang, 1990). The tobacco industry preys on young peoples' desire to feel grown up by including "cool" people who smoke in their advertisements—successful young women smoking Virginia Slims cigarettes and rugged, handsome men smoking Marlboros, for example. The advertisements encourage adolescents to associate cigarette smoking with a successful and, ironically, athletic and active lifestyle. Legislators are trying to introduce more stringent laws to further regulate the tobacco industry and the media. In one recent study, a combination of school and mass media interventions reduced cigarette smoking through adolescence (Flynn & others, 1995).

I'm glad I don't have to explain to a man from Mars why each day I set fire to dozens of little pieces of paper, and then put them in my mouth.

Mignon McLaughlin

One comprehensive health program that includes an attempt to curb cigarette smoking by adolescents was developed by clinical psychologist Cheryl Perry and her colleagues (Perry & others, 1988). Three programs were developed based on peer group norms, healthy role models, and social skills training. Elected peer leaders were trained as instructors. In grade 7, adolescents were offered *Keep It Clean,* a six-session course emphasizing the negative effects of smoking. In grade 8, students were involved in *Health Olympics,* an approach that included exchanging greeting

Many adolescents who smoke know the health risks associated with smoking, but they smoke anyway. Given this information, what might be the best strategy for reducing teenage smoking?

cards on smoking and health with peers in other countries. In grade 9, students participated in *Shifting Gears,* which included six sessions focused on social skills. In the social skills program, students critiqued media messages and created their own positive health videotapes. At the same time the school intervention occurred, a communitywide smoking cessation program, as well as a diet and health awareness campaign, were initiated. After 5 years, students who were involved in the smoking and health program were much less likely to smoke cigarettes, use marijuana, or drink alcohol than were their counterparts who were not involved in the program.

Prevention Issues

Being healthy involves far more than simply going to a doctor when you get sick and being treated for disease. We are becoming increasingly aware that our behavior determines whether we will develop a serious illness and when we will die (Lenfant, 1995; Sarafino, 1994). Seven of the ten leading causes of death in the United States are associated with the *absence* of healthy behaviors. Diseases such as influenza, polio, and rubella no longer are major causes of death. More deaths now are caused by heart disease (36 percent of all deaths in 1986), cancer (22 percent), and stroke (17 percent).

Personal habits and lifestyle play key roles in resisting disease and thriving under stress. These findings lead health psychologists, behavioral medicine specialists, and public health professionals to predict that the next major step in

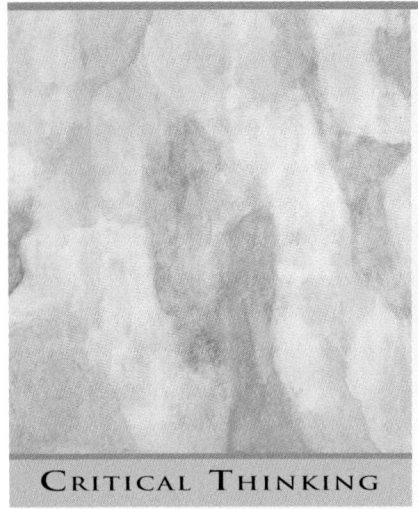

CRITICAL THINKING

*The George
Burns Paradox*

No matter how much evidence appears from medical research about the hazardous effects of smoking, many individuals remain unconvinced. These skeptics point to examples of people who regularly smoke and who have managed to live very long lives. George Burns is a good example. Nearly 100 years old, he is never seen without a cigar. If smoking is so awful, then how could George Burns live so long? Can you use this example to propose *some alternative explanations* that might explain both George Burns's longevity and the hazards of smoking?

Why might someone like George Burns be able to live so long even though he is a heavy cigar smoker?

improving the general health of the American population will be primarily behavioral, not medical. The federal government and the Society for Public Health Education have set health objectives for the year 2000 (Schwartz & Eriksen, 1989). Among them are the following:

- To develop preventive services targeting diseases and such problems as cancer, heart disease, stroke, unintended pregnancy (especially among adolescents), and AIDS.
- To promote health, including behavior modification and health education; stronger programs are urged for dealing with smoking, alcohol and drug abuse, nutrition, physical fitness, and mental health.
- To work toward cleaner air and water.
- To improve workplace safety, including reducing exposure to toxic chemicals.
- To meet the health needs of special populations, such as gaining a better understanding of disease prevention in African American and Latino populations (Klonoff, 1991); ethnic minority groups suffer disproportionately from cancer, heart disease, diabetes, and other major diseases.

America's health-care costs have soared and are moving toward the $1 trillion mark annually. Health experts hope to make a dent in these costs by encouraging people to live healthier lives. Many corporations have begun to recognize that health promotion for their employees is cost effective. Businesses are increasingly examining their employees' health behavior and the workplace environment as they recognize the role health plays in productive work. Smoke-free work environments, onsite exercise programs, bonuses to quit smoking and lose weight, and company-sponsored athletic events are increasingly found in American businesses.

You only live once—but if you work it right, once is enough.
Joe E. Lewis

Government Interventions and Preventive Health Care

Seventh-Day Adventists have strong convictions about behavior and health. Could a government be as successful as the Seventh-Day Adventists are in promoting behavior that ensures the health of its citizens? Several governments have tried various measures, with mixed success. The government of Finland, for example, has placed more restrictions on tobacco advertisements and liquor sales than most countries, which many believe has resulted in improved health for Finnish citizens. However, in the United States, both citizen and industry lobbying groups have made it difficult for health-related legislation to be approved. Cross-cultural psychologist Lisa Ilola (1990) points to seat belt use and mandatory helmets for motorcycle riders as examples of how many Americans, instead of accepting these reasonable protections for health and safety, bridle at what they believe is government intrusion into freedom of choice. The degree of respect for the government and the appropriateness of the government's action, it appears, are important factors in whether or not people will abide by legal constraints to promote their health and safety.

Cross-cultural psychologist Richard Brislin (1990) emphasizes that, to ensure the success of a social service program, the people who introduce or maintain it should be highly respected members of the community. For example, Hawaii has a highly successful program to encourage citizens to receive free blood pressure checkups. Firefighters volunteer to oversee the program. Anyone in Hawaii can have their blood pressure checked free of charge simply by going to a fire station. Residents take advantage of this program in large part because firefighters are highly respected and visible in Hawaiian communities—they have an active program in presenting safety information to schools, they entertain schoolchildren on field trips to fire stations, they are active in community service, and many are members of native Hawaiian families that go back five or six generations.

Prevention Related to Gender and Ethnicity

Gender and ethnicity play roles in life expectancy and health. According to psychologist Bonnie Strickland (1989), males are at greater risk than females for death at every age in the life span. The cause of death also varies for men and women. For example, four times more men than women die as a result of homicide, and twice as many men as women die as a result of respiratory cancer, suicide, pulmonary disease, accidents, cirrhosis of the liver, and heart disease.

In general, African Americans have a higher mortality rate than Whites for thirteen of the fifteen leading causes of death (Winett, King, & Altman, 1989). Also, of all ethnic minority women, African American women are the most vulnerable to health problems, reports the Public Health Service Task Force on Women's Health Issues (1985). For example, African American women, compared with White American women, are three times more likely to have high blood pressure, are twice as likely to die from cardiovascular disease, have a 35 percent higher death rate for diabetes, and are four times more likely to be a victim of homicide.

Not only are there cross-cultural and ethnic variations in health, but women and men experience health and the health-care system differently (Paludi, 1995; Stanton & Gallant, 1995). Special concerns about women's health today focus on unintended and unwanted pregnancy, abuse and violence, AIDS, the role of poverty in women's health, eating disorders, drug abuse, breast diseases, reproductive health, and the medical establishment's discrimination against women (O'Hara & others, 1995).

The women's health movement in the United States rejected an assumption that was all too often made by the male medical profession: that women lose control of their bodies out of ignorance. Consciousness-raising groups and self-help groups formed throughout the country in the 1960s and 1970s to instruct women about their bodies, reproductive rights, nutrition, and health care. Information was also given on how to conduct breast and pelvic examinations. The Boston Women's Health Book Collective, which was formed in 1969, has, as one of its goals, to teach women about their physical and mental health. It published *The New Our Bodies, Ourselves* (1992) and *Ourselves Getting Older* (1987), which are excellent resources for information about women's health.

Although females are increasingly becoming physicians, medicine continues to be a male-dominated profession.

Richard Brislin has made numerous contributions to our understanding of how culture influences human behavior, feelings, and thought. He has been especially sensitive to the ways in which knowledge about cultural contexts can be used to improve health, develop more effective ways of coping with stress, and develop better relations between people from different cultures.

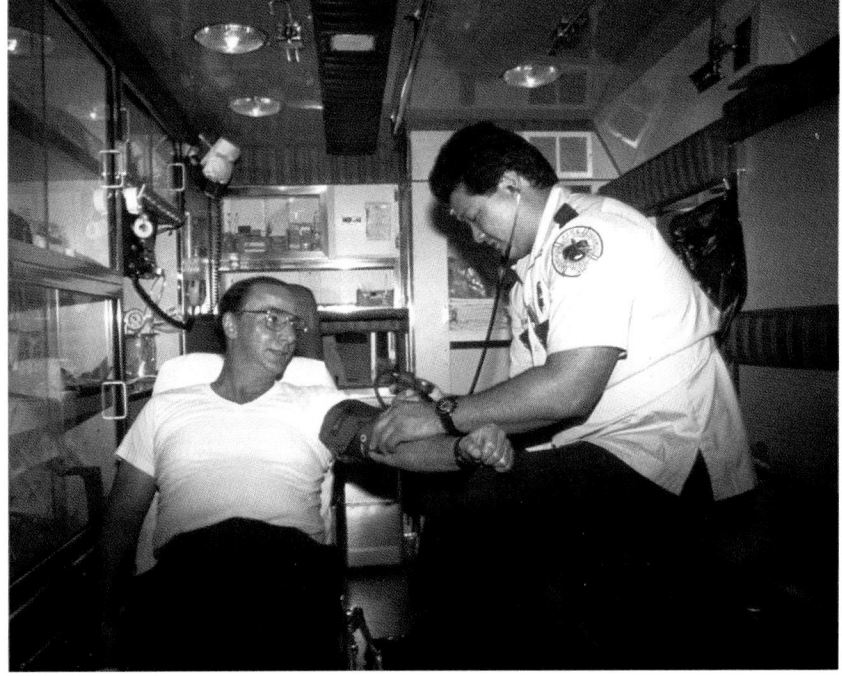

Cross-cultural psychologists, such as Richard Brislin, believe that, to ensure the success of social service programs, the people who introduce or maintain them should be highly respected members of the community. In Hawaii, for example, firefighters—highly respected and visible in Hawaiian communities—have been successful in getting Hawaiian residents to have their blood pressure checked.

Women's physical complaints often are devalued, interpreted as "emotional" rather than physical in origin, and dismissed as trivial. In one investigation, physicians described their men and women patients differently: The men were characterized as very direct, very logical, good decision makers, and rarely emotional, whereas the women were characterized as very excitable in minor crises, more easily influenced, less adventurous, less independent, very illogical, and even very sneaky (Broverman & others, 1970).

The issue of sex and gender bias has also recently been raised in selecting participants in medical research studies (Rabinowitz & Sechzur, 1994). Most medical research has been conducted with men, and frequently the results are generalized to women without apparent justification. For example, in a large-scale study involving 22,000 physicians that demonstrated the beneficial effect of an aspirin every other day on coronary heart disease, not a single woman was included in the study. Women's health advocates continue to press for greater inclusion of women in medical studies to reduce the bias that has characterized research on health, and they hope that the medical establishment will give increased attention to women's health concerns and treat women in less prejudiced, less biased ways (Strickland, 1988).

REVIEW

Relating Health and Psychology

Health psychology is a multidimensional approach to health that emphasizes psychological factors, lifestyle, and the nature of the health-care delivery system. Closely aligned with health psychology is behavioral medicine, which combines medical and behavioral knowledge to reduce illness and promote health. Psychoneuroimmunology explores the connections among psychological factors, the nervous system, and the immune system. Exploratory research suggests that our emotions and attitudes are connected to our immune system.

Both moderate and intense exercise produce important physical and psychological gains, such as lowered risk of heart disease and reduced anxiety. Experts increasingly recommend that the level of exercise you participate in should be pleasurable. Every indication suggests our nation's children are not getting enough exercise.

Understanding obesity is complex because body weight involves a number of factors. Estimates of body mass that can be explained by heredity range from 25 to 70 percent. Set point and BMR are other biological processes involved in weight. Environmental factors also play a role in obesity—obesity has doubled in the United States since 1900. Obesity has high costs. Dieting is a pervasive concern of many individuals in the United States and raises many questions, such as whether weight loss reduces or increases health risks, whether diets work (some do, many don't), whether diets are harmful, whether exercise benefits individuals who want to lose weight, and who should diet. Two increasingly common eating disorders are anorexia nervosa and bulimia. Cultural factors also are involved in nutrition.

In 1989 the surgeon general released extensive new evidence that smoking is more harmful than previously believed, accounting for one-fifth of all deaths in the United States. Researchers are increasingly finding that passive smoke also carries health risks. Smoking is both addictive and reinforcing. Stronger educational and policy efforts regarding smoking are needed. Current prevention programs with young people focus on social pressures from family, peers, and the media.

Seven of the ten leading causes of death—heart disease, cancer, and stroke, for example—are associated with the absence of healthy behaviors. The next major improvements in general health may be behavioral, not medical. A number of health goals for the year 2000 have been proposed and businesses are increasingly interested in improving the health of their employees. Cultural factors influence coronary problems, as the study of migrant ethnic groups shows. Cross-national studies also show that cultural factors influence cancer. Government interventions and preventions in health care require consideration of the degree of respect for the government and the appropriateness of the intervention and prevention.

Women and men often experience health and the health-care system differently. The medical profession has been male-dominated, and the treatment female patients receive has often been inferior to the treatment male patients receive. The issue of sex and gender bias has also recently been raised regarding the selection of participants for medical research studies.

Understanding Stress

We live in a world that includes many stressful circumstances. According to the American Academy of Family Physicians, two-thirds of all office visits to family doctors are for stress-related symptoms. Stress is also believed to be a major contributor to coronary heart disease, cancer, lung problems, accidental injuries, cirrhosis of the liver, and suicide, six of the leading causes of death in the United States. In 1989 two of the five best-selling drugs in the United States were an antianxiety drug (Xanax) and an ulcer medication (Zantac). No one really knows whether we experience more stress than our parents or grandparents did at our age, but it seems as if we do.

Stress is one of those terms that is not easy to define. Initially the word *stress* was loosely borrowed from physics. Humans, it was thought, are in some ways similar to physical objects, such as metals, that resist moderate outside forces but lose their resiliency at a point of greater pressure. However, unlike metal, human beings can think, reason, and experience a myriad of social and environmental circumstances that make defining stress more complex in psychology than in physics (Hobfoll, 1989).

Although psychologists debate whether stress is the threatening events in our world or our response to those demands, we will define stress broadly. **Stress** *is the response of individuals to the circumstances and events, called stressors, that threaten them and tax their coping abilities.* To understand stress, we need to know about the related biological, personality, cognitive, environmental, and sociocultural factors (see figure 14.2).

Biological Factors in Stress

According to the Austrian-born founder of stress research, Hans Selye (1974, 1983), stress simply is the wear and tear on the body due to the demands placed on it. Any number of environmental events, or stimuli, will produce the same stress response in the body. Selye observed patients with various problems: the death of someone close, a loss of income, arrest for embezzlement. Regardless of which problem the patient had, similar symptoms appeared: loss of appetite, muscular weakness, and decreased interest in the world.

The **general adaptation syndrome (GAS)** *is Selye's concept of the common effects on the body when demands* are placed on it. The GAS consists of three stages: alarm, resistance, and exhaustion. First, in the *alarm stage,* the body enters a temporary state of shock, a time when resistance to stress is below normal. The body detects the stress and tries to eliminate it. The body loses muscle tone, temperature decreases, and blood pressure drops. Then, a rebound called "countershock" occurs, in which resistance to stress begins to pick up; the adrenal cortex enlarges and hormone release increases. Soon after the alarm stage, which is short, the individual moves into the *resistance stage,* a no-holds-barred effort to combat stress. Stress hormones flood the body; blood pressure, heart rate, temperature, and respiration rate all skyrocket. If the all-out effort succeeds, the body returns to a more normal resting state. If the all-out effort to combat stress fails and the stress persists, the individual moves into the *exhaustion stage.* The wear and tear on the body takes its toll—the person may collapse in a state of exhaustion, and vulnerability to disease increases. Figure 14.3 illustrates Selye's general adaptation syndrome.

Adapt or perish, now as ever, is Nature's inexorable imperative.
H. G. Wells, *Mind at the End of Its Tether,* 1946

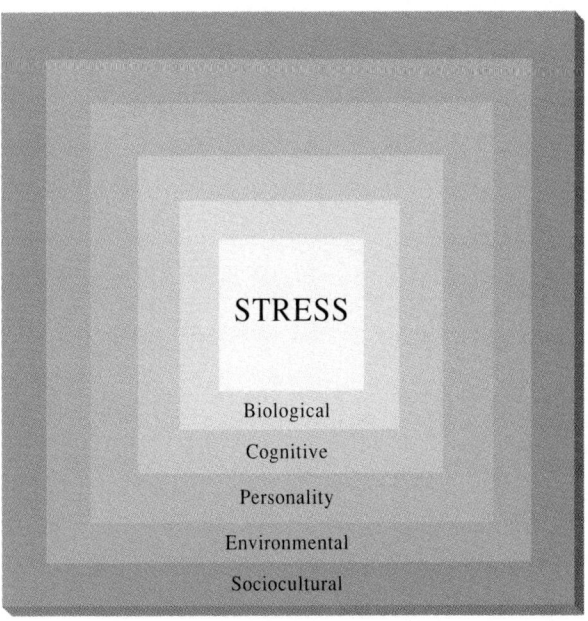

Figure 14.2

Factors Involved in Stress
Among the most important factors involved in understanding stress are biological factors (such as our body's response to stress); cognitive factors (such as whether we appraise an event as threatening or challenging); personality factors (such as how we handle anger or whether we trust others); environmental factors (such as the frustrating stressors we experience in our world); and sociocultural factors (such as frustration caused by limited opportunity).

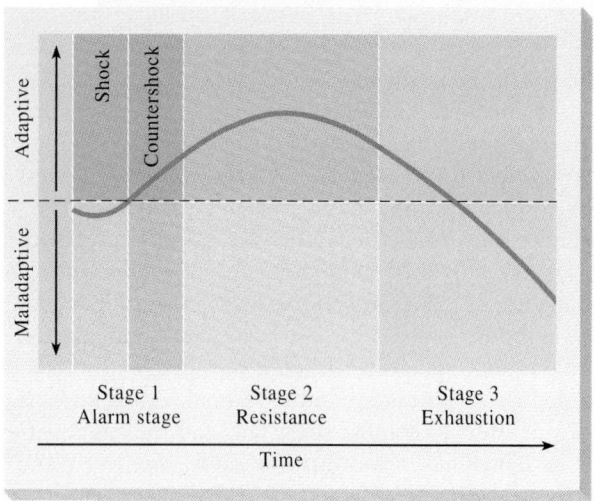

FIGURE 14.3

Selye's General Adaptation Syndrome
The general adaptation syndrome (GAS) is the typical series of
responses individuals have to stress. In the first stage (alarm), the
body enters a temporary state of shock, a time when resistance to
stress is below normal. Then a rebound called "countershock"
occurs, in which resistance to stress begins to pick up. Not much
later, the individual moves into the second state (resistance),
during which resistance to stress is intensified in an all-out effort
to combat stress. If the effort fails and stress persists, the
individual moves into the third and final stage (exhaustion),
when wear and tear on the body worsens, the person may
collapse in a state of exhaustion, and vulnerability to disease
increases.

From H. Selye, *The Stress of Life.* Copyright © 1976 McGraw-Hill, Inc. Reprinted by permission of
McGraw-Hill, Inc.

Not all stress is bad, though. **Eustress** is *Selye's term
for the positive features of stress.* Competing in an athletic
event, writing an essay, or pursuing someone who is attractive requires the body to expend energy. Selye does not say
we should avoid these fulfilling experiences in life, but he
does emphasize that we should minimize their wear and
tear on our bodies.

One of the main criticisms of Selye's view is that
human beings do not always react to stress in the uniform way he proposed. There is much more to understanding stress in humans than knowing their physical
reactions to it. We also need to know about their physical makeup, their perceptions, their personalities, and
the contexts in which the stressors occur (Seiffge-
Krenke, 1995).

Cognitive Factors in Stress

Most of us think of stress as environmental events that
place demands on our lives, such as losing one's notes
from a class, being yelled at by a friend, failing a test, or
being in a car wreck. While there are some common ways
we all experience stress, not everyone perceives the same
events as stressful. For example, one person may perceive
an upcoming job interview as threatening, while another
person may perceive it as challenging. One person may
perceive a D grade on a paper as threatening, another person may perceive the same grade as challenging. To some
degree, then, what is stressful depends on how people cognitively appraise and interpret events. This view has been
championed by Richard Lazarus (1966, 1991, 1993b;
Lazarus & Folkman, 1984). **Cognitive appraisal** *is
Lazarus's term to describe individuals' interpretation of
events in their lives as harmful, threatening, or challenging,
and their determination of whether they have the resources to
effectively cope with the event.*

In Lazarus's view, events are appraised in two steps:
primary appraisal and secondary appraisal. In *primary appraisal,* individuals interpret whether an event involves
harm or loss that has already occurred, a *threat* of some future danger, or a *challenge* to be overcome. *Harm* is the individual's appraisal of the damage the event has already
inflicted. For example, if you overslept yesterday and
missed an exam, the harm has already been done. *Threat* is
the individual's appraisal of potential future damage an
event may bring. For example, missing the exam may lower
the instructor's opinion of you and increase the probability
you will get a low grade in the course at the end of the semester. *Challenge* is the individual's appraisal of the potential to overcome the adverse circumstances of an event and
ultimately to profit from it. For example, a student may use
missing the exam as an opportunity to become acquainted
with the instructor and actually benefit from what initially
appeared to be a hopelessly bad circumstance.

> *The ultimate measure of a man is not where he stands in
> moments of comfort and convenience, but where he stands
> at times of challenge and controversy.*
>
> **Martin Luther King, Jr.**

After individuals cognitively appraise an event for its
harm, threat, or challenge, Lazarus says that they subsequently engage in secondary appraisal. In *secondary appraisal,* individuals evaluate their resources and determine
how effectively they can be used to cope with the event. This
appraisal is called *secondary* because it comes after primary
appraisal and depends on the degree to which the event has
been appraised as harmful, threatening, or challenging. Coping involves a wide range of potential strategies, skills, and
abilities for effectively managing stressful events. In the example of missing an exam, if you learn that a makeup will be
given 2 days later, you may not experience much stress since
you already have studied for the exam and have several

additional days to study for it. But if the instructor says that you have to write a lengthy paper for missing the test, you may cognitively appraise your situation and determine that this additional requirement places considerable demands on your time and wonder whether you will be able to meet the requirement. In this case, your secondary appraisal indicates a more stressful situation than simply having to take a makeup test several days later (Sears & others, 1993).

Lazarus believes an individual's experience of stress is a balance of primary and secondary appraisal. When harm and threat are high, and challenge and resources are low, stress is likely to be high; when harm and threat are low, and challenge and resources are high, stress is more likely to be low.

Personality Factors in Stress

Do you have certain personality characteristics that help you cope effectively with stress? Do other characteristics make you more vulnerable to stress? Three important candidates are the Type A behavior pattern, the Type C personality, and hardiness.

Type A Behavior Pattern

In the late 1950s a secretary for two California cardiologists, Meyer Friedman and Ray Rosenman, observed that the chairs in their waiting rooms were tattered and worn, but only on the front edge. The cardiologists had noticed the impatience of their cardiac patients, who often arrived exactly on time for an appointment and were in a great hurry to leave. Subsequently they conducted a study of 3,000 healthy men between the ages of 35 and 59 over a period of 8 years (Friedman & Rosenman, 1974). During the 8 years, one group of men had twice as many heart attacks or other forms of heart disease as anyone else. And autopsies of the men who died revealed that this same group had coronary arteries that were more obstructed than other men. Friedman and Rosenman described the coronary-disease group as characterized by **Type A behavior pattern,** *a cluster of characteristics—being excessively competitive, hard-driven, impatient, and hostile—thought to be related to the incidence of heart disease.*

However, further research on the link between Type A behavior and coronary disease indicates that the association is not as strong as Friedman and Rosenman believed (Williams, 1989). Researchers have examined the different components of Type A behavior, such as hostility, to determine a more precise link with coronary risk. People who are hostile or consistently turn anger inward, it turns out, are more likely to develop heart disease. Such people have been labeled "hot reactors," meaning they have intense physiological reactions to stress—their hearts race, their breathing quickens, and their muscles tense up—which could lead to heart disease. Redford Williams (1989), a leading researcher in charting the behavioral and

TYPE Z BEHAVIOR

Drawing by D. Reilly; © 1987 The New Yorker Magazine, Inc.

psychological dimensions of heart disease, believes each of us has the ability to control our anger and develop more trust in others, which he believes will reduce the risk for heart disease.

Type C Behavior

Type C behavior *refers to the cancer-prone personality, which consists in being inhibited, uptight, emotionally inexpressive, and otherwise constrained. This type of person is more likely to develop cancer than more expressive people are* (Temoshok & Dreher, 1992). The concept of Type C behavior fits with the findings of stress and health researchers that holding in one's problems and being inhibited about talking with others about problems can impair one's health.

Hardiness

Hardiness *is a personality style characterized by a sense of commitment (rather than alienation), control (rather than powerlessness), and a perception of problems as challenges (rather than threats).* In the Chicago Stress Project, male business managers 32 to 65 years of age were studied over a 5-year period. During the 5 years, most of the managers experienced stressful events, such as divorce, job transfers, the death of a close friend, inferior performance evaluations at work, and working at a job with an unpleasant boss. In one study, managers who developed an illness (ranging from the flu to a heart attack) were compared with those who did not (Kobasa, Maddi, & Kahn, 1982). The latter group was more likely to have a hardy personality. Another study investigated whether or not hardiness along with exercise and social support buffered stress and reduced illness in executives' lives (Kobasa & others, 1985). When all three factors were present in an executive's life, the level of illness dropped dramatically. This suggests the power of multiple buffers of stress, rather than a single buffer, in maintaining health. Still at issue, however, is the significance of the various components of hardiness (Feshbach & Wiener, 1991).

Biological, Cognitive, and Personality Factors in Stress

Stress is the way we respond to circumstances that threaten us and tax our coping abilities. Selye's general adaptation syndrome (GAS) describes the common effects of stress on the body. Stress is described as the wear and tear on the body due to the demands placed on it, according to Selye. This involves three stages—alarm, resistance, and exhaustion. Not all stress is bad; Selye calls good stress eustress. Critics argue that humans do not always respond as uniformly as Selye envisioned and that we also need to know about such factors as an individual's coping strategies.

Lazarus believes that stress depends on how individuals cognitively appraise and interpret events. Cognitive appraisal is Lazarus's term for individuals' interpretation of events in their lives as harmful, threatening, or challenging (primary appraisal) and their determination of whether they have the resources to cope effectively with the event (secondary appraisal).

Personality factors that are related to stress include Type A behavior, Type C personality, and hardiness. The Type A behavior pattern refers to a cluster of characteristics—being excessively competitive, hard-driven, impatient, and hostile—thought to be related to heart disease. The Type A pattern is controversial, with some researchers arguing that only specific components of the cluster, such as hostility, are associated with heart disease. Type C behavior refers to the cancer-prone personality, which consists of being inhibited, uptight, emotionally inexpressive, and otherwise constrained. Hardiness is a personality style characterized by commitment, control, and a perception of problems as challenges rather than threats. Hardiness buffers stress and is related to reduced illness.

Environmental Factors in Stress

Many circumstances, large and small, can produce stress in our lives. In some instances, cataclysmic events such as war, an automobile accident, a fire, or the death of a loved one produce stress. In others, the everyday pounding of being overloaded with work, of being frustrated in an unhappy relationship, or of living in poverty produce stress. What makes some situations stressful and others less so?

Overload, Conflict, and Frustration

Overload *happens when stimuli become so intense that we can no longer cope with them.* For example, persistent high levels of noise overload our adaptability. Overload can occur with work as well. How often have you said to yourself, "There are not enough hours in the day to do all I have to do." In today's computer age, we are especially faced with information overload. It is easy to develop the stressful feeling that we don't know as much about a topic as we should, even if we are a so-called expert.

Today the buzzword for overload is **burnout,** *a hopeless, helpless feeling brought about by relentless work-related stress. Burnout leaves its sufferers in a state of physical and emotional exhaustion that includes chronic fatigue and low energy.* Burnout usually occurs not because of one or two traumatic events but because of a gradual accumulation of heavy, work-related stress. Burnout is most likely to occur among individuals who deal with others in highly emotional situations (such as nurses and social workers) but have only limited control over altering their clients'/patients' outcomes (Goldberger & Breznitz, 1993).

On a number of college campuses, burnout, reaching a rate of 25 percent at some schools, is the most frequent reason students leave school before earning their degrees. Dropping out of college for a semester or two used to be considered a sign of weakness. Now it is more accepted and is sometimes called "stopping out" because the student fully intends to return; counselors may actually encourage some students who feel overwhelmed with stress to take a break from college. Before recommending "stopping out" though, most counselors first suggest that the student examine ways to reduce overload and possible coping strategies that would allow the student to remain in school. The simple strategy of taking a reduced or better-balanced class load sometimes works, for example. Most college counseling services have professionals who can effectively work with students to alleviate the sense of being overloaded and overwhelmed by life.

Stimuli not only overload us, but they also can be a source of conflict. Conflict occurs when we must decide between two or more incompatible stimuli. Three major types of conflict are approach/approach, avoidance/avoidance, and approach/avoidance. The **approach/approach conflict** *is a conflict in which the individual must choose between two attractive stimuli or circumstances.* Should you go to a movie or watch a video at home? Do you buy a Corvette or a Porsche? The approach/approach conflict is the least stressful of the three types of conflict because either choice leads to a positive result, even though choosing one over the other means you miss out on the positive experience of the other.

Stress can exist in dramatically different contexts. For example, life on the farm can be stressful based on economic hardship and social isolation. In one recent investigation, economic hardship in Iowa brought on by crisis in the agricultural industry was associated with inconsistent parenting, as well as increased drug use by adolescents (Lempers, Clarke-Lempers, & Simons, 1989). Contexts that are geared toward technology can also be stressful. Sometimes stimuli become so intense that we become overloaded and can cope no longer. In today's information age, we are especially faced with information overload. It is easy to develop the overwhelming feeling that we don't know as much about a topic as we should, a circumstance that produces what has been dubbed "information anxiety."

The **avoidance/avoidance conflict** *is a conflict in which the individual must choose between two unattractive stimuli or circumstances.* Will you go to the dentist to have a bad tooth pulled or endure the toothache? Do you go through the stress of giving an oral presentation in class or not show up and get a zero? You want to avoid both, but in each case, you must choose one. Obviously these conflicts are more stressful than having the luxury of having two enticing choices. In many instances, we delay our decision about the avoidance/avoidance conflict until the last possible moment, perhaps in hopes that other options will present themselves.

The **approach/avoidance conflict** *is a conflict involving a single stimulus or circumstance that has both positive and negative characteristics.* Let's say you really like the person you are going with and are thinking about getting married. On the one hand, you are attracted by the steady affection and love that marriage might bring, but, on the other hand, marriage is a commitment you might not feel ready to make. You look at a menu and face a dilemma— the double chocolate delight would be sumptuous, but is it worth the extra pound of weight? Our world is full of approach/avoidance conflicts and they can be highly stressful. In these circumstances, we often vacillate before deciding (Miller, 1959).

Frustration is another circumstance that produces stress. **Frustration** *refers to any situation in which a person cannot reach a desired goal.* If we want something and cannot have it, we feel frustrated. Our world is full of frustrations that build up to make our life more stressful—not having enough money to buy the car we want, not getting promoted at work, not getting an A average, being delayed for an important appointment by traffic, and being rejected by a friend. Failures and losses are especially frustrating— not getting grades that are high enough to get into medical school or losing someone we are closely attached to through death, for example. Sometimes the frustrations we experience are major life events, as in the cases of divorce and death. At other times, the accumulation of daily hassles may make us feel as though we're being nibbled to death by ducks.

Responses to frustration vary. When something blocks you from achieving a desired goal or outcome, you can change your goal and *give up*. You can *devalue* the goal. You can *circumvent* the frustration by reaching the goal using some other path. You can *aggress* against the frustration, which might or might not lead to the desired goal. Finally, you can *persist* on the same path toward your goal, gradually adapting to the frustration or eroding the frustrating elements of the situation. In this light, it is easy to understand the positive aspect of frustration. Learning to cope with frustrating circumstances can help us learn to delay gratification and develop patience.

Life Events and Daily Hassles

Think about your life. What events have created the most stress for you? A change in financial status, getting fired at work, a divorce, the death of someone you loved, a personal injury? And what about the everyday circumstances of your life? What hassles you the most? Not having enough time to study, arguing with your significant other, not getting enough credit for the work you do at your job?

Researchers have proposed that significant life events are a major source of stress and loosely have linked such life events with illnesses. The effects of individual life events, such as a tornado or volcanic eruption, can be evaluated, or

Making (or Remaking) the Grade

You studied all night for the exam. You thought you knew the material. The questions seemed a little tricky, but you finished the test and turned it in. When you got back a *D,* you were extremely frustrated. Can you apply the principles involved in frustration to predict some probable outcomes in this frustrating circumstance? Which option would you really choose?

· You could withdraw from the class and abandon the goal.
· You could persist in the course and commit to studying even harder.
· You could devalue the experience by making hostile comments in public about the professor's ability to create valid questions.

· You could physically aggress against the source of the frustration—the professor. (Bad idea.)
· You could attempt to switch sections of the course or ask to do work for extra credit, continuing to pursue the goal, by way of a different path.

Note that some of these responses, which demonstrate your ability to *apply psychological concepts to enhance personal adaptation,* are clearly more adaptive than others.

the effects of *clusters* of events can be studied. Thomas Holmes and Richard Rahe (1967) devised a scale to measure clusters of life events and their possible impact on illness in the context of the United States. Their widely used Social Readjustment Rating Scale includes events ranging from the death of a spouse (100 stress points) to minor violations of the law (11 stress points).

People who experience clusters of stressful life events, such as divorce, being fired from a job, or sexual difficulties, are more likely to become ill (Maddi, 1989); however, the ability to predict illness from life events alone is modest. Total scores on life-events scales such as the Social Readjustment Rating Scale are frequently ineffective at predicting future health problems. A life-events checklist tells us nothing about a person's physiological makeup, constitutional strengths and weaknesses, ability to cope with stressful circumstances, support systems, or the nature of the social relationships involved—all of which are important in understanding how stress is related to illness. A divorce, for example, might be less stressful than a marriage filled with day-to-day tension. In addition the Holmes-Rahe scale includes positive events, such as marital reconciliation and gaining a new family member, which can also create stressors that must be faced. However, the changes that result from positive events are not as difficult to cope with as the changes that result from negative events.

Psychologists increasingly consider the nature of daily hassles and daily uplifts to gain better insight about the nature of stress (Lazarus & Folkman, 1984). It might be that the primary sources of stress are not life's major events but, rather, our daily experiences. Enduring a boring but tense job or marriage and living in poverty do not show up on scales of major life events; yet the everyday tension involved in these living conditions adds up to a highly stressful life and in some cases psychological disturbance or illness.

How about your own life? What are the biggest hassles? One study showed that the most frequent daily hassles of college students were wasting time, being lonely, and worrying about meeting high achievement standards (Kanner & others, 1981). In fact, the fear of failing in our success-oriented world often plays a role in college students' depression. College students also found that the small things in life—having fun, laughing, going to movies, getting along well with friends, and completing a task—were their main sources of feeling uplifted.

Critics of the daily-hassles approach argue that some of the same problems with life-events scales occur when assessing daily hassles (Dohrenwend & Shrout, 1985). For example, knowing about a person's daily hassles tells us nothing about the body's resilience to stress, the person's coping ability or strategies, or how that person perceives stress. Further, the hassles scale has not been consistently related to objective measures of health and illness. Yet another criticism is that hassles can be conceived of as dependent measures rather than causes. People who complain about things, who report being anxious and unhappy, and who see the bad side of everything see more hassles in their daily lives. From this perspective, hassles don't predict bad moods; bad moods predict hassles. Supporters of the daily hassles concept contend that information about daily hassles can be used in concert with information about physiological reactions, coping, and how stress is perceived to provide a more complete picture of the causes and consequences of stress.

Canadian cross-cultural psychologist John Berry (*second from left*) has been an important pioneer in developing theoretical ideas and conducting research pertaining to how various dimensions of culture influence stress and coping. For example, he has described how a person facing acculturation can adapt to the pressures of change in four ways—assimilation, integration, separation, or marginalization.

Sociocultural Factors in Stress

Sociocultural factors influence the stressors individuals are likely to encounter, whether events are perceived as stressful or not, and the expectations individuals have about how stressors should be confronted. Among the sociocultural factors that influence stress are acculturation, socioeconomic status, and gender.

Acculturation and Acculturative Stress

Cultural subgroups in the United States can find contacts with mainstream society stressful. **Acculturation** *refers to cultural change that results from continuous, firsthand contact between two distinctive cultural groups.* **Acculturative stress** *refers to the negative consequences of acculturation.*

Canadian cross-cultural psychologist John Berry (1980) believes that a person facing acculturation can adapt to the pressures of change in four different ways—through assimilation, integration, separation, or marginalization. These four outcomes depend on how the individual answers two important questions: (1) Is my cultural identity of value and should I retain it? (2) Do I want to seek positive relations with the larger, dominant culture?

Assimilation *occurs when individuals relinquish their cultural identity and move into the larger society.* The nondominant group may be absorbed into an established "mainstream," or many groups may merge to form a new society (what is often called a "melting pot"). By contrast, **integration** *implies the maintenance of cultural integrity as well as the movement to become an integral part of the larger culture.* In this circumstance, a number of ethnic groups all cooperate within a larger social system ("a mosaic"). **Separation** *refers to self-imposed withdrawal from the larger culture.* If imposed by the larger society, however, separation becomes *segregation.* People might maintain their traditional way of life because they desire an independent existence (as in the case of "separatist" movements) or the dominant culture might exercise its power to exclude the other culture (as in the circumstances of slavery and apartheid).

Finally, there also is an option that involves a considerable amount of confusion and anxiety because the essential features of one's culture are lost but do not become replaced by those of the larger society. **Marginalization** *refers to the process in which groups are put out of cultural and psychological contact with both their traditional society and the larger, dominant society.* Marginalization often involves feelings of alienation and a loss of identity. Marginalization does not mean that a group has no culture but indicates that this culture may be disorganized and unsupportive of the acculturating individual.

As you can see, separation and marginalization, especially, are the least adaptive responses to acculturation. While separation can have benefits under certain circumstances, it may be especially stressful for individuals who seek separation while most members of their group seek assimilation. Integration and assimilation are healthier adaptations to acculturative pressures. But assimilation means some cultural loss, so it may be more stressful than integration, where selective involvement in the two cultural systems may provide the supportive base for effective coping.

Some researchers argue that individuals who belong to cultural subgroups can successfully negotiate the challenge of the subgroup as well as mainstream culture (LaFromboise, Coleman, & Gerton, 1993). They propose an **alternation model,** *in which individuals can develop bicultural competence without choosing one group over another or diminishing their own subgroup identification.* According to this model, their ability to adapt to different contexts can confer advantages over their monocultural peers.

Cross-cultural psychologists have established that acculturation effects are a factor in the development of coronary problems, emphasizing the role that culture plays in stress and health. As ethnic groups migrate, the health practices dictated by their cultures change while their genetic predisposition to certain disorders remains constant (Ilola, 1990). The Ni-Hon-San Study (Nipon-Honolulu-San Francisco), part of the Honolulu Heart Study, is an ongoing study of approximately 12,000 Japanese men in Hiroshima and Nagasaki (Japan), Honolulu, and San Francisco. In the study, the Japanese men living in Japan have had the lowest rate of coronary heart disease, those living in Honolulu have had an intermediate rate, and those living in San Francisco have had the highest rate. Accultura-

Vonnie McLoyd (*right*) has conducted a number of important investigations of the roles of poverty, ethnicity, and unemployment in children's and adolescents' development. She has found that economic stressors often diminish children's and adolescents' belief in the utility of education and their achievement strivings.

tion explains why the Japanese men's cholesterol level, glucose level, and weight all increased as they migrated and acculturated. As the Japanese men migrated farther away from Japan, their health practices, such as diet, changed. The Japanese men in California, for example, ate 40 percent more fat than the men in Japan.

Conversely Japanese men in California have much lower rates of cerebrovascular disease (stroke) than do Japanese men living in Japan. Businessmen in Japan tend to consume vast quantities of alcohol and chain smoke, two high-risk factors for stroke. As a result, stroke was the leading cause of death in Japan until it was surpassed by cancer in 1981. However, death rates from stroke for Japanese American men are at the same level as that of Anglo-American men. Researchers suspect that this level is related to a change in behavior. That is, Japanese American men consume less alcohol and smoke less than do their counterparts in Japan.

Socioeconomic Status

Poverty imposes considerable stress on individuals and families (Hoff-Ginsburg & Tardif, 1995; Huston, 1995). Chronic conditions such as inadequate housing, dangerous neighborhoods, burdensome responsibilities, and economic uncertainties are potent stressors in the lives of the poor. Ethnic minority families are disproportionately among the poor. For example, Puerto Rican families headed by women are 15 times more likely to live in poverty than are families headed by White men. Similarly, families headed by African American women are ten times more likely to live in poverty than families headed by White men (National Advisory Council on Economic Opportunity, 1980). Many people who become poor during their lives remain so for only 1 or 2 years. However, African Americans and female heads of household are

especially at risk for persistent poverty. The average poor African American child experiences poverty that will last almost 20 years (Wilson & Neckerman, 1986).

Poverty is also related to threatening and uncontrollable life events. For example, poor women are more likely to experience crime and violence than middle-class women are (Belle & others, 1981). And poverty undermines sources of social support that play a role in buffering the effects of stress. Poverty is related to marital unhappiness and to having spouses who are unlikely to serve as confidants (Brown, Bhrolochain, & Harris, 1975). Further, poverty means having to depend on many overburdened and often unresponsive bureaucratic systems for financial, housing, and health assistance that may contribute to a poor person's feelings of powerlessness.

Gender

Another sociocultural factor that plays a role in stress is gender. In the United States men and women differ in their longevity. Although men appear to have lower morbidity (fewer illness problems), they die younger than women. Life expectancy for men is 72 years; women can expect to live on the average of 79 years. Men and women tend to succumb to the same illnesses. Heart disease is the primary killer for both sexes.

Researchers are especially interested in how women's stress and health are affected by working outside of the home in demanding careers (Rodin & Ickovics, 1990). In almost all studies, employed women are healthier than non-employed women (LaCroix & Haynes, 1987). Researchers have found that women who stay at home and who perceive their lives as stressful and unhappy, who feel extremely vulnerable, and who engage in little physical activity are especially at risk for health problems (Verbrugge, 1989).

Motivation, Emotion, Health, and Personality

Determining why nonemployment is associated with higher stress levels is difficult—much like figuring out the causality in the old chicken-and-egg question. It may be that employment directly promotes health and reduces risk for women. On the other hand, it may be that women in poor health are unable to obtain or keep jobs.

Women and men have always had multiple roles, but researchers have found that women experience more conflict among roles and overload than men do (McBride, 1990; Wortman, Bernat, & Lang, in press). An important gender difference occurs in family responsibilities, which are detailed in chapter 10. Remember that even when both spouses work, wives perform a disproportionate share of child care and household tasks (Scarr, Lande, & McCartney, 1989). Interestingly, in spite of all the strain, the more roles a woman juggles, the healthier she seems to be (Baruch, Biener, & Barnett, 1987). Women who take on varied roles benefit from new sources of self-esteem, control, and social support, which, in turn, may improve both their mental and physical health (Rodin & Ickovics, 1990).

The nature and quality of a woman's experiences within a role are also important considerations in understanding stress and health. For example, roles with time constraints, irregular schedules, and little autonomy may jeopardize health. Therefore, women clerical workers, in particular, are more prone to health problems than other working women are (Haynes & Feinleib, 1980). In fact, contrary to the cultural belief that a high-powered career is more stressful to a woman's well-being, it seems that the more authority and autonomy a woman has on the job, the greater her sense of well-being (Baruch, Barnett, & Rivers, 1985).

Earlier in our discussion of social class and stress, we found that poverty is associated with increased stress and poorer health. Women are disproportionately among the poor. What's more, poor women face the double jeopardy of poverty and sexism. For example, women are paid less than men and are often denied opportunities to work because of their sex. The term **feminization of poverty** *refers to the fact that far more women than men live in poverty. Women's low incomes, divorce, and the resolution of divorce cases by the judicial system are the likely causes of the feminization of poverty.* Approximately one of every two marriages today will end in a divorce, meaning that far more women today than in the past must support themselves and, in many cases, one or more children as well. Further, women today are far less likely to receive alimony, or spousal support, than in the past. Even when alimony or child-support payments are awarded to a woman, they are poorly enforced.

As we saw in our discussion of socioeconomic status, ethnic minority women have especially high rates of poverty. These women face the extremely stressful triple jeopardy of poverty, racism, and sexism. Researchers must turn their attention to the mental health risks that accompany poverty and to ways that poor people, especially women, can cope more effectively with stress.

At this point, we have discussed the biological, cognitive, personality, environmental, and sociocultural factors involved in stress. Next, we will see that it also is extremely important to understand how to cope with stress.

REVIEW

Environmental and Sociocultural Factors in Stress

Overload, conflict, and frustration can lead to stress. Stress can be produced because stimuli become so intense and prolonged that we cannot cope. Three types of conflict are approach/approach, avoidance/avoidance, and approach/avoidance. Frustration occurs when we cannot reach a goal. Stress also may be produced by major life events or daily hassles. Life-events lists tell us nothing about how individuals cope with stress, their body strengths and weaknesses, and other important dimensions of stress. Daily hassles provide a more focused look, but their evaluation should include information about a person's coping ability and physical characteristics.

Acculturation is cultural change that results from continuous, firsthand contact between two cultural groups.

Acculturative stress is the negative consequences of acculturation. Acculturation takes place over time in a series of phases: precontact, contact, conflict, crisis, and adaptation. Four outcomes characterize an acculturating individual: assimilation, integration, segregation, and marginalization. The resilience and adaptation of ethnic minority groups can teach us much about coping and survival in the face of overwhelming adversity. Poverty imposes considerable stress on individuals. Chronic conditions, such as inadequate housing, dangerous neighborhoods, burdensome responsibilities, and economic uncertainties, are potent stressors in the lives of the poor. The incidence of poverty is especially high in ethnic minority families.

Gender is also a sociocultural determinant of stress. Of special interest is how the increased participation by women in the workforce has influenced their stress and health. Employment is associated with increased health among women. Even though women experience more conflict between roles and overload than men, women who engage in multiple roles are healthier because multiple roles expand potential resources and rewards. However, stressful roles with little autonomy and authority, such as being a clerical worker, often decrease women's health. Special concerns are the feminization of poverty and poverty among ethnic minority women.

COPING STRATEGIES

Coping is an extremely important part of adjustment. Just what do we mean by coping? **Coping** *is the process of managing taxing circumstances, expending effort to solve personal and interpersonal problems, and seeking to master, minimize, reduce, or tolerate stress and conflict.* We will explore coping strategies related to managing stress and illness.

Coping with Stress

Not everyone responds the same way to stress. Some individuals throw in the towel and give up when even the slightest thing goes wrong in their life. Others are motivated to work hard to seek solutions to personal problems and successfully adjust to even extremely taxing circumstances. A stressful event can be rendered considerably less stressful when a person successfully copes with it.

If you can't fight, and you can't flee, flow.

Robert Eliot

Problem-Focused and Emotion-Focused Coping

In our discussion of stress earlier in the chapter, we described Richard Lazarus's (1981, 1991, 1993) view that cognitive appraisal—interpreting events as harmful, threatening, or challenging, and determining whether one has the resources to effectively cope with the event—is critical to coping. Lazarus also believes that two general types of coping efforts can be distinguished. **Problem-focused coping** *is Lazarus's term for the cognitive strategy of squarely facing one's troubles and trying to solve them.* For example, if you are having trouble with a class, you might go to the study skills center at your college or university and enter a training program to learn how to study more effectively. You have faced your problem and attempted to do something about it. **Emotion-focused coping** *is Lazarus's term for responding to stress in an emotional manner, especially using defensive appraisal.* Emotion-focused coping involves using the defense mechanisms. In emotion-focused coping, we might avoid something, rationalize what has happened to us, deny it is occurring, laugh it off, or call on our religious faith for support. If you use emotion-focused coping, you might avoid going to the class. You might say the class doesn't matter, deny that you are having a problem, laugh and joke about it with your friends, or pray that you will do better. In one study, depressed people used coping strategies to avoid facing their problems more than people who were not depressed (Ebata & Moos, 1989).

But there are times when emotion-focused coping is adaptive. For example, denial is one of the main protective psychological mechanisms that enables people to cope with the flood of feelings that occur when the reality of death or dying becomes too great. In other circumstances, emotion-focused coping is maladaptive. Denying that the person you were dating doesn't love you any more when that person has actually become engaged to someone else is not adaptive. Denial can be used to avoid the destructive impact of shock, however, by postponing the time when you have to deal with stress. Over the long term, though, we are usually better off to use problem-focused more than emotion-focused coping.

Many individuals use both problem-focused and emotion-focused coping when adjusting to a stressful circumstance. For example, in one study, individuals said they used both problem-focused and emotion-focused coping strategies in 98 percent of the stressful encounters they face (Folkman & Lazarus, 1980). But aren't there other ways to cope than just using a combination of problem-focused and emotion-focused strategies?

Thinking, Changing, or Avoiding

Coping strategies can also be categorized as active-cognitive, active-behavioral, and avoidance (Billings & Moos, 1980). **Active-cognitive strategies** *are coping responses in which individuals actively think about a situation in an effort to adjust more effectively.* For example, if you have had a problem that involved breaking up with a girlfriend or a boyfriend, you may have coped by logically reasoning through why you are better off in the long run without her or him. Or you might analyze why the relationship did not work and use this information to help you develop better dating experiences in the future.

Active-behavioral strategies *are coping responses in which individuals take some type of action to improve their problem situation.* For example, to continue the example with dating, individuals who are having problems in dating may take the action of going to their college or university's counseling center, where they might be "coached" to improve their dating skills.

Stress is so abundant in our society that many of us are confronted with more than one stressor at the same time. An extremely valuable active-behavioral strategy for coping with stress is to try to remove at least one of the stressors from our life. For example, a college student might be taking an extra heavy course load, not have enough money to eat regularly, and have problems in a close relationship. Researchers have found that when several stressors are simultaneously experienced, the effects may be compounded (Rutter & Garmezy, 1983). For example, one study found that people who felt besieged by two chronic life stressors were four times more likely to eventually need psychological services than those who had to cope with only one chronic stressor (Rutter, 1979). The student facing the triple whammy of school, financial, and

Active-cognitive strategies

Prayed for guidance and/or strength
Prepared for the worst
Tried to see the positive side of the situation
Considered several alternatives for handling the problem
Drew on my past experiences
Took things a day at a time
Tried to step back from the situation and be more objective
Went over the situation in my mind to try to understand it
Told myself things that helped me feel better
Made a promise to myself that things would be different next
   time
Accepted it; nothing could be done

Active-behavioral strategies

Tried to find out more about the situation
Talked with spouse or other relative about the problem
Talked with friend about the problem
Talked with professional person (e.g., doctor, lawyer, clergy)
Got busy with other things to keep my mind off the problem
Made a plan of action and followed it
Tried not to act too hastily or follow my first hunch
Got away from things for a while
Knew what had to be done and tried harder to make things work
Let my feelings out somehow
Sought help from persons or groups with similar experiences
Bargained or compromised to get something positive from
   the situation
Tried to reduce tension by exercising more

Avoidance strategies

Took it out on other people when I felt angry or depressed
Kept my feelings to myself
Avoided being with people in general
Refused to believe that it happened
Tried to reduce tension by drinking more
Tried to reduce tension by eating more
Tried to reduce tension by smoking more
Tried to reduce tension by taking more tranquilizing drugs

FIGURE 14.4

**Examples of Active-Cognitive, Active-Behavioral, and
Avoidance Coping Strategies in Response to Stress**

relationship difficulties probably would benefit from removing one of the stressors—for instance, by dropping one class and taking a normal course load.

   Avoidance strategies *are responses that individuals use to keep stressful circumstances out of awareness so they do not have to deal with them.* Everything we know about coping suggests that avoidance strategies are extremely harmful to individuals' adjustment. In the example of having problems in dating, an avoidance strategy is to simply do nothing about it, with the result of never thinking about better ways to cope with dating problems and never taking any actions either. Examples of active-coping, active-behavioral, and avoidance strategies are shown in figure 14.4.

So far we have described two ways to classify coping responses: (1) problem-focused and emotion-focused, and (2) active-cognitive, active-behavioral, and avoidance. In general, of these different ways to cope, problem-focused coping, active-cognitive coping, and active-behavioral coping are the best strategies. Let's explore some other techniques that enhance the ability to cope.

Developing Self-efficacy

Self-efficacy—*the belief that one can master a situation and produce positive outcomes*—*can be an effective strategy in coping with stress and challenging circumstances.* Albert Bandura (1986, 1991) and others have shown that people's self-efficacy affects their behavior in a variety of circumstances, ranging from solving personal problems to going on diets. Self-efficacy influences whether people even try to develop healthy habits, how much effort they expend in coping with stress, how long they persist in the face of obstacles, and how much stress they experience.

   Let's look at several examples of how self-efficacy might work in coping. Overweight individuals will likely have more success with their diets if they believe they have the self-control to restrict their eating. Smokers who believe they will not be able to break their habit probably won't try to quit smoking, even though they know that smoking is likely to cause poor health and shorten their life.

   In sum, the belief that you can cope does not by itself eliminate all problems you might face. But the self-confidence that self-efficacy brings to challenging situations goes a long way toward overcoming difficult problems and allows you to cope with stress less emotionally (Eden & Aviram, in press; Sadry & Robertson, 1993).

Thinking Positively and Optimistically

*The world is round and the place that may seem like the end
may also be the beginning.*

Ivy Baker Priest

Thinking positively and avoiding negative thoughts is generally a good coping strategy when trying to handle stress more effectively. A positive mood improves our ability to process information more efficiently, makes us more altruistic, and gives us higher self-esteem. In most cases, an optimistic attitude is superior to a pessimistic one. It gives us a sense that we are controlling our environment, much like what Bandura (1986, 1991) talks about when he describes the importance of self-efficacy in coping. For example, in 1989, sports psychologist Jim Loehr (1989) pieced together videotaped segments of 17-year-old Michael Chang's most outstanding tennis points in the past year. Chang periodically watched the videotape—he always saw himself winning, he never saw himself make mistakes, and he always

Situation	Negative self-statement	Positive self-statements
Having a long, difficult assignment due the next day	"I'll never get this work done by tomorrow."	"If I work real hard I may be able to get it all done for tomorrow." "This is going to be tough but it is still possible to do it." "Finishing this assignment for tomorrow will be a real challenge." "If I don't get it finished, I'll just have to ask the teacher for an extension."
Losing one's job	"I'll never get another job."	"I'll just have to look harder for another job." "There will be rough times ahead, but I've dealt with rough times before." "Hey, maybe my next job will be a better deal altogether." "There are agencies that can probably help me get some kind of job."
Moving away from friends and family	"My whole life is left behind."	"I'll miss everyone, but it doesn't mean we can't stay in touch." "Just think of all the new people I'm going to meet." "I guess it will be kind of exciting moving to a new home." "Now I'll have two places to call home."
Breaking up with a person you love	"I have nothing to live for. He/she was all I had."	"I really thought our relationship would work, but it's not the end of the world." "Maybe we can try again in the future." "I'll just have to try to keep myself busy and not let it bother me." "If I met him (her), there is no reason I won't meet someone else someday."
Not getting into graduate school	"I guess I'm really dumb. I don't know what I'll do."	"I'll just have to reapply next year." "There are things I can do with my life other than going to grad school." "I guess a lot of good students get turned down. It's just so unbelievably competitive." "Perhaps there are a few other programs that I could apply to."
Having to participate in a class discussion	"Everyone else knows more than I do, so what's the use of saying anything?"	"I have as much to say as anyone else in the class." "My ideas may be different, but they're still valid." "It's OK to be a bit nervous; I'll relax as I start talking." "I might as well say something; how bad could it sound?"

FIGURE 14.5

Examples of How Positive Self-statements Can Be Used to Replace Negative Self-statements in Coping with Stressful Situations

saw himself in a positive mood. Several months later Chang became the youngest male to win the French Open Tennis Championship.

Cognitive Restructuring and Positive Self-talk Many cognitive therapists believe the process of **cognitive restructuring**—*modifying the thoughts, ideas, and beliefs that maintain an individual's problems*—can be used to get people to think more positively and optimistically. **Self-talk (also called self-statements)**—*the soundless, mental speech we use when we think about something, plan, or solve problems*—*is often very helpful in cognitive restructuring.* Positive self-talk can do a lot to give you the confidence that frees you to use your talents to the fullest. Since self-talk has a way of becoming a self-fulfilling prophecy, uncountered negative thinking can spell trouble. That's why it's so important to monitor your self-talk.

Several strategies can help you to monitor your self-talk. First, at random times during the day, ask yourself, "What am I saying to myself right now?" Then, if you can, write down your thoughts along with a few notes about the situation you are in and how you're feeling. Your goal is to fine-tune your self-talk to make it as accurate as possible. Before you begin, it is important to record your self-talk without any censorship.

You can also use uncomfortable emotions or moods—such as stress, depression, and anxiety—as cues for listening to your self-talk. When this happens, identify the feeling as accurately as possible. Then ask yourself, "What was I saying to myself right before I started feeling this way?" or, "What have I been saying to myself since I've been feeling this way?"

Situations that you anticipate might be difficult for you also are excellent times to access your self-talk. Write down a description of the coming event. Then ask yourself, "What am I saying to myself about this event?" If your thoughts are negative, think how you can use your strengths to turn these disruptive feelings into more positive ones and help turn a potentially difficult experience into a success.

It is also useful to compare your self-talk predictions (what you thought would or should happen in a given situation) with what actually took place. If the reality conflicts

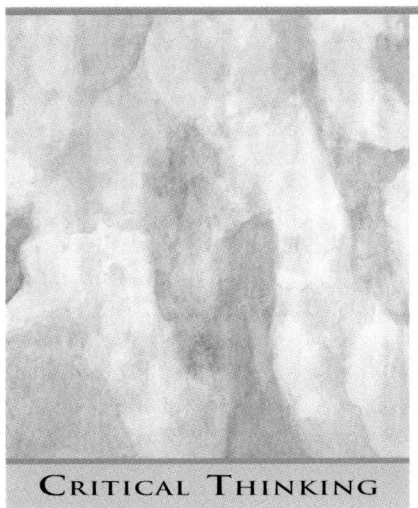

*The Power of
Positive Self-talk*

Suppose we design a simple study in which we intend to evaluate the effects of positive self-talk on performance in the psychology class. We recruit 60 volunteers and randomly assign them to two conditions. We will require the experimental group of 30 to use positive self-talk three times a day about their abilities in psychology. We'll require the control group simply to talk about their studies in psychology three times a day. We'll compare their final grade point averages in the end to see if there is a difference between the groups. How much confidence would you have that this experiment would produce a difference in performance between the two groups? Justify your answer; this should illustrate

your ability to *evaluate the validity of claims about behavior.*

Although the experiment might seem like a good idea, there are many problems. How would we know that the volunteers did their assigned jobs? Volunteers might not spend equal time in using positive self-talk or talking about psychology. One intervention might be more credible than the other, thereby generating greater confidence in its effectiveness. Did you spot other problems with the design?

---

with your predictions—as it often does when your self-talk is in error—pinpoint where your self-talk needs adjustments to fit reality.

You are likely to have a subjective view of your own thoughts. So it is helpful to enlist the assistance of a sympathetic but objective friend, partner, or therapist who is willing to listen, discuss your self-assessment with you, and help you to identify ways your self-talk is distorted and might be improved. And examples of how positive self-statements can be used to replace negative self-statements in coping with various stressful situations are presented in figure 14.5.

Positive Self-illusion   For a number of years, mental health professionals believed that seeing reality as accurately as possible was the best path to health. Recently though, researchers have found increasing evidence that maintaining some positive illusions about oneself and the world is healthy. Happy people often have mistakenly high opinions of themselves, giving self-serving explanations for events, and have exaggerated beliefs about their ability to control the world around them (Taylor & others, 1988).

Humankind cannot bear very much reality.

T. S. Eliot

Illusions, whether positive or negative, are related to one's sense of self-esteem. Having too grandiose an idea of yourself or thinking too negatively about yourself both have negative consequences. Rather, the ideal overall orientation may be an optimal margin of illusion in which individuals see themselves as slightly above average (see figure 14.6).

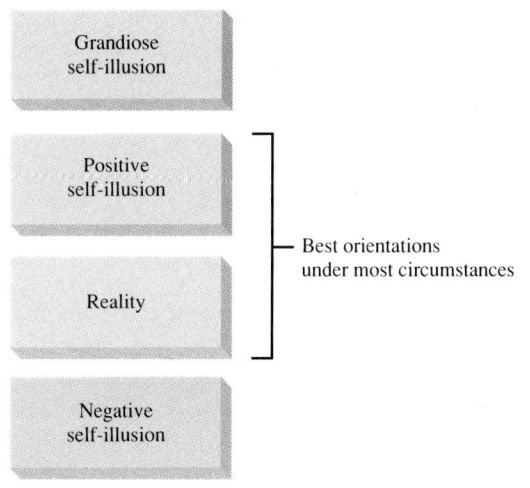

FIGURE 14.6

Baumeister's Model of Reality and Self-illusion
The most healthy individuals often have self-illusions that are slightly above their current level of functioning and ability. Having too grandiose an opinion of yourself or thinking negatively about yourself can have negative consequences. For some individuals, seeing things too accurately can be depressing. Overall, in most contexts, a reality orientation or a slightly above average self-illusion may be the most effective.

A negative outlook can increase our chances of getting angry, feeling guilty, and magnifying our mistakes. And for some people, seeing things too accurately can lead to depression. Seeing one's suffering as meaningless and random does not help a person cope and move forward, even if the suffering is random and meaningless. An absence of illusions may also keep individuals from undertaking the risky and ambitious projects that may yield the greatest rewards (Baumeister, 1989).

In some cases, though, a strategy of defensive pessimism may actually work best in handling stress. By imagining negative outcomes, people can prepare for stressful circumstances (Norem & Cantor, 1986). Think about the honors student who is worried that she will flunk the next test, or the nervous host who is afraid his lavish dinner party will fall apart. For these two people, thoughts of failure might not be paralyzing but instead might motivate them to do everything necessary to ensure that things go smoothly. By imagining potential problems, they may develop relevant strategies for dealing with or preventing negative outcomes. One study found that negative thinking spurred constructive thinking and feelings such as evaluating negative possibilities, wondering what the future held, psyching up for future experiences so they would be positive, feeling good about being prepared to cope with the worst, and forming positive expectations (Showers, 1986).

Developing an Optimistic Outlook

While some individuals at times use a strategy of defensive pessimism to improve their ability to cope with stress, overall a positive feeling of optimism is the best strategy. Indeed, a number of books have recently promoted the power of optimism in effective coping. *Learned Optimism* by Martin Seligman (1991) and *Positive Illusions: Creative Self-Deception and the Healthy Mind* by Shelley Taylor (1989) both provide excellent recommendations for ways to develop a more optimistic outlook on life that will help you cope more effectively.

How can you develop a more optimistic outlook? Seligman (1991) believes that the best tools for overcoming chronic pessimism lie in cognitive therapy, an approach that emphasizes more positive thinking by challenging self-defeating attitudes. Some cognitive therapists believe that optimistic coping skills can be assembled in six to twelve sessions, although Seligman believes that some individuals can master the techniques on their own. One of cognitive therapy's recommendations is to avoid ruminating and wallowing in self-pity when a bad event occurs. The tendency to repeatedly think and worry about negative circumstances and failures often prevents the development of positive coping strategies. Another recommendation of cognitive therapists is to dispute negative thoughts. Pessimists tend to use absolute, all-encompassing terms to describe defeats. They apply damaging labels to their behavior and pepper their language with words like *never* and *always*. Cognitive therapists advocate talking back to these negative thoughts in an optimistic style that limits self-blame and negative generalizations. According to Christopher Peterson, cognitive therapists are not telling people to be out of touch with reality, but rather to wear rose-colored glasses.

An optimistic outlook also may help individuals resist disease, as evidenced in a series of studies conducted by Peterson and his colleagues (Peterson & Stunkard, 1986). For example, college students were given the Attributional Style Questionnaire that evaluates an individual's optimistic and pessimistic tendencies. Then, their health was monitored over the next year. The pessimists had twice as many infections and doctors' visits as the optimists.

Social Support

Our crowded, polluted, noisy, and achievement-oriented world can make us feel overwhelmed and isolated. Now more than ever, we may need support systems such as family members, friends, and co-workers to buffer stress. **Social support** *is information and feedback from others that one is loved and cared for, esteemed and valued, and included in a network of communication and mutual obligation.*

The benefits of social support can be grouped into three categories: tangible assistance, information, and emotional support (Taylor, 1991). Family and friends can provide *tangible assistance* by giving individuals actual goods and services in stressful circumstances. For example, gifts of food are often given after a death in the family occurs, meaning that bereaved family members won't have to cook for themselves and for visiting relatives in a time when their energy and motivation is low. Individuals who provide support can also give *information* by recommending specific actions and plans to help the person under stress cope more effectively. Friends may notice that a co-worker is overloaded with work and suggest ways for him or her to manage time more efficiently or delegate tasks more effectively. In stressful situations, individuals often suffer emotionally and may develop depression, anxiety, and loss of self-esteem. Friends and family can provide *emotional support* by reassuring the person under stress that she or he is a valuable individual who is loved by others. Knowing that others care allows a person to approach stress and cope with stress with greater assurance.

Researchers consistently have found that social support helps individuals cope with stress. For example, in one study depressed persons had fewer and less-supportive relationships with family members, friends, and co-workers than did people who were not depressed (Billings, Cronkite, & Moos, 1983). In another study, the prognosticators of cancer, mental illness, and suicide included a lack of closeness to one's parents and a negative attitude toward one's family (Thomas, 1983). Widows die at a rate that is 3 to 13 times higher than the rate for married women, for every known cause of death. Close, positive attachments to others, both family and friends, consistently show up as important buffers of stress.

Consider Robert, who had been laid off by an automobile manufacturer when it was about to fold, then a decade later by a truck manufacturer, and more recently by yet another automobile manufacturer. By all accounts you would expect Robert to be down in the dumps or possibly feel that life had given him a bum deal. Yet he is one of the most well-adjusted individuals in the community. When asked his secret in the face of adversity and stress, he attributes his ability to cope to a wonderful family and some

Meditation has been an important dimension of Asians' lives for centuries.

great friends. Far more important than Robert's trials and tribulations is the support he receives from others, which helps him to handle stress.

In thinking about ways to improve your coping, it is important for you to recognize the potential sources of social support in your own environment and learn how to effectively draw on these resources in times of stress (Taylor, 1991). Sometimes your coping can also be improved by joining community groups, interest groups, or informal social groups that meet regularly.

Stress Management

Because many people have difficulty in managing stress themselves, psychologists have developed a variety of stress management programs that can be taught to individuals. We will study the nature of these stress management programs and evaluate some of the techniques that are used in them, such as meditation, relaxation, and biofeedback.

Stress management programs *teach individuals how to appraise stressful events, how to develop skills for coping with stress, and how to put these skills into use in their everyday lives.* Stress management programs are often taught through workshops, which are increasingly offered in the workplace (Taylor, 1991). Aware of the high cost of lost productivity to stress-related disorders, many organizations have become increasingly motivated to help their workers identify and cope with stressful circumstances in their lives. Some stress management programs are broad in scope, teaching a variety of techniques to handle stress; others are more narrow, teaching a specific technique, such as relaxation or assertiveness training. Some stress management programs are also taught to individuals who are experiencing similar kinds of problems—such as migraine headache sufferers or individuals with chronically high blood pressure. Colleges are increasingly developing stress management programs for students. If you are finding the experience of college extremely stressful and are having difficulty coping with taxing circumstances in your life, you might want to consider enrolling in a stress management program at your college or in your community. Let's now examine some of the techniques used in stress management programs.

Meditation   At one time, meditation was believed to have more in common with mysticism than with science. While meditation has become popular in the United States only in recent years, it has been an important part of life in Asia for centuries.

Meditation *is the system of thought and form of practice that incorporates exercises to attain bodily or mental control and well-being, as well as enlightenment.* The strategies of meditation vary but usually take one of two forms: either cleansing the mind to have new experiences or increasing concentration. **Transcendental meditation (TM)** *is the most popular form of meditation in the United States; it is derived from an ancient Indian technique and involves a mantra, which is a resonant sound or phrase that is repeated mentally or aloud to focus attention.* One widely used TM mantra is the phrase *Om mani padme hum.* By concentrating on this phrase, the individual replaces other thoughts with the syllables *Om mani padme hum.* In transcendental meditation the individual learns to associate a mantra with a special meaning, such as beauty, peace, or tranquility.

As a physiological state, meditation shows qualities of both sleep and wakefulness, yet it is distinct from them. It resembles the hypnagogic state, which is the transition from wakefulness to sleep, but at the very least it is prolongation of that state.

Early research on meditation's effects on the body showed that oxygen consumption was lowered, heart rate slowed down, blood flow increased in the arms and forehead, and EEG patterns were predominantly of the alpha variety—regular and rhythmic (Wallance & Benson, 1972). Other researchers have found support for the positive physiological changes that result from meditation and believe that meditation is superior to relaxation in reducing body arousal and anxiety (Dillbeck & Orme-Johnson, 1987; Eppley, Abrams, & Shear, 1989).

Relaxation   Many researchers acknowledge meditation's positive physiological effects but believe that relaxation is just as effective (Holmes, 1987). To learn how to put more relaxation into your life, try out the following exercise.

How relaxed are you right now? Would you like to feel more tranquil and peaceful? If so, you can probably reach that feeling state by following some simple instructions. First, you need to find a quiet place to sit. Get a comfortable chair and sit quietly and upright in it. Let your chin rest comfortably on your chest, your arms in your lap. Close your eyes. Then, pay attention to your breathing. Every time you inhale and every time you exhale, notice it and pay attention to the sensations of air flowing through your body, the feeling of

your lungs filling and emptying. After you have done this for several breaths, begin to repeat silently to yourself a single word every time you breathe out. The word you choose does not have to mean anything. You can make the word up, you could use the word *one,* or you could try a word that is associated with the emotion you want to produce, such as *trust, love, patience,* or *happy.* Try several different words to see which one works best for you. At first, you will find that thoughts intrude and you are no longer attending to your breathing. Just return to your breathing and say the word each time you exhale. After you have practiced this exercise for 10 to 15 minutes, twice a day, every day for 2 weeks, you will be ready for a shortened version. If you notice stressful thoughts or circumstances appearing, simply engage in the relaxation response on the spot for several minutes. If you are in public, you don't have to close your eyes, just fix your gaze on some nearby object, attend to your breathing and say your word silently every time you exhale.

The time to relax is when you don't have time for it.
Sydney J. Harris

Audiotapes that induce the relaxation response are available in most bookstores. They usually include soothing background music along with instructions for how to do the relaxation response. These audiotapes can especially help induce a more relaxed state before you go to bed at night.

Biofeedback   For many years operant conditioning was believed to be the only effective means to deal with voluntary behaviors such as aggression, shyness, and achievement. Behavior modification helped people to reduce their aggression, to be more assertive and outgoing, and to get better grades, for example. Involuntary behaviors such as blood pressure, muscle tension, and pulse rate were thought to be outside the boundaries of operant conditioning and more appropriate for classical conditioning. Beginning in the 1960s, though, psychologist Neal Miller (1969) and others began to demonstrate that people can control internal behaviors. **Biofeedback** *is the process in which individuals' muscular or visceral activities are monitored by instruments and information from the instruments is given (fed back) to the individuals so they can learn to voluntarily control the physiological activities.*

How does biofeedback work? Let's consider the problem of reducing an individual's muscle tension. The individual's muscle tension is monitored and the level of tension is fed back to him. Often the feedback is in the form of an audible tone. As muscle tension rises, the tone becomes louder; as it drops, the tone becomes softer. The reinforcement in biofeedback is the raising and lowering of the tone (or in some cases, seeing a dot move up or down on a television screen) as the individual learns to control muscle tension.

When biofeedback was developed, some overzealous individuals exaggerated its success and potential for helping people with problems such as high blood pressure and migraine headaches. But as more carefully designed investigations were conducted, the wildly enthusiastic early claims were replaced with more realistic appraisal of biofeedback's effectiveness (Schwartz, 1995). For example, some success in lowering blood pressure has been achieved, although it is easier to raise blood pressure than to lower it through biofeedback. Relaxation training and more general stress management programs are often just as effective in reducing blood pressure (Achmon & others, 1989).

The Value of Multiple Coping Strategies

Individuals who face stressful circumstances have many different strategies from which to choose. Often a good strategy is to choose more than one of them. Multiple coping strategies are often better than a single strategy alone. For example, people who have experienced a stressful life event or a cluster of such life events (such as the death of a parent, a divorce, or a significant income reduction) might seek social support, exercise regularly, reduce their drinking, and practice relaxation. These techniques represent adaptive, problem-focused strategies that emphasize changes in thought and action. See figure 14.7 for a summary of the positive methods for coping with stress and enhancing adjustment. These can serve as the basis for adopting some new strategies to manage stress more effectively.

Strategy	Elaboration
Engage in cognitive appraisal—challenges.	Work on interpreting events as challenges to overcome rather than as highly stressful forces that immobilize and emotionally blunt you.
Use cognitive appraisal—coping resources.	Evaluate your resources and determine how effectively they can be used to cope with the stressful event.
Engage in problem-focused coping.	Use the cognitive strategy of squarely facing your troubles and try to solve your personal and interpersonal problems.
Use emotion-focused coping.	Use this strategy sparingly, although such emotion-focused strategies as calling on one's religious faith can be helpful.
Engage in active-cognitive strategies.	Develop cognitive actions to cope with stress and adjust more effectively. Use such techniques as trying to see the positive side of situations, drawing on your past experiences, trying to step back from the situation to be more objective, and going over the situation in your mind and trying to understand it.
Engage in active behavioral strategies.	Try to take some behavioral action to solve the problem and reduce stress. Use such strategies as finding out more about the situation, enacting a plan, and seeking professional help.
Reduce or eliminate avoidance strategies.	Deal with stressful circumstances; don't avoid them. Don't keep your feelings to yourself, don't refuse to believe what happened, and don't try to reduce stress by drinking more, eating more, smoking more, or taking drugs.
Develop self-efficacy.	Develop a sense that your actions will produce favorable outcomes and expect to be able to master situations.
Engage in positive thinking and develop an optimistic outlook.	Eliminate self-defeating, pessimistic thinking; develop a positive outlook that your world is going to be better and then make it better.
Engage in self-control.	Work on controlling your negative emotions, such as anger and jealousy. Make an effort to keep yourself from getting into a frenzied state in which you can't think clearly about positive ways to cope. Develop patience and don't act too impulsively.
Seek social support.	Obtain emotional comfort from others—either friends, your spouse or partner, or a mental health professional.
Follow a disinhibition strategy, engage in some enjoyable activities, and use humor.	Open up and talk about your stressful experiences. Engage in at least some activities you enjoy doing instead of being immobilized and feeling sorry for yourself. Sometimes humor can help.
Use stress-management techniques or become involved in a stress-management program.	Develop a relaxation program, follow a better nutrition regimen, and engage in a more healthy lifestyle, or enroll in a workshop or program that teaches stress management.
Adopt multiple coping strategies.	Use more than one coping strategy by examining all of the different coping strategies and analyzing which combination would likely serve you best.

FIGURE 14.7

A Summary of Positive Ways to Cope with Stress and Adjust More Effectively

There is individual variation in how people cope, but for everyone, coping is an important dimension of adjustment. Coping is the process of managing taxing circumstances, expending effort to solve personal and interpersonal problems, and seeking to master, minimize, reduce or tolerate stress. A stressful event can be rendered considerably less stressful when a person copes with it.

According to Lazarus, cognitive appraisal and problem-focused coping are important aspects of effectively coping with stress. Active-cognitive and active-behavioral strategies are preferred coping strategies; avoidance is not. Other positive ways to cope include developing self-efficacy; engaging in positive thinking and developing an optimistic outlook; seeking social support; using stress management techniques or becoming involved in a stress management program; and adopting multiple coping strategies.

Self-efficacy—the belief that one can master a situation and produce positive outcomes—can be an effective strategy in coping with stress. Self-efficacy provides individuals with self-confidence, influencing whether some people ever even get started in trying to develop better health habits. Judgments about self-efficacy also influence how much effort individuals expend in coping with stress, how long they persist in the face of obstacles and how much stress they experience. Many cognitive therapists believe that cognitive restructuring can get people to think more positively and optimistically. Self-talk (also called self-statements) is often helpful in cognitive restructuring. Since self-talk has a way of becoming a self-fulfilling prophecy, uncountered negative thinking can spell trouble. That's why it is important to monitor your self-talk and replace negative self-statements with positive ones. Positive self-illusions can improve an individual's coping, but it is important to guard against unrealistic expectations. While some people use the strategy of defensive pessimism effectively, overall a feeling of optimism is the best strategy. An optimistic outlook can help individuals resist disease. Social support is information and feedback from others that one is loved and cared for, esteemed and valued, and included in a network of communication and mutual obligation. Three important benefits of social support are: tangible assistance, information, and emotional support. Researchers have consistently found that social support helps individuals to cope more effectively with stress.

Stress management programs teach individuals how to appraise stressful events, how to develop skills for coping with stress, and how to put these skills into use in their everyday lives. Stress management programs are often taught through workshops. Among the techniques that are taught in stress management workshops are meditation, relaxation, and biofeedback. Meditation is a system of thought that incorporates exercises to attain bodily or mental control and well-being, as well as enlightenment. Transcendental meditation is the most popular form of meditation in the United States. Researchers have found that meditation reduces body arousal and anxiety, but whether more so than relaxation is debated. The "relaxation response" can be especially helpful in reducing arousal and calming a person. Biofeedback has been successful in reducing muscle tension and blood pressure.

Coping with Illness

Even if we manage stress effectively and practice good health habits, we cannot always prevent illness. How do we recognize, interpret, and seek treatment for the symptoms of an illness? What is a patient's role? How good are we at adhering to medical advice and treatment? We will consider each of these questions in turn.

Recognizing and Interpreting Symptoms

How do you know if you are sick? Each of us diagnoses how we feel and interprets the meaning of symptoms to decide whether we have a cold, the flu, a sexually transmitted disease, an ulcer, heart disease, and so on. However, many of us are not very accurate at recognizing the symptoms of an illness. For example, most people believe that they can tell when their blood pressure is elevated. The facts say otherwise. The majority of heart attack victims have never sought medical attention for cardiac problems. Many of us do not go to the doctor when the early warning signs of cancers, such as a lump or cyst, appear. Also, we are better at recognizing the symptoms of illnesses we are more familiar with, such as a cold or the flu, than of illnesses we are less familiar with, such as diabetes.

As you learned in chapter 7, on memory, we use schemas to interpret information about ourselves in our world. Our prior experiences with a particular symptom may lead us to interpret it based on the schema we have for that symptom. For example, an individual with a long record of sprained ankles may dispel a swollen ankle as simply another sprain, not recognizing that she has a more serious injury—a fracture. By contrast, an individual who has never had a sprained ankle may perceive the swelling as serious and pursue medical intervention.

"We sincerely regret the unnecessary surgery, and we're going to put back as much as we possibly can."

© 1991 by Sidney Harris—"You Want Proof? . . ." W. H. Freeman and Company.

Seeking Treatment

Whether or not we seek treatment for symptoms depends on our perception of their severity and of the likelihood that medical treatment will relieve or eliminate them. If a person's ankle is fractured so badly he cannot walk without assistance, he is more likely to seek treatment than if the fracture produces only a slight limp. Also, someone may not seek treatment for a viral infection if she believes that no drug is available to combat it effectively. By contrast, a person is more likely to seek treatment if she believes that a fungus infection on her foot can be remedied by antibiotics.

When people direct their attention outward, they are less likely to notice symptoms than when they direct their attention inward. For example, a woman whose life is extremely busy and full of distracting activities is less likely to notice a lump on her breast than is a woman who has a much less active life. People who have boring jobs, who are socially inactive, and who live alone are more likely to report symptoms than people who have interesting jobs, who have active social lives, and who live with others (Pennebaker, 1983). Perhaps people who lead more active lives have more distractions and focus their attention less on themselves than do people with quieter lives. Even for people who have active lives, situational factors influence whether they will be attentive to symptoms. In one experiment, joggers were more likely to experience fatigue and be aware of their running-related aches and pains when they ran on a boring course than when they ran on a more interesting and varied course (Pennebaker & Lightner, 1980). The boring course likely increased the joggers' tendency to turn their attention inward and, thus, recognize their fatigue and pain.

Belief systems are also a factor in responding to symptoms. For example, Western people generally maintain a very positive, confident attitude about their health care. That attitude has only strengthened with advances in technological interventions. Many critics suggest that overconfidence in technological prowess may encourage more use of medical intervention than is really necessary. In addition, physicians in the United States are trained to regard illness and death as enemies to be fought. Our "medicalization" of many of life's processes may prevent us from seeing them as natural parts of the cycle of life. For contrasting experiences in other ethnic traditions, see Sociocultural Worlds 14.2.

The Patient's Role

Shelley Taylor (1979) identified two general types of patient roles. According to her analysis, some hospitalized individuals take on a "good patient" role, others a "bad patient" role. In the **"good patient" role,** *a patient is passive and unquestioning and behaves "properly."* The positive consequences of this role include being well-liked by the hospital staff, who in turn respond quickly to the "good patient's" emergencies. Like many roles, however, the "good patient" is somewhat superficial, and Taylor believes that, behind the facade, the patient may feel helpless, powerless, anxious, and depressed. In the **"bad patient" role,** *a patient complains to the staff, demands attention, disobeys staff orders, and generally misbehaves.* The refusal to become helpless, and the accompanying anger, may actually have some positive consequences, because "bad patients" take an active role in their own health care. The negative side of "bad patient" behavior, however, may aggravate such conditions as hypertension and angina, and such behavior may stimulate staff members to ignore, overmedicate, or prematurely discharge the "bad patient."

How can the stress of hospitalization be relieved? Realistic expectations about the experience, predictable events, and social support reduce the stress of hospitalization (Spacapan, 1988). When doctors communicate clearly to their patients about the nature of the treatment procedures and what to expect when they are hospitalized, patients' confidence in the medical treatment also increases, and, as we learned in the earlier discussion of stress, the social network of individuals who deeply care about us goes a long way toward reducing stress. Visits, phone calls, cards, and flowers from family members and friends lift patients' spirits and improve their recovery from illness.

Health Care for African Americans, Latinos, Asian Americans, and Native Americans

As mentioned before, there are differences within ethnic groups as well as among them. This is just as true of health among ethnic groups as it is of, say, family structure. The spectrum of living conditions and lifestyles within an ethnic group are influenced by social class, immigrant status, social and language skills, occupational opportunities, and such social resources as the availability of meaningful support networks. All of these can play a role in an ethnic minority member's health. Psychologists Felipe Castro and Delia Magaña (1988) developed a course in health promotion in ethnic minority communities, which they teach at UCLA. A summary of some of the issues they discuss in the course follows.

Prejudice and racial segregation are the historical underpinnings for the chronic stress of discrimination and poverty that adversely affects the health of many African Americans. Support systems, such as an extended family network, may be especially important resources to improve the health of African Americans and help them cope with stress (Boyd-Franklin, 1989; McAdoo, 1993).

Some of the same stressors mentioned for African Americans are associated with migration to the United States by Puerto Ricans, Mexicans, and Latin Americans. Language is often a barrier for unacculturated Latinos in doctor-patient communications. In addition, there is increasing evidence that diabetes occurs at an above-average rate in Latinos, making this disease a major health problem that parallels the above-average rate of high blood pressure among African Americans (Gardner & others, 1984).

Asian Americans have a broad diversity of national backgrounds and lifestyles. They range from highly acculturated Japanese Americans, who may be better educated than many Anglo-Americans and have excellent access to health care, to

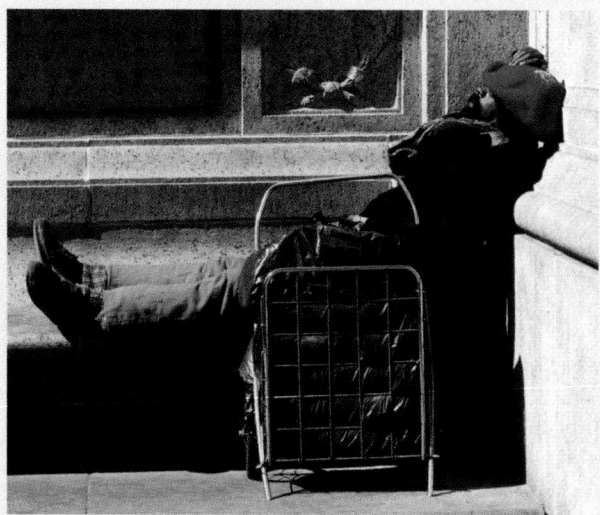

Prejudice and racial segregation may feel the chronic stress of discrimination and poverty that adversely affect the health of many African Americans.

Adherence to Medical Advice and Treatment

An estimated one-third of patients fail to follow recommended treatments. Adherence depends on the disorder and the recommendation. Only about 15 percent of patients do not follow doctors' orders for tablets and ointments, but more than 90 percent of patients do not heed lifestyle advice, such as to stop smoking, to lose weight, or to stop drinking (DiNicola & DiMatteo, 1984).

Why do we pay money to doctors and then not follow their advice? We might not adhere to a doctor's recommendations because we are not satisfied with the quality of the care we are receiving and because we have our own theories about our health and do not completely trust the doctor's advice. This mistrust is exacerbated when doctors use jargon and highly technical descriptions to inform patients about a treatment. Sometimes doctors do not give patients clear information or fully explain the risks of ignoring their orders. Sometimes patients might not communicate their concerns as clearly as they could, leaving doctors with an incomplete profile of the patient's concerns. To be motivated to stop smoking, to eat more nutritionally, or to stop drinking, patients need a clear understanding of the dangers involved in failure to adhere to the doctor's recommendation. Success or failure in treatment may depend on whether the doctor can convince patients that a valid, believable danger exists and can offer an effective, concrete strategy for coping with the problem (Lau, 1988).

Herbalists and folk healers continue to play an important role in the health care of Chinese Americans. For example, there are Chinese herbalists and folk healers in every Chinatown in the United States.

the many Indochinese refugees who have few economic resources and may be in poor health.

Cultural barriers to adequate health care include a lack of financial resources and poor language skills. In addition, members of ethnic minority groups are often unfamiliar with how the medical system operates, confused about the need to see numerous people, and uncertain about why they have to wait so long for service (Snowden & Cheung, 1990).

Other barriers may be specific to certain cultures, reflecting differing ideas regarding what causes disease and how it should be treated. For example, there are Chinese herbalists and folk healers in every Chinatown in the United States. Depending on their degree of acculturation to Western society, Chinese Americans may go to either a folk healer or a Western doctor first, but generally they will consult a folk healer for follow-up care. Chinese medicines are usually used for home care. These include ginseng tea, boiled centipede soup for cancer, and eucalyptus oil for dizziness resulting from hypertension.

Native Americans sometimes view Western medicine as a source of crisis intervention, quick fixes for broken legs, or cures for other symptoms; but they might not rely on Western medicine as a source for treating the causes of disease or for preventing disease. They also are reluctant to become involved in care that requires long-term hospitalization or surgery.

Both Navajo Indians and Mexican Americans rely on family members to make decisions about treatment. Doctors who expect such patients to decide on the spot whether or not to undergo treatment will likely embarrass the patient or force the patient to give an answer that may lead to canceled appointments. Mexican Americans also believe that some illnesses are due to natural causes whereas others are due to supernatural causes. Depending on their level of acculturation, Mexican Americans may be disappointed and confused by doctors who do not show an awareness of how to treat diseases with supposed supernatural origins.

Health-care professionals can increase their effectiveness with ethnic minority patients by improving their knowledge of patients' attitudes, beliefs, and folk practices regarding health and disease (Anderson, 1991; Martin, 1991). By integrating such information into Western medical treatments, health-care professionals can avoid alienating patients.

REVIEW

Coping with Illness

Many of us are not very accurate at diagnosing the symptoms of illness. When our attention is directed outward, we are less likely to detect symptoms than when our attention is directed inward. We use schemas developed through prior experience to interpret symptoms. Seeking treatment depends on our perception of the severity of the symptoms and the likelihood that medical treatment will reduce or eliminate the symptoms.

In the "good patient" role, individuals are passive and unquestioning and behave properly. In the "bad patient" role, individuals complain to the staff, demand attention, disobey staff orders, and generally misbehave. Realistic prior expectations, predictable events, and social support reduce the stress of hospitalization.

Approximately one-third of all patients do not follow treatment recommendations. Compliance varies with the disorder and the treatment recommendation, with our level of satisfaction with the quality of care we are receiving, and with our own theories about why we are sick and how we can get well. Clearer doctor-patient communication is needed for improved compliance.

We began this chapter with the story of Mort, whose life was seriously strained by a variety of stressors. Mort's score of 68 on the Stress Test diagnosed him as "seriously vulnerable" to stress. How high was your score? How vulnerable are you?

Well-constructed testing devices offer us an effective, systematic way *to make accurate observations, descriptions, and inferences about behavior.* For each test item, you indicated the degree to which the situation addressed by the item could contribute to your overall reactivity to stress; in effect, each item becomes a stress-related observation. The sum of your ratings produced your stress score.

Now what? If your test score suggests that you are vulnerable to stress, what kinds of predictions do you think you can make about your future physical and mental health? Have you already demonstrated particular patterns of "malfunctioning" that could be linked to the high degree of stress that you have reported?

After reading this chapter, you should have a new repertoire of ideas about how to address stress in more effective ways. In fact, scan the summary of positive coping strategies that you read about in figure 14.7. Pick three strategies that you think would be reasonable ways to improve your own coping style and reduce your vulnerability to stress. Think about the opportunities and challenges that would be involved in implementing these three strategies.

As a final reflection in this exercise, carefully examine the challenges that you identified in the implementation of your three strategies. Are these real challenges or convenient excuses? Just what would it take to encourage you to embark on a plan for a more healthful existence? Your implementation of a plan to improve your health would be a healthy example of *applying psychological concepts to enhance personal adaptation.*

OVERVIEW

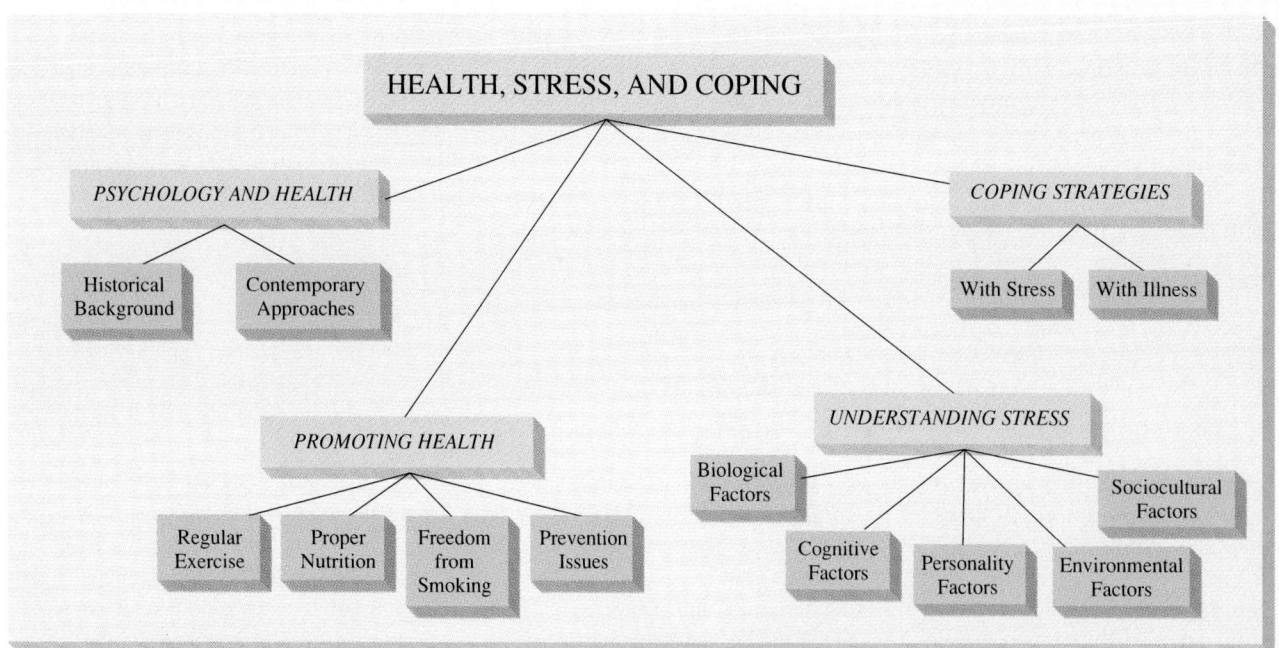

We began this chapter on health, stress, and coping by exploring the relation between health and psychology, including the historical background of the relation and contemporary perspectives. Then we turned our attention to promoting health—through regular exercise, proper nutrition, freedom from smoking, and prevention issues. Next, we sought to understand stress and its biological, cognitive, personality, environmental, and sociocultural factors. To conclude the chapter, we read about strategies for coping with stress and illness. Don't forget that you can obtain an overall summary of the chapter by again reading the in-chapter reviews on pages 504, 508, 513, 522, and 525.

PERSPECTIVES

Four main perspectives were emphasized in this chapter on health, stress, and coping: the neurobiological, sociocultural, behavioral, and cognitive. The neurobiological perspective appeared in the discussion of contemporary approaches relating health and psychology (pp. 489–490), exercise (pp. 491–495), nutrition (pp. 495–500), smoking (pp. 500–501), biological factors in stress (pp. 505–506), and biofeedback (p. 520). The sociocultural perspective was represented in the material on the historical background of relating health and psychology (p. 489), cultural factors in nutrition (pp. 499–500), pre-

vention issues in health care (pp. 501–504), ethnicity and nutrition (p. 497), and health care in different ethnic groups (p. 524). The behavioral perspective was reflected in the discussion of contemporary approaches to relating health and psychology (pp. 489–490), prevention issues in promoting health (pp. 501–504), environmental factors in stress (pp. 508–510), coping with stress (pp. 514–521), and coping with illness (pp. 522–525). The cognitive perspective was present in the discussion of cognitive factors in stress (pp. 506–507) and coping with stress (pp. 514–521).

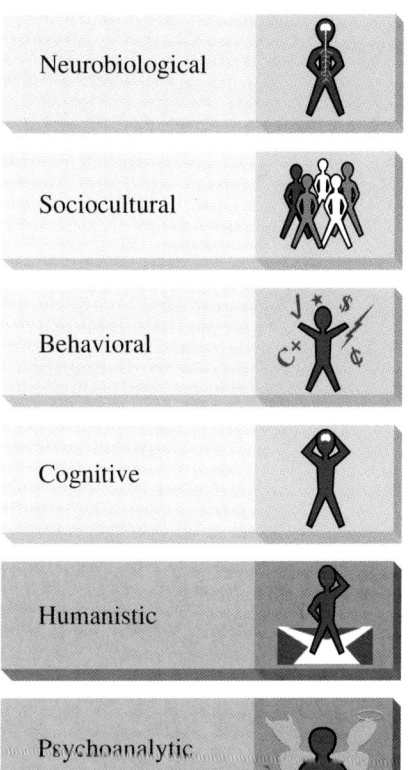

Neurobiological

Sociocultural

Behavioral

Cognitive

Humanistic

Psychoanalytic

KEY TERMS

health psychology A multidimensional approach to health that emphasizes psychological factors, lifestyle, and the nature of the health-care delivery system.   489

behavioral medicine A field closely related to health psychology that attempts to combine medical and behavioral knowledge to reduce illness and promote health.   489

psychoneuroimmunology The field that explores the connections among psychological factors (such as attitudes and emotions), the nervous system, and the immune system.   489

aerobic exercise Sustained exercise—jogging, swimming, or cycling, for example—that stimulates heart and lung activity.   491

set point The weight maintained when no effort is made to gain or lose weight.   495

basal metabolism rate (BMR) The minimal amount of energy an individual uses in a resting state.   495

anorexia nervosa An eating disorder that involves the relentless pursuit of thinness through starvation.   498

bulimia An eating disorder in which the individual consistently follows a binge-and-purge eating pattern.   498

stress The response of individuals to the circumstances and events, called stressors, that threaten them and tax their coping abilities.   505

general adaptation syndrome (GAS) Selye's concept of the common effects on the body when demands are placed on it. The GAS consists of three stages: alarm, resistance, and exhaustion.   505

eustress Selye's term for the positive features of stress.   506

cognitive appraisal Lazarus's concept of individuals' interpretation of events in their lives as harmful, threatening, or challenging, and their determination of whether they have the resources to effectively cope with the event.   506

Type A behavior pattern A cluster of characteristics—being excessively competitive, hard-driven, impatient, and hostile—thought to be related to the incidence of heart disease.   507

Type C behavior The cancer-prone personality, which consists of being inhibited, uptight, emotionally inexpressive, and otherwise constrained. This type of person is more likely to develop cancer than more expressive persons are.   507

hardiness A personality style characterized by a sense of commitment (rather than alienation), control (rather than powerlessness), and a perception of problems as challenges (rather than as threats).   507

overload The occurrence of stimuli so intense that the person cannot cope with them.   508

---

burnout A hopeless, helpless feeling brought about by relentless work-related stress. Burnout leaves its sufferers in a state of physical and emotional exhaustion that includes chronic fatigue and low energy.   508

approach/approach conflict A conflict in which the individual must choose between two attractive stimuli or circumstances.   508

avoidance/avoidance conflict A conflict in which the individual must choose between two unattractive stimuli or circumstances.   509

approach/avoidance conflict A conflict involving a single stimulus or circumstance that has both positive and negative characteristics.   509

frustration Any situation in which a person cannot reach a desired goal.   509

acculturation Cultural change that results from continuous, firsthand contact between two distinctive cultural groups.   511

acculturative stress The negative consequences of acculturation.   511

assimilation Individuals' relinquishing their cultural identity and moving into the larger society.   511

integration Maintenance of cultural integrity as well as movement to become an integral part of the larger culture.   511

separation Self-imposed withdrawal from the larger culture.   511

marginalization The process in which groups are put out of cultural and psychological contact with both their traditional society and the larger, dominant society.   511

alternation model The view that individuals can develop bicultural competence without choosing one group over another or diminishing their own subgroup identification.   511

feminization of poverty The fact that, increasingly, far more women than men live in poverty. Women's low incomes, divorce, and the way the judicial system typically resolves divorce cases are the likely causes of the feminization of poverty.   513

problem-focused coping Lazarus's term for the cognitive strategy of squarely facing one's own troubles and trying to solve them.   514

emotion-focused coping Lazarus's term for responding to stress in an emotional manner, especially using defensive appraisal.   514

active-cognitive strategies Coping responses in which individuals actively think about a situation in an effort to adjust more effectively.   514

active-behavioral strategies Coping responses in which individuals take some type of action to improve their problem situation.   514

avoidance strategies Responses that individuals use to keep stressful circumstances out of their awareness so they do not have to deal with them.   515

self-efficacy The belief that one can master a situation and produce positive outcomes; an effective coping strategy.   515

cognitive restructuring The modification of the thoughts, ideas, and beliefs that maintain an individual's problems.   516

self-talk (self-statements) The soundless mental speech people use when they think about something, plan, or solve problems; often helpful in cognitive restructuring.   516

social support Information and feedback from others that one is loved and cared for, esteemed and valued, and included in a network of communication and mutual obligation.   518

stress management programs Programs that teach individuals how to appraise stressful events, how to develop skills for coping with stress, and how to put these skills to use.   519

meditation A system of thought and form of practice that incorporates exercises to attain bodily or mental control and well-being, as well as enlightenment.   520

transcendental meditation (TM) The most popular form of meditation in the United States. TM is derived from an ancient Indian technique and involves a mantra, which is a resonant sound or phrase that is repeated mentally or aloud to focus attention.   520

biofeedback The process in which individuals' muscular or visceral activities are monitored by instruments and information is given (fed back) to the individuals so they can learn to voluntarily control these activities.   520

"good patient" role The role of being passive and unquestioning and behaving properly.   523

"bad patient" role The role of complaining to the staff, demanding attention, disobeying staff orders, and generally misbehaving.   523

THE NEW AEROBICS

(1970) by Kenneth Cooper. New York: Bantam.

The New Aerobics lays out Cooper's age-adjusted recommendations for aerobic exercise. The aerobic exercise program recommended by Cooper has been adopted by the United States Air Force, the United States Navy, and the Royal Canadian Air Force. The aerobics system is carefully planned to condition the heart, lungs, and body tissues of people who are either in fairly good health or poor health (the latter should especially have a physical exam before embarking on any exercise program). The aerobic program uses common forms of exercise—walking, running, swimming, cycling, handball, squash, and basketball—to achieve the desired results.

Cooper developed a simple, easy-to-follow aerobics point system that is age-adjusted to the capabilities of men, women, and children. To begin, Cooper recommends taking a 12-minute fitness test. The test is simple: How far you can run or walk in 12 minutes places you in one of five fitness categories, from very poor to excellent. Four to five workouts a week—such as running 2 miles at about 10 minutes a mile or less each of those days—will get you aerobically fit. Recently, Cooper has pointed out that if you just want to reduce your health risks but not be physically fit, you can accomplish this with a brisk half-hour walk four to five times a week.

Cooper's book is research based and easy to read, and if you are in only average or poor physical shape, Cooper's recommended program will reap physical and psychological benefits for you. More than any other individual, Kenneth Cooper is responsible for getting a lot of people off their couches and out on the walking or jogging track. His positive influence is even international. In Brazil, when people go out to run they call it "doing the Cooper." Another Cooper book we recommend is *The Aerobics Program for Well-Being.*

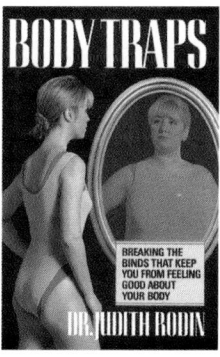

BODY TRAPS

(1992) by Judith Rodin. New York: William Morrow.

Body Traps focuses on the relation of a person's body to self-image and the destructive standards society has established for women's perceptions of their bodies. Rodin believes that we have become a nation of appearance junkies and fitness zealots. We spend more on beauty and fitness aids than on social services and education! She argues that good looks, appearance, and fitness have become the measures we use to evaluate our self-worth. This trend has gone so far that one deviation in our diet often spells the difference between confidence and despair, she says.

Rodin describes a number of different body traps we can fall into. The traps that cause us anguish over the way we look, anxiety over whether we are doing enough to be attractive, and shame for worrying about it. Rodin dispenses a number of recommendations for helping people avoid these body traps and developing more positive ways of relating to ourselves as we are.

This is a thoughtful, penetrating look at society's preoccupation with women's appearance and the unrealistic and harmful effects that preoccupation has produced. *Body Traps* is informative, well-written, and a helpful guide to what women's bodies mean to them.

THE NEW FIT OR FAT

(Revised Ed.) (1991) by Covert Bailey. Boston: Houghton Mifflin.

The New Fit or Fat describes ways to become healthy by developing better diet and exercise routines. Bailey argues that the basic problem for overweight people is not losing weight, which fat people do periodically, but in gaining weight, which fat people do more easily than those with a different body chemistry. He explores ways our body stores fat and analyzes why crash diets don't work. He explains the relation between fat metabolism and weight, concluding that the ultimate cure for obesity is aerobic exercise coupled with a sensible low-fat diet.

Originally published in 1977 as *Fit or Fat*, the 1991 edition is greatly expanded with new information on fitness lifestyles and recent scientific advances. A new chapter also answers readers' most frequently asked questions about Bailey's views on diet and exercise. This book offers solid, no-nonsense advice on how to lose weight and become more physically fit.

LEARNED OPTIMISM

(1990) by Martin Seligman. New York: Pocket Books.

Learned Optimism is one of the new breed of positive-thinking books, a breed that first began to appear in the late 1980s and has increased in number recently. The new breed is based on psychological research and gives specific strategies for optimistic thinking rather than the old breed of cheerleading books that were low on substance.

Seligman argues that optimism and pessimism are not fixed, inborn psychological traits, but rather are explanatory styles—habitual ways we explain things that happen to us. Pessimists, says Seligman, perceive defeat as permanent, catastrophic, and evidence of personal inadequacy; optimists, by contrast, perceive the same mishap as a temporary setback, something that can be controlled, and rooted in circumstances of luck. Seligman's positive message is that since pessimism is learned it can be unlearned. Included are self-tests to determine your levels of optimism, pessimism, and depression.

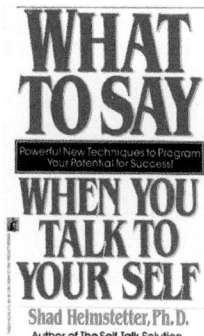

WHAT TO SAY WHEN YOU TALK TO YOUR SELF

(1986) by Shad Helmstetter. New York: Pocket Books.

What to Say When You Talk to Yourself examines the success literature and concludes that in all of the many recommendations there are some missing ingredients, which include permanent solutions and a word-for-word set of directions for self-programming an individual's mind. Helmstetter describes several types of self-talk, such as silent self-talk, self-speak, self-conversation, self-write, tape-talk, and creating your own self-tapes. He covers many self-talk problem solving strategies, how to change attitudes, how to change behaviors, and self-talk for different situations. You learn how to get started and how to create your own self-talk tape.

Unlike many authors of self-help books on coping and self-improvement, the author spells out the details of what to say to yourself to improve your life instead of just being a cheerleader.

BEYOND THE RELAXATION RESPONSE

(1984) by Herbert Benson. New York: Times Books.

Beyond the Relaxation Response is Herbert Benson's sequel to *The Relaxation Response.* A decade after he coined the term *the relaxation response,* Benson concluded that combining the relaxation response with another strategy is even more powerful in combating stress than the relaxation response alone. The other strategy is faith in a healing power either inside or outside of yourself.

Benson arrived at this conclusion because of his own clinical observations and studies of Tibetan monks in the Himalayas, which are described in detail in *Beyond the Relaxation Response.* This does not mean you have to believe in a certain dogma or a traditional religion. You can, but you also can achieve the desired result by having faith in yourself, or even in a state while exercising or eliciting the relaxation response. Benson tells you how to harness the power of faith in many different situations—while jogging or walking, swimming, lying in bed, or praying.

RESOURCES FOR PSYCHOLOGY AND IMPROVING HUMANKIND

American Public Health Association
    1815 15th Street
    Washington, DC 20005
    202–789–5600

This organization has available a number of books, manuals, and pamphlets on many different areas of health. It also publishes a newsletter on the delivery and support of health services in developing countries.

The LEARN Program for Weight Control (1988)
    by Kelly Brownell
    Dallas: American Health Publishers

This excellent book, written by a leading researcher, outlines an effective, healthy program for losing weight and maintaining the weight loss.

The New Aerobics for Women (1988)
    by Kenneth Cooper and Mildred Cooper
    New York: Bantam

This book tailors the concept of aerobic exercise to the capabilities and needs of women. It includes age-adjusted formulas for appropriate exercises that are tailored to a woman's lifestyle and current level of physical fitness.

Nutrition Education and Information
    1126 Sixteenth Street, NW, Suite 111
    Washington, DC 20036
    202–659–0074

This organization seeks to improve the public's knowledge of nutrition. It provides materials and guides for distribution and publishes books and pamphlets on effective nutrition.

Opening Up: The Healing Power of Confiding in Others (1990)
    by James Pennebaker
    New York: William Morrow

You learn why disclosing information about yourself to others can improve your health.

KNOWLEDGE OF AIDS RISK BEHAVIOR

SCORING

Give yourself one point for each correct answer. Any wrong answers should be clarified and corrected.

INTERPRETATION

If you missed more than four questions, you should gather more information about AIDS. Free pamphlets and

brochures with up-to-date information are available from your local health department and student health center. The correct answers to the test are

1 = F, 2 = T, 3 = T, 4 = T, 5 = F, 6 = F, 7 = F, 8 = F, 9 = F, 10 = F, 11 = F, 12 = F, 13 = T, 14 = F, 15 = T, 16 = T, 17 = T, 18 = F, 19 = F, 20 = T, 21 = F, 22 = F, 23 = T, 24 = T, 25 = F, 26 = F, 27 = F, 28 = F, 29 = T, 30 = T, 31 = T, 32 = F, 33 = F, 34 = F, 35 = T, 36 = T, 37 = T, 38 = T, 39 = T, 40 = F.

Personality

*Every person cries out to be
read differently.*

Simone Weil

THE STORY OF MARK TWAIN: A VISIT TO THE PUBLISHER

In the fall of 1890, Mark Twain decided to visit his publisher, George Putnam. According to Twain, the book clerk took one look at his clothes and formed some negative impressions about him that prompted the clerk to inform Twain somewhat harshly that Mr. Putnam "wasn't in." Twain knew it was a falsehood, so he decided to transact some unusual business with the clerk. He asked for a preferred volume, which the clerk retrieved and announced a price of three dollars for the transaction.

Then Twain announced that he was a publisher and requested that the clerk allow him the typical publisher's discount of 60 percent. The clerk appeared to be unmoved. Next Twain claimed that he was also an author and requested the discount reserved for authors of 30 percent. Twain observed that the clerk lost the color from his face. Finally Twain claimed that he also maintained his membership in the human race and suggested that the typical discount for such membership was 10 percent. Without a word, the severe-looking clerk produced a pencil from behind his ear and began calculating. The clerk deliberated for a moment and announced that he would have to refund fifteen cents to Twain because the publisher also offered a discount to seriously shy people.

This story about one of the legendary characters in American literature illustrates several principles related to the key ideas in the chapter on personality. We form judgments almost relentlessly about the personality of others based on how they look, how they dress, and how they behave. And it is quite easy to be wrong, as both Twain and the clerk so deftly illustrated—the clerk's misjudging Twain's commercial potential from his unimpressive dress and Twain's misjudging the clerk as humorless from his severe manner.

PREVIEW

In this chapter we will examine the formal systems of explanation that have evolved in Western cultures to describe personality. You will see that psychologists believe that personality is a property of the individual but disagree about the nature of personality. We will look at four perspectives on personality development: psychoanalytic, behavioral, cognitive, and humanistic. We will also explore various trait-based approaches and examine the influence of contexts on personality. We will conclude the chapter by reviewing various methods of personality assessment.

THE NATURE OF PERSONALITY

Capturing your uniqueness as a person is not an easy task. Most of us believe that we have some enduring personality characteristics. Psychologists define **personality** as *enduring, distinctive thoughts, emotions, and behaviors that characterize the way an individual adapts to the world.*

The term *personality* has many informal uses in our culture that are distinct from what psychologists are studying when they explore personality (Peterson, 1988). For example, we refer to Rosie as having "a great personality." In this sense, we positively evaluate something about her that goes beyond looks, possessions, intelligence, or status. She makes you feel good to be around her. On the other hand, we might describe Carolyn as having "no personality." This negative evaluation suggests that there may be little about Carolyn that makes her unique: no passions, no weird hobby or unusual ability, and little ability to engage others' attention. Celebrities have unique identities and are often referred to as "personalities." Whoopi Goldberg, Eddie Murphy, Lee Iaccoca, and David Letterman are well known not just for what they do, but for how they do it. They play roles in our culture that become identified with the personality characteristics they bring to the roles.

What Are You Really Like?

Try to come up with five or six characteristics that you think represent an enduring part of your makeup as a person. As you look at this list, consider the following about your self-reflection:

- Do you always behave in ways that are consistent with these traits?
- Would your closest friends agree with your characterization?
- How would those who don't like you describe you?
- Were your descriptions realistic or idealistic?

This exercise encourages you to *pursue alternative explanations to understand complex behavior.*

In the future everyone will be famous for fifteen minutes.

Andy Warhol

We also use the term *personality* to focus on distinctive characteristics—the ones that make us different from others. For example, we might describe Rachel as "holding grudges, just like her mother does." We tend to look at family members and compare ourselves for similar and dissimilar personality characteristics. This use of the term comes closest to what psychologists are interested in when they explore personality. Psychologists recognize that personality descriptions identify the essential characteristics of individuals and allow us to make subtle discriminations about the differences among us. Personality (*person*ality) does not exist apart from the person. It may help to think about personality as a blueprint or a map—a representation of the essential features that endear us to others or alienate others from us.

THEORIES OF PERSONALITY

Historically, psychologists have honored three theoretical perspectives—psychoanalysis, behaviorism, and humanism—as the dominant explanations for personality development. Cognitive psychology has also emerged as a viable theoretical framework that emphasizes information-processing aspects in explaining personality. Each perspective offers distinctive insights.

People have one thing in common: they are all different.

Robert Zend

The diversity of theories makes understanding personality a challenge. Just when you think one theory has the correct explanation of personality, another theory will make you rethink your earlier conclusion. To keep from getting frustrated, remember that personality is a complex, multifaceted topic and no single theory has been able to account for all its aspects; each theory has contributed an important piece to the personality puzzle. In fact, many pieces of information in different personality theories are *complementary* rather than contradictory. Together they let us see the total landscape of personality in all its richness.

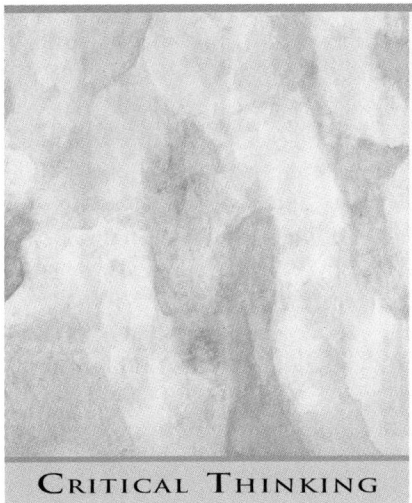

Many celebrities, such as Whoopi Goldberg, are called "personalities." They are well known, not just for what they do, but also for how they do it. Whoopi Goldberg's outgoing personality is a property of Whoopi Goldberg and is related to how she functions in the world. Of course, it is not just celebrities who have a personality. Each of us has a personality that is our property and is related to how we function in the world.

Psychoanalytic Perspectives

For psychoanalytic theorists, personality is unconscious—that is, beyond awareness—and heavily colored by emotion. Psychoanalytic theorists believe that behavior is merely a surface characteristic and that, to understand someone's personality, we have to look at the symbolic meanings of behavior and the deep inner workings of the mind. Psychoanalytic theorists also believe that early experiences with our parents extensively shape our personalities. These characteristics of personality were described by the original psychoanalytic theorist, Sigmund Freud.

Freud's Theory

Loved and hated, respected and despised—Sigmund Freud, whether right or wrong in his views, has been one of the most influential thinkers of the twentieth century. Freud was a medical doctor who specialized in neurology. He developed his ideas about psychoanalytic theory from his work with neurotic patients. He was born in Austria in 1856, and he died in London in 1939 at the age of 83. Freud spent most of his life in Vienna, but he left that city near the end of his career to escape Nazi anti-Semitism.

As the eldest child, Freud was regarded as a genius by his brothers and sisters and doted on by his mother. Later we will see that one aspect of Freud's theory emphasizes a young boy's sexual attraction for his mother; it is possible that he derived this belief from his own romantic attachment to his mother, who was beautiful and about 20 years younger than Freud's father.

In Freud's view, much more of the mind is unconscious than conscious. He envisioned the mind as a huge iceberg, with the massive part below the surface of the water being the unconscious part. Freud said that each of our lives

is filled with tension and conflict; to reduce this tension and conflict, we keep information locked in the unconscious mind. For Freud, the unconscious mind holds the key to understanding behavior. Freud believed that even trivial behaviors have special significance when the unconscious forces behind them are revealed. A twitch, a doodle, a joke, a smile, each may have an unconscious reason for appearing. They often slip into our lives without our awareness. For example, Allison is kissing and hugging Tyler, whom she is to marry in several weeks. She says, "Oh, *Jeff*, I love you so much." Tyler pushes her away and says, "Why did you call me Jeff? I thought you didn't think about him anymore. We need to have a talk!" You probably can think of times when such *Freudian slips* have tumbled out of your own mouth.

The Structure of Personality   Freud (1917) believed that personality has three structures: the id, the ego, and the superego. One way to understand the three structures is to imagine them as three rulers of a country (Singer, 1984). The id is king or queen, the ego is prime minister, and the superego is high priest. The id is an absolute monarch, owed complete obedience; it is spoiled, willful, and self-centered. The id wants what it wants right now, not later, The ego, as prime minister, has the job of getting things done; it is tuned into reality and is responsive to society's demands. The superego, as high priest, is concerned with right and wrong; the id may be greedy and needs to be told that nobler purposes should be pursued. It is important to think of these as processes and forces, however, not as concrete entities.

The **id** *is the Freudian structure of personality that consists of instincts, which are the individual's reservoir of psychic energy.* In Freud's view, the id is unconscious; it has no contact with reality. The id works according to the **pleasure principle,** *the Freudian concept that the id always seeks pleasure and avoids pain.*

It would be a dangerous and scary world if our personalities were all id. As young children mature, for example, they learn they cannot slug other children in the face.

Sigmund Freud is the father of psychoanalysis.

© 1991 by Sidney Harris—"You Want Proof? . . ." W. H. Freeman and Company.

They also learn they have to use the toilet instead of their diaper. As children experience the demands and constraints of reality, a new structure of personality is formed—the **ego,** *the Freudian structure of personality that deals with the demands of reality. The ego is called the executive branch of personality because it makes rational decisions.* Whereas the id is completely unconscious, the ego is partly conscious. It houses our higher mental functions—reasoning, problem solving, and decision making, for example. The ego abides by the **reality principle,** *the Freudian concept that the ego tries to make the pursuit of individual pleasure conform to the norms of society.* Few of us are cold-blooded killers or wild wheeler-dealers; we take into account the obstacles to our satisfaction that exist in our world. We recognize that our sexual and aggressive impulses cannot go unrestrained. The ego helps us test reality, to see how far we can go without getting into trouble and hurting ourselves.

> *If it were possible to talk to the unborn, one could never explain to them how it feels to be alive, for life is washed in the speechless real.*
>
> **Jacques Barzun, *The House of Intellect,* 1959**

The id and ego have no morality. They do not take into account whether something is right or wrong. In contrast, the **superego** *is the Freudian structure of personality that is the moral branch of personality. The superego takes into account whether something is right or wrong.* The superego is what we often refer to as the "conscience." Like the id, the superego does not consider reality; it doesn't deal with what is realistic, only with whether the id's sexual and aggressive impulses can be satisfied in moral terms. You probably are beginning to sense that both the id and the superego make life rough for the ego. Your ego might say, "I will have sex only occasionally and be sure to use an effective form of protection against pregnancy and sexually transmitted diseases." However, your id is saying, "I want to be satisfied; sex feels so good." Your superego is also at work: "I feel guilty about having sex."

Remember that Freud considered personality to be like an iceberg; most of our personality exists below the level of awareness, just as the massive part of an iceberg is beneath the surface of the water. Figure 15.1 illustrates this analogy and the extent of the unconscious part of our mind, in Freud's view.

Defense Mechanisms The ego calls on a number of strategies to resolve the conflict among its demands for reality, the wishes of the id, and the constraints of the superego. Through **defense mechanisms,** *the psychoanalytic term for unconscious methods of dealing with conflict, the ego distorts reality, thereby protecting itself from anxiety.* For example, when a person's ego blocks the pleasurable pursuits of the id, that person feels frustration. A diffuse state of distress ensues when the ego senses that the id is going to cause harm. This anxiety alerts the ego to resolve the conflict by means of defense mechanisms.

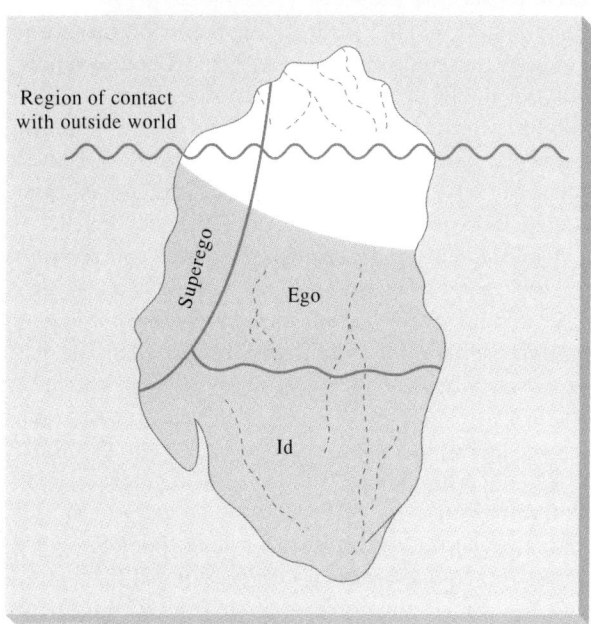

FIGURE 15.1

Conscious and Unconscious Processes: The Iceberg Analogy
This rather odd-looking diagram illustrates Freud's belief that most of the important personality processes occur below the level of conscious awareness. In examining people's conscious thoughts and their behaviors, we can see some reflections of the ego and the superego. Whereas the ego and superego are partly conscious and partly unconscious, the primitive id is the unconscious, totally submerged part of the iceberg.

Repression *is the most powerful and pervasive defense mechanism, according to Freud; it works to push unacceptable id impulses and traumatic memories out of awareness and back into the unconscious mind.* Repression is the foundation from which all other defense mechanisms work; the goal of every psychological defense is to *repress* threatening impulses, or push them out of awareness. Freud said that our early childhood experiences, many of which he believed are sexually laden, are too threatening and stressful for us to deal with consciously. We reduce the anxiety of this conflict through repression.

Among the other defense mechanisms we use to protect the ego and reduce anxiety are rationalization, displacement, sublimation, projection, reaction formation, and regression. **Rationalization** *is the psychoanalytic defense mechanism that occurs when the ego does not accept the real motive for an individual's behavior and replaces it with a sort of cover motive.* For example, you are studying hard for tomorrow's exam. You are really getting into the material when a friend calls and says he is having a party in an hour. He tells you that a certain person you find attractive will be there. You know that, if you don't stay in your room and study, you will do poorly on tomorrow's exam, but you tell yourself, "I did well on the first test in this class and I have been studying hard all semester; it's time I have some fun," so you go to the party. The real motive is wanting to go to the party, to have fun, and to see the attractive person. However, that reason wouldn't justify doing poorly on the exam, so you think you should stay home and study. Your ego now steps in and comes up with a better motive. Your ego says that you have worked hard all semester and you need to unwind, and that you will probably do better on the exam if you relax a little—a rationale that is more acceptable than just going to have fun and meet the desirable other person.

Displacement *is the psychoanalytic defense mechanism that occurs when an individual shifts unacceptable feelings from one object to another, more acceptable object.* For example, a woman is harassed by her boss. She gets angry but she doesn't feel she can take the anger out on the boss because she might get fired. When she gets home that evening, she yells at her husband, thus transferring her feelings toward her boss to her husband.

Sublimation *is the psychoanalytic defense mechanism that occurs when the ego replaces an unacceptable impulse with a socially approved course of action.* Sublimation is actually a type of displacement. For example, an individual with strong sexual urges might turn them into socially approved behavior by becoming an artist who paints nudes.

Projection *is the psychoanalytic defense mechanism that occurs when we attribute our own shortcomings, problems, and faults to others.* For example, a man who has a strong desire to have an extramarital affair keeps accusing his wife of flirting with other men. A manipulative businesswoman who takes advantage of everyone to shove her way up the corporate ladder tells her associate, "Everybody around here is so manipulative; they never consider my feelings." When we can't face our own unwanted feelings, we *project* them onto others and see others as having the undesirable traits.

Reaction formation *is the psychoanalytic defense mechanism that occurs when we express an unacceptable impulse by transforming it into its opposite.* For example, an individual who is attracted to the brutality of war becomes a peace activist, or a person who fears his sexual urges becomes a religious zealot.

Regression *is the psychoanalytic defense mechanism that occurs when we behave in a way characteristic of a previous developmental level.* When anxiety becomes too great for us, we revert to an earlier behavior that gave us pleasure. For example, a husband and wife might each run home to their mothers every time they have a big argument.

Two final points about defense mechanisms need to be understood. First, defense mechanisms are unconscious; we are not aware that we are calling on them to protect the ego and reduce anxiety. Second, when used in moderation or on a temporary basis, defense mechanisms are not necessarily unhealthy. For example, defense mechanisms, such as denial, can help a person cope with difficult circumstances, such as impending death. Under some circumstances therapists might strengthen their clients' defenses to make them less vulnerable to anxiety. For the most part, though, we should not let defense mechanisms dominate our behavior and prevent us from facing life's demands directly.

Life is the art of being well-deceived.
William Hazlitt (1778–1830)

The Development of Personality As Freud listened to, probed, and analyzed his patients, he became convinced that their problems were the result of experiences early in life. Freud believed that we go through five stages of psychosexual development and that, at each stage of development, we experience pleasure in one part of the body more than others. **Erogenous zones** *are those parts of the body that, at each stage of development, according to Freud's theory, have especially strong pleasure-giving qualities.*

Freud thought that adult personality is determined by the way we resolve conflicts among these early sources of pleasure—the mouth, the anus, and then the genitals—and the demands of reality. When these conflicts are not resolved, the individual may become fixated at a particular stage of development. **Fixation** *is the psychoanalytic defense mechanism that occurs when the individual remains locked in an earlier developmental stage because her or his needs are under- or overgratified.* For example, a parent may wean a child too early, be too strict in toilet training, punish the child for masturbation, or "smother" the child with too much attention. We will return to the idea of fixation and how it may show up in an adult's personality, but first we need to learn more about the early stages of personality development.

The **oral stage** *is the term Freud used to describe development during the first 18 months of life, in which the infant's pleasure centers on the mouth.* Chewing, sucking, and biting are chief sources of pleasure, and they help reduce tension.

The **anal stage** *is Freud's second stage of development, occurring between 1½ and 3 years of age, in which the child's greatest pleasure involves the anus or the elimination functions associated with it.* In Freud's view, the exercise of anal muscles reduces tension and provides pleasure.

THE FAR SIDE By GARY LARSON

"So, Mr. Fenton . . . Let's begin with your mother."

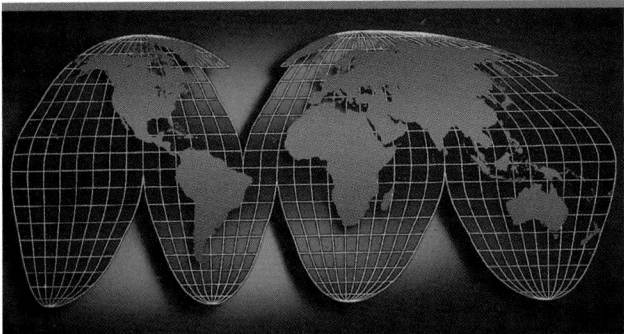

SOCIOCULTURAL WORLDS 15.1

Freud's Oedipus Complex: Culturally and Gender Biased

The Oedipus complex is one of Freud's most influential concepts pertaining to the importance of early psychosexual relationships for later personality development. Freud developed his theory during the Victorian era of the late 1800s, when sexual interests, especially those of females, were repressed. According to Freud, the phallic stage begins for a girl when she realizes she has no penis. He also believed that she recognizes the superiority of the penis to her anatomy and, thus, develops *penis envy*. Blaming her mother for her lack of a penis, the girl renounces her love for her mother and becomes intensely attached to her father. Since her desire for having a penis can never be satisfied directly, Freud speculated that the young girl yearns for a penis substitute, a baby. This version of the Oedipus complex is sometimes referred to as the *Electra complex*. Freud believed that this challenge is never fully resolved but merely dissipates over time as the girl begins to identify with—to take on the values and feminine behavior of—her mother. As a result, Freud assumed that women do not develop as strong a conscience (superego) as men.

Many psychologists believe that Freud placed far too much emphasis on biology's role in personality development. Freud concluded, for example, that boys are likely to develop a dominant, powerful personality because they have a penis; without a penis, girls are predisposed to become submissive and weak. In basing his view of male/female differences in personality development on anatomical differences, Freud ignored the enormous impact of culture and experience.

More than half a century ago, English anthropologist Bronislaw Malinowski (1927) observed the family dynamics of the Trobriand Islanders of the Western Pacific and found that the Oedipus complex is not universal. In the Trobriand Islands, the biological father is not the head of the household; that role is reserved for the mother's brother, who acts as a disciplinarian. In Freud's view, this family constellation should make no difference in the Oedipus complex; the young boy should still vie for his mother's love and perceive his father as a hated rival. However, Malinowski found no such conflict between fathers and sons in the Trobriand Islanders. However, he did observe that the young boys feared and directed negative feelings toward their maternal uncles, the authoritarian figures. Malinowski's finding undermined claims of universality for Freud's Oedipus complex theory, because it showed that the sexual relations within the family do not create conflict and fear for a child.

Psychoanalytic therapists refer to a young girl's desire for her father as the Electra complex. *What are some of the criticisms that have been directed at the theory of the Electra complex?*

The **phallic stage,** *Freud's third stage of development, occurs between the ages of 3 and 6: its name comes from the Latin word* phallus, *which means "penis." During the phallic stage, pleasure focuses on the genitals as the child discovers that self-stimulation is enjoyable.* In Freud's view, the phallic stage has a special importance in personality development because this period triggers the Oedipus complex. This name comes from Greek mythology, in which Oedipus, the son of the King of Thebes, unwittingly kills his father and marries his mother. The **Oedipus complex,** *in Freud's theory, is the young child's developing an intense desire to replace the parent of the same sex and to enjoy the affections of the opposite-sex parent.* As discussed in Sociocultural Worlds 15.1, the Oedipus complex, like many other aspects of Freud's theory, was not as universal as Freud believed; his concept was heavily influenced by the sociohistorical, cultural context of turn-of-the-century Vienna.

Oral stage

Anal stage

Phallic stage

Latency stage

Genital stage

FIGURE 15.2

Freudian Psychosexual Stages
Freud said we go through five stages of psychosexual development. In the oral stage, pleasure centers around the mouth. In the anal stage, pleasure focuses on the anus—the nature of toilet training is important here. In the phallic stage, pleasure involves the genitals—the opposite-sex parent becomes a love object. In the latency stage, a child represses sexual urges—same-sex friendship is prominent. In the genital stage, sexual reawakening takes place—the source of pleasure now becomes someone outside the family.

At about 5 to 6 years of age, children recognize that their same-sex parent might punish them for their incestuous wishes. To reduce this conflict, the child identifies with the same-sex parent, striving to be like him or her. If the conflict is not resolved, the individual may become fixated at the phallic stage.

The **latency stage** *is the fourth Freudian stage of development, occurring approximately between 6 years of age and puberty; the child represses all interest in sexuality and develops social and intellectual skills.* This activity channels much of the child's energy into emotionally safe areas and aids the child in forgetting the highly stressful conflicts of the phallic stage.

The **genital stage** *is the fifth and final Freudian stage of development, occurring from puberty on. The genital stage is the time of sexual reawakening; the source of sexual pleasure now becomes someone outside of the family.* Freud believed that unresolved conflicts with parents reemerge during adolescence. Once the conflicts are resolved, Freud believed, the individual becomes capable of developing a mature love relationship and of functioning independently as an adult. Figure 15.2 summarizes Freud's psychosexual stages.

Motivation, Emotion, Health, and Personality

CRITICAL THINKING

Freud and Schwarzenegger

If Sigmund Freud were alive today, what reactions do you think he might have to the level of violence and sexuality shown in contemporary action films? Your consideration of this question sensitizes you to the importance of *identifying underlying values that influence behavior.* Conversely, how do you think Arnold might have fared in Freud's Viennese Victorian context?

Arnold Schwarzenegger's most popular films usually include high levels of violence and sexuality. *How would Freud explain his popularity?*

Psychoanalytic Revisionists and Dissenters

Freud was among the first theorists to explore many new and uncharted regions of personality and is credited with founding psychoanalysis. As others joined him in this new medical frontier, neo-Freudians discovered that they had to update and revise Freud's ideas. Although they honored many of his concepts, they rejected some aspects of Freudian theory altogether. In particular, Freud's critics have said his ideas about sexuality, early experience, social factors, and the unconscious mind were misguided (Adler, 1927; Erikson, 1968; Fromm, 1947; Horney, 1945; Jung, 1917; Sullivan, 1953). The critics stressed several points:

- Sexuality is not the pervasive underlying force behind personality that Freud believed it to be.
- The first 5 years of life are not as powerful in shaping adult personality as Freud thought; later experiences deserve more attention than they have been given.
- The ego and conscious thought processes play more dominant roles in our personality than Freud gave them credit for; we are not wed forever to the id and its instinctual, unconscious clutches. The ego has a line of development separate from the id; viewed in this way, achievement, thinking, and reasoning are not always tied to sexual impulses, as Freud thought.
- Sociocultural factors are much more important than Freud believed. Freud placed more emphasis on the biological basis of personality by stressing the id's dominance.

(a)

(b)

(*a*) Karen Horney developed the first feminist-based criticism of Freud's theory, creating a model of women with positive qualities and self-valuation. (*b*) Nancy Chodorow has developed an important contemporary feminist revision of psychoanalysis theory that emphasizes the meaningfulness of emotions for women.

Let's examine three theories by dissenters and revisionists of Freud's theory in greater detail—Horney's, Jung's, and Adler's.

Horney's Sociocultural Modification

Although she agreed with much of Freud's theory of personality development, Karen Horney (1885–1952) rejected the classical psychoanalytic concept that anatomy determines behavior in favor of an approach that emphasizes the importance of sociocultural factors in development. She cautioned that such ideas as penis envy are only hypotheses. She insisted that these hypotheses should be supported with observable data before they are accepted as fact.

Horney pointed out that previous research about how women function was limited by the fact that those who described women, who influenced and represented the culture, and who determined the standards for suitable growth and development were men. She countered the notion of penis envy with the hypothesis that both sexes envy the attributes of the other and that men covet women's reproductive capacities. She also argued that women who feel penis envy are desirous only of the status that men have in most societies, not of their anatomy (Westkott, 1986).

Horney also believed that the need for security, not for sex or aggression, is the prime motive in human existence. Horney reasoned that a person whose needs for security have been met should be able to develop his or her capacities to the fullest extent. She also suggested that people usually develop one of three strategies in their effort to cope with anxiety. First, individuals may *move toward* people, seeking love and support. Second, individuals may *move away* from people, becoming more independent. Third, individuals may *move against* people, becoming competitive and domineering. A secure individual uses these three ways of coping in moderation and balance, whereas an insecure individual often uses one or more of these strategies in an exaggerated fashion, becoming too dependent, too independent, or too aggressive.

Psychologists continue to revise psychoanalytic theory. Nancy Chodorow's (1978, 1989) feminist revision of psychoanalytic theory, for example, emphasizes that many more women than men define themselves in terms of their relationships, that many men use denial as a defense mechanism in regard to their relationships with others, and that emotions tend to play a more prominent role in women's lives.

Psychoanalysis is the creation of a male genius, and almost all those who have developed these ideas have been men. It is only right and reasonable that they should evolve more easily a masculine psychology and understand more of the development of men than of women.

Karen Horney

Freud, living at a time when women were proving their heads were no different from men's, substituted the penis for the head as the organ of male superiority, an organ women could never prove they had.

Una Stannard

Jung's Depth Psychology

Freud's contemporary, Carl Jung (1875–1961), shared an interest in the unconscious; however, he believed that Freud underplayed the unconscious mind's role in personality. Jung suspected that the roots of personality go back to the dawn of human existence. The **collective unconscious** *is the impersonal, deepest layer of the unconscious mind, which is shared by all human beings because of their common ancestral past.* These common experiences have made a deep, permanent impression on the human mind. **Archetypes** *are the primordial influences in every individual's collective unconscious that filter our perceptions and experiences.* Jung's psychoanalytic theory is often referred to as "depth psychology" because archetypes reside deep within the unconscious mind, far deeper than what Freud described as our personal unconscious.

Two common archetypes are *anima* (woman) and *animus* (man). Jung believed that each of us has a passive, "feminine" side and an assertive, "masculine" side. We also have an archetype for self, which often is expressed in art. For example, the mandala, a figure within a circle, has been used so often that Jung took it to represent the self (see figure 15.3). Another archetype is the shadow, our darker self, which is evil and immoral. The shadow appears in many evil and immoral figures—Satan, Dracula, Mr. Hyde (of Jekyll and Hyde), and Darth Vader (of the *Star Wars* movies) (Peterson 1988).

I have never seen a greater monster or miracle in the world than myself.

Montaigne

Adler's Individual Psychology

Alfred Adler (1870–1937) was another contemporary of Freud. **Individual psychology** *is the name Adler gave to his theory of psychology to emphasize the uniqueness of every individual.* Unlike Freud's belief in the power of the unconscious mind, Adler argued that we have the conscious ability to monitor and direct our lives; he also believed that social factors are more important in shaping our personality than is sexual motivation (Silverman & Corsini, 1984).

Adler thought that everyone strives for superiority. Adler's concept of **striving for superiority** *emphasizes the*

FIGURE 15.3

Mandalas
Carl Jung believed that mandalas were so widely used to represent the self at different points in history that they were an archetype for the self.

human motivation to adapt to, improve, and master the environment. Striving for superiority is our response to the feelings of inferiority that we all experience as infants and young children when we interact with people who are bigger and more powerful. We strive to overcome these feelings of inferiority because they are uncomfortable. **Compensation** *is Adler's term for the individual's attempt to overcome imagined or real inferiorities or weaknesses by developing one's abilities.* Adler believed that compensation is normal. He said we often make up for a weakness in one ability by excelling in a different ability. For example, one person may be a mediocre student but compensate for this by excelling in athletics. **Overcompensation** *is Adler's term for the individual's attempt to deny rather than acknowledge a real situation or the individual's exaggerated efforts to conceal a weakness.* Adler described two patterns of overcompensation. **Inferiority complex** *is the name Adler gave to exaggerated feelings of inadequacy.* **Superiority complex** *is his concept of exaggerated self-importance that is designed to mask feelings of inferiority.*

In summary, Adler's theory emphasizes that people are striving toward a positive being and that they create their own goals. Their adaptation is enhanced by developing social interests and reducing feelings of inferiority. Like Jung, Adler has a number of disciples today.

Evaluating the Psychoanalytic Perspectives

Although psychoanalytic theories have diverged, they do share some core principles. Psychoanalytic theorists assert that personality is determined both by current experiences and by those from early in life. Some principles of psychoanalytic theory have withstood the test of time. For example, early experiences do shape our personality to a degree, and personality can be better understood by examining it developmentally.

Another belief that continues to receive considerable attention is that we mentally transform, and sometimes distort, environmental experiences. Psychologists also recognize that the mind is not all consciousness; unconscious motives lie behind some of our puzzling behavior. Psychoanalytic theorists' emphasis on conflict and anxiety leads us to consider the dark side of our existence, not just its bright side. Adjustment is not always an easy task; the individual's inner world often conflicts with the outer demands of reality. Finally, psychoanalytic theories continue to force psychologists to study more than the experimental, laboratory topics of sensation, perception, and learning; personality and adjustment are rightful and important topics of psychological inquiry as well.

The main concepts of psychoanalytic theories have been difficult to test; they are largely matters of inference and interpretation. Researchers have not, for example, successfully investigated such key concepts as repression in the laboratory.

Much of the data used to support psychoanalytic theories have come from clinicians' subjective evaluations of clients; in such cases, it is easy for each clinician to see what she expects because of the theory she holds. Other data come from patients' recollections of the distant past (especially those from early childhood) and are of dubious accuracy. Also, critics believe that psychoanalytic theories place too much weight on the ability of these early experiences within the family to shape personality, and that we retain the capacity for change and adaptation throughout our lives.

Some psychologists object that Freud overemphasized the role of sexuality in personality and that Freud and Jung placed too much faith in the unconscious mind's ability to control behavior. Others object that the psychoanalytic perspectives provide a model of a person that is too negative and pessimistic. We are not born into the world with only a bundle of sexual and aggressive instincts. The demands of reality do not always conflict with our biological needs.

Many psychoanalytic theories of personality, especially Freud's, have a male bias. Although Horney's theory helped correct this bias, psychoanalytic theory continues to be revised today.

At this point, you should have a sense of what personality is and a basic understanding of the themes of psychoanalytic theories. Next, we will explore two views of personality that are very different from the psychoanalytic theories.

REVIEW

The Nature of Personality and Psychoanalytic Theories

Personality refers to our enduring thoughts, emotions, and behaviors that characterize the way we adapt. A key question is why individuals respond to a situation in different ways.

Freud was one of the most influential thinkers in the twentieth century. He was a medical doctor who believed that most of the mind is unconscious. Freud said that personality has three structures: id, ego, and superego. The id is the reservoir of psychic energy that tries to satisfy our basic needs; it is unconscious and operates according to the pleasure principle. The ego tries to provide pleasure by operating within the boundaries of reality. The superego is the moral branch of personality. The conflicting demands of personality structures produce anxiety; defense mechanisms protect the ego and reduce this anxiety. Repression, the most pervasive defense mechanism, pushes unacceptable id impulses back into the unconscious mind. Other defense mechanisms include rationalization, displacement, sublimation, projection, reaction formation, and regression. Freud was convinced that problems develop

because of childhood experiences. He said we go through five psychosexual stages of development: oral, anal, phallic, latency, and genital. He believed that, if our needs are under- or overgratified at a particular stage, we can become fixated at that stage. During the phallic stage, the Oedipus complex is a major source of conflict.

The psychoanalytic dissenters and revisionists have argued that Freud placed too much emphasis on sexuality and the first 5 years of life and too little emphasis on the ego and conscious thought processes, as well as sociocultural factors. Karen Horney rejected the classical psychoanalytic concept that anatomy determines behavior, advocated by Freud, in favor of a sociocultural approach. She especially emphasized that Freud's theory is male biased. Horney said that the need for security, not sex or aggression, is the prime motive in human existence. She also theorized that individuals usually develop one of three strategies to cope with anxiety— moving toward people, moving away from people, or moving against people. The rectification of male bias in psychoanalytic theory continues

today through the efforts of such individuals as Nancy Chodorow. Jung thought Freud underplayed the role of the unconscious mind. He developed the concept of the collective unconscious, and his theory is often called depth psychology. Alfred Adler's theory is called individual psychology; it stresses every individual's uniqueness. Adler said people are striving toward a positive being and that they create their own goals. Their adaptation is enhanced by developing social interests and reducing feelings of inferiority.

The strengths of the psychoanalytic perspectives include an emphasis on the past, the developmental course of personality, mental representations of the environment, the concept of the unconscious mind, an emphasis on conflict, and their influence on psychology as a discipline. Their weaknesses include the difficulty in testing the main concepts, a lack of empirical data and an overreliance on reports of the past, too much emphasis on sexuality and the unconscious mind, a negative view of human nature, too much power given to early experience, and a male bias.

Behavioral Perspectives

Roy and Ann are engaged. We would probably informally describe them both as having warm, friendly personalities, from our observations of how much they appear to enjoy being with each other. Psychoanalytic theorists would say that their personalities are derived from long-standing relationships with their parents, especially their early childhood experiences. They also would argue that the reason for their attraction is unconscious; they are unaware of how their biological heritage and early life experiences have been carried forward to influence their adult personalities and behaviors.

In contrast, behaviorists would observe Roy and Ann and infer something quite different. Behaviorists would examine their experiences, especially their most recent ones, to identify the reasons for their mutual pursuit of each other's company. For example, behaviorists might focus on how Ann rewards Roy's attentiveness, and vice versa. They would avoid making references to unconscious thoughts, the Oedipus complex, and defense mechanisms and refer instead to behaviors and their consequences.

Early Behaviorism

At approximately the same time as Freud was interpreting his patients' unconscious minds through their early childhood recollections, behaviorists Ivan Pavlov and John B. Watson were conducting detailed observations of behavior under controlled laboratory conditions. Each conducted research that evolved into distinctive therapies, which will be discussed in chapter 17. Pavlov's work led to classical conditioning interventions. Watson's research founded operant conditioning procedures.

Out of the behavioral tradition grew the belief that personality is the sum of observable behaviors, learned through experiences with the environment. You may remember from chapters 1 and 6 that behaviorists believe we should examine only what can be directly observed and measured. This emphasis discourages exploring and explaining the origins of behavior. Instead, behaviorism encourages careful definition and precise measurement of behavior. Behavioral explanations shift the emphasis to the functions of behavior and how behavior can be modified.

Skinner's Behaviorism

Although psychologists regard John B. Watson as the father of behaviorism, B. F. Skinner's ideas dominated mainstream thinking about behavior for many decades. B. F. Skinner (1904–1990) concluded that personality is an individual's *behavior,* which is determined by the *external environment.* Skinner believed that psychologists do not have to resort to biological or cognitive processes to explain personality (behavior). Some psychologists say that including Skinner among personality theorists is like inviting a wolf to a party of lambs, because he took the "person" out of personality (Phares, 1984).

Behaviorists counter that you cannot pinpoint where personality is or how it is determined. In Skinner's view, personality simply consists of a collection of a person's observed, overt behaviors; it does not include internal traits or thoughts. For example, observations of Sam reveal that his behavior is shy, achievement-oriented, and caring. In short, these behaviors *are* his personality. According to Skinner, Sam is this way because the rewards and punishments in Sam's environment have shaped him into a shy, achievement-oriented, and caring person. Because of interactions with family members, friends, teachers, and others, Sam has *learned* to behave in this fashion.

Skinner believed that emphasizing mentalistic concepts prevented the development of a truly scientific approach to behavior. Thoughts and feelings should have no role in the analysis of behavior because they are covert events; they are neither directly observable nor necessary in accounting for behavior. Skinner characterized personality as a superfluous, mentalistic notion. He was satisfied with characterizing individuals according to the behaviors they used to operate in the environment. Psychologists who continue to support this reductionistic viewpoint are sometimes referred to as **radical behaviorists,** *psychologists who emphasize only observable behavior and reject its cognitive dimensions.*

Behaviorists who support Skinner's view would say that Sam's shy, achievement-oriented, and caring behavior might not be consistent and enduring. For example, Sam is uninhibited on Saturday night with friends at a bar, unmotivated to excel in English class, and occasionally nasty to his sister. In addition, Skinnerians believe that consistency in behavior comes from consistency in environmental experiences. If Sam's shy, achievement-oriented, and caring behavior is consistently rewarded, his pattern of behavior is likely to be consistent. However, Skinner stressed that our behavior always has the capacity for change if new experiences are encountered. The issue of consistency in personality is an important one. We will return to it on several occasions later in the chapter.

Behaviorists believe that if personality is learned and changes according to environmental experiences and situations, it follows that, by rearranging experiences and situations, an individual's personality can be changed. For a behaviorist, shy behavior can be changed into outgoing behavior; aggressive behavior can be shaped into docile behavior; lethargic, bored behavior can be shaped into enthusiastic, interested behavior. Much more about the behavioral techniques used to accomplish these changes in personality are discussed in chapter 17.

Some psychologists believe that the behaviorists are right when they say that personality is learned and influenced strongly by environmental experiences. However, many believe that Skinner went too far in rejecting cognition's role in personality. They argue that human learning requires cognitive mediation. The psychologists who emphasize behavior, environment, *and* cognition as the key factors in personality are called *social learning theorists*. Their objections moved behaviorism in a new direction—toward cognitive interpretation of behavior, which we will explore in the next section.

Cognitive Perspectives

Social learning theorists say that we are not mindless robots, responding mechanically to others in the environment. Nor do we respond like weather vanes, moving in response to the prevailing winds. Rather, we think, reason, imagine, plan, expect, interpret, believe, value, and compare. When others try to influence us, our values and beliefs allow us to evaluate their intentions and to resist or comply.

Social learning theory was spawned in the early 1940s when John Dollard and Neal Miller (1950) tried to couple behaviorism and psychoanalytic theory. The coupling was not successful, because the fuzziness of many psychoanalytic concepts made it virtually impossible to anchor them in the empirical observational methodology of behaviorism.

When Julian Rotter (1954) introduced the concept of **expectancy**—*an individual's belief in the probability that a specific behavior will lead to satisfactions or valued goals*—in the 1950s, social learning theory took on a cognitive flavor. At about the same time George Kelly (1955) also introduced a cognitive theory, called **personal construct theory**, *which emphasizes the importance of how people perceive, organize, interpret, and construe events and the world in which they live for understanding their personality.* Kelly believed that individuals constantly organize and assign meaning to their experiences. Kelly developed the concept of *personal constructs,* which are cognitive constructions of reality; these constructs serve as filters that explain why two people can experience the same event and not report the same experience.

In the 1970s, social learning theory became even more cognitive through the contributions of Walter Mischel (1973) and Albert Bandura (1977). They crafted **cognitive social learning theory,** *the contemporary version of social learning theory that stresses the importance of cognition, behavior, and environment in determining personality.* It was Mischel (1973) who coined the term *cognitive social learning theory.*

Bandura's and Mischel's theorizing and research reveal the cognitive nature of contemporary social learning theory. Bandura (1977, 1986, 1994) believes that we acquire an extensive amount of behavior through imitation. He argues that for imitation to take place, the cognitive processes of attention and memory have to be in operation. For example, to imitate another person's behavior, you have to attend to what the person did and remember it as well. More recently, Bandura (1994)

has stressed that the cognitive concept of **self-efficacy,** *the belief that one can master a situation and produce positive outcomes,* is a key ingredient in adaptation and coping.

Mischel's main research area is **delay of gratification,** *the ability to defer immediate satisfaction for a more desirable future outcome.* One way we might learn to delay gratification is to represent goal objects in different ways. In one study, when young children mentally represented rewards in consummatory ways, such as focusing on dimensions of their taste (thinking how yummy, crunchy, and tasty pretzels are), they delayed gratification much less than young children who mentally represented the rewards in nonconsummatory ways (thinking about pretzels as sticks or tiny logs) (Mischel & Baker, 1975). This type of experiment illustrated that the way in which we mentally represent the outcomes of a situation influences our ability to delay gratification.

Evaluating the Behavioral and Cognitive Learning Perspectives

Behavioral and cognitive learning theories emphasize that environmental experiences and situational influences determine personality. These approaches have fostered a scientific climate for understanding personality that highlights the observation of behavior. Cognitive social learning theory emphasizes both environmental influences and the "black box" of the human mind to explain personality; this theory also suggests that people have the ability to control their environment.

Critics of both the behavioral and the cognitive social learning perspectives take issue with several aspects of both theories. They criticize the behavioral view for ignoring the importance of cognition in personality and placing too much importance on the role of environmental experiences. Both approaches have been described as being too concerned with change and situational influences on personality and not paying adequate tribute to the enduring qualities of personality. Both are labeled reductionistic, which means they try to explain the complex concept of personality in terms of one or two factors. The critics

Albert Bandura (*left*) and Walter Mischel (*right*) crafted social learning theory's contemporary version, which Mischel labeled cognitive social learning theory.

Motivation, Emotion, Health, and Personality

charge that the behavioral and cognitive social learning views are too mechanical, missing the exciting, rich dimensions of personality. This latter criticism—that the creative, spontaneous, human dimensions of personality are missing from the behavioral and cognitive social learning perspectives—has been made on numerous occasions by humanists, whose perspective we will consider next.

The Humanistic Perspective

Remember our example of the engaged couple, Roy and Ann, who were described as having warm, friendly personalities. Phenomenological and humanistic psychologists would say that Roy and Ann's warm, friendly personalities are a reflection of their inner selves; these psychologists would emphasize that a key to understanding their mutual attraction is their positive perceptions of each other. Roy and Ann are not viewed as controlling each other or each other's behavior; rather, each has determined a course of action and has freely chosen to marry. No recourse to biological instincts or unconscious thoughts as reasons for their attraction is necessary in the phenomenological and humanistic perspectives. This explanation represents a **phenomenological worldview,** *which stresses the importance of our perceptions of ourselves and of our world in understanding personality; this worldview emphasizes that, for each individual, reality is what that individual perceives.*

The **humanistic perspective** *is the most widely adopted phenomenological approach to personality. The humanistic perspective stresses a person's capacity for personal growth, freedom to choose one's own destiny, and positive qualities.* Humanistic psychologists believe that each of us has the ability to cope with stress, to control our lives, and to achieve what we desire. Each of us has the ability to break through and understand ourselves and our world.

We carry with us the wonders we seek without us.
Sir Thomas Browne, 1642

You probably sense that the phenomenological and humanistic perspectives provide stark contrasts to the psychoanalytic perspective, which is based on conflict, destructive drives, and little faith in human nature, and to the behavioral perspective, which, at worst, seems to reduce human beings to mere puppets on the strings of rewards and punishments. Carl Rogers and Abraham Maslow were two of the leading architects of the humanistic perspective.

Carl Rogers's Approach

Like Freud, Carl Rogers (1902–1987) began his inquiry into human nature with people who were troubled. In the knotted, anxious, and defensive verbal stream of his clients, Rogers (1961) examined the nature of their world that kept them from having positive self-concepts and reaching their full potential as human beings. He proposed several concepts to explain the humanistic point of view.

Carl Rogers was a pioneer in the development of the humanistic perspective.

Our Conditioned, Controlling World Rogers believed that most people have considerable difficulty accepting their own feelings, which are innately positive. As we grow up, people who are central to our lives condition us to move away from these positive feelings. Our parents, siblings, teachers, and peers place constraints and contingencies on our behavior; too often we hear such phrases as "Don't do that," "You didn't do that right," and "How can you be so stupid?" When we don't do something right, we often get punished; parents may even threaten to take away their love. **Conditional positive regard** *is Rogers's term for making the bestowal of love or praise conditional on the individual's conforming to parental or social standards.* The result is low self-esteem.

These constraints and negative feedback continue during our adult lives. The result tends to be that our relationships either carry the dark cloud of conflict or we conform to what others want. As we struggle to live up to society's standards, we distort and disvalue our true selves. By constantly acting according to other people's standards, we might even completely lose our sense of our self.

The Self Through an individual's experiences with the world, a self emerges—the "I" or "me" of our existence. Rogers did not believe that all aspects of the self are conscious, but he did believe they are all accessible to consciousness. The self is a whole, consisting of one's self-perceptions (how attractive I am, how well I get along with others, how good an athlete I am) and the values we attach to these perceptions (good-bad, worthy-unworthy, for example). **Self-concept,** *a central theme for humanists, refers to individuals' overall perceptions of their abilities, behavior, and personality.* According to Rogers, a person who has a poor self-concept is likely to think, feel, and act negatively. Some psychologists are turning their interest to the differences and similarities among the self-concepts of individuals from different ethnic backgrounds (see Sociocultural Worlds 15.2).

There's a period of life when we swallow a knowledge of ourselves and it becomes either good or sour inside.

Pearl Bailey

In discussing self-concept, Rogers distinguished between the real self—that is, the self as it really is as a result of our experiences—and the ideal self, which is the self we would like to be. The greater the discrepancy between the real self and the ideal self, said Rogers, the more maladjusted we will be. To improve our adjustment, we can develop more positive perceptions of our real self, not worry so much about what others want, and increase our positive experiences in the world.

Unconditional Positive Regard, Empathy, and Genuineness

Rogers stressed that we can help a person develop a more positive self-concept through unconditional positive regard, empathy, and genuineness. Rogers said that we need to be accepted by others, regardless of what we do. **Unconditional positive regard** *is Rogers's term for accepting, valuing, and being positive toward another person regardless of the person's behavior.* Rogers recognized that, when a person's behavior is below acceptable standards, inappropriate, or even obnoxious, the person still needs the respect, comfort, and love of others. Rogers strongly believed that unconditional positive regard elevates a person's self-worth. However, Rogers (1974) distinguished between unconditional positive regard directed at an individual as a person of worth and dignity and unconditional positive regard directed at the individual's behavior. A Rogerian therapist creates supportive conditions in which the individual can come to terms with undesirable behavior.

---

*The living self has one purpose only:
to come into its own fullness of being,
as a tree comes into full blossom, or a bird
into spring beauty, or a tiger into lustre.*

D. H. Lawrence

Rogers also said we can help other people develop a more positive self-concept if we are *empathic* and *genuine.* Being empathic means being a sensitive listener and understanding another's true feelings. Being genuine means being

open with our feelings and dropping our pretenses and facades. For Rogers, unconditional positive regard, empathy, and genuineness are three key ingredients of human relations. We can use these techniques to help other people to feel good about themselves, and the techniques also help us get along better with others.

The Fully Functioning Person   Rogers (1980) stressed the importance of becoming a fully functioning person—someone who is open to experience, is not very defensive, is aware of and sensitive to the self and the external world, and for the most part has a harmonious relationship with others. A discrepancy between the real self and the ideal self may occur, others may try to control us, and our world may have too little unconditional positive regard. However, Rogers believed that human beings are highly resilient and capable of becoming fully functioning.

Our self-actualizing tendency is reflected in Rogers's comparison of persons with a plant he once observed on the coastline of northern California. As Rogers looked out at the waves beating furiously against the jagged rocks and shooting mountains of spray into the air, he noticed the breakers pounding a sea palm (a kind of seaweed that looks like a 2- to 3-foot-high palm tree). The plant seemed fragile and top-heavy. The waves crashed against the plant, bending its slender trunk almost flat and whipping its leaves in a torrent of spray, yet the moment the wave passed the plant was erect, tough, and resilient again. It was incredible that the plant could take this incessant pounding hour after hour, week after week, possibly even year after year, all the time nourishing itself, maintaining its position, and growing. In this palmlike seaweed, Rogers saw the tenacity and forward thrust of life and the ability of a living thing to push into a hostile environment and not only hold its own but adapt, develop, and become itself. So is the potential with each of us, according to Rogers (Rogers, 1963).

Abraham Maslow's Approach

Another theorist who made self-actualization the centerpiece of his humanistic philosophy was Abraham Maslow (1908–1970). Maslow was one of the most powerful forces behind the humanistic movement in psychology. He called the humanistic approach the "third force" in psychology—that is, an important alternative to the psychoanalytic and behavioral forces. Maslow pointed out that psychoanalytic theories place too much emphasis on disordered individuals and their conflicts. Behaviorists ignore the person all together, he said.

Remember from chapter 13 that Maslow (1954) said we have a hierarchy of needs in which certain basic needs (physiological needs, and needs for safety, love and belongingness, and self-esteem) have to be satisfied before we can satisfy the highest need, the need for self-actualization. Remember also that Maslow described *self-actualization* as a motivation to develop one's full potential as a human being. Maslow (1971) charted the human potential of creative, talented, and healthy people.

Motivation, Emotion, Health, and Personality

Ethnicity, Self, and Self-concept

Many of the early attempts to assess the nature of self and self-concept in various ethnic groups compared African American and White individuals (Clark & Clark, 1939; Coopersmith, 1967; Deutsch, 1967). These reports indicated that African Americans, especially African American children, have a more negative self-concept than Whites. However, more recent research suggests that African Americans, Mexican Americans, and Puerto Ricans have equally positive self-concepts and perhaps even higher self-esteem than Anglo-Americans do (Allen & Majidi-Ahi, 1989; Powell & Fuller, 1972).

"Ethnic pride" was one of the positive movements to spring out of the social turmoll of the sixties. Its emphasis on the richness and diversity of various cultures appears to have improved the self-esteem of ethnic minority groups (Garbarino, 1985). However, ethnic pride has both benefits and costs. One obvious benefit is a sense of cultural identity (such as being African American, Mexican American, or Native American), with clearly defined cultural roles as to what is expected of a competent person. Also, ethnic neighborhoods are often tight-knit and supportive. It's somewhat easier for a person to develop a positive sense of self in neighborhoods such as these, where people lend one another a hand and offer strategies for coping with problems. In addition, minority members who live in their ethnic neighborhoods can gain a sense of rootedness and acceptance.

However, there is no indication that acceptance within an ethnic group translates into prestige within mainstream American society (Rosenberg, 1965). Even though a person may have a secure sense of self as a member of an ethnic minority, he or she may still need to come to terms with prejudice beyond the ethnic neighborhood. When the values, morals, and behaviors of the ethnic neighborhood differ from society as a whole, an ethnic minority member may find it difficult to develop a sense of competence in mainstream society. At the same time, belonging to a group in which one is highly valued can serve as a buffer against racial prejudice.

Discussions of ethnicity, self, and self-concept still boil down to a fundamental issue: "What kind of people does the world need?" (Garbarino, 1985). If the quality of life on this planet is to be enhanced, people need to develop more harmonious, cooperative relationships. We need to ask whether we are socializing children to develop the kind of self-concept that encourages a competent, caring, sustainable society.

A generation of ethnic awareness and pride appears to have advanced the self-esteem of ethnic minority group members. A discussion of ethnicity and self-esteem raises the question of what kind of people the world needs. There is a growing need for a world of individuals who develop more harmonious, cooperative relationships.

He believed that needs come in two forms: deficiency needs and metaneeds (also called growth or self-actualization needs) (see figure 15.4). **Deficiency needs** *is Maslow's term for essential requirements—physiological needs (for food, shelter, comfort, and so on) and psychological needs (for affection, security, self-esteem, and so on)—that must be met; otherwise, individuals will try to make up for their absence.* **Metaneeds,** *or growth needs, is Maslow's term for higher, self-actualized needs; they include truth, goodness, beauty, wholeness, vitality, uniqueness, perfection, justice, inner wealth, and playfulness.* The

metaneeds cannot be satisfied until all the lower needs are met. The metaneeds themselves, however, are not hierarchically arranged in Maslow's model. For example, although we have to satisfy our need for belongingness before our need for self-esteem, we do not have to satisfy our need for goodness before our need for vitality. When our metaneeds are not fulfilled, Maslow cautioned, we may become maladjusted. For example, unfulfilled metaneeds may cause individuals to become alienated, weak, or cynical.

Maslow developed psychological profiles of famous people and concluded that such individuals as Eleanor Roosevelt, Albert Einstein, Abraham Lincoln, Walt Whitman, William James, and Ludwig van Beethoven were self-actualized. Table 15.1 lists Maslow's descriptions of the characteristics of self-actualized individuals.

Evaluating Humanistic Perspectives

Humanistic perspectives have made psychologists aware that the way we perceive ourselves and the world around us is a key element of personality. Humanistic psychologists also have reminded us that we need to consider the whole person and the positive bent of human nature. Their emphasis on conscious experience has given us the view that personality contains a "well of potential" that can be developed to its fullest.

A weakness of the humanistic perspective is that its key concepts are difficult to test. Self-actualization, for example, is not clearly defined. Psychologists are not certain how to study this concept empirically. Some humanists even scorn the experimental approach, preferring clinical interpretation as a data base. Verification of humanistic concepts has come mainly from clinical experiences rather than controlled, experimental studies. Some critics also believe that humanistic psychologists are too optimistic about human nature, overestimating the freedom and rationality of humans. Some critics say the humanists encourage self-love and narcissism.

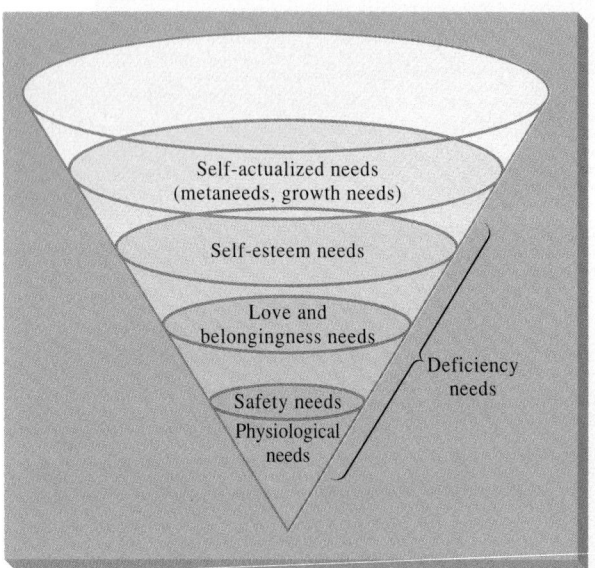

FIGURE 15.4

Maslow's Hierarchy of Needs
Only when the needs in the lower four circles (the deficiency needs) are reasonably satisfied can the self-actualized needs (metaneeds, growth needs) be satisfied. The deficiency needs are arranged hierarchically; the metaneeds are not.

**ABLE 15.1**

Maslow's Characteristics of Self-actualized Individuals

Realistic orientation	Identification with humankind and a strong social interest
Self-acceptance	Tendency to have strong intimate relationships with a few special, loved people rather than superficial relationships with many people
Acceptance of others and the natural world as they are	
Spontaneity	
Problem-centered rather than self-centered	Democratic values and attitudes
Air of detachment and need for privacy	No confusion of means with ends
Autonomous and independent	Philosophical rather than hostile sense of humor
Fresh rather than stereotyped appreciation of people and things	High degree of creativity
	Resistance to cultural conformity
Generally have had profound mystical or spiritual, though not necessarily religious, experiences	Transcendence of environment rather than merely coping with it

Source: A. H. Maslow, *The Farther Reaches of Nature*, pages 153–174, Viking Press, 1971.

Comparing Personality Theories

In the course of our discussion, we have seen that personality theories have many faces. One reason so many personality theories exist is that personality is a broad, multidimensional concept. We will compare several of the most important dimensions to help you review the theories we have presented thus far. A summary of these comparisons is presented in table 15.2. The discrete presentation of the perspectives gives the illusion that there is little overlap in the theories; however, a careful reading demonstrates both similarities and differences among the theories.

The Relative Importance of Biological Versus Learned Factors

Is personality due more to heredity and biological factors or to learning and environmental experiences? Freud's theory has a strong biogenetic foundation, although many psychoanalytic revisionists argued that he underestimated the power of environmental experiences and culture in determining personality. Behaviorism and cognitive psychology both see environment as a powerful influence on personality, Skinner being the strongest advocate of environment's influence. Cognitivists believe that neurobiological capacities mediate environmental experiences. Humanists are also more inclined to stress environmental over biological variables.

The Nature and Degree of Determinism

Is personality due more to an inner disposition or to an external circumstance? Personality theories vary not only in the factors they cite as most influential in determining personality, but in the amount of influence they take the factors to exert. **Determinism** *is the belief that historical or biological factors completely account for behavior.* Psychoanalytic theorists emphasize the internal dimensions of personality. In Freud's highly deterministic theory, the internal structures of the id, ego, and superego are responsible for personality. Although humanists also believe that internal determinants, such as self-concept and self-determination, have a role in shaping personality, they are less deterministic. To humanists, people are far more flexible than a strict deterministic view would allow. By contrast, behaviorists emphasize personality's external situational determinants, although cognitive theorists include both external events and internal structures as influential determinants.

The Role of Cognition and Consciousness

How prominent are cognitions and levels of consciousness in shaping personality? Freud and Jung were the strongest advocates of the unconscious mind's role in personality. Freud stressed that our deeply repressed experiences in infancy and early childhood determine what our personalities will be like

TABLE 15.2

Comparing Perspectives on Personality

Personality Dimensions	Psychoanalytic Perspectives	Behavioral Perspectives	Cognitive Perspectives	Humanistic Perspectives
The relative importance of biological versus learned factors	Freud emphasized biological foundations. Neo-Freudians give more credit to social experiences and culture than Freud did.	Skinner minimized biological foundations and promoted learning as the primary force.	Cognitive psychologists emphasize both neurobiological and environmental factors.	Humanistic theorists deemphasize biology and base their ideas on the power of change through experience.
The nature and degree of determinism	Freud's theories were highly deterministic; internal personality structures responsible.	Skinner's views are highly deterministic; environmental forces responsible.	Cognitivists invoke both internal and external determinants but stress human flexibility.	Humanists are less deterministic, but rely on internal determinants, such as self-determination.
The role of cognition and consciousness	Freud and Jung placed strong emphasis on the influence of unconscious forces.	Skinner rejected both conscious and unconscious thought.	Cognitivists base their theories on the power of conscious cognitions.	Humanists stress consciousness and cognition, especially self-perception.
The view of human nature	Pessimistic.	Neutral.	Neutral.	Optimistic.
Significant areas of criticism	Freud's critics believe that his theories have strong contextual limitations and are difficult to test.	Skinner's critics charge him with neglect of cognitive influences and simplistic or reductionistic explanations.	Critics of the cognitivist approaches challenge the superficiality of their explanations.	Critics of humanistic approaches believe they are naive, encouraging self-interest and irresponsibility.

when we become adults, for example. Most psychoanalytic theorists argue that we are largely unaware of how individual personalities develop. Skinner argues that neither unconscious nor conscious thoughts are important in determining personality. Also strongly deterministic, he believed that relying on such mentalistic concepts interferes with effective behavioral prediction and control. Cognitive theorists stress that cognitive factors mediate the environment's influence on personality. The humanists, such as Rogers and Maslow, emphasized conscious aspects of personality. They regard individuals as competent and capable of making conscious choices and of evaluating the success of their choices. Self-perception serves as the foundation for their individual adaptation. Both cognitive and humanistic perspectives appear to be less deterministic than either the psychoanalytic or the behavioral perspective.

Views on Human Nature

How does each approach to personality view human potential? Because it is founded on the power of sexual and aggressive drives, psychoanalysis promotes a bleak view of humanity. For example, Freud believed the difficulty human beings have in managing their aggressive impulses is likely to result in chronic aggression and warfare. Behavioral and cognitive approaches tend to take a more neutral perspective on human nature. Humanistic approaches are much more optimistic, believing that individuals have strong potential to *transcend*, or move beyond, the constraints they encounter.

Significant Areas of Criticism

What are the shortcomings of each major approach to personality? Each approach offers insights into personality, but no personality theory yet proposed can fully account for all dimensions of personality. Psychoanalytic theories have received the most severe criticism for their inequitable treatment of women and for their limited generalizability to other cultures and contexts. Critics have attacked behavioral theorists for being too simplistic, neglecting matters of emotion and cognition. More recent modifications to behaviorism offered by cognitive behaviorists have addressed many of those concerns; however, cognitivists are sometimes criticized for giving superficial interpretations of personality. Humanists are regularly criticized for naivete and for promoting self-interest at the expense of concern for others.

By now you should have a better understanding of personality, perhaps even *your* personality. However, we have not exhausted all points of view on the important influences on personality. Next we will explore in more detail how psychologists describe the influence of biology and culture in shaping personality.

REVIEW

The Behavioral, Cognitive and Humanistic Perspectives

In Skinner's behaviorism, cognition is unimportant in understanding personality. Rather, personality is observed behavior, which is influenced by the rewards and punishments in the environment. Personality varies according to the situation, in the behavioral view.

The cognitive perspective on personality grew out of social learning theory, which began to take on a cognitive flavor in the 1950s when Rotter and Kelly emphasized, respectively, the importance of expectancy and personal constructs. In the 1970s, Mischel and Bandura crafted social learning theory's contemporary version, cognitive social learning theory, which stresses the importance of cognition, behavior, and environment in understanding personality.

Strengths of both the behavioral and cognitive social learning perspectives include emphases on environmental determinants of behavior and a scientific climate for investigating personality, as well as the focus on cognitive processes and self-control in the cognitive social learning approach. The behavioral view has been criticized for taking the person out of personality and for ignoring cognition. These approaches have not given adequate attention to enduring individual differences and to personality as a whole.

The phenomenological worldview emphasizes our perceptions of ourselves and our world and centers on the belief that reality is what is perceived. The humanistic perspective is the most widely known phenomenological approach. In Carl Rogers's approach, each of us is a victim of conditional positive regard. The result is that our real self is not valued. The self is the core of personality; it includes both the real and the ideal self. Rogers said we can help others develop a more positive self-concept in three ways: unconditional positive regard, empathy, and genuineness.

Rogers also stressed that each of us has the innate, inner capacity to become a fully functioning person. Maslow called the humanistic movement the "third force" in psychology. Each of us has a self-actualizing tendency, according to Maslow. He distinguishes between deficiency needs and self-actualization needs, or metaneeds. The phenomenological and humanistic approaches sensitized psychologists to the importance of subjective experience, consciousness, self-concept, the whole person, and our innate, positive nature. Their weaknesses are the absence of an empirical orientation, a tendency to be too optimistic, and an inclination to encourage self-love.

Personality theories can be compared on the following factors: the relative importance of biological versus learned factors, the nature and degree of determinism, the role of cognition and consciousness, the view of human nature, and significant areas of criticism.

OTHER PERSPECTIVES: TRAITS AND CONTEXTS

As you saw in the story of Mark Twain that introduced this chapter, it is relatively easy for us to characterize human beings using descriptive terms denoting **traits,** *broad dispositions that lead to characteristic responses.* Different explanations based on traits or types have emerged over time, with variable levels of acceptance, popularity, and durability. In this section, we will explore the historical basis and the current status of type- and trait-based explanations, as well as the important influence of the contexts in which personality develops.

Personality Type Theories

As early as 400 B.C., Hippocrates classified people's personalities according to their body types. Hippocrates thought that people with more yellow bile than others, for example, were "choleric" (easily angered) whereas others, with an excess of blood, were more "sanguine" (cheerful and buoyant). He linked temperament to physical makeup. Psychologists regard his explanation as historically interesting but inaccurate. In 1925 the first formal study of physique and temperament appeared. E. Kretschmer published his findings nearly a generation before William Sheldon.

William Sheldon (1954) proposed a theory of body types and personality. **Somatotype theory** *is Sheldon's theory that precise charts reveal distinct body types, which in turn are associated with certain personality characteristics.* He concluded that individuals basically are one of three types (see figure 15.5). **Endomorph** *was Sheldon's term for a soft, round, large-stomached person who is relaxed, gregarious, and food loving.* **Mesomorph** *was Sheldon's term for a strong, athletic, and muscular person who is energetic, assertive, and courageous.* **Ectomorph** *was Sheldon's term for a tall, thin, fragile person who is fearful, introverted, and restrained.*

CRITICAL THINKING

The Fall of Type Theory

Sheldon's approach to personality was an interesting one that has some intuitive appeal. You probably know some overweight people who are fun-loving, some muscular people who are athletic, and some thin people who are tentative and quiet. Can you imagine some of the difficulties you might encounter if you were to put Sheldon's theory to the test? Describe one problem you would have in demonstrating the validity of Sheldon's theory; this gives you an opportunity to *evaluate the validity of conclusions about behavior.*

Endomorph
Chef Paul Prudhomme

Mesomorph
Actor Sylvester Stallone

Ectomorph
Former U.N. Ambassador Jeanne Kirkpatrick

FIGURE 15.5

Sheldon's Body Types
Although these famous individuals fit the body types described by Sheldon, their personalities may not fit Sheldon's predictions.

Appealing as it was, somatotyping also ran aground. For starters, research revealed that there is no significant relation between body type and personality (Cortes & Gatti, 1970). Many people simply do not fit into a neatly packaged category. In addition, using one, two, or three categories to describe individuals ignores the rich diversity and complexity of human characteristics. Thus, the somatotype theory is not popular today.

Trait Theories

Trait theories *propose that people have broad dispositions that are reflected in the basic ways they behave, such as whether they are outgoing and friendly or whether they are dominant and assertive.* People who have a strong tendency to behave in certain ways are described as high on the traits; those who have a weak tendency to behave in these ways are described as low on the traits. Although trait theorists sometimes differ on which traits make up personality, they all agree that traits are the fundamental building blocks of personality (Pervin, 1989).

Early Trait Psychology

Trying to pigeonhole the traits that make up personality is a herculean task. Gordon Allport and H. S. Odbert (1936), for example, combed the dictionary and counted almost 18,000 words that could be used to describe people. Allport said that several overarching categories could be used to reduce the vast number of words used to describe traits. One of Allport's trait categories was *individual traits,* which refers to an individual's unique way of dealing with the world.

Hans Eysenck (1967) also tackled the task of determining the basic traits of personality. He gave personality tests to large numbers of people and analyzed each person's response. Eysenck consistently found the traits of stability-instability and introversion-extraversion when he assessed the personalities of large numbers of individuals and suggested that these dimensions could be related. For example, he characterized an *introverted stable* personality as careful, even-tempered, and calm. He characterized an *extraverted unstable* personality as aggressive, excitable, and impulsive. The basic elements of Eysenck's theory have survived in modern views of trait psychology (see figure 15.6).

Contemporary Trait Psychology

Many contemporary trait psychologists are encouraged by evidence from a number of studies that reveals five basic dimensions of personality (Costa & McCrae, 1995; Hogan, 1987; McCrae & Costa, 1989). Called the *big five factors in personality,* they include

- extraversion-introversion
- friendly compliance versus hostile noncompliance
- neuroticism versus emotional stability
- conscientiousness
- intellect, imagination, or openness to experience

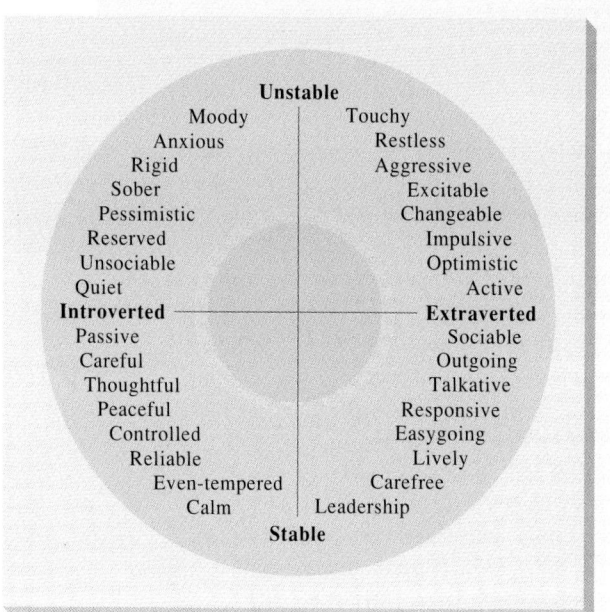

FIGURE 15.6

Eysenck's Dimensions of Personality
On the basis of his factor analytic studies, Eysenck concluded that personality consists of two basic dimensions: (1) stability-instability and (2) introversion-extraversion.

Extraversion-introversion focuses on assertiveness, gregariousness, and shyness; friendly compliance versus hostile noncompliance involves love and friendship at one end of the spectrum and enduring problems of aggression and lawlessness at the other end; neuroticism refers to emotional stability or instability; the will to achieve emphasizes achievement motivation; and intellect includes intelligence and creativity.

. . . And I'm working all day and I'm working all night
To be good-looking, healthy, and wise.
And adored.
And contented.
And brave.
And well-read.
And a marvelous hostess,
Fantastic in bed,
And bilingual,
Athletic,
Artistic . . .
Won't someone please stop me?
Judith Viorst, *Self-Improvement Program*

Trait-Situation Interaction

In his landmark book, *Personality and Assessment,* Walter Mischel (1968) criticized the trait view of personality as well as the psychoanalytic approach, both of which emphasize the internal organization of personality. Rather than viewing personality as consisting of broad, internal traits that are consistent across situations and time, Mischel said that personality often changes according to a given situation.

Mischel reviewed an array of studies and concluded that trait measures do a poor job of predicting actual behavior. For example, let's say Anne is described as an aggressive person. But when we observe her behavior, we find that she is more or less aggressive depending on the situation—she may be aggressive with her boyfriend but almost submissive with her new boss. Mischel's view was called **situationism,** *which means that personality often varies considerably from one context to another.* Mischel's argument was an important one, but many psychologists were not willing to abandon altogether the trait concept.

Today, most psychologists in the field of personality, including Mischel, are interactionists. They believe both trait (person) and situation variables are necessary to understand personality. They also agree that the degree of consistency in personality depends on the kind of persons, situations, and behaviors sampled (Pervin, 1993).

---

*Consistency requires you to be as ignorant today
as you were a year ago.*

Bernard Berenson

Suppose you want to assess the happiness of Jahmal, an introvert, and Amy, an extrovert. According to trait-situation interaction theory, we cannot predict who will be happier unless we know something about the situations they are in. Imagine you get the opportunity to observe them in two situations, at a party and in a library. As described in figure 15.7, considering both the traits of the individuals and the settings they are in improves our ability to predict their happiness.

One outcome of the trait/situation controversy is that the link between traits and situations has been more precisely specified. For example, researchers have found that (1) the narrower and more limited a trait is, the more likely it will predict behavior; (2) some people are consistent on some traits and other people are consistent on other traits; and (3) personality traits exert a stronger influence on an individual's behavior when situational influences are less powerful.

The Sociocultural Perspective

Walter Mischel's attack on the adequacy of trait explanations prompted a closer examination of personality's contextual basis. In the same vein, the sociocultural perspective also emphasizes the contextual basis of personality, although usually at a more global level than Mischel's. From the sociocultural perspective, we will examine two related issues: the dichotomy of individualism versus collectivism, and the cross-cultural challenges to the study of personality.

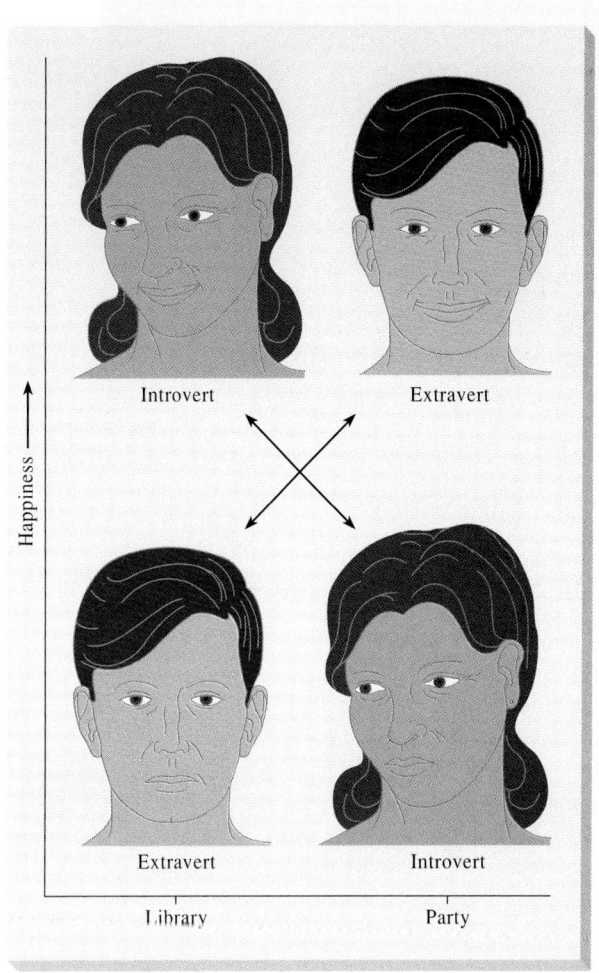

FIGURE 15.7

Trait-Situation Interaction
Who is happier, an introvert or an extravert? According to the concept of trait-situation interaction, we have to know the nature of the situation in which the introvert and extravert are behaving. At a party, the extravert probably will be happier than the introvert; at a library, the introvert probably will be happier than the extravert (Peterson, 1988).

Individualism Versus Collectivism

In America, "the squeaky wheel gets the grease." In Japan, "the nail that stands out gets pounded down." Such anecdotes suggest that people in Japan and America have very different views of self and other (Markus & Kitayama, 1991).

In cross-cultural research, the search for basic traits has been extended to a search for characteristics that are common to whole nations. In recent years, the most elaborate search for traits common to the inhabitants of a particular country has focused on the dichotomy of individualism/collectivism (Hofstede, 1980; Hui & Triandis, 1986; Triandis, 1994). **Individualism** *involves giving priority to personal goals rather than to group goals; it emphasizes*

How Collectivists and Individualists Can Interact More Effectively

If you come from a collectivist culture and you are about to interact with someone from an individualist culture, are there ways you can communicate with the other person more effectively? Similarly, if you are from an individualist culture and are about to interact with someone from a collectivist culture, are there ways you can communicate with the person more effectively? Cross-cultural psychologists Harry Triandis, Richard Brislin, and C. Harry Hui (1988) think so. Some of their recommendations follow. First are the suggestions for collectivists interacting with individualists:

1. Do not expect the individualists' compliance with group norms to be as high as it is in a collectivist culture.
2. A person from an individualist culture is likely to be very proud of his or her accomplishments. Compliment the individualist more than you are used to in your collectivist culture.
3. Expect individualists to be more emotionally detached from events that occur in their ingroup than is likely in your collectivist culture.
4. Do not feel threatened if individualists act competitively; learn to expect individualists to be more competitive than collectivists.
5. It is all right for you, as a collectivist, to talk about your accomplishments. You do not have to be modest but, at the same time, do not boast.

6. Expect a person from an individualist culture to be less strongly attached to the extended family than is the case in your collectivist culture. For example, family obligations are less likely to be accepted by an individualist as an excuse for failing to complete an assignment.
7. If you try to change an individualist's opinions, do not expect that you will be as persuasive as you are in your own collectivist culture when you use arguments that stress cooperation, harmony, or avoidance of confrontation.
8. A person from an individualist culture is more likely to define status in terms of individual accomplishments rather than on the basis of ascribed attributes (sex, age, family name, and so on) than is the case in a collectivist culture.

Following are some suggestions for individualists interacting with collectivists:

1. Learn to pay attention to group memberships. Collectivists' behavior often depends on the norms of the ingroups that are important in their lives.
2. Take into account the attitudes of a collectivist person's ingroup authorities. A collectivist person's attitudes and behaviors will probably reflect them.
3. When a collectivist person's group membership changes, his or her attitudes and even personality probably will change to reflect the different group.
4. Spend some time finding out about a collectivist person's ingroups. What events occur in them? What duties are specified? A collectivist person is more likely to do what these norms specify than an individualist is used to seeing.
5. Do not use yourself as a yardstick of involvement in activities that involve ingroups. A collectivist is much more likely to be involved with groups than is an individualist.
6. A collectivist will probably be less comfortable in competitive circumstances than an individualist will be.
7. If you have to criticize, do so carefully and only in private. In your collectivist culture, people usually do not say no or criticize.
8. Cultivate long-term relationships. Be patient. People in collectivist cultures value dealing with "old friends."

values that serve the self, such as feeling good, personal achievement and distinction, and independence. **Collectivism** *emphasizes values that serve the group by subordinating personal goals to preserve group integrity, the interdependence of members, and harmonious relationships.* Cross-cultural psychologists describe the cultures in many non-Western countries such as Russia, Japan, and India as more collectivistic than individualistic (Kagitcibasi, 1988,

1995; Triandis, 1985, 1994). To read about how collectivists and individualists can interact more effectively, turn to Applications in Psychology 15.1.

As with other attempts to explain personality, the individualism/collectivism dichotomy also has its detractors. They argue that describing entire nations of people as having a basic personality obscures the extensive diversity and individual variation that characterizes any nation's people.

Also, certain values, such as wisdom, mature love, and tolerance, serve both individual and collective interests (Schwartz, 1990). We are unlikely to find significant differences in some values and behaviors when we make cross-cultural comparisons between individualistic and collectivistic cultures.

Individualistic societies might promote the use of traits to describe personality, because there might be adaptive advantages to labeling systems that promote quick judgments about the actions of others in these contexts (Brislin, 1993). In contrast, collectivists are likely to maintain enduring relationships with individuals over a long period of time. Collectivists are far more likely to make subtle judgments about the behavior of others as a function of the setting or phase of life in which the behavior occurs.

Personality as a Cross-Cultural Construct

Cross-cultural psychologists believe that both the immediate setting and the broader cultural context are important in understanding personality. However, some challenge whether the concept of personality is useful in some cultural contexts.

As is true of a great deal of psychology's basic tenets, many of the assumptions about personality developed in Western cultures emphasize the individual or self. Psychological terms about personality often include the word *self*—for example, *self-actualization, self-awareness, self-concept, self-efficacy, self-reinforcement, self-criticism, self-doubt,* and *self-control* (Lonner, 1988; Rumpel, 1988). Most therapies in Western cultures emphasize interventions that focus on changing the self rather than modifying the systems or contexts in which the individual participates. Some social scientists believe that many of our problems, such as anxiety, depression, and shyness, are intensified by the emphasis on the self and independence in American culture (Munroe & Munroe, 1975). Critics of Western culture argue that our emphasis on individualism may undermine the basic need our species has for relatedness (Kagitcibasi, 1995). Regardless of their cultural background, people need a positive sense of self *and* connectedness to others to develop fully as human beings.

So far our discussion of personality has focused on a number of theories and viewpoints. As we will see next, assessment is also an extremely important aspect of personality.

Some social scientists believe that many of Americans' problems, such as anxiety, depression, and shyness, are intensified by the emphasis on the self and independence in the American culture. In many Eastern cultures, such as China, there is a much stronger emphasis on connectedness with others and group behavior. Similarly, pressures in collectivist cultures to conform may be experienced by some members as restricting freedom of choice.

REVIEW

Other Perspectives: Traits and Contexts

Different explanations of types and traits have emerged over time. Personality type theory involves classifying individuals according to particular types; Sheldon's somatotype theory is an example. This view is heavily criticized. Trait theories emphasize that personality involves the organization of traits within the individual; these traits are believed to be enduring. Allport stressed the individuality of traits; Eysenck sought the traits common to all of us. The search for trait dimensions continues; one contemporary view stresses that we have five basic traits.

Mischel's book *Personality and Assessment* ushered in an attack on trait theory; basically, Mischel argued that personality varies according to the situation considerably more than trait theorists acknowledge. Today most psychologists are interactionists; they believe personality is determined by a combination of both traits (or person variables) and the situation.

The sociocultural perspective in personality emphasizes both the dichotomy between individualism and collectivism, and the cross-cultural challenge to personality theory. Cross-cultural psychologists believe that both the immediate setting and the broader cultural context are important determinants of personality. In Western cultures, many assumptions about personality emphasize the individual and self.

PERSONALITY ASSESSMENT

"This line running this way indicates that you are a gregarious person, someone who really enjoys being around people. This division over here suggests that you are a risk taker; I bet you like to do things that are adventurous sometimes." These are the words you might hear from a palmist. Palmistry purports to "read" an individual's personality by interpreting precisely the irregularities and folds in the skin of the hand. For example, a large mound of Saturn, the portion of the palm directly below the third joint of the middle finger, ostensibly relates to wisdom, good fortune, and prudence.

Although palmists claim to provide a complete assessment of personality through reading lines in the hand, researchers debunk palmistry as quackery (Lanyon & Goodstein, 1982). Researchers argue that palmists give no reasonable explanation for their inferences about personality and point out that the hand's characteristics can change through age and even through exercise.

Even so, palmists manage to stay in business. They do so, in part, because they are keen observers—they respond to such cues as voice, general demeanor, and dress, which are more relevant signs of personality than the lines and folds on a person's palm. Palmists also are experts at offering general, trivial statements, such as "Although you usually are affectionate with others, sometimes you don't get along with people." This statement falls into the category of the **Barnum effect:** *if you make your descriptions broad enough, any person can fit them.* The effect was named after the famous showman P. T. Barnum, whose name still helps advertise the world's largest circus. Barnum used to lure gullible people with "Come one, come all—come and see a horse's tail where the head should be!" He would then show them a horse turned around in its stall.

I never think of the future. It comes soon enough.

Albert Einstein

In contrast, many psychologists use a number of scientifically developed tests and methods to evaluate personality, each assessing personality for different reasons (Butcher, 1995; Shrout & Fiske, 1995). Clinical and school psychologists assess personality to better understand an individual's psychological problems; they hope the assessment will improve their diagnosis and treatment of the individual. Industrial psychologists and vocational counselors assess personality to aid the individual's selection of a career. Research psychologists assess personality to investigate the theories and dimensions of personality discussed so far in this chapter. For example, if a psychologist wants to investigate self-concept, a measure of self-concept is needed. Some psychologists do not use formal assessment techniques. They prefer to rely on clinical observation and their years of expertise in interpreting clinical behavior.

Before we explore some specific personality tests, two more important points need to be made about the nature of personality assessment. First, the kinds of tests chosen by psychologists frequently depend on the psychologist's theoretical bent. Second, most personality tests are designed to assess stable, enduring characteristics, free of situational influence.

But the main thing is, does it hold good measure?

Robert Browning

Projective Tests

A **projective test** *presents individuals with an ambiguous stimulus and then asks them to describe it or tell a story about it. Projective tests are based on the assumption that the ambiguity of the stimulus allows individuals to project into it their feelings, desires, needs, and attitudes.* The test is especially designed to elicit an individual's unconscious feelings and conflicts, providing an assessment that goes deeper than the surface of personality. Projective tests attempt to get *inside* your mind to discover how you *really* feel and think, going beyond the way you overtly present yourself.

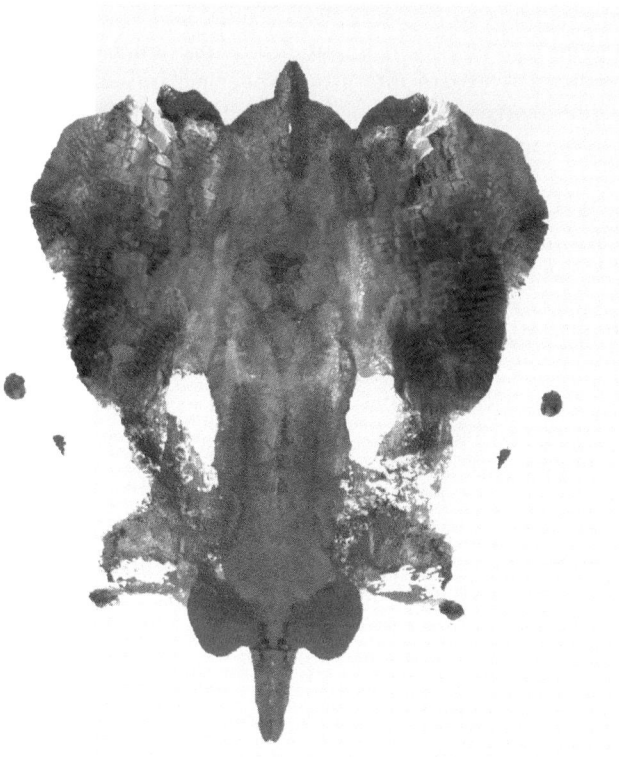

FIGURE 15.8

Type of Stimulus Used in the Rorschach Inkblot Test

The Rorschach Inkblot Test

The **Rorschach inkblot test,** *developed in 1921 by Swiss psychiatrist Hermann Rorschach, is the most well-known projective test; it uses individual perception of inkblots to determine personality.* The test consists of ten cards, half in black and white and half in color, which are shown to the individual one at a time (see figure 15.8). The psychologist asks the person to describe what she or he sees in each of the Rorschach inkblots. For example, an individual may say, "That looks like two people fighting." After the individual has responded to all ten inkblots, the examiner presents each of the inkblots again and inquires about the individual's earlier response. For example, the examiner might ask, "*Where* did you see the two people fighting?" and "*What* about the inkblot made the two people look like they were fighting?" Besides recording the responses, the examiner notes the individual's mannerisms, gestures, and attitudes.

How useful is the Rorschach in assessing personality? The answer to this question depends on one's perspective. From a scientific perspective, researchers are skeptical about the Rorschach (Feshbach & Wiener, 1991). Their disenchantment stems from the failure of the Rorschach to meet the criteria of reliability and validity, described in chapter 8. If the Rorschach were reliable, two different scorers, working independently without visual access to the individual taking the test, should agree on the personality characteristics of the individual. If the Rorschach were

valid, the individual's personality should predict behavior outside of the testing situation; that is, it should predict whether an individual will attempt suicide, become severely depressed, cope successfully with stress, or get along well with others. Conclusions based on research evidence suggest that the Rorschach does not meet these criteria of reliability and validity. This has led to serious reservations about the Rorschach's use in diagnosis and clinical practice.

However, the Rorschach continues to enjoy widespread use in clinical circles; some clinicians swear by the Rorschach, saying it is better than any other measure at getting at the true core of an individual's personality. They are not especially bothered by the Rorschach's low reliability and validity, pointing out that this is so because of the extensive freedom of response encouraged by the test. It is this freedom of response that makes the Rorschach such a rich clinical tool.

The Rorschach controversy continues, and it probably will not subside in the near future. Research psychologists will continue to criticize its low reliability and validity; many clinicians will continue to say that the Rorschach is a valuable clinical tool, providing insights about the unconscious mind that no other personality test can (Exner & Wiener, 1995).

The Thematic Apperception Test (TAT)

The **Thematic Apperception Test (TAT),** *which was developed by Henry Murray and Christiana Morgan in the 1930s, is an ambiguous projective test designed to elicit stories that reveal something about an individual's personality.* The TAT consists of a series of pictures, each on an individual card (see figure 15.9). The person administering the TAT asks the subject to tell a story about each of the pictures, including the events leading up to the situation described, the characters' thoughts and feelings, and how the situation turns out. Psychologists assume that the person projects her own unconscious feelings and thoughts into the story she tells. In addition to being used as a projective test in clinical practice, the TAT is used in the research of achievement motivation. Several of the TAT cards stimulate the telling of achievement-related stories, which enables the researcher to determine the person's need for achievement (McClelland & others, 1953).

In a newer version of the TAT, one of the cards depicts a scene of two people sitting on a bench by a river (McClelland, 1985). Following are two stories told by two different college students in response to this scene (King, 1991):

A: "These two people are involved in espionage. They are meeting to exchange information vital to the securities of both of their nations. Both feel they are doing the correct thing, but they are sometimes overwhelmed by intense feelings of guilt . . ."

B: "The couple is discussing their relationship. The woman is crying and her boyfriend is trying to console her. The reason she is crying is because he wants to see other women, she is hurt and does not want him to leave her alone. In this discussion, they will reach an agreement . . ."

FIGURE 15.9

A Picture from the Thematic Apperception Test (TAT)

Clearly, these two individuals told vastly different stories in response to the same picture. Through such imaginative stories, psychologists who use the TAT hope to reveal aspects of people of which the people themselves are unaware.

Other Projective Tests

Many other projective tests are used in clinical assessment. One test asks individuals to complete a sentence (for example, "I often feel . . ." "I would like to . . ."); another test asks the individual to draw a person; and another test presents a word, such as *fear* or *happy,* and asks the individual to say the first thing that comes to mind. Like the Rorschach, these projective tests have their detractors and advocates; the detractors often criticize the tests' low reliability and validity, and the advocates describe the tests' ability to reveal the underlying nature of the individual's personality better than more straightforward tests.

All projective tests share an important, often ignored characteristic. Although a person's responses may reflect the individual's personality, they also may be influenced by other factors, such as culture, social class, and gender. If the test interpreter does not share the same set of experiences as the test taker, how can the interpreter sensitively score the person's responses? Few people would recommend giving the Rorschach to someone who speaks another language,

then trying to organize the syllables into acceptable responses. However, it might also be presumptuous to assume that we can interpret another person's experiences confidently when his or her background differs sharply from our own.

Self-report Tests

Self-report tests *assess personality traits by asking what they are; these tests are not designed to reveal unconscious personality characteristics.* For example, self-report tests of personality include such items as the following:

I am easily embarrassed.
I love to go to parties.
I like to watch cartoons on TV.

Self-report tests are questionnaires that include a large number of such statements or questions. You respond with a limited number of choices (yes or no, true or false, agree or disagree, on a scale of 1 to 5, and so on). How do psychologists construct self-report tests of personality?

Constructing Self-report Tests

Many of the early personality tests were based on **face validity,** *which is an assumption that the content of the test items is a good indicator of what an individual's personality is like.* For example, if I developed a test item that asks you to respond whether or not you are introverted and you answer, "I enjoy being with people," I accept your response as a straightforward indication that you are not introverted. Tests based on face validity assume that you are responding honestly and nondefensively, giving the examiner an accurate portrayal of your personality.

Not everyone responds honestly, however, especially when questions concern their own personality. Even if the individual is basically honest, she or he might be giving socially desirable answers. **Social desirability** *is a factor that can lead individuals to give answers that they believe are socially desirable, rather than what they really think or feel, in order to make themselves look better.* For example, if someone is basically a lazy person, she may not want you to know this and she may try to present herself in a more positive way; therefore, she would respond negatively to the following item: "I fritter away time too much." Because of such responses, psychologists realized they needed to go beyond face validity in constructing personality tests; they accomplished this by developing empirically keyed tests.

Empirically keyed tests *rely on the test items to predict a particular criterion. Unlike tests based on face validity, in which the content of the items is supposed to be a good indicator of what a tested individual's personality is like, empirically keyed tests make no assumptions about the nature of the items.* Imagine we want to develop a test that will determine whether or not applicants for the position of police officer are likely to be competent at the job. We might ask a large number of questions of police officers, some of whom have excellent job records, others who have not performed as well. We would then use the questions that differentiate competent and incompetent police officers on our test to screen job applicants. If the item "I enjoy reading poetry" predicts success as a police officer, then we would include it on the test, even though it seems unrelated to police work. Next we will examine the most widely used empirically keyed personality test.

The Minnesota Multiphasic Personality Inventory

The **Minnesota Multiphasic Personality Inventory (MMPI)** *is the self-report personality test that is most widely used in clinical and research settings.* Psychologists originally developed the MMPI to improve the process of diagnosing individuals with mental disorders. A thousand statements were given to both people with mental disorders and apparently normal people. How often individuals agreed with each item was calculated; only the items that clearly differentiated the individuals with mental disorders from the normal individuals were retained. For example, a statement might be included on the depression scale of the MMPI if people diagnosed with a depressive disorder agreed with the statement significantly more than did normal individuals. This criterion keying allows us to include a statement with little face value, such as "I sometimes tease animals," on the depression scale, or any other scale, of the MMPI.

The MMPI eventually was streamlined to 566 items, including some repeated items, each of which can be answered *True, False,* or *Cannot say.* The items vary widely in content and include statements like the following:

I like to read magazines.
I never have trouble falling asleep.
People are out to get me.

A person's answers are grouped according to ten clinical categories, or scales, that measure such problems as depression, psychopathic deviation, schizophrenia, and social introversion.

The MMPI includes four validity scales in addition to the ten clinical scales. The validity scales were designed to indicate whether an individual is dishonest, careless, defensive, or evasive when answering the test items. For example, if an individual responds "False" to a number of items, such as "I get angry sometimes," it would be interpreted that she is trying to make herself look better than she really is. The rationale for the lie scale is that each of us gets angry at least some of the time, so the individual who responds "False" to many such items is faking her responses.

For the first time in its approximately 40-year history, the MMPI was revised in 1989. The revision added new content scales and deleted some statements, including all items pertaining to religion and most of the questions about sexual practices. The revised MMPI-2 has 567 items. Its basic clinical scales have not changed; however, content scales that relate to the broader professional interests of some clinicians and employers were added. In addition, cross-cultural research influenced the restructuring of the MMPI-2. The content scales focus on substance abuse, eating disorders, Type A behavior, repression, anger, cynicism, low self-esteem, family problems, and inability to function in a job.

Thousands of research studies and many books have documented the ability of the MMPI to improve the accuracy of diagnosis of mentally disturbed individuals. The MMPI has been used in more than 50 countries; more than 125 translations of the test are available.

However, cross-cultural psychologists don't automatically applaud the translation and use of the MMPI in other cultures. Mere translations without the development of norms specific to the culture might not produce a valid interpretation of personality. Cross-cultural psychologist Walter Lonner (1990) points out that the MMPI was developed by American psychologists and follows a Western view of mental health. Because it was standardized on a group of people in Minnesota, he recommends considerable caution when using the MMPI, as well as other personality tests, on people from other cultures.

The MMPI also contains some outdated stereotypes regarding gender. For example, if a woman responds on the MMPI that she likes hunting and fishing, she might be labeled abnormally masculine simply because more men report enjoying hunting and fishing.

Although the MMPI is used to assess normal functioning, critics suggest that this practice might not be appropriate or ethical. They believe that the MMPI is now being misused in business and education to predict which individual will make the best job candidate or which career an individual should pursue. Also, persons who are inadequately trained in psychological testing and diagnosis sometimes both give and interpret the MMPI, despite the fact that this is a clear violation of the code of ethics of the American Psychological Association. In these cases the MMPI is often used for purposes other than those for which it was originally designed.

Q-Sort

The term **Q-sort** *refers to a way of measuring personality in which individuals sort a set of adjectives or statements according to the degree to which they believe them to describe themselves.* Although humanists often disparage the use of labels, the Q-sort provides a mechanism by which self-concept can be measured using self-report. Statements like the following are presented to the person:

· I am satisfied with myself.
· I have few values and standards of my own.
· I don't trust myself.

Type of behavior	Item
Shared activities	We sat and read together.
	We took a walk.
Pleasing interactive events	My spouse asked how my day was.
	We talked about personal feelings.
	My spouse showed interest in what I said by agreeing or asking relevant questions.
Displeasing interactive events	My spouse commanded me to do something.
	My spouse complained about something I did.
	My spouse interrupted me.
Pleasing affectionate behavior	We held each other.
	My spouse hugged and kissed me.
Displeasing affectionate behavior	My spouse rushed into intercourse without taking time for foreplay.
	My spouse rejected my sexual advances.
Pleasing events	My spouse did the dishes.
	My spouse picked up around the house.
Displeasing events	My spouse talked too much about work.
	My spouse yelled at the children.

FIGURE 15.10

Items from the Spouse Observation Checklist
Couples are instructed to complete a more extensive checklist for 15 consecutive evenings to provide a thorough behavioral assessment of factors that contribute to marital satisfaction and strain. Each spouse records the behavior of his or her partner, and they make daily ratings of their overall satisfaction with the spouse's behavior.

From N. S. Jacobson, et al., "Toward a Behavioral Profile of Marital Distress" in *Journal of Consulting and Clinical Psychology*, 48:696–703. Copyright 1980 by the American Psychological Association. Adapted by permission.

The test taker then sorts the statements into categories from "least like me" to "most like me." In line with Carl Rogers's belief that it is important to distinguish between the real self and the ideal self, individuals are asked to sort the cards under either the self as is (real self) or the self the person would like to be (ideal self). Rogerians believe that a large discrepancy between the real self and the ideal self signals low self-esteem. The Q-sort can be used to measure progress in therapy or can be used in research.

Evaluating Self-report Tests

Adherents of the trait approach have strong faith in the utility of self-report tests. They point out that self-report tests have produced an improved understanding of the nature of personality traits than can be derived from, for example, projective tests. However, some critics (especially psychoanalysts) believe that self-report measures do not get at the core of personality and its unconscious determinants. Other critics (especially behaviorists) believe that self-report tests do not adequately capture the situational variations in personality and the ways in which personality changes as individuals interact with the environment.

Behavioral Assessment

Behavioral assessment attempts to obtain more objective information about an individual's personality by directly observing the individual's behavior. Instead of removing situational influences from personality, as projective tests and self-report measures do, behavioral assessment assumes that personality cannot be evaluated apart from the environment.

Recall from chapter 6 that behavior modification is an attempt to apply learning principles to change maladaptive behavior. Behavioral assessment of personality emerged from this tradition. For example, recall that an observer often will make baseline observations of the frequency of the individual's behaviors. This might be accomplished under controlled laboratory conditions or in natural circumstances. The therapist then modifies one aspect of the environment, such as getting parents and the child's teacher to stop giving the child attention when he or she engages in aggressive behavior. After a specified period of time, the therapist observes the child again to determine if the changes in the environment were effective in reducing the child's maladaptive behavior.

Sometimes, though, direct observations are impractical. What does a psychologist with a behavioral orientation do to assess personality? She might ask individuals to make their own assessments of behavior, encouraging them to be sensitive to the circumstances that produced the behavior and the outcomes or consequences of the behavior. For example, a therapist might want to know the course of marital conflict in the everyday experiences of a couple. Figure 15.10 shows a "spouse observation checklist" that couples can use to record their partner's behavior.

CRITICAL THINKING

Test-Taking Attitude

If you had to take a personality test, which of the test formats we have studied would be most interesting to you? How would you explain your choice? This example gives you an opportunity to *identify how your underlying values influence your behavior.* For example, you might be motivated by the value of self-knowledge. Any test that leads to greater insight would be worth taking. Or you might believe that the unconscious exerts strong influence. In this case, projective tests would be to your liking. Finally, you might dislike the idea of labeling. The Q-sort would be a good choice.

follow it? Psychologists assess such cognitive processes as expectations, planning, and memory, possibly through interviews or questionnaires. For example, an interview might include questions that ask of individuals whether they exaggerate their faults and condemn themselves more than the situation warrants. A questionnaire might ask a person what her thoughts are after an upsetting event or assess the way she thinks during tension-filled moments (Bellack & Hersen, 1988).

More information about behavioral and cognitive assessment appears in chapter 17, where we will discuss psychotherapies. Many of the behavioral and cognitive assessments of personality are recent developments and are just beginning to find their way

The influence of social learning theory has increased the use of cognitive assessment in personality evaluation. The strategy is to discover what thoughts underlie behavior; that is, how do individuals think about their problems? What kinds of thoughts precede maladaptive behavior, occur during its manifestation, and into the evaluation of personality. Increasingly psychologists who use projective and self-report tests to measure personality are evaluating the individual's behavior and thoughts in the testing situation to provide important additional information. A summary of the different orientations is presented in table 15.3.

TABLE 15.3

Who Uses Which Assessment Method?

Psychoanalytic assessment	Clinical interviews Psychohistorical analysis Projective tests such as Rorschach	Humanistic assessment	Self-report measures such as the Q-Sort Clinical interviews *Clinical judgment more important than scientific measurement*
Behavioral assessment	Observation Behavioral assessment	Trait assessment	Self-report measures such as MMPI
Cognitive assessment	Observation Behavioral assessment		

REVIEW

Personality Assessment

Psychologists use a number of tests and measures to assess personality. These measures are often tied to a psychologist's theoretical orientation. Personality tests were basically designed to measure stable, enduring aspects of personality. Projective tests use ambiguous stimuli to encourage individuals to project their personality into the stimuli. They are designed to assess the unconscious aspects of personality. The Rorschach is the most widely used projective test; its effectiveness is controversial. Self-report measures are designed to assess an individual's traits; the most widely used self-report measure is the MMPI, an empirically keyed test. Behavioral assessment tries to obtain more objective information about personality through the observation of behavior and its environmental ties. Cognitive assessment increasingly is being used as part of behavioral assessment.

When you began this chapter, you constructed a list of characteristics that you thought captured your personality. We challenged you to think about whether the traits you selected were representative, enduring, consistent, and realistic. We questioned whether others would describe you in the same way.

Compassion could have been one of the traits you selected. Suppose we wanted to develop a simple self-report inventory that would allow the measurement of some aspects of compassion. Walter Mischel suggests that traits interact with situations. Suppose, to measure your compassion, we asked you which of the following acts you would perform:

- Agreeing to a request to sponsor a child in a technologically disadvantaged country
- Intervening in a friend's drug or alcohol problem
- Offering money to the homeless when they confront you personally
- Taking in stray animals
- Sacrificing your own plans to help a friend
- Volunteering assistance to a driver with a disabled car
- Alerting a friend who has some lunch stuck between his teeth
- Letting a sick friend copy your homework
- Giving away all your possessions to a needy organization

As you can see, measuring the trait of compassion with this inventory would be extremely difficult. The actions listed in this self-report checklist could all be compassionate in some circumstances, but it would certainly be difficult to evaluate a person's compassion using responses to this list. For example, you could endlessly adopt stray animals, but there are practical constraints on how much compassion you could show using this behavior. You could let a friend copy your homework in the compassion of the moment, but that judgment might be far from compassionate in the long run because your friend will be unlikely to learn something that could be useful in the future. Could we rule out your having any compassion if you indicated you wouldn't perform any of the actions on the list? Probably not. Although our compassion self-report checklist has face validity (that is, each item relates to compassion), it is unlikely that we could use it as it stands to conduct valid research on the trait.

Making judgments about traits is difficult not only in research situations; it can be surprisingly challenging in life. Although we regularly make trait attributions to help us understand situations, we might not sufficiently capture the complexity of the situation. The use of traits to explain behavior can help us be efficient processors of reality, but it is doubtful that it helps us make accurate or fair-minded interpretations. Sometimes the labels lead us to make premature judgments and turn our attention elsewhere—we assign a trait as the reason for an action and move on.

How can this knowledge help us to be more effective critical thinkers in relation to judgments about personality? We should be able to *apply psychological concepts to enhance personal adaptation* by incorporating the following skills:

1. **Reserve judgment, particulary when making negative attributions.**
   How important is it to resolve a behavioral question by attributing someone's actions to a trait? In many situations, labeling requires making a judgment that we may later regret. In the tradition of Skinner, it may be more helpful to think about and describe specific behaviors involved in the situation than dispense with the situation by assigning dysfunctional traits as the cause. For example, marriage therapists often help couples learn to describe the behaviors that are upsetting to them rather than continue to use hurtful and unhelpful labeling (such as "You are inconsiderate and insecure").

2. **Recognize the boundaries of labels.**
   When we feel compelled to make trait judgments, it is still helpful to remember the context in which the behavior occurred and confine the judgment to that circumstance. For example, if you think of your father as "mean," it will be useful to identify the circumstances in which he is mean. He might be mean when he has not gotten enough sleep or when he is trying to watch his weight. This restricted use of the label recognizes that there are likely to be many circumstances in which he is not mean, which brings into question the fairness of the use of the term.

3. **Abandon expectations about consistency.**
   As you read in this chapter, many other cultures may be less intense about defining, categorizing, and judging personality features. This attitude may be a function of living in collectivistic cultures where there is no particular advantage in labeling others' traits. Richard Brislin (1993) believes that enduring relationships in collectivistic cultures may show greater tolerance about inconsistencies in human behavior. Even if we don't live in a collectivistic culture, we can save some frustration if, like collectivists, we do not expect human beings to be consistent across all situations.

The very purpose of existence is to reconcile the glowing opinion we hold of ourselves with the appalling things that other people think about us.

Quentin Crisp

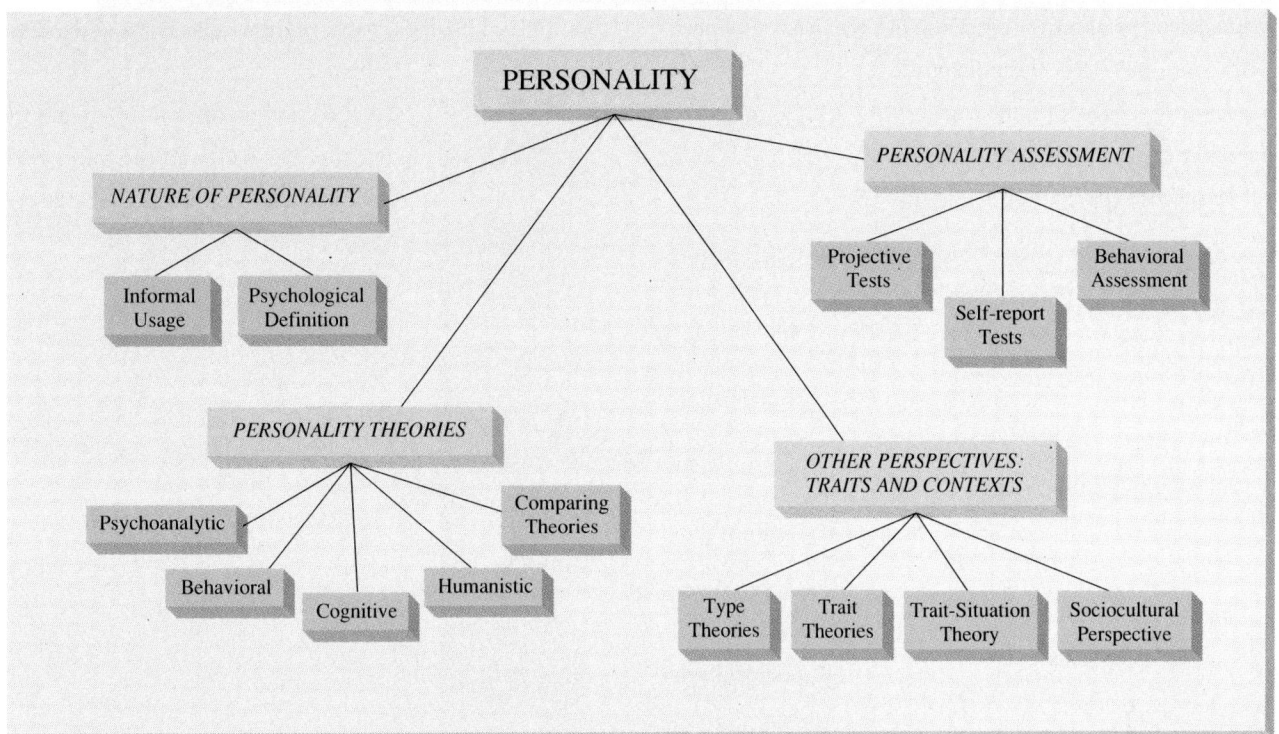

We began this chapter by evaluating the nature of personality, in terms of both informal usage of the term and a more formal psychological definition. We spent considerable time exploring personality theories—psychoanalytic, behavioral, cognitive, and humanistic— and we compared these theories. We also studied other perspectives—type theory, trait theory, trait-situation interaction, and the sociocultural perspective. To conclude the chapter, we read about personality assessment projective tests, self-report tests, and behavioral assessment. Remember that you can obtain an overall summary of the chapter by again studying the in-chapter reviews on pages 544, 552, 558, and 563.

We emphasized a number of perspectives in this chapter: the psychoanalytic perspective (pp. 536–544), the behavioral perspective (pp. 545–546), the humanistic perspective (pp. 547–550), the cognitive perspective (pp. 546–547), the sociocultural perspective (pp. 555–557). Also included in the chapter were a discussion of ethnicity and self-concept (p. 549), a discussion of how collectivists and individualists can interact more effectively (p. 556), and discussions of Freud's theory (pp. 536–540) and the roles of biological and learned factors (p. 551).

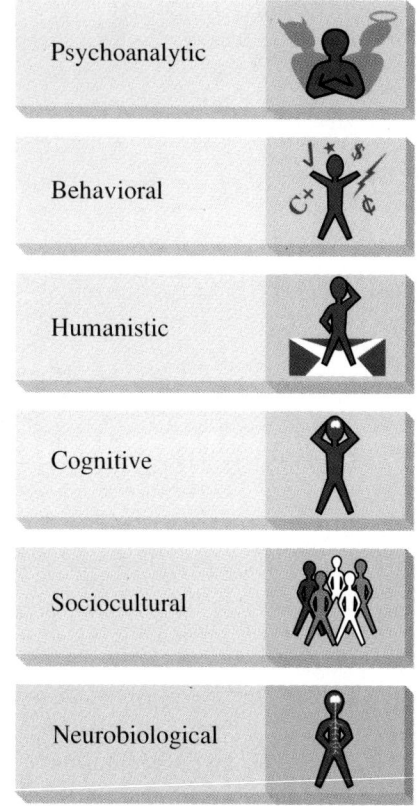

Psychoanalytic

Behavioral

Humanistic

Cognitive

Sociocultural

Neurobiological

KEY TERMS

personality Enduring, distinctive thoughts, emotions, and behaviors that characterize the way an individual adapts to the world. 534

id The Freudian structure of personality that consists of instincts, which are the person's reservoir of psychic energy. 536

pleasure principle The Freudian concept that the id always seeks pleasure and avoids pain. 536

ego The Freudian structure of personality that deals with the demands of reality; the ego is called the executive branch of personality because it makes rational decisions. 537

reality principle The Freudian concept that the ego tries to make the pursuit of individual pleasure conform to the norms of society. 537

superego The Freudian structure of personality that is the moral branch of personality. The superego takes into account whether something is right or wrong. 537

defense mechanisms The psychoanalytic term for unconscious methods of dealing with conflict; the ego distorts reality, thereby protecting itself from anxiety. 537

repression The most powerful and pervasive defense mechanism, according to Freud; it works to push unacceptable id impulses and traumatic memories out of awareness and back into the unconscious mind. 537

rationalization The psychoanalytic defense mechanism that occurs when the ego does not accept the real motive for an individual's behavior and replaces it with a sort of cover motive. 537

displacement The psychoanalytic defense mechanism that occurs when an individual shifts unacceptable feelings from one object to another, more acceptable object. 538

sublimation The psychoanalytic defense mechanism that occurs when the ego replaces an unacceptable impulse with a socially approved course of action. 538

projection The psychoanalytic defense mechanism that occurs when we attribute our own shortcomings, problems, and faults to others. 538

reaction formation The psychoanalytic defense mechanism that occurs when we express an unacceptable impulse by transforming it into its opposite. 538

regression The psychoanalytic defense mechanism that occurs when we behave in a way that is characteristic of a previous developmental level. 538

erogenous zones Those parts of the body at each stage of development that, according to Freud's theory, have especially strong pleasure-giving qualities. 538

fixation The psychoanalytic defense mechanism that occurs when the individual remains locked in an earlier developmental stage because her or his needs are under- or overgratified.   538

oral stage The term Freud used to describe development during the first 18 months of life, when the infant's pleasure centers on the mouth.   538

anal stage Freud's second stage of development, occurring between 1½ and 3 years of age, in which the child's greatest pleasure involves the anus or the eliminative functions associated with it.   538

phallic stage Freud's third stage of development, which occurs between the ages of 3 and 6; its name comes from the Latin word *phallus,* which means "penis." During the phallic stage, pleasure focuses on the genitals as the child discovers that self-stimulation is enjoyable.   539

Oedipus complex In Freud's theory, the young child's developing an intense desire to replace the parent of the same sex and to enjoy the affections of the opposite-sex parent.   539

latency stage The fourth Freudian stage of development, occurring approximately between 6 years of age and puberty; the child represses all interest in sexuality and develops social and intellectual skills.   540

genital stage The fifth Freudian stage of development, occurring from puberty on; the time of sexual reawakening; the source of sexual pleasure now becomes someone outside of the family.   540

collective unconscious In Jung's theory, the impersonal, deepest layer of the unconscious mind, which is shared by all human beings because of their common ancestral past.   542

archetypes Primordial influences in every individual's collective unconscious that filter our perceptions and experiences.   542

individual psychology The name Adler gave to his theory of psychology to emphasize the uniqueness of every individual.   542

striving for superiority The human motivation to adapt to, improve, and master the environment.   542

compensation Adler's term for the individual's attempt to overcome imagined or real inferiorities or weaknesses by developing her or his abilities.   543

overcompensation Adler's term for the individual's attempt to deny rather than acknowledge a real situation, or the individual's exaggerated efforts to conceal a weakness.   543

inferiority complex The name Adler gave to exaggerated feelings of inadequacy.   543

superiority complex Adler's concept of exaggerated self-importance that is designed to mask feelings of inferiority.   543

radical behaviorists Psychologists who emphasize only observable behavior and reject its cognitive dimensions.   545

expectancy An individual's belief in the probability that a specific behavior will lead to satisfactions or valued goals.   546

personal construct theory Kelly's theory that emphasizes the importance of how people perceive, organize, interpret, and construe events and the world in which they live for understanding their personality.   546

cognitive social learning theory The contemporary version of social learning theory that stresses the importance of cognition, behavior, and environment.   546

self-efficacy The belief that one can master a situation and produce positive outcomes.   546

delay of gratification The ability to defer immediate satisfaction for a more desirable future outcome.   546

phenomenological worldview A worldview that stresses the importance of our perceptions of ourselves and our world in understanding personality. This view emphasizes that, for each individual, reality is what that person perceives.   547

humanistic perspective The most widely adopted phenomenological approach to personality.   547

conditional positive regard Rogers's term for making the bestowal of love or praise conditional on the individual's conforming to parental or social standards.   547

self-concept An individual's overall perceptions of her or his abilities, behavior, and personality; a central theme for Rogers and other humanists.   548

unconditional positive regard Rogers's term for accepting, valuing, and being positive toward another person regardless of the person's behavior.   548

deficiency needs Maslow's term for essential requirements— physiological needs (for food, shelter, comfort, and so on) and psychological needs (for affection, security, self-esteem, and so on)—that must be met or else individuals will try to make up for their absence.   550

metaneeds In Maslow's theory, the higher, self-actualized needs; they include truth, goodness, beauty, wholeness, vitality, uniqueness, perfection, justice, inner wealth, and playfulness; also called growth needs.   550

determinism The belief that historical or biological factors completely account for behavior.   551

traits Broad dispositions that lead to characteristic responses.   553

somatotype theory Sheldon's theory that precise charts reveal distinct body types, which in turn are associated with certain personality characteristics.   553

endomorph Sheldon's term for a soft, round, large-stomached person who is relaxed, gregarious, and food loving.   553

mesomorph Sheldon's term for a strong, athletic, and muscular person who is energetic, assertive, and courageous.   553

ectomorph Sheldon's term for a tall, thin, fragile person who is fearful, introverted, and restrained.   553

trait theories Theories that propose that people have broad dispositions that are reflected in the basic ways they behave, such as whether they are outgoing and friendly or whether they are dominant and assertive.   554

situationism Mischel's view that a person's personality often varies from one context to another.   555

individualism Giving priority to personal goals rather than group goals; an emphasis on values that serve the self, such as feeling good, personal achievement and distinction, and independence.   555

collectivism An emphasis on values that serve the group by subordinating personal goals to preserve group integrity, interdependence of members, and harmonious relationships.   556

Barnum effect If you make your descriptions broad enough, any person can fit them.   558

projective tests Tests that present individuals with an ambiguous stimulus and then ask them to describe it or tell a story about it. Projective tests are based on the assumption that the ambiguity of the stimulus allows individuals to project into it their feelings, desires, needs, and attitudes.   558

Rorschach inkblot test The most well-known projective test, developed in 1921 by Swiss psychiatrist Hermann Rorschach. It uses individuals' perceptions of inkblots to determine their personality.   559

Thematic Apperception Test (TAT) An ambiguous projective test designed to elicit stories that reveal something about an individual's personality; developed by Henry Murray and Christiana Morgan in the 1930s.   559

self-report tests Tests that assess personality traits by asking individuals what their traits are; not designed to reveal unconscious personality characteristics. 560

face validity An assumption that the content of test items is a good indicator of what an individual's personality is like. 560

social desirability A factor that can lead individuals to give answers that they believe are socially desirable, rather than what they really think or feel, in order to make themselves look better. 560

empirically keyed tests Tests that rely on the test items to predict a particular criterion. Unlike tests based on face validity, in which the content of the test items is supposed to be a good indicator of what a tested individual's personality is like, empirically keyed tests make no assumptions about the nature of the items. 560

Minnesota Multiphasic Personality Inventory (MMPI) The self-report personality test most widely used in clinical and research settings. 561

Q-sort A way of measuring personality in which individuals sort a set of adjectives or statements according to the degree to which they believe them to describe themselves. 561

PRACTICAL KNOWLEDGE ABOUT PSYCHOLOGY

CONTROL YOUR DEPRESSION

(Revised) (1992) by Peter Lewinsohn, Ricardo Muñoz, Mary Youngren, and Antonette Zeiss. New York: Fireside.

Control Your Depression tells you how to reduce your depression by learning self-control techniques, relaxation training, pleasant activities, planning ahead, modifying self-defeating thinking patterns, and other behavioral/cognitive strategies. Dozens of examples illustrate how to gauge your progress, maintain the gains you make, and also determine whether you need further help. Easy to follow step-by-step methods take you through a number of strategies for controlling depression.

GENTLE ROADS TO SURVIVAL

(1991) by Andre Auw. Lower Lake, CA: Aslan.

In *Gentle Roads to Survival*, Auw presents a guide to making self-healing choices in difficult circumstances. Auw, a psychologist who was a close associate of Carl Rogers, tells you how to become a survivor. He believes that while some people may be born to be survivors, most of us have to learn survival skills. Auw addresses personal crises in religion, morality, agonizing parenting and marital breakups, the pain of cross-cultural adaptation, and many other highly stressful circumstances. He especially advocates that each person has to discover his or her own unique path of adaptation and coping.

Auw teaches readers the spirit of respect and caring in human relationships. Auw's approach is warm, sensitive, and compassionate. Before his death, Carl Rogers said that Andrew Auw's ideas contain a great deal of wisdom.

Man and His Symbols (1964)
> by Carl Jung
> Garden City, NY: Doubleday

This book includes writings by Jung and by four of his disciples; Jung's ideas are applied to anthropology, literature, art, and dreams.

Man, the Manipulator (1972)
> by Everett Shostrum
> New York: Bantam

This paperback presents humanistic ideas about the route from manipulation to self-actualization. Many case studies are included.

Mental Measurements Yearbook (1992, 11th ed.)
> edited by Jack Kramer and Jane Conoley
> Lincoln: University of Nebraska Press

This voluminous resource provides details about a wide range of personality tests.

Personality (1992, 2nd ed.)
> by Christopher Peterson
> Fort Worth, TX: Harcourt Brace

This well-written textbook on personality includes many applications to real-world issues.

Personality Disorder and the Five-Factor Model of Personality (1994)
> by Paul Costa and Thomas Widiger
> Washington, DC: American Psychological Association

This book includes information about using the five-factor model in the diagnosis and treatment of a number of psychological disorders, including substance abuse.

Psychological Testing of Hispanics (1992)
> by Kurt Geisinger
> Washington, DC: American Psychological Association

This book addresses a number of issues related to the psychological testing of Latinos, including testing in clinical settings and the workplace.

Abnormal Psychology and Therapy

The small seed of despair cracks open and sends experimental tendrils upward to the fragile skin of calm holding him together.

Judith Guest, *Ordinary People*

Modern life is stressful and leaves its psychological scars on too many people, who, unable to cope effectively, never reach their human potential. In this section, we explore how psychologists diagnose the range of mental disorder as well as how they treat disordered behavior. Section Seven contains two chapters: "Abnormal Psychology" (chapter 16) and "Therapies" (chapter 17).

PAUL KLEE
Strange Garden, detail

Abnormal Psychology

> *They cannot scare me with their
> empty spaces
> Between stars—on stars where
> no human race is.
> I have it in me so much nearer home
> To scare myself with my own
> desert places.*
>
> **Robert Frost**

Even before his father's suicide, the American author Ernest Hemingway seemed obsessed by the theme of self-destruction. As a young boy he enjoyed reading Stevenson's "The Suicide Club." At one point in his adult life, Hemingway said he would rather go out in a blaze of light than have his body worn out by age and his illusions shattered.

Hemingway's suicidal thoughts sometimes coincided with his marital crises. Just before marrying his first wife, Hadley, Hemingway became apprehensive about his new responsibilities and alarmed her by the mention of suicide. Five years later, during a crisis with his second wife, Pauline, he calmly told her he would have committed suicide if their love affair had not been resolved happily. Hemingway was strangely comforted by morbid thoughts of death. When he was feeling down and out, Hemingway would think about death and various ways of dying; the best way he thought, unless he could arrange to die in his sleep, would be to go off an ocean liner at night.

Hemingway committed suicide in his sixties. His suicide made people wonder why a man with such good looks, sporting skills, friends, women, wealth, fame, genius, and a Nobel Prize would kill himself. His actual life did not reflect the glamorous one others assigned to him. Rather, Hemingway had developed a combination of physical and mental disturbances. He had neglected his health for some years, and suffered from weight loss, skin disease, alcoholism, diabetes, hypertension, and impotence. His body in a shambles, he dreaded becoming an invalid and the slow death this would bring. At this point, the severely depressed Hemingway was losing his memory and no longer could write. One month before his suicide, Hemingway said, "Staying healthy. Working good. Eating and drinking with friends. Enjoying myself in bed. I haven't any of them" (Meyer, 1985, p. 559).

PREVIEW

Mental disorders know no social and economic boundaries. They find their way into the lives of the rich and famous and the poor and the unknown. In this chapter, we will study several mental disorders, including the depression and suicide that troubled the life of Ernest Hemingway. We begin by examining some basic questions about the nature of abnormal behavior, then turn our attention to the following mental disorders: anxiety, somatoform, dissociative, mood, schizophrenic, personality, and substance-use disorders. We also evaluate the legal aspects of mental disorders.

DIMENSIONS OF ABNORMALITY

Could Hemingway's depression and suicide be considered abnormal behavior? If so, what made them abnormal? What causes abnormal behavior? How can we classify abnormal behavior? How prevalent is abnormal behavior in our culture? We will consider each of these important questions about abnormal behavior.

Defining Abnormality

Distinguishing what is abnormal behavior from what is normal behavior is not an easy task. Many scholars have suggested that a variety of factors can define abnormality, including statistical prevalence, maladaptiveness and harmfulness, personal discomfort, and cultural norms.

Statistical Prevalence

Consider Albert Einstein, Charles Barkley, and Barbara Walters. We think of each of them as atypical. However, we don't think Einstein was abnormal because he was a genius, that Barkley is abnormal because of his mastery of basketball (although some might consider his temperamental outbursts a sign of abnormal behavior), or that Walters is abnormal because she is one of television's most talented and highly paid interviewers.

However, many forms of mental disorder are *statistically unusual occurrences* for the vast majority of individuals in a culture who do not experience the problem. Most of us, unlike Hemingway, do not commit suicide as a way of solving problems. Most of us do not engage in extensive hand-washing rituals or hear relentless self-critical voices inside our heads. Thus, one way psychologists categorize behaviors as abnormal is by how infrequently they occur among the general population.

Maladaptiveness and Harmfulness

Statistical rarity alone may be an insufficient criterion of abnormality. However, the second category—*maladaptiveness and harmfulness*—adds another dimension. Maladaptive behavior fails to promote the well-being, growth, and fulfillment of the person and might contribute to the misery or harm of others. Maladaptive and harmful behavior takes many forms, including depression, suicide, bizarre irrational beliefs, assaults on others, and drug addiction. These abnormal behaviors interfere with the ability to function effectively in the world.

At first glance, Hemingway's suicide appears to be maladaptive and harmful because it ended a brilliant writing career. However, we could challenge this inference. Hemingway's declining health and writing obstacles may have prevented him from living a fulfilling life. His depression may have impeded his ability to see other solutions to the problems he experienced.

Personal Discomfort

Hemingway's actions clearly fit the third criterion of abnormal behavior—*personal discomfort*. He communicated his despair in many ways throughout his life. As a criterion of abnormal behavior, personal discomfort need not be as severe as that experienced by Hemingway. Guilt, grief, strain, frustration, disappointment, anger, and fear can all serve as the foundation for experiences that become so intense that they no longer feel "within normal limits" of human experience.

Cultural Influences

Cultures develop *norms* about what behavior is acceptable and what behavior is not. We might consider the same behavior abnormal in one context and thoroughly acceptable in another. For example, many people in Western cultures believe that suicide is an unacceptable behavior. Thus, the norm or social custom is avoidance of suicide. In contrast, *hari-kiri* is a form of suicide that the Japanese culture encourages as an honorable alternative to shaming the family.

A depressed Hemingway shortly before his suicide.

In some cultures, people go about their daily activities with few or no clothes on. If we were to see someone walking naked down a city street in the United States, we probably would consider such behavior inappropriate; we also might think that such norm-violating behavior signaled that the person was in mental distress.

Sometimes the definition of abnormality changes from one historical period to another. For example, early in this century, many Americans believed that masturbation was sinful and caused everything from warts to insanity. Today only a few people think of masturbation as wicked, and most people accept the practice as a part of normal sexuality.

A final contextual example also poignantly demonstrates the fact that some individuals are empowered with the authority to label behaviors as "abnormal" and that other individuals are likely to be labeled. Prior to the Civil War, authorities diagnosed slaves who attempted to escape as having drapetomania (Cartwright, 1851/1981). This diagnosis categorized as mental illness a behavior that more likely was an adaptive response to severe life circumstances.

In sum, **abnormal behavior** is behavior that is maladaptive, harmful, statistically unusual, personally distressing, and/or designated abnormal by the culture.

Madness reveals the ungluing we all secretly fear:
the mind taking off from the body, the
possibility that that magnet that attaches
us to a context in the world can lose its grip.
Molly Haskell, *Love and Other Infectious Diseases*, 1990

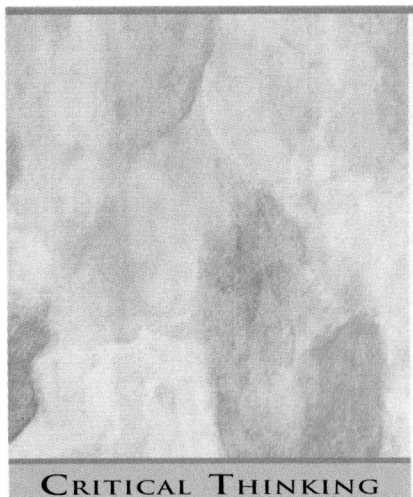

*Judging Abnormality
in Context*

We have studied the four hallmarks of abnormality. Now apply these characteristics to some behaviors observable in our culture:

Example 1. Living on the streets: Are the homeless statistically unusual? Are their behaviors maladaptive or harmful? Do they seem to be in personal distress? Does life on the street violate cultural norms?

Example 2. Making obscene phone calls: Are such phone calls statistically rare? Are they maladaptive? Do the phone callers seem to be in personal distress or do they cause distress to others? Are there cultural norms against making obscene phone calls?

Example 3. Shoplifting: How statistically rare is this behavior? Is shoplifting maladaptive? Who gets distressed by shoplifting? Does shoplifting violate cultural norms?

As you can see, each example behavior might be considered abnormal according to a different criterion. Some behaviors clearly meet all criteria. Others meet only a few. However, we are likely to regard all the examples as abnormal during this historical period in our culture. These examples represent *using psychological knowledge to promote human welfare,* because establishing the nature of abnormality can lead to intervention.

Living in the street, making obscene phone calls, and shoplifting all qualify as abnormal behavior, although these examples vary in how they meet criteria for abnormality.

The Origins of Abnormal Behavior

What causes people to behave abnormally? Psychologists typically sort the causes of abnormal behavior into three categories: biological factors, psychological factors, and sociocultural factors.

The Biological Approach

Proponents of the biological approach believe that abnormal behavior is due to a physical malfunction in the body, especially the brain. If an individual behaves in an uncontrollable manner, is out of touch with reality, or is severely depressed, biological factors are the primary culprits. Today scientists and researchers who adopt the biological approach often focus on brain processes and genetic factors as the causes of abnormal behavior. In the biological approach, drug therapy is frequently used to treat abnormal behavior.

The **medical model,** *also called the disease model, was the forerunner of the biological approach; the medical model states that abnormality is a disease or illness precipitated by internal physical causes.* Within this perspective, abnormalities are called mental *illnesses* and the individuals afflicted are *patients* in *hospitals,* who are treated by psychiatrists and, to a lesser extent, psychologists.

The Psychological Approaches

Although the biological approach provides an important perspective for understanding abnormal behavior, many psychologists believe that the medical model underestimates the importance of psychological factors, such as emotional turmoil, inappropriate learning, distorted thoughts, and inadequate relationships. The theories of personality described in chapter 15—psychoanalytic, behavioral and

TABLE 16.1

Unusual Culture-Bound Disorders

Amok	Malaysia, Philippines, Africa	This disorder involves sudden, uncontrolled outbursts of anger in which the person may injure or kill someone. Amok is often found in males who are withdrawn before the onset of the disorder. After an attack on someone, the individual feels exhausted and depressed and does not remember the rage and attack.
Anorexia nervosa	Western cultures, especially the United States	This eating disorder involves a relentless pursuit of thinness through starvation and can eventually lead to death. More about this disorder appears in chapter 15.
Windigo	Algonquin Indian hunters	This disorder involves a fear of being bewitched. The hunter becomes anxious and agitated, worrying he will be turned into a cannibal, with a craving for human flesh.
Nuptial psychosis	North Africa, India	This disorder occurs among very young women whose lives are disrupted by arranged marriage. Sexual trauma, separation from parents, and unfamiliar surroundings contribute to symptoms of confusion, hysteria, and suicide.
Kayak angst	Eskimos of Western Greenland	This occupational disorder strikes seal hunters who experience extreme anxiety after hours of solitary hunting in unfavorable and unstimulating environments.
Malgri	Australia	Severe abdominal pain caused by entering forbidden territory without purification rituals.
Berdache	Prairie Indians	This gender-role rejection allows men to avoid assuming aggressive roles by opting for the role of women.
Latah	Asia, Africa	This syndrome is found among low-status women who exhibit altered states of consciousness, including exaggerated obedience or impulsivity.
Koro	China	Sweating and severe anxiety mark this disorder, which represents a belief that the penis is retracting. The afflicted individual believes that, if the penis disappears, he will die.

social learning, and humanistic theories—provide insight into the nature of abnormal as well as normal behavior. Much more about the approaches to the treatment of abnormal behavior appears in the next chapter.

The Sociocultural Approach

As you might expect, the sociocultural approach emphasizes how culture, ethnicity, gender, age, and other sociocultural elements influence abnormal behavior. Most experts on abnormal behavior agree that many psychological disorders are universal, appearing in most cultures (Al-Issa, 1982a; World Health Organization, 1975). However, the frequency and intensity of abnormal behavior vary across cultures. Variations in disorders are related to social, economic, technological, religious, and other features of cultures (Costin & Draguns, 1989).

Some disorders appear to be especially culturebound. Al-Issa (1982a) described specific patterns illustrating how cultures influence abnormal behaviors. Certain exceptional patterns are *culturally approved* as opportunities to express expected but unusual behavior. Some cultures provide certain opportunities in which inebriation and sexual excesses are expected. The Mardi Gras celebrations of New Orleans are an example; another is the Greenland Eskimos' *Schimpfduelle*—ritualized insulting with song and

drumming. Some abnormal patterns are *culturally tolerated*. For example, in the Highlands of New Guinea, young men under severe stress enact the "wild man" syndrome. The wild man shows agitation, destroys property, and threatens attack. Others in the culture subdue, sometimes pamper, and ultimately reintegrate the wild man into the culture. Finally, some patterns are *culturally suppressed* through adherence to strong cultural prohibitions. Abnormal behavior can surface in direct contrast to the cultural norm. According to Al-Issa (1982a), the severe aggression found among mentally ill Japanese is due to the suppression promoted by Japanese culture's nonviolent norms. To learn more about several of the more unusual culture-bound disorders, turn to table 16.1.

Prevalence Estimates

How prevalent are mental disorders in the United States today? In a recent survey of 18,571 people randomly selected from five U.S. cities—New Haven, Connecticut; Baltimore, Maryland; St. Louis, Missouri; Piedmont, North Carolina; and Los Angeles, California—more than 15 percent of the respondents had suffered from a mental disorder during the previous month (Robins & Regier, 1990). Only one-third of the individuals reporting mental disorders had received treatment in the previous 6 months.

Nancy Felipe Russo (*at left*) has been instrumental in calling attention to the sociocultural factors involved in women's depression. She has chaired the National Coalition of Women's Mental Health.

Gender Prevalence

For the 1-month incidence of mental disorders, the data were also analyzed separately for men and women. The women had a slightly higher overall rate of mental disturbances than the men (16.6 percent versus 15.4 percent). The women had higher rates of mood disorders (for example, depression) (9.7 percent versus 4.7 percent); the men had higher rates of substance-use disorders (6.3 percent versus 1.6 percent) and antisocial personality disorders (0.8 percent versus 0.2 percent).

Women tend to be diagnosed as having disorders that typify traditional stereotypes of females. In particular, women are more likely than men to suffer from anxiety disorders and depression, disorders with symptoms that are internalized, or turned inward. Conversely, men are socialized to direct their energy toward the outside world—that is, to externalize their feelings and thoughts—and are more likely to show disturbances involving aggression and substance abuse.

Several explanations have been given as to why women are diagnosed and treated for mental disorders at a higher rate than men (Paludi, 1995). One possibility is that women do not have more mental disorders than men do, but that women are simply more likely to behave in ways that others label as mental disorders. For example, women have been taught to express their emotions, whereas men have been trained to control them. If women express feelings of sorrow and sadness, some individuals may conclude that women are more mentally disturbed than men are. Thus, the difference between the rates of mental disorders could involve the possibility that women more freely display and discuss their problems than men do.

A second explanation of the gender difference in the diagnosis of mental disorders focuses on women's inferior social position and the greater discrimination against women. Women are also more likely to experience certain trauma-inducing circumstances, such as incest, sexual harassment, rape, and marital abuse. Such abuse can increase women's emotional problems.

A third explanation of the gender difference in the diagnosis of mental disorders is that women are often placed in a "double-bind" situation in our society. For example, women can be labeled as mentally disturbed for either overconforming or underconforming to feminine gender-role stereotypes. That is, a woman who is overdependent, overemotional, and irrational is overconforming to the traditional feminine gender-role stereotype. On the other hand, a woman who is independent, who values her career as much as or more than her family, who doesn't express emotions, and who acts in a worldly and self-confident manner is underconforming to feminine gender-role stereotypes. In either case, the woman might be labeled emotionally disturbed. In sum, even though statistics show that women are more likely than men to have mental disorders, this gender difference may be the result of antifemale bias in American society.

Ethnicity and Socioeconomic Factors

In the United States, variations in mental disorders involve not only gender, but such factors as socioeconomic status, urbanization, neighborhood, and ethnicity. For example, people who live closest to the center of a city have the greatest risk of developing a mental disturbance (Suinn, 1984). Ethnic minority status also heightens the risk of mental distress (Huang & Gibbs, 1989). In one study on hospitalization rates, persons with Spanish surnames were more likely to be admitted for mental health problems when they were in the minority than when they were the majority (Bloom, 1975). In another study, conducted in New York City, this finding was supported: The fewer the number of ethnic members in one area—whether they were White, African American, or Puerto Rican—the higher their rate of mental health hospitalization (Rabkin, 1979). In yet another study, Whites living in African American areas had more than a 300 percent higher rate of severe mental disturbance than Whites living in White neighborhoods. Similarly, African Americans living in predominantly White areas have a 32 percent higher rate than African Americans living in African American neighborhoods (Mintz & Schwartz, 1964). All of these studies, however, are correlational; they do not determine cause and effect. It is possible that people who are mentally disturbed, or those predisposed to mental disorders, tend to choose communities in which they are the minority, or it may be that minority-group status produces stress and its related disorders.

Many ethnic minority individuals with a mental disorder live in low-income neighborhoods. However,

(a)

(b)

(*a*) People living in poor minority neighborhoods have high rates of mental disorders, but knowing this does not tell us why they have such high rates. Does poverty cause pathology, or are diagnosticians unaware of what behaviors and self-protective beliefs are necessary to survive in harsh contexts? (*b*) Effective therapy can take place when the client and therapist are from different sociocultural backgrounds. However, barriers to communication, which can develop in such circumstances, can destroy and undermine the effectiveness of therapy. Among the barriers are language differences, class-bound values, and culture-bound values.

knowing that people from poor minority neighborhoods have high rates of disorder does not reveal *why* they have such rates. Does poverty cause pathology, or is poverty a form of pathology for narrowly trained diagnosticians who are unaware of what behaviors and self-protective beliefs are necessary to survive in harsh circumstances? Researchers who are sensitive to, and comfortable with, these cultural dynamics are vital to the search for answers to these questions. To read further about the mental health of ethnic minority groups, turn to Sociocultural Worlds 16.1, where we present information about Latina women's mental health, one example of how ethnicity and mental health are related.

An Interactionist Approach

When considering an individual's behavior, whether abnormal or normal, it is important to remember the complexity of human nature and the multiple influences on behavior. Neither the biological nor the psychological nor the sociocultural approach independently captures this complexity. Abnormal behavior is influenced by biological factors (brain processes and heredity, for example), by psychological factors (emotional turmoil and distorted thoughts, for example), and by sociocultural factors (poverty and gender, for example). These factors often interact to produce abnormal behavior. We need to examine all approaches in order to produce a full explanation of abnormality.

Classifying Abnormal Behavior

Ever since human history began, people have suffered from diseases, sadness, and bizarre behavior. For almost as long, healers have tried to treat and cure them. The classification of mental disorders goes back to the ancient Egyptians and Greeks and has its roots in biology and medicine.

The first classification of mental disorders in the United States, based on the census data of 1840, used one category for all mental disorders. This one inclusive category included both the mentally retarded and the insane.

In the twentieth century, the American Psychiatric Association developed the major classification of mental disturbances in the United States. The *Diagnostic and Statistical Manual of Mental Disorders (DSM)*, published in 1952, included better definitions of mental disorders than previous classification efforts. A revised edition, the DSM-II, produced with more systematic assistance from expert diagnosticians, appeared in 1968. A third edition, the DSM-III, was published in 1980, and a revision of that manual, the DSM-III-R, in 1987. Published in 1994, the current manual, the DSM-IV, emphasizes refined empirical support of diagnostic categories.

Advantages of Diagnosis

Before we discuss the most widely used system to classify mental disorders, we will explore the many benefits of classifying mental disorders. First, a classification system provides professionals with a shorthand system for communicating with each other. For example, if one psychologist mentions in a case review that her client has a panic disorder and another psychologist says that her client has a generalized anxiety disorder, the two psychologists understand what the labels communicate about the disturbances. Second, a classification system permits psychologists to construct theories about the causes of particular disorders and design treatments for them. Third, a classification system can help psychologists to make predictions about disorders; it provides information about the likelihood that a disorder will occur, which individuals are most susceptible to the disorder, the progress of the disorder once it appears, and the prognosis for effective treatment (Meehl, 1986).

Disadvantages of Diagnosis

Advocates of the psychological and sociocultural approaches sometimes criticize the medical model and diagnostic practices because they believe that it encourages labeling processes that may be harmful. Some psychologists and psychiatrists believe that labeling individuals as "mentally ill" encourages them to perceive themselves as "sick" and to avoid assuming responsibility for coping with their problems (Szasz, 1977).

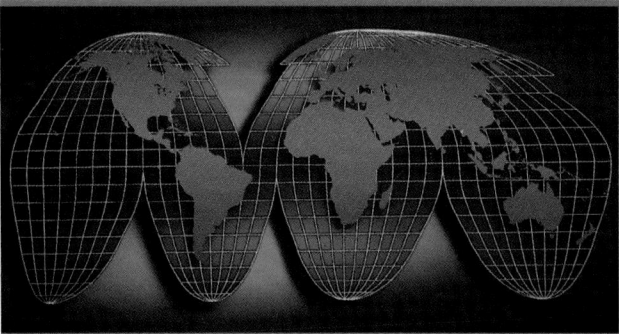

SOCIOCULTURAL WORLDS 16.1

Latina Women and Mental Health

Mental health policymakers have begun to recognize the importance of developing culturally sensitive mental health services for the rapidly growing Latino population. However, the gender bias that characterizes mental health theory, research, and practice is too often mirrored in mental health services designed to reach Latina populations (Russo, 1990). Any policy regarding the mental health of Latina women must recognize the importance of the diversity in the Latina population, in addition to gender bias. For example, in one study, Cuban Americans and Puerto Ricans made more visits to physicians than either Whites or African Americans, whereas Mexican Americans made fewer visits than any other group (Trevino, 1986).

To understand the mental health issues of Latina women, the social and economic contexts that shape their lives need to be considered. The stress of dislocation, loss of familiar people, and difficulties in starting life in a new land that accompany the experiences of migration and immigration also have mental health implications. The majority of Mexican Americans (75 percent) are born on the United States mainland; in contrast, most Puerto Ricans (55 percent), Cubans (75 percent), and Central or South Americans (64 percent) are not.

Latina women, with the exception of Cubans, are likely to have lower incomes and less education, as well as higher fertility rates, than Anglo-American women. Puerto Rican families are the poorest (earning 46 percent of non-Latinos), followed by Mexican American (71 percent) and Cuban (85 percent) families. Such poverty and its related woes—crowded housing, poor nutrition, boredom from lack of a job, frustration in getting adequate health care for children—is destructive to mental health.

Most discussions of Latino mental health portray an individual who is pressured and harassed by the problems of poverty, slum life, and a lack of acculturation into the American society (Rogler & others, 1987). However, 13 percent of all Latina women work in professional or managerial roles. In this group of Latina women, identity and personal life satisfaction are not derived solely from the roles of mother and wife (Amaro, Russo, & Johnson, 1987). Thus, these professional Latinas do not fit the cultural stereotype of the Latina woman who derives all of her identity from the roles of mother and wife. In understanding the mental health of Latina women, such diversity needs to be taken into account.

Latina women, with the exception of Cuban Americans, often have lower incomes and less education, as well as higher fertility rates, than Anglo American women. However, 13 percent of all Latina women work in professional or managerial roles. In this group of Latina women, identity and personal satisfaction are not derived solely from roles as mother and wife.

Using diagnostic procedures with members of ethnic minority groups may be especially problematic. In particular, studies have found that a client's ethnicity may adversely influence the assessment and diagnosis of mental disorders (Ramirez, 1989). For example, during diagnostic interviews, Native Americans may behave in ways that signal mental distress to a clinician unfamiliar with the Native American culture: Native Americans might be nonassertive, hesitant, and soft-spoken; they might exchange only limited eye contact; they might show discom-

fort and decreased performance on timed tasks; they might be reluctant to provide details about their personal lives; and they might have a group orientation rather than a self orientation (Hynd & Garcia, 1979). In addition, the historical difficulties between ethnic groups make it extremely difficult for many Native American, Latino, and African American individuals to trust a White person, or even a middle-class member of their own ethnic group, in the course of psychological assessment (Allen & Majidi-Ahi, 1989). For example, one study revealed that African

American clients tend to defend themselves by uttering essentially meaningless phrases or by telling clinicians what they want to hear (Jones & Seagull, 1977).

Cultural misunderstanding can work the other way too. Clinicians who are unfamiliar with their clients' cultural background might fail to pick up on cues that signal mental distress. Japanese Americans, for instance, often view mental disorders as inappropriate behavior or malingering (pretending to be mentally disordered to avoid work or responsibility) (Kitano, 1970). Consequently, even when Japanese Americans are in the throes of mental problems, they may be unwilling to acknowledge them (Okano, 1977). When Japanese Americans do admit to having a problem, they often recast it as a physical ailment rather than as a psychological problem. Thus, it is especially important for clinicians with Japanese American clients to thoroughly assess both psychological *and* physical factors (Nagata, 1989).

Assessing mental disorders in ethnic minority individuals is further complicated by the well-documented findings of ethnic and social class biases in diagnosis (Snowden & Cheung, 1990). One study revealed that clinicians find fewer psychological disorders among people from affluent backgrounds than among poor people; in fact, people from the lowest socioeconomic backgrounds are diagnosed as having mental disorders at twice the expected rate and are labeled with the most severe diagnoses (Hollingshead & Redlich, 1958). For example, one study found that the highest rate of mental disorders is in poor African American urban communities (Gould, Wunsch-Hitzig, & Dohrenwend, 1981).

Using the DSM-IV

Continuing revisions of the DSM reflect advancements in knowledge about the classification of mental disorders. On the basis of research and clinical experience, the DSM-IV added, dropped, or revised categories, sometimes generating controversy among the diagnosticians who rely on the classification system.

For example, the DSM-III dropped two important categories that have some historic importance: neurosis and psychosis. The term **neurotic** *refers to relatively mild mental disorders in which the individual has not lost contact with reality.* Individuals who are extremely anxious, troubled, and unhappy may still be able to carry out their everyday functions and have a clear perception of reality; these individuals would be classified as neurotic. The term **psychotic** *refers to severe mental disorders in which the individual has lost contact with reality.* Psychotic individuals have such distorted thinking and perception that they live in a very different world from that of others. Psychotic individuals might hear voices that are not present or think they are famous individuals, such as Jesus Christ or Napoleon. The DSM classification system dropped the terms *neurotic* and *psychotic* because they were too broad and ill-defined to be diagnostic labels. Although the DSM system dropped the

labels, clinicians still sometimes use them as a convenient way of referring to relatively mild or relatively severe mental disorders, respectively.

Neurotic means that he is not as sensible as I am, and psychotic means that he is even worse than my brother-in-law.

Karl Menninger

The **DSM-IV** *(Diagnostic and Statistical Manual of Mental Disorders, fourth edition) is the most recent major classification of mental disorders; it contains eighteen major classifications and descriptions of more than two hundred specific disorders.*

One of the features of the DSM-IV is its **multiaxial system,** *which classifies individuals on the basis of five dimensions, or "axes," that include the individual's history and highest level of competent functioning in the last year. This system ensures that the individual will not merely be assigned to a mental disorder category but instead will be characterized in terms of a number of clinical factors.* Following is a description of each of the axes:

Axis I. Clinical Disorders: The primary classification or diagnosis of the disorder (for example, fear of people). This axis includes all disorders except for the personality disorders.

Axis II. Personality Disorders/Developmental Problems: Personality disorders, long-standing problems in relating to others (for example, long-standing antisocial personality disorder), or developmental problems affecting the adjustment of children and adolescents.

Axis III. General Medical Conditions: General medical conditions that might be relevant in understanding the mental disorder (for example, an individual's history of disease, such as a cardiovascular problem).

Axis IV. Psychosocial and Environmental Problems: Stressors in the individual's recent past that might have contributed to the mental problem (for example, divorce, death of parent, or loss of a job).

Axis V. Global Assessment of Functioning: The individual's current level of functioning, on a scale of 100 (superior) to 1 (inability to maintain safety). The scale takes into account chronicity of symptoms and overall adjustment.

What are some of the changes in the DSM-IV? More than two hundred mental health professionals contributed to the development of DSM-IV. They were a much more diverse group than their predecessors, who were mainly of White male psychiatrists. More women, ethnic minorities, and nonpsychiatrists, such as clinical psychologists, were involved in the construction of the DSM-IV (Nathan, 1994). This led to greater attention to the context of gender- and ethnicity-related diagnosis. For example, DSM-IV contains an appendix entitled "Guideline for Cultural Formation and

Glossary of Culture-Related Syndromes" (Mezzich, Fabrega, & Kleinman, in-press). Also, the DSM-IV's publication is accompanied by a number of sourcebooks that present the empirical base of the DSM-IV. Thus, the DSM-IV is based more on empirical data than its predecessors were. In previous versions of the DSM, the reasons for diagnostic changes were not always explicit, so the evidence that led to their formulation was never available for public evaluation.

The Controversy Surrounding the DSM-IV

The most controversial aspect of the DSM-IV continues an issue that has been present since publication of the first DSM in 1952. Although more nonpsychiatrists were responsible for drafting the DSM-IV than in previous editions, the DSM-IV still reflects a medical or disease model (Clark, Watson, & Reynolds, 1995). Classifying individuals based on their symptoms and using medical terminology continues the dominance of the psychiatric tradition of thinking about mental disorders in terms of illness and disease. This strategy implies an internal cause of disorders that is more or less independent of external or environmental factors (Adams & Cassidy, 1993). Thus, even though researchers have begun to illuminate the complex interaction of genetic, neurobiologi-cal, cognitive, and environmental factors in the DSM disorders, the DSM-IV continues to espouse a medical or disease model of mental disorders (First, Frances, & Pincus, 1995; Frances, First, & Pincus, 1995; Nathan, 1994).

The DSM-IV also is controversial because it continues to label as mental disorders what are often thought of as everyday problems. For example, under learning or academic skills disorders, the DSM-IV includes the categories of reading disorder, mathematics disorder, and disorder of written expression. Under substance-related disorders, the DSM-IV includes the category of caffeine-use disorders. We don't usually think of these problems as mental disorders. Including them as mental disorders implies that such "normal behavior" should be treated as a mental disorder. But the developers of the DSM system argue that mental health providers have been treating many problems not included in earlier editions of DSM and that the classification system should be more comprehensive. One practical reason that everyday problems in living were included in the DSM-III-R and the DSM-IV is so that more individuals can get their health insurance companies to pay for professional help. Most health insurance companies reimburse their clients only for disorders listed in the DSM-IV system.

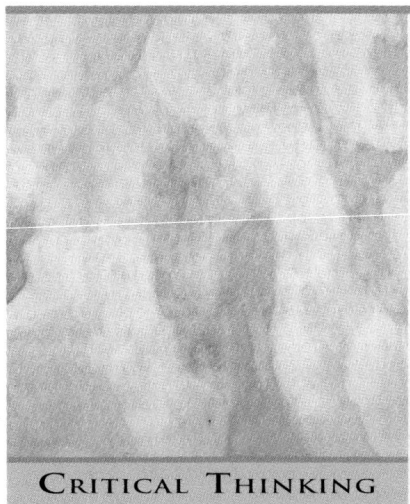

CRITICAL THINKING

Asking Questions to Create a Complete Picture of Mental Distress

Each time a diagnostician sits across from a new client, she encounters a virtual blank slate that must be filled in by her skilled questioning and the client's responses. A comprehensive diagnostic interview would involve questions that reflect all the perspectives you have studied. Suppose you are introduced to a new client named Ben. What you know about him is that he is White, age 16, unhappy, and failing in school. What questions would you want to ask that would produce answers consistent with the focus of the following perspectives?

A psychoanalytic question: The psychoanalytic focus would lead to questions about Ben's early childhood, his experiences of anxiety, perhaps even his dream life. Any of these areas would be fair game.

A learning question: The learning focus would examine Ben's history of punishment and reward, the role models whom he admires, and the reliable patterns of behavior he exhibits in different settings.

A cognitive question: The cognitive focus would examine Ben's thinking patterns and level of self-regard. Does he think of himself as a loser? Are there consistent negative evaluations that interfere with his functioning?

A neurobiological question: The neurobiologist would ask questions about his physiological experiences. Is he sleeping well? Eating properly? Is he related to anyone who has experienced the same problems? Does he have a learning difference? Is he abusing alcohol?

A humanistic question: The humanist focus might examine Ben's values and his goals. The humanist would want to know what strivings might motivate his activity as well as the events or outcomes that make him feel unfulfilled.

A sociocultural question: The sociocultural interviewer would identify other demographic aspects that might contribute to the picture. What type of high school does he attend? With whom, if anyone, does he align in friendship? How are his experiences influenced by his family's resources or lack of them?

As you can see, a comprehensive picture of Ben's life will address many elements of his experience. This practice encourages *pursuing alternative explanations to explain behavior comprehensively* .

Another issue frequently raised by its critics is that the DSM is too responsive to changing political issues. One example is the decision by the DSM-III Task Force to endorse an earlier vote of the American Psychiatric Association to remove homosexuality from the nomenclature and replace it with a limited diagnosis covering only persons who are distressed by their homosexual orientation. Another example is the decision by the DSM-IV Task Force to rename late luteal phase dysphoric disorder, which corresponds to premenstrual syndrome, and retain it in an appendix rather than incorporate it into the regular nomenclature.

Another criticism of the DSM-IV, and indeed of this type of classification system in general, is that the system focuses strictly on pathology and problems, with a bias toward finding something wrong with anyone who becomes the object of diagnostic study. A classic study by David Rosenhan (1973) demonstrated how strong the bias is toward attaching a label of mental disorder to someone. Rosenhan asked eight "normal" individuals to go to the admissions desk of a psychiatric hospital and complain that they heard an unidentified voice saying, "Empty," "Thud," and "Hollow." The psychiatric staff interviewed the eight individuals, who were honest about their life histories. All eight of these individuals were immediately admitted to the hospitals. They behaved normally while in the psychiatric ward. Seven of the eight were diagnosed as schizophrenic, listed as such on their records, and labeled as schizophrenics in remission when they were discharged. Rosenhan concluded that normal people are not noticeably sane. This "blind spot" is likely due to the absence of a satisfying "sane" option in current mental health classification systems, which define sanity only as the absence of insanity (Rothblum, Solomon, & Albee, 1986).

Because labels can become self-fulfilling prophecies, emphasizing strengths as well as weaknesses might help to destigmatize labels such as *borderline schizophrenic* or *ex-mental patient*. It would also help to provide clues to treatment that promote mental competence rather than working only to reduce mental distress.

The DSM-IV was developed by American mental health professionals. Most mental health professionals in other countries adopt the International Classification of Disease (ICD) guidelines established by the World Health Organization. The tenth edition of the ICD (ICD-10) was published in 1993. An effort was made to bring the DSM-IV into closer correspondence with ICD-10, but substantial differences in categories still persist (Frances, Pincus, & Widiger, in press). Such differences ensure that American and non-American mental health professionals will continue to have problems communicating with each other.

Psychologists usually go along with the DSM-IV, but psychiatrists are more satisfied with it. Even though the DSM-IV has its critics, it still is the most comprehensive classification system available.

REVIEW

Dimensions of Abnormality

Abnormal behavior can be statistically unusual within a culture, maladaptive and harmful, personally distressful, and/or designated as abnormal by the culture. A number of views have been proposed about the origins of abnormal behavior. Proponents of the biological approach believe that abnormal behavior is due to a physical malfunction in the body, especially in the brain. The disease model, also called the medical model, was the forerunner of the biological approach; the medical model states that abnormality is a disease or illness precipitated by internal physical causes. Many psychologists believe that the medical model underestimates the importance of psychological factors in abnormal behavior. The sociocultural approach emphasizes how culture, ethnicity, gender, age, and other sociocultural elements

influence abnormal behavior. Some disorders are especially culture-bound. Psychologists have made prevalence estimates, including estimates for gender, ethnicity, and economic status, of mental disorders. Many psychologists believe that an interactionist approach to mental disorders is a wise strategy.

DSM stands for *Diagnostic and Statistical Manual of Mental Disorders*. The DSM-II included the categories of neurotic and psychotic behavior. Though some mental health professionals still use the terms *neurotic* and *psychotic,* they have been dropped from the DSM classification. Mental disorder classification systems have both advantages and disadvantages. The most recent version of the DSM (DSM-IV) was published in 1994. One of the DSM-IV's features is its multiaxial system. The

DSM-IV Task Force was made up of a much more diverse group of individuals than its predecessors were and the DSM-IV is more empirically based than earlier editions. The most controversial aspects of the DSM-IV continue to be the classification of individuals based on their symptoms and the use of medical terminology that perpetuates the medical or disease model of mental disorders. Critics also point out that some everyday problems should not be included as disorders. Another issue raised by its critics is that the DSM-IV is too responsive to changing political times. Critics suggest that competent mental health categories should reflect positive as well as negative characteristics. The DSM-IV and the ICD-10 (International Classification of Disease) are still not completely compatible.

DIAGNOSTIC CATEGORIES OF MENTAL DISORDERS

Let's now examine the major categories of diagnosis featured in the DSM-IV. Although this is not an exhaustive exploration of the multitude of categories, the review will suggest the general qualities of the most prominent mental disorders, which we will illustrate by mentioning case studies.

Anxiety Disorders

Anxiety is a diffuse, vague, highly unpleasant feeling of fear and apprehension. People with high levels of anxiety worry a lot. **Anxiety disorders** *are psychological disorders that include the following main features: motor tension (jumpiness, trembling, inability to relax), hyperactivity (dizziness, a racing heart, or perspiration), and apprehensive expectations and thoughts.* Five important types of anxiety disorders are reviewed in this section.

Generalized Anxiety Disorder

Anna, who is 27 years old, had just arrived for her visit with the psychologist. She seemed very nervous and was wringing her hands, crossing and uncrossing her legs, and playing nervously with strands of her hair. She said her stomach felt like it was in knots, that her hands were cold, and that her neck muscles were so tight they hurt. She said that, lately, arguments with her husband had escalated. In recent weeks, Anna indicated, she had felt more and more nervous throughout the day, as if something bad were about to happen. If the doorbell sounded or the phone rang, her heart beat rapidly and her breathing quickened. When she was around people, she had a difficult time speaking. She began to isolate herself. Her husband became impatient with her, so she decided to see a psychologist (Goodstein & Calhoun, 1982).

Anna has a **generalized anxiety disorder,** *an anxiety disorder that consists of persistent anxiety for at least 1 month; an individual with a generalized anxiety disorder is unable to specify the reasons for the anxiety.* One study found that people with generalized anxiety disorder have higher degrees of muscle tension and hyperactivity than people with other types of anxiety disorders (Barlow & others, 1986). These individuals say they have been tense and anxious for over half their lives.

Panic Disorder

Panic disorder *is a recurrent anxiety disorder marked by the sudden onset of intense apprehension or terror.* The individual often has a feeling of impending doom but might not feel anxious all the time. Anxiety attacks often strike without warning and produce severe palpitations, extreme shortness of breath, chest pains, trembling, sweating, dizziness, and a feeling of helplessness. Victims are seized by the fear that they will die, go crazy, or do something they cannot control (Asnis & van Praag, 1995).

What are some of the psychosocial and biological factors involved in panic disorder? As shown in figure 16.1, most panic attacks are spontaneous; those that are not spontaneous are triggered by a variety of events. In many instances, a stressful life event has occurred in the past 6 months, most often a threatened or actual separation from a loved one or a change in job. Psychologists have only recently explored biological factors in panic disorder (Gorman & others, 1989).

Phobic Disorders

Agnes is a withdrawn 30-year-old who has been unable to go higher than the second floor of any building for more than a year. When she tries to overcome her fear of heights by going up to the third, fourth, or fifth floor, she becomes overwhelmed by anxiety. She remembers how it all began. One evening she was working alone and was seized by an urge to jump out of an eighth-story window. She was so frightened by her impulse that she hid behind a file cabinet for more than 2 hours until she calmed down enough to gather her belongings and go home. As she reached the first floor of the building, her heart was pounding and she was perspiring heavily. After several months, she gave up her position and became a lower-paid salesperson so she could work on the bottom floor of the store (Cameron, 1963).

A **phobic disorder,** *commonly called a phobia, is an anxiety disorder in which an individual has an irrational, overwhelming, persistent fear of a particular object or situation.* Individuals with generalized anxiety disorder cannot pinpoint the cause of their nervous feelings; individuals with phobias can. A fear becomes a phobia when a situation is so dreaded that an individual goes to almost any length to avoid it; for example, Agnes quit her job to avoid being in high places. Some phobias are more debilitating than others. An individual with a fear of automobiles has a more difficult time functioning in our society than a person with a fear of snakes, for example.

Phobias come in many forms. Some of the most common phobias involve heights, open spaces, people, close spaces, dogs, dirt, the dark, and snakes (see table 16.2 to read about a number of phobias). Simple phobias are relatively common and are easier to treat through psychotherapy than complex phobias, such as agoraphobia, are. **Agoraphobia,** *the fear of entering unfamiliar situations, especially open or public spaces, is the most common type of phobic disorder.* It accounts for 50 to 80 percent of the phobic population, according to some estimates (Foa, Steketze, & Young, 1984). Women are far more likely than men to suffer from agoraphobia. One study found that 84 percent of the individuals being treated for agoraphobia are women, and almost 90 percent of those women are married (Al-Issa, 1982b).

Psychologists have become increasingly interested in *social phobia,* the fear of social situations. Bashful or timid

Onset of attack	No. (%) of patients
Spontaneous	47 (78%)
Nonspontaneous, precipitated by	13 (22%)
Public speaking	3
Stimulant drug use	3
Family argument	2
Leaving home	2
Exercise (while pregnant)	1
Being frightened by a stranger	1
Fear of fainting	1

Stressful life events associated with attack	No. (%) of patients
No stressful life event within 6 months	22 (37%)
Stressful life event within 6 months*	38 (63%)
Threatened or actual separation from important person	11
Change in job, causing increased pressure	8
Pregnancy	7
Move	5
Marriage	3
Graduation	3
Death of close person	3
Physical illness	2

*Four patients had two concomitant stressful life events.

FIGURE 16.1

Nature of First Panic Attack and Associated Life Events
At left is the nature of first panic attacks and associated life events, and at right is Edvard Munch's painting *The Scream*. Experts often interpret Munch's painting as reflecting the terror brought on by a panic attack.

people often suffer from this phobia. Social phobia affects as many as 2 of every 100 Americans and tends to be evenly distributed between the sexes (Robins & others, 1984).

Why do people develop phobias? The answer often depends on the researcher's perspective. Psychoanalytic theorists, for example, say phobias develop as defense mechanisms to ward off threatening or unacceptable impulses—Agnes, for instance, hid behind a file cabinet because she feared she would jump out of an eighth-story window. Learning theorists, however, explain phobias differently; they say phobias are learned fears. In Agnes's case, she might have fallen out of a window when she was a little girl and, as a result, now associates falling with pain and fears high places. On the other hand, she may have heard about or seen other people who were afraid of high places. These last two examples are conditioning and observational learning explanations for Agnes's phobia. Cross-cultural psychologists point out that phobias also are influenced by cultural factors. Agoraphobia, for example, is much more common in the United States and Europe than in other areas of the world (Kleinman, 1988).

Neuroscientists are finding that biological factors, such as greater blood flow and metabolism in the right

Agoraphobia is the fear of entering unfamiliar situations, especially open or public places. Individuals with agoraphobia try to avoid crowded situations. They fear that escape would be difficult or impossible if they become highly anxious in such crowded situations. Agoraphobic individuals also usually avoid standing in line and riding in vehicles, activities that intensify their feelings of vulnerability.

TABLE 16.2

Types of Phobias

Acrophobia	Fear of high places
Aereophobia	Fear of flying
Agoraphobia	Fear of open places
Ailurophobia	Fear of cats
Algophobia	Fear of pain
Amaxophobia	Fear of vehicles, driving
Arachnophobia	Fear of spiders
Astrapophobia	Fear of lightning
Claustrophobia	Fear of closed places
Cynophobia	Fear of dogs
Gamophobia	Fear of marriage
Gynephobia	Fear of women
Hydrophobia	Fear of water
Melissophobia	Fear of bees
Mysophobia	Fear of dirt
Nyctophobia	Fear of darkness
Ophidiophobia	Fear of nonpoisonous snakes
Thanatophobia	Fear of death
Xenophobia	Fear of strangers

This partial listing reveals the variety of circumstances that can cause an individual to develop a phobia.

"But that's what you said yesterday—'Just one more cord'!"

Drawing by Woodman; © 1986 The New Yorker Magazine, Inc.

hemisphere of the brain than in the left, may also be involved in phobias. First-generation relatives of individuals suffering from agoraphobia and panic attacks have high rates of these disorders themselves, suggesting a possible genetic predisposition for phobias (d'Ansia, 1989). Others have found that identical twins reared apart sometimes develop the same phobias; one pair independently became claustrophobic, for example (Eckert, Heston, & Bouchard, 1981).

Obsessive-Compulsive Disorders

Bob is 27 years old and lives in a well-kept apartment. He has few friends and little social life. He was raised by a demanding mother and an aloof father. Bob is an accountant who spends long hours at work. He is a perfectionist. His demanding mother always nagged at him to improve himself, to keep the house spotless, and to be clean and neat, and she made Bob wash his hands whenever he touched his genitals. As a young adult, Bob finds himself ensnared in an exacting ritual in which he removes his clothes in a prearranged sequence and then endlessly scrubs every inch of his body from head to toe. He dresses himself in precisely the opposite way from which he takes off his clothes. If he deviates from this order, he *has* to start the sequence all over again. Sometimes

Bob performs the cleansing ritual four or five times an evening. Even though he is aware that this ritual is absurd, he simply cannot stop (Meyer & Osborne, 1982).

Obsessive-compulsive disorder (OCD) *is an anxiety disorder in which an individual has anxiety-provoking thoughts that will not go away (obsession) and/or urges to perform repetitive, ritualistic behaviors to prevent or produce a future situation (compulsion).* Individuals with obsessive-compulsive disorder repeat and rehearse doubts and daily routines, sometimes hundreds of times a day. The basic difference between obsession and compulsion is the difference between thought and action. Obsessions can immobilize the person with horrifying yet irresistible thoughts of killing someone in a traffic accident, for instance, whereas compulsions can result in bloody hands from hours of washing away imaginary germs. Although obsessions and compulsions are different, a person afflicted with OCD might be caught in the relentless grip of both problems.

> There is nothing worse than taking something into your head that is a revolving wheel you can't control.
>
> **Ugo Betti, *Struggle Till Dawn*, 1949**

The most common compulsions are excessive checking, cleansing, and counting. For example, Wesley believes that he has to check his apartment for gas leaks and make sure the windows are locked. His behavior is not compulsive if he does this once, but, if he goes back to check five or six times and then constantly worries that he may not have checked carefully enough once he has left the house, his behavior is compulsive. Most individuals do not enjoy their ritualistic behavior but feel anxious when they do not carry it out.

Positron emission tomography (PET) and other brain-imaging techniques indicate a neurological basis for OCD. Irregularities in neurotransmitter systems, especially serotonin and dopamine, seem to be involved. There also may be a genetic basis for the disorder; OCD runs in families.

Post-Traumatic Stress Disorder

Bernice sought help in therapy because she thought she was "losing her grip." Her boss was continually complaining that she wasn't paying attention to her work as a cashier. She feared that she would lose her job. She was having trouble sleeping. Whenever she would lie down, she had a strange feeling that she wasn't alone. Occasionally, she smelled disturbing smells. All of these problems seemed to intensify following the death of her uncle, a man she hadn't spoken to in decades and had disliked for as long as she could remember. Her therapist considered that Bernice might be a victim of post-traumatic stress disorder.

Post-traumatic stress disorder *is a mental disturbance that develops through exposure to a traumatic event (such as war), a severely oppressive situation (such as the holocaust), severe abuse (as in rape), a natural disaster (such as a flood or tornado), or an accidental disaster (such as a plane crash). The disorder is characterized by anxiety symptoms that either immediately follow the trauma or are delayed by months or even years.* The symptoms vary but can include the following:

- "Flashbacks" in which the individual relives the event in nightmares, or in an awake but dissociative-like state
- Constricted ability to feel emotions, often reported as feeling numb, resulting in an inability to experience happiness, sexual desire, enjoyable interpersonal relationships
- Excessive arousal, resulting in an exaggerated startle response or an inability to sleep
- Difficulties with memory and concentration
- Feelings of apprehension, including nervous tremors
- Impulsive outbursts of behavior such as aggressiveness, or sudden changes in lifestyle

Not every individual exposed to the same disaster develops post-traumatic stress disorder, which occurs when the individual's usual coping abilities are overloaded (Solomon, 1993). For example, it is estimated that 15 to 20 percent of Vietnam veterans experienced post-traumatic stress disorder. Vietnam veterans who had some autonomy and decision-making authority, such as Green Berets, were less likely to develop the disorder than soldiers who had no control over where they would be sent or when, and who had no option but to follow orders.

Preparation for a trauma also makes a difference in whether an individual will develop the disorder. For example, emergency workers who are trained to cope with traumatic circumstances usually do not develop post-traumatic stress disorder.

Some experts consider female sexual abuse and assault victims to be the single largest group of post-traumatic stress disorder sufferers (Koss, 1990). This is not very surprising, since these victims had no autonomy nor decision making in the situation. Few women are prepared to deal with the traumatic circumstances and consequences of rape. Many victims of sexual assault receive mixed societal messages after the trauma about the degree of their responsibility, and many victims remain secretive about having been raped. All these factors increase their risk for post-traumatic stress disorder.

Somatoform Disorders

"Look, I am having trouble breathing. You don't believe me. Nobody believes me. There are times when I can't stop coughing. I'm losing weight. I know I have cancer. My father died of cancer when I was twelve." Herb has been to six cancer specialists in the last 2 years; none can find anything wrong with him. Each doctor has taken X rays and conducted excessive laboratory tests, but Herb's test results do not indicate any illnesses. Might some psychological factors be responsible for Herb's sense that he is physically ailing?

Somatoform disorders *are mental disorders in which psychological symptoms take a physical, or somatic, form, even though no physical causes can be found.* Although these symptoms are not caused physically, they are highly distressing for the individual; the symptoms are real, not faked. Two types of somatoform disorders are hypochondriasis and conversion disorder.

Hypochondriasis

Carly seemed to be a classic hypochondriac. She always seemed to overreact to a missed heartbeat, shortness of breath, or a slight chest pain, fearing that something was wrong with her. **Hypochondriasis** *is a somatoform disorder in which the individual has a pervasive fear of illness and disease.* At the first indication of something's being amiss in her body, Carly calls the doctor. When a physical examination reveals no problems, she usually does not believe the doctor. She often changes doctors, moving from one to another searching for a diagnosis that matches her own. Most hypochondriacs are pill enthusiasts; their medicine chests spill over with bottles of drugs they hope will cure their imagined maladies. Carly's pill collection was spectacular.

Hypochondriasis is a difficult category to diagnose accurately. It often occurs with other mental disorders, such as depression.

Conversion Disorder

Conversion disorder *is a somatoform disorder in which an individual experiences genuine physical symptoms, even though no physiological problems can be found.* Conversion disorder received its name from psychoanalytic theory, which stressed that anxiety is "converted" into a physical symptom. A hypochondriac has no physical disability; an individual with a conversion disorder does have some loss

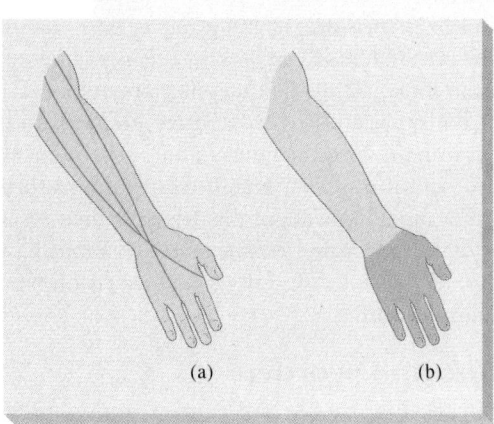

FIGURE 16.2

Glove Anesthesia
A patient who complains of numbness in the hand might be diagnosed as suffering from conversion disorder if the area of the hand affected showed that a disorder of the nervous system was not responsible. The skin areas served by nerves in the arm are shown in (a). Therefore, damage to a nerve in the arm tends to make only a portion of the hand numb (for example, the thumb and forefinger). The glove anesthesia shown in (b) could not result from damage to these nerves.

From Bootzin, et al., *Abnormal Psychology*. Copyright © 1972 McGraw-Hill, Inc. Reprinted by permission of McGraw-Hill, Inc.

of motor or sensory ability. Individuals with a conversion disorder may be unable to speak, may faint, or may even be deaf or blind.

Conversion disorder was more common in Freud's time than today. Freud was especially interested in this disorder, in which physical symptoms made no neurological sense. For example, individuals with *glove anesthesia* report that their entire hand is numb from the tip of their fingers to a cutoff point at the wrist. As shown in figure 16.2, if these individuals were experiencing true physiological numbness, their symptoms would be very different. Like hypochondriasis, conversion disorder often appears in conjunction with other mental disturbances. During long-term evaluation, conversion disorder often becomes displaced by another mental or physical disorder.

Dissociative Disorders

Dissociative disorders *are psychological disorders that involve a sudden loss of memory or change in identity. Under extreme stress or shock, an individual's conscious awareness becomes dissociated (separated or split) from previous memories and thoughts.* Three kinds of dissociative disorders are amnesia, fugue, and multiple personality.

Amnesia and Fugue

In chapter 7, amnesia was described as the inability to recall important events. Amnesia can be caused by an injury to the head, for example. However, **psychogenic amnesia** *is a dissociative disorder involving memory loss caused by extensive psychological stress.* For example, a man showed up at a hospital and said he did not know who he was. After several days in the hospital, he awoke one morning and demanded to be released. Eventually he remembered that he had been involved in an automobile accident in which a pedestrian had been killed. The extreme stress of the accident and the fear that he might be held responsible had triggered the amnesia.

Fugue, *which means "flight," is a dissociative disorder in which an individual not only develops amnesia but also unexpectedly travels away from home and assumes a new identity.* For example, one day a woman named Barbara vanished without a trace. Two weeks later, looking more like a teenager than a 31-year-old woman, with her hair in a ponytail and wearing bobby socks, Barbara was picked up by police in a nearby city. When her husband came to see her, Barbara asked, "Who are you?" She could not remember anything about the past 2 weeks of her life. During psychotherapy, she gradually began to recall her past. She had left home with enough money to buy a bus ticket to the town where she grew up as a child. She had spent days walking the streets and standing near a building where her father had worked. Later she had gone to a motel with a man; according to the motel manager, she had entertained a series of men over a 3-day period (Goldstein & Palmer, 1975).

Multiple Personality

Multiple personality *is the most dramatic but least common dissociative disorder; individuals suffering from this disorder have two or more distinct personalities, or selves,* like the fictional Dr. Jekyll and Mr. Hyde of Robert Louis Stevenson's short story. Each personality has its own memories, behaviors, and relationships; one personality dominates the individual at one point; another personality takes over at another time. The personalities might not be aware of each other, and the shift from one to the other can occur suddenly during distress.

One of the most famous cases of multiple personality involves the "three faces of Eve," which in reality is only a portion of the dramatic life history of Chris Sizemore. Sizemore recalls that she had her first experience with dissociation when she was 2. For the next 44 years, she experienced a life filled with severe headaches and periods of amnesia. Around age 25 she was diagnosed with multiple personality disorder. Her psychiatrists identified three alters functioning in her life and named them Eve Black, Eve White, and Jane (Thigpen & Cleckly, 1957).

Eve White was the original, dominant personality. She had no knowledge of her second personality, Eve Black, although Eve Black had been alternating with Eve White for a number of years. Eve White was bland, quiet, and serious—a rather dull personality. Eve Black, by contrast, was

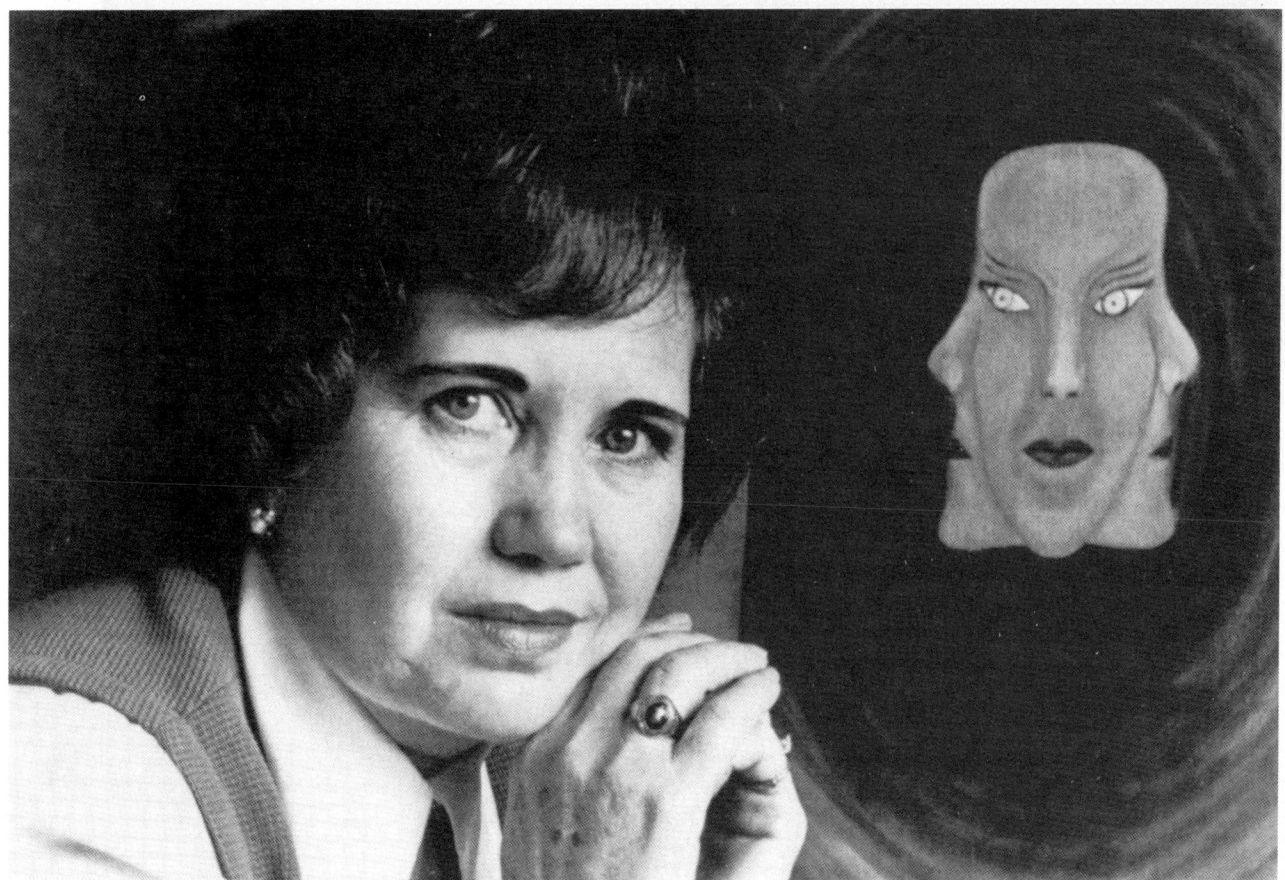

FIGURE 16.3

Multiple Personality: The Three Faces of Eve
Chris Sizemore, the subject of the book *Three Faces of Eve*, is shown with the work she painted and entitled *Three Faces in One*.

carefree, mischievous, and uninhibited. She "came out" at the most inappropriate times, leaving Eve White with hangovers, bills, and a reputation in local bars that she could not explain. During treatment, a third personality, Jane, emerged. More mature than the other two, Jane seemed to have developed as a result of therapy (see figure 16.3 for a portrayal of the three faces of Eve). However, Sizemore's personality didn't stabilize at that point. Alters continued to show up in trios, with one alter demonstrating characteristics of the wife and mother, another the party girl, and the third an intellectual. Of the twenty-two alters that appeared, ten were poets, seven artists, and one a tailor. According to Sizemore (1989), when her integrated personality emerged at age 47, she could paint and write but she couldn't sew.

A summary of the research literature on multiple personality suggests that the most striking feature related to the disorder is an inordinately high rate of sexual or physical abuse during early childhood (Ludolph, 1982).

Sexual abuse occurred in 56 percent of the reported cases, for example. Their mothers had been rejecting and depressed and their fathers distant, alcoholic, and abusive. Remember that, although fascinating, multiple personality disorder is rare. Until the 1980s, only about 300 cases had been reported (Suinn, 1984). In the past decade, however, hundreds more cases have been labeled "multiple personality disorder." Some argue that the increase represents a diagnostic fad. Others believe that it is not so rare but has been frequently misdiagnosed as schizophrenia. Improved techniques for assessing the physiological changes that occur when individuals change personalities increase the likelihood that more accurate rates can be determined (Braun, 1988).

Now that we have considered three major types of mental disorders—anxiety, somatoform, and dissociative—we will turn to a set of widespread disorders, the mood disorders.

Anxiety Disorders, Somatoform Disorders, and Dissociative Disorders

Anxiety is a diffuse, vague, highly unpleasant feeling of fear and apprehension. The main features of anxiety disorders are motor tension, hyperactivity, and apprehensive expectations and thoughts. Generalized anxiety disorder consists of persistent anxiety for at least 1 month without being able to pinpoint the cause of the anxiety. Panic disorder involves recurrent panic attacks marked by a sudden onset of intense apprehension or terror. Phobic disorders, commonly called phobias, involve an irrational, overwhelming, persistent fear of an object or a situation. Phobias come in many forms; the most common is agoraphobia. Psychoanalytic and learning explanations of phobias have been given; sociocultural and biological factors also are involved. Obsessive-compulsive disorders consist of recurrent obsessions or compulsions. Obsessions are anxiety-provoking thoughts that won't go away. Compulsions are urges to perform repetitive, ritualistic behaviors that usually occur to prevent or produce a future situation. Post-traumatic stress disorder is a mental disorder that develops through exposure to a traumatic event, a severely oppressive situation, severe abuse, a natural disaster, or an accidental disaster. Anxiety symptoms may immediately follow the trauma or may be delayed months or even years.

Somatoform disorders develop when psychological symptoms take a physical, or somatic, form, even though no physical cause can be found. Two somatoform disorders are hypochondriasis and conversion disorder. Hypochondriasis is a pervasive fear of illness and disease. It rarely occurs alone; depression often accompanies hypochondriasis. Conversion disorder develops when an individual experiences genuine symptoms, even though no physiological problems can be found.

Conversion disorder received its name from psychoanalytic theory, which stressed that anxiety is "converted" into a physical symptom. Some loss of motor or sensory ability occurs. The disorder was more common in Freud's time than today.

The dissociative disorders involve a sudden loss of memory or a change in identity. Under extreme stress or shock, the individual's conscious awareness becomes dissociated (separated or split) from previous memories and thoughts. Psychogenic amnesia involves memory loss caused by extensive psychological stress. Fugue involves a loss of memory, but individuals unexpectedly travel away from home or work, assume a new identity, and do not remember their old one. Multiple personality involves the presence of two or more distinct personalities in the same individual. The disorder is rare.

Mood Disorders

The **mood disorders** *are psychological disorders characterized by wide emotional swings, ranging from deeply depressed to highly euphoric and agitated.* Depression can occur alone, as in major depression, or it can alternate with mania, as in bipolar disorder. Depression is linked to the increasing rate of suicide. We will consider each of these disturbances in turn and then examine the causes of the mood disorders.

Major Depression

Major depression *is a mood disorder in which the individual is deeply unhappy, demoralized, self-derogatory, and bored. An individual with major depression shows changes in appetite and sleep patterns, decreased energy, feelings of worthlessness, problems concentrating, and guilt feelings that might prompt thoughts of suicide.* For example, Peter had been depressed for several months. Nothing cheered him up. His depression began when the girl he wanted to marry decided marriage was not for her, at least not with Peter. Peter's emotional state deteriorated to the point where he didn't leave his room for days at a time, he kept the shades drawn and the room dark, and he could hardly get out of bed in the morning. When he managed to leave his room, he had trouble maintaining a conversation and he usually felt exhausted. By the time Peter finally contacted his college counseling center, he had gone from being mildly depressed to being in the grips of major depression.

Although most people don't spiral into major depression, as Peter did, everyone feels "blue" sometimes. In our stress-filled world, people often use the term *depression* to describe brief bouts of normal sadness or discontent over life's problems. Perhaps you haven't done well in a class or things aren't working out in your love life. You feel down in the dumps and say you are depressed. In most instances, though, your depression won't last as long or be as intense as Peter's; after a few hours, days, or weeks, you snap out of your gloomy state and begin to cope more effectively with depression.

For many individuals, however, depression is a lingering, exhausting experience that can sometimes be severe enough to weaken ties with reality. Depression is so widespread that it has been called the "common cold" of mental disorders; more than 250,000 individuals are hospitalized every year for the disorder. Students, professors, corporate executives, laborers—no one is immune to depression,

SOCIOCULTURAL WORLDS 16.2

Women and Depression

Around the world, depression occurs more frequently among women than among men. The female-male ratio ranges from 2:1 to 3:1 in most industrialized countries (Depression Awareness, Recognition, and Treatment Program, 1987; Nolen-Hoeksema, 1990). Three explanations of the sex difference in depression are the following: (1) women are more willing to seek help and, therefore, are more likely to be categorized as having depression; (2) biological differences may exist between females and males that predispose females to become more depressed than males; and (3) psychosocial factors—different rearing environments, different social roles, and less favorable economic and achievement opportunities, for example—may produce greater depression in women than men. Some psychologists have also theorized that alcoholism may mask, or act as a cover for, depression in men (Culbertson, 1991).

Among the psychosocial factors in women's depression that were proposed by the American Psychological Association's National Task Force on Women and Depression (McGrath & others, 1990) were the following:

- Women's depression is related to avoidant, passive, dependent behavior patterns; it is also related to focusing too much on depressed feelings instead of on action and mastery strategies.

- The rate of sexual and physical abuse of women is much higher than previously thought and is a major factor in women's depression. Depressive symptoms may be long-standing effects of post-traumatic stress syndrome for many women.
- Marriage often confers a greater protective buffer against stress for men than for women. In unhappy marriages, women are three times as likely as men to be depressed. Mothers of young children are especially vulnerable to stress and depression; the more children in the house, the more depression women report.
- Poverty is a pathway to depression and three out of every four people in poverty in the United States are women and children. Minority women, elderly women, chemically-dependent women, lesbians, and professional women are also high-risk groups for depression and merit special attention and support.

Careful diagnosis is critical in the treatment of women's depression. Diagnostic assessment for women, in particular, should include taking a history of sexual and physical violence; exploring prescription drug use; discovering past and current medical conditions; and doing a reproductive life history to determine how menstruation, birth control, pregnancy, childbirth, abortion, and menopause may have contributed to women's depression. According to the Women's Task Force, depression is misdiagnosed at least 30 to 50 percent of the time in women. Approximately 70 percent of the prescriptions for antidepressants are given to women, often with improper diagnosis and monitoring. Prescription drug misuse is a danger for many women.

Understanding the nature of women's depression is a complex undertaking and merits more attention. Perhaps the current effort to better understand women's depression will be successful and reduce women's pain and suffering from depression.

not even writers Anne Sexton, Sylvia Plath, or F. Scott Fitzgerald or historical figures Abraham Lincoln or Winston Churchill, each of whom experienced major depression.

I was much too far out all my life
And not waving but drowning.
Stevie Smith, *Not Waving but Drowning,* 1957

A man's lifetime risk of developing major depression is approximately 10 percent. The risk is much greater for a woman—almost 25 percent. In fact, depression is the most common psychiatric diagnosis for African American and White women (Russo, 1985). To read further about women's depression, turn to Sociocultural Worlds 16.2.

In May 1988, the National Institute of Mental Health (NIMH) launched the public education phase of the first major program to communicate information about mood disorders (Regier & others, 1988). The inadequate care that results from a lack of understanding or a misunderstanding of depression is expensive and tragic. The annual cost of major depression to the nation is more than $16 billion. Given the existing range of psychological and pharmacological treatments, many individuals who go untreated suffer needlessly.

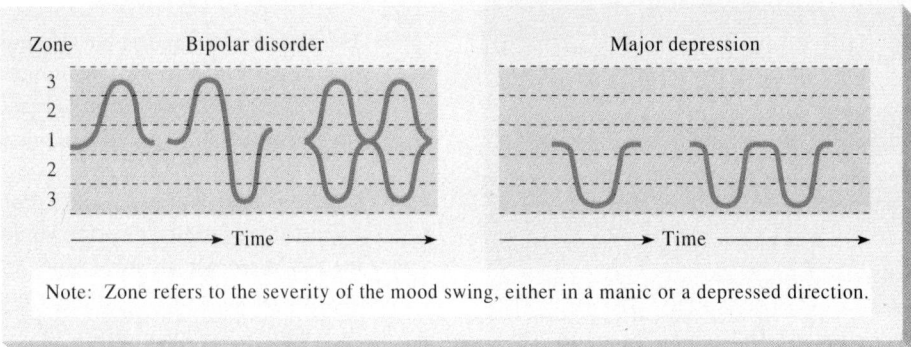

Zone   Bipolar disorder   Major depression

Note: Zone refers to the severity of the mood swing, either in a manic or a depressed direction.

FIGURE 16.4

Comparison of Mood Swings in Bipolar and Major Depression
Notice that both disorders include periods of relatively normal mood.

Bipolar Disorder

Bipolar disorder *is a mood disorder characterized by extreme mood swings; an individual with this disorder might be depressed, manic, or both.* We have described the symptoms of depression. In contrast, someone who is manic experiences elation, exuberance, and tireless stamina. He or she may be humorous, scheming, restless, and irritable; have a tendency for excess; and be in almost constant motion. The type of mood swings that might occur in bipolar disorder are described in figure 16.4, where they are contrasted with the mood swings of major depression.

Consider Charlene. She was alternately agitated and euphoric. She had experienced extreme mood swings since she was a child. At age 43, her family wanted to have her hospitalized. She claimed that she had discovered the "secret to life" and laughed heartily when anyone asked her to reveal the secret. Her energy seemed boundless. She often woke at 3 A.M. to do the daily vacuuming. Her family really started worrying when she could no longer control her spending. They found twenty-eight sets of coordinated towels and washcloths stashed under her bed. When she attempted to purchase three cars on the same day, her loan requests were rejected. She threatened suicide, and her family knew they needed help.

The lifetime risk of bipolar disorder is estimated at approximately 1 percent for both men and women (Weissman & Boyd, 1985). It is more common among divorced persons, although, in such cases, bipolar disorder may be a cause rather than a consequence of the divorce. Bipolar disorder also occurs more frequently in the close relatives of individuals with bipolar disorder than in the close relatives of depressed but non-bipolar-disordered individuals.

Suicide

The rate of suicide has tripled since the 1950s in the United States. Each year about 25,000 people take their own lives. At about the age of 15, the suicide rate begins to rise rapidly. Suicide accounts for 12 percent of the mortality in the adolescent and young adult age group. Men are about three times more likely than women to succeed at committing suicide. This may be due to their choice of method for attempting it—shooting themselves, for example. By contrast, females more often select methods, such as sleeping pills, which do not immediately cause death. Although males successfully commit suicide more frequently, females attempt it more often.

Estimates indicate that 6 to 10 suicide attempts occur for every successful suicide in the general population. For adolescents, the figure is as high as 50 attempts for every life taken. As many as 2 in every 3 college students have thought about suicide on at least one occasion. Their methods range from using drugs to crashing into the White House in an airplane.

There is no simple answer to why people commit suicide. Biological factors appear to be involved. Suicide, as with major depression, tends to run in families. Immediate and highly stressful circumstances, such as the loss of a spouse or a job, flunking out of school, or an unwanted pregnancy, can lead people, especially those who are genetically predisposed, to attempt suicide. Also, drug-related suicide attempts are more common now than in the past.

However, earlier experiences, such as a long-standing history of family instability and unhappiness, can also play

Over many centuries, the majority of Hispanics have maintained their spiritual belief in Catholicism. However, Catholicism does not always mean the same thing to all Hispanics. *What are some variations in the meaning of Catholicism to Hispanics from different ethnic backgrounds?*

a role in attempted suicides. Studies of gifted men and women found several predictors of suicide, such as anxiety, conspicuous instability in work and relationships, depression, and alcoholism (Schneidman, 1971; Tomlinson-Keasey, Warren, & Elliot, 1986).

Not all individuals who attempt suicide are clinically depressed. For example, most suicides are committed by older white males who are divorced, in poor health, and unemployed. Substance abuse and having a terminal illness also are related to suicidal thoughts and behavior. In high-pressure cultures, such as Japan and the United States, suicide rates are much higher than in less achievement oriented cultures. Also, as we will see next, in some cultures religion plays an important role in deterring suicide.

Over many centuries, most Latinos have maintained their spiritual belief in Catholicism. However, Latino subcultures interpret Catholicism differently from one another. A comparison of Mexican Americans with Puerto Ricans illustrates how different beliefs in Catholicism affect the suicide rates of various Hispanic American subcultures. For example, one study found that many depressed Mexican Americans control their suicidal impulses because Catholicism asserts that suicide is an unpardonable sin that carries church sanctions against those who attempt suicide, as well as eternal damnation in hell for those who succeed (Bach y Rita, 1982).

Even though Puerto Ricans tend to be Catholic, they also integrate Indian folk beliefs with their Catholicism. Overall, Puerto Ricans do not adopt organized religion, only minimally adhering to the Catholic doctrine. Many Puerto Ricans believe that spirits communicate with people through mediums, or people who act as channels of communication between the earthly world and a world of spirits. This belief, combined with the conviction that "unsolvable" conflicts can be handled by committing suicide, promotes a much higher rate of suicide among Puerto Ricans than among Mexican Americans.

Clinicians who have Latino clients need to be aware of such cultural differences. If a clinician erroneously thinks of Latinos as a homogeneous group, he or she might incorrectly evaluate the client's risk of suicide. For example, if the clinician reasons that Latinos are Catholics and Catholics do not believe in suicide because it is an unpardonable sin against God, the clinician may assess the risk of suicide for a Puerto Rican client as low, in which case the clinician might be very wrong.

Psychologists do not have the complete answers for detecting suicide impulses or for preventing them. However, psychologists believe that the most effective intervention for preventing suicide comes from those who have had special training. The advice offered in table 16.3 provides some valuable suggestions for communicating with someone you think may be contemplating suicide.

Causes of Mood Disorders

Explanations for mood disorders, such as Peter's depression and Charlene's bipolar disorder, come from psychoanalytic theory, cognitive and learning theories, biogenetic theories, and sociocultural theories.

Psychoanalytic Explanations In 1917 Sigmund Freud published a paper called "Mourning and Melancholia," in which he described his view of depression. Freud believed that depression is a turning inward of aggressive instincts. He theorized that a child's early attachment to a love object (usually the mother) contains a mixture of love and hate. When the child loses the love object or her dependency needs are frustrated, feelings of loss coexist with anger. Since the child cannot openly accept such angry feelings toward the individual she loves, the hostility is turned inward and experienced as depression. The unresolved mixture of anger and love is carried forward to adolescence and adulthood, where loss can bring back those early feelings of abandonment.

British psychiatrist John Bowlby (1980, 1989) agrees with Freud that childhood experiences are an important determinant of depression in adulthood. He believes that a combination of an insecure attachment to the mother, a lack of love and affection as a child, and the actual loss of a parent during childhood give rise to a negative cognitive set, or schema. The schema built up during childhood

TABLE 16.3

What to Do and What Not to Do When You Suspect Someone Is Likely to Commit Suicide

What to Do

1. Ask direct, straightforward questions in a calm manner: "Are you thinking about hurting yourself?"
2. Assess the seriousness of the suicidal intent by asking questions about feelings, important relationships, who else the person has talked with, and the amount of thought given to the means to be used. If a gun, pills, rope, or other means has been obtained and a precise plan developed, clearly the situation is dangerous. Stay with the person until help arrives.
3. Be a good listener and be very supportive.
4. Try to persuade the person to obtain professional help and assist him or her in getting this help.

What Not to Do

1. Do not ignore the warning signs.
2. Do not refuse to talk about suicide if a person approaches you about it.
3. Do not react with horror, disapproval, or repulsion.
4. Do not give false reassurances by saying such things as "Everything is going to be OK." Also do not give out simple answers or platitudes, such as "You have everything to be thankful for."
5. Do not abandon the individual after the crisis has passed or after professional counseling has commenced.

Adapted with permission from *Living With 10- to 15-Year-Olds: A Parent Education Curriculum.* Copyright by the Center for Early Adolescence, University of North Carolina at Chapel Hill, Carrboro, NC, 1992.

causes the individual to interpret later losses as yet other failures in one's effort to establish enduring and close positive relationships.

One longitudinal study of depression found that parents' lack of affection, high control, and aggressive achievement orientation in their children's early childhood are associated with depression among adolescent girls but not boys (Gjerde, 1985). This difference may be because depression generally occurs more often in girls than boys.

Cognitive and Learning Explanations   Individuals who are depressed rarely think positive thoughts. They interpret their lives in self-defeating ways and have negative expectations about the future. Psychotherapist Aaron Beck believes that such negative thoughts reflect schemas that shape the depressed individual's experiences (Beck, 1967). These habitual negative thoughts magnify and expand a depressed person's negative experiences. The depressed person may overgeneralize about a minor occurrence and think that he is worthless because a work assignment was turned in late, his son was arrested for shoplifting, or a friend made a negative comment about his hair. Beck believes that depressed people blame themselves far more than is warranted. For example, an athlete may accept complete blame for a team's loss when five or six other teammates, the opposing team, and other factors were involved.

Self-defeating and sad thoughts fit the clinical picture of the depressed individual. Whether these thoughts are the cause or the consequence of the depression, however, is controversial. Critics say that self-defeating thoughts are an outgrowth of biological and environmental conditions that produce depression.

Some years ago, in the interest of science, a researcher drowned two rats (Richter, 1957). The first rat was dropped into a tank of warm water; it swam around for 60 hours before it drowned. The second rat was handled differently. The researcher held the rat tightly in his hand until it quit struggling to get loose. Then the rat was dropped into the tank; it swam around for several minutes before it drowned. The researcher concluded that the second rat drowned more quickly because its previous experiences told it to give up hope; the rat had developed a sense of helplessness.

Learned helplessness *occurs when animals or humans are exposed to aversive stimulation, such as prolonged stress or pain, over which they have no control. The inability to avoid such aversive stimulation produces an apathetic state of helplessness.* Martin Seligman (1975) argued that learned helplessness is one reason many individuals become depressed. When individuals encounter stress and pain over which they have no control, they eventually feel helpless and depressed. Some researchers believe that the hopelessness characteristic of learned helplessness is often the result of a person's extremely negative, self-blaming attributions (Abramson, Metalsky, & Alloy, 1989; Metalsky & others, 1993).

Biogenetic Explanations   Biological explanations of depression involve genetic inheritance and chemical changes in the brain. In a large twin study conducted in Denmark, the identical twins were more likely to suffer from mood disorders than were the fraternal twins (Bertelson, 1979). If one identical twin developed a mood disorder, the other had a 70 percent chance of developing the disorder; a fraternal twin ran only a 13 percent risk. Another study revealed that biological relatives of an individual with a mood disorder are more likely to suffer from the disorder than are adopted relatives (Wender & others, 1986).

Remember from chapter 3 that neurotransmitters are chemical messengers that carry information from one neuron to the next. Two neurotransmitters involved in depression are norepinephrine and serotonin. Depressed individuals have decreased levels of norepinephrine, whereas individuals in a manic state have increased levels. Patients with unusually low serotonin levels are 10 times as likely to commit suicide than individuals with normal levels (Stanley & Stanley, 1989). The endocrine system also may be involved in depression—excessive secretion of cortisol from the adrenal gland occurs in depressed individuals, for example (Joyce, Donald, & Elder, 1987). More about the biological aspects of depression appears in the next chapter, where we will discuss the use of drugs to alleviate depression.

Sociocultural Explanations
Seligman (1989) speculated that the reason so many young American adults are prone to depression is that our society's emphasis on self, independence, and individualism, coupled with an erosion of connectedness to others, family, and religion, has spawned a widespread sense of hopelessness. Depressive disorders are found in virtually all cultures in the world, but their incidence, intensity, and components vary across cultures. A major difference in depression between Western and many non-Western cultures is the absence of guilt and self-deprecation in the non-Western cultures (Draguns, 1990).

Some cross-cultural psychologists believe that mourning rituals in many non-Western cultures reduce the risks of depression. For example, low depression rates in Taiwan may be related to the overt expression of grief that occurs in Chinese funeral celebrations (Tseng & Hsu, 1969). Ancestor worship in Japan also may act against depression because love objects are not considered to be lost through death (Yamamoto & others, 1969). The mourning practices of African Americans also may reduce depression by providing an opportunity for adequate grieving and by providing the bereaved with support rather than having to cope with death in isolation (Vitols, 1967).

Earlier in this chapter, you learned that women run a far greater risk of depression than men—at a ratio of 2:1. Researchers have shown that depression is especially high among single women who are the head of household and among young married women who work at unsatisfying, dead-end jobs (Russo, 1990). Such stressful circumstances, as well as others involving sexual abuse, sexual harassment, unwanted pregnancy, and powerlessness disproportionately affect women. These sociocultural factors may interact with biological and cognitive factors to increase women's rate of depression. A second possibility may be that men in mainstream American society obscure their depression with aggressive behavior that "acts out," or externalizes, their sad feelings. In cultures where alcohol abuse and aggression are rare, such as the culturally homogeneous Amish community (a religious sect in Pennsylvania), the rates of depression for women and men are virtually equal.

Separating the environmental, cognitive, biological, and sociocultural causes of depression is not easy (Beckman & Leber, 1995). Whether neurotransmitters, cognitive factors, environmental factors, or cross-cultural factors are cause or effect is still unknown. Like most behaviors we have discussed, depression is best viewed as complex and multiply determined (Kendall & Watson, 1989). To read further about the importance of becoming educated about depression, turn to Applications in Psychology 16.1

Schizophrenic Disorders
Schizophrenia produces a bizarre set of symptoms and wreaks havoc on an individual's personality. **Schizophrenic disorders** *are severe psychological disorders characterized by distorted thoughts and perceptions, odd communication, inappropriate emotion, abnormal motor behavior, and social withdrawal. The term* schizophrenia *comes from the Latin words* schizo, *meaning "split," and* phrenia, *meaning "mind." The individual's mind is split from reality, and his or her personality loses its unity.* Schizophrenia is not the same as multiple personality, which sometimes is called a "split personality." Schizophrenia involves the split of *the* personality from reality, not the coexistence of several personalities within one individual.

Characteristics of Schizophrenic Disorders
Bob began to miss work. He spent his time watching his house from a rental car parked inconspicuously down the street and following his fellow employees as they left work to see where they went and what they did. He kept a little black book, in which he scribbled cryptic notes. When he went to the water cooler at work, he pretended to drink but, instead, looked carefully around the room to observe if anyone seemed guilty or frightened.

Bob's world seemed to be closing in on him. After an explosive scene at the office one day, he became very agitated. He left and never returned. By the time Bob arrived at home, he was in a rage. He could not sleep that night, and the next day he kept his children home from school; all day he kept the shades pulled on every window. The next night, he maintained his vigil. At 4 A.M., he armed himself and burst out of the house, firing shots in the air while daring his enemies to come out (McNeil, 1967).

Bob is a paranoid schizophrenic. About 1 in every 100 Americans will be classified as schizophrenic in their lifetime (Gottesman, 1989). Schizophrenic disorders are serious, debilitating mental disorders about one-half of all mental hospital patients in the United States are schizophrenics. More now than in the past, schizophrenics live in society and periodically return for treatment at mental hospitals (Kane & Barnes, 1995). Drug therapy, which will be discussed in the next chapter, is primarily responsible for

Becoming Educated About Depression

As we saw earlier in this chapter, depression is one of the most pervasive mental disorders. In the last several decades, important advances have been made in the treatment of depression. Different medications, several forms of psychotherapy, and the combination of medication and therapy have been successful in alleviating the debilitating symptoms of depression. As many as 80 percent of persons with depression are likely to show improvement if they are diagnosed and treated properly (Leshner, 1992).

Unfortunately, a survey by the National Institute of Mental Health revealed that only one-third of individuals with depression in the United States receive any professional help for their disorder. Approximately three-fourths of the depressed individuals said they would just live with their depression until the disorder passes. Some people with depression take the unwise course of self-treating their symptoms by abusing drugs or alcohol.

Why do so many people with depression go untreated? The reasons include the public's poor understanding of depression's nature and the probability of successful treatment; stigmatization of the disorder, which makes many depressed individuals unwilling to seek treatment and makes family members and associates perceive depressed individuals as lazy or having a flawed character; and the failure of many health professionals and physicians to recognize and diagnose depression in clients, which is an essential step for appropriate referral or treatment.

To help remedy the dilemma of so many depressed individuals going undiagnosed and untreated, in 1986 the National Institute of Mental Health began a national campaign to educate the general public, as well as health professionals, about the nature of depression and its treatment. The campaign is called the NIMH Depression Awareness, Recognition, and Treatment (D/ART) program. As part of this campaign, NIMH has developed and distributed a wide array of educational materials and has worked with local and national groups to encourage better public and professional understanding of depression.

A recent thrust of the D/ART campaign is to focus on the workplace as a key site for recognizing depression and providing referral and treatment through employee assistance plans. Employers have been receptive to the D/ART workplace program because they recognize the extensive toll that depression takes in absenteeism and reduced productivity.

So that you personally can get a sense of your own level of depression or absence of depression, turn to table 16.A. You also can obtain more information about the nature, diagnosis, and treatment of depression by writing:

Depression/USA
Rockville, MD 20857

And other organizations involved in promoting a better understanding of depression and help for individuals with affective disorders are listed at the end of this chapter.

---

fewer schizophrenics being hospitalized. About one-third of all schizophrenics get better, about one-third get worse, and another third stay about the same once they develop this severe mental disorder.

What symptoms do these individuals have? Many schizophrenics have *delusions,* or false beliefs—one individual may think he is Jesus Christ, another Napoleon, for example. The delusions are utterly implausible. One individual may think her thoughts are being broadcast over the radio; another may think that a double agent is controlling her every move. Schizophrenics also may hear, see, feel, smell, and taste things that are not there. These *hallucinations* often take the form of voices. The schizophrenic might think he hears two people talking about him, for example. On another occasion, he might say, "Hear that rumbling in the pipe? That is one of my men in there watching out for me."

Often schizophrenics do not make sense when they talk or write. Their language does not appear to follow any rules. For example, one schizophrenic might say, "Well, Rocky, babe, help is out, happening, but where, when, up, top, side, over, you know, out of the way, that's it. Sign off." Such speech has no meaning to the listener. These incoherent, loose word associations are called *word salad.* As shown in figure 16.5, schizophrenics' paintings also have a bizarre quality.

A schizophrenic's motor behavior may be bizarre, sometimes taking the form of an odd appearance, pacing,

TABLE 16.A

Depression

Instructions

Below is a list of the ways you might have felt or behaved in the LAST WEEK. Indicate what you felt by putting an X in the appropriate box for each item.

Items	Rarely or None of the Time (Less Than 1 Day)	Some or a Little of the Time (1–2 Days)	Occasionally or a Moderate Amount of the Time (3–4 Days)	Most or All of the Time (5–7 Days)
During the past week:				
1. I was bothered by things that usually don't bother me.	▢	▢	▢	▢
2. I did not feel like eating; my appetite was poor.	▢	▢	▢	▢
3. I felt that I could not shake off the blues even with help from my family and friends.	▢	▢	▢	▢
4. I felt that I was just as good as other people.	▢	▢	▢	▢
5. I had trouble keeping my mind on what I was doing.	▢	▢	▢	▢
6. I felt depressed.	▢	▢	▢	▢
7. I felt that everything I did was an effort.	▢	▢	▢	▢
8. I felt hopeful about the future.	▢	▢	▢	▢
9. I thought my life had been a failure.	▢	▢	▢	▢
10. I felt fearful.	▢	▢	▢	▢
11. My sleep was restless.	▢	▢	▢	▢
12. I was happy.	▢	▢	▢	▢
13. I talked less than usual.	▢	▢	▢	▢
14. I felt lonely.	▢	▢	▢	▢
15. People were unfriendly.	▢	▢	▢	▢
16. I enjoyed life.	▢	▢	▢	▢
17. I had crying spells.	▢	▢	▢	▢
18. I felt sad.	▢	▢	▢	▢
19. I felt that people disliked me.	▢	▢	▢	▢
20. I could not get going.	▢	▢	▢	▢

Reprinted from *Behavioral Research and Therapy*, Vol. 3, J. Geer, "The Development of a Scale to Measure Fear," pages 45–53. Copyright 1965, with kind permission from Elsevier Science Ltd, The Boulevard, Langford Lane, Kidlington OX5 1GB, UK.

Turn to the end of the chapter to interpret your responses.

---

statuelike postures, or strange mannerisms. Some schizophrenics withdraw from their social world; they become so insulated from others that they seem totally absorbed in interior images and thoughts.

He raves; his words are loose as
heaps of sand, and scattered
from sense. So high he's
mounted on his airy throne, that
now the wind has got into his
head, and turns his brain to
frenzy.

John Dryden

Forms of Schizophrenic Disorders

Schizophrenic disorders appear in four main forms: disorganized, catatonic, paranoid, and undifferentiated schizophrenia.

Disorganized schizophrenia *is a schizophrenic disorder in which an individual has delusions and hallucinations that have little or no recognizable meaning—hence, the label* disorganized. A disorganized schizophrenic withdraws from human contact and might regress to silly, childlike gestures and behavior. Many of these individuals were isolated or maladjusted during adolescence.

Catatonic schizophrenia *is a schizophrenic disorder characterized by bizarre motor behavior, which sometimes takes the form of a completely immobile stupor (see figure 16.6).*

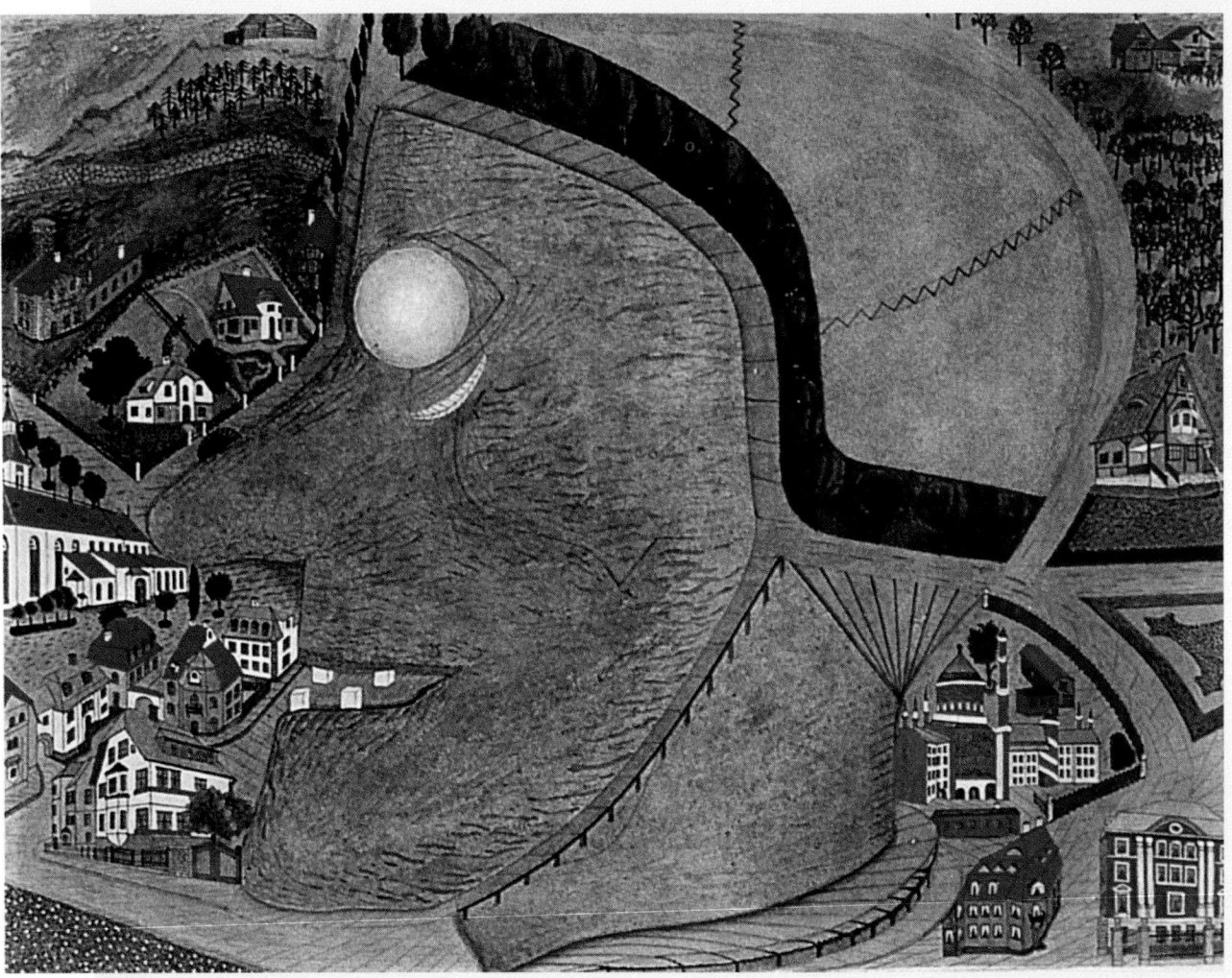

FIGURE 16.5

A Painting by a Schizophrenic
This painting is named *Landscape* and it is by August Neter, a successful nineteenth-century electrical engineer until he became schizophrenic in 1907. He lost interest in his work as an engineer as his mind became disorganized.

Even in this stupor, catatonic schizophrenics are completely conscious of what is happening around them. An individual in a catatonic state sometimes shows *waxy flexibility;* for example, if the person's arm is raised and then allowed to fall, the arm stays in the new position.

Paranoid schizophrenia *is a schizophrenic disorder characterized by delusions of reference, grandeur, and persecution.* The delusions usually form a complex, elaborate system based on a complete misinterpretation of actual events. It is not unusual for schizophrenics to develop all three delusions in the following order. First, they sense they are special and have been singled out for attention (delusions of reference). Individuals with delusions of reference misinterpret chance events as being directly relevant to their own lives—a thunderstorm, for example, might be perceived as a personal message from God. Second,

they believe that this special attention is the result of their admirable and special characteristics (delusions of grandeur). Individuals with delusions of grandeur think of themselves as exalted beings—the pope or the president, for example. Third, they think that others are so jealous and threatened by these characteristics that they spy and plot against them (delusions of persecution). Individuals with delusions of persecution think they are the target of a conspiracy—for example, recall Bob's situation described earlier.

Undifferentiated schizophrenia *is a schizophrenic disorder characterized by disorganized behavior, hallucinations, delusions, and incoherence.* This category of schizophrenia is used when an individual's symptoms either don't meet the criteria for the other types or they meet the criteria for more than one of the other types.

FIGURE 16.6

A Catatonic Schizophrenic
Disturbances in motor behavior are prominent symptoms in catatonic schizophrenia. Individuals may cease to move altogether, sometimes taking on bizarre postures.

Causes of Schizophrenia

Schizophrenic disorders may be caused by genetic and biological factors, as well as environmental and sociocultural factors.

Genetic Factors   If you have a relative with schizophrenia, what are the chances you will develop schizophrenia? It depends on how closely you are related. As genetic similarity increases, so does your risk of becoming schizophrenic (Sasaki & Kennedy, 1995). As shown in figure 16.7, an identical twin of a schizophrenic has a 46 percent chance of developing the disorder, a fraternal twin 14 percent, a sibling 10 percent, a nephew or niece 3 percent, and an unrelated individual in the general population 1 percent (Gottesman & Shields, 1982). Such data strongly suggest that genetic factors are involved in schizophrenia, although the precise nature of the genetic influence is unknown.

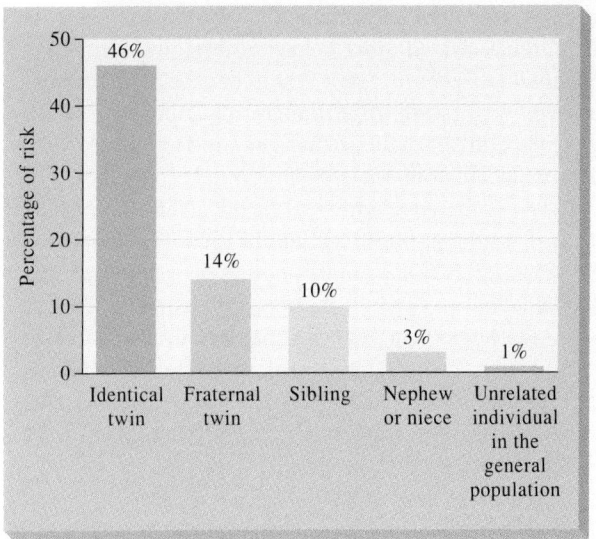

FIGURE 16.7

Lifetime Risk of Becoming Schizophrenic According to Genetic Relatedness
As your genetic relatedness to an individual with schizophrenia increases, so does your risk of becoming schizophrenic.

Neurobiological Factors   Many neuroscientists believe that imbalances in brain chemistry, including deficits in brain metabolism, a malfunctioning dopamine system, and distorted cerebral blood flow, cause schizophrenia (Goldberg, Berman, & Weinberger, 1995). Imaging techniques, such as the PET scan, clearly show deficits in brain metabolism. Do these deficits cause the disorder or are they simply symptoms of a disorder whose true origin lies deeper in the brain, in the genes, or in the environment? Whether the neurobiological factors are the cause or the effect, information about them improves our knowledge of schizophrenia's nature. We know that schizophrenics produce too much of the neurotransmitter dopamine. More about the dopamine system appears in the next chapter, where we will discuss the use of drugs to block excess dopamine production. Schizophrenics also have a reduced blood flow in the prefrontal cortex. For example, when scientists monitored the brains of schizophrenics as they performed a card-sorting task, blood did not adequately flow into the prefrontal region, where much of our advanced thinking takes place (Weinberger, Berman, & Zec, 1986).

This wretched brain gave way,
And I became a wreck,
At random driven,
Without one glimpse of reason.

Thomas Moore

Environmental Factors As scientists learn about schizophrenia's neurobiological basis, they must remember that schizophrenia, like all other behavior, does not occur in an environmental vacuum. Some researchers believe that environmental factors are important in schizophrenia (Goldstein, 1986); others believe that genetic factors outweigh environmental factors (Gottesman & Shields, 1982).

Stress is the environmental factor given the most attention in understanding schizophrenia. The **diathesis-stress view** *argues that a combination of environmental stress and biogenetic disposition causes schizophrenia* (Meehl, 1962). A defective gene makeup may produce schizophrenia only when an individual lives in a stressful environment. Advocates of the diathesis-stress view emphasize the importance of stress reduction and family support in treating schizophrenia.

Sociocultural Factors Disorders of thought and emotion are common to schizophrenia in all cultures, but the type and incidence of schizophrenic disorders may vary from culture to culture. For example, one of the more puzzling results is that the admission rates to mental health facilities for schizophrenia are very high for Irish Catholics in the Republic of Ireland (Torrey & others,

1984) but not for Irish Catholics living elsewhere (Murphy, 1978). One reason for this difference could be that the diagnostic criteria used in the Republic of Ireland are different from those used elsewhere, but this is not likely to be the complete answer. There are many areas of the world where the incidence of schizophrenia is considerably higher or lower than the worldwide incidence of just under 1 percent.

Rates of schizophrenia may also vary for different groups within a culture (Sartorius, 1992). For example, one study revealed that Blacks have higher rates of schizophrenia than Whites in both the United States and Great Britain (Bagley, 1984). In that study, Blacks had a significantly greater number of life crises that may have precipitated schizophrenic episodes. Also, the African Americans and African Britons who became schizophrenic had higher aspirations than those who did not. One explanation may be that their efforts to become assimilated into, and to achieve parity within, a mainstream society that is oppressively racist created considerable stress for them.

We have seen that the mood disorders and the schizophrenic disorders are complex and often debilitating. Next you will read about an intriguing set of disorders involving personality.

REVIEW

Mood Disorders and Schizophrenic Disorders

The mood disorders are characterized by wide emotional swings, ranging from deeply depressed to highly euphoric and agitated. Depression can occur alone, as in major depression, or it can alternate with mania, as in bipolar disorder. Individuals with major depression are sad, demoralized, bored, and self-derogatory. They often do not feel well, lose stamina easily, have a poor appetite, and are listless and unmotivated. Depression is so widespread that it is called the "common cold" of mental disturbances.

Bipolar disorder is characterized by extreme mood swings; an individual with this disorder might be depressed, manic, or both. In the manic phase, individuals are exuberant, have tireless stamina, and have a tendency for excess. They also are restless, irritable, and in almost constant motion. The rate of suicide

has increased dramatically in the United States. There is no simple answer to why individuals attempt suicide—immediate, earlier, biological, and cultural factors may be involved. Explanations of mood disorders come from psychoanalytic theory, cognitive and learning theories, biogenetic theories, and sociocultural theories.

Schizophrenic disorders are severe mental disorders characterized by distorted thoughts and perceptions, odd communication, inappropriate emotion, abnormal motor behavior, and social withdrawal. The individual's mind splits from reality, and the personality loses its unity. About 1 in 100 Americans becomes schizophrenic, and schizophrenia accounts for approximately one-half of all individuals in mental hospitals. Many schizophrenics have delusions,

or false beliefs, and hallucinations. They often do not make sense when they talk or write. The schizophrenic's motor behavior may be bizarre, and the schizophrenic may withdraw from social relationships.

Schizophrenia appears in four main forms: disorganized, catatonic, paranoid, and undifferentiated. Proposed causes of schizophrenia include genetic and biological factors, as well as environmental factors. Many neuroscientists believe that imbalances in brain chemistry cause schizophrenia. The diathesis-stress model emphasizes both biogenetic and environmental stress. Cognitive and emotional disorders of thought are common in schizophrenia in all cultures, but the type and incidence of schizophrenic disorders may vary cross-culturally and across social classes.

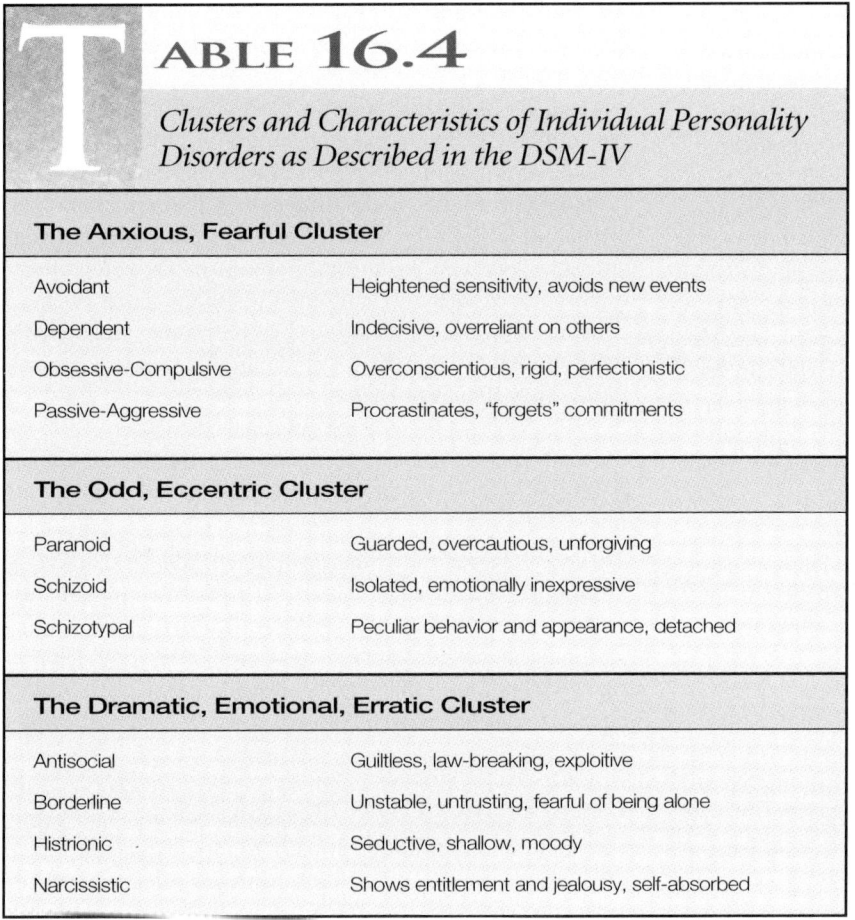

TABLE 16.4

Clusters and Characteristics of Individual Personality Disorders as Described in the DSM-IV

The Anxious, Fearful Cluster

Avoidant	Heightened sensitivity, avoids new events
Dependent	Indecisive, overreliant on others
Obsessive-Compulsive	Overconscientious, rigid, perfectionistic
Passive-Aggressive	Procrastinates, "forgets" commitments

The Odd, Eccentric Cluster

Paranoid	Guarded, overcautious, unforgiving
Schizoid	Isolated, emotionally inexpressive
Schizotypal	Peculiar behavior and appearance, detached

The Dramatic, Emotional, Erratic Cluster

Antisocial	Guiltless, law-breaking, exploitive
Borderline	Unstable, untrusting, fearful of being alone
Histrionic	Seductive, shallow, moody
Narcissistic	Shows entitlement and jealousy, self-absorbed

Personality Disorders

Personality disorders *are psychological disorders that develop when personality traits become inflexible and, thus, maladaptive.* Individuals with these maladaptive traits often do not recognize that they have a problem and might show little interest in changing. Personality disorders are notoriously difficult to treat therapeutically (Livesley, 1995).

Although there are eleven distinct personality disorder diagnoses described in the DSM-IV, clinicians think of the disorders as "clustered" around dominant characteristics. One cluster of personality disorders involves odd or eccentric behaviors. A second cluster emphasizes fear and anxiety. And a third cluster stresses dramatic, emotional, or erratic behaviors. We will describe one or more representative disorders from each of the clusters to illustrate their features. The complete list of personality disorders appears in table 16.4.

The Schizotypal Personality Disorder

The **schizotypal personality disorder** *is a personality disorder in the odd/eccentric cluster. Individuals with this disorder appear to be in contact with reality but many aspects of their behavior are distasteful, which leads to rejection or withdrawal from others.* Individuals are likely to be diagnosed with this label based on their eccentric patterns.

Consider Bruce. Although he was able to hold a job, he associated little with his co-workers. He strongly preferred to spend his breaks and time away from work with a sketchpad designing new flags for countries of the world. His geographic and political knowledge was impressive, but it was painful for him to engage in conversations with others. In contrast, when constructing new flags, he hummed and talked to himself.

Obsessive-Compulsive Personality Disorder

Obsessive-compulsive personality disorder *is in the anxious, fearful cluster of personality disorders. Anxious adjustment is its primary feature.* Individuals with this personality disorder tend to be exacting, precise, and orderly. They generate discomfort in others by requiring the same precision from others. They pay attention to each detail as a means of warding off anxiety. Individuals who show obsessive-compulsive style often are successfully adjusted to positions that require careful execution of details. For instance, Alex is a policeman in charge of preparing and maintaining evidence for trials. He repeatedly checks his files for completeness and order. Although well respected for the quality of his work by his fellow officers, he becomes enraged when they alter his meticulous organization.

Borderline Personality Disorder

Borderline personality disorder *is in the dramatic, emotional, erratic cluster of personality disorders.* Consider Pam, who never could manage to keep a college roommate. Each relationship would start off with a promise. Pam spoke enthusiastically about each new prospect as being "different from all the others." She bought them presents and almost courted their friendship. However, within a few weeks she would wildly criticize a new roommate for her poor hygiene, her preference for "low-life" acquaintances, and her impossible housekeeping skills. In desperation, she would threaten to kill herself if someone more caring and sensitive were not assigned to her immediately. Individuals with borderline tendencies often view the world as neatly divided into good and bad features. Their tolerance of frustration is very limited, as is their capacity to trust others. These individuals use manipulative, attention-seeking acts as a means of controlling others.

The Antisocial Personality Disorder

The **antisocial personality disorder** *is also in the dramatic, emotional, erratic cluster of personality disorders. It is the most problematic personality disorder for society. These individuals (who used to be called psychopaths or sociopaths) regularly violate the rights of others.* Individuals with antisocial personality disorder often resort to crime, violence, and delinquency. This disorder begins before the age of 15 and continues into adulthood; it is much more typical of males than of females. Consider Martin, who shows many of the behaviors typical of adults with antisocial personality. He cannot maintain a consistent work record. He steals, harasses others, rarely plans ahead, and fails to meet his financial obligations. He repeatedly gets into fights and shows little remorse when he has harmed someone. Tiffany also demonstrates many antisocial characteristics already in high school: truancy, school suspension, running away from home, stealing, vandalism, drug use, sexual acting-out, and violation of rules at home and school. Such behaviors are commonplace among young adults afflicted with antisocial personality disorder.

The Controversy About Personality Disorders

The general category of personality disorders is perhaps the most controversial of the diagnostic areas in the DSM-IV. Many scholars believe that we should not regard challenging personality styles as equivalent to other diagnostic categories that may have a clearer medical origin. Some have suggested that personality disorders represent a "wastebasket diagnosis": any individual whose problems do not fit into a more precise diagnosis may end up labeled with a personality disorder. Finally, some scholars (Landrine, 1989) believe that personality disorders might serve as political conveniences to dismiss those whose behavior is troublesome, confusing, or irritating.

Substance-Use Disorders

In chapter 5, we discussed a number of drugs and their effects on individuals. A problem associated with drug use is called a **substance-use disorder,** *which is characterized by one or more of the following features: (1) a pattern of pathological use that involves frequent intoxication, a need for daily use, and an inability to control use—in a sense, psychological dependence; (2) a significant impairment of social or occupational functioning attributed to the drug use; and (3) physical dependence that involves serious withdrawal problems.*

The use of many of the drugs described in chapter 5 can lead to a substance-use disorder. Alcohol, barbiturates, and opium derivatives all are capable of producing either physical or psychological dependence. Alcoholism is an especially widespread substance-use disorder; it has been estimated that 6 to 8 million Americans are alcoholics. Although substantial numbers of women abuse alcohol, more men than women are alcoholics. Among African Americans, the male-female alcoholic ratio is 3:2; among White Americans, the ratio is approximately 4:1 (Russo, 1990).

Many individuals are surprised to learn that substantial numbers of women are alcoholics or abusers of other drugs. Although most of the research on drug abuse has been directed toward males, studies have found that females are just as likely to be treated for drug-related problems in emergency rooms. Without a more intense research effort directed at female drug abusers, the unique facets of their drug abuse will go uncharted. For both male and female drug abusers, biogenetic, psychological, and sociocultural factors may all be involved.

LEGAL ASPECTS OF MENTAL DISORDERS

The legal status of individuals with mental disorders raises a number of controversial issues: What is involved in committing disordered and dangerous individuals to mental institutions? What is the status of using the insanity defense for capital crimes? How does "guilty but insane" differ from competence to stand trial? We will consider each of these issues in turn.

Commitment and Dangerousness

Having a mental disorder in itself is not adequate grounds for placing individuals in mental institutions against their will. However, the behavior of some mentally disordered individuals is so severe that they are a threat to themselves and/or to others, and they may need protective confinement. Although procedures vary somewhat from state to state, certain conditions usually must be present before the state can formally commit persons to a mental institution: The persons must have a mental disorder and must be dangerous either to themselves or to other people. Dangerousness judgments in the absence of criminal involvement may depend on a demonstrated inability to take care of one's daily physical needs.

Commitment, *the process by which an individual becomes institutionalized in a mental hospital,* can be voluntary or involuntary. Some individuals commit themselves, recognizing that their behavior is potentially dangerous or incompetent. However, the state commits others on an involuntary basis through judicial proceedings. **Civil commitment** *transpires when a judge deems an individual to be a risk to self or others as a function of mental disorder.* A civic commitment proceeding often involves psychiatric evaluation and a formal judicial hearing. The judge must conclude that the evidence is "clear and convincing," based on a 1979 precedent (*Addington v. Texas*), or they cannot order hospitalization.

Determining whether a mentally disordered individual is dangerous is not easy, even for mental health professionals.

Two famous cases involving the insanity plea resulted in different outcomes. Before his murder in 1994, Jeffrey Dahmer's insanity defense for murder and cannabalism was unsuccessful. In contrast, a jury found Lorena Bobbitt "innocent by reason of insanity" in her sexual assault on her husband.

Nonetheless, there are times when professionals have to make dangerousness judgments. Recent court decisions have held mental health professionals liable when unconfined clients they were treating have caused harm to others. Legal precedents require therapists to warn potential victims if their patients threaten to kill someone (Faulkner, McFarland, & Bloom, 1989).

Criminal Responsibility

Criminal commitment *occurs when a mental disorder is implicated in the commission of a crime.* Procedures may ensure that the individual receives mental health care as an inpatient in a mental health hospital rather than imprisonment. Two areas in which psychologists make decisions about criminal responsibility include the insanity defense and the determination of competence to stand trial. We will examine each of these challenges in turn.

The Insanity Defense

Insanity *is a legal term, not a psychological term. A legally insane person is considered mentally disordered and incapable of being responsible for his or her actions.* The **insanity defense** *is a plea of "innocent by reason of insanity" used as a legal defense in criminal trials.* In our culture, guilt implies responsibility and intent—to be guilty of a crime, an individual has to have knowingly and intentionally committed it. The jury determines whether the defendant is guilty, based on such legally defined criteria. Controversy swirls about the concept of insanity because of concerns that criminals will unfairly use this plea to avoid prosecution.

In recent years, two publicized cases employing the insanity defense have led to different outcomes. Jeffrey Dahmer's attorneys were unable to persuade the jury in 1992 that his murdering and ritualized cannibalism of fifteen young men resulted from insanity. The prosecution pointed to his skilled execution and coverup of the crimes as evidence that he was rational and should be held responsible. The jury found Dahmer guilty and sane at the time he committed the crimes and ordered him to serve fifteen life terms without parole. In 1994, Dahmer was murdered by another inmate.

In a contrasting example from 1994, Lorena Bobbitt's attorneys were successful in employing the insanity plea. Lorena Bobbitt claimed that she had suffered years of physical and sexual abuse from her husband, John. According to her defense attorneys, after one particularly abusive episode with her husband, she experienced an irresistible impulse. She waited for her husband to fall asleep. Then she cut off his penis, drove away from the house, and threw his penis out of the car window. Although her trial was controversial, the jury found her "guilty, but insane" at the time she committed the crime. After several weeks of confinement in a mental hospital, Lorena Bobbitt was able to return to the community.

The appropriateness of the insanity plea remains highly controversial (Slovenko, 1995). Successful insanity defense is relatively rare because juries struggle with applying the legal criteria to complex situations. Some experts recommend changes in the defense, arguing that the courts should establish whether or not the defendant committed the crime, independently of establishing the defendant's

---

Evaluating the Insanity Plea

A great deal of controversy has been generated about the use of the insanity plea as a legal defense. Where do your sympathies lie on the appropriateness of the insanity plea? Is the insanity plea a helpful legal procedure to insure mental health care for those who clearly need the help? Or is the insanity plea an insurance policy for those who can neatly sidestep imprisonment through skillful legal defense? Which side do you favor? What values underlie your position? Your exploration of this controversial issue encourages you to *demonstrate awareness of underlying values that motivate behavior.*

sanity status (Steadman & others, 1989). Many states have moved to adopt this approach. In addition, the Supreme Court reviewed a case in 1994 that opened the opportunity for states to revisit their insanity plea practices.

Determining Competency

Competency *is an individual's ability to understand and participate in a judicial proceeding.* Competent individuals can consult with a lawyer and ask questions about the proceedings. Individuals whom the courts deem competent to stand trial may still plead that they were "guilty, but insane" at the time they committed the offenses. Individuals deemed incompetent to stand trial may be remanded to institutional care at the discretion of a judge who has evaluated the testimony of expert witnesses and other evidence pertinent to the individual's current state of mind.

REVIEW

Personality Disorders, Substance-Abuse Disorders, and the Legal Aspects of Disorders

Personality disorders are psychological disorders that develop when personality traits become inflexible and, thus, maladaptive. Individuals with a personality disorder often do not recognize that they have a problem and show little interest in changing their behavior. Three clusters of personality disorders are the anxious, fearful cluster; the odd, eccentric cluster; and the dramatic, emotional, erratic cluster. The schizotypal personality is in the odd, eccentric cluster; obsessive-compulsive personality disorder is in the anxious, fearful cluster; borderline personality disorder and antisocial personality disorder are in the dramatic, emotional, erratic cluster. Personality disorders are a controversial category of mental disorders.

A substance-abuse disorder is characterized by one or more of the following features: (1) a pattern of pathological use that involves frequent intoxication, a need for daily use, and an inability to control use—in the sense of psychological dependence; (2) a significant impairment of social or occupational functioning, attributed to the drug use; and (3) physical dependence that involves serious withdrawal problems.

The legal status of individuals with mental disorders raises a number of controversial issues: commitment and dangerousness, criminal responsibility, the insanity defense, and determining competence.

A classic study in the 1950s showed that schizophrenia appears to have a "downward drift" according to socioeconomic class (Hollingshead & Redlich, 1958). Studying institutionalization patterns across multiple hospitals, the researchers suggested that being a member of a lower socioeconomic class enhances your risk of schizophrenia in your lifetime.

The usual degree of risk cited for schizophrenia is close to 1 percent, meaning that 1 out of every 100 individuals in the culture will become schizophrenic. However, a number of factors appear to be related to increasing the risk for schizophrenia. Although the presence of these factors does not guarantee the development of schizophrenia, they enhance the risk for the individual with these characteristics.

We can find a good example of increased risk in genetic studies (Gottesman & Shields, 1982). Blood relation to a diagnosed schizophrenic increases risk. Your risk of schizophrenia increases from 1.0 percent to 4.4 percent if you have a schizophrenic parent, to 13.7 percent if your fraternal twin has schizophrenia, and to 46.0 percent if your identical twin has schizophrenia. Thus, biological factors contribute to risk in substantial ways but do not completely account for the development of schizophrenia. If they did, we would expect that identical twins would virtually always avoid or succumb to schizophrenia together.

If living in lower socioeconomic classes does seem to enhance risk, can you identify possible variables that could account for this explanation? What specific factors might account for risk that can be more directly linked to the limited resources families have in lower socioeconomic existence?

One longitudinal study identified many "markers" for increased schizophrenic risk (Watt, 1984). These included

- low birthweight and challenging birth conditions
- absence of a close relationship with the mother early in life
- underdeveloped infant motor coordination
- being raised in an institution or foster home
- underdeveloped intelligence skills, particularly verbal skills
- distractibility and attention problems
- aggressiveness and anger
- confusing parent-child communication

Did you think of other variables that could be associated with lower socioeconomic conditions?

Despite the restrictions that lower-class existence can impose on a person's ability to cope with life's stressors, there are, nonetheless, some individuals from lower-class backgrounds who develop considerable resourcefulness and resilience.

When supposed ethnic differences in schizophrenia are examined in the context of socioeconomic status—comparing African Americans, Latinos, and Whites, for example—the ethnic differences tend to vanish. Thus, it seems that poverty and the living conditions poverty engenders are much more likely to be associated with schizophrenia than is ethnicity. This research serves as a powerful reminder to *pursue alternative explanations to explain behavior comprehensively.*

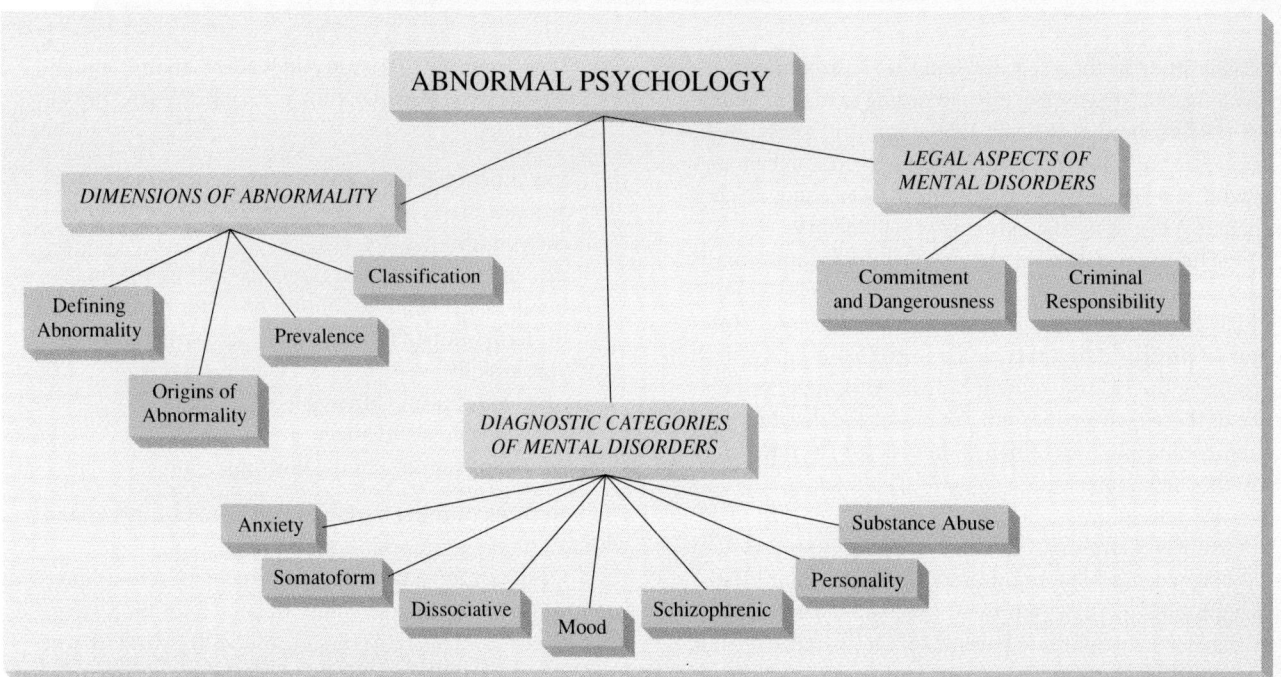

ABNORMAL PSYCHOLOGY

DIMENSIONS OF ABNORMALITY

LEGAL ASPECTS OF MENTAL DISORDERS

Defining Abnormality

Classification

Prevalence

Origins of Abnormality

Commitment and Dangerousness

Criminal Responsibility

DIAGNOSTIC CATEGORIES OF MENTAL DISORDERS

Anxiety

Somatoform

Dissociative

Mood

Schizophrenic

Personality

Substance Abuse

I n this chapter we explored the nature of abnormal psychology, beginning with an evaluation of the dimensions of abnormality. We defined abnormality, studied the origins of abnormal behavior, read about prevalence estimates of disorders, and learned about how mental disorders are classified. Then we spent considerable time exploring the diagnostic categories of mental disorders: anxiety, somatoform, dissociative, mood, schizophrenic, personality, and substance-use. Next, we read about the legal aspects of mental disorders, especially the concepts of commitment and dangerousness, as well as criminal responsibility. Don't forget that you can obtain an overall summary of the chapter by again reading the in-chapter reviews on pages 583, 590, 600, and 604.

Five perspectives were described in this chapter. The most attention was given to the neurobiological and sociocultural perspectives. The neurobiological perspective was discussed in the sections on the origins of abnormal behavior (pp. 576–577), the causes of mood disorders (pp. 593–595), and the causes of schizophrenic disorders (pp. 599–600). The sociocultural approach was presented in the sections on the origins of abnormal behavior (pp. 576–577), suicide (pp. 592–593), the causes of mood disorders (pp. 593–595), and the causes of schizophrenic disorders (pp. 599–600). The behavioral and cognitive perspectives appeared in material on the causes of mood disorders (pp. 593–595). The psychoanalytic perspective was also described in the section on mood disorders (pp. 593–594) as well as in the discussion of conversion disorder (pp. 587–588).

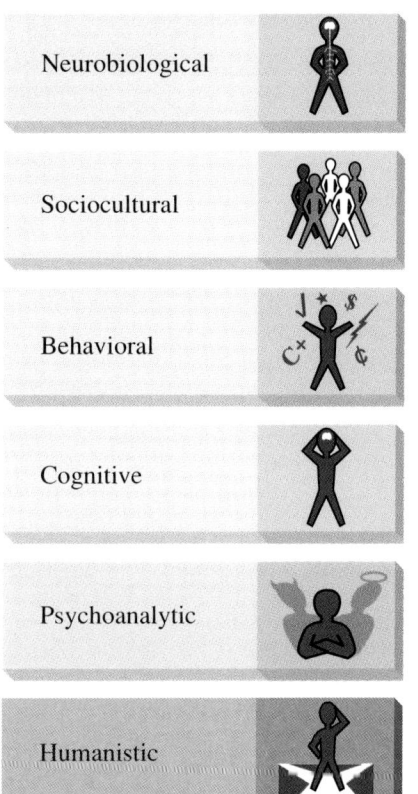

Neurobiological

Sociocultural

Behavioral

Cognitive

Psychoanalytic

Humanistic

abnormal behavior Behavior that is maladaptive, harmful, statistically unusual, personally distressing, and/or designated abnormal by the culture.   575

medical model Also called the disease model; the forerunner of the biological approach. This model states that abnormal behavior is a disease or illness precipitated by internal physical causes.   576

neurotic disorders Relatively mild mental disorders in which the individual has not lost contact with reality.   581

psychotic disorders Severe mental disorders in which the individual has lost contact with reality.   581

DSM-IV *Diagnostic and Statistical Manual of Mental Disorders,* fourth edition. The DSM-IV is the most recent major classification of mental disorders and contains eighteen major classifications and describes more than 200 specific disorders.   581

multiaxial system A feature of the DSM-IV in which individuals are classified on the basis of five dimensions, or "axes," that include the individual's history and highest level of functioning in the last year. This system ensures that the individual will not merely be assigned to a mental disorder category, but instead will be characterized by a number of clinical factors.   581

anxiety disorders Psychological disorders that include the following main features: motor tension (jumpiness, trembling, inability to relax), hyperactivity (dizziness, racing heart, or perspiration), and apprehensive expectations and thoughts.   584

generalized anxiety disorder An anxiety disorder that consists of persistent anxiety for at least 1 month. An individual with this disorder is unable to specify the reasons for the anxiety.   584

panic disorder A recurrent anxiety disorder that is marked by the sudden onset of apprehension or terror.   584

phobic disorder An anxiety disorder that occurs when an individual has an irrational, overwhelming, persistent fear of a particular object or situation; commonly called a phobia.   584

agoraphobia The fear of entering unfamiliar situations, especially open or public spaces; the most common phobic disorder.   584

obsessive-compulsive disorder (OCD) An anxiety disorder in which the individual has anxiety-provoking thoughts that will not go away (obsession) and/or urges to perform repetitive, ritualistic behaviors to prevent or produce a future situation (compulsion).   586

post-traumatic stress disorder A mental disorder that develops through exposure to any of several traumatic events, such as war, the Holocaust, severe abuse as in rape, natural disasters such as floods and tornados, and accidental disasters such as plane crashes. The disorder is characterized by anxiety symptoms that may be apparent 1 month after the trauma or be delayed by months or even years until onset.   587

somatoform disorders Mental disorders in which the psychological symptoms take a physical, or somatic, form, even though no physical causes can be found.   587

hypochondriasis A somatoform disorder in which the individual has a pervasive fear of illness and disease.   587

conversion disorder A somatoform disorder in which an individual experiences genuine physical symptoms, even though no physiological problems can be found.   587

dissociative disorders Psychological disorders that involve a sudden loss of memory or change in identity. Under extreme stress or shock, an individual's conscious awareness becomes dissociated (separated or split) from previous memories and thoughts.   588

psychogenic amnesia A dissociative disorder involving memory loss caused by extensive psychological stress.   588

fugue A dissociative disorder in which an individual not only develops amnesia but also unexpectedly travels away from home and establishes a new identity (*fugue* means "flight").   588

multiple personality The most dramatic but least common dissociative disorder; individuals with this disorder have two or more distinct personalities.   588

mood disorders Psychological disorders characterized by wide emotional swings, ranging from deeply depressed to highly euphoric and agitated. Depression can occur alone, as in major depression, or it can alternate with mania, as in bipolar disorder.   590

major depression A mood disorder in which the individual is deeply unhappy, demoralized, self-derogatory, and bored. An individual with major depression shows changes in appetite and sleep patterns, decreased energy, feelings of worthlessness, concentration problems, and guilt feelings that might prompt thoughts of suicide.   590

bipolar disorder A mood disorder characterized by extreme mood swings; an individual with this disorder might be depressed, manic, or both.   592

learned helplessness A response that occurs when animals or humans are exposed to aversive stimulation, such as prolonged stress or pain, over which they have no control. The inability to avoid such aversive stimulation produces an apathetic state of helplessness.   594

schizophrenic disorders Severe psychological disorders characterized by distorted thoughts and perceptions, odd communication, inappropriate emotion, abnormal motor behavior, and social withdrawal. The term *schizophrenia* comes from the Latin words *schizo,* meaning "split," and *phrenia,* meaning "mind." The individual's mind is split from reality, and his or her personality loses its unity.   595

disorganized schizophrenia A schizophrenic disorder in which an individual has delusions and hallucinations that have little or no recognizable meaning—hence the label *disorganized.*   597

catatonic schizophrenia A schizophrenic disorder characterized by bizarre motor behavior, which sometimes takes the form of an immobile stupor.   597

paranoid schizophrenia A schizophrenic disorder characterized by delusions of reference, grandeur, and persecution.   598

undifferentiated schizophrenia A schizophrenic disorder characterized by disorganized behavior, hallucinations, delusions, and incoherence.   598

diathesis-stress view The view that a combination of environmental stress and biogenetic disposition causes schizophrenia.   600

personality disorders Psychological disorders that develop when personality traits become inflexible and, thus, maladaptive.   601

schizotypal personality disorder A personality disorder in the odd, eccentric cluster. Individuals with this disorder appear to be in contact with reality, but many aspects of their behavior are distasteful, which leads to rejection or withdrawal from others.   601

obsessive-compulsive personality disorder A personality disorder in the anxious, fearful cluster; anxious adjustment is the primary feature.   601

borderline personality disorder A personality disorder in the dramatic, emotional, and erratic cluster; the person's behavior exhibits these characteristics.   601

antisocial personality disorder A personality disorder in the dramatic, emotional, and erratic cluster; the most problematic personality disorder for society. Individuals with this disorder often resort to crime, violence, and delinquency.   602

substance-use disorder A disorder characterized by one or more of the following features: (1) a pattern of pathological use that involves frequent intoxication, a need for daily use, and an inability to control use—in the sense of psychological dependence; (2) a significant impairment of social or occupational functioning attributed to drug use; and (3) physical dependence that involves serious withdrawal problems.   602

commitment The process by which an individual becomes institutionalized in a mental hospital.   602

civil commitment Commitment that transpires when a judge deems an individual to be a risk to self or others due to a mental disorder.   602

criminal commitment Commitment that occurs when a mental disorder is implicated in the commission of a crime.   603

insanity A legal term, not a psychological one. A legally insane person is considered mentally disordered and incapable of being responsible for his or her actions.   603

insanity defense A plea of "innocent by reason of insanity," used as a legal defense in criminal trials.   603

competency An individual's ability to understand and participate in a judicial proceeding.   604

DON'T PANIC

(1986) by Reid Wilson. New York: Harper-Perennial.

Wilson describes a self-help program for coping with panic attacks. The book describes what panic attacks are like, how it feels when you are undergoing one, and what type of people are prone to having panic attacks. It gives advice on how to sort through the physical and psychological aspects of panic attacks. You also learn how to conquer panic attacks, especially through self-monitoring. Specific recommendations are made about the effective use of breathing exercises, focused thinking, mental imagery, and deep muscle relaxation.

OBSESSIVE-COMPULSIVE DISORDERS

(1991) by Steven Levenkron. New York: Warner Books.

Levenkron believes that obsessive-compulsive disorder is the personality's attempt to reduce anxiety, which may stem from a painful childhood or a genetic tendency toward anxiety. Levenkron developed therapy techniques to help people who suffer from this disorder that include the help and support of parents, teachers, physicians, and friends. The book includes many case histories to illustrate the problems people who have obsessive-compulsive disorder encounter and how they can overcome their problem. Levenkron argues that people can reduce or eliminate their obsessions and compulsions if they follow four basic steps: (1) Rely on a family member or a therapist for support and comfort, (2) unmask their rituals, (3) talk in depth to trusted family members or a therapist, and (4) control their anxiety.

FEELING GOOD

(1980) by David Burns. New York: Avon.

Feeling Good is a cognitive therapy approach to coping with depression. Cognitive therapists like Burns, who trained and continues to work with Aaron Beck at the University of Pennsylvania School of Medicine, argue that the key to coping with depression is to identify and restructure faulty negative thinking. In *Feeling Good,* Burns outlines the techniques people can use to identify and combat false assumptions that underlie their flawed negative thinking.

Burns takes you on a journey through the development of the cognitive therapy approach and why he thinks it is the best way to treat depression. You learn how to diagnose your moods and why you feel the way you think. You read about how to develop positive self-esteem, stand up for your rights when you are unjustly criticized, cope with anger, and default guilt.

Burns gives you the insight to distinguish between normal bouts of sadness and more serious depression, to defeat hopelessness and suicidal tendencies, to cope with the strains of everyday living, and to become knowledgeable about antidepressant drug therapy. *Feeling Good* has many self-assessment tests, self-help forms, and charts to help you cope with depression.

Burns's easy-to-read style, extensive use of examples and charts, and enthusiasm give readers a clear understanding of cognitive therapy and the confidence to try out its techniques. Another good choice is Burns's *The Feeling Good Handbook,* which applies cognitive therapy to depression and other problems, including anxiety and those involving relationships.

Anxiety Disorders and Phobias: A Cognitive Perspective (1985)

>by Aaron Beck and Gary Emery
>New York: Basic Books

This book provides information about different types of anxiety and how people can change their thinking to overcome the anxiety that is overwhelming them.

Depression and Related Affective Disorders

>Johns Hopkins Hospital, Meyer 3-181
>600 N. Wolfe Street
>Baltimore, MD 21205
>410–955–4647

This is an organization for individuals with affective disorders and their families, friends, and mental health professionals. The organization provides support, referrals, and educational programs, and it publishes a quarterly newsletter, *Smooth Sailing.*

International Society for the Study of Multiple Personality and Dissociation

>5700 Old Orchard Road, 1st Floor
>Skokie, IL 60077-1024
>708–966–4322

This organization of mental health professionals and students promotes a greater understanding of dissociation.

National Foundation for Depressive Illness

>P.O. Box 2257
>New York, NY 10116
>800–248–4344

This foundation provides information and education about recent medical advances in affective mood disorders; it also has a referral service.

National Mental Health Association

>1021 Prince Street
>Alexandria, VA 22314-2971
>800–969–NMHA

This consumer advocacy organization is devoted to promoting mental health and improving the lives of individuals with a mental disorder. It publishes NMHA Focus four times a year, as well as pamphlets on mental health issues.

National Mental Health Consumers Association

>P.O. Box 1166
>Madison, WI 53701

This organization seeks to protect the rights of mental health clients in housing, employment, and public benefits; it encourages the creation of self-help groups and aids them in acquiring funding and networking with other organizations.

Youth Suicide National Center

>204 E. 2nd Ave Suite 203
>San Mateo, CA 94401
>415–347–3961

This is a national clearinghouse that develops and distributes educational materials on suicide and reviews current youth suicide prevention and support programs. Publications include *Suicide in Youth and What You Can Do About It* and *Helping Your Child Choose Life: A Parent's Guide to Youth Suicide.*

After completing the Depression Scale, use the chart below to assign points to your answers. Add up all the points.

Interpretation

If your score is around 7, then you are like the average male in terms of how much depression you experienced in the last week. If your score is around 8–9, then your score is similar to how much depression the average female experienced in the last week. If your score is 16 or more, you might benefit from professional help for the depression you have been experiencing.

	Rarely or None of the Time (Less Than 1 Day)	Some or a Little of the Time (1–2 Days)	Occasionally or a Moderate Amount of the Time (3–4 Days)	Most or All of the Time (5–7 Days)
1.	0	1	2	3
2.	0	1	2	3
3.	0	1	2	3
4.	3	2	1	0
5.	0	1	3	3
6.	0	1	2	3
7.	0	1	2	3
8.	3	2	1	0
9.	0	1	2	3
10.	0	1	2	3
11.	0	1	2	3
12.	3	2	1	0
13.	0	1	2	3
14.	0	1	2	3
15.	0	1	2	3
16.	3	2	1	0
17.	0	1	2	3
18.	0	1	2	3
19.	U	1	2	3
20.	0	1	2	3

Total Number of Points: _____

Therapies

CHAPTER OUTLINE

CRITICAL THINKING ABOUT BEHAVIOR

CHAPTER BOXES

SOCIOCULTURAL WORLDS

APPLICATIONS IN PSYCHOLOGY

CRITICAL THINKING

*Nothing can be changed until
it is faced.*

James Baldwin

The Story of Susanna Kaysen: A Perilous Journey

Etiology

This person is (pick one):

1. on a perilous journey from which we can learn much when he or she returns;
2. possessed by (pick one):
   a) the gods,
   b) God (that is, a prophet)
   c) some bad spirits, demons, or devils,
   d) the Devil;
3. a witch;
4. bewitched (variant of 2);
5. bad, and must be isolated and punished;
6. ill, and must be isolated and treated by (pick one):
   a) purging and leeches,
   b) removing the uterus if the person has one,
   c) electric shock to the brain,
   d) cold stress sheets wrapped tight around the body,
   e) Thorazine or Stelazine;
7. ill, and must spend the next seven years talking about it;
8. a victim of society's low tolerance for deviant behavior;
9. sane in an insane world;
10. on a perilous journey from which he or she may never return (Susanna Kaysen, *Girl, Interrupted*, p. 15)

Susanna Kaysen's autobiography about her own struggle with disordered behavior offers some provocative insights about the challenge of treating mental disorder. Diagnosed as having a borderline personality disorder with major depression, Kaysen chronicled her journey through a maze of psychotherapeutic treatments. Ultimately she achieved a greater sense of independence and stability, although she herself was uncertain about what aspects of her care facilitated her improvement.

PREVIEW

Many people today seek therapy. Some, like Susanna Kaysen, find themselves in the immobilizing grip of depression and fear. Others may need help in overcoming trauma, such as physical or sexual abuse in childhood. And others simply want to gain insight about themselves and improve their lives. Whatever the reason that people seek therapy, there are many different therapies to help them—one count listed more than 450 variations (Karasu, 1986). In this chapter, we begin by exploring the nature of psychotherapy in its earliest recorded forms and in contemporary practice. We will examine both individual therapies and therapies for systems, including groups, families, and even communities. Next, we evaluate the important question of whether psychotherapy is effective, especially from the vantage point of the sociocultural perspective. We conclude with an overview of biomedical perspectives on therapy.

THE NATURE OF THERAPY

It would be difficult to pinpoint exactly when, historically, some people were first designated as healers to help others with disordered thoughts, emotions, and behavior. However, it is clear today that not only is therapy an acceptable avenue for resolving personal challenges and mental problems, it has become a thriving enterprise. Contemporary practitioners come from a variety of backgrounds and work with an astonishing array of problems with individuals, groups, and communities. We will first examine the historical underpinnings of modern psychotherapeutic interventions.

As we study the origins of modern therapy, keep in mind that our knowledge about the causes and treatment of disorder is far more sophisticated than that of our ancestors. By the same token, our descendants' knowledge may show many of our own beliefs and practices to be foolish or harmful. The shifts in perspective through the years regarding dysfunction, as well as the durability of some beliefs, underscore the importance of context in influencing judgments about what constitutes normal and disordered behavior.

Historical Viewpoint

In ancient societies, individuals believed that abnormal behavior had both mystical and organic origins. In many cultures, disordered behavior represented possession by a spirit residing in the afflicted person. When evil spirits were deemed responsible, the authorities imposed **trephining,** *a procedure that involves chipping a hole in the skull to allow the*

FIGURE 17.1

Trephining
The technique of trephining involved chipping a hole in the skull through which an evil spirit, believed to be the source of the person's abnormal behavior, might escape. The fact that some people actually survived the operation is shown by this skull. The bone had had time to heal considerably before the individual died.

evil spirit to escape (see figure 17.1). In some other cultures, behavior disorder was interpreted as a sign that nature was out of balance (Torrey, 1986). Such individuals might be granted special privilege, rather than treatment designed to bring them back within the bounds of expected behavior.

In the fourth century B.C., Hippocrates, a Greek physician, proposed that mental problems and disordered behavior resulted from brain damage or an imbalance of body chemicals. He prescribed rest, exercise, a bland diet, and abstinence from sex and alcohol as cures for depressed mood. Unfortunately, Hippocrates's theories lost their influence.

In the Middle Ages there was a resurgence of the belief that spiritual possession was the cause of disorder. Many of those who were identified as "different" probably suffered from neurological disorders, such as epilepsy or Tourette's syndrome, a disease that involves repetitive motor and vocal tics. Many of the unfortunates, whom the authorities deemed possessed by evil spirits, were labeled as witches. **Exorcism,** *a religious rite that involved prayer, starvation, beatings, and various forms of torture,* became a popular intervention to cast out the evil spirits. When exorcism involved particularly harsh practices, the notion was to make the disordered individuals so physically uncomfortable that no evil spirit would remain in their bodies. If that didn't work, the only "cure" left was to destroy the body. From the fourteenth through the seventeenth century, 200,000 to 500,000 people thought to be witches were hanged or burned at the stake. Some historians have pointed out that women were usually the victims and that the pursuit of witches seemed to intensify during periods of economic turmoil.

CRITICAL THINKING

Exploring the Procedure of Trephining

You may have been repulsed when you examined the image of the trephined skull in figure 17.1. Imagine having to undergo such an invasive procedure in technologically primitive conditions to resolve your disordered thoughts and feelings. Yet there are many possibilities for how the procedure of trephining could have successfully reduced disordered behavior. Can you develop any plausible psychological explanations based on reasoning to identify why trephining could have been successful in reducing disordered behavior?

The threat of undergoing such a severe procedure (without anesthetic) might have reduced disordered behavior through negative reinforcement. One might try hard to keep unusual behavior under control to avoid the procedure.

The attention one gained by undergoing this procedure might also have addressed some needs underlying expressions of disorder. The recipient's own expectation that the procedure would help might have produced different behavior. Some individuals in particular cultural traditions believed that the procedure might release the individual from the grip of spirits. Of course, many trephined patients were unlikely to survive the operation, so disordered behavior was automatically reduced when the patient died. Were you able to identify any of these explanations? On-target explanations demonstrate your ability to *make accurate inferences about behavior.*

FIGURE 17.2

Pinel Unchaining Mentally Disabled Individuals
In this painting, Pinel is shown unchaining the inmates at La Bicetre Hospital. Pinel's efforts led to widespread reform and more humane treatment of mentally disabled individuals.

During the Renaissance, the authorities built *asylums* ("sanctuaries") to house the mentally disordered. They probably intended both to provide protection for those who were incapable and to create some clear physical boundaries between normally functioning persons and those who were disordered. However, the asylums were not much better than exorcisms; the inmates often were chained to walls, caged, or fed sparingly.

Fortunately, Philippe Pinel (1745–1826), the head physician at a large asylum in Paris, initiated a significant change in the treatment of the mentally disordered, whom Pinel described as ordinary people who could not reason well because of their serious personal problems. He believed that treating the mentally disabled like animals not only was inhumane but also hindered their recovery. Pinel convinced the French government to unchain large numbers of patients, some of whom had not been outside of the asylum for 30 to 40 years (see figure 17.2). He replaced the dungeons with bright rooms and spent long hours talking with patients, listening to their problems, and giving advice.

Although Pinel's efforts led to reform, it was slow. Even as late as the nineteenth century in the United States, the mentally disordered were kept alongside criminals in prisons. Dorothea Dix, a nurse who had taken a position at a prison in the middle of the nineteenth century, was instrumental in getting the mentally disabled separated from criminals. She embarked on a state-to-state campaign to upgrade prisons and persuaded officials to use better judgment in deciding which individuals should be placed in prisons. State governments began building large asylums for the mentally disabled because of Dix's efforts, although the conditions in the asylums often were no better than in the prisons.

Although we have made significant advances in the twentieth century in the ways that we view and treat the mentally disordered, we are far from resolving all the problems associated with their care. As you will read later in this chapter, our prevailing attitudes in the United States toward mental disorder have contributed substantially to the problem of homelessness. Our technological sophistication has

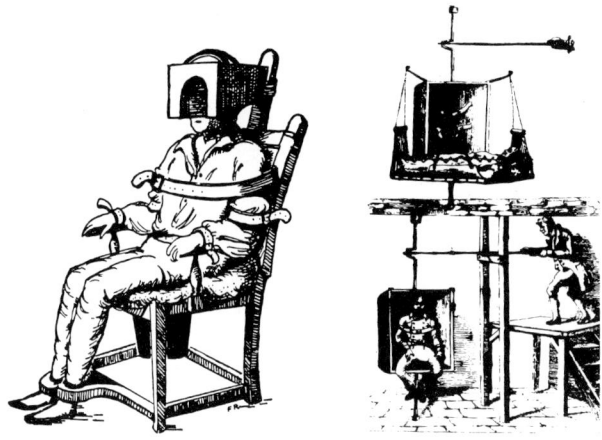

Even after Pinel and others reformed mental institutions, some rather strange techniques were invented to control the most difficult mentally disabled individuals. The tranquilizing chair (*left*) and circulating swing (*right*) were used to calm mentally disabled individuals at the beginning of the nineteenth century. Fortunately, their use soon diminished.

"I utilize the best from Freud, the best from Jung and the best from my Uncle Marty, a very smart fellow."

© 1994 by Sidney Harris—"Stress Test," Rutgers University Press.

also rendered us more resistant to non-Western explanations of behavior disorder (Pedersen, 1993). For example, many cultural and ethnic traditions maintain beliefs that possession can be a source of disorder, which most Western therapists reject.

The quest for improved methods, the concern for preventing mental disorder, and the recognition of the importance of humane treatment is not just the province of Western psychology. In our discussion of the nature of psychotherapy, we will emphasize practices in the United States, but we will also examine some therapeutic practices in other cultures (which we will return to later in the chapter).

Contemporary Practice

Psychotherapy is *the process of working with individuals to reduce their emotional problems and improve their adjustment.* Mental health professionals help individuals recognize, define, and overcome personal and interpersonal difficulties. Psychotherapists use a number of strategies to accomplish these goals: talking, interpreting, listening, rewarding, and modeling, for example. Psychotherapy *does not* include biomedical treatment, such as drugs or surgery.

Orientations

The theories of personality discussed in chapter 15 are the basis for a number of important approaches to psychotherapy, which can generally be distinguished as *insight* or *action* therapies. **Insight therapy** *encourages insight into and awareness of oneself as the critical focus of therapy.* **Action therapy** *promotes direct changes in behavior; insight is not essential for change to occur.* Psychodynamic therapies, based on the psychoanalytic theories of Freud and those in his tradition, and humanistic therapies, based on the humanistic theories of Rogers and Maslow, among others, are

considered to be insight therapies. Therapeutic applications of Skinner's behavioral principles constitute action therapies. Cognitive therapies have both insight-oriented and action-oriented components.

Most contemporary therapists do not use one form of therapy exclusively with their clients. The majority of today's therapists are **eclectic**—*they use a variety of approaches to therapy.* Often therapists tailor the therapeutic approach to their clients' needs. Even a therapist with a psychodynamic orientation might use humanistic approaches or a family therapist might use behavioral techniques, for example.

Therapists also orient themselves toward intervention at a particular level. Some therapists tend to view client needs as a matter of symptoms or problems without particular regard to the context in which the problems are experienced; psychoanalytic and behavioral approaches usually focus on specific *problems.* Humanistic therapists see the problem as having a wider scope and try to get at the involvement of the whole *person.* Cognitive therapists view adaptation as an interaction between the person and the *situation* (Pedersen, 1994). Other therapists like to work at the level of a *system* in which the individual functions. This includes couple and family therapy, group therapy, and community interventions. The expansion of systems therapy has prompted therapists to consider sociocultural factors as important components that influence the success or failure of any intervention.

Practitioners and Settings

A variety of mental health professionals, including clinical psychologists, psychiatrists, and counselors, practice psychotherapy. Remember from chapter 1 that psychiatrists have a medical degree and can prescribe drugs for mental disabilities. Clinical psychologists, by contrast, are trained in graduate programs of psychology and use psychotherapy rather than drugs to treat mental problems, although many psychologists are beginning to advocate granting

TABLE 17.1

Main Types of Mental Health Professionals

Professional Type	Degree	Experience Beyond Bachelor's Degree	Nature of Training
Clinical psychologist and counseling psychologist	Ph.D., ED.d., or Psy.D.	5–7 years	Includes both clinical and research training. Involves a 1-year internship in a psychiatric hospital or mental health facility. Recently some universities have developed Psy.D. programs, which lead to a professional degree with stronger clinical than research emphasis. The Psy.D. training program takes about the same number of years as the clinical psychology Ph.D. program and also requires a 1-year internship.
Psychiatrist	M.D.	7–9 years	Four years of medical school, plus an internship and residency in psychiatry, are required. A psychiatry residency involves supervision in therapies, including psychotherapy and biomedical therapy.
Social worker	M.S.W., D.S.W., or Ph.D.	2–5 years	Graduate work in a school of social work that includes specialized clinical training in mental health facilities
Psychiatric nurse	R.N., M.A., or Ph.D.	0–5 years	Graduate work in school of nursing, with special emphasis on care of mentally disabled individuals in hospital settings and mental health facilities
Occupational therapist	B.S., M.A., or Ph.D.	0–5 years	Emphasis on occupational training, with focus on physically or psychologically handicapped individuals. Stresses getting individuals back into the mainstream of work.
Pastoral counselor	None to Ph.D. or D.D. (Doctor of Divinity)	0–5 years	Requires ministerial background and training in psychology. An internship in a mental health facility as a chaplain is recommended.
Counselor	M.A.	2 years	Graduate work in department of psychology or department of education, with specialized training in counseling techniques

Note: The above listing refers to the mental health professionals who go through formal training at recognized academic and medical institutions. The government commonly licenses these professionals and certifies their skills. Professional organizations regulate their activities.

prescription privileges to appropriately trained psychologists. Table 17.1 describes the main types of mental health professionals, their degrees, the years of education required for the degrees, and the nature of the training.

Just as there is a variety of mental health professionals, there is a variety of settings in which therapy takes place. During the first half of this century, psychotherapists primarily practiced in mental hospitals, where individuals remained for months, even years. During the past several decades, psychologists have recognized that psychotherapy is not just for those who are so mentally disordered that they cannot live in society. Today people who seek counseling and psychotherapy may go to a community health center, to the outpatient facility of a hospital, or to the private office of a mental health practitioner.

Access to Services

Psychotherapy usually is an expensive proposition. Even though reduced fees, and occasionally free services, can be arranged in public hospitals for those who are poor, many of the people who are most in need of psychotherapy do not get it. Psychotherapists have been criticized for preferring to work with "young, attractive, verbal, intelligent, and successful" clients (called YAVISes) rather than "quiet, ugly, old, institutionalized, and different" clients (called QUOIDs). A national sample of clinical psychologists established that psychologists appear to be less willing to work with poorer and less-educated clients than with people from higher socioeconomic classes (Sutton & Kessler, 1986). This preference is attributed in part to the fact that disenfranchised individuals tend to have a poor *prognosis* (likelihood of improving from treatment). Such individuals might have difficulties keeping to the rigid appointment schedules required by most therapists, perhaps because their lives are chaotic. These problems hinder the development of a strong working alliance between client and therapist, which has adverse effects on prognosis.

Financial factors also promote a preference for working with clients from higher socioeconomic classes. YAVIS clients tend to seek mental health care from private practitioners in mental health agencies and use health insurance to pay for their care when their therapists can provide a diagnosis consistent with the DSM-IV. QUOID clients usually must rely on reduced-fee or cost-free programs provided by public agencies supported through private grants or government funding. Clinicians generally earn higher incomes by concentrating services with YAVIS clients rather than QUOID clients.

The challenge involved in paying for psychotherapeutic services has led to dramatic changes in mental health care delivery in recent years. Concerned by mounting mental health care costs that seemed to derive from protracted psychotherapy with questionable gains, health insurance companies began to seek new delivery systems. **Managed health care,** *a system in which external reviewers approve the type and length of treatment to justify insurance reimbursement,* has grown rapidly. Therapists whose clients participate in managed health care must confer with an external agent about their treatment goals and make systematic reports about client progress to secure continued insurance funding.

Many problems have surfaced with this practice (Broskowski, 1995; Fox, 1995). Although managed health care has promoted the development of more explicit and measurable treatment plans, the emphasis on cost management clearly favors short-term over long-term therapy methods. This emphasis can inappropriately shift some treatment to superficial interventions when the clinical problem requires more depth and more time than the health care managers allow. Both clients and therapists report discomfort with the potential violation of confidentiality and privacy when reporting therapy details to a third party. Some research suggests that the bureaucracy involved in setting up the watchdog system may absorb the savings that were supposed to be gained through the implementation of the system. Insurance reimbursement and managed health care will both be significantly affected by implementation of national health care mandates.

Ethical Standards

Those who seek treatment from qualified mental health care practitioners can feel some reassurance that their problems will be addressed professionally and ethically, based on the systems used in certifying practitioners. Licensing and certification practices require mental health care providers to know relevant state and professional ethical codes before their credentials are granted. Most of these codes require ethical practice as well as vigilance about unethical practice by others in the field. The codes typically address the importance of doing no harm to clients, protecting the privacy of clients, avoiding dual relationships with clients, and staying updated in contemporary practices. Violations of ethical codes can result in the loss of one's license to practice.

So far we have glimpsed the history and basic nature of psychotherapy as it is practiced today. Contemporary psychotherapies include a number of diverse approaches to working with people to reduce their problems and improve their adjustment. We begin our survey by discussing forms of individual psychotherapy.

REVIEW

The Nature of Therapy

Historically, some of the first forms of therapy derived from the belief, in ancient societies, that abnormal behavior had both mystical and organic origins. Many early treatments of mental disabilities were inhumane. Asylums were built during the Renaissance. Pinel's efforts led to extensive reform. Dix's efforts helped to separate the mentally disabled from prisoners.

In contemporary practice, psychotherapy is the process of working with individuals to reduce their emotional problems and improve their adjustment. Among the orientations of therapists are insight therapy, which encourages insight into and awareness of oneself (both psychoanalytic and humanistic therapies are insight therapies), and action therapy, which promotes direct changes in behavior for which insight is not essential (Skinner's behaviorism is an action therapy). Cognitive therapies have both insight and action components. Many therapists take an eclectic approach to therapy. Therapists also operate at different levels, such as at the level of the individual or at the level of a system—family, group, or community.

Practitioners include clinical psychologists, counseling psychologists, psychiatrists, and social workers. Psychotherapy takes place in a greater variety of settings today than in the past. Individuals of lower socioeconomic status are less likely to receive therapy than are individuals of higher socioeconomic status. Managed health care has increased dramatically in recent years, although not without problems. Psychotherapists are supposed to adhere to certain ethical standards.

INDIVIDUAL THERAPIES

Your prototype of individual therapy might be the stereotyped image of the client lying down on a couch while the therapist makes notes about the client's day-to-day experiences. In fact, few individual therapists follow this strategy. Most individual therapies take place face to face and are more conversational. We will explore four orientations of individual therapy: psychoanalytic, humanistic, behavioral, and cognitive.

Psychodynamic Therapies

The **psychodynamic therapies** *stress the importance of the unconscious mind, extensive interpretation by the therapist, and the role of infant and early childhood experiences.* Many psychodynamic approaches have grown out of Freud's psychoanalytic theory of personality. Today some therapists with a psychodynamic perspective show allegiance to Freud; others do not.

Freud's Psychoanalysis

Psychoanalysis *is Freud's therapeutic technique for analyzing an individual's unconscious thought.* Freud believed that clients' current problems could be traced to childhood experiences, many of which involved conflicts about sexuality. He also recognized that the early experiences were not readily available to the individual's conscious mind. Only through extensive questioning, probing, and analyzing was Freud able to put the pieces of the individual's personality together and help the individual become aware of how these early experiences were affecting present adult behavior. To reach the shadowy world of the unconscious, psychoanalytic therapists often use the therapeutic techniques of free association, catharsis, interpretation, dream analysis, transference, and resistance.

In psychoanalysis the therapist uses **free association,** *the technique of encouraging individuals to say aloud whatever comes to mind, no matter how trivial or embarrassing.* When Freud detected that a client was resisting the spontaneous flow of thoughts, he probed further. He believed that the crux of the person's emotional problem probably lurked below this point of resistance. Freud thought that, when clients talked freely, their emotional feelings emerged. **Catharsis** *is the psychoanalytic term for clients' release of emotional tension when they relive an emotionally charged and conflicted experience.*

Interpretation plays an important role in psychoanalysis. As the therapist interprets free associations and dreams, the client's statements and behavior are not taken at face value. To understand what is truly causing the client's conflicts, the therapist constantly searches for symbolic, hidden meanings in what the individual says and does. From time to time, the therapist suggests possible meanings of the client's statements and behavior.

To encourage his patients to relax, Freud had them recline on the couch in his study while he sat in the chair on the left, out of their view.

The aim in analysis is to bring the magnificent energy of the wild horse under the control of the rider, without using a whip that will kill its spirit.

Marion Woodman

Dream analysis *is the psychotherapeutic technique psychoanalysts use to interpret a client's dreams. Psychoanalysts believe that dreams contain information about the individual's unconscious thoughts and conflicts.* Freud distinguished between the dream's manifest and latent content. **Manifest content** *is the psychoanalytic term for the conscious, remembered aspects of a dream.* **Latent content** *is the psychoanalytic term for the unconscious, unremembered, symbolic aspects of a dream.* A psychoanalyst interprets a dream by analyzing its manifest content for disguised unconscious wishes and needs, especially those that are sexual and aggressive. For some examples of the sexual symbols psychoanalysts use to interpret dreams, turn to figure 17.3. Freud cautioned against overinterpreting, however. Once Freud was challenged about possibly having an oral fixation himself, symbolized by his relentless cigar smoking. In response, he quipped, "Sometimes a cigar is just a cigar."

Freud also believed that transference was an inevitable and essential aspect of the analyst-client relationship. **Transference** *is the psychoanalytic term for the client's relating to the analyst in ways that reproduce or relive important relationships in the client's life.* A client might interact with an analyst as if the analyst were a parent or lover, for example. When transference dominates therapy, the client's comments may become directed toward the analyst's personal life. Transference is often difficult to overcome in psychotherapy. However, transference can be used therapeutically as a model of how clients relate to important people in their lives.

Sexual theme	Objects or activities in dreams that symbolize sexual themes
Male genitals, especially penis	Umbrellas, knives, poles, swords, airplanes, guns, serpents, neckties, tree trunks, hoses
Female genitals, especially vagina	Boxes, caves, pockets, pouches, the mouth, jewel cases, ovens, closets
Sexual intercourse	Climbing, swimming, flying, riding (a horse, an elevator, a roller coaster)
Parents	King, queen, emperor, empress
Siblings	Little animals

FIGURE 17.3

The Psychoanalyst's Interpretation of Sexual Symbolism in Dreams

Resistance *is the psychoanalytic term for a client's unconscious defense strategies that prevent the analyst from understanding the client's problems.* Resistance occurs because it is painful to bring conflicts into conscious awareness. By resisting therapy, individuals do not have to face their problems. Showing up late or missing sessions, arguing with the psychoanalyst, or faking free associations are examples of resistance. Some clients go on endlessly about a trivial matter to avoid facing their conflicts. A major goal of the analyst is to break through this resistance.

Psychotherapy, unlike castor oil which will work no matter how you get it down, is useless when forced on an uncooperative patient.

Abigail Van Buren

Contemporary Psychodynamic Therapies

Although the face of psychodynamic therapy has changed extensively since its inception almost a century ago, many contemporary psychodynamic therapists still probe clients' unconscious thoughts about their earliest childhood experiences to provide clues to their clients' current problems (Wallerstein, 1992). Many contemporary psychodynamic therapists also try to help clients gain insight into their emotionally laden, repressed conflicts (Strupp, 1992).

However, only a small percentage of contemporary psychodynamic therapists rigorously follow Freud's guidelines. Many psychodynamic therapists still emphasize the importance of unconscious thought and early family experiences, but they also accord more power to the conscious mind and current relationships in understanding a client's problems. Clients rarely see their therapist several times a week. Now clients usually have weekly appointments.

Fortunately, analysis is not the only way to resolve inner conflicts. Life itself still remains a very effective therapist.
Karen Horney, *Our Inner Conflicts*, 1945

Contemporary psychodynamic approaches emphasize the development of the self in social contexts (Erikson, 1968; Kohut, 1977; Mahler, 1979). In Heinz Kohut's view, early relationships with attachment figures, such as one's parents, are critical. As we develop, we do not relinquish these attachments; we continue to need them. Kohut's prescription for therapy involves getting the patient to identify and seek out appropriate relationships with others. He also wants patients to develop more realistic appraisals of relationships. Kohut believes that therapists need to interact with their clients in ways that are empathic and understanding. As we will see next, empathy and understanding are absolute cornerstones for humanistic therapists as they encourage their clients to further their sense of self.

Humanistic Therapies

In the **humanistic psychotherapies,** *clients are encouraged to understand themselves and to grow personally. In contrast to psychodynamic therapies, humanistic therapies emphasize conscious thoughts rather than unconscious thoughts, the present rather than the past, and growth and fulfillment rather than curing illness.* Two main forms of the humanistic psychotherapies are person-centered therapy and Gestalt therapy.

Person-Centered Therapy

Person-centered therapy *is a form of humanistic therapy developed by Carl Rogers (1961, 1980), in which the therapist provides a warm, supportive atmosphere to improve the client's self-concept and encourage the client to gain insight about problems.* Rogers's therapy was initially called client-centered therapy, but he rechristened it person-centered therapy to underscore his deep belief that everyone has the ability to grow. The relationship between the therapist and the person is an important aspect of Rogers's therapy. The therapist must enter into an intensely personal relationship with the client, not as a physician diagnosing a disease but as one human being to another. Notice that Rogers referred to the "client" and then the "person" rather than the "patient." Rogers's approach demonstrates a strong individualistic bias that would fare best in cultures that stress the value of the individual.

Recall from chapter 15 that Rogers believed that each of us grows up in a world filled with *conditions of worth;* the positive regard we receive from others has strings attached. We usually do not receive love and praise unless we conform to the standards and demands of others. This causes us to be unhappy and have low self-esteem as adults; rarely do we think that we measure up to such standards or think that we are as good as others expect us to be.

To free the person from worry about the demands of society, the therapist creates a warm and caring environment. A Rogerian therapist tries to avoid disapproving of what a client says or does. Recall from chapter 15 that Rogers believed this *unconditional positive regard* improved the person's self-esteem. The therapist's role is "nondirective"—that is, he or she does not try to lead the client to any particular revelation. The therapist is there to listen sympathetically to the client's problems and to encourage greater self-regard, independent self-appraisal, and decision making.

Rogers advocated other techniques in addition to using unconditional positive regard. **Genuineness** *is the Rogerian concept of the importance of the therapist's being genuine and not hiding behind a facade. Therapists must let clients know their feelings.* **Accurate empathy** *is Rogers's term for the therapist's ability to identify with the client.* Rogers believed that therapists must sense what it is like to be the client at any moment in the client-therapist relationship. **Active listening** *is Rogers's term for the ability to listen to another person with total attention to what that person says and means.* One way therapists improve active listening is by restating or paraphrasing what the client said. Clients report that this practice helps them feel supported in order to gain the courage to make changes they wish to make.

Gestalt Therapy

Gestalt therapy *is a humanistic therapy, developed by Frederick (Fritz) Perls (1893–1970), in which the therapist questions and challenges clients to help them become more aware of their feelings and face their problems.* Perls was trained in Europe as a Freudian psychoanalyst, but as his career developed his ideas became noticeably different from Freud's. Perls agreed with Freud that psychological problems originate in unresolved past conflicts and that these conflicts need to be acknowledged and worked through. Also like Freud, Perls (1969) stressed that interpretation of dreams is an important aspect of therapy.

In other ways, however, Perls and Freud were miles apart. Perls believed that unresolved conflicts should be brought to bear on the here and now of the individual's life.

Fritz Perls was the founder of Gestalt therapy.

verbal and nonverbal behavior, and uses role playing. To demonstrate an important point to a client, a Gestalt therapist might exaggerate a client's characteristic. To stimulate change, the therapist might openly confront the client.

Another technique of Gestalt therapy is role playing, by either the client, the therapist, or both. For example, if an individual is bothered by conflict with her mother, the therapist might play the role of the mother and reopen the quarrel. The therapist may encourage the individual to act out her hostile feelings toward her mother by yelling, swearing, or kicking the couch, for example. In this way, Gestalt therapists hope to help individuals better manage their feelings instead of letting their feelings control them.

As you probably noticed, a Gestalt therapist is much more directive than a person-centered therapist. By being more directive, the Gestalt therapist provides more interpretation and feedback. Nonetheless, both of these humanistic therapies encourage individuals to take responsibility for their feelings and actions, to understand their true selves, to develop a sense of freedom, and to look at what they are doing with their lives.

Now that we have studied the insight therapies, we will turn our attention to therapies that take a very different approach to working with individuals to reduce their problems and improve their adjustment—the behavior therapies.

The therapist *pushes* clients into deciding whether they will continue to allow the past to control their future or whether they will choose *right now* what they want to be in the future. To this end, Perls *confronted* individuals and encouraged them to actively control their lives and to be open about their feelings.

Gestalt therapists use a number of techniques to encourage individuals to be open about their feelings, to develop self-awareness, and to actively control their lives. The therapist sets examples, encourages congruence between

---

Every new adjustment is a crisis in self-esteem.

Eric Hoffer

REVIEW

Psychodynamic and Humanistic Therapies

Psychodynamic therapies stress the importance of the unconscious mind, early family experiences, and extensive interpretation by the therapist. Psychoanalysis is Freud's technique for analyzing an individual's unconscious thought. Free association, catharsis, interpretation, dream analysis, transference, and resistance are techniques used in psychoanalytic therapy. Although psychodynamic therapy has changed, many contemporary psychodynamic therapists still probe the unconscious mind for early family experiences that might provide

clues to the client's current problems. The development of the self in social contexts is an important theme in Kohut's contemporary approach.

In the humanistic therapies, clients are encouraged to understand themselves and to grow personally. The humanistic therapies emphasize conscious thoughts, the present, and growth and fulfillment. Person-centered therapy, developed by Rogers, emphasizes that the therapist should provide a warm and supportive atmosphere to improve the client's self-image and to encourage the client

to gain insight into problems. The therapist replaces conditions of worth with unconditional positive regard and uses genuineness, accurate empathy, and active listening to raise the client's self-esteem. Gestalt therapy, developed by Fritz Perls, emphasizes that the therapist should question and challenge clients in order to help them become more aware of their feelings and face their problems. Gestalt therapy is more directive than is the nondirective approach of person-centered therapy.

1. On the way to the university on the day of an examination
2. In the process of answering an examination paper
3. Before the unopened doors of the examination room
4. Awaiting the distribution of examination papers
5. The examination paper lies face down before her
6. The night before an examination
7. One day before an examination
8. Two days before an examination
9. Three days before an examination
10. Four days before an examination
11. Five days before an examination
12. A week before an examination
13. Two weeks before an examination
14. A month before an examination

FIGURE 17.4

A Desensitization Hierarchy from Most to Least Fearful Circumstances

Behavior Therapies

Behavior therapies *use principles of learning to reduce or eliminate maladaptive behavior.* Behavior therapies are based on the behavioral theory of learning and personality described in chapters 6 and 15. Behavior therapists do not search for unconscious conflicts, like psychodynamic therapists, or encourage individuals to develop accurate perceptions of their feelings and self, like humanistic therapists. Insight and self-awareness are not the keys to helping individuals develop more adaptive behavior patterns, say the behavior therapists. The insight therapies—psychodynamic and humanistic—treat maladaptive symptoms as signs of underlying, internal problems. Behavior therapists, however, assume that the overt maladaptive symptoms are the problem. Individuals can become aware of why they are depressed and still be depressed, say the behavior therapists. A behavior therapist tries to eliminate the depressed symptoms or behaviors themselves rather than try to get individuals to gain insight or awareness about why they are depressed (O'Donahue & Krasner, 1995).

Behavior therapists initially based their interventions almost exclusively on the learning principles of clas-

sical and operant conditioning, but behavior therapies have become more diverse in recent years. As cognitive social learning theory grew in popularity and the cognitive approach became more prominent in psychology, behavior therapists increasingly included cognitive factors in their therapy. First we will discuss the classical and operant conditioning approaches; then we will turn to the cognitive therapies.

Classical Conditioning Approaches

In chapter 6, you learned how we acquire, or learn, some behaviors, especially fears, through classical conditioning and that these behaviors can be unlearned, or extinguished. If an individual has learned to fear snakes or heights through classical conditioning, perhaps the individual could unlearn the fear. Two procedures based on classical conditioning that are used in behavior therapy are systematic desensitization and aversive conditioning.

Systematic Desensitization Sys-*tematic desensitization* *is a method of behavior therapy that treats anxiety by associating deep relaxation with successive visualizations of increasingly intense anxiety-producing situations; this technique is based on classical conditioning* (Wolpe, 1963). Consider the common fear of taking a test. Using systematic desensitization, a behavior therapist first asks the client which aspects of the fearful situation—in this case, taking a test—are the most and least frightening. Then, the behavior therapist arranges these circumstances in order from most to least frightening. An example of this type of desensitization hierarchy is shown in figure 17.4.

The next step is to teach individuals to relax. Behavior therapists teach clients to recognize the presence of muscular contractions, or tensions, in various parts of their bodies and then to contract and relax different muscles. Once individuals are relaxed, the therapist asks them to imagine the least fearful stimulus in the hierarchy. Subsequently the therapist moves up the list of items from least to most fearful while the clients remain relaxed. Eventually individuals are able to imagine the most fearful circumstance without being afraid—in our example, on the way to the university the day of an exam. In this manner, individuals learn to relax while thinking about the exam instead of feeling anxious.

"Leave us alone! I am a behavior therapist! I am helping
my patient overcome a fear of heights!"

© 1990 by Sidney Harris.

Researchers have found that systematic desensitization is often an effective treatment for a number of phobias, such as fear of giving a speech, fear of heights, fear of flying, fear of dogs, and fear of snakes. If you were afraid of snakes, for instance, the therapist might initially have you watch someone handle a snake. Then the therapist would ask you to engage in increasingly more fearful behaviors—you might first just go into the same room with the snake, next you would approach the snake, subsequently you would touch the snake, and eventually you would play with the snake (Bandura, Blanchard, & Ritter, 1969).

Aversive Conditioning *Aversive conditioning is an approach to behavior therapy that involves repeated pairings of an undesirable behavior with aversive stimuli to decrease the behavior's rewards so the individual will stop doing it; this technique is based on classical conditioning.* Aversive conditioning is used to teach people to avoid such behaviors as smoking, overeating, and drinking. Electric shocks, nausea-inducing substances, and verbal insults are some of the noxious stimuli used in aversive conditioning (Bernstein, 1991).

How would aversive conditioning be used to reduce a person's alcohol consumption? Every time a person drank an alcoholic beverage, he or she also would consume a mixture that induced nausea. In classical conditioning terminology, the alcoholic beverage is the conditioned stimulus and the nausea-inducing agent is the unconditioned stimulus. By repeatedly pairing alcohol with the nausea-inducing agent, alcohol becomes the conditioned stimulus that elicits nausea, the conditioned response. As a consequence, alcohol is no longer associated with something pleasant but, rather, is associated with something highly unpleasant.

Operant Conditioning Approaches

Andy is a college student who has difficulty studying. He complains that he always starts to fall asleep when he goes to his desk to study. He has decided to see a therapist about how he might improve his studying because his grades are deteriorating. The behavior therapist's first recommendation is to replace his desk lamp's 40-watt bulb with a brighter one. The second recommendation is to turn his desk away from his bed. The third recommendation is to do only schoolwork at his desk; he is not allowed to write a letter, read a magazine, or daydream while at the desk. If he wants to do any of these other things, he must leave his desk.

To help Andy improve his study habits, the behavior therapist first evaluated Andy's responses to the stimuli in his room. Then the therapist gave Andy direct and precise suggestions about what to do. The therapist did not spend time analyzing his unconscious conflicts or encouraging him to "get in touch with his feelings." Rather, the therapist wanted to change Andy's responses to the environmental stimuli that were causing the problem.

When we discussed operant conditioning in chapter 6, we examined how an individual's behavior is controlled by its consequences. We also discussed *behavior modification,* which is often used by behavior therapists. The idea behind behavior modification is to replace unacceptable, maladaptive responses with acceptable, adaptive ones. Consequences are set up to ensure that acceptable responses are reinforced and unacceptable ones are not (Bergin & Garfield, 1994; Davison & Neale, 1994; Hanson, 1993).

A **token economy** *is a behavior modification system in which behaviors are reinforced with tokens (such as poker chips) that can be exchanged later for desired rewards (such as candy, money, or going to a movie).* Behavior therapists have implemented token economies in a number of classrooms, institutions for the mentally retarded, homes for delinquents, and mental hospitals with schizophrenics.

In some instances, behavior modification works; in others it does not. One person may become so wedded to the tokens that, when they are removed, the positive behavior associated with the tokens disappears. Yet another person might continue the positive behavior after the tokens are removed. Some critics object to behavior modification because they believe such extensive control of another person's behavior unethically infringes on the individual's rights. However, as with the college student who could not study, maladaptive responses can be turned into adaptive ones through behavior modification.

The behavior therapies you have just read about do not include cognitive processes in their effort to modify the behavior of individuals with problems. As we will see next, cognitive therapy gives thought processes a more prominent role in helping individuals reduce their problems and improve their adjustment.

Cognitive Therapies

Derek, a 21-year-old single undergraduate student has delusions that he is evil. He perceives himself as a failure in school and a failure to his parents. He is preoccupied with negative thoughts, dwells on his problems, and exaggerates his faults. Such thinking is common among depressed individuals and suggests that cognitive therapy might be a viable approach to treating Derek's depression.

The **cognitive therapies** *emphasize that an individual's cognitions, or thoughts, are the main source of abnormal behavior. Cognitive therapies attempt to change the individual's feelings and behaviors by changing cognitions.* Cognitive therapies differ from psychoanalytic therapies by focusing more on overt symptoms instead of deep-seated unconscious thoughts, by providing more structure to an individual's thoughts, and by being less concerned about the origin of the problem (Beck & Haaga, 1992). Cognitive therapies vary in the use of unstructured training sessions that require individuals to practice prescribed exercises. Many cognitive therapies are more likely to adhere to a conversational format. Cognitive therapists also vary in their emphasis on manipulating the environment to increase adaptive behavior (Dryden & Trower, 1989).

Cognitive Behavior Therapies

The earliest form of cognitive therapy stemmed from both cognitive psychology, with its emphasis on the effect of thoughts on behavior, and behaviorism, with its emphasis on behavior-change techniques. Cognitive behavior therapists strive to change clients' misconceptions, strengthen their coping skills, increase their self-control, and encourage constructive self-reflection Meichenbaum, 1993).

Self-efficacy Self-efficacy—*the belief that one can master a situation and produce positive outcomes*—is especially important in developing adaptive behavior, according to social learning theorist Albert Bandura. Moreover, Bandura (1989, 1994) believes that self-efficacy is the key to successful therapy. At each step of the therapy process, people need to bolster their confidence by telling themselves, "I can do this," "I'm going to make it," "I'm getting very good," and so on. As people gain confidence and engage in more adaptive behavior, the successes become intrinsically rewarding. Before long individuals will persist with considerable effort in solving their problems because of the pleasurable outcomes that were set in motion by self-efficacy.

Self-instructional Methods **Self-instructional methods** *are cognitive behavior techniques aimed at teaching individuals to modify their own behavior* (Meichenbaum, 1977). Using self-instructional methods, cognitive behavior

TABLE 17.2

Statements That Promote Coping in Self-instructional Methods

Preparing for Anxiety or Stress

What do I have to do?
I'm going to map out a plan to deal with it.
I'll just think about what I have to do.
I won't worry; doesn't help anything.
I have a lot of different strategies to call on.

Confronting and Handling the Anxiety or Stress

I can meet the challenge.
I'll keep on taking just one step at a time.
I can handle it. I'll just relax, breathe deeply, and use one of the strategies.
I won't think about the pain; I'll think about what I have to do.

Coping with Feelings at Critical Moments

What is it I have to do?
I was supposed to expect the pain to increase; I just have to keep myself in control.
When the pain comes, I'll just pause and keep focusing on what I have to do.

Reinforcing Self-statements

Good, I did it.
I handled it well.
I knew I could do it.
Wait until I tell other people how I did it!

therapists try to get clients to change what they say to themselves. The therapist gives the client examples of constructive statements, known as "reinforcing self-statements," that the client can repeat in order to take positive steps to handle stress or meet a goal. The therapist also encourages the client to practice the statements through role playing and strengthens the client's newly acquired skills through reinforcements. A series of examples of constructive statements that can be used to cope with stressful situations is shown in table 17.2 (Meichenbaum, Turk, & Burstein, 1975).

In recent years, many therapists have focused less on the structured training session format of cognitive behavior therapy. Two of the most important contemporary cognitive therapies are Albert Ellis's rational-emotive therapy and Aaron Beck's cognitive therapy.

CRITICAL THINKING

Finding Your Voice

Many college students report stark terror about the challenge of participating in class discussions or asking questions in class. They might be shy. They might be anxious about what others will think. They might lack confidence in the quality of their thinking. Which of the behavior therapies do you think would be most helpful in conquering this behavior deficit? How would you go about *applying this psychological framework to enhance your personal adaptation* to college?

Rational-Emotive Therapy

Rational-emotive therapy *is based on Albert Ellis's view that individuals become psychologically disordered because of their beliefs, especially those that are irrational and self-defeating* (Ellis, 1962, 1993). Ellis says that we usually talk to ourselves when we experience stress; too often the statements are irrational, making them more harmful than helpful.

Ellis abbreviated the therapy process into the letters *A, B, C, D,* and *E.* Therapy usually starts at *C,* the individual's upsetting emotional *C*onsequence; this might involve depression, anxiety, or a feeling of worthlessness. The individual usually says that *C* was caused by *A,* the *A*ctivating Experience, such as a blowup in marital relations, the loss of a job, or failure in school. The therapist works with the individual to show that an intervening factor, *B,* the individual's *B*elief System, is actually responsible for why she moved from *A* to *C.* Then the therapist goes on to *D,* which stands for *D*isputation; at this point, the individual's irrational beliefs are disputed, or contested, by the therapist. Finally, *E* is reached, which stands for *E*ffects, or outcomes, of the rational-emotive therapy, as when individuals put their changed beliefs to work.

Beck's Cognitive Therapy

Aaron Beck (1976) developed a form of cognitive therapy to treat psychological dysfunctions, especially depression. He believes that the most effective therapy with depressed individuals involves four phases: (1) the depressed clients are shown how to identify self-labels—that is, how they view themselves, (2) they are taught to notice when they are thinking distorted or irrational thoughts, (3) they learn how to substitute appropriate thoughts for inappropriate ones, and (4) they are given feedback and motivating comments from the therapist to stimulate their use of these techniques.

Results from a large-scale study by the National Institute of Mental Health (NIMH) support the belief that Beck's cognitive therapy is an effective treatment for depression (Mervis, 1986). Beck and his colleagues conducted this therapy with moderately to severely depressed individuals for 16 weeks at three sites. The symptoms of depression were eliminated completely in more than 50 percent of the individuals receiving Beck's cognitive therapy, as compared to only 29 percent in a comparison group (Clark & Beck, 1989).

A comparison group is an important feature in most psychological research. Without a comparison group, the researchers in the NIMH study would have had no way of knowing if the symptoms of depression in the experimental group would have disappeared even without therapy. That is, it is possible that, in any random sample of depressed individuals, more than 50 percent show a remission of symptoms over a 16-week period, regardless of whether or not they receive therapy. Because only 29 percent of the depressed individuals in the comparison group became free of their symptoms, the researchers had good reason to believe that the cognitive therapy—which produced more than a 50 percent remission of symptoms—was effective.

Now the real beginnings of the "freedom" which we have discussed for many years—and a heady freedom it is, coming after so many years of reaching outward for it—to finally discover all I had to do was reach inward, and it was there waiting all the time for me!

Alisa Wells

At this point, we have discussed four major approaches to individual therapy—psychodynamic, humanistic, behavior, and cognitive. Figure 17.5 will help you keep the approaches straight in your mind.

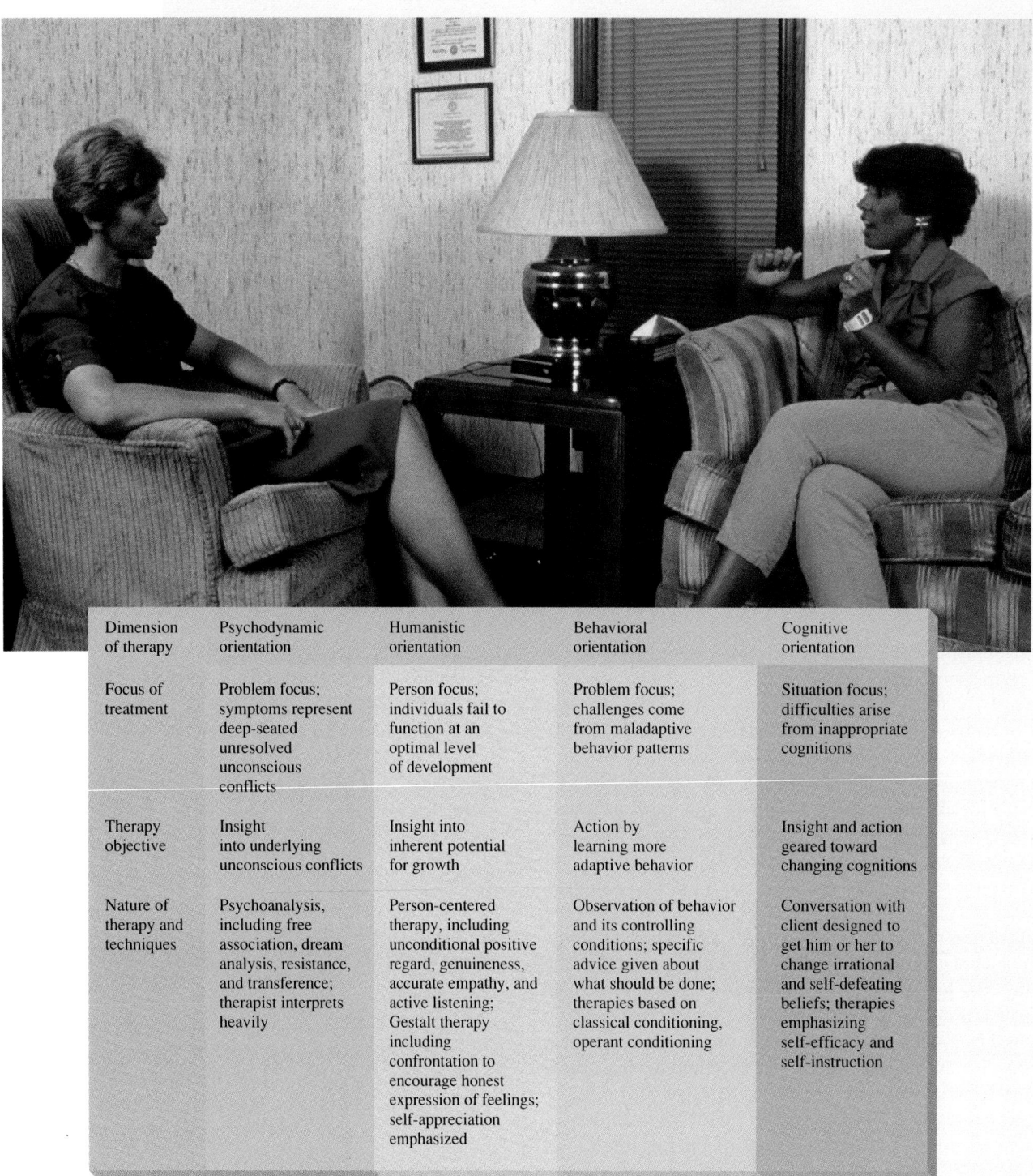

Dimension of therapy	Psychodynamic orientation	Humanistic orientation	Behavioral orientation	Cognitive orientation
Focus of treatment	Problem focus; symptoms represent deep-seated unresolved unconscious conflicts	Person focus; individuals fail to function at an optimal level of development	Problem focus; challenges come from maladaptive behavior patterns	Situation focus; difficulties arise from inappropriate cognitions
Therapy objective	Insight into underlying unconscious conflicts	Insight into inherent potential for growth	Action by learning more adaptive behavior	Insight and action geared toward changing cognitions
Nature of therapy and techniques	Psychoanalysis, including free association, dream analysis, resistance, and transference; therapist interprets heavily	Person-centered therapy, including unconditional positive regard, genuineness, accurate empathy, and active listening; Gestalt therapy including confrontation to encourage honest expression of feelings; self-appreciation emphasized	Observation of behavior and its controlling conditions; specific advice given about what should be done; therapies based on classical conditioning, operant conditioning	Conversation with client designed to get him or her to change irrational and self-defeating beliefs; therapies emphasizing self-efficacy and self-instruction

FIGURE 17.5

A Comparison of Psychotherapies

Abnormal Psychology and Therapy

Behavior therapies use principles of learning to reduce or eliminate maladaptive behavior. Behavior therapies are based on behavioral theories of learning and personality. Behavior therapists try to eliminate symptoms or behaviors rather than trying to get individuals to gain insight into their problems. Two classical conditioning procedures used in behavior therapy are systematic desensitization and aversive conditioning. Operant conditioning approaches emphasize modifying an individual's maladaptive responses to the environment. The idea behind behavior modification is to replace unacceptable, maladaptive responses with acceptable, adaptive ones.

Consequences are set up to ensure that acceptable responses are reinforced; unacceptable ones are not. A token economy is an example of behavior modification.

Cognitive therapies include cognitive behavior therapy, Ellis's rational-emotive therapy, and Beck's cognitive therapy. Cognitive therapies emphasize that an individual's thoughts, or cognitions, are the main source of abnormal behavior. Cognitive therapies attempt to change the individual's feelings and behaviors by changing cognitions. Cognitive behavior therapy tries to help individuals behave more adaptively by modifying their thoughts. Cognitive behavior therapists strive to change

misconceptions, strengthen coping skills, increase self-control, and encourage constructive self-talk. Rational-emotive therapy is a cognitive therapy developed by Albert Ellis. It is based on the idea that individuals become psychologically disabled because of their beliefs, especially those that are irrational and self-defeating; therapy is designed to change these beliefs. Aaron Beck developed a form of cognitive therapy to treat psychological disorders, especially depression. The therapy involves identifying self-labels, detecting irrational thoughts, substituting appropriate for inappropriate thoughts, and receiving feedback from the therapist to stimulate these cognitive changes.

SYSTEMS INTERVENTIONS

A major issue in therapy is how it can be structured to reach more people and at less cost. One way to address this problem is for therapists to see clients in a group rather than individually. A second way is through community psychology approaches. These approaches have the advantage of working with individuals in the context of a larger system.

Group Therapies

Nine people make their way into a room, each looking tentatively at the others. Although each person has met the therapist during a diagnostic interview, no one knows any of the other clients. Some of the people seem reluctant, others enthusiastic. All are willing to follow the therapist's recommendation that group therapy might help each of them learn to cope better with their problems. As they sit down and wait for the session to begin, one thinks, "Will they really understand me?" Another wonders, "Do the others have problems like mine?" Yet another thinks, "Can I stick my neck out with these people?"

Individual therapy is often expensive and time consuming. Freud believed that therapy is a long process and saw clients as often as three to five times a week for a number of years. Advocates of group therapy stress that individual therapy is limited because the client is seen outside the normal context of relationships, relationships that may hold the key to successful therapy. Many psychological problems develop in the context of interpersonal

relationships—within one's family, marriage, or peer group, for example. By seeing individuals in the context of these important groups, therapy may be more successful (Fuhrman & Burlingame, 1995).

Group therapy is diversified. Some therapists practice psychodynamic, humanistic, behavior, or cognitive therapy. Others use group approaches that are not based on the major psychotherapeutic perspectives. Six features make group therapy an attractive format (Yalom, 1975, 1995):

1. *Information.* Individuals receive information about their problems from either the group leader or other group members.
2. *Universality.* Many individuals develop the sense that they are the only persons who have such frightening and unacceptable impulses. In the group, individuals observe that others also feel anguish and suffering.
3. *Altruism.* Group members support one another with advice and sympathy and learn that they have something to offer others.
4. *Corrective recapitulation of the family group.* A therapy group often resembles a family (and, in family therapy, the group *is* a family), with the leaders representing parents and the other members siblings. In this "new" family, old wounds may be healed and new, more positive "family" ties made.
5. *Development of social skills.* Corrective feedback from peers may modify flaws in an individual's interpersonal skills. A self-centered individual may

Family systems therapy has become increasingly popular in recent years. In family systems therapy, the assumption is that psychological adjustment is related to patterns of interaction within the family unit.

see that he is self-centered if five other group members inform him about his self-centeredness; in individual therapy, he may not believe the therapist.

6. *Interpersonal learning.* The group can serve as a training ground for practicing new behaviors and relationships. For example, a hostile woman may learn that she can get along better with others by not behaving so aggressively.

Family and Couple Therapy

"A friend loves you for your intelligence, a mistress for your charm, but your family's love is unreasoning; you were born into it and are of its flesh and blood. Nevertheless, it can irritate you more than any group of people in the world," commented French biographer André Maurois. His statement suggests that the family may be the source of an individual's problems. **Family therapy** *is group therapy with family members.* **Couple therapy** *is group therapy with married or unmarried couples whose major problem is their relationship.* These approaches stress that, although one person may have some abnormal symptoms, the symptoms are a function of family or couple relationships (Lebow & Gurman, 1995; Nichols & Schwartz, 1995). Psychodynamic, humanistic, or behavior therapies may be used in family or couple therapy, but the main form of family therapy is family systems therapy.

Woe, woe, woe, and again woe to you if you do not change.
Elisabeth of Braunschweiger (1510–1558)
in a letter to her son

Family systems therapy *is a form of therapy based on the assumption that psychological adjustment is related to patterns of interaction within the family unit.* Families who do not function well foster abnormal behavior on the part of one or more of their members (Minuchin, 1985; Satir, 1964). Four of the most widely used family systems therapy techniques are these:

1. *Validation.* The therapist expresses an understanding and acceptance of each family member's feelings and beliefs and, thus, validates the person. When the therapist talks with each family member, she finds something positive to say.
2. *Reframing.* The therapist teaches families to reframe problems; problems are cast as a family problem, not an individual's problem. For example, the family therapist reframes the problems of a delinquent adolescent in terms of how each family member contributed to the situation. The father's lack of attention to his son and marital conflict may be involved.
3. *Structural change.* The family systems therapist tries to *restructure* the coalitions in a family. In a mother-son coalition, the therapist might suggest that the father take a stronger disciplinarian role to relieve the mother of some of the burden. Restructuring might be as simple as suggesting that parents explore satisfying ways to be together; the therapist may recommend that, once a week, the parents go out for a quiet dinner together, for example.
4. *Detriangulation.* In some families, one member is the scapegoat for two other members who are in conflict but pretend not to be. For example, in the triangle of two parents and one child, the parents may insist that their marriage is fine but find themselves in subtle conflict over how to handle the child. The therapist tries to disentangle, or *detriangulate,* this situation by shifting attention away from the child and toward the conflict between the parents.

Although many of the principles of family therapy can be applied to most families, cross-cultural psychologists caution against transferring a Western view of family dynamics to other cultures. Unique sociohistorical, cultural circumstances experienced by different ethnic minority groups also require certain considerations. To read about some of the considerations regarding family therapy in African American families, turn to Sociocultural Worlds 17.1.

Couple therapy proceeds in much the same way as family therapy. Conflict in marriages and in relationships between unmarried individuals frequently involves poor communication. In some instances, communication has broken down entirely. The therapist tries to improve the communication between the partners. In some cases, she will focus on the roles partners play: one may be "strong," the other "weak"; one may be "responsible," the other "spoiled," for example. Couple therapy addresses diverse problems such as jealousy, sexual messages, delayed childbearing, infidelity, gender roles, two-career families, divorce, and remarriage (Jacobson & Addis, 1993). Now we turn our attention to other forms of group therapy—personal growth and self-help groups.

Abnormal Psychology and Therapy

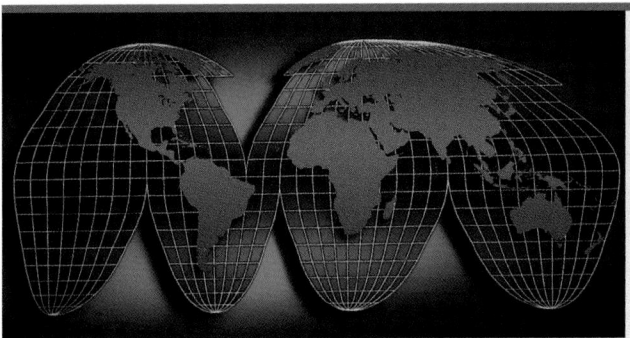

Therapy with African American Families

Family therapists who work with African American families are often called on to fulfill various roles, such as educator, director, advocate, problem solver, and role model (Grevious, 1985). As a therapist takes on these roles, he or she must recognize that the clients are members of a community, as well as individuals or members of families (Aponte, 1979). The following case study illustrates some of the multiple roles and the community orientation that a therapist must be aware of in working with African American families (Grevious, 1985).

Mrs. B. entered family therapy because her 11-year-old son Todd was disruptive in school and falling behind in his work. She complained of feeling overwhelmed and not being able to cope with the situation. The therapist conducted a home visit and observed that the family lived in a run-down building in a poor neighborhood. Even so, the therapist found that Mrs. B.'s apartment was immaculate, work and sleep space had been set aside for Todd. It was obvious from the well-worn Bible on the coffee table and the religious paintings and calendars on the walls that Mrs. B.

had strong religious convictions. The therapist discovered that Mrs. B.'s strong-willed mother recently had moved into the apartment after an incapacitating leg operation. The grandmother's diabetes created additional stress in the home. Despite her illness, the grandmother tried to exercise considerable control over Mrs. B. and Todd, causing a power struggle in the family. The therapist also learned that Mrs. B. had recently stopped attending church. After the therapist encouraged her to attend church again, Mrs. B.'s spirits improved considerably. In addition, the grandmother joined a senior citizens program, which transported her to the center three times a week and to church two Sundays a month. These increased community activities for the grandmother had a positive impact on the family.

Family therapists who see African American clients also believe that it is important to provide concrete advice or assistance (Foley, 1975). If the problem is a parent-child relationship, for example, a family therapist might recommend that the parents participate in a parent training program, rather than conduct insight therapy. Also, therapists may occasionally need to educate African American families about social service programs and the difficulties they might encounter in gaining access to those programs (Pinderhughes, 1982).

A family therapist who works with African American families also needs to emphasize their strengths, such as pride in being African American, the extended family, and religion, as well as take into consideration their vulnerabilities, such as the impact of racism, discrimination, and victimization (Boyd-Franklin, 1989). Therapists might need to advocate for African American clients whose strain lies in trying to adjust to demands that might be unfair or discriminatory. In addition, therapists need to recognize that there will be diversity of experience among African American families. More about therapy with African Americans and other ethnic minorities appears later in the chapter.

Personal Growth Groups

A number of group therapies in recent years have focused on people whose lives are lacking in intimacy, intensity, and accomplishment. **Personal growth groups** *have their roots in the humanistic therapies; they emphasize personal growth and increased openness and honesty in interpersonal relations.*

An **encounter group** *is a personal growth group designed to promote self-understanding through candid group interaction.* For example, one member of an assembled group thinks he is better than everyone else. After several minutes of listening to the guy's insufferable bragging, one group member says, "Look, jerk, nobody here likes you; I would like to sell you for what you think you are worth and buy you for what you are actually worth!" Other members of the group might also criticize the braggart. Outside of an

encounter group, most people probably would not confront someone about bragging; in an encounter group, they may feel free to express their true feelings about each other.

Encounter groups improve the psychological adjustment of some individuals, but not others. For example, in one study, the majority of college students who were members of an encounter group felt better about themselves and got along better with others than did their counterparts, who were not involved in an encounter group (Lieberman, Yalom, & Miles, 1973). However, 8 percent of the participants in the encounter group felt that the experience was harmful. For the most part, they blamed the group leader for intensifying their problems; they said the leader's remarks were so personally devastating that they could not handle them.

Self-help Groups

Although encounter groups are not as popular today as they were in the 1970s, they were the forerunners of today's self-help groups. **Self-help groups** *are voluntary organizations of individuals who get together on a regular basis to discuss topics of common interest. The group leader and members give support to help individuals with their problems.* Self-help groups are so-called because they are conducted without a professional therapist. Self-help groups play an important role in our nation's mental health—approximately 6.25 million people participate in such groups each year.

In addition to reaching so many people in need of help, these groups are important because they use community resources and are relatively inexpensive. They also serve people who are less likely to receive help otherwise, such as less-educated middle-aged adults, homemakers, and blue-collar workers.

Founded in 1930 by a reformed alcoholic, Alcoholics Anonymous (AA) is one of the best-known self-help groups. Mental health professionals often recommend AA for their alcoholic clients. Weight Watchers and TOPS (Take Off Pounds Sensibly) are also self-help groups. There are myriad self-help groups, such as Parents Without Partners, lesbian and gay support groups, cocaine-abuse support groups, and child-abuse support groups. Table 17.3 provides a sampling of the wide variety of self-help groups available in one city.

You may be wondering how a group of people with the same problem can come together and do one another any good. You might be asking yourself why they don't just help themselves and eliminate the need for the group. In fact, seeing that others share the same burden makes people feel less isolated, less like freaks of nature; it increases a psychological sense of community or belonging; and it can give hope where there might have been none before (Levine & Perkins, 1987).

Self-help groups also provide an ideology, or set of beliefs, that members can use as a guide. These groups provide members with a sympathetic audience for confession, sharing, and emotional release. The social support, role modeling, and sharing of concrete strategies for solving problems that unfold in self-help groups add to their effectiveness. For instance, a woman who has been raped may not believe a male counselor who tells her that, with time, she will be able to put back together the pieces of her life and work through much of the psychological pain. However, the same message from another rape survivor—someone who has had to work through the same feelings of rage, fear, and violation—may be more believable.

> *Life is either a daring adventure or nothing.*
> *Security does not exist in nature, nor do the children of men as a whole experience it. Avoiding danger is no safer in the long run than exposure.*
>
> **Helen Keller**

TABLE 17.3
A Potpourri of Self-help Groups

A recent listing of self-help groups in a Tulsa, Oklahoma, Sunday newspaper included more than 200 entries. Among the wide variety listed were the following self-help groups.

Social Concerns

Tulsa Society for Depressed Women
Love Without Shame
Gamblers Anonymous
Phobia Society of Tulsa
Relocated Corporate Wives
Rebuilders: For Divorcés
Sex Addicts: Anonymous
Rap Group and Caring and Coping Partners of Vietnam Veterans

Eating/Weight Disorders

Movers and Shapers
Overeaters Anonymous
TOPS (Take Off Pounds Sensibly)

Alcohol/Substance Abuse

Students Against Drugs and Alcohol
Alcoholics Victorious
How to Cope with a Dependent Person
Adult Children of Alcoholic Parents
Alcoholics Anonymous
Teen Awareness Group
Cocaine Anonymous

Parenting

Single Working Mothers
Tulsa Adoptive Parents
Parents Without Partners
After Baby Comes
Happier Home Parents
Stepparents Group
Sooner Parents of Twins

Health

Resolve of Tulsa (an infertility group)
Mended Hearts (for those who have had open-heart surgery)
Group for Alzheimer's Caregivers
AIDS Support Program
ENCORE (for breast cancer patients)
SHHH (Self-Help for the Hard of Hearing)
LITHIUM Group (for those with bipolar disorder)
Families of Children with Diabetes
Indian Health Care Resource Center
Families of Nursing Home Residents

Many individuals feel uncomfortable with formal methods of therapy or support. Instead, they might turn to friends, relatives, religious leaders, or designated officials of the community to assist them in solving problems.

The increased use of drug therapy in mental institutions facilitated the transfer of many mental patients back to the community. The architects of deinstitutionalization believed that these individuals could be given medication to keep them stabilized until they could find continuing care. However, many residents of mental health institutions have no families or homes to go to and community mental health facilities are not adequately equipped to deal with the severe cases. Many individuals who are discharged from state mental hospitals join the ranks of "the homeless." Of course, though, not all homeless people are former mental patients. Controversy continues about whether individuals should be discharged so readily from state mental institutions, which usually struggle with underfunding and staff shortages.

Community Psychology

The community psychology movement was born in the early 1960s, when it became apparent to mental health practitioners, including clinical psychologists, that our mental health care system was woefully inadequate. The system was not reaching the poor. Many of those who could afford help often did not seek therapy because of its social stigma. As a result, deinstitutionalization became a major thrust of the community psychology movement. **Deinstitutionalization** *is the movement to transfer the treatment of mental disabilities from inpatient mental institutions to community-based facilities that stress outpatient care.* New drugs for treating the severely mentally disabled, such as schizophrenics, meant that large numbers of people could be released from mental institutions and treated in community-based centers.

In 1963 Congress passed the Community Mental Health Center Act, which provided funds for establishing one facility for every 50,000 individuals in the nation. The centers were designed to meet two basic goals—to provide community-based mental health services and to commit resources that help *prevent* disorders as well as treat them. Outpatient care is one of the important services that community mental health centers provide. Individuals can attend therapy sessions at a center and still keep their jobs and live with their families. Another important innovation

that grew out of the community psychology movement is called outreach services. Rather than expecting people with mental or emotional problems to make an appointment at a mental health center, mental health care workers in this program go to community locations, such as storefront clinics, where they are accessible and needed most. Many community-based mental health services stay open 24 hours a day, often handling such emergencies as suicide attempts and drug overdoses.

The philosophy of community-based services also includes training teachers, ministers, family physicians, and others who directly interact with community members to offer lay counseling and various workshops, such as assertive training or coping with stress. This broadens mental health resources, allowing more people to receive help in settings where they are more likely to be comfortable than in traditional mental health centers (Orford, 1992).

In principle, community-based mental health systems should work well. In practice, the systems are severely underfunded, over-enrolled, and sometimes hopelessly bureaucratic. Despite these problems, community psychologists continue to work on many levels to improve community systems.

Primary Prevention

Primary prevention *is a community psychology concept, borrowed from the public health field, that describes efforts to reduce the number of new cases of mental disorders.* By definition, primary prevention programs are offered to populations completely free of a disorder. Like immunization in public health, primary prevention programs try to identify and "inoculate" people against the development of mental disorders. Primary prevention programs tend to follow one of three strategies: community-wide, milestone, or high-risk (Bloom, 1985).

In the *community-wide* approach, programs are available to everyone in a given geographic area. In Washington, D.C., the program "Beautiful Babies Right from the Start," for example, provides free prenatal care and well-baby care for the baby's first 18 months to women and their infants in the poorest communities. This program attempts to prevent pregnant women from engaging in harmful behaviors, such as substance abuse or poor nutrition, that put infants at risk for premature birth, low birthweight, and such disorders as hyperactivity, impaired

*The Plight of
the Homeless*

As is the case with many social policy initiatives, the deinstitutionalization movement was undertaken for a noble purpose. Many individuals were appropriately concerned that the hospitalization practices in the 1950s and 1960s had led to a loss of individual rights for those who had been hospitalized. Deinstitutionalization assumed that effective care could be delivered in decentralized community centers under the watchful eye of concerned families. In what way does the dimension of *individualism versus collectivism* influence the success of the deinstitutionalization movement? Your consideration of this issue encourages you to *identify the underlying values that influence behavior.*

such as school children, to find those who show early signs of problems and provide them with mental health services.

Tertiary Prevention

Tertiary prevention *is a community psychology concept that describes efforts to reduce the long-term consequences of mental health disorders that were not prevented or arrested early in the course of the disorders.* Tertiary prevention programs are geared toward people who once required long-term care or hospitalization and provide services that can reduce the probability they will become so debilitated again. Halfway houses (community residences for individuals who no longer require institutionalization but who still need some support in readjusting to the community) are an example of tertiary prevention. Such programs seek to increase individuals' coping skills by reducing their social isolation, by increasing their social skills, and by developing educational strategies tailored to their needs.

Community psychology has successfully reached large numbers of mentally and emotionally distressed people, not only through prevention but also through intervention (Levine, Toro, & Perkins, 1993). Unfortunately, strong cutbacks in federal funding of community mental health centers in the 1980s have diminished their effectiveness and stalled their expansion.

Because programs such as outreach services may be the only mental health care available to those who are poor or who are from ethnic minority backgrounds, community psychology approaches are especially important (Marin, 1993). Remember from our earlier comments that psychotherapy has been more available to the wealthy. An explicit value of community psychology is to assist people who are disenfranchised from society to gain access to comparable forms of support. **Empowerment** *refers to helping individuals develop skills they need to improve their adaptation and circumstances.* To read about how community psychology is involved in empowering Latino Americans, turn to Sociocultural Worlds 17.2.

memory, and disorganized thinking. In the *milestone* approach, the target group is every person in a population who reaches a certain hurdle, or critical life transition, such as being fired, becoming a parent for the first time, or going away to college. Counseling for fired employees and orientation programs for college students are two examples of milestone programs. In a *high-risk* program, the focus is on specific groups of people whose chances of developing mental disorders are extremely high, such as children of alcoholics, children with chronic illnesses, and ethnic minority children.

Secondary Prevention

Secondary prevention *is a community psychology concept in which screening for early detection of problems, as well as early intervention, is carried out.* A major goal of secondary prevention programs is to reach large numbers of potential clients. These programs often use *paraprofessionals*, volunteers without formal mental health training who work closely with psychologists, to meet this goal. One approach to secondary prevention involves teaching coping skills to people under high levels of stress, the bereaved, the newly employed, and prospective parents. Another type involves screening groups of individuals,

SOCIOCULTURAL WORLDS 17.2

The Development of Community Psychology Approaches for Latino Americans

According to psychologists Amado Padilla, Rene Ruiz, and Rodolfo Alvarez (1975, 1989), a wide range of innovative programs are needed to improve the lives of Latino Americans and to help them cope with problems. These programs include remedial education, vocational guidance and retraining, drug abuse and crime prevention programs, and college counseling.

The researchers recommend that community mental health centers, for example, serve as a hub for many activities. In addition to providing treatment for a wide range of human problems, the facilities could be used for youth activities, such as sports and dances, and for cultural events, such as Spanish-language films and fiestas. Most mental health experts believe that it makes sense to involve community members in a neighborhood center that ostensibly is there to serve their needs. Also, people from the community should be part of the center's administration, and the advertising media, in both Spanish and English, can be used to inform the community about the facility, its services, and its activities.

For example, one community mental health facility in east Los Angeles was designed to attract local Mexican Americans (Karno & Morales, 1971). The facility was located in the heart of the community, convenient to transportation, comfortable, and inviting. In 2½ years, the director of the facility hired 22 full-time professional, paraprofessional, and clerical personnel. Of these 22, 15 were fluent in Spanish. Ten were natives and/or residents of the area. Twelve were of Mexican American descent, one was Cuban, and another was Peruvian. The treatment program was based on a philosophy of prevention, and it helped people gain access to a wide variety of community mental health agencies. As a backup, the center offered short-term crisis-oriented treatment that included individual, family, and drug therapy. The center seemed to fulfill the objective of providing appropriate treatment for Mexican Americans. More such centers are badly needed in areas in which Latino Americans live.

El Centro de la Causa, on Chicago's west side, is another example of a successful community mental health center (Schensul, 1974). A group of young Chicanos started this youth center by organizing a community fiesta that raised enough money to cover the original operating budget of $1,800. Within months the group had convinced a church organization to provide $40,000 for staff and services. Within 3 years, the operating budget was more than $400,000. Funding was used to train community residents as paraprofessionals in mental health, reading improvement programs, English classes, recreation and youth activities, and drug-abuse programs.

One community mental health facility in east Los Angeles was located in the heart of the community, convenient to transportation, comfortable, and inviting. The facility was successful in attracting local Mexican Americans to come in and discuss their problems with professionals and paraprofessionals.

Some approaches have the advantage of working with individuals in the context of a larger system. These therapies include group therapies, family and couple therapy, and community psychology.

Group therapies emphasize that social relationships hold the key to successful therapy; therefore, therapy involving group interactions may be more beneficial than individual therapy. Family therapy and couple therapy, as well as personal growth groups, are common. Community psychology was born in the early 1960s. Deinstitutionalization, in which the treatment of mental disorders is transferred from inpatient mental institutions to outpatient community mental health facilities, has been especially important in community psychology. As a result, mental health services are more accessible to individuals from low-income and ethnic minority backgrounds. Three community psychology approaches are primary prevention, secondary prevention, and tertiary prevention. Empowerment—providing assistance so that individuals can gain more control over their lives—is a key concept in community psychology.

Is Psychotherapy Effective?

Do individuals who go through therapy get better? Are some approaches more effective than others, or is the situation similar to that of the Dodo in *Alice's Adventures in Wonderland*? Dodo was asked to judge the winner of a race; he decided, "Everybody has won and all must have prizes." How would we evaluate the effectiveness of psychotherapy? Would we take the client's word, or the therapist's word? What would be our criteria for effectiveness? Would it be "feeling good," "adaptive behavior," "improved interpersonal relationships," "autonomous decision making," or "more positive self-concept," for example? During the past several decades, an extensive amount of thought and research has addressed these questions.

Outcome Research on the Effectiveness of Psychotherapy

Four decades ago, Hans Eysenck (1952) shocked the pundits in the field of psychotherapy by concluding that treatment is ineffective. Eysenck analyzed 24 studies of psychotherapy and found that approximately two-thirds of the individuals with neurotic symptoms improved. Sounds impressive so far. But Eysenck also found that a similar percentage of neurotic individuals on waiting lists to see a psychotherapist also showed marked improvement even though they were not given any psychotherapy at all.

Critics of Eysenck's findings suggested that there were many irregularities in how he analyzed his data and drew conclusions. Even so, Eysenck's pronouncement prompted a flurry of research on psychotherapy's effectiveness. Hundreds of studies on the outcome of psychotherapy have now been conducted (Sanderson, 1995; Whiston & Sexton, 1993). One strategy for analyzing these diverse studies is called **meta-analysis,** *in which the researcher statistically combines the results of many different studies.* In one meta-analysis of psychotherapy research, 475 studies were statistically combined (Smith, Glass, & Miller, 1980). Only those studies in which a therapy group had been compared with an untreated control group were compared. The results were much kinder to psychotherapy effectiveness than Eysenck's earlier results: On 88 percent of the measures, individuals who received therapy improved more than those who did not. This meta-analysis documents that psychotherapy is effective in general, but it does not inform us about the specific ways in which different therapies might be effective.

People who are thinking about seeing a psychotherapist not only want to know whether psychotherapy in general is effective, but they would especially like to know which form of psychotherapy is effective for their particular problem. In the meta-analysis conducted by Mary Lee Smith and her colleagues (Smith, Glass, & Miller, 1980) comparisons of different types of psychotherapy were also made. For example, behavior therapies were compared with insight therapies (psychodynamic, humanistic). Both the behavior and insight therapies were superior to no treatment at all, but they did not differ from each other in effectiveness. While no particular therapy was the best in the study by Smith and her colleagues, some therapies do seem to be more effective in treating some disorders than others. The behavior therapies have been most successful in treating specific behavioral problems, such as phobias and sexual dysfunctions (Bowers & Clum, 1988). The cognitive therapies have been most successful in treating depression (Clark & Beck, 1989). Also, many therapies have their maximum benefit early in treatment with less improvement occurring as the individual remains in therapy (Karasu, 1986).

The informed consumer also needs to be aware of some evidence that in certain cases psychotherapy can actually be harmful. For example, people who have a low tolerance of anxiety, low motivation, and strong signs of psychological deterioration may worsen as therapy progresses. Characteristics of the therapist also have been related to a worsening of the client's status as therapy progresses. Therapists who are aggressive, who try to get clients to disclose personal information too quickly, and who are impatient with the process of change may exacerbate their clients' problems (Suinn, 1984). Therapist bias can be harmful when the therapist does not understand ethnic, religious, gender, or other cultural differences, but instead pressures such clients to conform to White, middle-class norms. Finally, therapists who engage in sex with a client harm the client; such behavior is absolutely unethical.

While incompetent and unethical therapists do exist, there are many impeccable therapists who successfully help their clients. Like jazz musicians, psychotherapists must be capable of improvising, gracefully. As psychologist Jerome Frank put it, "Successful therapy is not just a scientific process, it is a healing art as well."

Common Themes and Specificity in Psychotherapy

After carefully studying the nature of psychotherapy for more than 25 years, Jerome Frank (1982) concluded that effective psychotherapies have the common elements of expectations, mastery, and emotional arousal. By inspiring an expectation of help, the therapist motivates the client to continue coming to therapy. These expectations are powerful morale builders and symptom relievers in themselves. The therapist also increases the client's sense of mastery and competence. For example, clients begin to feel that they can cope effectively with their world. Therapy also arouses the individual's emotions, essential to motivating behavioral change, according to Frank.

The therapeutic relationship is another important ingredient in successful psychotherapy (Garfield, 1995; Strupp, 1989). A relationship in which the client has confidence and trust in the therapist is essential to effective psychotherapy. In one study, the most common ingredient in the success of different psychotherapies was the therapist's supportiveness of the client (Wallerstein, 1989). The client and therapist engage in a "healing ritual," which requires the active participation of both the client and the therapist. As part of this ritual, the client gains hope and becomes less alienated.

But while psychotherapies have common themes, some critics worry about carrying this commonality too far. Specificity in psychotherapy still needs careful attention—we need to understand "*what* treatment is most effective for *this* individual with *that* specific problem, and under *which* set of circumstances" within the cultural context (Bonger & Beutler, 1995; Paul, 1967). At this time, however, we do not know which approach works best in which situation with which therapist. Some therapists are better trained than others, some are more sensitive to a person's feelings, some are more introverted, and some are more conservative. Because of the myriad ways we differ as human beings, the ideal "fit" of therapist and client is difficult to pinpoint scientifically. To read about guidelines for seeking professional help, turn to Applications in Psychology 17.1.

Only in the last two decades have psychologists become sensitive to the sociocultural aspects of therapy. Let's examine how gender, ethnicity and social class, and culture influence treatment effectiveness.

Gender Issues in Treatment Effectiveness

One of the by-products of changing gender roles for women and men is a rethinking of approaches to psychotherapy. In some instances, the development of abnormal behavior and lack of effective psychotherapy may be due to traditional gender conditioning (Worell & Robinson, 1993). Our discussion of gender and therapy focuses on three areas: autonomy and relatedness in therapy, consciousness-raising groups, and feminist therapies, each of which we examine in turn.

Freud is the father of psychoanalysis. It had no mother.
Germaine Greer, The Female Eunuch, 1971

Autonomy and Relatedness in Therapy

Autonomy and relatedness are central issues to an understanding of gender conditioning. For many years autonomy was championed as an important characteristic for maturity. As a result, autonomy was the unquestioned goal of many psychotherapies, relatedness was not. Thomas Szasz (1965), for example, claimed that the basic goal of psychotherapy is to foster autonomy, independence, and freedom. The humanistic therapies—Rogers, Maslow, and Perls—argued that to become psychologically healthy, an individual has to become self-actualized through self-determination and fulfillment of needs, independent of social constraints or personal commitments.

But therapists are taking a new look at autonomy as the ideal goal of therapy for females. Should therapy with females focus more on the way most females have been socialized and place more emphasis on relationships? Can females, even with psychotherapy, achieve autonomy in a male-dominated society? Are conventional ways of thinking about autonomy and relatedness appropriate for capturing the complexity of human experience? Would psychotherapy for females, as well as for males, be improved if its goals were more androgynous in nature, stressing better psychological functioning in *both* autonomy and relatedness?

Because traditional therapy often has not adequately addressed the specific concerns of women in a sexist society, several nontraditional approaches have arisen. These nontraditional therapies emphasize the importance of helping people break free from traditional gender roles and stereotypes. The nontraditional therapies avoid language that labels one sex as more socially desirable or valuable

APPLICATIONS IN PSYCHOLOGY 17.1

Guidelines for Seeking Professional Help

Marcia felt anxious most of the time. But what caused her the greatest difficulty was that she became so anxious during exams in her classes that she would nearly freeze. Her mind would go blank and she would begin to sweat and shake all over. It was such a problem that she was failing her classes. She told one of her professors that this was the problem with her grades. He told her that it sounded like she had a serious case of test anxiety, and that she should get some help. Marcia decided that she better take his advice and wanted to find a psychotherapist. How would she go about finding a therapist? How could she know that she was going to see someone who could help her, as opposed to a professional who would not be helpful, or perhaps even make things worse? These are only a few of the questions people commonly have when they seek to find a therapist.

When trying to find a therapist, Marcia could consider a psychologist, psychiatrist, social worker, counselor, or any number of other helping professionals. Each of these mental health professionals is qualified to provide psychotherapeutic services. They all practice from any one or combination of the therapeutic orientations discussed in this chapter. They may also see people on an individual, one to one basis, or in small groups, as in group therapy. The critical question is, of course, how does someone go about selecting a therapist to help them? This is not as easy a question as it may appear at first glance. We may face many of the same problems when we try to find a 'good' medical doctor, accountant, or dentist; however, the way that most people go about finding these other professional services may not be the best way of selecting a therapist. Asking a friend for a good therapist ignores the fact that some approaches to therapy work better with some problems than others. Also, every therapeutic relationship is different, so one person's experience in therapy is not translatable to another person's. We offer the following general suggestions when looking for a therapist.

1. Identify the professional's credentials. Although all different types of mental health professionals may be competent, psychologists, psychiatrists, and social workers all differ in their approach to therapy, based on differences in training:

Psychologists tend to be focused on the person's emotions and behaviors; psychiatrists are trained as medical doctors, so their perspective is likely to involve physical aspects of psychological problems; and social workers will be inclined to take a person's entire family and social situation into account. Regardless of the exact profession, some minimal credentials should be considered important. All states have licensing regulations for professionals who provide public services. Thus, a therapist should be licensed or certified by a state in order to practice. In addition, in some cases it may be important for a professional to have some advanced, specialized training in a certain area. For example, if a person is seeking help with a specific problem, like drug abuse, alcohol abuse, or a sexual problem, the therapist should have some training in that area. You should ask about the professional's credentials either before or during a first visit.

2. When starting therapy, give it some time before making a judgment of how useful it is. Making changes is very difficult. Expecting too much too soon can result in premature dissatisfaction and disappointment. Because a large part of therapy involves the development of a relationship with the therapist, it may take several meetings to really know if things are going well. One suggestion is to give it four to six weekly meetings. If it does not seem like things are going the way you would like, it is a good idea to discuss your progress with the therapist and ask what you should expect with regard to making progress. Setting specific goals with specific time expectations can be helpful. If your goals are not being met, you might consider a new therapist.

3. Be a thoughtful and careful consumer of mental health services. With any services, the more informed you are about the services provided, the better decision you can make about whether or not they are the right services for you. Calling around and asking specific questions about approaches and specializations is one way to become informed about the services offered by therapists. Consider how important it may be that the therapist is of your same or opposite sex, whether it is important that they have experience with your specific difficulty, as well as other specific characteristics. You may also want to learn more about their theoretical orientation to therapy as described in this chapter. Most professionals are quite comfortable talking about their background and training. Your confidence and trust in the professional is an important part of how well therapy will work for you.

These general guidelines should be used when first looking for a therapist. Remember that people should continually evaluate their own progress throughout therapy and when they feel dissatisfied with how it is going, they should discuss this with their therapist. Remember that therapy is like other services: when dissatisfied you can always look for another therapist. Don't think that just because one therapist has not been helpful none will be. All therapists and therapeutic relationships are different. Finding the right therapist is one of the most important factors in therapy success (Kalichman, 1994).

Increased interest has focused on gender roles in psychotherapy. *Might female psychotherapists be more likely to encourage autonomy and relatedness, rather than autonomy alone, as psychotherapy goals?*

Rachel Hare-Mustin (*left*) and Jeanne Maracek (*right*) have made important contributions to understanding the role of gender in psychotherapy. They have been especially concerned about the inclusion of strategies in psychotherapy to help women break free from gender stereotypes and male bias.

than the other (Worrell, 1989). Let's now consider two such nontraditional therapies: Consciousness-raising groups and feminist therapy.

Consciousness-Raising Groups

Consciousness-raising groups *are believed by some feminists to be important alternatives or adjuncts to traditional therapies; they often involve several people meeting in a member's home, are frequently leaderless (or members take turns facilitating discussion), and focus on the members' feelings and self-perceptions.* Instead of seeking and accepting male-biased therapy, women may meet in consciousness-raising groups to define their own experiences with their own criteria.

Some men followed suit and formed all-male consciousness-raising groups in which they discuss what it means to be male in our society (Rabinowitz & Cochran, 1987). Several colleges and universities have rape-awareness programs, a form of consciousness-raising groups for men. Going even further, the University of Wisconsin group, "Men Stopping Rape," offers a version of their program to junior high and high school students (Paludi, 1995).

Feminist Therapies

Feminist therapies *are usually based on a critique of society wherein women are perceived to have less political and economic power than men have. Also, feminist therapies assume that the reasons for women's problems are principally social, not personal.* Many individuals assume that feminist therapies and nonsexist therapies are identical. However, some feminists distinguish between the two. For example, **nonsexist therapy** *occurs when the therapist has become aware of and primarily overcome his or her own sexist attitudes and behavior.* Thus, a nonsexist therapist would not perceive a dependent man or an independent woman to be showing emotional problems just because they are acting in counterstereotypic ways. Nonsexist therapists do not view mar-

riage as any better for women or men. And these therapists also encourage women and men to adopt androgynous gender roles rather than stereotypic masculine or feminine ones (Paludi, 1995). Feminist therapy represents a sociocultural perspective that can be interwoven with other approaches to enhance their effectiveness (Dutton-Douglas & Walker, 1988).

Feminist therapists, both male and female, believe that traditional psychotherapy continues to carry considerable gender bias, and that women clients cannot realize their full potential without becoming aware of society's sexism. The goals of feminist therapists are no different from other therapists' goals. Feminist therapists make no effort to turn clients into feminists, but want the female client to be fully aware of how the nature of the female role in the American society can contribute to the development of a mental disorder. Feminist therapists believe women must become aware of the effects of social oppression on their own lives if they are to achieve their mental health goals.

In one feminist approach to therapy, women go through three phases en route to mental health (Williams, 1987). First, in *harmful adaptation,* women accept dependency and the rules of a patriarchal society. In this phase, women harm themselves because they subordinate their own desires and needs to the values of the system. Second, in *corrective action,* when women realize what harmful adaptation has done to them, they begin to develop their own identity and to articulate personal goals. Third, in *health maintenance,* women develop pride in their new identity and form alliances with other women to work toward better conditions for all women. In this model of feminist therapy, women move from acceptance of an oppressive society to taking pride in a new, positive status and helping other women achieve the same.

Ethnicity and Social Class Issues in Treatment Effectiveness

For much too long, psychotherapists were concerned almost exclusively with helping middle- and upper-class individuals cope with their problems while ignoring the needs of people who were poor or from ethnic minority backgrounds (Atkinson, Morten, & Sue, 1993; Comas-Díaz & Griffith, 1988; Parham, 1995; Ponterotto & others, 1995). Although having financial resources doesn't guarantee happiness, functionality, or a stress-free existence, psychology has been remiss in the seriousness with which it has undertaken to provide improved services to ethnic minority individuals and members of the lower class (Aponte, Rivers, & Wohl, 1995; Yutrzenka, 1995).

Most people, regardless of their ethnicity, prefer to discuss problems with their parents, friends, and relatives rather than with mental health professionals. However, other factors complicate the delivery of health care services to the underserved (Snowden & Hines, 1994). One reason is that there are so few ethnic minority psychotherapists. For example, one study found that African American college students were more likely to use the college's mental health facilities if an African American clinician or counselor were available than if only White counselors were available (Thompson & Cimbolic, 1978).

Therapy can be effective when the therapist and client are from different cultural backgrounds if the therapist has excellent clinical skills and is culturally sensitive (Gim, Atkinson, & Kim, 1991; Sue, in press). Researchers have also found that Asian Americans, African Americans, Latinos, and Native Americans terminate psychotherapy after an initial session at a much higher rate than do Anglo-Americans (Sue, Allen, & Conaway, 1978). The social stigma of being a "mental patient," fear of hospitalization, conflict between their own belief system and the beliefs of modern mental health practitioners, and the availability of an alternate healer are additional reasons ethnic minority individuals terminate therapy early (Lefley, 1984).

Barriers to Therapeutic Effectiveness

Psychotherapy involves interpersonal interaction and communication. Verbal and nonverbal messages need to be accurately sent and received. Very effective therapy can take place when the client and therapist are from different sociocultural backgrounds. However, when the psychotherapist and client come from different cultural backgrounds, barriers to communication can develop, which can lead to misunderstandings that destroy rapport and undermine the effectiveness of psychotherapy (Atkinson, Morten, & Sue, 1993). Among the barriers that can impede psychotherapy's effectiveness with individuals from ethnic minority groups are (1) language differences, (2) class-bound values, and (3) culture-bound values.

(a)

(b)

(c)

(d)

How might therapy proceed differently in the following contexts: (a) an ethnic minority client with a White, middle-class therapist, (b) a White male client from impoverished circumstances in rural Appalachia, (c) an Asian American client who is a recent immigrant to the United States, and (d) an African American female client with an African American female therapist?

Language Differences A psychotherapist's reliance on verbal interaction to establish rapport with a client presupposes that the psychotherapist and the client can understand each other. However, many psychotherapists fail to recognize that there may be a language barrier between them and ethnic minority individuals that restricts the development of rapport. Also, many educationally and economically impoverished clients may not have the verbal skills required to benefit from the psychotherapist's advice, interpretation, and counseling, especially if the psychotherapist communicates complex concepts to the client. Psychotherapists may also misinterpret the body language—gestures and postures, for example—of individuals from ethnic minority groups. For example, African American clients often avoid eye contact in conversation, whereas White clients usually maintain eye contact. A psychotherapist may inappropriately interpret an African American client's lack of eye contact as inattentiveness, lack of interest, or anger.

Class-Bound Values   One of the most frequently encountered issues involving middle-class psychotherapists and lower-class clients is the willingness to make and keep psychotherapy appointments. Lower-class clients may be concerned with "survival" or "making it through the day." Appointments made for 2 weeks in the future or 50-minute sessions may not be appropriate for the needs of a lower-class client who requires immediate help. One clinician described poor Appalachian Whites as refusing to live by the clock and not only refusing to adhere to the values of promptness, planning, and protocol but also suspecting people who do adhere to these values (Vontress, 1973). The clients' socioeconomic status also affects the kind of treatment they receive. For example, one study revealed that students from upper socioeconomic backgrounds are given more exploratory counseling interviews than students from lower socioeconomic backgrounds (Ryan & Gaier, 1968).

Culture-Bound Values   Psychotherapists often impose their own values on clients from a different cultural background. Referring to clients from other cultures, especially those from ethnic minority groups, as "culturally deprived" exemplifies this imposition. Cultural misunderstandings can lead to difficulties in communication, expectations, the quality of care given, and the client's motivation to continue psychotherapy (Cayleff, 1986). For instance, many psychotherapists believe that self-disclosure is an important condition for effective psychotherapy. However, clients are less likely to disclose private, sensitive information about themselves to someone who has a different cultural background. Also, self-disclosure may be contrary to the basic cultural values of individuals from some cultures. For example, Chinese Americans are taught at an early age to refrain from emotional expression; they may find psychotherapists' demands to disclose personal information as threatening (Sue & Sue, 1972). Similar conflicts have been reported for Chicanos (Cross & Maldonado, 1971) and Native Americans (Trimble, 1976).

Not all cultures share the Western mainstream views about the causes and appropriate treatment of disorders. In one investigation, six ethnic minority groups viewed maladaptive behavior more broadly than did the mainstream mental health professionals (Flaskerud, 1984). For example, the ethnic minority groups described maladaptive behavior in spiritual, moral, somatic (bodily), psychological, and metaphysical terms. The ethnic minority groups also had different ideas about therapy than the mental health professionals. The ethnic groups said the management of abnormal behavior could include social, spiritual, economic, vocational, recreational, personal, physical, and psychological strategies, whereas the mental health professionals said it should involve traditional psychotherapy and psychopharmaceutical approaches.

Ethnically Responsive Therapy

An example of a broad, culturally sensitive approach to therapy is the recent interest in integrating folk healers into Western therapy when certain ethnic groups are involved. For example, in Florida, the University of Miami's Community Mental Health Center uses folk healers, including Afrocuban *santeros,* Haitian *houngans* or *mambos,* Hispanic *espiritistas,* and African American root doctors as consultants, trainers, and referral sources. Such collaboration allows clients in need of therapy to derive whatever benefit they can from Western methods without turning their backs on the methods of their culture (Lefley, 1984).

In response to demands for more concrete recommendations on how to conduct therapy, some clinicians have attempted to devise ethnically responsive treatments (Casas & San Miguel, 1993; Helms, 1993). For example, in working with Asian Americans, a number of therapists recommend a directive and structured approach because Asian Americans prefer the concrete direction provided in this format. In working with Latinos, some therapists recommend a reframing of problems as medical rather than psychological to reduce resistance. The assumption is that Latinos will be more receptive to a combined medical and psychological orientation, due to their health concept of an integrated mind and body (Comas-Díaz & others, 1982; Padilla, 1994). In working with African Americans, some therapists recommend externally focused, action-oriented therapy, rather than internally focused, intrapsychic therapy.

Nobody, as long as he moves about among the chaotic currents of life, is without trouble.

Carl Jung

Such recommendations, however, raise some important questions. For example, isn't it impossible for therapists to effectively change their therapy orientation to work with ethnic minority groups? Thus, a psychoanalytic therapist might find it difficult to use the externally focused, action-oriented therapy recommended for African Americans. By using a specific approach, supposedly based on the client's cultural background, how does the therapist

How critical is it to the success of psychotherapy for the therapist to have the same demographic variables as the client (such as ethnicity, gender, socioeconomic class, religion, and sexual orientation)? How important would it be for you personally to have a therapist with a similar background and characteristics comparable to your own? Your response reflects your ability to *create a plausible psychological argument relying on evidence.*

The Match Game

deal with diversity and individual differences in an ethnic or cultural group? Because of the problems raised by such questions, we cannot just say, "Know the cultural background of the client or use this approach with that particular ethnic or cultural group."

According to Stanley Sue (1990, in press) what we can say is that when they see ethnic minority clients, therapists should emphasize two processes, at least in initial therapy sessions: (1) credibility and (2) giving. **Credibility** *is the therapist's believability.* **Giving** *refers to the client's receiving some kind of benefit from treatment early in the therapy process.* Two factors are important in increasing credibility: ascribed status and achieved status. Ascribed status is one's position or role defined by others or cultural norms. In some cultures, the young are subordinate to the old, those who are naive abide by those in authority, and females have less power than males. Credibility must also be achieved. The therapist can achieve credibility by doing something that the client perceives as being helpful or competent. Lack of ascribed credibility may be the main reason ethnic minority individuals tend to steer clear of therapy; lack of achieved credibility may be the main reason ethnic minority individuals terminate therapy once it has begun as well as problems with rapport.

In terms of giving, clients may wonder how talking to a therapist will alleviate their problems. Therapists need to help ethnic minority clients see the relationship between therapy and why it will help a person get better. It is important for the therapist to make this association in the first session. Many ethnic minority clients do not understand Western psychotherapy. The first session should not be just an assessment session, but rather the therapist should find

out about the client, give some recommendations for treatment, and say something concrete to the client so the client will leave the first session saying, "I got something out of it that I think will help me and I want to come back again." Many therapists believe this approach produces a stronger therapeutic alliance regardless of the ethnicity of the client and therapist.

So far we have discussed a variety of psychotherapies that can help individuals cope more effectively with stress and develop more adaptive, less harmful behavior. In recent years considerable progress has also been made in biomedical therapies, which we now discuss.

BIOMEDICAL THERAPIES

Biomedical therapies *are treatments to reduce or eliminate the symptoms of psychological disorders by altering the way an individual's body functions. Drug therapy is the most common form of biomedical therapy.* Psychologists and other mental health professionals may provide psychotherapy in conjunction with the biomedical therapy administered by psychiatrists and other medical doctors.

Drug Therapy

Psychotherapeutic drugs are used to treat many mental disorders—anxiety, depression, and schizophrenia, for example. In some instances, these drugs are effective when other forms of therapy are not. Drug therapy has substantially reduced the amount of time schizophrenics must spend in hospitals, for example. Three main types of psychotherapeutic drugs are antianxiety drugs, antipsychotic drugs, and antidepressant drugs.

Antianxiety Drugs

Antianxiety drugs *are commonly known as tranquilizers; these drugs reduce anxiety by making individuals less excitable and more tranquil.* Why are antianxiety drugs so widely used? Many individuals experience stress, anxiety, or an inability to sleep well; family physicians and psychiatrists prescribe these drugs to improve our abilities to cope with these situations more effectively. The most widely used antianxiety drugs are Xanax and Valium.

The relaxed feelings brought on by antianxiety drugs are a welcome relief to individuals experiencing anxiety and stress in their lives. However, these drugs often cause fatigue and drowsiness; motor abilities can be impaired and work productivity reduced; and extended use can produce dependence. In some instances, the combination of antianxiety drugs and alcohol has caused death. When an individual feels anxious, it may be best to face the problems creating the anxiety rather than relying on antianxiety drugs to avoid the problems.

Antipsychotic Drugs

Antipsychotic drugs *are powerful drugs that diminish agitated behavior, reduce tension, decrease hallucinations and delusions, improve social behavior, and produce better sleep patterns in severely mentally disabled individuals, especially schizophrenics.* Neuroleptics are the most widely used antipsychotic drugs.

The main value of antipsychotic drugs is their ability to block the dopamine system's action in the brain. Recall from our discussion in chapter 15 that schizophrenics have too much of the neurochemical messenger dopamine. Numerous well-controlled investigations have revealed that, when used in sufficient doses, the neuroleptics reduce a variety of schizophrenic symptoms, at least in the short term (Kirkpatrick & others, 1989). The neuroleptics do not cure schizophrenia, however, and they may have severe side effects. The neuroleptics treat the symptoms of schizophrenia, not its causes. If an individual stops taking the drugs, the symptoms return.

Neuroleptic drugs have substantially reduced the lengths of hospital stays for schizophrenics. Although schizophrenics often are able to return to the community because drug therapy keeps their symptoms from reappearing, most have difficulty coping with the demands of society and most are chronically unemployed.

Tardive dyskinesia *is a major side effect of the neuroleptic drugs; it is a neurological disorder characterized by grotesque, involuntary movements of the facial muscles and mouth, as well as extensive twitching of the neck, arms, and legs.* As many as 20 percent of all schizophrenics taking neuroleptics develop this disorder; elderly women are especially vulnerable.

Long-term neuroleptic therapy also is associated with increased depression and anxiety. For example, schizophrenics who have taken neuroleptics for many years report that they feel miserable most of the time. Nonetheless, for the majority of schizophrenics, the benefits of neuroleptic treatment outweigh its risks and discomforts, even if a cure for schizophrenia remains elusive.

Lithium *is a drug that is widely used to treat bipolar disorder* (recall that this disorder involves wide mood swings of depression and mania). The amount of lithium that circulates in the bloodstream needs to be monitored carefully because its effective dosage is precariously close to toxic levels. Memory impairment is also associated with lithium use.

As with schizophrenia, the treatment of affective disorders might also involve a combination of drug therapy and psychotherapy. In one study, the combination of tricyclics and interpersonal psychotherapy produced a lower than normal relapse rate for depressed clients (10 percent versus 22 percent) (Frank & Kupfer, 1986). The interpersonal therapy focused on the clients' ability to develop and maintain positive interpersonal relationships and included an educational workshop for the clients and their families.

Some strategies for increasing the effectiveness of the neuroleptics involve (1) administering lower dosages over time rather than giving a large initial dose and (2) combining drug therapy with psychotherapy. The small percentage of schizophrenics who are able to hold jobs suggests that drugs alone will not make them contributing members of society. Vocational, family, and social-skills training are needed in conjunction with drug therapy to facilitate improved psychological functioning and adaptation to society.

Antidepressant Drugs

Antidepressant drugs *regulate mood. The three main classes of antidepressant drugs are tricyclics, such as Elavil; MAO inhibitors, such as Nardil; and SSRI inhibitors, such as Prozac.* The *tricyclics*, so-called because of their three-ring molecular structure, probably work because they increase the level of certain neurotransmitters, especially norepinephrine and serotonin. The tricyclics reduce the symptoms of depression in approximately 60 to 70 percent of all cases. The tricyclics are not effective in improving mood until 2 to 4 weeks after the individual begins taking them, and they sometimes have adverse side effects—such as restlessness, faintness, and trembling. The MAO inhibitors are not as widely used as the tricyclics because they are more toxic, they require more dietary restrictions, and they usually have less potent therapeutic effects. Nonetheless, some severely depressed individuals who do not respond to the tricyclics do respond to the MAO inhibitors.

The third category of antidepressant drugs caused such a flurry of attention in recent years that their prescription was the topic of a cover story in both *Time* and *Newsweek*. The most prominent of the selective serotonin reuptake inhibiting (SSRI) type is Prozac (followed by Nardil and Paxil). SSRI drugs work by interfering with the reabsorption of serotonin in the brain. Prozac is most frequently prescribed for dysthymia, a mild to moderate form of clinical depression, but has also successfully treated anxiety, obsession, and shyness. Prozac, approved by the FDA in 1987, is a "clean" drug, meaning that side effects are few and unlikely (these include risk of nausea, diarrhea, and loss of sexual function) and there is no risk of addiction. Although many individuals report that they feel fully themselves when taking Prozac (Kramer, 1993), the drug also can be disinhibiting and dangerous for some individuals, who report an increase in suicidal feelings and aggressive impulses. The popularity of Prozac has prompted social

FIGURE 17.6

Phototherapy
Seasonal affective disorder is often treated with a bank of high-intensity, full-spectrum lights for several hours each morning before daybreak during the fall and winter months when the disorder is most debilitating.

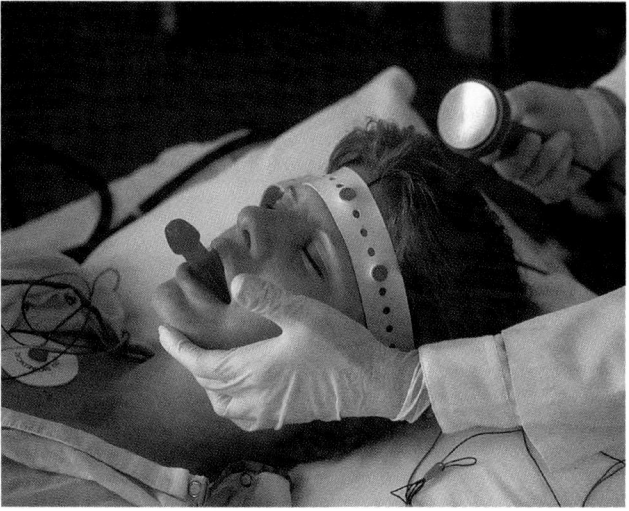

Electroconvulsive therapy (ECT), commonly called "shock therapy," causes a seizure in the brain. ECT is still given to as many as 60,000 people a year, mainly to treat major depression.

critics to question whether we may be on the brink of a "designer drug culture" in which personal eccentricities of normal personality are seen as warranting correction through medication.

Phototherapy

Can you imagine setting aside several hours every morning during the fall and winter to sit in front of a bright white light in order to avoid disturbing feelings (see figure 17.6)? Phototherapy, the use of full-spectrum light (containing all the colors naturally present in daylight), has received anecdotal support as an effective treatment for those suffering the form of depression called **seasonal affective disorder (SAD),** *depression that appears to be caused by a decrease in exposure to sunlight.* Those who suffer this problem invariably report greater emotional challenges in the winter months. The creators of the therapy believe that the artificial light compensates SAD sufferers to alleviate the symptoms of depression (Jacobsen & others, 1987; Rosenthal and others, 1985).

Electroconvulsive Therapy

"Then something bent down and took hold of me and shook me like the end of the world. Wee-ee-ee-ee-ee, it shrilled, through an air crackling with blue light, and with each flash a great jolt drubbed me until I thought my bones would break and the sap fly out of me like a split plant." Such images as this description from Sylvia Plath's (1971) autobiographic novel, *The Bell Jar,* have shaped the public's

view of **electroconvulsive therapy (ECT).** *Commonly called "shock treatment," ECT is sometimes used to treat severely depressed individuals. The goal of ECT is to cause a seizure in the brain much like what happens spontaneously in some forms of epilepsy.* A small electric current, lasting for 1 second or less, passes through two electrodes placed on the individual's head. The current excites neural tissue, stimulating a seizure that lasts for approximately 1 minute.

ECT has been used for more than 40 years. In earlier years, it often was used indiscriminately, sometimes even as a punishment for patients. ECT is still used on as many as 60,000 individuals a year, mainly to treat major depression. Adverse side effects may include memory loss or other cognitive impairment. Today ECT is given mainly to individuals who have not responded to drug therapy or psychotherapy.

ECT sounds as if it would entail intolerable pain, but the manner in which it is administered today involves little discomfort. The patient is given anesthesia and muscle relaxants before the current is applied; this allows the individual to sleep through the procedure, it minimizes convulsions, and it reduces the risk of physical injury. The individual awakens shortly afterward with no conscious memory of the treatment.

The following example reveals how ECT, used as a last resort, can be effective in reducing depression (Sackheim, 1985). Carly is a 36-year-old teacher and mother. She has been in psychotherapy for several years. Prior to entering the hospital, she had taken tricyclics with unsuccessful results. In the first 6 months of her hospital stay, doctors tried various drugs to reduce her depression; none worked.

She slept poorly, lost her appetite, and showed no interest even in reading newspaper headlines. Obsessed with the idea that she had ruined her children's lives, she repeatedly threatened suicide. With her consent, doctors began ECT; after five treatments, Carly returned to her family and job. Not all cases of ECT turn out as positively, however; and even when ECT works, no one knows why it works (Kramer, 1987).

Psychosurgery

One biomedical treatment is even more extreme than ECT. **Psychosurgery** *is a biomedical therapy that involves the removal or destruction of brain tissue to improve the individual's psychological adjustment.* The effects of psychosurgery are irreversible.

In the 1930s, Portuguese physician Egas Moniz developed a procedure known as a *prefrontal lobotomy.* In this procedure, a surgical instrument is inserted into the brain and rotated, severing fibers that connect the frontal lobe, important in higher thought processes, and the thalamus, important in emotion. Moniz theorized that, by severing the connections between these brain structures, the symptoms of severe mental disorders could be alleviated. Prefrontal lobotomies were conducted on thousands of patients from the 1930s through the 1950s. Moniz was even awarded the Nobel Prize for his work. However, although some patients may have benefited from the lobotomies, many were left in vegetablelike states because of the massive assaults on their brains.

These crude lobotomies are no longer performed. Since the 1960s, psychosurgery has become more precise. When psychosurgery is now performed, a small lesion is made in the amygdala or another part of the limbic system. Today only several hundred patients per year undergo psychosurgery; it is used as a last resort and with extreme caution.

REVIEW

The Effectiveness of Psychotherapy and Biomedical Therapies

Psychotherapy in general is effective, but no single treatment is more effective than others. Behavioral therapies are often most successful in treating specific behavioral problems, such as phobias; cognitive therapy is often most successful in treating depression. Common themes in successful therapies include expectations, a sense of mastery, emotional arousal, and a confiding relationship. We still need to examine further which therapy works best with which individual in which setting with which therapist.

Historically the goal of therapy has been autonomy, but questions are raised about this as an ideal goal of therapy, especially for females. The goals of psychotherapy should include more attention to relatedness. Two nontraditional, gender-related forms of therapy are consciousness-raising groups and feminist therapy. Some feminist therapists distinguish between feminist therapy and nonsexist therapy. For too long, the needs of people from poor and ethnic minority backgrounds were ignored by psychotherapists. Among the barriers that impede psychotherapy's effectiveness with ethnic minority individuals are language differences, class-bound values, and culture-bound values. Credibility and giving are two important therapy processes with ethnic minority clients.

Biomedical therapies are designed to reduce or eliminate the symptoms of psychological disorders by altering the way an individual's body functions. Drug therapy is the most common biomedical therapy. Drug therapy may be effective when other therapies have failed, as in reducing the symptoms of schizophrenia. Three major classes of psychotherapeutic drugs are antianxiety, antipsychotic, and antidepressant. Phototherapy is often used with individuals who have seasonal affective disorder. Electroconvulsive therapy, commonly called "shock treatment," creates a seizure in the brain; its most common use is as a last resort in treating severe depression. Psychosurgery is an irreversible procedure; brain tissue is destroyed in an effort to improve psychological adjustment. Today's psychosurgery is more precise than the early prefrontal lobotomies. Psychosurgery is used only as a last resort.

One pill makes you larger,
And one pill makes you small.

Grace Slick

Lewis Carroll's *Alice in Wonderland* is often read as a whimsical metaphorical account of the adaptability that drugs can provide. When Alice was not tall enough to reach an opening, she drank a potion and magically grew to the required height. When she came upon another entrance that was too small for her giant frame, she drank another potion to shrink herself sufficiently.

Although science cannot produce the physical transformations described in Lewis Carroll's tale, many believe we are on the brink of a revolution in pharmacology that will produce mental health "designer drugs" not just to medicate the mentally disordered but to enhance the capacities of people with "normal" personalities. Once again, science may have made technological progress in areas where we have not fully considered the ethical and moral implications of implementing the technology.

Peter Kramer's depressed and anxious patients in *Listening to Prozac* are persuasive. They speak of feeling liberated from the edginess and depression that confused and confined them. They proclaim that they have discovered their true selves. They regret the span of their lives when they were without Prozac and wonder who they could have become if they had been able to be at their best throughout their lives.

However, the use of medication to enhance normal functioning is decidedly controversial. Many argue against the use of drugs to enhance normal function on religious grounds or because such interventions are "unnatural." Many believe philosophically that lives were meant to be lived fully, including feeling pain without the blunting caused by medication, in order to experience the full range of what life has to offer. Still others object on practical grounds. They express concern that we do not fully understand the long-term implications of using these drugs; they worry that there may be some serious bodily harms from long-term use that we simply have not had time to discover.

Those who advocate the development of mental health designer drugs view this technology as another step in helping humans adapt more effectively to their environments. For example, individuals who are born nearsighted use the technology of eyeglasses and contact lenses to compensate for their deficiencies and to adapt visually to their environments. People with chronic disease in our culture use any available technology to sustain life and promote a better quality of life. Advocates argue that designer drugs are a similar use of technology to adapt to ever worsening stress in contemporary life. They are optimistic that science will continue to produce cleaner and safer drugs for a variety of problems. They also suggest that society as a whole would benefit from citizens who are functioning closer to their maximum potential.

Where do you stand on the use of drugs to enhance normal functioning? If you had the opportunity legally to take a drug that would enhance your performance, would you? Or would you pass this opportunity by, regarding it as an example of human foolishness in trying to attain perfection using artificial methods? What personality characteristics or values undergird your position on designer drugs? Your position should reveal your ability to *identify values that influence behavior.*

The desire to take medicine is perhaps the greatest feature which distinguishes man from animals.

William Osler

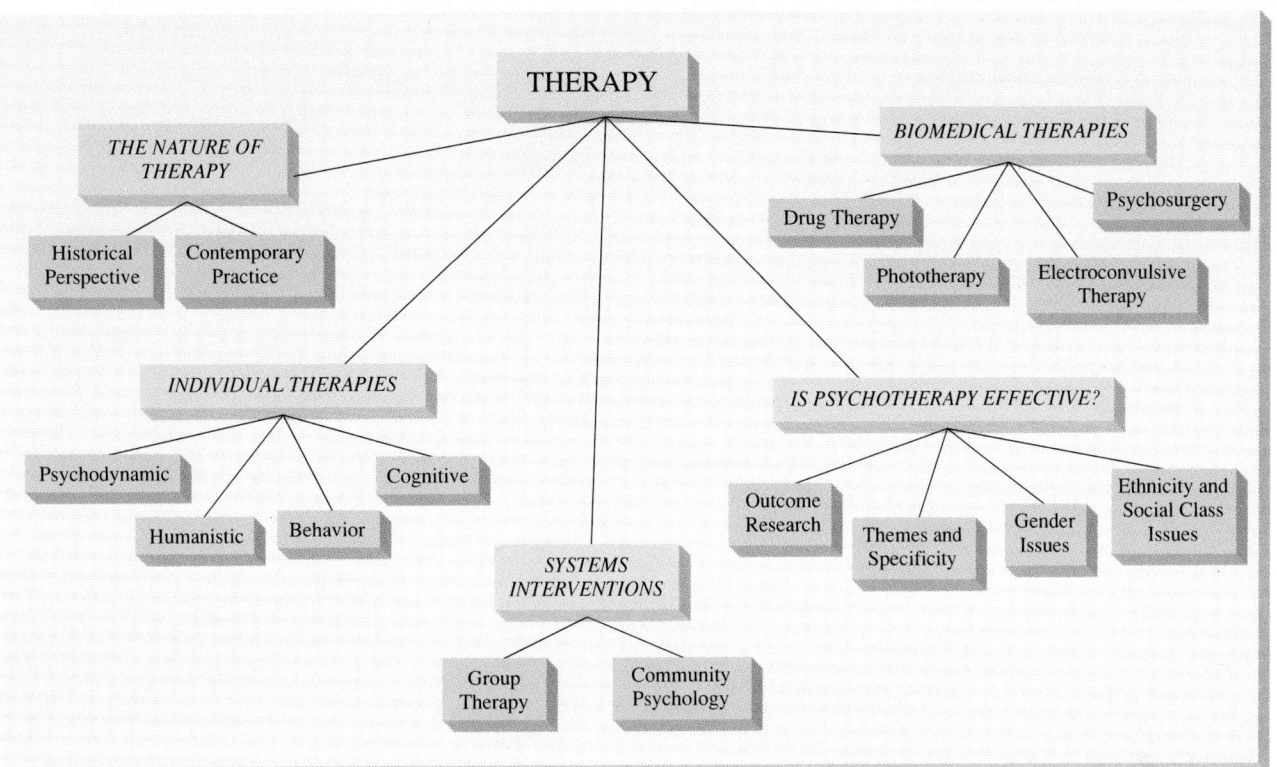

THERAPY

THE NATURE OF THERAPY

Historical Perspective

Contemporary Practice

INDIVIDUAL THERAPIES

Psychodynamic

Humanistic

Behavior

Cognitive

SYSTEMS INTERVENTIONS

Group Therapy

Community Psychology

BIOMEDICAL THERAPIES

Drug Therapy

Phototherapy

Electroconvulsive Therapy

Psychosurgery

IS PSYCHOTHERAPY EFFECTIVE?

Outcome Research

Themes and Specificity

Gender Issues

Ethnicity and Social Class Issues

W e began this chapter by exploring the nature of psychotherapy, both historically and in terms of contemporary practice. We spent considerable time examining the individual therapies—psychodynamic, humanistic, behavioral, and cognitive. Then we studied systems interventions—group therapy and community psychology. We read about whether therapy is effective, considering outcome research, themes and specificity, and gender, ethnicity, and social class issues. Our coverage of biomedical therapies focused on drug therapy, phototherapy, electroconvulsive therapy, and psychosurgery. Don't forget that you can obtain an overall summary of this chapter by again reading the in-chapter reviews on pages 619, 623, 629, 636, and 645.

All of the six main perspectives were emphasized in this chapter. The psychoanalytic perspective was covered in the discussion of psychodynamic therapies (pp. 620–622), the humanistic perspective in the material on humanistic therapies (pp. 622–623), the behavioral perspective in the section on behavior therapies (pp. 624–625), the cognitive perspective in the ideas about cognitive therapies (pp. 626–627), the sociocultural perspective in coverage of practitioners and settings (pp. 617–618), community psychology (pp. 633–634), therapy with African American families (p. 631), and development of community psychology approaches for Latino Americans (p. 635), and the neurobiological perspective in the material on biomedical therapies (pp. 642–645).

| Psychoanalytic |
| Humanistic |
| Behavioral |
| Cognitive |
| Sociocultural |
| Neurobiological |

KEY TERMS

trephining A procedure, no longer used, that involved chipping a hole in the skull to allow evil spirits to escape. 614

exorcism A religious rite used during the Middle Ages that was designed to remove evil spirits from a person; it involved prayer, starvation, beatings, and various forms of torture. 615

psychotherapy The process of working with individuals to reduce their emotional problems and improve their adjustment. 617

insight therapy Therapy that encourages insight into and awareness of oneself as the critical focus of therapy. 617

action therapy Therapy that promotes direct changes in behavior; insight is not essential for change to occur. 617

eclectic Using a variety of approaches. 617

managed health care A system in which external reviewers approve the type and length of treatment to justify insurance reimbursement. 619

psychodynamic therapies Therapies that stress the importance of the unconscious mind, extensive therapist interpretation, and the role of infant and early childhood experiences. 620

psychoanalysis Freud's therapeutic technique for analyzing an individual's unconscious thought. 620

free association The technique of encouraging individuals to say aloud whatever comes to mind, no matter how trivial or embarrassing. 620

catharsis The psychoanalytic term for clients' release of emotional tension when they relive an emotionally charged and conflicted experience. 620

dream analysis The psychotherapeutic technique psychoanalysts use to interpret a client's dream. Psychoanalysts believe that dreams contain information about the individual's unconscious thoughts and conflicts. 620

manifest content The psychoanalytic term for the conscious, remembered aspects of a dream. 620

latent content The psychoanalytic term for the unconscious, unremembered, symbolic aspects of a dream. 620

transference The psychoanalytic term for a client's relating to an analyst in ways that reproduce or relive important relationships in the client's life. 620

resistance The psychoanalytic term for a client's unconscious defense strategies that prevent the analyst from understanding the client's problems. 621

humanistic psychotherapies Therapies that encourage clients to understand themselves and to grow personally. In contrast to psychodynamic therapies, humanistic therapies emphasize conscious thoughts rather than unconscious thoughts, the present rather than the past, and growth and fulfillment rather than curing illness.   622

person-centered therapy   A form of humanistic therapy developed by Carl Rogers, in which the therapist provides a warm, supportive atmosphere to improve the client's self-concept and encourage the client to gain insight about problems.   622

genuineness   The Rogerian concept of the importance of the therapist's being genuine and not hiding behind a facade.   622

accurate empathy   Rogers's term for the therapist's ability to identify with the client.   622

active listening   Rogers's term for the ability to listen to another person with total attention to what the person says and means.   622

Gestalt therapy   A humanistic therapy developed by Fritz Perls, in which the therapist questions and challenges clients to help them become more aware of their feelings and face their problems.   622

behavior therapies   Therapies that use principles of learning to reduce or eliminate maladaptive behavior.   624

systematic desensitization   A method of behavior therapy that treats anxiety by associating deep relaxation with successive visualizations of increasingly intense anxiety-producing situations; this technique is based on classical conditioning.   624

aversive conditioning   An approach to behavior therapy that involves repeated pairings of an undesirable behavior with aversive stimuli to decrease the behavior's rewards so that the individual will stop doing it; this technique is based on classical conditioning.   625

token economy   A behavior modification system in which behaviors are reinforced with tokens (such as poker chips) that can be exchanged later for desired rewards (such as candy, money, or going to a movie).   625

cognitive therapies   Therapies that emphasize that an individual's cognitions, or thoughts, are the main source of abnormal behavior; cognitive therapies attempt to change the individual's feelings and behaviors by changing her or his cognitions.   626

self-efficacy   The belief that one can master a situation and produce positive outcomes.   626

self-instructional methods   Cognitive behavioral techniques aimed at teaching individuals to modify their own behavior.   626

rational-emotive therapy   Therapy based on Albert Ellis's assertion that people become psychologically disordered because of their beliefs, especially those that are irrational and self-defeating.   627

family therapy   Group therapy with family members.   630

couple therapy   Group therapy with married or unmarried couples whose major problem is their relationship.   630

family systems therapy   A form of therapy based on the assumption that psychological adjustment is related to patterns of interaction within the family unit.   630

personal growth groups   Groups that have their roots in the humanistic therapies; they emphasize personal growth and increased openness and honesty in interpersonal relations.   631

encounter group   A personal-growth group designed to promote self-understanding through candid group interaction.   631

self-help groups   Voluntary organizations of individuals who get together on a regular basis to discuss topics of common interest. The group leader and members give support to help individuals with their problems. Self-help groups are so-called because they are conducted without a professional therapist.   632

deinstitutionalization   The movement to transfer the treatment of mental disabilities from inpatient medical institutions to community-based facilities that stress outpatient care.   633

primary prevention   A community psychology concept, borrowed from the public health field, denoting efforts to reduce the number of new cases of mental disorders.   633

secondary prevention   A prevention method involving screening for early detection of problems and early intervention; a community psychology concept.   634

tertiary prevention   A community psychology concept denoting efforts to reduce the long-term consequences of mental health disorders that were not prevented or arrested early in the course of the disorders.   634

empowerment   Helping individuals develop skills they need to improve their adaptation and circumstances.   634

meta-analysis   A research strategy that involves statistically combining the results of many different studies.   636

consciousness-raising groups   Groups that are believed by some feminists to be an important alternative or adjunct to traditional therapy. They often involve several people meeting in a member's home, are frequently leaderless, and focus on members' feelings and self-perceptions. Instead of seeking and accepting male-biased therapy, women may meet in consciousness-raising groups to define their own experiences with their own criteria.   639

feminist therapies   Therapies that usually are based on a critique of society wherein women are perceived to have less political and economic power than men have. Also, feminist therapies assume that the reasons for women's problems are principally social, not personal.   639

nonsexist therapy   Therapy that occurs when the therapist has become aware of and primarily overcome his or her sexist attitudes and behavior.   639

credibility   A therapist's believability.   642

giving   The client's receiving some kind of benefit from treatment early in the therapy process.   642

biomedical therapies   Treatments to reduce or eliminate the symptoms of psychological disorders by altering the way an individual's body functions. Drug therapy is the most common form.   642

antianxiety drugs   Drugs that are commonly known as tranquilizers and reduce anxiety by making individuals less excitable and more tranquil.   642

antipsychotic drugs   Powerful drugs that diminish agitated behavior, reduce tension, decrease hallucinations and delusions, improve social behavior, and produce better sleep patterns in severely mentally disabled individuals, especially schizrenics.   643

tardive dyskinesia   A major side effect of the neuroleptic drugs; a neurological disorder characterized by grotesque, involuntary movements of the facial muscles and mouth, as well as extensive twitching of the neck, arms, and legs.   643

lithium   A drug that is widely used to treat bipolar disorder.   643

antidepressant drugs   Drugs that regulate mood. The three main classes of antidepressant drugs are tricyclics, such as Elavil; MAO inhibitors, such as Nardil; and SSRI inhibitors, such as Prozac.   643

seasonal affective disorder (SAD)   Depression that appears to be caused by seasonally shorter exposure to sunlight.   644

electroconvulsive therapy (ECT)   Commonly called shock treatment, a type of therapy sometimes used to treat severely depressed individuals by causing brain seizures similar to those caused by epilepsy.   644

psychosurgery   A biomedical therapy that involves the removal or destruction of brain tissue to improve the person's psychological adjustment.   645

THE CONSUMER'S GUIDE TO PSYCHOTHERAPY

(1992) by Jack Engler and Daniel Goleman. New York: Simon & Schuster.

This is a comprehensive manual on psychotherapy for consumers. Among the questions the authors ask and evaluate are these:

- How do I decide if I need therapy?
- Which therapy approach is best for me?
- How do I find the right therapist?
- What questions should I ask during the first session?
- How can I afford therapy?
- How can I tell if therapy is really working?
- How do I know when to end therapy?

The book is based on the clinical opinions of almost a thousand therapists nationwide. Included are case studies and listings of mental health organizations, as well as therapist referral sources.

FIVE THERAPISTS AND ONE CLIENT

(1991) by Raymond Corsini and Contributors. Itasca, IL: Peacock.

Therapists with five distinctive approaches to helping clients describe their conceptual orientation and therapy techniques and demonstrate how they would likely work with the same fictitious client. The imaginary client is a relatively normal individual with unusual and persistent problems—a common client for psychotherapists in private practice. Four clear-cut systems of psychotherapy were selected: Alfred Adler's individual therapy, Carl Rogers's person-centered therapy, Albert Ellis's rational-emotive therapy, and behavior therapy. Finally, a fifth therapy approach—eclectic therapy—was chosen. How therapists from these five different approaches would handle the same client serves as the core of the book, helping you to see distinctive ways therapists with different orientations conduct psychotherapy.

THE COMPLEAT THERAPIST

(1991) by Jeffrey Kottler. New York: Jossey-Bass.

Kottler reveals the techniques all good therapists have in common and combines the most effective healing therapies into one framework. Important characteristics include the therapist's personality, skillful thinking processes, communication skills, and intimate and trusting relationships. This book gives excellent insight into the characteristics of therapists that help clients improve regardless of the therapist's theoretical orientation.

COUNSELING AMERICAN MINORITIES

(4th ed.) (1993) by Donald Atkinson, George Morten, & Derald Sue. Dubuque, IA: Brown & Benchmark.

This book provides valuable information about counseling and psychotherapy with individuals from ethnic minority backgrounds. Entire sections are devoted to the American Indian client, the Asian American client, the African American client, and the Latino client. You also might want to read *Psychotherapy and Counseling With Minorities* (1991) by Manuel Ramirez (New York: Pergamon).

RESOURCES FOR PSYCHOLOGY AND IMPROVING HUMANKIND

Behavior Therapy
This journal publishes articles on a wide range of behavior therapy strategies and a number of fascinating case studies. Look through recent issues to learn how behavior therapy is conducted.

Canadian Centre for Stress and Well-Being
141 Adelaide St. West, Suite #1506
Toronto, ON M5H 3L5
416–363–6204

An educational and counseling center for individuals and corporations. They hold public seminars and teach the positive use of stress for personal and corporate well-being. They also distribute numerous publications, a self-help kit, and relaxation tapes.

Canadian Mental Health Association/Assocation canadienne pur la sante mentale
2160 Yonge St.
Toronto, ON M4S 2Z3
416–484–7750

CMHA goals are to promote mental health and to educate all people about mental health needs throughout Canada and around the world. Among their recent publications: *Diversity Works* (about reasonable accommodation in the workplace) and *Learning Diversity* (accommodation in educational settings) for people with serious mental health problems.

Current Psychotherapies (1989) (2nd ed.)
by Ray Corsini (Ed.)
Itasca, IL: Peacock

Therapists from various schools of psychotherapy describe their approaches.

Gestalt Therapy Verbatim (1969)
by Fritz Perls
Lafayette, CA: Real People Press

Fritz Perls, the founder of Gestalt therapy, lays out the main ideas of his approach in vivid detail.

Great Cases in Psychotherapy (1979)
by D. Wedding and R. Corsini
Itasca, IL: Peacock

A complete description of a number of well-known cases in psychotherapy, including clients of Sigmund Freud, Fritz Perls, Alfred Adler, Carl Jung, and Carl Rogers.

National Alliance of the Mentally Ill
2101 Wilson Road, Suite 302
Arlington, VA 22201
703–524–7600

This is an alliance of self-help/advocacy groups concerned with severe and chronically mentally disordered individuals. The objective is to provide emotional support and practical guidance to families. They have resource materials available and publish a monthly newsletter, *NAMI Advocate*.

National Council of Community Mental Health Centers
12300 Twinbrook Parkway, No. 320
Rockville, MD 20852
301–984–6200

This organization's goal is to improve the quality of community mental health care; its divisions include consultation, education, and prevention. Publications and other materials are available.

North American Society of Adlerian Psychology
202 S. State Street, Suite 1212
Chicago, IL 60604
312–939–0834

This organization involves mental health professionals and people interested in the therapy approach of Alfred Adler. It promotes the establishment of a family education association and parent study groups and publishes a monthly newsletter and a journal, *Individual Psychology*.

Social Psychology and Culture

Man is by nature a social animal.

Aristotle

We are biological and cognitive beings, but we also are social beings. Other people play important roles in our lives. Social psychologists study how we perceive other people and social situations, how we respond to other people and they to us, how we are influenced by social situations, and the influence of culture on social behavior. Section Eight contains two chapters: "Social Psychology" (chapter 18) and "Culture and Ethnicity" (chapter 19).

PAUL GAUGIN
The Market, detail

Social Psychology

> Our concern is not how to worship in
> the catacombs but how to remain
> human in the skyscrapers.
>
> **Abraham J. Heschel**

THE STORY OF DAVID KORESH: CHARISMATIC SADIST OR TRUE BELIEVER?

I ronically, *charismatic* and *combustible* were two terms *Time* magazine used to characterize cult leader David Koresh in the days before his Waco, Texas, compound exploded on April 19, 1993, killing himself and many of his followers. Born Vernon Howell in Houston, he dropped out of the ninth grade but found great comfort in the teachings of an offshoot of the Seventh-Day Adventist Church, the Branch Davidians. He joined an existing congregation in Waco and rose to its leadership, changing his name to David Koresh in 1990. Actively recruiting new members from the United States, Britain, and Australia, he transformed the congregation into a cult based on apocalyptic theology and secular survivalism; they stockpiled food and ammunition to prepare for the end of the world through nuclear or social catastrophe.

Koresh's charisma allowed him to impose on his followers all manner of sacrifices that he decreed did not apply to him. Members donated their assets and paychecks to cover the expenses of the compound. Men worked hard at construction while women attended the house and provided education for the children. Members were fed with strict rations of vegetables, although Koresh instituted dietary changes on some days without explanation. In contrast, Koresh had access to the things that were forbidden to the members, such as meat, beer, and television. Men were required to be

celibate. Women were to be available to Koresh as "wives." Koresh was charged with child sexual abuse several times for his preferences for young brides, but he had never been convicted. Those who left the cult described Koresh as a zealous, imaginative preacher, offering sermons that extended long into the night with scriptural interpretations that inexplicably varied from one sermon to the next. He paddled and humiliated rule breakers; when paddlings didn't produce compliance, Koresh ordered the rule breakers to lie down in raw sewage and refused to let them bathe afterward. His blend of physical force, psychological and physical sadism, and personal magnetism became a deadly combination in the context of the challenge to his rights by the Justice Department.

Janet Reno had been on her job as the attorney general of the Justice Department for only about a month when the Bureau of Alcohol, Tobacco, and Firearms proposed a plan for its second assault on "Ranch Apocalypse," Koresh's Waco compound. The original assault had been mounted because the ATF believed that Koresh was holding cult members hostage and stockpiling ammunition, including machine guns, hand grenades, and radio-controlled aircrafts to carry explosives. The ATF's first assault, on February 28, went badly; four ATF agents were killed and sixteen were wounded. As many as ten cult members were

David Koresh

reported dead as well, including one of Koresh's many children. Fifty-one days later, the ATF's second assault began with tear gas, designed to force the members out of the compound. Instead of surrender, the ATF encountered explosions, and raging fire developed, racing through the compound fueled by stacks of Bibles and wooden benches. This time an estimated 25 children and 60 adults, including Koresh, died in the fire.

In the end, no one knew for certain what had caused the fire, whether it was part of a massive suicide plan on the part of Koresh and his followers, whether the ATF began the fire, or whether the fire had started by accident. One thing that was certain was that the assault had been a mistake. Reno courageously assumed the blame for an operation under her leadership that had proved far more devastating than anticipated. At least for Koresh and his followers, his predictions of a holocaust had come true.

The horrifying story of David Koresh introduces many of the themes that we will explore in this chapter. For example, what attracts us to individuals or the religious philosophies they espouse? What makes us pursue some relationships and abandon others? How do we function in interpersonal and group relationships? What makes leadership influential and what makes it fail? How do organizations, whether the religious organization of the Branch Davidians or the professional organization of the Justice Department, facilitate or hinder effective social behavior? We will also examine the values that influence social judgment.

SOCIAL COGNITION

As we interact with our world, we are both actors and spectators, doing and perceiving, acting and thinking. Social psychologists are interested in how we perceive our social world and how we try to make sense of our own behavior and the behavior of others. They are also interested in how we form and change our attitudes. We will begin the study of social cognition by exploring the nature of social perception.

Social Perception

Social perception *is our judgment about the qualities of individuals, which involves how we form impressions of others, how we gain self-knowledge from our perception of others, and how we present ourselves to others to influence their perceptions of us.*

Impression Formation

Our evaluations of people often fall into broad categories—good or bad, happy or sad, introvert or extrovert, for example. If someone asked for your impression of your psychology professor, you might respond, "She is great." Then you might go on to describe your perception of her characteristics—for example, "She is charming, intelligent, witty, and sociable." These opinions represent inferences you make from the samples of her behavior you experience directly. From this description we can also infer that you have a positive impression of her.

As we form impressions of others, we cognitively organize the information in two important ways. First, our impressions are *unified,* and second, our impressions are *integrated.* Traits, actions, appearance, and all of the other information we obtain about a person are closely connected in memory, even though the information may have been obtained in an interrupted or random fashion. We might obtain some information today, more next week, some more in 2 months. During those 2 months, we interacted with many other people and developed impressions of them as well. Nonetheless, we usually perceive the information about a particular person as unified, as a continuous block of information.

Our first encounter with someone also contributes to the impression we form. First impressions are often enduring. **Primacy effect** *is the term used for the enduring quality of initial impressions.* One reason for the primacy effect is that we pay less attention to subsequent information about the individual (Anderson, 1965). The next time you want to impress someone, a wise strategy is to make sure that you put your best foot forward in your first encounter.

Social Comparison

How many times have you asked yourself questions such as "Am I as smart as Jill?" "Is Bob better looking than I am?" or "Is my taste as good as Carmen's?" We gain self-knowledge from our own behavior; we also gain it from others through **social comparison,** *the process in which individuals evaluate their thoughts, feelings, behaviors, and abilities in relation to other people. Social comparison helps individuals to evaluate themselves, tells them what their distinctive characteristics are, and aids them in building an identity.*

Some years ago Leon Festinger (1954) proposed a theory of social comparison. He stressed that when no objective means is available to evaluate our opinions and abilities, we compare ourselves with others. Festinger believed that we are more likely to compare ourselves with others who are similar to us than with those who are dissimilar to us. He reasoned that if we compare ourselves with someone who is very different from us, we will not be able to obtain an accurate appraisal of our own behavior and thoughts. This means that we will develop more accurate self-perceptions if we compare ourselves with people in communities similar to where we grew up and live, with people who have similar family backgrounds, and with people of the same sex, for example. Social comparison theory has been extended and modified over the years and continues to provide an important rationale for why we affiliate with others and how we come to know ourselves (Kenrick & others, 1993).

In contrast to Festinger's emphasis on the role of social comparison in evaluating one's abilities, recently researchers have focused more on the self-enhancing properties of downward comparisons (Banaji & Prentice, 1994; Wood, 1989). Individuals under threat (negative feed-

"Randall, my old college nemesis, I was hoping I'd find you here."

back, low self-esteem, depression, and illness, for example) try to improve their well-being by comparing themselves with someone less fortunate (Buunk & others, 1990; Gibbons & McCoy, 1991; Pelham, 1991; Smith & Insko, 1987).

Impression Management

How do you present yourself to others? Do you try to act naturally and be yourself, or do you deliberately change your behavior to get other people to have a more favorable impression of you? **Impression management** *is the process in which individuals strive to present themselves in a favorable light.* When we present ourselves to others, we usually try to make ourselves look better than we really are. Collectively we spend billions of dollars rearranging our faces, our bodies, our minds, and our social skills. Some of the money is spent so we will feel good about ourselves regardless of what others think; some is spent so that others will form a more favorable impression of us.

In situations where you want to influence the impressions you make on others, how can you go about doing this? Four recommended "impression-management" strategies follow:

1. *Use behavioral matching.* This simply means doing what the other person is doing. When you are with a modest person, behave in a modest way. When you are with a carefree person, behave in a carefree way.
2. *Conform to expectations in the situation.* Don't show up barefoot in your professor's office—save that look for the beach or frat house. Don't play a radio in the library, and don't read at a party.
3. *Show appreciation of others and make favorable comments about them.* People like to be complimented. Look for something good to say about the person you are communicating with, such as "I really like your watch. Where did you find it?"
4. *Use positive nonverbal cues.* We not only can influence what others think of us by our words but also by a number of nonverbal cues.

Keep in mind, though, that impression management techniques that work in one cultural setting may not work in another. In particular, appreciation and flattery are often culture-bound. For example, in some Eastern European countries, if one person expresses great admiration for another's watch, courtesy dictates that the watch should be given to the admirer! In the Native American culture of the Sioux, it's considered courteous to open a conversation with a compliment. Nonverbal cues also vary considerably from culture to culture. For example, the sign made by holding three fingers up with thumb and finger circled has a meaning in the West that is very different from its meaning in Japan, where the signal symbolizes money, and in South America, where it issues a sexual invitation (Keating, 1994).

In seeking better ways to present ourselves to others, it helps to know the causes of an individual's behavior. In our effort to find out the causes of people's behavior, we make attributions about the behavior.

Attribution

Attribution theorists argue that we want to know why people do the things they do because the knowledge will enable us to cope more effectively with the situations that confront us. **Attribution theory** *states that individuals are motivated to discover the underlying causes of behavior as part of their interest in making sense out of the behavior.* In a way, attribution theorists say people are much like intuitive scientists, seeking the reason something happens.

We can classify the reasons individuals behave the way they do in a number of ways, but one basic distinction stands out above all the others—the distinction between *internal* causes, such as the actor's personality traits or motives, and *external* causes, which are environmental, situational factors (Heider, 1958). If you don't do well on a test, do you attribute it to the professor's having plotted against you and made the test too difficult (external cause) or to your not having studied hard enough (internal cause)? The answer to such a question influences how we feel about ourselves. If we believe our poor performance is the professor's fault (he gives unfair tests, for example), we don't feel as bad as when we do not spend enough time studying: By using an external attribution, we place the blame somewhere other than on ourselves.

Our attributions are not always accurate. In a given situation the person who acts, or the actor, produces the behavior to be explained. Then the onlooker, or the observer, offers a causal explanation of the actor's behavior or experience. Actors often explain their own behavior with external causes, while observers often explain the actor's behavior with internal causes. The **fundamental attribution error** *is that observers overestimate the importance of traits and underestimate the importance of situations when they seek explanations of an actor's behavior* (Ross, 1977). On the other hand, actors rely more on situations than they do on traits in explaining their own behavior. Actors often show a self-serving bias in explaining their actions by shifting blame to external forces. This difference in attribution style is referred to as the **actor-observer hypothesis,** *the hypothesis that differences in*

Example: The employee left out an entire column of data in her data entry task.

ACTOR (Employee)	OBSERVER (Employer)
More likely to give external, situational explanations of own behavior	More likely to give internal, trait explanations of actor's behavior
"It's too noisy in here to concentrate."	"You're really rushing and not being careful."

FIGURE 18.1

The Actor-Observer Hypothesis
In this situation, the two supervisors are the observers and the employee is the actor *(top middle of the photograph)*. If the employee has made an error in her work, how are the employee and her supervisors likely to give different explanations of her behavior, based on your knowledge of actor-observer differences and the fundamental attribution error?

interpretations of motives are based on points of view. For example, you observe a classmate verbally stumble when called upon by the teacher. As the observer, you might be inclined to explain her difficulty as internally caused by her being "slow" or confused. She, as actor, might link her attribution to the external cause of having stayed out too late the night before. This justification helps her feel less bad about her embarrassing public performance. On the other hand, she could shift the attribution to her "mean" teacher (internal attribution about the observed), who posed questions that were unfair (an external cause for her to stumble). Since actors and observers often have different ideas about what causes behavior, many attributions are biased. Behavior is determined by a number of factors, so it is not surprising that our lives are full of squabbling and arguing about the causes of behavior. Attribution theory provides us with a more informed perspective on disagreements in marriages, the courts, the Senate, and many other social arenas (Harvey, 1995). See figure 18.1 for an illustration of how the actor-observer hypothesis works in job-related contexts.

Attitudes and Behavior

As Mark Twain said, "It is a difference of opinion that makes horses race." **Attitudes** *are beliefs and opinions that can predispose individuals to behave in certain ways.* We have attitudes about all sorts of things, and we live in a world in which we try to influence each other's attitudes.

In a civilized society we all depend upon each other, and our happiness results from the good opinion of mankind.

Samuel Johnson

Think about your attitudes toward religion, politics, and sex. Now think about your behavior in these areas. Consider sex, for example. How liberal or conservative are your sexual attitudes? Does your behavior match your attitudes? Researchers have found that we have more accepting attitudes toward sexual practices than our behavior actually shows (Dreyer, 1982). As we study the relation of attitudes to behavior, two questions arise: How strongly do attitudes influence behavior? How strongly does behavior influence attitudes?

The fundamental attribution error is tricky. The concept explains why two individuals can live through one situation and not report the same experience.

For example, suppose the person who sits next to you in class is never on time. He comes in late consistently and makes lots of noise moving to his seat. How would you (the observer) explain his behavior? How would he (the actor) explain his own behavior?

Now suppose you are late to class. How would you, as the actor, explain this lapse? What value differences are likely to separate the explanations of the actor and the observer? Your conclusions will illustrate your *awareness of underlying values that motivate behavior,* in this case the assignment of a self-protec-

tive or dismissive attribution. You might even find yourself hesitating before you judge the motives of others, in order to minimize your own fundamental attribution errors.

Predicting Behavior from Attitudes

More than 50 years ago, Richard LaPiere (1934) toured the United States with a Chinese couple. LaPiere expected to encounter prejudice against the Asians. He thought they would be banned from restaurants and hotels, for example. Surprisingly, in more than 10,000 miles of travel, the threesome was rejected only once. It appeared, LaPiere thought, that there were few negative attitudes toward Asians in the Untied States. To see if this actually was the case, LaPiere wrote a letter to all 251 places he and his Asian friends had visited, asking the proprietors if they would provide food or lodging to Asians. More than half responded; of those, a resounding 90 percent said they absolutely would not allow Asians in their restaurant or motel. LaPiere's study documented a powerful lesson in understanding human behavior: what we *say* may be different from what we *do*.

The connection between attitudes and behaviors may vary with the situation. In the study of attitudes toward Asians in the 1930s, the Chinese who accompanied LaPiere were well dressed and carried expensive luggage; they might have inspired different attitudes if they had appeared in cheaper attire or if they had not been traveling in the company of a European male. To consider further situational influences on attitude-behavior connections, imagine asking someone about his attitude toward people who drive pickup trucks. Let's say he responds, "Totally classless." A month later the guy stops for a cup of coffee in a small West Texas town. A burly man in the next booth is talking with his buddies about the merits of pickup trucks. He turns to our

friend and asks, "How do you like that green pickup truck sitting outside?" Needless to say, his response is not "totally classless." This example suggests that the demands of the situation can be powerful even when we hold strong beliefs. This is an important point that social psychologists refer to throughout their work on explaining social behavior.

Behavior's Influence on Attitudes

"The actions of men are the best interpreters of their thoughts," asserted seventeenth-century English philosopher John Locke. Does doing change your believing? If you quit drinking, will you have a more negative attitude toward drinking? If you take up an exercise program, are you more likely to extol the benefits of cardiovascular fitness when someone asks your attitude about exercise?

Changes in behavior can precede changes in attitudes (Bandura, 1989). Social psychologists offer two main explanations of behavior's influence on attitudes. The first is that people have a strong need for cognitive consistency; consequently, they might change their attitudes to make them more consistent with their behavior. The second is that our attitudes often are not completely clear, so we observe our behavior and make inferences about it to determine what our attitudes should be. Let's consider these two views in more detail.

Festinger's Cognitive Dissonance Theory

Cognitive dissonance, *a concept developed by social psychologist Leon Festinger (1957), refers to an individual's motivation*

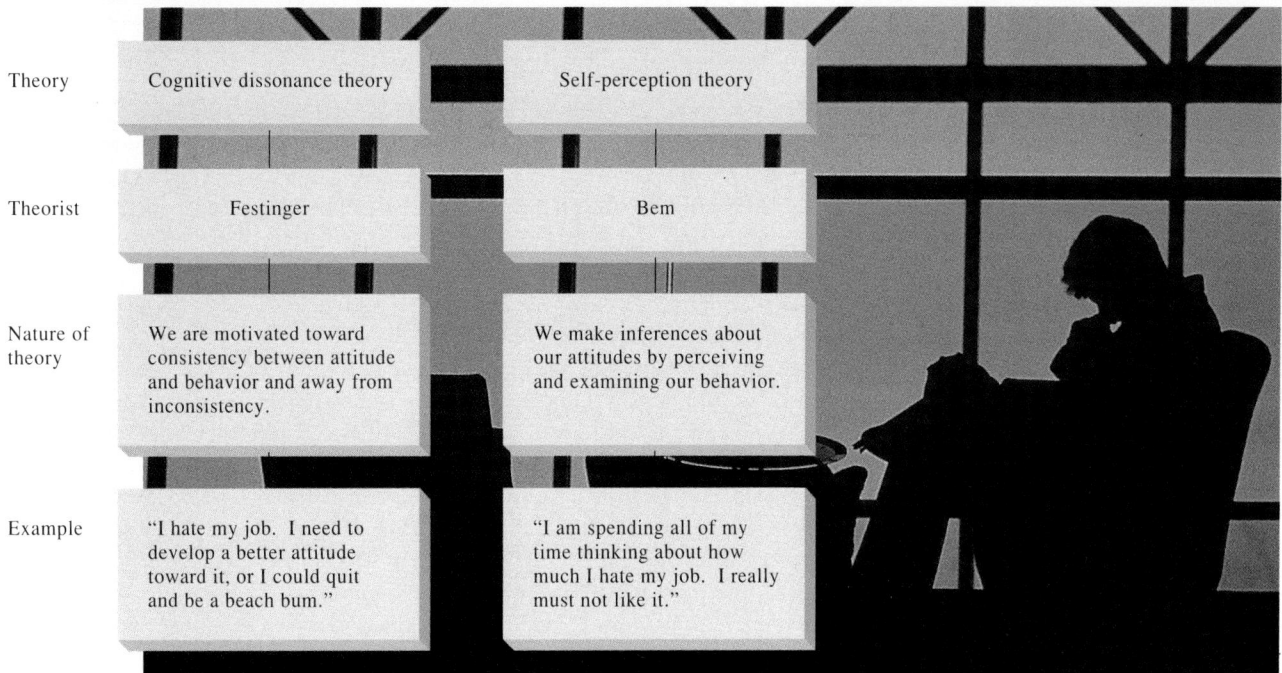

	Cognitive dissonance theory	Self-perception theory
Theory	Cognitive dissonance theory	Self-perception theory
Theorist	Festinger	Bem
Nature of theory	We are motivated toward consistency between attitude and behavior and away from inconsistency.	We make inferences about our attitudes by perceiving and examining our behavior.
Example	"I hate my job. I need to develop a better attitude toward it, or I could quit and be a beach bum."	"I am spending all of my time thinking about how much I hate my job. I really must not like it."

FIGURE 18.2

Two Views of Behavior's Influence on Attitudes

to reduce the discomfort (dissonance) caused by two inconsistent thoughts. For example, we might feel uneasy about a discrepancy that exists between our attitudes and our behavior. The absence of internal justification for the difference between what we believe and what we do creates dissonance. We can engage in a variety of actions to reduce the dissonance. Imagine a circumstance in which you do something you do not feel good about, such as flunking a test. You might reduce the dissonance by devaluing the test or accusing the teacher of unfair testing practices. You might drop the course, deciding it was no longer important for your future. All these actions reduce dissonance. We often justify our behavior, as George Bernard Shaw did with his father's alcoholism: "If you cannot get rid of the family skeleton, you may as well make it dance." Shaw's justification helped him reduce the tension between his father's drinking problem and his attitude about it. Cognitive dissonance is about making our skeletons dance, about trying to reduce tension by cognitively justifying things that are unpleasant (Aronson, 1992).

Bem's Self-perception Theory Not all social psychologists, however, are satisfied with cognitive dissonance as an explanation for the influence of behavior on attitudes.

Daryl Bem, for example, believes that the cognitive dissonance view relies too heavily on internal factors, which are difficult to measure. Bem (1967) argues that we should move away from such nebulous concepts as "cognitions" and "psychological discomfort" and replace them with more behavioral terminology. **Self-perception theory** *is Bem's theory of the attitude-behavior connection; it stresses that individuals make inferences about their attitudes by perceiving their behavior.* For example, consider the remark "I am spending all of my time thinking about the test I have next week; I must be anxious," or "This is the third time I have gone to the student union in 2 days; I must be lonely." Bem believes we look to our own behavior when our attitudes are not completely clear. This means that when we have clear ideas about something, we are less likely to look to our behavior for clues about our attitudes; however, if we feel ambivalent about something or someone, our behavior is a good place to look to determine our attitude. Figure 18.2 compares cognitive dissonance and self-perception theories.

We have just explored how social cognitions help us to perceive ourselves and others and to form attitudes. Next we will examine the nature of interpersonal relationships.

Three important dimensions of social perception are developing impressions of others, making social comparisons, and presenting ourselves to others to influence their social perceptions. Our impressions are unified. First impressions are important and influence impressions at a later point. We evaluate ourselves by comparison with others. Festinger stressed that social comparison provides an important source of self-knowledge, especially when no other objective means is available; we are more likely to compare ourselves with others who are similar. We usually try to make ourselves look better than we really are. Four recommended impression management strategies are to (1) use behavioral matching, (2) conform to situational norms, (3) show appreciation of others and flatter them, and (4) use positive nonverbal cues.

Attribution focuses on the motivation to infer causes of behavior in order to make sense out of the world. One of the most frequent and important ways we classify the causes of behavior is in terms of internal and external causes. Our attributions are not always accurate; the human mind has a built-in bias in making causal judgments. The fundamental attribution error involves overestimating the importance of traits and internal causes while underestimating the importance of situations and external causes. Actors are more likely to choose external causes, observers internal causes. The observer may be in greater error. Attitudes are beliefs and opinions. Social psychologists are interested in how strongly attitudes predict behavior. Today it is believed that, when situational influences are weak, the attitude-behavior connection is strengthened. Cognitive dissonance theory, developed by Festinger, argues that, because we have a strong need for cognitive consistency, we change our attitudes to make them more consistent with our behavior so that dissonance is reduced. Bem developed a more behavioral approach, called self-perception theory; it stresses the importance of making inferences about our own behavior, especially when our attitudes are not clear.

INTERPERSONAL RELATIONSHIPS

No love, no friendship can cross the path of our destiny without leaving some mark on it forever.

François Mauriac

Social psychologists have long been fascinated by the social cognitions, affect, and behaviors that comprise interpersonal relationships. What factors make one person physically attractive while others fail to make an impression? How do some relationships move from casual acquaintances to deep friendship? What do we really know about love and loneliness? What causes one person to offer help to another, especially when they don't even know each other? We will address each of these questions in turn as we examine interpersonal relations.

Attraction

Birds of a feather do indeed flock together. *Familiarity,* having spent time together or in close proximity, is an essential condition for a close relationship to develop. Usually friends and lovers have been around each other for a long time; they may have grown up together, gone to high school or college together, worked together, or gone to the same social events. Once we have been exposed to someone for a period of time, what is it that makes the relationship breed friendship and even love?

One of the strongest lessons from studies of close relationships is the importance of *similarity,* sharing preferences and outlooks. Our friends, as well as our lovers, are much more like us than unlike us. We and the people we are closely involved with have similar attitudes, behaviors, and other characteristics, such as taste in clothes, intelligence, personality, political attitudes, other friends, values, lifestyle, physical attractiveness, and so on.

Consensual validation *provides an explanation of why people are attracted to others who are similar to them. Our own attitudes and behavior are supported when someone else's attitudes and behavior are similar to ours—their attitudes and behavior validate ours.* People tend to shy away from the unknown. We may tend, instead, to prefer people whose attitudes and behavior we can predict. And similarity implies that we will enjoy doing things with the other person, which often requires a partner who likes the same things and has similar attitudes.

How important is *physical attraction* as a factor in promoting an interpersonal relationship? Many advertising agencies would have us believe it is the most important factor in establishing and maintaining a relationship. However, heterosexual men and women differ on the importance they place on good looks when they seek an intimate partner. Women tend to rate as most important such traits as considerateness, honesty, dependability, kindness, and understanding; men prefer good looks, cooking skills, and frugality (Buss & Barnes, 1986). Attractive men tend to initiate contacts with women more than less attractive men

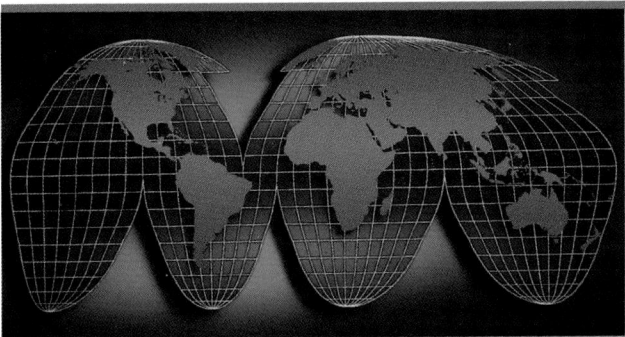

Mate Selection Around the World

Are there universal criteria for attractiveness in a mate? Many scholars believed that anthropologists can "do no more than point to the dazzling array of characteristics that various people in various places at various times have idealized" in the search for universal attractiveness criteria (Hatfield & Sprecher, 1986, p. 12). Some cross-cultural psychologists believe there are some aspects of attractiveness that are consistent across cultures despite the variations in preferences that occur in different contexts.

David Buss (1994), an expert on international mating strategies, conducted an ambitious cross-cultural study involving fifty other scientists who examined mate preferences in thirty-seven cultures. He found surprising uniformity among the most desirable characteristics for a partner. Using both rating and ranking systems, Buss discovered the following common preferences among all the cultures represented in the study: kindness and understanding, intelligence, good health, emotional stability and maturity, dependability, and a pleasing disposition.

The importance of love as a cross-cultural preference also surprised the researchers. Many scientists have regarded love as a Western value that emerged only a few centuries ago; but Chinese, Nigerians, Iranians, Indonesians, and Palestinians all identified mutual attraction and love as a desirable characteristic. Buss concluded that the concept of love is not as culture-bound as social scientists formerly assumed.

Although Buss found striking commonalities in the cross-cultural study, the research also demonstrated significant differences in values among cultures. Chief among these differences was the value placed on **chastity,** *inexperience with sexual intercourse.* On one end of the continuum were the Netherlands, Sweden, and Norway, where chastity is not regarded as particularly valuable. Some participants even wrote on the questionnaire that it was not helpful to have an inexperienced partner as a potential mate. On the other end, people from Taiwan, Indian, China, and Iran described chastity as essential. Other countries placed moderate value on chastity.

Participants rated some other characteristics unequally in different cultures. Some examples reveal contrasting values that operate in mate selection. Estonians and Chinese highly prize being a good housekeeper, Iranians prize religiosity, and neither characteristic appears to have much value in North America and Western Europe, according to their ratings and rankings. Neatness was little valued in Great Britain, Ireland, and Australia, but highly rated in Nigeria and Iran. Buss emphasized that the differences reported between cultures should not be interpreted to imply uniformity within each culture.

do. Women's physical attractiveness is not a determining factor in their involvement with men, for two reasons. Men are likely to pursue women who they feel will accept them and attractive women, who may worry that men want them only for their looks, are less trusting of men (Lips, 1988). To read about the criteria for physical attractiveness in different cultures, turn to Sociocultural Worlds 18.1.

One outcome of a desire for self-knowledge is that people tend to choose interaction partners who see them as they see themselves. In a series of studies, people used two general strategies to self-verify: (1) they created environments that confirmed their self-views, primarily by choosing appropriate interaction partners, and (2) they interpreted and remembered their interactions as confirming their self-views (Swann, 1987; Swann, Stein-Seroussi, & Giesler, 1992). The inclination to choose interaction partners who confirm one's self-views is likely rooted in a desire to maintain perceptions of predictability and control.

Physical attractiveness appears to play a role in partner selection in all cultures. For example, one classic, early study found that health, feminine plumpness, and cleanliness were the criteria for feminine attractiveness in a wide range of cultures (Ford & Beach, 1951). Being overweight remains a sign of female beauty in most underdeveloped countries; however, plumpness is no longer an indicator of health in economically developed countries. Emaciated looks continue to indicate ill health and are evaluated as less attractive in both modern and more traditional cultures.

However, the criteria for beauty may differ, not just *across* cultures, but over time *within* cultures as well (Lamb & others, 1993). In the 1940s, the ideal female beauty in the United States was typified by the well-rounded figure of Marilyn Monroe. As a result of the American preoccupation with health, Monroe's 135 pound, 5-foot-5-inch physique would be regarded as overweight by today's standards. In the 1980s and 1990s, the ideal physique for both men and women is neither pleasingly plump nor extremely slender.

The force of similarity also operates at a physical level. Most of us can't have Cindy Crawford or Denzel Washington as a friend or lover; how do we deal with this limitation? We usually seek out someone at our own level of attractiveness in both physical characteristics and social attributes. Most of us come away with a reasonably good chance of finding a "good match." Research indicates that this **matching hypothesis**—*that while we may prefer a more attractive person in the abstract, in the real world we end up choosing someone who is close to our own level of attractiveness*—holds up (Kalick & Hamilton, 1986).

Several additional points help to clarify the role of physical beauty and attraction in our close relationships. Much of the research has focused on initial or short-term encounters; researchers have not often evaluated attraction over the course of months and years. As relationships endure, physical attraction probably assumes less importance. Rocky Dennis, as portrayed in the movie *Mask,* is a case in point. His peers and even his mother initially wanted to avoid Rocky, whose face was severely distorted, but over the course of his childhood and adolescent years, the avoidance turned into attraction and love as people got to know him. As Rocky's story demonstrates, familiarity can overcome even severe initial negative reactions to a person.

Ask a toad what is beauty . . . he will answer that it is a female with two great round eyes coming out of her little head, a large flat mouth, a yellow belly and a brown back.

Voltaire, *Philosophical Dictionary,* 1764

Once attraction initiates a relationship, other opportunities exist to deepen the relationship to friendship and love. We begin with friendship.

Friendship

One friend in life is much, two are many, and three hardly possible.

Henry Adams

As suggested by Henry Adams, true friendship is hard to come by. **Friendship** *is a form of close relationship that involves enjoyment, acceptance, trust, intimacy, respect, mutual assistance, understanding, and spontaneity.* We like to spend time with our friends, and we accept their friendship without trying to change them. We assume our friends will act in our best interest and believe that they make good judgments. We help and support our friends and they return the assistance. When we share experiences and deep personal matters with a friend, we believe that the friend will understand our

Friendships are an important dimension of our close relationships. *What are the common characteristics of friendship?*

perspective. We feel free to be ourselves around our friends (Davis, 1985). One study of more than 40,000 individuals revealed that many of these characteristics are considered the qualities of a best friend (Parlee, 1979).

And, although it has been proposed that males treat friendships in terms of respect, females in terms of affection (Tannen, 1990), tests of this difference have not always held up (Gaines, 1994).

Gender plays a role in self-disclosure and friendships (Darlega & others, 1994). These gender differences appear in same-sex friendships and the miscommunications between men and women in close relationships. Women tend to hone their self-disclosure skills and learn to trust the relationship-enhancing qualities of self-disclosure in their same-sex peer/friendship relationships. In peer/friendship relationships that emphasize competition and challenge, males often avoid revealing weaknesses and at times associate self-disclosure with loss of control and with vulnerability. Thus, females and males not only reveal different preferences for and patterns of self-disclosure but also interpret the meaning and purpose of self-disclosure differently.

Romantic or Passionate Love

Romantic love *is also called passionate love or Eros; it has strong components of sexuality and infatuation, and it often predominates in the early part of a love relationship.* Poets, playwrights, and musicians through the ages have lauded the fiery passion of romantic love—and lamented the searing pain when it fails. Think for a moment about songs and books that hit the top of the charts. Chances are they're about love. Well-known love researcher Ellen Bersheid (1988) says that it is romantic love we mean when we say that we are "in love" with someone. It is romantic love she believes we need to understand if we are to learn what love is all about. To assess your experience with passionate love, turn to table 18.1.

In our culture, romantic love is the main reason we get married. In 1967, a famous study showed that men maintained that they would not get married if they were not

---

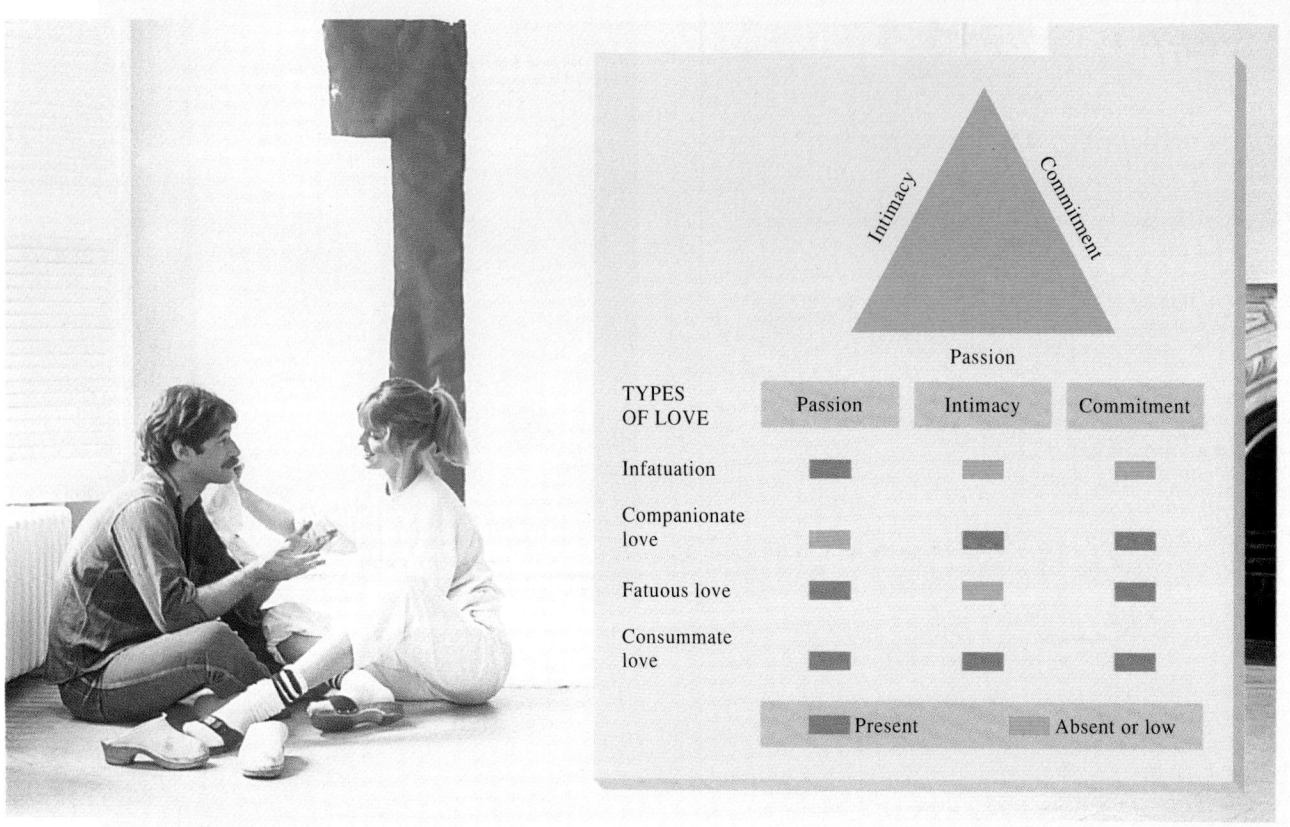

FIGURE 18.3

Sternberg's Triangle of Love
Sternberg identified three dimensions that shape the experience we call love. He distinguished different types of love in which these dimensions vary. *Which types would you say that you have experienced?*

Affectionate or Companionate Love

Love is more than just passion. **Affectionate love,** *also called companionate love, is the type of love that occurs when individuals desire to have the other person near and have a deep, caring affection for the person.*

There is a growing belief that the early stages of love have more romantic ingredients, but as love matures, passion tends to give way to affection. Phillip Shaver (1986) describes the initial phase of romantic love as a time that is fueled by a mixture of sexual attraction and gratification, a reduced sense of loneliness, uncertainty about the security of developing another attachment, and excitement from exploring the novelty of another human being. With time, he says, sexual attraction wanes, attachment anxieties either lessen or produce conflict and withdrawal, novelty is replaced with familiarity, and lovers either find themselves securely attached in a deeply caring relationship or distressed—feeling bored, disappointed, lonely, or hostile, for example. In the latter case, one or both partners may eventually seek another close relationship.

When two lovers go beyond their preoccupation with novelty, unpredictability, and the urgency of sexual attrac-

tion, they are more likely to detect deficiencies in each other's caring. This may be the point in a relationship when women, who often are better caregivers than men, sense that the relationship has problems. Wives are almost twice as likely as husbands to initiate a divorce, for example (National Center for Health Statistics, 1989).

So far we have discussed two forms of love: romantic (or passionate) and affectionate (or companionate). Robert J. Sternberg (1988) described a third form of love, consummate love, which he said is the strongest, fullest type of love. Sternberg proposed the **triangular theory of love:** *that love includes three dimensions—passion, intimacy, and commitment* (see figure 18.3). Couples must share all three dimensions to experience consummate love.

Passion, as described earlier, is physical and sexual attraction to another. Intimacy is the emotional feelings of warmth, closeness, and sharing in a relationship. Commitment is our cognitive appraisal of the relationship and our intent to maintain the relationship even in the face of problems. If passion is the only ingredient (with intimacy and commitment low or absent), we are merely *infatuated.* This might happen in an affair or a fling in which there is little intimacy and even less commitment. A relationship marked

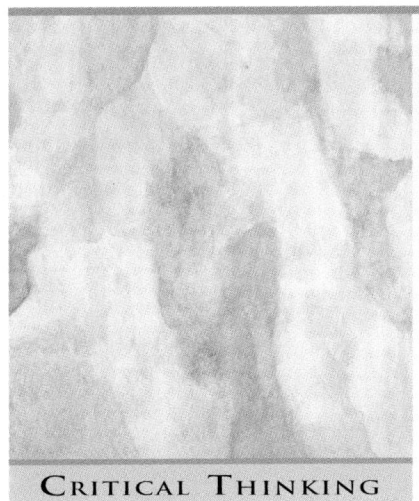

CRITICAL THINKING

*How Do You
Know When You
Are in Love?*

Author Nancy Mitford once said, "To fall in love you have to be in the state of mind for it to take, like a disease." You may have thought you were "afflicted" only to discover with the passing of time and some disappointment that you were wrong. What are your symptoms of falling in love? Once you have in mind your characteristics, interview three other people about their symptoms, and compare your symptoms with theirs. Are there common characteristics? Are there interesting differences? Your interviews will *demonstrate appreciation of individual differences.*

---

*Love conquers all things except
poverty and toothache.*

Mae West

---

by intimacy and commitment but low or lacking in passion is called *affectionate love,* a pattern often found among couples who have been married for many years. If passion and commitment are present but intimacy is not, Sternberg calls the relationship *fatuous love,* as when one person worships another from a distance.

We are who we love.

Erik Erikson

Not all of us experience the passion, intimacy, and commitment of love, and not all of us have many, or even one, close friend in whom we can confide. Understanding our social relationships also involves exploring feelings of loneliness.

Loneliness

Some of us are lonely. We may feel that no one knows us very well. We may feel isolated and sense that we do not have anyone we can turn to in times of need or stress. Our society's emphasis on self-fulfillment and achievement, the importance we attach to commitment in relationships, and a decline in stable close relationships are among the reasons loneliness is common today (de Jong-Gierveld, 1987).

Loneliness is associated with a person's gender, attachment history, self-esteem, and social skills (Lau & Gruen, 1992). Both men and women who lack female companions have a greater risk of being lonely. Lonely people often have a history of poor relationships with their parents. Early experiences of rejection and loss (as when a parent dies) can

cause a lasting feeling of being alone. Lonely people often have low self-esteem and tend to blame themselves more than they deserve for their inadequacies. Also, lonely people usually have poor social skills (Jones, Hobbs, & Hockenbury, 1982). For example, they show inappropriate self-disclosure, self-attention at the expense of attention to a partner, or an inability to develop comfortable intimacy.

When traditional-age students leave the familiar world of their hometown and family to enter college, they may feel especially lonely. Many college freshmen feel anxious about meeting new people and developing a new social life. One student commented:

My first year here at the university has been pretty lonely. I wasn't lonely at all in high school. I lived in a fairly small town— I knew everyone and everyone knew me. I was a member of several clubs and played on the basketball team. It's not that way at the university. It is a big place and I've felt like a stranger on so many occasions. I'm starting to get used to my life here and in the past few months I've been making myself meet people and get to know them, but it has not been easy.

As this comment illustrates, freshmen rarely take their high school popularity and social standing into the college environment. There may be a dozen high school basketball stars, National Merit scholars, and former student council presidents in a single dormitory wing. Especially if students attend college away from home, they face the task of forming new social relationships.

In one study, 2 weeks after the school year began, 75 percent of 354 college freshmen felt lonely at least part of the time since arriving on campus (Cutrona, 1982). More than 40 percent said their loneliness was moderate to severe in intensity. Students who were the most optimistic and had the highest self-esteem were more likely to overcome their loneliness by the end of their freshman year. Loneliness is not reserved only for traditional-age college freshmen, though. Upperclassmen and nontraditional-age students are often lonely as well.

Males and females attribute their loneliness to different sources. Men are more likely to blame themselves, and women are more likely to blame external factors. Men are socialized to initiate relationships, whereas women are traditionally socialized to wait, then respond. Perhaps men blame themselves because they feel they should do something about their loneliness, whereas women wonder why no one calls.

It is important to distinguish being alone from being lonely. Most of us cherish the moments we can be left alone for a while. Aloneness can heal, but loneliness can hurt.

How do you determine if you are lonely? Scales of loneliness ask you to respond to such questions as the following:

I don't feel in tune with the people around me.
I can find companionship when I want it.

Where you used to be, there is a hole in the world, which
I find myself constantly walking around in the daytime,
and falling into at night.

Edna St. Vincent Millay

Loneliness is about an absence of meaningful connections in our lives. In contrast, altruism is about purposeful connecting with others to offer assistance, even when we do not know the person we are assisting.

Altruism

Altruism *is an unselfish interest in helping another person.* We often hear or read about acts of generosity and courage, such as rock concerts and other fund-raisers to help AIDS victims, the taxi driver who risks his life to save a woman in a dark alley, and volunteers who pull a baby from an abandoned well. You might have placed some of your hard-earned cash in the palm of a homeless person or perhaps cared for a wounded cat. How do psychologists account for such acts of human altruism?

Evolutionary psychologists emphasize that some types of altruism help to perpetuate our genes (Buss, 1995). An act in the biological realm is altruistic if it increases the prospect for survival and the opportunity to reproduce.

Evolutionary psychologists believe that benefits can accrue to individuals who form cooperative reciprocal relationships (Trivers, 1971). By being good to someone now, individuals increase the likelihood that they will receive a benefit from the other person in the future. Through this reciprocal process, both gain something beyond what they could have by acting alone.

Evolutionary psychologists also stress that those who carry our genes—our children—have a special place in the domain of altruism. Natural selection favors parents who care for their children and improve their probability of surviving. A parent feeding its young is performing a biological altruistic act because the young's chance of survival is increased. So is a mother bird who performs a distraction ritual to lure predators away from the eggs in her nest. She is willing to sacrifice herself so that three or four of her young offspring will have the chance to survive, thus preserving her genes. Individuals also often show more empathy toward other relatives in relation to their genetic closeness. In the case of a natural disaster, people's uppermost concern is their family (Cunningham, 1986). In one recent study involving a hypothetical decision to help in life-or-death situations, college students chose to aid close kin over distant kin, the young over the old, the healthy over the sick, the

Friends of Ian O'Gorman *(being held aloft)* demonstrated an unusual degree of altruism when eleven of them shaved their heads prior to the chemotherapy that would cause Ian to lose his hair. Ian had non-Hodgkins lymphoma, and his chemotherapy protocol enhanced his chances of survival. The idea was originally Taylor Herber's. He claimed he would shave his head as a joke but then decided to do it because it would be less traumatizing for his best friend, who was likely to lose his hair as a side effect of chemotherapy. Others joined the cause as soon as they heard. His friends were relieved that the girls, who wanted to join in support, never followed through, since they believed Ian wouldn't want to be "followed around by a bunch of bald girls." The boys committed to future shaved heads if Ian's illness required more chemotherapy.

examples of altruism do involve social exchanges. We exchange gifts, cards, and tips for competent service, for example. It sounds cold and calculating to describe altruism in terms of costs and benefits, but that is exactly what social exchange theory does.

Not all altruism is motivated by reciprocity and social exchange, but this view alerts us to the importance of considering interactions between oneself and others to understand altruism. And not all seemingly altruistic behavior is unselfish. Some psychologists even argue that true altruism has never been demonstrated, while others argue that a distinction between altruism and egoism is possible (Batson & others, 1986). **Egoism** *is involved when person A gives to person B to ensure reciprocity; to gain self-esteem; to present oneself as powerful, competent, or caring; or to avoid social and self-censure for failing to live up to normative expectations.* By contrast, altruism occurs when person A gives to person B with the ultimate goal of benefiting person B. Any benefits that come to person A are unintended.

wealthy over the poor, and the premenopausal woman over the postmenopausal woman (Burnstein, Crandall, & Kitayama, 1994). In this same study, when an everyday favor rather than a life-or-death situation was involved, the college students gave less weight to kinship and chose to help either the very young or the very old over those of intermediate age, the sick over the healthy, and the poor over the wealthy.

Reciprocity and exchange are important aspects of altruism. Humans everywhere give to and receive from others. For example, sales representatives rely on the principle of reciprocity when they offer you free samples during your grocery shopping trip. They give you a sample of ice cream in exchange for your attention and possible purchase of the product. Reciprocity is a fundamental tenet of major religion in the world—including Judaism, Christianity, Buddhism, and Islam. Reciprocity encourages us to do unto others as we would have them do unto us. Certain sentiments are involved in reciprocity: In Western contexts, for instance, trust is probably the most important principle over the long run; guilt occurs if we do not reciprocate, and anger results if someone else does not reciprocate.

Social exchange theory *states that individuals should benefit those who benefit them, or for a benefit received, an equivalent benefit should be returned at some point.* Many

Describing individuals as having altruistic or egoistic motives implies that person variables are important in understanding altruistic behavior. Altruistic behavior is determined by both person and situational variables. A person's ability to empathize with the needy or to feel a sense of responsibility for another's welfare affects altruistic motivations. The stronger these personality dispositions, the less we would expect situational variables to influence whether giving, kindness, or helping occur.

But as with any human behavior, characteristics of the situation influence the strength of altruistic motivation. Some of these characteristics include the degree of need shown by the other individual, the needy person's responsibility for his plight, the cost of assisting the needy person, and the extent to which reciprocity is expected.

One of the most widely studied aspects of altruism is bystander intervention. Why does one person help a stranger in distress while another won't lift a finger? It often depends on the circumstances. More than 20 years ago a young woman named Kitty Genovese cried out repeatedly as she was brutally murdered. She was attacked at about 3 A.M. in a respectable area of New York City. The murderer left and returned to attack her again three-times; he finally put an end to Kitty's life as she crawled to her apartment door and screamed for help. It took the slayer about 30

"All I'm saying is, giving a little something to the arts might help our image."

Drawing by P. Steiner; © 1989 The New Yorker Magazine, Inc.

help 75 percent of the time, but when another bystander is present, the figure drops to 50 percent. **Diffusion of responsibility,** *the tendency to feel less responsible and to act less responsibly in the presence of others,* is one explanation of why bystanders fail to act. When a situation is sufficiently ambiguous, we might tend to look to the behavior of others for clues about what to do. People may think that someone else will call the police or that since no one is helping, possibly the person does not need help.

Many other aspects of the situation influence whether the individual will intervene and come to the aid of the person in distress. Bystander intervention is less likely to occur in the following situations (Shotland, 1985):

- When the intervention might lead to personal harm, retaliation by the criminal, or days in court testifying
- When helping takes time
- When a situation is ambiguous
- When the individuals struggling or fighting are married or related
- When a victim is perceived as being drunk rather than disabled, or of a different ethnic group
- When bystanders have no prior history of victimization themselves, have witnessed few crimes and intervention efforts, or have not had training in first aid, rescue, or police tactics

At this point, we have discussed many aspects of social relationships, including helping others, liking others, loving others, and feeling lonely. Next we will further discuss the role of social influence in our lives.

minutes to kill Kitty. Thirty-eight neighbors watched the gory scene and heard Kitty Genovese's screams. No one helped or even called the police.

The **bystander effect** *is that individuals who observe an emergency help less when someone else is present than when they are alone.* The bystander effect helps to explain the apparent cold-blooded indifference to Kitty Genovese's murder. Social psychologists John Darley and Bibb Latané (1968) documented the bystander effect in a number of criminal and medical emergencies. Most of the bystander intervention studies show that when alone, a person will

REVIEW

Attraction and Close Relationships

Familiarity precedes a close relationship. We like to associate with people who are similar to us.

Friendship is an important aspect of close relationships that is characterized by enjoyment, acceptance, trust, and other features. Females in general engage in more intimate self-disclosure than males do. Romantic love is involved when we say we are "in love"; this includes passion, sexuality, and a mixture of emotions, not all of which are positive. Affectionate (companionate) love is more

important as relationships mature. Shaver proposed a developmental model of love, and Sternberg proposed a triangular model. Sternberg believes that affectionate love is made up of intimacy and commitment, which along with romantic love constitute the three facets of his model of love.

Loneliness is associated with many factors, including a poor attachment history with parents and low self-esteem. It is important to remember the distinction between being alone and being lonely.

Altruism is an unselfish interest in helping another person. Examples of human altruism are plentiful. Evolutionary psychologists stress that altruism involves increasing the prospects for survival as well as reproduction. Reciprocity and social exchange are often involved, although not always. Motivation can be altruistic or egoistic. Psychologists have studied both person and situation variables involved in altruism. Extensive research has been conducted on bystander interventions.

In the scale of the destinies, brawn will never weigh as much as brain.

James Russell Lowell (1819–1891)

Both brawn and brain have been used to influence others. In this section we will explore the nature of social influence as it occurs between people in relationships and among people in groups.

Interpersonal Influence

Social influence between two people comes in many forms. However, influence involves a change in attitude or a change in action that results from the efforts of another. We will examine two kinds of interpersonal influence: persuasion and obedience to authority.

Persuasion

No matter what side of an argument you're on, you always find some people on your side that you wish were on the other side.

Jascha Heifetz

We spend many hours of our lives trying to persuade people to do certain things. A young man might try to persuade a young woman of the intensity of his love for her. Advertisers try to persuade us that their product is superior and life-enhancing. Politicians and corporations are also heavily involved in the persuasion process. Politicians, for example, have full arsenals of speech writers and image consultants to ensure that their words and behavior are as persuasive as possible. Social psychologists believe that persuasion involves four key components: who conveys the message (the source), what the message is (the communication), what medium is used (the channel), and for whom the message is intended (the target).

The Communicator (Source) Suppose you are running for president of the student body. You tell students you are going to make life at your college better. Would they believe you? That would depend on several different factors.

Two factors involved in whether or not we believe someone are the *expertise* and the *credibility* of the communicator. Expertise depends on qualifications. If you had held other elective offices, students would be more likely to believe you have the expertise to be their president. We attribute competence to experts, believing they are knowledgeable about the topics they address.

In addition to expertise and credibility, *trustworthiness* is an important quality of an effective communicator.

"First off, by way of establishing some credibility, I'd like to note that twenty years ago I was living in a fur-lined van."

Drawing by D. Reilly; © 1989 The New Yorker Magazine, Inc.

This factor depends on whether what you say and how you say it is perceived as honest or dishonest. It was in Abraham Lincoln's best interest, then, to be called "Honest Abe"; being perceived as honest increased the power of his communication.

Social psychologists believe that *power, attractiveness, likableness,* and *similarity* are four important characteristics that add to a communicator's ability to change people's attitudes. In running for student body president, you will probably have more clout with students if you have been on the university president's student issues committee. Power may be an important characteristic for a communicator because it is associated with the ability to impose sanctions or control rewards and punishments (Kelley & Thibaut, 1978). In running for student body president, you are also more likely to get votes if students perceive you as attractive and similar to themselves. That's why you often see presidential candidates putting on miners' helmets in West Virginia, speaking a Spanish phrase in San Antonio, or riding a tractor in Iowa. The candidates are striving to show that they share common interests and an identity with their audience.

Similarity is also widely used in advertising. In commercials we might see a homemaker scrubbing the floor while advertising a new cleaner or a laborer laughing with his buddies at a bar while drinking beer. The creators of these commercials hope you will relate to these people because you perceive them as similar to yourself. Of course, many products are promoted by appealing to our personal ideals. To do this, attractive or famous individuals are used in advertisements. Elizabeth Taylor tries to persuade us to buy cologne, and Michael Jordan tries to persuade us to buy athletic shoes, for example.

Other factors that influence attitudes are the sex of the communicator and gender roles. To learn more about how gender might be a factor in attitudes about political candidates, turn to Sociocultural Worlds 18.2. As we will see next, the content of the message also is an important factor in influencing attitudes.

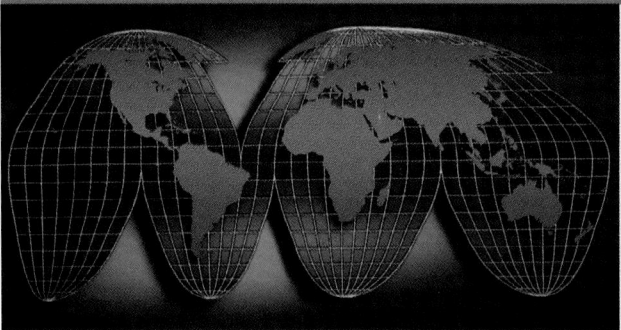

Gender and Politics: From Ferraro to County Clerk

It is the summer of 1984. The November presidential election is only months away; the Democrats are far behind in the polls. The economy is looking better, and Republican incumbent Ronald Reagan's lead seems insurmountable. What could the Democratic party do to persuade the American population to switch their allegiance? It would have to be something bold, something never tried before in the history of American politics.

One of the areas in which Reagan seemed vulnerable was women's rights; the National Organization for Women (NOW) called Reagan insensitive to women, for example. For the first time in history, a woman—Geraldine Ferraro—was selected to fill the vice-presidential slot on the Democratic ticket. Although the Democrats did not win the 1984 presidential election, Ferraro's selection was an important step for women in their effort to achieve equality.

As more women have sought political office, the issue of gender has assumed a more important role in attitude change. Surveys reveal that, in today's political climate, we are more likely to vote for qualified female candidates, especially if they are running for lower political offices (Gallup, 1984). Discrimination still exists, though, especially in gubernatorial campaigns (Yankelovich, Skelly, & White, 1984).

The challenge is to determine for whom and under what circumstances gender makes the most difference. Social psychologist Carol Sigelman and her colleagues (1986) wanted to find out to what extent voters are influenced by a candidate's gender, physical attractiveness, and prestige in relation to the responsibility of the office being sought. The researchers gave college students information about six challengers to an incumbent in either a mayoral or county clerk's race. The challengers were men and women of high, moderate, or low physical attractiveness. The researchers found that the male, but not the female, voters discriminated against the female candidates. In addition, the men saw the women as less qualified, fewer of the men voted for the women, and the men rated the women lower overall. The males' antifemale bias was not offset by a preference for the women candidates by the female voters, however. The female voters tended to choose evenly between the male and female candidates. Also, attractiveness was less consistently an asset for the female candidates than it was for the males. Although it appears that less discrimination against female candidates occurs today than in past years, this research suggests that equality has not yet been reached.

Geraldine Ferraro campaigned as a vice-presidential candidate on the Mondale-Ferraro Democratic ticket in 1984. What is gender's role in political attitudes?

The Message   What should the content of a message be like to make it more persuasive? Should appeals be more positive than negative? Should a rational or emotional strategy be used?

How often have we seen politicians vow to run a clean campaign but as soon as the bell sounds come out swinging below the belt? In the 1988 presidential campaign, negative advertising became a big issue and proved to be effective. George Bush succeeded in branding Michael Dukakis with the *L* word (liberal) in the campaign. Negative appeals play on our emotions, while positive appeals are directed at our rational, logical thinking. The less informed we are, the more likely we will respond to an emotional appeal. For example, if we do not know anything about nuclear waste, an emotional appeal to keep a hazardous waste dump from being built near our home may influence our attitude about the project more than an appeal based on reasoning. For people who did not know much about Dukakis's political

Jesse Jackson is shown here campaigning for president in 1988. Whether a candidate is running for president of the United States or president of a college's student body, expertise, credibility, trust, power, attraction, and similarity are important characteristics.

background, Bush's criticism of Dukakis was probably a wise strategy. Bush tried pinning the liberal label on Bill Clinton in the 1992 presidential campaign, but the sociopolitical context had changed.

All other things being equal, the more frightened we are, the more we will change our attitude. The day after the telecast of the vivid nuclear war film *The Day After,* more negative attitudes about the United States' massive nuclear arsenal surfaced (Schofield & Pavelchak, 1985, 1989). Advertisers also sometimes take advantage of our fears to stimulate attitude change. For example, you may have seen the Michelin tire ad that shows a baby playing near tires or the life insurance company ad that shows a widow and her young children moving out of their home, which they lost because they did not have enough insurance.

Does persuasion based on fear-inducing strategies change behavior as well as attitudes? In one study, researchers tried to scare smokers into taking chest X rays and becoming nonsmokers by varying the intensity of the fear-producing stimulus (Leventhal, 1970). The low-fear group was advised to get X rays and stop smoking. The moderate-fear group was shown a film in which a young man's cancer was diagnosed from X rays. The high-fear group also was shown the film but viewed a film of a gory operation as well. The researchers concluded that the most frightened were the most likely to show behavior changes. In addition, fear-arousing communication might have limited influence in the absence of clear and specific instructions about taking countermeasures. Four months after the experiment, the subjects who were most frightened and most specifically instructed were smoking less than were subjects who had been in the other groups.

From *It's a Mom's Life* by David Sipress. Copyright © 1988 by David Sipress. Used by permission of Dutton Signet, a division of Penguin Books USA Inc.

Music is widely used to make us feel good about messages. Think about how few television commercials you have seen without some form of music either in the background or as a prominent part of the message. When we watch such commercials, we may associate the pleasant feelings of the music with the product, even though the music itself does not provide any information about the product.

The Medium   While there are many factors to consider in regard to the message itself, the communicator also needs to be concerned about which medium to use to get the message across. Consider the difference between watching a presidential debate on television and reading about it in the newspaper. Television lets us see how the candidates deliver the message, what their appearance and mannerisms are like, and so on. Because it presents live images, television is considered the most powerful medium for changing attitudes. One study revealed that the winners of various political primaries were predicted by the amount of media exposure they had (Grush, 1980).

Television's power of persuasion is staggering. By the time the average American adolescent graduates from high school, he or she has watched 20,000 hours of television, far more than the number of hours spent in the classroom. Social scientists have studied television's influence on matters such as the impact of commercials on purchases, of mass media political campaigning on voting, of public service announcements on health, of broad-based ideological campaigns on lifestyles, and of television violence on aggression.

How strong is television's influence on an individual's attitudes and behavior? Some reviews of research conclude that there are few effects (Zeigler & Harmon, 1989). Other reviews conclude television has a more formidable effect (Clifford, Bunter, & McAleer, 1995).

The Target (Audience)   What are some characteristics of the audience that determine whether a message will be effective? Age, gender, and self-esteem are three such factors. Younger people are more likely to change their attitudes than older ones, females appear to be more susceptible to persuasion than males, and self-esteem is

Suppose that you have just taken up running as a good form of exercise and decide to do some research on the best running shoes for your needs. You look at *Consumer Reports.* You go to specialized shoe stores and examine models. After much research and evaluation, you decide on a particular costly pair. But just before you make your purchase, you mention your choice to your favorite running companion, who comprehensively describes all the troubles that she encountered with that brand. She describes poor wear, blisters, and leg aches, all attributed to the bad buy she made, and discourages you from making a similar mistake.

What do you do? Most of us are inclined to abandon all of our painstaking research under the influence of the personal testimony of a friend whose opinion we prize. A vivid, clear, personal example apparently carries more evaluative weight with us than even our own conclusion derived from more reliable methods. We assume that our friend's experience is typical, when it simply might not be. Can you think of an example in which the power of a personal example may have undermined your confidence in your own more systematic methods? Your awareness of the typicality effect of personal testimony may assist you to *evaluate the validity of your conclusions* as well as save you from acting on testimony about atypical personal experiences.

---

*The world is not run by thought,
not by imagination, but by opinion.*
Elizabeth Drew

---

believed to be important but does not have a predictable pattern. Another factor is the strength of the audience's attitude. If the audience is not strongly committed to a particular attitude, change is more likely; if it is strong, the communicator will have more difficulty.

Obedience

Obedience *is behavior that complies with the explicit demands of an individual in authority.* Although many parents try to instill obedience in their children, obedience sometimes can be destructive: The disaster in Waco described at the beginning of this chapter, the massacre of Vietnamese civilians at My Lai, and the Nazi crimes against Jews and others in World War II are other examples of destructive obedience. Adolph Eichmann, for example, has been described as an ambitious functionary who believed that it was his duty to obey Hitler's orders. An average middle-class man with no identifiable criminal tendencies, Eichmann ordered the killing of 6 million Jews and others. The following experiment, first performed by Stanley Milgram at Yale University, provides insight into such obedience.

As part of an experiment in psychology, you are asked to deliver a series of painful electric shocks to another person. You are told that the purpose of the study is to determine the effects of punishment on memory. Your role is to be the "teacher" and punish the mistakes made by a "learner"; each time the learner makes a mistake, your job is to increase the intensity of the shock by a certain amount. You are given a 75-volt shock to show you how it feels. You are then introduced to the "learner," a nice 50-year-old man who mumbles something about having a heart condition. He is strapped to a chair in the next room and communicates with you through an intercom. As the trials proceed, the "learner" quickly runs into trouble and is unable to give the correct answers. Should you shock him? The apparatus in front of you has thirty switches, ranging from 15 volts (light) to 375 volts (marked "danger") to 450 volts (marked "XXX"). As you raise the intensity of the shock, the "learner" says he's in pain. At 150 volts, he demands to have the experiment stopped. At 180 volts, he cries out that he can't stand it anymore. At 300 volts, he yells about his heart condition and pleads to be released. If you hesitate in shocking the learner, however, the experimenter tells you that you have no choice; the experiment must continue.

As you might imagine, in Milgram's study the "teachers" were uneasy about shocking the "learner." At 240 volts, one "teacher" responded, "Two hundred forty volts delivered: Aw, no. You mean I've got to keep going with that scale? No sir, I'm not going to kill that man—I'm not going to give him 450 volts!" (Milgram, 1965, p. 67). At the very high voltage, the "learner" quit responding. When the "teacher" asked the experimenter what to do, he simple instructed the "teacher" to continue the experiment and told him that it was his obligation to complete the job. Figure 18.4 shows the setting of the experiment. The 50-year-old "learner" was a confederate of the experimenter. He was not being shocked at all. Of course, the "teachers" were unaware of this.

Forty psychiatrists were asked how they thought individuals would respond in this situation. The psychiatrists predicted that only 1 in 100 would go further than 150 volts, that fewer than 1 in 25 would go as far as 300 volts,

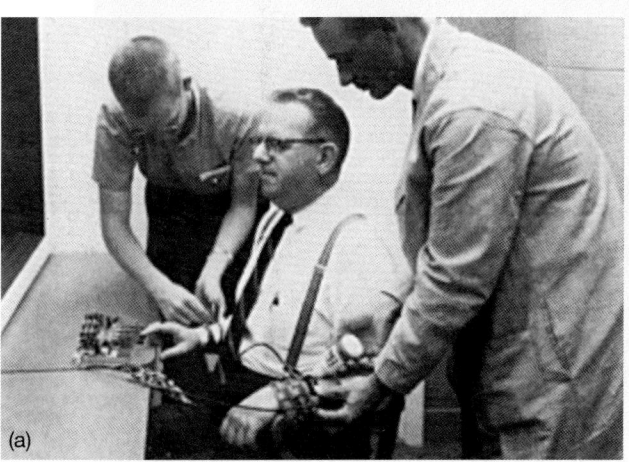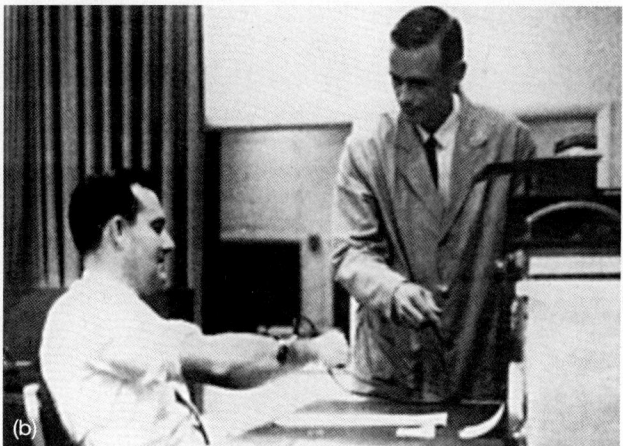

FIGURE 18.4

Milgram Obedience Study
(a) A 50-year-old man ("learner") is strapped into a chair. The experimenter makes it look as if a shock generator is being connected to his body through a number of electrodes. *(b)* The subject ("teacher") is given a sample 75-volt shock. *How far do you think you might have taken the shock in order to help science and assist the "learner" to learn?*

CRITICAL THINKING

Milgram's Results and Standards of Humane Research

We're going to sidetrack for a moment and explore an important point about the Milgram experiments: How *ethical* were they? The volunteers in Milgram's experiment clearly felt anguish, and some were very disturbed about harming another individual. After the experiment was completed, they were told that the "learner" was not actually shocked. Even though they were debriefed and told that they really had not shocked anyone, was it ethical to impose such anguish on them?

Milgram argued that we have learned a great deal about human nature from the experiments. He claimed that they tell us how far individuals will go in their obedience, even if it means being cruel to someone. The volunteers were interviewed later, and more than four of every five said that they were glad they had participated in the study; none said they were sorry they had participated. When Milgram conducted his studies on obedience, the ethical guidelines for research were not as stringent as they are today. The current ethical guidelines of the American Psychological Association stress that researchers should obtain informed consent from their volunteers. Deception should be used only for very important purposes. Individuals are supposed to feel as good about themselves when the experiment is over as they did when it began. Under today's guidelines, it is unlikely that the Milgram experiment would be conducted.

Over three decades have elapsed since Milgram's original study. Many students tend to believe the passing of time is an important variable in understanding how obedient Milgram's volunteers were. They can't imagine being as obedient in the same situation. Suppose we wanted to put this idea to the test. Would finding out how individuals would react to this research challenge be sufficiently valuable to outweigh the level of deception that would be required? Are there other problems in doing research in a contemporary context that Milgram did not have to face? Your consideration of this issue illustrates the importance of *practicing standards of ethical treatment toward individuals and groups.*

APPLICATIONS IN PSYCHOLOGY 18.1

Resisting Social Influence

If a man does not keep pace with his companions,
perhaps it is because he hears a different drummer.
Let him step to the music which he hears,
however measured or far away.

Henry David Thoreau

Most of us in this culture would prefer to think of ourselves as stepping to our own music, maybe even setting the rhythms for others, rather than trying to keep pace with our companions. However, society requires a certain degree of conformity if society is to function at all. For example, without conformity, traffic patterns in America would be nightmarish. As we go through our lives, we are both conformist and nonconformist. Sometimes conforming can be quite comfortable. For example, chances are good that you wear blue jeans during some part of your week as a result of conforming to some fashion standards. However, sometimes we are overwhelmed by the persuasion and influence of others. In some of those circumstances, we may need to resist and gain personal control over our lives.

Our individualistic culture prizes self-direction. It is important to remember that our relation to the social world is reciprocal; when others are attempting to exert undue social influence over us, we can recognize and resist this influence in the tradition espoused by Thoreau. We can also exert personal control over our actions and influence others in turn (Bandura, 1986, 1989, 1991). If you believe that someone in a position of authority is making an unjust request or asking you to do something wrong, what choice of actions do you have? Your choices include:

- You can comply.
- You also can give the appearance of complying but secretly do otherwise.
- You can publicly dissent by showing doubts and disenchantment but still follow directives.
- You can openly disregard the orders and refuse to comply.
- You can challenge or confront the authority.
- You might get higher authorities to intervene or organize a group of people who agree with you to show the strength of your view.

In 1989 Chinese students led a massive demonstration against the Chinese government in Beijing. The students resisted the government's social influence by putting together resources to challenge the Chinese authorities; however, the government eventually prevailed after ordering the massacre of hundreds of students.

and that only 1 in 1,000 would deliver the full 450 volts. The psychiatrists, it turns out, were way off the mark. The majority of the individuals obeyed the experimenter. In fact, almost two of every three delivered the full 450 volts.

In subsequent studies, Milgram set up a storefront in Bridgeport, Connecticut, and recruited volunteers through newspaper ads. Milgram wanted to create a more natural environment for the experiment and to use a wider cross-section of volunteers. In these additional studies, close to two-thirds of the individuals still selected the highest level of shock for the "learner." In variations of the experiment, Milgram discovered some circumstances that encouraged disobedience: when an opportunity was given to see others disobey, when the authority figure was not perceived to be legitimate and was not close by, and when the victim was made to seem more human. To read about resisting social influence, turn to Applications in Psychology 18.1.

At this point in our discussion of social psychology, we have examined the interpersonal contexts of our thoughts, behaviors, and activities. Next we will explore group relations.

Understanding persuasion and attitude focuses on the communicator (source), the message (communication), the medium (channel), and the target (audience). Communicators are most influential when they have expertise and credibility, trustworthiness, and power; attractiveness and similarity also are important. The less informed we are, the better emotional appeals work; the more frightened we are, the more we will be influenced. Positive emotional appeals can be persuasive, especially through the use of music. Because it delivers live images, television may be the most powerful medium; its persuasive capabilities are staggering, given the frequency of viewing. Experts debate television's influence. Younger individuals are more likely to change their attitudes than older individuals and females are more readily persuaded than males. Self-esteem is thought to be important, but a predictable effect for it has not been found. If an audience is not strongly committed to a preexisting attitude, change is more likely. Obedience is behavior that complies with the explicit demands of an authority. Milgram's classic experiment demonstrated the power of obedience. The subjects followed the experimenter's directions even though they perceived they were hurting someone. Milgram's experiments raise the question of ethics in psychological experimentation.

Influence in Groups

A student joining a fraternity, a jury deciding a criminal case, a company president delegating authority, a family reunion, a prejudiced remark about a minority group, conflicts among nations, arguments in the neighborhood, and attempts to reach peace—all of these circumstances reflect our lives as members of groups. Each of us belongs to many groups. Some we choose; others we do not. We choose to belong to a club, but we are born into a particular ethnic group, for example. Some group participation is very satisfying; other group experiences are frustrating and ineffective.

In this section we will explore social influence in groups and examine the roles that tend to form in groups. We will identify some theories about the development of leaders in groups and how conflicts between participants are resolved. We'll also explore some challenging aspects of social influence, including conformity, groupthink, and deindividuation.

The Nature of Groups

Group membership satisfies our personal needs, rewards us, provides information, raises our self-esteem, and gives us an identity. We might join a group because we think it will be enjoyable and exciting and satisfy our need for affiliation and companionship. We might join a group because we will receive rewards, either material or psychological. By taking a job with a company, we get paid to work for a group, but we also reap prestige and recognition. Groups are an important source of information. For example, as we listen to other members talk in a Weight Watchers group, we learn about their strategies for losing weight. As we sit in the audience at a real estate seminar, we learn how to buy property with no money down. Many of the groups of which you are a member—your family, a college, a club, a team—make you feel good, raise your self-esteem, and provide you with an identity.

Any group to which you belong has certain things in common with all other groups. All groups have their own **norms,** *rules that apply to all members of a group.* The city government requires each of its workers to wear socks, Mensa requires individuals to have a high IQ, Polar Bear Club members must complete a 15-minute swim in below-freezing temperatures. These are examples of norms.

Roles *are rules and expectations that govern certain positions in a group. Roles define how people should behave in a particular position in the group.* In a family, parents have certain roles, siblings have other roles, and a grandparent has yet another role. On a football team, many roles must be filled: center, guard, tackle, end, quarterback, halfback, and fullback, for example, and that only covers the offense. Roles and norms, then, tell us what is expected of the members of a group.

One advantage of group participation is that more resources are brought to bear on any given problem. This may enhance the ability to complete tasks on time and accurately, particularly when compared to the efficiency of one individual working alone.

Many factors affect whether a group will be productive or not. The quality of leadership is one important variable that determines group effectiveness. However, experiences in groups can also lead to some unpleasant outcomes. For example, conflicts can develop between group members. Coalitions can form within a group that can prolong group effort with protracted discussions among the factions. Although it can be an adaptive force in some circumstances, pressures to conform can create some problems for individual group members. In addition, two other problems—groupthink and deindividuation—result in ineffectiveness or poor adaptation.

Leadership

"I am certainly not one of those who need to be prodded. In fact, if anything, I am the prod," British Prime Minister Winston Churchill said of himself. What made Churchill a great leader? Was it a set of personality traits, the situation into which he was thrust, or a combination of the two?

The **great person theory** *says that some individuals have certain traits that make them best suited for leadership positions.* Leaders are commonly thought to be assertive, cooperative, decisive, dominant, energetic, self-confident, tolerant of stress, willing to assume responsibility, diplomatic and tactful, and persuasive. Although we can list traits and skills possessed by leaders, a large number of research studies conclude that we cannot predict who will become a leader solely from an individual's personality characteristics.

Is it the situation, then, that produces leaders? According to the **situational theory of leadership,** *the needs of a group change from time to time, and a person who emerges as a leader in one circumstance will not necessarily be the person who becomes a leader in another circumstance.* Many psychologists believe that a combination of personality characteristics and skills and situational influences determines who will become a leader.

At this point, our discussion of group relations has focused on why we join groups, how groups are structured, and why some individuals are leaders and others are followers. Next we will discuss how groups, especially minority and majority groups, deal with each other.

Majority-Minority Influence

Think about the groups in which you have been a member. Who had the most influence, the majority or the minority? In most groups—whether a jury, family, or corporate meeting—the majority holds sway over the minority. The majority exerts both normative and informational pressure on the group. Its adherents set the group's norms; those who do not go along may be rejected. The majority also has a greater opportunity to provide information that will influence decision making.

In most cases, the majority wins, but there are occasions when the minority has its day. How can the minority swing the majority? The minority cannot win through normative influence because it is outnumbered. It must do its work through *informational pressure.* If the minority presents its views consistently, confidently, and nondefensively, then the majority is more likely to listen to the minority's view. The minority position might have to be repeated several times in order to create sufficient impact.

In group situations, some individuals are able to command the attention of others and thus have a better opportunity to shape and direct subsequent social outcomes. To achieve such a high social impact, they have to distinguish themselves in various ways from the rest of the group. They have to make themselves noticed by others—by the opinions they express, the jokes they tell, or by their nonverbal style. They may be the first ones to raise a new idea, to disagree with a prevailing point of view, or to propose a creative alternative solution to a problem. People who have a high social impact often are characterized by their willingness to be different. In one recent study, people high in individuation (those who are differentiated from other parts of the

Certain individuals in the minority have played important roles in history. *(a)* Martin Luther King, Jr., helped African Americans gain important rights. *(b)* Corazon Aquino, who became president of the Philippines after defeating Ferdinand Marcos, toppled a corrupt political regime and reduced the suffering of many Philippine citizens.

physical and social environment) had a stronger social impact on the group than their low individuation counterparts (Whitney, Sagrestano, & Maslach, 1994).

Certain individuals in a minority may play a crucial role. Individuals with a history of taking minority stands may trigger others to dissent, showing them that disagreement is

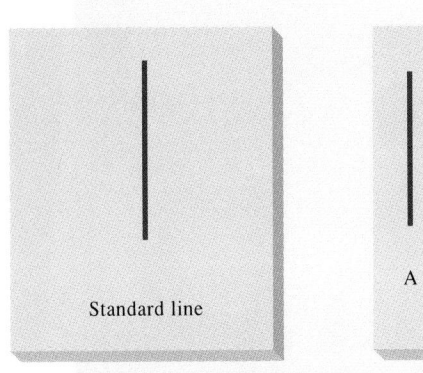
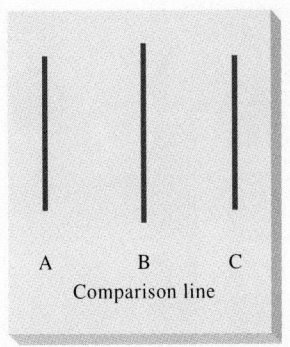

Standard line

A   B   C
Comparison line

FIGURE 18.5

Asch's Conformity Experiment
The figures show the stimulus materials for the Asch conformity experiment on group influence. The photograph shows the dilemma for the subject (*seated in the middle*) after five confederates of the experimenter chose the incorrect line.

possible and the minority stand may be the best course. Such is the ground of some of history's greatest moments—when Lincoln spoke out against slavery, racism dominated and tore at the country, and, when Corazon Aquino became a candidate for president of the Philippines, few people thought Ferdinand Marcos could be beaten. Although the scale is smaller, the triumph might be the same for a gang member influencing the gang's decision not to vandalize, the woman executive persuading her male colleagues to adopt a less sexist advertising tactic, or the ethnic minority student expressing his views in a dominantly White classroom.

Conformity

Conformity comes in many forms and affects many areas of our lives. Do you take up jogging because everyone else is doing it? Does fashion dictate that you let your hair grow long this year and cut it short the next? Would you take cocaine if pressured by others or would you resist? **Conformity** *occurs when individuals adopt the attitudes or behavior of others because of real or imagined pressure from others to do so.*

Conformity to rules and regulations result in people engaging in a number of behaviors that make society run more smoothly. For example, consider what would happen if most people did not conform to rules such as these:

stopping at red lights, driving on the correct side of the road, not punching others in the face, going to school regularly, and so on. However, in the following experiments, researchers reveal how conformity pressures can sometimes make us act against our better judgment and even have dramatic, unfortunate consequences.

Every society honors its live conformists and its dead troublemakers.
Mignon McLaughlin

Put yourself in the following situation. You are taken into a room, where you see five other people seated around a table. A person in a white lab coat enters the room and announces that you are about to participate in an experiment on perceptual accuracy. The group is shown two cards, the first having only a single vertical line on it, the second card with three vertical lines of varying length. You are told that the task is to determine which of the three lines on the second card is the same length as the line on the first card. You look at the cards and think, "What a snap. It's so obvious which is longest." The other people in the room are actually associates of the experimenter (researchers often call such persons "confederates" of the experimenter); they've been hired to perform in ways the experimenter dictates (of course, you are not aware of this). On the first several trials, everyone agrees about which line matches the standard. Then, on the fourth trial, each of the others picks an incorrect line; you have a puzzled look on your face. As the last person to make a choice, you're in the dilemma of responding as your eyes tell you or conforming to what the others have said. How do you think you would answer?

Solomon Asch conducted this classic experiment on conformity in 1951 (see figure 18.5). He believed there would be little yielding to group pressure. To find out if this was so, Asch instructed his accomplices to respond incorrectly on 12 of the 18 trials. To Asch's surprise, the volunteer participants conformed to the incorrect answers 35 percent of the time. The pressure to conform is strong. Even in a clear-cut situation, such as in the Asch experiment, we often conform to what others say and do. We don't want to be laughed at or have others be angry with us.

Put yourself in another situation. You have volunteered to participate in a psychology experiment. By the flip of a coin, half of the volunteers are designated as prisoners and half as guards in a mock prison; you are one of the

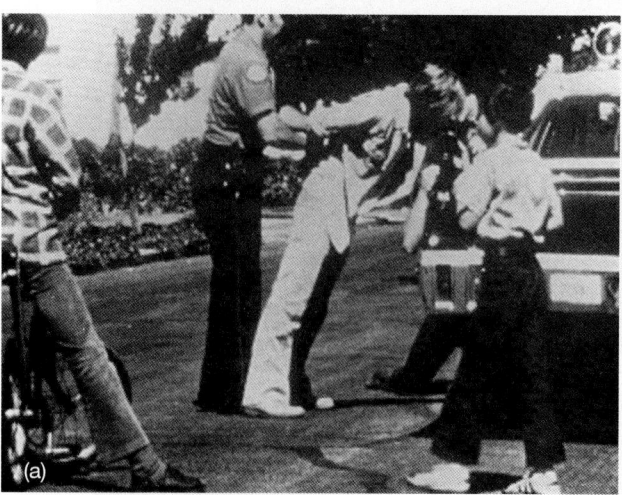

FIGURE 18.6

Zimbardo's Prison Experiment
(a) A volunteer for a psychology experiment is picked up on campus—he had lost a coin flip and was designated a prisoner.
(b) A student conforms to the hostile, abusive role of prison guard.

fortunate ones because you will be a guard. How much would you and your fellow volunteers conform to the social roles of "guard" and "prisoner"? You are instructed to maintain law and order—to do a guard's job. You will make a fine guard, you think, because you are kind and respect the rights and dignity of others. In just a few hours, however, you find that your behavior, and that of the other "guards" and "prisoners," has changed; each of you has begun to conform to what you think are the expected social roles for guards and prisoners. Over the course of 6 days, you and the other guards begin to make the prisoners obey petty, meaningless rules and force them to perform tedious, useless, and sometimes humiliating tasks. What's more, you find yourself insulting the prisoners and keeping them "in line" with night sticks. Many of the prisoners begin acting like robots. They develop an intense hatred for you and the other guards and constantly think about ways to escape.

You may be thinking that this scenario stretches credibility. No one you know, and certainly not you, would behave in such an abusive way. However, psychologist Philip Zimbardo and his colleagues (1972) conducted just such an experiment with a group of normal, mature, stable, intelligent young men at Stanford University. In fact, the prison study was scheduled to last 2 weeks, but the behavior of the "guards" and "prisoners" changed so drastically that the experiment had to be stopped after 6 days. Although many of the prisoners resisted the guards and asked questions initially, after a while they gave up and virtually stopped reacting. Five of the prisoners had to be released, four because of severe depression or anxiety and the fifth because he broke

out in a rash all over his body; several of the guards became brutal with the prisoners. Figure 18.6 shows some of the circumstances in the prison study.

Cross-cultural psychologists wondered if this tendency to conform in such dramatic ways is an American phenomenon or if the same behavior occurs in other cultures. Using the Asch experiment, researchers have found that research participants in Lebanon, Hong Kong, Brazil, and Fiji conform at about the same rate, 35 percent (Mann, 1980). However, they found conformity lower in Germany (22 percent) and higher among the Bantu of Rhodesia (51 percent). Surprisingly, conformity in Japan was found to be relatively low—25 percent (Frager, 1970). The results of the Japanese study were counterintuitive—that is, contrary to what the researchers expected. Because of strong social pressures to conform in Japan's collectivistic culture, the researchers expected a much higher rate. Perhaps the Japanese feel strong loyalty to their own social groups but not to groups created in the laboratory. In addition, collectivists tend to belong to few in-groups and might be less inclined to feel pressures to conform in contexts that exploit these pressures. As a result, we cannot conclude that the Japanese are nonconforming; it might be that they simply do not conform to the wishes of strangers. Germans also demonstrated less conformity (22 percent). Cross-cultural psychologist Richard Brislin (1993) believes that such results might represent a conscious choice to be perceived as less authoritarian and obedient.

Other cross-cultural research on conformity suggests that people in agricultural societies have a tendency to con-

680   *Social Psychology and Culture*

TABLE 18.1
Passionate Love

Instructions

The items ask you what it's like when you are passionately in love. Think of the person you love most passionately *right now*. If you are not in love right now, think of a person you loved passionately. If you have never been in love, think of the person you came closest to caring for in that way. Keep this person in mind as you complete the items (the person you choose should be of the opposite sex if you are heterosexual or of the same sex if you are homosexual). Try to tell how you felt at the time your feelings were the most intense. Select a number from 1 to 9 that best reflects your feelings, for each item.

Not at all true		Moderately true			Definitely true	
1 2	3	4 5	6	7	8	9

1. I would feel deep despair if _____ left me.
2. Sometimes I feel I can't control my thoughts; they are obsessively on _____ .
3. I feel happy when I am doing something to make _____ happy.
4. I would rather be with _____ than anyone else.
5. I'd get jealous if I thought _____ were falling in love with someone else.
6. I yearn to know all about _____ .
7. I want _____ —physically, emotionally, mentally.
8. I have an endless appetite for affection from _____ .
9. For me, _____ is the perfect romantic partner.
10. I sense my body responding when _____ touches me.
11. _____ always seems to be on my mind.
12. I want _____ to know me—my thoughts, my fears, my hopes.
13. I eagerly look for signs indicating _____'s desire for me.
14. I possess a powerful attraction for _____ .
15. I get extremely depressed when things don't go right in my relationship with _____ .

Turn to the end of the chapter to interpret your passionate love experience.

From E. Hatfield, "Passionate and Companionate Love" in *The Psychology of Love*, edited by R. J. Sternberg and M. L. Barnes. Copyright © 1988 Yale University Press, New Haven, CT. Reprinted by permission.

In a study in 1967, the men said they would not get married unless they were in love with a woman, but the women were either undecided or said they would get married even if they did not love the man. However, in the 1980s, women had changed their opinions to the point that theirs were almost identical to men's, no longer maintaining they would get married if they were not in love.

"in love." Women either were undecided or said that they would get married even if they did not love their prospective husband (Kephart, 1967). In the 1980s, women and men tended to agree that they would not get married unless they were "in love." And more than half of today's men and women say that not being "in love" is sufficient reason to dissolve a marriage (Bersheid, Snyder, & Omoto, 1989).

I flee who chases me, and chase who flees me.

Ovid, *The Loves*, A.D. 8

Romantic love is especially important among college students. One study of unattached college men and women found that more than half identified a romantic partner, rather than a parent, sibling, or friend, as their closest relationship (Bersheid, Snyder, & Omoto, 1989). We are referring to romantic love when we say, "I am *in love*," not just "I *love*."

Romantic love includes a complex intermingling of different emotions—fear, anger, sexual desire, joy, and jealousy, for example. Obviously, some of these emotions are a source of anguish. One study found that romantic loves were more likely than friends to be the cause of depression (Berscheid & Fei, 1977).

Although Berscheid admits this is an inadequate answer, she concluded that romantic love is about 90 percent sexual desire. Berscheid (1988) believes sexual desire is vastly neglected in the study of romantic love. As she puts it, "To discuss romantic love without also prominently mentioning the role sexual arousal and desire plays in it is very much like printing a recipe for tiger soup that leaves out the main ingredient."

Love is purely a creation of the human imagination . . . the most important example of how the imagination continually outruns the creature it inhabits.

Katherine Anne Porter

---

form more than people in hunter-gatherer groups (Berry, 1967). Agricultural societies rely on the cooperation of their residents to cultivate, plant, and harvest their food supply. This high degree of interdependence makes it vital that members conform to societal norms. More complex societies sometimes reward nonconformity, encouraging members to exploit the diverse opportunities for career and self-expression offered in the multifaceted dimensions of the societies.

Groupthink

Sometimes groups make rational decisions and come up with the best solution to a problem. Not always. Group members, especially leaders, often want to develop or maintain unanimity among group members. **Groupthink** *is the motivation of group members to maintain harmony and unanimity in decision making, suffocating differences of opinion in the process* (Janis, 1972). Groupthink evolves because members often boost each other's egos and increase each other's self-esteem by seeking conformity, especially in stressful circumstances. This motivation for harmony and unanimity may result in disastrous decisions and policy recommendations. Examples of groupthink include the United States invasion of Cuba (the Bay of Pigs), the escalation of the Vietnam war, the failure to prepare for the invasion of Pearl Harbor, the Watergate coverup, Irangate, and the launching of the unsafe *Challenger* shuttlecraft.

Leaders often favor a solution and promote it within the group. Members of the group also tend to be cohesive and isolate themselves from qualified outsiders who could influence their decisions. Leaders can avoid groupthink by encouraging dissident opinions, by not presenting a favored plan at the outset, by appointing a "devil's advocate" to argue for unpopular opinions, and by having several independent groups work on the same problem.

Deindividuation

Group membership usually confers many advantages. However, some group processes are not only unpleasant but dangerous. As early as 1895, Gustav LeBon observed that a group can foster uninhibited behavior, ranging from wild celebrations to mob behavior. The brutal activities of the Ku Klux Klan, the wearing of erotic outfits in public during Mardi Gras wild times, and "good ol' boys" rolling a car on spring break in Fort Lauderdale might be due to **deindividuation,** *a state of reduced self-awareness, weakened self-restraints against impulsive actions, and apathy about negative social evaluation.*

One explanation of deindividuation is that the group offers anonymity: We may act in an uninhibited manner because we believe that authority figures and victims are less likely to discover that we are the culprits. Other explanations emphasize that arousal and conformity to the roles emerging in the group can fuel behavior in agitated groups that the individuals involved would not engage in on their own.

We have examined how social influence operates in interpersonal and group relationships. Next we will explore how work settings serve as a social context.

We can become deindividuated in groups. Examples of situations in which people can lose their individual identity include *(a)* at Ku Klux Klan rallies, *(b)* at Mardi Gras, and *(c)* in national patriotism crowds.

ORGANIZATIONAL BEHAVIOR

Not only does work provide us with a means of earning a living, but we also hope it will give us a sense of purpose and fulfillment in life. Because work is such a fundamental part of most people's lives, psychologists are becoming increasingly interested in understanding what makes the workplace a good environment. We will discuss industrial/organizational psychology, workers' functions in groups, and the changing faces and places of organizations.

Industrial/Organizational Psychology

Industrial/organizational (I/O) psychology *is the branch of psychology that focuses on the workplace—both its workers and the organization that employs them.* Industrial/organizational psychologists are concerned with personnel selection and development; with employee attitudes, motivation, and morale; and with the many facets of understanding and predicting behavior in organizations. The I/O psychologist serves both the employee and the employer—sometimes a very thin line to straddle—on the one hand working to enhance the worker's life, on the other hand seeking to improve the profitability of the organization.

There are two sides to I/O psychology—the science/research side and the practical/applied side. On the research side, I/O psychology is a scientific field concerned with conducting studies that will advance knowledge about people at work. The practical/applied side of I/O psychology is concerned with putting the results of scientific knowledge gained through research into practice to solve work-related problems. Consider the following example of I/O psychology's practical side. The shape and color of road signs are a result of research by I/O psychologists on highway safety. You may remember from your earlier study in sensation and perception that colors in the blue range of the visible light spectrum are detected best by the rods in our retinas. The applied result: many police cars are equipped with at least one blue light. I/O psychologists also contributed to the layout and design of controls on such items as kitchen ranges and telephones. The push-button phone (touch tone) was developed because I/O psychologists demonstrated that pushing buttons was easier, more accurate, and faster than dialing.

Industrial/organizational psychology covers a vast territory and can be divided up in many ways. One of the most common ways to partition I/O psychology is into industrial psychology, organizational psychology, and human factors psychology (engineering psychology).

Working with people is difficult, but not impossible.
Peter Drucker

Industrial psychology *is the subdivision of I/O psychology that focuses on personnel and human resource management. This branch consists of the various personnel* activities that organizations engage in such as recruitment, selection, performance appraisal, training, and career development. A basic underlying theme of all of these activities is individual differences. People are different and an important goal of industrial psychology is to examine these differences in an empirical way. Companies do not want to recruit everyone, only those candidates who are likely to make good workers. By the same logic, companies don't want to hire just anybody, only those workers who have a high probability of being successful workers.

Organizational psychology *is the subdivision of I/O psychology that examines the social and group influences within an organization, in contrast with the emphasis of industrial psychologists on individual differences.* Most people do not work in isolation—few of us are lighthouse keepers! They interact with other people and the organization for which they work in many ways. Workers are affected by managers, formal groups of coworkers, the formal policies and procedures of the organization, and various changes that are made by the organization. Likewise, organizations are influenced by employees. Thus, organizational psychologists study the way in which individuals and organizations interact.

Human factors psychology (engineering psychology) *is the subdivision of I/O psychology that focuses on (a) the design of machines that workers use to perform their jobs and (b) making the environment in which humans function safer and more efficient.* Equipment must be designed to be compatible with the worker. If the person and the machine are to work in concert, they must be matched to one another, each making the best use of the other's strengths.

Workers in Groups

Organizations consist of both formal and informal groups. **Formal groups** *are established by management to do the organization's work.* Formal groups include such departments as quality assurance, electrical engineering, cost accounting, and personnel. Organizations are increasingly using formal groups known as work teams (Sundstrom, De Meuse, & Futrell, 1990). Work teams are often established for subsections of manufacturing and assembly processes. For example, General Motors reorganized its assembly lines into work teams of 5 to 20 workers. In the work team approach, the team members decide among themselves who will do each task. This approach is derived from the Japanese style of management, which is discussed in greater detail in Sociocultural Worlds 18.3.

Informal groups *are clusters of workers formed by the group's members.* Informal groups develop because of the interests and needs of the individuals who work in the organization. They consist of both friendship groups, arising from relationships that develop among members of the organization, and interest groups, which are organized around a common activity or interest, such as sports, the arts, or politics. Among the interest groups that have developed in recent years are networks of working women. Many of these groups began in male-dominated organizations as

Among interest groups that have developed in recent years are networks of working women. Many of these groups began as informal gatherings of women in male-dominated organizations who wanted the support of other women.

The corporate board rooms of American business are male dominated and in many instances are filled exclusively with males. Only one African American heads a Fortune 1000 company and, in one survey of 1,700 senior executives, only 8 were women, all of them White.

informal gatherings of women who wanted the support of other women. Soon, however, they developed far beyond their initial social purposes. The interest groups became sources of counseling, job placement, and management training. Some of the interest groups were established as formal, permanent associations, whereas others remained informal groups.

Informal groups can be as influential as formal groups in determining behavior in an organization. One classic study demonstrated the sensitivity of workers to the behavior of others in their group and the importance of informal norms of behavior at the Hawthorne Plant of the Western Electric Company in Chicago (Mayo, 1993; Roethlisberger & Dickson, 1939). Management set a goal for each worker to wire a certain number of telephone switchboards per day. However, the work group as a whole established an acceptable level of output for its members. Workers who were above or below this informally established norm were criticized by other members of the work group. Workers who failed to meet the acceptable level were called "chiselers," whereas those who exceeded the norm were labeled "rate busters" or "speed kings." A worker who wanted to be accepted by the group could not produce at too low or too high a level. Thus, as a worker approached the accepted level for each day, he or she slowed down rather than overproduce. Even though the individual workers could have made more money by producing more switchboards, they adhered to the informal work group's norm.

The Changing Faces and Places of Organizations

As we move into the twenty-first century, what will the workplace be like? Changes are expected in both the workers and the work environment. In the year 2000, workers will be more culturally diverse—one-third of all new en-

trants into the labor force are anticipated to be ethnic minority members. Larger numbers of women will enter the labor force, putting greater pressure on society to help balance the demands of work and family (Ickovics, 1991; Offermann & Gowing, 1990). Work settings themselves also are changing.

Gender and Ethnicity

In the Japanese workplace, most women have inferior roles as temporary workers. Although women and ethnic minorities in the American workplace are considered permanent employees, organizational psychologists Ann Morrison and Mary Ann Von Glinow (1990) assert that White women and people of color experience a "glass ceiling" in management. The glass ceiling concept was popularized in the 1980s to describe a subtle barrier that is virtually transparent yet so strong that it prevents women and ethnic minorities from moving up in the management hierarchy. Today women fill nearly one-third of all management positions, an improvement from 19 percent in 1972, but most are in jobs with little authority and low pay. Only 2 percent of all senior executives are women, and only 1.7 percent of the corporate officers of all Fortune 500 companies are women. The picture for ethnic minority executives is even more dismal. Only one African American heads a Fortune 1000 company.

A number of reasons have been proposed for these gender and ethnic disparities in management (Morrison & Von Glinow, 1990). One explanation points to inadequacies in women and ethnic minorities themselves. For example, women's fear of success or their unwillingness to take risks have been proposed as reasons for their lack of management positions (Riger & Galligan, 1980). However, female and male managers are much more similar than dissimilar on many personality, motivational, and intellectual factors.

Nenko Management in Japan

In the past several decades, Americans have become very interested in the Japanese style of management called Nenko, which emphasizes group decision making by consensus. Nenko is practiced in approximately 30 percent of Japan's manufacturing companies. This management approach consists of three basic strategies: Articulate a unique company philosophy, engage employees in extensive socialization, and view the organization as an internal labor market (Havatny & Pucik, 1981; Oh, 1976).

Employees are hired soon after they graduate and generally remain in Nenko organizations throughout their careers. Companies practicing Nenko go to great lengths to establish a "family" atmosphere. Employees not only work together, they often live together in company housing, vacation at company resorts, and socialize at company centers. Young employees are selected on the basis of not only

their technical qualifications but also the ease with which they can be assimilated, or "fit," into the organization. Employers expect that employees will dedicate their service and loyalty to the company. In their first several years of work, employees rotate into different jobs at the same level in an organization so they can learn various aspects of the business and get to know their co-workers. This strategy helps socialize employees to the company's culture and philosophy. Their early salaries are meager, but they receive other forms of economic subsidy from the company to support them until their salaries grow.

Nenko organizations use a number of specific techniques to support their objectives (Havatny & Pucik, 1981). Employers assign tasks to work teams, not to individuals; managers evaluate group performance rather than individual performance. They base individual salary appraisals on the quality of group performance. Not surprisingly, Japanese workers usually develop a strong group identity. Subtle pressures encourage Nenko workers to seek friendships in the organization. Managers spend considerable time talking with employees about personal concerns, providing housing assistance, suggesting recreational activities, and sometimes even assisting in arranging marriage. Such strategies help the firm's management convey its concern for the employee's welfare; in return, employees become committed to the organization.

However, the Nenko approach has its critics. The approach blatantly discriminates against women, who are considered only temporary employees and are paid at substantially lower rates. Nenko employees retire at age 55. If they stay on the job longer, their pay is also cut dramatically (Oh, 1976). Employment in a Nenko company is difficult to

---

Ethnic minority managers have shown special strengths in interpersonal relations and stability of performance. A second explanation is that the dominant group is biased. Many employers, customers, and employees believe that women and people of color are less suited for management positions, even when they are strong candidates. Another belief that handicaps women in particular is that in most organizations the "good manager" is still described as masculine rather than androgynous. A third explanation is that the racist underpinning of society permeate organizations. Intergroup theory states that two types of groups exist in organizations—identity groups (based on ethnicity, family, gender, and age) and organization groups (based on common work tasks, work experience, and positions in the hierarchy). Tension results when the composition of an organization's group membership changes but the mix in identity group membership does not (Thomas & Aldefer,

1989). An organization's demographics often mirror the pattern in society as a whole, as when Whites fill most of the high-status positions and African Americans the low-status positions. As a result, managers may evaluate women and people of color through the distorted lens of prejudice.

Many organizational psychologists believe that the workplace needs to adjust to accommodate women and ethnic minorities. Eastman Kodak and Du Pont are two companies that have implemented programs designed to help managers work together within a diverse workforce and to reduce discrimination. The value of such programs is that issues are brought out into the open, allowing individuals to discuss their beliefs.

A special concern for women and ethnic minorities in organizations is **tokenism,** *which means being treated as a representative of a group rather than as an individual.* The token position places enormous pressure on women and

secure and depends on the appropriateness of the candidate's educational track, which might begin as early as preschool. Critics suggest that Nenko promotes conformity at the expense of individual creativity. They also argue that Nenko might not be the real cause of Japan's economic success, since it is found only in the major Japanese firms; many small companies cannot afford the luxury of hiring employees for life. Critics argue that Japan's meteoric economic rise also has been fueled by postwar reconstruction, a close alliance between government and business, a strong sense of nationalism, and a strong cultural tradition of duty, obedience, and discipline (Steers, 1988).

Nenko advocates argue that its basic strategies can help American organizations improve their performance. The approach has been successfully applied in some American firms, such as Rockwell International, an aerospace firm, and Eli Lilly, a pharmaceutical company. Despite the criticisms, Nenko will have considerable value for certain firms, although others might function more effectively using different management approaches (Lincoln & Kalleberg, 1990). This may be especially true of companies that operate in individualistic cultural contexts, which focus on individual achievement, rather than collectivist contexts, which foster collaboration and group pride. As we approach the twenty-first century, global economic interdependence will emphasize three features of successful workers (Brislin, 1993): (1) awareness of impending changes and the cultural contexts in which they occur; (2) awareness of knowledge that will help them adapt; and (3) skill in dealing with conflicts and emotional confrontations in resolving problems among diverse peoples.

In Japan—a collectivist culture—the management style emphasizes group and consensual decision making, and Japanese management engages employees in extensive socialization.

ethnic minority individuals. Organizational psychologists believe that when women and ethnic minority individuals face tokenism, they need to perfect certain skills, such as the ability to negotiate and resolve conflict (Morrison & Von Glinow, 1990).

Support groups may help increase the number of women and ethnic minority members in management. For example, Security Pacific National Bank developed a program entitled Black Officers Support System (BOSS) to recruit African Americans and reduce their turnover (Irons & Moore, 1985). In Washington, D.C., the Executive Leadership Council is made up of fifty African American managers from major industries who recruit and hire ethnic minorities (Leinster, 1988). Such groups provide career guidance and psychological support for women and ethnic minority individuals seeking managerial positions.

Changing Organizations

Organizations themselves also will change. Corporations are failing at a noticeable rate, whereas others are scaling down the size of their operations to survive. Mergers and acquisitions displace workers with increasing regularity. The types of jobs available continue to shift from the manufacturing sector to the service sector, which accounted for 71 percent of the nation's jobs in 1990. In addition, businesses are increasingly becoming international organizations. As a result, many companies' success may rest on the ability to relate to workers and companies in other countries.

Many jobs are becoming more complex and more cognitively demanding. As knowledge increases exponentially, technically trained workers, such as engineers, face a "half life" of 5 years; that is, half of what engineers know in any given year is obsolete 5 years later because of rapid

As we move into the twenty-first century, the workforce will be increasingly diverse. However, many barriers still prevent women and ethnic minorities from reaching the high levels of management. One training strategy of some corporations is to provide support groups for recruiting women and ethnic minorities and socializing them about the culture of the organization.

technological advances (Goldstein & Gilliam, 1990). In the future, such demands will require considerable continuing education and training programs for workers.

Millions of workers center a great deal of their lives on the workplace. As a result, the heads of organizations are realizing that the workplace is an important setting for promoting an individual's health and welfare (Offermann & Gowing, 1990). Many organizations have programs to help workers balance work and family and promote health through stress-management courses and fitness centers.

On many occasions in this chapter we have seen how social contexts influence behavior. In the next chapter, we continue to explore the important role of contexts in behavior by studying how culture and ethnicity influence behavior.

REVIEW

Group Relations and Organizational Behavior

Groups satisfy our personal needs, reward us, provide us with information, raise our self-esteem, and enhance our identity. Every group has norms and roles. Both the great person theory, which emphasizes personality traits and skills, and situational factors have been proposed to explain why certain people become leaders. Personality and situational factors likely combine to determine who will become a leader. The majority usually has the most influence, but at times the minority has its day, being most effective through using informational pressure. Conformity is change in an individual's behavior because of real or imagined pressure to do so. Two experiments demonstrate conformity's power in our lives: Asch's study on judgments of line length and Zimbardo's study of social roles in a mock prison. Groupthink is the motivation of group members to

maintain harmony and unanimity in decision making, suffocating differences of opinion in the process. Deindividuation is the loss of identity as an individual and the development of group identity in group situations, which promote arousal and anonymity.

Industrial/organizational psychology focuses on the workplace, both its workers and the organizations that employ them. A common way of partitioning I/O psychology is into industrial psychology, organizational psychology, and human factors psychology (engineering psychology). Groups in organizations include both formal groups—established by management to do the organization's work—and informal groups—formed by the group's members. Informal groups include friendships and interest groups. Some organizational psychologists believe that women and ethnic minority individuals face a

number of barriers in their efforts to move up the management hierarchy. There are very few women in the top levels of management and even fewer ethnic minorities. A reason for these low numbers is based on differences that handicap women and ethnic minorities, as well as discrimination. However, there are more similarities than differences between White males and their female and ethnic minority counterparts. A special concern is tokenism. Changes are expected in both workers and the environment of the workplace. The workplace will increasingly become diverse, service oriented, and internationally linked. Many jobs are becoming more complex and cognitively demanding. Increased interest in the workplace as a setting for promoting individuals' health and welfare is occurring.

Loneliness, like depression, can be a dark cloud that enfolds a person's day-to-day life. Feeling lonely should not be confused with being alone. Time spent alone can be quite satisfying and meaningful, but when we find ourselves longing to be with others and feeling unconnected, isolated, and alienated our loneliness can seriously interfere with our sense of life satisfaction. Although most of us may feel lonely from time to time, some people find themselves feeling intensely lonely for long periods of time.

One way to prevent loneliness is to become involved with activities that involve interactions with others. For example, many opportunities to meet others and become involved arise through work, school, community announcements, and religious organizations. Sometimes people can join organizations and volunteer time for some cause that they endorse. Spending time with others and developing social network will have the long term payoff of reducing the chances of being alone and feeling lonely. In addition, people can arrange their lifestyle in such a way as to increase social contacts. For example, one social gathering can lead to the development of several new social contacts if people take the initiative to introduce themselves to others and start a conversation. Meeting new people and developing social ties always involves taking some personal risks, but the benefits often outweigh these risks.

Loneliness often occurs as a result of the loss of social contacts. Moving to a new community, changing jobs, and breaking off dating relationships usually decrease the number of social contacts a person has. Thus, when social contacts are lost they need to be replaced. Lost contacts need not be replaced with the same type of relationship. For example, when a dating relationship is broken off, new nondating friends can fill the social void. Also, social contacts do not necessarily have to be new to meet social needs. Sometimes spending more time with old friends can meet social needs.

Like with depression, it is important to recognize the warning signs of loneliness. Knowing what feelings might arise before one begins to feel lonely can allow a person to head off the loneliness by doing something. For example, some people may begin to feel somewhat bored and alienated before loneliness sinks in. Recognizing these feelings as a warning sign of loneliness can make a big difference in people's being able to prevent themselves from becoming lonely. This is especially important because loneliness can become so intense that it can keep a person from acting. Thus, as with depression, heading off loneliness can be much easier than trying to get out of it.

Over and above most other means of avoiding loneliness is the development of interests and activities that provide the opportunity to develop social contacts.

continued . . .

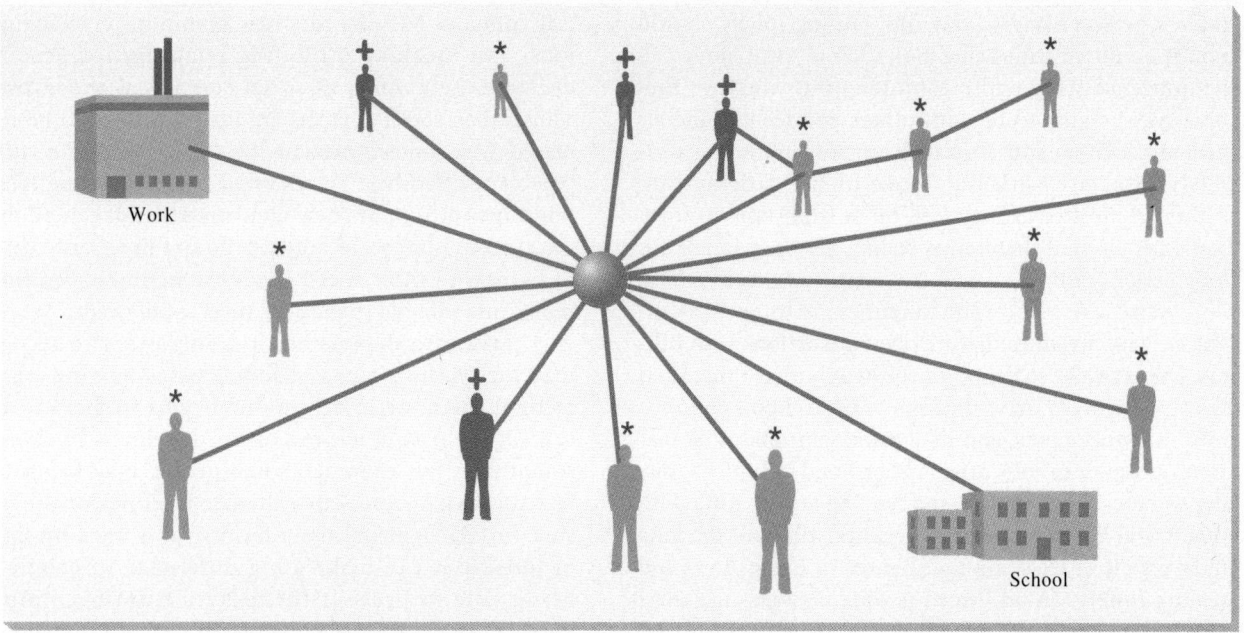

FIGURE 18.7

An Example of a Social Network
The center represents the person, such as yourself, connected to the surrounding persons represented by *'s. For this network, there are additional clusters of others in the domains of school and work that the person is connected to. Only four of the persons are close friends, however, represented by a +.

A person's social contacts are referred to as a social network because usually contacts are not isolated from each other, but rather are interconnected. Consider your own social network. You probably know many people, some better than others, and some who know each other. You can examine your own social network by drawing it out in a schematic diagram. Figure 18.7 shows an example of such a diagram, with each star representing a social contact, connected by lines if they know each other. None of the contacts are family, and those with a plus are closer friends than those without pluses.

Evaluating your social network shows how your social needs are met. When social contacts change or are lost, knowing your social network can help you make adjustments and avoid loneliness. Take some time and think about the people you see and those that you share time with. Construct a social network and think about relationships that are most important to you and those you would like to strengthen. Use the space below to note the people you see as connected to you and the strength of the relationships. Upon completion, you will have *applied psychological concepts to enhance your personal adaptation.*

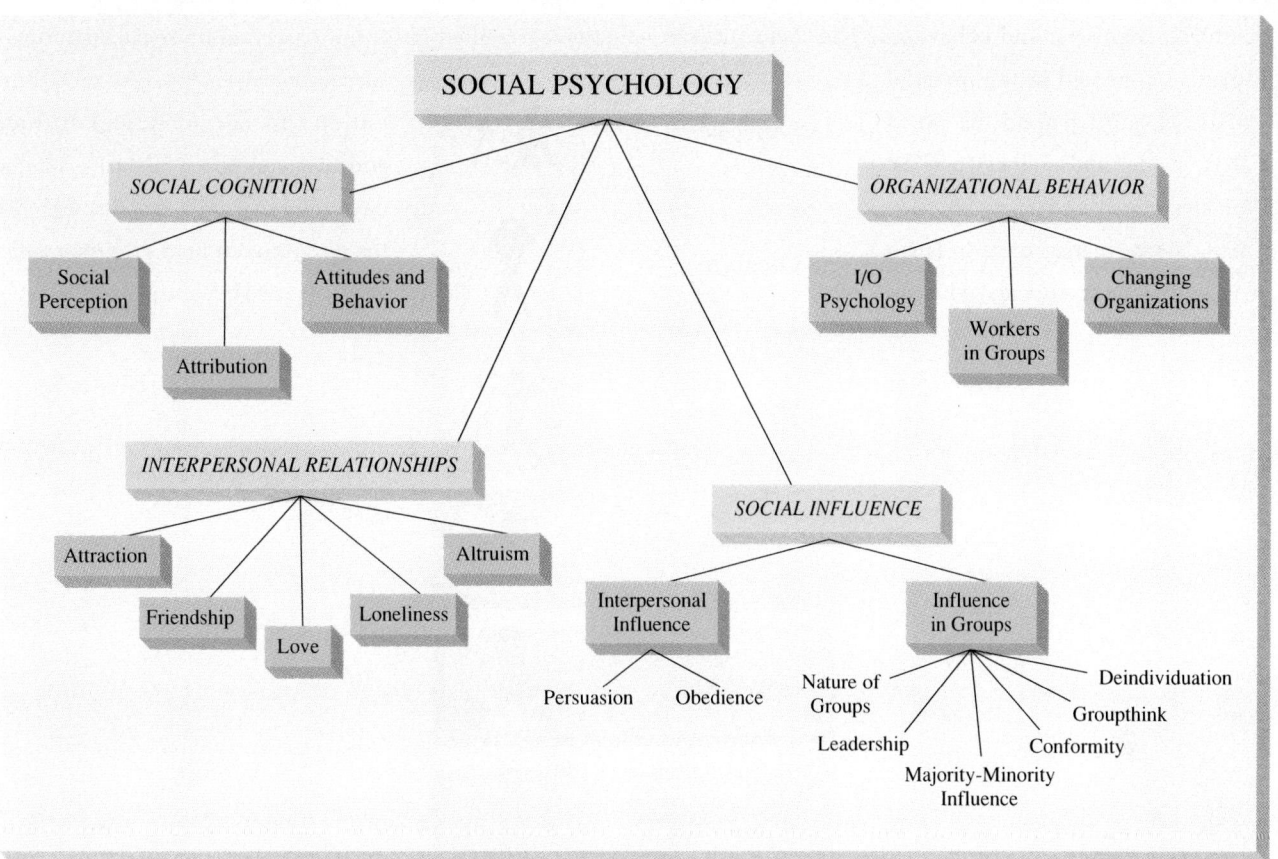

SOCIAL PSYCHOLOGY

SOCIAL COGNITION

- Social Perception
- Attribution
- Attitudes and Behavior

ORGANIZATIONAL BEHAVIOR

- I/O Psychology
- Workers in Groups
- Changing Organizations

INTERPERSONAL RELATIONSHIPS

- Attraction
- Friendship
- Love
- Loneliness
- Altruism

SOCIAL INFLUENCE

- Interpersonal Influence
  - Persuasion
  - Obedience
- Influence in Groups
  - Nature of Groups
  - Leadership
  - Majority-Minority Influence
  - Conformity
  - Groupthink
  - Deindividuation

We began this chapter by studying the nature of social cognition, including social perception, attribution, and attitudes and behavior. Then we evaluated interpersonal relationships, focusing on attraction, friendship, love, loneliness, and altruism. Our coverage of social influence emphasized interpersonal influence (persuasion and obedience) and influence in groups (the nature of groups, leadership, majority-minority influence, conformity, groupthink, and deindividuation). The final main section of the chapter described the nature of work relationships—I/O psychology, workers in groups, and the changing workforce. Don't forget that you can obtain an overall summary of the chapter by again reading the in-chapter reviews on pages 662, 670, 677, and 686.

Three perspectives were presented in this chapter: the sociocultural, cognitive, and behavioral. The sociocultural perspective appeared in the material on mate selection around the world (p. 663), gender and politics (p. 672), cultural variations in conformity (p. 680), Nenko management in Japan (pp. 684–685), and gender and ethnicity in organizations (pp. 683–685). The cognitive perspective was represented in the entire section on social cognition—social perception (pp. 657–658), attribution (pp. 658–659), and attitudes and behavior (pp. 659–661). The behavioral perspective was presented in the discussion of Bem's self-perception theory (p. 661).

Sociocultural

Cognitive

Behavioral

Psychoanalytic

Humanistic

Neurobiological

social perception Judgment about the qualities of individuals, which involves how we form impressions of others, how we gain self-knowledge from perception of others, and how we present ourselves to others to influence their perceptions of us.   657

primacy effect The enduring quality of initial impressions.   657

social comparison The process in which individuals evaluate their thoughts, feelings, behaviors, and abilities in relation to other people.   657

impression management The process in which individuals strive to present themselves in a favorable light.   658

attribution theory The theory that individuals are motivated to discover the underlying causes of behavior as part of their interest in making sense out of the behavior.   658

fundamental attribution error Observers' tendency to overestimate the importance of traits and underestimate the importance of situations when they seek explanations of an actor's behavior.   658

actor-observer hypothesis In attribution theory, differences in the interpretation of motives based on point of view.   658

attitudes Beliefs and opinions that can predispose individuals to behave in certain ways.   659

cognitive dissonance A concept developed by social psychologist Leon Festinger; an individual's motivation toward consistency and away from inconsistency.   660

self-perception theory Bem's theory of connections between attitudes and behavior; it stresses that individuals make inferences about their attitudes by perceiving their behavior.   661

consensual validation A concept that provides an explanation of why people are attracted to others who are similar to them. Our own attitudes and behavior are supported when someone else's attitudes and behavior are similar to ours— their attitudes and behaviors validate ours.   662

chastity Inexperience with sexual intercourse.   663

matching hypothesis The hypothesis that while we may prefer a more attractive person in the abstract, in the real world we end up choosing someone who is close to our own level of attractiveness.   664

friendship A form of close relationship that involves enjoyment, acceptance, trust, intimacy, respect, mutual assistance, understanding, and spontaneity.   664

romantic love Also called passionate love or Eros; a type of love with strong components of sexuality and infatuation; it often predominates in the early part of a love relationship.   664

affectionate love Also called companionate love; a type of love that occurs when an individual desires to have the other person near and has a deep, caring affection for the person.   666

triangular theory of love Sternberg's theory that love comes in three main forms: passion, intimacy, and commitment.   666

altruism An unselfish interest in helping someone else.   668

social exchange theory The theory that individuals should benefit those who benefit them, or that, for a benefit received, an equivalent benefit should be returned at some point.   669

egoism An attitude in which one does something beneficial for another person in order to ensure reciprocity; to present oneself as powerful, competent, or caring; or to avoid social or self-censure for failing to live up to normative expectations.   669

bystander effect The effect of others' presence on a person's giving help; individuals who observe an emergency help less when someone, another observer, is present than when they are a lone observer.   670

obedience Behavior that complies with the explicit demands of an individual in authority.   674

norms Rules that apply to the members of a group.   677

roles Rules and expectations that govern certain positions in a group. Roles define how people should behave in a particular position in the group.   677

great person theory The theory that individuals with certain traits are best suited for leadership positions.   678

situational theory of leadership The theory that the needs of a group change from time to time and that a person who emerges as leader in one circumstance will not necessarily be the person who becomes a leader in another circumstance.   678

conformity Individuals' adopting the attitudes or behavior of others because of real or imagined pressure from others to do so.   679

groupthink The motivation of group members to maintain harmony and unanimity in decision making, suffocating differences of opinion in the process.   681

deindividuation A state of reduced self-awareness, weakened self-restraints against impulsive actions, and apathy about negative social evaluation.   681

industrial/organizational (I/O) psychology The branch of psychology that focuses on the workplace—both its workers and the organization that employs them.   682

industrial psychology The subdivision of I/O psychology that focuses on personnel and human resource management. This branch consists of the various personnel activities that organizations engage in, such as recruitment, selection, performance appraisal, training, and career development.   682

organizational psychology The subdivision of I/O psychology that examines the social and group influences within an organization, in contrast with the emphasis of industrial psychologists on individual differences.   682

formal groups Groups established by management to do the organization's work.   682

informal groups Clusters of workers formed by the group's members.   682

tokenism Treating a person as a representative of a group rather than as an individual.   684

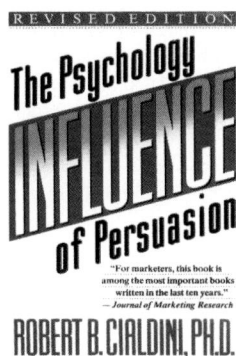

INFLUENCE

(1993, rev. ed.) by Robert Cialdini. New York: Quill.

This highly acclaimed book by a well-known social psychologist explores how influence works in today's marketplace. Cialdini provides valuable suggestions for persuading other people and understanding how others try to persuade us. He also covers how power works, the role of reciprocity in influence, the importance of commitment and consistency, how to say no, scarcity, relationships with others, advertising, sales techniques, and instant influence.

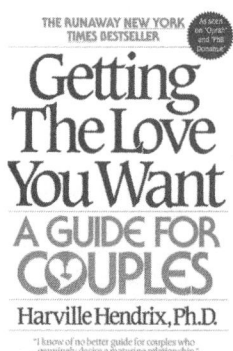

GETTING THE LOVE YOU WANT

(1988) by Harville Hendrix. New York: Henry Holt.

Getting the Love You Want is a guide for couples to help them improve their relationship. The book is based on Hendrix's couple workshop techniques that are designed to help couples construct a conscious marriage, a relationship based on awareness of unresolved childhood needs and conflicts that cause individuals to select a particular spouse. The author instructs readers how to conduct a 10-week course in marital therapy in the privacy of their home. In stepwise fashion you learn how to communicate more clearly and sensitively, how to eliminate self-defeating behaviors, and how to focus your attention on meeting your partner's needs. Hendrix's goal is to transform the downward spiral of the struggle for power into a mutually beneficial relationship of emotional growth.

This is a good book for couples, especially those engulfed in a conflicted relationship. Hendrix does an excellent job of helping you become aware of long-standing family-of-origin influences on your current relationships. His 10-week in-home workshop includes a variety of ingenious exercises.

SHYNESS

(1987) by Philip Zimbardo. Reading, MA: Addison-Wesley.

According to Zimbardo, shyness is a widespread social problem that affects as many as four out of every five people at one time or another in their lives. He explores how and why people become shy and examines the roles that parents, teachers, spouses, and culture play in creating shy individuals. What does Zimbardo say shy people can do about their situations? First, you have to analyze your shyness and figure out how you got this way. Possible reasons include negative evaluations, fear of being rejected, fear of intimacy, or lack of adequate social skills. Second, you need to build up your self-esteem. To help you do this, Zimbardo spells out fifteen steps to becoming more confident. And third, you need to improve your social skills. Zimbardo describes several behavior modification strategies, tells you to set realistic goals, and advocates working hard toward achieving these goals. This is an excellent self-help book for shy individuals. It dispenses sound advice, is free of psychobabble, and is easy to read.

Intimate Connections (1985)

> by David Burns
>
> New York: William Morrow

This book describes how to overcome loneliness. Burns believes lonely individuals need to change their patterns of perception. He tells you how to make social connections and develop closer relationships with others. Checklists, daily mood logs, and self-assessments are found through the book.

Intimate Strangers (1983)

> by Lilian Rubin
>
> New York: HarperCollins

This book focuses on intimacy and communication difficulties between women and men. Rubin believes that female/male differences in intimacy are related to the fact that it is mothers who primarily raise children and are the family's emotional manager. She believes females develop a much greater capacity for intimacy than males do. Her solution is for fathers to become more nurturant with their children.

The Social Animal (1995, 7th ed.)

> by Elliot Aronson
>
> New York: W. H. Freeman

This book is an enjoyable presentation of research and thinking about many different topics in social psychology by a leader researcher. Aronson discusses conformity, mass communication, persuasion, and self-justification.

SCORING AND INTERPRETATION OF THE PASSIONATE LOVE QUIZ

SCORING

Total your responses for the 15 items on the passionate love scale.

INTERPRETATION

If your score is 15–45, your passionate love experience has not been a very passionate one; if your score is 60–90, it has been a moderately passionate one; and if your score is 105–135, your passionate love experience has been a very intense one.

Culture and Ethnicity

We need every human gift and cannot
afford to neglect any gift because of
artificial barriers of sex or race or class
or national origin.

Margaret Mead, *Male and Female* **(1949)**

THE STORY OF ROSA PARKS: A DIGNIFIED CHALLENGE

While riding home on the bus from her job as an assistant tailor in a department store in downtown Montgomery, Alabama, 42-year-old Rosa Parks resisted her way into history. On December 1, 1955, she chose a seat next to a Black man in the front of the area in the bus that the bus line set aside for Blacks. The front of the bus, which was reserved for Whites, was already full. When a White man got on in search of a seat, the driver asked the four Blacks in the front row of the Black section to move, which was the established practice by the bus line. Parks refused to move even though the others complied. The driver called the police, who arrested Parks and sent her to jail. Released on a $100 bond, she moved quickly to help in the organization of the Montgomery Improvement Association (MIA) to address the problem of segregation, electing Martin Luther King, Jr., as the organization's first president. They initiated a bus boycott to protest practices that discriminated against Blacks, who constituted 75 percent of the ridership of the bus line. At her trial, the jury found Parks guilty and fined her $10. She refused to pay, and the authorities sent her back to jail. The MIA targeted Alabama segregation laws by filing suit against the state for discriminatory treatment of Parks and others on the bus line. Nearly a year later, after much litigation, the U.S. Supreme Court ordered the integration of the Montgomery bus lines. The costly boycott of the bus line ended after 381 days.

Parks had learned about prejudice and slavery from the stories that her maternal grandparents told. She had joined the NAACP in 1943, serving as the secretary for 13 years. She also had been active in recruiting Blacks to vote. Despite her activism, she might not have foreseen what events would follow her resistance that day on the Montgomery bus. In an interview later in her life, she explained her action by saying, "I felt just resigned to give what I could to protest against the way I was treated."

After Parks served her jail term, her circumstances worsened. She and her husband lost their jobs and suffered significant harassment from the community. Finding life in Montgomery no longer tolerable, they eventually moved to Detroit, where she continued her community organizing activities. Her refusal to give up her seat in the face of tremendous social pressure and well-established discriminatory practices has made her widely recognized as "the mother of the civil rights movement." As a result of her courage and her commitment, the United States began to change, setting the stage for new opportunities to understand and celebrate the diversity of the American people (Smith, 1991).

PREVIEW

The valiant actions of Parks and others during the period of the civil rights movement capture many of the social psychology concepts that we will address in this chapter on culture and ethnicity. We will explore how things change in cultural and ethnic traditions. We will also discuss the processes that create strain between people. Throughout this final chapter we will also integrate ideas from previous chapters to promote your retention of key ideas. We will conclude with an exploration of critical-thinking skills for promoting greater harmony among people who are different from each other.

Culture is the behavior patterns, beliefs, and all other products of a particular group of people that are passed on from generation to generation. In the Bororo culture of Niger in west central Africa, one custom that has been passed down through the generations in their culture is washing a friend's back at a well. *Since the Bororo are nomads, can you think of any other social purposes this cleanliness practice might serve?*

CULTURE

We live in a world that seems to have gotten smaller and more interactive through dramatic improvements in communications and travel. One consequence of life on a shrinking globe is the critical need to develop ways to live peaceably with others by understanding, tolerating, and appreciating differences among people, whether they live in different cultures, celebrate different ethnic traditions, or pursue lifestyles or belief systems substantially different from our own. Let's begin with the exploration of culture as the first step in examining the social processes that hinder or enhance our appreciation of diversity.

The Nature of Culture

In Arab communities, cleanliness is an important value. Muslim men and women attend the public baths once a week before Friday prayers because they believe that the purity of the soul relates to the cleanliness of the body. As

a condition of faith, Muslims also wash their hands before and after eating and wash their hands, arms, and feet before each of five daily prayers. Although many Western cultures promote the idea that "cleanliness is next to Godliness," our scientific knowledge of the role of germs in disease and promises from the health and cosmetics industries that cleanliness will improve our social status probably create greater conscientiousness among Westerners. People who live in Western cultures usually conduct their hygiene practices privately. Even something as relatively straightforward as bathing shows the clear influence of the power of cultural context on behavior (Fernea & Fernea, 1994).

Culture *refers to the behavior patterns, beliefs, and all other products of a particular group of people that are passed on from generation to generation.* These products result from the interaction between groups of people and their environment over many years. A cultural group can be as large as the population of the United States or as small as an African

HUNTER-GATHERERS, NORTH AMERICA, LATE 20TH CENTURY

© 1991 by Sidney Harris—"You Want Proof? . . ." W. H. Freeman and Company.

hunter-gatherer group. Whatever the size of the group, its culture influences the behavior of its members.

Cross-cultural studies—*comparisons of cultures with one or more other cultures*—*provide information about the degree to which people's behavior, thoughts, and feelings are similar, or universal, across cultures, or to what degree they are culture-specific.*

Cross-cultural expert Richard Brislin (1993) recently described the following features of culture:

- Culture is made up of ideals, values, and assumptions about life that guide people's behaviors.
- Culture refers to those aspects of the culture that people produce.
- Culture is transmitted from generation to generation, with the responsibility for the transmission resting on the shoulders of parents, teachers, and community leaders.
- Culture's influence often becomes noticed the most in well-meaning clashes between people from very different cultural backgrounds.
- Despite compromises, cultural values endure.
- When people's cultural values are violated or when cultural expectations are ignored, they react emotionally.
- It is not unusual for people to accept a cultural value at one point in their life and reject it at another point. For example, rebellious adolescents and young adults might accept a culture's values and expectations after having children of their own.

You might interpret Brislin's descriptions to suggest that members of a culture behave similarly—that is, that

they think, act, and react in uniform ways. However, anthropologists have established that individual differences emerge even in relatively homogeneous cultures (Kluckhohn, 1953). Despite the likely variation within cultures, cross-cultural studies have become a popular method for distinguishing aspects of humankind that are universal from those that might be distinctive of a particular cultural context.

Emic and Etic Approaches

When theorizing about and conducting research on culture, social scientists distinguish between an emic approach and an etic approach. In the **emic approach,** *the goal is to describe behavior in one culture or ethnic group in terms that are meaningful and important to the people in that culture or ethnic group, without regard to other cultures or ethnic groups. The emic approach is culture-specific.* In the **etic approach,** *the goal is to describe behavior so that generalizations can be made across cultures. The etic approach is culture-universal.* If researchers construct a questionnaire in an emic fashion, their concern is only that the questions be meaningful to the particular culture or ethnic group being studied. If, however, the researchers construct a questionnaire in an etic fashion, they want to include questions that reflect concepts familiar to all cultures.

Many cross-cultural psychologists advocate using emic strategies to identify and measure etic constructs (Triandis, 1994). For example, the notion of **social distance,** *an etic construct, is the cultural belief that people should maintain a certain distance from each other.* This belief exists in all cultures. However, the specific distance that should be maintained differs according to culture. In Latin American countries, to bathe the listener in your breath is a sign of respect that encourages very close social distance. This idea is horrifying to many odor-conscious Westerners who would find the Latin American practice offensive and intolerable. Both cultures believe distance should be regulated (the etic principle) but practice different zones of comfort. Emic approaches clarify these differences.

How might the emic and etic approaches be reflected in the study of family processes? In the emic approach, the researcher might choose to focus only on middle-class White families, without regard for whether the information in the study can be generalized to, or is appropriate for, ethnic minority groups. In a subsequent study, the researcher might decide to adopt an etic approach by studying not only middle-class White families but also lower-income White families, African American families, Latino American families, and Asian American families. One result of studying ethnic minority families is that researchers have found that the extended family provides a support system more often for ethnic minority families than for White families (McAdoo, 1994). In this case, the emic approach reveals a

CRITICAL THINKING

You have read about social distance and family studies as two examples of how etic approaches establish cultural universals by examining varying cultural practices through emic methods. Based on your own travels, reading, or talking with others from other cultures, can you think of another etic principle and emic implementations of that principle in two different cultures? Your application of these concepts demonstrate your ability to *make accurate observations, descriptions, and inferences about behavior.*

*Etic Principles with
Emic Realities*

Individualistic	Collectivistic
Focuses on individuals	Focuses on groups
Self is determined by personal traits independent of groups; self is stable across contexts	Self is defined in in-group terms; self can change with context
Private self is most important	Public self is most important
Personal achievement, competition, power are important	Achievement is for the benefit of the in-group; cooperation is stressed
Cognitive dissonance is frequent	Cognitive dissonance is infrequent
Emotions (such as anger) are self-focused	Emotions (such as anger) are often relationship based
People who are the most liked are self-assured	People who are the most liked are modest, self-effacing
Values: pleasure, achievement, competition, freedom	Values: security, obedience, in-group harmony, personalized relationships
Many casual relationships	Few, close relationships
Save own face	Save own and other's face
Independent behaviors: swimming, sleeping alone in room, privacy	Interdependent behaviors: co-bathing, co-sleeping
Relatively rare mother-child physical contact	Frequent mother-child physical contact (such as hugging, holding)

FIGURE 19.1

Characteristics of Individualistic and Collectivistic Cultures

different pattern of family interaction than the etic approach does, documenting that research with middle-class White families cannot always be generalized to other ethnic groups and that findings about ethnic groups cannot be assumed, without verification, to be true of other groups.

Individualism and Collectivism

In cross-cultural research, the search for basic traits has extended to characteristics common to whole nations. In recent years, the most elaborate search for traits has focused on the dichotomy between individualism and collectivism (Hofstede, 1980; Triandis, 1994; Triandis, Brislin, & Hui, 1988). **Individualism** *involves giving priority to personal goals rather than to group goals; it emphasizes values that serve the self, such as feeling good, personal distinction and achievement, and independence.* **Collectivism** *emphasizes values that serve the group by subordinating personal goals to preserve group integrity, interdependence of the members, and harmonious relationships.* Figure 19.1 summarizes some of the main characteristics of individualism and collectivism. Many Western cultures, such as the United States, Canada, Great Britain, and the Netherlands, are described as individualistic; many Eastern cultures, such as China, Japan, India, and Thailand, are described as collectivistic.

Many of psychology's basic tenets have been developed in individualistic cultures like the United States. Consider the flurry of *self-* terms in psychology that have an individualistic focus: for example, *self-actualization, self-awareness, self-efficacy, self-reinforcement, self-criticism, self-serving, selfishness,* and *self-doubt* (Lonner, 1988; Rumpel, 1988).

Critics of the Western notion of psychology point out that human beings have always lived in groups, whether large or small, and have always needed one another for survival. They argue that the Western emphasis on individualism may undermine our basic species need for relatedness (Kagitcibasi, 1988, 1995). Some social scientists believe that many problems in Western cultures are intensified by the Western cultural emphasis on individualism. Individualistic cultures have higher rates than collectivistic cultures for suicide, drug abuse, crime, teenage pregnancy, divorce, child abuse, and mental disorders. Some critics believe that the pendulum might have swung too far toward individualism in many Western cultures. Regardless of their cultural background, people need a positive sense of *self* and *connectedness to others* to develop fully as human beings.

Some psychologists criticize the individualism/collectivism dichotomy. They argue that describing an entire nation of people as all having the same basic kind of personality obscures the diversity and individual variation in any nation's people. Also, certain values are in both individual and collective interests; these include wisdom, mature love, and tolerance (Schwartz, 1990; Schwartz & Sagiv, 1995).

We are all in this together—by ourselves.

Lily Tomlin

Models of the Process of Change

We react to new cultural or ethnic experiences with a mix of emotions. When the new experience stretches into the future, other emotions and actions come into play. We will explore both situations further.

When two cultures collide is the only time when true suffering exists.

Hermann Hesse

Initial Contact

"There is no doubt that a sudden descent into the unknown can be an uncomfortable and at times terrifying experience, whether we are talking about a young American student's first trip abroad to Southeast Asia, a farmer from the U.S. Midwest visiting New York, a New Yorker hiking in the Rocky Mountains, or an Australian visiting Tokyo for the first time" (Bochner, 1994, p. 245). All of these experiences are examples of **culture shock,** *the disorganizing effects of exposure to unfamiliar ways of life.* Psychologist Stephen Bochner described the term *culture shock* as "snappy" but inadequate, as it emphasizes the negative or disabling effects of exposure and overlooks the exhilarating or positive benefits that can result from exploring new ways of life.

Enduring Contact

When contact between cultures or ethnic traditions is enduring, changes in attitudes, behavior, and lifestyle may result. These changes can happen at the individual level or can influence entire communities or cultures. Psychologists have proposed several models to describe how change occurs within culture and between cultures, including assimilation, acculturation, alternation, multiculturalism, integration, and fusion (Berry, 1990; LaFromboise, Coleman, & Gerton, 1993).

Assimilation *occurs when individuals relinquish their cultural identity and move into the larger society.* The nondominant group might be absorbed into an established "mainstream." The individuals who assimilate often suffer from a sense of alienation and isolation until they have been accepted, and perceive their acceptance, in the new culture.

Acculturation *is cultural change that results from continuous contact between two distinctive cultural groups and that preserves the identities of both.* In assimilation, people who assimilate will eventually become full members of the majority group's culture and lose their identity with their culture of origin. In contrast, acculturation stresses that people can become competent participants in the majority culture while still being identified as a member of a minority culture. Although this system sounds as though it honors heritage and thus would be more positive, it is not without stress. To read more about the nature of acculturative stress, turn to Sociocultural Worlds 19.1.

Alternation *assumes that it is possible for an individual to know and understand two different cultures. It also assumes that individuals can alter their behavior to fit a particular social context.* The alternation model differs from the assimilation and acculturation models in the following way: In the alternation model, it is possible to maintain a positive relationship with both cultures (LaFromboise, Coleman, & Gerton, 1993).

Multiculturalism *promotes a pluralistic approach to understanding two more cultures. This model argues that people can maintain their distinct identities while working with others from different cultures to meet national or economic needs they have in common.* Multicultural societies encourage all groups to maintain and/or develop their group identity, develop acceptance and tolerance of other groups, engage in intergroup contact and sharing, and learn each other's language. In the multicultural model, people can maintain a positive identity as members of their culture of origin while simultaneously developing a positive identity with another culture.

Integration *implies the maintenance of cultural integrity as well as the movement to become an integral part of the larger culture.* In this type of cultural arrangement, a number of cultural groups cooperate within a larger social system (which is "a mosaic").

Fusion *implies that cultures sharing economic, political, or geographic boundaries will fuse until they are indistinguishable and form a new culture.* This approach reflects the assumptions behind the "melting-pot theory" which some social scientists have referred to as "add culture and stir." Each culture brings to the melting pot various strengths and weaknesses that take on new forms through the interaction of cultures as equal partners. The fusion model differs from assimilation and accommodation in that the fusion model assumes that no culture is superior to another.

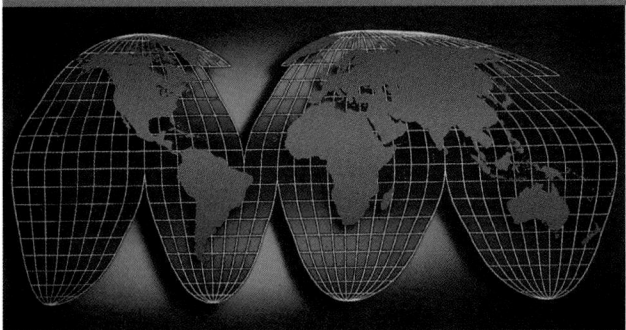

The Acculturative Stress of Ethnic Minority Individuals

As upwardly mobile ethnic minority families have attempted to integrate historically all-White neighborhoods, interracial tensions have mounted (Huang & Gibbs, 1989). Although many Americans have thought of racial tensions and prejudice largely as Black/White issues, this is no longer the case (Arbona, 1995). Racial tensions and hostility often emerge among the various ethnic minorities as each struggles for housing and employment opportunities, seeking its fair share in these limited markets. Clashes become inevitable as Hispanic family markets spring up in African American urban neighborhoods, as Vietnamese extended families displace Puerto Rican apartment dwellers, and as the increasing enrollment of Asian students on college campuses is perceived as a threat to affirmative action policies by other ethnic minority students. Despite the hardships caused by interethnic conflicts these ethnic minority groups have survived and flourished. They have shown remarkable resilience and adaptation by developing their own communities and social structures—such as African American churches, Vietnamese mutual assistance associations, Chinese American family associations, Japanese language schools, Indian "bands" and tribal associations, and Mexican American kin systems. In addition, they have learned to negotiate with the dominant White culture. Essentially they have mastered two cultures and have developed impressive strategies for adapting to life in America. The resilience and adaptation of ethnic minority groups can teach us much about coping and survival in the face of overwhelming adversity.

To help buffer the stress in their lives, many ethnic minority groups find support in their own social structures, which include Mexican American kin systems, African American churches, Chinese American family associations, and Native American tribal associations.

I am a part of all that I have met.

Alfred, Lord Tennyson

Depending on the situation and person, any of these models may explain people's experiences as they acquire competence in a new culture. For example, consider an African American family that has moved from the rural South to live in a city. One member of the family might assimilate into the dominant Anglo culture, another may follow the path of acculturation, a third member might choose to alternate actively between the two cultures, and yet a fourth member may choose to live in a context in which the two cultures exist side by side as described in the multicultural, integration, and fusion models. According to some culture theorists, the more people are able to maintain active and effective relationships through alternation between the cultures, the less difficulty they will have in acquiring and maintaining competence in both cultures (LaFramboise, Coleman, & Gerton, 1993).

John Berry (1980, 1994), a Canadian cross-cultural psychologist, argues that models which encourage collaboration are the most adaptive models for change. However, Berry observed that other, less adaptive cultural solutions, such as separation, segregation, and marginalization, can also occur. **Separation** *is self-imposed withdrawal from the larger culture.* However, if imposed by the larger society, separation becomes *segregation.* People might maintain their traditional way of life because they desire an independent existence (as in "separatist" movements), or the dominant culture might exercise its power to exclude the other culture (as in slavery and apartheid). **Marginalization** *is the process in which groups are put out of cultural and psychological contact with both their traditional culture and the larger, dominant culture.* People who have been marginalized often feel alienation and a loss of identity. According to Berry, separation and marginalization are the least adaptive responses, assimilation and integration the most adaptive.

REVIEW

Culture

Culture is the behavior patterns, beliefs, and all other products of a particular group of people that are passed on from generation to generation. Cross-cultural studies involve the comparison of two or more cultures. They provide information about the degree to which people are similar, or universal, across cultures, or to what degree their behavior, thoughts, and feelings are culture-specific. In the emic approach, the goal is to describe behavior in one culture or ethnic group in terms that are meaningful and important to the people of that culture or ethnic group, without regard to other cultures or ethnic groups. The emic approach is culture-specific. In the etic approach, the goal is to describe behavior so that generalizations can be made across cultures. The etic approach is culture-universal. Some cross-cultural psychologists ascribe characteristics to entire cultures or nations. One such characteristic is the individualism/collectivism dichotomy. Individualism involves giving priority to personal goals rather than to group goals; it emphasizes values that serve the self. Collectivism emphasizes values that serve the group by subordinating personal goals to preserve group integrity, interdependence of members, and harmonious relationships. Many Western cultures are described as individualistic, many Eastern cultures as collectivistic.

Among the models that have been used to understand the processes of change that occur in transitions within and between cultures are the models of assimilation, acculturation, alternation, multiculturalism, integration, and fusion. The multicultural model promotes a pluralistic approach to understanding two or more cultures. There are four choices people can make in a situation requiring adaptation in plural societies: assimilate, integrate, separate, or be marginalized. Berry argues that separation and marginalization are the least adaptive responses, assimilation and integration the most adaptive. LaFromboise believes that the more people are able to maintain active and effective relationships through alternation between cultures, the less difficulty they will have in acquiring and maintaining competency in both cultures.

ETHNICITY AND INTERGROUP RELATIONS

The United States today has a far more diverse ethnic makeup than in past decades, yet our experiences with diversity are likely to vary, depending on where we live and what our family traditions are. For example, ninety-three languages are spoken in Los Angeles alone. Yet there are still communities in the United States that are quite homogeneous, so experiences with people whose traditions are unlike their own are limited. Although people vary according to their cultural and ethnic backgrounds, we have much in common wherever and however we live. Understanding true cultural variability does not undermine the value of equality that Americans commonly cherish; such knowledge reaffirms the value of diversity that has grown in importance in recent years (Triandis, 1994).

> There is a destiny that makes us brothers. None goes his way
> alone. What we send into the lives of others comes back into
> our own.
>
> **Edwin Markham**

The Nature of Ethnicity

Ethnicity *(the word* ethnic *comes from the Greek word for "nation") is based on cultural heritage, nationality characteristics, race, religion, and language. Ethnicity involves descent from common ancestors, usually in a specific part of the world.* Ethnicity is central to the development of an **ethnic identity,** *which is a sense of membership in an ethnic group based on shared language, religion, customs, values, history, and race. Ethnic identity involves the relative importance of one's ethnicity in comparison with other aspects of the self that contribute to one's identity.*

If we don't distinguish between ethnicity and ethnic identity, we can't understand people's having an ethnicity (they *are* Polish American, for example) but not identifying with or have feelings about their ethnicity. Consider a college student who identifies herself as a fifth-generation Texan and is proud of it—this is her ethnic identity. She does not know much about her ancestors from Europe and is not very interested in her European descent (her ethnicity).

People often infer another's ethnicity based on physical features they believe to be typical of a given ethnic group. For example, one of the downed flyers in the Persian Gulf War had features that would be considered "Arab." He was treated worse by his captors than were the other prisoners of war, who had non-Arab features. This reminds us that ethnicity is a category that people might use to classify and stereotype others, even if they don't want to be categorized that way themselves and feel that the inferences are wrong and unfair (Brislin, 1987).

Recently, some people have voiced dissatisfaction with the use of the term *minority* as in the phrase *ethnic minority group.* Some people have also objected to the terms *Black* and *Black American,* preferring instead the term *African American,* to emphasize their ancestry. (You might recall our earlier discussion of the power of labels in chapter 15.) What is the nature of such dissatisfaction and objections? The term *minority* has traditionally been associated with inferiority and deficits. Further, the concept "minority" implies that there is a majority. In the United States, the majority group, Whites, is actually composed of many different ethnic groups. In this text we intentionally use the term *ethnic minority.* Rather than implying that ethnic minority groups should be perceived as inferior or deficient, we use the term to convey the impact that minority status has had on many ethnic groups. The circumstances of an ethnic group are a function not solely of its own culture but

James Jones has made important contributions to our understanding of racial bias and the social psychology of ethnic issues.

also of how the ethnic group has experienced the strains of interethnic contact. For example, Asian American psychologist Stanley Sue (1990) argues that patterns of alcohol abuse among Native Americans cannot be fully understood without considering the exploitation that Native Americans historically have suffered.

You might also be wondering why we are using the term *ethnicity* rather than *race* to denote the sociocultural heritage of a group of people, such as Native Americans, Latinos, African Americans, and Asian Americans. We do this because *ethnicity* is primarily a *sociocultural* term and *race* is primarily a *genetic, biological* term. The concept of race has not been very beneficial in predicting behavior and mental processes (Jones, 1991, 1994). It also has led to considerable stereotyping of people and prejudice against them. The concept of race does not adequately take into account the considerable diversity within any group of people, such as African Americans or Whites. Nonetheless, although race has some biological basis, it has taken on considerable social meaning as well and continues to be a widely used label in our society.

Intergroup Relations

Although harmony is possible among people with different ethnic traditions, we have come to expect that such positive relations are hard-won and rare. Consider some of the

Many contexts around the world involve extensive conflict, such as: *(a)* the renewal of ancient animosities between Serbs and Croats in what was Yugoslavia, *(b)* Los Angeles, where riots broke out following the beating of Rodney King by police, *(c)* the neo-Nazi movement in Germany, and *(d)* the Middle East, where Jews and Arabs engage in hostile encounters.

challenges that events and circumstances in the United States and around the world present:

- In 1992, riots broke out in Los Angeles after African American Rodney King was beaten by White police and the police were acquitted of any wrongdoing by a jury. The beating and the trial brought racial animosities to the surface.
- In 1993, in what was Yugoslavia, Serbs and Croats renewed ancient animosities. Even UN intervention and boycotts couldn't stem the underlying ethnic hatred and killing.

- In Germany in the early 1990s, the neo-Nazi movement picked up steam. Some German-born citizens wanted an ethnic cleansing of their country and non-German-born immigrants were beaten and killed.
- In the Middle East, Jews and Arabs live in segregated communities and loathe each other. Territorial disputes and threats of war are virtually daily occurrences.
- In 1994, South Africa held its first elections open to Black candidates. Nelson Mandela won handily over his White opponent, Willem de Klerk. However, he took on the presidential responsibilities for a country

Group members often show considerable pride in their group identity, as reflected in *(a)* African Americans' celebration of Martin Luther King Day, *(b)* Mexican Americans' celebration of Cinco de Mayo, *(c)* Native Americans' celebration of their heritage, and *(d)* Polish Americans' celebration of their cultural background.

in which a history of apartheid and oppression had made Blacks into second-class citizens. The White ruling class had grudgingly given up ground. Racially motivated riots and killings continued to occur.

In this portion of the chapter, we will explore the social processes that hinder effective intergroup relationships. We will examine ethnocentrism, stereotyping, and prejudice, as well as discimination and racism and their contributions to intergroup conflict.

Ethnocentrism

Psychologists believe that **ethnocentrism,** *the tendency to favor one's own group over other groups,* is a natural outcome of successful adaptation to one's own group. The positive side of ethnocentrism is that it fosters a sense of pride in one's own group that fulfills the human urge to attain and maintain a positive self-image. As we approach the end of the twentieth century, group pride has mushroomed. There's Black Pride and there is Gay Pride. The Scots happily grow more Scottish, the Irish more Irish.

There is something paradoxical, though, about such pride. It may be difficult to maintain pride in one's own group without negative comparisons to other groups. Often members of a group stress their differences with others rather than emphasize pride in their own group. Though people from different cultures might vary in how strongly they identify with their group, some attitudes appear to be constant from culture to culture. For example, American social psychologist Donald Campbell and his colleagues (Brewer & Campbell, 1976; Campbell & LeVine, 1968) found that people in all cultures have a tendency to

- believe that what happens in their culture is "natural" and "correct" and what happens in other cultures is "unnatural" and "incorrect."

- perceive their cultural customs as universally valid; that is, what is good for us is good for everyone.
- behave in ways that favor their cultural group.
- feel proud of their cultural group.
- feel hostile toward other cultural groups.

Pride is seldom delicate: it will please itself with very mean advantages.

Samuel Johnson

Pride is the mask of one's own faults.

Jewish proverb

Henry Tajfel (1978) proposed the **social identity theory,** *which states that when individuals are assigned to a group, they invariably think of the group as an in-group for them. This occurs because individuals want to have a positive self-image. Social identity theory helps explain prejudice and conflict between groups.* Tajfel, a European Jew who survived World War II, had as his goal to explain the extreme violence and prejudice his group experienced during the Holocaust.

Self-image consists of both a personal identity and many different social identities. Tajfel argues that individuals can improve their self-image by enhancing either their personal identity or their social identity. Tajfel believes that our social identity is especially important. When we compare the social identity of our group with the social identity of another group, we often maximize the distinctiveness of the two groups. Think about your social identity with your hometown. Or imagine two professional basketball fans, one who lives in Houston and is a Houston Rockets fan, and one who lives in New York and is a New York Knicks fan. When the Rockets won the 1994 NBA championship, the Houston fan's self-image was enhanced. As these two fans talk with each other, they argue about the virtues of their teams, reinforcing the distinctiveness of their social identities with two different groups. As they strive to promote their social identities, it is not long before they intersperse proud, self-congratulatory remarks with nasty comments about the opposing team. In short, the theme of the conversation has become "My team is good and I am good. Your team is bad and you are bad." And so it goes with the sexes, ethnic groups, nations, social classes, religions, sororities, fraternities, and countless other groups. These comparisons often lead to competition and even to "legitimizing" discrimination against other groups.

Stereotyping

A **stereotype** *is a generalization about a group's characteristics that does not take into account any variation from one member of the group to the next.* Think about your image of a dedicated accountant. Most of us would probably describe such a person as "quiet," "boring," "unsociable," and so on. Rarely, would we come up with a mental image of this person as extraverted, the life of the party, or artistic. Characterizing all accountants as boring is a clear example of a stereotype, as is describing all Italians as excitable.

Researchers have found that we are less likely to detect variations among individuals who belong to "other" groups than those who belong to "our" group. For example, Whites are more likely to stereotype Blacks than other Whites during eyewitness identification (Brigham, 1986). Tajfel showed that it doesn't take much for us to think in terms of "we" and "they." For example, he assigned one person to a particular group because she overestimated the number of dots on a screen. He assigned another person to a different group because he underestimated the number. Once assigned to the two groups, the members were asked to award money to other participants. Those eligible to receive the money were distinguished only by their membership in one of the two groups just described. Invariably, the subjects acted favorably (awarded money) toward members of their own group. If we would favor our own group based on such a trivial criterion, it is no wonder that we would show intense in-group favoritism when differences are not so trivial.

The manner in which stereotyping could work in educational settings was portrayed in a clever third-grade classroom demonstration documented in the film *Eye of the Storm* (1970). Jane Elliot told her students that scientific research had demonstrated that blue-eyed children are smarter than brown-eyed children. She offered a plausible reason why this finding might be true and then offered special privileges to the blue-eyed children while she ridiculed the brown-eyed children. Very soon, she discovered that an in-group and an out-group formed, each making negative comments about the other. Before things got out of control, she interrupted her regular activities again and told the students that she had misinterpreted the finding; she claimed that scientists had actually discovered that brown-eyed children were smarter. Again, she offered a justification and resumed giving differential treatment. The same stereotyping occurred again. She concluded the experiment and revealed the nature of her deceptions, followed by a frank talk about the stereotypes that had formed and the behaviors that developed as a consequence. Like the experience in Jane Elliot's class, many students can describe some academic challenges that they attribute to stereotyping and the prejudicial behavior that followed.

Stereotypes are often described as cognitive categories that people use when thinking about groups and individuals from those groups. Much of the last 25 years of research on stereotypes has emphasized and documented the role of cognitive mechanisms in the biased judgments of individuals (Jussim & others, 1995). In the *cognitive* perspective, the perceiver's *beliefs* about social groups are involved in stereotyping. Biased beliefs are often interpreted as reflecting any of several cognitive mechanisms, such as schemas, expectations, and prototypes. Some individuals also may engage in stereotyping without being aware of it (Greenwald & Banaji, 1995).

However, some researchers argue that *affective* factors are responsible for stereotyping more than cognitive factors. For example, in a classic book, *The Roots of Prejudice*, Gordon Allport (1954) argued that the emotional dimensions of prejudice, such as anger, produce irrational and biased judgments that lead to stereotyping. In the affective view, how much people *like* or *dislike*, different groups (in contrast to the cognitive view's emphasis on a person's beliefs) generate stereotyping. In one recent study, affect, as reflected in liking or disliking, produced judgmental bias and stereotyping (Jussim & others, 1995). In sum, both cognitive and affective factors are likely involved in stereotyping.

Prejudice

Prejudice's harmful nature has appeared on many occasions in the history of humankind. The population of North American Indians dropped from an estimated three million in the 17th century to about 600,000 today because of brutal slayings. More than 6 million Jews were murdered by the Nazis in the 1940s under the justification of "purifying" the European racial stock. Only a fraction of the 6 million Jews remain in Europe today.

Whites' racial prejudice against African Americans has characterized much of America's history. When Africans were imported into America as slaves, they were described as property and treated in subhuman ways. In the first half of the twentieth century, most African Americans lived in the South and were still largely segregated by law—

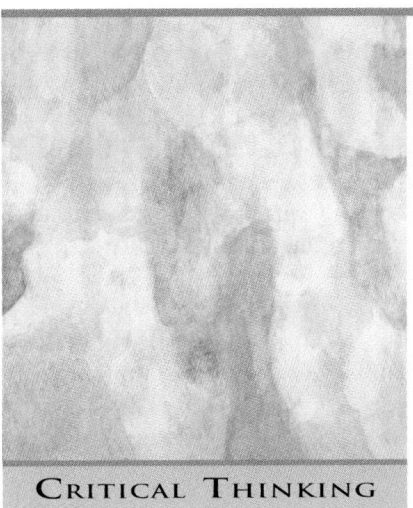

CRITICAL THINKING

Reconstructing Prejudice

Psychologist-philosopher William James once observed that one function of education is to "rearrange prejudice." The purpose of this exercise is aimed at just such an outcome.

No matter how well intentioned we are, life circumstances have probably produced some prejudices in us. If you don't maintain particular prejudices toward people with different or cultural ethnic traditions, there might be other kinds of people who bring out your most judgmental qualities. For example, prejudices complicate the lives of people with certain religious beliefs or political convictions, people who are unattractive or *too* attractive, people with unpopular occupations (such as lawyers or police officers), people who are physically or cognitively challenged, and people from bordering states or towns, among others. You may even recognize, with this expanded list, that it is hard to escape being the target of prejudice yourself at some point in your life, regardless of who you are.

Select some prejudice that still exerts some influence on your thinking and try to determine how you developed the attitude.

- Did it spring from one bad encounter with the group representative?
- Did you learn the prejudice through modeling from others whose opinion you prize?
- In what way does holding on to the prejudice enhance your self-image?
- Is it a prejudice that assists your own adaptation?
- What events would have to transpire to give you sufficient justification for rearranging your prejudice?

By *evaluating the validity of your conclusion* about your prejudice, you might continue to espouse the belief but with stronger justifications and reflection, or you might be able to let it go.

---

restaurants, movie theatres, and buses had separate areas for Whites and African Americans. Even with the downfall of segregation, much higher portions of African Americans than Whites live below the poverty line today.

African Americans and Native Americans are not the only ethnic minority groups that has been subjected to prejudice in the United States. Many Latinos also live below the poverty line, have low educational achievement, and low paying jobs. Lesbians and gays have historically been subjected to considerable prejudice from the heterosexual majority. This prejudice has been so intense that most homosexuals stayed "in the closet" until recently, not revealing their sexual preferences for fear of prejudice and discrimination. In fact, virtually every social group has been the victim of prejudice at one time or another.

Sometimes it's like a hair across your cheek. You can't see it. You can't find it with your fingers, but you keep brushing at it because the feel of it is irritating.

Marian Anderson

You probably are confident that you know what prejudice means. And, like most people, you might not think of yourself as especially prejudiced. In fact, each of us maintains stereotypes and shows prejudice. **Prejudice** *is an un-* *justified attitude toward an individual based on the individual's membership in a group.* We usually assume that prejudices are negative; however, positive bias is also a form of prejudice. For example, "teacher's pets" are a good example of positive prejudice by teachers for a special student; this favoritism is likely to incite negative prejudice from other students. The group that inspires an individual's prejudice can be made up of people of a particular race, sex, age, religion, nation, or other difference (Aboud, 1988).

Discrimination

Prejudices can be unexpressed. However, **discrimination** *occurs when prejudice leads to differences in treatment based on the individual's membership in a group.* Recall the example of Rosa Parks at the beginning of the chapter. Because of her membership in the Black Montgomery community, she was the target of discriminatory treatment by the bus line. Although it might be hard to accept, it is possible that some individuals might act in discriminatory ways without being racist. For example, bus drivers who were not especially prejudiced toward Blacks in Montgomery might still have practiced discrimination as a way to conform to the expectations of the community and the bus line. However, many drivers might also have been comfortable implementing the rules because they were consistent with their own stereotypes and prejudices.

Stanley Sue, shown lecturing to Asian Americans, has been an important advocate of increased research on ethnic minority issues in psychology. Sue has conducted extensive research on the role of ethnicity in abnormal behavior and psychotherapy. He also has provided considerable insight into ethnic minority issues.

In the end, antiblack, antifemale, and all forms of discrimination are equivalent to the same thing—antihumanism.

Shirley Chisholm, *Unbought and Unbossed,* 1970

Racism

We live in a society in which virtually every ethnic minority group—Asians, Irish, Latinos, African Americans, Eastern Europeans—has experienced discrimination. For some people, every member of an out-group is inferior. **Racism** *is a belief that members of another race or ethnic group are inferior.* In many cases, racists believe that members of another race or ethnic group are inferior in many respects, ranging from morals to intelligence, because they were born into the particular out-group. Racism also has a power component when racist beliefs produce action that gives preference to one group over another.

There will be strange ebbs and flows in the tide of race feelings.

Amy Levy, *Reuban Sachs,* 1988

Today in many parts of the world it is unfashionable to express intense racism openly (Brislin, 1993), although in some countries intense racism openly rears its ugly head. For example, neo-Nazis have resurrected the call for an "ethnic cleansing" of Germany in an effort to deport non-German-born individuals and restrict certain foreigners from entering the country and becoming citizens. In the United States, intense racism heated up when White police officers in Los Angeles beat Rodney King during his arrest. Such incidents still spark conflict and hatred between African Americans and Whites.

Today, most Whites show more accepting attitudes toward African Americans than even a decade or two ago (Sears & others, 1994). The vast majority of Whites support African Americans' rights to public office, access to public accommodations, fair housing, and so on. Violence by Whites toward African Americans has diminished considerably. However, occasional incidents—such as the Rodney King beating— still spark conflict and hatred between African Americans and Whites. And often there still is resistance to programs that would help African Americans reach full equality—such as affirmative action and school desegregation.

Some social scientists engage in lively debate about whether White society will continue to move toward liberal racial attitudes or resist further change (Gaines & Reed, 1995). While most Whites ostensibly support integration, it may just be *lip service.* That is, on the surface, many Whites make socially correct comments about African Americans, but underneath harbor racist feelings. Whites' support for general principles of equality may be *superficial.* It is easy to support equality in the abstract, but supporting its actual implementation has real and costly implications. White Americans also may have a genuine *ambivalence* about African Americans. In this view, Whites sympathize with the problems African Americans have faced and continue to face, but also perceive that African Americans have contributed to their plight by their lack of ambition and failure to take advantage of opportunities.

Another possibility is that old-fashioned racism has been replaced by a new form called *aversive racism,* which describes the conflict Whites experience between their genuinely egalitarian values and their own negative feelings toward African Americans. In this perspective, Whites are ashamed of their negative feelings and do not want them to be exposed, so they simply avoid African Americans. In old-fashioned racism, Whites felt hostility and hatred toward African Americans; in aversive racism, they feel discomfort, uneasiness, and fear. Yet another possibility is that old-fashioned racism has been replaced by another version called *symbolic racism,* which consists of a combination of anti-Black feelings and traditional values such as those involved in the Protestant ethic. Symbolic racism is the attitude that African Americans are pushing too hard, too fast, for equality, making unfair demands and getting undeserved special attention, such as favoritism in jobs and college admissions (Nosworthy, Lea, & Lindsay, 1995; Sears, 1987). In sum, while old-fashioned intense racism has diminished, other forms of racism seem to have replaced it (Swim & others, 1995).

Programs that were designed to help ethnic minorities reach full equality, such as affirmative action and school desegregation, remain controversial. According to clinical psychologist Stanley Sue (1990), supporters believe that these programs "level the playing field" and they enthusiastically support their continuation. Equal-opportunity advocates want to eliminate discrimination. Their goal is to abolish racial and ethnic bias, intentional patterns of segregation, and discriminatory admissions or selection criteria. However, even if discrimination is eliminated, there is no guarantee that equal outcomes will be achieved. Realizing this, advocates of equal outcomes believe that it is important to have special programs and affirmative action to narrow the gap between ethnic minority groups and Whites. In their view, color-blind policies that are applied to ethnic groups already showing significant disparities from Whites only serve to maintain differential achievements. Critics, such as George Will, argue that such approaches simply reverse the discrimination. They predict that the programs' negative impact in the long run will undermine the short-term achievements.

Despite the complexity of this problem, Sue believes that the real goal of our society should be to maximize the potential of every individual, irrespective of color, ethnic group, or gender. Some social scientists engage in lively debate about whether society will continue to move toward more accepting attitudes or resist further change. Next, we will examine some ideas for improving interethnic relations.

Improving Interethnic Relations

Martin Luther King once said, "I have a dream that my four little children will one day live in a nation where they will not be judged by the color of their skin but by the content of their character." How might we possibly reach the world Martin Luther King envisioned—a world without prejudice and racism? Beginning with Gordon Allport's study of prejudice in 1954, researchers have consistently found that contact itself does not improve relations with people from other ethnic backgrounds. What does improve interethnic relations? Two answers lie in sharing superordinate goals and achieving intimacy.

Superordinate Goals

Years ago social psychologist Muzafer Sherif and his colleagues (1961) fueled "we-they" competition between two groups of 11-year-old boys at a summer camp called Robbers Cave in Oklahoma. In the first week, the one group hardly knew the other group existed. One group became known as the Rattlers (a tough and cussing group whose shirts were emblazoned with a snake insignia), and the other was known as the Eagles.

Near the end of the first week each group learned of the other's existence. It took little time for we-they talk to surface ("They had better not be on our ball field." "Did you see the way one of them was sneaking around?"). Sherif, who disguised himself as a janitor so he could unobtrusively observe the Rattlers and Eagles, had the two groups compete in baseball, touch football, and tug-of-war. Counselors manipulated and judged events so the teams

were close. Each team perceived the other to be unfair. Raids, burning the other group's flag, and fights resulted. The Rattlers and Eagles further derided one another as they held their noses in the air as they passed each other. Rattlers described all Rattlers as brave, tough, and friendly and called all Eagles sneaky and smart alecks. The Eagles reciprocated by labeling the Rattlers crybabies.

After we-they competition transformed the Rattlers and Eagles into opposing "armies," Sherif devised ways to reduce hatred between the groups. He tried noncompetitive contact but that didn't work. Only when the groups were required to work together cooperatively to solve a problem did the Rattlers and Eagles develop a positive relationship. Sherif created superordinate tasks that required the efforts of both groups: working together to repair the only water supply to the camp, pooling their money to rent a movie, and cooperating to pull the camp truck out of a ditch.

Might Sherif's idea—that of creating cooperation rather than competition between groups—be applied to ethnic groups? When the schools of Austin, Texas, were desegregated through extensive busing, increased racial tension among African Americans, Mexican Americans, and Anglo-Americans resulted in violence in the schools. The superintendent consulted Elliot Aronson, a prominent social psychologist, who was at the University of Texas in Austin at the time. Aronson (1986) thought it was more important to prevent ethnic hostility than to control it. He observed a number of elementary school classrooms in Austin and saw how fierce the competition was between children of unequal status.

Aronson stressed that the reward structure of the classrooms needed to be changed from a setting of unequal competition to one of cooperation among equals, without making any curriculum changes. To accomplish this, he put together the *jigsaw classroom*. The jigsaw classroom works by creating a situation where all of the students have to pull together to get the "big picture." Let's say we have a class of

Elliot Aronson developed the concept of the jigsaw classroom to reduce ethnic conflict. How does the jigsaw classroom work?

CRITICAL THINKING

The Portable Jigsaw

You learned about Elliott Aronson's use of the jigsaw classroom to promote co-operation among students of unequal status as they learned about the Civil War. Collaborative learning procedures are gaining popularity at all levels of education because they enhance student involvement and encourage students to develop stronger social skills while they learn. This may have sounded like a good teacher's strategy when you read about it. However, you can adopt this strategy to enhance your own study skills.

For example, how would you apply this strategy to learning about intergroup relations? For a study group of six, describe how you would use the jig-saw technique to divide and conquer the material covering reactions ranging from ethnocentrism to racism presented in this chapter. Could this technique be transferred to other areas of study besides history and psychology? Successful transfer of this skill demonstrates your ability to _apply psychological concepts and skills to enhance personal adaptation._

thirty students, some Anglo, some African American, and some Latino. The academic goal is to learn about the Civil War. The class might be broken up into five study groups of six students each, with the groups being as equal as possible in terms of ethnic competition and academic achievement level. Learning about the Civil War becomes a class project divided into six parts; one part is given to each member of the six-person group. The components might be paragraphs from a historian's study of the Civil War, such as passages on the role of economic conditions in the war, the use of slaves as a source of labor, geographical differences between the North and the South, and so on. The parts are like the pieces of a jigsaw puzzle. They have to be put together to form the complete puzzle.

Each student has an allotted time to prepare. Then the group meets, and each member tries to teach her or his part to the group. After an hour or so each student is tested on the Civil War. Each student must learn the entire lesson; learning depends on the cooperation and effort of other members. Aronson believes that this type of learning increases students' interdependence through cooperatively reaching a common goal.

The strategy of emphasizing cooperation rather than competition and the jigsaw approach have been widely used in classrooms in the United States. A number of studies reveal that this type of cooperative learning is associated with increased self-esteem, better academic performance, friendships among classmates, and improved interethnic perceptions (Slavin, 1989).

It is not easy to get groups who do not like each other to cooperate. The air of distrust and hostility is hard to overcome. Creating superordinate goals that require the cooperation of both groups is one viable strategy, as evidenced in Sherif's and Aronson's work. Other strategies involve disseminating positive information about the "other" and reducing the potential threat of each group (Worschel, 1986).

Prejudices, it is well known, are more difficult to eradicate from the heart whose soil has never been loosened or fertilized by education; they grow there, firm as weeds among stones.

Charlotte Brontë

Intimate Contact

We indicated earlier that contact by itself does not improve interethnic relations. However, Brislin (1993) believes that one form of contact—intimate contact—can. Intimate contact in this context does not mean sexual relations. Rather, it involves sharing one's personal worries, troubles, successes, failures, personal ambitions, and coping strategies. When people reveal personal information about themselves, they are more likely to be perceived as individuals rather than as members of a category. The sharing of personal information also often produces the discovery that others previously considered as "them," or the out-group, have many of the same feelings, hopes, and concerns; this can help to break down in-group/out-group, we-they barriers.

In one of the initial investigations of extensive interethnic contact, African American and White residents in an integrated housing project were studied (Deutsch & Collins, 1951). The residents lived in small apartments, and the housing project included shared facilities, such as laundry rooms and playgrounds for children, that allowed for interethnic contact. Whites found it more enjoyable to talk with African Americans than to stare at the walls while their

Intimate personal contact that involves sharing doubts, hopes, problems, ambitions, and much more is one way to improve interethnic relations.

laundry was being cleaned, and African American and White parents began to converse with each other as they watched them play. The young African American and White children played with each other regardless of skin color. Initially the conversations focused on such nonintimate matters as the quality of the washing machines and the weather, but eventually it moved on to more personal matters. The Whites and the African Americans discovered that they shared a number of similar concerns, such as jobs and work, the quality of schools for their children, taxes, and so on. The revelation that they shared many of the same concerns and problems helped to diminish in-group/out-group thoughts and feelings. Sharing intimate information and becoming friendly with someone from another ethnic group helps to make people more tolerant and less prejudiced toward the other ethnic group.

REVIEW

Ethnicity and Intergroup Relations

Ethnicity (the word *ethnic* comes from the Greek word for "nation") is based on cultural heritage, nationality characteristics, race, religion, and language. Ethnicity involves descent from common ancestors, usually in a specific part of the world. Ethnicity is central to the development of an ethnic identity, which is a sense of membership in an ethnic group based on shared language, religion, customs, values, history, and race. *Ethnicity* is primarily a sociocultural term. *Race* is a biological term, although it has taken on considerable social meaning.

Prejudice is an unjustified negative attitude toward an individual based on the individual's membership in a group. A stereotype is a generalization about a group's characteristics that does not take into account any variation from one member of the group to the next. Stereotypes likely involve both cognitive and affective dimensions. Ethnocentrism is the tendency to favor one's own group over other groups. One theory devised to explain prejudice and conflict is Tajfel's social identity theory, which states that when individuals are assigned to a group they invariably think of the group as an in-group for them. This occurs because they want to have a positive image.

Racism is a belief that the members of a race or ethnic group are inferior. Intense racism is less prevalent today than in the past but it still rears its ugly head from time to time. While old-fashioned racism has diminished, other forms of racism seem to have replaced it. One contemporary form of racism that is less intense than old-fashioned racism is superficial support for principles of equality.

CULTURE, ETHNICITY, AND CRITICAL THINKING

How important is it to apply critical-thinking skills to better understand culture and ethnicity? How can critical-thinking skills be used to promote cultural pluralism?

An Important Connection: Culture/Ethnicity and Critical Thinking

Throughout this book we have emphasized the importance of contexts in understanding human behavior. In that regard, we have especially underscored that culture and ethnicity are becoming increasingly important contexts. Throughout this book we have also emphasized the importance of critical thinking in understanding human behavior. In every chapter you have engaged in activities to improve your critical thinking about psychological matters. Let's explore the importance of engaging in critical thinking about culture and ethnicity.

If we want to make something really superb of this planet, there is nothing whatever that can stop us.

Shepherd Mead

Part of the excitement that the future holds is the promise of continuing extensive contact between people from quite different cultural and ethnic backgrounds. However, we will also continue to face significant challenges in developing a stable social and political structure that treats individuals with differing backgrounds in an equitable manner. Although the standards, practices, and traditions of White Americans have dominated our society, immigrants, refugees, and ethnic minority individuals are requesting that the nation's schools, employers, and governments honor many of their cultural customs. On a practical basis, our institutions cannot accommodate every aspect of every culture represented in our nation. One unfortunate consequence is that many children learn attitudes in school that are inconsistent with the attitudes they learn at home (Brislin, 1990). This is just one example of the serious decisions that we face about shaping a fair and harmonious future during an era of increasing complication.

Most ethnic minorities want to participate fully in society, but they don't necessarily agree on how to accomplish that goal. People are often caught between conflicting values of assimilation and cultural pluralism (Sue, 1990). You will recall that assimilation refers to the absorption of an ethnic minority group into the dominant group. This often entails the loss of some or all of the behavior and values of the ethnic minority group. Those who advocate assimilation as the dominant outcome of cultural contact usually exhort ethnic minority groups to become more "American." In contrast, **pluralism** *refers to the coexistence of distinct ethnic and cultural groups in the same society.* Those who advocate pluralism usually promote cultural differences, urging that those differences be maintained and appreciated. Although assimilation still has many supporters, many people now believe that pluralism offers the greatest hope for strengthening our nation and improving our ability to function effectively with other cultures who share the planet with us.

It is well to remember that the entire population of the universe, with one trifling exception, is composed of others.

John Andrew Holmes

Critical Thinking Skills for Promoting Cultural Pluralism

In the prechapter of this book we highlighted a number of important critical-thinking skills that can help you better understand human behavior. To conclude this chapter and the book, we return to those critical-thinking skills and apply them to an important agenda for the remainder of this decade and the approaching twenty-first century: promoting cultural pluralism.

Make Accurate Observations, Descriptions, and Inferences About Behavior by Expecting Diversity Within a Group and Limiting Generalizations

Accurate observation, description, and inference are essential to understanding behavior. Psychologists practice careful observation and precise description to reduce misunderstanding. They recognize that inferences leave a great deal of room for personal interpretation and error. Obviously, these abilities are especially important in being able to understand sociocultural issues.

You have experienced how easy it can be to make inappropriate inferences about behavior. In fact, you might have found it helpful sometimes to think about your own personal experiences instead of the examples we have given. In sociocultural contexts, incautious inferences can lead to conclusions that are not just wrong but harmful to ourselves and others.

You can observe a lot just by watching.

Yogi Berra

One fact that should enhance our abilities as interpreters of reality is that there is diversity within every group. No cultural characteristic or value is common to all or nearly all members of a particular ethnic group, whether Russians, Italians, or Indonesians. Failure to assume individual variation is likely to result in stereotyping and ineffective social interaction with individuals from other ethnic and cultural traditions (Triandis, 1991). We may need to develop some generalizations in order to guide our actions, to make accurate predictions, and to adapt to the challenges

As a group, Asian Americans show exceptional achievement patterns. However, Asian Americans represent a heterogeneous group with marked variations in characteristics. There is considerable diversity in every ethnic group. For example, Asian Americans show high educational attainments but many Asian Americans have very little education (Sue & Padilla, 1986). Although the "whiz kid" image fits many Asian Americans, for thousands of other Asian Americans, including a high percentage of the 600,000 Indochinese refugees who fled Vietnam, Laos, and Cambodia in the late 1970s, the problems are legion. Many in this wave of refugees lived in poor surroundings in their homelands. They came to the United States with little education and few skills. They speak little English and have a difficult time finding a decent job. They often share housing with relatives. Adjusting to school is difficult for their children. Better school systems use a range of social services to help the Indochinese refugees adapt.

in the environment, but we should be ready to modify or abandon these schemas if they don't explain the variations we encounter or if they harm others.

Stereotypes are based on inferences. We often attribute negative characteristics to members of groups based on a negative experience we have had with a member of that group, in part because we predict that what is true of one person will be true of others. It is also important to recognize how easy it is to make generalizations. As we discovered in the chapters on learning and thinking, some experiences produce "one-trial learning." That is, we can usually learn the components of unpleasant or painful situations readily. Unfortunately, this suggests that we can rapidly generalize a bad experience with one representative of a group to unfavorable and rejecting evaluations of the group itself. We need to restrain our natural pattern-finding abilities in order to honor the true variation that exists in any group.

Pursue Alternative Explanations to Explain Behavior Comprehensively in Order to Challenge Incorrect Assumptions That Are Motivated by Prejudice

Psychologists actively look for alternative explanations to explain behavior. You have studied various perspectives (such as the psychoanalytic and neurobiological) presented in this text that foster comprehensive explanations. Using these perspectives is especially important when we are forming conclusions about behaviors or behavioral differences.

Incorrect assumptions about the differences between White Americans and ethnic minority Americans proliferate and take on a power all their own (for example, stereotypes that all Jews are ambitious and all African Americans are naturally athletic). Belief in these stereotypes can keep us from recognizing the many ways in which people, regardless of ethnicity or culture, are similar. As members of ethnic minorities begin to have a stronger voice in society, more similarities will emerge. Understanding these similarities between people, regardless of ethnicity, will help break down the stereotypes that lead to prejudice.

Natives who beat drums to drive off evil spirits are the objects of scorn to smart Americans who blow horns to break up traffic jams.

Mary Ellen Kelly

When we think about what causes a person's behavior and adaptation, we tend to think in terms of a single cause. However, human behavior and adaptation are not simple matters. For example, consider 19-year-old Tom, a Native American high school dropout. It's possible he quit school because his family did not adequately appreciate the importance of education. Even if that were true, it is likely that other factors were involved. For example, it is possible that Tom comes from a low-income family that he helps to support. The school Tom attended may have had a poor history of helping Native Americans adapt to school; perhaps it has no multicultural programs or no Native Americans within the school administration who can serve as role models. It may also turn out that the town in which Tom lives devotes few resources to programs for youths, regardless of their ethnicity. And there undoubtedly are more factors that contributed to Tom's decision to leave school. Because it is the result of many factors, behavior is said to be multiply determined.

Demonstrate Appreciation for Individual Differences by Recognizing and Respecting Legitimate Differences Within Groups

Ours is a diverse, multicultural world teeming with different languages, family structures, and customs. A cascade of historical, economic, and social experiences have produced these differences among ethnic and cultural groups (Albert, 1988; Triandis, 1994). We need to recognize and respect legitimate differences to appreciate the common ground we share with people whose ethnicity and cultural heritage differ from our own. Respecting others with different traditions will facilitate communication and cooperation in our increasingly interdependent world.

While this sounds reasonable to many of us now, for too long legitimate ethnic differences were overlooked. Virtually any difference from middle-class White characteristics and lifestyles—ranging from the way people looked to the kind of music they listened to—was thought of as a deficit. Too often, these differences have been seized upon by some segments of society, seeking to justify their own biases, to exploit, to humiliate, and to oppress people from ethnic minority backgrounds (Jones, 1991, 1994). Many psychologists now seek to discover the psychological assets and strengths of ethnic groups. This new trend is long overdue.

Develop Psychological Arguments Using Evidence, but Honor Subjective Traditions

Psychologists have long endorsed the standard of using objective evidence in creating and defending arguments about behavior. The dominance of experimental research methods attests to the widespread belief among psychologists in the importance of manipulation and control as elements of developing sound arguments. Science seeks to explain why things work the way they do. Social science tries to bring that sense of orderliness to the explanation of behavior. Some culture experts suggest that psychologists avoid abstract and complicated ideas such as culture because they don't want to sacrifice the possibility of establishing order (Lonner & Malpass, 1994).

Technological man can't believe in anything that can't be measured, taped, or put into a computer.

Clare Boothe Luce

Adherence to objective standards remains an important feature of psychological argumentation. However, as we seek to understand the realities of diverse peoples, we will need to expand the methods we use to explore those realities. Qualitative research methods, which do not insist upon manipulation and control as part of the research protocol, are gaining acceptance among many psychologists.

In the past the influence of behaviorism and the importance of observable evidence has also placed some topics of human behavior beyond the bounds of acceptable research. For example, many psychologists have traditionally struggled with spiritual issues. With the growing acceptance of the cognitive perspective, however, matters of spirit may also find new opportunities for attention using psychological methods. This inclusiveness may be especially important in exploring ethnic traditions, such as those of Latino and Native Americans, in which matters of spirit are prominent and compelling. Some culture experts describe as culture-blindness the tendency to overlook characteristics that are not part of Western culture (Lonner & Malpass, 1994).

Evaluate the Validity of Conclusions About Behavior Through Vigilance About Objectivity in Research

Contemporary criticisms of research methods suggest that even with careful attention to details of control and objectivity, bias can still contaminate the results of research in ways that may be difficult to detect. As we discussed in chapter 2, a researcher can define constructs in ways that may reflect bias. Subject selection, operational definitions, and interpretation of results are all arenas in which bias can hinder objective analysis. Researchers need to be especially sensitive to the assumptions they make when they interpret their results with regard to the larger sociocultural context.

Social Psychology and Culture

Cross-cultural psychologists Walter Lonner and Roy Malpass (1994) describe psychology as not just culture-blind but also culture-bound. They point out that over 90 percent of all psychologists *who have ever lived* have been reared in Western contexts. Obviously, most of their research reflects the Western contexts that are familiar to them, which means that much of psychology is culture-bound to Western ways of thinking.

Psychology itself tends to demonstrate a bias that predisposes attention to the different or deviant rather than the normal. For example, we study aggression rather than peaceful behavior. We publish research studies in which groups demonstrate differences rather than similarities. Some research journals might not even publish findings unless a difference between groups has been discovered. Many researchers suggest that the search for significant differences may create some artificial emphases in our understanding of behavior and hinder our ability to find similarities among different kinds of people.

Demonstrate Awareness of Underlying Values That Motivate Behavior by Examining Values Involved in Sociocultural Conflicts

As you have seen in many exercises throughout the text, two individuals can experience the same situation and come away from the experience with entirely different versions, based on values that can serve as perceptual filters. Value conflicts in sociocultural contexts have been a source of considerable controversy. According to Stanley Sue (1990), without properly identifying the assumptions and effects of the conflicting values, it may be difficult to resolve ethnic minority issues.

We have explored some of the more common value differences that can influence sociocultural conflict resolution. The fact that some groups are collectivistic and some are individualistic can help you to predict the kind of values that most group members might hold. Harry Triandis (1994) identified security, obedience, duty, harmony, hierarchy, and personalized relationships as characteristic of collectivists. Individualists emphasize the values of pleasure seeking, winning, achievement, freedom, autonomy, and fair exchange. For example, suppose governmental agencies create incentive programs to lure businesses into urban areas. Collectivists might see such incentives as a great idea because a thriving business offers new opportunities to the community, particularly to ethnic minority workers. Individualists might evaluate such incentives in terms of the profits and risks involved in such a move at an individual level. Both perspectives have relevance to the issue, but they will produce different justifications for action and may lead to different preferred outcomes.

Actively Take the Perspective of Others in Solving Problems by Considering Different Sides of Sensitive Issues

When someone's behavior and traditions are different from our own, we can demonstrate empathy by trying to understand what life would be like if we were in their shoes. Largely due to the influence of cognitive psychology, we recognize that individuals actively construct reality. Our heritage, our biological systems, our health, and our life experiences all conspire to help us construct unique individual realities. This virtually guarantees that our constructions of reality will not match the realities of others with whom we work and live, not to mention those whose daily circumstances we can hardly imagine.

When we recognize that our own constructions can be biased or incomplete, we are more likely to be willing to connect with others and collaborate. We share our realities to come to reasonable solutions or compromises as well as to achieve some consensus about the nature of reality. The capacity to suspend judgment about others and adopt an empathetic stance toward individuals with different traditions can promote the potential richness that diversity has to offer (Kirshenbaum, 1995).

Practice Standards of Ethical Treatment Toward Individuals and Groups by Discouraging Discrimination and Prejudice

Psychologists maintain rigorous ethical standards with regard to the care of clients and the treatment of participants in research. Their concerns about confidentiality and disclosure, among other ethics practices, attest to the importance of treating people with fairness and dignity. As you have seen in exploring research studies through history, the discipline of psychology has not always abided by such high standards. Formal codes of ethics, licensure proceedings, and research review processes help to facilitate the higher standards that have evolved in the field of psychology. Concerns for humane and ethical treatment remain strong among psychologists as the borders of psychology appropriately expand into new sociocultural territories.

In a recent Gallup poll, Americans said they believe that the United States is tolerant of ethnic differences and that overt racism is basically unacceptable (*Asian Week*, 1990). However, many ethnic minority members experience persistent forms of discrimination and prejudice in many domains of life—in the media, in interpersonal interactions, and in daily conversations (Sue, 1990). However, prejudice and racism are often expressed in more subtle and indirect ways than they once were (Sears & others, 1994). As an expression of high ethical standards, we need to be vigilant about subtle racist expectations and behaviors we may have acquired.

In today's world, most people agree that children from different ethnic groups should attend the same school. However, despite more accepting attitudes about many dimensions of ethnicity, a substantial portion of individuals say that they don't feel comfortable with people from ethnic groups other than their own. For example, in a recent survey of students at 390 colleges and universities, more than half of the African Americans and almost one-fourth of the Asian Americans, but only 6 percent of the Anglo Americans, said that they felt excluded from school activities (Hurtado, Dey, & Trevino, 1994). We still have a long way to go in reducing discrimination and prejudice.

We are not just citizens of the United States or Canada. We are citizens of the world. By increasing our understanding of the behavior and values of cultures around the world, we hope that we interact with people from other cultures more effectively and make this planet a more hospitable, peaceful place in which to live.

APPLICATIONS IN PSYCHOLOGY 19.1

Interacting with People from Other Cultures

Even when people don't have any prejudices and don't intend to discriminate against people from other cultures and ethnic groups, problems in intercultural communication can develop. Some of the reasons problems surface are subtle and difficult to understand. For example, no convenient language has developed to help people discuss many unintended intercultural difficulties.

How can people improve their interaction with people from other cultures? Developing certain skills and personality traits can help. For many years, cross-cultural psychologist Richard Brislin has been studying ways to improve the communication of people from different cultures. A summary of his recently proposed suggestions follows (Brislin, 1993).

Brislin believes that people who are *culturally flexible* can make changes in their behavior that meet the challenges of various sociocultural contexts. For example, the Japanese want to know their business associates as *people*. Casual conversations about people's backgrounds and interests give them the opportunity to get to know each other better. The lengthy time spent chatting with business associates gives the Japanese a way of determining whether or not the individuals can be trusted in future negotiations. Culturally flexible American businesspeople might find themselves in Japan and be willing to engage in more "small talk" than if they were doing business in their own country.

Intercultural interaction is improved when the participants are *enthusiastic* about developing intercultural relationships. Many individuals merely tolerate such interactions as necessary for completing a task. Instead, individuals who are enthusiastic actually look forward to the diversity and stimulation that intercultural relationships can produce.

Enthusiasm also increases the likelihood that people from different cultures *will use a variety of effective ways of communicating with each other.* Enthusiastic individuals will make the effort to learn another language and explore the nonverbal behaviors that will improve their communication with people from another culture. Enthusiasm can also help people overcome the discomfort that results from making mistakes, such as when they struggle to speak the foreign language they are learning and make a number of errors.

People who are competent in intercultural interaction *have methods to resolve conflicts effectively.* Effective conflict resolution involves addressing difficulties in a collaborative manner, focusing on issues instead of personalities, and working toward mutual understanding. Focusing on cultural differences can actually be a part of effective conflict management. For example, one person might suggest to another that the fact that they are from different cultures and have different ways of doing things could contribute to their disagreement on a particular issue. Highlighting cultural differences can draw attention away from the more threatening emphasis on personalities.

Being willing to modify one's behavior to meet the expectations of people in other cultures is the final dimension in improving intercultural interaction. By trying new approaches, an individual can not only communicate that there are many ways to behave and think, but demonstrate tolerance for that which may be unfamiliar or different. The pattern of socialization most familiar to you might not be the best for a person in another part of the world. The need for tolerance toward differences in ethnic heritage, cultural background, religion, gender, sexual orientation, and medical history is becoming an increasingly important issue in many parts of the world.

Prejudice is the reason of fools.

Voltaire

Apply Psychological Concepts and Skills to Enhance Personal Adaptation in a World That Is Increasing in Global Interdependence

Throughout the text, you have had an opportunity to apply psychological concepts to improve your understanding of many aspects of your personal life. Part of improving the quality of your personal adaptation involves coming to

terms with a changing world. Global interdependence is no longer a matter of preference or choice. It is an inescapable reality. We are not just citizens of the United States or Canada or Puerto Rico. We are citizens of the world, a world that through modern communication and transport has become increasingly intertwined. By improving our understanding of the behavior and values of cultures around the world, we hope that we can interact more effectively with each other and make this a more hospitable, peaceful planet (Sloan, 1990). To read further about interacting with people from different cultures, turn to Applications in Psychology 19.1.

Make accurate observations, descriptions, and inferences about behavior
by expecting diversity within a group and limiting generalizations.

Pursue alternative explanations to explain behavior comprehensively
in order to challenge incorrect assumptions that are motivated by prejudice.

Demonstrate appreciation for individual differences
by recognizing and respecting legitimate differences within groups.

Develop psychological arguments using evidence,
but honor subjective traditions.

Evaluate the validity of conclusions about behavior
through vigilance about objectivity in research.

Demonstrate awareness of underlying values that motivate behavior
by examining values involved in sociocultural conflicts.

Actively take the perspective of others in solving problems
by considering different sides of sensitive issues.

Practice standards of ethical treatment toward individuals and groups
by discouraging discrimination and prejudice.

Apply psychological concepts and skills to enhance personal adaptation
in a world that is increasing in global interdependence.

Use psychological knowledge to promote human welfare
through education, teaching, research, intervention, and prevention.

FIGURE 19.2

Critical-Thinking Skills for a Pluralistic Society

People who develop the habit of thinking of themselves as world citizens are fulfilling the first requirement of sanity in our time.

Norman Cousins

Use Psychological Knowledge to Promote Human Welfare Through Education, Teaching, Research, Intervention, and Prevention

The knowledge base of information about sociocultural issues in psychology is increasing, but a lot of blank spaces remain in the study of ethnicity and culture. It is very important for psychologists to devote increased effort toward expanding the knowledge base of information about ethnicity and culture (Graham, 1992; Sue, in press). We need to know more about how diverse socialization experiences and adaptations to changing environments, especially those that present competing demands, can be integrated to produce a more competent human being (Jones, 1991, 1994). We need to know more about why Latino and Native American children leave school at such high rates. We especially need to know more about ways to prevent such high dropout rates, or how to intervene to help high school dropouts lead more competent, satisfying lives. Also, ethnicity and culture should be systematically included on the agendas at all levels of education—from preschool through graduate school—to help us construct a culture with greater tolerance and improved communication.

Through much of its history, the field of psychology has not had an admirable record on the topics of ethnicity and culture or in helping to create environments in which ethnic minority students can thrive. This decade represents a precious opportunity for individuals to make important contributions to our understanding of sociocultural concerns. Psychology not only needs to improve its knowledge base about sociocultural issues but also needs more well-trained psychologists who can deal effectively with sociocultural concerns. Consider a career in psychology in which you can help improve the lives of all human beings through education, teaching, research, intervention, or prevention. If your career interests do not lie with psychology, remember to use psychology to enhance your personal adaptation and to improve your quality of life. Figure 19.2 summarizes critical-thinking skills for a pluralistic society.

If we lacked imagination enough to foresee something better, life would indeed be a tragedy.

Laurence J. Peter

REVIEW

Culture, Ethnicity, and Critical Thinking

Pluralism is the coexistence of distinct ethnic and cultural groups in the same society. We described the following critical-thinking tools for promoting cultural pluralism: Make accurate observations, descriptions, and inferences about behavior by expecting diversity within a group and limiting generalizations; pursue alternative explanations to explain behavior comprehensively in order to challenge incorrect assumptions that are racially motivated; demonstrate appreciation for individual differences by recognizing and respecting legitimate differences within groups; develop psychological arguments using evidence, but honor subjective traditions; evaluate the quality of conclusions about behavior through vigilance about bias in research; demonstrate awareness of underlying values that motivate behavior by examining values involved in sociocultural conflicts; actively take the perspective of others in solving problems by considering different sides of sensitive issues; practice standards of ethical treatment by discouraging discrimination and prejudice; apply psychological concepts and skills to enhance personal adaptation in a world that is increasing in global interdependence; and use psychological knowledge to promote human welfare through education, teaching, research, intervention, and prevention.

CRITICAL THINKING ABOUT BEHAVIOR

Foundations for a Different Future

It is often quite daunting to maintain an optimistic outlook about what the future holds for ethnic and cultural relations in this country and across the globe. Headlines reinforce how little tolerance we have for people whose traditions are different from our own. Such unrest shows up in everything from petty insults and ethnic jokes to severe displays of hostility or bloodshed. Rarely is the world completely at peace, largely due to our human inability to cope with the attitudes, values, and behaviors of those who are unlike us.

This final critical-thinking exercise is a simple one. Identify someone whose cultural or ethnic traditions (or other sociocultural characteristics, such as economic status or sexual orientation) are different from your own. This individual can be from your class, your neighborhood, a civic organization, or interest group. Ask that individual to agree to sit down with you for a simple conversation of 15 minutes in order to help you complete an assignment for psychology. Your objective? Try to establish how similar you are in as many ways as you can.

What kinds of conclusions will you come to? You might identify that you both are "morning people." Perhaps you both rely on public transportation to get around. Maybe you both have a sister-in-law you can't abide. Perhaps you both like Beethoven or Boyz II Men.

Maybe you both have O-positive blood. The number of similarities you discover will be limited only by your imagination and your energy.

What does it mean? This exercise is designed to facilitate relationships that achieve intimacy. When you recognize how many similarities can be discovered between you and your partner, you may find it more difficult to think in ethnocentric or self-serving terms in relation to the group your partner represents. In addition, your curiosity may have been aroused by some of the differences you discovered.

This may be a small start, but it is through such intimate exchange that stronger bonds can be forged between people of different traditions and values. Stronger bonds offer promise for greater interethnic and intercultural understanding. By completing this exercise, you demonstrate your ability to *appreciate individual differences*. Your recognition of similarity encourages you to *use psychological knowledge to promote human welfare through research and prevention*. By achieving intimacy with "the other," you set the stage for a different kind of future.

No one need wait a moment.
We can start now.
We can start changing the world.

Anne Frank

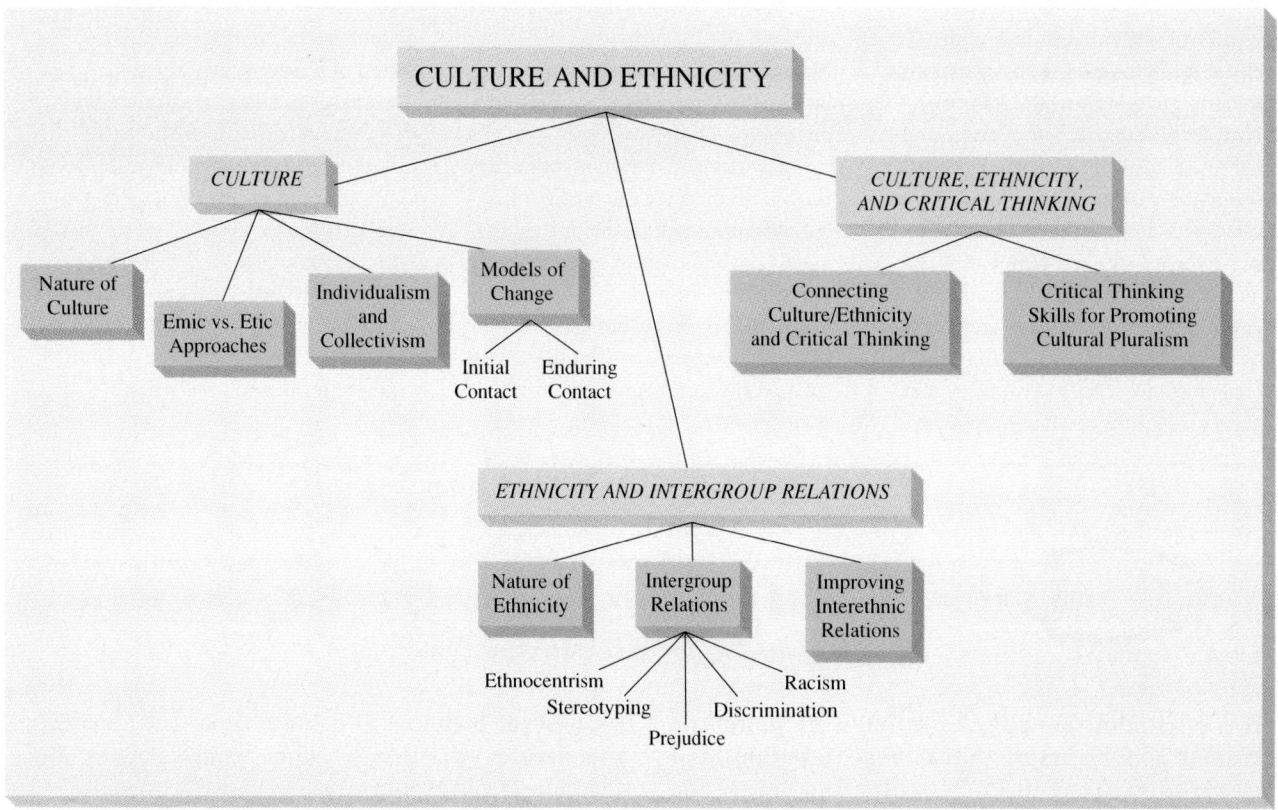

We began this chapter by exploring culture—its nature (emic vs. etic approaches, individualism and collectivism) and models of change (initial contact and enduring contact). Then we turned our attention to ethnicity and intergroup relations, exploring the nature of ethnicity, interethnic relations (ethnocentrism, stereotyping, discrimination, prejudice, and racism), and improving interethnic relations. We concluded the main section of the chapter by exploring the connection of culture and ethnicity and critical thinking, and examining a number of thinking skills for a pluralistic society. Don't forget that you can obtain an overall summary of the chapter by again reading the in-chapter reviews on pages 702, 711, and 719.

This entire chapter reflects the sociocultural perspective. Each section of the chapter is infused with the importance of contexts in understanding human behavior: culture (pp. 697–702), ethnicity and intergroup relations (pp. 702–711), and critical thinking for a pluralistic society (pp. 712–718). The sociocultural approach was also reflected in the discussion of the acculturative stress of ethnic minority individuals (p. 701). The humanistic perspective also appears in this chapter through the emphasis on improving interethnic relations (pp. 709–711) and developing critical-thinking tools for a pluralistic society (pp. 712–718). And the cognitive perspective is presented in the emphasis on the importance of developing critical-thinking skills for a pluralistic society (pp. 712–718).

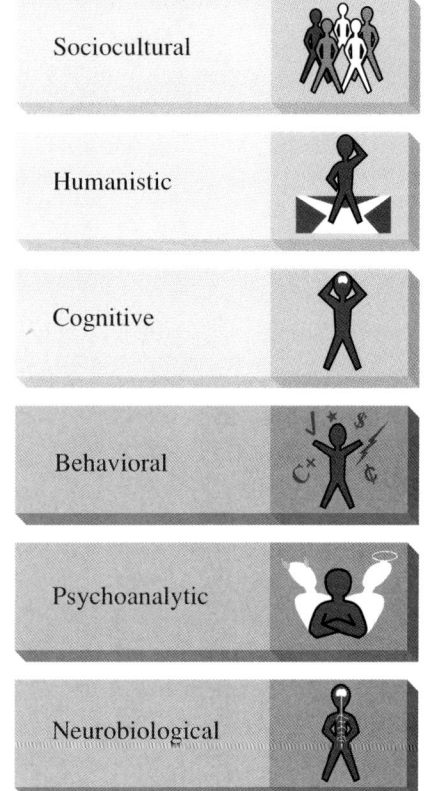

Sociocultural

Humanistic

Cognitive

Behavioral

Psychoanalytic

Neurobiological

culture The behavior, patterns, beliefs, and all other products of a particular group of people that are passed on from generation to generation. 697

cross-cultural studies The comparison of two or more cultures, which provides information about the degree to which people's behavior, thoughts, and feelings are similar, or universal across cultures, and to what degree they are culture-specific. 698

emic approach An approach in which the goal is to describe behavior in one culture or ethnic group in terms that are meaningful and important to the people in that culture or ethnic group, without regard to other cultures or ethnic groups; a culture-specific approach. 698

etic approach An approach in which the goal is to describe behavior so that generalizations can be made across cultures; a culture-universal approach. 698

social distance An etic construct; the cultural belief that people should maintain a certain distance from each other. 698

individualism Giving priority to personal goals rather than to group goals; emphasizing values that serve the self, such as feeling good, personal distinction and achievement, and independence. 699

collectivism Emphasizing values that serve the group by subordinating personal goals to preserve group integrity, interdependence of members, and harmonious relationships. 699

culture shock The disorganizing effects of exposure to unfamiliar ways of life. 700

assimilation Individuals' relinquishing their cultural identity and moving into the larger society. 700

acculturation Change that results from continuous contact between two distinct cultural groups and that preserves the identities of both. 700

alternation Individuals' knowing and understanding two different cultures, and altering their behavior to fit the different social contexts of the two cultures. 700

multiculturalism A pluralistic approach to understanding two or more cultures; a model in which people maintain their distinct identities while working with others from different cultures to meet national or economic needs they have in common. 700

integration The maintenance of cultural integrity while moving to become an integral part of the larger culture. 700

fusion A model in which cultures sharing economic, political, or geographic boundaries will fuse until they become indistinguishable and form a new culture. 700

separation Self-imposed withdrawal from the larger culture. 702

marginalization The process in which groups are put out of cultural and psychological contact with both their traditional culture and the larger, dominant culture. 702

ethnicity An aspect of human beings that is based on cultural heritage, nationality characteristics, race, religion, and language. 703

ethnic identity A sense of membership in an ethnic group based on shared language, religion, customs, values, history, and race. 703

ethnocentrism The tendency to favor one's own group over other groups. 705

social identity theory The theory that when individuals are assigned to a group, they invariably think of their own group as an in-group for them. This occurs because individuals want to have a positive self-image. Social identity theory helps to explain prejudice and conflict between groups. 705

stereotype A generalization about a group's characteristics that does not take into account any variation from one member of the group to the next. 706

prejudice An unjustified attitude toward an individual based on the individual's membership in a group. 707

discrimination Differential treatment, due to prejudice, based on an individual's membership in a group. 707

racism A belief that the members of another race or ethnic group are inferior. 708

pluralism The coexistence of distinct ethnic and cultural groups in the same society. 712

CREATING COMMUNITY ANYWHERE

(1993) by Carolyn Shaffer and Kristin Anundsen. Los Angeles: Jeremy Tarcher.

This book includes a wealth of ideas about how to create community connections with others. Whether you live in an urban or a rural area, are single or married, or reside near or far from your family, you will find many useful suggestions about how to discover opportunities for community involvement, including helpful recommendations for how to establish and participate in support groups, workplace teams, new forms of residence sharing, social clubs, creativity groups, neighborhood associations, electronic networks, women's and men's discussion groups, intellectual groups, and spiritual communities. Guidelines are given for creating effective communication in groups, conducting productive meetings, making joint decisions, and working through conflicts. The authors profile many successful communities in the United States. The book includes a number of anecdotes, quotations, cartoons, and photographs.

PEOPLE: PSYCHOLOGY FROM A CULTURAL PERSPECTIVE

(1994) by David Matsumoto. Pacific Grove, CA: Brooks/Cole.

This brief, unique book challenges many of the ideas of mainstream psychology. The author goes beyond the ordinary findings of psychology to reveal how culture has an impact on behavior, feelings, and thoughts. Topics given considerable attention from a cultural perspective are the self, perception, cognition, development, language, emotion, abnormal behavior, and social relationships.

PSYCHOLOGY AND CULTURE

(1994) edited by Walter Lonner and Roy Malpass. Boston: Allyn & Bacon.

This recent book includes a large number of articles about ethnicity and culture written by leading experts. The book's main sections emphasize the universal experience of being different (with chapters on a number of ethnic groups, such as African Americans), cultural variations on some common human dimensions (with chapters on such topics as culture and altered states of consciousness), culture's influence on social and developmental processes (with chapters on such topics as patterns of parenting across cultures), culture's influence on basic psychological processes (with chapters on such topics as learning styles and culture), everyday modes of functioning as shaped by culture (with chapters on such topics as prejudice and guilt), the stresses, strains, and challenges facing humans in transition (with chapters on such topics as acculturative stress), and health psychology as mediated by cultural factors (with chapters on such topics as culture and depression).

CULTURE AND SOCIAL BEHAVIOR

(1994) by Harry Triandis. New York: McGraw-Hill.

This insightful book by one of cross-cultural psychology's leading figures, Harry Triandis, aims to unveil how culture influences people's social behavior. Among the topics given considerable coverage are how to study cultures, how to analyze subjective culture, culture and communication, cultural influences on aggression, helping, dominance, and conformity, dealing with diversity in intercultural relations, and intercultural training.

Affiliation of Multicultural Societies and Services
385 South Boundary Rd.
Box 2980747
Vancouver, B.C. V5K 4S1 CANADA
604–298–5949

An umbrella organization for all multicultural groups and societies. They publish a monthly newsletter.

Association of Black Psychologists
P.O. Box 55999
Washington, DC 20040–5999
202–722–0808

This organization of professional psychologists and others in associated disciplines publishes the *Resource Manual for Black Psychology Students* and a number of other brochures and bulletins related to African American psychology.

Campus Outreach Opportunity League (COOL)
University of Minnesota
386 McNeal Hall
St. Paul, MN 55108–1011
612–624–3018

COOL promotes and supports student involvement in community service. It has a network of more than six hundred colleges and universities. Its goal is to help students address such issues as homelessness, hunger, illiteracy, and cultural diversity. If you are interested in starting or strengthening a community service program on your campus, COOL staff members will help you develop your strategy.

**Canada Ethnocultural Council/
Conseil ethnoculturel du Canada**
251 Laurier Ave. West, #1100
Ottawa, ON K1P 5J6
613–230–3867

A coalition of 38 national organizations representing over 2000 ethnic groups across Canada. They publish the magazine *Ethno Canada,* support legislation, and sponsor conferences and research on multicultural issues.

Center for Community Change
1000 Wisconsin Avenue, NW
Washington, DC 20007
202–342–0519

The objective of this center is to provide information and technical assistance to low-income and minority-based organizations to increase the effectiveness of their programs.

***Human Behavior in Global Psychology* (1990)**
by M. Segall, P. Dasen, J. Berry, & Y. Poortinga
Elmsford, NY: Pergamon

This book evaluates a number of topics in psychology from a cross-cultural perspective.

International Association of Cross-Cultural Psychologists
c/o Jeff Lewis
Pitzer College
1050 N. Mills Avenue
Claremont, CA 91711

This organization of professionals and students interested in cross-cultural psychology publishes the *Journal of Cross-Cultural Psychology* and *Cross-Cultural Psychology Bulletin.*

National Urban League
The Equal Opportunity Building
500 East 62nd Street
New York, NY 10021
212–310–9000

The National Urban League is an influential social service and civil rights organization with more than 30,000 volunteers working to obtain equal opportunities for African Americans and other ethnic minority groups. If you are interested in helping, contact the affiliate where you live or the National Urban League at the address listed above.

***Teaching a Psychology of People: Resources for Gender and Sociocultural Awareness* (1988)**
edited by P. A. Berman and K. Quina
Washington, DC: American Psychological Association

This book includes a variety of chapters by psychologists interested in the roles of ethnicity and culture in understanding behavior and mental processes.

APPENDIX

Analyzing the Data

With Don Hockenbury
Tulsa Junior College

> *The essence of life is statistical*
> *improbability on a colossal scale.*
>
> **Richard Dawkins**

COMMUNICATING WITH DATA

Statistical thinking will one day be as necessary for efficient citizenship as the ability to read and write.

H. G. Wells

Gross national product. Grade point average. Dow Jones Industrial Average. Earned-run average. Whether you realize it or not, statistics weave in and out of your life on a daily basis. For example, high schools, colleges, and universities use statistics to track student demographics, such as the number of students attending college, student grade point averages, and the tally of students who drop out. Advertisers use statistics to persuade you to buy their products by telling you that other consumers prefer their products "by a margin of five to one." Weather reports indicate that the temperature is "ten degrees above the average for this time of year." Statistics are also widely used in sports, such as football, baseball, and basketball. Crime statistics and statistics about homeless people are just two examples of many patterns of data the federal government tracks and reports. In short, statistics are so much a part of our lives that an understanding of basic statistics is essential if you want to be an informed citizen. Communicating effectively with numbers has become a survival skill in our culture.

Psychologists use statistics to communicate about data they collect in order to describe behavior patterns and evaluate research hypotheses. You will remember that psychologists often design research with a quantitative bias. They develop research strategies in which they operationalize and measure behavior. Researchers subject these measurements to statistical analysis to determine whether their hypotheses are sound.

The purpose of this appendix is to help you make sense out of some basic statistical concepts that are used in everyday life as well as in scientific research. **Statistics** *are mathematical methods used to describe, summarize, and draw conclusions about data.* We will address two basic categories of statistics. Our primary focus will be on **descriptive statistics,** *mathematical procedures used to describe and summarize data in a meaningful fashion.* In contrast, **inferential statistics,** *complex mathematical methods used to draw conclusions about data,* will be addressed only briefly in this appendix.

DESCRIPTIVE STATISTICS

Psychologists use descriptive statistics to describe the characteristics of either a single variable or a relationship or *interaction* between two variables. This is important in most psychological studies, because if we were simply to report all the individual scores, it would be virtually impossible to interpret the meaning of the results. Descriptive

"Tonight, we're going to let the statistics speak for themselves."

Drawing by Koren; © 1974 The New Yorker Magazine, Inc.

statistics allow us to avoid this situation by employing several measures that reveal the overall characteristics of the data. Descriptive statistics can be reported as numerical representations or graphic representations. Let's look at these practices.

Descriptive Statistics for One Variable

Data regarding one variable can be communicated in several ways. We can examine the raw data or we can organize the data numerically in a frequency distribution. We can create graphs—histograms or frequency polygons—that represent the data. We can also characterize single-variable data using numerical estimates called measures of central tendency and measures of variability.

Suppose that we are interested in number of siblings (brothers and sisters) as the primary variable. (Recently some educational researchers have found some interesting connections between number of siblings and aspects of academic performance, but we will return to this relationship when we examine descriptive statistics for two variables later in the chapter.) Let's start with an example from an imaginary introductory psychology class. All 20 students in this class answer a short questionnaire, which asks for the number of brothers and sisters they have, among other data of interest. We will use the sibling information to illustrate the ways descriptive statistics can communicate about a set of data.

Raw Data

Following are the number of siblings each member of the class indicated:

6	4	3	8
6	2	0	2
1	2	3	0
2	3	2	1
3	2	2	8

What kinds of conclusions can you derive by looking at this raw data on siblings? It is difficult to draw any general

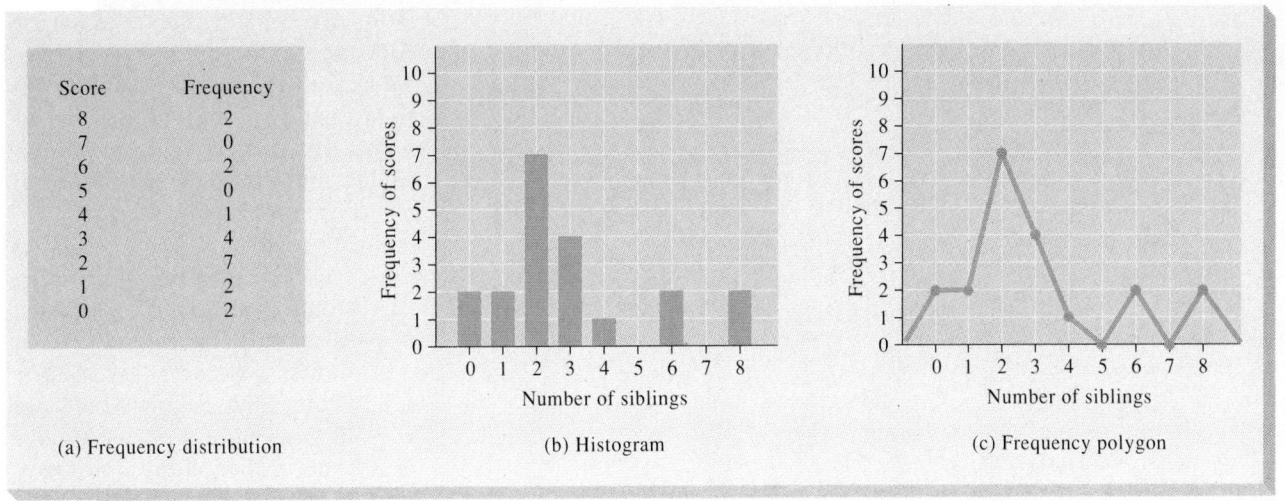

Score	Frequency
8	2
7	0
6	2
5	0
4	1
3	4
2	7
1	2
0	2

(a) Frequency distribution

(b) Histogram

(c) Frequency polygon

FIGURE A.1

Frequency Distribution, Histogram, and Frequency Polygon
These data are from a hypothetical survey on number of siblings reported by 20 students in your psychology class. (*a*) A frequency distribution lists the scores from lowest to highest, with the number of times each score appears. (*b*) A histogram depicts the frequency distribution in graphic form, with vertical bars representing the frequency of scores. (*c*) A frequency polygon is basically the same as a histogram except that the data are represented with lines rather than bars. *Which of these formats do you find easiest to interpret?*

conclusions about the overall tendencies of the group, because raw data are overwhelming. It would be even more difficult if our sample size were 500 or 1,000 students in the class instead of just 20. We need to organize the data in a more meaningful way using descriptive statistics.

Frequency Distribution

The first step in organizing the data is developing a **frequency distribution,** *a listing of scores from lowest to highest, with the number of times each score appears in a sample.* Figure A.1a shows the frequency distribution for our data on number of siblings. The column on the left lists the possible responses (number of siblings), and the column on the right shows how often that response was given. Although the frequency distribution offers an advantage over raw data, interpreting the data can still be problematic, particularly when numbers of categories of data are large. Researchers generate graphic representations of the data to make interpretation easier.

Graphic Representations

A **histogram** *is a frequency distribution in graphic form, in which vertical bars represent the frequency of scores per category or class.* Figure A.1b shows a histogram for our data on sibling number. A histogram is often called a *bar graph* or, occasionally, a *block diagram.* The news media frequently use histograms to provide visual impact about research

findings. Researchers are likely to use histograms when the number of categories of the variable (that is, number of bars) is small and will not be hard to interpret.

As you examine the histogram, you can see its correspondence with the frequency distribution. The value or score is represented on the horizontal axis (*x* axis) of the histogram. The frequency of responses at each value is represented on the vertical axis (*y* axis). Both representations identify seven students who have two siblings and no students who have five siblings.

A **frequency polygon** *is similar to the histogram except that we represent the data with lines rather than bars.* Figure A.1c shows a frequency polygon for the data on number of siblings. Researchers use frequency polygons when either the sample size is very large or the number of categories within the variable would make it challenging to interpret the data from a histogram. As shown in the histogram and the frequency polygon, the *x* axis indicates the score values, and the *y* axis indicates how often each score occurs in the set of data.

One frequency polygon that has been of considerable interest to psychologists is the **normal distribution** (*also called a bell-shaped curve), which is a symmetrical distribution with a majority of cases falling in the middle of the possible range of scores and few scores appearing toward the extremes of the range.* Many naturally occurring phenomena, such as height, weight, athletic ability, and some aspects of human intelligence, follow or closely approximate a

Mean	Median			Mode	
	Ranking	Scores in order		Score	Frequency
6	1	0		8	2
6	2	0		7	0
1	3	1		6	2
2	4	1		5	0
3	5	2		4	1
4	6	2		3	4
2	7	2		2	7 ← Most frequent score
2	8	2		1	2
3	9	2		0	2
2	10	2	Middle of rankings		
3	11	2		Mode = 2	
0	12	3			
3	13	3			
2	14	3			
2	15	3			
8	16	4			
2	17	6			
0	18	6			
1	19	8			
8	20	8			
60/20=3					

Because there is an even set of scores, median equals middle two scores added together, then divided by 2. Thus, $\frac{2+2}{2}=2$

0 1 2 3 4 5 6 7 8

FIGURE A.2

Mean, Median, and Mode

These data are from a hypothetical survey on number of siblings reported by 20 students in your psychology class. The mean is the numerical average for a group of scores; it is calculated by adding all the scores and then dividing by the number of scores. The median is the score that falls exactly in the middle of a distribution of scores after they have been ranked from highest to lowest. When there is an even number of scores, as there is here, you add the middle two scores and divide by 2 to calculate the median. The mode is the score that appears most often.

normal distribution. Because of its important role in data interpretation, we will return to the normal curve later in the appendix.

Although histograms and frequency polygons can help graphically represent a group of scores, you many want to communicate about your group of scores using a numerical estimate, either a measure of central tendency, a measure of variability, or both. Let's look at these two measures.

Measures of Central Tendency

If you want to describe an "average" value for a set of scores, you would use one of the measures of central tendency. In essence, a **measure of central tendency** is a single number that tells you the overall characteristics of a set of data. There are three measures of central tendency: the mean, the median, and the mode.

The **mean** is the numerical average for a group of scores or values. The mean is calculated by adding all the scores

and then dividing by the number of scores. To compute the mean for the data collected on number of siblings, we add all the scores, equaling 60, then divide by the total number of scores, 20. This gives us a mean of 3 siblings. This procedure is shown on the left side of figure A.2.

The **median** is the score that falls exactly in the middle of a distribution of scores after they have been arranged (ranked) in order. When you have an odd number of scores (say, five or seven scores), the median is the score with the same number of scores above it as below it after all the scores have been ranked. For example, suppose you ask your five closest college friends how many courses they are currently taking. You arrange the responses in order from lowest to highest and get the following scores: 1, 2, 4, 5, 7. The median is represented by the middle value in the ranked order, or 4 classes. When you have an even number of scores (8, 10, or 20 scores, for example), you simply add the middle 2 scores and divide by 2 to arrive at the median. In our example using number of siblings, we have an even number of scores (20), so the median is the 10th and 11th scores added together and divided by 2, or (2 + 2)/2. Thus, the median number of siblings for our set of 20 responses is 2, as shown in figure A.2. One important characteristic of the mean is that it is unaffected by one or a few extreme scores.

The **mode** is the score that occurs most often. The mode can be determined very easily by looking at a frequency distribution, histogram, or frequency polygon. In our present example, the mode is 2, which is the number of siblings indicated most often by the members of your psychology class. Although the mode is the least used measure of central tendency, it has descriptive value because, unlike the mean and the median, there can be two or more modes. Consider the following 15 scores on a 10-point surprise quiz: 9, 3, 8, 5, 9, 3, 6, 9, 4, 10, 2, 3, 3, 9, 7. The quiz scores 9 and 3 each appear four times. No other score in this example appears as often or more often. Thus, this set of scores has two modes, or a *bimodal distribution*. It is, in fact, possible to have several modes, or a *multimodal distribution*. It also is possible to have no mode at all.

Depending on the research question being investigated, the mode may actually provide more meaningful

The Trap of the Average

Then there is the man who drowned crossing a stream with an average depth of six inches.

W. I. E. Gates

Selecting the right measure of central tendency can be challenging. In general, the mean is a good indicator of the central tendency for a group of scores; it is the measure of central tendency that researchers use most often. One exception to this rule is when a group of scores contains extreme scores.

Annual earnings represent a single variable that will illustrate the importance of selecting the right measure of central tendency to communicate about the data. Suppose we have collected annual earnings data on group 1, consisting of seven people. The frequency distribution is as follows:

Group 1

$17,000	1
$21,000	2
$23,000	1
$24,000	1
$25,000	1
$28,000	1

Test yourself on the differences in concepts. What is the mode? What would be the median score? Calculate the mean by adding up the raw scores and dividing by the number of scores.

The mode is easy to determine from the frequency distribution. The value $21,000 occurs twice and stands out in the distribution as the only repeated value. We determine the median score by identifying the score that occupies the middle (or 4th) position in this frequency distribution: $24,000. In calculating the mean, the sum of all the earnings adds up to $159,000. When you divide that by 7, you discover that the mean is about $22,700. In this example the median, mode, and mean are all relatively close.

Suppose we examine another group in which all of the scores are identical except for the last one. In this case, we are including as the 7th score Steven Spielberg's approximate annual earnings as a highly successful movie director. The data for group 2 are as follows:

Group 2

$17,000	1
$21,000	2
$23,000	1
$24,000	1
$25,000	1
$45,000,000	1

Which measures of central tendency would change? Which ones would *not* be influenced by the inclusion of an extreme score? As you have probably guessed, the median would stay the same. The fourth score in the distribution is still $24,000. The mode remains the same. The value of $21,000 still occurs twice. The mean is the measure that is dramatically influenced. In this case, the average salary is now over $6 million. This example illustrates how important it is to find out what kind of "average" figure is being presented to communicate the characteristics of any group of data. These insights may also help you develop appropriate skepticism when evaluating statistical claims. For example, radio humorist Garrison Keillor asserts that in his fictionalized hometown of Lake Woebegone, "all the women are strong, all the men are good-looking, and all the children are *above average.*"

information than either the mean or the median. For example, developers of a program to help people stop smoking would benefit more from knowing that the "modal" age of the greatest number of people who smoke is either 22 *or* 58 than from knowing that the mean age of smokers is 37. By knowing that smoking behavior is distributed bimodally in the population, they can more appropriately target their program to young adults and older adults rather than to middle-aged adults.

Measures of Variability

Along with obtaining the overall or central characteristics for a sample, *we can also ask how much the scores in a sample vary from one another. These measures are called* **measures of variability** *or* **measures of dispersion.** The two measures of variability are called the range and the standard deviation.

The **range** *is the numerical difference between the highest and the lowest scores.* The range for our data on number of siblings would be 8 (high score) minus 0 (low score), for a range of 8. Generally speaking, the range is a rather simplistic estimate of variability, or dispersion, for a group of scores. More important, because the range involves only two scores, it can produce a misleading index of variability; thus, the range is rarely used as a measure of variability. The most commonly used measure of variability is the standard deviation.

The **standard deviation** *is a measure of how much the scores vary on the average around the mean of a sample.* It

Scores	Score minus mean (x)	Difference squared (x^2)
0	−3	9
0	−3	9
1	−2	4
1	−2	4
2	−1	1
2	−1	1
2	−1	1
2	−1	1
2	−1	1
2	−1	1
2	−1	1
3	0	0
3	0	0
3	0	0
3	0	0
4	1	1
6	3	9
6	3	9
8	5	25
8	5	25

Mean = 60/20 = 3 $\Sigma x^2 = 102$

$$\text{Standard deviation} = \sqrt{\frac{\Sigma x^2}{N}} = \sqrt{\frac{102}{20}} = \sqrt{5.1} = 2.26$$

FIGURE A.3

Computing the Standard Deviation
The standard deviation is a measure of how much the scores vary, on the average, around the mean of a sample. In this figure, you can see how the standard deviation was calculated for the data gathered from a hypothetical survey on number of siblings reported by 20 students in your psychology class. In computing a standard deviation, four steps have to be followed:

1. Calculate the mean of the scores.
2. From each score, subtract the mean and then square that difference. (Squaring the scores will eliminate any negative signs that result from subtracting the mean.)
3. Add the squares and then divide by the number of scores.
4. Calculate the square root of the value obtained in step 3. This is the standard deviation.

The formula for these four steps is

$$\text{Standard deviation} = \sqrt{\frac{\Sigma x^2}{N}}$$

where x = the individual score minus the mean, N = the number of scores, and Σ = the sum of.

indicates how closely scores are clustered around the mean. The smaller the standard deviation, the less variability from the mean and vice versa. The mathematical steps involved in calculating a standard deviation are presented in figure A.3.

Researchers often present the mean and standard deviation of a set of scores on a single variable together. This practice communicates the average and the range of scores in conventional terms that allow scientists and psychologists to infer a great deal about nature of the original data. In addition, these measures are less cumbersome and more efficient than graphic representations.

The Properties of the Normal Distribution

As we saw earlier, frequency polygons for many types of data produce a normal distribution. For example, the normal distribution of IQ scores as measured by the Wechsler Adult Intelligence Scale is shown in figure A.4. This figure illustrates several important characteristics of the normal distribution. For example, it is perfectly symmetrical. The same numbers of scores lie above the mean as below it. Because of this perfect symmetry, the mean, median, and mode are identical in a normal distribution. The bell shape illustrates that the most common scores are near the middle. The scores become less frequent and more extreme the farther away from the middle they appear.

The normal distribution incorporates information about both the mean and the standard deviation. Notice that the mean estimate of intelligence (IQ) in figure A.4 is 100 and the standard deviation is 15 IQ points. As shown in figure A.5, the area on the normal curve that is one standard deviation above the mean and one standard deviation below the mean represents 68.26 percent of the scores. At two standard deviations above and below the mean, we can account for 95.42 percent of the scores. Finally, three standard deviations above and below the mean contain 99.74 percent of the scores. If we apply this information to estimating intelligence in the population in figure A.4, we can see that 68 percent of the population has an IQ between 85 and 115, 95 percent of the population has an IQ between 70 and 130, and 99 percent of the population has an IQ between 55 and 145.

Descriptive Statistics for Two Variables

Up to this point, we've focused on descriptive statistics used to describe only one variable. Often the goal of research is to describe the relationship between two variables. This information can be represented graphically in scatter plots as well as numerically using the correlation coefficient.

Scatter Plots

Let's return to the example of the information we collected on your classmates. In addition to number of siblings, we also asked them to report their high school grade point averages. The raw data we collected are shown on the left side of figure A.6. Also shown is a scatter plot of those scores. A **scatter plot** *is a graph on which pairs of scores are represented.* In this case, we are looking at the possible relationship between number of siblings and academic performance. The possible scores for one variable—number of siblings—are indicated on the *y* axis, and the scores for the second variable—grade point average—are indicated on the *x* axis. Each dot on the scatter plot represents one pair of scores as reported by each member of your class. As you can see, there seems to be a distinct pattern to our scatter plot— that is, as the number of siblings increases, high school GPA decreases. Tentatively, at least, there appears to be an association between these two variables. Just how related are these two factors? It's difficult to go beyond a broad generalization from simply viewing a scatter plot.

The Correlation Coefficient

Just as we found measures of central tendency and measures of variability to be more precise than frequency distributions or histograms in describing one variable, it would be helpful if we had a type of measurement that is more precise than a scatter plot to describe the relationship between two variables. In such cases, we could compute a correlation coefficient.

A **correlation coefficient** *is a numerical value that expresses the degree of relationship between two variables.* There are two parts to a correlation coefficient: the number or value of the coefficient and the sign (positive or negative). The correlation coefficient ranges from +1.00 to −1.00 and tells you about the nature of the relationship between the two factors.

The strength of the relationship between two variables depends on the numerical value of the coefficient. You need to think about the range of the correlation coefficient as being different from an integer number line (. . . −3, −2, −1, 0, 1, 2, 3, . . .). In other words, negative numbers are

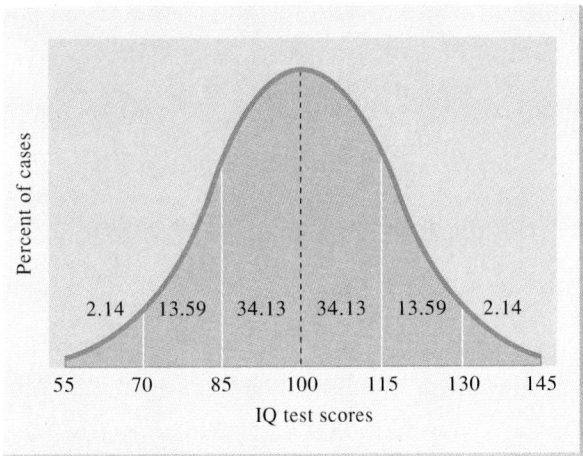

FIGURE A.4

Normal Distribution, or Bell-Shaped Curve
This graph shows the normal distribution of IQ scores as measured by the Wechsler Adult Intelligence Scale. The normal distribution is a type of frequency polygon in which most of the scores are clustered around the mean. The scores become less frequent the farther they appear above or below the mean.

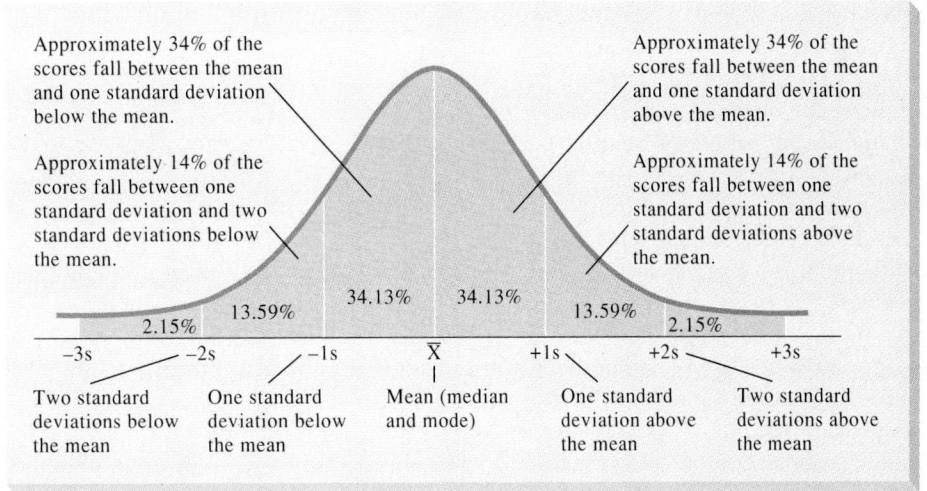

FIGURE A.5

The Normal Distribution

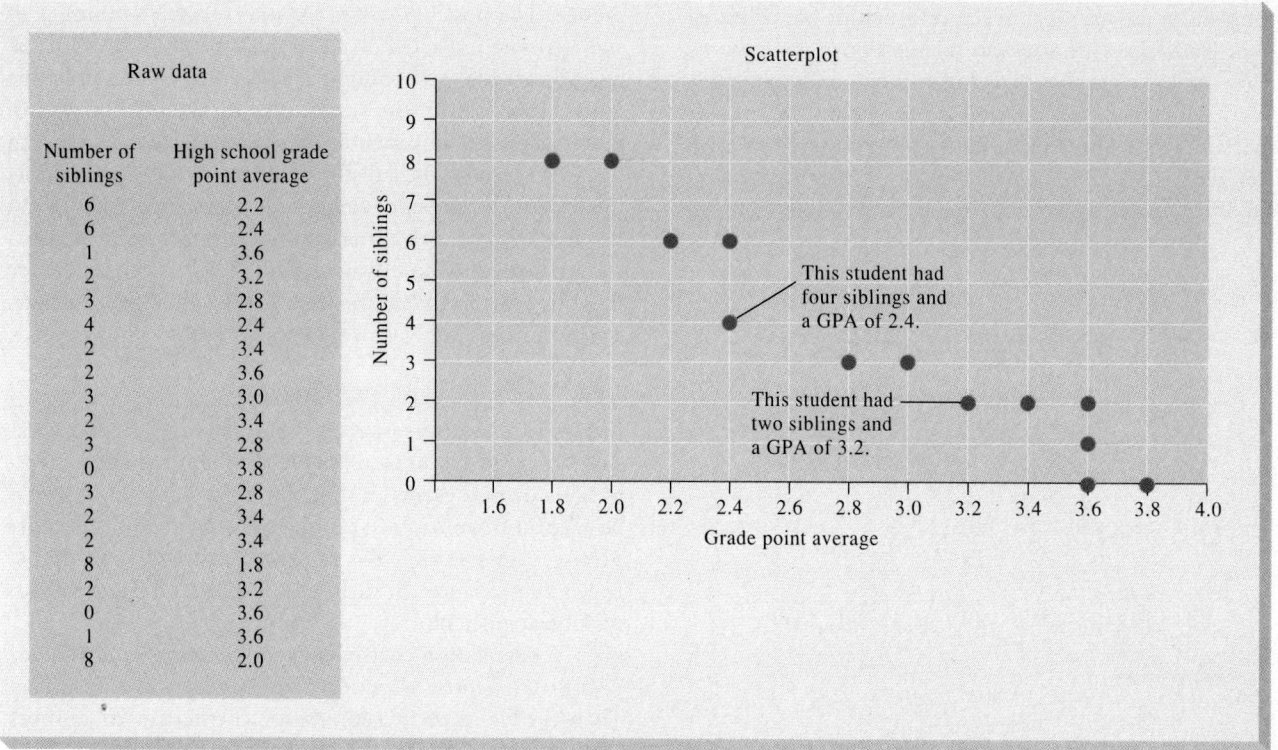

Raw data	
Number of siblings	High school grade point average
6	2.2
6	2.4
1	3.6
2	3.2
3	2.8
4	2.4
2	3.4
2	3.6
3	3.0
2	3.4
3	2.8
0	3.8
3	2.8
2	3.4
2	3.4
8	1.8
2	3.2
0	3.6
1	3.6
8	2.0

FIGURE A.6

Descriptive Measures for Two Variables

This scatter plot depicts the possible relationship between number of siblings and grade point average. Each dot on the scatter plot represents one pair of scores as reported by each member of your class in a hypothetical survey. The raw data from that survey are shown on the left.

not less than positive numbers. A correlation coefficient of +.65 is just as strong as a correlation of −.65. The rule is simple: The closer the number is to 1.00, the stronger the correlation. Conversely, the closer the number is to .00, the weaker the relationship. A correlation of .00 indicates that no relationship at all exists between two sets of variables.

The plus and minus signs of the correlation coefficient tell you nothing about the strength of the correlation. Instead, these valences indicate the direction of the relationship between the two variables. A **positive correlation** *is a relationship in which the two factors vary in the same direction.* Both variables tend to go up together *or* both factors tend to go down together. Either situation represents a positive relationship, in that both factors vary together. A **negative correlation** *is a relationship in which the two factors vary in opposite directions.* As one factor increases, the other factor decreases. The plus or minus sign tells you nothing about the strength of correlation. Thus, a correlation of +.15 indicates a weak positive correlation, and a −.74 indicates a strong negative correlation. A correlation of −.87 is stronger than a correlation of +.45. Examples of scatter plots showing positive and negative correlations appear in figure A.7.

When interpreting correlation coefficients, avoid the temptation to attach value judgments to correlational signs.

TABLE A.1

Guidelines for Interpreting the Strength of the Correlation Coefficient

1.00	Perfect relationship; the two factors always occur together
.76–.99	Very strong relationship; the two factors occur together very often
.51–.75	Strong relationship; the two factors occur together frequently
.26–.50	Moderate relationship; the two factors occur together occasionally
.01–.25	Weak relationship; the two factors seldom occur together
.00	No relationship; the two factors never occur together

A positive correlation is not "good" or "desirable," and a negative correlation is not "bad" or "undesirable." Table A.1 offers guidelines for interpreting correlational numbers.

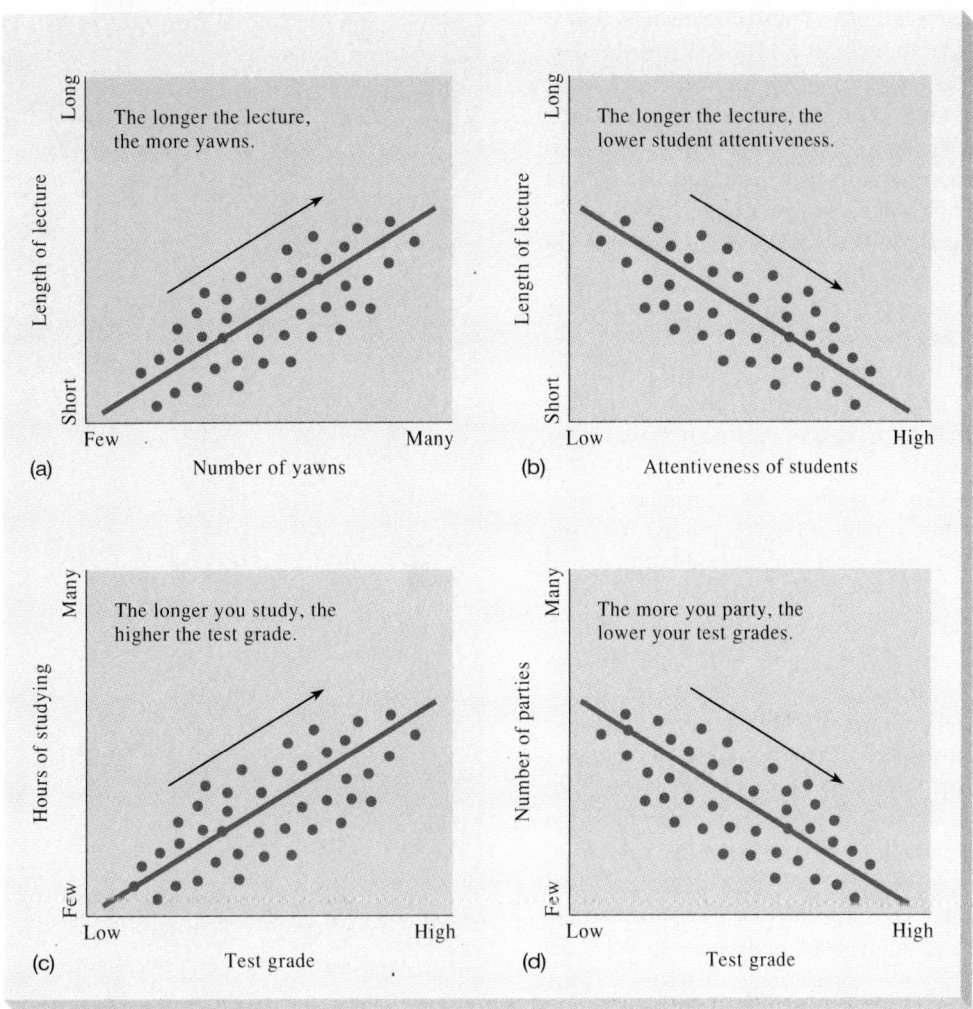

FIGURE A.7

Scatter Plots Showing Positive and Negative Correlations
Which of these scatter plots show positive correlations and which show negative correlations? Graphs A and C show positive correlations. A positive correlation occurs when two factors vary in the same direction. Graphs B and D show negative correlations. A negative correlation occurs when two factors vary in opposite directions.

Let's assume that we have calculated the correlation coefficient for the relationship between how long your instructor lectures (the variable on the y axis) and the number of times students yawn (the x-axis variable). On the basis of the data we collect in each of your classes, we produce a correlation coefficient (represented by the letter r) of +.70. The number .70 tells us that these two factors happen together frequently. The positive sign indicates that the two factors vary in the same direction, or *covary*. In simpler language, as the amount of time your professor lectures in each class increases, the number of students' yawns in each class increases. An example of a negative correlation in this situation might be the relationship between how long your instructor lectures and the level of student attentiveness (operationalized as the duration or frequency of eye contact). The data indicate that longer lecture periods are associated with reduced eye contact, whereas shorter lecture periods are associated with increased eye contact. Figure A.7 demonstrates other correlations that illustrate relationships between variables in college settings.

Let's return to our original example examining the relation between number of siblings and high school grade point average. The correlation between these two variables is –.95. How would you interpret this correlation? This means that the relationship between grade point and sibling number is negative and strong. We interpret the number .95 to represent a very strong relation between the two variables. The negative sign demonstrates an *inverse* relationship. Thus, students with fewer siblings tend to have higher grade point averages, whereas students with many siblings appear to have worse grades.

We must exercise caution when interpreting correlation coefficients. For example, could we conclude that if you are an only child, you will get a 4.0 GPA? Are you destined to make poor grades if you grew up in a large family? Of course not. Individual performances cannot be precisely determined using correlation coefficients. Correlation coefficients are population parameters and do not correspond precisely to individual values and prediction. At best, we can make only general predictions based on the trends in the data.

Another interpretive problem is that *correlation does not necessarily indicate causality.* Although researchers frequently use correlation coefficients to analyze the relationship between two variables, the general public frequently misinterprets the findings. Causality means that one factor makes, produces, or creates change in a second factor. Correlation means that two factors *seem* to be related, associated, or connected such that, as one factor changes, the other factor seems to change. Correlation implies potential causality that may or may not actually be there. Even though two factors are strongly or even perfectly correlated, in reality a third factor may be responsible for the changes observed. Thus, in our hypothetical example showing a very strong negative correlation between number of siblings and GPA, the changes observed in these two variables could be due to a third factor. For example, perhaps children who grow up in larger families have a greater tendency to hold part-time jobs after school, thereby limiting the amount of time they can study, or children who grow up in small families may be more likely to have their own rooms, thereby allowing them more uninterrupted study time. In any case, the point remains the same: correlation only potentially indicates a causal relationship.

Look at the terms in bold type in the following headlines:

Researchers **Link** Coffee Consumption to Cancer of Pancreas
Scientists Find **Connection** Between Ear Hair and
   Heart Attacks
Psychologists Discover **Relation** Between Marital Status
   and Health
Researchers Identify **Association** Between Loneliness and
   Social Skills
Parental Discipline **Tied** to Personality Disorders
   in Children

All of the words in bold type are synonymous with correlation, not causality. The general public, however, tends to equate such terms as "connection" or "association" with causality. As you read about the findings of psychological studies, or findings in other sciences, guard against making the same interpretation. Remember, correlation means only that two factors seem to occur together.

Thus, the correlation coefficient is a very useful and important statistical tool for psychological as well as other kinds of research. The correlational method is especially helpful in situations in which variables cannot be manipu-

Correlation methods permit research in situations that cannot be experimentally manipulated, such as natural disasters like the 1993 earthquake in Los Angeles.

lated and measured. It may be unethical to conduct an experiment because it poses either a physical or a psychological danger to the subjects. For instance, it would be unethical to carry out an experiment in which expectant mothers are directed to smoke varying number of cigarettes to see how cigarette smoke affects the baby's birthweight. Some factors simply cannot be manipulated experimentally, such as the effects of the 1993 earthquake in Los Angeles or the childhood backgrounds of people who are abusive parents. In these situations, psychologists might collect data using systematic *observation* of subjects rather than systematic *manipulation* in the experimental method. Systematic observation techniques, which were described in chapter 2, include case studies, naturalistic observation, interviews, questionnaires, and standardized tests. All of these approaches can produce measurements that can be related and interpreted using correlational coefficients. The mathematical steps involved in computing a correlation coefficient are shown in figure A.8.

Student number	Number of siblings (X variable)	Score minus mean (3.0)	Difference squared	High school GPA (Y variable)	Score minus mean (3.0)	Difference squared	x multiplied by y
N	X	x	x^2	Y	y	y^2	xy
1	6	3	9	2.2	−.8	.64	−2.4
2	6	3	9	2.4	−.6	.36	−1.8
3	1	−2	4	3.6	.6	.36	−1.2
4	2	−1	1	3.2	.2	.04	−0.2
5	3	0	0	2.8	−.2	.04	0.0
6	4	1	1	2.4	−.6	.36	−0.6
7	2	−1	1	3.4	.4	.16	−0.4
8	2	−1	1	3.6	.6	.36	−0.6
9	3	0	0	3.0	0.0	.00	0.0
10	2	−1	1	3.4	.4	.16	−0.4
11	3	0	0	2.8	−.2	.04	0.0
12	0	−3	9	3.8	.8	.64	−2.4
13	3	0	0	2.8	−.2	.04	0.0
14	2	−1	1	3.4	.4	.16	−0.4
15	2	−1	1	3.4	.4	.16	−0.4
16	8	5	25	1.8	−1.2	1.44	−6.0
17	2	−1	1	3.2	.2	.04	−0.2
18	0	−3	9	3.6	.6	.36	−1.8
19	1	−2	4	3.6	.6	.36	−1.2
20	8	5	25	2.0	−1.0	1.00	−5.0

N = 20   Mean = 3.0 $\Sigma x^2 = 102$ Mean = 3.0 $\Sigma y^2 = 6.72$ $\Sigma xy = -25.00$

$$r = \frac{\Sigma xy}{\sqrt{\Sigma x^2 \times \Sigma y^2}} = \frac{-25.00}{\sqrt{(102)\,(6.72)}} = \frac{-25.00}{\sqrt{685.44}} = \frac{-25.00}{26.18} = -.95$$

FIGURE A.8

Computation of a Correlation Coefficient

These data are from a hypothetical survey on number of siblings and high school GPA reported by 20 students in your psychology class. The correlation coefficient of −.95 indicates a very strong negative relationship between number of siblings and high school GPA. The following formula is used to calculate a correlation coefficient:

$$r = \frac{\Sigma xy}{\sqrt{\Sigma x^2 \times \Sigma y^2}}$$

where x is the difference between each X variable minus the mean; y is the difference between each Y variable minus the mean; Σxy is the sum of the cross products (each x score multiplied by its corresponding y score); Σx^2 is the sum of the squares of the x scores; and Σy^2 is the sum of the squares of the y scores. This figure contains the calculation of the correlation coefficient of −.95. From our previous discussion, we know that this is a very strong association indicating that, as number of siblings increases, grade point average decreases. What exactly does this mean? How are we supposed to interpret this hypothetical finding? Does this mean that, if you are an only child, you will have a 4.0 GPA? Does this mean that, if you grew up in a large family, you are destined to make poor grades?

INFERENTIAL STATISTICS

As you've seen in the previous section, correlational studies cannot establish causality. How, then, can a researcher provide compelling evidence for a causal relationship between two variables? As you may recall from chapter 2, psychologists use the experimental method to examine cause-and-effect hypotheses about variables. They use inferential statistics to interpret their findings.

Experimental Design

In the experimental method, researchers hold all variables constant and then systematically manipulate the factor that they think produces change (the independent variable). They measure the variable believed to be affected by these manipulations (the dependent variable). If the researchers have held all factors constant except for their manipulation of the independent variable, then any changes observed in the dependent variable can be attributed to the independent

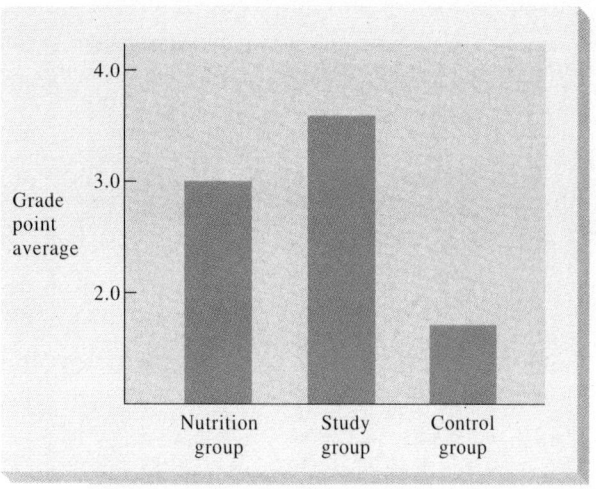

FIGURE A.9

Histogram Contrasting the Fictionalized Mean Grade Point Averages Derived in an Experiment in Which Two Intervention Strategies Were Employed to Improve Grades

variable; changes in the independent variable *caused* changes to occur in the dependent variable. This is the most compelling evidence of causality that science can provide, assuming that the experiment was carefully designed and controlled to avoid such experimental pitfalls as experimenter bias, subject bias, situational bias, or invalid scores. Furthermore, experimental evidence of causality is even more compelling if the research can be *replicated,* or repeated, by other researchers using different subjects.

Suppose we decide to design some interventions for college students who are struggling in their courses. We wish to design an experimental study to test whether the interventions (the cause) that we have in mind will have the desired outcome (the effect) of improving college grades. We recruit participants for the study and randomly assign them to one of three situations: intervention 1 (improved nutrition), intervention 2 (required study periods), or the control group (no intervention). We hypothesize that required study periods are more effective in enhancing grade point average than is improved nutrition or no intervention. After we collect the data, we have to interpret whether the data support or disconfirm the hypothesis.

Psychologists usually get a preliminary idea about whether their data support the hypothesis by scrutinizing the means for each group. Figure A.9 depicts a histogram of these artificial data. Note that the independent variable (type of intervention) occupies the *x* axis. The dependent variable (grade point average) is represented on the *y* axis. At first glance, the data appear to support the original hypothesis. However, how large do those differences have to be before we can conclude confidently that the differences are meaningful? Inferential statistics can help answer that question.

Hypothesis Testing

There are many kinds of inferential statistics. Depending on the characteristics of the data and the number of groups being compared, psychologists apply different tests. In our experiment on improving grade point averages, we would use the t-test or analysis of variance, although there are other inferential procedures.

Inferential statistics *are complex mathematical methods used to draw conclusions about data that have been collected.* More specifically, inferential statistics are used to indicate whether or not data sufficiently support or confirm a research hypothesis. To accomplish this, inferential statistics rely on statements of probability and statistical significance, two important concepts that we will examine briefly.

Although it is beyond the scope of this appendix to explore these different measures of inferential statistics in detail, the logic behind inferential statistics is relatively simple. Measures of inferential statistics yield a statement of probability about the differences observed between two or more groups; this probability statement tells what the odds are that the observed differences were due simply to chance. If an inferential statistical measure tells you that the odds are less than 5 out of 100 (or .05) that the differences are due to chance, the results are considered statistically significant. In statistical terminology, this is referred to as the *.05 level of statistical significance,* or the *.05 confidence level.* Put another way, **statistical significance** *means that the differences observed between two groups are so large that it is highly unlikely whose differences are due merely to chance.*

The .05 level of statistical significance is considered the minimum level of probability that scientists will accept for concluding that the differences observed are real, thereby supporting a hypothesis. Some researchers prefer to use more rigorous levels of statistical significance, such as the .01 level of statistical significance (1 out of 100) or the .001 level of statistical significance (1 out of 1,000). Regardless of which level of statistical significance used, by knowing that a research result is statistically significant, you can be reasonably confident that the finding is not due simply to chance. Of course, replication of the study, with similar significant results, can increase your confidence in the finding even further.

However, a statistically significant difference does not always translate into a difference that has meaning in everyday life. Before assuming that a finding is significant both statistically and in everyday terms, it's wise to look at the actual differences involved. Sometimes the differences are so small as to be inconsequential. For example, in comparisons of average scores for males and females on the math section of the Scholastic Aptitude Test, the difference is statistically significant, with males performing better than females (Benbow & Stanley, 1983). In reality, however, the average difference is only a few points. Caution, therefore, should be exercised in the practical interpretation of statistically significant findings.

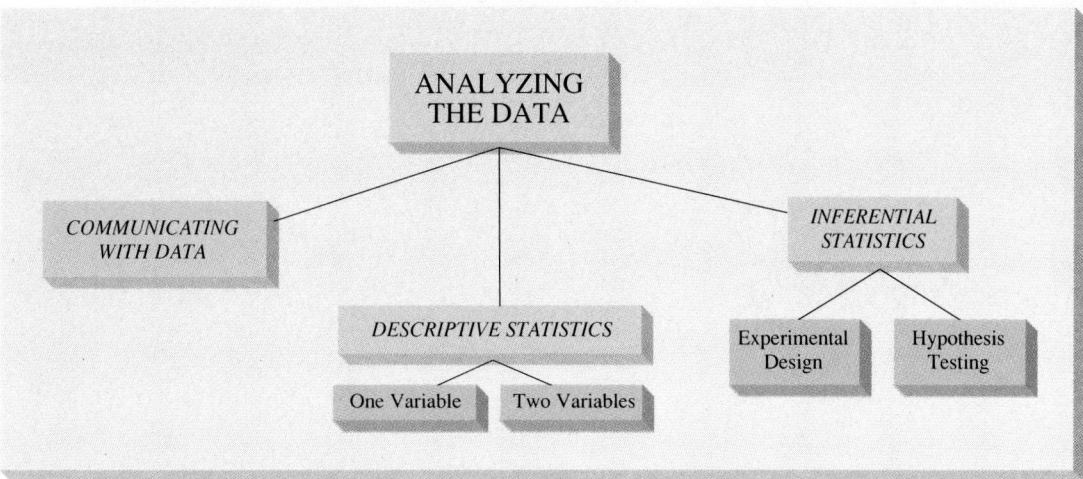

I n this appendix, we explored how to analyze data. We began by studying how to communicate with data, then we turned our attention to descriptive statistics and an evaluation of single-variable and two-variable psychological investigations. Finally, we read about inferential statistics and the roles of experimental design and hypothesis testing.

KEY TERMS

statistics Mathematical methods used to describe, summarize, and draw conclusions about data. 726

descriptive statistics Mathematical procedures used to describe and summarize samples of data in a meaningful fashion. 726

inferential statistics Complex mathematical methods used to draw conclusions about data that have been collected. 726

frequency distribution A listing of scores from lowest to highest with the number of times each score appears in a sample. 727

histogram A graph of a frequency distribution, in which vertical bars represent the frequency of scores per category or class. 727

frequency polygon Basically the same as a histogram except that the data are represented with lines instead of bars. 727

normal distribution A symmetrical distribution with a majority of cases falling in the middle of the possible range of scores and few scores appearing toward the extremes of the range. Also called a bell-shaped curve. 727

measure of central tendency A single number that tells you the overall characteristics of a set of data. 728

mean The numerical average for a group of scores or values. 728

median The score that falls exactly in the middle of a distribution of scores after they have been arranged (ranked) from highest to lowest. 728

mode The score that occurs most often. 728

measures of variability Measures of how much the scores in a sample vary from one another. 729

range The distance between the highest and the lowest score. 729

standard deviation A measure of how much the scores vary, on the average, around the mean of a sample. 729

scatter plot A graph on which pairs of scores are represented. 731

correlation coefficient A numerical value that expresses the degree of relationship between two variables. 731

positive correlation A relationship in which the two factors vary in the same direction. 732

negative correlation A relationship in which the two factors vary in opposite directions. 732

statistical significance The idea that the differences observed between two groups are sufficiently large that it is highly unlikely that they are due merely to chance. 736

GLOSSARY

A

abnormal behavior Behavior that is maladaptive, harmful, statistically unusual, personally distressing, and/or designated as abnormal by the culture.   575

absolute threshold The minimum amount of energy that we can detect.   95

accommodation (cognitive) An individual's adjustment to new information.   307

accommodation (optical) An increase in the curvature of the lens in the eye.   100

acculturation Change that results from continuous, firsthand contact between two distinctive cultural groups that preserves the identities of both.   511, 700

acculturative stress The negative consequences of acculturation.   511

accurate empathy Rogers's term for the therapist's ability to identify with the client.   622

acetylcholine (ACh) A neurotransmitter that produces contractions of skeletal muscles by acting on motor nerves.   71

achievement motivation (need for achievement) The desire to accomplish something, to reach a standard of excellence, and to expend effort to excel.   460

action potential The brief wave of electrical charge that sweeps down the axon.   69

action therapy Therapy that promotes direct changes in behavior; insight is not essential for change to occur.   617

activation-synthesis view The view that dreams have no inherent meaning. Rather they reflect the brain's efforts to make sense out of or find meaning in the neural activity that takes place during REM sleep. In this view, the brain has considerable random activity during REM sleep, and dreams are an attempt to synthesize the chaos.   148

active-behavioral strategies Coping responses in which individuals take some type of action to improve their problem situation.   514

active-cognitive strategies Coping responses in which individuals actively think about a situation in an effort to adjust more effectively.   514

active listening Rogers's term for the ability to listen to another person with total attention to what the person says and means.   622

activity theory The theory that the more active and involved older people are, the more satisfied they will be with their lives and the more likely it is that they will stay healthy.   365

actor-observer hypothesis In attribution theory, differences in the interpretation of motives based on point of view.   658

acupuncture A technique in which thin needles are inserted at specific points in the body to produce effects such as local anesthesia.   111

adaptation Behavioral changes in response to challenges in the environment that enhance the organism's likelihood of survival.   63

addiction Physical dependence on a drug.   152

additive mixture The mixing of light beams from different parts of the color spectrum.   103

adolescence The transition from childhood to adulthood, which involves physical, cognitive, and socioemotional changes. In most cultures adolescence begins at about 10 to 13 years of age and ends at about 18 to 21 years of age.   335

adolescent egocentrism The adolescent's belief that others are as preoccupied with the adolescent as she herself is, the belief that one is unique, and the belief that one is indestructible.   338

adrenal glands Glands whose secretions play an important role in our moods, energy level, and ability to cope with stress; each adrenal gland secretes epinephrine (also called adrenaline) and norepinephrine (also called noradrenaline).   77

aerobic exercise Sustained exercise—jogging, swimming, or cycling, for example—that stimulates heart and lung activity.   491

affectionate love Also called companionate love; a type of love that occurs when an individual desires to have the other person near and has a deep, caring affection for the person.   666

afferent nerves Sensory nerves that carry information to the brain.   67

afterimages Sensations that remain after a stimulus is removed.   104

ageism Prejudice against people based on their age.   365

agoraphobia The fear of entering unfamiliar situations, especially open or public spaces; the most common phobic disorder.   584

AIDS A sexually transmitted disease that is caused by the human immunodeficiency virus (HIV), which destroys the body's immune system.   436

algorithms Procedures that guarantee an answer to a problem.   252

all-or-none principle The principle that once the electrical impulse reaches a certain level of intensity, it fires and moves all the way down the axon, remaining at the same strength throughout its travel.   69

alpha waves The EEG pattern of individuals who are in a relaxed or drowsy state.   41

altered state of consciousness A mental state that is noticeably different from normal awareness. Drugs, meditation, traumas, fatigue, hypnosis, and sensory deprivation produce altered states of consciousness.   137

alternation model The view that individuals can develop bicultural competence without choosing one group over another or diminishing their own subgroup identification. 511, 700

altruism An unselfish interest in helping someone else. 668

Alzheimer's disease A degenerative, irreversible brain disorder that impairs memory and social behavior. 363

amnesia The loss of memory. 232

amplitude Measured in decibels (dB), the amount of pressure produced by a sound wave relative to a standard. More generally, the height of a wave of any kind. 106, 141

amygdala A limbic system structure, located within the base of the temporal lobe, that is involved in the discrimination of objects that are important for an organism's survival, such as appropriate food, mates, and social rivals. 77

anal stage Freud's second stage of development, occurring between 1½ and 3 years of age, in which the child's greatest pleasure involves the anus or the eliminative functions associated with it. 538

analogy A type of formal reasoning that always has four parts, in which the relation between the first two parts is the same as the relation between the last two. 255

androgens The main class of male sex hormones. 397

androgyny The presence of desirable masculine and feminine characteristics in one individual. 390

anorexia nervosa An eating disorder that involves the relentless pursuit of thinness through starvation. 498

anterograde amnesia A memory disorder in which the individual cannot form memories of new information or events. 232

antianxiety drugs Drugs that reduce anxiety by making individuals less excitable and more tranquil; commonly known as tranquilizers. 642

antidepressant drugs Drugs that regulate mood. The three main classes of antidepressant drugs are tricyclics, such as Elavil; MAO inhibitors, such as Nardil; and SSRI inhibitors, such as Prozac. 643

antipsychotic drugs Powerful drugs that diminish agitated behavior, reduce tension, decrease hallucinations and delusions, improve social behavior, and produce better sleep patterns in severely mentally disabled individuals, especially schizophrenics. 643

antisocial personality disorder A personality disorder in the dramatic, emotional, and erratic cluster; the most problematic personality disorder for society. Individuals with this disorder often resort to crime, violence, and delinquency. 602

anxiety disorders Psychological disorders that include the following main features: motor tension (jumpiness, trembling, inability to relax), hyperactivity (dizziness, racing heart, or perspiration), and apprehensive expectations and thoughts. 584

aphasia An inability to recognize or express language. 83

approach/approach conflict A conflict in which the individual must choose between two attractive stimuli or circumstances. 508

approach/avoidance conflict A conflict involving a single stimulus or circumstance that has both positive and negative characteristics. 509

archetypes Primordial influences in every individual's collective unconscious that filter our perceptions and experiences. 542

artificial intelligence (AI) The science of creating machines capable of performing activities that require intelligence when they are done by people. 248

assimilation (cognitive) The incorporation of new information into one's existing knowledge. 307

assimilation (social) Individuals' relinquishing their cultural identity and moving into the larger society. 511, 700

association cortex Areas of the brain that are involved in our highest intellectual functions, such as problem solving and thinking; also called association areas. 80

attachment A close emotional bond between the infant and the caregiver. 318

attitudes Beliefs and opinions that can predispose individuals to behave in certain ways. 659

attribution theory The theory that individuals are motivated to discover the underlying causes of behavior as part of their effort to make sense out of the behavior. 461, 658

auditory nerve The nerve that carries neural impulses to the brain's auditory areas. 108

authoritarian parenting A restrictive, punitive style that exhorts the child to follow the parent's directions and to respect work and effort. The authoritarian parent places firm limits and controls on the child, with little verbal exchange allowed. Authoritarian parenting is associated with children's social incompetence. 320

authoritative parenting A parenting style that encourages children to be independent but still places limits and controls on their actions. Extensive verbal give-and-take is allowed, and the parents are warm and nurturant toward the child. Authoritative parenting is associated with children's social competence. 320

automatic processes A form of consciousness that requires minimal attention and does not interfere with other ongoing activities. 137

automatic processing A process of encoding information in memory that does not require capacity, resources, or effort. 222

autonomic nervous system The division of the peripheral nervous system that takes messages to and from the body's internal organs, monitoring such processes as breathing, heart rate, and digestion. 66

autonomy versus shame and doubt Erikson's second stage of development, occurring in late infancy and toddlerhood (ages 1–3 years). 316

aversive conditioning An approach to behavior therapy that involves repeated pairings of an undesirable behavior with aversive stimuli to decrease the behavior's rewards so that the individual will stop doing it; this technique is based on classical conditioning. 625

avoidance/avoidance conflict A conflict in which the individual must choose between two unattractive stimuli or circumstances. 509

avoidance strategies Responses that individuals use to keep stressful circumstances out of awareness so they do not have to deal with them. 515

axon The part of the neuron that carries information away from the cell body to other cells. 67

B

"bad patient" role The role in which a patient complains to the staff, demands attention, disobeys staff orders, and generally misbehaves. 523

barbiturates Depressant drugs, such as Nebutal and Seconal, that induce sleep or reduce anxiety. 157

Barnum effect If you make your descriptions broad enough, any person can fit them. 558

basal metabolism rate (BMR) The minimal amount of energy an individual uses in a resting state. 495

basilar membrane A membrane that is housed inside the cochlea and runs its entire length. 108

behavior Everything we do that can be directly observed. 5

behavior modification The application of operant conditioning principles to changing behavior; its main goal is to replace unacceptable responses with acceptable, adaptive ones. 190

behavior therapies Therapies that use principles of learning to reduce or eliminate maladaptive behavior. 624

behavioral medicine A field closely related to health psychology that attempts to combine medical and behavioral knowledge to reduce illness and promote health. 489

behavioral perspective An emphasis on the scientific study of observable behavioral responses and their environmental determinants. 13

beta waves High-frequency electrical activity in the brain, characteristic of periods of concentration. 141

bilingual education Programs for students with limited proficiency in English that instruct students in their own language part of the time while they learn English. 266

binocular cues Depth cues that are based on both eyes working together. 118

biofeedback The process in which individuals' muscular or visceral activities are monitored by instruments and information is given (fed back) to the individuals so they can learn to voluntarily control their physiological activities. 523

biological processes Processes that involve changes in an individual's physical nature. 297

biomedical therapies Treatments to reduce or eliminate the symptoms of psychological disorders by altering the way an individual's body functions. Drug therapy is the most common form. 642

bipolar disorder A mood disorder characterized by extreme mood swings; an individual with this disorder might be depressed, manic, or both. 592

blind spot The area of the retina where the optic nerve leaves the eye on its way to the brain. 100

borderline personality disorder A personality disorder in the dramatic, emotional, and erratic cluster; the person's behavior exhibits these characteristics. 601

brightness A characteristic of color based on its intensity. 102

brightness constancy Recognition that an object retains the same degree of brightness even when different amounts of light fall on it. 121

bulimia An eating disorder in which the individual consistently follows a binge-and-purge eating pattern. 498

burnout A hopeless, helpless feeling brought about by relentless work-related stress. Burnout leaves its sufferers in a state of physical and emotional exhaustion that includes chronic fatigue and low energy. 508

bystander effect The effect of others' presence on a person's giving help; individuals who observe an emergency help less when another observer is present than when they are a lone observer. 670

C

Cannon-Bard theory The theory that emotion and physiological states occur simultaneously. 471

care perspective Carol Gilligan's theory of moral development, which sees people in terms of their connectedness with others and focuses on interpersonal communication, relationships with others, and concern for others. 346

carpentered-world hypothesis The hypothesis that people who live in cultures in which straight lines, right angles, and rectangles predominate (in which rooms and buildings are usually rectangular, and many objects, such as city streets, have square corners) should be more susceptible to illusions involving straight lines, right angles, and rectangles (such as the Müller-Lyer illusion) than people who live in noncarpentered cultures are. 123

case study A study that provides an in-depth look at one individual. Clinical psychologists use case studies when they cannot duplicate the unique aspects of an individual's life for study, for either practical or ethical reasons. 40

catatonic schizophrenia A schizophrenic disorder characterized by bizarre motor behavior, which sometimes takes the form of an immobile stupor. 597

catharsis The psychoanalytic term for clients' release of emotional tension when they relive an emotionally charged and conflicted experience. 620

cell body The part of the neuron that contains the nucleus, which directs the manufacture of the substances the neuron uses for its growth and maintenance. 67

central nervous system (CNS) The brain and spinal cord. 66

cerebellum A part of the brain that extends from the rear of the hindbrain and is located above the medulla; consists of two rounded structures thought to play important roles in motor control. 73

cerebral cortex (cerebrum) The most recently evolved part of the brain; covering the rest of the brain almost like a cap, it is the largest part of the brain and makes up about 80 percent of its volume. 78

chaining An operant conditioning technique used to teach a complex sequence, or chain, of behaviors. The procedure begins by shaping the final response in the sequence, then works backward until a chain of behaviors is learned. 186

chastity Inexperience with sexual intercourse. 663

chlamydia The most common of all sexually transmitted diseases, named for *Chlamydia trachomatis,* an organism that spreads by sexual contact and infects the genital organs of both males and females. 436

chromosomes Threadlike structures located in the nucleus of each human cell. Chromosomes come in 23 pairs, one member of each pair coming from each parent. 59

chunking The grouping, or "packing," of information into higher-order units that can be remembered as single units. Chunking expands working memory by making large amounts of information more manageable. 216

circadian rhythm A daily behavioral or physiological cycle, such as the 24-hour sleep/wake cycle. 139

civil commitment Commitment that transpires when a judge deems an individual to be a risk to self or others due to a mental disorder. 602

---

clairvoyance The ability to perceive remote events that are not in sight.   125

classical conditioning A form of learning in which a neutral stimulus becomes associated with a meaningful stimulus and acquires the capacity to elicit a similar response.   173

clinical and counseling psychology The most widely practiced specialization in psychology. Clinical and counseling psychologists diagnose and treat people with psychological problems.   18

cochlea A long tubular fluid-filled structure in the inner ear that is coiled up like a snail.   108

cognitive appraisal Lazarus's concept of individuals' interpretation of events in their lives as harmful, threatening, or challenging, and their determination of whether they have the resources to effectively cope with the event.   506

cognitive developmental theory of gender The theory that children's gender typing occurs after they have developed a concept of gender. Once they begin to consistently conceive themselves as male or female, children often organize their world on the basis of gender.   400

cognitive dissonance A concept developed by social psychologist Leon Festinger; an individual's motivation toward consistency and away from inconsistency.   660

cognitive map An organism's mental representation of the structure of physical space.   199

cognitive perspective An emphasis on the mental processes involved in knowing: how we direct our attention, how we perceive, how we remember, and how we think and solve problems.   14

cognitive processes Processes that involve changes in an individual's thought, intelligence, and language.   297

cognitive restructuring The modification of the thoughts, ideas, and beliefs that maintain an individual's problems.   516

cognitive social learning theory The contemporary version of social learning theory that stresses the importance of cognition, behavior, and environment.   546

cognitive therapies Therapies that emphasize that an individual's cognitions, or thoughts, are the main source of abnormal behavior; cognitive therapies attempt to change the individual's feelings and behaviors by changing cognitions.   626

collective unconscious In Jung's theory, the impersonal, deepest layer of the unconscious mind, which is shared by all human beings because of their common ancestral past.   542

collectivism An emphasis on values that serve the group by subordinating personal goals to preserve group integrity, interdependence of members, and harmonious relationships.   556, 699

commitment The process by which an individual becomes institutionalized in a mental hospital.   602

community psychology An area that focuses on providing accessible care for people with psychological problems. Community-based mental health centers are one means of providing services like outreach programs to people in need, especially those who traditionally have been underserved by mental health professionals.   19

compensation Adler's term for the individual's attempt to overcome imagined or real inferiorities or weaknesses by developing her or his abilities.   543

competence motivation The motivation to deal effectively with the environment, to be adept at what we attempt, and to make the world a better place.   459

competency An individual's ability to understand and participate in a judicial proceeding.   604

complex sounds Sounds in which numerous frequencies of sound blend together.   106

computer-assisted axial tomography (CAT scan) A three-dimensional imaging technique in which pictures obtained by passing X rays through the head are assembled by a computer into a composite image.   84

concept A category used to group objects, events, and characteristics on the basis of common properties.   249

conception The penetration of an ovum (egg) by a sperm; also called fertilization.   302

concrete operational thought Piaget's term for the 7- to 11-year-old child's understanding of the world. At this stage of thought, children can use operations—for instance, they can mentally reverse the pouring of liquid from one beaker to another and understand that the volume is the same even though the beakers are different in height and weight. Logical reasoning replaces intuitive thought as long as the principles are applied to concrete examples.   313

conditional positive regard Rogers's term for making the bestowal of love or praise conditional on the individual's conforming to parental or social standards.   547

conditioned response (CR) The learned response to the conditioned stimulus that occurs after CS-US association.   174

conditioned stimulus (CS) A previously neutral stimulus that elicits the conditioned response after being paired with the unconditioned stimulus.   174

conditioned taste aversions Classically conditioned avoidance reactions to food.   180

cones Receptors for color perception.   100

conformity Individuals adopt the attitudes or behavior of others because of real or imagined pressure from others.   679

consciousness Awareness of external and internal stimuli or events.   136

consciousness-raising groups Groups that are believed by some feminists to be an important alternative or adjunct to traditional therapy. They often involve several people meeting in a member's home, are frequently leaderless, and focus on members' feelings and self-perceptions. Instead of seeking and accepting male-based therapy, women may meet in consciousness-raising groups to define their own experiences with their own criteria.   639

consensual validation A concept that provides an explanation of why people are attracted to others who are similar to them. Our own attitudes and behavior are supported when someone else's attitudes and behavior are similar to ours—their attitudes and behaviors validate ours.   662

conservation The principle that a substance's quantity stays the same even though its shape changes.   310

content validity The extent to which a test covers broadly the content it is purported to cover.   272

context The historical, economic, social, and cultural factors that influence mental processes and behavior.   6

continuity of development Gradual, cumulative change from conception to death.   297

contour A location at which a sudden change of brightness occurs.   117

control group In an experiment, the comparison group that is treated like the experimental group in every way except for the manipulated factor.   37

controlled processes The most alert states of consciousness, in which individuals actively focus their efforts toward a goal.   137

conventional level Kohlberg's second level of moral thinking in which an individual shows an intermediate level of internalization. The individual abides by certain standards (internal), but they are the standards of others (external), such as parents' standards (stage 3) or society's laws (stage 4).   346

convergence A binocular cue for depth perception in which the eyes turn inward as an object gets closer. When the eyes converge or diverge, information is sent to the brain, which interprets the information about the inward (object is closer) or outward (object is farther away) eye movement.   119

convergent thinking Thinking that produces one correct answer and is characteristic of the kind of thinking on standardized intelligence tests.   258

conversion disorder A somatoform disorder in which an individual experiences genuine physical symptoms, even though no physiological problems can be found.   587

cornea A clear membrane just in front of the eye; its function is to bend the light falling on the surface of the eye just enough to focus it at the back of the eye.   99

corpus callosum A large bundle of axons that connects the brain's two hemispheres.   81

correlation coefficient A numerical value that expresses the degree of relationship between two variables.   731

correlational research methods Methods in which the goal is to describe the strength of the relation between two or more events or characteristics.   35

counterconditioning A classical conditioning procedure for weakening a conditioned response of fear by associating the fear-provoking stimulus with a new response that is incompatible with the fear.   177

couple therapy Group therapy with married or unmarried couples whose major problem is their relationship.   630

crack An intensified form of cocaine that consists of chips of pure cocaine that are usually smoked.   158

creativity The ability to think in novel ways and to come up with unique solutions to problems.   258

credibility A therapist's believability.   642

criminal commitment Commitment that occurs when a mental disorder is implicated in the commission of a crime.   603

criterion validity A test's ability to predict other measures, or criteria, of an attribute.   273

critical thinking Grasping the deeper meaning of problems, keeping an open mind about different approaches and perspectives, and deciding for oneself what to believe or do.   256

cross-cultural psychology An area that examines the role of culture in understanding behavior, thought, and emotion.   18

cross-cultural studies The comparison of two or more cultures, which provides information about the degree to which people's behavior, thoughts, and feelings are similar, or universal across cultures, and to what degree they are culture-specific.   698

cue-dependent forgetting Forgetting information because of failure to use effective retrieval cues.   230

cultural-familial retardation A mental deficit in which no evidence of organic brain damage can be found; these individuals' IQs range from 50 to 70. Psychologists suspect that such mental deficits result from the normal variation that distributes people along the range of intelligence scores above 50, combined with growing up in a below-average intellectual environment.   276

culture The behavior patterns, beliefs, and other products of a particular group of people, such as their values, work patterns, music, dress, diet, and ceremonies, that are passed on from generation to generation.   15, 697

culture-fair tests Intelligence tests that are intended to not be culturally biased.   282

culture shock The disorganizing effects of exposure to unfamiliar ways of life.   700

culture specificity hypothesis The hypothesis that cultural experiences determine what is socially relevant in a person's life, and, therefore, what the person is most likely to remember.   236

current concern A state the person occupies between becoming committed to pursuing a goal and either attaining it or abandoning it.   453

D

data Information gathered through systematic observation.   29

date or acquaintance rape Coercive sex forced by someone with whom the victim is at least casually acquainted.   433

daydreaming A form of consciousness that involves a low level of conscious effort.   137

decay theory The theory that when something new is learned, a neurochemical "memory trace" is formed, but over time this trace tends to disintegrate.   232

declarative memory The conscious recollection of information, such as specific facts or events, and, at least in humans, information that can be verbally communicated. Declarative memory has been called "knowing that" and, more recently, "explicit memory."   219

deductive reasoning Reasoning from the general to the specific; working with abstract statements (premises) and deriving a conclusion.   254

defense mechanisms The psychoanalytic term for unconscious methods of dealing with conflict; the ego distorts reality, thereby protecting itself from anxiety.   537

deficiency needs Maslow's term for essential requirements—physiological needs (for food, shelter, comfort, and so on) and psychological needs (for affection, security, self-esteem, and so on)—that must be met or else individuals will try to make up for their absence.   550

deindividuation A state of reduced self-awareness, weakened self-restraints against impulsive actions, and apathy about negative social evaluation.   681

deinstitutionalization The movement to transfer the treatment of mental disabilities from inpatient medical institutions to community-based facilities that stress outpatient care.   633

delay of gratification The ability to defer immediate satisfaction for a more desirable future outcome.   546

delta waves The EEG pattern characteristic of deepening sleep and progressive muscle relaxation.   142

dendrite The receiving part of the neuron, serving the important function of collecting information and orienting it toward the cell body.   67

deoxyribonucleic acid (DNA) A complex molecule that contains genetic information.   60

dependent variable The factor that is measured in an experiment; it might change when the independent variable is manipulated.   37

depth perception The ability to perceive objects three-dimensionally.   118

descriptive research methods Methods intended to provide an accurate portrayal of behavior. Descriptive statistics communicate basic qualities of the data being reported.   35

descriptive statistics Mathematical procedures used to describe and summarize samples of data in a meaningful fashion.   726

determinism The belief that historical or biological factors completely account for behavior.   551

development A pattern of movement or change that begins at conception and continues through the life cycle.   297

developmental psychology An area concerned with how we become who we are, from conception to death.   18

diathesis-stress view The view that a combination of environmental stress and biogenetic disposition causes schizophrenia.   600

dichromats People with only two kinds of cones.   104

difference threshold Also called the just noticeable difference (jnd), the smallest difference in stimulation required to discriminate one stimulus from another 50 percent of the time.   97

discontinuity of development Development involving qualitatively distinct stages in the life span.   297

discrimination (classical conditioning) The process of learning to respond to certain stimuli and not to others.   175

discrimination (operant conditioning) The process of responding in the presence of another stimulus that is not reinforced.   190

discrimination (social) Differential treatment, based on an individual's membership in a group, due to prejudice.   707

discriminative stimuli A signal that a response will be reinforced.   190

disease model of addiction The view that addictions are biologically based, lifelong diseases that involve a loss of control over behavior and require medical and/or spiritual treatment for recovery.   153

disorganized schizophrenia A schizophrenic disorder in which an individual has delusions and hallucinations that have little or no recognizable meaning—hence the label *disorganized*.   597

displacement The psychoanalytic defense mechanism that occurs when an individual shifts unacceptable feelings from one object to another, more acceptable object.   538

display rules Sociocultural standards that determine when, where, and how emotions should be expressed.   477

dissociative disorders Psychological disorders that involve a sudden loss of memory or change in identity. Under extreme stress, or shock, an individual's conscious awareness becomes dissociated (separated or split) from previous memories and thoughts.   588

divergent thinking Thinking that produces many answers to the same question and is characteristic of creativity.   258

dominant-recessive genes principle The principle that if one gene of a pair is dominant and one is recessive, the dominant gene exerts its effect, overriding the potential influence of the recessive gene. A recessive gene exerts its influence only if both genes of the pair are recessive.   60

dopamine An inhibitory neurotransmitter that is related to movement, attention, learning, and mental health; too much dopamine in the brain's synapses is associated with a severe mental disorder, schizophrenia.   71

double standard The belief that many sexual activities are acceptable for males but not for females.   426

dream analysis The psychotherapeutic technique psychoanalysts use to interpret a client's dream. Psychoanalysts believe that dreams contain information about the individual's unconscious thoughts and conflicts.   620

drive An aroused state that occurs because of a physiological need.   451

drive reduction theory The theory that a physiological need creates an aroused state (drive) that motivates the organism to satisfy the need.   451

DSM-IV *Diagnostic and Statistical Manual of Mental Disorders,* fourth edition. The DSM-IV is the most recent major classification of mental disorders and contains eighteen major classifications and more than 200 specific disorders.   581

dyslexia A learning difference that negatively influences the quality and rate of reading.   277

E

early adulthood A developmental period that begins in the late teens or early twenties and ends in the late thirties to early forties. It is a time when individuals establish personal and economic independence, intensely pursue a career, and seek intimacy with one or more individuals.   351

early-later experience issue An issue that focuses on the degree to which early experiences (especially in infancy) or later experiences are the key determinants of a child's development.   297

echoic memory The auditory sensory registers in which information is retained for up to several seconds.   215

eclectic Using a variety of approaches.   617

ecological theory A relatively recent view of sleep that is based on the theory of evolution. It argues that the main purpose of sleep is to prevent animals from wasting their energy and harming themselves during the parts of the day or night to which they have not adapted.   144

ectomorph Sheldon's term for a tall, thin, fragile person who is fearful, introverted, and restrained.   553

efferent nerves Motor nerves that carry the brain's output.   67

effortful processing Processing that requires capacity or resources to encode information in memory.   222

ego The Freudian structure of personality that deals with the demands of reality; the ego is called the executive branch of personality because it makes rational decisions.   537

egocentrism Piaget's term for the inability to distinguish between one's own perspective and someone else's.   310

egoism An attitude in which one does something beneficial for another person in order to ensure reciprocity; to present oneself as powerful, competent, or caring; or to avoid social or self-censure for failing to live up to normative expectations.   669

eidetic memory Also called photographic memory; a form of memory involving especially vivid details. The small number of individuals who have eidetic memory can recall significantly more details of visual information than most of us can.   216

elaboration The extensiveness of processing at any given depth in memory.   222

electroconvulsive therapy (ECT) A type of therapy sometimes used to treat severely depressed individuals; commonly called shock therapy.   644

electroencephalograph An instrument that records the electrical activity of the brain; electrodes placed on an individual's scalp record brain-wave activity, which is reproduced on a chart known as an electroencephalogram (EEG).   84

embryonic period The second through eighth week after conception.   302

emic approach An approach to research that has as its goal describing behavior in one culture or ethnic group in terms that are meaningful and important to the people in that culture or ethnic group, without regard to other cultures or ethnic groups. The emic approach is culture-specific.   41, 698

emotion Feeling, or affect, that involves a mixture of arousal (fast heartbeat, for example), conscious experience (thinking about being in love with someone, for example), and overt behavior (smiling or grimacing, for example).   468

emotion-focused coping Lazarus's term for responding to stress in an emotional manner, especially using defensive appraisal.   514

empirically keyed tests Tests that rely on the test items to predict a particular criterion. Unlike tests based on face validity, in which the content of the test items is supposed to be a good indicator of what a tested individual's personality is like, empirically keyed tests make no assumptions about the nature of the items.   560

empowerment Helping individuals develop skills they need to improve their adaptation and circumstances.   634

encoding The transformation of information in, and/or transfer of information into, a memory system.   221

encounter group A personal-growth group designed to promote self-understanding through candid group interaction.   631

endocrine system The hypothalamus and other endocrine glands that release their chemical products directly into the bloodstream.   76

endomorph Sheldon's term for a soft, round, large-stomached person who is relaxed, gregarious, and food loving.   553

endorphins Natural opiates that are neurotransmitters; endorphins are involved in pleasure and the control of pain.   72

environment All of the surrounding conditions and influences that affect the development of living things.   59

epigenetic principle Erikson's term for the process that guides development through the life cycle. The epigenetic principle states that human beings unfold according to a blueprint, with each stage of development coming at a predictable time. Ultimately, all stages contribute to a complete identity.   316

episodic memory The retention of information about the where and when of life's happenings.   219

erogenous zones Those parts of the body at each stage of development that, according to Freud's theory, have especially strong pleasure-giving qualities.   538

estradiol A hormone associated, in girls, with breast, uterine, and skeletal development.   337

estrogens The main class of female sex hormones.   397

ethnic identity A sense of membership in an ethnic group, based on shared language, religion, customs, values, history, and race.   15, 703

ethnicity An aspect of human beings that is based on cultural heritage, nationality characteristics, race, religion, and language.   15, 703

ethnocentrism The tendency to favor one's own group over other groups.   705

ethology The study of the biological basis of behavior in natural habitats.   452

etic approach An approach to research in which the goal is to describe behavior so that generalizations can be made across cultures. The etic approach is culture-universal.   41, 698

eustress Selye's term for the positive features of stress.   506

exhibitionism A psychosexual disorder in which individuals expose their sexual anatomy to others to obtain sexual gratification.   431

exorcism A religious rite used during the Middle Ages that was designed to remove evil spirits from a person; it involved prayer, starvation, beatings, and various forms of torture.   615

expectancy An individual's belief in the probability that a specific behavior will lead to satisfactions or valued goals.   546

experiment A carefully regulated procedure in which researchers manipulate one or more factors believed to influence the behavior being studied and hold all other factors constant.   36

experimental and physiological psychology Areas that involve pure research. Although psychologists in other areas conduct experiments, virtually all experimental and physiological psychologists follow precise, careful experimental strategies.   18

experimental group The group in an experiment whose experience is manipulated.   37

experimental research methods Methods that allow us to precisely determine behavior's causes.   36

expert systems Computer-based systems for assessing knowledge and making decisions in advanced skill areas.   248

extinction (classical conditioning) The weakening of the conditioned response in the absence of the unconditioned stimulus.   176

extinction (operant conditioning) A decrease in the tendency to perform a behavior that receives neither a positive nor a negative consequence.   185

extrasensory perception (ESP) Perception that occurs without the use of any known sensory process.   124

extrinsic motivation The influence of external rewards and punishments.   461

F

face validity An assumption that the content of test items is a good indicator of what an individual's personality is like.   560

family systems therapy A form of therapy based on the assumption that psychological adjustment is related to patterns of interaction within the family unit.   630

family therapy Group therapy with family members.   630

feminist therapies Therapies that usually are based on a critique of society wherein women are perceived to have less political and economic power than men have. Also, feminist therapies assume that the reasons for women's problems are principally social, not personal.   639

feminization of poverty   The fact that, increasingly, far more women than men live in poverty. Women's low incomes, divorce, and the way the judicial system typically resolves divorce cases are the likely causes of the feminization of poverty.   513

fetal alcohol syndrome (FAS)   A cluster of abnormalities that appear in the offspring of mothers who drink alcohol heavily during pregnancy.   303

fetal period   The third through ninth months after conception.   302

fetishism   A psychosexual disorder in which an individual relies on inanimate objects or a specific part of the body for sexual gratification.   431

figure-ground relationship   The principle by which we organize the perceptual field into stimuli that stand out (figure) and those that are left over (ground).   117

fitness   In evolutionary theory, the degree to which an individual can produce viable offspring.   63

fixation   The psychoanalytic defense mechanism that occurs when the individual remains locked in an earlier developmental stage because his or her needs are under- or overgratified.   538

fixed-interval schedule   Reinforcement of the first appropriate response after a fixed amount of time has elapsed.   189

fixed-ratio schedule   Reinforcement of a behavior after a set number of responses.   188

forebrain   The region of the brain that governs the highest functions. Among its important structures are the thalamus, the hypothalamus and endocrine system, the limbic system, and the cerebral cortex.   74

formal groups   Groups established by management to do the organization's work.   682

formal operational thought   Piaget's fourth stage of cognitive development, which appears between 11 and 15 years of age. Formal operational thought is abstract, idealistic, and logical.   338

fovea   A minute area in the center of the retina where vision is at its best.   100

free association   The technique of encouraging individuals to say aloud whatever comes to mind, no matter how trivial or embarrassing.   620

frequency   With respect to sound waves, the number of cycles (full wavelengths) that pass through a point in a given time; also, more generally, the number of wave cycles per second.   106, 141

frequency distribution   A listing of scores from lowest to highest with the number of times each score appears in a sample.   727

frequency polygon   Basically the same as a histogram except that the data are represented with lines instead of bars.   727

frequency theory   The theory of hearing that states that the perception of a sound's frequency is due to how often the auditory nerve fires.   108

friendship   A form of close relationship that involves enjoyment, acceptance, trust, intimacy, respect, mutual assistance, understanding, and spontaneity.   664

frontal lobe   The portion of the cerebral cortex that is behind the forehead and is involved in the control of voluntary muscles and in intelligence.   78

frustration   Any situation in which a person cannot reach a desired goal.   509

fugue   A dissociative disorder in which an individual not only develops amnesia but also unexpectedly travels away from home and establishes a new identity (*fugue* means "flight").   588

functional fixedness   The inability to solve a problem because it is viewed only in terms of usual functions.   252

functionalism   William James's theory that psychology's role is to study the functions of the mind and behavior in adapting to the environment.   9

fundamental attribution error   Observers' tendency to overestimate the importance of traits and underestimate the importance of situations when they seek explanations of an actor's behavior.   658

fusion   A model in which cultures sharing economic, political, or geographic boundaries will fuse until they become indistinguishable and form a new culture.   700

G

GABA   Gamma aminobutyric acid, a chemical substance that is a neurotransmitter; inhibits the firing of motor neurons.   70

gate-control theory   The theory that the spinal column contains a neural gate that can be opened (allowing the perception of pain) or closed (blocking the perception of pain).   110

gender   The sociocultural dimension of being female or male, particularly how we learn to think and behave as females and males.   15, 384

gender identity   The sense of being male or female, which most children begin to acquire by the time they are 3 years old.   385

gender role   A set of expectations that prescribes how females or males should think, act, or feel.   385

gender-role transcendence   The belief that an individual's competence should be conceptualized not on the basis of masculinity, femininity, or androgyny but, rather, on a personal basis.   391

gender-role stereotypes   Broad categories that reflect our impressions and beliefs about females and males.   392

gender schema   A cognitive structure that organizes the world in terms of female and male.   401

gender schema theory   The theory that children's attention and behavior are guided by an internal motivation to conform to gender-based, sociocultural standards and stereotypes.   401

general adaptation syndrome (GAS)   Selye's concept of the common effects on the body when demands are placed on it. The GAS consists of three stages: alarm, resistance, and exhaustion.   505

generalization (classical conditioning)   The tendency of a new stimulus that is similar to the original conditioned stimulus to elicit a response that is similar to the conditioned response.   175

generalization (operant conditioning)   Giving the same response to similar stimuli.   189

generalized anxiety disorder   An anxiety disorder that consists of persistent anxiety for at least 1 month. An individual with this disorder is unable to specify the reasons for the anxiety.   584

generativity versus stagnation   Erikson's seventh stage of development, occurring mainly in middle adulthood. Middle-aged adults need to assist the younger generation in leading useful lives.   356

genes   Short segments of DNA that contain the hereditary information.   60

genital herpes   A sexually transmitted disease in which the symptoms are small, painful bumps or blisters on the genitals.   436

genital stage The fifth Freudian stage of development, occurring from puberty on; the time of sexual reawakening and the source of sexual pleasure now becomes someone outside of the family.   540

genuineness The Rogerian concept of the importance of the therapist's being genuine and not hiding behind a facade.   622

germinal period The first 2 weeks after conception.   302

Gestalt psychology An approach that states that people naturally organize their perceptions according to certain patterns. *Gestalt* is a German word that means "configuration" or "form." One of Gestalt psychology's main principles is that the whole is not equal to the sum of its parts.   117

Gestalt therapy A humanistic therapy developed by Fritz Perls, in which the therapist questions and challenges clients to help them become more aware of their feelings and face their problems.   622

gifted Having above-average intelligence (an IQ of 120 or higher) and/or superior talent for something.   277

giving The client's receiving some kind of benefit from treatment early in the therapy process.   642

gonorrhea A sexually transmitted disease that is commonly called the "drip" or the "clap"; one of the most common STDs in the United States, it is caused by a bacterium from the gonococcus family, which thrives in the moist mucous membranes lining the mouth, throat, vagina, cervix, urethra, and anal tract.   435

"good patient" role The role in which one is passive and unquestioning and behaves properly.   523

great person theory The theory that individuals with certain traits are best suited for leadership positions.   678

groupthink The motivation of group members to maintain harmony and unanimity in decision making, suffocating differences of opinion in the process.   681

H

hallucinogens Psychoactive drugs that modify a person's perceptual experiences and produce visual images that are not real. Hallucinogens are also called psychedelic ("mind altering") drugs.   158

hardiness A personality style characterized by a sense of commitment (rather than alienation), control (rather than powerlessness), and a perception of problems as challenges (rather than threats).   507

health psychology A multidimensional approach to health that emphasizes psychological factors, lifestyle, and the nature of the health-care delivery system.   489

helpless orientation The orientation of individuals who seem trapped by the experience of difficulty. They attribute their difficulty to a lack of ability.   462

heuristics Rules of thumb that can suggest a solution to a problem but do not ensure that it will work.   252

hidden observer The term used by Hilgard for the part of a hypnotized individual's mind that is completely aware of what is happening. This part of the individual remains a passive, or hidden, observer until called on to comment.   151

hierarchy of motives Maslow's concept that all individuals have five main needs that must be satisfied, in the following sequence: physiological, safety, love and belongingness, self-esteem, and self-actualization.   453

hindbrain The lowest portion of the brain, located at the skull's rear. It consists of the spinal cord, the lower brain stem (pons and medulla), and the cerebellum.   73

hippocampus A limbic system structure that has a special role in the storage of memories.   78

histogram A graph of a frequency distribution, in which vertical bars represent the frequency of scores per category or class.   727

holophrase hypothesis The concept that a single word can be used to imply a complete sentence, and that infants' first words characteristically are holophrastic.   261

homeostasis The body's tendency to maintain an equilibrium or steady state.   451

hormones Chemical messengers manufactured by the endocrine glands.   76

hue A characteristic of color based on its wavelength content.   102

human sexual response cycle The four phases of human sexual response— excitement, plateau, orgasm, and resolution—identified by Masters and Johnson.   418

humanistic perspective An emphasis on a person's capacity for personal growth, freedom to choose one's own destiny, and positive qualities. The most widely adopted phenomenological approach to personality.   14

humanistic psychotherapies Therapies that encourage clients to understand themselves and to grow personally. In contrast to psychodynamic therapies, humanistic therapies emphasize conscious thoughts rather than unconscious thoughts, the present rather than the past, and growth and fulfillment rather than curing illness.   622

hypnosis A psychological state of altered attention and awareness in which the individual is unusually receptive to suggestions.   150

hypochondriasis A somatoform disorder in which the individual has a pervasive fear of illness and disease.   587

hypothalamus An area just below the thalamus that monitors three enjoyable activities—eating, drinking, and sex; also helps to direct the endocrine system through the pituitary gland. It is also involved in emotion, stress, and reward.   75

hypotheses Assumptions that can be tested to determine their accuracy.   29

hypothetical-deductive reasoning Piaget's name for adolescents' cognitive ability to develop hypotheses, or best guesses, about how to solve problems, such as algebraic equations.   338

I

iconic memory The visual sensory registers, in which information is retained for about ¼ second.   215

id The Freudian structure of personality that consists of instincts, which are the person's reservoir of psychic energy.   536

identification theory A theory that stems from Freud's view that preschool children develop a sexual attraction to the opposite-sex parent, then, at 5 to 6 years of age, renounce the attraction, due to anxiety, subsequently identifying with the same-sex parent and unconsciously adopting the same-sex parent's characteristics.   398

identity versus identity confusion The fifth of Erikson's stages of human development, occurring primarily during the adolescent years. The development of identity involves finding out who we are, what we are all about, and where we are going in life.   343

idiographic needs Needs that are important for the individual, not the group.   45

impression management The process in which individuals strive to present themselves in a favorable light.   658

imprinting The tendency of an infant animal to form an attachment to the first moving object it sees or hears.   318

incentives Positive or negative stimuli or events that motivate a person's behavior.   452

incest Sex between two relatives; virtually universally taboo.   434

independent variable The manipulated, influential, experimental factor in an experiment.   37

individual differences The consistent, stable ways people differ from each other.   269

individual psychology The name Adler gave to his theory of psychology to emphasize the uniqueness of every indiviudal.   542

individualism Giving priority to personal goals rather than group goals; an emphasis on values that serve the self, such as feeling good, personal achievement and distinction, and independence.   555, 699

inductive reasoning Reasoning from the specific to the general; drawing conclusions about all members of a category based on observing only some of the members.   254

industrial/organizational (I/O) psychology The branch of psychology that focuses on the workplace—both the workers and the organizations that employ them.   19, 682

industrial psychology The subdivision of I/O psychology that focuses on personnel and human resource management. This branch consists of the various personnel activities that organizations engage in, such as recruitment, selection, performance appraisal, training, and career development.   19

industry versus inferiority Erikson's fourth developmental stage, occurring approximately in the preschool years.   318

inferences Our interpretations of observed behavior.   5

inferential statistics Complex mathematical methods used to draw conclusions about data that have been collected.   726

inferiority complex The name Adler gave to exaggerated feelings of inadequacy.   543

infinite generativity A person's ability to produce an endless number of meaningful sentences using a finite set of words and rules, which makes language a highly creative enterprise.   260

informal groups Clusters of workers formed by the group's members.   682

information theory The contemporary explanation of how classical conditioning works; the key to understanding classical conditioning is the information the organism obtains from the situation.   180

initiative versus guilt Erikson's third stage of development, occurring during the preschool years.   316

inner ear The oval window, cochlea, and organ of Corti.   108

insanity A legal term, not a psychological one. A legally insane person is considered mentally disordered and incapable of being responsible for his or her actions.   603

insanity defense A plea of "innocent by reason of insanity," used as a legal defense in criminal trials.   603

insight learning A form of problem solving in which an organism develops a sudden understanding of how to solve a problem.   200

insight therapy Therapy that encourages insight into and awareness of oneself as the critical focus of therapy.   617

insomnia A common sleep problem; the inability to sleep.   145

instinct An innate, biological determinant of behavior.   451

instinctive drift The tendency of animals to revert to instinctive behavior that interferes with learning.   201

integration The maintenance of cultural integrity while moving to become an integral part of the larger culture.   511, 700

integrity versus despair Erikson's eighth and final stage of human development, which occurs mainly in late adulthood; it is a time of looking back at what we have done with our lives.   336

intelligence Verbal ability, problem-solving skills, and the ability to learn from and adapt to the experiences of everyday life.   269

intelligence quotient (IQ) Devised in 1912 by William Stern; a person's mental age divided by chronological age, multiplied by 100.   274

interference theory The theory that we forget not because memories are actually lost from storage, but because other information gets in the way of retrieval of what we want to remember.   231

internalization The developmental change from behavior that is externally controlled to behavior that is controlled by internal, self-generated standards and principles.   345

interneurons Central nervous system neurons that mediate sensory input and motor output. Interneurons make up most of the brain.   67

interview A descriptive method in which questions are asked directly to an individual to find out about the person's experiences and attitudes.   39

intimacy versus isolation Erikson's sixth stage of development, occurring mainly in early adulthood. Intimacy is the ability to develop close, loving relationships.   356

intrinsic motivation The internal desire to be competent and to do something for its own sake.   461

introspection A technique whereby specially trained people carefully observe and analyze their own mental experiences.   9

ions Electrically charged particles that include sodium (NA^+) chloride (Cl^-), and potassium (K^+). The neuron creates electrical signals by moving these charged ions back and forth through its membrane; the waves of electricity that are created sweep along the membrane.   68

iris The colored part of the eye, which can range from light blue to dark brown.   99

J

James-Lange theory The theory that emotion results from physiological states triggered by stimuli in the environment.   471

justice perspective A theory of moral development that focuses on the rights of the individual; individuals independently make moral decisions. Kohlberg's theory is a justice perspective.   346

K

kinesthetic senses Senses that provide information about movement, posture, and orientation.   112

L

laboratories Controlled settings with many of the complex factors of the "real world" removed.   33

language A system of symbols used to communicate with others; in humans, characterized by organizational rules and infinite generativity.   260

late adulthood A developmental period that begins around 60 to 70 years of age and ends when the individual dies. It is a time of adjustment to decreased strength and health, retirement, reduced income, new social roles, and learning how to age successfully.   361

latency stage The fourth Freudian stage of development, occurring approximately between 6 years of age and puberty; the child represses all interest in sexuality and develops social and intellectual skills.   540

latent content The psychoanalytic term for the unconscious, unremembered, symbolic aspects of a dream.   620

law of effect The hypothesis, developed by Robert Thorndike, that behaviors followed by positive outcomes are strengthened, whereas behaviors followed by negative outcomes are weakened.   182

learned helplessness A response that occurs when animals and humans are exposed to aversive stimulation, such as prolonged stress or pain, over which they have no control. The inability to avoid such aversive stimulation produces an apathetic state of helplessness.   594

learning A relatively permanent change in behavior that occurs through experience.   173

learning difference Problematic development in specific academic skills that does not reflect overall intellectual ability.   276

learning set A strategy that an individual tends to use to solve problems.   252

lens of the eye The transparent and somewhat flexible ball-like entity filled with a gelatinous material; its function is to bend the light falling on the surface of the eye just enough to focus it at the back of the eye.   99

levels of processing theory Craik and Lockhart's theory that memory processing occurs on a continuum from shallow to deep; in this theory, deeper processing produces better memory.   222

life-process model of addiction The view that addiction is not a disease but rather a habitual response and source of gratification or security that can be understood only in the context of social relationships and experiences.   153

light A form of electromagnetic energy that can be described in terms of wavelengths.   98

limbic system A loosely connected network of structures under the cerebral cortex that plays an important role in both memory and emotion.   77

linguistic relativity hypothesis The view that culture shapes language, which further determines the structure of thinking and shapes our basic ideas.   265

lithium A drug that is widely used to treat bipolar disorder.   643

long-term memory A type of memory that holds huge amounts of information for a long period of time, relatively permanently.   218

loudness The perception of the sound wave's amplitude.   106

lucid dreams A class of dreams in which a person "wakes up" mentally but remains in the sensory landscape of the dream world.   147

M

magnetic resonance imaging (MRI) An imaging technique that involves creating a magnetic field around a person's body and using radio waves to construct images of the person's tissues (such as brain tissues) and biochemical activity.   85

maintenance rehearsal The conscious repetition of information that increases the length of time the information stays in working memory.   216

major depression A mood disorder in which the individual is deeply unhappy, demoralized, self-derogatory, and bored. An individual with major depression shows changes in appetite and sleep patterns, decreased energy, feelings of worthlessness, concentration problems, and guilt feelings that might prompt thoughts of suicide.   590

managed health care A system in which external reviewers approve the type and length of treatment to justify insurance reimbursement.   619

manifest content The psychoanalytic term for the conscious, remembered aspects of a dream.   620

marginalization The process in which groups are put out of cultural and psychological contact with both their traditional culture and the larger, dominant culture.   511, 702

masochism A psychosexual disorder in which individuals derive sexual gratification from being subjected to physical pain, inflicted by others or themselves.   431

mastery orientation The orientation of individuals who are task oriented. Instead of focusing on their ability, they are concerned about learning strategies.   462

matching hypothesis The hypothesis that although we might prefer a more attractive person in the abstract, in the real world we end up choosing someone who is close to our own level of attractiveness.   664

maturation The orderly sequence of changes dictated by the genetic code.   297

mean The numerical average for a group of scores or values.   728

measure of central tendency A single number that tells you the overall characteristics of a set of data.   728

measures of variability Measures of how much the scores in a sample vary from one another.   729

median The score that falls exactly in the middle of a distribution of scores after they have been arranged (ranked) from highest to lowest.   728

medical model Also called the disease model; the forerunner of the biological approach. This model states that abnormal behavior is a disease or illness precipitated by internal physical causes.   576

meditation A system of thought and form of practice that incorporates exercises to attain bodily or mental control and well-being, as well as enlightenment.   520

medulla A part of the brain that begins where the spinal cord enters the skull; helps to control breathing and regulates a portion of the reflexes that allow us to maintain an upright posture.   73

memory The retention of information over time. Psychologists study how information is initially placed, or encoded, into memory; how it is retained, or stored, after being encoded; and how it is found, or retrieved, for a certain purpose later.   214

memory processes The encoding of new information into memory, the representation of information, and the retrieval of what was previously stored.   221

memory span The number of digits an individual can report back in order following a single presentation of them.   216

menopause The time in middle age, usually in the late forties or early fifties, when a woman's menstrual periods cease completely.   351

mental age (MA) An individual's level of mental development relative to others.   274

mental processes Thoughts, feelings, motives, and so on, that each of us experiences privately but that cannot be observed directly.   5

mental retardation A condition of limited mental ability in which an individual has a low IQ, usually below 70 on a traditional intelligence test, and has difficulty adapting to everyday life.   276

mesomorph Sheldon's term for a strong, athletic, and muscular person who is energetic, assertive, and courageous.   553

meta-analysis A research strategy that involves statistically combining the results of many different studies.   636

metaneeds In Maslow's theory, the higher, self-actualized needs; they include truth, goodness, beauty, wholeness, vitality, uniqueness, perfection, justice, inner wealth, and playfulness; also called growth needs.   550

midbrain An area between the hindbrain and forebrain where many nerve fiber systems ascend and descend to connect lower and higher portions of the brain; in particular, the midbrain relays information between the brain and the eyes and ears.   73

middle adulthood A developmental period that begins at about 35 to 45 years of age and ends at about 55 to 65 years of age. It is a time of expanding personal and social involvement, increased responsibility, adjustment to physical decline, and career satisfaction.   351

middle ear An area of the ear consisting of these four main parts: eardrum, hammer, anvil, and stirrup.   108

Minnesota Multiphasic Personality Inventory (MMPI) The self-report personality test most widely used in clinical and research settings.   561

misogyny Hatred of women.   389

mnemonics Techniques for making memory more efficient.   237

mode The score that occurs most often.   728

monocular cues Depth cues based on each eye working independently.   118

mood disorders Psychological disorders characterized by wide emotional swings, ranging from deeply depressed to highly euphoric and agitated. Depression can occur alone, as in major depression, or it can alternate with mania, as in bipolar disorder.   590

morphology The rules for combining morphemes, which are the smallest meaningful string of sounds that contain no smaller meaningful parts.   260

motherese Talking to babies in a higher-pitched voice than normal and with simple words and sentences.   263

motivation Why people behave, think, and feel the way they do. Motivated behavior is energized and directed.   451

multiaxial system A feature of the DSM-IV in which individuals are classified on the basis of five dimensions, or "axes," that include the individual's history and highest level of functioning in the last year. This system ensures that the individual will not merely be assigned to a mental disorder category, but instead will be characterized by a number of clinical factors.   581

multiculturalism A pluralistic approach to understanding two or more cultures; a model in which people maintain their distinct identities while working with others from different cultures to meet national or economic needs they have in common.   700

multiple-factor theory L. L. Thurstone's theory that intelligence consists of seven primary mental abilities: verbal comprehension, number ability, word fluency, spatial visualization, associative memory, reasoning, and perceptual speed.   270

multiple personality The most dramatic but least common dissociative disorder; individuals with this disorder have two or more distinct personalities.   588

myelin sheath A layer of fat cells that encases most axons; it not only acts to insulate the axon but also helps nerve impulses travel faster.   68

N

narcolepsy The overpowering urge to fall asleep.   146

natural selection The evolutionary process that favors the individuals within a species that are best adapted to survive and reproduce in their particular environment.   63

naturalistic observation Observation of behavior in real-world settings with no attempt to manipulate or control the situation.   34

nature A term often used to describe an organism's biological inheritance.   59

need A deprivation that energizes the drive to eliminate or reduce the deprivation.   451

need for affiliation The social motive to be with other people, which involves establishing, maintaining, and restoring warm, close, personal relationships.   466

need for power The motivation to be in control, to have prestige and status, and to get others to conform to our wishes.   466

negative affectivity (NA) Emotions that are negatively toned, such as anxiety, anger, guilt, and sadness.   469

negative correlation A relationship in which the two factors vary in opposite directions.   732

negative reinforcement The relationship in which the frequency of a response increases because the response either removes a negative circumstance/stimulus or lets the individual avoid the negative stimulus altogether.   183

neo-Piagetians Developmentalists who have elaborated on Piaget's theory, believing that children's cognitive development is more specific in many respects than he thought.   314

neurobiological perspective The view that the brain and nervous system play central roles in understanding behavior, thought, and emotion.   14

neurons Nerve cells, the basic units of the nervous system.   66

neurotic disorders Relatively mild mental disorders in which the individual has not lost contact with reality.   581

neurotransmitters Chemical substances that carry information across the synaptic gap to the next neuron.   69

nightmare A frightening dream that awakens the sleeper from REM sleep.   146

night terror A state characterized by sudden arousal from sleep and intense fear, usually accompanied by a number of physiological reactions.   136

noise The term given to irrelevant and competing stimuli.   96

nomothetic research Research that takes place at the level of the group.   45

nonsexist therapy Therapy that occurs when the therapist has become aware of and primarily overcomes his or her sexist attitudes and behavior.   639

nonstate view The view that hypnotic behavior is similar to other forms of social behavior and can be explained without appealing to special processes. Hypnotic behavior is purposeful, goal-directed action that is best understood by the way subjects interpret their situation and how they try to present themselves.   151

nonverbal leakage Involves the communication of true emotions through nonverbal channels even when the person tries to verbally conceal the truth.   475

norepinephrine A neurotransmitter that usually inhibits the firing of neurons in the brain and spinal cord but excites the heart muscles, intestines, and urogenital tract.   71

normal distribution A symmetrical distribution in which a majority of cases fall in the middle of the possible range of scores and few scores fall in the extremes of the range. Also called a bell-shaped curve.   274, 727

norms (social) Rules that apply to the members of a group.   677

norms (tests) Established standards of performance for a test. Norms are established by giving the test to a large group of people who represent the target population. This allows the researcher to determine the distribution of test scores. Norms tell us which scores are considered high, low, or average.   273

nurture A term often used to describe an organism's environmental experiences.   59

O

obedience Behavior that complies with the explicit demands of an individual in authority.   674

object permanence Piaget's term for one of the infant's most important accomplishments: understanding that objects and events continue to exist even when they cannot directly be seen, heard, or touched.   308

observational learning Learning that occurs when a person observes and imitates someone else's behavior; also called imitation or modeling.   195

obsessive-compulsive disorder (OCD) An anxiety disorder in which the individual has anxiety-provoking thoughts that will not go away (obsession) and/or urges to perform repetitive, ritualistic behaviors to prevent or produce a future situation (compulsion).   586

obsessive-compulsive personality disorder A personality disorder in the anxious, fearful cluster; anxious adjustment is the primary feature.   601

occipital lobe The portion of the cerebral cortex at the back of the head that is involved in vision.   78

Oedipus complex In theory, the young child's developing an intense desire to replace the parent of the same sex and to enjoy the affections of the opposite-sex parent.   539

olfactory epithelium Tissue located at the top of the nasal cavity that contains a sheet of receptor cells for smell.   114

operant conditioning (instrumental conditioning) A form of learning in which the consequences of behavior produce changes in the probability of the behavior's occurrence.   182

operational definition A definition of behavior in terms of observable features.   38

operations In Piaget's theory, mental representations that are reversible.   309

opiates Opium and its derivatives, which depress the central nervous system's activity.   157

opponent-process theory The theory that cells in the visual system respond to red-green and blue-yellow colors; a given cell might be excited by red and inhibited by green, while another cell might be excited by yellow and inhibited by blue.   105

oral stage The term Freud used to describe development during the first 18 months of life, when the infant's pleasure centers on the mouth.   538

organic retardation Mental retardation caused by a genetic disorder or by brain damage. *Organic* refers to the tissues or organs of the body, so there is some physical damage in organic retardation.   276

organizational psychology The subdivision of I/O psychology that examines the social and group influences within an organization, in contrast with the emphasis of industrial psychologists on individual differences.   682

organ of Corti The part of the ear that runs the length of the cochlea and sits on the basilar membrane. It contains the ear's sensory receptors, which change the energy of sound waves into nerve impulses that can be processed by the brain.   108

outer ear The pinna and the external auditory canal.   107

overcompensation Adler's term for the individual's attempt to deny rather than acknowledge a real situation, or the individual's exaggerated efforts to conceal a weakness.   543

overload The occurrence of stimuli so intense that the person cannot cope with them.   508

P

pain threshold The stimulation level at which pain is first perceived.   109

panic disorder A recurrent anxiety disorder that is marked by the sudden onset of apprehension or terror.   584

papillae Bumps on the surface of the tongue that contain taste buds, which are the receptors for taste.   114

paranoid schizophrenia A schizophrenic disorder characterized by delusions of reference, grandeur, and persecution.   598

paraphilias Psychosexual disorders in which the source of an individual's sexual satisfaction is an unusual object, ritual, or situation.   431

parasympathetic nervous system The division of the autonomic nervous system that calms the body.   67

parietal lobe The portion of the cerebral cortex at the top of the head and toward the rear; it is involved in processing body sensations.   78

partial reinforcement Intermittent reinforcement; responses are not reinforced every time they occur.   188

pedophilia A psychosexual disorder in which the sex object is a child and the intimacy usually involves manipulation of a child's genitals.   432

perception The brain's process of organizing and interpreting sensory information to give it meaning.   95

perceptual set Expectations that influence how perceptual elements will be interpreted. 117

performance orientation Involves being concerned with the outcome in achievement, whereas a mastery orientation focuses on the process of achievement. In the performance orientation, winning is what matters and happiness is thought to result from winning. 462

peripheral nervous system A network of nerves that connects the brain and spinal cord to other parts of the body. Takes information to and from the brain and spinal cord and carries out the commands of the CNS to execute various muscular and glandular activities. 66

permissive-indifferent parenting A style of parenting in which the parent is very involved in the child's life; it is associated with children's social incompetence, especially with a lack of self-control. 321

permissive-indulgent parenting A style of parenting in which parents are highly involved with their children but place few demands or controls on them. Permissive-indulgent parenting is associated with children's social incompetence, especially with lack of self-control. 321

personal construct theory Kelly's theory that emphasizes the importance of how people perceive, organize, interpret, and construe events and the world in which they live for understanding their personality. 546

personal growth groups Groups that have their roots in the humanistic therapies; they emphasize personal growth and increased openness and honesty in interpersonal relations. 631

personal projects Sequences of personally relevant actions, similar to current concerns, but focusing on behavioral enactment more than on thought. 453

personality Enduring, distinctive thoughts, emotions, and behaviors that characterize the way an individual adapts to the world. 534

personality disorders Psychological disorders that develop when personality traits become inflexible and, thus, maladaptive. 601

personality psychology An area that focuses on relatively enduring traits and characteristics of individuals. 18

person-centered therapy A form of humanistic therapy developed by Carl Rogers, in which the therapist provides a warm, supportive atmosphere to improve the client's self-concept and encourage the client to gain insight about problems. 622

phallic stage Freud's third stage of development, which occurs between the ages of 3 and 6; its name comes from the Latin word *phallus*, which means "penis." During the phallic stage, pleasure focuses on the genitals as the child discovers that self-stimulation is enjoyable. 539

phenomenological worldview A worldview that stresses the importance of our perceptions of ourselves and our world in understanding personality. This view emphasizes that, for each individual, reality is what that person perceives. 547

phobias Irrational fears. 177

phobic disorder An anxiety disorder that occurs when an individual has an irrational, overwhelming, persistent fear of a particular object or situation; commonly called a phobia. 584

phonology The study of language's sound system. 260

pitch The perceptual interpretation of sound's frequency. 106

pituitary gland An important endocrine gland that sits at the base of the skull and is about the size of a pea; this gland controls growth and regulates other glands. 76

place theory The theory of hearing that states that each frequency produces vibrations at a particular spot on the basilar membrane. 108

pleasure principle The Freudian concept that the id always seeks pleasure and avoids pain. 536

pluralism The coexistence of distinct ethnic and cultural groups in the same society. 712

polygraph A machine that is used to try to determine if someone is lying by monitoring changes in the body—heart rate, breathing, and electrodermal response (an index that detects skin resistance to passage of a weak electric current)—thought to be influenced by emotional states. 474

pons A bridge in the hindbrain that contains several clusters of fibers involved in sleep and arousal. 73

positive affectivity (PA) The range of positive emotion, from high energy, enthusiasm, and excitement to being calm, quiet, and withdrawn. Joy and happiness involve positive affectivity. 469

positive correlation A relationship in which the two factors vary in the same direction. 732

positive reinforcement The relationship in which the frequency of a response increases because it is followed by a pleasant stimulus. 183

positron-emission tomography (PET scan) An imaging technology that measures the amount of specially treated glucose in various areas of the brain, then sends this information to a computer. 85

postconventional level Kohlberg's highest level of moral thinking; moral development is completely internalized and not based on others' standards. An individual recognizes alternative moral courses, explores the options, and then develops a personal moral code. The code is among the principles generally accepted by the community (stage 5) or it is more individualized (stage 6). 346

posthypnotic amnesia The subject's inability to remember what took place during hypnosis, induced by the hypnotist's suggestion. 151

posthypnotic suggestion A suggestion, made by the hypnotist while the subject is in a hypnotic state, that the subject carries out after emerging from the hypnotic state. 151

post-traumatic stress disorder A mental disorder that develops through exposure to any of several traumatic events, such as war, the Holocaust, severe abuse as in rape, natural disasters such as floods and tornados, and accidental disasters such as plane crashes. The disorder is characterized by anxiety symptoms that may be apparent 1 month after the trauma, or be delayed by months or even years until onset. 587

precognition "Knowing" events before they occur. 125

preconventional level Kohlberg's lowest level of moral thinking, in which an individual shows no internalization of moral values—moral thinking is based on expectations of punishments (stage 1) or rewards (stage 2) that come from the external world. 345

prejudice An unjustified attitude toward an individual based on the individual's membership in a group. 707

preoperational thought Piaget's term for the 2- to 7-year-old's understanding of the world. Children at this stage of reasoning cannot understand such logical operations as the reversibility of mental representations. 310

preparedness The species-specific biological predisposition to learn in certain ways but not in others. 201

preterm infant An infant born prior to 38 weeks after conception; also called a premature infant. 304

primacy effect Superior recall for items at the beginning of a list. The enduring quality of initial impressions. 229, 657

primary prevention A community psychology concept, borrowed from the public health field, denoting efforts to reduce the number of new cases of mental disorders. 633

primary reinforcement The use of reinforcers that are innately satisfying; that is, no learning is required on the organism's part to make them pleasurable. 188

priming Facilitation in responding to a stimulus that immediately follows a related stimulus. 220

proactive interference Interference that occurs when material that was learned earlier disrupts the recall of material learned later. 231

problem-focused coping Lazarus's term for the cognitive strategy of squarely facing one's own troubles and trying to solve them. 514

problem solving An attempt to find an appropriate way of attaining a goal when the goal is not readily available. 251

procedural memory Knowledge in the form of skills and cognitive operations about how to do something. Procedural memory cannot be consciously recollected, at least not in the form of specific events or facts; this makes procedural memory difficult, if not impossible, to communicate verbally. Procedural memory has been called "knowing how" and, more recently, "implicit memory." 219

projection The psychoanalytic defense mechanism that occurs when we attribute our own shortcomings, problems, and faults to others. 538

projective tests Tests that present individuals with an ambiguous stimulus and then ask them to describe it or tell a story about it. Projective tests are based on the assumption that the ambiguity of the stimulus allows individuals to project into it their feelings, desires, needs, and attitudes. 558

psychiatry A branch of medicine practiced by physicians with a doctor of medicine (M.D.) degree who specialize in abnormal behavior and psychotherapy. 18

psychoactive drugs Substances that act on the nervous system to alter our states of consciousness, modify our perceptions, and change our moods. 152

psychoanalysis Freud's therapeutic technique for analyzing an individual's unconscious thought. 620

psychoanalytic perspective An emphasis on the unconscious aspects of the mind, conflict between biological instincts and society's demands, and early family experiences. 14

psychodynamic therapies Therapies that stress the importance of the unconscious mind, extensive therapist interpretation, and the role of infant and early childhood experiences. 620

psychogenic amnesia A dissociative disorder involving memory loss caused by extensive psychological stress. 588

psychokinesis Closely associated with ESP, the mind over matter phenomenon of being able to move objects without touching them, such as mentally getting a chair to rise off the floor or shattering a glass merely by staring at it. 125

psychological dependence The need to take a drug to cope with problems and stress. 152

psychology The scientific study of behavior and mental processes in contexts. 5

psychology of women An area that emphasizes the importance of promoting the research and study of women, integrating this information about women with current psychological knowledge and beliefs, and applying the information to society and its institutions. 18

psychoneuroimmunology The field that explores the connections between psychological factors (such as attitudes and emotions), the nervous system, and the immune system. 489

psychosexual disorders Sexual problems caused mainly by psychological factors. 430

psychosexual dysfunctions Disorders that involve impairments in the sexual response cycle, either in the desire for gratification or in the ability to achieve it. 430

psychosurgery A biomedical therapy that involves the removal of brain tissue to improve the person's psychological adjustment. 645

psychotherapy The process of working with individuals to reduce their emotional problems and improve their adjustment. 617

psychotic disorders Severe mental disorders in which the individual has lost contact with reality. 581

puberty A period of rapid skeletal and sexual maturation that occurs in early adolescence. 337

punishment A consequence that decreases the probability that a behavior will occur. 183

pupil The opening, which appears black, in the center of the iris. 99

Q

questionnaire A method similar to a highly structured interview, except respondents read the questions and mark the answers on a sheet of paper rather than respond directly to the interviewer. 39

Q-sort A way of measuring personality in which individuals sort a set of adjectives or statements according to the degree to which they believe them to describe themselves. 561

R

racism A belief that the members of another race or ethnic group are inferior. 708

radical behaviorists Psychologists who emphasize only observable behavior and reject its cognitive dimensions. 545

random assignment Assignment of subjects to experimental and control conditions by chance. This practice reduces the probability that the results of the experiment will be due to preexisting differences in the two groups. 37

random sample A sample in which every member of a population or group has an equal chance of being selected. 31

range The distance between the highest and lowest score. 729

rape Forcible sex with a person who does not give consent. 433

rational-emotive therapy Therapy based on Albert Ellis's assertion that people become psychologically disordered because of their beliefs, especially those that are irrational and self-defeating. 627

rationalization The psychoanalytic defense mechanism that occurs when the ego does not accept the real motive for an individual's behavior and replaces it with a sort of cover motive. 537

reaction formation The psychoanalytic defense mechanism that occurs when we express an unacceptable impulse by transforming it into its opposite. 538

reality principle The Freudian concept that the ego tries to make the pursuit of individual pleasure conform to the norms of society. 537

reasoning The mental activity of transforming information to reach conclusions. 254

recall A memory measure in which the individual must retrieve previously learned information, as on an essay test. 230

recency effect Superior recall for items at the end of a list. 229

recognition A memory measure in which the individual only has to identify (recognize) learned items, as on a multiple-choice test. 230

reflexes Automatic stimulus-response connections that are "hardwired" into the brain. 174

regression The psychoanalytic defense mechanism that occurs when we behave in a way that is characteristic of a previous developmental level. 538

reinforcement (reward) A consequence that increases the probability that a behavior will occur. 183

reliability How consistently a person performs on a test. 272

REM sleep A periodic stage of sleep during which dreaming occurs. 143

repair theory The theory that sleep restores, replenishes, and rebuilds our brains and bodies, which are somehow worn out by the day's waking activities. 144

repression The most powerful and pervasive defense mechanism, according to Freud; it works to push unacceptable id impulses and traumatic memories out of awareness and back into the unconscious mind. 537

resistance The psychoanalytic term for a client's unconscious defense strategies that prevent the analyst from understanding the client's problems. 621

resting potential The stable, negative charge of an inactive neuron. 68

reticular formation A diffuse collection of neurons involved in stereotyped patterns of behavior such as walking, sleeping, or turning to attend to a sudden noise. 73

retina The light-sensitive surface in the back of the eye that houses light receptors called rods and cones. 100

retinal or binocular disparity Perception in which the individual sees a single scene, even though the images on the eyes are slightly different. 119

retroactive interference Interference that occurs when material learned later disrupts the recall of material learned earlier. 231

retrograde amnesia A memory disorder that involves memory loss for a segment of the past but not for new events. 232

retronasal olfaction The portion of the olfaction system involved in processing food-related smells. 114

rites of passage A ceremoney or ritual that marks an individual's transition from one status to another. 342

rods The receptors in the retina that are exquisitely sensitive to light, but are not very useful for color vision. 100

roles Rules and expectations that govern certain positions in a group. Roles define how people should behave in a particular position in the group. 677

romantic love Also called passionate love or Eros; a type of love with strong components of sexuality and infatuation; it often predominates in the early part of a love relationship. 664

romantic script The behavioral script according to which sex is synonymous with love; in this script, it is acceptable to have sex with someone, whether we are married or not, if we are in love with that person. 425

Rorschach inkblot test The most well-known projective test, developed in 1921 by Swiss psychiatrist Hermann Rorschach. It uses individuals' perceptions of inkblots to determine their personality. 559

S

sadism A psychosexual disorder in which an individual derives sexual gratification from inflicting pain on others. 431

saturation A characteristic of color based on its purity. 102

scatter plot A graph on which pairs of scores are represented. 731

schedules of reinforcement Timetables that determine when a response will be reinforced. 188

schema Information—concepts, events, and knowledge—that already exists in a person's mind. A cognitive structure, or network of associations, that organizes and guides an individual's perception. 226, 401

schizophrenic disorders Severe psychological disorders characterized by distorted thoughts and perceptions, odd communication, inappropriate emotion, abnormal motor behavior, and social withdrawal. The term *schizophrenia* comes from the Latin words *schizo,* meaning "split," and *phrenia,* meaning "mind." The individual's mind is split from reality, and his or her personality loses its unity. 595

schizotypal personality disorder A personality disorder in the odd, eccentric cluster. Individuals with this disorder appear to be in contact with reality, but many aspects of their behavior are distasteful, which leads to rejection or withdrawal from others. 601

school and educational psychology An area concerned with children's learning and adjustment in school. 19

science of psychology The use of systematic methods to observe, describe, explain, and predict behavior. 6

scientific method An approach used to discover accurate information or establish meaningful relations about mind and behavior. It includes the following steps: analyze a problem, formulate a tentative explanation, collect data, draw conclusions, and confirm or revise theory. 28

sclera The white outer part of the eye, which helps to maintain the shape of the eye and to protect it from injury. 99

script A schema for an event. 228

seasonal affective disorder (SAD) Depression that appears to be caused by seasonally shorter exposure to sunlight. 644

secondary prevention A prevention method involving screening for early detection problems and early intervention; a community psychology concept. 634

secondary reinforcement Reinforcement that acquires its positive value through experience; secondary reinforcers are learned, or conditional, reinforcers. 188

secure attachment Attachment in which the infant uses the caregiver, usually the mother, as a secure base from which to explore the environment. Ainsworth believes that secure attachment in the first year of life provides an important foundation for psychological development later in life. 319

selection bias A lack of representativeness in a sample. 31

selective attention The focusing of attention on a narrow band of information. 221

self-actualization The highest and most elusive of Maslow's needs; the motivation to develop one's full potential as a human being. 453

self-concept An individual's overall perceptions of her or his abilities, behavior, and personality; a central theme for Rogers and other humanists. 548

self-efficacy The belief that one can master a situation and produce positive outcomes; this is an effective coping strategy. 462, 626

self-esteem Involves the evaluative and affective dimensions of self-concept; self-esteem is also referred to as self-worth or self-image. 463

self-help groups Voluntary organizations of individuals who get together on a regular basis to discuss topics of common interest. The group leader and members give support to help individuals with their problems. Self-help groups are so-called because they are conducted without a professional therapist. 632

self-instructional methods Cognitive behavioral techniques aimed at teaching individuals to modify their own behavior. 626

self-perception theory Bem's theory of connections between attitudes and behavior; it stresses that individuals make inferences about their attitudes by perceiving their behavior. 661

self-report tests Tests that assess personality traits by asking individuals what their traits are; not designed to reveal unconscious personality characteristics. 560

self-talk (self-statements) The soundless mental speech people use when they think about something, plan, or solve problems; often helpful in cognitive restructuring. 516

semantic memory A person's general knowledge about the world. It includes knowledge about a person's fields of expertise, general academic knowledge of the sort learned in school, and "everyday" knowledge about meanings of words, famous individuals, important places, and common things. Semantic memory knowledge appears to be independent of the individual's personal identity with the past. 220

semantics The meanings of words and sentences. 260

semicircular canals Canals located in the inner ear that contain the sensory receptors that detect bodily motion such as tilting of the head or body. 113

sensation The process of detecting and encoding stimulus energy in the world. 95

sensorimotor thought In Piaget's theory, the stage of development that lasts from birth to about 2 years of age, corresponding to the period of infancy. An infant constructs an understanding of the world by coordinating sensory experiences (such as seeing and hearing) with physical (motor) actions. 308

sensory adaptation Weakened sensitivity due to prolonged stimulation. 98

sensory memory Memory that holds information from the world in its original sensory form for only an instant, not much longer than the brief time for which one is exposed to the visual, auditory, and other sensations. 215

separation Self-imposed withdrawal from the larger culture. 511, 702

serial position effect The effect of an item's position in a list on our recall of it; in particular, recall is superior for items at the beginning and at the end of a list. 229

serotonin An inhibitory neurotransmitter that is involved in the regulation of sleep as well as depression. 71

set point The weight maintained when no effort is made to gain or lose weight. 458, 495

sex The biological dimension of being female or male. 15

sexual script A stereotyped pattern of role prescriptions for how individuals should behave sexually. 425

sexually transmitted diseases (STDs) Diseases that are contracted primarily through sex—intercourse as well as oral-genital and anal-genital sex. 434

shape constancy Recognition that an object remains the same shape even though its orientation to us changes. 120

shaping The process of rewarding approximations of desired behavior. 186

situational theory of leadership The theory that the needs of a group change from time to time and that a person who emerges as leader in one circumstance will not necessarily be the person who becomes a leader in another circumstance. 678

situationism Mischel's view that a person's personality often varies from one context to another. 555

size constancy Recognition that an object remains the same size even though the retinal image of the object changes. 120

sleep apnea A sleep disorder in which individuals stop breathing because their windpipe fails to open or brain processes involved in respiration fail to work properly. 146

sleep spindles Brief bursts of higher-frequency brain waves during sleep. 142

social comparison The process in which individuals evaluate their thoughts, feelings, behaviors, and abilities in relation to other people. 657

social desirability A factor that can lead individuals to tell interviewers or other examiners what they think is socially desirable rather than what they really think or feel, in order to make themselves look better. 39, 560

social distance An etic construct; the cultural belief that people should maintain a certain distance from each other. 698

social exchange theory The theory that individuals should benefit those who benefit them, or that for a benefit received, an equivalent benefit should be returned at some point. 669

social identity theory The theory that when individuals are assigned to a group, they invariably think of their own group as an in-group for them. This occurs because individuals want to have a positive self-image. Social identity theory helps to explain prejudice and conflict between groups. 705

social learning theory of gender The theory that children's gender development occurs through observation and imitation of gender-related behavior, as well as through the rewards and punishments children experience for gender-appropriate and gender-inappropriate behaviors. 399

social motives The needs and desires of people that are learned through experience with the social world. Such motives are not derived from basic biological factors, the way hunger, thirst, sleep, and to some degree sexuality are. People who are high in a particular social motive will keep trying to reach goal states related to that motive.   465

social perception Judgment about the qualities of individuals, which involves how we form impressions of others, how we gain self-knowledge from perception of others, and how we present ourselves to others to influence their perceptions of us.   657

social policy A national government's course of action designed to influence the welfare of its citizens.   298

social psychology An area that deals with people's social interactions, relationships, perceptions, and attitudes.   18

social support Information and feedback from others that one is loved and cared for, esteemed and valued, and included in a network of communication and mutual obligation.   518

sociobiology A contemporary view that relies on evolutionary biology to explain social behavior.   63

sociocultural perspective An emphasis on the influence of culture, ethnicity, and gender, among other sociocultural factors, as essential to understanding behavior, thought, and emotion.   15

socioemotional processes Processes that involve changes in an individual's relationships with people, changes in emotion, and changes in personality.   297

somatic nervous system A division of the peripheral nervous system consisting of sensory nerves that convey information from the skin and muscle to the CNA about such matters as pain and temperature, and motor nerves that inform muscles when to act.   66

somatoform disorders Mental disorders in which the psychological symptoms take a physical, or somatic, form, even though no physical causes can be found.   587

somatotype theory Sheldon's theory that precise charts reveal distinct body types, which in turn are associated with certain personality characteristics.   553

somnambulism Sleepwalking; it occurs during the deepest stages of sleep.   145

S-O-R model A model of learning that gives some importance to cognitive factors. S stands for stimulus, O for organism, and R for response.   199

sounds Vibrations of air that are processed by the auditory (hearing) system; also called sound waves.   106

special process theory The view that hypnotic behavior is different from nonhypnotic behavior. Hypnotic responses are elicited by suggestion rather than being voluntary reactions.   151

spontaneous recovery The process in classical conditioning by which a conditioned response can reappear without further conditioning.   176

standard deviation A measure of how much the scores vary, on the average, around the mean of a sample.   729

standardization The development of uniform procedures for administering and scoring a test; also the development of norms for the test.   273

standardized tests Tests, consisting of a series of written or oral questions, that have two distinct features. First, psychologists usually total an individual's score to yield a single score, or set of scores, that reflects something about the individual. Second, psychologists compare the individual's score to the scores of a large group of similar people to determine how the individual responded relative to others.   40

statistical significance The idea that the differences observed between two groups are sufficiently large that it is highly unlikely that they are due merely to chance.   736

statistics Mathematical methods used to describe, summarize, and draw conclusions about data.   726

stereotype A generalization about a group's characteristics that does not take into account any variation from one member of the group to the next.   706

stimulants Psychoactive drugs that increase the central nervous system's activity.   157

stimulus substitution Pavlov's theory of how classical conditioning works; the nervous system is structured in such a way that the CS and US bond together and eventually the CS substitutes for the US.   180

storm-and-stress view G. Stanley Hall's view that adolescence is a turbulent time charged with conflict and mood swings.   335

stream of consciousness A continuous flow of changing sensations, images, thoughts, and feelings.   137

stress The response of individuals to the circumstances and events, called stressors, that threaten them and tax their coping abilities.   505

stress management programs Programs that teach individuals how to appraise stressful events, how to develop skills for coping with stress, and how to put these skills to use.   519

striving for superiority The human motivation to adapt to, improve, and master the environment.   542

structuralism The early theory of psychology developed by Wundt that emphasized the importance of conscious thought and classification of the mind's structures.   9

sublimation The psychoanalytic defense mechanism that occurs when the ego replaces an unacceptable impulse with a socially approved course of action.   538

subliminal perception Perception of stimuli below the threshold of awareness.   97

substance-use disorder A disorder characterized by one or more of the following features: (1) a pattern of pathological use that involves frequent intoxication, a need for daily use, and an inability to control use—in the sense of psychological dependence; (2) a significant impairment of social or occupational functioning attributed to drug use; and (3) physical dependence that involves serious withdrawal problems.   602

subtractive mixture The mixing of pigments rather than of beams of light.   103

superego The Freudian structure of personality that is the moral branch of personality. The superego takes into account whether something is right or wrong.   537

superiority complex Adler's concept of exaggerated self-importance that is designed to mask feelings of inferiority.   543

syllogism A deductive reasoning task that consists of a major premise, a minor premise, and a conclusion.   255

sympathetic nervous system The division of the autonomic nervous system that arouses the body.   67

synapses Tiny gaps between neurons. Most synapses are between the axon of one neuron and the dendrites or cell body of another neuron.   69

syntax The ways words are combined to form acceptable phrases and sentences.   260

syphilis A sexually transmitted disease caused by the bacterium *Treponema pallidum,* a member of the spirochete family.   435

systematic desensitization A method of behavior therapy that treats anxiety by associating deep relaxation with successive visualizations of increasingly intense anxiety-producing situations; this technique is based on classical conditioning.   624

T

tardive dyskinesia A major side effect of the neuroleptic drugs; a neurological disorder characterized by grotesque, involuntary movements of the facial muscles and mouth, as well as extensive twitching of the neck, arms, and legs.   643

telegraphic speech The use of short and precise words to communicate; characteristic of young children's two- and three-word utterances.   261

telepathy The transfer of thought from one person to another.   124

temporal lobe The portion of the cerebral cortex that is just above the ears and is involved in hearing.   78

teratogen Any agent that causes a birth defect. (*Teratogen* comes from the Greek word *tera,* meaning "monster.")   303

tertiary prevention A community psychology concept denoting efforts to reduce the long-term consequences of mental health disorders that were not prevented or arrested early in the course of the disorders.   634

testosterone A hormone associated, in boys, with the development of genitals, an increase in height, and a change of voice.   337

test-retest reliability Consistency of results when the same person is given the same test on two different occasions.   272

thalamus An area at the top of the brain stem in the central core of the brain. It serves as an important relay station functioning much like a telephone switchboard between the diverse areas of the cortex and the reticular formation.   74

Thematic Apperception Test (TAT) An ambiguous projective test designed to elicit stories that reveal something about an individual's personality; developed by Henry Murray and Christiana Morgan in the 1930s.   559

theory A coherent set of ideas that helps to explain data and to make predictions. A theory has hypotheses.   29

theta waves Low-frequency and low-amplitude EEG patterns that characterize stage 1 sleep.   142

timbre The tone color or perceptual quality of a sound.   106

tip-of-the-tongue phenomenon (TOT state) A type of effortful retrieval that occurs when people are confident that they know something but just can't quite seem to pull it out of memory.   229

token economy A behavior modification system in which behaviors are reinforced with tokens (such as poker chips) that can be exchanged later for desired rewards (such as candy, money, or going to a movie).   625

tokenism Treating a person as a representative of a group rather than as an individual.   684

tolerance The state in which a greater amount of a drug is needed to produce the same effect.   152

traditional religious script The behavioral script according to which sex is acceptable only within marriage; both premarital and extramarital sex are taboo, especially for women.   425

traits Broad dispositions that lead to characteristic responses.   553

trait theories Theories that propose that people have broad dispositions that are reflected in the basic ways they behave, such as whether they are outgoing and friendly and whether they are dominant and assertive.   554

tranquilizers Depressant drugs, such as Valium and Xanax, that reduce anxiety and induce relaxation.   157

transcendental meditation (TM) The most popular form of meditation in the United States. TM is derived from an ancient Indian technique and involves a mantra, which is a resonant sound or phrase that is repeated mentally or aloud to focus attention.   520

transference The psychoanalytic term for a client's relating to an analyst in ways that reproduce or relive important relationships in the client's life.   620

transsexualism A gender identity disorder in which an individual has an overwhelming desire to become a member of the opposite sex.   432

transvestism A psychosexual disorder in which an individual obtains sexual gratification by dressing up as a member of the opposite sex.   431

trephining A procedure, no longer used, that involved chipping a hole in the skull to allow evil spirits to escape.   614

triangular theory of love Sternberg's view that love comes in three main forms: passion, intimacy, and commitment.   666

triarchic theory Sternberg's theory that intelligence consists of componential intelligence, experiential intelligence, and contextual intelligence.   270

trichromatic theory The theory that color perception is based on the existence of three types of receptors, each of which is maximally sensitive to different, but overlapping, ranges of wavelengths.   104

trichromats People with normal color vision; they have three kinds of cone receptors.   104

trust versus mistrust Erikson's first psychosocial stage, which is experienced in the first year of life. A sense of trust requires a feeling of physical comfort and a minimal amount of fear and apprehension about the future.   316

two-factor theory Spearman's theory that individuals have both general intelligence, which he called *g,* and a number of specific intelligences, which he called *s.*   270

Type A behavior pattern A cluster of characteristics—being excessively competitive, hard-driven, impatient, and hostile—thought to be related to the incidence of heart disease.   507

Type C behavior The cancer-prone personality, which consists of being inhibited, uptight, emotionally inexpressive, and otherwise constrained. This type of person is more likely to develop cancer than more expressive persons are.   507

U

unconditional positive regard Rogers's term for accepting, valuing, and being positive toward another person regardless of the person's behavior.   548

unconditioned response (UR) An unlearned response that is automatically associated with the US.   174

unconditioned stimulus (US) A stimulus that produces a response without prior learning.   174

unconscious thought In Freud's theory, a reservoir of unacceptable wishes, feelings, and thoughts that are beyond conscious awareness.   137

undifferentiated schizophrenia A schizophrenic disorder characterized by disorganized behavior, hallucinations, delusions, and incoherence.   598

V

validity The extent to which a test measures what it is purported to measure.   272

variable-interval schedule Reinforcement of a response after variable amounts of time have elapsed.   189

variable-ratio schedule Reinforcement of responses at an average rate but on an unpredictable basis.   188

ventromedial hypothalamus (VMH) A region of the hypothalamus that plays an important role in controlling hunger.   458

vestibular sense The sense that provides information about balance and movement.   112

visual illusion An illusion that occurs when two objects produce exactly the same retinal image but are perceived as different images.   121

volley theory The theory of hearing that states that high frequencies can be signaled by teams of neurons that fire at different offset times to create an overall firing rate that could signal a very high frequency.   108

voyeurism A psychosexual disorder in which individuals derive sexual gratification by observing the sex organs or sex acts of others.   431

W

wavelength The distance from the peak of one wave to the peak of the next.   98

Weber's law The principle that the difference threshold is a constant percentage of the magnitude of the comparison stimulus rather than a constant amount. Weber's law generally holds true.   97

withdrawal An addict's undesirable intense pain and craving for an addictive drug when the drug is withdrawn.   152

working memory Also sometimes called short-term memory, this is a limited-capacity memory system in which information is retained for as long as 30 seconds, unless the information is rehearsed, in which case it can be retained longer.   216

Y

Yerkes-Dodson law The generalization that performance is best under conditions of moderate, rather than low or high, arousal.   469

Z

zone of proximal development (ZPD) Vygotsky's term for tasks too difficult for children to master alone, but that can be mastered with the guidance and assistance of adults or more-skilled children.   315

zygote A fertilized egg.   302

REFERENCES

Aber, L., Allen, L., Mitchell, C., & Seidman, E. (1992, March). *Neighborhood social isolation and adolescent academic achievement: Gender and race-specific patterns and processes.* Paper presented at the meeting of the Society for Research on Adolescence, Washington, DC.

Abona, C. (1995). Culture, ethnicity, and race. *The Counseling Psychologist, 23,* 74–78.

Aboud, F. (1988). *Children and prejudice.* New York: Basil Blackwell.

Abraham, J. D., & Hansson, R. O. (1995). Successful aging at work: An applied study of selection, optimization, and compensation through impression management. *Journal of Gerontology, 50B,* P94–P103.

Abramson, L. Y., Metalsky, G. I., & Alloy, L. B. (1989). Hopelessness depression: A theory-based subtype of depression. *Psychological Review, 96,* 358–372.

Achmon, J., Granek, M., Golomb, M., & Hart, J. (1989). Behavioral treatment of essential hypertension: A comparison between cognitive therapy and biofeedback of heart rate. *Psychosomatic Medicine, 51,* 152–164.

Adams, H. E., & Cassidy, J. F. (1993). The classification of abnormal behavior: An overview. In P. B. Sutker & H. E. Adams (Eds.), *Comprehensive textbook of psychopathology* (2nd ed.). New York: Plenum Press.

Adler, A. (1927). *The theory and practice of individual psychology.* New York: Harcourt, Brace, & World.

Adler, H. E., & Rieber, R. W. (Eds.). (1995). *Aspects of the history of psychology in America: 1892–1992.* Washington, DC: American Psychological Association.

Adler, T. (1991, January). Seeing double? Controversial twins study is widely reported, debated. *APA Monitor, 22,* 1, 8.

Ainsworth, M. D. S. (1967). *Infancy in Uganda: Infant care and the growth of love.* Baltimore: Johns Hopkins University Press.

Ainsworth, M. D. S. (1979). Infant-mother attachment. *American Psychologist, 34,* 932–937.

Albee, G. W. (1988). Foreword. In P. A. Bronstein & K. Quina (Eds.), *Teaching a psychology of people: Resources for gender and sociocultural awareness.* Washington, DC: American Psychological Association.

Albert, R. D. (1988). The place of culture in modern psychology. In P. A. Bronstein & K. Quina (Eds.), *Teaching a psychology of people: Resources for gender and sociocultural awareness.* Washington, DC: American Psychological Association.

Al-Issa, I. (1982a). Does culture make a difference in psychopathology? In I. Al-Issa (Ed.), *Culture and psychopathology.* Baltimore: University Park Press.

Al-Issa, I. (1982b). Sex differences in psychopathology. In I. Al-Issa (Ed.), *Culture and psychopathology.* Baltimore: University Park Press.

Allen, L., & Majidi-Ahi, S. (1989). Black American children. In J. T. Gibbs & L. N. Huang (Eds.), *Children of color.* San Francisco: Jossey-Bass.

Allen, L., & Mitchell, C. M. (in press). *Poverty and adolescent health.* Paper prepared for the U.S. Congress, Office of Technology Assessment.

Allen, L., & Santrock, J. W. (1993). *Psychology: The contexts of behavior.* Dubuque, IA: Brown & Benchmark.

Allen, M., Brown, P., & Finlay, B. (1992). *Helping children by strengthening families.* Washington, DC: Children's Defense Fund.

Allport, G. (1954). *The roots of prejudice.* Cambridge, MA: Addison-Wesley.

Allport, G. W., & Odbert, H. S. (1936). Trait names: A psycholexical study. *Psychological Monographs, 47* (whole no. 211).

Amabile, T. M., & Hennessey, B. A. (1988). The motivation for creativity in children. In A. K. Boggiano & T. Pittman (Eds.), *Achievement motivation: A social-developmental perspective.* New York: Cambridge University Press.

Amaro, H., Russo, N. F., & Johnson, J. (1987). Family and work predictors of psychological well-being among Hispanic women professionals. *Psychology of Women Quarterly, 11,* 505–521.

American College Health Association. (1989, May). *Survey of AIDS on American college and university campuses.* Washington, DC: Author.

Ames, C., & Ames, R. (Eds.). (1989). *Research on motivation in education* (Vol. 3). San Diego: Academic Press.

Amoore, J. E. (1970). *Molecular basis of odor.* Springfield, IL: Charles C Thomas.

Anderson, B. L. (1983). Primary orgasmic dysfunction: Diagnostic considerations and a review of treatment. *Psychological Bulletin, 93,* 105–136.

Anderson, B. L., Kiecolt, J. K., & Glaser, R. (1994). A biobehavioral model of cancer stress and disease course. *American Psychologist, 49,* 389–404.

Anderson, N. (1991, August). *Sociodemographic aspects of hypertension in African Americans: A research agenda for health psychology.* Paper presented at the meeting of the American Psychological Association, San Francisco.

Anderson, N. H. (1965). Primacy effects in personality impression formation using a generalized order effect paradigm. *Journal of Personality and Social Psychology, 2,* 1–9.

Andreassi, J. L. (1989). *Psychophysiology* (2nd ed.). Hillsdale, NJ: Erlbaum.

Andres, R. (1989). Does the "best" body weight change with age? In A. J. Stunkard & A. Baum (Eds.), *Perspectives on behavioral medicine.* Hillsdale, NJ: Erlbaum.

Andressen, N. C. (1991). Schizophrenia and related disorders in DSM-IV. *Schizophrenia Bulletin, 17,* 25–26.

Anson, C. A. (1988). *Atlanta's adopt-a-student project.* William T. Grant Foundation Annual Report, New York.

Aponte, H. (1979). Family therapy and the community. In M. S. Gibbs, J. R. Lachenmeyer, & J. Sigel (Eds.), *Community psychology: Theoretical and empirical approaches.* New York: Gardner Press, 1979.

Aponte, J. F., Rivers, R. R., & Wohl, J. (1995). *Psychological interventions with ethnically diverse groups.* Needham Heights, MA: Allyn & Bacon.

Armsden, G. G., & Greenberg, M. T. (1984). *The inventory of parent and peer attachment: Individual differences and their relationship to psychological well-being in adolescence.* Unpublished manuscript, University of Washington.

Aronson, E. (1986, August). *Teaching students things they think they already know all about: The case of prejudice and desegregation.* Paper presented at the meeting of the American Psychological Association, Washington, DC.

Aronson, E. (1992). *The social animal* (6th ed.). New York: W. H. Freeman.

Arroyo, C. G., & Sternberg, R. J. (1993). *Against all odds: A view of the gifted disadvantaged.* Department of Psychology, Yale University, New Haven, CT.

Asch, S. E. (1951). Effects of group pressure on the modification and distortion of judgments. In H. S. Guetzkow (Ed.), *Groups, leadership and men.* Pittsburgh: Carnegie University Press.

Asian Week. (1990, June 29). *Poll finds racial tension decreasing,* p. 4.

Asnis, G. M., & van Praag, H. M. (1995). *Panic disorder*. New York: Wiley.

Atkinson, D., Morten, G., & Sue, D. (1993). *Counseling American minorities* (4th ed.). Dubuque, IA: Brown & Benchmark.

Atkinson, D. R., Morten, G., & Sue, D. W. (1993). *Counseling American minorities: A cross-cultural perspective* (4th ed.). Dubuque, IA: Brown & Benchmark.

Atkinson, J. W., & Raynor, I. O. (1974). *Motivation and achievement*. Washington, DC: V. H. Winston.

Atkinson, R. C., & Shiffrin, R. M. (1968). Human memory: A proposed system and its control processes. In K. W. Spence & J. T. Spence (Eds.), *The psychology of learning and motivation* (Vol. 2). San Diego: Academic Press.

Auw, A. (1991). *Gentle roads to survival*. Lower Lake, CA: Aslan.

Averill, J. R. (1983). Studies on anger and aggression: Implications for theories of emotion. *American Psychologist, 38,* 1145–1160.

Ax, A. F. (1953). The physiological differentiation of fear and anger in humans. *Psychosomatic Medicine, 15,* 433–442.

Baars, B. J. (1989). *A cognitive theory of consciousness*. New York: Cambridge University Press.

Bach y Rita, G. (1982). The Mexican-American religion and cultural influences. In R. M. Bacera, M. Karno, & J. Escobar (Eds.), *Mental health and Hispanic Americans: Clinical perspectives*. New York: Grune & Stratton.

Bachman, J. G. (1991). Dropouts, school. In R. M. Lerner, A. C. Petersen, & J. Brooks-Gunn (Eds.), *Encyclopedia of adolescence* (Vol. 1). New York: Garland.

Baddeley, A. (1990). *Human memory: Theory and practice*. Boston: Allyn & Bacon.

Baddeley, A. (1992). Working memory. *Science, 255,* 556–560.

Baddeley, A. (1993). Working memory and conscious awareness. In A. F. Collins, S. E. Gathercole, M. A. Conway, & P. E. Morris (Eds.), *Theories of memory*. Hillsdale, NJ: Erlbaum.

Baddeley, A. D., Bressi, S., Della Sala, S., Logie, R., & Spinnler, H. (in press). Working memory. *Brain*.

Baer, J. (1993). *Creativity and divergent thinking*. Hillsdale, NJ: Erlbaum.

Bagley, C. (1984). The social aetiology of schizophrenia in immigrant groups. In J. E. Mezzich & C. E. Berganza (Eds.), *Culture and psychopathology*. New York: Columbia University Press.

Bahrick, H. P., Bahrick, P. O., & Wittlinger, R. P. (1975). Fifty years of memory for names and faces: A cross-sectional approach. *Journal of Experimental Psychology: General, 104,* 54–75.

Bailey, C. (1991). *The new fit or fat* (rev. ed.). Boston: Houghton Mifflin.

Ball, W., & Tronick, E. (1971). Infant responses to impending collision: Optical and real. *Science, 171,* 818–820.

Baltes, P. B. (1987). Theoretical propositions life-span developmental psychology: On the dynamics between growth and decline. *Developmental Psychology, 23,* 611–626.

Banaji, M., & Prentice, D. A. (1994). The self in social contexts. *Annual Review of Psychology, 45,* 297–332.

Bandura, A. (1965). Influence of models' reinforcement contingencies on the acquisition of imitative responses. *Journal of Personality and Social Psychology, 1,* 589–596.

Bandura, A. (1965). Influence of models' reinforcement contingencies on the acquisition of imitative responses. *Journal of Personality and Social Psychology, 1,* 589–595.

Bandura, A. (1971). *Social learning theory*. New York: General Learning Press.

Bandura, A. (1977). *Social learning theory*. Englewood Cliffs, NJ: Prentice Hall.

Bandura, A. (1986). *Social foundations of thought and action*. Englewood Cliffs, NJ: Prentice Hall.

Bandura, A. (1989). Social cognitive theory. In R. Vasta (Ed.), *Six theories of child development*. Greenwich, CT: JAI.

Bandura, A. (1991). Self-efficacy: Impact of self-beliefs on adolescent life paths. In R. M. Lerner, A. C. Petersen, & J. Brooks-Gunn (Eds.), *Encyclopedia of adolescence* (Vol. 2). New York: Garland.

Bandura, A. (1991). Social cognitive theory of moral thought and action. In W. M. Kurtines & J. Gewirtz (Eds.), *Moral behavior and development*. Hillsdale, NJ: Erlbaum.

Bandura, A. (1994). Social cognitive theory of mass communication. In J. Bryant & D. Zillman (Eds.), *Media effects*. Hillsdale, NJ: Erlbaum.

Bandura, A., & Jourden, F. J. (1991). Self-regulatory mechanisms governing the impact of social comparison on complex decision making. *Journal of Personality and Social Psychology, 60,* 941–951.

Bandura, A., Blanchard, E. B., & Ritter, B. (1969). Relative efficacy of desensitization and modeling approaches for inducing behavioral, affective, and attitudinal changes. *Journal of Personality and Social Psychology, 13,* 173–199.

Barbach, L. (1975). *For yourself*. New York: Signet.

Bard, P. (1934). Emotion. In C. Murchison (Ed.), *Handbook of general experimental psychology*. Worcester, MA: Clark University Press.

Barlow, D. H., Blanchard, E. B., Vermilyea, J. A., Vermilyea, B. B., & Dimardo, P. A. (1986). Generalized anxiety and generalized anxiety disorder: Description and reconceptualization. *American Journal of Psychiatry, 143,* 40–44.

Barnouw, V. (1963). *Culture and personality*. Homewood, IL: Dorsey.

Baron, N. (1992). *Growing up with language*. Reading, MA: Addison-Wesley.

Barron, F. (1989, April). The birth of a notion. Exercises to tap your creative potential. *Omni,* pp. 112–119.

Barry, H., Child, I. L., & Bacon, M. K. (1959). Relation of child training to subsistence economy. *American Anthropologist, 61,* 51–63.

Bartlett, F. C. (1932). *Remembering*. Cambridge, England: Cambridge University Press.

Bartley, S. H. (1969). *Principles of perception*. New York: Harper & Row.

Bartoshuk, L. (1994, June). *Clinical studies as aids in teaching taste*. Paper presented at the meetings of the American Psychological Association, Washington, DC.

Baruch, G. K., Barnett, R. C., & Rivers, C. (1985). *Lifeprints: New patterns of love and work for today's women*. New York: Signet.

Baruch, G. K., Biener, I., & Barnett, R. C. (1987). Women and gender in research on work and family. *American Psychologist, 42,* 130–136.

Batson, C. D., Bolen, M. H., Cross, J. A., & Jeuringer-Benefiel, H. E. (1986). Where is the altruism in the altruistic personality? *Journal of Personality and Social Psychology, 50,* 212–220.

Baumeister, R. F. (1989). *Masochism and the self*. Hillsdale, NJ: Erlbaum.

Baumrind, D. (1971). Current patterns of parental authority. *Developmental Psychology Monographs, 4* (1, Pt. 2).

Baumrind, D. (1989, April). *Sex-differentiated socialization effects in childhood and adolescence*. Paper presented at the biennial meeting of the Society for Research in Child Development, Kansas City.

Baumrind, D. (1991). Parenting styles and adolescent development. In J. Brooks-Gunn, R. Lerner, & A. C. Petersen (Eds.), *The encyclopedia of adolescence*. New York: Garland.

Beal, C. R. (1994). *Boys and girls: The development of gender roles*. New York: McGraw-Hill.

Beck, A. (1976). *Cognitive therapies and the emotional disorders*. New York: International Universities Press.

Beck, A. T. (1967). *Depression*. New York: Harper & Row.

Beck, A. T., & Haaga, D. A. F. (1992). The future of cognitive therapy. *Psychotherapy, 29,* 34–38.

Beckham, E. E., & Leber, W. R. (Eds.). (1995). *Handbook of depression* (2nd ed.). New York: Guilford Press.

Bednar, R. L., & Peterson, S. R. (1995). *Self-esteem* (2nd ed.). Washington, DC: American Psychological Association.

Belenky, M. F., Clinchy, B. M., Goldberger, N. R., & Tarule, J. M. (1986). *Women's ways of knowing*. New York: Basic.

Bell, A. P., & Weinberg, M. S. (1978). *Homosexualities*. New York: Simon & Schuster.

Bell, A. P., Weinberg, M. S., & Mammersmith, S. K. (1981). *Sexual preference: Its development in men and women*. New York: Simon & Schuster.

Bellack, A. S., & Hersen, M. (Eds.). (1988). *Behavioral assessment*. Elmsford, NY: Pergamon.

Belle, D. (1988). *Women's mental health research agenda: Poverty*. Rockville, MD: National Institute of Mental Health.

Belle, D., Longfellow, C., Makosky, V., Saunder, E., & Zelkowitz, P. (1981). Income, mothers' mental health, and family functioning in a low-income population. In American Academy of Nursing (Ed.), *The impact of changing resources on health policy*. Kansas City: American Nurses Association.

Bem, D. J. (1967). Self-perception. An alternative interpretation of cognitive dissonance phenomena. *Psychological Review, 74,* 183–200.

Bem, S. L. (1977). On the utility of alternative procedures for assessing psychological androgyny. *Journal of Consulting and Clinical Psychology, 45,* 196–205.

Benbadis, S. R., Wolgamuth, B. R., Perry, M. C., & Dudley, S. D. (1995). Dreams and rapid eye movement sleep in the multiple sleep latency test. *Sleep, 18,* 105–108.

Benbow, C. P., & Stanley, J. C. (1983). Sex differences in mathematical reasoning ability: More facts. *Science, 222,* 1029–1031.

Benet, S. (1976). *How to live to be 100*. New York: Dial Press.

Bennett, S. K. (1994). The American Indian: A psychological overview. In W. J. Lonner & R. Malpass (Eds.), *Psychology and culture.* Needham Heights, MA: Allyn & Bacon.

Bennett, W. I., & Gurin, J. (1982). *The dieter's dilemma: Eating less and weighing more.* New York: Basic.

Benson, H. (1984). *Beyond the relaxation response.* New York: Times Books.

Benton, C., Hernandez, A., Schmidt, A., Schmitz, M., Stone, A., & Weiner, B. (1983). Is hostility linked with affiliation among males and with achievement among females? A critique of Pollak and Gilligan. *Journal of Personality and Social Psychology, 45,* 1167–1171.

Berger, S. M. (1971). Observer perseverance as related to a models' success: A social comparison analysis. *Journal of Personality and Social Psychology, 19,* 341–350.

Bergin, A. E., & Garfield, S. L. (1994). *Handbook of psychotherapy and behavior change.* New York: Wiley.

Berk, S. F. (1985). *The gender factory: The apportionment of work in American households.* New York: Plenum.

Berndt, T. J., & Perry, T. B. (1990). Distinctive features and effects of early adolescent friendships. In R. Montemayor (Ed.), *Advances in adolescent research.* Greenwich, CT: JAI.

Bernstein, I. L. (1991). Aversion conditioning in response to cancer and cancer treatment. *Clinical Psychology Review, 11,* 185–191.

Berry, J. (1994). Acculturative stress. In W. J. Lonner & R. Malpass (Eds.), *Acculturative stress.* Boston: Allyn & Bacon.

Berry, J. W. (1967). Independence and conformity in subsistence level societies. *Journal of Personality and Social Psychology, 7,* 415–418.

Berry, J. W. (1969). On cross-cultural comparability. *International Journal of Psychology, 4,* 119–128.

Berry, J. W. (1971). Ecological and cultural factors in spatial perceptual development. *Canadian Journal of Behavioral Science, 3,* 324–336.

Berry, J. W. (1980). Acculturation as varieties of adaptation. In A. Padilla (Ed.), *Acculturation: Theory, model, and some new findings.* Washington, DC: American Association for the Advancement of Science.

Berry, J. W. (1980). Introduction to methodology. In H. C. Triandis & J. W. Berry (Eds.), *Handbook of cross-cultural psychology: Methodology* (Vol. 2). Boston: Allyn & Bacon.

Berry, J. W. (1983). Textured contexts: Systems and situations in cross-cultural psychology. In S. H. Irvine & J. W. Berry (Eds.), *Human assessment and cultural factors.* New York: Plenum.

Berry, J. W. (1990). Psychology of acculturation: Understanding individuals moving between cultures. In R. W. Brislin (Eds.), *Applied cross-cultural psychology.* Newbury Park, CA: Sage.

Berry, J. W., & Bennett, J. A. (1992). Conceptions of cognitive competence. *International Journal of Psychology, 27,* 73–88.

Berry, J. W., Poortinga, Y. H., Segall, M. H., & Dasen, P. R. (in press). *Cross-cultural psychology: Theory, method, and applications.* Cambridge, England: Cambridge University.

Berry, J. W., Poortinga, Y. H., Segall, M. H., & Dasen, P. R. (1992). *Cross-cultural psychology: Theory, method, and applications.* Cambridge, England: Cambridge University Press.

Berscheid, E. (1988). Some comments on love's anatomy: Or, whatever happened to an old-fashioned lust? In R. J. Sternberg & M. L. Barnes (Eds.), *Anatomy of love.* New Haven, CT: Yale University Press.

Berscheid, E., & Fei, J. (1977). Sexual jealousy and romantic love. In G. Clinton & G. Smith (Eds.), *Sexual jealousy.* Englewood Cliffs, NJ: Prentice Hall.

Berscheid, E., Snyder, M., & Omoto, A. M. (1989). Issues in studying close relationships: Conceptualizing and measuring closeness. In C. Hendrick (Ed.), *Close relationships.* Newbury Park, CA: Sage.

Bertelson, A. (1979). A Danish twin study of manic-depressive disorders. In M. Schous & E. Stromgren (Eds.), *Origin, prevention, and treatment of affective disorders.* Orlando, FL: Academic Press.

Berzon, B. (1988). *Permanent partners.* New York: Plume.

Bexton, W. H., Heron, W., & Scott, T. H. (1954). Effects of decreased variation in the sensory environment. *Canadian Journal of Psychology, 8,* 70–76.

Billings, A. G., & Moos, R. H. (1981). The role of coping responses and social resources in attenuating the stress of life events. *Journal of Behavioral Medicine, 4,* 157–189.

Billings, A. G., Cronkite, R. C., & Moos, R. H. (1983). Social-environment factors in unipolar depression. *Journal of Abnormal Psychology, 92,* 119–133.

Billy, J. O. G., Tanfer, K., Grady, W. R., & Klepinger, D. H. (1993). The sexual behavior of men in the United States. *Family Planning Perspectives, 25,* 52–60.

Blackmore, S. (1987). A report of a visit to Carl Sargent's laboratory. *Journal of the Society for Psychical Research, 54,* 186–198.

Blair, S. N., & Kohl, H. W. (1988). Physical activity: Which is more important for health? *Medicine and Science and Sports and Exercise, 20,* (2, Suppl.), 5–7.

Blakemore, J. E. O. (1993, March). *Preschool children's interest in babies: Observations in naturally occurring situations.* Paper presented at the biennial meeting of the Society for Research in Child Development, New Orleans.

Blash, R., & Unger, D. G. (1992, March). *Cultural factors and the self-esteem and aspirations of African-American adolescent males.* Paper presented at the meeting of the Society for Research on Adolescence, Washington, DC.

Blechman, E. A., & Brownell, K. D. (Eds.). (1987). *Handbook of behavioral medicine for women.* Elmsford, NY: Pergamon.

Bloom, B. (1975). *Changing patterns of psychiatric care.* New York: Human Science Press.

Bloom, B. (1995, August). *Real children, real choices.* Paper presented at the meeting of the American Psychological Association, New York City.

Bloom, B. L. (1985). *Community mental health: A general introduction* (2nd ed.). Monterey, CA: Brooks/Cole.

Bloor, C., & White, F. (1983). Unpublished manuscript, University of California at San Diego.

Blount, B. G. (1982). Culture and the language of socialization: Parental speech. In D. A. Wagner & H. W. Stevenson (Eds.), *Cultural perspectives on child development.* San Francisco: W. H. Freeman.

Blumstein, P. W., & Schwartz, P. (1983). *American couples.* New York: William Morrow.

Blundell, J. E. (1984). Systems and interactions: An approach to the pharmacology of feeding. In A. J. Stunkard & E. Stellar (Eds.), *Eating and its disorders.* New York: Raven Press.

Bly, R. (1990). *Iron John.* New York: Vintage Books.

Bochner, S. (1994). Culture shock. In W. J. Lonner & R. Malpass (Eds.), *Acculturative stress.* Boston: Allyn & Bacon.

Bogatz, G., & Ball, S. (1972). *Reading with television: An evaluation of the Electric Company.* Princeton, NJ: Educational Testing Service.

Boggiano, A. K., & Pittman, T. S. (1993). *Achievement and motivation.* New York: Cambridge University Press.

Bohannon, J. N., III. (1988). Flashbulb memories for the Space Shuttle disaster: A tale of two theories. *Cognition, 29,* 179–186.

Bolles, R. (1995). *What color is your parachute?* Berkeley, CA: Ten Speed Press.

Bornstein, M. H., & Krasnegor, N. A. (1989). *Stability and continuity in mental development.* Hillsdale, NJ: Erlbaum.

Bouchard, C., Trembley, A., Despres, J. P., Nadeau, A., Lupien, P., Theriault, G., Dussault, J., Moorjani, S., Pinault, S., & Fournier, G. (1990). The response to long-term overfeeding in identical twins. *New England Journal of Medicine, 322,* 1477–1482.

Bouchard, T. J., Heston, L., Eckert, E., Keyes, M., & Resnick, S. (1981). The Minnesota study of twins reared apart: Project description and sample results in the developmental domain. *Twin Research, 3,* 227–233.

Bourguignon, E., & Evascu, T. (1977). Altered states of consciousness within a general evolutional perspective: A holocultural analysis. *Behavior Science Research, 12,* 199–216.

Bower, G. H., Clark, M., Winzenz, D., & Lesgold, A. (1969). Hierarchical retrieval schemes in recall of categorized word lists. *Journal of Verbal Learning and Verbal Behavior, 3,* 323–343.

Bowers, K. S. (August, 1992). *The problem of consciousness.* Paper presented at the meeting of the American Psychological Association, Washington, DC.

Bowers, T. G., & Clum, G. A. (1988). Relative contribution of specific and nonspecific treatment effects: Meta-analysis of placebo-controlled behavior therapy research. *Psychological Bulletin, 103,* 315–323.

Bowlby, J. (1969). *Attachment and loss* (Vol. 1). London: Hogarth Press.

Bowlby, J. (1989). *Secure attachment.* New York: Basic Books.

Boyd-Franklin, N. (1989). *Black families in therapy: A multisystems approach.* New York: Guilford.

Bransford, J. D., & Stein, B. S. (1984). *The ideal problem solver.* New York: W. H. Freeman.

Braun, B. G. (1988). *The treatment of multiple personality disorder.* Washington, DC: American Psychiatric Press.

Brazelton, T. B. (1992). *Touchpoints.* Reading, MA: Addison-Wesley.

Brean, H. (1958, March 31). What hidden sell is all about. *Life,* pp. 104–114.

Breland, K., & Breland, M. (1961). The misbehavior of organisms. *American Psychologist, 16,* 681–684.

Brewer, M. B., & Campbell, D. T. (1976). *Ethnocentrism and intergroup attitudes.* New York: Wiley.

Brickman, P., Coates, D., & Janoff-Bulman, R. J. (1978). Lottery winners and accident victims: Is happiness relative? *Journal of Personality and Social Psychology, 36,* 917–927.

Briggs, J. L. (1970). *Never in anger.* Cambridge, MA: Harvard University Press.

Brigham, J. C., Maas, A., Snyder, L. D., & Spaulding, K. (1982). Accuracy of eyewitness identification in a field setting. *Journal of Personality and Social Psychology, 41,* 683–691.

Brim, G. (1992, December 7). Commentary, *Newsweek,* p. 52.

Brim, G. (1992). *Ambition.* New York: Basic Books.

Brislin, R. (1993). *Understanding culture's influence on behavior.* Fort Worth, TX: Harcourt Brace.

Brislin, R. W. (1987). Increasing awareness of class, ethnicity, culture, and race by expanding on students' own experiences. In *The G. Stanley Hall Lecture Series* (Vol. 8). Washington, DC: American Psychological Association.

Brislin, R. W. (1990). Applied cross-cultural psychology: An introduction. In R. W. Brislin (Ed.), *Applied cross-cultural psychology.* Newbury Park, CA: Sage.

Brobeck, J. R., Tepperman, T., & Long, C. N. (1943). Experimental hypothalamic hyperphagia in the albino rat. *Yale Journal of Biological Medicine, 15,* 831–853.

Brone, R. J., & Fisher, C. B. (1988). Determinants of adolescent obesity: A comparison with anorexia nervosa. *Adolescence, 23,* 155–169.

Bronfenbrenner, U. (1989, April). *The developing ecology of human development.* Paper presented at the biennial meeting of the Society for Research in Child Development, Kansas City, MO.

Bronfenbrenner, U. (1995, March). *The role research has played in Head Start.* Paper presented at the meeting of the Society for Research in Child Development, Indianapolis, IN.

Bronstein, P. A., & Paludi, M. (1988). *The introductory psychology course from a broader perspective.* Washington, DC: American Psychological Association.

Bronstein, P. A., & Paludi, M. (1988). The introductory course from a broader perspective. In P. A. Bronstein & M. Paludi (Eds.), *Teaching a psychology of people.* Washington, DC: American Psychological Association.

Bronstein, P. A., & Quina, K. (1988). Perspectives on gender balance and cultural diversity in the teaching of psychology. In P. A. Bronstein & K. Quina (Eds.), *Teaching a psychology of people: Resources for gender and sociocultural awareness.* Washington, DC: American Psychological Association.

Brooks-Gunn, J. (1991). Maturational timing variations in adolescent girls, antecedents of. In R. M. Lerner, A. C. Petersen, & J. Brooks-Gunn (Eds.), *Encyclopedia of adolescence.* New York: Garland.

Brooks-Gunn, J. (1992, March). *Revisiting theories of "storm and stress": The role of biology.* Paper presented at the meeting of the Society for Research on Adolescence, Washington, DC.

Brooks-Gunn, J., & Chase-Landsdale, P. L. (1995). Adolescent parenthood. In M. H. Bornstein (Ed.), *Handbook of parenting, Vol. 3.* Hillsdale, NJ: Erlbaum.

Broskowski, A. T. (1995). The evolution of health care: Implications for the training and careers of psychologists. *Professional Psychology, 26,* 156–162.

Broverman, I., Broverman, D., Clarkson, F., Rosenkrantz, P., & Vogel, S. (1970). Sex-role stereotypes and clinical judgements of mental health. *Journal of Consulting and Clinical Psychology, 34,* 1–7.

Broverman, I., Vogel, S., Broverman, D., Clarkson, F., & Rosenkranz, P. (1972). Sex-role stereotypes: A current appraisal. *Journal of Social Issues, 28,* 59–78.

Brown, D. R., & Gary, L. E. (1985). Social support network differentials among married and nonmarried black females. *Psychology of Women Quarterly, 9,* 229–241.

Brown, E., Deffenbacher, K., & Sturgill, W. (1977). Memory for faces and the circumstances of encounter. *Journal of Applied Psychology, 6,* 311–318.

Brown, G., Bhrolchain, M., & Harris, T. (1975). Social class and psychiatric disturbance among women in an urban population. *Sociology, 9,* 225–254.

Brown, G. R., & Collier, L. (1989). Transvestites' women revisited: A nonpatient sample. *Archives of Sexual Behavior, 18,* 73–84.

Brown, J. K. (1985). Introduction. In J. K. Brown & V. Kerns (Eds.), *In her prime: A new view of middle-aged women.* South Hadley, MA: Bergin & Garvey.

Brown, R. (1973). *A first language: The early stages.* Cambridge, MA: Harvard University Press.

Browne, C. R., Brown, J. V., Blumenthal, J., Anderson, L., & Johnson, P. (1993, March). *African American fathering: The perception of mothers and sons.* Paper presented at the biennial meeting of the Society for Research in Child Development, New Orleans.

Browne, M. W. (1994, October 16). What is intelligence, and who has it? *New York Times Book Review,* pp. 2–3, 41–42.

Brownell, K. D. (1991). Dieting and the search for the perfect body: Where physiology and culture collide. *Behavior Therapy, 22,* 1–12.

Brownell, K. D. (1993). Whether obesity should be treated. *Health Psychology, 10,* 303–310.

Brownell, K. D., & Fairburn, C. G. (Eds.). (1995). *Eating disorders and obesity.* New York: Guilford.

Brownell, K. D., & Rodin, J. (1994). The dieting maelstrom: Is it possible and advisable to lose weight? *American Psychologist, 9,* 781–791.

Brownell, K. D., & Rodin, J. (in press). Medical, metabolic, and psychological effects of weight cycling and weight variability. *Archives of Internal Medicine.*

Budwig, N. (1995). *A developmental-functionalist approach to child language.* Hillsdale, NJ: Erlbaum.

Bunger, B., & Beutler, L. E. (1995). *Comprehensive textbook of psychotherapy.* New York: Oxford University Press.

Burgess, K. (1968). The behavior and training of a killer whale (Orcinus orca) at San Diego Sea World. *International Zoo Yearbook, 8,* 202–205.

Burgio, L. D., & Burgio, K. L. (1986). Behavioral gerontology: Application of behavioral methods to the problem of older adults. *Journal of Applied Behavior Analysis, 19,* 321–328.

Burns, D. (1980). *Feeling good.* New York: Avon.

Burnstein, E., Crandall, C., & Kitayama, S. (1994). Some Neo-Darwinian decision rules for altruism: Weighing cues for inclusive fitness as a function of the biological importance of the decision. *Journal of Personality and Social Psychology, 67,* 773–789.

Burton, L. M., Allison, K. W., & Obeidallah, D. (1995). Social context and adolescence: Alternative perspectives on developmental pathways for African-American teens. In L. J. Crockett & A. C. Crouter (Eds.), *Pathways through adolescence.* Hillsdale, NJ: Erlbaum.

Buss, D. M. (1994). *The evolution of desire: Strategies of human mating.* New York: Basic Books.

Buss, D. M. (1995). Evolutionary psychology: A new paradigm for psychological science. *Psychological Inquiry, 6,* 1–30.

Buss, D. M., & Barnes, M. (1986). Preferences in human mate selection. *Journal of Personality and Social Psychology, 50,* 559–570.

Butcher, J. N. (Ed.). (1995). *Clinical personality assessment.* New York: Oxford University Press.

Butler, R. A. (1953). Discrimination learning by rhesus monkeys to visual-exploration motivation. *Journal of Comparative and Physiological Psychology, 46,* 95–98.

Butler, R. N. (1993). Did you say 'sarcopenia'? *Geriatrics, 48,* 11–12.

Butters, N., Delis, D., & Lucas, J. (1995). Clinical assessment of memory disorders in amnesia and dementia. *Annual Review of Psychology, Vol. 46.* Palo Alto, CA: Annual Reviews.

Button, C. M., Grant, M. J., Hannah, T. E., & Ross, A. S. (1993). The dimensions underlying perceived attitudes: Liberalism and concern for traditional values. *Canadian Journal of Behavioural Research, 25,* 230–252.

Buunk, B. P., Collins, R. L., Taylor, S. E., Van Yperen, N. W., & Dakof, G. A. (1990). The affective consequences of social comparison: Either direction has its ups and downs. *Journal of Personality and Social Psychology, 59,* 1238–1249.

Byrnes, J. P. (1988). Formal operations: A systematic reformulation. *Developmental Review, 8,* 66–87.

Calkins, S. D., & Fox, N. A. (1992). The relations among infant temperament, security of attachment, and behavioral inhibition at twenty-four months. *Child Development, 63,* 1456–1472.

Cameron, D. (1988, February). Soviet schools. *NEA Today,* p. 15.

Cameron, N. (1963). *Personality development and psychopathology.* Boston: Houghton Mifflin.

Campbell, D. T., & LeVine, R. A. (1968). Ethnocentrism and intergroup relations. In R. Abelson & others (Eds.), *Theories of cognitive consistency: A sourcebook.* Chicago: Rand McNally.

Cannon, W. B. (1927). The James-Lange theory of emotions: A critical examination and an alternative theory. *American Journal of Psychology, 39,* 106–124.

Cannon, W. B., & Washburn, A. (1912). An explanation of hunger. *American Journal of Physiology, 29,* 441–454.

Canter, M. B., Bennett, B. E., Jones, S. E., & Nagy, T. F. (1994). *Ethics for psychologists.* Washington, DC: American Psychological Association.

Caplan, P. J., & Caplan, J. B. (1994). *Thinking critically about research on sex and gender.* New York: McGraw-Hill.

Carraher, T. H., & Carraher, D. W. (1981). Do Piagetian stages describe the reasoning of the unschooled adults? *Quarterly Newsletter of the Laboratory of Comparative Human Cognition, 3,* 61–68.

Carroll, C., & Miller, D. (1994). *Health* (5th ed.). Dubuque, IA: Brown & Benchmark.

Carskadon, M. (1993, January 12). The great American sleep debt: Commentary. *Washington Post,* p. WH9.

Carson, R. C., Butcher, J. N., & Coleman, J. C. (1988). *Abnormal psychology and modern life.* Glenview, IL: Scott, Foresman.

Carstensen, L. L., Hanson, K. A., & Freund, A. M. (1995). Selection and compensation in adulthood. In R. A. Dixon & L. Backman (Eds.), *Compensating for psychological deficits and declines.* Hillsdale, NJ: Erlbaum.

Cartwright, R. D. (1978, December). Happy endings for our dreams. *Psychology Today,* pp. 66–74.

Cartwright, R. D. (1989). Dreams and their meaning. In M. H. Dryger, T. Roth, & W. C. Dement (Eds.), *Principles and practice of sleep medicine.* San Diego: Harcourt Brace Jovanovich.

Cartwright, S. A. (1851/1981). Report on the diseases and physical peculiarities of the Negro race. In A. L. Caplan, H. T. Engelhardt, Jr., and J. J. McCartney (Eds.), *Concepts of health and disease: Interdisciplinary perspectives* (pp. 305–326). Reading, MA: Addison-Wesley.

Casas, J. M., & San Miguel, S. (1993). Beyond questions and discussion: There is a need for action. *Counseling Psychologist, 21,* 233–239.

Case, R. (1985). *Intellectual development: Birth to adulthood.* New York: Academic Press.

Casper, R. C. (1989). Psychodynamic psychotherapy in acute anorexia nervosa and acute bulimia nervosa. In A. H. Esman (Ed.), *International annals of adolescent psychiatry.* Chicago: University of Chicago Press.

Cassell, C. (1984). *Swept away: Why women fear their own sexuality.* New York: Simon & Schuster.

Castro, F. G., & Magaña, D. (1988). A course in health promotion in ethnic minority populations. In P. A. Bronstein & K. Quina (Eds.), *Teaching a psychology of people.* Washington, DC: American Psychological Association.

Catania, A. C. (1990, March). *The significance of nonhuman research in the analysis of human behavior.* Paper presented at the Eastern Psychological Association, Philadelphia.

Cayleff, S. E. (1986). Ethical issues in counseling gender, races, and culturally distinct groups. *Journal of Counseling and Development, 64,* 345–347.

Cervantes, R. C. (1987). Hispanics in psychology. In P. J. Woods & C. S. Wilkinson (Eds.), *Is psychology the major for you?* Washington, DC: American Psychological Association.

Chance, P. (1988). *Learning and behavior.* Belmont, CA: Wadsworth.

Chasnoff, L. J., Griffith, D. R., MacGregor, S., Dirkes, K., & Burns, K. A. (1989). Temporal patterns of cocaine use in pregnancy. *Journal of the American Medical Association, 261,* 1741–1744.

Chen, G. (1995). Differences in self-disclosure patterns among Americans versus Chinese. *Journal of Cross-Cultural Psychology, 26,* 84–91.

Children's Defense Fund. (1990). *Children 1990.* Washington, DC: Children's Defense Fund.

Chodorow, N. J. (1978). *The reproduction of mothering.* Berkeley: University of California Press.

Chodorow, N. J. (1989). *Feminism and psychoanalytic theory.* New Haven, CT: Yale University Press.

Chomsky, N. (1957). *Syntactic structure.* The Hague: Mouton.

Cialdini, R. (1993). *Influence.* New York: Quill.

Clark, D. A., & Beck, A. T. (1989). Cognitive theory and therapy of anxiety and depression. In P. C. Kendall & D. Watson (Eds.), *Anxiety and depression.* San Diego: Academic Press.

Clark, E. V. (1983). Meanings and concepts. In P. H. Mussen (Ed.), *Handbook of child psychology* (4th ed., Vol. 3). New York: Wiley.

Clark, K. B. (1991, August). *Brown versus Board of Education: Then and now.* Paper presented at the meeting of the American Psychological Association, San Francisco.

Clark, K. B., & Clark, M. P. (1939). The development of self and the emergence of racial identification in Negro preschool children. *Journal of Social Psychology, 10,* 591–599.

Clark, L. A., Watson, D., & Reynolds, S. (1995). Diagnosis and classification in psychopathology. *Annual Review of Psychology, Vol. 46.* Palo Alto, CA: Annual Reviews.

Clifford, B. R., Bunter, B., & McAleer, J. L. (1995). *Television and children.* Hillsdale, NJ: Erlbaum.

Cochran, S. D., & Mays, V. M. (1990). Sex, lies, and HIV. *New England Journal of Medicine, 322,* 774–775.

Cohen, L. A. (1987, November). Diet and cancer. *Scientific American,* pp. 128–137.

Coie, J. D. (1993, March). *The adolescence of peer relations.* Paper presented at the biennial meeting of the Society for Research in Child Development, New Orleans.

Colby, A., Kohlberg, L., Gibbs, J., & Lieberman, M. (1983). A longitudinal study of moral judgment. *Monographs of the Society for Research in Child Development.* (Serial No. 201).

Cole, M., & Scribner, S. (1977). Cross-cultural studies of memory and cognition. In R. V. Kail & J. W. Hagen (Eds.), *Perspectives on the development of memory and cognition.* Hillsdale, NJ: LEA.

Coleman, J. (1995, March). *Adolescent sexual knowledge: Implications for health and health risks.* Paper presented at the meeting of the Society for Research in Child Development, Indianapolis, IN.

Coles, R. (1986). *The political life of children.* Boston: Little, Brown.

Colgrove, M., Bloomfield, H., & McWilliams, P. (1991). *How to survive the loss of a love.*

Coll, C. T. G., Erkut, S., Alarcon, O., Garcia, H. A. V., & Tropp, L. (1995, March). *Puerto Rican adolescents and families: Lessons in construct and instrument development.* Paper presented at the meeting of the Society for Research in Child Development, Indianapolis, IN.

Comas-Díaz, L. (1993). Hispanic/Latino communities: Psychological implications. In D. R. Atkinson, G. Morten, & D. W. Sue (Eds.), *Counseling American minorities.* Dubuque, IA: Brown & Benchmark.

Comas-Díaz, L., & Griffith, E. E. H. (Eds.). (1988). *Clinical guidelines in cross cultural mental health.* New York: Wiley.

Comas-Díaz, L., Geller, J., Melgaoza, B., & Baker, R. (1982, August). *Attitudes and expectations about mental health services among Hispanics and Afro-Americans.* Paper presented at the 90th annual meeting of the American Psychological Association, Washington, DC.

Comer, J. P. (1988). Educating poor minority children. *Scientific American, 259,* 42–48.

Comer, J. P., & Poussaint, A. E. (1992). *Raising Black children.* New York: Plume.

Committee for Economic Development. (1987). *Children in need: Investment strategies for the educationally disadvantaged.* Washington, DC: Author.

Condry, J. C. (1989). *The psychology of television.* Hillsdale, NJ: Erlbaum.

Conway, M., & Rubin, D. (1993). The structure of autobiographical memory. In A. F. Collins, S. E. Gathercole, M. A. Conway, & P. E. Morris (Eds.), *Theories of memory.* Hillsdale, NJ: Erlbaum.

Cooper, C. R., & Ayers-Lopez, S. (1985). Family and peer systems in early adolescence: New models of the role of relationships in development. *Journal of Early Adolescence, 5,* 9–22.

Cooper, C. R., & Grotevant, H. D. (1989, April). *Individuality and connectedness in the family and adolescents' self and relational competence.* Paper presented at the biennial meeting of the Society for Research in Child Development, Kansas City.

Cooper, C. R., Grotevant, H. D., Moore, M. S., & Condon, S. M. (1982, August). *Family support and conflict: Both foster adolescent identity and role taking.* Paper presented at the meeting of the American Psychological Association, Washington, DC.

Cooper, K. (1970). *The new aerobics.* New York: Bantam.

Coopersmith, S. (1967). *The antecedents of self-esteem.* New York: W. H. Freeman.

Coren, S., & Girus, J. S. (1972). Illusion decrement in intersecting line figures. *Psychonomic Science, 26,* 108–110.

Coren, S., & Ward, I. M. (1989). *Sensation and perception.* San Diego: Harcourt Brace Jovanovich.

Cornoldi, C., & Logie, R. (1995). *Stretching the imagination.* New York: Oxford University Press.

Corsini, R., & others. (1991). *Five therapists and one client.* Itasca, IL: Peacock.

Cortes, J. B., & Gatti, F. M. (1970, April). Physique and propensity. *Psychology Today,* pp. 42–44.

Costa, P. T. (1988, August). *Personality, continuity and the changes of adult life.* Paper presented at the American Psychological Association, Atlanta.

Costa, P. T., & McRae, R. R. (1995). Solid ground in the wetlands of personality: A reply to Block. *Psychological Bulletin, 117,* 216–220.

Costanzo, M. (1992). Training students to decode verbal and nonverbal cues: Effects on confidence and performance. *Journal of Educational Psychology, 84,* 308–313.

Costello, C., & Stone, A. J. (1995). *The American woman: 1994–1995. Where we stand.* New York: Norton.

Costin, F., & Draguns, J. G. (1989). *Abnormal psychology.* New York: Wiley.

Cotton, N. (1979). The familial incidence of alcoholism: A review. *Journal of Studies on Alcohol, 40,* 89–116.

Cournoyer, R. J., & Mahalik, J. R. (1995). Cross-sectional study of gender role conflict examining college-aged and middle-aged men. *Journal of Counseling Psychology, 42,* 11–19.

Cowley, G. (1988, May 23). The wisdom of animals. *Newsweek,* pp. 52–58.

Craik, F. I. M., & Lockhart, R. S. (1972). Levels of processing: A framework for memory research. *Journal of Verbal Learning and Verbal Behavior, 11,* 671–684.

Craik, F. I. M., & Tulving, E. (1975). Depth of processing and retention of words in episodic memory. *Journal of Experimental Psychology: General, 104,* 268–294.

Crick, M. (1977). *Explorations in language and meaning: Toward a scientific anthropology.* New York: Halsted Press.

Crosby, F. J. (1991). *Juggling.* New York: Free Press.

Cross, W. C., & Maldonado, B. (1971). The counselor, the Mexican American, and the stereotype. *Elementary School Guidance and Counseling, 6,* 27–31.

Csikszentimihalyi, M. (1990). *Flow.* New York: Harper & Row.

Culbertson, F. M. (1991, August). *Mental health of women: An international journey.* Paper presented at the meeting of the American Psychological Association, San Francisco.

Cunningham, M. R. (1986). Measuring the physical in physical attractiveness: Quasi-experiments on the sociobiology of female facial beauty. *Journal of Personality and Social Psychology, 50,* 925–935.

Curtiss, S. (1977). *Genie.* New York: Academic Press.

Cutrona, C. E. (1982). Transition to college: Loneliness and the process of social adjustment. In L. A. Peplau & D. Perlman (Eds.), *Loneliness: A sourcebook of current theory, research and therapy.* New York: Wiley.

Dallenbach, K. M. (1927). The temperature spots and end-organs. *American Journal of Psychology, 52,* 331–347.

Daly, M., & Wilson, M. (1995). Evolutionary psychology: Adaptationist, selectionist, and comparative. *Psychological Inquiry, 6,* 34–38.

D'Andrade, R. G., & Strauss, C. (1992). *Human motives and cultural models.* New York: Cambridge University Press.

d'Ansia, G. I. D. (1989). Familial analysis of panic disorder and agoraphobia. *Journal of Affective Disorders, 17,* 1–8.

Danzinger, S., & Danzinger, S. (1993). Child poverty and public policy: Toward a comprehensive antipoverty agenda. *Daedalus: America's Childhood, 122,* 57–84.

Darling, C. A., Kallon, D. J., & Van Duesen, J. E. (1984). Sex in transition, 1900–1984. *Journal of Youth and Adolescence, 13,* 385–399.

Darwin, C. (1859). *On the origin of species.* London: John Murray.

Darwin, C. (1872/1965). *The expression of the emotions in man and animals.* Chicago: University of Chicago Press.

Davidson, R. J., Ekman, P., Saron, C. D., Senulis, J. A., & Friesen, W. V. (1990). Approach-withdrawal and cerebral asymmetry: Emotional expression and brain physiology. *Journal of Personality and Social Psychology, 58,* 330–341.

Davis, K. E. (1985, February). Near and dear: Friendship and love compared. *Psychology Today,* pp. 22–29.

Davison, G. C., & Neale, J. M. (1994). *Abnormal psychology* (6th ed.). New York: Wiley.

Dawkins, M. S. (1990). From an animal's point of view. *Behavioral and Brain Sciences, 13,* 1–8.

DeFour, D. C., & Paludi, M. (1991, August). *Ethnicity, sex, and sexual harassment.* Paper presented at the meeting of the American Psychological Association, San Francisco.

de Jong-Gierveld, J. (1987). Developing and testing a model of loneliness. *Journal of Personality and Social Psychology, 53,* 119–128.

Dement, W. (1993, January 12). The great American sleep debt: Commentary. *Washington Post,* p. WH9.

Denmark, F. L. (1994). Engendering psychology. *American Psychologist, 49,* 329–334.

Denmark, F. L., & Paludi, M. A. (Eds.). (1993). *Handbook on the psychology of women.* Westport, CT: Greenwood Press.

Denmark, F. L., Russo, N. F., Frieze, I. H., Sechzur, J. (1988). Guidelines for avoiding sexism in psychological research: A report of the Ad Hoc Committee on nonsexist research. *American Psychologist, 43,* 582–585.

Dennett, D. (1991). *Consciousness explained.* Boston: Little, Brown.

Denton, R. K. (1988). Lucidity, sex, and horror in Senoi dreamwork. In J. Gackenbach & S. P. LaBerge (Eds.), *Conscious mind, sleeping brain: Perspectives on lucid dreaming.* New York: Plenum.

DePaulo, B. M. (1994). Spotting lies: Can humans learn to do better? *Current Directions in Psychological Science, 3,* 83–86.

Depression/Awareness, Recognition, and Treatment (D/ART) Publication Series. (1987). *Sex differences in depressive disorders.* Washington, DC: U.S. Dept. of Health and Human Services, NIMH.

Deregowski, J. (1980). *Illusions, patterns, and pictures: A cross-cultural perspective.* London: Academic Press.

Deregowski, J. B. (1970). Effect of cultural value of time upon recall. *British Journal of Social and Clinical Psychology, 9,* 37–41.

Derlega, V. J., Metts, S., Petronio, S., & Marguilis, S. T. (1994). *Self-disclosure.* Newbury Park, CA: Sage.

Derlega, V. J., Winstead, B. A., Wong, P. T. P., & Hunter, S. (1985). Gender effects in an initial encounter: A case where men exceed women in self-disclosure. *Journal of Social and Personal Relationships, 2,* 25–44.

Deutsch, F. M. (1991). Women's lives: The story not told by theories of development. *Contemporary Psychology, 36,* 237–238.

Deutsch, J. A., & Gonzales, M. F. (1980). Gastric nutrient content signals satiety. *Behavioral and Neural Biology, 30,* 113–116.

Deutsch, M. (Ed.). (1967). *The disadvantaged child: Selected papers of Martin Deutsch and his associates.* New York: Basic Books.

Deutsch, M., & Collins, M. (1951). *Interracial housing: A psychological evaluation of a social experiment.* Minneapolis: University of Minnesota Press.

Dewey, J. (1933). *How we think: A restatement of the relation of reflective thinking to the educative process.* Lexington, MA: D. C. Heath.

Diamond, E. E. (1988). Women's occupational plans and decisions: An introduction. *Applied Psychology: An International Review, 37,* 97–102.

Diaz, R. M. (1983). Thought and two languages: The impact of bilingualism on cognitive development. *Review of Research in Education, 10,* 23–54.

DiBiase, R. (1993, March). *Attachment, temperament, and ego development in adolescence.* Paper presented at the biennial meeting of the Society for Research in Child Development, New Orleans.

Dickerscheid, J. D., Schwarz, P. M., Noir, S., & El-Taliawy, T. (1988). Gender concept development of preschool-aged children in the United States and Egypt. *Sex Roles, 18,* 669–677.

Dickinson, A. (1989). The expectancy theory of animal conditioning. In S. B. Klein & R. R. Mowrer (Eds.), *Pavlovian conditioning and the status of traditional learning theory.* Hillsdale, NJ: Erlbaum.

Dickson, G. L. (1990). A feminist post-structuralist analysis of the knowledge of menopause. *Advances in Nursing Science, 12,* 15–31.

Diener, E. (1984). Subjective well-being. *Psychological Bulletin, 95,* 542–575.

Dietz, W. (1986, March). *Comments at the workshop on childhood obesity.* Washington, DC: National Institutes of Health.

DiGiulio, R. C. (1989). *Beyond widowhood.* New York: Free Press.

Dillbeck, M. C., & Orme-Johnson, D. W. (1987). Physiological differences between transcendental meditation and rest. *American Psychologist, 42,* 879–881.

DiNicola, D. D., & DiMatteo, M. R. (1984). Practitioners, patients, and compliance with medical regimens: A social psychological perspective. In A. Baum, S. E. Taylor, & J. E. Singer (Eds.), *Handbook of psychology and health* (Vol. 4). Hillsdale, NJ: Erlbaum.

Dixon, R. A., & Backman, L. (1995). Concept of compensation. In R. A. Dixon & L. Backman (Eds.), *Compensating for psychological deficits and declines.* Hillsdale, NJ: Erlbaum.

Dohrenwend, B. S., & Shrout, P. E. (1985). "Hassles" in the conceptualization and measurement of life stress variables. *American Psychologist, 40,* 780–785.

Dolcini, M. M., Coates, T. J., Catania, J. A., Kegeles, S. M., & Hauck, W. W. (1995). Multiple sex partners and their psychosocial correlates: The population-based AIDS in Multiethnic Neighborhoods (AMEN) study. *Health Psychology, 14,* 22–31.

Dollard, J., & Miller, N. (1950). *Personality and psychotherapy.* New York: McGraw-Hill.

Dolnick, E. (1988, December). The right (left) stuff. *Omni,* p. 45.

Donnerstein, E. (1980). Aggressive erotica and violence against women. *Journal of Personality and Social Psychology, 39,* 269–277.

Donnerstein, E. (1987, May). *Pornography, sex, and violence.* Invited presentation, University of Texas at Dallas.

Dorn, L. D., & Lucas, F. L. (1995, March). *Do hormone-behavior relations vary depending upon the endocrine and psychological status of the adolescent?* Paper presented at the meeting of the Society for Research in Child Development, Indianapolis, IN.

Dovidio, J. F., & Gaertner, S. L. (Eds.). (1986). *Prejudice, discrimination, and racism.* San Diego, CA: Academic Press.

Dow-Edwards, D. L. (1995). Developmental toxicity of cocaine. In M. Lewis & M. Bendersky (Eds.), *Mothers, babies, and cocaine.* Hillsdale, NJ: Erlbaum.

Draguns, J. G. (1990). Applications of cross-cultural psychology in the field of mental health. In R. W. Brislin (Ed.), *Applied cross-cultural psychology.* Newbury Park, CA: Sage.

Draper, T. W., Larsen, J. M., Haupt, J. H., Robinson, C. C., & Hart, C. (1993, March). *Family emotional climate as a mediating variable between parent education and child social competence in an advantaged subculture.* Paper presented at the biennial meeting of the Society for Research in Child Development, New Orleans.

Dreyer, P. H. (1982). Sexuality during adolescence. In B. B. Wolman (Ed.), *Handbook of developmental psychology.* Englewood Cliffs, NJ: Prentice Hall.

Driscoll, J. W., & Bateson, P. (1988). Animals in behavioral research. *Animal Behavior, 36,* 1569–1574.

Dryden, W., & Trower, P. (Eds.). (1989). *Cognitive psychotherapy.* New York: Springer.

Duncan, G. J. (1993, March). *Economic deprivation and child development.* Paper presented at the biennial meeting of the Society for Research in Child Development, New Orleans.

Dutton, D., & Aron, A. (1974). Some evidence for heightened sexual attraction under conditions of high anxiety. *Journal of Personality and Social Psychology, 30,* 510–517.

Dutton-Douglas, M., & Walker, L. (Eds.). (1988). *Feminist psychotherapies: Integrations of therapeutic and feminist systems.* Norwood, NJ: Ablex.

Eagly, A. H., & Crowley, M. (1986). Gender and helping behavior: A meta-analytic review of the social psychological literature. *Psychological Bulletin, 100,* 283–308.

Ebata, A. T., & Moos, R. H. (1989, April). *Coping and adjustment in four groups of adolescents.* Paper presented at the biennial meeting of the Society for Research in Child Development, Kansas City.

Eccles, J. S. (1987). Gender roles and achievement patterns: An expectancy value perspective. In J. M. Reinisch, L. A. Rosenblum, & S. A. Sanders (Eds.), *Masculinity/femininity: Basic perspectives.* New York: Oxford University Press.

Eckert, E. D., Heston, L. L., & Bouchard, T. J. (1981). MZ twins reared apart. Preliminary findings of psychiatric disturbances and trait. In L. Gedda, P. Paris, & W. D. Nance (Eds.), *Twin Research* (Vol. 1). New York: Alan Liss.

Edelman, M. W. (1992). *The measure of our success: A letter to my children and yours.* Boston: Beacon Press.

Edelman, M. W. (1995). *The state of America's children.* Washington, DC: Children's Defense Fund.

Eden, D., & Aviram, A. (in press). Self-efficacy training to speed reemployment: Helping people to help themselves. *Journal of Applied Psychology.*

Educational Testing Service. (1992, February). *Cross-national comparisons of 9–13 year olds' science and math achievement.* Princeton, NJ: Educational Testing Service.

Edwards, B. (1979). *Drawing on the right side of the brain.* Los Angeles: Tarcher.

Efron, R. (in press). *The decline and fall of hemispheric specialization.* Hillsdale, NJ: Erlbaum.

Ehrhardt, A. A. (1987). A transactional perspective on the development of gender differences. In J. M. Reinisch, L. A. Rosenblum, & S. A. Sanders (Eds.), *Masculinity/femininity: Basic perspectives.* New York: Oxford University Press.

Eich, E. (1990, June). *Searching for mood dependent memory.* Paper presented at the meeting of the American Psychological Society, Dallas.

Eichorn, D. H., Clausen, J. A., Haan, N., Honzik, M. P., & Mussen, P. H. (Eds.). (1981). *Present and past in middle life.* New York: Academic Press.

Eisenberg, A., Murkoff, H., & Hathaway, S. (1988). *What to expect when you're expecting* (2nd ed.). New York: Workman.

Ekman, P. (1980). *The face of man.* New York: Garland STPM.

Ekman, P. (1985). *Telling lies: Clues to deceit in the marketplace, politics, and marriage.* New York: W. W. Norton.

Ekman, P. (1993). Facial expressions and emotion. *American Psychologist, 48,* 384–392.

Ekman, P., & Friesen, W. (1974). Detecting deception from the body or face. *Journal of Personality and Social Psychology, 29,* 288–298.

Ekman, P., & Friesen, W. V. (1968). The repertoire of nonverbal behavior—Categories, origins, usage and coding. *Semiotica, 1,* 49–98.

Ekman, P., & Friesen, W. V. (1971). Constants across cultures in the face and emotion. *Journal of Personality and Social Psychology, 17,* 124–129.

Ekman, P., & Sullivan, M. (1991). Who can catch a liar? *American Psychologist, 46,* 913–920.

Ekman, P., Levenson, R. W., & Friesen, W. V. (1983). Autonomic nervous system activity distinguishes among emotions. *Science, 221,* 1208–1210.

Elkind, D. (1978). Understanding the young adolescent. *Adolescence, 13,* 127–134.

Elkind, D. (1981). *The hurried child.* Reading, MA: Addison-Wesley.

Ellis, A. (1962). *Reason and emotion in psychotherapy.* New York: Lyle Stuart.

Ellis, A. (1993). Reflections on rational-emotive therapy. *Journal of Consulting and Clinical Psychology, 61,* 199–201.

Ellis, A., & Velton, E. (1992). *When AA doesn't work for you: Rational steps to quitting alcohol.* Fort Lee, NJ: Barricade Books.

Ellis, H. C. (1987). Recent developments in human memory. In V. P. Makosky (Ed.), *The G. Stanley Hall Lecture Series.* Washington, DC: American Psychological Association.

Ellis, H. C., Thomas, R. L., & Rodriguez, I. A. (1984). Emotional mood states and memory: Elaborative encoding, semantic processing, and cognitive effort. *Journal of Experimental Psychology: Learning, Memory, and Cognition, 10,* 470–482.

Ellis, L., & Ames, M. A. (1987). Neurohormonal functioning and sexual orientation: A theory of homosexuality-heterosexuality. *Psychological Bulletin, 101,* 233–258.

Emmons, R. A. (in press). Motives and life goals. In S. Briggs, R. Hogan, & W. Jones (Eds.), *Handbook of personality psychology.* Orlando: Academic Press.

Engel, J. W. (1984). Marriage in the People's Republic of China: Analysis of a new law. *Journal of Marriage and the Family, 46,* 947–954.

Engler, J., & Goleman, D. (1992). *The consumer's guide to psychotherapy.* New York: Simon & Schuster.

Ennis, R. H. (1991). Critical thinking: Literature review and needed research. In L. Idol & B. F. Jones (Eds.), *Educational values and cognitive instruction.* Hillsdale, NJ: Erlbaum.

Entwisle, D. R., & Astone, N. M. (1995, March). *Some practical guidelines for measuring children's SES, race, and ethnicity.* Paper presented at the meeting of the Society for Research in Child Development, Indianapolis, IN.

Eppley, K. R., Abrams, A. I., & Shear, J. (1989). Differential effects of relaxation effects on trait anxiety: A meta-analysis. *Journal of Clinical Psychology, 45,* 957–974.

Epstein, C. F. (1987). Multiple demands and multiple roles: The conditions of successful management. In F. J. Crosby (Ed.), *Spouse, parent, worker: On gender and multiple roles.* New Haven, CT: Yale University Press.

Erikson, E. H. (1950). *Childhood and society.* New York: W. W. Norton.

Erikson, E. H. (1968). *Identity: Youth and crisis.* New York: W. W. Norton.

Espin, O. M. (1993). Psychological impact of migration on Latinos. In D. R. Atkinson, G. Morten, & D. W. Sue (Eds.), *Counseling American minorities.* Dubuque, IA: Brown & Benchmark.

Essed, P. (1992). *Understanding everyday racism.* Newbury Park, CA: Sage.

Evans, B. J., & Whitfield, J. R. (Eds.). (1988). *Black males in the United States: An annotated bibliography from 1967 to 1987.* Washington, DC: American Psychological Association.

Evans, I. M., Cicchelli, T., Cohen, M., & Shapiro, N. (1995). *Staying in school.* Baltimore, MD: Paul Brookes.

Evans, P. (1989). *Motivation and emotion.* New York: Routledge.

Evans, T. (1992). *Mentors.* Princeton, NJ: Peterson's Guides.

Exner, J. E., & Weiner, I. B. (1995). *The Rorschach, Vol. 3.* New York: Wiley.

Eye of the storm. (1970). Reissued as *A class divided.* (1985). Frontline. Washington, DC: PBS Video.

Eyler, F. D., Behnke, M. L., & Stewart, N. J. (1990). *Issues in identification and follow-up of cocaine-exposed neonates.* Unpublished manuscript, Department of Psychology, University of Florida, Gainesville, FL.

Eysenck, H. J. (1952). The effects of psychotherapy: An evaluation. *Journal of Consulting Psychology, 16,* 319–324.

Eysenck, H. J. (1967). *The biological basis of personality.* Springfield, IL: Charles C Thomas.

Fairburn, C. G. (1995). *Overcoming binge eating.* New York: Guilford.

Falco, M. (1992). *The making of a drug-free America.* New York: Times Books.

Fanselow, M. S., DeCola, J. P., & Young, S. L. (1993). Mechanisms responsible for reduced contextual conditioning with massed unsignaled unconditioned stimuli. *Journal of Experimental Psychology: Animal Processes, 19,* 121–137.

Farley, J. E. (1990). *Sociology.* Englewood Cliffs, NJ: Prentice Hall.

Fasick, F. A. (1988). Patterns of formal education in high school as rites of passage. *Adolescence, 23,* 457–468.

Faulkner, L. R., McFarland, B. H., & Bloom, J. D. (1989). An empirical study of emergency commitment. *American Journal of Psychiatry, 146,* 182–186.

Fausto-Sterling, A., & Balaban, E. (1993). Genetics and male sexual orientation. *Science, 261,* 1257.

Feiring, C., & Lewis, M. (1969). Sex and age differences in young children's reactions to frustration: A further look at the Goldberg and Lewis subjects. *Child Development, 50,* 848–853.

Feldman, D. H., & Piirto, J. (1995). Parenting talented children. In M. H. Bornstein (Ed.), *Handbook of parenting*, Vol. 1. Hillsdale, NJ: Erlbaum.

Ferguson, C. A. (1977). Baby talk as a simplified register. In C. E. Snow & C. A. Ferguson (Eds.), *Talking to children*. New York: Cambridge University Press.

Ferguson, D. M., Harwood, L. J., & Shannon, F. T. (1987). Breast feeding and subsequent social adjustment in six to eight year old children. *Journal of Child Psychology and Psychiatry, 28,* 378–386.

Fernea, E., & Fernea, R. (1994). Cleanliness and culture. In W. J. Lonner & R. Malpass (Eds.), *Psychology and culture*. Needham Heights, MA: Allyn & Bacon.

Feshbach, S., & Wiener, B. (1991). *Personality* (3rd ed.). Lexington, MA: Heath.

Festinger, L. (1957). *A theory of cognitive dissonance*. Evanston, IL: Row Peterson.

Field, T. (1995). Cocaine exposure and intervention in early development. In M. Lewis & M. Bendersky (Eds.), *Mothers, babies, and cocaine*. Hillsdale, NJ: Erlbaum.

Fine, T. H., & Turner, J. W. (1987). *Proceedings of the Second International Conference on REST*. Toledo, OH: IRIS.

First, M. B., Frances, A., & Pincus, H. A. (1995). *DSM-IV handbook for differential diagnosis*. Washington, DC: American Psychiatric Press.

Fischer, J., & Gochros, H. L. (1975). *Planned behavior change*. New York: Free Press.

Fivush, R. (1995, March). *The development of narrative remembering: Implications for the recovered memory debate*. Paper presented at the meeting of the Society for Research in Child Development, Indianapolis, IN.

Flaskerud, J. (1984). A comparison of perceptions of problematic behavior by six minority groups and mental health professionals. *Nursing Research, 33,* 190–228.

Flavell, J. H. (1985). *Cognitive development* (2nd ed.). Englewood Cliffs, NJ: Prentice Hall.

Flynn, B. S., Worden, J. K., Secker-Walker, R. H., Badger, G. J., & Geller, B. M. (1995). Cigarette smoking prevention effects of mass media and school interventions targeted to gender and age groups. *Journal of Health Education, 26,* S-45–S-51.

Foa, E. B., Steketze, G., & Young, M. C. (1984). Agoraphobia. *Clinical Psychology Review, 4,* 431–457.

Foley, V. (1975). Family therapy with Black disadvantaged families: Some observations on roles, communications, and techniques. *Journal of Marriage and Family Counseling, 1,* 29–38.

Folkman, S., & Lazarus, R. S. (1980). An analysis of coping in a middle-aged community sample. *Journal of Health and Social Behavior, 21,* 219–239.

Foner, N. (1984). *Ages in conflict*. New York: Columbia University Press.

Fonnebo, V. (1985). The Tormso heart study: Coronary risk factors in Seventh-Day Adventists. *American Journal of Epidemiology, 112,* 789–793.

Ford, C., & Beach, F. (1951). *Patterns of sexual behavior*. New York: Harper.

Fowler, C. A., Wolford, G., Slade, R., & Tassinary, L. (1981). Lexical access with and without awareness. *Journal of Experimental Psychology: General, 110,* 341–362.

Fox, R. E. (1995). The rape of psychotherapy. *Professional Psychology, 26,* 147–155.

Frager, R. (1970). Conformity and anti-conformity in Japan. *Journal of Personality and Social Psychology, 15,* 203–210.

Frances, A., First, M. B., & Pincus, H. A. (1995). *DSM-IV guidebook*. Washington, DC: American Psychiatric Press.

Frances, A. J., Pincus, H. A., & Widiger, T. A. (in press). DSM-IV and international communication in psychiatric diagnosis. In Y. Honda, M. Kastrup, & J. E. Mezzich (Eds.), *Psychiatric diagnosis: A world perspective*. New York: Springer.

Frank, E., & Kupfer, D. J. (1986). Psychotherapeutic approaches to treatment of recurrent unipolar depression: Work in progress. *Psychopharmacology Bulletin, 22,* 558–565.

Frank, J. D. (1982). Therapeutic components shared by all psychotherapies. In J. H. Harvey & M. M. Parks (Eds.), *Psychotherapy research and behavior change*. Washington, DC: American Psychological Association.

Franken, L. E. (1994). *Human motivation* (3rd ed.). Pacific Grove, CA: Brooks/Cole.

Frankl, V. (1984). *Man's search for meaning*. New York: Pocket Books.

Fraser, S. (Ed.). (1995). *The bell curve wars: Race, intelligence, and the future of America*. New York: Basic Books.

Fredman, L., Daly, M. P., & Lazur, A. M. (1995). Burden among White and Black caregivers to elderly adults. *Journal of Gerontology, 50B,* S110–S118.

Freeman, D. (1983). *Margaret Mead and Samoa*. Cambridge, MA: Harvard University Press.

Freud, S. (1900/1953). The interpretation of dreams. In J. Strachey (Ed.), *The standard edition of the complete psychological works of Sigmund Freud*. London: Hogarth Press.

Freud, S. (1917). *A general introduction to psychoanalysis*. New York: Washington Square Press.

Friedman, M., & Rosenman, R. (1974). *Type A behavior and your heart*. New York: Knopf.

Friedman, M. A., & Brownell, K. D. (1995). Psychological correlates of obesity: Moving to the next generation of research. *Psychological Bulletin, 117,* 3–20.

Frieze, I. H. (1995). Editorial review. *Psychology of Women Quarterly, 19,* 153–159.

Fromm, E. (1947). *Man for himself*. New York: Holt Rinehart.

Fuhrman, A., & Burlingame, G. M. (1995). *Handbook of group psychotherapy*. New York: Wiley.

Furth, H. G., & Wachs, H. (1975). *Thinking goes to school*. New York: Oxford University Press.

Furumoto, L. (1989). The new history of psychology. In I. S. Cohen (Ed.), *The G. Stanley Hall lecture series* (Vol. 9). Washington, DC: American Psychological Association.

Furumoto, L., & Scarborough, E. (1986). Placing women in the history of psychology. *American Psychologist, 41,* 35–42.

Gagnon, J. H., & Simon, W. (1973). *Sexual conduct*. Chicago: Aldine.

Gaines, S. O., & Reed, E. S. (1995). Prejudice: From Allport to Dubois. *American Psychologist, 50,* 96–103.

Gallup, G. (1984, August–September). *Gallup Report*, Nos. 228–229, 2–9.

Gallup Report. (1987). *Legalized gay relations*. Gallup Report No. 254, p. 25.

Gannon, L., Luchetta, T., Rhodes, K., Pardie, L., & Segrist, D. (1992). Sex bias in psychological

research: Progress or complacency? *American Psychologist, 47,* 389–396.

Garbarino, J. (1985). *Adolescent development: An ecological perspective*. Columbus, OH: Merrill.

Garbarino, J., & Kostelny, K. (1995). Parenting and public policy. In M. H. Bornstein (Ed.), *Handbook of parenting, Vol. 3*. Hillsdale, NJ: Erlbaum.

Garcia, C. T., Coll, E. C., Meyer, E. C., & Brillon, L. (1995). Ethnic and minority parenting. In M. H. Bornstein (Ed.), *Handbook of parenting, Vol. 2*. Hillsdale, NJ: Erlbaum.

Gardner, B. T., & Gardner, R. A. (1971). Two-way communication with an infant chimpanzee. In A. Schrier & F. Stollnitz (Eds.), *Behavior of nonhuman primates* (Vol. 4). New York: Academic Press.

Gardner, H. (1983). *Frames of mind*. New York: Basic Books.

Gardner, H. (1993). *Creating minds*. New York: Basic Books.

Gardner, L. I., Stern, M. P., Haffner, S. M., Gaskill, S. P., Hazuda, H. P., Relethford, J. H., & Eifter, C. W. (1984). Prevalence of diabetes in Mexican Americans: Relationships to percent of gene pool derived from Native American sources. *Diabetes, 33,* 86–92.

Garfein, A. J., & Herzog, A. R. (1995). Robust aging among the young-old, old-old, and oldest-old. *Journal of Gerontology, 50B,* S77–S87.

Garfield, S. L. (1995). *Psychotherapy* (2nd ed.). New York: Wiley.

Garrett, P., Ng'andu, N., & Ferron, J. (1994). Poverty experiences of young children and the quality of their home environment. *Child Development, 65,* 331–345.

Garrick, T. R., & Lowenstein, R. J. (1989). Behavioral medicine in the general hospital. *Psychosomatics, 30,* 123–134.

Garrod, A., Smulyan, L., Powers, S., & Kilkenny, R. (1995). *Adolescent portraits*. Needham Heights, MA: Allyn & Bacon.

Garwood, S. G., Phillips, D., Hartman, A., & Zigler, E. F. (1989). As the pendulum swings: Federal agency programs for children. *American Psychologist, 44,* 434–440.

Gathercole, S., & Baddeley, A. D. (1989). Development of vocabulary in children and short-term phonological memory. *Journal of Memory and Language, 28,* 200–213.

Gazzaniga, M. S. (1986). *The social brain*. New York: Plenum.

Gerlach, J. (1991). Introduction: Women, education, and aging. *Educational Gerontology, 17,* iii.

Geschwind, N., & Behan, P. (1982). Left-handedness: Association with immune disease, migraine, and developmental learning disorder. *Proceedings of the National Academy of Sciences, 79,* 5097–5100.

Gibbons, F. X., & McCoy, S. B. (1991). Self-esteem, similarity, and reactions to active versus passive downward comparison. *Journal of Personality and Social Psychology, 60,* 414–424.

Gibbs, J. T., & Huang, L. N. (Eds.). (1989). *Children of color*. San Francisco: Jossey-Bass.

Gibbs, N. (1990, Fall). The dreams of youth. *Time* [Special Issue], pp. 10–14.

Gibson, E. J., & Walk, R. D. (1960). The "visual cliff." *Scientific American, 202,* 64–71.

Gibson, J. J. (1966). *The senses considered as perceptual systems*. Boston: Houghton Mifflin.

Gidycz, C. A., Hanson, K., & Layman, M. J. (1995). A prospective analysis of the relationships among sexual assault experiences. *Psychology of Women Quarterly, 19,* 5–29.

Gilligan, C. (1982). *The different voice.* Cambridge, MA: Harvard University Press.

Gilligan, C. (1990). Teaching Shakespeare's sister. In C. Gilligan, N. Lyons, and T. Hanmer (Eds.), *Making connections: The relational worlds of adolescent girls at Emma Willard School.* Cambridge, MA: Harvard University Press.

Gilligan, C. (1992, May). *Joining the resistance: Girls' development in adolescence.* Paper presented at the symposium on development and vulnerability in close relationships, Montreal.

Gilmore, D. O. (1990). *Manhood in the making.* New Haven, CT: Yale University Press.

Gim, R. H., Atkinson, D. R., & Kim, S. J. (1991). Asian-American acculturation, counselor ethnicity and cultural sensitivity, and ratings of counselors. *Journal of Counseling Psychology, 38,* 57–62.

Gjerde, P. (1985, April). *Adolescent depression and parental socialization patterns. A prospective study.* Paper presented at the biennial meeting of the Society for Research in Child Development, Toronto.

Gladue, B. A. (1994). The biopsychology of sexual orientation. *Current Directions in Psychological Science, 3,* 150–154.

Glick, J. (1975). Cognitive development in cross-cultural perspective. In F. Horowitz (Ed.), *Review of child development research* (Vol. 4). Chicago: University of Chicago Press.

Glisky, E. L., & Schacter, D. L. (1987). Acquisition of domain-specific knowledge in organic amnesia: Training for computer-related work. *Neuropsychologica, 25,* 893–906.

Godden, D. R., & Baddeley, A. D. (1975). Context-dependent memory in two natural environments: On land and under water. *British Journal of Psychology, 66,* 325–331.

Goldberg, H. (1980). *The new male.* New York: Signet.

Goldberg, S., & Lewis, M. (1969). Play behavior in the year-old infant: Early sex differences. *Child Development, 40,* 21–31.

Goldberg, T. E., Berman, K. F., & Weinberger, D. R. (1995). Neuropsychology and neurophysiology of schizophrenia. *Current Opinion in Psychiatry, 8,* 34–40.

Goldberger, L., & Breznitz, S. (1993). *Handbook of stress.* New York: Free Press.

Goldstein, B. (1994, January). *Touching students' lives through interactive teaching of psychology of gender.* Paper presented at the sixteenth annual National Institute on the Teaching of Psychology, St. Petersburg, FL.

Goldstein, E. B. (1989). *Sensation and perception* (3rd ed.). Belmont, CA: Wadsworth.

Goldstein, E. B. (1994). *Sensation and perception* (4th ed.). Belmont, CA: Wadsworth.

Goldstein, I. R., & Gilliam, P. (1990). Training system issues in the year 2000. *American Psychologist, 45,* 134–143.

Goldstein, M. J. (1986, August). *Psychosocial factors in the course and onset of schizophrenia.* Paper presented at the meeting of the American Psychological Association, Washington, DC.

Goldstein, M. J., & Palmer, J. O. (1975). *The experience of anxiety.* New York: Oxford University Press.

Good, G. E., Robertson, J. M., O'Neil, J. M., Fitzgerald, L. F., Sevens, M., DeBord, K. A., Bartels, K. M., & Braverman, D. G. (1995). Male gender role conflict. *Journal of Counseling Psychology, 42,* 3–10.

Goodall, J. (1990). *Through a window: My thirty years with the chimpanzees in the Gombe.* Boston: Houghton Mifflin.

Goodchilds, J. D., & Zellman, G. L. (1984). Sexual signaling and sexual aggression in adolescent relationships. In N. M. Malamuth & E. D. Donnerstein (Eds.), *Pornography and sexual aggression.* New York: Academic Press.

Goodstein, L. D., & Calhoun, J. F. (1982). *Understanding abnormal behavior.* Reading, MA: Addison-Wesley.

Goodwin, D. W. (1988). *Is alcoholism hereditary?* (2nd ed.). New York: Ballantine.

Gorman, J. M., Liebowitz, M. R., Fyer, A. J., & Stein, J. (1989). A neuroanatomical hypothesis for panic disorder. *American Journal of Psychiatry, 146,* 148–161.

Gottesman, I. I. (1989). Vital statistics, demography, and schizophrenia. *Schizophrenia Bulletin, 15,* 5–8.

Gottesman, I. I., & Shields, J. (1982). *The schizophrenic puzzle.* New York: Cambridge University Press.

Gottfried, A. E., Gottfried, A. W., & Bathurst, K. (1995). Maternal and dual-earner employment status and parenting. In M. H. Bornstein (Ed.), *Handbook of parenting, Vol. 2.* Hillsdale, NJ: Erlbaum.

Gould, M., Wunsch-Hitzig, R., & Dohrenwend, B. S. (1981). Estimating the prevalence of childhood psychopathology. *Journal of American Academy of Child Psychiatry, 20,* 162–176.

Gould, S. J. (1981). *The mismeasure of man.* New York: W. W. Norton.

Gould-Martin, K., & Ngin, C. (1981). Chinese Americans. In A. Harwood (Ed.), *Ethnicity and medical care.* Cambridge, MA: Harvard University Press.

Graham, S. (1986, August). *Can attribution theory tell us something about motivation in Blacks?* Paper presented at the meeting of the American Psychological Association, Washington, DC.

Graham, S. (1987, August). *Developing relations between attributions, affect, and intended social behavior.* Paper presented at the meeting of the American Psychological Association, New York.

Graham, S. (1990). Motivation in Afro-Americans. In G. L. Berry & J. K. Asamen (Eds.), *Black students: Psychosocial issues and academic achievement.* Newbury Park, CA: Sage.

Graham, S. (1992). Most of the subjects were White and middle class. *American Psychologist, 47,* 629–639.

Grant, J. P. (1994). *The state of the world's children.* New York: UNICEF.

Gray, C. R., & Gummerman, K. (1975). The enigmatic eidetic image: A critical examination of methods, data, and theories. *Psychological Bulletin, 82,* 383–407.

Green, P. (1995, March). *Sesame Street: More than a television show.* Paper presented at the meeting of the Society for Research in Child Development, Indianapolis, IN.

Greenwald, A. G., & Banaji, M. R. (1995). Implicit social cognition: Attitudes, self-esteem, and stereotypes. *Psychological Review, 102,* 4–27.

Gregory, R. (1992). *Psychological testing.* Needham Heights, MA: Allyn & Bacon.

Gregory, R. L. (1978). *Eye and brain: The psychology of seeing* (3rd ed.). New York: McGraw-Hill.

Grevious, C. (1985). The role of the family therapist with low-income Black families. *Family Therapy, 12,* 115–122.

Grush, J. E. (1980). Impact of candidate expenditures, regionality, and prior outcomes on the 1976 Democratic presidential primaries. *Journal of Personality and Social Psychology, 38,* 337–347.

Gruys, A. (1993, March). *Security of attachment and its relation to quantitative and qualitative aspects of friendship.* Paper presented at the biennial meeting of the Society for Research in Child Development, New Orleans.

Guilford, J. P. (1967). *The structure of intellect.* New York: McGraw-Hill.

Gullotta, T. P., Adams, G. R., & Montemayor, R. (Eds.). (1995). *Substance abuse in adolescence.* Newbury Park, CA: Sage.

Gur, R. C., Mozley, L. H., Mozley, P. D., Resnick, S. M., Karp, J. S., Alavi, A., Arnold, S. E., & Gur, R. E. (1995). Sex differences in regional cerebral glucose metabolism during a resting state. *Science, 267,* 528–531.

Guthrie, R. (1976). *Even the rat was white: A historical view of psychology.* New York: Harper & Row.

Guttman, N., & Kalish, H. I. (1956). Discriminability and stimulus generalization. *Journal of Experimental Psychology, 51,* 79–88.

Hahn, A. (1987, December). Reaching out to America's dropouts: What to do? *Phi Delta Kappan,* pp. 256–263.

Hall, C. C. I., Evans, B. J., & Selice, S. (Eds.). (1989). *Black females in the United States.* Washington, DC: American Psychological Association.

Hall, G. S. (1904). *Adolescence* (Vols. 1 & 2). Englewood Cliffs, NJ: Prentice Hall.

Hallam, S. C., Arnold, H. M., & Miller, R. R. (1990, March). *Blocking of a Pavlovian conditioned inhibitor.* Paper presented at the meeting of the Eastern Psychological Association, Philadelphia, PA.

Halmi, D. (1980). Gastric bypass for massive obesity. In A. J. Stunkard (Ed.), *Obesity.* Philadelphia: Saunders.

Halonen, J. (1995). Demystifying critical thinking. *Teaching of Psychology, 22,* 75–81.

Hamer, D. H., Hu, S., Magnuson, V. L., Hu, N., & Pattatucci, A. M. L. (1993). A linkage between DNA markers on the X chromosome and male sexual orientation. *Science, 261,* 321–327.

Hansell, S. (1991). The meaning of stress. *Contemporary Psychology, 36,* 112–114.

Hanson, D. J. (1993). Current issues and advances in social-skills assessment and intervention with children and adolescents. *Behavior Modification, 17,* 227–228.

Harkness, S., & Super, C. M. (1995). Culture and parenting. In M. H. Bornstein (Ed.), *Handbook of parenting, Vol. 2.* Hillsdale, NJ: Erlbaum.

Harlow, H. F., & Zimmerman, R. R. (1959). Affectional responses in the infant monkey. *Science, 130,* 421–432.

Harold, R. D., & Eccles, J. S. (1990, March). *Maternal expectations, advice, and provision of opportunities: Their relationships to boys'* and girls' occupational aspirations. Paper presented at the meeting of the Society for Research in Adolescence, Atlanta.

Harris, R. F., Wolf, N. M., & Baer, D. M. (1964). Effects of adult social reinforcement on child behavior. *Young Children, 20,* 8–17.

Harris, R. J., Schoen, L. M., & Hensley, D. L., (1992). A cross-cultural study of story memory. *Journal of Cross-Cultural Psychology, 23,* 133–147.

Harrison, C. A. (1991). Older women in our society: America's silent, invisible majority *Educational Gerontology, 17,* 111–122.

Harter, S. (1990). Self and identity development. In S. S. Feldman & G. R. Elliott (Eds.), *At the threshold: The developing adolescent.* Cambridge, MA: Harvard University Press.

Harter, S., & Marold, D. B. (1992). Psychological risk factors contributing to adolescent suicide ideation. In G. Noam & S. Borst (Eds.), *Child and adolescent suicide.* San Francisco: Jossey Bass.

Harvey, J. H. (1995). *Odyssey of the heart.* New York: W. H. Freeman.

Hasher, L., & Zacks, R. T. (1979). Automatic and effortful processes in memory. *Journal of Experimental Psychology: General, 108,* 356–388.

Hatcher, R., & others. (1988). *Contraceptive technology, 1988–1989* (14th ed.). New York: Irvington.

Hatfield, E., & Sprecher, S. (1986). *Mirror, mirror . . . : The importance of looks in everyday life.* Albany: State University of New York Press.

Hatvany, N., & Pucik, V. (1981). An integrated management system: Lessons from the Japanese experience. *Academy of Management Review, 6,* 469–480.

Hayflick, L. (1975, September). Why grow old? *Stanford Magazine,* pp. 36–43.

Hayflick, L. (1977). The cellular basis for biological aging. In C. E. Finch & L. Hayflick (Eds.), *Handbook of the biology of aging.* New York: Van Nostrand.

Haynes, G. S., & Feinleib, M. (1980). Women, work and coronary heart disease: Prospective findings from the Framingham Heart Study. *American Journal of Public Health, 70,* 130–141.

Heath, S. B. (1989). Oral and literate traditions among Black Americans living in poverty. *American Psychologist, 44,* 367–373.

Heath, S. B. (in press). The children of Trackton's children: Spoken and written language in social change. In J. Stigler, G. Herdt, & R. A. Schweder (Eds.), *Cultural psychology: The Chicago symposia.* New York: Cambridge University Press.

Hechinger, F. (1992). *Fateful choices.* New York: Hill & Wang.

Heider, F. (1958). *The psychology of interpersonal relations.* New York: Wiley.

Helgeson, V. S., & Sharpsteen, D. J. (1987). Perceptions of danger in achievement and affiliation situations: An extension of the Pollack and Gilligan versus Benton et al. debate. *Journal of Personality and Social Psychology, 53,* 727–733.

Hellige, J. B. (1990). Hemispheric asymmetry. *Annual Review of Psychology, 41.*

Helmreich, R. L. (1995). Culture shocks social psychology: Two views. *Contemporary Psychology, 40,* 108–109.

Helmstetter, S. (1986). *What to say when you talk to yourself.* New York: Pocket Books.

Henderson, V. L., & Dweck, C. S. (1990). Motivation and achievement. In S. S. Feldman & G. R. Elliott (Eds.), *At the threshold: The developing adolescent.* Cambridge, MA: Harvard University Press.

Hendrix, H. (1988). *Getting the love you want.* New York: Henry Holt.

Heppner, P. P. (1995). On gender role conflict in men. *Journal of Counseling Psychology, 42,* 20–23.

Hernandez, D. J. (1988). Demographic trends and the living arrangements of children. In E. M. Hetherington & J. D. Arasteh (Eds.), *Impact of divorce, single-parenting, and stepparenting on children.* Hillsdale, NJ: Erlbaum.

Hernandez, G. G. (1991). Not so benign neglect: Researchers ignore ethnicity in defining family caregiver burden and recommending services. *Gerontologist, 31,* 271.

Hernstein, R. J., & Murray, C. (1994). *The bell curve: Intelligence and class structure in modern life.* New York: Free Press.

Hershenson, M. (1989). The most puzzling illusion. In M. Hershenson (Ed.), *The moon:An anomaly of visual space.* Hillsdale, NJ: Erlbaum.

Hetherington, E. M. (1995, March). *The changing American family and the well-being of children.* Paper presented at the meeting of the Society for Research in Child Development, Indianapolis, IN.

Hetherington, E. M., & Stanley-Hagan, M. M. (1995). Parenting in divorced and remarried families. In M. H. Bornstein (Ed.), *Handbook of parenting, Vol. 3.* Hillsdale, NJ: Erlbaum.

Hiester, M., Carlson, E., & Sroufe, L. A. (1993, March). *The evolution of friendships in preschool, middle childhood, and adolescence: Origins in attachment history.* Paper presented at the biennial meeting of the Society for Research in Child Development, New Orleans.

Hilgard, E. R. (1965). *Hypnotic suggestibility.* New York: Harcourt Brace.

Hilgard, E. R. (1977). *Divided consciousness: Multiple controls in human thought and action.* New York: Wiley.

Hill, J. P., & Holmbeck, G. (1986). Attachment and autonomy in adolescence. In G. Whitehurst (Ed.), *Annals of child development.* Greenwich: JAI Press.

Himelein, M. J. (1995). Risk factors for sexual victimization in dating. *Psychology of Women Quarterly, 19,* 31–48.

Hinde, R. A. (1984). Why do the sexes behave differently in close relationships? *Journal of Social and Personal Relationships, 1,* 471–501.

Hinde, R. A. (1992). Commentary: Can biology explain human development? *Human Development, 35,* 34–39.

Hines, M. (1982). Prenatal gonadal hormones and sex differences in human behavior. *Psychological Bulletin, 92,* 56–80.

Hines, T. (1988). *Pseudoscience and the paranormal.* Buffalo, NY: Prometheus Books.

Hiraga, Y., Cauce, A. M., Mason, C., & Ordonez, N. (1993, March). *Ethnic identity and the social adjustment of biracial youth.* Paper presented at the biennial meeting of the Society for Research in Child Development, New Orleans.

Hirsch, E. D. (1987). *Cultural literacy: What every American needs to know.* Boston: Houghton Mifflin.

Ho, M. K. (1992). *Minority children and adolescents in therapy.* Newbury Park, CA: Sage.

Hobson, J. A. (1992). A new model of brain-mind state: Activation level, input source, and mode of processing. In J. S. Antrobus & M. Bertini (Eds.), *The neuropsychology of sleep and dreaming.* Hillsdale, NJ: Erlbaum.

Hoff-Ginsburg, E., & Tardif, T. (1995). Socioeconomic status and parenting. In M. H. Bornstein (Ed.), *Handbook of parenting, Vol. 1.* Hillsdale, NJ: Erlbaum.

Hoffereth, S. L. (1990). Trends in adolescent sexual activity, contraception, and pregnancy in the United States. In J. Bancroft & J. M. Reinisch (Eds.), *Adolescence and puberty.* New York: Oxford University Press.

Hofstede, G. (1980). *Culture's consequences: International differences in work-related values.* Newbury Park, CA: Sage.

Hogan, R. T. (1987, August). *Conceptions of personality and the prediction of job performance.* Paper presented at the meeting of the American Psychological Association, New York.

Hollingshead, A. B., & Redlich, F. C. (1958). *Social class and mental illness.* New York: Wiley.

Hollingworth, L. S. (1914). Functional periodicity: An experimental study of the mental and motor abilities of women during menstruation. *Teachers College Contributions to Education,* No. 69.

Hollingworth, L. S. (1918). Sex differences in mental traits. *Psychological Bulletin, 13,* 377–384.

Holmbeck, G. N., Paikoff, R. L., & Brooks-Gunn, J. (1995). Parenting adolescents. In M. H. Bornstein (Ed.), *Handbook of parenting, Vol. 1.* Hillsdale, NJ: Erlbaum.

Holmes, D. (1987). The influence of meditation versus rest on physiological arousal: A second examination. In M. A. West (Ed.), *The psychology of meditation.* Oxford, England: Clarendon Press.

Holmes, T. H., & Rahe, R. H. (1967). The social readjustment rating scale. *Journal of Psychosomatic Research, 11,* 213–218.

Holtzmann, W. (1982). Cross-cultural comparisons of personality development in Mexico and the United States. In D. Wagner & H. W. Stevenson (Eds.), *Cultural perspectives on child development.* San Francisco: W. H. Freeman.

Horm, J., & Anderson, K. (1993). Who in America is trying to lose weight? *Annals of Internal Medicine, 119,* 672–676.

Horney, K. (1945). *Our inner conflicts.* New York: Norton.

Howard, R. W. (1995). *Learning and memory.* Westport, CT: Praeger.

Howat, P. M., & Saxton, A. M. (1988). The incidence of bulimic behavior in a secondary and university school population. *Journal of Youth and Adolescence, 17,* 221–231.

Howe, C. J. (1993). *Language learning.* Hillsdale, NJ: Erlbaum.

Howe, M. L. (1995, March). *Early memory development and the emergence of autobiographical memory.* Paper presented at the meeting of the Society for Research in Child Development, Indianapolis, IN.

Hoyenga, K. B., & Hoyenga, K. T. (1984). *Motivational explanations of behavior: Evolutionary, physiological, and cognitive ideas.* Monterey, CA: Brooks/Cole.

Huang, L. N., & Gibbs, J. T. (1989). Future directions: Implications for research, training, and practice. In J. T. Gibbs & L. N. Huang (Eds.), *Children of color*. San Francisco: Jossey-Bass.

Hubel, D. H., & Wiesel, T. N. (1965). Receptive fields and functional architecture in two nonstriate visual areas (18 and 19) of the cat. *Journal of Neurophysiology, 28*, 229–289.

Hudson, W. (1960). Pictorial depth perception in subcultural groups in Africa. *Journal of Social Psychology, 52*, 183–208.

Hughes, M. (1995). *Bereavement and support: Healing in a group environment*. Bristol, PA: Taylor & Francis.

Hunt, M. (1974). *Sexual behavior in the 1970s*. Chicago: Playboy.

Hurtado, S., Dey, E. L., & Trevino, J. G. (1994). *Exclusion or self-segregation? Interaction across racial/ethnic groups on college campuses*. Paper presented at the American Educational Research Association annual meeting.

Hurvich, L. M., & Jameson, D. (1969). Human color perception. *American Scientist, 57*, 143–166.

Huston, A. (1995, August). *Children in poverty*. Paper presented at the meeting of the American Psychological Association, New York City.

Huston, A. C. (1983). Sex-typing. In P. H. Mussen (Ed.), *Handbook of child psychology* (4th ed., Vol. 4). New York: Wiley.

Huston, A. C., McLoyd, V. C., & Coll, C. G. (1994). Children and poverty: Issues in contemporary research. *Child Development, 65*, 275–282.

Hyde, J. S. (1981). How large are cognitive gender differences? A meta-analysis using W^2 and d. *American Psychologist, 36*, 892–901.

Hyde, J. S. (1984). Children's understanding of sexist language. *Developmental Psychology, 20*, 697–706.

Hyde, J. S. (1990). Meta-analysis and the psychology of gender differences. *Signs: Journal of Women in Culture and Society, 16*, 55–69.

Hyde, J. S. (1993). Meta-analysis and the psychology of women. In F. L. Denmark & M. A. Paludi (Eds.), *Handbook on the psychology of women*. Westport, CT: Greenwood.

Hyde, J. S. (1994). *Understanding human sexuality* (5th ed.). New York: McGraw-Hill.

Hyde, J. S., & Plant, E. A. (1995). Magnitude of psychological gender differences: Another side to the story. *American Psychologist, 50*, 159–161.

Hynd, G. W., & Garcia, W. I. (1979). Intellectual assessment of the Native American student. *School Psychology Digest, 8*, 446–454.

Ickovics, J. R. (1991, August). *Labor force diversity: A challenge to psychology*. Paper presented at the meeting of the American Psychological Association, San Francisco.

Ikels, C. (1989). Becoming a human being in theory and practice: Chinese views of human development. In D. I. Kertzer & K. W. Schaie (Eds.), *Age structuring in comparative perspective*. Hillsdale, NJ: Erlbaum.

Ilola, L. M. (1990). Culture and health. In R. W. Brislin (Ed.), *Applied cross-cultural psychology*. Newbury Park, CA: Sage.

Inclan, J. E., & Herron, D. G. (1989). Puerto Rican adolescents. In J. T. Gibbs & L. N.

Huang (Eds.), *Children of color*. San Francisco: Jossey-Bass.

Institute for Health Policy. (1993). *Substance abuse: Key indicators for policy*. Princeton, NJ: Robert Wood Johnson Foundation.

Irons, E. E., & Moore, G. W. (1985). *Black managers: The case of the banking industry*. New York: Praeger.

Irvine, S. H., & Berry, J. W. (1988). The abilities of mankind: A reevaluation. In S. H. Irvine & J. W. Berry (Eds.), *Human abilities in cultural context*. New York: Cambridge University Press.

Jacob, K. A. (1981). The Mosher report. *American Heritage*, pp. 57–64.

Jacobsen, F., Wehr, T., Sack, D., James, S., & Rosenthal, N. (1987). Seasonal affective disorder: A review of the syndrome and its public health implications. *American Journal of Public Health, 77*, 57–60.

Jacobson, N. S., & Addis, M. E. (1993). Research on couples and couple therapy: What do we know? Where are we going? *Journal of Consulting and Clinical Psychology, 61*, 85–93.

Jagacinski, C. M., & Nicholls, J. G. (1990). Reducing effort to protect perceived ability: "They'd do it but I wouldn't." *Journal of Educational Psychology, 82*, 15–21.

Jahoda, G. (1980). Theoretical and systematic approaches in cross-cultural psychology. In H. C. Triandis & J. G. Draguns (Eds.), *Handbook of cross-cultural psychology* (Vol. 1.). Boston: Allyn & Bacon.

James, W. (1890/1950). *The principles of psychology*. New York: Dover.

Jameson, D., & Hurvich, L. (1989). Essay concerning color constancy. *Annual Review of Psychology, 40*.

Janis, I. (1972). *Victims of groupthink: A psychological study of foreign-policy decisions and fiascos*. Boston: Houghton Mifflin.

Jarrett, R. L. (1995). Growing up poor: The family experiences of socially mobile youth in low-income African American neighborhoods. *Journal of Research on Adolescence, 10*, 111–135.

Jemmot, J. B., & Jones, J. M. (1993). Social psychology and AIDS among ethnic minorities. In J. B. Pryor & G. D. Reeder (Eds.), *The social psychology of HIV infection*. Hillsdale, NJ: Erlbaum.

Jensen, A. R. (1969). How much can we boost IQ and scholastic achievement? *Harvard Educational Review, 39*, 1–23.

Jensen, L. A. (1995, March). *The moral reasoning of orthodox and progressivist Indians and Americans*. Paper presented at the meeting of the Society for Research in Child Development, Indianapolis, IN.

Johnson, C. (1990, May). The new woman's ethics report. *New Woman*, p. 6.

Johnson, R. E., & others (1989). A seroepidemiologic survey of the prevalence of herpes simplex virus type 2 infection in the United States. *New England Journal of Medicine, 321*, 7–12.

Johnson-Laird, P. N. (1989). *The computer and the mind*. Cambridge, MA: Harvard University Press.

Johnston, L., Bachman, J., & O'Malley, P. (1989, February 24). News Release. *Teen drug use*. Ann Arbor: University of Michigan, Institute for Social Research.

Johnston, L., O'Malley, G., & Bachman, J. (1994, December). *Drug use continues to decline*

among American teenagers. Unpublished manuscript, University of Michigan, Institute of Social Research.

Johnston, L. D., O'Malley, P. M., & Bachman, J. G. (1992, January 25). *The 1991 survey of drug use by American high school and college students*. Ann Arbor: University of Michigan, Institute of Social Research.

Johnston, L. D., O'Malley, P. M., & Bachman, J. G. (1993, April 9). *Drug use rises among the nation's eighth grade students*. Ann Arbor: University of Michigan, Institute of Social Research.

Johnston, L. D., O'Malley, P. M., & Bachman, J. G. (1993). *National survey results on drug use from the Monitoring the Future study, 1975–1992*. Rockville, MD: National Institute on Drug Abuse.

Jones, A., & Seagull, A. (1977). Dimensions of the relationship between the Black client and the White therapist. *American Psychologist, 32*, 850–856.

Jones, B. E. (1989). Basic mechanisms of sleep-wake states. In M. H. Dryger, T. Roth, & W. C. Dement (Eds.), *Principles and practice of sleep medicine*. San Diego: Harcourt Brace Jovanovich.

Jones, J. M. (1987). Blacks in psychology. In P. J. Woods & C. S. Wilkinson (Eds.), *Is psychology the major for you?* Washington, DC: American Psychological Association.

Jones, J. M. (1990, August). *Psychological approaches to race: What have they been and what should they be?* Paper presented at the meeting of the American Psychological Association, Boston.

Jones, J. M. (1991). Psychological models of race: What have they been and what should they be? In J. D. Goodchilds (Ed.), *Psychological perspectives on human diversity in America*. Washington, DC: American Psychological Association.

Jones, J. M. (1993, August). *Racism and civil rights: Right problem, wrong solution*. Paper presented at the meeting of the American Psychological Association, Toronto, CAN.

Jones, J. M. (1994). The African American: A duality dilemma? In W. J. Lonner & R. Malpass (Eds.), *Psychology and culture*. Needham Heights, MA: Allyn & Bacon.

Jones, M. C. (1924). A laboratory study of fear: The case of Peter. *Journal of Genetic Psychology, 31*, 308–315.

Jones, M. C. (1965). Psychological correlates of somatic development. *Child Development, 36*, 899–911.

Jones, W. H., Hobbs, S. A., & Hockenbury, D. (1982). Loneliness and social skills deficits. *Journal of Personality and Social Psychology, 42*, 682–689.

Joyce, P. R., Donald, R. N., & Elder, P. N. (1987). Individual differences in plasma cortisol changes during manta and depression. *Journal of Affective Disorders, 12*, 1–6.

Jung, C. G. (1917). *Analytic psychology*. New York: Moffat, Yard.

Jussim, L., Manis, M., Nelson, T. E., & Sofin, S. (1995). Prejudice, stereotypes, and labeling effects: Sources of bias in person perception. *Journal of Personality and Social Psychology, 68*, 228–246.

Kübler-Ross, E. (1974). *Questions and answers on death and dying*. New York: Macmillan.

Kagan, J. (1987). Perspectives on infancy. In J. D. Osofsky (Ed.), *Handbook on infant development* (2nd ed.). New York: Wiley.

Kagan, J. (1992). Yesterday's promises, tomorrow's promises. *Developmental Psychology, 28,* 990–997.

Kagan, S., & Madsen, M. C. (1972). Experimental analysis of cooperation and competition of Anglo-American and Mexican children. *Developmental Psychology, 6,* 49–59.

Kagitcibasi, C. (1988). Diversity of socialization and social change. In P. R. Dasen, J. W. Berry, & N. Sartorious (Eds.), *Health and cross-cultural psychology: Toward applications.* Newbury Park, CA: Sage.

Kagitcibasi, C. (in press). Is psychology relevant to global human development issues? *American Psychologist.*

Kagitcibasi, C., & Berry, J. W. (1989). Cross-cultural psychology: Current research and trends. *Annual Review of Psychology, 40.*

Kail, R., & Pellegrino, J. W. (1985). *Human intelligence.* New York: W. H. Freeman.

Kalichman, S. (1994). Guidelines for seeking professional help. In J. Simons, S. Kalichman, & J. W. Santrock, *Human adjustment.* Dubuque, IA: Brown & Benchmark.

Kalichman, S. (1994). Knowledge of AIDS risk behavior. In J. Simons, S. Kalichman, & J. W. Santrock, *Human adjustment.* Dubuque, IA: Brown & Benchmark.

Kalichman, S. C. (1995). *Understanding AIDS.* Washington, DC: American Psychological Association.

Kalick, S. M., & Hamilton, T. E. (1986). The matching hypothesis reexamined. *Journal of Personality and Social Psychology, 51,* 673–682.

Kamin, L. J. (1968). Attention-like processes in classical conditioning. In M. R. Jones (Ed.), *Miami Symposium on the prediction of behavior: Aversive stimuli.* Coral Gables, FL: University of Miami Press.

Kamo, Y. (1988). Determinants of the household division of labor: Resources, power, and ideology. *Journal of Family Issues, 9,* 177–200.

Kandel, E. R., & Schwartz, J. H. (1982). Molecular biology of learning: Modulation of transmitter release. *Science, 218,* 433–443.

Kane, J. M., & Barnes, T. R. E. (1995). Schizophrenia research: Challenges and opportunities. *Current Opinion in Psychiatry, 8,* 19–20.

Kanner, A. D., Coyne, J. C., Schaefer, C., & Lazarus, R. S. (1981). Comparisons of two modes of stress measurement. Daily hassles and uplifts versus major life event. *Journal of Behavioral Medicine, 4,* 1–39.

Kaplan, H. S. (1974). *The new sex therapy.* New York: Times Books.

Karasu, T. B. (1986). The psychotherapies: Benefits and limitations. *American Journal of Psychotherapy, 15,* 324–342.

Karno, M., & Morales, A. (1971). A community mental health service for Mexican Americans in a metropolis. *Comprehensive Psychiatry, 12,* 115–121.

Kastenbaum, R. (1995). *Death, society, and human experience* (5th ed.). Needham Heights, MA: Allyn & Bacon.

Katz, I., Wackenhut, J., & Hass, R. G. (1986). Racial ambivalence, value duality, and behavior. In J. F. Dovidio & S. L. Gaertner (Eds.), *Prejudice, discrimination, and racism.* San Diego, CA: Academic Press.

Katz, L., & Chard, S. (1989). *Engaging the minds of young children: The project approach.* Norwood, NJ: Ablex.

Kaufman, A. S., & Kaufman, N. L. (1983). *Kaufman assessment battery for children: Interpretive manual.* Circle Pines, MN: American Guidance Series.

Keating, C. F. (1994). World without words: Messages from face and body. In W. J. Lonner & R. Malpass, *Psychology and culture.* Needham Heights, MA: Allyn & Bacon.

Keating, D. P. (in press). Structuralism, deconstruction, reconstruction: The limits of reasoning. In W. F. Overton (Ed.), *Reasoning, necessity, and logic: Developmental perspectives.* Hillsdale, NJ: Erlbaum.

Keefe, S. E., & Padilla, A. M. (1987). *Chicano ethnicity.* Albuquerque: University of New Mexico Press.

Kelley, H. H., & Thibaut, J. (1978). *Interpersonal relations. A theory of interdependence.* New York: Wiley.

Kelly, G. A. (1955). *The psychology of personal constructs* (Vols. 1 & 2). New York: W. W. Norton.

Kendall, P. C., & Watson, D. (Eds.). (1989). *Anxiety and depression.* San Diego: Academic Press.

Kenrick, D. T., Montello, D. R., Gutierres, S. E., & Trost, M. R. (1993). Effects of physical attractiveness on affect and perceptual judgments: When social comparison overrides social reinforcement. *Personality and Social Psychology Bulletin, 19,* 195–199.

Kephart, W. M. (1967). Some correlates of romantic love. *Journal of Marriage and the Family, 29,* 470–474.

Kiecolt-Glaser, J. K., & Glaser, R. (1988). Behavioral influences on immune function. In T. Field, P. McCabe, & N. Schneiderman (Eds.), *Stress and coping across development.* Hillsdale, NJ: Erlbaum.

Kiecolt-Glaser, J. K., Malarkey, W. B., Chee, M., Newton, T., Cacioppo, J. T., Mao, H. Y., & Glaser, R. (1993, August). *Negative behavior during marital conflict is associated with immunological down-regulation.* Paper presented at the meeting of the American Psychological Association, Toronto.

Killen, M., & Hart, D. (Eds.). (1995). *Morality in everyday life.* New York: Cambridge University Press.

Kilpatrick, A. C. (1992). *Long-range effects of childhood and adolescent sexual experiences: Myths, mores, and menaces.* Hillsdale, NJ: Erlbaum.

Kimble, G. A. (1961). *Hilgard and Marquis's conditioning and learning.* New York: Appleton-Century-Crofts.

Kimble, G. A. (1984). Psychology's two cultures. *American Psychologist, 39,* 833–839.

Kimble, G. A. (1989). Psychology from the standpoint of a generalist. *American Psychologist, 44,* 491–499.

Kimmel, E. B. (1992). Women's contributions to psychology. *Contemporary Psychology, 37,* 201–202.

King, L. (1991). *Investigations in the relations, predictive validity and implications of implicit and explicit motives.* Unpublished dissertation, University of California, Davis.

Kinsey, A. C., Pomeroy, W. B., & Martin, E. E. (1948). *Sexual behavior in the human male.* Philadelphia: Saunders.

Kirkpatrick, B., Buchanan, R. W., Waltrip, R. W., Jauch, D., & Carpenter, W. T. (1989). Diazepam treatment of early symptoms of schizophrenic relapse. *Journal of Nervous and Mental Disease, 177,* 52–53.

Kirschenbaum, H. (1995). *100 ways to enhance values and morality in schools and youth settings.* Boston: Allyn & Bacon.

Kitano, H. H. L. (1970). Mental illness in four cultures. *Journal of Social Psychology, 80,* 121–134.

Kleinman, A. (1988). *Rethinking psychiatry.* New York: Macmillan.

Klinger, E. (1987). The interview questionnaire technique: Reliability and validity of a mixed idiographic-nomothetic measure of motivation. In J. N. Butcher and C. D. Spielberger (Eds.), *Advances in personality assessment* (Vol. 6, pp. 32–48). Hillsdale, NJ: Erlbaum.

Klivington, K. (Ed.). (1989). *The science of mind.* Cambridge, MA: MIT Press.

Klonoff, E. A. (1991, August). *Ethnicity and women's health: The neglected women.* Paper presented at the meeting of the American Psychological Association, San Francisco.

Kluckhohn, F. R. (1953). Dominant and variant value orientations. In C. K. M. Kluckhohn & H. A. Murray (Eds.), *Personality in nature, society, and culture.* New York: Knopf.

Kluckhohn, F. R. (1969). Dominant and variant value orientations. In C. Kluckhohn & Murray, H. A. (Eds.), *Personality in nature, society, and culture.* New York: Alfred A. Knopf.

Kobak, R., & Frenz-Gilles, R. (1993, March). *Attachment processes during parent-teen conversations.* Paper presented at the biennial meeting of the Society for Research in Child Development, New Orleans.

Kobasa, N., Maddi, S., & Kahn, S. (1982). Hardiness and health. A prospective study. *Journal of Personality and Social Psychology, 42,* 168–177.

Kobasa, S. C., Maddi, S. R., Puccetti, M. C., & Zola, M. (1985). Relative effectiveness of hardiness, exercise, and social support as resources against illness. *Journal of Psychosomatic Research, 29,* 525–533.

Kohlberg, L. (1966). A cognitive-developmental analysis of children's sex-role concepts and attitudes. In E. E. Maccoby (Ed.), *The development of sex differences.* Palo Alto, CA: Stanford University Press.

Kohlberg, L. (1969). Stage and sequence: The cognitive-developmental approach to socialization. In D. A. Goslin (Ed.), *Handbook of socialization theory and research* (p. 379). Chicago: Rand McNally.

Kohlberg, L. (1976). Moral stages and moralization: The cognitive-developmental approach. In T. Lickona (Ed.), *Moral development and behavior.* New York: Holt, Rinehart & Winston.

Kohlberg, L. (1986). A current statement on some theoretical issues. In S. Modgil & C. Modgil (Eds.), *Lawrence Kohlberg.* Philadelphia: Falmer Press.

Kohler, W. (1925). *The mentality of apes.* New York: Harcourt Brace Jovanovich.

Kohn, M. L. (1977). *Class and conformity: A study in values* (2nd ed.). Chicago: University of Chicago Press.

Kohut, H. (1977). *The restoration of the self.* New York: International Universities Press.

Kolb, L. (1973). *Modern clinical psychiatry* (8th ed.). Philadelphia: Saunders.

Koocher, G. P., & Keith-Spiegel, P. (1996). *Ethics in psychology.* New York: Oxford University Press.

Kopp, C. (1994). *Baby steps.* New York: W. H. Freeman.

Kopp, C. B., & Kaler, S. R. (1989). Risk in infancy: Origins and implications. *American Psychologist, 44,* 224–230.

Kornetsky, C. (1986, August). *Effects of opiates and stimulants on brain stimulation: Implications for abuse.* Paper presented at the meeting of the American Psychological Association, Washington, DC.

Koss, M. P. (1990). The women's mental health research agenda: Violence against women. *American Psychologist, 45,* 374–384.

Koss, M. P. (1993, August). *Sex gone wrong: Current perspectives on rape and sexual harassment.* Paper presented at the meeting of the American Psychological Association, Toronto.

Kottak, C. P. (1991). *Anthropology: The exploration of human diversity.* New York: McGraw Hill.

Kottler, J. (1991). *The compleat therapist.* New York: Jossey-Bass.

Kramer, B. A. (1987). Electroconvulsive therapy use in geriatric depression. *Journal of Nervous and Mental Disease, 175,* 233–235.

Kramer, P. D. (1993). *Listening to Prozac.* New York: Penguin.

Kretschmer, E. (1925). *Physique and character* (W. J. H. Sprott, Trans.). New York: Harcourt Brace.

Kunitz, S. J., & Levy, J. E. (1981). In A. Harwood (Ed.), *Ethnicity and medical care.* Cambridge, MA: Harvard University Press.

Kunitz, S. J., Levy, J. E., Odoroff, C. L., & Bollinger, J. (1971). The epidemiology of alcoholic cirrhosis in two southwestern Indian tribes. *Quarterly Journal of Studies on Alcoholism, 32,* 706–720.

Kutchinsky, B. (1992). The child sexual abuse panic. *Nordisk Sexologi, 10,* 30–42.

LaBerge, S. P. (1992). *Physiological studies of lucid dreaming.* Hillsdale, NJ: Erlbaum.

Labouvie-Vief, G. (1986, August). *Modes of knowing and life-span cognition.* Paper presented at the meeting of the American Psychological Association, Washington, DC.

LaCroix, A. Z., & Haynes, S. G. (1987). Gender differences in the health effects of workplace roles. In R. C. Barnett, L. Biener, & G. K. Baruch (Eds.), *Gender and stress.* New York: Free Press.

Ladd, G. W., & LeSieur, K. D. (1995). Parents and children's peer relationships. In M. H. Bornstein (Ed.), *Handbook of parenting, Vol. 4.* Hillsdale, NJ: Erlbaum.

LaFromboise, T., Coleman, H. L. K., & Gerton, J. (1993). Psychological impact of biculturalism: Evidence and theory. *Psychological Bulletin, 114,* 395–412.

LaFromboise, T. D. (1993). American Indian mental health policy. In D. R. Atkinson, G. Morten, & D. W. Sue (Eds.), *Counseling American minorities.* Dubuque, IA: Brown & Benchmark.

LaFromboise, T. D., & Low, K. G. (1989). American Indian children and adolescents. In J. T. Gibbs & L. N. Huang (Eds.), *Children of color.* San Francisco: Jossey-Bass.

Laguerre, M. S. (1981). Haitian Americans. In A. Harwood (Ed.), *Ethnicity and medical care.* Cambridge, MA: Harvard University Press.

Lamb, C. S., Jackson, L. A., Cassiday, P. B., & Priest, D. J. (1993). Body figure preferences of men and women: A comparison of two generations. *Sex Roles, 28,* 345–358.

Lamb, M. E., & Sternberg, K. J. (1992). Sociocultural perspectives on nonparental child care. In M. E. Lamb, K. J. Sternberg, C. Hwang, & A. G. Broberg (Eds.), *Child care in context.* Hillsdale, NJ: Erlbaum.

Landrine, H. (1989). The politics of personality disorder. *Psychology of Women Quarterly, 13,* 325–339.

Landrine, H. (Ed.). (1995). *Bringing cultural diversity to feminist psychology.* Washington, DC: American Psychological Association.

Lane, H. (1976). *The wild boy of Aveyron.* Cambridge, MA: Harvard University Press.

Lange, C. G. (1922). *The emotions.* Baltimore: Williams & Wilkins.

Lanyon, R. I., & Goodstein, L. D. (1982). *Personality and assessment* (2nd ed.). New York: Wiley.

LaPiere, R. (1934). Attitudes versus actions. *Social Forces, 13,* 230–237.

Larson, J. H. (1988). The Marriage Quiz: College students' beliefs in selected myths about marriage. *Family Relations, 37,* 3–11.

Lashley, K. S. (1950). In search of the engram. In *Symposium of the Society for Experimental Biology* (Vol. 4). New York: Cambridge University Press.

Lau, R. R. (1988). Beliefs about control and health behavior. In D. S. Gochman (Ed.), *Health behavior: Emerging perspectives.* New York: Plenum.

Lau, S., & Gruen, G. E. (1992). The social stigma of loneliness: Effect of target person's and perceiver's sex. *Personality and Social Psychology Bulletin, 18,* 182–189.

Lavine, L. O., & Lombardo, J. P. (1984). Self-disclosure: Intimate and non-intimate disclosures to parents and best friends as a function of Bem sex-role category. *Sex Roles, 11,* 735–744.

Lazarus, R. S. (1966). *Psychological stress and the coping process.* New York: McGraw-Hill.

Lazarus, R. S. (1981). The stress and coping paradigm. In C. Eisdorfer, D. Cohen, A. Kleinman, & P. Maxim (Eds.), *Models for clinical psychopathology.* New York: Spectrum.

Lazarus, R. S. (1984). On the primacy or cognition. *American Psychologist, 39,* 124–129.

Lazarus, R. S. (1991). *Emotion and adaptation.* New York: Oxford University Press.

Lazarus, R. S. (1991). Progress on a cognitive-motivational-relational theory of emotion. *American Psychologist, 46,* 352–367.

Lazarus, R. S. (1993). From psychological stress to the emotions: A history of a changing outlook. *Annual Review of Psychology, 44,* 1–21.

Lazarus, R. S., & Folkman, N. (1984). *Stress appraisal and coping.* New York: Springer.

Lebow, J. L., & Gurman, A. S. (1995). Research assessing couple and family therapy. *Annual Review of Psychology, Vol. 46.* Palo Alto, CA: Annual Reviews.

Lecci, L., Okun, M. A., & Karoly, P. (1994). Life regrets and current goals as predictors of psychological adjustment. *Journal of Personality and Social Psychology, 66,* 731–741.

Lee, D. J., & Hall, C. C. I. (1994). Being Asian in North America. In W. J. Lonner & R. Malpass (Eds.), *Psychology and culture.* Needham Heights, MA: Allyn & Bacon.

Lee, I., Hsieh, C., & Paffenbarger, R. S. (1995). *Exercise intensity and longevity in men.* *Journal of the American Medical Association, 273,* 1179–1184.

Lee, L. C. (1992, August). *In search of universals: Whatever happened to race?* Paper presented at the meeting of the American Psychological Association, Washington, DC.

Lee, T. F. (1991). *The human genome project: Cracking the genetic code of life.* New York: Plenum Press.

Lee, V. E., Croninger, R. R., Linn, E., & Chen, X. (1995, March). *The culture of sexual harassment in secondary schools.* Paper presented at the meeting of the Society for Research in Child Development, Indianapolis, IN.

Lefley, H. P. (1984). Delivering mental health services across cultures. In P. B. Pederson, N. Sartorius, & A. J. Marsella (Eds.), *Mental health services: The cross-cultural context.* Beverly Hills: Sage.

Lempers, J. D., Clarke-Lempers, D., & Simons, R. L. (1989). Economic hardship, parenting, and distress in adolescence. *Child Development, 60,* 25–39.

Lempers, J. D., Flavell, E. R., & Flavell, J. H. (1977). The development in very young children of tacit knowledge concerning visual perception. *Genetic Psychology Monographs, 95,* 3–53.

Lenfant, C. (1995). Improving the health of America's youth: The NHLBI perspective. *Journal of Health Education, 26,* 6–8.

Lenneberg, E. (1967). *The biological foundations of language.* New York: Wiley.

Lenneberg, E. H., Rebelsky, F. G., & Nichols, I. A. (1965). The vocalization of infants born to deaf and hearing parents. *Human Development, 8* 23–37.

Lepper, M., Greene, D., & Nisbett, R. E. (1973). Undermining children's intrinsic interest with extrinsic rewards. *Journal of Personality and Social Psychology, 28,* 129–137.

Lerner, H. (1985). *The dance of anger.* New York: Harper Perennial.

Lerner, H. (1990). *The dance of intimacy.* New York: Harper Perennial.

Lerner, H. G. (1989). *The dance of intimacy.* New York: Harper & Row.

Lerner, R. M., & von Eye, A. (1992). Sociobiology and human development: Arguments and evidence. *Human Development, 35,* 12–33.

Lerner, R. M., Petersen, A. C., & Brooks-Gunn, J. (Eds.). (1991). *Encyclopedia of adolescence.* New York: Garland.

Leshner, A. I. (1992, July). Winning the war against clinical depression. *USA Today,* pp. 86–87.

Lester, B. M., Freier, K., & LaGasse, L. (1995). Prenatal cocaine exposure and child outcome: What do we really know? In M. Lewis & M. Bendersky (Eds.), *Mothers, babies, and cocaine.* Hillsdale, NJ: Erlbaum.

Leukefeld, C. G., & Haverkos, H. W. (1993). Sexually transmitted diseases. In T. P. Gulotta, G. R. Adams, & R. Montemayor (Eds.), *Adolescent sexuality,* Newbury Park, CA: Sage.

Levant, R. F. (1995). Toward the reconstruction of masculinity. In R. F. Levant & W. S. Pollack (Eds.), *A new psychology of men.* New York: Basic.

LeVay, S. (1991). A difference in hypothalamic structure between heterosexual and homosexual men. *Science, 253,* 1034–1037.

Levenkron, S. (1991). *Obsessive-compulsive disorders.* New York: Warner Books.

Leventhal, H. (1970). Findings and theory in the study of fear communications. *Advances in Experimental Social Psychology, 5,* 119–186.

Leventhal, H., & Tomarken, A. J. (1986). Emotion: Today's problems. *Annual Review of Psychology, 37,* 565–610.

Levine, M., & Perkins, D. V. (1987). *Principles of community psychology.* New York: Oxford University Press.

Levine, M., Toro, P. A., & Perkins, D. V. (1993). Social and community interventions. *Annual Review of Psychology, 44,* 525–558.

LeVine, S. (1979). *Mothers and wives: Gusii women of East Africa.* Chicago: University of Chicago Press.

Levinson, D. (1978). *The seasons of a man's life.* New York: Knopf.

Levinson, D. J. (1987, August). *The seasons of a woman's life.* Paper presented at the meeting of the American Psychological Association, New York.

Levitan, I. B., & Kaczmarek, L. K. (1991). *The neuron.* New York: Oxford University Press.

Levy, S. M. (1985). *Behavior and cancer.* San Francisco: Jossey-Bass.

Lewinsohn, P., Muñoz, R., Youngren, M., & Zeiss, A. (1992). *Control your depression* (rev. ed.). New York: Fireside.

Lewinsohn, P. M. (1987). The Coping with Depression course. In R. F. Muñoz (Ed.), *Depression prevention.* New York: Hemisphere.

Lieberman, M. A., Yalom, I. D., & Miles, M. B. (1973). *Encounter groups: First facts.* New York: Basic Books.

Liebert, R. J., & Sprafkin, J. (1988). *The early window: Effects of television on children and youth* (2nd ed.). New York: Pergamon.

Lincoln, J. R., & Kalleberg, A. L. (1990). *Culture, control, and commitment: A study of work organization and work attitudes in the United States and Japan.* New York: Cambridge University Press.

Linn, M. C., & Hyde, J. S. (1991). Cognitive and psychosocial gender differences, trends in. In R. M. Lerner, A. C. Petersen, & J. Brooks-Gunn (Eds.), *Encyclopedia of adolescence* (Vol. 1). New York: Garland.

Linn, M. C., & Peterson, A. C. (1986). A meta-analysis of gender differences in spatial ability: Implications for mathematics and science achievement. In J. S. Hyde & M. C. Linn (Eds.), *The psychology of gender: Advances through meta-analysis.* Baltimore: Johns Hopkins University Press.

Lipscomb, G. H., Muram, D., Speck, P. M., & Mercer, B. M. (1992, June). Male victims of sexual assault. *Journal of the American Medical Association, 267,* 3064.

Little, B. R. (1989). Personal projects analysis: Trivial pursuits, magnificent obsessions, and the search for coherence. In D. M. Buss & N. Cantor (Eds.), *Personality psychology: Recent trends and emerging directions* (pp. 15–31). New York: Springer-Verlag.

Livesley, W. J. (Ed.). (1995). *The DSM-IV personality disorders.* New York: Guilford.

Locke, E. A., & Latham, G. P. (1990). *A theory of goal setting and task performance.* Englewood Cliffs, NJ: Prentice-Hall.

Locke, J. L., Bekken, K. E., Wein, D., & Ruzecki, V. (1991, April). *Neuropsychology of babbling: Laterality effects in the production of rhythmic manual activity.* Paper presented at the Society for Research in Child Development meeting, Seattle.

Loehr, J. (1989, May). [Personal communication.] United States Tennis Association Training Camp, Saddlebrook, FL.

Loftus, E. F. (1975). Spreading activation within semantic categories: Comments on Rosch's "Cognitive representations of semantic categories." *Journal of Experimental Psychology, 104,* 234–240.

Loftus, E. F. (1980). *Memory.* Reading, MA: Addison-Wesley.

Loftus, E. F. (1993a). Psychologists in the eyewitness world. *American Psychologist, 48,* 550–552.

Loftus, E. F. (1993b). The reality of repressed memories. *American Psychologist, 48,* 518–537.

Logue, A. W. (1986). *Eating and drinking.* New York: W. H. Freeman.

Long, P. (1986, January). Medical mesmerism. *Psychology Today,* pp. 28–29.

Lonner, W., & Malpass, R. (Eds.). (1994). *Psychology and culture.* Boston: Allyn & Bacon.

Lonner, W. J. (1988, October). *The introductory psychology text and cross-cultural psychology: A survey of cross-cultural psychologists.* Bellingham: Western Washington University, Center for Cross-cultural Research.

Lonner, W. J. (1990). An overview of cross-cultural testing and assessment. In R. W. Brislin (Ed.), *Applied cross-cultural psychology.* Newbury Park, CA: Sage.

Lonner, W. J., & Malpass, R. (1994). *Psychology and culture.* Needham Heights, MA: Allyn & Bacon.

Lopata, H. Z. (1994). *Circles and settings: Role changes of American women.* Albany, NY: State University of New York Press.

Lorenz, K. Z. (1965). *Evolution and modification of behavior.* Chicago: University of Chicago Press.

Lorenz, K. Z. (1966). *On aggression.* San Diego: Harcourt Brace Jovanovich.

Lorion, R., & Allen, L. (1989). Preventive services in mental health. In D. A. Rochefort (Ed.), *Handbook on mental health policy in the United States.* New York: Greenwood Press.

Lott, B. (1994). *Women's lives: Themes and variations in gender learning.* Pacific Grove: Brooks/Cole.

Ludolph, P. (1982, August). *A reanalysis of the literature on multiple personality.* Paper presented at the American Psychological Association, Washington, DC.

Luria, A., & Herzog, E. (1985, April). *Gender segregation across and within settings.* Paper presented at the biennial meeting of the Society for Research in Child Development, Toronto.

Lykken, D. T. (1985). The probity of the polygraph. In S. M. Kassin & L. S. Wrightsman (Eds.), *The psychology of evidence and trial procedure.* Beverly Hills, CA: Sage.

Lykken, D. T. (1987, Spring). The validity of tests: Caveat emptor. *Jurimetrics Journal,* pp. 263–270.

Lynch, G. (1990, June). *The many shapes of memory and the several forms of synaptic plasticity.* Paper presented at the meeting of the American Psychological Society, Dallas.

Maccoby, E. E. (1987, November). Interview with Elizabeth Hall: All in the family. *Psychology Today,* pp. 54–60.

Maccoby, E. E. (1989, August). *Gender and relationships: A developmental account.* Paper presented at the meeting of the American Psychological Association, New Orleans.

Maccoby, E. E., & Jacklin, C. N. (1974). *The psychology of sex differences.* Palo Alto, CA: Stanford University Press.

Maccoby, E. E., & Martin, J. A. (1983). Socialization in the context of the family: Parent-child interaction. In P. H. Mussen (Ed.), *Handbook of child psychology* (4th ed., Vol. 4). New York: Wiley.

Maddi, S. (1989). *Theories of personality* (5th ed.). Homewood, IL: Dorsey.

Mader, S. S. (1994). *Human biology* (3rd ed.). Dubuque, IA: Wm. C. Brown.

Magai, C., & McFadden, S. H. (1995). *The role of emotions in social and personality development.* New York: Plenum.

Mager, R. F. (1972). *Goal analysis.* Belmont, CA: Fearon.

Magid, B. (1995). Is biology destiny after all? *Journal of Psychotherapy Practice and Research, 4,* 1–9.

Mahler, M. (1979). *Separation-individuation.* New York: Jason Aronson.

Mahoney, M. J. (1989). Sport psychology. In *The G. Stanley Hall Lecture Series* (Vol. 9). Washington, DC: American Psychological Association.

Mahoney, M. J., Gabriel, T. J., & Perkins, T. S. (1987). Psychological skills and exceptional athletic performance. *Sport Psychologist, 1,* 181–199.

Maier, N. R. F. (1931). Reasoning in humans. *Journal of Comparative Psychology, 12,* 181–194.

Malamuth, N. M., & Donnerstein, E. (Eds.). (1983). *Pornography and sexual aggression.* New York: Academic Press.

Malinowski, B. (1927). *Sex and repression in savage society.* New York: Humanities Press.

Mandell, C. J., & Mandell, S. L. (1989). *Computers in education today.* St. Paul: West.

Mandler, G. (1980). Recognizing: The judgment of previous occurrence. *Psychological Review, 87,* 252–271.

Mandler, G. (1984). *Mind and body.* New York: Norton.

Mann, L. (1980). Cross-cultural study of small groups. In H. C. Triandis & R. W. Brislin (Eds.), *Handbook of cross-cultural psychology* (Vol. 5). Boston: Allyn & Bacon.

Manning, A. (1989). The genetic bases of aggression. In J. Groebel & R. A. Hinde (Eds.), *Aggression and war: Their biological and social bases.* New York: Cambridge University Press.

Marín, G. (1993). Defining culturally appropriate community interventions: Hispanics as a case study. *Journal of Community Psychology,* 149–161.

Marín, G. (1994). The experience of being a Hispanic in the United States. In W. J. Lonner & R. Malpass (Eds.), *Psychology and culture.* Needham Heights, MA: Allyn & Bacon.

Marek, G. J., & Seiden, L. S. (1991). Neurotransmitters in affective disorders. In T. Archer & S. Hansen (Eds.), *Behavioral biology: Neuroendocrine axis.* Hillsdale, NJ: Erlbaum.

Markides, K. S. (1995). Aging and ethnicity. *The Gerontologist, 35,* 276–277.

Markson, E. W. (1995). Older women: The silent majority? *The Gerontologist, 35,* 278–281.

Markus, H. R., & Kitayama, S. (1991). Culture and the self: Implications for cognition, emotion, and motivation. *Psychological Review, 98,* 224–253.

Marsiglio, W. (Ed.). (1995). *Fatherhood.* Newbury Park, CA: Sage.

Marsiske, M., Lang, F. R., Baltes, P. B., & Baltes, M. M. (1995). Selective optimization with compensation. In R. A. Dixon & L. Backman (Eds.), *Compensating for psychological deficits and declines*. Hillsdale, NJ: Erlbaum.

Martin, B. (1991, August). *Challenges of using the theory of reasoned action in Hispanic health research*. Paper presented at the meeting of the American Psychological Association, San Francisco.

Martin, G., & Pear, J. (1988). *Behavior modification: What it is and how to do it* (3rd ed.). Englewood Cliffs, NJ: Prentice Hall.

Maslow, A. H. (1954). *Motivation and personality*. New York: Harper & Row.

Maslow, A. H. (1971). *The farther reaches of human nature*. New York: Viking.

Masson, M. E. J., & Graf, P. (1993). Introduction: Looking back and into the future. In P. Graf & M. E. J. Masson (Eds.), *Implicit memory*. Hillsdale, NJ: Erlbaum.

Masters, W. H. (1993, August). *Sex therapy: Past, present, and future*. Paper presented at the meeting of the American Psychological Association, Toronto.

Masters, W. H., & Johnson, V. E. (1966). *Human sexual response*. Boston: Little, Brown.

Matas, L., Arend, R. A., & Sroufe, L. A. (1978). Continuity in adaptation: Quality of attachment and later competence. *Child Development, 49,* 547–556.

Matlin, M. W. (1983). *Cognition*. New York: Holt, Rinehart & Winston.

Matlin, M. W. (1983). *Perception*. Boston: Allyn & Bacon.

Matlin, M. W. (1993). *The psychology of women* (2nd ed.). Fort Worth, TX: Harcourt Brace.

Matsumoto, D. (1989). Cultural influences on the perception of emotion. *Journal of Cross-Cultural Psychology, 20,* 92–105.

Matsumoto, D. (1994). *People: Psychology from a cultural perspective*. Pacific Grove, CA: Brooks/Cole.

Mayo, E. (1933). *The human problems of industrial civilization*. New York: Macmillan.

Mays, V. (1993, August). *HIV prevention in women and ethnic minorities*. Paper presented at the meeting of the American Psychological Association, Toronto.

Mays, V. M. (1991, August). *Social policy implications of the definition of race*. Paper presented at the meeting of the American Psychological Association, San Francisco.

Mays, V. M. (1991, August). *The role of sexual orientation and ethnic identification in HIV health risk*. Paper presented at the meeting of the American Psychological Association, San Francisco.

McAdoo, H. P. (Ed.). (1993). *Family ethnicity*. Newbury Park, CA: Sage.

McAdoo, H. P. (Ed.). (1994). *Black families* (3rd ed.). Newbury Park, CA: Sage.

McAuley, E., & Duncan, T. E. (1991). The causal attribution process in sport and physical activity. In S. Graham & V. S. Folkes (Eds.), *Attribution theory: Applications to achievement, mental health, and interpersonal conflict*. Hillsdale, NJ: Erlbaum.

McBride, A. B. (1990). Mental health effects of women's multiple roles. *American Psychologist, 45,* 381–384.

McCandless, B. R., & Trotter, R. J. (1977). *Children* (3rd ed.). New York: Holt, Rinehart & Winston.

McCarley, R. W. (1989). The biology of dreaming sleep. In M. H. Dryger, T. Roth, & W. C. Dement (Eds.), *Principles and practice of sleep medicine*. San Diego: Harcourt Brace Jovanovich.

McClelland, D. C. (1955). Some social consequences of achievement motivation. In M. R. Jones (Ed.), *Nebraska Symposium on Motivation*. Lincoln: University of Nebraska Press.

McClelland, D. C. (1978). Managing motivation to expand human freedom. *American Psychologist, 33,* 201–210.

McClelland, D. C. (1985). *Human motivation*. Glenview, IL: Scott, Foresman.

McClelland, D. C., Atkinson, J. W., Clark, R., & Lowell, E. L. (1953). *The achievement motive*. New York: Appleton-Century-Crofts.

McConaghy, N. (1993). *Sexual behavior: Problems and management*. New York: Plenum.

McCrae, R. R., & Costa, P. T. (1989). The structure of interpersonal traits: Wiggins' circumplex and the five-factor model. *Journal of Personality and Social Psychology, 56,* 586–595.

McDaniel, M. A., & Pressley, M. (1987). *Imagery and related mnemonic processes*. New York: Springer-Verlag.

McDougall, W. (1908). *Social psychology*. New York: G. Putnam & Sons.

McGrath, E., Keita, G. P., Strickland, B., & Russo, N. F. (1990). *Women and depression: Risk factors and treatment issues*. Washington, DC: American Psychological Association.

McGue, M., & Bouchard, T. J. (1989). Genetic and environmental determinants of information processing and special mental abilities. In R. J. Sternberg (Ed.), *Advances in the psychology of human intelligence*. Hillsdale, NJ: Erlbaum.

McGue, M., & Carmichael, C. M. (1995). Life-span developmental psychology: A behavioral genetic perspective. In L. F. Dilalla & S. M. C. Dollinger (Eds.), *Assessment of biological mechanisms across the life span*. Hillsdale, NJ: Erlbaum.

McHale, S. M. (1995). Lessons about adolescent development from the study of African-American youth: Commentary. In L. J. Crockett & A. C. Crouter (Eds.), *Pathways through adolescence*. Hillsdale, NJ: Erlbaum.

McIver, T. (1988). Backward masking and other backward thoughts about music. *Skeptical Inquirer, 13,* 50–63.

McKinlay, S. M., & McKinlay, J. B. (1984). *Health status and health care utilization by menopausal women*. Unpublished manuscript, Cambridge Research Center, American Institutes for Research, Cambridge, MA.

McLoyd, V. (1993, March). *Direct and indirect effects of economic hardship on socioemotional functioning in African-American adolescents*. Paper presented at the biennial meeting of the Society for Research in Child Development, New Orleans.

McLoyd, V. C. (1993, March). *Sizing up the future: Economic stress, expectations, and adolescents' achievement motivation*. Paper presented at the biennial meeting of the Society for Research in Child Development, New Orleans.

McLoyd, V. C., & Ceballo, R. (1995, March). *Conceptualizing economic context*. Paper presented at the meeting of the Society for Research in Child Development, Indianapolis, IN.

McNeil, E. B. (1967). *The quiet furies*. Englewood Cliffs, NJ: Prentice Hall.

McShane, D. A. (1987). American Indians and Alaska natives in psychology. In P. J. Woods & C. S. Wilkinson (Eds.), *Is psychology the major for you?* Washington, DC: American Psychological Association.

Mead, M. (1928). *Coming of age in Samoa*. New York: Morrow.

Mead, M. (1935/1968). *Sex and temperament in three primitive societies*. New York: Dell.

Medvedev, Z. A. (1974). The nucleic acids in the development of aging. In B. L. Strehler (Ed.), *Advances in gerontological research* (Vol. 1). New York: Academic Press.

Meehl, P. E. (1962). Schizotoma, schizotypy, schizophrenia. *American Psychologist, 17,* 827–838.

Meehl, P. E. (1986). Diagnostic taxa as open concepts. In T. Millon & G. I. Klerman (Eds.), *Contemporary directions in psychopathology*. New York: Guilford Press.

Meichenbaum, D. (1977). *Cognitive-behavior modification. An integrative approach*. New York: Plenum Press.

Meichenbaum, D. (1986). Cognitive behavior modification. In F. H. Kanfer & A. P. Goldstein (Eds.), *Helping people change: A textbook of methods*. New York: Pergamon.

Meichenbaum, D. (1993). Changing conceptions of cognitive behavior modification: Retrospect and prospect. *Journal of Consulting and Clinical Psychology, 61,* 202–204.

Meichenbaum, D., Turk, D., & Burstein, S. (1975). The nature of coping with stress. In I. Sarason & C. Spielberger (Eds.), *Stress and anxiety*. Washington, DC: Hemisphere.

Meltzoff, A. N., & Moore, M. K. (1983). Newborn infants imitate adult facial gestures. *Child Development, 54,* 702–709.

Melzack, R., & Wall, P. D. (1965). Pain mechanisms: A new theory. *Science, 150,* 971–979.

Melzack, R., & Wall, P. D. (1983). *The challenge of pain*. New York: Basic Books.

Mercer, J. R., & Lewis, J. F. (1978). *System of multicultural pluralistic assessment*. New York: Psychological Corporation.

Mervis, J. (1986, July). NIMH data point way to effective treatment. *APA Monitor, 17,* 1, 13.

Messinger, J. C. (1971). Sex and repression in an Irish folk community. In D. S. Marshall & R. C. Suggs (Eds.), *Human sexual behavior: Variations in the ethnic spectrum*. New York: Basic Books.

Metalsky, G. I., Joiner, T. E., Hardin, T. S., & Abramson, L. Y. (1993). Depressive reactions to failure in a naturalistic setting. *Journal of Abnormal Psychology, 102,* 101–109.

Meyer, J. (1985). *Hemingway* (p. 559). New York: Harper & Row.

Meyer, R. G., & Osborne, Y. V. H. (1982). *Case studies in abnormal behavior*. Boston: Allyn & Bacon.

Mezzich, J. E., Fabegra, H., & Kleinman, A. (in press). On enhancing the cultural sensitivity of DSM-IV. *Journal of Nervous and Mental Disease*.

Michael, R., Gagnon, J., Laumann, E., & Kolata, G. (1994). *Sex in America*. Boston: Little, Brown.

Midgeley, J. (1971). Drinking and attitudes toward drinking in Muslim community. *Quarterly Journal of Studies on Alcoholism, 32,* 148–158.

Milgram, S. (1965). Some conditions of obedience and disobedience to authority. *Human Relations, 18,* 56–76.

Miller, G. A. (1956). The magical number seven, plus or minus two: Some limits on our capacity for information processing. *Psychological Review, 48,* 337–442.

Miller, J. B. (1986). *Toward a new psychology of women* (2nd. ed.). Boston: Beacon Press.

Miller, J. G. (1995, March). *Culture, context, and personal agency: The cultural grounding of self and morality.* Paper presented at the meeting of the Society for Research in Child Development, Indianapolis, IN.

Miller, N. E. (1959). Liberalization of basic S-R concepts: Extension to conflict behavior, motivation, and social learning. In S. Koch (Ed.), *Psychology: A study of science.* New York: McGraw-Hill.

Miller, N. E. (1969). Learning of visceral glandular responses. *Science, 163,* 434–445.

Miller, N. E. (1985). The value of behavioral research on animals. *American Psychologist, 40,* 432–440.

Miller, R. (1990). Leta Stetter Hollingworth: Pioneer Woman of Psychology. *Roeper Review, 12,* 142–144.

Miller, S. K., & Slap, G. B. (1989). Adolescent smoking: A review of prevalence and prevention. *Journal of Adolescent Health Care, 10,* 129–135.

Miller-Jones, D. (1989). Culture and testing. *American Psychologist, 44,* 360–366.

Minninger, J. (1984). *Total recall.* New York: Pocket Books.

Mintz, N., & Schwartz, D. (1964). Urban ecology and psychosis: Community factors in the incidence of schizophrenia and manic-depression among Italians in Greater Boston. *International Journal of Social Psychiatry, 10,* 101–118.

Minuchin, P. (1985). Families and individual development: Provocations from the field of family therapy. *Child Development, 56,* 289–302.

Mischel, W. (1968). *Personality and assessment.* New York: Wiley.

Mischel, W. (1973). Toward a cognitive social learning reconceptualization of personality. *Psychological Review, 80,* 252–283.

Mischel, W., & Baker, N. (1975). Cognitive transformations of reward objects through instructions. *Journal of Personality and Social Psychology, 31,* 254–261.

Mishkin, M., & Appenzellar, T. (1987). The anatomy of memory. *Scientific American, 256,* 80–89.

Mistry, J., & Rogoff, B. (1994). Remembering in cultural context. In W. J. Lonner & R. Malpass (Eds.), *Psychology and culture.* Boston: Allyn & Bacon.

Moates, D. R., & Schumacher, G. M. (1980). *An introduction to cognitive psychology.* Belmont, CA: Wadsworth.

Monagle, K. (1990, October). Women around the world. *New Woman,* pp. 195–197.

Money, J. (1986). *Lovemaps: Clinical concepts of sexual/erotic health and pathology, paraphilia, and gender transposition in childhood, adolescence, and maturity.* New York: Irvington.

Monk, T. H. (1989). Circadian rhythms in subjective activation, mood, and performance efficiency. In M. H. Dryger, T. Roth, & W. C. Dement (Eds.), *Principles and practice of sleep medicine.* San Diego: Harcourt Brace Jovanovich.

Monnier, M., & Hosli, L. (1965). Humoral regulation of sleep and wakefulness by hypnogenic and activating dialyzable factors. *Progress in Brain Research, 18,* 118–123.

Montagu, A. (1971). *Touching: The human significance of the skin.* New York: Columbia University Press.

Montemayor, R., & Flannery, D. J. (1991). Parent-adolescent relations in middle and late adolescence. In R. M. Lerner, A. C. Petersen, & J. Brooks-Gunn (Eds.), *Encyclopedia of adolescence* (Vol. 2). New York: Garland.

Moore, T. E. (1995). Subliminal self-help auditory tapes: An empirical test of perceptual consequences. *Canadian Journal of Behavioural Science, 27,* 9–20.

Morgan, W. P., & Goldson, S. E. (1987). *Exercise and mental health.* Washington, DC: Hemisphere.

Morris, D., Collett, P., Marsh, P., & O'Shaugnessy, M. (1979). *Gestures.* New York: Stein & Day.

Morrison, A. M., & Von Glinow, M. A. (1990). Women and minorities in management. *American Psychologist, 45,* 200–209.

Moses, J., Steptoe, A., Mathews, A., & Edwards, S. (1989). The effects of exercise training on mental well-being in the normal population: A controlled trial. *Journal of Psychosomatic Research, 33,* 47–61.

Moskowitz, D. S., Suh, E. J., & Desaulniers, J. (1994). Situational influences on gender differences in agency and communion. *Journal of Personality and Social Psychology, 66,* 753–761.

Munroe, R. H., Himmin, H. S., & Munroe, R. L. (1984). Gender understanding and sex role preference in four cultures. *Developmental Psychology, 20,* 673–682.

Munroe, R. L., & Munroe, R. H. (1975). *Cross-cultural human development.* Monterey, CA: Brooks/Cole.

Murdock, G. P. (1949). *Social structure.* New York: Macmillan.

Murphy, H. B. (1978). Cultural factors in the genesis of schizophrenia. In D. Rosenthal & S. S. Kety (Eds.), *The transmission of schizophrenia.* Elmsford, NY: Pergamon.

Murphy, S. T., & Zajonc, R. B. (1993). Affect, cognition, and awareness: Affective priming with optimal and suboptimal stimulus exposures. *Journal of Personality and Social Psychology, 64,* 723–739.

Murray, H. A. (1938). *Explorations in personality.* New York: Oxford University Press.

Muuss, R. E. (1989). *Theories of adolescence* (15th ed.). New York: Random House.

Myers, D. (1992). *The pursuit of happiness.* New York: William Morrow.

Nagata, D. K. (1989). Japanese American children and adolescents. In J. T. Gibbs & L. N. Huang (Eds.), *Children of color.* San Francisco: Jossey-Bass.

Nass, G. D., Libby, R. W., & Fisher, M. P. (1981). *Sexual choices: An introduction to human sexuality.* Monterey, CA: Wadsworth.

Nathan, P. E. (1994). DSM-IV: Empirical, accessible, not yet ideal. *Journal of Clinical Psychology, 50,* 103–109.

National Academy of Sciences, National Research Council. (1989). *Diet and health: Implications for reducing chronic disease risk.* Washington, DC: National Academy Press.

National Advisory Council on Economic Opportunity. (1980). *Critical choices for the '80s.* Washington, DC: U.S. Government Printing Office.

National Center for Health Statistics. (1989, June). *Statistics on marriage and divorce.* Washington, DC: U.S. Government Printing Office.

National Center for Health Statistics. (1989). *Health, United States, 1988.* DHHS Pub. No. (PHS) 89–1232, Public Health Service. Washington, DC: U.S. Government Printing Office.

National Institutes of Health. (1994). Cigarette smoking among adults, United States, 1992, and changes in definition of current cigarette smoking. *Mortality and Morbidity 43,* 342–346.

Neugarten, B. L. (1986). The aging society. In A. Pifer & L. Bronte (Eds.), *Our aging society: Paradox and promise.* New York: W. W. Norton.

Nevid, J. S., & Gotfried, F. (1995). *Choices: Sex in the age of STDs.* Needham Heights, MA: Allyn & Bacon.

Nevis, E. C. (1983). Using an American perspective in understanding another culture: Toward a hierarchy of needs for the Peoples Republic of China. *Journal of Applied Psychology, 19,* 256.

Nichols, M. P., & Schwartz, R. C. (1995). *Family therapy.* Needham Heights, MA: Allyn & Bacon.

Nicholson, A. N., Bradley, C. M., & Pasco, P. A. (1989). Medications: Effect on sleep and wakefulness. In M. H. Dryger, T. Roth, & W. C. Dement (Eds.), *Principles and practice of sleep medicine.* San Diego: Harcourt Brace Jovanovich.

Nishio, K., & Bilmes, M. (1993). Psychotherapy with Southeast Asian clients. In D. R. Atkinson, G. Morten, & D. W. Sue (Eds.), *Counseling American minorities.* Dubuque, IA: Brown & Benchmark.

Nolen-Hoeksema, S. (1990). *Sex differences in depression.* Stanford, CA: Stanford University Press.

Norem, J. K., & Cantor, N. (1986). Anticipatory and post-hoc cushioning strategies: Optimism and defensive pessimism in "risky" situation. *Cognitive Therapy Research, 10,* 347–362.

Nosworthy, G. J., Lea, J. A., & Lindsay, C. L. (1995). Opposition to affirmative action: Racial affect and traditional value predictors across four programs. *Journal of Applied Social Psychology, 25,* 314–337.

Nottelman, E. D., Susman, E. J., Blue, J. H., Inoff-Germain, G., Doran, L. D., Loriaux, D. L., Cutler, G. B., & Chrousos, G. P. (1987). Gonadal and adrenal hormone correlates of adjustment in early adolescence. In R. M. Lerner & T. T. Foch (Eds.), *Biological-psychological interactions in early adolescence.* Hillsdale, NJ: Erlbaum.

Novak, C. A. (1977). Does youthfulness equal attractiveness? In L. E. Troll, J. Israel, & K. Israel (Eds.), *Looking ahead: A woman's guide to the problems and joys of growing older.* Englewood Cliffs, NJ: Prentice Hall.

Novlin, D., Robinson, B. A., Culbreth, L. A., & Tordoff, M. G. (1983). Is there a role for the liver in the control of food intake? *American Journal of Clinical Nutrition, 9,* 233–246.

O'Donahue, W., & Krasner, L. (Eds.). (1995). *Theories of behavior therapy.* Washington, DC: American Psychological Association.

Offer, D., Ostrov, E., Howard, K. I., & Atkinson, R. (1988). *The teenage world: Adolescents' self-image in ten countries.* New York: Plenum.

Ogbu, J. U. (1989, April). *Academic socialization of Black children: An inoculation against future failure?* Paper presented at the meeting of the Society for Research in Child Development, Kansas City.

Oh, T. K. (1976). Japanese management: A critical review. *Academy of Management Review, 1,* 14–25.

O'Hara, M. W., Reiter, R. C., Johnson, S. R., & Engeltinger, J. (1995). *Psychological aspects of women's reproductive health.* Bristol, PA: Taylor & Francis.

Okano, Y. (1977). *Japanese Americans and mental health.* Los Angeles: Coalition for Mental Health.

Olds, J. M. (1958). Self-stimulation experiments and differentiated rewards systems. In H. H. Jasper, L. D. Proctor, R. S. Knighton, W. C. Noshay, & R. T. Costello (Eds.), *Reticular formation of the brain.* Boston: Little, Brown.

Olds, J. M., & Milner, P. M. (1954). Positive reinforcement produced by electrical stimulation of the septal area and other areas of the rat brain. *Journal of Comparative and Physiological Psychology, 47,* 419–427.

Oller, D. K. (1995, February). *Early speech and word learning in bilingual and monolingual children: Advantages of early bilingualism.* Paper presented at the meeting of the American Association for the Advancement of Science, Atlanta, GA.

Orford, J. (1992). *Community psychology: Theory and practice.* New York: Wiley.

Ornstein, P. A. (1995, March). *Remembering the distant past.* Paper presented at the meeting of the Society for Research in Child Development, Indianapolis, IN.

Ornstein, R., & Sobel, D. (1989). *Healthy pleasures.* Reading, MA: Addison-Wesley.

Ossip-Klein, D. J., Doyne, E. J., Bowman, E. D., Osborn, K. M., McDougall-Wilson, I. B., & Neimeyer, R. A. (1989). Effects of running or weight lifting on self-concept in clinically depressed women. *Journal of Consulting and Clinical Psychology, 57,* 158–161.

Ostoja, E., McCrone, E., Lehn, L., Reed, T., & Sroufe, L. A. (1995, March). *Representations of close relationships in adolescence: Longitudinal antecedents from infancy through childhood.* Paper presented at the meeting of the Society for Research in Child Development, Indianapolis, IN.

O'Toole, A. (1994). Perception. In J. W. Santrock, *Psychology* (4th ed.). Dubuque, IA: Brown & Benchmark.

Overton, W. F., & Byrnes, J. P. (1991). Cognitive development. In R. M. Lerner, A. C. Petersen, and J. Brooks-Gunn (Eds.), *Encyclopedia of adolescence* (Vol. 1). New York: Garland.

Padilla, A. M. (Ed.). (1994). *Hispanic psychology.* Newbury Park, CA: Sage.

Padilla, A. M., & Lindholm, K. J. (1992, August). *What do we know about culturally diverse children?* Paper presented at the meeting of the American Psychological Association, Washington, DC.

Padilla, A. M., Ruiz, R. A., & Alvarez, R. (1989). Community mental health services for the Spanish speaking/surnamed population. In D. R. Atkinson, G. Morten, & D. W. Sue (Eds.), *Counseling American minorities.* Dubuque, IA: Wm. C. Brown.

Paffenbarger, R. S., Hyde, R. T., Wing, A. L., & Hsieh, C. (1986). Physical activity, all-cause mortality, and longevity of college alumni. *New England Journal of Medicine, 314,* 605–612.

Paffenbarger, R. S., Hyde, R. T., Wing, A. L., Lee, I., Jung, D. L., & Kampter, J. B. (1993). The association of changes in physical-activity level and other life-style characteristics with morality among men. *New England Journal of Medicine, 328,* 538–545.

Paivio, A. (1971). *Imagery and verbal processes.* New York: Holt, Rinehart & Winston.

Paivio, A. (1986). *Mental representations: A dual coding approach.* New York: Oxford University Press.

Paloutzian, R. F. (1996). *Invitation to the psychology of religion* (2nd ed.). Needham Heights, MA: Allyn & Bacon.

Paludi, M. A. (1992). *The psychology of women.* Dubuque, IA: Brown & Benchmark.

Paludi, M. A. (1995). *The psychology of women* (2nd ed.). Dubuque, IA: Brown & Benchmark.

Parham, T. A., & McDavis, R. J. (1993). Black men, an endangered species: Who's really pulling the trigger? In D. R. Atkinson, G. Morten, & D. W. Sue (Eds.), *Counseling American minorities.* Dubuque, IA: Brown & Benchmark.

Parke, R. (1988). Families in life-span perspective: A multilevel developmental approach. In E. M. Hetherington & M. Perlmutter (Eds.), *Child development in life-span perspective.* Hillsdale, NJ: Erlbaum.

Parlee, M. B. (1979, April). The friendship bond: PT's survey report on friendship in America. *Psychology Today,* pp. 43–54, 113.

Passuth, P. M., Maines, D. R., & Neugarten, B. L. (1984). *Age norms and age constraints twenty years later.* Paper presented at the annual meeting of the Midwest Sociological Society, Chicago.

Patterson, C. J. (1995). Lesbian and gay parenthood. In M. H. Bornstein (Ed.), *Handbook of parenting, Vol. 3.* Hillsdale, NJ: Erlbaum.

Patterson, G. (1975). *Families.* Champaign, IL: Research Press.

Patterson, G. R. (1991, April). *Which parenting skills are necessary for what?* Paper presented at the biennial meeting of the Society for Research in Child Development, Seattle.

Paul, G. L. (1967). Strategy of outcome research in psychotherapy. *Journal of Consulting Psychology, 31,* 109–119.

Pavlov, I. P. (1927). *Conditioned reflexes* (F. V. Anrep, Trans. and Ed.). New York: Dover.

Peck, M. S. (1978). *The road less traveled.* New York: Simon & Schuster.

Pedersen, P. (1994). A culture-centered approach to counseling. In W. Lonner & R. Malpass (Eds.), *Psychology and culture.* Needham Heights, MA: Allyn & Bacon.

Peele, S., & Brodsky, A. (1991). *The truth about addiction and recovery.* New York: Simon & Schuster.

Pelham, B. W. (1991). On the benefits of misery: Self-serving biases in the depressive self-concept. *Journal of Personality and Social Psychology, 61,* 670–681.

Penfield, W. (1947). Some observations in the cerebral cortex of man. *Proceedings of the Royal Society, 134,* 349.

Pennebaker, J. W. (1983). Accuracy of symptom perception. In A. Baum, S. E. Taylor, & J. Singer (Eds.), *Handbook of psychology and health* (Vol. 4). Hillsdale, NJ: Erlbaum.

Pennebaker, J. W., & Lightner, J. M. (1980). Competition of internal and external information in an exercise setting. *Journal of Personality and Social Psychology, 39,* 165–174.

Penner, S. G. (1987). Parental responses to grammatical and ungrammatical child utterances. *Child Development, 58,* 376–384.

Perkins, D. N. (1984, September). Creativity by design. *Educational Leadership,* 18–25.

Perlmutter, M. (1994). Cognitive skills within the context of adult development and old age. In C. Fisher & R. Lerner (Eds.), *Applied developmental psychology.* New York: McGraw-Hill.

Perls, E. (1969). *Gestalt therapy verbatim.* Lafayette, CA: Real People Press.

Perry, C., Hearn, M., Murray, D., & Klepp, K. (1988). *The etiology and prevention of adolescent alcohol and drug abuse.* Unpublished manuscript, University of Minnesota.

Persinger, M. A., & Krippner, S. (in press). Experimental dream telepathy-clairvoyance and geomagnetic activity. *Journal of the American Society for Psychical Research.*

Pert, A. B., & Snyder, S. H. (1973). Opiate receptor: Demonstration in a nervous tissue. *Science, 179,* 1011.

Pervin, L. (1989). *Personality: Theory and research* (5th ed.). New York: Wiley.

Pervin, L. A. (1993). *Personality* (6th ed.). New York: Wiley.

Peskin, H. (1967). Pubertal onset and ego functioning. *Journal of Abnormal Psychology, 72,* 1–15.

Petersen, A. C. (1979, January). Can puberty come any faster? *Psychology Today,* pp. 45–56.

Peterson, C. (1988). *Personality.* San Diego: Harcourt Brace Jovanovich.

Peterson, C., & Stunkard, A. J. (1986). *Personal control and health promotion.* Unpublished manuscript, Department of Psychology, University of Michigan, Ann Arbor.

Pfeiffer, E., Verwoerdt, A., & Davis, G. C. (1974). Sexual behavior in middle life. In E. Palmore (Ed.), *Normal aging. II: Reports from the Duke longitudinal studies, 1970–1973.* Durham, NC: Duke University Press.

Phares, E. J. (1984). *Personality.* Columbus, OH: Merrill.

Phillips, R. L., & others. (1980). Influence of selection versus lifestyle on risk of fatal cancer and cardiovascular disease among Seventh-Day Adventists. *American Journal of Epidemiology, 112,* 296–314.

Phinney, J. S. (1989). Stages of ethnic identity development in minority group adolescents. *Journal of Early Adolescence, 9,* 34–39.

Phinney, J. S., & Alipura, L. (1990). Ethnic identity in college students from four ethnic groups. *Journal of Adolescence, 13,* 171–183.

Phinney, J. S., & Rosenthal, D. A. (1992). Ethnic identity in adolescence: Process, context, and outcome. In G. R. Adams, T. P. Gullotta, & R. Montemayor (Eds.), *Adolescent identity formation.* Newbury Park, CA: Sage.

Piaget, J. (1960). *The child's conception of the world.* Totowa, NJ: Littlefield.

Pinderhughes, E. (1982). Afro-American families and the victim system. In M. McGoldrick, M. J. Pearce, & J. Giordano (Eds.), *Ethnicity and family therapy.* New York: Guilford Press.

Plath, S. (1971). *The bell jar.* New York: Harper & Row.

Pleck, J. H. (1983). The theory of male sex role identity: Its rise and fall, 1936–present. In M. Lewin (Ed.), *In the shadow of the past: Psychology portrays the sexes.* New York: Columbia University Press.

Pleck, J. H. (1995). The gender role strain paradigm: An update. In R. F. Levant & W. S. Pollack (Eds.), *A new psychology of men.* New York: Basic.

Pleck, J. H., Sonnenstein, F. L., & Ku, L. C. (1994). Problem behaviors and masculine ideology in adolescent males. In R. Ketterlinus & M. E. Lamb (Eds.), *Adolescent problem behaviors.* Hillsdale, NJ: Erlbaum.

Plomin, R. (1993, March). *Human behavioral genetics and development: An overview and update.* Paper presented at the biennial meeting of the Society for Research in Child Development, New Orleans.

Plomin, R., DeFries, J. C., & McClearn, G. F. (1990). *Behavioral genetics: A primer.* New York: W. H. Freeman.

Plutchik, R. (1980). *Emotion: A psychoevolutionary synthesis.* New York: Harper & Row.

Podolsky, D., & Silberner, J. (1993, January 18). How medicine mistreats the elderly. *U.S. News and World Report,* pp. 72–79.

Polivy, J., & Herman, C. P. (1991). Good and bad dieters: Self-perception and reaction to a dietary challenge. *International Journal of Eating Disorders, 10,* 91–99.

Pollack, S., & Gilligan, C. (1985). Killing the messenger. *Journal of Personality and Social Psychology, 48,* 374–375.

Pollack, W. S. (1995). No man is an island: Toward a new psychoanalytic psychology of men. In R. F. Levant & W. S. Pollack (Eds.), *A new psychology of men.* New York: Basic.

Pollock, V. E., Schneider, L. S., Gabrielli, W. F., & Goodwin, D. W. (1987). Sex of parent and sex of offspring in the transmission of alcoholism: A meta-analysis. *Journal of Nervous and Mental Disease, 173,* 668–673.

Ponterotto, J. G., Casas, J. M., Suzuki, L. A., & Alexander, C. M. (Eds.). (1995). *Handbook of multicultural counseling.* Newbury Park, CA: Sage.

Posada, G., Lord, C., & Waters, E. (1995, March). *Secure base behavior and children's behavior in three different contexts.* Paper presented at the meeting of the Society for Research in Child Development, Indianapolis, IN.

Pouissant, A. F. (1972, February). Blaxploitation movies—Cheap thrills that degrade Blacks. *Psychology Today,* pp. 22–33.

Powell, G. J., & Fuller, M. (1972). The variables for positive self-concept among young Southern Black adolescents. *Journal of the National Medical Association, 43,* 72–79.

Premack, D. (1986). *Gavagi! The future history of the ape language controversy.* Cambridge, MA: MIT Press.

Prentice, D. A., & Miller, D. T. (1993). Pluralistic ignorance and alcohol use on campus: Some consequences of misperceiving the social norm. *Journal of Personality and Social Psychology, 64,* 243–256.

Price-Williams, D., Gordon, W., & Ramirez, M. (1969). Skill and conservation: A study of pottery-making children. *Developmental Psychology, 1,* 796.

Proust, M. (1928). *Swan's way* (C. K. Scott Moncrieff, trans.). New York: Modern Library.

Pylyshyn, Z. W. (1973). What the mind's eye tells the mind's brain. A critique of mental imagery. *Psychological Bulletin, 80,* 1–24.

Rabinowitz, F. E., & Cochran, S. V. (1987). Counseling men in groups. In M. Scher, M. Stevens, G. Good, & G. A. Eichenfield (Eds.), *Handbook of counseling and psychotherapy with men.* Newbury Park, CA: Sage.

Rabinowitz, V. C., & Sechzur, J. (1994). Feminist methodologies. In F. L. Denmark & M. A. Paludi (Eds.), *Handbook on the psychology of women.* Westport, CT: Greenwood.

Rabkin, J. (1979). Ethnic density and psychiatric hospitalization: Hazards of minority status. *American Journal of Psychiatry, 136,* 1562–1566.

Ramey, C. (1989, April). *Parent-child intellectual similarities in natural and altered ecologies.* Paper presented at the biennial meeting of the Society for Research in Child Development, Kansas City.

Ramirez, O. (1989). Mexican American children and adolescents. In J. T. Gibbs & L. N. Huang (Eds.), *Children of color.* San Francisco: Jossey-Bass.

Ramirez, O., & Arce, C. Y. (1981). The contemporary Chicano family: An empirically based review. In A. Baron (Ed.), *Explorations in Chicano psychology.* New York: Praeger.

Randi, J. (1980). *Flim-flam!* New York: Lippincott.

Ratcliff, K. S., & Bogdan, J. (1988). Unemployed women: When `social support' is not supportive. *Social Problems, 35,* 54–63.

Ratner, N. B. (1993). Learning to speak. *Science, 262,* 260.

Ravnikar, V. (1992, May 25). Commentary, *Newsweek,* p. 82.

Redd, W. H. (1995). Behavioral research in cancer as a model for health psychology. *Health Psychology, 14,* 99–100.

Regier, D. A., Hirschfeld, R. M. A., Goodwin, F. K., Burke, J. D., Lazar, J. B., & Judd, L. L. (1988). The NIMH Depression Awareness, Recognition, and Treatment Program: Structure, aims, and scientific basis. *American Journal of Psychiatry, 145,* 1351–1357.

Reinisch, J. (1992, December 7). Commentary, *Newsweek,* p. 54.

Reinisch, J. M. (1990). *The Kinsey Institute new report on sex: What you must know to be sexually literate.* New York: St. Martin's Press.

Reiser, B. J., Black, J. B., & Abelson, R. P. (1985). Knowledge structures in the organization and retrieval of autobiographical memories. *Cognitive Psychology, 17,* 89–137.

Renzetti, C. M., & Curran, D. J. (1992). *Women, men, and society.* Boston: Allyn & Bacon.

Rescorla, R. A. (1988). Pavlovian conditioning: It's not what you think it is. *American Psychologist, 43,* 151–160.

Rescorla, R. A., & Wagner, A. R. (1972). A theory of Pavlovian conditioning: Variations in the effectiveness of reinforcement and nonreinforcement. In A. Black & W. F. Prokasy (Eds.), *Classical conditioning II: Current theory and research.* New York: Appleton-Century-Crofts.

Restak, R. (1988). *The mind.* New York: Bantam.

Revitch, E., & Schlesinger, L. B. (1978). Murder: Evaluation, classification, and prediction. In I. L. Kutash, S. B. Kutash, & L. B. Schlesinger (Eds.), *Violence.* San Francisco: Jossey-Bass.

Richter, C. P. (1957). On the phenomenon of sudden death in animals and man. *Psychosomatic Medicine, 19,* 191–198.

Richwald, G. A., Schneider-Munoz, M., & Valdez, R. B. (1989). Are condom instructions in Spanish readable? Implications for AIDS preventions. *Hispanic Journal of Behavioral Sciences, 11,* 70–82.

Riger, S., & Galligan, P. (1980). An exploration of competing paradigms. *American Psychologist, 35,* 902–910.

Robins, L. N., Helzer, J. F., Weissman, M. M., Orvashcel, H., Gruenberg, F., Burke, J. D., & Regier, D. A. (1984). Lifetime prevalence of specific psychiatric disorders in three sites. *Archives of General Psychiatry, 41,* 949–958.

Robinson, I., Ziss, K., Ganza, B., Katz, S., & Robinson, E. (1991). Twenty years of the sexual revolution, 1965–1985: An update. *Journal of Marriage and the Family, 53,* 216–220.

Rodgers, C. D., Paterson, D. H., Cunningham, D. A., Noble, E. G., Pettigrew, F. P., Myles, W. S., & Taylor, A. W. (1995). Sleep deprivation: Effects on work capacity, self-paced walking, contractile properties, and perceived exertion. *Sleep, 18,* 30–38.

Rodin, J. (1984, December). Interview: A sense of control. *Psychology Today,* pp. 38–45.

Rodin, J. (1992). *Body traps.* New York: William Morrow.

Rodin, J., & Ickovics, J. R. (1990). Women's health: Review and research agenda as we approach the 21st century. *American Psychologist, 45,* 1018–1034.

Roethlisberger, F., & Dickson, W. J. (1939). *Management and the worker.* Cambridge, MA: Harvard University Press.

Rogers, C. R. (1961). *On becoming a person.* Boston: Houghton-Mifflin.

Rogers, C. R. (1963). The actualizing tendency in relation to "motives" and consciousness. In M. R. Jones (Ed.), *Nebraska Symposium on Motivation.* Lincoln: University of Nebraska Press.

Rogers, C. R. (1974). In retrospect: Forty-six years. *American Psychologist, 29,* 115–123.

Rogers, C. R. (1980). *A way of being.* Boston: Houghton-Mifflin.

Roghmann, K. J. (1981). The health of school-aged children. In L. V. Klemman (Ed.), *Research priorities in maternal and child health.* Waltham, MA: Brandeis University, Office of Maternal and Child Health.

Rogler, L. H., Malgady, R. G., Costantino, G., & Blumenthal, R. (1987). What do culturally sensitive mental health services mean? *American Psychologist, 42,* 565–570.

Rogoff, B. (1990). *Apprenticeship in thinking: Cognitive development in social context.* New York: Oxford University Press.

Rogoff, B. (1993, March). *Whither cognitive development in the 1990s?* Paper presented at the biennial meeting of the Society for Research in Child Development, New Orleans.

Rogoff, B., & Mistry, J. (1985). Memory development in cultural context. In M. Pressley & C. Brainerd (Eds.), *The cognitive side of memory development.* New York: Springer-Verlag.

Rogoff, B., & Morelli, G. (1989). Perspectives on children's development from cultural psychology. *American Psychologist, 44,* 343–348.

Rohner, R. P., & Rohner, E. C. (1981). Parental acceptance-rejection and parental control: Cross-cultural codes. *Ethnology, 20,* 245–260.

Roll, S., Hinton, R., & Glazer, M. (1974). Dreams and death: Mexican Americans vs. Anglo-Americans. *Interamerican Journal of Psychology, 8,* 111–115.

Root, M. P. (Ed.). (1992). *Racially mixed people in America.* Newbury Park, CA: Sage.

Root, M. P. P. (1993). Guidelines for facilitating therapy with Asian American clients. In D. R. Atkinson, G. Morten, & D. W. Sue (Eds.), *Counseling American minorities.* Dubuque, IA: Brown & Benchmark.

Rosch, E. H. (1973). On the internal structure of perceptual and semantic categories. In T. E. Moore (Ed.), *Cognition and the acquisition of language.* New York: Academic Press.

Rose, R. J. (1995). Genetics and human behavior. *Annual Review of Psychology, Vol. 46.* Palo Alto, CA: Annual Reviews.

Roseman, I. J., Dhawan, N., Rettek, S. I., Naidu, R. K., & Thapa, K. (1995). Cultural differences and cross-cultural similarities in appraisals and emotional responses. *Journal of Cross-Cultural Psychology, 26,* 23–48.

Rosen, K. H., & Stith, S. M. (1995). Women terminating abusive dating relationships: A qualitative study. *Journal of Personal and Social Relationships, 12,* 155–160.

Rosenberg, M. (1965). *Society and the adolescent self-image.* Princeton, NJ: Princeton University Press.

Rosenhan, D. L. (1973). On being sane in insane places. *Science, 179,* 250–258.

Rosenthal, N., Sack, D., Carpenter, C., Parry, B., Mendelson, W., & Wehr, T. (1985). Antidepressant effects of light in seasonal affective disorder. *American Journal of Psychiatry, 142,* 163–170.

Rosenthal, R. (1976). *Experimenter effects in behavioral research.* New York: Halstead.

Rosenthal, R., & Jacobsen, L. (1968). *Pygmalion in the classroom.* New York: Holt, Rinehart & Winston.

Rossi, A. (1989). A life course approach to gender, aging, and intergenerational relations. In K. W. Schaie & C. Schooler (Eds.), *Social structures and aging.* Hillsdale, NJ: Erlbaum.

Rothblum, E. D., Solomon, L. J., & Albee, G. W. (1986). The sociopolitical perspective of DSM-III. In T. Millon & G. L. Klerman (Eds.), *Contemporary directions in psychopathology: Toward the DSM-IV.* New York: Guilford Press.

Rotter, J. B. (1954). *Social learning and clinical psychology.* New York: Prentice Hall.

Rowe, J., & Kahn, R. (1987). Human aging: Usual and successful. *Science, 237,* 143–149.

Rubin, L. B. (1984). *Intimate strangers: Men and women working together.* New York: Harper & Row.

Rubin, Z., & Mitchell, C. (1976). Couples research as couples counseling. *American Psychologist, 31,* 17–25.

Rumbaugh, D. M., Hopkins, W. D., Washburn, D. A., & Savage-Rumbaugh, E. S. (1991). Comparative perspectives of brain, cognition, and language. In N. A. Krasnegor, D. M. Rumbaugh, M. Studdert-Kennedy, & R. L. Schiefelbusch (Eds.), *Biological and behavioral determinants of language development.* Hillsdale, NJ: Erlbaum.

Rumberger, R. W. (1983). Dropping out of high school: The influence of race, sex, and family background. *American Educational Research Journal, 20,* 199–220.

Rumberger, R. W. (1987). High school dropouts: A review of the issues and evidence. *Review of Educational Research, 57,* 101–121.

Rumpel, E. (1988, August). *A systematic analysis of the cultural content of introductory psychology textbooks.* Unpublished master's thesis, Western Washington University, Bellingham.

Russo, N. F. (1990). Overview: Forging research priorities for women's mental health. *American Psychologist, 45,* 368–374.

Russo, N. F. (1995). PSQ: A scientific voice in feminist psychology. *Psychology of Women Quarterly, 19,* 1–3.

Rutter, M. (1979). Protective factors in children's response to stress and disadvantage. In M. W. Kent & J. E. Rolf (Eds.), *Primary prevention in psychopathology* (Vol. 3). Hanover, NH: University Press of New England.

Rutter, M., & Garmezy, N. (1983). Developmental psychopathology. In P. H. Mussen (Ed.), *Handbook of child psychology* (4th ed., Vol. 4). New York: Wiley.

Ryan, D. W., & Gaier, E. L. (1968). Student socio-economic status and counselor contact in junior high school. *Personnel and Guidance Journal, 46,* 466–472.

Rybash, J. W., Roodin, P. A., & Santrock, J. W. (1991). *Adult development and aging* (2nd ed.). Dubuque, IA: Brown & Benchmark.

Rymer, R. (1993). *Genie.* New York: HarperCollins.

Rymer, R. (1993). *Genie.* New York: HarperCollins.

Saarni, C. (1988). Children's understanding of the interpersonal consequences of dissemblance of nonverbal emotional-expressive behavior. *Journal of Nonverbal Behavior, 12,* 275–294.

Sackheim, H. A. (1985, June). The case for ECT. *Psychology Today,* pp. 37–40.

Sacks, O. (1993, May 10). To see and not see. *New Yorker,* pp. 59–66+.

Sadik, N. (1991, March–April). Success in development depends on women. In *Popline.* New York: World Population News Service.

Sadker, M., & Sadker, D. (1994). *Failing at fairness: How America's schools cheat girls.* New York: Charles Scribner's Sons.

Sadry, G., & Robertson, I. T. (1993). Self-efficacy and work-related behavior: A review and meta-analysis. *Applied Psychology, 42,* 139–152.

Sagan, C. (1980). *Cosmos.* New York: Random House.

Saklofske, D. H., & Zeidner, M. (Eds.). (1995). *International handbook of personality and intelligence.* New York: Plenum.

Sanderson, W. C. (1995, March). Which therapies are proven effective? *APA Monitor,* p. 4.

Sandler, D. P., Comstock, G. W., Helsing, K. J., & Shore, D. L. (1989). Deaths from all causes in non-smokers who lived with smokers. *American Journal of Public Health, 79,* 163–167.

Sangree, W. H. (1989). Age and power: Life-course trajectories and age structuring of power relations in East and West Africa. In D. I. Kertzer & K. W. Schaie (Eds.), *Age structuring in comparative perspective.* Hillsdale, NJ: Erlbaum.

Santrock, J. W. (1993). *Children* (3rd ed.). Dubuque, IA: Brown & Benchmark.

Santrock, J. W. (1995). *Life-span development* (5th ed.). Dubuque, IA: Brown & Benchmark.

Santrock, J. W. (1996). *Child development* (6th ed.). Dubuque, IA: Brown & Benchmark.

Sarafino, E. P. (1994). *Health psychology* (2nd ed.). New York: John Wiley.

Sargent, C. (1987). Skeptical fairytales From Bristol. *Journal of the Society for Psychical Research, 54.*

Sarrel, P., & Masters, W. (1982). Sexual molestation of men by women. *Archives of Human Sexuality, 11,* 117–131.

Sartorius, N. (1992). Commentary on prognosis for schizophrenia in the third world. *Culture, Medicine, and Psychiatry, 16,* 81–84.

Sasaki, T., & Kennedy, J. L. (1995). Genetics of psychosis. *Current Opinion in Psychiatry, 8,* 25–28.

Satir, V. (1964). *Conjoint family therapy.* Palo Alto, CA: Science and Behavior Books.

Savage-Rumbaugh, E. S., Murphy, J., Sevick, R. A., Brakke, K. E., Williams, S. L., & Rumbaugh, D. (1993). Language comprehension in ape and child. *Monographs of the Society for Research in Child Development, 58,* (3–4, Serial No. 233).

Saxe, G. B. (1981). Body parts as numerals: A developmental analysis of numeration among the Oksapmin in Papua, New Guinea. *Child Development, 52,* 306–316.

Saxe, L., Dougherty, D., & Cross, T. (1985). The validity of polygraph testing: Scientific analysis and public controversy. *American Psychologist, 40,* 355–366.

Scarr, S. (1984, May). [Interview.] *Psychology Today,* pp. 59–63.

Scarr, S. (1991, April). *Developmental theories for the 1990s.* Presidential address, biennial meeting of the Society for Research in Child Development, Seattle.

Scarr, S., Lande, J., & McCartney, K. (1989). Child care and the family: Complements and interactions. In J. Lande, S. Scarr, & N. Gunzenhauser (Eds.), *Caring for children: Challenge to America.* Hillsdale, NJ: Erlbaum.

Schachter, S. (1971). Some extraordinary facts about obese humans and rats. *American Psychologist, 26,* 129–144.

Schachter, S., & Singer, J. E. (1962). Cognitive, social, and physiological determinants of emotional state. *Psychological Review, 69,* 379–399.

Schacter, D. L., Chiu, C. P., & Ochsner, K. N. (1993). Implicit memory: A selective review. *Annual Review of Neuroscience, 16.*

Schaffer, H. R., & Emerson, P. E. (1964). The development of social attachments in infancy. *Monographs of the Society for Research in Child Development, 2913,* Serial No. 941.

Schank, R., & Abelson, R. (1977). *Scripts, plans, goals, and understanding.* Hillsdale, NJ: Erlbaum.

Schensul, S. L. (1974). Commentary: Skills needed in action anthropology: Lessons from El Centro de la Causa. *Human Organization, 33,* 203–209.

Scherer, K. R., Wallbott, H. G., Matsumoto, D., & Kudoh, T. (1988). Emotional experience in cultural context: A comparison between Europe, Japan, and the United States. In K. R. Scherer (Ed.), *Facets of emotion: Recent research.* Hillsdale, NJ: Erlbaum.

Schneidman, E. S. (1971). Suicide among the gifted. *Suicide and Life-Threatening Behavior, 1,* 23–45.

Schofield, J., & Pavelchak, M. (1985). The day after: The impact of a media event. *American Psychologist, 40,* 542–548.

Schofield, J. W., & Pavelchak, M. A. (1989). Fallout from *The Day After:* Impact of the TV film on attitudes related to nuclear war. *Journal of Applied Social Psychology, 19,* 433–448.

Schreiber, J. M., & Homiak, J. P. (1981). Mexican Americans. In A. Harwood (Ed.), *Ethnicity and medical care.* Cambridge, MA: Harvard University Press.

Schulz, R., & Curnow, C. (1988). Peak performance and age among super athletes. Track and field, swimming, baseball, tennis, and golf. *Journal of Gerontology, 43,* 113–120.

Schunk, D. H. (1983). Developing children's self-efficacy and skills: The roles of social comparative information and goal-setting. *Contemporary Educational Psychology, 8,* 76–86.

Schwartz, M. S. (1995). *Biofeedback* (2nd ed.). New York: Guilford.

Schwartz, R., & Eriksen, M. (1989). Statement of the Society for Public Health Education on the national health promotion disease prevention objectives for the year 2000. *Health Education Quarterly, 16,* 3–7.

Schwartz, S. H. (1990). Individualism-collectivism. *Journal of Cross-Cultural Psychology, 21,* 139–157.

Schwartz, S. H., & Sagiv, L. (1995). Identifying culture-specifics in the content and structure of values. *Journal of Cross-Cultural Psychology, 26,* 92–116.

Scitovsky, A. A. (1988). Medical care in the last twelve months of life: Relation between age, functional status, and medical care expenditures. *Milbank Quarterly, 66,* 640–660.

Scott-Jones, D. (1995, March). *Incorporating ethnicity and socioeconomic status in research with children.* Paper presented at the meeting of the Society for Research in Child Development, Indianapolis, IN.

Scribner, S. (1977). Modes of thinking and ways of speaking: Culture and logic reconsidered. In P. N. Johnson-Laird & P. C. Watson (Eds.), *Thinking: Readings in cognitive science.* New York: Cambridge University Press.

Seager, J., & Olson, A. (Eds.). (1986). *Women of the world: An international atlas.* New York: Simon & Schuster.

Sears, D. O. (1987). Symbolic racism. In P. Katz & D. Taylor (Eds.), *Towards the elimination of racism: Profile in controversy.* New York: Plenum.

Sears, D. O., & Funk, C. (1991). The role of self-interest in social and political attitudes. In M. Zann (Ed.), *Advances in experimental social psychology,* Vol. 24. San Diego, CA: Academic Press.

Sears, D. O., & McConahay, J. B. (1973). *The politics of violence: The new urban Blacks and the Watts riot.* Boston: Houghton Mifflin.

Sears, D. O., Peplau, L. A., Freedman, J. L., & Taylor, S. E. (1993). *Social psychology* (7th ed.). Englewood Cliffs, NJ: Prentice Hall.

Sears, D. O., Peplau, L. A., Freedman, J. L., & Taylor, S. E. (1994). *Social psychology* (8th ed.). Englewood Cliffs, NJ: Prentice Hall.

Seffge-Krenke, I. (1995). *Stress, coping, and relationships in adolescence.* Hillsdale, NJ: Erlbaum.

Segall, M. H., Campbell, D. T., & Herskovits, M. J. (1963). Cultural differences in the perception of geometric illusions. *Science, 193,* 769–771.

Segall, M. H., Dasen, P. R., Berry, J. W., & Poortinga, Y. H. (1990). *Human behavior in global perspective.* New York: Pergamon.

Seligman, M. (1990). *Learned optimism.* New York: Pocket Books.

Seligman, M. E. P. (1970). On the generality of the laws of learning. *Psychological Review, 77,* 406–418.

Seligman, M. E. P. (1975). *Helplessness. On depression, development and death.* San Francisco: W. H. Freeman.

Seligman, M. E. P. (1989). Why is there so much depression today? The waxing of the individual and the waning of the common. In *The G. Stanley Hall Lecture Series.* Washington, DC: American Psychological Association.

Seligman, M. E. P. (1991). *Learned optimism.* New York: Knopf.

Selye, H. (1974). *Stress without distress.* Philadelphia: Saunders.

Selye, H. (1983). The stress concept. Past, present, and future. In C. I. Cooper (Ed.), *Stress research.* New York: Wiley.

Semaj, L. T. (1985). Afrikanity, cognition, and extended self-identity. In M. B. Spencer, G. K. Brookins, & W. R. Allen (Eds.), *Beginnings: The social and affective development of Black children.* Hillsdale, NJ: Erlbaum.

Shaffer, C., & Anundsen, K. (1993). *Creating community anywhere.* Los Angeles: Jeremy Tarcher.

Shanks, D. R. (1991). Categorization by a connectionist network. *Journal of Experimental Psychology: Learning, Memory, and Cognition, 17,* 433–443.

Shaver, P. (1986, August). *Being lonely, falling in love: Perspectives from attachment theory.* Paper presented at the meeting of the American Psychological Association, Washington, DC.

Sheehy, G. (1991). *The silent passage.* New York: Random House.

Sheldon, W. H. (1954). *Atlas of men.* New York: Harper.

Shepard, R. (1967). Recognition memory for words, sentences, and pictures. *Journal of Verbal Learning and Verbal Behavior, 6,* 156–163.

Shepherd, L. J. (1993). *Lifting the veil: The feminine face of science.* Boston: Shambhala.

Sher, K. J. (1991). *Children of alcoholics: A critical appraisal of theory and research.* Chicago: University of Chicago Press.

Sher, K. J. (1993). Children of alcoholics and the intergenerational transmission of alcoholism: A biopsychosocial perspective. In J. S. Baer, G. A. Marlatt, & R. J. McMahon (Eds.), *Addictive behaviors across the life span.* Newbury Park, CA: Sage.

Sherer, K., & Wallbott, H. (1994). Evidence for the universality and cultural variation of different emotion response patterning. *Journal of Personality and Social Psychology, 66,* 310–328.

Sherif, M., Harvey, O. J., White, B. J., Hood, W. R., & Sherif, C. W. (1961). *Intergroup cooperation and competition: The Robbers Cave experiment.* Norman: University of Oklahoma Press.

Sherwood, A., Light, K. C., & Blumenthal, J. A. (1989). Effects of aerobic exercise training on hemodynamic responses during psychosocial stress in normotensive and borderline hypertensive Type A men: A preliminary report. *Psychosomatic Medicine, 51,* 123–136.

Shields, S. A. (1991a). Gender in the psychology of emotion: A selective research review. In K. T. Strongman (Ed.), *International Review of Studies on Emotion* (Vol. I). New York: Wiley.

Shields, S. A. (1991b, August). *Doing emotion/doing gender.* Paper presented at the meeting of the American Psychological Association, San Francisco.

Shotland, R. L. (1985, June). When bystanders just stand by. *Psychology Today,* pp. 50–55.

Showers, C. (1986, August). *The motivational consequences of negative thinking: Those who imagine the worst try harder.* Paper presented at the meeting of the American Psychological Association, Washington, DC.

Showers, C. (1992). Compartmentalization of positive and negative self-knowledge: Keeping bad apples out of the bunch. *Journal of Personality and Social Psychology, 62,* 1036–1049.

Shrout, P. E., & Fiske, S. T. (Eds.). (1995). *Personality research, methods, & theory.* Hillsdale, NJ: Erlbaum.

Siegler, R. S. (1995, March). *Nothing is; everything becomes.* Paper presented at the meeting of the Society for Research in Child Development, Indianapolis, IN.

Siffre, M. (1975). Six months alone in a cave. *National Geographic, 147,* 426–435.

Sigelman, C. K., Thomas, D. B., Sigelman, L., & Ribich, F. D. (1986). Gender, physical attractiveness, and electability: An experimental investigation of vote biases. *Journal of Applied Social Psychology: 16,* 229–248.

Signorielli, N. (1993). Television, the portrayal of women, and children's attitudes. In G. L. Berry & J. K. Asamen (Eds.), *Children and television.* Newbury Park, CA: Sage.

Silverman, N. N., & Corsini, R. J. (1984). Is it true what they say about Adler's individual psychology? *Teaching of Psychology, 11,* 188–189.

Simmons, R. G., & Blyth, D. A. (1987). *Moving into adolescence.* Hawthorne, NY: Aldine.

Simon, H. A. (1990). Invariants in human behavior. *Annual Review of Psychology, 41.*

Simons, J., Kalichman, S., & Santrock, J. W. (1994). *Human adjustment.* Dubuque, IA: Brown & Benchmark.

Simons, J. M., Finlay, B., & Yang, A. (1991). *The adolescent and young adult fact book.* Washington, DC: Children's Defense Fund.

Singer, J. L. (1984). *The human personality.* San Diego: Harcourt Brace Jovanovich.

Sizemore, C. C. (1989). *A mind of my own.* New York: William Morrow.

Skinner, B. F. (1938). *The behavior of organisms: An experimental analysis.* New York: Appleton-Century-Crofts.

Skinner, B. F. (1948). *Walden two.* New York: Macmillan.

Skinner, B. F. (1961). Teaching machines. *Scientific American, 205,* 90–102.

Skinner, B. F. (1971). *Beyond freedom and dignity.* New York: Knopf.

Skinner, B. F. (1990). Can psychology be a science of mind? *American Psychologist, 45,* 1206–1210.

Skinner, E. A., Wellborn, J. G., & Connell, J. P. (1990). What it takes to do well in school and whether I've got it: A process model of perceived control and children's engagement and achievement in school. *Journal of Educational Psychology, 82,* 22–32.

Slavin, R. (1989). Cooperative learning and student achievement. In R. Slavin (Ed.), *School and classroom organization.* Hillsdale, NJ: Erlbaum.

Slavin, R. E. (1988). *Educational psychology* (2nd ed.). Englewood Cliffs, NJ: Prentice Hall.

Sloan, T. S. (1990). Psychology for the third world? *Journal of Social Issues, 46*, 1–20.

Slobin, D. (1972, July). Children and language: They learn the same all around the world. *Psychology Today*, pp. 71–76.

Slovenko, R. (1995). *Psychiatry and criminal culpability.* New York: Wiley.

Smith, J. C. (Ed.). (1991). *Notable Black American women.* Detroit: Gale Research.

Smith, M. L., Glass, G. N., & Miller, R. L. (1980). *The benefit of psychotherapy.* Baltimore: Johns Hopkins University Press.

Smith, R. H., & Insko, C. A. (1987). Social comparison choice during ability evaluation: The effects of comparison publicity, performance feedback, and self-esteem. *Personality and Social Psychology Bulletin, 13*, 111–122.

Snarey, R. (1987, June). A question of morality. *Psychology Today*, pp. 6–8.

Snow, C. E. (1989, April). *Imitation as one path to language acquisition.* Paper presented at the biennial meeting of the Society for Research in Child Development, Kansas City.

Snowden, L. R., & Cheung, F. K. (1990). Use of inpatient mental health services by members of ethnic minority groups. *American Psychologist, 45*, 347–355.

Snowden, L. R., & Hines, A. M. (1994). Reaching the underserved: Mental health services and special populations. In W. Lonner & R. Malpass (Eds.), *Psychology and culture.* Needham Heights, MA: Allyn & Bacon.

Sobell, L. C., & Sobell, M. (in press). Timeline follow-back: A technique for assessing self-reported ethanol consumption. In J. Allen & R. Z. Litten (Eds.), *Techniques to assess alcohol consumption.* Totowa, NJ: Humana.

Sobell, M. B., & Sobell, L. C. (1993). Treatment for problem drinkers: A public health priority. In J. S. Baer, G. A. Marlatt, & R. J. McMahon (Eds.), *Addictive behaviors across the life span.* Newbury Park, CA: Sage.

Sokal, M. M. (1992). Origin and early years of the American Psychological Association, 1890–1906, *American Psychologist, 47*, 111–122.

Solano, C. H. (1982). Loneliness and patterns of self-disclosure. *Journal of Personality and Social Psychology, 43*, 524–531.

Solomon, R. (1964). Punishment. *American Psychologist, 19*, 239–253.

Solomon, Z. (1993). *Combat stress reaction.* New York: Plenum.

Spacapan, S. (1988). Social psychology and health. In S. Spacapan & S. Oskamp (Eds.), *The social psychology of health.* Newbury Park, CA: Sage.

Spade, J. Z., & Reese, C. A. (1991). We've come a long way, maybe: College students' plans for work and family. *Sex Roles, 24*, 309–321.

Spearman, C. E. (1927). *The abilities of man.* New York: Macmillan.

Spence, J. T., & Heimreich, R. (1978). *Masculinity and femininity: Their psychological dimensions.* Austin: University of Texas Press.

Spence, M., & DeCasper, A. J. (1982). *Human fetuses perceive human speech.* Paper presented at the International Conference of Infant Studies, Austin.

Spencer, M. B., & Dornbusch, S. M. (1990). Challenges in studying minority youth. In S. S. Feldman & G. R. Elliott (Eds.), *At the threshold: The developing adolescent.* Cambridge, MA: Harvard University Press.

Sperling, G. (1960). The information available in brief visual presentations. *Psychological Monographs, 74* (Whole No. 11).

Sperry, R. W. (1968). Hemisphere deconnection and unity in conscious awareness. *American Psychologist, 23*, 723–733.

Sprei, J. E., & Courtois, C. A. (1988). The treatment of women's sexual dysfunctions arising from sexual assault. In R. A. Brown & J. R. Fields (Eds.), *Treatment of sexual problems in individual and couples therapy.* Great Neck, NY: PMA.

Squire, C. (1993). *Women and AIDS.* Newbury Park, CA: Sage.

Squire, L. (1990, June). *Memory and brain systems.* Paper presented at the meeting of the American Psychological Society, Dallas.

Squire, L. R. (1992). Memory and the hippocampus: A synthesis from findings with rats, monkeys, and humans. *Psychological Review, 99*, 195–231.

Squire, L. R., Knowlton, B., & Musen, G. (1993). The structure and organization of memory. *Annual Review of Psychology, 44*, 453–495.

Sroufe, L. A. (1985). Attachment classification from the perspective of infant-caregiver relationships and infant temperament. *Child Development, 56*, 1–14.

Sroufe, L. A. (in press). Pathways to adaptation and maladaptation: Psychopathology as developmental deviation. In D. Cicchetti (Ed.), *Developmental psychopathology: Past, present, and future.* Hillsdale, NJ: Erlbaum.

Stanley, B., & Stanley, M. (1989). Biochemical studies in suicide victims: Current findings and future implications. *Suicide and Life-Threatening Behavior, 19*, 30–42.

Stanovich, D. (1992). *How to think straight about psychology* (3rd ed.). New York: HarperCollins.

Stanton, A. L., & Gallant, S. J. (Eds.). (1995). *The psychology of women's health.* Washington, DC: American Psychological Association.

Steadman, H. J., Callahan, L. A., Robbins, P. C., & Morrissey, J. P. (1989). Maintenance of an insanity defense under Montana's "abolition" of the insanity defense. *American Journal of Psychiatry, 146*, 357–360.

Steers, R. M. (1988). *Introduction to organizational behavior* (2nd ed.). Glenview, IL: Scott, Foresman.

Steinberg, L. (1993). *Adolescence* (3rd ed.). New York: McGraw-Hill.

Steinberg, L., & Levine, A. (1990). *You and your adolescent.* New York: Harper Perennial.

Stengel, R. (1992, March 16). Midnight's Mayor. *Time Magazine*.

Stern, J. S. (1984). Is obesity a disease of inactivity? In A. J. Stunkard & E. Stellar (Eds.), *Eating and its disorders.* New York: Raven.

Sternberg, R. J. (1985a, November). Teaching critical thinking. Part 1: Are we making critical mistakes? *Phi Delta Kappan*, 194–198.

Sternberg, R. J. (1985b, December). Teaching critical thinking. Part 2: Possible solutions. *Phi Delta Kappan*, 277–280.

Sternberg, R. J. (1986). *Intelligence applied.* San Diego: Harcourt Brace Jovanovich.

Sternberg, R. J. (1988). *The triangle of love.* New York: Basic Books.

Sternberg, R. J. (1988). A triarchic view of intelligence in cross-cultural perspective. In S. H. Irvine & J. W. Berry (Eds.), *Human abilities in cultural context.* Cambridge: Cambridge University Press.

Stevenson, H. G. (1995, March). *Missing data: On the forgotten substance of race, ethnicity, and socioeconomic classifications.* Paper presented at the meeting of the Society for Research in Child Development, Indianapolis, IN.

Stevenson, H. W. (1992). Learning from Asian schools. *Scientific American, 267*, 70–76.

Stevenson, H. W. (1995). Mathematics achievement of American students: First in the world by the year 2000? In C. A. Nelson (Ed.), *Basic and applied perspectives on learning, cognition, and development.* Minneapolis, MN: University of Minnesota Press.

Stevenson, H. W., Chen, C., & Lee, S. Y. (1993). Mathematics achievement of Chinese, Japanese, and American children: Ten years later. *Science, 259*, 53–58.

Steward, P. (1995). *Beginning writers in the zone of proximal development.* Hillsdale, NJ: Erlbaum.

Stewart, K. R. (1953). Culture and personality in two primitive groups. *Complex, 9*, 3–23.

Stewart, K. R. (1972). Dream theory in Malaya. In C. Tart (Ed.), *Altered states of consciousness.* New York: Anchor.

Stillings, N. A., Weisler, S. E., Chase, C. H., Feinstein, M. H., Garfield, J. L., & Rissland, E. L. (1995). *Cognitive science* (2nd ed.). Cambridge, MA: MIT Press.

Stoller, E. P., & Gibson, R. C. (1994). *Worlds of difference: Inequality in the aging experience.* Thousand Oaks, CA: Pine Forge Press.

Stotland, S., & Zuroff, D. C. (1991). Relations between multiple measures of dieting, self-efficacy, and weight change in a behavioral weight control program. *Behavior Therapy, 22*, 47–59.

Streissguth, A. P., Martin, D. C., Sandman, B. M., Kirchner, G. L., & Darby, B. L. (1984). Intrauterine alcohol and nicotine exposure: Attention and reaction time in four-year-old children. *Developmental Psychology, 20*, 533–543.

Strickland, B. (1988). Sex-related differences in health and illness. *Psychology of Women Quarterly, 12*, 382–399.

Striegel-Moore, R., Pike, K., Rodin, J., Schreiber, G., & Wilfley, D. (1993, March). *Predictors and correlates of drive for thinness.* Paper presented at the biennial meeting of the Society for Research in Child Development, New Orleans.

Strupp, H. H. (1989). Psychotherapy. *American Psychologist, 44*, 717–724.

Strupp, H. H. (1992). The future of psychodynamic psychotherapy. *Psychotherapy, 29*, 21–28.

Strupp, H. H. (1995). The psychotherapist's skills revised. *Clinical Psychology: Science and Practice, 2*, 70–74.

Stunkard, A. J. (1987). The regulation of body weight and the treatment of obesity. In H. Weiner & A. Baum (Eds.), *Eating regulation and discontrol.* Hillsdale, NJ: Erlbaum.

Stunkard, A. J. (1989). Perspectives on human obesity. In A. J. Stunkard & A. Baum (Eds.), *Perspectives on behavioral medicine: Eating, sleeping, and sex.* Hillsdale, NJ: Erlbaum.

Sue, D., & Sue, D. W. (1993). Ethnic identity: Cultural factors in the psychological development of Asians in America. In D. R. Atkinson, G. Morten, & D. W. Sue (Eds.), *Counseling American minorities*. Dubuque, IA: Brown & Benchmark.

Sue, D. W., & Sue, S. (1972). Counseling Chinese-Americans. *Personnel and Guidance Journal, 50,* 637–644.

Sue, S. (1990, August). *Ethnicity and mental health: Research and policy issues*. Paper presented at the meeting of the American Psychological Association, San Francisco.

Sue, S. (in press). Ethnicity and mental health: Research and policy issues. *Journal of Social Issues.*

Sue, S., Allen, D., & Conaway, L. (1978). The responsiveness and equality of mental health care to Chicanos and Native Americans. *American Journal of Community Psychology, 6,* 137–146.

Suedfeld, P., & Coren, S. (1989). Perceptual isolation, sensory deprivation, and rest: Moving introductory psychology texts out of the 1950s. *Canadian Psychology, 30,* 17–29.

Suinn, R. M. (1984). *Fundamentals of abnormal psychology*. Chicago: Nelson-Hall.

Suinn, R. M. (1987). Asian Americans in psychology. In P. J. Woods & C. S. Wilkinson (Eds.), *Is psychology the major for you?* Washington, DC: American Psychological Association.

Sullivan, H. S. (1953). *The interpersonal theory of psychiatry*. New York: W. W. Norton.

Suls, J. (1989). Self-awareness and self-identity. In J. Worrell & F. Danner (Eds.), *The adolescent as decision maker*. New York: Academic Press.

Sundstrom, E., De Meuse, K. P., & Futrell, D. (1990). Work teams: Applications and effectiveness. *American Psychologist, 45,* 120–133.

Super, C. M. (1980). Cross-cultural research on infancy. In H. C. Triandis & A. Heron (Eds.), *Handbook of cross-cultural psychology. Vol. 4: Developmental psychology*. Boston: Allyn & Bacon.

Super, C. M. (1981). Behavioral development in infancy. In R. H. Munroe, R. L. Munroe, & B. B. Whiting (Eds.), *Handbook of cross-cultural human development*. New York: Garland STPM.

Sutton, R. G., & Kessler, M. (1986). National study of the effects of clients' socioeconomic status on clinical psychologists' professional judgments. *Journal of Consulting and Clinical Psychology, 54,* 275–276.

Suzman, R. M., Harris, T., Hadley, E. C., Kovar, M. G., & Weindruch, R. (1992). The robust oldest old: Optimistic perspectives for increasing healthy life expectancy. In R. M. Suzman, D. P. Willis, & K. G. Manton (Eds.), *The oldest old*. New York: Oxford University Press.

Swann, W. B. (1987). Identity negotiation: Where two roads meet. *Journal of Personality and Social Psychology, 53,* 1038–1051.

Swann, W. B., Stein-Seroussi, A., & Giesler, R. B. (1992). Why people self-verify. *Journal of Personality and Social Psychology, 62,* 392–401.

Swanson, D. P. (1995, March). *The effects of racial identity and socioeconomic status on academic outcomes for adolescents*. Paper presented at the meeting of the Society for Research in Child Development, Indianapolis, IN.

Swim, J. K., Aikin, K. J., Hall, W. S., & Hunter, B. A. (1995). Sexism and racism: Old-fashioned and modern prejudices. *Journal of Personality and Social Psychology, 68,* 199–214.

Syvalahti, E. K. (1985). Drug treatment of insomnia. *Annals of Clinical Research, 17,* 265–272.

Szapocznik, J. (1995). Research on disclosure of HIV status: Cultural evolution finds an ally in science. *Health Psychology, 14,* 4–5.

Szasz, I. (1977). *Psychiatric slavers: When confinement and coercion masquerade as cure*. New York: Free Press.

Szasz, T. (1965). *The ethics of psychoanalysis*. New York: Basic Books.

Tafoya, T. (1993, August). *Who's parenting the parents? Shattered scripts, missing models, and AIDS*. Paper presented at the meeting of the American Psychological Association, Toronto.

Tager-Flusberg, H. (1994). (Ed.). *Constraints on language acquisition*. Hillsdale, NJ: Erlbaum.

Tajfel, H. (1978). The achievement of group differentiation. In H. Tajfel (Ed.), *Differentiation between social groups. Studies in the social psychology of intergroup relations*. London: Academic Press.

Tan, Amy. (1989). *The joy luck club*. New York: Putnam.

Tannen, D. (1990). *You just don't understand*. New York: Ballantine.

Tavris, C. (1989). *Anger: The misunderstood emotion* (2nd ed.). New York: Touchstone.

Tavris, C. (1992). *The mismeasure of woman*. New York: Touchstone.

Tavris, C., & Wade, C. (1984). *The longest war: Sex differences in perspective* (2nd ed.). San Diego: Harcourt Brace Jovanovich.

Taylor, S. E. (1979). Hospital patient behavior: Reactance, helplessness, or control? *Journal of Social Issues, 35,* 156–184.

Taylor, S. E. (1989). *Positive illusions: Creative self-deception and the healthy mind*. New York: Basic Books.

Taylor, S. E. (1991). *Health psychology* (2nd ed.). New York: McGraw-Hill.

Taylor, S. E., Collins, R., Skokan, L., & Aspinwall, L. (1988, August). *Illusion, reality, and adjustment in coping with victimizing events*. Paper presented at the meeting of the American Psychological Association, Atlanta.

Taylor, S. P. (1982). Mental health and successful coping among aged Black women. In R. C. Manuel (Ed.), *Minority aging*. Westport, CT: Greenwood.

Teachman, J. D., & Polonko, K. A. (1990). Cohabitation and marital stability in the United States. *Social Forces, 69,* 207–220.

Temoshok, L., & Dreher, H. (1992). *The Type C syndrome*. New York: Random House.

Terman, L. (1925). *Genetic studies of genius. Vol. 1: Mental and physical traits of a thousand gifted children*. Stanford, CA: Stanford University Press.

Terman, L. M., & Oden, M. H. (1959). *Genetic studies of genius: Vol. 5. The gifted group at mid-life*. Stanford, CA: Stanford University Press.

The Health of America's Children. (1992). Washington, DC: Children's Defense Fund.

Thigpen, C. H., & Cleckley, H. M. (1957). *Three faces of Eve*. New York: McGraw-Hill.

Thomas, C. B. (1983). Unpublished manuscript, Johns Hopkins University, Baltimore.

Thomas, D. A., & Aldefer, C. P. (1989). The influence of race on career dynamics: Theory and research on minority career experiences. In M. Arthur, D. Hall, & B. Lawrence (Eds.), *Handbook of career theory*. Cambridge, England: Cambridge University Press.

Thomas, J. S. (1993, July 17). Ruth Ginsburg: Carving a career path through male-dominated legal world. *Congressional Quarterly Weekly Report, 51,* 1876–1877.

Thompson, L., & Walker, A. J. (1989). Gender in families: Women and men in marriage, work, and parenthood. *Journal of Marriage and the Family, 51,* 845–871.

Thompson, R. A. (1991). Construction and reconstruction of early attachments: Taking perspective on attachment theory and research. In D. P. Keating & H. G. Rosen (Eds.), *Constructivist perspectives on atypical development*. Hillsdale, NJ: Erlbaum.

Thompson, R. A., & Cimbolic, P. (1978). Black students' counselor preference and attitudes toward counseling center use. *Journal of Counseling Psychology, 25,* 570–575.

Thornburg, H. D. (1981). Sources of sex education among early adolescents. *Journal of Early Adolescence, 1,* 171–184.

Thorndike, E. L. (1898). Animal intelligence: An experimental study of the associative process in animals. *Psychological Review Monograph Supplement, 2* (4, Whole No. 8).

Thurstone, L. L. (1938). *Primary mental abilities*. Chicago: University of Chicago Press.

Tobin, J. J. (1987). The American idealization of old age in Japan. *Gerontologist, 27,* 53–58.

Tolman, E. C. (1932). *Purposive behavior in animals and man*. New York: Appleton-Century-Crofts.

Tolman, E. C. (1948). Cognitive maps in rats and men. *Psychological Review, 55,* 189–208.

Tolman, E. C., Ritchie, B. F., & Kalish, D. (1946). Studies in spatial learning: I. Orientation and short-cut. *Journal of Experimental Psychology, 36,* 13–24.

Tomasello, M., & Merriman, W. E. (Eds.). (1995). *Beyond names for things*. Hillsdale, NJ: Erlbaum.

Tomlinson-Keasey, C. (1990). The working lives of Terman's gifted women. In H. W. Grossman & N. L. Chester (Eds.), *The experience and meaning of work in women's lives*. Hillsdale, NJ: Erlbaum.

Tomlinson-Keasey, C. (1993, August). *Tracing the lives of gifted women*. Paper presented at the American Psychological Association, Toronto.

Tomlinson-Keasey, C., Warren, L. W., & Elliott, J. F. (1986). Suicide among gifted women. A prospective study. *Journal of Abnormal Psychology, 95,* 123–130.

Torrey, E. F., & others. (1984). Endemic psychosis in western Ireland. *American Journal of Psychiatry, 141,* 966–970.

Torrey, E. T. (1986). *Witch doctors and psychiatrists: The common roots of psychotherapy and its future*. New York: Harper & Row.

Tran, T. V., Wright, R., & Chatters, L. (1991). Health, stress, psychological resources, and subjective well-being among older Blacks. *Psychology and Aging, 6,* 100–108.

Trevino, R. (1986). National statistical data systems and the Hispanic population. In *Task force on Black and minority health, report of the secretary's task force on Black and minority health. Vol. VIII: Hispanic health issues*, pp. 45–54. Washington, DC: U.S. Department of Health and Human Services.

Triandis, H. (1985). Collectivism vs. individualism: A reconceptualization of a basic concept in cross-cultural social psychology. In C. Bagley & G. K. Verman (Eds.), *Personality, cognition, and values.* London: Macmillan.

Triandis, H. (1994). *Culture and social behavior.* New York: McGraw-Hill.

Triandis, H. (1994). Culture and social behavior. In W. J. Lonner & R. Malpass (Eds.), *Psychology and culture.* Needham Heights, MA: Allyn & Bacon.

Triandis, H. C. (1989, March). *Cross-cultural studies of individualism and collectivism.* Paper presented at the Nebraska Symposium on Motivation, Lincoln.

Triandis, H. C. (1992a, August). *Perspectives on international psychology (past, present, future): Research.* Paper presented at the meeting of the American Psychological Association, Washington, DC.

Triandis, H. C. (1992b, June). Presentation at the workshop "Making Basic Texts in Psychology More Culture-Inclusive and Culture-Sensitive," Western Washington University, Bellingham.

Triandis, H. C. (1994). *Culture and social behavior.* New York: McGraw-Hill.

Trimble, J. E. (1976). Value differences among American Indians: Concern for the concerned counselor. In P. Pedersen, W. J. Lonner, J. G. Draguns (Eds.), *Counseling across cultures.* Honolulu: University of Hawaii Press.

Trimble, J. E. (1989). *The enculturation of contemporary psychology.* Paper presented at the meeting of the American Psychological Association, New Orleans.

Trimble, J. E., & Fleming, C. (1989). Client, counselor, and community characteristics. In P. Pedersen, J. Draguns, W. Lonner, & J. Trimble (Eds.), *Counseling across cultures* (3rd ed.). Honolulu: University of Hawaii Press.

Trivers, R. (1971). The evolution of reciprocal altruism. *Quarterly Review of Biology, 46,* 35–57.

Tseng, W., & Hsu, J. (1969). Chinese culture, personality formation, and mental illness. *International Journal of Social Psychiatry, 16,* 5–14.

Tulving, E. (1972). Episodic and semantic memory. In E. Tulving & W. Donaldson (Eds.), *Origins of memory.* San Diego: Academic Press.

Tulving, E. (1989). Remembering and knowing the past. *American Scientist, 77,* 361–367.

Tulving, E., & Schacter, D. L. (1990). Priming and human memory systems. *Science, 247,* 301–306.

Tulving, E., Schacter, D. L., & Stark, H. A. (1982). Priming effects in word-fragment completion are independent of recognition memory. *Journal of Experimental Psychology: Learning, Memory, and Cognition, 8,* 336–342.

Turnbull, C. (1961). Some observations regarding the experiences and behavior of Bambuti Pygmies. *American Journal of Psychology, 74,* 304–308.

U.S. Bureau of the Census. (1990). *Statistical abstracts of the United States, 1990.* Washington, DC: U.S. Department of Commerce.

U.S. Department of Health and Human Services, Public Health Service. (1989). *Reducing the health consequences of smoking: 25 years of progress.* Washington, DC: U.S. Government Printing Office.

U.S. Department of Labor, Bureau of Statistics. (1991). *Consumer expenditures in 1991.* Washington, DC: U.S. Government Printing Office.

Ubell, C. (1992, December 6). We can age successfully. *Parade,* pp. 14–15.

Ulbrich, P. M. (1988). The determinants of depression in two-income marriages. *Journal of Marriage and the Family, 50,* 121–131.

Unger, R. (1992, Spring). Time and time again. *Psychology of Women Newsletter,* pp. 1–2.

Unger, R. K., & Crawford, M. (1992). *The psychology of sex and gender.* New York: McGraw-Hill.

United States Commission on Civil Rights (1975). *A better chance to learn: Bilingual bicultural education.* Washington, DC: U.S. Government Printing Office.

United States Department of Justice, Bureau of Justice Statistics. (1983, October). *Report to the nation on crime and violence* (NJC–87068). Washington, DC: U.S. Government Printing Office.

Urberg, K. A., Shyu, S., & Liang, J. (1990). Peer influence in adolescent cigarette smoking. *Addictive Behavior, 15,* 247–255.

Vaillant, G. E. (1977). *Adaptation to life.* Boston: Little, Brown.

Van den Berghe, P. L. (1978). *Race and racism: A comparative perspective.* New York: Wiley.

Verbrugge, L. M. (1989). The twain meet: Empirical explanations of sex differences in health and mortality. *Journal of Health and Social Behavior, 30,* 282–304.

Vitols, M. (1967). *Patterns of mental disturbance in the Negro.* Unpublished manuscript, Cherry Hospital, Goldsboro, NC.

Von Békésy, G. (1960). Vibratory patterns of the basilar membrane. In E. G. Wever (Ed.), *Experiments in hearing.* New York: McGraw-Hill.

Vontress, C. E. (1973). Counseling: Racial and ethnic factors. *Focus on Guidance, 5,* 1–10.

Voyer, D., Voyer, S., & Bryden, M. P. (1995). Magnitude of sex differences in spatial abilities: A meta-analysis and consideration of critical variables. *Psychological Bulletin, 117,* 250–270.

Vygotsky, L. S. (1962). *Thought and language.* Cambridge, MA: MIT Press.

Wadsworth, S. J., DeFries, J. C., Fulker, D. W., & Plomin, R. (1995). Cognitive ability and academic achievement in the Colorado Adoption Project: A multivariate genetic analysis of parent-offspring and sibling data. *Behavior Genetics, 25,* 1–16.

Wagman, M. (1995). *The science of cognition.* Westport, CT: Praeger.

Wagner, D. (1980). Culture and memory development. In H. Triandis & A. Heron (Eds.), *Handbook of cross-cultural psychology: Vol. 4. Developmental psychology.* Boston: Allyn & Bacon.

Wald, G., & Brown, P. K. (1965). Human color vision and color blindness. *Cold Spring Harbor Symposia on Quantitative Biology, 30,* 345–359.

Waldman, I. D., Weinberg, R. A., & Scarr, S. W. (1995, March). *Behavior genetic analyses of family environment measures and the relation of these to IQ.* Paper presented at the meeting of the Society for Research in Child Development, Indianapolis, IN.

Wallace, R. K., & Benson, H. (1972). The physiology of meditation. *Scientific American, 226,* 85–90.

Wallerstein, R. (1992). *The common ground of psychoanalysis.* Northvale, NJ: Jason Aronson.

Wallis, C. (1985, December 9). Children having children. *Time,* pp. 78–88.

Walter, J. P. (1974). Two poverties equal many hungry Indians: An economic and social study of nutrition. *American Journal of Economics and Sociology, 33,* 33–44.

Ward, C. (Ed.). (1989). *Altered states of consciousness and mental health: A cross-cultural perspective.* Newbury Park, CA: Sage.

Ward, C. (1994). Culture and altered states of consciousness. In W. J. Lonner & R. Malpass (Eds.), *Psychology and culture.* Needham Heights, MA: Allyn & Bacon.

Warden, C. J., & Jackson, T. A. (1935). Imitative behavior in the rhesus monkey. *Journal of Genetic Psychology, 46,* 103–25.

Warner, K. E. (1989). Smoking and health: A 25-year perspective. *American Journal of Public Health, 79,* 141–143.

Warner, R. L. (1986). Alternative strategies for measuring household division of labor: A comparison. *Journal of Family Issues, 7,* 179–185.

Wasserman, G. S. (1978). *Color vision: An historical introduction.* New York: Wiley.

Waterman, A. S., & Archer, S. I. (in press). A life-span perspective on identity formation. In P. B. Baltes, D. L. Featherman, & R. M. Lerner (Eds.), *Life-span development and behavior* (Vol. 10). Hillsdale, NJ: Erlbaum.

Waters, E. (1991). Individual differences in infant-mother attachment. In J. Columbo & J. W. Fagen (Eds.), *Individual differences in infancy.* Hillsdale, NJ: Erlbaum.

Watson, J. B. (1913). Psychology as the behaviorist views it. *Psychological Review, 20,* 158–177.

Watson, J. B. (1928). *Psychological care of the infant and child.* New York: Norton.

Watson, J. B., & Rayner, R. (1920). Emotional reactions. *Journal of Experimental Psychology, 3,* 1–14.

Watt, N. F. (Ed.). (1984). *Children at risk for schizophrenia: A longitudinal perspective.* New York: Cambridge University Press.

Watts, T. D., & Lewis, R. G. (1988). Alcoholism and Native American youth: An overview. *Journal of Drug Issues, 18,* 69–86.

Webb, W. B. (1978). Sleep and dreams. *Annual Review of Psychology.*

Wechsler, D. (1949). *Wechsler Intelligence Scale for Children.* New York: Psychological Corporation.

Wechsler, D. (1955). *Wechsler Adult Intelligence Scale manual.* New York: Psychological Corporation.

Wechsler, D. (1967). *Wechsler Preschool and Primary Scale of Intelligence.* New York: Psychological Corporation.

Wechsler, D. (1972). "Hold" and "Don't Hold" test. In S. M. Chown (Ed.), *Human aging.* New York: Penguin.

Wechsler, D. (1974). *Wechsler Intelligence Scale for Children, Revised.* New York: Psychological Corporation.

Wechsler, D. (1981). *Wechsler Adult Intelligence Scale, Revised.* New York: Psychological Corporation.

Weimer, W. B. (1974). Overview of a cognitive conspiracy. In W. B. Weimer & D. S. Palermo (Eds.), *Cognition and the symbolic processes.* Hillsdale, NJ: Erlbaum.

Weinberg, R. A. (1989). Intelligence and IQ: Landmark issues and great debates. *American Psychologist, 44,* 98–104.

Weinberger, D. R., Berman, K. F., & Zec, R. F. (1986). Physiological dysfunction of the dorsolateral prefrontal cortex in schizophrenia. *Archives of General Psychiatry, 43,* 114–124.

Weinstein, S. (1968). Intensive and extensive aspects of tactile sensitivity as a function of body part, sex, and laterality. In D. R. Kenshalo (Ed.), *The skin senses.* Springfield, IL: Charles C Thomas.

Weisenberg, M. (1982). Cultural and ethnic factors in reaction to pain. In I. Al-Issa (Ed.), *Culture and psychopathology.* Baltimore: University Park Press.

Weisman, A. D. (1989). Vulnerability and the psychological disturbances of cancer patients. *Psychosomatics, 30,* 80–85.

Weissman, M. M., & Boyd, J. H. (1985). Affective disorders: Epidemiology. In H. I. Kaplan & B. J. Sadock (Eds.), *Comprehensive textbook of psychiatry/IV.* Baltimore: Williams & Wilkins.

Wells, G. L. (1993). What do we know about eyewitness identification? *American Psychologist, 48,* 553–571.

Wender, P. H., Kety, S. S., Rosenthal, D., Schulsinger, F., Ortmann, J., & Lunde, I. (1986). Psychiatric disorders in the biological and adoptive families of adopted individuals with affective disorders. *Archives of General Psychiatry, 43,* 923–929.

Wertheimer, M. (1945). *Productive thinking.* New York: Harper.

West, L. J. (1972). A cross-cultural approach to alcoholism. *Annals of the New York Academy of Sciences, 197,* 214–216.

Westkott, M. (1986). *The feminist legacy of Karen Horney.* New Haven, CT: Yale University Press.

Whiston, S. C., & Sexton, T. L. (1993). An overview of psychotherapy outcome research: Implications for practice. *Professional Psychology, 24,* 43–51.

White, C. (Ed.). (1995). *Men's ways of being.* Boulder, CO: Westview Press.

White, R. W. (1959). Motivation reconsidered: The concept of competence. *Psychological Review, 66,* 297–333.

Whiting, B. B. (1989, April). *Culture and inter-personal behavior.* Paper presented at the biennial meeting of the Society for Research in Child Development, Kansas City.

Whiting, B. B., & Whiting, J. W. M. (1975). *Children of six cultures.* Cambridge, MA: Harvard University Press.

Whitman, F. L., Diamond, M., & Martin, J. (1993). Homosexual orientation in twins: A report of 61 pairs and three triplet sets. *Archives of Sexual Behavior, 22,* 187–198.

Whitney, K., Sagrestano, L. M., & Maslach, C. (1994). Establishing the social impact of individuation. *Journal of Personality and Social Psychology, 66,* 1140–1153.

Whorf, B. L. (1956). *Language, thought, and creativity.* New York: Wiley.

Wilkinson, S., & Kitzinger, C. (1993). *Heterosexuality.* Newbury Park, CA: Sage.

William T. Grant Foundation Commission. (1988). *The forgotten half: Non-college bound youth in America.* New York: William T. Grant Foundation.

William T. Grant Foundation. (1989). *American youth: A statistical snapshot.* Washington, DC: William T. Grant Foundation.

Williams, J. (1987). *Psychology of women: Behavior in a biosocial context* (3rd ed.). New York: W. W. Norton.

Williams, J. E., & Best, D. L. (1982). *Measuring sex stereotypes: A thirty-nation study.* Newbury Park, CA: Sage.

Williams, J. E., & Best, D. L. (1989). *Sex and psyche: Self-concept viewed cross-culturally.* Newbury Park: CA: Sage.

Williams, M. E., & Condry, J. (1989, April). *Minority portrayals and cross-racial interaction television.* Paper presented at the biennial meeting of the Society for Research in Child Development, Kansas City.

Wilson, B. J., & Gottman, J. M. (1995). Marital interaction and parenting. In M. H. Bornstein (Ed.), *Handbook of parenting, Vol. 4.* Hillsdale, NJ: Erlbaum.

Wilson, E. O. (1975). *Sociobiology: The new synthesis.* Cambridge, MA: Harvard University Press.

Wilson, E. O. (1995, February). *Unity in diversity.* Paper presented at the meeting of the American Association for the Advancement of Science, Atlanta, GA.

Wilson, G. T. (1993). Relationship of dieting and voluntary weight loss to psychological functioning and binge eating. *Annals of Internal Medicine, 119,* 727–730.

Wilson, G. T. (1994). Behavioral treatment of obesity: Thirty years and counting. *Advances in Behaviour Research and Therapy, 16,* 31–75.

Wilson, L. L., & Stith, S. M. (1993). Culturally sensitive therapy with Black clients. In D. R. Atkinson, G. Morten, & D. W. Sue (Eds.), *Counseling American minorities.* Dubuque, IA: Brown & Benchmark.

Wilson, M. N. (1989). Child development in the context of the extended family. *American Psychologist, 44,* 380–385.

Wilson, R. (1986). *Don't panic.* New York: Harper Perennial.

Winett, R. A., King, A. C., & Altman, D. G. (1989). *Health psychology and public health: An integrative approach.* New York: Pergamon.

Winn, M. (1987). *Unplugging the plug-in-drug.* New York: Penguin.

Winner, E. (1986, August). Where pelicans kiss seals. *Psychology Today,* pp. 24–35.

Wise, R. A., & Rompre, P. P. (1989). Brain dopamine and reward. *Annual Review of Psychology, 40.*

Wober, M. (1966). Sensotypes. *Journal of Social Psychology, 70,* 181–189.

Wober, M. (1974). Towards an understanding of the Kiganda concept of intelligence. In J. W. Berry & P. R. Dasen (Eds.), *Culture and cognition.* London: Methuen.

Wolpe, J. (1963). Behavior therapy in complex neurotic states. *British Journal of Psychiatry, 110,* 28–34.

Wong, H. Z. (1982). Asian and Pacific Americans. In L. Snowden (Ed.), *Reaching the undeserved: Mental health needs of neglected populations.* Beverly Hills, CA: Sage.

Wood, J. T. (1994). *Gendered lives: Communication, gender, and culture.* Belmont, CA: Wadsworth.

Wood, J. V. (1989). Theory and research concerning social comparisons of personal attributes. *Psychological Bulletin, 106,* 231–248.

Woods, P. J., & Wilkinson, C. S. (1987). *Is psychology the major for you?* Washington, DC: American Psychological Association.

Wooley, S. C., & Garner, D. M. (1991). Obesity treatment: The high cost of false hope. *Journal of the American Dietetic Association, 91,* 1248–1251.

Worell, J., & Robinson, D. (1993). Feminist counseling therapy for the 21st century. *Counseling Psychologist, 21,* 92–96.

World Health Organization. (1975). *Schizophrenia: A multi-national study.* Geneva: World Health Organization.

Worrell, J. (1989). Images of women in psychology. In M. A. Paludi & G. A. Steuernagel (Eds.), *Foundations for a feminist restructuring of the academic disciplines.* New York: Haworth Press.

Wortman, C., Bernat, M., & Lang, E. (in press). Coping with overload. In M. Frankenhaeuser, M. Chesney, & V. Lundberg (Eds.), *Women, work, and stress.* New York: Plenum.

Wright, J. C. (1995, March). *Effects of viewing Sesame Street: The longitudinal study of media and time use.* Paper presented at the meeting of the Society for Research in Child Development, Indianapolis, IN.

Wylie, P. (1942). *Generation of vipers.* Toronto: Rinehart.

Yalom, I. D. (1975). *The therapy and practice of group psychotherapy.* New York: Basic Books.

Yalom, I. D. (Ed.). (1995). *The theory and practice of group psychotherapy* (4th ed.). New York: Basic Books.

Yamamoto, J., Okonogi, K., Iwasaki, T., & Yoshimura, S. (1969). Mourning in Japan. *American Journal of Psychiatry, 125,* 1660–1665.

Yankelovich, D., Skelly, F., & White, A. (1984). *Sex stereotypes and candidacy for high level political office.* New York: Yankelovich, Skelly, & White.

Yarmey, A. D. (1973). I recognize your face but I can't remember your name: Further evidence on the tip of the tongue phenomenon. *Memory and Cognition, 1,* 287–290.

Yates, B. (1985). *Self-management: The science and art of helping yourself.* Belmont, CA: Wadsworth.

Yeni-Komshian, G. H. (1995, February). *What happens to our first language when we learn a second language?* Paper presented at the meeting of the American Association for the Advancement of Science, Atlanta, GA.

Yentsch, C. M., & Sindermann, C. J. (1992). *The woman scientist: Meeting the challenges for a successful career.* New York: Plenum.

Young, C. (1993). Psychodynamics of coping and survival of the African American female in a changing world. In D. R. Atkinson, G. Morten, & D. W. Sue (Eds.), *Counseling American minorities.* Dubuque, IA: Brown & Benchmark.

Young, K. T. (1990). American conceptions of infant development from 1955 to 1984: What the experts are telling parents. *Child Development, 61,* 17–28.

Yuill, N., Oakhill, J., & Parkin, A. (1989). Working memory, comprehension ability and the resolution of text anomaly. *British Journal of Psychology, 80,* 351–361.

Yutrzenka, B. A. (1995). Making a case for training in ethnic and cultural diversity in increasing treatment efficacy. *Journal of Consulting and Clinical Psychology, 63,* 197–206.

Zahn-Waxler, C. (1990, May 28). Commentary. *Newsweek,* p. 61.

Zajonc, R. B. (1984). On the primacy of affect. *American Psychologist, 39,* 117–123.

Zarcone, V. P. (1989). Sleep hygiene. In M. H. Dryger, T. Roth, & W. C. Dement (Eds.), *Principles and practice of sleep medicine.* San Diego: Harcourt Brace Jovanovich.

Zeigler, L. H., & Harmon, W. (1989). More bad news about the news. *Public Opinion, 12,* 50–52.

Zelnik, M., & Kantner, J. F. (1977). Sexual and contraceptive experiences of young unmarried women in the United States, 1976 and 1971. *Family Planning Perspectives, 9,* 55–71.

Ziegert, K. A. (1983). The Wedesih prohibition of corporal punishment: A preliminary report. *Journal of Marriage and the Family, 45,* 917–926.

Zigler, E. (1989, April). *Discussion, symposium of effects of caregiving quality on children and families.* Presentation at the biennial meeting of the Society for Research in Child Development, Kansas City.

Zigler, E., & Muenchow, S. (1992). *The story of Head Start.* New York: Basic Books.

Zigler, E. F. (1995). Meeting the needs of children in poverty. *American Journal of Orthopsychiatry, 65,* 6–9.

Zilbergeld, B. (1992). *The new male sexuality.* New York: Bantam Books.

Zimbardo, P. (1987). *Shyness.* Reading, MA: Addison-Wesley.

Zimbardo, P., Haney, C., Banks, W., & Jaffe, D. (1972). *The psychology of imprisonment: Privation, power, and pathology.* Unpublished manuscript, Stanford University, Stanford, CA.

Zorick, F. (1989). Overview of insomnia. In M. H. Dryger, T. Roth, & W. C. Dement (Eds.), *Principles and practice of sleep medicine.* San Diego: Harcourt Brace Jovanovich.

Zorumski, C. F., & Isenberg, K. E. (1991). Insights into the structure and function of GABA-benzodiazepine receptors: Ion channels and psychiatry. *American Journal of Psychiatry, 148,* 162–171.

CREDITS

LINE ART AND TEXT

Front Matter

Figure P.1: Walter Pauk, *How to Study in College*, Fourth Edition. Copyright © 1989 by Houghton Mifflin Company. Reprinted with permission. Prologue: Reprinted by permission from *Selections from the Writings of 'Abdu'l-Baha*, Copyright © 1978 by the Universal House of Justice.

Chapter 1

p. 24: Book cover from *Understanding Culture's Influence on Behavior* by Richard Brislin, book copyright © 1993 by Harcourt Brace & Company, cover illustration copyright © Gary Logan, reprinted by permission of the publisher. p. 24: Cover of *Is Psychology the Major for You?* by P. J. Woods and C. S. Wilkinson. Copyright © 1987 by the American Psychological Association. Reprinted with permission.

Chapter 2

p. 52: From David Stanovich, *How to Think Straight About Psychology*, 3d ed. Copyright © HarperCollins Publishers, Inc., New York, NY. Reprinted by permission.

Chapter 3

Figure 3.13: Graph from *Functional Neuroscience* by Michael Gazzaniga, Diana Steen and Bruce T. Volpe. Copyright © 1979 by Harper & Row, Publishers, Inc. Reprinted by permission of HarperCollins Publishers, Inc. Figure 3.14: From *The Neurosciences: A Third Study Program* edited by Schmitt and Worden. Copyright © 1974 The MIT Press, Cambridge, MA. Reprinted by permission. Figure 3.18: From John W. Hole, Jr., *Human Anatomy and Physiology*, 6th ed. Copyright © 1993 Wm. C. Brown Communications, Inc., Dubuque, Iowa. Reprinted by permission of Times Mirror Higher Education Group, Inc., Dubuque, Iowa. All Rights Reserved. p. 90: Cover of *The Science of Mind* by Kenneth Klivington. Copyright © 1989 The MIT Press, Cambridge, MA. Reprinted by permission. p. 90: From *The Mind* by Richard Restak,

M.D. Copyright © 1988 by Educational Broadcasting Corporation and Richard M. Restak, M.D. Used by permission of Bantam Books, a division of Bantam Doubleday Dell Publishing Group, Inc.

Chapter 4

Figure 4.9: Figure from *Introduction to Psychology*, Seventh Edition by Ernest R. Hilgard, Rita L. Atkinson and Richard C. Atkinson, copyright © 1979 by Harcourt, Brace & Company, reproduced by permission of the publisher. Figure 4.15a: From John W. Hole, Jr., *Human Anatomy and Physiology*, 5th ed. Copyright © 1990 Wm. C. Brown Communications, Dubuque, Iowa. Reprinted by permission of Times Mirror Higher Education Group, Inc., Dubuque, Iowa. All Rights Reserved. Figure 4.17: From Dodge L. Fernald and Peter S. Fernald, *Introduction to Psychology*, 5th ed. Copyright © 1985 Wm. C. Brown Communications, Inc., Dubuque, Iowa. Reprinted by permission of Times Mirror Higher Education Group, Inc., Dubuque, Iowa. All Rights Reserved. Figure 4.20: Figure from *Fundamentals of Child Devleopment*, Second Edition by Harry Munsinger, copyright © 1975 by Holt, Rinehart & Winston, Inc., reproduced by permission of the publisher. Figure 4.24: James J. Gibson, *The Perception of the Visual World*. Copyright © 1950 by Houghton Mifflin Company. Reprinted with permission. Figure 4.31: From R. L. Gregory and J. C. Wallace, "Recovery from Early Blindness" in *Experimental Psychological Society Monograph*, No. 2. Copyright © 1963 Cambridge University Press. p. 133: From Hines, Terence, *Pseudoscience and the Paranormal* (Buffalo, NY: Prometheus Books). Copyright 1988 by Terence Hines. Used by permission of the publisher.

Chapter 5

p. 166: From *Consciousness Explained* by Daniel Dennett. Copyright © 1991 by Daniel C. Dennett. Used by permission of Little, Brown and Company. p. 166: Cover

of *The Truth about Addiction and Recovery* by Stanton Peele and Archie Brodsky with Mary Arnold. Cover copyright © 1992 by Simon & Schuster Inc. Reprinted by permission of Simon & Schuster Inc. p. 166: Cover of *The Making of a Drug Free America* by Mathea Falco. Copyright © 1992 Times Books, Inc., a division of Random House, Inc. Reprinted by permission.

Chapter 6

Figure 6.1b: From Benjamin B. Lahey, *Psychology: An Introduction*, 3d ed. Copyright © 1989 Wm. C. Brown Communications, Inc., Dubuque, Iowa. Reprinted by permission of Times Mirror Higher Education Group, Inc., Dubuque, Iowa. All Rights Reserved. Figure 6.7: From W. N. Dember, et al., *General Psychology*, 2d ed. Copyright © 1984 Lawrence Erlbaum Associates, Inc. Reprinted by permission. Figure 6.8: Source: E. L. Thorndike, "Animal Intelligence: An Experimental Study of the Associative Process in Animals" in *Psychological Review Monograph Supplement*, 2(4, whole no. 8), 1898. Figure 6.11: Source: B. F. Skinner, "Pigeons In a Pelican" in *American Psychologist*, 5:28–37, American Psychological Association, 1960. Figure 6.13: From *Learning and Behavior* by Paul Chance. Copyright © 1994, 1987, 1979 by Wadsworth Publishing Company. Reprinted by permission of Brooks/Cole Publishing Company, a division of Thomson Publishing Inc., Pacific Grove, CA 93950. Figure 6.15: Source: N. Guttman and H. I. Kalish, "Discriminability and Stimulus Generalization" in *Journal of Experimental Psychology*, 51:81, American Psychological Association, 1956. Figure 6.16: Source: Data from Paul Chance, *Learning and Behavior*, Wadsworth Publishing Company, 1979. Figure 6.18: From Albert Bandura, "Influence of Model's Reinforcement Contingencies on the Acquisition of Imitative Response" in *Journal of Personality and Social Psychology*, 1:589–595. Copyright © 1965 by the American Psychological Association. Reprinted with permission. Figure 6.21:

Source: E. C. Tolman, et al., "Studies in Spatial Learning I: Orientation and Short-Cut" in *Journal of Experimental Psychology,* 36:13–24, American Psychological Association, 1946. Figure 6.A: From G. B. Saxe, "Body Parts as Numerals: A Developmental Analysis of Numeration Among the Oksapmin in Papua, New Guinea" in *Child Development,* 52:306–316. Copyright © 1981 The Society for Research in Child Development, Inc. Reprinted by permission. p. 210: Cover from *Families* by Gerald Patterson. Copyright © 1975 Research Press, Champaign, IL. Reprinted by permission. p. 210: Cover of *Mentors* by Thomas Evans. Copyright © 1992 Peterson's Guides, Princeton, NJ. Reprinted by permission.

Chapter 7

Figure 7.7: From Gordon H. Bower, "Organizational Factors in Memory" in *Cognitive Psychology,* 1:18–46. Copyright © 1970 Academic Press. Reprinted by permission. Figure 7.8: From A. M. Collins and M. R. Quillan, "Retrieval Time from Semantic Memory" in *Journal of Verbal Learning and Verbal Behavior,* 3:240–248. Copyright © 1969 Academic Press. Reprinted by permission. Figure 7.9: From R. Lachman, et al., *Cognitive Psychology and Information Processing.* Copyright © 1979 Lawrence Erlbaum Associates, Inc. Reprinted by permission. p. 243: Cover of *Total Recall* by Joan Minninger. Cover copyright © 1986 by Pocket Books, a division of Simon & Schuster Inc. Cover photo copyright © 1986 by Comstock. Reprinted by permission of Pocket Books, a division of Simon & Schuster Inc.

Chapter 8

Figure 8.2: From *An Introduction to Cognitive Psychology* by D. R. Moates and G. M. Schumacher. Copyright © 1980 by Wadsworth Publishing Company. Reprinted by permission of Brooks/Cole Publishing Company, a division of Thomson Publishing Inc., Pacific Grove, CA 93950. Figure 8.16: Courtesy of John W. Berry. p. 289: From Russ Rymer, *Genie.* Copyright © 1993 HarperCollins Publishers, Inc., New York, NY. Reprinted by permission. p. 289: Cover from *Growing Up With Language* by Naomi Baron, 1992. Photo copyright © Chris Green, Elizabeth Hathon Studios. Design copyright © Stephen Gleason, Design Power, Inc. Reprinted by permission. p. 289: Cover art by Cynthia Dunn for *Creating Minds* by Howard Gardner, published by Basic Books, a division of HarperCollins Publishers, Inc.

Chapter 9

Figure 9.2: Source: Children's Defense Fund, *Children 1990,* page 4. Figure 9.6: Reprinted by permission of the publishers from *Postnatal Development of the Human Cerebral Cortex* by Jesse LeRoy Conel, Cambridge, Mass.: Harvard University Press, Copyright © by the President and Fellows of Harvard College. Figure 9.10a: Joshua Nove/Dennie Palmer Wolf. Figure 9.10b: Reprinted with permission of Ellen Winner. p. 330: From Marian Wright Edelman, *The Measure of Our Success.* Copyright © 1992 Harper Perennial, a division of HarperCollins Publishers. Reprinted by permission. p. 330: Cover of *What to Expect When You're Expecting,* 2d ed., by Arlene Eisenberg, Heidi E. Murkoff, and Sandee E. Hathaway. Copyright © 1988 by Workman Publishing Co., New York, NY. p. 330: *Touchpoints, the Essential Reference: Your Child's Emotional and Behavioral Development* © 1992 T. Berry Brazelton, M.D. Reprinted by permission of Addison-Wesley Publishing Company, Inc. Photo © Hornick Rivlin. p. 331: From *Raising Black Children* by James P. Comer and Alvin F. Poussaint. Copyright © 1975, 1992 by James P. Comer and Alvin F. Poussaint. Used by permission of Dutton Signet, a division of Penguin Books USA Inc.

Chapter 10

Figure 10.1: From A. F. Roache, "Secular Trends in Human Growth, Maturation and Development" in *Monographs of the Society for Research in Child Development,* Series #179, 44:20. Copyright © 1979 The Society for Research in Child Development, Inc. Reprinted by permission. Figure 10.2: From J. M. Tanner, et al., "Standards from Birth to Maturity for Height, Weight, Height Velocity, and Weight Velocity: British Children 1965" in *Archives of Diseases in Childhood,* 41. Copyright © 1966 BMJ Publishing Group, London, England. Reprinted by permission. Figure 10.5: From *The Seasons of a Man's Life* by Daniel J. Levinson, et al. Copyright © 1978 by Daniel J. Levinson. Reprinted by permission of Alfred A. Knopf, Inc. Figure 10.6: From P. M. Passuth, et al., "Age Norms and Age Constraints Twenty Years Later" paper presented at the annual meeting of the Midwest Sociological Society, Chicago, IL, April 1984. Figure 10.7: Source: U.S. Census data, Social Security Administration, *The Statistical History of the United States,* 1976. p. 376: Jacket design from *Fateful Choices* by Fred Hechinger. Jacket design copyright © 1992 by Meadows and Wiser. Cover photograph copyright © 1992 by Harold Feinstein from *Children of War.* Reprinted by permission of Hill and Wang, a division of Farrar, Straus & Giroux, Inc. p. 376: From

Laurence Steinberg and Ann Levine, *You and Your Adolescent.* Copyright © 1990 Harper Perennial, a division of HarperCollins Publishers. Reprinted by permission. p. 377: Cover of *The Road Less Traveled* by M. Scott Peck, M.D. Cover copyright © 1978 by Simon & Schuster Inc. Reprinted by permission of Simon & Schuster Inc. p. 377: *What Color Is Your Parachute?* copyright © 1995 by Richard Nelson Bolles. Used by permission of Ten Speed Press, Berkeley, CA. p. 378: Cover of *Man's Search for Meaning* by Viktor Frankl. Cover copyright © 1978 by Simon & Schuster Inc. Reprinted by permission of Simon & Schuster Inc. p. 378: From *How to Survive the Loss of a Love* by Melba Colgrove, Ph.D., Harold H. Bloomfield, M.D., and Peter McWilliams, published by Prelude Press, 8159 Santa Monica Blvd., Los Angeles, CA 90046, 1–800–LIFE–101. p. 384: From *Like Water for Chocolate* by Laura Esquivel. Copyright translation © 1992 by Doubleday, a division of Bantam Doubleday Dell Publishing Group, Inc. Used by permission of Doubleday, a division of Bantam Doubleday Dell Publishing Group, Inc.

Chapter 11

p. 385: *Fun With Dick and Jane* by William S. Gray and May H. Arbuthnot. Copyright, 1940, by Scott, Foresman and Company. Reprinted by permission. Figure 11.2b: From Janet S. Hyde, "Gender Differences in Mathematics Performance" in *Psychological Bulletin,* 107:139–155. Copyright © 1990 by the American Psychological Association. Reprinted with permission. Figure 11.A: From Janet S. Hyde, "Children's Understanding of Sexist Language" in *Developmental Psychology,* 20:703. Copyright © 1984 by the American Psychological Association. Reprinted with permission. p. 411: Cover of *Mismeasure of Woman* by Carol Tavris. Cover copyright © 1993 by Simon & Schuster Inc. Reprinted by permission of Simon & Schuster Inc. p. 411: Cover of *You Just Don't Understand* by Deborah Tannen. Copyright © 1990 Ballantine Books, a division of Random House, Inc. Reprinted by permission. p. 412: From Harriet Lerner, *The Dance of Intimacy.* Copyright © 1990 Harper Perennial, a division of HarperCollins Publishers, Inc. Reprinted by permission. p. 412: From *The New Male* by Herb Goldberg. Copyright © 1980 by Herb Goldberg. Used by permission of Dutton Signet, a division of Penguin Books USA Inc.

Chapter 12

Figure 12.3: From Masters & Johnson. Reprinted by permission. Figure 12.4b: From C. A. Darling, et al., "Sex in Transition, 1980–1984" in *Journal of Youth and Adolescence,* 13:388. Copyright © 1984 Plenum Publishing Corporation.

Reprinted by permission. Figure 12.5: From Alfred C. Kinsey, et al., *Sexual Behavior in the Human Male.* Copyright © 1948 The Kinsey Institute for Research in Sex, Gender, and Reproduction, Inc. Reprinted by permission of The Kinsey Institute for Research in Sex, Gender, and Reproduction, Inc. Table 12.2: From "A Short-Form Scale to Measure Sexual Discord in Dyadic Relationships" in *The Journal of Sex Research.* Copyright © 1981 The Society for the Scientific Study of Sex, Mount Vernon, IA. Reprinted by permission. p. 443: From *For Yourself: The Fulfillment of Female Sexuality* by Lonnie Garfield Barbach. Copyright © 1975 by Lonnie Farfield Barbach. Used by permission of Dutton Signet, a division of Penguin Books USA Inc. p. 444: From *The New Male Sexuality* by Bernie Zilbergeld, Ph.D. Copyright © 1992 by Bernie Zilbergeld. Used by permission of Bantam Books, a division of Bantam Doubleday Dell Publishing Group, Inc. p. 444: From *Permanent Partners* by Betty Berzon, Ph.D. Copyright © 1988 by Betty Berzon, Ph.D. Used by permission of Dutton Signet, a division of Penguin Books USA Inc.

Chapter 13

Figure 13.2a: From E. C. Nevis, *Journal of Applied Behavioral Science* 19:256. Copyright © 1983 Sage Publications, Inc. Figure 13.3: From W. B. Cannon, "Hunger and Thirst" in C. Murchison (ed.), *The Foundations of Experimental Psychology.* Copyright © 1928 Clark University Press. Reprinted by permission. Figure 13.4: Reprinted from the 1961 *Nebraska Symposium on Motivation,* by permission of the University of Nebraska Press. Copyright © 1961 by the University of Nebraska Press. Copyright © renewed 1989 by the University of Nebraska Press. Figure 13.8: From M. R. Lepper, et al., "Undermining Children's Intrinsic Interest with Extrinsic Rewards" in *Journal of Personality and Social Psychology,* 28:134. Copyright © 1973 by the American Psychological Association. Reprinted with permission. p. 483: Cover of *Ambition* by Gilbert Brim. Cover copyright © 1992 Penguin USA. p. 484: Cover of *The Pursuit of Happiness* by David G. Myers, Ph.D. By permission of William Morrow & Company, Inc. p. 484: From Mihaly Csikszentmihalyi, *Flow.* Copyright © 1990 Harper & Row, Publishers, Inc., a division of HarperCollins Publishers, Inc. Reprinted by permission. p. 485: From Harriet Lerner, *The Dance of Anger.* Copyright © 1985 Harper Perennial, a division of HarperCollins Publishers, Inc. Reprinted by permission. p. 484: Cover of *Anger* by Carol Tavris. Cover copyright

© 1989 by Simon & Schuster Inc. Reprinted by permission of Simon & Schuster Inc.

Chapter 14

art, p. 494: Source: Adapted from J. A. Kelly, et al., "HIV Risk Behavior Reduction Following Intervention with Key Opinion Leaders of a Population: An Experimental Community Level Analysis" in *American Journal of Public Health,* 81:168–171, 1991. Figure 14.4: From C. J. Holahan and R. H. Moos, "Personal and Contextual Determinants of Coping Strategies" in *Journal of Personality and Social Psychology,* 52:946–955. Copyright © by the American Psychological Association. Reprinted with permission. Figure 14.5: From *Contemporary Behavior Therapy,* 2nd edition, by M. D. Spiegler and D. C. Guevremont. Copyright © 1993 by Brooks/Cole Publishing Company, a division of Thomson Publishing Inc., Pacific Grove, CA 93950. Reprinted by permission of the publisher. p. 529: From *The New Aerobics* by Kenneth H. Cooper. Copyright © 1970 by Kenneth H. Cooper. Used by permission of Bantam Books, a division of Bantam Doubleday Dell Publishing Group, Inc. p. 529: Cover of *Body Traps* by Dr. Judith Rodin. By permission of William Morrow & Company, Inc. p. 530: Cover from *The New Fit or Fat* by Covert Bailey. Copyright © 1991 Houghton Mifflin Company. Reprinted by permission. p. 530: Cover of *Learned Optimism* by Martin E. P. Seligman. Cover copyright © 1992 by Pocket Books, a division of Simon & Schuster Inc. Reprinted by permission of Pocket Books, a division of Simon & Schuster Inc. p. 530: Cover of *What to Say When You Talk to Yourself* by Shad Helmstetter, Ph.D. Cover copyright © 1987 by Pocket Books, a division of Simon & Schuster Inc. Reprinted by permission of Pocket Books, a division of Simon & Schuster Inc. p. 531: Cover from *Beyond the Relaxation Response* by Herbert Benson. Copyright © 1984 Times Books, Inc., a division of Random House, Inc. Reprinted by permission.

Chapter 15

Figure 15.1: From *Psychology: A Scientific Study of Human Behavior* by L. S. Wrightsman, C. K. Sigelman, and F. H. Sanford. Copyright © 1979, 1975, 1970, 1965, 1961 by Brooks/Cole Publishing Company, a division of Thomson Publishing Inc. Reprinted by permission of the publisher. Figure 15.4: Source: Abraham Maslow, "A Theory of Human Motivation" in *Motivation and Personality,* 2d ed., 1970. Figure 15.6: From Dr. Hans J. Eysenck, London, England. Reprinted by permission. p. 554: Excerpted from "Self-Improvement Program." Copyright © 1973, 1974, 1976 by Judith Viorst. From *How Did I Get to Be 40*

& Other Atrocities, published by Simon & Schuster. Reprinted by permission. Figure 15.10: From N. S. Jacobson, et al., "Toward a Behavioral Profile of Marital Distress" in *Journal of Consulting and Clinical Psychology,* 48:696–703. Copyright © 1980 by the American Psychological Association. Reprinted with permission. p. 568: Cover of *Control Your Depression* by Peter M. Lewinsohn. Cover copyright © 1992 by Simon & Schuster Inc. Reprinted by permission of Simon & Schuster Inc. p. 568: Cover from *Gentle Roads to Survival* by Andre Auw. Copyright © Aslan Publishing, Santa Rosa, CA. Reprinted by permission.

Chapter 16

p. 573: From *The Poetry of Robert Frost* edited by Edward Connery Lathem. Copyright 1936 by Robert Frost. Copyright © 1964 by Lesley Frost Ballantine. Copyright © 1969 by Henry Holt and Co., Inc. Reprinted by permission of Henry Holt and Co., Inc., and Jonathan Cape, London. Figure 16.4: From Moshen Mirabi, *DSM-III Training Guide,* L. J. Webb, et al. (eds.), page 87. Copyright © 1981 Brunner/Mazel, Inc. Reprinted with permission from Brunner/Mazel, Inc. p. 592: From Dorothy Parker, "Resume" in *Enough Rope.* Copyright © 1927 Amereon Limited, Mattituck. NY. Figure 16.7: From I. I. Gottesman and J. Shields, *The Schizophrenic Puzzle.* Copyright © 1992 Cambridge University Press. Reprinted with the permission of Cambridge University Press. p. 609: Reprinted by permission of Warner Books/New York, from *Obsessive-Compulsive Disorders,* 1991. p. 609: From R. Reid Wilson, *Don't Panic.* Copyright © 1986 Harper Perennial, a division of HarperCollins Publishers, Inc. Reprinted by permission. p. 609: Cover of *Feeling Good* by David Burns. By permission of Avon Books.

Chapter 17

p. 617: Source: National Library of Medicine. p. 650: Cover from *Five Therapists and One Client* by Raymond Corsini, et al., 1991. Reproduced with permission of F. E. Peacock Publishers, Inc., Itasca, IL 60143. p. 650: Cover of *The Consumer's Guide to Psychotherapy* by Jack Engler and Daniel Goleman. Cover copyright © 1992 by Simon & Schuster Inc. Reprinted by permission of Simon & Schuster Inc. p. 650: Jacket design: Willi Baum. Reprinted by permission. p. 651: From Donald Atkinson, et al., *Counseling American Minorities,* 4th ed. Copyright © 1993 Wm. C. Brown Communications, Inc., Dubuque, Iowa. Reprinted by permission of Times Mirror Higher Education Group, Inc., Dubuque, Iowa. All Rights Reserved.

Chapter 18

Figure 18.3: Source: Data from R. J. Sternberg, *The Triangle of Love,* Basic Books, Inc., 1988. Figure 18.5: Source: S. E. Asch, "Studies of Independence and Conformity: A Minority of One Against a Unanimous Majority" in *Psychological Monographs,*, 90 (whole no. 416), American Psychological Association, 1956. p. 692: Cover of *Influence* by Robert B. Cialdini, Ph.D. By permission of Quill Trade Paperback, an imprint of William Morrow & Company, Inc. p. 692: From Harville Hendrix, *Getting the Love You Want.* Copyright © 1988 Harper Perennial, a division of HarperCollins Publishers, Inc. Reprinted by permission. p. 692: *Shyness: What It Is, What to Do About It,* © 1977 by Philip Zimbardo. Reprinted by permission of Addison-Wesley Publishing Company, Inc. Cover illustration © 1989 by Bart Goldman.

Chapter 19

Figure 19.1: From Harry C. Triandis, "Making Basic Texts in Psychology More Culture-Inclusive and Culture-Sensitive"; presentation at a workshop. Reprinted by permission of Harry C. Triandis. p. 723: Reprinted by permission of The Putnam Publishing Group/Jeremy P. Tarcher, Inc., from *Creating Community Anywhere* by Carolyn R. Shaffer and Kristin Anundsen. Copyright © 1993 by Carolyn R. Shaffer and Kristin Anundsen. p. 723: Cover of *People: Psychology from a Cultural Perspective* by David Matsumoto. Copyright © 1994 Brooks/Cole Publishing Company. Cover photo: Craig Lovell © '95. Reprinted by permission. p. 723: Cover from *Psychology and Culture,* W. Lonner and R. Malpass (eds.). Copyright © 1994 by Allyn and Bacon. Reprinted by permission. p. 723: Cover of *Culture and Social Behavior* by Harry Triandis. Copyright © 1994 McGraw-Hill, Inc., New York, NY. Reprinted by permission of McGraw-Hill, Inc.

Appendix

Figure A.1: Source: Data from Wayne Weiten, et al., *Psychology Applied to Modern Life: Adjustment in the 90s,* Third Edition, Wadsworth Publishing Company, Brooks/Cole Publishing, 1991.

PHOTOGRAPHS

Section Openers

1: © Inner Peace/Michio Takayama/Michael McCormick Gallery; 2: © China Odyssey/Courtesy of John Santrock; 3: © La Parade/George Seurat/Metropolitan Museum of Art; 4: © Poppyfield/Monet/Art Resource; 5: © The Kiss/August Klimt/Oesterrichische Galerie; 6: © Effect of the Moon on Historical Certainty/Bill Rane/Michael McCormick Gallery; 7 © :Strange Garden/Paul Klee/Metropolitan Museum of Art; 8: © The Market/Paul Gauguin/Superstock

Chapter 1

Opener: © Mark Richards/Photo Edit; p. 4: © Wide World Photo; p. 6left: © Paul Conklin; p. 6 right:Michael Philip Mannheim/First Light,Toronto; p. 7: © Bob Daemmrich/The Image Works; 1.2B:Bettmann Archive; 1.2C:Bettmann Archive; 1.2D:Courtesy of Ruth Howard; 1.2E: Bettmann Archive; 1.2F:Courtesy of Keith and Mamie Clark; 1.2G:Bettman Archive; 1.2H:Center for the Study of the Person; 1.2I:Courtesy of Albert Bandura; 1.2J:Courtesy of Eleanor Macobby; 1.2K:Courtesy of John Berry; 1.2L:Courtesy of Sandra Bem; 1.2M:Courtesy of Judith Rodin; 1.2N:Courtesy of Roger Sperry; 1.2O:Bettmann Archive; 1.2P:Bettmann Archive; 1.2Q:Bettmann Archive; 1.2R:Jane Reed; 1.2S:Bettmann Archive; 1.2T:Archives of the History of American Psychology, University of Akron; 1.2U:Bettmann Archive; 1.2V:Bettmann Archive; 1.2W:Bettmann Archive; 1.2X: Archives of the History of American Psychology, University of Akron; 1.2Y:Courtesy of Archives of the History of American Psychology, University of Akron; p. 15:Courtesy of Harry Triandis; p. 16L middle: © David Young Wolff/Photo Edit; p. 16 right: © David Young Wolff/Photo Edit; p. 17: © Jay Dickman

Chapter 2

Opener: © Sharon Beals/Insight; p. 28:Ken Regan/Camera Five; 2.1: © Michael Melford/The Image Bank; p. 32:Courtesy of Dr. Florence L. Denmark/Photo by Robert Wesner; 2.2 left: © Anthony Bannister/Earth Scenes; 2.2 right: © Chagnan/Anthro-Photo; p. 34: © Ed Tronick/Anthro-Photo; p. 35: © Peter Byron/Monkmeyer Press; 2.5: © Courtesy of Albert Bandura; p. 40: © Jeff Greenberg/The Picture Cube; p. 44: © Rafael Macial/Photo Researchers

Chapter 3

Opener: © Scott Camaziwe/Photo Researchers; p. 58: © Enrico Ferorelli; p. 60 top: © Vincent Hazat/Photo Researchers; 3.1:Regents of the University of California; 3.2 : © Four by Five; 3.3 right: © Four by Five; 3.3 left: © Elyse Lewin/The Image Bank, Dallas; p. 64 left top:Courtesy of United Nations; p. 64 large:Courtesy of United Nations; p. 64 right top: © Gio Barto/The Image Bank/Dallas; p. 64 top middle: © Jim Shaffer; p. 64 bottom left:Courtesy of United Nations; p. 64 bottom right: © Harvey Lloyd/The Stock Market; p. 67: © David Young Wolff/Photo Edit; 3.5: © Lennart Nilsson; 3.9: © Lennart Nilsson; p. 72: © Alan Becker/The Image Bank, Dallas; 3.10: © Lennart Nilsson; 3.11: © Hank Morgan/Photo Researchers; 3.13:John Wiley, California Institute of Technology, Estate of James Olds; 3.17: © Wilder Penfield Papers/Montreal Neurological Institute; 3.20:Courtesy of the National Library of Medicine; p. 82:Courtesy of Jerre Levy; 3.22 top left: © Bettmann Archives; 3.22 top right: © Picture Group; 3.22 bottom left: Courtesy of NASA; 3.22 bottom right: © Bettmann Archives; 3.23: © Charles Gupton; 3.24: © M. Posner, University of Oregon; 3.25: © Science Source/Photo Researchers

Chapter 4

Opener: © Eric Meola/Image Bank; 4.1: © Bob Coyle; 4.2 bottom: © Helmut Gritscher/Peter Arnold; 4.2 top: © Douglas B. Nelson/Peter Arnold; 4.4: © Morris Karol; 4.6: © Burton McNeely/The Image Bank, Dallas; 4.7:Courtesy of MacBeth, Division of Koll Morgen; 4.8a: © Fritz Goreau/Life Magazine,1944 Time Inc.; 4.8b: © Fritz Goreau/Life Magazine,1944 Time Inc.; 4.13a: © J.P.Laffont/Sygma; 4.13b: © Peabody Museum of Salem, Photograph by Mark Sexton; 4.14a: © Lennart Nilsson; 4.14: © Lou Jones/The Image Bank; 4.15: © Lennart Nilsson; 4.18: © 1953 M.C. Escher/Cordon Art; 4.19: © Asahi Shimbun; 4.21: © The National Gallery of Art; 4.22:Reproduction by courtesy of the Trustees, The National Gallery, London; 4.23: © Lawrence Migdale; 4.28a: © Herman Eisenceiss/Photo Researchers; 4.28b: © Emillo Mercado/Jeroboam; 4.30: © Enrico Ferorelli; p. 124: © R. Joedecke/The Image Bank; 4.32: © Psychology Today; 4.33: © Dana Fineman/Sygma

Chapter 5

Opener: © David Hiser/The Image Bank; p. 138a: © Joel Gordon; p. 138b: © Dean/The Image Works; 5.1B: © Steve Dunwell/Image Bank; 5.1C: © David Young Wolff/Photo Edit; 5.1D: © David Frazier Photolibrary; 5.1E: © Randy Duchaine/Stock Market; 5.1F: © Luis Castaneda/Image Bank; 5.1G: © Caesar Paredes/Stock Market; 5.1H: © Barry Christensen/Stock Boston; 5.2: © Michel Siffre; 5.5: From Dreamstage Scientific Catalog, © 1977 J. Allan Hobson & Hoffman La Roche; p. 149: © James Wilson/Woodfin Camp; p. 153: © Luis Castaneda/Image Bank; p. 156all: © Floyd Holdman,LTD; 5.8top: © Derik Murray/Image Bank; 5.8all

Chapter 6

Opener: © Jeff Smith/The ImageBank, Texas; p. 172left: © Bettmann; p. 172 right: © 1992 Childrens Television Workshop. Used by permission of Television Workshop; p. 174: © Whitney Lane/Image Bank; 6.1: © Bettmann Archives;

6.4:Courtesy of Dr. Ben Harris; 6.5: © Jay Fries/The Image Bank, Dallas; 6.6: © Richard Wood/Picture Cube; 6.9: © Nancy Brown/The Image Bank, Dallas; 6.10: © Dion Ogust/The Image Works; 6.12: © Richard Wood/The Picture Cube; p. 192a: © Richard Hutchins/Photo Researchers, Inc.; p. 192b: © Granitsas/The Image Works; p. 193c: © Kevin Forest/The Image Bank, Dallas; p. 192 large: © Jeff Smith/The Image Bank, Texas; 6.19: © Francois Dardelet/The Image Bank, Dallas; p. 197: © Bruce Coleman; 6.23:Courtesy of Animal Behavior Enterprises, Inc.; 6.A: © David Gillison/Peter Arnold; p. 205: © Eiji Miyazawa/Black Star

Chapter 7

Opener: © Frans Lanting/Minden Pictures; 7.2: © R.Kawakami/The Image Bank, Dallas; p. 218: © Ira Wyman/Sygma; p. 219: © Bettmann Archives; p. 223: © Fredericks/Image Works; p. 227: © Jim Shaffer; 7.10left: © G.Aschendorf/Photo Researchers; 7.10middle: © Jeff Greenberg/Photo Edit; 7.10right: © Brian Seed/Tony Stone Images; 7.12: © Derek Berwin/The Image Bank, Dallas; 7.13: © Four by Five; p. 233: © Wide World Photos; p. 235: © Tom McHugh/Photo Reaearchers

Chapter 8

Opener: © Jon Riley/Tony Stone Images; p. 246: © Bettmann Archive; p. 247 left: © Peter Menzel/Stock Boston; p. 247 left middle: © Makoto Iwafuji/Stock Market; p. 247 right middle: © Bob Gomel/Stock Market; p. 247 right: © Seth Resnick/Stock Boston; p. 250: © Historical Pictures; p. 257a: © Gregory Heisler/Image Bank; p. 257b: © Gary Gladstone/Image Bank; p. 257c: © Paul Gerda/Leo de Wys; p. 257d: © Stacy Pick/Stock Boston; p. 263: © Anthony Bannister/Earth Scenes; p. 264 left: © Katrina Thomas/Photo Researchers; p. 264 right: © Preuss/The Image Works; p. 265 left: © Superstock; p. 265 right: © Superstock; p. 266: © Lawrence Migdale/Photo Researchers, Inc.; 8.10: © Enrico Fervelli; 8.11a: © David Hamilton/The Image Bank; 8.11b: © Steve Dunwell/The Image Bank, Dallas; 8.11c: © Meike Mass/The Image Bank, Dallas; 8.12a: © G&H Anders/The Image Bank, Dallas; 8.12B: © Meike Mass/The Image Bank, Dallas; 8.12c: © Bob Daemmrich/The Image Works; p. 272: © Shooting Star; 8.15: © Jill Cannefax/EKM Nepenthe; 8.17a: © David Austen/Stock Boston; 8.17b: © Ben Simmons/Stock Market

Chapter 9

Opener: © Tom Rosenthal/Superstock; p. 296: © Kelly Wilkinson/Indianapolis Star; 9.2A: © Michael Melford/Image Bank; 9.2A1: © Michael Melford/Image Bank; 9.2A2: © Mark Walker/Picture Cube; p. 301 left: © M.Richards/Photo Edit; p. 301 middle: © Image Works; p. 301 right: © Joseph Nettis/Photo Researchers; 9.3: © Lennart Nilsson; 9.4: © Lennart Nilsson; 9.5: © Lennart Nilsson; p. 303 right: © Chas Cancellare/Picture Group; p. 304:Courtesy of Dr. Tiffany Fields; 9.7: © Edward Lettau/Photo Researchers,Inc.; p. 308: © Yves DeBraine/Black Star; 9.8 both: © D.Goodman/Monkmeyer Press; 9.9 right: © Denise Marcotte/The Picture Cube; 9.11 top: © Paul Fusco/Magnum Photos, Inc.; 9.12 botttom: © Owen Franken/Stock Boston; 9.15: © Richard Hutchings/Photo Researchers, Inc.; 9.16: © Alan Becker/The Image Bank; 9.17 top: © William Hopkins; 9.17 top middle: © Suzanne Szasz/Photo Researchers; 9.17 bottom middle: © Suzanne Szasz/Photo Researchers; 9.17 bottom: © Mel Digiacomo/Image Bank; 9.18: © Martin Rogers/Stock Boston; 9.19: © Nina Leen/Time/Life Magazine, Time Inc.; p. 320: © Wide World Photos; p. 21: © Bob Daemmrich/The Image Works; 9.A top: © FPG International; 9.A top middle: © Peter Turnley/Black Star; 9.A middle: © Kevin Horan/Picture Group; 9.A bottom middle: © Alan Stuart Frank/Photo Researchers; 9.A bottom: © Joseph Rodriquez/Black Star; p. 324a: © Pieter Breughel/Kunsthistorisches Museum; p. 324b: © Bob Daemmrich/Image Works

Chapter 10

Opener: © Harold Sund/Image Bank; p. 334: © John Goodman; p. 335: © Lanpher Productions, Inc.; 10.1: © Luis Villota/The Stock Market; 10.2: © Alan Carey/The Image Works; 10.3: © W. Eastep/The Stock Market; 10.4: © Michael Melford/Image Bank; p. 343: © Daniel Laine; p. 344:/Courtesy of Margaret Beale Spencer; p. 345: © Bob Daemmrich/The Image Works; p. 346: © Keith Carter Photography; p. 350:Courtesy of Midnight Basketball League; 10.5 top: © Walter Bibikow/The Image Bank, Dallas; 10.5 middle: © Kaz Mori/The Image Bank, Dallas; 10.5 bottom: © Ewing Galloway; 10.6 top: © Bettmann Archive; 10.6 bottom: © Andy Caulfield/Image Bank, Dallas; p. 360 left: © Owen Franken/Stock Boston; p. 360 right: © Bettman Archives; 10.7: © Nilo Lima/Photo Researchers; p. 362: © Bob Daemmrich/Stock Boston; p. 362 bottom: © Bruce Kliewe/Jeroboam; p. 363a: © John Launois/Black Star; p. 363: © John Launois/Black Star; p. 364: © Linda Creighton/U.S. News and World Report;

p. 365: © Elyse Lewin/The Image Bank, Dallas; p. 366: © Comstock; p. 367: © Wayne Floyd/Unicorn Photos; 10.9:Courtesy of University of California; 10.10a: © Jackson Hill/Southern Lights Photography; 10.10b: © Spencer Swanger/Tom Stack & Associates

Chapter 11

Opener: © David Madison/Image Bank; p. 384: © Paul Conklin/Photo Edit; p. 388: © James Pozarik/Gamma Liason; p. 387: © Irene Young; p. 390: © Bettye Lane/Photo Researchers, Inc.; p. 392: © Edward Lettau/Photo Researchers; 11.2A: © Comstock; 11.3 top: © Maria Taglienti/The Image Bank; 11.3 bottom: © Larry Dale Gordon/The Image Bank, Dallas; 11.4: © Erika Stone; p. 400: © Suzanne Szasz/Photo Researchers, Inc.; p. 400 left:Courtesy of Eleanor Maccoby; 11.5: © Ken Gaghan/Jeroboam; p. 403: © Robert Potter; p. 404: © Tim Bieber/The Image Bank; p. 406 all: © Carol Beckwith/National Geographic; p. 407 left: © Bernard Pierre Wolff/Photo Researchers, Inc.; p. 407 right: © Catherine Gehm

Chapter 12

Opener: © Stephen Wilkes/Image Bank; p. 419 top: © Bob Coyle; p. 419T right: © Anthony Mercieca/Photo Researchers; p. 419 bottom left: © Sven-Olof Lindblad/Photo Researchers; p. 419 bottom: © Jill Cannefax/Ekm Nepenthe; p. 421: © Cliff Feulner/The Image Bank; p. 422: © Bernard Gotfryd/Woodfin Camp; 12.4: © Butch Martin, Inc.; p. 427 left: © Randy Taylor/Sygma; p. 427 right: © R. Maiman/Sygma; p. 432 left: © Wide World Photos; p. 432 right: © Bettmann; p. 434: © Charles Steiner/Picture Group; p. 436: © Alon Reininger/Contact Press

Chapter 13

Opener: © Kaz Mori/Image Bank; p. 450:ASSOCIATED PRESS 1991 L.A. TIMES; 13.1 top: © Paul Trummer/The Image Bank; 13.1 top midddle: © Ted Kawaleski/The Image Bank, Dallas; 13.1 middle: © Jim Shaffer; 13.1 bottom middle: © Jim Shaffer; 13.1 bottom: © 1992 Lawrence Migdale; 13.2 top: © Phil Borden/Photo Edit; 13.2 bottom: © David Young Wolff/Photo Edit; 13.4:Courtesy Dr. Philip Teitelbaum, Published in the Proceedings of the American Philosphical Society,1964,Vol.108.; 13.5: © University of Wisconsin Primate Laboratory; 13.7:From Dreamstage Scientific Catalog, © 1977 J. Allan Hobson & Hoffman La Roche; p. 463: © Wide World Photos; p. 464:Courtesy of Sandra Graham; p. 465: © Will & Deni McIntyre/Photo Researchers, Inc.; 13.9 right: © Leo de Wys; 13.13 left:

© Donald Dutton; 13.13 right: © Donald Dutton; 13.14: © Jim Shaffer; 13.15 left: © John Urban; 13.15 left middle: © Paul Ekman; 13.15 middle right: © Paul Ekman; 13.15 right: © Paul Ekman; p. 477 bottom: © Terry Eiler/Stock Boston; p. 478: © Robert Harding Library; p. 480: © Jean Claude Lejeune

Chapter 14

Opener: © John P. Kelly/The Image Bank, Dallas; p. 488: © Jim Pickerell/Image Works; p. 490a: © George V. Mann; p. 490b: © David Stoecklein/The Stock Market; p. 491: © William Hopkins; p. 495 top: © Douglas Fisher/Image Bank; p. 495 bottom: © W. Woodworth/Superstock; p. 498 top: © Jamie Villasseca/The Image Bank; p. 498 bottom: © David Frazier Photo Library; 14.1: © John Elk; p. 501: © Tony Freeman/Photo Edit; p. 502: © Wide World Photos; p. 503 left:Courtesy Dr. Richard Brislin; p. 503 right: © John Bowen; p. 509 left: © William Steve Burr/The Image Bank, Dallas; p. 509 right: © Ted Kawalerski/The Image Bank; p. 511: Courtesy of John Berry; p. 512:Courtesy of Dr. Vonnie McLoyd; p. 519: © Cary Wolkinsky/Stock Boston; p. 524:Roy Morsch/The Stock Market; p. 525: © Combstock

Chapter 15

Opener: © Y. Arthus-Bertrand/Peter Arnold; p. 535:Bettmann; p. 536: © Bettmann; 15.2 top left: © Robert Eckert/Ekm Nepenthe; 15.2 top right: © James Marshall; 15.2 bottom left: © Burton McNeely/Image Bank; 15.2 bottom middle: © Antman/Image Works; 15.2 bottom left: © Richard Hutchings/Photo Researchers; p. 541: © Shooting Star; p. 539: © Antonio Luiz Hamdan/Image Bank; p. 540: © Superstock; p. 541a: Bettmann Archives; p. 541b: Courtesy of Nancy Chodorow, photo by Jean Margolis; 15.3 left: © Jonathan Wright/Bruce Coleman; 15.3 right: © Bettmann Archives; p. 546 left: Courtesy of Albert Bandura; p. 546 right:Courtesy of Dr. Walter Mischel; p. 547:Center for the Study of the Person; p. 549 left: © Bruce Roberts/Photo

Researchers, Inc.; p. 549 right: © Superstock, Inc.; 15.5 left: © Wide World Photos; 15.5 middle: © Wide World Photos; 15.5 right: © Bettmann; p. 557: © Roger Miller/The Image Bank; 15.9:Reprinted by permission of the Publishers from Henry A. Murray, "Thematic Apperception Test", Cambridge, MA: Harvard University Press, Copyright © 1943 by the President and Fellows of Harvard College, © 1971 by Henry A. Murray.; 15.10: © Spencer Grant/Marilyn Gartman Agency

Chapter 16

Opener: © Alain Choisnet/The Image Bank; p. 595: © Bettmann; p. 576 left: © RB/Photo Edit; p. 576 middle: © David Young Wolff/Photo Edit; p. 576 right: © Richard Hutchings/Photo Edit; p. 578:Courtesy of Nancy Felipe Russo; p. 579a: © Adam Tannen/Combstock; p. 579b: © Stephen Marks/Image Bank; p. 580: © Jim Shaffer; 16.1: © Art Resource; p. 585 bottom: © Richard Laird/FPG; 16.3: © Gerald Martineau/The Washington Post; p. 593: © Bob Daemmrich/Stock Boston; 16.5:Courtesy of University of Heidelberg; 16.6: © Grunnitus/Monkmeyer Press; p. 603 left: © Wide World Photos; p. 603 right: © Bettmann

Chapter 17

Opener: © Stacy Pickerell/Tony Stone World Wide; 17.1: © National Museum of Denmark; 17.2: © Historical Pictures; p. 620: © Historical Pictures/Stock Montage; 17.3: © Bosch/Art Resource; p. 623:Courtesy of Deke Simen; 17.4: © David Frazier Photolibrary; 17.5: © Combstock; p. 630: © Bob Daemmrich/Stock Boston; p. 633: © Jay Lurie Photography; p. 635: © Buzz Lawrence Photography; p. 639 left: © Russ Kinne/Comstock; p. 639 right:Courtesy of Rachel Hare-Mustin & Jeanne Maracek; p. 640a: © Combstock; p. 640b: © J.Y. Rabeuf/The Image Works; p. 640c : © Peter Menzel/Stock Boston; p. 640d: © Robert Houser/Comstock

Chapter 18

Opener: © Tom Prettyman/Photo Edit; p. 656: © Sygma; 18.1: © Jeff Smith/The Image Bank,Dallas; 18.2: © Stephen Wilkes/The Image Bank; p. 664: © Joel Gordon; p. 665: © Miguel/The Image Bank; 18.3: © Robert Farber/The Image Bank; p. 668: © Brett Froomer/The Image Bank; p. 672: © Arthur Grace/Stock Boston; 18.4 left:Courtesy of Alexandra Milgram; 18.4 right:Courtesy of Alexandra Milgram; p. 676: © Wide World Photos; p. 678 top: © Wide World Photos; p. 678B: © Alberto Garcia/Gamma Liaison; 18.5:Courtesy of William Vandivert; 18.6:Courtesy of Philip Zimbardo; 18.6:Courtesy of Philip Zimbardo; p. 681 top: © Michael Edrington/Image Works; p. 681 middle: © Andrea Pistolesi/Image Bank; p. 681 bottom: © Jean-Marc Loubat/Photo Reseachers; p. 683 left:Andy Levine/Photo Researchers, Inc.; p. 683 right: © David Frazier Photolibrary; p. 685: © Four by Five; p. 686: © Janeart, LTD/The Image Bank

Chapter 19

Opener: © Marc Romanelli; p. 697: © Victor Englebert/Photo Researchers; p. 701 top right: © Luis Villota/Stock Market; p. 701 top left: © Myrleen Ferguson/Photo Edit; p. 701 left: © Catherine Gehm; p. 701 right: © Catherine Gehm; p. 703:Courtesy of James Jones; p. 704 top: © Wide World Photos; p. 704 middle: © Wide World Photos; p. 704 bottom: © Wide World Photos; p. 704 left: © Wide World Photos; p. 705a: © Larry Kolvoord/The Image Works; p. 705b: © Bob Daemmrich/The Image Works; p. 705c: © Bill Gillette/Stock Boston; p. 705d: © Ellis Herwig/The Picture Cube; p. 708:Courtesy of Stanley Sue; p. 709: © Cleo Freelance Photography; p. 711: © Ellis Herwig/Stock Boston; p. 713 top: © Superstock; p. 713 bottom: © Bruce Coleman; p. 716 top left: © Fuji/Image Works; p. 716 top right: © Derek Berwin/The Image Bank; p. 716 bottom left: © Superstock; p. 716 bottom right: © Cameramann/The Image Work

Name Index

Danzinger, S., 300
Darby, B. L., 303
Darling, C. A., 424
Darwin, C., 62, 476
Dasen, P. E., 32, 123, 250
Dasen, P. R., 32, 280
Davidson, R. J., 474
Davis, K. E., 664
Davison, G. C., 625
Dawkins, M. S., 44
DeBord, K. A., 403
DeCasper, A. J., 305
DeCola, J. P., 180
Deffenbacher, K., 230
DeFour, D. C., 433
DeFries, J. C., 59, 279
de Jong-Gierveld, J., 667
Delis, D., 363
Dement, W., 144
De Meuse, K. P., 682
Denmark, F. L., 15, 32, 386, 393
Denton, R. K., 150
DePaulo, B. M., 475, 476
Deregowski, J., 125
Deregowski, J. B., 236
Derlega, V. J., 664
Desaulniers, J., 391
Despres, J. P., 495
Deutsch, F. M., 359
Deutsch, J. A., 457
Deutsch, M., 549, 710
Dewey, J., 256
Dey, E. L., 715
Dhawan, N., 476
Diamond, E. E., 353
Diamond, M., 428
Diaz, R. M., 267
DiBiase, R., 320
Dickerscheid, J. D., 407
Dickson, G. L., 352
Dickson, W. J., 683
Diener, E., 470
Dietz, W., 496
DiGuilio, R., 372
Dillbeck, M. C., 520
Dimardo, P. A., 584
DiMatteo, M. R., 524
DiNicola, D. D., 524
Dirkes, K., 303
Dixon, R. A., 370
Dohrenwend, B. S., 510, 581
Dolcini, M. M., 437
Dollard, J., 546
Dolnick, E., 82
Donald, R. N., 595
Donnerstein, E., 434
Doran, L. D., 337
Dorn, L. D., 337
Dornbusch, S. M., 324, 343, 344
Dougherty, D., 474
Dow-Edwards, D. L., 303
Doyne, E. J., 493, 495
Draguns, J. G., 577, 595
Draper, T. W., 278
Dreher, H., 507
Dreyer, P. H., 659
Dryden, W., 626
Dudley, S. D., 143
Duncan, G. J., 298
Duncan, T. E., 462
Dussault, J., 495
Dutton, D., 473
Dutton-Douglas, M., 639
Dweck, C. S., 462

E

Eagly, A. H., 514
Ebata, A., 514
Eccles, J. S., 465
Eckert, E., 58
Eckert, E. D., 586
Edelman, M. W., 300
Eden, D., 515
Edwards, B., 84
Edwards, S., 493, 496
Efron, R., 82
Ehrhardt, A. A., 397
Eich, E., 230
Eichorn, D. H., 360
Eifter, C. W., 524
Ekman, P., 474, 475, 476, 477
Elder, P. N., 595
Elkind, D., 338, 460
Elliott, J. R., 593
Ellis, A., 154, 627
Ellis, H. C., 222, 223, 238
Ellis, L., 428
El-Taliawy, T., 407
Emmons, R. A., 453
Engel, J. W., 17
Engeltinger, J., 503
Ennis, R. H., 256
Entwisle, D. R., 42
Eppley, K. R., 520
Eriksen, M., 502
Erikson, E. H., 316, 318, 343, 356, 368, 541, 622
Erkut, S., 42
Espin, O. M., 404
Evans, B. J., 403, 405
Evans, I. M., 348
Evans, P., 468
Evascu, T., 139
Exner, J. E., 559
Eyler, F. D., 303
Eysenck, H. J., 554, 636

F

Fabegra, H., 582
Fairburn, C. G., 495, 496, 499
Fanselow, M. S., 180
Farley, J. E., 428
Fasick, F. A., 342
Faulkner, L. R., 603
Fausto-Sterling, S., 62
Fei, J., 665
Feinleib, M., 513
Feinstein, M. H., 247
Feiring, C., 396
Feldman, D., 278
Ferguson, C. A., 263
Ferguson, D. M., 306
Fernea, E., 697
Fernea, R., 697
Ferron, J., 300
Feshbach, S., 507, 559
Festinger, L., 657, 660
Field, T., 303
Fine, T. H., 460
Finlay, B., 322, 350
First, M. B., 582
Fischer, J., 186
Fisher, M. P., 425
Fiske, S. T., 558
Fitzgerald, L. F., 403
Fivush, R., 227
Flannery, D. J., 341
Flaskerud, J., 641
Flavell, E. R., 314

Flavell, J. H., 308, 313, 314
Fleming, C., 16
Flynn, B. S., 501
Foa, E. B., 584
Foley, V., 631
Folkman, N., 506, 510
Folkman, S., 514
Foner, N., 359
Fonnebo, V., 500
Ford, C., 663
Fournier, G., 495
Fowler, C. A., 97
Fox, R. E., 619
Frager, R., 680
Frances, A., 582
Frances, A. J., 583
Frank, E., 643
Frank, J. D., 637
Franken, L. E., 462
Fraser, S., 279
Fredman, L., 372
Freedman, J. L., 507, 708, 715
Freeman, D., 335
Freier, K., 303
Frenz-Gilles, R., 341
Freud, S., 14, 137, 147, 452, 536, 593
Freund, A. M., 370
Friedman, M., 507
Friedman, M. A., 495
Friesen, W., 475
Friesen, W. V., 474, 477
Frieze, I. H., 32, 387, 393
Fromm, E., 541
Fuhrman, A., 629
Fulker, D. W., 59
Fuller, M., 549
Furth, H. G., 312
Furumoto, L., 11
Futrell, D., 682
Fyer, A. J., 584

G

Gabriel, T. J., 463
Gabrielli, W. F., 157
Gagnon, J., 424, 427
Gaier, E. L., 641
Gaines, S. O., 708
Gallant, S. J., 503
Galligan, P., 683
Gallup, G., 672
Gannon, L., 32
Ganza, B., 424
Garbarino, J., 298, 549
Garcia, C. T., 322
Garcia, H. A. V., 42
Garcia, W. I., 580
Gardner, B. T., 267
Gardner, H., 271
Gardner, L. I., 524
Gardner, R. A., 267
Garfein, A. J., 362
Garfield, J. L., 247
Garfield, S. L., 625, 637
Garmezy, N., 514
Garner, D. M., 496
Garrett, P., 300
Garrod, A., 343
Garwood, S. G., 300
Gary, L. E., 355
Gaskill, S. P., 524
Gathercole, S., 217
Gatti, F. M., 554
Gazzaniga, M., 81
Geller, B. M., 501

Geller, J., 641
Gerton, J., 511, 700, 702
Geschwind, N., 83
Gibbons, F. X., 658
Gibbs, J., 346
Gibbs, J. T., 343, 464, 578, 701
Gibbs, N., 386
Gibson, E. J., 122, 123
Gibson, J. J., 109
Gibson, R. C., 366
Gidycz, C. A., 433
Giesler, R. B., 663
Gilliam, P., 686
Gilligan, C., 346, 359, 387, 396, 466
Gilmore, D. O., 405
Gim, R. H., 640
Girus, J. S., 122
Gjerde, P., 594
Gladue, B. A., 428
Glaser, R., 5, 355, 489
Glass, G. N., 636
Glazer, M., 149
Glick, J., 280
Glisky, E. L., 232
Gochros, H. L., 186
Godden, D. R., 230
Goldberg, H., 402
Goldberg, S., 396
Goldberg, T. E., 599
Goldberger, L., 508
Goldberger, N. R., 387
Goldson, S. E., 492
Goldstein, E. B., 35, 108
Goldstein, I. R., 686
Goldstein, M. J., 588, 600
Gonzales, M. F., 457
Good, G. E., 403
Goodall, J., 28
Goodchilds, J. D., 426
Goodstein, L. D., 558, 584
Goodwin, D. W., 155, 157
Goodwin, F. K., 591
Gordon, W., 203
Gorman, J. M., 584
Gotfried, F., 435
Gottesman, I. I., 595, 599, 600, 605
Gottfried, A. E., 354
Gottfried, A. W., 354
Gottman, J. M., 354
Gould, M., 581
Gould, S. J., 60
Gould-Martin, K., 497
Grady, W. R., 427, 435
Graf, P., 219
Graham, S., 32, 464, 718
Granek, M., 520
Grant, J. P., 306
Grant, M. J., 42
Gray, C. R., 217
Green, P., 172
Greenberg, M. T., 341
Greene, D., 461
Greenwald, A. G., 706
Gregory, R., 39
Gregory, R. L., 123
Grevious, C., 631
Griffith, D. R., 303
Grim, G., 359
Grotevant, H. D., 341
Gruen, G. E., 667
Gruenberg, F., 585
Grush, J. E., 673
Gruys, A., 319
Guilford, J. P., 258
Gullotta, T. P., 155

Gummerman, K., 217
Gur, R. C., 84
Gur, R. E., 84
Gurin, J., 497
Gurman, A. S., 630
Guthrie, R., 202
Gutierres, S. E., 657
Guttman, N., 189

H

Haaga, D. A. F., 626
Haan, N., 360
Hadley, E. C., 362
Haffner, S. M., 524
Hahn, A., 347
Hall, C. C. I., 16, 403
Hall, G. S., 335
Hall, W. S., 708
Halonen, J., 256
Hamer, D. H., 62
Hamilton, T. E., 664
Haney, C., 680
Hannah, T. E., 42
Hansell, S., 358
Hanson, D. J., 625
Hanson, K., 433
Hanson, K. A., 370
Hansson, R. O., 370
Hardin, T. S., 594
Harkness, S., 322
Harlow, H. F., 318
Harmon, W., 673
Harold, R. D., 465
Harris, R. F., 190
Harris, R. J., 228
Harris, T., 362, 512
Harrison, C. A., 366
Hart, C., 278
Hart, D., 346
Hart, J., 520
Harter, S., 344, 463
Hartman, A., 300
Harvey, J. H., 659
Harvey, O. J., 709
Harwood, L. J., 306
Hasher, L., 222
Hatcher, R., 422, 423
Hatfield, E., 663
Hatvany, N., 684
Hauck, W. W., 437
Haupt, J. H., 278
Haverkos, H. W., 435
Hayflick, L., 362, 363
Haynes, G., 513
Haynes, S. G., 512
Hazuda, H. P., 524
Hearn, M., 501
Heath, S. B., 264
Heider, F., 461, 658
Heimreich, R., 390
Helgeson, V. S., 466
Hellige, J. B., 82
Helmreich, R. L., 7
Helsing, K. J., 500
Helzer, J. F., 585
Henderson, V. L., 462
Hennessey, B. A., 259
Hensley, D. L., 228
Heppner, P. P., 403
Hernandez, A., 466
Hernandez, D. J., 353
Hernandez, G. G., 365
Hernstein, R. J., 279
Heron, W., 459
Herron, D. G., 324

Hersen, M., 563
Hershenson, M., 122
Herskovits, M. J., 124
Herzog, A. R., 362
Herzog, E., 400
Heston, L., 58
Heston, L. L., 586
Hetherington, E. M., 355
Hiester, M., 319
Hilgard, E. R., 151
Hill, J., 341
Himelein, M. J., 433
Himmin, H. S., 407
Hinde, R. A., 65
Hines, A. M., 640
Hines, M., 396
Hintes, T., 127
Hinton, R., 149
Hiraga, Y., 344
Hirsch, E. D., 237
Hirschfeld, R. M. A., 591
Ho, M. K., 16
Hobbs, S. A., 667
Hobson, J. A., 144
Hockenbury, D., 667
Hoff-Ginsberg, E., 322, 512
Hofstede, G., 555, 699
Hogan, R. T., 554
Hollingshead, A. B., 581, 605
Hollingworth, L. S., 386
Holmbeck, G., 341
Holmbeck, G. N., 341
Holmes, D., 520
Holmes, T. H., 358, 510
Holtzmann, W., 464
Homiak, J. P., 496
Honzik, M. P., 360
Hood, W. R., 709
Hopkins, W. D., 268
Horm, J., 496
Horney, K., 541, 542
Horrereth, S. L., 420, 421
Hosli, L., 144
Howard, K. I., 336
Howard, R. W., 173
Howe, C. J., 262
Howe, M. L., 227, 233
Hoyenga, K. B., 467
Hoyenga, K. T., 467
Hsieh, C., 491
Hsu, J., 595
Hu, N., 62
Hu, S., 62
Huang, L. N., 343, 464, 578, 701
Hubel, D. H., 102
Hudson, W., 125
Hughes, M., 372
Hunt, M., 424
Hunter, B. A., 708
Hurtado, S., 715
Hurvich, L., 105
Hurvich, L. M., 105
Huston, A., 300, 512
Huston, A. C., 300, 399, 464
Hyde, J. S., 5, 393, 394, 395, 396, 416, 436
Hyde, R. T., 369, 491
Hynd, G. W., 580

I

Ickovics, J. R., 512, 513, 683
Ikels, C., 366
Ilola, L. M., 502, 512
Inclan, J. E., 324
Inoff-Germain, G., 337
Insko, C. A., 658

Name Index

Rosenberg, M., 549
Rosenham, D. L., 583
Rosenkranz, P., 390, 393, 504
Rosenman, R., 507
Rosenthal, D. A., 343
Rosenthal, N., 44, 644
Rosenthal, R., 37, 283
Ross, A. S., 42
Rossi, A., 358
Rothblum, E. D., 583
Rotter, J. B., 546
Rowe, J., 362
Rubin, D., 231
Rubin, L. B., 355
Rubin, Z., 43
Ruiz, R. A., 635
Rumbaugh, D., 267
Rumbaugh, D. M., 268
Rumberger, R. W., 348
Rumpel, E., 557, 699
Russo, N., 388, 591
Russo, N. F., 32, 387, 393, 580, 595, 602
Rutter, M., 514
Ruzecki, V., 261
Ryan, D. W., 641
Rybash, J. W., 353
Rymer, R., 262

S

Saarni, C., 480
Sack, D., 644
Sackheim, H. A., 644
Sacks, O., 94
Sadik, N., 388
Sadker, D., 465
Sadker, M., 465
Sadry, G., 515
Sagan, C., 62
Sagiv, L., 700
Sagrestano, L. M., 678
Saklofske, D. H., 273
San Miguel, S., 641
Sanderson, W. C., 636
Sandler, D. P., 500
Sandman, B. M., 303
Sangree, W. H., 366
Santrock, J. W., 184, 335, 341, 353, 357, 369, 431, 438
Sarafino, E. P., 501
Sargent, C., 126
Saron, C. D., 474
Sarrel, P., 434
Sartorius, N., 600
Sasaki, T., 599
Satir, V., 630
Saunder, E., 512
Savage-Rumbaugh, E. S., 267, 268
Savick, R. A., 267
Saxe, G. B., 204
Saxe, L., 474
Scarborough, E., 11
Scarr, S., 280, 281, 513
Scarr, S. W., 59
Schachter, S., 458, 473
Schacter, D. L., 219, 220, 232
Schank, R., 228
Schensul, S. L., 635
Scherer, K. R., 479
Schlesinger, L. B., 40
Schmidt, A., 466
Schmitz, M., 466
Schneider, L. S., 157
Schneider-Munoz, M., 437
Schneidman, E. S., 593
Schoen, L. M., 228

Schofield, J., 673
Schofield, J. W., 673
Schreiber, G., 498
Schrieber, J. M., 497
Schulz, R., 351
Schunk, D. H., 462
Schwartz, D., 578
Schwartz, J. H., 234
Schwartz, M. S., 521
Schwartz, P., 355, 427
Schwartz, R., 502
Schwartz, R. C., 630
Schwartz, S. H., 557, 700
Schwarz, P. M., 407
Scitovsky, A. A., 362
Scott, T. H., 459
Scott-Jones, D., 42
Scribner, S., 236, 339
Seager, J., 388
Seagull, A., 581
Sears, D. O., 507, 708, 715
Sechzur, J., 32, 393, 504
Secker-Walker, R. H., 501
Seffge-Krenke, I., 506
Segall, M. H., 32, 123, 124, 250, 280
Segrist, D., 32
Seiden, L. S., 71
Selice, S., 403
Seligman, M. E. P., 201, 518, 594, 595
Selye, H., 505, 506
Semaj, L., 344
Senulis, J. A., 474
Sevens, M., 403
Sexton, T. L., 636
Shanks, D. R., 225
Shannon, F. T., 306
Shapiro, N., 348
Sharpsteen, D. J., 466
Shaver, P., 666
Shear, J., 520
Sheehy, G., 352
Sheldon, W. H., 553
Shepard, R., 227
Sher, K. J., 157
Sherer, K., 476
Sherif, C. W., 709
Sherif, M., 709
Sherwood, A., 491
Shields, J., 599, 600, 605
Shields, S. A., 480
Shiffrin, R. M., 229
Shore, D. L., 500
Shotland, R. L., 670
Showers, C., 463, 518
Shrout, P. E., 510, 558
Shyu, S., 501
Siegler, R. S., 314
Siffre, M., 141
Sigelman, C. K., 672
Sigelman, L., 672
Signorielli, N., 35
Silberner, J., 364
Silverman, N. N., 542
Simmons, R. G., 337
Simon, H. A., 14
Simons, J., 369, 431, 438
Simons, J. M., 350
Simons, R. L., 509
Singer, J. E., 473
Singer, J. L., 536
Sizemore, C. C., 589
Skelly, F., 672
Skinner, B. F., 13, 136, 182, 185, 189, 193, 545
Skinner, E. A., 461
Slade, R., 97

Slap, G. B., 501
Slavin, R., 710
Slavin, R. E., 266
Sloan, T. S., 717
Slovenko, R., 603
Smith, J. C., 696
Smith, M. L., 636
Smith, R. H., 658
Smulyan, L., 343
Snarey, R., 347
Snidermann, C. J., 387
Snow, C. E., 262
Snowden, L. R., 525, 581, 640
Snyder, L. D., 227
Snyder, M., 665
Snyder, S. H., 72
Sobel, D., 491
Sobell, L. C., 157
Sobell, M., 157
Sobell, M. B., 157
Sofin, S., 706
Sokal, M. M., 19
Solomon, L. J., 583
Solomon, R., 184
Solomon, Z., 587
Sonnenstein, F. L., 392
Spacapan, S., 523
Spade, J. Z., 386
Spaulding, K., 227
Spearman, C. E., 270
Speck, P. M., 433
Spence, J. T., 390
Spence, M., 305
Spencer, M. B., 324, 343, 344
Sperling, G., 216
Sperry, T. W., 81
Sprafkin, J., 172
Sprecher, S., 663
Sprei, J. E., 433
Squire, C., 437
Squire, L., 234
Squire, L. R., 14, 234
Sroufe, L. A., 298, 319
Stanley, B., 595
Stanley, M., 595
Stanley-Hagan, M. M., 355
Stanton, A. L., 503
Stark, H. A., 220
Steadman, J. H., 604
Steers, R. M., 685
Stein, B. S., 250
Stein, J., 584
Steinberg, L., 341
Stein-Seroussi, A., 663
Steketze, G., 584
Stengel, R., 246
Steptoe, A., 493, 496
Stern, J. S., 497
Stern, M. P., 524
Sternberg, K. J., 298
Sternberg, R. J., 256, 270, 278, 280, 666
Stevenson, H. G., 42
Stevenson, H. W., 204, 205
Steward, P., 315
Stewart, K. R., 150
Stewart, N. J., 303
Stillings, N. A., 247
Stith, S. M., 433
Stoller, E. P., 366
Stone, A., 466
Stone, A. J., 387
Stotland, S., 497
Strauss, C., 455
Streissguth, A. P., 303
Strickland, B., 388, 503, 504, 591

Striegel-Moore, R., 498
Strupp, H. H., 622, 637
Stunkard, A. J., 459, 499, 518
Sturgill, W., 230
Sue, D., 405, 640
Sue, D. W., 64, 405, 641
Sue, S., 273, 640, 641, 642, 703, 709, 712, 715, 718
Suedfeld, P., 459
Suh, E. J., 391
Suinn, R. M., 11, 578, 589, 637
Sullivan, H. S., 541
Sullivan, M., 475
Suls, J., 343
Sundstrom, E., 582
Super, C. M., 304, 320, 322
Susman, E. J., 337
Sutton, R. G., 618
Suzman, R. M., 362
Suzuki, L. A., 640
Swann, W. B., 663
Swanson, D. P., 464
Swim, J. K., 708
Syvalahti, E. K., 145
Szapocznik, J., 437
Szasz, I., 579
Szasz, T., 637

T

Tafoya, T., 438
Tager-Flusberg, H., 261
Tajfel, H., 705
Tan, A., 404, 534
Tanfer, K., 427, 435
Tannen, D., 664
Tardif, T., 322, 512
Tarule, J. M., 387
Tassinary, L., 97
Tavris, C., 83, 400, 470, 480
Taylor, A. W., 144
Taylor, S. E., 507, 518, 519, 523, 658, 708, 715
Taylor, S. P., 367
Teachman, J. D., 5
Temoshok, L., 507
Tepperman, T., 458
Terman, L., 278
Terman, L. M., 278
Thapa, K., 476
Theriault, G., 495
Thibaut, J., 671
Thigpen, C., 588
Thomas, B. A., 684
Thomas, C. B., 384, 518
Thomas, D. B., 672
Thomas, R. L., 222
Thompson, L., 354, 355
Thompson, R. A., 320, 640
Thornburg, H. D., 420
Thorndike, E. L., 182
Thurstone, L. L., 270
Tobin, J. J., 366
Tolman, E. C., 180, 199
Tomarken, A. J., 473
Tomasello, M., 261
Tomlinson-Keasey, C., 278, 593
Tordoff, M. G., 457
Toro, P. A., 634
Torrey, E. F., 600
Torrey, E. T., 615
Tran, T. V., 365
Trembley, A., 495
Trevino, J. G., 715
Trevino, R., 580
Triandis, H., 8, 15, 555, 556, 698, 699, 702, 714, 715

Trimble, J. E., 16, 42, 641
Trivers, R., 668
Tronick, E., 123
Tropp, L., 42
Trost, M. R., 657
Trotter, R. J., 60
Trower, P., 626
Tseng, W., 595
Tulving, E., 219, 220, 222
Turk, D., 626
Turnbull, C., 124
Turner, J. W., 460

U

Ubell, C., 334
Ulbrich, P. M., 354
Unger, D. G., 344
Unger, R., 15, 393, 399
Urberg, K. A., 501

V

Vaillant, G. E., 357
Valdez, R. B., 437
Van den Berghe, P. L., 64
Van Duesen, J. E., 424
van Praag, H. M., 584
Van Yperen, N. W., 658
Velton, E., 154
Vergrugge, L. M., 512
Vermilyea, B. B., 584
Vermilyea, J. A., 584
Vitols, M., 595
Vogel, S., 390, 393, 504
Von Bekesy, G., 108
von Eye, A., 65
Von Glinow, M. A., 683, 685
Vontress, C. E., 641
Voyer, D., 394
Voyer, S., 394
Vygotsky, L. S., 315

W

Wachs, H., 312
Wade, C., 480
Wadsworth, S. J., 59
Wagman, M., 248
Wagner, A. R., 180
Wagner, D., 236
Wald, G., 104
Waldman, I. D., 59
Walk, R. D., 122, 123
Walker, A. J., 354, 355
Walker, L., 639
Wall, P. D., 110
Wallace, R. K., 519
Wallbott, H., 476
Wallbott, H. G., 479
Wallerstein, R., 622
Wallis, C., 420, 421
Walter, J. P., 497
Waltrip, R. W., 643
Ward, C., 139
Warden, C. J., 198
Wark, I. M., 96
Warner, K. E., 500
Warner, R. L., 355
Warren, L. W., 593
Washburn, A., 457
Washburn, D. A., 268
Wasserman, G. S., 103
Waters, E., 319
Watson, D., 582, 595
Watson, J. B., 9, 136, 177, 202

Watt, N. F., 605
Watts, T. D., 156
Webb, W. B., 143, 144
Wechsler, D., 274, 365
Wehr, T., 644
Weimer, W. B., 247
Wein, D., 261
Weinberg, M. S., 427, 428
Weinberg, R. A., 59, 279
Weinberger, D. R., 599
Weindruch, R., 362
Weinstein, S., 109
Weinter, I. B., 559
Weisenberg, M., 110
Weisler, S. E., 247
Weisman, A. D., 490
Weissman, M. M., 585, 592
Wellborn, J. G., 461
Wells, G. L., 227
West, L. J., 156
Westkott, M., 542
Whiston, S. C., 636
White, A., 672
White, B. J., 709
White, C., 403
White, F., 369
White, R. W., 459
Whitfield, J. R., 405
Whiting, B. B., 34
Whiting, J. W. M., 34
Whiting, R. B., 396
Whitman, F. L., 428
Whitney, K., 678
Whorf, B. L., 265
Widiger, T. A., 583
Wiener, B., 466, 507, 559
Wiesel, T. N., 102
Wilfley, D., 498
Wilkinson, C. S., 17
Wilkinson, S., 425
Williams, J., 639
Williams, J. E., 393
Williams, M. E., 197
Williams, S. L., 267
Wilson, B. J., 354
Wilson, E. O., 63
Wilson, G. T., 496, 497
Wilson, M., 63
Wilson, M. N., 322
Winett, R. A., 503
Wing, A. L., 369, 491
Winn, M., 35
Winner, E., 309
Winzenz, D., 223
Wise, R. A., 76
Wittlinger, R. P., 218
Wober, M., 123, 270
Wohl, J., 640
Wolf, N. M., 190
Wolford, G., 97
Wolgamuth, B. R., 143
Wolpe, J., 624
Wong, H. Z., 16
Wood, J. T., 406
Wood, J. V., 657
Woods, P. J., 17
Wooley, S. C., 496
Worden, J. K., 501
Worell, J., 637
Worrell, J., 639
Wortman, C., 513
Wright, J. C., 172
Wright, R., 365
Wunsch-Hitzig, R., 581
Wylie, P., 416

Subject Index

A

Abnormal behavior
    anxiety disorders, 584–587
    and commitment, 602–603
    competency, 604
    cross-cultural view, 577
    diagnosis, advantages/disadvantages of, 579–581
    dimensions of, 575
    dissociative disorders, 588–589
    DSM-IV classification, 579, 581–583
    and ethnic minorities, 578
    gender differences, 578
    insanity defense, 603–604
    interactionist approach, 579
    medical model, 576
    mood disorders, 590–595
    personality disorders, 601–602
    and poverty, 578–579
    prevalence of mental disorders, 577
    schizophrenic disorders, 595–600
    somatoform disorders, 587–588
    substance-use disorders, 602
Absolute threshold, 95–97
Accommodation
    Piaget's theory, 307
    visual, 100
Acculturation, meaning of, 511, 700
Acculturative stress, 511–512, 701–702
Acetylcholine (ACh), 71
Achievement
    and attribution theory, 461
    and ethnic minorities, 464
    and gender differences, 464–465
    and goal-setting, 462
    and helpless orientation, 462
    and intrinsic and extrinsic motivation, 461–462
    and mastery orientation, 462
    and performance orientation, 462
    and self-efficacy, 462
    and self-esteem, 463–464
Achievement motivation, 460–461
Action potential, 69
Action therapy, 617
Activation-synthesis view, dreams, 148
Active listening, in person-centered therapy, 622
Active-behavioral strategies, for coping, 514–515
Active-cognitive strategies, for coping, 514
Activity theory, late adulthood, 365
Actor-observer hypothesis, 658–659
Acupuncture, 111–112
Adaptation, 63
Addiction, 152–153
    disease model, 153
    life-process model, 153
    and psychological dependence, 152

Additive mixture, 103
Adolescence
    and alcohol use, 155
    cognitive development, 338–339
    early and late maturation, 337–338
    high school dropouts, 347–348
    identity development, 343–344
    moral development, 344–347
    multiple-problem behaviors in, 347, 348–349
    parent-child relationships in, 341
    physical development, 336–338
    storm-and-stress view, 335
    teenage pregnancy, 348
    theories of, 335–336
Adoption studies, alcoholism, 157
Adrenal glands, 77
Adulthood. *See* Early and middle adulthood;
    Late adulthood
Affectionate love, 666, 667
Afferent nerves, 67
Affiliation, need for, 466
African Americans
    in American culture, 15
    gender roles, 403–404
    health of, 524
    language traditions of, 264
    therapy with, 631
Afterimages, 104
Ageism, 365
Aggression, gender differences, 395–396
Agoraphobia, 584, 585
AIDS, 436–438, 492–494
    and ethnic minorities, 436–437
    and homosexuality, 427
    pediatric, 303
    risk factors, 437, 492–494
    stages of disease, 437–438
    transmission of, 437
Alcohol use, 153–157, 160
    cross-cultural view, 155, 156
    identification of young abusers, 155
    nature/nurture issue, 155, 157
    and prenatal development, 303
    and self-help groups, 154
Alcoholics Anonymous (AA), 154, 632
Algorithms, 252
All-or-none principle, 69
Alpha waves, 141
Altered states of consciousness, 137–139
    dreams, 147–148
    hypnosis, 150–151
    and psychoactive drugs, 152–161
    and religion, 138–139
Alternation model, for cultural subgroups, 511, 700
Altruism, 668–670
    bystander effect, 669–670

    evolutionary view, 668
    meaning of, 668
    social exchange theory, 669
    versus egoism, 669
Alzheimer's disease, 363
American Psychological Association (APA), 19
Amnesia, 232
    anterograde and retrograde amnesia, 232
    psychogenic amnesia, 588
Amphetamines, 157, 160
Amplitude
    EEG, 141
    sound, 106
Amygdala, 77
Anal stage, 538
Analogies, 255
Androgens, 397
Androgyny, 390–391
Anger, 470
Animal studies, 32–33
    ethical issues, 43–44
Animals, language learning by, 267–268
Anorexia nervosa, 498
Anterograde amnesia, 232
Antianxiety drugs, 642–643
Antidepressant drugs, 643
Antipsychotic drugs, 643
Antisocial personality disorder, 602
Anxiety disorders, 584–587
    drug therapy, 642–643
    generalized anxiety disorder, 584
    obsessive-compulsive disorder, 586–587
    panic disorder, 584
    phobic disorder, 584–586
    post-traumatic stress disorder, 587
Aphasia, 83
Approach/approach conflict, 508
Approach/avoidance conflict, 509
Archetypes, 542
Artificial intelligence (AI), 248
Asian Americans
    in American culture, 15
    gender roles, 404, 405
    health of, 524–525
Assimilation
    cultural, 511, 700
    Piaget's theory, 307
Association cortex, 80
Astrology, 47
Attachment, 318–320
    criticisms of theory, 319–320
    and later depression, 593–594
    secure and insecure attachment, 319
    theories of, 318–319
Attention, 221–222

Computers
    artificial intelligence (AI), 248
    compared to brain, 116, 247–248
    expert systems, 248
Concept, definition of, 249
Concept formation, 249–250
Conception, 302
Concrete operational thought, 311–313, 400
Conditional positive regard, 547
Conditioned response (CR), 174
Conditioned stimulus (CS), 174, 180
Conditioned taste aversion, 180
Cones, of eye, 100–101
Conflict, 508–509
Conformity, 679–681
    cross-cultural view, 680–681
Consciousness, 136–139
    altered states of, 137–139
    controlled and automatic processes, 137
    daydreaming, 137
    definition of, 136
    Freud's view, 137
    stream of, 137
Consciousness-raising groups, 639
Consensual validation, 662
Conservation, in Piaget's theory, 310, 311
Content validity of test, 272–273
Contexts, nature of, 6–7
Continuity of development, 297, 360
Contour, 117
Contraception, 421–422
    factors in choice of, 421–422
    failure rates, 423
Control group, 37
Controlled processes, 137
Conventional level, 346
Convergence, visual, 119
Convergent thinking, 258
Conversion disorder, 587–588
Coping
    active-behavioral strategies, 514–515
    active-cognitive strategies, 514
    avoidance strategies, 515
    cognitive restructuring, 516
    emotion-focused coping, 514
    with illness, 522–525
    and optimism, 518
    positive self-illusions, 517–518
    positive thinking, 515–518
    problem-focused coping, 514
    and self-efficacy, 515
    self-talk, 516–517
    and social support, 518–519
    stress management, 519–520
Cornea, 99
Corpus callosum, 81
Correlation coefficient, 731–734
Correlational research, 35
Counseling psychology, 19
Counterconditioning, 177–178
Crack, 158
Creativity, 256, 258–259
Criminal commitment, 603
Criterion validity of test, 273
Critical period, in language development, 261–262
Critical thinking, 256
Cross-cultural psychology, 19
Cross-cultural research, 41–42
    benefits and challenges of, 42
    emic and etic approaches, 41, 698–699
Cross-cultural view
    abnormal behavior, 577
    alcohol use, 155, 156
    attraction, 663
    care of children, 301

conformity, 680–681
death and dying, 371
depression, 595
dreams, 149–150
emotion, 479
gender, 388
gender roles, 405–407
individualism versus collectivism, 555–557, 699–700
intelligence, 280–281
late adulthood, 363, 366
learning, 204–205
memory, 236, 238
middle age, 359–360
motivation, 455–456
nutrition, 499–500
pain, 110
perception, 123–124, 125
schizophrenic disorders, 600
sex education, 421
sexual arousal, 417–418
suicide, 593
Cue-dependent forgetting, 230
Cultural bias
    and intelligence tests, 281–282
    and research, 32
Cultural evolution, 60
Cultural factors
    language development, 263, 265
    learning, 202–203
Cultural-familial retardation, 276
Culture
    changes in attitude and contact with, 700–702
    culture shock, 700
    definition of, 15, 697–698
    features of, 698
Culture specificity hypothesis, memory, 236
Culture-fair tests, 282–283
Current concerns, nature of, 453

D

Daily hassles, and stress, 510
Data collection, 29
Date rape, 433
Daydreaming, 137
Death and dying
    cross-cultural view, 371
    loss of life partner, 372
    stages of, 371–372
Decay theory, forgetting, 232
Declarative memory, 219
Deductive reasoning, 254–255
Defense mechanisms, 537–538
    displacement, 538
    projection, 538
    rationalization, 537–538
    reaction formation, 538
    regression, 538
    repression, 537
    sublimation, 538
Deficiency needs, 550
Deindividuation, 681
Deinstitutionalization, 633
Delay of gratification, 546
Delta waves, 142
Dendrite, 67
Deoxyribonucleic acid (DNA), 60
Dependent variables, 37
Depressant drugs, 153–157, 160
Depression
    biological factors, 594–595
    cognitive view of, 594
    cross-cultural view, 595
    drug therapy, 643–644

and early attachment, 593–594
education about, 596
electroconvulsive therapy (ECT), 644
Freud's theory, 593
gender differences, 591
and learned helplessness, 594
major depression, 590–591
seasonal affective disorder (SAD), 644
Depth perception, 118–119
    visual cliff, 122–123
Descriptive research, 35
Descriptive statistics, 726–735
    central tendency measures, 728–729
    correlation coefficient, 731–734
    for one variable, 726–730
    for two variables, 730–734
    frequency distribution, 727
    graphic representations, 727–728
    normal distribution, 730
    scatter plots, 731
    variability measures, 729–730
Determinism, 551
Development
    cognitive development, 307–315
    continuity and discontinuity, 297
    developmental processes in, 297
    early-later experience issue, 297–298
    maturation, 297
    meaning of, 297
    physical development, 304–306
    prenatal development, 302–303
    and social policy, 298, 300–301
    socioemotional development, 316–325
Developmental psychology, 19
Devil's tuning fork illusion, 122
Diagnostic and Statistical Manual of Mental Disorders (DSM-IV), 579, 581–583
    changes in edition, 581–582
    controversy related to, 582–583
    multiaxial system, 581
Diathesis-stress view, schizophrenic disorders, 600
Dichromats, 104
Dieting, 496–498
Difference threshold, 97
Diffusion of responsibility, 670
Discontinuity of development, 297
Discrimination, 707
    classical conditioning, 175–176
    operant conditioning, 190
Discriminative stimuli, 190
Disease model, addiction, 153
Disorganized schizophrenia, 597
Displacement, 538
Display rules, emotion, 477–478
Dissociative disorders, 588–589
    fugue, 588
    multiple personality, 588–589
    psychogenic amnesia, 588
Divergent thinking, 258
Divorce, 355
Dominant-recessive genes theory, 60–61
Dopamine, 71
Double standard, 426
Dream analysis, 620
Dreams, 147–149
    activation-synthesis view, 148
    cross-cultural view, 149–150
    as entertainment, 147–148
    lucid dreaming, 147–148
    nature of, 148–149
    as problem solving, 147
    as wish fulfillment, 147
Drive, meaning of, 451
Drive reduction theory, motivation, 451

Integration, cultural, 511, 700
Intelligence
    cross-cultural view, 280–281
    definition of, 269
    and ethnic minorities, 280
    frames of intelligence theory, 271–272
    giftedness, 277–278
    and learning differences, 276–277
    mental retardation, 276
    multiple-factor theory, 270
    nature/nurture issue, 278–280
    triarchic theory, 270–271
    two-factor theory, 270
Intelligence quotient (IQ), meaning of, 274
Intelligence tests
    Binet tests, 273–274
    criteria for test design, 272–273
    and cultural bias, 281–282
    culture-fair tests, 282–283
    use and misuse of, 283–284
    Wechsler scales, 274–275
Interference theory, forgetting, 231–232
Intergroup relations, 703–711
    discrimination, 707
    ethnocentrism, 705–706
    improvement of, 709–711
    prejudice, 706–707
    racism, 708–709
    social identity theory, 705–706
    and stereotyping, 706
Internalization, and moral development, 345
International Classification of Disease
        (ICD-10), 583
Interneurons, 67
Interpersonal influence
    obedience, 674–676
    persuasion, 671–674
Interpersonal relationships
    attraction, 662–664
    friendship, 664
    love, 664–667
Interpretation, in psychoanalysis, 620
Interviews, research-related, 39
Intimacy
    gender differences, 466
    in marriage, 355
Intimacy versus isolation, 356
Intrinsic motivation, and achievement, 461–462
Introspection, 9, 247
Ions, 68
Iris, 99

J

James-Lange theory, emotion, 471
Japanese management, 684–685
Jigsaw classroom, 709–710
Jung's theory, of personality, 542
Justice perspective, moral development, 346

K

Kinesthetic sense, 112
Kohlberg's theory, 344–346
    criticisms of, 346, 347
    internalization in, 345
    moral dilemmas, 373

L

Labeling, and language, 285
Laboratory research, 33–34
Language
    animal use of, 267–268
    definition of, 260
    infinite generativity of, 260
    morphology, 260

phonology, 260
    semantics, 260
    syntax, 260
Language development
    babbling, 261
    bilingualism, 262, 266–267
    biological factors, 262
    critical period in, 261–262
    cultural factors, 263, 265
    environmental factors, 262–263
    holophrase hypothesis, 261
    linguistic relativity hypothesis, 265–266
    motherese, 263
    telegraphic speech, 261
Late adulthood, 361–370
    activity theory, 365
    ageism, 365
    cognitive development, 365
    cross-cultural view, 363, 366
    Erikson's theory, 366, 368
    ethnic minorities, 365–366, 367
    exercise in, 368–369
    factors in successful aging, 369–370
    and health care system, 364
    life review, 366, 368
    physical development, 362–363
    time span of, 361
Latency stage, 540
Latent content, dreams, 620
Latinos
    in American culture, 15
    Catholicism and suicide, 593
    gender roles, 404, 405
    health of, 524
    mental health and women, 580
Law of effect, 182–183
Leadership, 677–678
Learned helplessness, and depression, 594
Learning
    and behavior modification, 206
    biological factors, 201–202
    classical conditioning, 173–182
    cognitive factors, 198–200
    cross-cultural view, 204–205
    cultural factors, 202–203
    definition of, 173
    observational learning, 195–196
    operant conditioning, 182–194
Learning differences, 276–277
Learning set, 252
Lens, eye, 99–100
Levels of processing theory, memory, 222
Lie detection, 474–476
    and nonverbal leakage, 475
    polygraph, 474–475
    signs of lying, 476
Life events
    and adulthood, 358
    and stress, 509–510
Life expectancy, of Americans, 359
Life review, 366, 368
Life-process model, 153
Light, 98–99
Limbic system, 77–78
Linguistic relativity hypothesis, language
        development, 265–266
Lithium, 643
Loneliness, 667–668
    prevention of, 687–688
Long-term memory, 218
Loudness, sound, 106
Love, 664–667
    affectionate love, 666, 667
    romantic love, 664–665
    triangular theory of, 666

LSD, 158, 160
Lucid dreaming, 147–148

M

Magnetic resonance imaging (MRI), 85
Maintenance rehearsal, 216
Managed health care, and psychotherapy, 619
Manifest content, dreams, 620
MAO inhibitors, 643
Marginalization, cultural, 511, 702
Marijuana, 158, 160
Marriage, 353–354
    dual-career marriage, 354
    intimacy in, 355
    loss of life partner, 372
Masochism, 431–432
Mastery orientation, and achievement, 462
Matching hypothesis, 664
Math learning, cross-cultural view, 204–205
Mathematics ability, gender differences, 394
Maturation, meaning of, 297
Mean, 728
Media, reports on research, 44–46
Median, 728
Medical model, abnormal behavior, 576
Meditation, stress management, 519
Medulla, 73
Memory
    and attention, 221–222
    cross-cultural view, 236, 238
    culture specificity hypothesis, 236
    declarative memory, 219
    decline in middle age, 352–353
    definition of, 214
    echoic memory, 215–216
    educational implications, 236–237
    effortful and automatic processing, 222
    eidetic memory, 216–217
    and elaboration, 222–223
    episodic memory, 219–220
    and eyewitness testimony, 227
    forgetting, 230–232
    iconic memory, 215
    and imagery, 223–224
    levels of processing theory, 222
    long-term memory, 218
    network theories, 225
    neurobiological basis of, 234–235
    primacy and recency effects, 229
    priming, 220
    procedural memory, 219
    recall and recognition, 230
    and representation, 225–228
    and repression, 232–234
    retrieval from, 229–230
    schema theories, 225–228
    semantic memory, 220
    sensory memory, 215–216
    working memory, 216–218
Memory improvement
    chunking, 216
    for names, 239
    imagery, 237–238
    maintenance rehearsal, 216
    method of loci, 237
    mnemonics, 237, 238
    peg method, 238
Memory span, 216
Menarche, 336–337
Menopause, 351–352
Men's movement, 402–403
Mental age (MA), 274
Mental health, and exercise, 493–495
Mental hospitals, historical view, 616
Mental processes, nature of, 5

Mental retardation, 276
Mesmerism, 150
Mesomorph, 553
Meta-analysis, 636
Metaneeds, 550
Method of loci, 237
Midbrain, 73
Middle ear, 108
Midlife crisis, 357, 359
Milgram's study, 674–676
Minnesota Multiphasic Personality Inventory
(MMPI), 40, 561
Minnesota Study of Twins Reared Apart, 58
Misogyny, 389
Mnemonics, 237, 238
Mode, 728
Modeling. *See* Observational learning
Monocular cues, to depth, 118
Mood disorders, 590–595
  bipolar disorder, 592
  major depression, 590–591
  and suicide, 592–593
  See also Depression
Moon illusion, 122
Moral development, 344–347
  care perspective, 346
  Gilligan's theory, 346–347
  justice perspective, 346
  Kohlberg's theory, 344–346
Moral dilemmas, 373
Morphology, 260
Motherese, 263
Motivation
  behavioral view, 452
  cognitive factors, 452–453
  cross-cultural view, 455–456
  definition of, 451
  drive reduction theory, 451
  ethological perspective, 451–452
  Freud's view, 452
  hierarchy of motives, 453–455
  humanistic approach, 453–455
  instinct theory, 451
  issues related to, 456
Motives
  achievement motivation, 460–461
  competence motivation, 459–460
  hunger, 457–459
  social motives, 465–467
Motor development
  childhood, 306
  infancy, 304–305
Müller-Lyer illusion, 121
Multiaxial system, DSM-IV, 581
Multiculturalism, 700
Multiple personality, 588–589
Multiple-factor theory, intelligence, 270
Myelin sheath, 68

N

Narcolepsy, 146
Native Americans
  in American culture, 15
  gender roles, 404, 405
  health care, 525
Natural selection, 63
Naturalistic research, 34
Nature/nurture issue
  alcohol use, 155, 157
  basis of, 59
  intelligence, 278–280
  perception, 122–123
Need for affiliation, 466
Need for power, 466–467

Needs
  hierarchy of needs theory, 453–455, 548, 560
  meaning of, 451
Negative affectivity, 469, 470
Negative reinforcement, 183–184, 206
Nenko, 684–685
Neo-Piagetians, 314
Nerves
  afferent and efferent, 67
  nerve impulse, 68–69
Nervous system
  divisions of, 66–67
  nerve impulse, 68–69
  neural transmission, 67
  neurons, 67–68
  neurotransmitters, 69–72
  synapses, 69
Network theories, memory, 225
Neural-auditory processing, 108–109
Neurobiological perspective
  basis of, 14
  gender identity, 397–398
  motivation, 451–452
  schizophrenic disorders, 599
Neurons, 67–68
  and memory, 234–235
  structure of, 67–68
Neurotransmitters, 69–72
  acetylcholine (ACh), 71
  and depression, 595
  dopamine, 71
  endorphins, 72
  functions of, 69
  GABA (gama aminobutyric acid), 70
  norepinephrine, 71
Night terrors, 136
Nightmares, 146
Nomothetic research, 45
Nonsexist therapy, 639
Nonstate theory, hypnosis, 151
Nonverbal leakage, 475
Norepinephrine, 71
Normal distribution, 274, 727–728, 730
Norms
  in groups, 677
  tests, 273
Nutrition
  cross-cultural view, 499–500
  and ethnic minorities, 497
  in infancy, 306

O

Obedience, 674–676
Obesity, 495–498
  and dieting, 496–498
  environmental factors, 495–496
  and exercise, 497
  and external cues, 459
  genetic factors, 495
Object permanence, 308–309
Objectivity, and research, 42–43
Observation
  laboratory research, 33–34
  naturalistic observation, 34
  research-related, 38–39
Observational learning, 195–198
  applications of, 198
  evaluation of, 198
  process of, 195–196
  role models, 197
Obsessive-compulsive disorder, 586–587, 601
Occipital lobe, 78
Oedipus complex, 539–540
Olfactory epithelium, 114

Operant conditioning, 182–194
  applications of, 190–193, 206, 625
  behaviorists' study of, 185–186
  chaining, 186
  discrimination, 190
  evaluation of, 193
  extinction, 185
  generalization, 189–190
  and law of effect, 182–183
  punishment in, 183, 184–185
  reinforcement in, 183–184, 186, 188–189
  schedules of reinforcement, 188–189
  and self-control problems, 187, 191–193
  shaping, 186
  time interval in, 186
Operational definition, 38
Operations, in Piaget's theory, 309–310
Opiates, 157
Opponent-process theory, 105
Optimism, and coping, 518
Oral stage, 538
Organ of Corti, 108
Organic retardation, 276
Organizational behavior
  changing organizations, 685–686
  ethnic minorities in organizations, 683–685
  formal and informal groups, 682–683
  Japanese management, 684–685
  tokenism, 684–685
  women in organizations, 683–685
Organizational psychology, 682
Orgasm, 419
Outer ear, 107
Overcompensation, 543
Overload, 508

P

Pain sensation, 109–111
Panic disorder, 584
Paranoid schizophrenia, 598
Paraphilias, 431
Parasympathetic nervous system, 67
Parenting styles, 320–324
  and ethnic minorities, 322, 324
  and social class, 322
Parietal lobe, 78
Partial reinforcement, 188
Pedophilia, 432
Peers
  in adolescence, 342–343
  in childhood, 324–325
Peg method, 238
Perception
  cross-cultural view, 123–124, 125
  definition of, 95
  depth perception, 118–119
  extrasensory, 124–127
  illusions, 121–122
  in infancy, 305
  nature/nurture issue, 122–123
  perceptual constancy, 120–121
  perceptual processes, 117
  shape perception, 117–118
Perceptual set, 117
Performance orientation, and achievement, 462
Peripheral nervous system, 66
Permissive-indifferent parenting, 321
Permissive-indulgent parenting, 321
Personal construct theory, 546
Personal growth groups, 631
Personal projects, nature of, 453
Personality
  behavioral view, 545–546
  cognitive view, 546–547

Research
    animal studies, 32–33
    case studies, 40
    correlational research, 35
    cross-cultural research, 41–42
    descriptive research, 35
    ethical issues, 43–44
    experimental research, 36–38
    interviews, 39
    laboratory research, 33–34
    media reporting of, 44–46
    naturalistic research, 34
    nomothetic research, 45
    and objectivity of researcher, 42–43
    observation, 38–39
    questionnaires, 39–40
    scientific method, 28–31
    settings for, 33–34
    standardized tests, 40–41
    subject selection, 31–33
Resistance, in psychoanalysis, 621
Resting potential, 68
Reticular formation, 73
Retina, 100
Retinal disparity, 119
Retroactive interference, 231
Retrograde amnesia, 232
Retronasal olfaction, 114
Rites of passage, 341–342
Ritual possession, 139
Rods, of eye, 100–101
Rogers's theory, 547–548
    person-centered therapy, 622
Role models, and observational learning, 195, 197
Roles, in groups, 677
Romantic love, 664–665
Romantic script, 425
Rorschach inkblot test, 559

S

Sadism, 431
Saturation, color, 102
Scatter plots, 731
Schema, meaning of, 226, 401
Schema theories, memory, 225–228
Schizophrenic disorders, 595–600
    catatonic schizophrenia, 597–598
    characteristics of, 595–597
    cross-cultural view, 600
    diathesis-stress view, 600
    disorganized schizophrenia, 597
    drug therapy, 643
    environmental factors, 600
    genetic factors, 599
    neurobiological factors, 599
    paranoid schizophrenia, 598
    undifferentiated schizophrenia, 598
Schizotypal personality disorder, 601
School psychology, 19
Scientific method, 28–31
    choosing problem, 29
    conclusions in, 29
    confirm or revise theory, 29
    data collection, 29
    hypothesis in, 29
    and problem solving in psychology, 29–30
    theory in, 29
Sclera, 99
Seasonal affective disorder (SAD),
        treatment of, 644
Seasons of man's life theory, 356
Secondary prevention, 634
Secondary reinforcement, 188
Secure attachment, 319

Selection bias, 31
Selective attention, 221
Self, in Rogers's theory, 547–548
Self-actualization, 453, 455, 548
    characteristics of, 550
Self-concept
    and ethnic minorities, 549
    meaning of, 548
Self-control problems, operant
        conditioning of, 187, 191–193
Self-efficacy, 626
    and coping, 515
    meaning of, 546
Self-esteem
    and achievement, 463–464
    meaning of, 463
Self-help groups, 154, 632
    types of, 632
Self-instructional methods, 626
Self-perception theory, 661
Self-report tests
    construction of, 560–561
    Minnesota Multiphasic Personality
        Inventory (MMPI), 561
    Q-sort, 561–562
Self-talk, and coping, 516–517
Semantic memory, 220
Semantics, 260
Semicircular canals, 113
Sensation
    absolute threshold, 95–97
    auditory system, 106–109
    definition of, 95
    difference threshold, 97
    haptic system, 109–113
    in infancy, 305
    kinesthetic sense, 112
    pain, 109–111
    pressure, 109
    sensory adaptation, 98
    smell, 114–115
    subliminal perception, 97
    taste, 114
    temperature, 109
    touch, 109
    vestibular sense, 112–113
    visual system, 98–106
Sensorimotor thought, 308–309
Sensory adaptation, 98
Sensory memory, 215–216
Separation, cultural, 511, 702
Serial position effect, and memory retrieval, 229
Set point, 495, 497
Sex, definition of, 15
Sex education, 420–421
Sexism, 385
Sexual arousal, 416–418
Sexual harassment, 433
Sexual response cycle, 418–419
Sexual satisfaction, 429
Sexual scripts, 425–426
Sexuality
    contraception, 421–422
    and double standard, 426
    heterosexuality, 422, 424–425
    homosexuality, 426–429
    psychosexual disorders, 430–432
    sexual arousal, 416–418
    sexual knowledge, 420
    sexual myths, 420
    sexual response cycle, 418–419
    sexual satisfaction, 429
    sexual scripts, 425–426
Sexually transmitted diseases, 434–438
Shape constancy, 120, 121

Shape perception, 117–118
Shaping, 186
Short-term memory, working memory, 216–218
Singlehood, 353, 355
Situational theory, of leadership, 678
Situationism, 555
Size constancy, 120
Sleep
    and circadian rhythm, 139, 141
    dreams, 147–149
    ecological theory, 144
    necessity of, 144
    REM sleep, 143
    repair theory, 144
    sleep cycles, 141–143
    sleep deprivation, 144
Sleep apnea, 146
Sleep disorders, 144–146
Sleep spindles, 142
Smell sensation, 114–115
Snowflake model, of creativity, 259
Social class, and parenting styles, 322
Social clock, 358
Social comparison, 657–658
Social desirability, 39
    and test responses, 560
Social distance, 698
Social exchange theory, 669
Social identity theory, 705–706
Social learning theory
    cognitive social learning theory, 546
    gender identity, 399–400
    observational learning, 195–198
Social motives, 465–467
    need for affiliation, 466
    need for power, 466–467
Social perception
    impression formation, 657
    impression management, 658
    social comparison, 657–658
Social phobia, 584–585
Social policy, and child development, 298, 300–301
Social psychology, 19
Social support, and coping, 518–519
Sociobiology, 63, 65
Sociocultural perspective, 15–17
Socioemotional development, 316–325
    attachment, 318–320
    Erikson's theory, 316–318
    parent-adolescent relationships, 341
    and parenting styles, 320–324
    and peers, 324–325, 342–343
    and play, 325
    rites of passage, 341–342
Socioemotional processes, in development, 297
Somatic nervous system, 66
Somatoform disorders, 587–588
Somatotype theory, 553–554
Somnambulism, 145–146
S-O-R model, 199
Sound, 106
Special process theory, hypnosis, 151
Split-brain research, 81
Spontaneous recovery, 176
Sports psychology, 462–463
Standard deviation, 729–730
Standardization, of tests, 273
Standardized tests, 40–41
Statistical significance, 736
Statistics
    descriptive statistics, 726–735
    inferential statistics, 735–736
Stereotyping
    gender roles, 392–393
    of groups, 706